The Moral of the Story

AN INTRODUCTION TO ETHICS

Ninth Edition

NINA ROSENSTAND

San Diego Mesa College

THE MORAL OF THE STORY: AN INTRODUCTION TO ETHICS, NINTH EDITION

Published by McGraw Hill LLC, 1325 Avenue of the Americas, New York, NY 10121. Copyright © 2021 by McGraw Hill LLC. All rights reserved. Printed in the United States of America. Previous editions © 2017, 2013, and 2009. No part of this publication may be reproduced or distributed in any form or by any means, or stored in a database or retrieval system, without the prior written consent of McGraw Hill LLC, including, but not limited to, in any network or other electronic storage or transmission, or broadcast for distance learning.

Some ancillaries, including electronic and print components, may not be available to customers outside the United States.

This book is printed on acid-free paper.

1 2 3 4 5 6 7 8 9 LCR 24 23 22 21 20

ISBN 978-1-259-23119-3 (bound edition)
MHID 1-259-23119-4 (bound edition)
ISBN 978-1-260-83890-9 (loose-leaf edition)
MHID 1-260-83890-0 (loose-leaf edition)

Product Developer: *Alexander Preiss*
Marketing Manager: *Nancy Baudean*
Content Project Manager: *Danielle Clement*
Buyer: *Susan K. Culbertson*
Design: *Beth Blech*
Content Licensing Specialist: *Brianna Kirschbaum*
Cover Image: *The Metropolitan Museum of Art, New York, The Berggruen Klee Collection, 1987*
Compositor: *SPi Global*

All credits appearing on page or at the end of the book are considered to be an extension of the copyright page.

Library of Congress Cataloging-in-Publication Data

Names: Rosenstand, Nina, author.
Title: The moral of the story : an introduction to ethics / Nina
    Rosenstand, San Diego Mesa College.
Description: Ninth edition. | New York : McGraw-Hill Education, 2020. |
    Audience: Ages 18+
Identifiers: LCCN 2020004776 | ISBN 9781259231193 (hardcover)
Subjects: LCSH: Ethics–Textbooks.
Classification: LCC BJ1012 .R59 2020 | DDC 170–dc23
LC record available at https://lccn.loc.gov/2020004776

The Internet addresses listed in the text were accurate at the time of publication. The inclusion of a website does not indicate an endorsement by the authors or McGraw Hill LLC, and McGraw Hill LLC does not guarantee the accuracy of the information presented at these sites.

mheducation.com/highered

For Craig and my parents

Immorality may be fun, but it isn't fun enough to take the place of 100 percent virtue and three square meals a day.

—Design for Living

Contents

PART 3

How Should I Be? Virtue Ethics

Preface

The ninth edition of *The Moral of the Story* represents 25 years of editions, with the publication year of the first being 1994. It has been a humbling experience for me to contemplate the fact that I have been privileged to teach as well as write about issues that have concerned us for over a quarter of a century—some issues reflecting the changing times and others being timeless discussions about moral issues rooted in our common human nature.

Like the previous editions of *The Moral of the Story,* the ninth edition is a combination of classical questions in ethical theory and contemporary issues. The general concept remains the same: that discussions about moral issues can be facilitated using stories as examples, as a form of ethics lab where solutions can be tried out under controlled conditions. The book is written primarily for such college courses as Introduction to Ethics; Moral Philosophy; and Introduction to Philosophy: Values. Many textbooks in value theory or ethics choose to focus on problems of social importance, such as abortion, euthanasia, and capital punishment. This book reflects my own teaching experience that it is better for students to be introduced to basic ethical theory before they are plunged into discussions involving moral judgments. Consequently, *The Moral of the Story* provides an overview of influential classical and contemporary approaches to ethical theory. However, without practical application of the theories, there can be no complete understanding of the problems raised, so each chapter includes examples that illustrate and explore the issues. As in previous editions, each chapter concludes with a section of examples—summaries and excerpts—taken from the world of fiction, novels and films in particular. The final chapter provides a sampler of discussions within Applied Ethics.

Within the last three decades, narrative theory has carved out a niche in American and European philosophy as well as in other academic disciplines. It is no longer unusual for ethicists and other thinkers to include works of fiction in their courses as well as in their professional papers, not only as examples of problem solving, but also as illustrations of an epistemological phenomenon: Humans are, in Alasdair MacIntyre's words, storytelling animals, and we humans seem to choose the narrative form as our favorite way to structure meaning as we attempt to make sense of our reality. The narrative trend is making itself felt in other fields as well: The medical profession is looking to stories that teach about doctor–patient relationships; psychotherapists recommend that patients watch films to achieve an understanding of their own situation, and have patients write stories with themselves as the lead character. The court system is making use of films and novels to reach young people in trouble with the law. The U.S. military is partnering up with authors to anticipate possible scenarios for future assaults on American interests. NASA is teaming up with science fiction writers and Hollywood in an attempt to once again make space exploration exciting for new generations of readers, and judging from the success of recent films, that approach is working. And neuroscientists tell us that we understand the world by superimposing narrative order on the chaos we experience. It seems that new fields are constantly being added to the list of professions that are discovering, or rediscovering, the potential of stories.

Organization

Like the previous editions, the ninth edition of *The Moral of the Story* is divided into three major sections. Part 1 introduces the topic of ethics and places the phenomenon of storytelling within the context of moral education and discussion. Part 2 examines the conduct theories of ethical relativism, psychological and ethical egoism, altruism, utilitarianism, and Kantian deontology, and explores the concepts of personhood, rights, and justice. Part 3 focuses on the subject of virtue theory and contains chapters on Socrates and Plato, Aristotle, contemporary virtue theories in America, theories of authenticity in the Continental tradition, and gender theory. The virtues of courage, compassion, loyalty, and gratitude are examined in detail, and the book concludes with a more detailed discussion of a broad selection of moral issues, applying theories introduced in previous chapters. Each chapter concludes with a set of study questions, a section of Primary Readings with excerpts from classical and contemporary texts, and a section of Narratives, a collection of stories that illustrate the moral issues raised in the chapter. The Primary Readings are selected for their value as discussion topics; they don't necessarily reflect my own views, and I have made no attempt to select readings that cover all possible angles, because of space limitations. The Narratives will be described in more detail below.

Major Changes to the Ninth Edition

Throughout the ninth edition, all examples and discussions reflecting moral and social issues in the news have been updated wherever an update seemed reasonable. However, because of the particularly volatile and adversarial political climate we are currently experiencing, I have opted for minimizing references to the current political situation in the United States as much as possible, rather than plunging into the debate. Whenever it has been unavoidable, I have made every effort to present issues in a fair and nonpartisan manner, true to the (at least approximated) evenhanded style of previous editions. Major changes to the ninth edition include the following: As with every new edition, **Chapter One** has been revised, with a new introduction, reflecting the fact that we still live in a "50/50 nation," morally and politically. The section "Good and Evil" has been updated and expanded to examine current stories of egregiously evil behavior as well as extraordinary selflessness. Finally, the Narratives section now includes a summary of the film *The Eichmann Story*, reflecting the discussion in the chapter about the "banality of evil."

Chapter Two has been updated with current examples of films and television shows illustrating moral problems, including the videogame *Red Dead Redemption 2*. New boxes feature the Superhero phenomenon in entertainment and an update on the moral complexities of the HBO series *Game of Thrones*.

Chapter Three has a new introduction discussing the case of a young American missionary losing his life as a result of intruding on another culture, and updates of other current issues.

Chapter Four updates the actions of individuals giving up their lives to save students and co-workers in mass shootings and acts of terrorism. In addition, the Narratives section now includes a summary of John Steinbeck's classic novel *The Winter of Our Discontent*, a chilling exploration of fundamental selfishness as well as its antidote.

Chapter Five has a new box on utilitarianism and the Enlightenment, as well as a box on the trolley problem, seen from a utilitarian perspective, and the Narrative section now includes a companion story, the "Trolley Problem" episode from the television series *The Good Place*.

Chapter Six has a new box featuring an illustration of the categorical imperative taken from a classic episode of *The Simpsons*, "Bart's Inner Child." In addition, a new box on treating others merely as a means to an end provides examples from current debates including the #MeToo movement.

Chapter Seven has been updated with discussions about cloning and personhood, a reference to recent shootings, a new box on the issue of siblings being organ donors, and a new section on equity. A new Primary Reading has been added, an excerpt from John Rawls' "The Priority of Rights and Ideas of the Good." The Narratives section has a new story, the Academy Award-winning film *Green Book*.

Chapter Eight has a new box Stoicism and its connection to Platonism.

Chapter Nine has a new Primary Reading by Tom Chatfield, *A Balanced Life*.

Chapter Ten now includes a discussion of the college admissions scandal of 2019 as well as updates in the Nietzsche section.

Chapter Eleven has a new box on the virtue (or vice) of *loyalty*, and the Mexican Academy Award-winning film *Roma* has been selected to illustrate the concept.

Chapter Twelve has been updated with references to current discussions concerning gender equality and gender identity as well as a box on Plato's feminism in dispute, and a box on the #MeToo movement. The Narrative section now includes the novel (with reference to the TV series) *The Handmaid's Tale*.

Chapter Thirteen has several thoroughly revised sections, including the renewed debate about abortion in the United States, as well as updates regarding euthanasia, media ethics, just war, animal rights, environmental issues, and the death penalty. A few new boxes have been added, including a box on profit vs. pets (the melamine scandal) and one on Artificial Intelligence. In addition, a new section now addresses the issue of gun control and gun rights.

I would like to mention an issue that has been in effect since the eighth edition: the field of textbook publishing is changing, and some changes have impacted this ninth edition of *The Moral of the Story.* Those readers who have used this book through several editions will notice some changes in the Primary Readings and Narratives sections: Some texts have disappeared, or have been replaced with public-domain translations, paraphrased summaries, and short excerpts. These decisions have been necessary due to the fact that permissions to include lengthy text excerpts in textbooks have become much harder or downright impossible to obtain, and I had no choice but to exclude some texts despite them being a staple in the book for many editions. In addition, I've had to abandon the inclusion of several new, planned primary readings, such as an excerpt from Mary Midgley's "Mythology of Selfishness." As a compromise I have chosen to maintain the presence of such texts in the book by placing detailed descriptions and short excerpts into the chapter text itself, or in the case of narratives (particularly the novels), paraphrasing the stories and keeping brief excerpts of an essential paragraph or two allowed under the public domain notion. I hope I have done those texts justice. In addition, some cartoons have been replaced by others—in some cases because fresh material seemed like a good idea, but in other cases because the cartoons from previous editions were no longer available.

Using the Narratives

The Narratives have been chosen from a wide variety of sources ranging from epic prose, poems, and novels to films, one graphic novel, and new to this edition, a narrative videogame at the request of many students (despite the fact that I am admittedly not a gamer). I wish to emphasize that from a literary and artistic point of view, summaries and excerpts do not do the originals justice; a story worth experiencing, be it a novel, short story, or film, can't be reduced to a mere plot outline or fragment and still retain all of its essence. As Martha Nussbaum says, the form is an inherent part of the story content. Usually, there is more to the story than the bare bones of a moral problem, and in writing these summaries I have had to disregard much of the richness of story and character development. Nevertheless, I have chosen the summary or excerpt format in order to discuss a number of different stories and genres as they relate to specific issues in ethics. Because I believe it is important to show that there is a cross-cultural, historic tradition of exploring moral problems through telling a story, I have opted for a broad selection of Narratives. Each chapter has several Narratives, and some additional narratives—or narratives from previous editions—now appear in boxes within the chapter text, but it is not my intention that the instructor should feel obligated to cover all of them in one course; rather, they should be regarded as options that can be alternated from semester to semester—a method I like to use myself for the sake of variety. There are, of course, other ways than summaries in which stories and ethical theory can be brought together; one might, for instance, select one or two short stories or films in their original format for class discussion, or make them available to the students for extra credit. I hope that instructors will indeed select a few stories—novels, short stories, or films—for their classes to experience firsthand. However, the Narratives are written so that firsthand experience should not be necessary to a discussion of the problem presented by the story. The summaries and excerpts give readers just enough information to enable them to discuss the moral problem presented. I hope that some readers will become inspired to seek out the originals on their own. In most cases, the ending is important to the moral significance of a story, and whenever that is the case, I include that ending. In cases where the ending is not significant to the moral drama, I have done my best to avoid giving it away because I don't want to be a spoiler.

Because space is limited, I have not been able to include more than a sampling of stories, and I readily admit that my choices are subjective ones; I personally find them interesting as illustrations and effective in a classroom context where students come from many different cultural backgrounds. Because I am a naturalized U.S. citizen, originally a native of Denmark, I have chosen to include a few references to the Scandinavian literary and film tradition. I am fully aware that others might choose other stories or even choose different ethical problems to illustrate, and I am grateful to the many users of the previous eight editions, instructors as well as students, who have let me know about their favorite stories and how they thought this selection of stories might be expanded and improved. The new Narratives reflect some of those suggestions.

As in previous editions, I emphasize that I wholeheartedly welcome e-mails from students as well as instructors who use this book, with relevant comments and suggestions for new stories as well as additional philosophical perspectives: nrosenst@sdccd.edu.

Mc Graw Hill connect®

The ninth edition of *The Moral of the Story* is now available online with Connect, McGraw-Hill Education's integrated assignment and assessment platform. Connect also offers SmartBook for the new edition, which is the first adaptive reading experience proven to improve grades and help students study more effectively. All of the title's website and ancillary content is also available through Connect, including:

- A full Test Bank of multiple-choice questions that test students on central concepts and ideas in each chapter.
- An Instructor's Manual for each chapter with full chapter outlines, sample test questions, and discussion topics.

You're in the driver's seat.

Want to build your own course? No problem. Prefer to use our turnkey, prebuilt course? Easy. Want to make changes throughout the semester? Sure. And you'll save time with Connect's auto-grading too.

65%

Less Time Grading

Laptop: McGraw-Hill; Woman/dog: George Doyle/Getty Images

They'll thank you for it.

Adaptive study resources like SmartBook® 2.0 help your students be better prepared in less time. You can transform your class time from dull definitions to dynamic debates. Find out more about the powerful personalized learning experience available in SmartBook 2.0 at **www.mheducation.com/highered/ connect/smartbook**

Make it simple, make it affordable.

Connect makes it easy with seamless integration using any of the major Learning Management Systems— Blackboard®, Canvas, and D2L, among others—to let you organize your course in one convenient location. Give your students access to digital materials at a discount with our inclusive access program. Ask your McGraw-Hill representative for more information.

Padlock: Jobalou/Getty Images

Solutions for your challenges.

A product isn't a solution. Real solutions are affordable, reliable, and come with training and ongoing support when you need it and how you want it. Our Customer Experience Group can also help you troubleshoot tech problems— although Connect's 99% uptime means you might not need to call them. See for yourself at **status. mheducation.com**

Checkmark: Jobalou/Getty Images

FOR STUDENTS

Effective, efficient studying.

Connect helps you be more productive with your study time and get better grades using tools like SmartBook 2.0, which highlights key concepts and creates a personalized study plan. Connect sets you up for success, so you walk into class with confidence and walk out with better grades.

Study anytime, anywhere.

Download the free ReadAnywhere app and access your online eBook or SmartBook 2.0 assignments when it's convenient, even if you're offline. And since the app automatically syncs with your eBook and SmartBook 2.0 assignments in Connect, all of your work is available every time you open it. Find out more at **www.mheducation.com/readanywhere**

> *"I really liked this app—it made it easy to study when you don't have your text-book in front of you."*
>
> - Jordan Cunningham, Eastern Washington University

No surprises.

The Connect Calendar and Reports tools keep you on track with the work you need to get done and your assignment scores. Life gets busy; Connect tools help you keep learning through it all.

Calendar: owattaphotos/Getty Images

Learning for everyone.

McGraw-Hill works directly with Accessibility Services Departments and faculty to meet the learning needs of all students. Please contact your Accessibility Services office and ask them to email accessibility@mheducation.com, or visit **www.mheducation.com/about/accessibility** for more information.

Top: Jenner Images/Getty Images, Left: Hero Images/Getty Images, Right: Hero Images/Getty Images

Acknowledgments

As always, I first want to thank my students in the classes Introduction to Philosophy: Values, Philosophy of Women, Reflections on Human Nature, Human Nature and Society, and Philosophy and Literature for their enthusiastic cooperation in suggesting good stories and discussing drafts of the stories and study questions with me—an invaluable help in fine-tuning the summaries and questions. Since 2017 I have been teaching online classes in Introduction to Philosophy: Values in addition to my on-campus classes, and the feedback I have received from online students reflecting issues in *The Moral of the Story* has been a tangible reality-check as well as a morale-boost for me. I have learned much about what students find compelling, what has needed additional explanations, and what has appeared outdated. I appreciate all my students' candor and eagerness to participate with their suggestions and analyses.

Next, I would like to thank the project team at McGraw-Hill Higher Education for excellent, quick communication and support, in particular Development Editor Adina Lonn for her thorough, prompt, upbeat, and helpful emails and suggestions. Thanks also to Brianna Kirschbaum, Content Licensing Specialist, for seeking solutions with energy and sensitivity, and Janet Robbins, R&P Project Manager, for terrific research and helpful ideas. Many thanks to the entire team at McGraw-Hill Education, including Product Developer Alexander Preiss, Marketing Manager Nancy Baudean, Content Project Manager Danielle Clement, and Designer Beth Blech. I also wish to thank the following reviewers, and six anonymous reviewers, for their suggestions:

Irene J. Byrnes, SUNY Broome Community College

Susan Cosby Ronnenberg, Viterbo University

Gina Teel, Southeast Arkansas College

My colleagues at the Social Sciences Department at San Diego Mesa College, which includes professors, adjuncts, and professors emeritus/emerita of philosophy, history, political science, and geography, are a wonderful support group—many of us come from different professional fields and have different outlooks on many things, but we all cherish the ambience of professional integrity in our workplace and find time to discuss ethics-related issues on a regular basis: Thank you to my colleagues from the Social Sciences Department as well as other departments for supporting me through nine editions and 25 years of periodic, recurring work on *The Moral of the Story*: In particular I wish to thank Department Chair John Crocitti, Jonathan McLeod, Donald Abbott, Dwight Furrow, and Dean Charles Zappia. In addition, I would like to express my appreciation to Josef Binter for sharing his ongoing research into Nietzsche at the Nietzsche Archive, Heidelberg with me, and to Tony Pettina for being an advance reader on the section on Asian moral philosophy. I would like to thank my colleague Ian Duckles for his invaluable help in steering me through the maze of narrative open-ended video games with a moral aspect, and I also want to extend my appreciation to my colleague Mary Gwin with whom I share a fascination for the potential of stories as moral laboratories, and an interest in the life quality of companion animals.

At Mesa College, we have a biannual *Meeting of the Minds* tradition where philosophy faculty, contract as well as adjuncts, meet and share our thoughts about teaching and engage in debates about classical and current philosophical topics. I want to express my appreciation for the professional enthusiasm of all the philosophy faculty who participate regularly in these meetings. My colleague John Berteaux, philosophy professor at Monterey State University, deserves my heartfelt thanks for being an old friend and colleague from the adjunct days who shares my concerns for issues in social ethics and who has generously shared his work, including his archive of newspaper columns with me. A special word of appreciation goes to my friend and colleague Harold Weiss, professor of philosophy at Northampton Community College who has been enormously helpful in suggesting new material for past as well as the current edition, including several films I would otherwise not have thought of including. I would like to extend my gratitude to Michael Schwartz, Royal Melbourne Institute of Technology, Australia, a supportive friend and a source of inspiration over several editions. I appreciate his bold thought that readers of the anniversary issue of *Research in Ethical Issues in Organizations* of which he is joint editor might be interested in reading about my journey through 25 years and 8 editions of *The Moral of the Story*. In addition, I can't express enough relief and thankfulness for the guidance and advice from game master Jessica Humphrey when I was trying to get a grip on the concept of videogames as well as *Dungeons & Dragons* games. She steered me through the conceptual maze of *Red Dead Redemption 1* and *2* and made me understand the potential moral richness of the new story medium.

Because this edition builds upon the previous eight editions, I would like to acknowledge the generous support and suggestions I have received in the past from a very large number of people—friends, colleagues, and other professionals from a wide variety of fields—who have graciously given me their time and assistance. Your input has been invaluable to me, and I am profoundly grateful to you all.

My father, Finn Rosenstand, *raconteur par excellence*, frequently mentioned that if given the choice, he would like to live every single day all over again—something that Nietzsche would have appreciated as a sign that one truly loves life and is not a nay-sayer. Throughout my career as a philosophy instructor, and writer of textbooks and other works, he tirelessly looked for material I might be able to use. As I have mentioned in previous editions, he was instrumental in opening my mind to intellectual curiosity, human compassion, and a passion for history, literature, and film. My appreciation for what he has meant to me has no boundaries.

Most of all, I want to thank my husband, Craig R. Covner, for his strength and loving support. We share a love of American and world history as well as film history, and I appreciate being able to run impressions and ideas by him, and being sure to get a thoughtful and honest response. For four decades, he has put up with my periodic writer's work-mode, always being there for me with patience and a wonderful sense of humor.

Chapter One
Thinking About Values

The Best of Times, the Worst of Times?

Entering into the third decade of the twenty-first century, a future that to some seemed fairly predictable 10 years ago is anything but. A snapshot of the beginning of 2020: the unemployment rate in the United States down to 3.6 percent; the GDP growth rate advancing 2.3 percent, and the S&P 500 (the stock market), while undergoing fluctuation and adjustments, hitting 29,348.10 in February of 2020. American troops coming home from Syria and Afghanistan, with just a small peace-keeping force left; the militant group ISIS, a huge threat to the Middle Eastern region and even the world, seemingly close to being defeated. The commitment to space exploration back on the agenda, both from the U.S. government (NASA) and from the private sector (SpaceX), as well as around the world. In other words, peace and prosperity. And yet, a new virus spreading across the globe, with subsequent stock market unrest; populations on the move from Central America toward the United States, causing border unrest; school shootings and other mass shootings in the United States; weather patterns apparently changing, requiring massive human responses and commitment; the United Kingdom having gone through "Brexit," leaving the European Union, reflecting deep internal political and existential disagreements; funding for science programs in the United States down, and a profound sense of political disagreement within the United States, with an impeached—and acquitted—president, a divided press, and even private citizens of a different political opinion having a hard time engaging in a civil discourse.

Charles Dickens' words from his 1859 novel, *A Tale of Two Cities,* "It was the best of times, it was the worst of times," referred to the era of the French Revolution, but once again they seem appropriate for today. Our quick snapshot does not evoke the enormous upheavals of a recession, or a world conflict, or the threats of terror that we have become so familiar with in the first decades of the twenty-first century (upheavals that may again be on the horizon, of course), but instead we see fears of a pandemic, and the political climate of hostility within the United States has reached levels not seen in a generation. We are, once again, aptly described as a "50-50 Nation." The presidential elections in 2000 and 2016 were particularly close. In 2016, the Republican candidate Donald Trump became our 45th president as the clear winner of the electoral vote, while Democratic candidate Hillary Clinton won the popular vote. And at the time of writing this, a new presidential election is underway.

Even if we have "blue states" and "red states" showing up on the electoral map, there are blue and red areas within each state. This is of course politics, and our main topic is going to be ethics and values, but there is a relevant connection: There is a set of moral values commonly associated with Democratic policies, such as being pro-choice/pro-abortion, increased gun control, LGBTQ rights, and scaling back military operations, and another associated with Republican politics generally advocating pro-life policies, pro-gun ownership rights, and strong support for the military as well as border security. A theory has been voiced by several commentators that there seems to be a drift toward the "left" in the American public, with the gradual acceptance of same-sex marriage, women in combat roles, and concern for intersex equity, but that some viewpoints, often identified as conservative, remain strong, such as support for the 2nd Amendment (gun rights) and border security. These stereotypes don't always hold up, and in addition there is a growing movement of Independents, voters who decline to state a party affiliation on their voter registration form. So it may be misleading to say that the nation is divided down the middle—but it is a clear indication that across this nation we just don't all agree on the details of how one should be a good citizen, other than it is a good thing to have a form of government where the people have the opportunity to vote. So if we're looking for a code of ethics to live by, and even to promote, we should expect that not everyone is going to agree. But what is also commonplace is that we tend to think that those who disagree with us are either stupid, ignorant, or perhaps even evil. Social media are full of such assumptions. And that lends itself to thinking that we, perhaps in fact, are citizens of two cultures within the United States, the culture of liberal values and the culture of conservative values (a pattern known in many other countries with a Western tradition of democracy and right to free speech). Some call it a *culture war*. It has even been labeled a "cold Civil War." So here I have a little recommendation—an introduction of a moral value, if you will: For the sake of a good discussion, whether in the classroom, online, or perhaps just as an internal dialogue with yourself, it may be useful not to jump to the immediate conclusion that people who disagree with you are stupid, ignorant, or evil. As we strive to become a nation of successful diversity, we sometimes forget that *moral and political diversity* also deserves a place alongside diversity of gender, race, religion, economic background, sexual orientation, and so forth. In other words, people have a right to have a wide variety of opinions, and some of these opinions are arrived at through honest and conscientious deliberation. This is where this textbook, true to its previous eight editions, will champion the concept of open-mindedly listening to what the "other side" has to say, even as we may remain convinced of the rationality of our own view. We have little chance of being able to talk with one another and even learn from one another if we keep thinking that everybody who doesn't agree with us is automatically wrong or wrongheaded.

On the other hand, an acceptance of the fact that people disagree on moral issues doesn't have to lead to a moral relativism, or an assumption that there is always another side to everything. Despite our moral differences in this culture, most reasonable people are going to agree on some basic values: In my experience, the majority of Americans are in favor of justice and equality, and against murder, child abuse, racism, sexism, slavery, animal torture, and so forth. In Chapter 3 you'll find a discussion of ethical relativism, and in Chapter 11 you'll find a further discussion of the search for common values in a politically diverse culture.

Living in Interesting Times

Sometimes we hear about an old Chinese saying, *May you live in interesting times*, and, according to tradition, it is meant as a curse, not a benign wish. As a matter of fact, there doesn't seem to actually be such an ancient Chinese expression; the one that comes closest seems to be 1600 century Chinese writer Feng Menlong's opinion that it is "Better to be a dog in a peaceful time than a human in a chaotic world," and the "interesting times" expression seems to have been introduced by Western writers in the 1930s. But whether or not it really is an ancient Chinese curse, or an idea concocted by sarcastic Westerners and attributed to Chinese wisdom, it strikes a chord in many hearts these days. As much as we in the Western modern world have been used to thinking that an exciting life is a good life, there is an ancient cross-cultural wisdom present in the saying, echoed in famous French seventeenth century philosopher René Descartes's personal motto, *Bene vixit qui bene latuit*, "One lives well who hides well": a quiet life, safe from turmoil and violent death, has been the dream of many a human being who has fled destruction and persecution, or kept a low profile hoping that the tide of violence might pass them by. And here we are, in our various cities and regions of the West and around the world, living two kinds of lives these days, our normal lives with their normal hopes for our families, our health and our jobs, and a New Normal life where we are constantly reminded that we are vulnerable, to a degree that few of us had imagined only a few decades ago. The threat of climate change, pandemics, terrorism, and random violence haunts us, and "hiding well" is no guarantee that sudden disaster will pass us by. All this unpredictability takes its toll; even people from cultures that have previously registered high on the "happiness" scale are registering lower than before. Many of us are worried about tomorrow, overall. Some people predict that we in the next half-century may be facing challenges, environmental as well as financial and political, never seen before in recorded human history.

And yet: Human beings are amazingly resilient. Humans have been through plagues, famine, natural disasters, and wholesale abuse by fellow human beings. In other words, we have *always* lived in "interesting times." And perhaps our current era is actually even less "interesting" than earlier centuries. As American-Canadian cognitive scientist and linguist Steven Pinker stresses, statistically we live in far less violent times now than for instance the Middle Ages. In *The Better Angels of Our Nature* (2011) Pinker says,

> "We now know that native peoples, whose lives are so romanticized in today's children's books, had rates of death from warfare that were greater than those of our world wars. The romantic visions of medieval Europe omit the exquisitely crafted instruments of torture and are innocent of the thirtyfold greater risk of murder in those times. The centuries for which people are nostalgic were times in which the wife of an adulterer could have her nose cut off, children as young as eight could be hanged for property crimes, a prisoner's family could be charged for easement of irons, a witch could be sawn in half, and a sailor could be flogged to a pulp. The moral commonplaces of our age, such as that slavery, war, and torture are wrong, would have been seen as saccharine sentimentality, and our notion of universal human rights almost incoherent. . . . The forces of modernity—reason, science, humanism, individual rights—have not, of course, pushed steadily in one direction; nor will they ever bring about a utopia or end the frictions and hurts that come with being human. But on top of all the benefits that modernity has brought us in health, experience, and knowledge, we can add its role in the reduction of violence."

So are we moving toward a kinder, gentler, more peaceful world, because we, as Pinker thinks, are paying more attention to the voice of reason and common sense? An opposing view has been voiced by British political philosopher John Gray who finds Pinker's optimism naive. For Gray, civilization is a fragile entity. In "Steven Pinker is wrong about violence and war" Gray says, "Improvements in civilization are real enough, but they come and go. While knowledge and invention may grow cumulatively and at an accelerating rate, advances in ethics and politics are erratic, discontinuous and easily lost. Amid the general drift, cycles can be discerned: peace and freedom alternate with war and tyranny, eras of increasing wealth with periods of economic collapse. Instead of becoming ever stronger and more widely spread, civilization remains inherently fragile and regularly succumbs to barbarism." So who is right? Are we teetering on the brink of some kind of cultural collapse, or are we just *in medias res* (in the middle of things), looking at chaotic life from the inside, unable to see the bigger and fairly reassuring picture?

As I frequently mention to my students, and I will pass it on to you, the reader, the future envisioned in overall positive terms by Pinker and in negative terms by Gray is, in many ways, in your hands. You may not have the actual power to mold the future, but you will have the power to help inspire and even mold reactions of fellow human beings to whatever challenges are waiting for us, up ahead in the stream of time, through social media, and whatever other kind of media we may have in the future. Being forearmed with knowledge, not only of the past, but with the *values* of both past and present, will help you in your decision-making. And so we embark on this journey into *The Moral of the Story*, examining moral value systems of primarily the Western culture in contemporary and modern times as well as past centuries—because each new idea is generally a reaction to older ideas that have somehow become inadequate. The book, however, is not a chronological journey. It moves through modern moral problems, to equivalents in the past, and back to contemporary scenarios.

The fact is that we all encounter issues involving moral values on an everyday basis; sometimes they involve small decisions, sometimes large ones. Some everyday issues that are in the news are questions about **Internet file sharing**/copying/downloading of copyrighted material. Some find it is rightfully illegal, while others find it to be completely acceptable and even a morally decent thing—sharing new ideas with others. Another issue that you may have been engaged in discussing is the ethics of **texting and communication** on social media such as Instagram and Facebook. What exactly is an appropriate level of intimacy and sharing of information if it risks getting into the wrong hands? And what is the kind of information we can, in all decency, text to each other—is it acceptable to break up through a text message? "Sext"—send sexy pictures taken with or without the portrayed person's permission? Share gossip? All these questions involve an underlying code of ethics. So, too, do the major moral issues we as a society are struggling with: Some of the big questions and even conflicts we have dealt with during the first decade of this century have involved the **right to marry** whomever you choose, including a person of your own gender; the question of the appropriate **response to terrorism** (through the civil courts, or military actions and tribunals); the use of **torture in interrogations** of presumed terrorists; the right to have access to **euthanasia;** the continued question about the moral status of **abortion** (both of these topics are featured in Chapter 13); the periodically resurfacing discussion about the right to **gun ownership;** the moral status of **pets** as property or family members; and other such issues that involve both moral and legal perspectives. This book will deal with some of those issues, but perhaps more important, it will deal with the values underlying those issues—the moral theories explaining those values. Later in this chapter we look at the terms of *values, morals,* and *ethics.* Some questions involving values focus on **how we ought to behave** vis-à-vis other living beings; any moral theory that involves a focus on action, on *what to do,* is known as an *ethic of conduct,* and we will look at various theories of ethics of conduct from Chapter 3 through Chapter 7. However, there is a different kind of moral philosophy that focuses on **developing a good character,** on *how to be,* generally referred to as *virtue ethics,* and that is our topic for Chapters 8 through 11. Of the remaining chapters, this chapter and Chapter 2 explore the current spectrum of moral discussions and the influence of storytelling as a tool for both teaching and learning about moral values. Chapter 12 looks at various models of ethics as seen by feminists, and Chapter 13 represents what is known as "applied ethics," moral philosophies applied to specific cases or scenarios, such as the abortion issue, euthanasia, media ethics, just-war theory, animal rights, and environmental ethics.

For each of the issues mentioned above there is generally a side promoting it and a side arguing against it. We're used to that kind of debate in a free society, and you'll see some of those questions discussed in this book, in particular in Chapters 7 and 13.

Values, Morals, and Ethics

In its most basic sense, what we value is something we believe is set apart from things that we don't value or that we value less. When do we first begin to value something? As babies, we live in a world that is divided into what we like and what we don't like—a binary world of plus and minus, of yes and no. Some psychoanalysts believe we never really get over this early stage, so that some people simply divide the world into what they like or approve of and what they dislike or disapprove of. However, most of us add to that a justification for our preferences or aversions. And this is where the concept of *moral values* comes in. Having values implies that we have a moral code that we live by, or at least that we tell ourselves we try to live by, a set of beliefs about what constitutes *good conduct and a good character.* Perhaps equally important, having values implies that we have a conception of what *society* should be, such as a promoter of values we consider good, a safety net for when things go wrong, an overseer that punishes bad behavior and rewards good behavior, a caregiver for all our basic needs, or a minimalist organization that protects the people against internal and external enemies but otherwise leaves them alone to pursue their own happiness. In Chapter 7 we examine several of these conceptions of social values.

When they hear I teach ethics, people who are unfamiliar with how college classes in the subject are taught say, "Good! Our college students really need that!" That response always makes me pause: What do they think I teach? Right from wrong? Of course, we do have discussions about right and wrong, and we can, from time to time, even reach agreement about some moral responses being *preferable* to other moral responses. If students haven't acquired a sense of values by the time they're in college, I fear it's too late: Psychologists say a child must develop a sense of values *by the age of seven* to become an adult with a conscience. If the child hasn't learned by the second grade that other people can feel pain and pleasure, and that one should try not to harm others, that lesson will probably never be truly learned. Fortunately, that doesn't mean everyone must be taught the *same* moral lessons by the age of seven—as long as we have *some* moral background to draw on later, as a sounding board for further ethical reflections, we can come from morally widely diverse homes and still become morally dependable people. A child growing up in a mobster type of family will certainly have acquired a set of morals by the age of seven—but it isn't necessarily the same set of morals as those acquired by a child in a liberal, secular, humanist family or in a Seventh-Day Adventist family. The point is that all these children will have their "moral center" activated and can expand their moral universe. A child who has never been taught *any* moral lessons may be a sociopath of the future, a person who has no comprehension of how other people feel, no empathy. A case that garnered attention some years ago, and introduced a new concept, "affluenza," was the 2013 case of Ethan Couch, then 16 years old, whose drunk driving resulted in the deaths of four people. At his trial, a psychologist testified for the defense that growing up in a very affluent, permissive family had not taught him right from wrong. Whether or not this argument was just a lawyer's clever trick, it highlighted the possibility that we indeed have to be exposed to ideas of right and wrong as children in order to recognize them as significant later in life. And with the attempted flight of Couch and his mother to Mexico in 2015, it seemed clear that Couch's lack of understanding that one must take responsibility for one's actions was something that his mother may not have sufficiently understood, either. In 2016 a Texas judge ordered him to serve 2 years in prison, 180 days for each of the four victims. Couch was released in April 2018, but in January 2020 he was again arrested for violation of his probation.

If having moral values has to do with brain chemistry, and with simple likes and dislikes, why don't we turn to the disciplines of neuroscience and psychology for an understanding of values? Why is philosophy the discipline that examines the values issue? That question goes to the core of what philosophy is: Neuroscience can tell us about the physical underpinnings of our mental life and possibly whether our mental reactions have a correlation to the world we live in, but as you will see below, it can't tell us whether our mental processes are socially appropriate or inappropriate, morally justified or unjustified, and so forth. Neuroscience has recently identified areas in the brain where moral decisions involving empathy take place, but that doesn't mean that neuroscientists can tell us *which* moral decisions are more correct than others. Psychology can tell us only what people believe and possibly why they believe it; it can't make a statement about whether people are justified in believing it. Philosophy's job, at least in this context, is to *question* our values; it forces us to provide *reasons,* and preferably good reasons, for giving our moral approval to one type of behavior and disapproving of another. Philosophy asks the fundamental question *Why?,* in all its fields, including the field of value theory/ethics. (Box 1.1 gives an overview of the classic branches within philosophy.) Why do we have the values we have? Why do values make some people give up their comfort, even their lives, for a cause, or for other people's welfare? Why do some people disregard the values of their society for a chosen cause or for personal gain? Is it ever morally appropriate to think of yourself and not of others? Are there ultimate absolute moral values, or are they a matter of personal or cultural choices? Such fundamental questions can be probed by philosophy in a deeper and more fundamental way than by neuroscience or psychology, and we will explore such questions in the upcoming chapters.

Box 1.1 THE FOUR CLASSIC BRANCHES OF PHILOSOPHY

In the chapter text, you read that philosophy traditionally asks the question *Why?* This is one of the features that has characterized Western philosophy from its earliest years in Greek antiquity.

The word "philosophy" itself comes from Greek: *Philo* = love, and *sophia* = wisdom. So someone who loves wisdom is essentially a philosopher, at least according to the ancient Greeks. Notice that they didn't call it "love of knowledge." You might ask yourself, why? Does the search for knowledge always result in wisdom?

We generally date Western philosophy from approximately seven hundred years B.C.E./B.C. ("before the common era"/"before Christ"), when some Greek thinkers, such as Thales, Heraclitus, and Parmenides, began to ask questions about what *reality* truly consists of: Is it the way we perceive it through the senses, or is there an underlying true reality that our intellect can understand? Thales believed the underlying reality was water; Heraclitus believed that it was a form of ever-changing energy; and Parmenides saw true reality as being an underlying realm of permanence, elements that don't change. We call this form of philosophy *metaphysics;* in Chapter 8 you will read a brief introduction to Plato's famous theory of metaphysics, but otherwise the topic of metaphysics has only indirect bearing on the topic of this book. A few centuries after Thales, the next area of philosophy that manifested itself was *ethics,* with Socrates' questioning of what is the right way to live (see chapter text). Two generations later the third area of philosophy was introduced, primarily through the writings of Aristotle: *logic,* the establishing of rules for proper thinking as opposed to fallacious thinking. But the fourth area of Western philosophy didn't really take hold in the minds of thinkers until some two

thousand years later, in the seventeenth century, when René Descartes began to seriously explore what the mind can know: *epistemology,* or theory of knowledge. All four branches of philosophy are represented today in school curricula and enjoy vibrant debates within the philosophical community. The only branch to have languished somewhat is metaphysics, since modern science has answered some of its ancient questions: We now know about the subnuclear reality of quantum mechanics. But a classical question of metaphysics remains unanswered by science (even if most scientists have an opinion about the question): What is the nature of the human mind? Do we have a soul that outlives our bodies, or will our self be extinguished with the demise of our brain?

Until the mid–twentieth century, philosophy was usually taught in the West with the underlying assumption that philosophy as such was, by and large, a Western phenomenon. That rather ethnocentric attitude has changed considerably over the last decades. It is now recognized unequivocally among Western scholars that Asian philosophy has its own rich traditions of exploration of metaphysics and ethics in particular; and some philosophers point out that in a sense, all cultures have metaphysics and ethics, even if they have no body of philosophical literature, because their legends, songs, and religious stories will constitute the culture's view of reality as well as the moral rules and their justifications. As for logic and epistemology, they are not as frequently encountered in non-Western cultures: Indian philosophy has established its own tradition of logic, but epistemology remains a Western philosophical specialty, according to most Western scholars.

To the four classic branches, philosophy has added a number of specialized fields over the centuries, such as philosophy of art (aesthetics), social philosophy, philosophy of religion, political philosophy, philosophy of sports, philosophy of human nature, philosophy of gender, and philosophy of science. What makes these fields philosophical inquiries is their special approach to their subjects; they investigate not only the nature of art, social issues, religion, politics, and so on, but also the theoretical underpinnings of each field, its hidden assumptions and agendas, and its future moral and social pitfalls and promises.

If having values is such an important feature of our life, should elementary schools teach values, then? It may be just a little too late, if indeed a child's moral sense is developed by the age of seven, but at least there is a chance it might help; and for children whose parents have done a minimal job of teaching them respect for others, school will probably be the only place they'll learn it. Some elementary schools are developing such programs. Problems occur, however, when schools begin to teach values with which not all parents agree. We live in a culture of diversity, and although some parents might like certain topics to be on the school agenda, others certainly would not. Some parents want their children to have early access to sex education, whereas others consider it unthinkable as a school subject. There is nothing in the concept of values that implies we all have to subscribe to exactly the same ones, no matter how strongly we may feel about our own. So, beyond teaching basic values such as common courtesy, perhaps the best schools can do is make students aware of values and value differences and let students learn to argue effectively for their own values, as well as to question them. Schools, in other words, should focus on *ethics* in addition to *morality.*

So what is the difference between *ethics* and *morality? Ethics* comes from Greek (*ethos,* character) and *morality* from Latin (*mores,* character, custom, or habit). Today, in English as well as in many other Western languages, both words refer to some form of proper conduct. Although we, in our everyday lives, don't distinguish clearly between morals and ethics, there is a subtle difference: Some people think the word *morality* has negative connotations, and in fact it does carry two different sets of associations for most of us. The positive ones are guidance, goodness, humanitarianism, and so forth. Among the negative associations are repression, bigotry, persecution—in a word, *moralizing.* Suppose the introductory ethics course on your campus was labeled "Introduction to Morals." You would, in all likelihood, expect something different from what you would expect from a course called "Introduction to Ethics" or "Introduction to Values." The word *morality* has a slightly different connotation from that of the terms *ethics* and *values.* That is because *morality* usually refers to *the moral rules we follow,* the values that we have. *Ethics* is generally defined as *theories about those rules;* ethics questions and justifies the rules we live by, and, if ethics can find no rational justification for those rules, it may ask us to abandon them. Morality is the stuff our social life is made of—even our personal life—and ethics is the ordering, the questioning, the awareness, the investigation of what we believe: Are we justified in believing it? Is it consistent? Should we remain open to other beliefs or not? If we live by a system of moral rules, we may or may not have understood them or even approved of them, but if we have a code of ethics, we signal to the world that we stand by our values, understand them, and are ready to not only act on them but also defend them with words and deeds.

In other words, it is not enough just to have moral rules; we should, as moral, mature persons, be able to justify our viewpoints with ethical arguments or, at the very least, ask ourselves why we feel this way or that about a certain issue. Ethics, therefore, is much more than a topic in a curriculum. As moral adults, we are required to think about ethics all the time.

Most people, in fact, do just that, even in their teens, because it is also considered a sign of maturity to question authority, at least to a certain extent. If a very young adult is told to be home at 11 P.M., she or he will usually ask, "Why can't I stay out till midnight?" When we have to make up our minds about whether to study over the weekend or go hiking, we usually try to come up with as many pros and cons as we can. When someone we have put our trust in betrays that trust, we want to know why. All those questions are practical applications of ethics: They question the rules of morality and the breaking of those rules. Although formal training in ethical questions can make us better at judging moral issues, we are, as adult human beings, already quite experienced just because we already have asked "Why?" a number of times in our lives.

Good and Evil

You have probably heard the "E-word" (evil) recently, in conversation or in the media. And *good* is surely one of the most frequently used words in the English language. But interestingly, for most of the previous century ethicists preferred to use terms such as "morally acceptable and unacceptable," or "right versus wrong," rather than good versus evil. That pattern seems to be changing, and we'll talk about why in this section.

Tham Luang Rescue Operation Center/AP Images

For 18 days in June and July 2018, twelve boys between 11 and 16 years of age from a junior football team and their 25-year-old coach were trapped deep in a system of caves in Thailand by rising waters. What was supposed to have been an outing after football practice became a nightmare in the dark. After nine days, they were located by two British divers, all alive, but the rescue mission was in itself a challenge. The boys had to be taught how to stay calm during the long trek out, some of it under water. The world was watching on TV as the boys emerged, one by one over several days, in time before the next heavy rainfall. All the boys and their coach were rescued, but one rescuer, a former Thai Navy SEAL, died from asphyxiation, and another Thai SEAL died later from blood poisoning, a result of the rescue ordeal. Thailand opened the Tham Luang caves to tourism in November of 2019.

When terrible things happen to ordinary people, including natural disasters as well as calamities of human origin, we frequently hear stories of people who are not only victims of the disaster, but also subsequent victims of human schemes of violence or fraud. But we also hear about people who go out of their way to help others. In 2015, three young American males, two service members and a college student, thwarted a terrorist attack on a high-speed passenger train headed for Paris by tackling and subduing the terrorist, risking their lives in the process. In October 2017, a shooter targeted a concert audience in Las Vegas; from his windows at a high-rise hotel, he shot 58 people to death and wounded more than 400. Several people in the audience went out of their way to help others to safety. Among them was Jonathan Smith, who helped 30 individuals get out of harm's way. He was himself injured but survived. In June 2018, twelve boys between 11 and 16 years of age and their 25-year-old leader were trapped in a cave in Thailand, with waters rising. After nine days in the cold and dark cave, they were discovered by two divers, but it took almost two weeks for the boys to be rescued because of the very difficult layout of the cave system. A team of Thai SEALs brought them all out safely over the course of three days, but it cost the lives of two of the SEALs (see the photo on p.8). And in New Zealand in March 2019, Abdul Aziz, having immigrated from Afghanistan, confronted and attacked the gunman who had just murdered 50 worshipers at two mosques, and forced him into fleeing, making it possible for two local police officers to apprehend him.

Such stories (of which you will hear more in Chapter 4 where we will discuss the phenomena of selfishness and altruism) remind us that dreadful things can happen in the blink of an eye, sometimes due to natural disasters and sometimes due to deliberate actions by fellow human beings, but also that there are extraordinary people who will rise to the occasion and make decisions that may cost them their lives for the sake of others. That, to most of us, may be the ultimate form of goodness, but the everyday kindness of a helping hand or a considerate remark shouldn't be discounted, even if the kind person isn't endangering his or her life.

There is hardly a word with a broader meaning in the English language than *good*—we can talk about food tasting good, test results being good, a feeling being good, but also, of course, of actions being good and persons being good, and we mean something different in all these examples. In Box 1.2 you'll find a discussion of moral and nonmoral values, and "good" fits right into that discussion: It is a value term because it expresses approval, but it can be an approval that has to do with moral issues (such as actions and a person's character) or it can be unrelated to moral issues, such as judging the result of a quiz, or a medical test, or something we approve of because of its aesthetic qualities (it looks good, tastes good, sounds good). If we assume that we're interested mostly in the moral value of "good," we have only narrowed it down somewhat, because now we have to define what, in our context and in our culture, is considered a morally good act. It could be acting according to the rules of one's culture's religion; it could be acting with compassion or with foresight as to the overall consequences of one's actions; or it could be simply doing one's duty. A "good person" could be someone who is simply nice by nature, but it could also be someone who struggles to do the right thing, perhaps even against his or her nature. Or it could be simply someone we approve of, based on our cultural rules. That particular moral attitude will be discussed in Chapter 3, *Ethical Relativism*.

Box 1.2 MORAL AND NONMORAL VALUES

What is a *value?* Most often the word refers to a moral value, a judgment of somebody's behavior according to whether or not it corresponds to certain moral rules (for example, "Madison is a wonderful person; she always stays after the party to help with the dishes"). However, some value judgments have nothing to do with moral issues, and so they are called *nonmoral,* which is not the same as *immoral* (breaking moral rules) or *amoral* (not having any moral standards). Such nonmoral value judgments can include statements about taste (such as "The new gallery downtown has a collection of exquisite watercolors"; "I really dislike Ramon's new haircut"; and "Finn makes a great jambal-aya"), as well as statements about being correct or incorrect about facts (such as "Lois did really well on her last math test" and "You're wrong; last Saturday we didn't go to the movies; that was last Sunday"). Like moral value judgments, nonmoral value judgments generally refer to something being right or wrong, good or bad; but, unlike moral value judgments, they don't refer to morally right or wrong behavior. Non-moral value concepts abound in our present-day society: What we call *aesthetics*, art theory, is a form of nonmoral value theory, asking questions such as, Are there objective rules for when art is good? and Is it bad, or is it a matter of personal taste or of acculturation? If you dis-like hip-hop music, or like Craftsman-style archi-tecture, are there valid objective justifications for your likes and dislikes, or are they relative to your time and place? Art theory even has an additional values concept: the relationship between light and dark colors in a painting. But the most prevalent nonmoral value concept in our everyday world surely has to do with getting *good value*—with buying something for less than it is worth. That prompted a political commen-tator, Michael Kinsley, who was fed up with the political talk about moral values a few years ago, to quip, "When I want values, I go to Wal-Mart." And McDonald's has been running a commer-cial suggesting that parents who want *family val-ues* should take their kids to McDonald's for the Value Meal, appealing to the perennial parental guilt. In other words, satirists and copywriters can have a field day doing a switcheroo on our conception of values, from nonmoral to moral and back again, and what we readers and con-sumers can do is stay on our toes so we aren't manipulated.

In our everyday life, we encounter the term *evil* frequently in the media and entertainment, and most of us use it regularly. We even have a character in a popular series of comic movies about retro hero Austin Powers, Dr. Evil, who really is quite evil, and enjoying it. Entire film franchises and book series are centered around the fight against evil, such as the *Harry Potter* series, *X-Men, Lord of the Rings,* and perhaps more than any other story franchise, *Star Wars.* But entertainment is one thing that we can leave behind. Real life is another thing: Survivors of massacres will carry those memories with them for the remainder of their lives, and friends and relatives of victims lost to violence will feel that loss forever. The first decades of the twenty-first century have been marred and punctuated by deliberate acts of harm toward what most of us would call "innocents"—people, including children, who have never in their lives committed any acts that would warrant any aggressive action toward them. There have been acts of terror against entire communities, from the terror attacks of 9/11, 2001, to the Boston Marathon bombings of 2013, the mass murders in San Bernardino in 2015, and the synagogue shooting in Pittsburgh in 2018. There have also been numerous school shootings over the years, such as at Virginia Tech in 2007, at Sandy Hook Elementary School in Newtown, CT, in 2012, and the Parkland, FL school shooting in 2018, prompting school administrations around the country to take measures and train school personnel in "Active Shooter" scenarios.

And then we have the media favorites: the serial-killer stories where killers manage to evade the law for months, sometimes even decades, preying on young or otherwise vulnerable members of society—children, prostitutes, and drug addicts. From the BTK (Bind, Torture, Kill) killer Dennis Rader, to Joseph Duncan, who killed an entire family in Idaho so he could abduct and abuse the two youngest children (of whom only the little girl survived, to become an excellent and clear-minded witness against him) to the Golden State Killer, captured in 2018 and accused of 12 murders and 40 rapes over a period of 30 years. In Austria Josef Fritzl was arrested for having kept his own daughter captive in a hidden room in the basement for twenty-four years, raping her and fathering seven children with her. In Perris, California David and Louise Turpin pleaded guilty to shackling and torturing their 13 children. They are serving a 25-year-to-life sentence. And in Minnesota, 13-year-old Jayme Closs was kidnapped and kept prisoner by a man who had killed her parents so he could abduct her. After almost 3 months she managed to escape, and her kidnapper was caught. Bottom line: Extreme wrongdoing, with devastating consequences for victims, doesn't have to be on a grand scale such as mass murders and serial killings; victimizing defenseless children also qualifies.

The question we need to ask here is this: Are such people who victimize others—humans or animals—evil? Or should we just say that their *actions* are evil? Or should we use another term entirely, such as being *morally wrong*?

What do the professionals—the ethicists who make a living teaching theories of moral values and writing papers, monographs, and textbooks—say? For centuries scholars distinguished between *natural evil* (disasters) and *moral evil,* referring to human choices going against the will of God. Until the end of the nineteenth century it was still quite common for philosophers to talk about moral evil, but for most of the twentieth century ethicists preferred to talk about issues such as selfishness and unselfishness, informed consent, group rights versus individual rights, as well as moral right and wrong, even occasionally moral *goodness,* but up until recently we rarely heard professional ethicists mention the concept of *evil.* Exceptions would be American philosophers such as Philip Hallie and Richard Taylor and the British philosopher Mary Midgley. However, times are changing, and even in the philosophical debate today the term *evil* is seeing a resurgence. So why were so few philosophers up until very recently interested in talking about good and evil, when it was one of the key topics in centuries past? For one thing, there has been an underlying assumption that good and evil are *religious* concepts, and as we shall see, the philosophical discussions about ethics and values have generally tended to steer clear of the religious connection to ethics. For another, talking about good and evil generally implies that we *pass judgment* on what is good and what is evil—which means that we take sides. We no longer analyze concepts in some lofty realm of objectivity, we engage ourselves in seeking good and shunning evil. It also means that we condemn those who are labeled evil and praise those we call good. In other words, we engage in what some would call *moralizing,* and most ethicists have for decades tried to avoid just that, with some exceptions. However, since September 11, 2001, the concept of evil has been part of our political vocabulary, spearheaded by President Bush, who labeled nations supporting terrorism as an *axis of evil* and referred to the terrorists of 9/11 and others as *evildoers.* A precedent was created when President Reagan labeled the Soviet Union "The Evil Empire" in the 1980s. Although that terminology, to some critics, is far too close to a religious vocabulary for comfort, for other Americans there is great relief and, indeed, comfort in being able to use a word with the weight of tradition behind it to describe something most of us consider dreadful acts committed by people with no consideration for human decency, and the more of such acts we see perpetrated on what we might call innocent people, the more we're likely to use the "E-word." But what exactly do we call evil? Is evil a force that exists outside human beings—is there a source of evil such as the devil, some satanic eternal power that tempts and preys on human souls? Or is it, rather, a force within the human mind, disregarding the needs and interests of other human beings just to accomplish a goal? Or might it perhaps be a *lack of* something essential, similar to what medieval scholars called *privatio,* absence of goodness? Maybe a blind spot in the human mind, a lack of a sense of community, belonging, empathy for others? In that case, might we explain the acts of evildoers as those of sick individuals? But wouldn't that entail that they can't be *blamed* for what they do, because we don't usually blame people for their illnesses? Those are questions that involve religion, psychology, and ethics, and there is to this day no consensus among scholars as to how "evil" should be interpreted. Some see terrorists, serial killers, and child molesters as evil, but we may not agree on what makes them evil—a childhood deprived of love, a genetic predisposition, a selfish choice that involves disregard for other people's humanity, a brainwashing by an ideology that distinguishes between "real" people and throwaway people, an outside superhuman evil force that chooses a human vehicle? For the German philosopher Immanuel Kant, whom you'll meet in Chapter 6, there was no doubt what evil is: the self-serving choice that individuals make freely, even when they know full well the moral law they ought to be following.

Kant's view comes out of the eighteenth century, however, and as you have seen above, philosophers of the twentieth century generally steered away from calling people or actions evil, with one notable exception, and that exception started a trend that continues to this day: the introduction of the concept "the Banality of Evil," a term coined by German philosopher Hannah Arendt in 1963 in her book *Adolf Eichmann in Jerusalem: A Report on the Banality of Evil.*

Fred Stein Archive/Archive Photos/Getty Images

Hannah Arendt (1906–1975) was a Jewish-German philosopher who narrowly escaped the Holocaust of World War II. She left Germany in 1933, the year Hitler came into power, and spent some time in Switzerland and France, but with the Nazi occupation of Northern France in 1941, and the subsequent collaboration by the French government, she was interned in a labor camp with French Jews. She was released and able to emigrate to the United States, where she became a naturalized citizen in 1950. Her major works are *The Origins of Totalitarianism* (1951), *The Human Condition* (1958), and *Eichmann in Jerusalem: A Report on the Banality of Evil* (1963). Her life was chronicled in the 2012 film, *Hannah Arendt.*

Arendt was living in Germany when Hitler came to power, but she managed to flee to Paris before the Holocaust: She was a German Jew, and would undoubtedly have been swept up in the extermination process. Years after the war she was tormented not only by the thought of the atrocities perpetrated in the death camps but also by the knowledge that so many human beings either stood by and let the Holocaust happen or actively participated in the torture and death of other human beings. (And, for the record, the Holocaust *did* happen—13 million people perished in the Nazi death camps on the orders of Hitler and his henchmen Himmler and Eichmann, and those who deny that fact are playing political games. Enough said.) The conclusion reached by Arendt and published in her book from 1963 after having witnessed Eichmann's trial in Jerusalem is that the German public who had an inkling of what was going on and the Nazis who were actively engaged in the *Endlösung*, or the "Final Solution," were not evil in the sense that they (or most of them) deliberately sought to gain personal advantage by causing pain and suffering to others. Rather, it was more insidious: Little by little, they came to view the atrocities they were asked to perform, or disregard, as a duty to their country and their leader, as something their victims deserved, or simply as a normal state of affairs and not something hideous or depraved. They became *banal*, everyday acts, corrupting the minds of the victimizers. In Arendt's words about Eichmann's execution for his participation in the Holocaust:

It was as though in those last minutes he was summing up the lesson that this long course in human wickedness had taught us—the lesson of the fearsome, word-and-thought- defying *banality of evil.* . . . The trouble with Eichmann was precisely that so many were like him, and that the many were neither perverted nor sadistic, that they were, and still are, terribly and terrifyingly normal. From the viewpoint of our legal institutions and of our moral standards of judgment, this normality was much more terrifying than all the atrocities put together, for it implied—as had been said at Nuremberg over and over again by the defendants and their counsels—that this new type of criminal . . . commits his crimes under circumstances that make it well-nigh impossible for him to know or to feel that he is doing wrong. . . .

With Arendt's introduction of the banality—or normalcy—of evil, the philosophical discussion of moral wrongdoing took a new turn. Could it be that horrendous acts of harm done by ordinary people should be seen as "not really their fault"? As something they were brainwashed into doing? Arendt herself seems to lean in that direction by viewing Eichmann himself merely a bureaucrat who was somehow swept up by an ideology, but as German philosopher Bettina Stangneth mentions in her book *Eichmann Before Jerusalem: The Unexamined Life of a Mass-Murderer* (2014), Eichmann was anything but a victim, he was truly the mastermind behind much of the Holocaust, knowing full well what he did, and how it affected the lives of fellow Germans. According to Stangneth, in her desire to show that ordinary people can be manipulated into doing horrible things, Arendt ended up casting her net too wide, and making apologies for the truly malicious indiuals, the manipulators themselves. But regardless of whether Arendt was right or wrong about Eichmann himself, her notion of Banality of Evil allowed philosophers to once again engage in discussions about evil, without having to deal with any religious context, and the term "evil" once again found a home in moral debates, in a limited way, and it has turned out to be eminently useful in explaining group pressures and bullying, even among children. In the Narratives section at the end of the chapter, we look at a film depicting the trial of Adolf Eichmann, *The Eichmann Show,* which raises the question whether we might all be capable of doing monstrous things to innocent fellow human beings.

In addition, coming out of the concept of evil becoming everyday-like, banal, there is an implication: that it is possible to fight the group-pressures or pressures from authorities that may result in a Banality-of-evil scenario. Many of you have heard of Stanley Milgram's obedience experiments at Yale University in the 1960s, wherein Professor Milgram showed that if you are under the influence of an authority who takes responsibility for your actions, you are likely to be willing to commit acts of atrocity toward other human beings; he demonstrated that test subjects, believing themselves to be assisting with an experiment, would overcome their unwillingness to give electric shocks to test subjects in another room (in reality actors who weren't being harmed at all) to the point of killing them, as long as they were told they had to do it, and it was not their responsibility. A film, *Experimenter* (2015), explores Milgram's obedience experiments and their impact on our self-image. The other infamous experiment that you may have heard of is the Stanford Prison Experiment in 1971, conducted by psychologist professor Philip Zimbardo, wherein a group of experimental subjects—ordinary male college students—were divided into "prisoners" and "prison guards," in order to examine why conditions would deteriorate so quickly in a real prison setting. Before long the "prison guards" began treating the "prisoners" with abusive cruelty, believing that such behavior was somehow warranted to maintain authority, and Zimbardo had to terminate the experiment within less than a week. Both an American film, *The Stanford Prison Experiment*, and a German version, titled *The Experiment,* are chilling reenactments of the experiment. Some see such an event as proof that human nature is fundamentally bad—it doesn't take much for the veneer of civilization to wear thin, and our true, evil nature surfaces. For others, all this means is that there are all kinds of reasons why people do what they do; some of what we call evil is based on a moral choice, and some of it is an outcome of environmental pressures or brain anomalies.

In 2007 Zimbardo published a book, *The Lucifer Effect,* in which he drew parallels between the experiment and the Abu Ghraib incident of 2004 in which American military personnel guarding suspected terrorists in Iraq subjected them to psychological torture, focusing specifically on the power of humans to resist the pressure from authorities, find enough moral fortitude, and say no to allowing acts of harm to escalate into some kind of permitted, normal, banal behavior. In his own words, "Three decades earlier, I had witnessed eerily similar scenes as they unfolded in a project I directed, of my own design: naked, shackled prisoners with bags over their heads, guards stepping on prisoners' backs as they did push-ups, guards sexually humiliating prisoners, and prisoners suffering from extreme stress. . . . As the project's principal investigator, I designed the experiment that randomly assigned normal, healthy, intelligent college students to enact the roles of either guards or prisoners in a realistically simulated prison setting." Zimbardo sees a similar group mentality being responsible for both the Stanford Prison experiment and the American soldiers at Abu Ghraib in Iraq in 2004.

But before we begin to assume that all evil acts are of the kind that may lurk in ordinary people's hearts, let us just remind ourselves that not all evil acts are banal. Surely, the deliberate torturing and killing of children is not the kind of evil that ordinary people are periodically persuaded to perform under extraordinary circumstances, and neither are deliberate mass murders. For such acts involving deliberate choices directly intending and resulting in harm to innocent people we may want to reserve the terms *egregious* or *extreme evil*. If we want to adopt the vocabulary of "evil," in addition to "morally wrong" and "misguided," we must also recognize that there are *degrees* of evil, ranging from reluctantly causing pain (such as in the Milgram experiments) to humiliating other human beings, to abusing, torturing, and killing them with deliberation and gusto. And perhaps it is a disservice to our sense of evil to assume that "we're all capable of doing evil." Some forms of evil are the result not of ordinary people being seduced into insensitivity but of some people's deliberate choices to cause harm—such as Adolf Eichmann. A study by Allan Feinigstein in *Theory and Psychology* (2015) points out that most Nazi perpetrators actually didn't show any remorse, and some even seemed to relish the torture and suffering they inflicted—so they actually didn't fall under the "banality of evil" category at all. And on the other hand, even in the Stanley Milgram experiment some test subjects refused to push the shock lever. In Chapter 11, in the section about the philosopher Philip Hallie, you'll read a story that goes into detail about rising up against evil: the story of a French village that rebelled against the Nazis. Hallie presents this story as an "antidote to cruelty," and you will find an additional reference to Philip Zimbardo and his coining of a new term, "the banality of heroism," a theory that claims that if evil is a possibility in our hearts, so, too, are heroism and altruism—in other words, inherent *goodness*.

Even if we have now taken a look at some different meanings of the term *evil*, we have of course by no means exhausted the topic, but a further discussion would be outside the scope of an introductory chapter. We might continue talking about where we think evil originates—as a failing to see others as equal human beings, maybe even a brain deficiency that excludes empathy? Or is it willful selfishness? In Chapter 4 we look at the concepts of selfishness and unselfishness. Or is it just a matter of perspective—one culture's evil is another culture's goodness? And does it matter whether a deliberate, harmful act is committed in the name of a political or religious cause? Would that make the act less or maybe more evil? We look at the question of different cultural values in Chapter 3. Or we might also ask the question that has troubled many cultures for thousands of years, generally known as the *Problem of Evil:* If there is a god, and he, she, or it is a well-intended, all-powerful being, then why do terrible things happen to good people? That question, profound as it may be, belongs within *Philosophy of Religion* and lies beyond the scope of this textbook. That doesn't mean you're not welcome to think about its implications.

Debating Moral Issues from Religion to Neurobiology and Storytelling

Every functional society on earth has had a philosophy of what one should do or be in order to be considered a good person. Sometimes that moral code is expressed orally in stories and songs, and sometimes it is expressed in writing. When it is expressed as a set of rules with explanations justifying the rules, we may call it a *code of ethics*. For it to become a philosophical discipline, we must add the practice of examining and questioning the rules.

The Socratic Beginnings of Ethics

The Greek philosopher Socrates (fifth century B.C.E.) is often credited with being the first philosopher in the Western tradition to focus on ethics. That can be a reasonable observation, provided we don't confuse ethics with morals. It would, of course, be preposterous to claim that any one person, including a famous philosopher, should get credit for inventing morals. Every society since the dawn of time has had a moral code, even if all it consisted of was "respect the chief and your elders." Without a communal moral code you simply can't maintain a society, and in every generation parents have been the primary teachers of the continuity of morality. In addition, as we'll see in the next section, every society on the planet seems to have had a religion of some sort, and into every religion is built a moral code. So what did Socrates contribute, if he didn't invent morals? He elevated the discussion of morals to the level of an academic, critical examination, exploration, and justification of values. It became an abstract discussion that was, for the first time in the West, removed from both religious dogma and social rules, at the same time becoming a personal matter of growth and wisdom. Most of our knowledge of Socrates comes from the works of the philosopher Plato, one of his students. In his series of *Dialogues,* conversations between Socrates and various friends, students, and enemies, Plato has Socrates observe, on his final day before being executed for crimes against the Athenian state (see Chapter 8), that "the unexamined life is not worth living," and that the ultimate question for every human being is, "How should one live?" Acquiring moral wisdom is thus a requirement for a person who doesn't want to go through life with blinders on. Although we can imagine that wise old men and women may have taught the same lesson throughout human time, Socrates was the first that we know of to incorporate critical questions about moral values into a study of philosophical issues for adults. In other words, Socrates became the inventor of ethics as an *academic discipline,* not just a critical lifestyle. And for over 2000 years, philosophers in the West have included the study of ethics in their curricula, including the notion that to be a morally mature person you must engage in a personal critical examination of your own values and the values of your society. The famed *Socratic* or *dialectic method* has two major points: that if you approach an issue rationally, other rational minds will be able to accept your conclusion, and that a useful approach is a conversation, a *dialogue,* between teacher and student. The teacher will guide the student through a series of questions and answers to a rational conclusion, rather than give the student the answer up front. The method is to this day a favorite among philosophy instructors, psychotherapists, and law school professors.

Moral Issues and Religion

Cultures developing independently of the Western tradition have experienced a similar fascination for the subject of acting and living right. Socrates' version remains unique among ancient thinkers because he encouraged critical thinking instead of emphasizing being an obedient citizen. In China, Confucius expressed his philosophy of proper moral conduct as a matter of obedience to authorities and, above all, respect for one's elders at approximately the same time that Socrates was teaching students critical thinking in the public square in Athens. In Africa, tribal thinkers developed a strong sense of morality that stressed individuals' sense of responsibility to the community and the community's understanding of its responsibility to each individual—a philosophy that has become known to the West in recent years through the proverb "It takes a village to raise a child." Among American Indian tribes, the philosophy of harmony between humans and their environment—animate as well as inanimate nature—has been part of the moral code. (We take a look at traditional Chinese values in Chapter 11, and in Chapter 8 we return to traditional African as well as American Indian value systems.)

For all cultures, however, there is a common denominator: Go back far enough in time and you'll find a connection between the social life of the culture, its *mores,* and its religion. In some cultures the connection is clear and obvious to this day: Religion is the key to the moral values of the members of the community, and any debate about values usually takes place within the context of that religion. In other cultures, such as large parts of Europe, Canada, Australia, and to some extent the United States, the connection to religion has become more tenuous and has in some cases all but vanished; public social life has become secularized, and moral values are generally tied to the question of social coexistence rather than to a religious basis. That doesn't mean that individual people can't feel a strong connection to the religious values of their family and their community. This raises several questions, all depending on one's viewpoint and personal experience.

If you have grown up in a culture where religion is a predominant cultural phenomenon, or if you have grown up in a religious family, or if you find yourself deeply connected to a religious community today, do you regard your moral values as being inextricably tied to your religion? Do you regard moral values as being closely connected to religion as such? If that is your background, then chances are that you'll answer yes.

And if you have grown up in a Western, largely secularized culture such as big-city USA, and have not grown up in a religious family, or have distanced yourself from religion for some reason or other, do you view the question of religion as irrelevant for moral values in a modern society and for your own moral decisions? Chances are that you'll answer yes, if this description applies to you.

Here, in a nutshell, is the problem when talking about religion and values. In this diverse world—diverse not just because of nationalities, ethnicity, gender, and religion but also because of the vast variety of moral and political views even within one community—it is very hard for us to reach any kind of consensus or find common ground about values if we seek answers exclusively in our religion. Chances are that if you have a religion, it is not shared by a large number of people you associate with. If you stick exclusively to the group you share your faith (or nonfaith) with, of course you will feel fortified by the confirmation of your views through your religion, and your ideas aren't going to be challenged; but if you plan to be out and about in the greater society of this Western culture, you can't expect everyone to agree with you. (In Chapter 3 we discuss the issue of how to approach the subject of moral differences.) So how does moral philosophy approach this issue? Interestingly, you'll find religious as well as nonreligious moral philosophers in modern times. Go back to the nineteenth century and beyond, and you will find that almost all the Western moral philosophers were religious—Christian or Jewish. In the twentieth century there was a sharp increase in moral philosophers who chose a secular basis of reasoning for their ethics, and that remains a feature of today's ethical debates. But even in centuries past, most philosophers who argued about ethics and who professed to be religious tended to avoid using their religion as the ultimate justification for their moral values. Because, how can you argue with faith? Either you share the faith or you don't. But argue on a basis of rationality, and you have a chance of reaching an understanding of values, even if you disagree about religion—or at least you may gain an understanding of where the other person is coming from. *Reason* as a tool of ethics can be a bridge builder between believers, atheists, and agnostics. For agnostics and atheists, there can be no turning to religion for unquestioned moral guidance, because they view religion itself as an unknown or nonexistent factor. Agnostics claim that they do not know whether there is a God or that it is impossible to know. Atheists claim that there is no God. Both the agnostic and the atheist may find that religion suggests solutions to their problems, but such solutions are accepted not because they come from religion but because they somehow make sense.

For a philosophical inquiry, the requirement that a solution make sense is particularly important; although religion may play a significant role in the development of moral values for many people, a philosophical investigation of moral issues must involve more than faith in a religious authority. Regardless of one's religious belief or lack thereof, such an investigation must involve reasoning because, for one thing, philosophy teaches that one must examine issues without solely relying on the word of authority. For another thing, a rational argument can be a way for people to reach an understanding in spite of having different viewpoints on religion. Accordingly, a good way to communicate about ethics for both believers and nonbelievers is to approach the issue through the language of *reason*.

Moral Issues and Logic

As we saw at the end of the section on moral issues and religion, it has been a choice of philosophers from the earliest times to argue about moral issues on the basis of reasoning rather than religious faith, regardless of their own religious affiliations. That means that the classical philosophical field of *logic* is considered a valuable tool for discussing moral issues, because if philosophers can agree on anything, it is usually whether or not an argument violates the rules of logic.

An "argument" in philosophy is not a heated discussion or a screaming contest but a certain type of communication that strives to convince a listener that something is true or reasonable. Here is an ultrashort account of the basic principles of logic: An argument has at least one premise, and usually several premises, followed by a conclusion. Such an argument can be either *inductive* or *deductive*. The conclusion of an inductive argument is based on a gathering of evidence (such as "Tom probably won't say thank you for the birthday present—he never does"), but there is no certainty that the conclusion is true, only that it is probable. On the other hand, in a deductive argument the premises are supposed to lead to a certain conclusion. A *valid* deductive argument is a deductive argument whose conclusion follows necessarily from its premise or premises. (For example, "All dogs are descendents of wolves; Fluffy is a dog; therefore, Fluffy is a descendent of wolves." This is valid whether or not dogs actually are descendents of wolves, which *inductive* evidence shows they probably are.) A *sound* deductive argument is an argument that is valid and whose premises are also factually true (such as "On the vernal [spring] equinox, night and day are of equal length all over the planet. So, on the vernal equinox, the day is twelve hours long in Baghdad as well as in Seattle").

Logical fallacies invalidate a moral viewpoint just as they do any other kind of viewpoint. Have you heard someone claim that because she has been cheated by two auto mechanics, no auto mechanics can be trusted? That's the fallacy of *hasty generalization.* Have you heard someone who is an expert in one field claim to be an authority in another—or people referring to some vague "expert opinion" in defense of their own views? That is the fallacy of *appeal to authority.* When someone tries to prove a point just by rephrasing it, such as "I'm right, because I'm never wrong," that is the fallacy of *begging the question,* a circular definition assuming that what you are trying to prove is a fact. How about a bully arguing that if you don't give him your seat/purse/ car, he will harm you? That's the *ad baculum* (Latin for "by the stick") fallacy, the fallacy of using physical threats. And if someone says, "Well, you know you can't believe what Fred says—after all, he's a guy," that's an *ad hominem* ("to the man") fallacy, which assumes that who a person is determines the correctness or incorrectness of what he or she says. And a politician declaring "If we continue to allow women to have abortions, then pretty soon nobody will give birth, and the human race will die out" offers a *slippery slope* argument, which assumes that drastic consequences will follow a certain policy. Closely related is the *straw man* fallacy, inventing a viewpoint so radical that hardly anyone holds it, so you can knock it down: "Gun advocates want to allow criminals and children to own weapons, so we should work toward a gun ban." And if you claim that "it is my way or the highway," then you are *bifurcating*—you are creating a *false dichotomy* (unless, of course, we're really talking about a situation with no third possibility, such as being pregnant—you can't be a little bit pregnant; it's either/or).

Another fallacy is the famed *red herring,* familiar to every fan of mystery and detective stories. A "red herring" is placed on the path to confuse the bloodhound. In other words, it is a deflection away from the truth. In an everyday setting, this can be accomplished by changing the subject when it gets too uncomfortable ("Why did you get an F on your test, Kevin?" "Mom, have I ever told you you're prettier than all my friends' moms?"). The notoriety of the red herring fallacy in court cases is well known, such as attacking a rape victim's sexual history to deflect attention away from the defendant. A fallacy most of us who make our living teaching are very familiar with is the fallacy of *ad misericordiam,* appeal to pity: "Please, can I get an extension on my paper? My backpack was stolen, my cat ran away, my grandma is in the hospital, and I've got these really painful hangnails." Or is it hangovers, perhaps? We've heard them all, all the bad excuses. But an excuse becomes an *ad misericordiam* fallacy only if it is nothing but an excuse. Sometimes a person truly deserves special consideration because of individual hardship, of course. Those and other logical fallacies are rampant in media discussions, and part of proper moral reasoning consists in watching out for the use of such flawed arguments, in one's own statements as well as in those of others.

Moral Issues and the Neurobiological Focus on Emotions

But is logic all there is to a good moral argument? Some philosophers would say yes, even today: The force of a moral viewpoint derives from its compelling logic. But increasingly, other voices are adding that a good moral argument is compelling not just because of its logic but also because it makes sense *emotionally.* If we have no feeling of moral approval or outrage, then do we really *care* about whether something is morally right or wrong? If we don't *feel* that it's wrong to harm a child, then how is logic going to persuade us? A classic answer has been an appeal to the logic of the Golden Rule: You wouldn't want someone to harm *you,* would you? But, say some, that's an appeal to how you'd *feel* in the same situation. An appeal to pure feeling isn't going to be enough, because feelings can be manipulated, and appeals to emotions don't solve conflicts if we don't share those emotions; but combined with the logic of reasoning emotions can form the foundation of a forceful moral argument, according to some modern thinkers. And they find support from a group of researchers who normally haven't had much occasion, or inclination, to converse with philosophers: neuroscientists.

In 1999 researchers at the University of Iowa led by neuroscientist Antonio Damasio found that a general area of the brain, the prefrontal cortex, plays a pivotal role in our development of a moral sense. And in 2007 came a new conclusion, also published by Damasio with other scientists in the journal *Nature,* that the human brain contains an area that enables us to think about other people's lives with empathy. And while Damasio is not a philosopher, he has a keen understanding of, and an interest in the history of philosophy and the philosophical and moral implications of his findings. Damasio sees human beings as primarily emotional beings, not predominantly rational beings. For generations philosophers have relied on the power of *reason* and logic to come up with solutions to moral problems; now that is being challenged by neuroscientists such as Damasio, and philosophers such as Martha Nussbaum (below), claiming that there is more to a good moral decision than relying exclusively on logic. But laypeople, without having much knowledge of the more elaborate moral theories expressed by philosophers, have generally relied on their moral and religious upbringing as well as their *moral intuition*: Some actions have just seemed obviously right, and some obviously wrong, based on each person's cultural and religious background (in Chapter 3 we discuss whether there might be universal moral values). Now neuroscientists are telling us that the old controversial assumption that we have a moral intuition is not far wrong—most of us seem to be born with a capacity for understanding other people's plights, which means that naturalism as a moral philosophy is staging a strong comeback (Box 1.3 explores the new interest in *moral naturalism* as a result of the latest findings in neuroscience). But that doesn't mean we always automatically know the right thing to do, or the proper way to be, especially when the world changes dramatically within a generation. Scientists tell us that much of what goes on within our moral intuition is based on the way humans used to live together thousands of years ago when we were living in small tribal groups consisting of perhaps 100 members, all of whom we knew personally. Our sense of duty, our concern for others, our joys of friendship, and our sense of fairness have for tens of thousands of years evolved within such small groups, and we have not yet adjusted to the world of relationships being so much bigger and more complex. But we all (at least those of us who are born with an undamaged brain) come equipped with a sense of empathy. While not exactly a "moral center" (Damasio has been careful to point that out), the normal function of that area of the brain will result in a reluctance to cause harm to others, even if greater harm to a majority could thereby be avoided. This study dovetailed with previous research and speculations by other scientists: On the basis of a study of thirty people, out of whom six had suffered damage to their ventromedial frontal lobes, the neuroscientists concluded that we humans have an area in the brain that, when undamaged, makes us hesitate if faced with a tough decision involving other people's lives. We have, from ancient times, developed an emotional reluctance to make decisions that will cause the death of other people, even if it is for the common good. The research subjects with damage to that specific part of the brain had no problem making moral decisions that would save many but cause the deaths of one or a few humans. These subjects did not come across as callous, unfeeling people and were absolutely not classified as sociopaths. They would no more sell their daughters into sex slavery or torture an animal than would the "normal" subjects. However, when asked to make decisions that would cost human lives, they showed much less reluctance than the subjects with no damage to that part of the brain. Questions such as "Would you divert a runaway vehicle so that it will kill one person instead of the five people in its current path?" were answered affirmatively. (You will encounter that scenario below, in the notorious trolley problem.) The researchers concluded that the "normal" brain has evolved to recognize the value of a human life emotionally, probably because we are social beings and need to be able to have emotional ties to the people in our group.

Box 1.3 THE RETURN OF MORAL NATURALISM

Over the course of the twentieth century and the beginning of the twenty-first, ethicists (moral philosophers) have been divided as to the nature and origin of moral values. Some have claimed that, somehow, values are embedded in the human psyche and that every human being within the normal range, psychologically, has a set of values. Although such values will evidently differ somewhat from culture to culture, according to this theory values will not differ radically from culture to culture, since we all come equipped with a moral intuition, hardwired from birth. Such viewpoints are referred to by the general term **of moral naturalism.** Others have claimed that our value systems are exclusively a matter of social convention, convenient systems for living in groups, so they can be completely different from culture to culture. Yet others have held that our morals, although not hardwired, are not relative but a result of rational deliberation. In upcoming chapters we look at the theories of cultural and ethical relativism as well as the entire question of which values we ought to have—values that simply reflect the culture we live in, values that we feel naturally drawn to, or values that reflect a timeless rational system of ethics regardless of our cultural affiliation.

In a manner of speaking, both the view that morals are relative and the view that we have a moral intuition have found support in twenty-first-century science: The relativist points to the vast knowledge amassed by anthropology over a hundred years showing that, indeed, moral values differ dramatically all over the planet; in addition, psychology has shown how flexible the mind of the human child is, ready to adapt to any social convention favored by the group it grows up within. And yet, moral intuitionism has seen a boost from neuroscientists within the last few years, and in the chapter text you'll see how the studies performed by Antonio Damasio and others have provided support for philosophers who think our sense of right and wrong is somehow hard-wired into our nature: What makes us flourish as a social group is *good for us,* and as such deemed good by the society in question. But the idea is not new—twenty-four centuries ago Aristotle (see Chapter 9) had similar thoughts.

This study has made waves for several reasons. For one, it corroborated that we do appear to have been equipped with some sort of *moral intuition* from birth. For another, it weighed in on an ancient debate in moral philosophy: Are our moral decisions primarily emotional or primarily logical? And *should* they be primarily emotional or primarily logical? The vast majority of philosophers since the time of Socrates and Plato have argued that the more we are able to disregard our personal emotions when we make moral decisions, the better our decisions will be. As you will see in several chapters in this book, philosophers (such as Plato, Chapters 4 and 8; Jeremy Bentham, Chapter 5; and Immanuel Kant, Chapter 6) have argued that moral decisions ought to be either exclusively or predominantly rational, logical, and unemotional. It is a rare exception to read a philosopher who argues either that our moral decisions *are in fact* emotional (such as David Hume does; see Chapter 4) or that they *should be* emotional (argued by Richard Taylor; see Chapter 11). A handful of thinkers from Aristotle (Chapter 9) to Martha Nussbaum (in this chapter) argue that we shouldn't make moral decisions without using our reason but that we shouldn't disregard our emotions either. In Chapter 11 philosopher Jesse Prinz discusses whether we need moral empathy to make moral decisions. Box 1.4 discusses the British philosopher Philippa Foot's so-called trolley problem and its implications for our understanding of emotional and rational responses to moral dilemmas.

Box 1.4 THE TROLLEY PROBLEM AND EMOTION VS. REASON

The famous (or infamous) trolley problem is a so-called *thought experiment* first envisioned in 1967 by British philosopher Philippa Foot (see Chapter 10) and later developed further by American philosopher Judith Jarvis Thomson. In Foot's version, a trolley (or "tram") is headed straight for five workers on the track. You are the trolley conductor, and you can divert it to another track, but on that track there is one worker. Either way, someone is going to die. Foot's question is not only, *Could* you make yourself divert the trolley, but *should* you? Foot's point was, for one thing, to bring up the issue of whether there is a difference between "killing and letting die," and for another, to illustrate various responses based on different moral philosophies (which we look at in upcoming chapters), and in particular to show that an exclusive focus on the well-being of many [as in the philosophy of utilitarianism (Chapter 5)] is not a satisfactory moral response. We take a closer look at the trolley problem in Chapter 5. However, Thomson's version is even more challenging: Imagine that the only way you can stop the trolley is by pushing "a fat man" next to you in front of the tracks. Here, she says, you're not just deflecting harm, you are causing additional harm, to someone with rights (although her point is also that pulling the lever and diverting the trolley to the track with the person is also taking responsibility for a life).

Subsequent versions have various numbers of people on the tracks versus having to sacrifice a larger or smaller number of people to save them—including imagining that the person you must sacrifice is someone you love, such as your mother or your son. Such questions are good at illustrating a variety of moral concerns about rights, equality, and consequences, but very few people will ever have to make such agonizing "Sophie's choices," the term deriving from the film classic *Sophie's Choice* where a mother captured by the Nazis during World War II has to choose life for one of her two children and death for the other. However, the trolley problem has also been picked up on by experimental philosophers (philosophers believing that practical experience and experiments should dictate our philosophical theories) Joshua Green and Jonathan Cohen. What they found under lab conditions was that even if the test subjects know that they can save five by killing one, the emotional response conflicts with the rational response. We just don't want to harm that one person, even if we can save five. And Damasio, in his 2007 study, adds to the result: Most of us have a natural empathy that makes us reluctant to cause harm, even if reason tells us it is the only logical way. The philosophical question here is, of course, whether it sometimes makes sense to override our empathy and be rational—and save the many by sacrificing the few. The popular television series *The Good Place* dedicated an episode in its second season to this question, and we discuss the trolley problem further in Chapter 5, as well as the episode from *The Good Place*.

The neuroscientists' study seems to say that a healthy human brain will intuitively incorporate emotions in its moral decisions involving other people's lives—which would mean that all the philosophers who have argued that emotions should be avoided in moral decision making are somehow wrong and are even advocating something inhumane. So is that all we need to disprove them? Hardly. Neuroscientists can tell us *where* in the brain our moral decisions take place, and evolutionary psychologists can tell us how the whole field of ethics has evolved, and some scientists even claim that when we make big complex decisions we tend to rely on our emotions, while smaller, simpler questions are typically solved rationally. These findings may be enlightening to the field of moral philosophy (and I personally think they are fascinating and not to be disregarded). However, these scientists can't necessarily tell us which moral decisions are *better*. But what may be even more important is that the classical philosophical point of arguing in favor of reason and against emotion is that even if it is hard to disregard our emotions in key moral decisions, then that is perhaps precisely what we ought to do from time to time? We may feel reluctant or squeamish about sacrificing one life to save a hundred, but that may be what is required of us in extreme situations, not because it is easy, or because we enjoy it, but because it is *necessary*. The difficulty with this approach is that such arguments have been used, through time, to enslave countless innocent human beings, or use them as cannon fodder, or exterminate them, all in the name of reason. But it is also the only argument we have to justify shooting a plane full of passengers down if it has been hijacked and is headed for the Capitol, or to not forget about the law when a serial killer of children shows contrition in court and claims he has had a horrible life of abuse himself. At a less dramatic level, reason's override of emotions is what we need when our child is crying because she doesn't want to go to the dentist or to kindergarten; you will encounter this question again in Chapter 5. So, again, the neuroscientists can tell us what are normal and abnormal brain reactions, but without further philosophical discussion they can't tell us what is *morally right*. Furthermore, if we take into account the results of the Stanley Milgram obedience experiments and Zimbardo's Stanford Prison Experiment, we can't conclude that humans will not harm one another—they may be reluctant, normally, to harm one another, but that reluctance can be overridden by other factors, such as threats, fear for their own safety, ambitions, and a wish to please their superiors. It takes a moral philosopher (with or without academic credentials) to engage in that discussion.

And that is precisely what moral philosophers do. Some, such as Patricia Churchland and Joshua Green, focus on the biology of the brain to get a more complete picture of where moral decisions originate and how they work within human evolution and human social life. Others, like Martha Nussbaum, look at human behavior in general, to get a sense of how we understand our norms and values from a point of view that includes human emotions. We return to Nussbaum shortly.

Moral Issues and Storytelling

All cultures tell stories, and all cultures have codes for proper behavior. Very often those codes are taught through stories, but stories can also be used to *question* moral rules and to examine morally ambiguous situations. A fundamental premise of this book is that stories sometimes can serve as shortcuts to understanding and solving moral problems. Many literature professors may be inclined to tell us that people don't read anymore, that the novel is dead, or that nobody appreciates good literature these days. I myself am rather disappointed when students are unfamiliar with the classics of literature or have grown to hate them through high school manglings. However, it just isn't true that people don't read novels—bestsellers are flourishing as never before. And an element has been added to our appreciation of good stories: *movies*. The American film industry has been in existence for over a hundred years and TV dramas have become increasingly morally and psychologically complex. It should be no surprise to anyone that as much as films and TV dramas can provide simple entertainment, they can also give us in-depth, unforgettable views of human life, including moral issues. This book makes use of that treasure trove of movie stories as well as novels, short stories, epic poems, graphic novels, television shows, and plays as illustrations of moral problems and solutions.

Using stories here has two purposes. One is to supply a foundation for further debate about the application of the moral theories presented in the chapter; the other is to inspire you to experience these stories in their original form, through print or video, since they are, of course, richer and more interesting than any outline can possibly show.

Martha Nussbaum: Stories, Ethics, and Emotions

For the greater part of the twentieth century most Western philosophers had a tacit agreement that stories were best left in the nursery, but times have changed: There is now a growing interest in the cultural and philosophical importance of storytelling, in technological as well as pretechnological cultures, and stories are becoming shortcuts to understanding ourselves on an individual as well as a cultural level. One of the most influential voices speaking for narratives as a way to communicate about values is Martha Nussbaum (b. 1947), a philosopher and a professor of law and ethics; her main interest is not the intellectual value of storytelling as much as the emotional force of narratives.

Nussbaum believes there was a time when philosophers understood the value of narratives. The Greek thinker Aristotle (whom she greatly admires) believed that experiencing a drama unfold teaches the viewer basic important lessons about having the proper feelings at the proper time—lessons about life and virtue in general. As modern Western philosophy took shape, however, the idea of emotions seemed increasingly irrelevant. But within the past decade American philosophers, sometimes inspired by the new findings in neurobiology and sometimes on their own, have increasingly argued that emotions are not only a legitimate, but also an essential part of moral decision making—not the only important part, because reason is also crucial, but something that can't be ignored. In a sense you're getting the end of the story here before you're treated to the beginning, because in the upcoming chapters you'll be hearing much about the philosophical tradition of past centuries where emotions have been considered more or less irrelevant for moral decisions (such as Chapters 5 and 6 in particular), but the interesting thing is that philosophers today who do want to regard emotions as an essential part of thinking about ethics are in a sense revising a viewpoint that was introduced by Aristotle himself 2,400 years ago: relevant emotions, in the proper measure, are indeed essential to our sense of moral right and wrong. Martha Nussbaum has found inspiration in the literary tradition. In the late twentieth century Nussbaum was one of the first voices for a reevaluation of emotions in moral philosophy with her book *Love's Knowledge* (1990) and she has explored the concept of rational emotions in her later work, *Upheavals of Thought: The Intelligence of Emotions* (2001), *Hiding from Humanity* (2004), *Frontiers of Justice* (2004), and *From Disgust to Humanity: Sexual Orientation and Constitutional Law* (2010). She points out that emotions weren't excluded from philosophy because they did not yield *knowledge;* in other words, it is not because of any lack of *cognitive value* that philosophers have refused to investigate emotions. There is actually much cognitive value in emotions, for emotions are, on the whole, quite *reasonable* when we look at them in context. When do we feel anger? When we believe that someone has deliberately injured us or someone we care about—in other words, when we feel the situation warrants it. Feelings such as disappointment, elation, grief, and even love are all responses to certain situations. They develop according to some inner logic; they don't strike at random. How do we know? Because if we realize that we were wrong about the situation, our anger slowly disappears. Imagine this situation (which is an example of my own concoction, not Nussbaum's!): You own a pair of expensive "AirPods" (ear buds). You go to the school library to do some research, and for some reason leave your bag unattended for a few minutes, with somebody sitting at the computer station next to you. The AirPods case is in your bag. You come back, take your bag, and leave. Later you look for your AirPods, and the case isn't where it is supposed to be. Oh no! You think back to the moment where you left your bag unattended. Somebody must have stolen it! And you hightail it back to the library where the same person is still sitting there, doing research, so in anger you accuse him or her of having stolen your AirPods. He or she denies any knowledge of your device, and a confrontation ensues. Your bag is shuffled around, and all of a sudden out pops the case from another pocket. It was never stolen—you just didn't look carefully enough. So now, if you are a rational being, what becomes of your anger? It would have been righteous if your AirPods had indeed been stolen, but now you have egg on your face. So do you apologize? Or do you leave, sneering and convinced that person surely must have had something to do with it after all? If your anger fades away and turns into embarrassment, then you have an example of a rational emotion with moral relevance. If you still feel somewhat angry, then the feeling is irrational—unless you're angry at yourself. The film *Smoke Signals,* discussed at the end of the chapter, is an example of exactly this type of emotion when a main character's strong feelings of anger and envy are transformed through a confrontation with reality. And most feelings have such an element of rationality—if they are responses to real situations, they are usually somewhat logical—except love, says Nussbaum. Perhaps love is not that easy to analyze—people in love don't seem to respond logically to situations that ought to change their feelings of love. (The person you love is seeing someone else, and what do you do? Continue to be helplessly in love.) But even love responds to such challenges in a way; we probably realize that our feelings are, somehow, out of place.

Why, then, have so many philosophers refused to deal seriously with emotions? Not because emotions lack cognitive value, but because they show how we react to situations outside our control. When we are emotional, we are not *self-sufficient,* and most philosophers have, according to Nussbaum, preferred to investigate a more autonomous part of the human character, our reason. (Of course, some philosophers and psychoanalysts have pointed out that reason is not immune to outside influence, either, but Nussbaum is addressing the trends in traditional philosophy before the twentieth century, when the idea of reason being affected by the Unconscious was not yet commonly accepted.) So Nussbaum makes two major points that are important for our discussion about using stories to illustrate moral problems:

(*1*) *Emotions can be morally relevant in moral discussions if they are reasonable*, i.e., they reflect the reality of the situation.

(*2*) *One of the best ways to investigate such moral emotions is to read fiction.*

Roberto Serra – Iguana Press/Getty Images

Martha Nussbaum (b. 1947), American philosopher. The author of *Love's Knowledge, Upheavals of Thought, Hiding from Humanity, Frontiers of Justice,* and *From Disgust to Humanity: Sexual Orientation and Constitutional Law,* she suggests that novels are supremely well suited to explore moral problems. Through novels we have the chance to live more than our own lives and to understand human problems from someone else's point of view. Since others can read the same novels, we can share such knowledge and reach a mutual understanding.

For Nussbaum, emotions provide access to values, to human relationships, and to understanding ourselves, so they must be investigated. And where do they manifest themselves most clearly? In narratives. Stories are actually emotions put into a structure. When we are children and adolescents, we learn how to manipulate objects and relate to others; we learn cognitive skills and practical skills, and among the skills we learn are when to feel certain kinds of emotions. The prime teacher of emotions is the story. That means, of course, that different societies may tell different stories teaching different lessons, so we must retain a certain amount of social awareness and social criticism when reading stories from any culture, including our own. People in their formative years are not just empty vessels into which stories are poured. Nussbaum maintains there is no rule saying that people must accept everything their culture teaches them, so those who don't approve of the stories being told or who think the stories haven't been told right will begin to tell their own stories. Important as emotions are, alongside our reason, in shaping our moral values, Nussbaum has of late found it necessary to specify that two particular emotions should not be considered conducive to moral understanding: *disgust* and *shame*. Here Nussbaum enters the political arena by claiming that some emotions are more morally and politically appropriate than others. When we say we are disgusted with something or someone, we set ourselves on a pedestal as being better and purer, says Nussbaum, and that to her is an unrealistic assessment that does nothing more than create an us-versus-them environment.

To understand emotions we must read stories, but that ought to come easily to us, Nussbaum believes, since we already enjoy doing just that. She does stress, however, that we have to read the entire story, not just rely on a synopsis. There is an integral relationship between the form and the content of a story. As she says in her book *Love's Knowledge,* we can't skip "the emotive appeal, the absorbing plottedness, the variety and indeterminacy of good fiction" without losing the heart of the experience. So in a sense Nussbaum does not specifically advocate *using stories to illustrate moral problems,* as we will be doing in this book. Instead, she supports reading stories as a way of *sharing basic experiences of values* and using philosophy as a tool for analyzing that experience. For her, the story comes first, and then the analysis can follow. In the Primary Readings section, you'll find an excerpt from *Love's Knowledge.*

Why use stories, though? Why can't we approach moral issues by more traditional avenues, such as examples that are "made to order" by philosophers? Because, says Nussbaum, they lack precisely the rich texture that makes the story an experience we can relate to. Besides, such examples are formulated in such a way that the conclusion is obvious. Novels tend to be quite open-ended, a feature that Nussbaum believes is valuable. Novels preserve "mystery and indeterminacy," just like real life. Let's take a quick look at her theory, because, as luck (and planning) will have it, you're already well acquainted with a "philosophical example" of the kind Nussbaum had in mind, a couple of pages back: the trolley problem. So let us apply her criticism to that famous example. The original version by Philippa Foot is indeed terse. There is no "particularity, emotive appeal, absorbing plottedness, variety or indeterminacy" of a good story, quoting from Nussbaum's own text in the Primary Readings section. There is just the basic question of saving five people and killing one, or saving the one and letting five people die. They might as well be faceless stick figures—they have no story. It takes the subsequent versions of the trolley problem to add the human element; in other words, story lines are added, and the moral dilemma comes to life. What if the person on the track is your daughter? Your beloved? May they not seem more important than 5 strangers? But what if the five strangers are top scientists, on the verge of a universal cancer cure? Stories add a moral dimension, so in that respect Nussbaum is right: stories create an emotional appeal that may well be relevant in a moral decision process.

However, here we must not forget that Philippa Foot didn't intend the trolley problem to present a solution to any moral conundrum; she wanted to point out the *bones* of a moral problem and how a seemingly easy solution may not be so simple after all. Sometimes a straightforward little philosophical example is indeed all that we need—not an entire novel, short story, or movie.

Why not just rely on your own experiences to learn about life? Some of them must certainly contain both mystery and indeterminacy. To some extent we do that already; we draw on our own experience as much as we possibly can when judging concrete and abstract cases. But the trouble is, one human life is just not enough for understanding the myriad ways of being. As Nussbaum says,

> We have never lived enough. Our experience is, without fiction, too confined and too parochial. Literature extends it, making us reflect and feel about what might otherwise be too distant for feeling. . . . All living is interpreting; all action requires seeing the world *as* something. So in this sense no life is "raw" and . . . throughout our living we are, in a sense, makers of fictions. The point is that in the activity of literary imagining we are led to imagine and describe with greater precision, focusing our attention on each word, feeling each event more keenly—whereas much of actual life goes by without that heightened awareness, and is thus, in a certain sense, not fully or thoroughly lived.

Furthermore, it is much harder to talk about events in your own life than it is to discuss events in a story. We may not want to share our deepest feelings, or we may not be able to express them. But if we talk with friends about a passage in a favorite book or film, we can share both an emotional and a moral experience. One final word about Nussbaum's theory: It is important that we remember that she has no wish to replace the traditional rational approach to moral issues with an emotional approach—to her, emotions can be relevant in moral decision making, but that doesn't make reason irrelevant. But we have a fuller understanding of being human, and making moral decisions, if we allow our focus to include relevant emotions as well as reason.

Today? An Assessment

One might ask how Nussbaum's two suggestions have played out since she launched them in 1990. Are philosophers using more stories to illustrate moral issues? Most definitely. Whether inspired by her, or arriving at their own conclusions, a great many philosophers today find that stories—novels, short–stories, movies, TV shows, and even graphic novels and narrative video games—can be a great asset to a discussion about moral values, particularly in the classroom and online, and that topic is what we are going to explore in Chapter 2. But what about her other suggestion, that emotions can be morally relevant if they are reasonable? When she suggested as much in *Love's Knowledge*, the tendency in moral philosophy was, as it had been for a very long time, to regard *reason*, not emotion, as the golden road to making moral decisions, but over the last few decades a different trend has emerged—not just in moral philosophy, but in the public debate in general: that it is how you *feel* that matters. Reality has, in many cases, become a matter of emotional interpretation (we return that that phenomenon at the end of Chapter 7). That goes far beyond what Nussbaum suggests in her book from 1990, because her focus on emotions specifies that they have to be reasonable and rational—they have to have their origin in some factual situation, not just reacting to a perception. So one might say that the trend has gone in favor of emotions in moral decision making in a far more radical way that Nussbaum had in mind.

At the end of the chapter you'll find a narrative that illustrates Nussbaum's theory of storytelling as a key to understanding ourselves and one another and of emotion as having a rational component: *Smoke Signals* shows the character development of an angry young man who learns that the cause of his anger against his father was mainly in his own head.

Furthermore, the narrative *The Eichmann Show* serves two purposes: to illustrate Arendt's concept of the *banality of evil*, and also to illustrate Nussbaum's point that sometimes we understand a moral problem better by experiencing a story with "particularity and emotion," rather that reading about it as an event in a history book.

In this book we will follow Martha Nussbaum's suggestion and, at the end of each chapter, look at a variety of stories, each with their own moral problem and possible solution. The chapter text itself will have philosophical examples and real-life events, too, for good measure.

Study Questions

1. Would you consider it a reasonable excuse for wrongdoing (such as drunk, reckless driving) that the perpetrator was never taught moral values as a child due to the sense of privilege and affluence of his or her family? Why or why not? (Incidentally, a similar argument was first used in the infamous Leopold and Loeb case in 1924 by famous lawyer Clarence Darrow.)

2. In your opinion, should children learn values in elementary school? Explain why or why not, and craft an argument for and against the idea as it might be presented by a teacher and a parent.

3. Give three examples of statements about moral issues, illustrating three logical fallacies.

4. In your view, does evil exist? If yes, is it a force outside, or inside of humans? Is there a difference between *being* evil and *doing* evil? Explain.

5. Comment on Nussbaum's statement that "We have never lived enough. Our experience is, without fiction, too confined and too parochial. Literature expands it, making us reflect and feel about what might otherwise be too distant for feeling." What does she mean? Do you agree? Why or why not?

6. Would you agree with Nussbaum that the well-written story does a better job of enlightening us about moral issues than the philosophical example or the real-life event? Explain.

Primary Reading and Narratives

The Primary Reading is from *Love's Knowledge* by Martha Nussbaum, explaining why fictional stories are better at teaching moral lessons than real-life stories and little made-to-order philosophical examples are. The first Narrative is a summary and short excerpt from Shirley Jackson's short story "The Lottery," an American classic about the banality of evil in a fictional society with traditions. The second Narrative is a summary of the film *Smoke Signals* linking up with the Nussbaum excerpt. Two young American Indian males embark on a journey on which one, Thomas, grows as a storyteller, and the other, Victor, loses his anger toward his father and his jealousy of Thomas. The final Narrative is the television film *The Eichmann Show*, depicting the Eichmann 1961 trial seen from the point of view of the television crew shooting the a documentary of the trial and broadcasting it to the world.

 Primary Reading

Love's Knowledge

MARTHA NUSSBAUM

Excerpt, 1990.

In this excerpt, Nussbaum argues that novels, short stories, and dramas are very well suited to providing an emotional lesson in moral issues because of the brevity of human life: We just can't experience everything ourselves, so fiction provides a shortcut to understanding the range of human emotions. She also explains why such philosophical examples as those you will encounter in this book (such as Kant's example of the killer at the door looking for your friend, see Chapter 6) aren't good enough to teach the same lesson. You may be interested to know that in Nussbaum's later books she also considers films a valid medium for discussing moral issues.

> Not only novels prove appropriate, because (again, with reference only to these particular issues and this conception) many serious dramas will be pertinent as well, and some biographies and histories—so long as these are written in a style that gives sufficient attention to particularity and emotion, and so long as they involve their readers in relevant activities of searching and feeling, especially feeling concerning their own possibilities as well as those of the characters. . . .

> But the philosopher is likely to be less troubled by these questions of literary genre than by a prior question: namely, why a literary work at all? Why can't we investigate everything we want to investigate by using complex examples of the sort that moral philosophers are very good at inventing? In reply, we

must insist that the philosopher who asks this question cannot have been convinced by the argument so far about the intimate connection between literary form and ethical content. Schematic philosophers' examples almost always lack the particularity, the emotive appeal, the absorbing plottedness, the variety and indeterminacy, of good fiction; they lack, too, good fiction's way of making the reader a participant and a friend; and we have argued that it is precisely in virtue of these structural characteristics that fiction can play the role it does in our reflective lives. As [novelist Henry] James says, "The picture of the exposed and entangled state is what is required." If the examples do have these features, they will, themselves, be works of literature. Sometimes a very brief fiction will prove a sufficient vehicle for the investigation of what we are at that moment investigating; sometimes, as in "Flawed Crystals" (where our question concerns what is likely to happen in the course of a relatively long and complex life), we need the length and complexity of a novel. In neither case, however, would schematic examples prove sufficient as a substitute. (This does not mean that they will be totally dismissed; for they have other sorts of usefulness, especially in connection with other ethical views.)

We can add that examples, setting things up schematically, signal to the readers what they should notice and find relevant. They hand them the ethically salient description. This means that much of the ethical work is already done, the result "cooked." The novels are more open-ended, showing the reader what it is to search for the appropriate description and why that search matters. (And yet they are not so open-ended as to give no shape to the reader's thought.) By showing the mystery and indeterminacy of "our actual adventure," they characterize life more richly and truly—indeed, more precisely—than an example lacking those features ever could; and they engender in the reader a type of ethical work more appropriate for life.

But why not life itself? Why can't we investigate whatever we want to investigate by living and reflecting on our lives? Why, if it is the Aristotelian ethical conception we wish to scrutinize, can't we do that without literary texts, without texts at all—or, rather, with the texts of our own lives set before us? Here, we must first say that of course we do this as well, both apart from our reading of the novels and (as [French novelist Marcel] Proust insists) in the process of reading. In a sense Proust is right to see the literary text as an "optical instrument" through which the reader becomes a reader of his or her own heart. But, why do we need, in that case, such optical instruments?

One obvious answer was suggested already by Aristotle: we have never lived enough. Our experience is, without fiction, too confined and too parochial. Literature extends it, making us reflect and feel about what might otherwise be too distant for feeling. The importance of this for both morals and politics cannot be underestimated. *The Princess Casamassima* [1886, a novel by Henry James]—justly, in my view—depicts the imagination of the novel-reader as a type that is very valuable in the political (as well as the private) life, sympathetic to a wide range of concerns, averse to certain denials of humanity. It cultivates these sympathies in its readers.

We can clarify and extend this point by emphasizing that novels do not function, inside this account, as pieces of "raw" life: they are a close and careful interpretative description. All living is interpreting; all action requires seeing the world *as* something. So in this sense no life is "raw," and (as James and Proust insist) throughout our living we are, in a sense, makers of fictions. The point is that in the activity of literary imagining we are led to imagine and describe with greater precision, focusing our attention on each word, feeling each event more keenly—whereas much of actual life goes by without that heightened awareness, and is thus, in a certain sense, not fully or thoroughly lived. Neither James nor Proust thinks of ordinary life as normative, and the Aristotelian conception concurs: too much of it is obtuse, routinized, incompletely sentient. So literature is an extension of life not only horizontally, bringing the reader into contact with events or locations or persons or problems he or she has not otherwise met, but also, so to speak, vertically, giving the reader experience that is deeper, sharper, and more precise than much of what takes place in life.

Study Questions

1. Is Nussbaum right that philosophical examples don't work as well as fictional stories when it comes to conveying a moral point? Why or why not?

2. What does she mean by "no life is 'raw'"? Is she right in saying the "We have never lived enough"?

3. Nussbaum's theory of moral discussion through fiction also includes films; can you think of a film, not mentioned in this chapter, which would teach a lesson that is both a "horizontal and a vertical extension of life"?

  Narrative

The Lottery

SHIRLEY JACKSON

***Short story, 1948. Excerpt and Summary.* Short film, 1969. Larry Yust (Director and Screenwriter)**

The first narrative in this book is an American classic that shocked its readers when it was published in *The New Yorker,* June 26, 1948. "The Lottery" is a short story with a moral message, and readers have often compared it to Hannah Arendt's book *Eichmann in Jerusalem* even though it predates Arendt's book by fifteen years, because it, too, deals with what we now have become accustomed to calling the **banality of evil.**

It is a nice sunny morning, June 27, in a world that sounds like small-town America of the mid-twentieth century. (Astute readers would notice that the fateful date in the story would be the day after the publication of the short story.) Everybody in the little village is gathering in the square between the post office and the bank for the annual tradition of the lottery, a tradition that reaches far, far back in time, not just in the village, but in the entire extended community where the story takes place. The beginnings are lost in time, but the village elders still hold on to a very old box, replacing even older boxes, where the wooden lottery pieces used to be kept, but nowadays they have been replaced by folded-up pieces of paper, one for each member of the community, young and old. Everybody is anxious to get the lottery over with because they have plans for the day and want to get home early. In anticipation, some are filling their pockets with stones. There used to be rituals of some kind associated with the lottery, but now everybody is just sworn in, and one of the businessmen in town, Mr. Summers, a man without a family, is ready to conduct the lottery. One of the last people to arrive is Mrs. Hutchinson who didn't want to leave her home and join her family at the lottery before she'd finished the dishes.

The lottery begins; everybody draws for themselves if they are adults; a family member draws for those who are home sick or are too young to draw. People talk among themselves in the crowd, about a neighboring village where they've given up on the lottery, and one of the older men, Mr. Warner, who has taken part in seventy-six lotteries, dismisses the idea as socially dangerous.

Where would they be without the lottery? Headed for total chaos. Nobody would want to work anymore, he says, and everybody would be living in caves. Eventually all lots are drawn, and now comes the time to open up the pieces of paper to see who has "got it." It turns out to be Bill Hutchinson. His wife Tessie, who arrived late, protests and says he didn't get enough time to draw a lot, but her husband tells her bluntly to shut up. Everybody took the same chance. Now the drawing has to be narrowed down between Bill and Tessie and their three underage children. Each of the little kids gets to pick his or her own paper, and Tessie and Bill reach in and pick their own. The kids open their papers and are overjoyed to discover they're blank. And Bill's is blank as well, which means that Tessie got the one with the black spot on it. Bill holds it up for everyone to see. Mr. Summers tells the crowd to finish quickly, and without delay, everybody moves over to the pile of stones gathered for the lottery purpose.

> The children had stones already. And someone gave little Davy Hutchinson a few pebbles.

> Tessie Hutchinson was in the center of a cleared space by now, and she held her hands out desperately as the villagers moved in on her. "It isn't fair," she said. A stone hit her on the side of the head. Old Man Warner was saying, "Come on, come on, everyone." Steve Adams was in the front of the crowd of villagers, with Mrs. Graves beside him.

> "It isn't fair, it isn't right," Mrs. Hutchinson screamed, and then they were upon her.

Study Questions

1. Is Tessie Hutchinson right that the lottery was not *fair*? Was it not conducted according to the rules? If so, why is she saying it wasn't fair? Is her statement essentially a lament that life isn't fair, or does it have another meaning? And what does she mean by saying it isn't *right*?

2. What is the significance that "little Davy Hutchinson" is forced to participate in stoning his own mother to death?

3. What would you say is the moral message of this story, if any? Might there be several messages?

4. How can this story be said to illustrate the "banality of evil"? Compare "The Lottery" to Hannah Arendt's analysis of Nazi atrocities, Stanley Milgram's obedience experiments, and Philip Zimbardo's Stanford Prison experiment.

5. Since 1948, American fiction has seen a number of stories with a similar scenario of rituals involving the suffering of innocents, from Ursula Le Guin's "The Ones Who Walk Away from Omelas" (see Chapter 6) to the movies *The Island* (see Chapter 7), *The Purge,* and *The Hunger Games*. If you are familiar with these (or other) stories with the same motif of ritual sacrifice for the community, comment on the similarities and differences between them and "The Lottery."

Narrative

Smoke Signals

SHERMAN ALEXIE (SCREENWRITER)

CHRIS EYRE (DIRECTOR)

Film, 1998. Based on the short-story collection by Sherman Alexie, **The Lone Ranger and Tonto Fist-fight in Heaven.** *Summary.*

Thomas and Victor are young Coeur d'Alene Indians living on the reservation in Idaho in the late 1990s. They grew up together and share the story of one fateful night when they were babies. On that night Thomas's parents' house burned down, with Thomas, his parents, and Victor inside. Someone saved Victor, and Thomas's parents threw their baby to safety out the second-story window while they themselves burned to death. Thomas was caught in midair by Victor's father, Arnold. Since then, Thomas has lived with his grandmother.

The selection of this movie is intended to illustrate Martha Nussbaum's theory of rational emotions. One might say (and this is your author's interpretation) that Victor has three major issues. One is his deep-seated anger toward his father, a violent drunk who left the family, presumably never to return. Another is an equally deep-seated jealousy toward Thomas, because Arnold saved him from the fire, and not his own son. And last is a fear-mixed resentment of the white culture surrounding the reservation, based on hundreds of years of history plus Arnold's casual jabs against "white people who should go back where they belong." These issues are at least partially emotion based, and in the course of the film we watch as they are each challenged and modified by reality checks.

Not much happens on the reservation; everyone knows everyone else, and the height of excitement seems to be playing basketball at the gym. One of the young Indians remarks, "Sometimes it is a good day to die—other times it is a good day to play basketball." Sometimes they watch Westerns on TV and discuss whether the cowboys always win or whether the Indians sometimes win. Thomas remarks, with a grin, that there is nothing more pathetic than Indians on TV—except Indians watching Indians on TV!

Thomas is a seer and a storyteller; everything he has experienced in his short life turns into stories—and his stories contain a considerable amount of pure fantasy too. That irritates Victor, who wants him just to tell the truth. Much about Thomas irritates Victor: Thomas braids his long hair very tightly; Victor wears his long hair free-flowing. Thomas always wears a dark three-piece suit, whereas Victor wears blue jeans and T-shirts. And Victor cultivates a warrior's inscrutable face, whereas Thomas has a ready smile for everyone. What irritates Victor most is Thomas's stories about Victor's father, Arnold. Victor knows him as a man who got drunk and beat him and his mother. Thomas sees Arnold as his hero, a magic man—the man who not only saved his life but also took him to a breakfast at Denny's in Spokane once. They met on the footbridge across the Spokane Falls, and somehow Thomas has associated Arnold with that spot ever since; it has become a power place to him. And Arnold was a storyteller, like Thomas—with a love for a *good* story rather than a *true* story. But Arnold is no longer around for Thomas to tell new stories about—he left his family in anger when Victor was a child.

Their quiet life is interrupted by a phone call from Phoenix: A woman named Suzy calls Victor's mother with the news that Arnold is dead. He lived in a trailer close to her, and his things are still there, including his truck. Someone needs to get him and his belongings. Victor is reluctant to go because he harbors immense resentment toward his father for leaving him, but Thomas puts up the money for the ticket from his piggy bank under one condition: that he gets to go to Phoenix too.

On the bus, Thomas and Victor have a variety of encounters with the world of the whites, not all of them pleasant. For instance, a pair of rednecks take their seats and force them to move. But Victor is not very pleasant either. He calls a young girl a liar for embellishing her one life story: her near chance of going to the Olympics. And he gets on Thomas's case for not knowing how to be an Indian: He must have watched *Dances with Wolves* two hundred times, says Victor, and he still doesn't know how to act like he's come home from the buffalo hunt. Thomas protests that their people weren't buffalo hunters but fishermen. Victor replies that there is nothing glorious about coming home from fishing—the movie wasn't called "Dances with Salmon"!—and we get a sense that perhaps it is Victor, not Thomas, who feels uncomfortable about his role and his culture.

Photo 12/Alamy Stock Photo

In *Smoke Signals* (1998) Victor (Adam Beach, left) and Thomas (Evan Adams) from the Coeur d'Alene Indian reservation in Idaho are on their way to pick up the ashes of Victor's father Arnold in Arizona. Thomas irritates Victor because he wears his hair in tight braids, wears a three-piece suit—and was rescued as a baby by Arnold, whereas Victor believes his own father didn't care about him.

After days of traveling nonstop, they finally arrive in Phoenix and walk to the desert hideout of Arnold and Suzy. She turns out to be a hospital administrator and much younger than Arnold, but for years she has had a close relationship with him—"We kept each other's secrets," she says. The three of them share her frybread, traditional American Indian fare, and Thomas tells a wonderful story of how Victor's mother fed a hundred Indians with only fifty frybreads—which turns out to be not quite true, although it is a good story. Suzy has heard about Victor and Thomas and all the basketball games Arnold played with Victor. And she has heard the true story about the night of the fire. After Thomas has fallen asleep, Suzy tells Victor the story that he has never heard, about the night of the fire: What had haunted Arnold for all those years was that he set the fire by accident in a drunken stupor. He left his family because he couldn't stand his own memories, but he never intended to stay away forever. But now that Victor hears the truth, he also hears something he dares not believe: that Arnold ran back into the burning house to save him. For years, Victor has resented Thomas for being the one saved by Arnold. And now he has to revise all his resentments. Coming face-to-face with the loss of his father, Victor grieves in the traditional Indian way: He cuts his long hair.

The next morning, Victor and Thomas leave in Arnold's truck, taking with them only Arnold's ashes and his basketball. Victor is in a panicked, angry rush to get home, but there is yet another trial ahead for him. Late that night, on a dark desert road, he and Thomas crash the truck, barely avoiding ramming into two cars that had collided moments before the boys' arrival. The driver of the car that caused the accident, a white man, is drunk and obnoxious, and his wife is desperately apologetic. But down in the ravine is a car with two injured women, and the nearest town is twenty miles away. Victor's truck is disabled, but he doesn't hesitate for a moment: He must run for help. And he starts out running into the night, with the long stride of his ancestor warriors. He runs until his side hurts and his vision blurs, and by dawn he collapses. But he is close enough to a town to be seen by a road repair crew, and he gets the message about the injured motorists through.

As Victor and the women—who might have died if it hadn't been for his heroic run—are recovering in the hospital, Thomas is standing by, and we can tell that he has the material for many future stories. One woman says they are heroes, coming to the rescue just like the Lone Ranger and Tonto—and the boys answer that they're more like Tonto and Tonto. One snag develops, though: The man who caused the accident has filed false charges against the boys for assault and causing the accident, and Victor and Thomas are taken to the police station. All the old fear and resentment of the white power structure descend on the boys, who feel they won't be believed—but not everyone outside the reservation is like the drunken white driver. His wife, for one, has issued a statement against her husband, and the two women who were in the other car side with the boys, too. And the police chief, a white man, has good sense and sends the boys on their way.

Six days after leaving Idaho, Victor and Thomas are back with Arnold's ashes. The one who has undergone the most profound change is Victor; he now understands that his dad never planned to leave and that he just hadn't gotten around to going home yet. Now he understands the ghosts his father lived with year after year. So he barely picks on Thomas anymore and even offers him the deepest gesture he can think of: *He shares his father's ashes with him.* So (again, your author's interpretation) one might conclude that Victor's three issues have been resolved in the light of reason. His anger toward his father turned out to be somewhat unfounded (although Arnold would of course still be remembered as a father who was a violent, heavy drinker), and his emotions changed accordingly. His jealousy of Thomas was completely unfounded, and the jealousy becomes a sense of brotherhood instead. And the resentment toward "white people"? On their journey some white people were unpleasant, and some were understanding and helpful. It doesn't take away centuries of justified resentment, but it helps modify Victor's feelings toward the world outside the "rez." At last, Victor gets to scatter Arnold's ashes where both he and Thomas feel Arnold's spirit belongs: over the Spokane Falls. Meanwhile, in a voice-over, Thomas leaves us with thoughts about forgiving our fathers: "How do we forgive our fathers? Maybe in a dream? . . . Do we forgive our fathers for leaving us too often when we were little, or scaring us with unexpected rage or making us nervous because there never seems to be any rage at all? . . . Shall we forgive them for their excesses of warmth, or coldness, shall we forgive them for pushing, or leaning, for shutting doors, for speaking through walls, or being silent? . . . If we forgive our fathers, what is left?"

Study Questions

1. What do you think made Victor come to terms with his father's disappearance and death? How has Victor changed? Why didn't Thomas change as much?

2. Thomas can make any mundane situation into an interesting, magical time by telling stories about it—but the stories are not always true. Is this morally acceptable? Why or why not?

3. Apply Martha Nussbaum's theory of the rationality of emotions to Victor's situation: Was Victor's anger at his father rational? Why or why not? How can we tell? (Clue: What happened to Victor's anger when he learned the truth about his father?) Why did his jealousy toward Thomas disappear? And what happened to his resentment of "white people"?

4. Why do Western movies play such a big role in Thomas's and Victor's lives? Do you think it is a positive or a negative role?

5. What is funny about the boys' remark that they are more like Tonto and Tonto?

 Narrative

The Eichmann Show

SIMON BLOCK (TELEPLAY)
PAUL ANDREW WILLIAMS (DIRECTOR)

BBC Television film, 2015. Summary

Based on the Fruchtman-Hurwitz documentary series, *Eichmann on Trial*, 1961.

The Eichmann Show, a British television docudrama, qualifies as a story suited to raise a moral issue according to Martha Nussbaum's criterion for a biography and/or a history because it contains "particularity and emotive appeal." In addition, it features an analysis of evil that matches what you have read earlier in this chapter, inspired by the very same event witnessed by Hannah Arendt, after which she gave the world the concept "banality of evil." The film blends authentic footage from the 1961 documentary with filmed sequences telling the story of the television production, and we see the Eichmann trial through the lenses of the cameras in addition to following the discussion between the producer and the director about what was most important, the documenting of Nazi atrocities for the world to see and remember, or an analysis of Eichmann himself and his inner motivations and emotions.

It is 1961, and Adolf Eichmann, the brain behind the Holocaust, has just been captured in Argentina and transported to Israel where he is about to stand trial. American TV producer Milton Fruchtman hopes to be given permission to televise the trial live to the world, and contacts Hollywood documentary director Leo Hurwitz, who has been blacklisted by the 1950s hunt for communists and communist sympathizers, the phenomenon we today know as McCarthyism. Hurwitz is happy to be offered the job, and they meet in Jerusalem. The trial judges aren't yet on board with the project, but once they see that camera can be totally hidden from view, they give their permission. Leo Hurwitz meets his Israeli camera crew and gives them an introductory speech about what they are about to witness: the trial of a man who has done monstrous things.

> Hurwitz: "I don't believe in monsters, but I believe that men are responsible for monstrous things. What transformed this ordinary man [Eichmann] into someone who was capable of sending hundreds of thousands of children to their deaths, and then going home every evening and kissing his own children goodnight? A human being like any of us?"
>
> Yaakov Jonilowicz, one of the camera crew, speaks up: "He is not like us. I am not Eichmann."
>
> Hurwitz: "Under the circumstances anyone is capable of fascist behavior."
>
> Yaakov: "Not I."

Later on in the film, we find out Yaakov's background, and his reason for being so adamant.

The trial begins, with Eichmann in a glass enclosure. Fruchtman is committed to reaching a worldwide audience, but people's TVs are tuned to the developing crisis in Cuba known as the "Bay of Pigs," and the first man in space, the Russian cosmonaut Juri Gagarin. Fruchtman predicts that once the witness testimonies start, the audiences will return. And he is right.

Eyewitness after eyewitness is presented in court (here we see the actual footage from the trial): One man, a Jew who was a death camp prisoner but ordered to be a gravedigger, tells how he witnessed truckloads of Jews arriving at the death camp and being gassed inside the trucks. The trucks were then driven to a mass grave site where the bodies were dumped. Among the bodies he had to bury were his own wife and their two children. Another witness, a Jewish woman, tells how she escaped a mass shooting. Everybody was forced to strip naked and herded to a pit, and there they were gunned down, including babies. She was not mortally wounded, and managed to crawl out from under the mounds of bodies. Yet another witness recounts how four trucks arrived from Paris with Jews—1,000 children and 200 adults in each truck, all dead. One witness is overcome with emotion at his own testimony, and collapses in court. Another witness tells of how he was forced to work in Auschwitz as 14-year-old, and being so cold that he hid out inside the warm crematorium with bodies still in the ovens. Furthermore, he was forced to spread the ashes of the dead on the paths so the Nazis wouldn't slide. We learn that overall, 112 survivors and eyewitnesses bear testimony against Eichmann. Eichmann is listening to it all, and we watch his face (the real footage from 1961), and there is hardly any reaction. A smirk, a drawn corner of his mouth, but no emotional reaction that would indicate that he feels anything at all.

Under the testimonies Yaakov is beginning to feel ill, and several of the younger men in the camera crew have to leave the room, overwhelmed with disgust and emotional turmoil. It becomes clear to Fruchtman and Hurwitz that Yaakov has been in a death camp himself, and is suffering from what we today call PTSD, posttraumatic stress disorder—and this is why his denial of having any fascist tendencies was so heartfelt. He says that he wants to continue with the production because this is the first time after the war that survivors feel they can speak out and be believed. The same thought is expressed by Hurwitz's landlady in Jerusalem, hotel and restaurant owner Mrs. Landau, who also survived a concentration camp. She tells Hurwitz that the survivors haven't talked about their traumatic experiences because nobody was willing to believe them, but now that the trial is being transmitted, people are willing to listen—because of him. And she gives him a piece of chocolate cake, on the house.

While the trial is being filmed and transmitted, an argument erupts between Fruchtman and Hurwitz, because Hurwitz was focusing the camera on Eichmann's unemotional face, and missed the collapse of the witness. Fruchtman accuses Hurwitz of conducting "a personal investigation of the nature of evil" instead of doing what he is paid to do, filming the whole trial. Hurwitz insist that they can do both, but Fruchtman says that the two visions get in the way of each other. Hurwitz is waiting for a sign in Eichmann's face that he is cracking up—that somehow, the horror of the stories will affect him emotionally so much that he will have a breakdown. And it will be the face of a person confronting his own evil deeds. Fruchtman says Eichmann probably isn't going to crack, because he has been trained in watching atrocities, but it really doesn't matter if he cracks or not, because the story of Nazi atrocities will be exposed to the world regardless of Eichmann's reactions. The two completely different moral narratives—exposing the Nazi atrocities, and exposing one man's struggle with himself, are competing for attention in the TV production. Even on a day off, Hurwitz can't stop thinking and talking about Eichmann, and he explains to one of the young TV crew that it is important that people watch the TV coverage of Eichmann so they will see that we are all capable of it, and how we can resist the temptation to submit to authority pressure and prejudice.

The cross-examination of Eichmann begins, and Hurwitz watches for any emotional reaction. Eichmann, as well as the entire world through television, watches films shot at the liberation of the death camps, with emaciated prisoners, piles of bodies, all the atrocities documented for the world to see. We see how the camera crew (the actors) and the audience at the trial (in 1961) react in horror and revulsion. But Eichmann still isn't reacting.

Behind the scenes Hurwitz and Fruchtman have another talk, less confrontational than the previous scene. Hurwitz wants to leave, quit, and go home, even if his wife is there to provide moral support. He feels that he has failed because his camera hasn't picked up any change in Eichmann's demeanor. Fruchtman responds, "Because you couldn't find any humanity in Eichmann? Maybe because it isn't there?" It is the filming of the trial that is the important story, and it is unfolding successfully. The Nazi horrors are now documented and will never be forgotten or explained away.

And in the end Eichmann caves: He denies ever having given orders resulting in torture and deaths; he claims he has been following orders (from heads of security and others) and that he is not responsible. But in a certain case where Jewish prisoners were forced on a long march to their deaths, he concedes that it was he who *proposed* it. The judges now pronounce him guilty of the murders of millions of Jews, Poles, Gypsies, and other people targeted for extermination by the Nazis, and sentence him to death by hanging, claiming that even if he blindly followed orders, he should still have refused. (The following year, 1962, Eichmann was indeed executed by hanging.)

Milton Fruchtman's and Leo Hurwitz's television coverage was the first global documentary series, and it ends with these words, spoken by Fruchtman himself:

> "For each of us who has ever felt that God created us better than any other human being has stood on the threshold where Eichmann once stood. And each of us who allowed the shape of another person's nose, or the color of their skin, or the manner in which they worship their God to poison our feeling toward them, have known the loss of reason that led Eichmann to his madness. For this is how it all began, for those who did these things."

Study Questions

1. This story features two competing moral narratives, one where the evils of the Nazi reign need to be exposed to the world so we will never forget, and the other being the attempted insight into a person responsible for many of those evils, trying to gauge the depths of his heart and his conscience. Which story do you think it more important? Do they really "get in the way of each other"?

2. Hannah Arendt's concept "the banality of evil" is never mentioned in the film, but even so, one might say it provides the foundation for some of the statements from Hurwitz and the judges. Identify which ones.

3. Is Fruchtman right that each of us could be standing on the threshold of fascism if we think we are better than others? Is Yaakov, and victims like him, an exception (remember he says, "He is not like us. I am not Eichmann!")? Explain.

4. The defense "I was just following orders" has been considered unacceptable in Western courts ever since the Nuremberg trials of Nazi war criminals in the late 1940s, because it is assumed that we ought to have enough character to refuse to follow orders that go against our common sense of humanity. Can you think of a case where someone might claim to just having been following orders, committing some atrocity, and the court might take it under consideration?

5. How might Martha Nussbaum evaluate the value of this story as a way to discuss moral issues?

Chapter Two
Learning Moral Lessons from Stories

We may think that the most powerful moral lessons are learned from events in our childhood (when we are caught doing something we aren't supposed to do, or when we *aren't* caught), but chances are the most powerful lessons we carry with us are lessons we learn from the *stories* we have read or that were read to us.

Didactic Stories

Many of you may recognize this typical, unpleasant event from childhood: Your authority figure takes you aside to tell you Aesop's fable "The Boy Who Cried Wolf." A lad was tending sheep at the outskirts of town, and he thought it might be fun to give the village a scare, so he cried, "The wolf is here! The wolf is here!" And the villagers came running, but there was no wolf. The boy tricked the town again and again, until that fateful day when the wolf really did come. The boy cried for his life, "The wolf is here!" but nobody believed him anymore. The wolf ate the sheep and the shepherd too. At least, that is the way the story was told to me when I was five years old.

Why are children told such a gruesome story? Because adults deem it necessary to teach children a moral lesson. Even a child understands the message: "The shepherd boy lied and suffered the consequences. You don't want to be like him, do you?" It is a powerful lesson. Indeed, the appeal of the story seems to go beyond European and American traditions: I have a colleague from India who tells me that when she was a little girl in Calcutta, she was told the story of the boy who cried tiger.

Stories that are told to teach a moral lesson are called *didactic* stories. These instructional stories may well be as old as humanity. When giving a keynote address about stories in ethics at a philosophical retreat in Denmark some years ago, I asked the audience, a mixed group of several hundred people ranging from their teens to their eighties, if they had been told the story of "The Boy Who Cried Wolf" when they were kids; a forest of hands went up, young smooth hands alongside gnarled old hands, and all of a sudden it seemed to me that I was looking down the corridor of time, from these living generations backward to the other generations long gone, each one of them telling their children about the lying shepherd boy—in all likelihood a story so old that it predates Aesop's version.

The New Interest in Stories Across the Professions

The interest in using stories (narratives) to explore moral problems is increasing, for stories can serve as a laboratory in which moral solutions can be tried out before any decisions are made. Here are some examples of how stories are being used as moral laboratories today.

- In an op-ed piece in the *New York Times,* "Practicing Medicine Is Grimm Work," medical student Valerie Gribben tells how she deals with difficult situations as a prospective medical doctor by keeping in mind the lessons in human nature she believes she has learned from reading the fairytales collected by the Brothers Grimm:

The Grimm fairy tales once seemed as if they took place in lands far, far away, but I see them now in my everyday hospital rotations. I've met the eternal cast of characters. I've taken down their histories (the abandoned prince, the barren couple) or seen their handiwork (the evil stepmother, the lecherous king).

Fairy tales are, at their core, heightened portrayals of human nature, revealing, as the glare of injury and illness does, the underbelly of mankind. Both fairy tales and medical charts chronicle the bizarre, the unfair, the tragic. And the terrifying things that go bump in the night are what doctors treat at 3 A.M. in emergency rooms.

So I now find comfort in fairy tales. They remind me that happy endings are possible. . . . They also remind me that what I'm seeing now has come before. Child endangerment is not an invention of the Facebook age. Elder neglect didn't arrive with Gen X. And discharge summaries are not always happy; "Cinderella" originally ended with a blinding, and Death, in his tattered shroud, waits at the end of many journeys.

She is not alone. For the past few decades medical students have been increasingly exposed to not only case studies involving medical ethics but also to stories of fiction, such as Leo Tolstoy's "The Death of Iván Ilyich" (1886) and the 1994 film *Philadelphia,* that deal with medical problems. The students seem to feel better equipped to deal with "real" problems because of this exploratory background. Why? Because no matter how many case histories she examines or how many colleagues she talks to, a medical student may not be able to understand a patient from the inside quite as well as when a great writer tells the story from the patient's point of view. The New York University School of Medicine's Literature, Arts, and Medicine Database is a website dedicated to listing films and works of literature that may be of help as a resource for medical personnel, such as *And the Band Played On, Awakenings, Gattaca, Lorenzo's Oil, The English Patient, The Doctor,* and even *Million Dollar Baby,* with its euthanasia theme. Books include Christy Brown's *My Left Foot,* Camus's *The Plague,* and Jane Austen's *Emma.* The AllhealthCare website lists 10 recommended movies with medical themes, including *Patch Adams* and *My Own Country,* and Scrubsmag.com has its own list, including both tearjerkers and comedies. The Literature and Medicine program in Maine has since 1997 gathered health care professionals around the concept that reading and discussing literature can improve their professional skills and help them understand their patients and clients. In addition, patients with psychological issues have occasionally been encouraged to use movies as a sort of self-treatment, but such advice should always be followed up with a discussion. There are no quick fixes to our psychological, social, and moral problems; good stories can help us begin to explore an issue—but they can't be a substitute for insight or discussion. That also means that the stories you encounter in this book are meant to illustrate typical moral problems and possible solutions, but they aren't meant to stand alone as problem solvers.

- Some psychologists are advocating a method called *bibliotherapy* to facilitate communication between parents and children. Through reading stories with their children, parents may find it easier to explain difficult issues, because together, through the fictional universe, they can explore issues and emotions that may be more difficult to approach on either an abstract or a highly personal level. For example, it's hard to explain death to children—either as a concept or as a real event in a family. Perhaps a story about the death of a pet could help focus the discussion. Of course, this may be just an easy way out for parents who don't have a clue how to relate to their children, but ideally the sharing of stories is a positive way to make the child understand about arrivals of new siblings, a move to a new home, deaths in the family, and other traumatic events. (It may sound like a brand new idea, but in the next section you will see that this is in effect how myths and fairy tales used to work in traditional societies.) An offshoot of bibliotherapy is the new field of *cinematherapy*, advocating not only viewing TV series and movies to de-stress, but even to binge-watch, in order to chase the stress components of one's life away from one's immediate attention. Critics have pointed out, however, that once the bingeing is over, the stress factors tend to reappear.

- The criminal justice system is experimenting with the use of stories. The *ABA Journal* has a dedicated website, "The 25 Greatest Legal Movies," updated regularly, topped by *To Kill a Mockingbird* and including *12 Angry Men, My Cousin Vinny, Anatomy of a Murder, Inherit the Wind, A Few Good Men*, and *Witness for the Prosecution*. The interest in the didactic value of such films to the legal community is no longer something that just happens by accident after someone goes to the movies and sees a connection to real-life cases—it is now something that is an accepted and established form of learning. But this isn't just of abstract interest to scholars and lawyers: Increasingly, the courts in the Western world are experimenting with exposing convicted criminals to novels and films that may cause them to rethink their own lives and understand the severity of their crimes. Case in point: A poacher in Missouri who had been arrested for illegally killing hundreds of deer, cutting off their heads and leaving their bodies to rot, was sentenced by a judge to one year in prison, *and* to watch the Disney movie *Bambi* at least once a month.

- Psychotherapists are having patients tell about their own lives as if they were stories or asking them to select a famous fairy tale as a model or template of the way they see their own lives. The idea of telling one's own story as a form of therapy and moral education is something we will look at in detail in the final chapter.

- Stories have been found to have great potential for promoting cross-cultural or multicultural understanding. They can highlight cultural differences in a way that presents them as exciting and worth exploring, while emphasizing the fundamental human similarities underneath the surface differences.

- NASA and Tor/Forge Books have teamed up in an attempt to create exciting stories about space exploration. NASA's hope is that such novels, written with both scientific accuracy and imagination, can awaken an interest in space and science in general among young people, similar to the way science-fiction novels in the 1950s and 60s inspired an entire generation of space scientists and astronauts. We'll have to wait a couple of decades, though, to see if the idea has caught on, but evidence is in that the 2015 film *The Martian* and the 2018 film *Ad Astra* have reawakened the interest in space exploration, and NASA has followed up with the release of a series of "travel posters" depicting future space destinations such as Mars. JPOL strategic visualist Dan Goods says, "Imagination is so critical to creating a future you want to be part of. Many of the things we are doing today were imagined by artists and science fiction writers decades ago. These destinations are all actual places that we know about, and one day, perhaps humans can go to them in the future."

- Last on this list, but not least: An increasing number of *philosophers* are now looking to stories as a way not only to explain difficult theories to their freshman students but also to explore the philosophical richness of literature and films in itself. The venerable publishing house Blackwell has had enormous success with its expanding series of philosophy books featuring a work of fiction, such as *The Ultimate Star Trek and Philosophy, Game of Thrones and Philosophy, Lord of the Rings and Philosophy, Harry Potter and Philosophy,* all the way to *The Good Place and Philosophy*. Active on the social network Twitter, Blackwell has solicited public participation, asking for new movie/graphic novel/novel title recommendations to add to their series. Unthinkable a few decades ago, such a success doesn't happen in a vacuum: There is a genuine

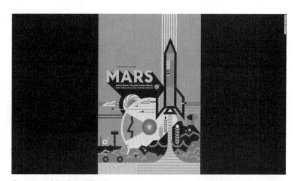

Courtesy NASA/JPL-Caltech

NASA is actively hoping to recruit a new generation of space-interested young people by supporting realistic stories of space exploration such as *The Martian* and releasing posters such as this one, designed by NASA's Jet Propulsion Laboratory (JPL) Studio, imagining Mars as a habitable world. In addition, NASA is sending out a call to college students to consider applying for astronaut training, in particular for a future mission to Mars.

professional interest in reading philosophy into fiction, and interpreting fiction through philosophy these days, to the enthusiastic applause of some, and head-scratching of others.

Until recently, most American philosophers have been suspicious of using stories as illustrations of moral problems for several reasons. Some have felt that using stories would cause readers to be concerned with *specific* cases rather than with seeing the general picture. Others have worried that telling stories might manipulate readers' emotions instead of appealing to their reason: Such stories would perhaps lead people to *do* the right thing, but they wouldn't lead people to *think* about moral issues, because a story is not a logical argument but, rather, a persuasion—a story is not logic but rhetoric. And the danger would, of course, also be that the reader might be seduced into doing the *wrong* thing—either by emulating one of the "evil" characters in the story, or by being sucked into the universe of a story going against mainstream values. We look at such possibilities below, and in Chapter 3 we examine the possibility of values being relative to different cultures.

Interestingly, literature professors have been just as reluctant to strike up a conversation with philosophers, fearing that the formal demands of a quality work of fiction would be compromised if there is too much focus on some underlying truth or message—novels aren't supposed to be "preachy," in other words. But with the new bridges being built in recent years between literature and philosophy some of those fears are being put aside, and literature and philosophy scholars such as Charles Johnson (see end of chapter) and Stephen George have been collaborating on an emerging field: *Philosophy of fiction.* And stories don't have to be preachy in order to be philosophical: There is a difference between stories that moralize and stories that discuss moral problems. In the past, philosophers seem to have assumed that stories illustrating moral problems are always of the moralizing kind. Now a different attitude seems to be growing among ethics scholars; they recognize that stories need not be moralizing to illustrate a moral point. Such stories may express a moral point of view, and then that point of view can be open for discussion. Or a story may have an open-ended conclusion, one in which the moral issues are not resolved. Even moralizing stories may have their proper role to play from time to time, and stories are an excellent way to illustrate how difficult a moral problem can be. As noted in Chapter 1, the field of philosophy is also slowly warming up to the old idea that feelings are not irrelevant in moral discussions. The psychologist Carol Gilligan argues for the legitimacy of emotions in moral decision making. As you know, Martha Nussbaum points out that emotions are not a matter of something uncontrollable, like hunger, but instead involve decision making and rational choices. Another philosopher, Philip Hallie, states that without feelings for the victims of evildoing, we can't hope to understand what a moral sense is all about. Jonathan Bennett, another contemporary philosopher, insists that although certain moral principles may be admirable, others may be warped: The Nazi exterminators had firm moral principles, but they were principles most people don't approve of today. Without sympathy for other people, our principles may go astray. One of the ways in which we can engage both our sympathy and our moral principles is through stories.

Some of the stories in this book are didactic (they teach a lesson), and some of them are more open-ended. It seems that, usually, we prefer learning from stories that were *not* written especially to teach a lesson. That may be one of the secrets of literature: We may forgive a good story for preaching a little, but we can't forgive a bad story for preaching. In other words, we are most accepting of a moral lesson if it is not too obvious, if it appears only between the lines and is subordinate to the plot and the characters. The stories that are most effective in teaching lessons may be those that are not obviously intended to do so. Examples of extreme didactic films would be the 1915 classic *The Birth of a Nation* (the Civil War seen from the Southern viewpoint) and *Reefer Madness,* a film generally viewed today as a propaganda film against the use of marijuana. Stories with more dimensions to them, and thus more interesting to a modern audience, might be films such as *Monster's Ball* and *Mystic River* or the anti-drug films *Drugstore Cowboy, Requiem for a Dream,* and *Fear and Loathing in Las Vegas.*

Of course, real-life events and discussions of those events are essential to our understanding of moral issues, but using stories is an alternative way of talking about these issues, because a story can serve as a slice of life that we are invited to share in.

The Value of Stories Across Time and Space

Why do we tell stories? And why is it relevant for moral philosophy? What we do know is that all cultures have narratives, and most cultures operate with some story types that are fictional. Apparently we can't help telling stories with a beginning, a middle, and an ending. We are truly what the Scottish philosopher Alasdair MacIntyre has called us, "story-telling animals." And recently, neuroscientists have begun to weigh in on why humans are so prone to storytelling. Neuroscientist Michael Gazzaniga, University of California, Santa Barbara, has proposed a theory based on years of research into the two brain hemispheres: Our left brain hemisphere attempts to make sense out of our feelings and experiences as well as our conscious and subconscious thoughts by putting a story together about them, a cause-and-effect story which helps us get a sense of who we are, and how to cope with life and the unexpected. Other researchers have found that we tend to identify with protagonists in stories, and we react to stories with the same brain regions that are engaged when we react to real-life events. And good stories make us *feel good*—there is a release of oxytocin in the brain that may actually make us slightly addicted to good stories. The immediate evolutionary benefits to such a phenomenon seem to include a kind of social bonding or glue—we get hooked on telling each other the same stories, and that helps us survive as a group. On the flip side, that may also open up for the possibility of manipulation and brainwashing by those who have the social power to tell the official versions of the stories, so it is a double-edged sword to have the capacity for storytelling. It may make us live better, and make more sense of our lives, but it may also facilitate power plays.

There are of course many reasons for telling stories, for reading and writing novels and short stories, and for making and watching films. It seems that in early, pretechnological cultures the purpose of storytelling was twofold: On the *human* side, the purpose was to knit the tribe firmly together by setting up the rules and boundaries that would establish a group identity. Besides, storytelling helped to pass the time on rainy days, and it kept the children occupied for a while. On the *cosmic* side, the purpose was to establish the story of the beginning of time, when everything was created, so if a symbolic re-creation seemed necessary (and it did, periodically), one could tell and enact the "beginning" stories and in that way "renew" the cosmos. Storytelling has never been more important than it was in those ancient times, for in telling the story people helped re-create the universe, put the sun in its right place, and made sure that the seasons followed one another in the proper order.

The strength of storytelling is no less apparent in many religions. Periodically (usually once a year), believers remind themselves of an important time in the history of their religion: the creation of the world, the creation of the religion itself, or the establishment of the believers' identity through a religious event. Usually a story is told about that event, and even if it is supposed to be a reminder rather than a re-creation, it is still a sacred and powerful vehicle.

In ancient times the storytellers were the primary teachers of morals. Of course, parents have always had a hand in moral education, but in pretechnological cultures (what used to be called "primitive" cultures), those who knew the legends were the ones who, in effect, represented the social institutions of religion, school, and government. The myths surrounding the origin of the world, of society, of food items, and of love and death and the stories of the important men and women in the tribe's past provided rules for the tribe to live by—moral structures that could be used in everyday life to make decisions about crops, marriages, warfare, and so forth. The way to teach children how to become good members of the tribe was to tell the old stories.

The question of *how long* humans have been telling stories has until recently been a matter of guesswork. We have cave paintings dating back 60,000 years and further, and sometimes they look like panels in a graphic novel, so we assume that they refer to some kind of story, perhaps about a hunt or a battle. And according to neuroscience, humans are hard-wired to tell stories so as to make sense of our lives. So perhaps we humans have been storytellers as long as we have had language, which takes us back at least 300,000 years when humanity consisted of a small group of Homo Sapiens struggling to survive in Africa, before spreading out into the world. But some scholars have now taken it upon themselves to provide solid proof of the age of some of the stories we still know today, such as Beauty and the Beast, by comparing the languages in which they're told in a *phylogenetic* analysis, an analysis of the rate of changes in languages with a common origin, and they've found that some stories within the Indo-European tradition go back at least 6000 years. We take a closer look at that research in the section on fairy tales below.

In ancient times, stories apparently had the moral function of assuring the members of the community that there was a clear difference between right and wrong. In our technological world we no longer have such a body of ready-made prescriptions for moral conduct—at least, we don't think we do. In fact, however, we still tell stories, we still listen to stories, and we still take moral lessons from them. Some people read the Bible, the Torah, the Quran, or other religious books and seek comfort in their stories of human frailty and perseverance. Some people keep their Marvel comic-book collections and dive into the old stories from time to time for some basic moral reinforcement. Some people read biographies of remarkable men and women and are inspired by the stories of courage and bravery. Adults may not read fairy tales anymore, but we read novels—classics, bestsellers, or even graphic novels. And if we don't read novels, we go to the movies or watch TV, including Netflix and YouTube. And as my students like to point out, today's computer games have graduated from being simple target practice to stories with deeply involved plots and complex characters. Wherever we turn we find *stories*—some are real and some fictional, some are too outdated or too radical for us to relate to, but we find at least some stories that have served as our moral guideposts. Even if you are not a great reader or movie-goer, you probably can recall at least one story that has moved you.

Fact, Fiction, or Both?

In the secular world we usually tell stories of two kinds: those that we believe to be historically true and those that we know never took place but that have their own special truth to them, a *poetic* truth. The fairy tale "Little Red Riding Hood" is not a historical account, but children may enjoy it if they are old enough to deal with their fear of the wolf, who comes to a gruesome end. Parents enjoy telling it, because they can smuggle home a lesson: Don't talk to strangers, and watch out for "wolves" in disguise. Box 2.1 looks at reality TV—which purports to be fact, not fiction.

Box 2.1 REALITY SHOWS: WHERE DID THE STORY GO?

Although the academic interest in stories has been on the increase, some story aficionados worry that the public interest in stories may be on the wane, considering the popularity of *reality shows*. TV shows such as *Survivor* and *The Bachelor* have scored top ratings, but that's not all: The public's interest in the lives of "public figures," whether they be celebrities, criminals, or just ordinary people caught up in some media circus, has also been on the rise. An entire TV channel, HGTV, is producing stories of buying, selling, and renovating homes, featuring real-estate and designer professionals who, in turn, have become famous for playing themselves on TV. Some media analysts claim there is a decreasing interest in made-up stories these days, and an increased interest in real stories. There are two things we can say about that: For one thing, "reality shows" aren't really real—sorry to burst that bubble. As much as they feature "real people," they are scripted to a great extent and their content and structure are heavily edited. That means that even if they don't have a clear plot structure laid out beforehand, they are still narratives—stories that interest us. For another, perhaps there is a reason why the stories of "real people" attract attention these days. As we shall see in a later chapter, there are even philosophical theories about why we all of a sudden care so much about these strangers. The positive spin, as we shall see in Chapter 4, is that we extend the feelings we have for friends and relatives to these strangers, for a while. The negative spin, which I will suggest here, is that our world, presented to us by the media, has started to seem overwhelming to us. Our brains have evolved, through hundreds of thousands of years, into tribal brains, focusing on interacting intimately with a group of people probably no bigger than about one hundred members, mostly relatives and neighbors. That meant close interaction, with lots of talk and gossip about those relatives and neighbors. But most of us no longer live in such communities—we don't know our neighbors, and we have little connection to our relatives. But we still have the need for tribal gossip and concern—so we turn to those new neighbors of ours, the TV people. And the more "real" they seem, the more we (or some of us) feel engaged in their destinies. One needs to think of the success of the Kardassian family, being at first the center of a reality show, and ending up being propelled to popular culture status. Some people would say, "Then get a life!" But this *is* our life in the modern world, for better or worse. The upside is that our horizon literally expands, through the stories of others, factual as well as fictional, introducing moral issues we would never have related to or even imagined in previous times. We have all now been educated in the unethical: insider trading, child molestations by priests, religious fanatics kidnapping children and brainwashing them, red herrings introduced in court cases to confuse juries, and so forth. The downside is, of course, that this expanded interest may be nothing but a thirst for titillation, a ghoulish rubbernecking taken to an extreme. Another downside may be that, as some psychologists have concluded, our natural empathy may actually be eroded by reality shows because we end up thinking of the characters as fictional rather than real. How much should we engage ourselves in other people's problems, and to what extent should the media report them? We return to such issues in Chapter 13.

What about accounts that we don't know to be either historical or poetic? The story of Zorro, for example, is not a historical account, although there may have been an outlaw in Old California who vaguely resembled the Zorro character. Some readers feel cheated if they find out that a story is more legend than history, but others find it all the more fascinating because it is a mixture of what we think happened and what we wish had happened. It may not tell us much about history, but it tells us a great deal about people, including ourselves, who *wish* that Zorro were real.

Even stories that we believe to be factual, such as the story of the battle of the Alamo or the sinking of the *Titanic,* are not usually simple reports of facts; such stories must have a beginning, a middle, and an ending, and most often we choose the beginning and the ending according to what we feel makes the most *sense.* In actual life, the stream of events goes on, usually with little indication that here begins something new or here a story comes to an end—except in the case of someone's birth or death. Even in the latter case, the story goes on without the person who has died. So even "true" stories have an element of *poetic creativity,* in that we choose what to include in the story, what is *relevant* to the story (not every meal or visit to the bathroom is important in order for us to understand the life and times of Gandhi, or Muhammed Ali, or Princess Diana), and where to begin and end the story. Even eyewitness accounts, often regarded as the one true record of events, are full of creativity. Two persons observing the same event will very likely come up with slightly different versions of it; they notice different things because they are standing in different spots and because they are different people with different interests in life. If eyewitnesses are asked to tell about an event long past, some of their memories will be sharper than others, some will mirror exactly what they saw, and some will mirror what they felt or what they feel now, which turns their stories into personal interpretations of the event. At best, any account of a past event can only approximate what happened. We can never truly reproduce the event.

Religious legends reveal the same tension between fact and fiction. If believers suspect that events described in the legends never happened or that they happened in a different and more "everyday" way than is described in the religious text, they may experience a general disappointment with their religion, or they may elect to deny the possibility that the religious stories are less than fact-based, or they may deny the plausibility of new interpretations of the old stories—such as we saw in the aftermath of the fictional novel by Dan Brown, *The DaVinci Code* (see below). Other believers, however, may see the stories as being rich with poetry and telling human truths that are on a higher, more spiritual level. Aristotle, who was intensely interested in the relationship between history and poetry, said that history may deal with facts, but poetry deals with Truth.

Folktales and Other Traditional Stories

The term *folktales* is a generic term for stories told orally within any given culture (and then written down at a later time in history). Often there is a fantastic or supernatural element in the story, and they usually carry some kind of social or religious message—a moral to the story.

Myths

We don't know anything about the first stories ever told, but if we are to judge from ancient myths and legends, there is a good chance that they served as reminders of proper conduct. The Cherokees tell of Grandmother Spider's way of making clay pots, and it seems to be (among other things) a lesson for Cherokee women in how to make pots the correct way. Myths in general have two main purposes: to strengthen the social bonding among people and to fortify the individual psychologically. *Traditional myths* work on those two levels at once by presenting stories of gods, goddesses, and culture heroes who tell their society about the ideal social behavior and individuals about the proper role models to follow. In a sense, traditional myths are a successful combination of *ethics of conduct* and *virtue ethics,* giving answers to age-old questions within the category of "What should I do?" as well as "How should I be?" (See Chapters 1 and 8.)

The myth of the loss of immortality told by the Trobriand people of New Guinea is such a story. It tells us that once humans could rejuvenate themselves; they could shed their skins and become young again. A grandmother took her granddaughter to the river and then went off by herself to shed her skin. When she came back, the granddaughter didn't recognize her (she appeared to be a young girl) and shooed her away. Upset, the grandmother went back and put her old skin on again. The granddaughter told her that she had chased a young girl, an impostor, away. The grandmother said, "Just because you refused to recognize me, nobody will be able to be young again. We shall all die of old age now." Aside from the fact that the story unfairly places the immense burden of causing mortality on an ignorant young girl—myths often blame a major disaster on a small event, as when Eve eats the fruit from the Tree of Knowledge—the lesson is that we humans are mortal and there is nothing we can do about it. The story also seems to say that humans, far from being victims, are very important beings, since they can cause such a cosmic calamity as the loss of immortality!

Fairy Tales

Another ancient category of stories with moral lessons is the *fairy tale*. As you read above, new research has shown that some folktales date back thousands of years as an oral tradition. Researchers Jamshid Tehrani and Sarah Graca da Silva have shown, in "Comparative Phylogenic Analyses Uncover the Ancient Roots of Indo-European Folktales" (2016) that stories such as *Beauty and the Beast* and *Rumplestiltskin* have been told from generation to generation in various versions for the past 4000 years, some of them dating back as far as 6000 years. The fairy tales collected by the Grimm brothers in early-nineteenth-century Germany reflect what has now been proven to be a very old tradition of stories with morals, and they are not just for children; the stories were told originally to both young and old. And furthermore, it seems to be worldwide. The Trobriand people distinguish between three kinds of stories. First, there are the "myths," which are sacred stories about the beginning of the world and of society. They must be taken very seriously. Second, there are the "true legends," semihistorical accounts of heroes in the past and their travels. They are supposed to be taken at face value, for the most part. Last, there are the "fairy tales," stories to be told in the rainy season, usually with some point of teaching the young about the customs of the people but also with the intent of pure entertainment. They are recognized as never having happened.

Most cultures acknowledge that there is a difference between stories in which the good are rewarded and the evil are punished and stories of everyday life. The fairy tale has been described by psychoanalysts as pure wishful thinking, but many fairy tales involve gruesome events that are hardly wish fulfillments, because they often happen to characters who don't "deserve" them. Such events do serve a purpose, though, in making the punishment of the evil characters seem justified (for a discussion of the concept of evil, see Chapter 1).

Literature scholars believed until recently that the tale of Little Red Riding Hood was a product of the literary elite, not a folktale, but Tehrani and da Silva have shown that it, too, is several thousand years old, and has obviously been thriving because of its didactic power. "Hansel and Gretel" is a folklore classic with much the same lesson: Don't go with strangers, and don't let them feed you candy! But the most famous fairy tales from the Grimm brothers' collection today are probably those that have been revised for modern audiences by Walt Disney Studios, such as *Cinderella* and *Snow White and the Seven Dwarfs*. The cartoon versions are known by several generations of moviegoers, videotape purchasers, DVD collectors and their children, and subscribers to Internet video channels. The animated Disney *Cinderella* (1950) is an upbeat story of the poor orphan girl who lives with her wealthy stepmother and stepsisters in a huge old house, where she is treated like an unpaid servant or a slave. When the king of the country invites all unmarried young women to a grand ball at the castle to meet the prince so he can choose a wife, the evil stepsisters sabotage Cinderella's dream of going to the ball. They tear to pieces the dress that her little friends the mice and the birds have made for her, and leave her in tears as they depart for the ball. But Cinderella's fairy godmother appears in a swirl of sparkles and transforms her into a radiant princess, with glass slippers. A pumpkin becomes a magic chariot, and her mice friends become horses, her dog becomes a valet, and her old horse becomes a coachman, but only for the evening. She must leave the ball before midnight, because then everything reverts to the way it was. You probably know the rest of the story: She meets the prince, and he falls in love with her, but midnight is approaching, so she runs away—leaving one glass slipper behind. And next day, the prince's servant scours the countryside to find the girl whose foot can fit into the glass slipper. Despite new attempts at sabotage from Cinderella's stepmother and the sisters, Cinderella emerges as the mystery woman from the ball, and she marries the prince and lives happily ever after. No punishment is meted out to her stepfamily for torturing her. That is the version most of us know. And although a child may rejoice that Cinderella is never going back to the harsh life of work and no love, there is perhaps a slight letdown that she magnanimously forgives her tormentors. Disney's 2015 version stayed by-and-large true to the general plot of the animated classic, with a few intrigue twists, and a lot of computer-generated imagery (CGI). Also, here Cinderella forgives her evil stepmother who is not punished for her scheming.

But if you ever sit down with a copy of *Grimm's Fairy Tales,* you'll encounter quite a different version. In the original story, Cinderella's father isn't dead; he is just oblivious to the torture his new wife and her pretty daughters put his daughter through. Her friends the doves and the pigeons are the ones with magic powers: There is no fairy godmother. While she is crying at her mother's grave under a magic tree, the birds bring her a gold party dress, as well as gold slippers. The essential plot of Cinderella meeting the prince and losing the slipper is the same as that of the modern version—but the aftermath is far more bloody. Since the sisters' feet are much bigger than Cinderella's, they try to fit into the slipper presented by the prince, in person, by cutting their heels and toes off, with blood seeping through the gold fabric. And when Cinderella marries the prince, the evil sisters are punished: They walk up the aisle as bridesmaids behind the bride, and Cinderella's pigeons peck their eyes out. "And so they were condemned to go blind for the rest of their days because of their wickedness and falsehood," as the story concludes.

An interesting variation on the theme that actually reaches back to the older version is the film *Ever After* (1998), in which one of Cinderella's evil sisters and the stepmother are in fact punished after Cinderella marries the prince—in a way that seems utterly appropriate to a modern mindset: They are sentenced to work in the laundry of the castle so they can understand the life they had forced Cinderella to live before her life changed. The shoe is now on the other foot (without cutting any toes or heels), and the moral lesson of *karma* is learned: What goes around, comes around.

What is interesting here is the development of the moral lessons embedded in the old story. Fairy tales at the time when the Grimm brothers collected the stories were folktales, told primarily by adults for adults, and the moral lessons were harsh and severe: Evil stepmothers, brothers, and sisters, or whoever tortured the good boy or girl, met a horrific end, a painful death or dismemberment, whereas the good person was rewarded with wealth and fame. In the Disney cartoons of the mid–twentieth century, the moral lesson seems to be not for the evil family members but for the suffering hero: Hang in there with fortitude, and things will change! Both *Ever After* and *Cinderella* (2015) reflect the changing times: Cinderella is a woman of initiative, action, and intellect, not someone who needs to be rescued, but in *Ever After* the stepsisters end up being punished in a way that will rehabilitate them and change them for the better!

The drastic revenge theme from the folklore of times past, not just in the West, but around the globe, has been interpreted by psychoanalysts as having a *cathartic*, cleansing function, perhaps even more so than putting an evil stepsister to work in the laundry: Some psychoanalysts today maintain that the real value of such stories—which, they say, children should not be protected from but, rather, exposed to—is that children can get rid of their aggressions toward their parents through the stories. (As we shall see in an upcoming section, Aristotle would have agreed with this psychoanalytic point of view.) In addition, the child is exposed to evil but at the same time acquires a dose of hopeful strength and learns that evil can be dealt with. In other words, the most horrible, gruesome, bloody fairy tales may be the ones with the most positive message for the impressionable reader: Yes, there are terrible things out there, but with fortitude we can vanquish them.

Parables

For 2000 years, Christians have found moral support in parables such as those of the Good Samaritan and the prodigal son.

The *parable* is an allegorical story for adults; it is supposed to be understood as a story about ourselves and what we ought to do. Although the purpose of the fairy tale seems to be primarily to entertain and secondarily to teach a moral lesson, the purpose of the parable is *primarily* to teach a moral and religious lesson. Christianity is not the only religion with parables; the Islamic, Hebrew, and Buddhist traditions contain such stories.

What fascinated the early readers of Jesus of Nazareth's parables was that they were so hard to live up to—not just because it was hard to be good, but also because the moral demands of Jesus himself usually ran counter to what society demanded of its citizens or what it viewed as proper moral conduct. What was so difficult for Jesus' contemporaries to understand? He demanded not only that we be compassionate toward all in need but also that we consider *every* person a fellow human being, not just those from our own village, country, or culture, and especially not just those who show compassion toward us.

The parable of the prodigal son (Luke 15:11–32) has been one such lesson that people with ordinary common sense and good manners find hard to follow. The "bad" son who has squandered his inheritance comes home and is sorry. The father makes a fuss over the bad son and slaughters the fattened calf for him. The good son, who has stayed with his father, is upset, for he has never received any recognition of his stability from his father, and yet now it seems that the bad son is more important. And he is, to Jesus, for he has been on a longer journey than the good son: all the way to perdition and back. Christians, therefore, ask themselves if that means we should go on a binge and then repent rather than never go on a binge at all. The answer may be that the story is supposed to be judged from the point of view not of the good or the bad brother but of the *father*. Indeed, the secret to many of the parables is to find out whose viewpoint they express. The parable of the Good Samaritan (Luke 10:30–34) is about a victim of highway robbery and mugging. As he lies wounded at the roadside, he is ignored by several upstanding citizens but is helped by a social outcast, the Samaritan. (The story is outlined in Chapter 11.) This parable is told from the wounded man's point of view ("who is my neighbor"), not from the point of view of the Samaritan.

Nicku/Shutterstock

The Trial of Abraham's Faith (plate by Gustave Doré, 1866). Abraham, having received the command from God to sacrifice his only son, Isaac, dutifully takes Isaac up the mountain to the place of sacrifice. Isaac, unaware that it is he himself who is to be the victim, is carrying the firewood that Abraham will use to light the sacrificial fire.

A Story of Sacrifice: Abraham and Isaac

Although it is not classified as a parable, the Old Testament story of Abraham being told to sacrifice his son Isaac (Genesis 22:1–19) has had the same kind of effect on its listeners. It is one of the hardest stories for a religion that believes in a loving God, be it from a Jewish or a Christian point of view, to explain. Abraham and his wife Sarah are childless until they have Isaac very late in their lives, through God's intervention. (Abraham already has another son, Ishmael, by Sarah's maid Hagar, conceived with Sarah's blessing to make up for her own inability to have children, but Isaac, being the legitimate son according to the tradition, now supersedes his older half-brother, who is eventually sent away by Abraham, along with Hagar.) God tells Abraham that his descendants through Isaac will be as numerous as the stars in the sky and the grains of sand in the desert. When Isaac is a half-grown boy, however, God tells Abraham to take Isaac up the mountain and sacrifice him like a sheep. Abraham leads Isaac away, heavyhearted but obedient to God. The boy believes they are on their way to sacrifice an animal to God, until his father ties him to the sacrificial stone and is about to stab him the ritual way when God's voice stops him, saying the request was just a test of Abraham's piety. God supplies a ram for Abraham to sacrifice instead.

The implications of this story have confounded believers and nonbelievers for over 2000 years. A God who commands such a thing must be a cruel God, critics say, cruel and with a strange sense of humor. The philosopher Søren Kierkegaard (see Chapter 11) sees the story as an illustration of the *limitations of ethics:* Ethically speaking, what Abraham was about to do was wrong; he had no business killing his son, because that is not how people are supposed to behave. But for Abraham, as for any believer, there is a law that is higher than the moral laws of society, and that is the law of *faith*—not faith that God will save his child, but faith that it really *is* God who is requiring him to sacrifice Isaac and that we can't know God's purpose. Kierkegaard saw Abraham's ordeal as a test of his faith in God rather than of his morals, and a "leap of faith" is, for the Lutheran Kierkegaard, a matter between the individual and God and nobody else. The opinion of society does not enter into the picture at all. Other interpretations of the story see no split between morality and faith but view it as an illustration of God's absolute demands on his people. Yet others see it as justification for sacrificing everything one holds dear if a higher law demands it. With this last interpretation it really is irrelevant that God stopped Abraham at the last moment. For all Christians, the parallel to a later time when God did not stop himself from sacrificing his own son to save the world is a close one. (See Box 2.2 for Franz Kafka's interpretation of this parable.)

A recent critique of the old story has been suggested by anthropologist Carol Delaney in her book *Abraham on Trial: The Social Legacy of Biblical Myth.* Delaney asks, Why should faith in God be illustrated best by a father's willingness to sacrifice his son? Why couldn't the test of faith instead be measured by a parent's willingness to *protect* his or her child, not sacrifice it? The story has been told as if Abraham is the sole parent, with sole rights and responsibilities, and the biblical writers obviously didn't see Isaac's mother, Sarah, as someone with a right to her opinion about the matter. Delaney isn't criticizing the male-dominated ways of the Old Testament so much as asking why nobody since then, of all the commentators in Judeo-Christian

Box 2.2 KAFKA'S ABRAHAM

In his nonfiction piece "Abraham," the Austrian-Czech novelist Franz Kafka (1883–1924) interprets the story of Abraham and Isaac in ways that are rather different from the traditional one. For one thing, he says, there was no need for any "leap of faith" for Abraham to accept the word of God, because if Abraham were to prove himself, then something precious to him had to be put on the line. If Abraham had so much—riches, a son, and a prophecy that he would become the father of the Jewish people—then he could be tested only by the threat of having something taken away from him. This is logical, says Kafka; it requires no leap of faith at all. What *would* require a leap of faith is if Abraham had been a different sort of person. Suppose he truly wanted to please God by performing the sacrifice but was a person of low self-esteem? He really wants to do what is right, like Cervantes' Don Quixote, but he can't quite believe that he can be the one God was speaking to because he believes he is unworthy. He is afraid that if he proceeds with the sacrifice, it will turn out that the command was just a joke, and he will be a laughingstock, like Quixote, who always tried to do the heroic thing but ended up fighting windmills. For this Abraham, being laughed at would make him even more unworthy of being called by God. It would be as though a worthy person had been called, but this grungy, unworthy Abraham showed up instead, foolishly believing himself to be the worthy one. Now this, says Kafka, would indeed require a leap of faith.

history, has thought to ask whether Sarah might have had something relevant to say about the murder of her son as a proof of faith in God. Delaney actually echoes Kierkegaard's idea here that Abraham's willingness to kill Isaac would be completely *immoral,* but she doesn't agree with his further step that morals and faith are different things altogether. In the section below called "The Bargain," you'll meet another story from the Bible, that of a father who sees parenthood as a lesser duty: the story of Jephtha's daughter.

Fables and Counterfables

In the eighteenth and nineteenth centuries, adults finally began to notice that children were not just small and inadequate adults, and children's literature was invented as a literary genre. The gory fairy tale was toned down to suit the nursery, and another kind of story, which had previously been enjoyed by adults, was introduced to children: the *fable.* Aesop's and La Fontaine's fables became very popular as moral lessons for children. "The Mouse and the Lion" (the lion spares the mouse and later the mouse saves the lion's life) taught that you had better not disregard someone unimportant, for he or she might be of help to you some day, and "The Sour Grapes" (the fox can't reach the grapes, and declares that they are probably sour anyway) taught that if someone claims something is not worth having, it may be because he or she can't have it. The main reason adults told these fables to children was, of course, that the grown-ups wanted their children to become good citizens, and the stories seemed an efficient way to press home the point. Those early stories for children said, in essence, "Behave, or else"; they provided little opportunity for children's imagination to take flight. An important exception is the work of Hans Christian Andersen (1805–1875), who, throughout his fairy tales and stories, insisted that children's imaginations should be left unfettered by the sour realism of grown-ups. In fact, Andersen's stories have a true poetic quality and carry multiple meanings; they are not really children's stories at all. Children can enjoy them, to be sure, but they will enjoy them much more when they are older and capable of reading between the lines. For Andersen, not only was the imagination of the children in danger of being stifled by adults, but also the imagination of the adults themselves was in danger of withering away. Andersen's moral lesson is one of openness. He tells us to listen to the world and not just respond to it with preconceived notions; if we do, we will encounter only what we expect, and we will never again see the magic and splendor of the world the way children do.

Other stories with moral lessons were being written for children during that same time period. Didactic stories took up the thread of the fables and taught children how to behave: to obey their parents, to be kind to animals, to finish their porridge, and to not make fun of people who looked different. Although today the lessons of those stories may seem, for the most part, quite inoffensive, the stories themselves often reveal sexism, racism, and a general naive belief that the writer had all the wisdom in the world. Those "moral stories" not only present a moral problem but also *moralize.* This tendency to teach moral lessons enraged Mark Twain to the extent that he wrote a parody called "About Magnanimous-Incident Literature" (to which *Mad* magazine and an entire genre of comedy films such as the *Naked Gun* series, *Top Secret,* and *Airplane* are indebted, taking an idea to its logical, comic extreme). Twain's parody gives us the "true" ending to the little moral stories. In one story, the scruffy little homeless dog that the kindly village doctor cures comes back the next day with another scruffy little dog to be cured, and the doctor praises God for the chance to heal another unfortunate creature. End of moral story; here comes Twain: The next day there are four scruffy dogs outside the doctor's office, and the following week there are hundreds of howling mutts waiting to be treated. The original mutt is going crazy from all this helpfulness and bites the doctor, who wishes he had shot it in the first place.

Stories with Role Models

What kind of people do we like to hear stories about? And after the story, do we go out and do the same thing as the hero in the book, the TV show, or the movie?

When we talk about fictional characters who somehow teach a moral lesson, we are talking about *role models.* Cartoon superhero characters such as Superman and Spiderman may have certain qualities that we identify with and would like to emulate. But if we include Batman, we encounter an interesting twist: Batman is not a wholesome character; he has a psychological problem (which has been cleverly explored in recent films). Not all heroic characters are completely virtuous. If we look at fictional heroes in Western popular literature, from King Arthur, Lancelot, and Robin Hood to D'Artagnan, Scarlett O'Hara, and even Harry Potter, we see that most of these people are morally flawed. The tendency in the twentieth century had been to depict them as being as morally flawed as possible, something that may reflect a certain sense of cynicism. In the early twenty-first century, however, we see a trend in stories for young adults of returning to the idea of the main characters being fundamentally good, but misunderstood and even shunned by society, from *X-Men* to *Twilight* and *The Hunger Games* (although some characters may certainly display a dark personality).

Being drawn to the dark side of characters in stories is not a new phenomenon; in the medieval churches of Europe, peasant congregations were spellbound by murals depicting biblical scenes that sometimes covered the entire inside of the church. The murals kept them occupied during the long hours while the priest spoke in Latin, which the peasants did not understand. The moral lesson of that artwork was obvious, but it was expressed through depictions not of good people so much as of *bad* people; scenes illustrating people going to hell are usually much more vivid and artistically interesting than are scenes of people going to heaven. Perhaps the artists thought it was more fun to depict horrors than bland happiness. It does seem to be a human trait that we dwell on stories with a dark element, rather than on those with happy endings. Yet these stories can certainly teach a moral lesson. We must conclude, therefore, that not all moral lessons involve role models to be emulated; rather, a considerable number of moral lessons are negative rather than positive: *Don't.* Sometimes characters who show themselves to be morally flawed become our heroes not because they are good but because they are like us, or worse. If these "bad good people" see the folly of their ways in the end, we especially take them to our hearts. Perhaps we do this because we hope that we will be loved too, even if we make mistakes. It seems that, on the whole, we have the heroes we deserve, as it has sometimes been said. A cautious time has cautious heroes; a violent time has violent heroes. During the time that we accept them as our heroes, we let their images guide our actions; when their day is done, we can still learn from them—they can teach us about the way we once were.

Some stories are moral investigations of a flawed character, such as Joseph Conrad's Lord Jim (see the Narrative in Chapter 9), who makes a fatal, cowardly decision in his youth and tries to live it down for the rest of his life. In Victor Hugo's *Les Misérables,* Jean Valjean morally rises above the crimes of his youth only to be haunted by them until the end of his life. Fyodor Dostoyevsky's *Crime and Punishment* examines the philosophical deliberations of Raskolnikov as he imagines the right of the extraordinary individual to do whatever he wants, including committing murder. Gustave Flaubert's *Madame Bovary* traces Emma's deterioration through boredom and through fantasies (brought on by reading novels!). A work by the Danish author J. P. Jacobsen, *Marie Grubbe,* in some ways parallels *Madame Bovary.* It investigates the downfall of a noble lady through three marriages: to a nobleman, to a soldier, and finally to a drunk. The cause of her deterioration seems to be the same as Emma's: sensualism and boredom. The last time we encounter Marie, she is tending the ferry that runs between two small towns, to support her drunkard husband. The irony of the story is that in this squalor Marie finally finds the happiness that eluded her when she was a "fine lady."

Stories such as these are not written with the intention of sending their readers out on any heroic errands. They are, primarily, explorations of fascinating human characters. They also serve as moral evaluations by asking whether the characters redeem themselves somehow, even in their degradation. At times a character's redeeming act or quality goes against mainstream morality, as in the story of Marie Grubbe, and then the story forces us to ask which value is the ultimate moral value. Do we agree with society that Marie's life was wasted, full of missed opportunities? Or do we agree with the author that life, and morality, have many faces and that there is some intrinsic value in staying true to yourself, no matter how much that sentiment may differ from the public ethos? If such characters serve as a warning not to emulate them, we call them *negative role models.* We meet this concept again in Chapter 10 in an extended discussion about role models and virtue ethics.

Some Fantastic Tales for Grown-Ups

The stories that have affected Western culture are too numerous to count, but a few stand out as *archetypes,* models that we seem to return to over and over again. In this section we will look at three themes (or, in the language of literary criticism, *tropes,* or in Internet lingo, *memes*) that keep showing up in the world of fiction: *the bargain, the good twin and the bad twin,* and *the quest.*

The Bargain

There is a certain genre of stories that continually fascinates the adult imagination: the story in which some- one bargains with fate (or with gods or devils) to gain some advantage—or doesn't literally bargain, but simply puts his or her life and happiness on the line to obtain what he or she wants most.

Research into the origin of folktales which you've read about earlier in this chapter has shown that the Bar- gain trope in particular is very ancient, dating back to the Indo-European bronze age of 6000 years ago. Researchers Tehrani and De Silva refer to this trope as "The Smith and the Devil":

> The basic plot of this tale—which is stable throughout the Indo-European speaking world, from India to Scandi- navia—concerns a blacksmith who strikes a deal with a malevolent supernatural being (e.g. the Devil, Death, a jinn, etc.). The smith exchanges his soul for the power to weld any materials together, which he then uses to stick the villain to an immovable object (e.g. a tree) to renege on his side of the bargain.

Tehrani and De Silva speculate that the story reflects fascination with forging metals, a new invention 6000 years ago. They link the story to theories about ancient migrations and development of metals, but the main point for us is the "bargain" theme: The ancient smith who makes a deal with the devil to get supernatural powers is the great-grandfather of all our stories of hopeful or desperate people making deals—or trying to make deals—with higher powers. The smith is successful in outsmarting the devil, but not all bargain stories have such a happy ending.

Why do such stories continue to intrigue us? Perhaps it is because we recognize the single-mindedness of some individuals, and their success, and wonder what price they may have to pay (perhaps even hoping that they have to pay a price). Or perhaps it is because we, in desperate situations, also try to bargain with fate: If you let me live, I'll give up smoking/be kinder to my spouse/stop gambling/stop eating junk food, and so on. If you let me pass the test, I promise I'll be a good student from now on. If you let me win the battle, I promise you I will sacrifice the first living thing that approaches me when I come home. That is the bargain in the biblical horror story of **Jephtha's daughter**. Jephtha, a leader of the army of the Israelites, is losing a battle and asks God to grant him victory, and in return he promises to make a sacrifice. And indeed he wins the battle—but that is when the nightmare begins. According to some scholars, Jephtha may have expected to be met by a dog or a servant, but it is his virgin daughter who comes to greet him. What does he do? Does he resolve to cheat God and save his daughter? No, he gives her a month to "grieve for her virginity", and then he sacrifices her. (In this case, God does not step in to prevent it as he did for Abraham.) And let us not forget that Jephtha *asked* for a bargain with God, whereas Abraham was chosen to be tried. So was Jephtha a good man? That depends on what time period we're in, and how moral issues differ: In the Old Testament, Jephtha upholds his end of the bargain, hard as it is for him, and is thus an honorable man. We may grieve for his daughter (who doesn't even have a name in the story), but she is, essentially, his property, and he has a right, even a duty, to sacrifice her because of a promise made to God. Seen from a modern, secular perspective, Jephtha is probably condemned by most of us because he tries to make a bargain without foreseeing the consequences, but also because he is a terrible father, betraying the trust of his daughter, believing that his higher duty is his promise to God, rather than his obligation to his family. Sometimes, like Jephtha, we keep our bargains with fate, but most often we don't. Stories in which a bargain has been made with the devil, however, usually cast him as a reliable businessman: He keeps his end of the deal, and he expects you to keep yours.

One might think that the story in Homer's *Iliad* of the sacrifice of King Agamemnon's daughter Iphigenia so the Greek fleet will get a fair wind to Troy would come under the bargain trope, but here Agamemnon sacrifices his adult daughter first—an action that will later cost him his life—and does indeed get a good breeze to fill his sails. He doesn't "bargain" with the higher powers in the same manner that Jephtha does, he makes his "payment" to the gods first, probably in much the same way that human sacrifice has been conducted for much of human history.

Probably the best known of all devil bargains is the **story of Dr. Faust**, the main character in Johann Wolfgang von Goethe's masterpiece, *Faust.* There was, in Württemberg, Germany, in the sixteenth century, an actual man named Johann Faust; he was an astrologer and a magician at a time when science, astrology, and magic were only just beginning to be separated, conceptually and practically. "Alchemists" were undertaking experiments based in part on scientific evidence and in part on magical formulae; such practices usually were outlawed as heresy by the Catholic Church. The Spanish Inquisition disposed of many an early scientist for being a heretic well into the seventeenth century. Even before *Faust,* though, stories appeared with the same motif: the necromancer (sorcerer) who sells his soul. Those stories have been fused with the legend of Faust because of that frequent representation in literature. Around 1589 (some 50 years after the death of the actual Dr. Faust), Marlowe wrote the *Tragical History of Dr. Faustus,* but it was Goethe's 1800s version that became the ultimate metaphor for the scientist who will do anything, including sell his soul, for pure knowledge (in Faust's case, to secure the formula for turning base metals into gold). (Later in this chapter you'll find an early story by Goethe, *The Sorrows of Young Werther,* about a young man who dies from unrequited love—the novel that made Goethe instantly famous.) The story of Faust was made into an American tale by Stephen Vincent Benét, "The Devil and Daniel Webster," but with a twist: Webster outwits the devil. (This is actually a whole subgenre by itself—the outwitting of the devil.) In the 1940s, Nobel Prize winner Thomas Mann modernized the original story in his novel *Dr. Faustus,* which explores the mind-set of a man of the times; in Mann's book the obsession is not science but art.

Through the Faust story runs a moralizing thread: *Faust does wrong in selling his soul.* There are folklore and fairy-tale stories that are in complete accordance with that view. One story that has spread from country to country in different versions is the folktale of the boy who wanted to play the fiddle like no one else, and the devil taught him to play so sweetly that the fish would jump out of the river to listen, the birds would stop singing, and all the girls the boy ever wanted would flock to him. The trouble was that every time he wanted to put the fiddle down, he couldn't. In other words, the devil made him do it and he played himself to death. Some musicians might say it was worth it. Case in point: a modern legend featuring the blues guitarist Robert Johnson tells that his incredible talent came from selling his soul to the devil at a crossroads.

The Faustian theme also has been explored in films from time to time, as in *The Picture of Dorian Gray*, where Dorian's painting ages, but not he himself, and *Angel Heart,* in which a character realized something he had forgotten—that he sold his soul—and there is no help or redemption for him in the end. Another such bargain-film is *Ghost Rider,* in which a young man sells his soul to save his father's life. The short film *Beat the Devil* (2001) by Tony Scott explores the same theme. At the end of this chapter you will find a summary of the film *Pulp Fiction.* One of the study questions hints at a possible interpretation—did the gangster boss sell his soul to the devil? But perhaps the Faustian bargain theme most familiar to millennials these years is that of Tom Riddle from the Harry Potter series, seeking secret, forbidden knowledge at the peril of losing his soul. Another character who indeed loses his—to the Dark Side—in return for power is Anakin Skywalker of the *Star Wars* prequels. But since he was trying to save his wife, it isn't as obvious a self-centered deal as in most Faustian stories.

The Good Twin and the Bad Twin

A story that is closely related to that of Dr. Faust, but with an added element, is Robert Louis Stevenson's 1886 story of *Dr. Jekyll and Mr. Hyde.* As with Goethe's story, Stevenson's is loosely based on a real person—in this case an eighteeth-century Scottish cabinetmaker and city councillor by day and a burglar by night. The kindly Dr. Jekyll becomes the evil Mr. Hyde by drinking his own invention, a personality-changing drug intended, the story goes, to distill goodness from evil in the human character. Jekyll, who is not so kindly after all given that he throws away his life and *respectability* (a notion nineteenth-century readers found particularly problematic) for the sake of finding knowledge, parallels Dr. Faust in that obsession—but here the story departs from the Faustian pattern. Not only is the devil absent (he is manifested only in the "well-deserved" death of Jekyll/Hyde), but also another theme is introduced: the *double character.* After all, Jekyll and Hyde are the same man, and the symbolism is easy to read: We all have a beast "hyding" in us, an alter ego, and we must not let it loose no matter how much we would like to. The reason Jekyll keeps returning to his Hyde persona is that it feels good, it amuses him; he gets to do things that Victorian England frowned upon, such as going out on the town. Of course, he exceeds even the tolerance of any time period when he tortures and kills. The moral lesson is broad and completely in tune with nineteenth-century Victorian mores, as well as with most of the Christian tradition: Keep your inner beast in check, and don't give in to your physical desires.

When we look at the theme of twin souls, we generally have two versions: one person with two personalities, such as Jekyll and Hyde, and two persons who are inextricably linked but very different, such as good and evil twins, a theme that we will return to below. A famous story from the early twentieth century of one person with two "natures" is Herman Hesse's *Steppenwolf,* the tale of Harry Haller, a middle-aged, middle-class man who is contemplating suicide at fifty because he sees nothing positive in life any longer—and his dual nature, the Steppenwolf, a sarcastic, lonely being still thirsty for the outrageous experience. Another story is the popular animated film *Shrek:* The haughty, beautiful Princess Fiona has a deep secret; at night she is transformed into a green-skinned ogre. One hundred years before *Shrek,* Hans Christian Andersen wrote his story of "The Swamp King's Daughter," a serious, symbolic tale of the daughter of a beautiful Egyptian princess and the vicious king of the swamp: In daylight she is a beautiful but evil woman; but at night she is a sweet, gentle, compassionate soul trapped in the body of a giant toad. The dual-nature stories are easily interpreted as the battle between our "angel" side and our "devil" side—or, as the Christian tradition has generally viewed it, our spirit and our flesh. But as Herman Hesse says, "The division into wolf and man, flesh and spirit, by means of which Harry tries to make his destiny more comprehensible to himself is a very great simplification. . . . Harry consists of a hundred or a thousand selves, not of two. His life oscillates, as everyone's does, not merely between two poles, such as the body and the spirit, the saint and the sinner, but between thousands and thousands."

The stories of twins are sometimes harder to interpret, but interestingly, they often work along the same symbolic lines: One twin (or sibling or friend) generally represents "good," or the spiritual life, and the other twin represents "evil," or the world of physical desires. Often the author's purpose is to describe two sides of any one of us, just as the dual-nature stories do. Where the story gets interesting, such as in John Steinbeck's novel *East of Eden*, which focuses on the twins Cal and Aron, is the point at which the good twin, Aron, suddenly seems to have an evil streak, and the "bad" twin, Cal, reveals a higher moral nature, and we begin to doubt the stereotypes. A twist to the "Twin trope" is the TV series *Game of Thrones*, where the fraternal Lannister twins Cersei (female) and Jaime (male) start out as both being cruel and selfish, but over 8 seasons morph into different characters: Cersei becomes obsessed with creating a legacy for her family through her children, while Jaime finds a deeper level of decency and humanity inside himself. But of course, life rarely imitates fiction, except for a few infamous cases, including one California court case in the 1990s where a woman actually hired a hit man to kill her twin sister because she wanted to take over her life—because her sister was admired for her goodness and kindness. The plot was foiled, and the "good" sister testified against her "evil" sister in court and got her convicted. And in 2017 a Peruvian criminal, Alexander Delgado Herrera, escaped prison where he was serving a 16-year sentence for child sexual abuse and robbery by drugging his visiting twin brother, putting on his clothes, and walking out of the prison. He was recaptured the following year.

The Quest

The first quest story that we know of is that of Gilgamesh, the king of Uruk, actually the first written story in the Western tradition. Gilgamesh loses his only friend, Enkidu, to a withering disease. This brings home to Gilgamesh the fact that all humans are mortal, and he is seized by a terrible fear. So he sets out to find the secret of immortality. This story has been told by Sumerians since at least approximately 1500 B.C.E. Gilgamesh goes to the ends of the earth and finds the oldest living humans, Utnapishtim and his wife, who survived the big flood by the grace of the gods. (They were safe in a wooden box that floated on the waters—an *ark*.) Utnapishtim's rescue, however, was a one-time deal, and Gilgamesh must look elsewhere for his own rescue from death. In the end he finds the plant that gives immortality, picks it, and drops it in the water. Gilgamesh must go under the sea where the monster snake lives; into its gaping maw he must crawl to get the weed—but he can't retrieve it. Gilgamesh had immortality for a while, but then he lost it, for it is the fate of humans to be mortal.

Gilgamesh's quest was a failure, but it was heroic nevertheless, because it embodied a human longing to live forever, as well as the acknowledgment that we can't, even if we are the king of Uruk. The quest motif is one of the most moving in the history of literature and film, precisely because even if the hero doesn't find what he or she sets out to find, the search itself remains the most important part of the story. The quest forces the hero to mature and makes him or her realize the true importance, or lack of importance, of the quest's object.

Myths and legends abound with quest stories. The Navajo goddess Grandmother Spider searches for the sun in the early days when the land is in darkness. She finds it and steals a piece and puts it into her clay pot to bring home. In the Greek legend of Jason and the Golden Fleece, Jason and his argonauts go on a quest for a sheepskin made of gold. Egyptian legend tells of the goddess Isis, who searches for the remains of her husband, Osiris, who was murdered. Some searchers even go to the underworld to find what they are looking for: Ulysses goes to the realm of the dead to speak with the wise Teresias. Orpheus goes to the underworld to try to retrieve his beloved wife, Eurydice, from the dead. The Native American Modoc culture hero Kumokum goes to the land of the dead in search of his daughter. Ishtar, the all-powerful goddess of the Middle East, finds that her powers are limited when her young lover, Tammuz, dies, and she goes to the underworld to buy him back. The earth goddess Demeter goes to the kingdom of the dead to get back her daughter, Persephone, who has been abducted by Hades, the king of the underworld.

These stories confirm what we know: that we would go to the ends of the earth and the land of the dead if it could bring back those we love. We also know that it would be to no avail; Gilgamesh's lesson is one that every human learns.

Some quests are of a happier nature. In the African folktale about the girl Wanjiru, Wanjiru's family sacrifices her so that the rains will come, but a young warrior goes to the underworld to fetch her back. He carries her on his back to the world of the living and hides her until she is strong again; then he displays her at the great dance. Her family is now ashamed of the way they treated her, and the warrior and Wanjiru are married.

Two quest motifs have, each in its own right, come to epitomize the *search*. One is *Moby Dick*, and the other is the legend of the Holy Grail.

Herman Melville's *Moby Dick* (1851) has become the American model for the quest, but with a special angle: The searcher is mad, and the quest is meaningless, except to Captain Ahab himself. In many stories, although the object of the quest may be out of reach, it usually is something to which the reader can relate. In the case of *Moby Dick*, though, the reader identifies not with the searcher but with an observer, Ishmael. The quest itself is seen as pointless, and quite mad. Eventually, Captain Ahab finds his white whale but he and the rest of the crew die, except for Ishmael, who alone "survived to tell thee."

Hollywood came up with a modern version of the whale search for a society that reveres whales but dislikes sharks. In *Jaws* the symbolism is stronger than in the Melville story; the gigantic shark is a more obvious representation of inhuman evil. However, the sense of ambiguity present in *Moby Dick* is missing in *Jaws*. The Melville story makes us wonder if Ahab's quest was worth the passion and trouble; in *Jaws* we know the quest was ill-advised.

In a sense, there is one Hollywood story that is much more closely related to *Moby Dick* than is *Jaws*. In one of its most superb productions, John Ford's film *The Searchers*, Hollywood created a folklore version of the mad quest. As the title indicates, in the movie it is the search, more than the object of the search, that matters. For eight years Ethan and Marty look all over the western United States for Ethan's niece Debbie, who was captured by the Comanche Indians. Marty is the observer we identify with, the "Ishmael" of the story. Marty tries to reason with Ethan, who is obsessed with revenge rather than rescue and as time passes he comes to consider his niece "contaminated" by living with the Comanches, and resolves to kill her. Ethan finds his "white whale," the Comanche chief responsible for murdering Ethan's family and kidnapping Debbie, but he realizes, in the nick of time, that his motives were misguided. Ethan is redeemed and returned to sanity through human love, as he brings his niece home to the settlers' community. However, he has traveled too far on the road to obsession and human loneliness and is doomed to wander alone. We return to *The Searchers* in Chapter 10.

The search for the *Holy Grail*, part of Arthurian legend, is a quest that succeeds only symbolically, if at all. Several years after the glorious time of the Round Table, Arthur's knights become obsessed with finding the cup from the Last Supper of Christ, the Grail. They each go through trials to find the cup, but only Galahad (or sometimes Percival) succeeds in seeing the Grail, and even he is denied any further access. Since the time that the tale was first told, the quest for the Grail has become a symbol of the search for a profound truth, a holy revelation, for the meaning of life, if you will. (Box 2.3 looks at some grail quests in film.) Even when the search is unsuccessful and even futile, as it is for Cervantes' Don Quixote, who searches far and wide for the "impossible dream," the search itself nevertheless lends the searcher a cloak of heroism, no less than it did for Gilgamesh. The grail theme can encompass any kind of quest, not just a search for a cup or an item. One of the surprise bestsellers in the early years of the twenty-first century was Dan Brown's *The Da Vinci Code*, a story set in the contemporary world and featuring a hunt for the truth behind the legend of the Holy Grail. To many readers' surprise—even shock—the grail turns out to be not a cup, but—a person! A woman who, according to the speculative theory, gave birth to a child of Jesus Christ: Mary Magdalene. She, and the bloodline, are the Holy Grail or, in French, not the *San Greal* (Holy Grail) but the *Sang Real* (Royal Bloodline). *The Da Vinci Code*, the book as well as the film, spawned a veritable cottage industry of TV specials and interpretive books, but in fact the theory had been floated decades earlier in the controversial book *Holy Blood, Holy Grail* by Baigent, Leigh, and Lincoln. (Baigent even sued Brown for plagiarism, but lost the lawsuit.) Although the plot captures the imagination of many, it remains speculation without solid evidence, according to most historians.

Box 2.3 THE HOLY GRAIL IN THE MOVIES

Aside from the movie based on Dan Brown's book *The Da Vinci Code*, the grail theme has been explored in films such as *Quest for Fire*, the hominid adventure story with gibberish dialogue by Anthony Burgess, and in out-and-out adventure stories such as *Raiders of the Lost Ark*. *Indiana Jones and the Last Crusade* is about the hunt for the Grail itself. The science fiction classic *2001: A Space Odyssey* is a grail quest for the ultimate mystery, the black, ancient monolith. *The Fisher King* is another film that uses the grail motif. It presents a realistic portrayal of homelessness and teaches the lesson that anything is worthy of being the object of a quest if that quest is undertaken in the spirit of love. In other films, such as *Stanley and Livingstone* and *The Mountains of the Moon,* people traverse the jungles of Africa seeking out other people, the source of the Nile, or a better understanding of themselves and their role in the scheme of things.

Stories that involve a search for an antidote may incorporate both the grail element and an element of catharsis (a spiritual cleansing). Finding the grail is the cure for the ailment, but it also may serve as a liberating, spiritual healing process. Tolkien's *Lord of the Rings* is in fact a reversed grail story, because it has to do not with *finding* a special object, but with *getting rid of it.* The Ring that Frodo has to take to Mordor in order to destroy it is the source of evil, and a great temptation for everyone, including Frodo. As in the Holy Grail legend, it is only Galahad who is of sufficient spiritual purity to even have a vision of the Grail, so Frodo is the only one whose heart is pure enough to undertake the journey (although, as many fans of the trilogy will want to point out, without the unselfish courage of Samwise Gamgee, his friend, the Ring would never have been destroyed).

The quest can thus be for something sublime, something ideal, or not of this world, or it can be for something as down-to-earth as money. Regardless of whether the story takes the high path or the low path, the quest as a story type seems to be very enduring.

Contemporary Story Genres

Sometimes the moral lesson in a story is hard to find; we may be blind to it, or it may be somewhat dated, having evolved in another era. There is a scene in Aldous Huxley's novel *Brave New World* (1932) in which the young "savage," John, who has grown up on a nature reservation unaffected by the modern era of eugenics, total sexual liberty, and test-tube babies, introduces his friend, the scientist Helmholtz, to Shakespeare. He reads from *Romeo and Juliet,* certain that the moral drama of the young lovers who can't have each other will move his modern friend. Helmholtz, however, doubles up laughing, because he can't for the life of him see that there is a problem: If Romeo and Juliet want each other, why don't they just have sex and let it go at that, instead of making such an embarrassing fuss about it? He is blind to the social and moral structures of the past, and the savage is very upset that ethical communication seems impossible in a new era that has done away with family relationships, birth, siblings, and spouses and that refuses to recognize the phenomenon of death.

In a similar way, stories depicting unwanted pregnancies struck a deep chord in times past but haven't had the same resonance since the advent of legal abortion and safe birth control. Old Hollywood films about the trials of two lovers who can't get a divorce from their spouses also sometimes require us to stretch a bit in order to empathize with the characters. Stories praising the glory of war, which were quite successful until the early twentieth century, have not done well with the majority of modern readers and viewers for quite some time now. But popular story genres depicting human hard choices and deep emotions continue to flourish, from narratives of war, to stories of the Old West, to science fiction and fantasy stories, to crime stories, and even what we might call "pseudo-historical fantasy," such as in the series of novels and television series *Game of Thrones* (see Box 2.4). Below we take a closer look at those genres and their moral focal points.

Box 2.4 ALTERNATIVE HISTORY, WITH DRAGONS: *GAME OF THRONES*

HBO/Kobal/Shutterstock

Main characters in Game of Thrones Daenerys Targaryen (Emilia Clarke) and Jon Snow (Kit Harrington) finally meet in the 7th season and reach a tentative alliance, but their relationship is not resolved until the final, 8th, season, with some twists that only diehard GoT connoisseurs had predicted.

There are of course other genres of fiction than the ones mentioned in this section, such as horror, comedy, docudramas (or mockumentaries), historical fiction, animation such as manga and anime, and fantasy. But what about "pseudo-historical fantasy"? The book series by George R.R. Martin, *A Song of Ice and Fire*, better known under the title *Game of Thrones* (GoT) which it shares with its HBO 8-season television version, would qualify as such a hybrid category: set in a fictional universe very similar to Europe in the fifteenth century, we are treated to multiple story lines involving seven kingdoms vying for power over the realm of Westeros. Seen from one perspective it is a morality tale about profound selfishness and equally profound human decency and innocence in a

political world where the power structure is crumbling, and civil war is sweeping all the rules away. Thomas Hobbes's political theory (Chapter 4) fits the GoT universe very well. But seen from another perspective it is a fantasy story about dragons and dark powers of magic. No favorite character is safe—the one man we think is going to be the hero of the series, Eddard Stark, head of House Stark, a person with a deep sense of duty, loses his life at the end of Vol. 1/Season 1. His son, the rash young Robb Stark who challenges the family responsible for the killing, the all-powerful House Lannister, meets his own end at the hands of a traitor at a time when the readers/viewers least expect it. And the shrewd head of the Lannister family, Tywin, is himself not safe from a righteously vindictive member of his own family.

Game of Thrones is a treasure trove of characters with moral flaws, but also with moral backbone, and sometimes the flaws and the backbone belong to the same person, such as one of the main characters, Tyrion Lannister. You could take almost every chapter in this book, and find one or several characters in GoT exemplifying that exact theory of right and wrong. Here are some samples: Who is the perfect image of an **ethical egoist**, someone who thinks everyone should look after themselves (Chapter 4)? Petyr Baylish, "Littlefinger." An **altruist**, only thinking about helping others, never himself (Chapter 4)? Samwell Tarly. A **Kantian deontologist**, always being concerned about their duty (Chapter 6)? Eddard Stark himself, but also his "bastard son" Jon Snow. And a **utilitarian**, trying to create the maximum amount of happiness for the maximum number, whatever the means (Chapter 5)? Surprisingly, the eunuch Lord Varys. Who might be a **soft universalist** (Chapter 3), trying to unite cultures with very different values under one core value of freedom? The Khaleesi, Daeneyris Targarian—up to a point. And then she appears to change character, and a ruthless streak appears! And somebody representing **virtue ethics** (Chapters 8 and 9) with a strong, loyal character that can bear any adversity? Brienne of Tarth. And of course there are a variety of very **evil** characters (Chapter 1). In addition, the story has a **Bargain** trope (Stannis Baratheon and Melisandre), a **Quest** trope (Daeneyris, Arya Stark), and a **Twin** trope, with a twist (Jaime and Cersei Lannister).

(The list is your author's vision, not the TV producers' or Martin's! Feel free to disagree, of course.)

In 2019, the 8-season series came to an end, with mixed reactions from viewers worldwide who, in many cases, had been dedicated to watching and discussing the series for a decade. What everybody could agree on was the impressive production value, but that was where the agreement ended. Was the story handled properly? Did the characters act according to their character? And (let's not forget the CGI animals) was the plot fair to both dragons and direwolves? Were the actions of the main characters justified? And above all, did the right person end on the Iron Throne? For a great many viewers everything came to a satisfying conclusion, but over a million others petitioned to have the entire Season 8 reshot. Passions ran high. *A Game of Thrones* had become a popular tale speaking to multiple generations, both as a series of books and as a TV production, reflecting aspects of human nature we are proud of, and some we are less proud of, and making viewers reconsider the idea of moral choices. Whether one thinks the wrap-up of one of the most intriguing and enduring entertainment narratives of today was rushed or appropriate, the character Tyrion Lannister's words may help put the importance of the series into perspective:

"What unites people? Armies? Gold? Flags? *Stories.* There is nothing in the world more powerful than a good story. Nothing can stop it. No enemy can defeat it."

Wartime Stories: Duty and Honor

Wartime stories with moral lessons were common in past eras when it seemed that each generation of young men was expected to be initiated into manhood through some local armed conflict. But the idea of war as a natural arena for the exercise of masculine virtues received a serious blow in World War I, with its murky reasons for fighting and its wholesale slaughter of entire squadrons—young men from the same family or village or the same university, dying side by side in the trenches from mustard gas and machine gun fire, and leaving villages and colleges empty of an entire generation of male youth. That agonizing era has been portrayed ever since in films such as *All Quiet on the Western Front* and *Gallipoli, A Very Long Engagement,* and the acclaimed British television series *Crimson Field.* The soldier on the white horse with a feather plume in his helmet, dying gloriously for his country, became one of the images left behind in the nineteenth century, giving way to twentieth-century bitterness. For many people the entire idea of glory in war has become nothing but propaganda, invented by the leaders to inspire their legions to march unquestioningly off to the front as cannon fodder. In 2018, the centennial of the end of World War I, "The Great War," a technically cutting-edge movie by Peter Jackson, *They Shall Not Grow Old*, used restored silent footage from the war to bring home an experience of the increasingly distant time that made it feel shockingly contemporary, and in 2019 audiences were treated to another World War I film, *1917,* telling its story in 'real time" with a seemingly continuously filming camera.

Entertainment Pictures/Alamy Stock Photo

In *Indiana Jones and the Last Crusade* (1989), the archaeologists Indiana Jones (Harrison Ford) and his father (Sean Connery) search for the ultimate treasure in the Christian tradition: the Holy Grail, presumably the cup used by Jesus Christ at the Last Supper. Here Jones and Jones are barely escaping with their lives from a fire in a Nazi stronghold.

However, the image of the warrior as stalwart and honorable is so deeply imbedded in most human cultures that it shouldn't be dismissed as merely the result of the manipulation of gullible people by poets, propagandists, monarchs, and generals. It seems to resonate with something deep in us that identifies us as social beings, with a loyalty to our own people, for better or worse. Some would say it is a specifically *male* resonance; others see it as a *class* identification, which should be uprooted in a global community—but many see it as a part of a natural love for where we grew up and whom we grew up with, regardless of class and gender, and not infrequently a love for the principles we have been taught.

For some pacifists, any story of war is a distasteful reminder of human nature at its worst—but even for many pacifists, a wartime story can be meaningful in its focus, not on the glory of war, but on humans under pressure, displaying devotion to duty and their comrades. The classic definition of a **just war** (see Chapter 13) is that a war can't be fought for territory, or for glory, but strictly for defending one's country or preventing future genuine threats. That means a war can be fought only if no other option seems reasonable or practical. A story about a just war must show that war is the last moral option and that the goal is peace. In addition, it must demonstrate a clear vision of who is right and who is wrong.

World War II spawned thousands of novels and films telling the story of good triumphing over evil. Some films attempt factually to depict actual wartime events, such as *The Longest Day, A Bridge Too Far, Enola Gay, Hamburger Hill,* and *Heroes of Telemarken*. Others spin fictional elements and characters into a story with a message about the experience of war, such as *Twelve O'Clock High, Memphis Belle, Midnight Clear, Saving Private Ryan, The Thin Red Line, We Were Warriors,* and the acclaimed HBO series *Band of Brothers* and *The Pacific*. The Korean War has been depicted by the *M*A*S*H* film and television series, the Vietnam War by a number of films from *The Green Berets* to *Apocalypse Now* to *Born on the Fourth of July;* the Gulf War is featured in *Jarhead; Black Hawk Down* tells a story from our involvement in Somalia, and September 11 is the topic of *The World Trade Center, United 93,* and—seen from a child's point of view—*Incredibly Close and Extremely Loud*. The war in Afghanistan is an element of the novel and film *The Kite Runner* as well as the film *Brothers,* the television series *Combat Hospital,* and—from a female perspective—the novel *A Thousand Splendid Suns,* which is featured in the Narrative section in Chapter 12. The growing number of films featuring the war in Iraq include *Stop Loss, The Hurt Locker, The Green Zone, American Sniper, In the Valley of Elah,* and the made-for-TV movie *Act of Honor.*

The Moral Universe of Westerns: Hard Choices

Stories of the American West, called *Westerns,* have served as moral lessons for both the American public and a worldwide audience for more than a hundred years. All nations seem to go through periods when they "rediscover" their past, but the American West as a historical period is both recent and very short: from 1865 to about 1885—from the end of the Civil War to the end of the open cattle range, which resulted from the advent of barbed wire and the bad winters of the 1880s. There have probably been more stories told about the Old West than could ever have happened. Even when the Old West was still alive, those in the East were reading dime novels that glamorized the West; the first Western films were shot outside New York City in the early 1900s. The process of creating a legend about the recent past was very rapid and even involved actual cowboys and gunfighters who moved from the plains and the deserts to Hollywood to lend a hand. Wyatt Earp himself, of Tombstone fame, went to Hollywood, and when he died, Tom Mix, the Western film hero, was one of his pallbearers.

Pictorial Press Ltd/Alamy Stock Photo

Quentin Tarantino's Western *Django Unchained* (2012) shows the adaptability of the Western genre. It is not the first Western film where African Americans have played major roles, but *Django Unchained,* set in the 1850s, is seen from the point of view of Django, played by Jamie Foxx. A slave who has been promised his freedom if he helps track down outlaws, Django is also on a quest to find and free his wife, now the property of the brutal slave owner Calvin Candie (Leonardo DiCaprio). Tarantino is paying homage to the genre by having Django travel through locations that have been used in numerous Westerns.

Making entertainment out of recent history was one way to draw people to the theaters. If that were all, though, the Western never would have endured as long as it has. Part of its allure seems to have been its exoticism; the West is, still, a unique landscape. And then there is wishful thinking: Perhaps the Old West was never the way it appears in movies, but we wish it had been. An even greater appeal is the *moral potential* of a Western. For Western aficionados, it is almost like watching a ritual. The story usually is one we are familiar with, even if we are seeing it for the first time: There have to be good guys and bad guys, and horses, and they have to do a lot of riding back and forth among rocks in a gorgeous landscape. Then there is usually a good girl and sometimes also a bad girl. And there is a threat, either from Indians or the railroad or rustlers or (in later Westerns) big business, which is warded off by the strength and wit of Our Hero, sometimes even reluctantly. (He often has to be dragged into the fight.) When the problem is solved, the hero rarely settles down but rides off into the sunset so that he doesn't get entangled in the peace and prosperity of the society he helped stabilize. In later Westerns, the good guys are Native Americans/Indians or blacks or a gang of outlaws and the bad guys are the army or other Indians or the law; the stable society becomes a negative rather than a positive image. Traditionally, though, the general pattern is the same: The power of the individual (the Good) rises above the threat of a larger force (the Evil). Sometimes the individual paves the way for civilization, but in the process makes himself superfluous, as in what may be the best Western ever made,

The Searchers (see p. 55 and Chapter 10). Sometimes the individual accomplished his moral triumph in spite of the community that lets him down, as in another classic, *High Noon* (see Chapter 6). And sometimes the individual stands up for what he believes in but is sacrificed by the community who rejects his values, as in the underrated masterpiece *The Life of Tom Horn*.

A concept, *The Code of the West*, embodies the underlying values of many Westerns, including integrity, honesty, and reliability, sometimes expressed as "Riding for the Brand." The "Brand" (originally the mark branded into the hides of the livestock) is the symbol of the ranch you're riding for, but it can also mean the values you support. "Riding for the Brand" has transitioned from a nineteenth-century ranch-hand code of ethics to a twenty-first-century loyalty to basic core values.

Why do people watch Westerns if they already know what will happen? Because the movie experience (or TV experience) itself is a *moral event.* People take part in the story by watching it, and they feel that when the problems on the screen are solved, the general problems of life are, in some symbolic way, put to rest at the same time. The moviegoer may not even be aware of this psychological process.

One might think that if the Western had a moral message, it would seem pretty dated, and sometimes even offensive, to modern audiences. After all, the first generation of Westerns left the overall impression that it was fine to kill Indians, that women were weak and had to be protected, that blacks were nonexistent, that the land was there only to be developed, that animal life and suffering were irrelevant, and so on. However, some themes were timeless, such as courage versus cowardice, and the Western developed a potential to change with the changing times. There were still good guys and bad guys, but in each period they reflected the problems of the contemporary world, at least in a symbolic sense. In the 1950s the Western began to reflect a growing unease with the stereotype of townspeople conquering the wilderness; the sixties saw an increasing sympathy for the outlaw. The Western of the seventies was influenced by the Vietnam War and began to address problems of discrimination, overdevelopment, and pollution. In the eighties the Western seemed to have nothing more to say, but in the nineties it acquired a voice once again; current Westerns often deal with cross-cultural and cross-racial issues in the American melting pot, such as *Hostiles* (2017) (See Box 2.5 for an overview of how the messages of Westerns have changed.) The Western, being the one narrative genre that is truly American, shows an amazing potential for being able to introduce many kinds of social and moral problems in a single framework in which people have to make big, moral decisions in a land where they are dwarfed by rocks, mountains, and deserts. These stories of momentous decisions appeal not just to Americans but to people all over the world. This makes the Western much more than just a movie genre. It has become a transcultural story told in a universal moral language.

Box 2.5 THE CHANGING MESSAGES OF WESTERNS

Western films have from the early days managed to integrate modern problems into the period plot. The classic film (and book) *The Oxbow Incident* focused on mass hysteria, cowardice, and lynching. The Vietnam War era had its "Vietnam Westerns" in which massacred Indians symbolized the Vietnamese and the army symbolized the U.S. Army in Vietnam (*Soldier Blue, Little Big Man*). Post-Watergate Westerns showed corrupt politicians and greedy railroad tycoons (*Young Guns I* and *II*). Westerns of the 1990s explored the issue of violence and its justification. *Tombstone* and *Wyatt Earp* both examine the effects of violence on a township and on the individual (Earp) who tries to put an end to it, and *Unforgiven* probably makes the strongest antiviolence statement of all newer Westerns, reflecting on the loss of humanity in the life of a gunfighter.

With the return of the Western, there has been a growing sensitivity not only to historical accuracy but also to a multiethnic presence in the Old West. African Americans have found a heroic identity in the Western landscape (*Silverado, Lonesome Dove, Django Unchained*), and American Indians have emerged from old stereotypes such as devils or angels to become real people with their own language and their own problems and jokes (*Dances with Wolves, The Last of the Mohicans, Geronimo, Hostiles*). Strong female characters in Westerns are still rare, although there have been a few of them over the years in the films *Johnny Guitar, Rio Bravo,* and *High Noon,* the television movie *Lonesome Dove,* and the television series *Dr. Quinn, Medicine Woman. The Ballad of Little Jo,* about a woman passing herself off as a man to get by in life; *Open Range,* featuring a female character who, in her determination, is as strong as the male "hero"; and the Netflix series *Godless* and *Strange Empire*, all help to dispel the impression that Westerns are exclusively about men and for men. Both the original (1969) and the remake (2010) of *True Grit* feature a spunky teenage girl as the main character, set on avenging her father's death—although, in both films, the boozing, talkative one-eyed U.S. Marshal Rooster Cogburn gets most of the camera attention.

Critics were divided about the 2005 Western *Brokeback Mountain.* The film, based on the short story by Annie Proulx, was about two young male sheepherders who find sex during a lonely summer on the range, and a conflicted love for the rest of their lives as cowboys in Wyoming and Texas. It was hailed, or deplored, as the first "gay Western," but in fact other Westerns have experimented with the topic. The first Western film with an openly gay theme was

Andy Warhol's experimental 1974 film *Lonesome Cowboys;* another Western with minor gay characters portrayed in a positive light is *Tombstone,* the acclaimed (otherwise straight) Western from 1993. Critics familiar with Western films pointed out, however, that *Brokeback Mountain* really was not so much a Western as a love story, about lovers who can't find happiness because of the world they live in, in the tradition of *Romeo and Juliet,* and that the outer accessories (the cowboy hats, the horses, the pickup trucks) were incidental.

A new twist to the Western movies has been added in recent years, what we might call the "serious spoof." Movies such as the animated *Rango* and the comedy *A Million Ways to Die in the West* use traditional Western backdrops and story lines, but add a novelty perspective; sometimes it works, giving the genre fresh blood and a fresh perspective, such as in *Rango* which may have funny, animated characters, but really works as a traditional Old West morality tale about greed, courage, and community spirit. And then there is the offbeat *Cowboys and Aliens* which is exactly what it sounds like, a cowboy movie with an alien invasion plot, but instead of being a hokey affront to both the Western and the Sci-Fi genre it manages to pull off a great and entertaining cross-genre tale of the human spirit under extreme pressure. Quentin Tarantino's *Django Unchained* (2012) is yet another innovative take on the old genre, with the story of the black slave Django liberating himself and seeking to find and free his wife in a Western "Quest" type of story. In 2015, Tarantino followed up with another Western, *The Hateful Eight,* staying closer to the traditional Western plot, but with his own brand of what reviewers have called "over-the-top violence."

TV Western series are a chapter unto themselves. In the 1950s and 1960s, there were Western television series running every day on all three network channels, as successful and ubiquitous as cop shows have been in the last few decades. Shows such as *Rawhide, Have Gun Will*

Travel, The Rifleman, Wagon Train, Wanted: Dead or Alive, and *Gunsmoke* were collective forms of entertainment as well as moral lessons for an entire generation of young Americans. Later decades looked elsewhere for entertainment value, but in the 2000s the Western television series has made an interesting comeback, such as the award-winning HBO series *Deadwood* (2004-6). A parable of politics and human greed versus compassion, rather than a traditional Western series, the show turned many fans of Western movies away because of its raunchy language but won many viewers over through its intriguing psychological portrayals of characters in a society rising from the mud of a mining camp, and a wrap-up movie was aired on HBO in 2019, due to popular demand, providing an ending to the story which had been left in limbo on cancellation in 2016. A fresh element to the TV Western was added with the series *Longmire,* based on the successful novels by Craig Johnson about Sheriff Walt Longmire. The series is set in contemporary Wyoming and blends classic Western values with contemporary sensitivities, in particular American Indian issues. Another contemporary Western series dealing with modern issues is *Yellowstone*. In common for most stories set in the West, whether it be the Old or the New West, is a focus on humans having to make hard choices according to a code of values.

Add to the universe of Westerns: videogames. The phenomenon of videogames with storylines now includes some of the most popular games ever, such as *Red Dead Revolver* and *Red Dead Redemption 2*. The latter is featured in the Narratives section at the end of the chapter.

Science Fiction: What Future Do We Want?

Like the Western, science fiction was born as a literary genre in the nineteenth century. The French author Jules Verne astounded the world with his fantasies of men on the moon and journeys to the center of the earth and the bottom of the sea. Even Hans Christian Andersen predicted, in one of his lesser-known stories, that in "thousands of years" Americans would be flying in machines to Europe to visit the Old World. Verne's stories contained an element that has blossomed in modern science fiction: a *moral awareness*. His stories reveal an awareness of the possible repercussions of the inventions, as well as a general political consciousness, which makes his books much more than mere entertainment. In England, the works of H. G. Wells combined science fantasy and social comment in the same way.

Box 2.6 DO WE NEED SUPERHEROES?

For years popular media have been inundating us with stories of "living dead"—zombies attempting to take over the world. But a viewer scrolling through the available movies and TV shows on Netflix and other cable channels at the beginning of the twenty-twenties may notice that a new trend has taken over. Exit zombies, and enter the **superheroes**! To be sure, superhero stories aren't new, but they seem to capture the imagination of movie makers at the entrance to the third decade of our twenty-first century, perhaps as a reflection of Marvel Comics having played an important role in the early life of contemporary movie makers. And they are going way beyond the straightforward tales of the near-invincibility of a Superman. From *Black Panther* to *Spiderman* to *The Incredibles*, the psychology of the outsider is explored—the outsider who has in her or his power to help society, but who has been rejected by society. Trying to fit in and hide their powers, they eventually find their niche as well as acceptance in a society that realizes that it needs what they have to offer. So what is it that seems so attractive about superheroes? For one thing, it may simply reflect that a new generation of young viewers has grown up with animated superhero stories on TV and in videogames, but the concept of a superhero reaches deeper into a young mind than that. At a certain age, haven't most of us felt awkward and misunderstood? Haven't we felt that we had to put on a façade in order to fit into our environment? And haven't we wished we had the power to overcome our obstacles and become accepted? So the attraction may be related to the sense of alienation that many adolescents feel, trying to get used to living in an adult world. But there may be an additional side to the superhero story: some of them, from Superman to Captain Marvel, are not outsiders as much as individuals with a hidden, extraordinary power that enables them to solve problems that are too difficult for ordinary people—and perhaps the rise of superhero stories reflects the feeling, shared by many young people today, that the problems of the world are becoming overwhelming, and a helping hand from more-than-human beings would be a welcome thing. Perhaps not a yearning for "saviors" in a religious sense, but a reflection of a hope that somewhere out there, hiding behind the mask of an ordinary citizen, is someone who can steer us through the maze of twenty-first-century challenges.

In the twentieth century, science fiction became a major genre of entertainment, from pulp magazines and comic books to serious novels and films of high quality. Their subjects range from the pure fantasy of magical universes to hard-core thought experiments of exploratory science. Although science fiction need not always involve ethical issues, it has proved to be one of the most suitable genres for exploring them, especially such problems as we believe may lurk in our future. (Box 2.6 explores the superheroes phenomenon in movies and television shows.)

In a category by itself is the end-of-civilization type of science fiction, sometimes referred to as "cyberpunk." The civilized world is destroyed by a nuclear war or a giant meteor strike or pollution or the advent of hostile aliens or an epidemic disease. Although this type of story affords the author a chance to present many scenes of gruesome death or terrible disaster, the most serious problems usually occur in the relationships among the survivors. Will they degenerate into a "war of everybody against everybody," as the philosopher Thomas Hobbes would say, or will the human spirit of compassion for one's fellow beings triumph? This form also allows us to discuss how the characters got into such dire situations in the first place. If it is through human folly or neglect, such as climate change or pollution, the stories can serve as powerful moral *caveats,* or warnings. Famous dystopia or cyberpunk films include *Fahrenheit 451* (excellent novel and film, see below), *A Clockwork Orange, Blade Runner, Soylent Green, X-Files: Fight the Future, Gattaca* (see Chapter 7), *Children of Men, Code 46, Armageddon, Starship Troopers, The Postman* (great novel, so-so film), *Minority Report, The Island* (see Chapter 7), both the original *The Day the Earth Stood Still* and its 2010 remake, and *V for Vendetta.* The young-adult trilogy of novels, *The Hunger Games, Catching Fire*, and *Mockingjay* have captured the imagination of many young readers with the stories of young people being chosen by a future controlling government to fight to the death in the annual games. The film trilogy has gone on to become a hugely popular and well-crafted illustration of a popular series. Added to the cyberpunk universe has been the sub-genre of zombie or "living dead" stories, possibly as a response to a fear that other people seem increasingly dehumanized in our postmodern world.

Entertainment Pictures/Alamy Stock Photo

The Day After Tomorrow tells a story of instant global weather disaster, brought about by global warming. Here New York City is being hit by a gigantic tsunami, right before the big chill sets in and plunges the East into a new ice age. Critics praised the special effects but weren't kind to the plot or the science behind it.

Interestingly enough, there is a "counterfable" to the end-of-the-world scenario. It is the story of the Happy Future—not a future without problems, but a future in which some of today's pressing problems have been solved. Such stories present a world without nuclear threat, without racism or sexism, without nationalistic chauvinism—a world in which science has acquired a humanistic face and politics on earth, as well as in space, is conducted with a democratic spirit and common sense. The original *Star Trek* television series pioneered that hopeful fantasy of the future. The sequel, *Star Trek: The Next Generation,* showed that the Happy Future scenario was as welcome as ever, not in a naive sense, but as a vision of a maturing humanity that, free from the fears, deprivations, and resentments of the modern age, may be able to turn its energy toward new frontiers and challenges. The current *Star Trek* film series, set in an alternative timeline, has to some extent abandoned the vision of the Happy Future, but stays true to the personalities of the characters, while new *Star Trek* television series on cable channels, one starring the captain of the immensely popular *Star Trek: TNG,* keep the original dream alive.

Another great series of science fiction stories that has also proved to have staying power is the *Star Wars* franchise, perhaps the most enduring of all American science fiction fantasies, and now owned and backed by the Disney corporation. But in the *Star Wars* universe we find no Federation of civilized planets as in *Star Trek;* on the contrary, the evil forces are organized into an evil Empire, and the heroes, the Jedi Knights, are guerrillas battling the overwhelming military power—and its bureaucracy. Scholars and journalists have spent time analyzing this interesting opposition of space-opera scenarios—a benevolent Federation and an evil Empire—and some have pronounced *Star Trek* to be the fantasy of liberals preferring big government, and *Star Wars* the fantasy of conservatives fighting for individual freedoms in the face of the bureaucracy. With the return of *Star Wars* in 2015 with Episode VI, and concluded in 2019 with episode IX, *The Rise of Skywalker,* as well as a television series, *Star Wars: Resistance,* a new generation is now growing up with the moral universe of *Star Wars*—like their parents and grandparents!

Be that as it may, both series have created enduring stories that, in many ways, have become part of our American mythology, and both occasionally approach the question of what it really means to be human: **Who (or what) counts as a person?** In *Star Trek* we have the half-human, half-Vulcan Mr. Spock, the android Data, and the hologram The Doctor, all on the edge of humanity, all counting as persons and yet having their person-hood placed in doubt time and time again. In *Star Wars* we have a multitude of characters who are considered persons but not human, such as Chewbacca the Wookie, the 'droids, Yoda, Jar-Jar Binks, and the wise woman in the third trilogy, Maz Kanata. The question of who counts as a person is especially popular in science fiction novels: Several sci-fi authors have specialized in this issue, among them Cordwainer Smith, Octavia Butler, Rebecca Ore, Ursula K. Le Guin, and C. J. Cherryh. In stories about genetically altered chimps and other animals who do the dirty work for humans (Smith), humans adopted by aliens (Butler, Ore), and lone human envoys to alien societies (Le Guin and Cherryh), we are invited to explore (1) what makes us human and (2) how we treat those we think don't qualify. In Chapter 7 we take a closer look at the issue of person-hood and discuss the film *Gattaca,* about challenges to the concepts of personhood and rights.

The *golem* may be the oldest character in the science fiction genre. It comes from the Eastern European Jew-ish tradition, in which it was said that a man might create an artificial person out of clay, a golem, but if he weren't careful to keep this creature in check with certain magical acts and formulas, the clay man would grow and eventually take over and kill him. One story tells of a rabbi creating a golem to help the Jews protest false accusations of blood-sacrificing of Christians during Passover. This particular golem helped the Jewish people for years by exposing Christian plots to plant dead bodies of Christians in Jewish homes. But the golem became too strong and powerful for the rabbi to handle, so in the end the rabbi had to turn him back into the clay from which he had been created. In another version of the story, the rabbi turned the golem back into clay because his job was done and there was no reason to keep him around anymore. (And the character *Gollum* in *Lord of the Rings* wasn't named by accident—he is, in effect, a creation of the Ring, originally a hob-bit-type creature transformed by its evil power.) In the early nineteenth century, Mary Wollstonecraft Shelley (the daughter of famed philosopher Mary Wollstonecraft, see Chapter 12) created a similar artificial person, the monster of Frankenstein. Shelley's theme was the same as that of the golem story: human arrogance and invention run wild. In a strange sense we might say that the golem story is very traditional: If you exceed your boundaries, your creation will come back to haunt you. In a broader sense, though, the story teaches us to evaluate our actions from a moral perspective. In the movies, the artificial monster has taken on a number of guises, from the maniacal computer HAL in *2001: A Space Odyssey* and the Arnold Schwarzenegger char-acter in the *Terminator* movies to the corrupted robots in *I, Robot*. Sometimes there is a twist to the story, though: In some science fiction stories, the monster is not the *creation* but the *creators,* such as in *Artificial Intelligence: AI,* in which a robot child is rejected by his human family. The innocent victim is here the hapless robot created as a thing for humans to use, a slave to the whims of humans.

In any event, the artificial person serves well not just as a topic for discussion about what to do if artificial beings become viable in our society but also as a figurative image of ourselves. (Box 2.7 discusses the human qualities of the artificial person.) The artificial person makes us realize what it is to be human and what we ought to be like to be *more* human; it provides an excursion into our own descriptive and normative concepts of humanity and provokes us to explore **how we should treat the *Other***. (In philosophy the person who is dif-ferent from oneself is often referred to as the Other. The term signifies that one is facing something or some-one that one is fundamentally unfamiliar with. It can mean a stranger, a person of the other sex or of another race, or it can mean other people or beings as such, as opposed to oneself and one's own experiences. Some-times it signifies someone complementary to oneself, but it may also mean that the Other is not as complete, worthy, or important as oneself and one's own kind. You will encounter the concept again in Chapter 10.)

Box 2.7 THE NONHUMAN WHO WANTS TO BECOME HUMAN

Artificial persons in fiction and films often yearn to become human. Frankenstein's monster suffers from that yearning, but he is not allowed to become what he wishes to be. Data, the android in *Star Trek: The Next Generation,* does not have the capability to feel human emotions, but he is intellectually curious about what causes humans to act passionately or maliciously. He longs to be human the way a child longs to grow up. The replicants in *Blade Runner* are ready to kill for a chance to become full-dimensional humans. *Wall-e* is a robot with more humanity that the devolved humans who have left the planet and gotten comfortable in space, not bothering to use their legs to move around anymore. And *D9* also ends up representing the human spirit although he/it is essentially just a stuffed burlap sack on a robotic frame. In a sense, these robots who long for a human heart are of course all descendants of the Tin Man in *The Wizard of Oz.* And the robot Sonny in *I, Robot* awakens to consciousness and becomes the visionary liberator of all

of his kind—the artificial beings created as servants without rights. The artificial human in *Terminator 2* displays definite human characteristics; he bonds with a small boy and sacrifices himself for the sake of humankind. And the little robotic boy David in *Artificial Intelligence: AI* (which should probably have been called *Artificial Emotion* instead) has been designed to bond with his human family and love them unconditionally. The tragedy arises when they see no obligation to return his love, because he isn't human, and try to dispose of him like a used tissue. His dream is to become a real boy so his mother will love him. Just as the monster side of the artificial person is symbolized by the golem, the wanting-to-be-human side is epitomized by Pinocchio, the wooden puppet who wants to become a real boy. As the story of Pinocchio teaches, you don't become a "real" boy by doing the bad-boy things. If you do the bad-boy things (have fun and skip school), you become what bad boys become: an ass. *Pinocchio* is for all intents and purposes a very moralistic fable.

The dangerous, serious golem has a strange, lighthearted counterpart in the Roman tradition that has, so to speak, acquired a life of its own in popular culture: Ovid's story of Pygmalion, the sculptor who created a statue of a goddess, Aphrodite (in some versions Galatea), and fell in love with it. Aphrodite the statue came to life, and she and Pygmalion got married. The story has appeared in numerous versions in Western literature since then, most famously in George Bernard Shaw's 1912 play *Pygmalion.* The play (later made into a film) tells the story of a professor of phonetics, Professor Higgins, who makes a bet with a friend that he can transform the street vendor Eliza into a proper lady with upper-class English pronunciation and vocabulary. The classic musical and film *My Fair Lady* was the next step in the popularization of the story. Another version was added with the film *Educating Rita* (1983). A digital film fantasy of an artificially created dream woman who acquires a life of her own, *Simone* (2002) and *Her* (2015), brought the theme full circle back to the golem, the artificial person. All the women "come to life" in this female golem-trope have one feature in common: that they can't be controlled by their makers—in addition to a life, each develops a *will* of her own—but fortunately for the sculptor or the scientist (a male), she usually ends up loving him in spite of his shortcomings. (For another twist, read about *Ex Machina* in Chapter 7.) One might say that the Pygmalion story is the male fantasy of creating life—not as a father, but as a master and lover—and the golem story is the male fantasy of creating life as a master and partner. Both story types involve the illusion of *control* and the loss of that control. Interestingly, there is at this point no direct female counterpart to the golem or Pygmalion stories: The literary tradition has no female sculptor, painter, scientist, or witch who "creates" a male to do her dirty work, or to become her lover—perhaps because (1) women already create life on a regular basis and need no fantasy to fulfill the need for creativity, or (2) most stories have, until the twentieth century, been told from the male perspective. However, if we broaden the Pygmalion trope to include women who shape their lover or husband to become the man they want him to be, then world literature abounds with female Pygmalions!

Be that as it may, golem and Pygmalion stories may symbolize fundamental human longings to create and fears that their creation may run amok, out of control. And essentially, this may be the very nature of the human experience, regardless of gender: Some of us have children; some of us teach children; some of us teach young adults and adults; some of us create art; some of us invent new technologies, weapons, devices, medicines; some of us blaze trails or give the world new paradigms and templates to change our self-comprehension. But do we know where these creations of ours will go once we have relinquished control or once control has been taken away from us? The golem and Pygmalion stories illustrate two aspects of the creative process: One is the fear that our creation will wreak havoc, and the other is the hope that our creation will love us, and be a success, and enrich the world. Parents, teachers, artists, inventors—we all have these hopes and fears. They are two sides of the same experience, the yin and the yang. The stories help us come to terms with them. A variation of the theme of the golem, with an element of Pygmalion, can be found in Charles Johnson's short story "The Education of Mingo." Antebellum farmer Moses Green, a lonely old white man, buys a black slave, Mingo, not for the work, but mainly so that Moses can have company. Since Mingo has no knowledge of Western culture, Moses educates Mingo as if he were a child—but instead of becoming a companion, Mingo develops into a mental copy of Moses, even to the point where Mingo reads Moses' subconscious intentions and acts on them. Instead of a partner or a son, Mingo has become an alter ego, a golem that Moses can't control. You can read a summary of this story in the Narrative section.

And then we have science fiction stories about the *value of stories,* such as Ray Bradbury's famous science fiction novel (and films) *Fahrenheit 451,* in which the fire department no longer puts out fires, but sets them, whenever the government has discovered another illegal private stash of novels and other books, in a future society where the written word has become outlawed. Bradbury's solution? Each book lover memorizes his or her favorite novel or nonfiction masterpiece and recites it to new generations until the day comes when reading will again be a treasured activity. The other side of the debate about the value of stories may be represented by the comedy *Galaxy Quest,* in which an alien race has followed our space opera series with great interest, believing that they are "historical documents." They don't understand that such shows are fiction, created for entertainment. So is fiction the same as lies, without value? As the film speculates, even the silly stories of a low-budget television series may make us rise to the occasion and act more nobly than we ever thought possible!

Mystery and Crime: The Fight Against Evil

As some surveys have found, we modern humans have developed a deep sense of vulnerability—even before the terror attacks of 9/11/2001, at a time when the crime rate was dropping, people still felt that everyday life was full of dangers. Perhaps that accounts for the perennial popularity of detective stories. Cop shows and murder mysteries give us some semblance of a feeling that something can actually be done to control the forces we feel are threatening us.

More than in any other genre, the attention centers on the issue of *good and evil*—not in an abstract sense, but as personified on the streets. We may generalize somewhat and say that science fiction deals with desirable versus undesirable futures, Westerns deal with hard choices, and war movies deal with questions of duty, but crime stories above all specialize in questions of good and evil—and what to do about evil. Sometimes we follow the story to its ending with a great deal of hope: Something can be done. At other times, it seems as if forces of good are trying to empty the ocean with a slotted spoon. What makes this genre so compelling is that evil acquires a face: the face of the bad guy (male or female). And when that person is caught, sentenced, or killed, the greater formless threat of Evil seems to have been vanquished for a while too. Even when the bad guy wins, as he has so often in recent movies, we still have a sense that the fight against evil is not fruitless or without merit. As such, this genre has an inside angle on moral narratives: Regardless of whether the good guys or the bad guys win, or whether you can tell the difference between the good guys and bad guys (as in some movies from the 1970s), or whether the good guys are really bad guys (as in stories of corrupt cops), there is a subtext of a moral discussion going on: What is good? What is evil? And what can be done about it?

The first acknowledged detective story with a "whodunit" focus, "The Murders in the Rue Morgue," was written by American author Edgar Allan Poe in 1841. In England, Sir Arthur Conan Doyle followed shortly after with his stories about the sleuth Sherlock Holmes. In France, Georges Simenon created the police detective Maigret in 1931. Major heroic fictional detectives—mostly private investigators—in the literary tradition include characters such as Mike Hammer, Sam Spade, Dick Tracy, Lord Peter Wimsey, Philip Marlowe, Paul Drake (from *Perry Mason*), Nero Wolfe, Miss Marple, and Easy Rawlins. At the movies, we've followed the puzzle-solving efforts of police detectives and private eyes from Nick and Nora Charles (*The Thin Man* films) to Dirty Harry to the detectives of *L.A. Confidential, Mulholland Falls,* the *Die Hard* and *Lethal Weapon* films, *48 Hours,* and *Devil in a Blue Dress.* Television has given us cop shows such as *Dragnet, Adam 12, Columbo, Barney Miller, Hill Street Blues, NYPD Blue, Law and Order, Homicide, NCIS,* and *CSI.* A borderline mystery/sci-fi series that reached almost mythic proportions in the late 1990s was *The X-Files,* with its two-person team of FBI agents attempting to solve crimes that, in some cases, were "out of this world." Mulder (the believer) and Scully (the skeptic) revealed conspiracies within conspiracies, only to have their results sealed by yet another cover-up; the driving force behind Mulder's idealism was that "the truth is out there." With the successful return of *The X Files* in 2016 as a six-part miniseries, the series both spoofed itself and added an additional dimension of twenty-first-century cynicism. The shows *CSI: Crime Scene Investigation* and *NCIS* and their spin-offs have in some sense taken over where *The X-Files* left off, in popularity and influence on our popular culture: With their highly glamorized stories of forensic crime scene research, the network shows have educated an entire TV-watching nation to the point that it has become commonplace among laypeople (including jurors!) to expect that electronic forensics plus DNA, hair, and fiber will be found at each crime scene and will point unequivocally to a suspect—and that is, of course, not always the case.

While most readers are used to considering crime and police detective stories quintessentially American, the genre is thriving with homegrown authors in many other countries. Especially Scandinavian authors have taken to the gritty, noir-style stories of law enforcement, private detectives, or journalists going up against depraved individuals preying on the physically or socially vulnerable—the classic battle between good and evil in a hypermodern setting. Authors who have made American readers sit up and take notice are Swedish Stieg Larsson with his *Girl with the Dragon Tattoo* trilogy, Swedish Henning Mankell, Norwegian Jo Nesbø, and Danish Sara Blaedel. Interesting to Scandinavian critics, these stories have a high level of individualism, even within a setting typical for Scandinavia where everybody feels that they belong to a society where the government watches over you, like (generally) benign aunts and uncles, and there is virtually no tradition of vigilantism (except for the fierce resistance in Norway and Denmark against the Nazis during World War II). But even so, the crime stories that flourish today have individuals who take it upon themselves to cut through red tape and catch the bad guys when the government is too slow, fails to see the true picture, or even collaborates with the shady characters, such as in Larsson's trilogy. The Scandinavian genre of crime stories, despite the cultural differences, seems to resonate with American readers, perhaps precisely because of the "individual against red tape" theme.

Like Westerns and science fiction, the mystery genre reflects changing mores: For the longest time, law-enforcement officers were depicted as the good guys and criminals as the bad guys. And if the law wasn't the hero, at least the detective was. As modern cynicism increased, it became common for novels and films to depict the criminal as an "antihero" and the establishment as the evil power. In the Primary Readings section you'll find an excerpt from Raymond Chandler's classic essay on the detective story "The Simple Art of Murder." Lately, the patterns have merged into the good cop/detective/FBI agent fighting a two-front battle against both the bad guys on the streets and the bad guys in administration or the Internal Affairs Division. An example of this is the acclaimed film (and novel) *L.A. Confidential,* in which the truly bad guy is not the mobster or a street gang member but a high-ranking police officer. This story model reflects something that we the audience don't particularly like to see anymore—the criminal given the hero treatment, and we don't automatically buy into the idea that perps are poor misguided souls who would have been upstanding citizens if they'd had a decent childhood. On the other hand, today's audience doesn't believe that law-enforcement officers are all knights in shining armor either. We do still want to believe, however, that somebody competent and committed is out there fighting crime. So the story model of the cop fighting criminals *and* superiors strikes a realistic, as well as a hopeful, chord for a modern audience.

AMC/Photofest

Breaking Bad's Walter White in the middle of his drug empire. The series challenges our sense of right and wrong; we simultaneously root for a dying man who has been shoved aside by the world and (some of us, anyway) feel repulsed at the world of power which he creates.

Particularly shocking to cable TV audiences was the Showtime crime series *Dexter*—because the hero of the series was also what under other circumstances would be called the villain, a serial killer. But with dark humor the series won over the viewers by having Dexter kill (mostly) other serial killers who prey on the defenseless and innocent. Dexter lives by a code, The Code of Harry, bequeathed to him by his adoptive father who knew Dexter's dark side, his bloodlust: (1) Never get caught, and (2) Never kill an innocent. Other rules include, "Never make a scene," and "Fake emotion" to appear normal, because Dexter doesn't have feelings like other human beings—at least not in the first seasons of the show. Even so, because of his dedication to taking out the vicious killers that the justice system somehow failed to hold accountable, we find ourselves rooting for perhaps the most prolific and skillful fictional killer of them all—which makes for an interesting moral twist to the story. An equally shocking, and even more critically acclaimed, television series was the five-season show *Breaking Bad,* with its main character, Walter White, transforming himself from a mild-mannered chemistry teacher dying of cancer to a ruthless producer of meth.

As with *Dexter,* the sympathies and values of the audience are taken for a roller coaster ride. The television format of crime series has been "tweaked" in recent years by cable TV series breaking with some standards—frequently because they could, not being bound by network limitations. The series *True Detective,* Season 1, inventing a ten-episode-long storyline with a cinema-quality plot and direction, set new standards. (You'll find another reference to *True Detective* Season 1 in Chapter 13.) And the TV series *Fargo,* inspired by the 1998 film, has blended sophisticated humor and extreme violence in a manner usually reserved for movie screens. As Netflix, Amazon Prime, and other subscription Internet providers begin to influence viewing patterns world-wide by offering quality entertainment, we are already seeing new movies and series exploring crime story potentials.

Are Stories Harmful? A New and Ancient Debate

And now: from exploring current forms of entertainment we go back in time, to a time when classic forms of entertainment in the Western culture were being shaped; and what we find is that some of the debates surrounding those emerging art forms were actually quite similar to the debates about the influence of entertainment that we have today.

In 1774 *The Sorrows of Young Werther,* a novel, was published in Germany. The author was 24-year-old Johann Wolfgang von Goethe, who would later write the definitive version of *Faust.* In the novel—incidentally, one of the first modern novels as we know it, with a story line involving the emotional development of a main character during the course of a happy or an unhappy encounter—young Werther suffers so dramatically from unrequited love that he takes his own life. (See the Narrative at the end of the chapter.) In the wake of the book's publication, Germany, and later all of Europe, witnessed a rash of suicides being committed or attempted by young readers of *Werther.* Why did they do it? Goethe certainly never intended his book to be a suicide manual. This is one of the first examples in modern times of a work of fiction inspiring its readers to take drastic action. This book, along with other works of literature, art, and philosophy, ushered in the new Age of Romanticism, when the ideal person was perceived as an *emotional* rather than a *rational* being, and men, as well as women, acted on their emotions, often in public. The decision of young Werther was seen as a romantic option and had a powerful emotional effect; even some famous poets of the day chose to end their lives, and the rest of Europe woke up to the dangers, and the thrill, of literature.

Since then, scholars of literature have discussed why Goethe's book had such an effect; it was not the first tragic story printed, and poems and songs of unrequited love had been common since the Middle Ages. Several factors seem to have been involved. First, *mass printing* and distribution of literature were now under way. Second, the era known as the *Enlightenment was coming to an end*, and its effects were beginning to be felt. There was a focus on the rights and capacities of the individual, including the right (for boys) to receive an education. That meant that the common man, as well as many women, was now able to read. Third, the theme of the story, Werther's emotions, seemed to strike a chord in the young readers who were moving away from the idealization of reason, which had been central to the lives of their parents and grandparents, to the Age of Romanticism, with an *idealization of emotions*—so we are talking about a kind of generational rebellion. All in all, you might say that this was a book that appeared at exactly the right time. And its fame landed Goethe a job with the royal court at 26 years of age. But for the rest of his long life, he was disturbed at the effect his book had on its young readers.

The aftermath of *Werther* was not the first time in Western culture that the topic of the effects of an artistic work had arisen. In ancient Greece, Plato and Aristotle had debated whether art was a good or a bad psychological influence. Plato claimed that art, especially drama, was bad for people because it inspired violent emotions; people watching a play with a violent theme would be inspired to commit violence themselves. For Plato; the ideal life was spent in complete balance and harmony; if the balance was upset, that life would be less perfect. Reason helped keep a person in balance; if emotions took over, reason would be diminished, and imbalance would occur. And since art helped stir emotions, then art was dangerous. At the end of this chapter, you'll find an excerpt from Plato's *Republic* expressing that theory. Ironically, Plato himself had been an aspiring playwright before encountering Socrates, and would have known about what makes a popular dramatic play—he had attempted to write those very plays himself when he was young. (One might even say that Plato did become a playwright, in the service of Philosophy, writing more than 20 "Dialogues" consisting of lively conversations between Socrates and friends as well as enemies.) And when he has Socrates say (see p. 83) that going to the theater can corrupt "even men of high character," we get a sense that Plato may be recalling an actual conversation with Socrates, or at least sharing the lesson he'd learned himself when turning away from the theater. But Plato's student Aristotle had a different view of the theater: He was born in northern Greece, the same area where his favorite playwright Euripides came from, and was very familiar with his tragedies. Aristotle seems to have thoroughly enjoyed going to the theater, for its moral value as well as for entertainment, to the extent that he wrote two books about the theater, parts 1 and 2 of *The Poetics*. Part 1 was dedicated to an analysis and, literally, a prescription for writing good tragedies, and Part 2 focused on the proper writing of comedies. His book on tragedy has survived to this day (see the excerpt at the end of this chapter), but his book on comedy has been lost since the early Middle Ages. (At the end of the chapter you'll find a Primary Reading from Umberto Eco's novel *The Name of the Rose* featuring the fantasy of Aristotle's book on comedy resurfacing in the High Middle Ages).

Aristotle believed that art, and especially drama, was good for people because it allowed them to act out their emotions vicariously; a good play would thus cleanse the spectator of disturbing emotions, and he or she could return home a calmer person: The exposure to strong feelings and to a considerable amount of stage violence would have a *cathartic* effect. Aristotle claimed that feeling pity and fear for the victim of the tragedy cleanses us by making us understand that tragedy could happen to anyone, including ourselves. In his book on tragedy, *Poetics* (see the excerpt at the end of the chapter), Aristotle makes it clear that the best tragic plays are those in which misfortune happens not to a very good person but to an ordinary person who made a monumental error in judgment. And since most of us are ordinary persons, the play becomes a moral learning experience—a moral laboratory in which we can see our inner urges acted out and learn from the tragic consequences. (Box 2.8 explores the debate between reason and emotion.)

Box 2.8 REASON OR EMOTION? APOLLO VERSUS DIONYSUS

Goethe's novel *The Sorrows of Young Werther* came as a harbinger of a cultural sea change from the dominant worldview of the eighteenth century, the Age of Reason, to the new age that was dawning, the Age of Romanticism. Goethe himself embraced the philosophy of the Age of Reason—the belief that reason, not emotion, is the true problem solver—but others took their cue from *Werther* and let the age of emotions roll in. Interestingly, these shifts of focus between rationality and emotion have happened at other times. In some ways one can say such a shift took place on a small scale between the 1950s and the late 1960s, and we are seeing a similar trend today with the neuroscientific research into the fundamental nature of emotions. But much earlier that same transformation had swept through a society in which intellectuals—perhaps purely by chance—had also been debating about the dangers and value of stories: Plato's and Aristotle's Greece.

The Greek theater was only a couple of generations old by the time Plato warned against its emotional pull, yet it had already developed a rich tradition of annual plays and prizes, all in honor of a god imported from the Middle East, Dionysus. The older gods such as Zeus, Athena, and Apollo were still worshiped, especially in Athens, but a religious battle was brewing during the lifetime of Plato and Aristotle for the souls of all Greeks: Whereas the old gods, in particular Apollo and Athena, symbolized reason and self-control (a principle that is predominant in Socrates' and Plato's way of thinking), Dionysus was the god of wine and excess. You may know him under his Roman name, Bacchus. This philosophical battle between self-control and emotional abandon was won by Plato: His writings have endured, with their praise of reason, whereas nobody is a true worshiper of Dionysus anymore. Within the ancient Greek world itself, however, one can say that Dionysus won: The theater flourished, with the moral support of Aristotle, who himself was from the north where they worshiped Dionysus. And today movies and television shows, the ultimate legacy of the Dionysian religion, are being produced and enjoyed all over the world.

One might wonder what kind of plays the ancient Greeks watched at the time of Plato and Aristotle that led to such different evaluations of the experience of drama from these two thinkers. For one thing, Greek drama had been around for only a couple of generations. It seems to have begun in the form of religious pageants at the annual festival of Dionysus in Athens and developed rapidly into a contest among playwrights of tragedies, comedies, and satyr plays (wild farces with sexual themes), with much prestige for the winners. More than fifteen thousand spectators might see one performance of any play at the theater in Athens. The oldest surviving Greek play is *The Persians* by Aeschylus (ca. 472 B.C.E.); by that time, the emphasis on religious themes in the plays had already waned, and stories depicting the human condition (with some divine intervention) became popular.

Just what was it about drama that Plato found so dangerous and Aristotle so uplifting? One of the stories in the Narratives section is a Greek tragedy, Euripides' *Medea,* in which a woman kills her children to get revenge on her estranged husband. Another, perhaps the most famous, example of Greek tragedy is the story of *Oedipus Rex* by Sophocles. At Oedipus's birth, his parents, the king and queen of Thebes, are told that their baby son will grow up to kill his father and marry his mother, so to thwart the fates, they have him placed on the ground in the mountains for the animals to dispose of. But his life is saved by a passing shepherd, who takes him to the court of the king and queen of Corinth to be raised as their son. As a young adult, Oedipus inquires about his future—and is told by the oracle that he is destined to kill his father and marry his mother. He flees his homeland, fearing that he might harm his beloved parents (who never told him that he was adopted). At a crossroads he meets a man who won't give way to him, so Oedipus fights and kills him. Later he marries the widowed queen of the land and becomes king. But after years of happily married life, Oedipus and his wife learn the truth: that he did indeed fulfill the prophecy and kill his natural father—the unknown man at the crossroads—and marry his natural mother. His wife/mother commits suicide, and Oedipus gouges out his eyes in grief and shame.

Other stories watched avidly by the Athenian audiences include *The Bacchae,* a lesser-known story by Euripides in which a mother, in a religious frenzy, tears her own son's head off, believing him to be a mountain lion; and Aeschylus's tragedy *Agamemnon,* about the king who leads the Greeks into the battle of Troy, only to lose his life on his homecoming at the hands of his wife and her lover (see p. 52).

The common denominators in these tragedies were strong family passions, speculations on the nature of fate, and a considerable amount of bloodshed. In the excerpt from *Poetics* (at the end of the chapter), Aristotle points out that the quality of the tragedy is far superior if the producers don't rely on (in modern terminology) special effects but on the elements of the story itself: If it is well written, the audience will be shocked to the bone by the mere telling of the story—no stagecraft can make it more effective.

The debate is still with us, although it now takes a somewhat different form. We now must consider whether violence in movies and on television inspires people (and especially children) to commit violence or whether it allows them to act out their aggressions in a safe environment. Psychologists who believe that violent fairy tales can be good for children clearly belong to the Aristotelian tradition, although they may not support the excessive violence portrayed in movies and on TV. Video and computer games have come under increasing scrutiny for the very same reasons: Children and immature adult players may be influenced by the violence of the games. Whereas the early video and computer games were games of speed and skill, but without any (or with a very simple) story line, these games are today increasingly complex. Their plot lines not only involve the player/players but also are designed so that the players, through their skills and choices, may experience a slightly different story each time they play the game. Game series such as the *Jedi Knight,* the *Call of Duty,* the *Half Life,* and *The Sims* have entered a new level of entertainment wherein the player is, to some extent, coauthor of the plot, within a range of possible plot lines. Even regular television shows are now experimenting with the audience being involved in choosing plot lines; the British dramatic series *Black Mirror* surprised its audience by introducing the episode "Bandersnatch," in which viewers select the plot line to follow, as in a videogame. That gives the old phenomenon of storytelling a new twist—although stories have always been around, the storytellers have been celebrated unique individuals, in recognition of the truth that not everyone can tell a good yarn. If we can design our own stories now, will we have patience with stories that others have written? And will we be able to recognize a *good* story when we see it? (Box 2.9 discusses the present and future of virtual reality and narrative videogames.)

Box 2.9 VIRTUAL REALITY—A NEW NARRATIVE FORMAT?

With the recent developments of Virtual Reality for gaming, new aspects are opening up for the field of VR, including what is known as **Narrative Immersion**: the feeling of being immersed in the story you are "watching," and even determining its course, becoming a coauthor of events. For videogames a whole new level of engagement is predicted; your author has, admittedly, not played a videogame since the 1990s, but frequent conversations with gamers as well as reading up on the advances in gaming indicate to me that games have become increasingly narrative as well as interactive, with alternative plotline options, such as *Witcher 3, The Sword of Destiny, Star Wars: Knights of the Old Republic, Chrono Trigger, Metroid*, and *Fables*. Narrative videogames should thus be regarded as one of the available narrative media in addition to novels, short stories, graphic novels, live theater plays, movies, TV shows, and Internet streaming of stories. Add to that the VR experience, and we may indeed be looking at a new form of narrativity. While some gamers believe this will spell the end of not only two-dimensional (2D) videogaming, but even 2D movies and TV, because of the intensity of the immersion experience as well as the control over the story which the player will have (or seem to have), voices of skeptics are already being heard.

Will the printed media stories disappear because of VR? Probably not, because our imagination is still a very powerful tool, and the way we envision characters in a novel is still a form of personal creativity that some of us are very fond of. And besides, some of us actually prefer to read a good story that someone else, with more talent than us, has served up for us. But how about the visual media? Will movies and TV stories, and even documentaries and news shows, now become VR, or extinct? Must we feel immersed in everything we watch? For one thing, some of us don't even like 3D, and prefer the "flat view." And some of us would definitely enjoy VR, but not for every media experience. Some media experiences are probably better kept at a distance!

The upside of VR is precisely the immersion: One might say we can enhance our lives by adding these new experiences of places and people and eras we would never experience in our "regular" life. The downside is precisely the same: that an immersion in a fake reality may be more interesting than our own, and thus addictive, like a brain drug. Neuroscientists have already told us that listening to stories releases oxytocin in the brain, so we can just imagine the amplified effect of VR. The ever-prescient world of Sci-Fi has even explored that idea decades ago.

And the relevance for ethics? Obviously, a VR narrative can present wonderful moral dilemmas, just like any other fictional world, especially since we'll be in the middle of the story and actually feel what it might be like to be confronted with the "banality of evil," or being tempted by the self-serving "Dark Side of the Force." We might even reach a new level in Experimental Philosophy (see Chapter 1) and have people make choices about, for instance, the Trolley Problem in a VR setting, such as the television series *The Good Place* has experimented with, throwing one of its characters, Chidi, into a simulated reality where he had to choose among five workers on one trolley track and one on the other (see Chapter 5). But it will probably also illustrate that our reactions may be more influenced by emotions and less by reason, the more "immersed" we feel, which could be a problem if the situation required a cool head. And how will frequent immersion games affect our sense of reality when we are on our own in our real world, and people can get hurt, and don't come back to life? In 2018 in Mississippi, a 9-year-old boy shot and killed his 13-year-old sister for not handing him the game control. Was that a case of extreme bad behavior or a lack of comprehension that the world outside of the game is real? Will the lack of profound consequences in a world of VR games affect our moral compass in the real world with no reset options? And, which is probably the worst moral problem: if one prefers the VR world to one's own, is one opting out of the moral, and even physical relationships with real people?

However, what video and computer games have become notorious for in recent years is their increasing emphasis on (and some would say glorification of) violence. In several school shootings, a connection between the shooters and their preference for violent video games has been brought up. For many, that is a preposterous assumption; for others, the association is obvious.

Movies that have acquired a reputation for inspiring copycats are *The Program* (where young people challenge each other by positioning themselves in the middle of a heavily trafficked street), the television series *Beavis and Butthead* (an arson episode), *The Burning Bed* (an abused wife kills her husband), *The Getaway* (robbers observe the schedule of money transports), *Stand By Me* (kids knock down mailboxes), *Taxi Driver* (said to have inspired John Hinckley in his attempt to assassinate President Reagan in order to impress Jodie Foster, who starred in the film), *Heat* (a bank robbery in L.A.), and *Set It Off* (a film about female bank robbers that served as a blueprint for a gang of two adult women and three teen girls who robbed banks in the state of Washington in 1998). The 1994 film *Natural Born Killers* may have inspired both a bank robbery and the massacre of high school students in Littleton, Colorado, in 1999. The Columbine High massacre has also been linked to the film *The Basketball Diaries.* In Los Angeles, a 16-year-old boy and two male cousins who stabbed the boy's mother to death told detectives that they had been inspired by *Scream* and *Scream 2.* In Michigan, a group of teens tried to make a *Blair Witch Project*–type horror video by kidnapping a young woman. And in 2007 a home invasion in Connecticut resulted in the strangulation murder of a mother and her two daughters who died in an arson fire. One of the home invaders was sentenced to death in 2010; the other, standing trial the following year, told the court that his co-defendant took out twenty-four fictional books on violent murders, rape, and arson while in prison, preparing for the crime. An Internet phenomenon in its own class is the *Slender Man,* a fictional character who stabs his victims. The character became an urban myth, retold by Internet users, and has so far inspired several acts of violence by teenage girls, including attempted murder and arson. In 2919 the Netflix film *Bird Box* inspired a teenage driver in Utah to drive blindfolded, taking the "Bird Box challenge" having gone viral on the Internet. Predictably, she crashed the car. (On the positive side I might mention that Madisyn Kestell, a 10-year-old girl from Wisconsin, saved her mother's life in 2011 by giving her artificial respiration as she had seen done in the drama series *Grey's Anatomy*, and in 2019 a young mechanic in Arizona, Cross Scott, saved a woman's life by using the resuscitation technique he had seen in an old episode of *The Office.* In addition, according to researchers from the University of Buffalo, reading Harry Potter stories and the Twilight series boosts young readers' feelings of empathy for others.)

Even if we might feel tempted to do something we've seen in a film, most of us refrain because our common sense, experience, or conscience tells us it is not a smart thing to do. We believe we have a choice; we have the free will to decide whether or not to do things. Thus the question is, Should society play it safe and make sure that nobody has access to violent or suggestive stories because a few will imitate the action? In other words, should we allow censorship? Or should we let people take responsibility for what they watch and for what their children watch? Should we trust them to be their children's guides rather than hand the job over to the government?

Plato believed in censorship in his ideal state because he didn't trust people to know what was good or bad for them. Was Plato correct in saying that it can be dangerous to be exposed to emotion-stirring dramas? It seems so, under certain circumstances; but are those circumstances enough to justify imposing censorship on all viewers, even those who would never let their balance be disturbed?

On the other hand, is Aristotle right that it is beneficial overall to a mind under a great deal of tension to be exposed to violent fictional dramas? Given that television sets in American homes are on several hours a day on the average and that a great many shows during those hours will bring violence into the home, television and Internet movie viewing are not necessarily a good prescription for a modern stressed-out person seeking relaxation, despite what the theory of cinematherapy says (see p. 38). We should remember that the drama Aristotle recommended as beneficial was not available twenty-four hours a day, as it is on a TV set; Greek dramas were originally performed once a year in connection with religious festivals, and Aristotle's philosophy in general advocates *moderation* in all things. In Chapter 9 you'll read about his theory of the *Golden Mean*: nothing to excess, but in the right amount, between too much and too little. If he could have taken part in the modern debate, he most certainly would have advised against overdoing the exposure to violence on TV, the Internet, and in movies. At the end of the chapter, in the Primary Readings section, you will find an excerpt from one of Plato's works and one of Aristotle's—and a summary of a novel by contemporary philosopher Umberto Eco, *The Name of the Rose,* in which he pits the tradition of Plato against the words of Aristotle. Plato advised against the use of fiction, and Aristotle advocated enjoying fiction in moderation—comedy as well as tragedy. According to Eco, the Western world would have been a happier place had Aristotle's views prevailed! (For more on Plato and Aristotle, see Box 2.10.)

Box 2.10 SOCRATES, PLATO, AND ARISTOTLE

Plato (427?–347 B.C.E.) was a student of Socrates, the man who is sometimes called the father of Western philosophy. He studied with Socrates in Athens for over 20 years, and after Socrates' execution (see Chapter 8) he left Athens in anger and grief. A few years later he returned and became a teacher in his own right. While running his own school of philosophy he wrote numerous books, *Dialogues,* about the teachings of Socrates. Among his students was a young man from the province of Stagira, Aristotle (384–322 B.C.E.). Deeply influenced by Plato, Aristotle nevertheless developed his own approach to philosophy. For that and other reasons, Aristotle was not chosen as leader of the school when Plato died, so he left Athens for other jobs, including tutoring the young prince Alexander of Macedonia (Alexander the Great). But like Plato after his exile, Aristotle returned to Athens, opened up his own school, and began a short but immensely influential career of teaching and writing about philosophy and science. We talk about Socrates and Plato in detail in Chapter 8 and about Aristotle in Chapter 9.

Of course, children and adults are exposed to violence not just on TV and on film; fictional violence is on the increase in comic books, in video games and computer games, in social media videos, and in the lyrics to music often favored by teens. The framework for this chapter, however, is the influence of stories, so I've chosen to focus on violence in the visual media in general.

Whether we agree with Plato or with Aristotle, the fact remains that stories—both in written and in visual form—affect us. Some societies have reacted by banning certain works or by conducting what to me is one of the foulest displays of cultural censorship: book burning. Other societies support the right of their citizens to decide for themselves what they wish to read or view.

Most influential works were never intended as moral guidebooks for the public except in the broadest sense. Goethe didn't write his *Werther* to persuade dozens of young, lovesick Germans to kill themselves—quite possibly, he intended for young Germans to examine their lives and loves more closely. Few authors would want their readers to imitate the actions of their fictional characters, although most would like to think their story has at least been food for thought. In the nineteenth century, there was as much concern about novels having a bad influence on readers as we today worry about movies and video games tempting immature minds with fictional universes. While many scholars today, such as Martha Nussbaum, think that novels can provide great opportunities for personal growth, in a positive way, we're only just getting started viewing other narrative media in the same light.

Stories considered good learning tools in twenty-first-century America will in all likelihood be different from didactic stories in other times and places. It is a separate and very interesting question whether there is such a thing as universally morally commendable stories; we take a look at the subject of ethical relativism in Chapter 3.

Is it appropriate to talk about the impact of stories as if they take place in a vacuum, with vacuous people as receptacles? Of course not. Children and adults have a certain background that helps them process the stories they are exposed to, and this is where the influence of parents becomes important: If parents and children usually communicate about the stories the children are exposed to—or if parents are the ones telling their children the stories—ideally the children acquire a critical stance from the stories they will hear and watch as adults. That critical stance lowers the risk of their running out mindlessly to emulate some action that may look "cool" on the screen. It lowers the risk both that we take stories too seriously and that we don't take them seriously enough. Indeed, we don't even have to agree on which stories are morally valuable and which ones are misguided, or even nefarious propaganda. But whatever our political views, we relate to stories as having the potential for expressing moral values. So in the final analysis, those of us who, like me, love stories and like to use them as moral lessons should remember to approach any story cautiously. Do stories create moral saints? No. Do they create moral sinners? No, not without cooperation from their audience. We must process the stories we are exposed to and ask questions such as, *Do we understand its lesson? Do we want its lesson? Would we want the children in our lives to learn from the story?* And if we say no, rather than trying to ban the story we should perhaps encourage others to acquire that same critical distance. Even if the story may not have a valuable lesson to teach children, it may still be an interesting story for adults! And if the story presents a challenge to the moral universe of some adult readers, such as *Fifty Shades of Grey* (or even hardcore pornography, for that matter) might be perceived, or stories of extreme violence, such as the *Saw* movies, we need to ask ourselves if the freedom of the artist to create, and the consumer to take in, should outweigh the risks to society that provocative stories might entail, and how they may lead immature minds in wrong directions. We know what Plato would say—and we know Aristotle's answer.

All the stories in this book are examples of how natural it is for humans to think in terms of stories when they want to discuss a moral problem. At this point, though, I would like to repeat something I mentioned earlier. These summaries of stories are by no means a sufficient substitute for reading the stories or watching the films yourself; the outlines merely provide a basis for discussing the specific problems explored in the stories in light of the theories presented in this book. If a certain narrative appeals to you, then read the original book or watch the original film. In this way you will add another set of "parallel lives" to your own life experience. Besides, it's not a bad idea to let the characters in films and novels make some of our mistakes for us, as long as we don't forget to make ourselves the central character in some stories of our own now and again.

Throughout this book you will see examples of stories being the bearers of moral values. Of course, we have not even scratched the surface of the treasure of stories available to us, and I hope that our discussion will inspire you to experience and evaluate other narratives in light of the theories of ethics you'll encounter in this book.

Study Questions

1. Name three didactic stories, describe their plots, and explain their moral lessons. Do you agree with those lessons? Why or why not?

2. Give an example of a story with a quest or a bargain and explain its philosophical significance: Does the quest have a deeper meaning than what the story plot entails? Can the bargain be viewed as a metaphor for a common life experience? Can you relate either type of story to something in your own experience?

3. Discuss the phenomenon of Goethe's novel about Werther, who commits suicide because of unrequited love: What were the effects of the publication? Why did that phenomenon happen? Do you think something similar could happen today, inspired by a film, a novel, or some other medium of fiction? If yes, what should be done to prevent it, if anything? If no, why not?

4. Compare and contrast Plato's and Aristotle's views on whether watching a dramatic play (or, today, perhaps a film) has a positive influence. Compare their viewpoints with the current discussion on the subject of violence in films and on television. In your opinion, is one viewpoint more correct than the other? Why or why not?

5. If you are familiar with narrative video games, would you say that they can effectively present profound moral problems with a variety of solutions? Is it possible to learn about moral decision-making from video games? Why or why not?

Primary Readings and Narratives

This chapter concludes with four Primary Readings mixing ancient and modern views on fiction and five Narratives. In a section from Plato's *Republic,* you will read, in his own words, his argument that drama is bad for the mind; next, you will read Aristotle's argument that drama can be beneficial; the section is taken from his *Poetics.* The third Primary Reading is a summary and short excerpt from a novel, Umberto Eco's *The Name of the Rose,* in which Eco gives us an idea of how he thinks the lost part of Aristotle's *Poetics* might have read. The final Primary Reading is an excerpt from a classic text by one of the most famous writers of detective fiction, Raymond Chandler, who analyzes the core components of the detective story.

The first Narrative is a summary and excerpt of a drama, written more than 2000 years ago: Euripides' *Medea,* about a mother killing her two children to avenge herself on her unfaithful husband; the second is an excerpt from Goethe's novel *The Sorrows of Young Werther* from 1774 about a young man overcome with grief over being jilted by his girlfriend; the third Narrative belongs to the twenty-first century, but is a videogame set in 1899 in the Old West, *Red Dead Redemption 2;* the fourth Narrative is an excerpt and summary of Charles Johnson's golem/Pygmalion story "The Education of Mingo"; and the final Narrative is a summary of a scene from Quentin Tarantino's classic movie *Pulp Fiction.*

Primary Reading

Republic

PLATO

Excerpt from Book X, **The Republic,** *fourth century* B.C.E. **Plato. The Republic of Plato, 3e.** *Translated by Benjamin Jowett. London: Oxford University Press, 1888.*

In this excerpt from Plato's dialogue *The Republic,* Socrates (*right*) is having a conversation with Plato's brother Glaucon about the nature of art and of drama in particular. Glaucon is supplying the "Yes"s, and Socrates is supplying the rest of the conversation. You'll find additional excerpts from *The Republic* in Chapters 4 and 8. At that time you will be familiar with a theory of Socrates', the "tripartite soul," but in order to get as much as possible out of this excerpt you need to know that Socrates speculates that we have three parts of the soul: *reason, willpower (or passion), and appetites,* and reason ought to enlist willpower in the task of controlling our appetites or desires at all times. The end result is a rational person who is in mental balance.

We may state the question thus:—Imitation imitates the actions of men, whether voluntary or involuntary, on which, as they imagine, a good or bad result has ensued, and they rejoice or sorrow accordingly. Is there anything more?

No, there is nothing else.

But in all this variety of circumstances is the man at unity with himself—or rather, as in the instance of sight there was confusion and opposition in his opinions about the same things, so here also is there not strife and inconsistency in his life? Though I need hardly raise the question again, for I remember that all this has been already admitted; and the soul has been acknowledged by us to be full of these and ten thousand similar oppositions occurring at the same moment?

And we were right, he said.

Yes, I said, thus far we were right; but there was an omission which must now be supplied.

What was the omission?

Were we not saying that a good man, who has the misfortune to lose his son or anything else which is most dear to him, will bear the loss with more equanimity than another?

Yes.

But will he have no sorrow, or shall we say that although he cannot help sorrowing, he will moderate his sorrow?

The latter, he said, is the truer statement.

Tell me: will he be more likely to struggle and hold out against his sorrow when he is seen by his equals, or when he is alone?

It will make a great difference whether he is seen or not. When he is by himself he will not mind saying or doing many things which he would be ashamed of any one hearing or seeing him do?

True.

There is a principle of law and reason in him which bids him resist, as well as a feeling of his misfortune which is forcing him to indulge his sorrow?

True.

But when a man is drawn in two opposite directions, to and from the same object, this, as we affirm, necessarily implies two distinct principles in him?

Certainly.

One of them is ready to follow the guidance of the law?

How do you mean?

Digital image courtesy of the Getty's Open Content Program

The law would say that to be patient under suffering is best, and that we should not give way to impatience, as there is no knowing whether such things are good or evil; and nothing is gained by impatience; also, because no human thing is of serious importance, and grief stands in the way of that which at the moment is most required.

What is most required? he asked.

That we should take counsel about what has happened, and when the dice have been thrown order our affairs in the way which reason deems best; not, like children who have had a fall, keeping hold of the part struck and wasting time in setting up a howl, but always accustoming the soul forthwith to apply a remedy, raising up that which is sickly and fallen, banishing the cry of sorrow by the healing art.

Yes, he said, that is the true way of meeting the attacks of fortune.

Yes, I said; and the higher principle is ready to follow this suggestion of reason?

Clearly.

And the other principle, which inclines us to recollection of our troubles and to lamentation, and can never have enough of them, we may call irrational, useless, and cowardly?

Indeed, we may.

And does not the latter—I mean the rebellious principle—furnish a great variety of materials for imitation? Whereas the wise and calm temperament, being always nearly equable, is not easy to imitate or to appreciate when imitated, especially at a public festival when a promiscuous crowd is assembled in a theatre. For the feeling represented is one to which they are strangers.

Certainly.

Then the imitative poet who aims at being popular is not by nature made, nor is his art intended, to please or to affect the rational principle in the soul; but he will prefer the passionate and fitful temper, which is easily imitated ?

Clearly.

And now we may fairly take him and place him by the side of the painter, for he is like him in two ways: first, inasmuch as his creations have an inferior degree of truth—in this, I say, he is like him; and he is also like him in being concerned with an inferior part of the soul; and therefore we shall be right in refusing to admit him into a well-ordered State, because he awakens and nourishes and strengthens the feelings and impairs the reason. As in a city when the evil are permitted to have authority and the good are put out of the way, so in the soul of man, as we maintain, the imitative poet implants an evil constitution, for he indulges the irrational nature which has no discernment of greater and less, but thinks the same thing at one time great and at another small—he is a manufacturer of images and is very far removed from the truth.

Exactly.

But we have not yet brought forward the heaviest count in our accusation—the power which poetry has of harming even the good (and there are very few who are not harmed), is surely an awful thing?

Yes, certainly, if the effect is what you say.

Hear and judge: The best of us, as I conceive, when we listen to a passage of Homer, or one of the tragedians, in which he represents some pitiful hero who is drawling out his sorrows in a long oration, or weeping, and smiting his breast—the best of us, you know, delight in giving way to sympathy, and are in raptures at the excellence of the poet who stirs our feelings most.

Yes, of course I know.

But when any sorrow of our own happens to us, then you may observe that we pride ourselves on the opposite quality—we would fain be quiet and patient; this is the manly part, and the other which delighted us in the recitation is now deemed to be the part of a woman.

Very true, he said.

Now can we be right in praising and admiring another who is doing that which any one of us would abominate and be ashamed of in his own person?

No, he said, that is certainly not reasonable.

Nay, I said, quite reasonable from one point of view.

What point of view?

If you consider, I said, that when in misfortune we feel a natural hunger and desire to relieve our sorrow by weeping and lamentation, and that this feeling which is kept under control in our own calamities is satisfied and delighted by the poets;—the better nature in each of us, not having been sufficiently trained by reason or habit, allows the sympathetic element to break loose because the sorrow is another's; and the spectator fancies that there can be no disgrace to himself in praising and pitying any one who comes telling him what a good man he is, and making a fuss about his troubles; he thinks that the pleasure is a gain, and why should he be supercilious and lose this and the poem too? Few persons ever reflect, as I should imagine, that from the evil of other men something of evil is communicated to themselves. And so the feeling of sorrow which has gathered strength at the sight of the misfortunes of others is with difficulty repressed in our own.

How very true!

And does not the same hold also of the ridiculous? There are jests which you would be ashamed to make yourself, and yet on the comic stage, or indeed in private, when you hear them, you are greatly amused by them, and are not at all disgusted at their unseemliness;—the case of pity is repeated;—there is a principle in human nature which is disposed to raise a laugh, and this which you once restrained by reason, because you were afraid of being thought a buffoon, is now let out again; and having stimulated the risible faculty at the theatre, you are betrayed unconsciously to yourself into playing the comic poet at home.

Quite true, he said.

And the same may be said of lust and anger and all the other affections, of desire and pain and pleasure, which are held to be inseparable from every action—in all of them poetry feeds and waters the passions instead of drying them up; she lets them rule, although they ought to be controlled, if mankind are ever to increase in happiness and virtue.

I cannot deny it.

Therefore, Glaucon, I said, whenever you meet with any of the eulogists of Homer declaring that he has been the educator of Hellas, and that he is profitable for education and for the ordering of human things, and that you should take him up again and again and get to know him and regulate your whole life according to him, we may love and honour those who say these things—they are excellent people, as far as their lights extend; and we are ready to acknowledge that Homer is the greatest of poets and first of tragedy writers; but we must remain firm in our conviction that hymns to the gods and praises of famous men are the only poetry which ought to be admitted into our State. For if you go beyond this and allow the honeyed muse to enter, either in epic or lyric verse, not law and the reason of mankind, which by common consent have ever been deemed best, but pleasure and pain will be the rulers in our State.

That is most true, he said.

And what shall be their education? Can we find a better than the traditional sort? —and this has two divisions, gymnastic for the body, and music for the soul.

True.

Shall we begin education with music, and go on to gymnastic afterwards?

By all means.

And when you speak of music, do you include literature or not ?

I do.

And literature may be either true or false?

Yes.

And the young should be trained in both kinds, and we begin with the false?

I do not understand your meaning, he said.

You know, I said, that we begin by telling children stories which, though not wholly destitute of truth, are in the main fictitious; and these stories are told them when they are not of an age to learn gymnastics.

Very true.

That was my meaning when I said that we must teach music before gymnastics.

Quite right, he said.

You know also that the beginning is the most important part of any work, especially in the case of a young and tender thing; for that is the time at which the character is being formed and the desired impression is more readily taken.

Quite true.

And shall we just carelessly allow children to hear any casual tales which may be devised by casual persons, and to receive into their minds ideas for the most part the very opposite of those which we should wish them to have when they are grown up?

We cannot.

Then the first thing will be to establish a censorship of the writers of fiction, and let the censors receive any tale of fiction which is good, and reject the bad; and we will desire mothers and nurses to tell their children the authorized ones only. Let them fashion the mind with such tales, even more fondly than they mould the body with their hands; but most of those which are now in use must be discarded.

Of what tales are you speaking? he said.

You may find a model of the lesser in the greater, I said; for they are necessarily of the same type, and there is the same spirit in both of them.

Very likely, he replied; but I do not as yet know what you would term the greater.

Those, I said, which are narrated by Homer and Hesiod, and the rest of the poets, who have ever been the great storytellers of mankind.

But which stories do you mean, he said; and what fault do you find with them?

A fault which is most serious, I said; the fault of telling a lie, and, what is more, a bad lie.

But when is this fault committed?

Whenever an erroneous representation is made of the nature of gods and heroes,—as when a painter paints a portrait not having the shadow of a likeness to the original.

Yes, he said, that sort of thing is certainly very blameable; but what are the stories which you mean?

First of all, I said, there was that greatest of all lies in high places, which the poet told about Uranus, and which was a bad lie too,—I mean what Hesiod says that Uranus did, and how Cronus retaliated on him. The doings of Cronus, and the sufferings which in turn his son inflicted upon him, even if they were true, ought certainly not to be lightly told to young and thoughtless persons; if possible, they had better be buried in silence. But if there is an absolute necessity for their mention, a chosen few might hear them in a mystery, and they should sacrifice not a common [Eleusinian] pig, but some huge and unprocurable victim; and then the number of the hearers will be very few indeed.

Why, yes, said he, those stories are extremely objectionable.

Study Questions

1. Is Plato right that a well-balanced, emotionally stable character is rarely the main focus of a fictional drama? Can you think of any dramatic story involving an even-tempered person as the main character (or one of the main characters)? I have often asked my students this question, and I'll let you be the judge of some of my students' suggestions: How about Verbal Kint from *The Usual Suspects*? Hannibal Lecter from *The Silence of the Lambs*? Spock from *Star Trek*? James Bond? How about Special Agent Leroy Jethro Gibbs from *NCIS*? Or Walter White from *Breaking Bad?* Are these characters even-tempered, emotionally balanced, in other words, unflappable? And if so, are they still interesting as lead characters? Can you think of a female lead character who would fit the description?

2. Do you agree with Plato that having your emotions stirred on behalf of a character in a story undermines your ability to control your own emotions?

3. In your opinion, should we always be able to control our emotions in public? Why or why not?

4. Relate Plato's viewpoint to the current debate about violence in entertainment.

5. In Plato's view, what is the danger in watching comedies? Do you agree? Why or why not?

6. Evaluate the view expressed by Socrates that censorship is appropriate in our ideal state. Do you agree? Why or why not?

Primary Reading

Poetics

ARISTOTLE

Excerpts from Chapters 6, 13, and 14, Poetics, fourth century B.C.E. Aristotle, **On the Art of Poetry.** *Translated by Ingram Bywater, with a preface by Gilbert Murray. London: Oxford University Press, 1920.*

In these two excerpts from Aristotle's *Poetics,* he has just explained that delight in poetry (fiction in general) is natural for humans because fiction is an imitation of life, and so we learn about life from fiction—and to Aristotle, knowledge is always a good thing. Here he proceeds to tell us what makes a good tragic story.

> A tragedy, then, is the imitation of an action that is serious and also, as having magnitude, complete in itself; in language with pleasurable accessories, each kind brought in separately in the parts of the work; in a dramatic, not in a narrative form; with incidents arousing pity and fear, wherewith to accomplish its catharsis of such emotions . . . .

> We assume that, for the finest form of Tragedy, the Plot must not be simple but complex; and further, that it must imitate actions arousing fear and pity, since that is the distinctive function of this kind of imitation. It follows, therefore, that there are three forms of Plot to be avoided. (1) A good man must not be seen passing from happiness to misery, or (2) a bad man from misery to happiness. The first situation is not fear inspiring or piteous, but simply odious to us. The second is the most untragic that can be; it has not one of the requisites of Tragedy; it does not appeal either to the human feeling in us, or to our pity, or to our fears. Nor, on the other hand, should (3) an extremely bad man be seen falling from happiness into misery. Such a story may arouse the human feeling in us, but it will not move us to either pity or fear; pity is occasioned by undeserved misfortune, and fear by that of one like ourselves; so that there will be nothing either piteous or fear-inspiring in the situation. There remains, then, the intermediate kind of personage, a man not pre-eminently virtuous and just, whose misfortune, however, is brought upon him not by vice and depravity but by some error of judgment, of the number of those in the enjoyment of great reputation and prosperity; e.g. Oedipus, Thyestes, and the men of note of similar families. The perfect Plot, accordingly, must have a single, and not (as some tell us) a double issue; the change in the hero's fortunes must be not from misery to happiness, but on the contrary from happiness to misery; and the cause of it must lie not in any depravity, but in some great error on his part; the man himself being either such as we have described, or better, not worse, than that. Fact also confirms our theory. Though the poets began by accepting any tragic story that came to hand, in these days the finest tragedies are always on the story of some few houses, on that of Alcmeon, Oedipus, Orestes, Meleager, Thyestes, Telephus, or any others that may have been involved, as either agents or sufferers, in some deed of horror. The theoretically best tragedy, then, has a Plot of this description. The critics, therefore, are wrong who blame Euripides for taking this line in his tragedies, and giving many of them an unhappy ending. It is, as we have said, the right line to take. The best proof of this: on the stage, and in the public performances, such plays, properly worked out, are seen to be the most truly tragic; and Euripides, even if his execution be faulty in every other point, is seen to be nevertheless the most tragic certainly of the dramatists. After this comes the construction of Plot which some rank first, one with a double story (like the *Odyssey*) and an opposite issue for the good and the bad personages. It is ranked as first only through the weakness of the audiences; the poets merely follow their public, writing

as its wishes dictate. But the pleasure here is not that of Tragedy. It belongs rather to Comedy, where the bitterest enemies in the piece (e.g. Orestes and Aegisthus) walk off good friends at the end, with no slaying of any one by any one.

The tragic fear and pity may be aroused by the Spectacle; but they may also be aroused by the very structure and incidents of the play—which is the better way and shows the better poet. The Plot in fact should be so framed that, even without seeing the things take place, he who simply hears the account of them shall be filled with horror and pity at the incidents; which is just the effect that the mere recital of the story in *Oedipus* would have on one. To produce this same effect by means of the Spectacle is less artistic, and requires extraneous aid. Those, however, who make use of the Spectacle to put before us that which is merely monstrous and not productive of fear, are wholly out of touch with Tragedy; not every kind of pleasure should be required of a tragedy, but only its own proper pleasure.

The tragic pleasure is that of pity and fear, and the poet has to produce it by a work of imitation; it is clear, therefore, that the causes should be included in the incidents of his story. Let us see, then, what kinds of incident strike one as horrible, or rather as piteous. In a deed of this description the parties must necessarily be either friends, or enemies, or indifferent to one another. Now when enemy does it on enemy, there is nothing to move us to pity either in his doing or in his meditating the deed, except so far as the actual pain of the sufferer is concerned; and the same is true when the parties are indifferent to one another. Whenever the tragic deed, however, is done within the family—when murder or the like is done or meditated by brother on brother, by son on father, by mother on son, or son on mother—these are the situations the poet should seek after.

Study Questions

1. Would you agree with Aristotle that the best kind of dramatic fiction involves an ordinary man who experiences misfortune because of an error in judgment? Think of modern films and novels that might fit this pattern (involving ordinary men *and* women).

2. What is "catharsis of emotions"? Do you agree with Aristotle that it can be obtained by experiencing dramatic fiction?

3. As we have seen, Plato disapproves of a dramatic story, whereas Aristotle approves of it. In view of the fact that Plato wrote in quite a dramatic way about the downfall of Socrates (see Chapter 8), do you think Aristotle would have viewed Plato's story as an example of cathartic literature?

4. Aristotle says a good tragedy shouldn't need any "Spectacle" if the story is enough to make people shudder with fear and pity. In the *Poetics* he defines it as the actual, physical appearance of actors on the stage, but as you see in this excerpt he also specifies that the Spectacle is unnecessary if the audience can imagine the situation through a good narration on stage. We could perhaps take that to mean a good dramatic performance doesn't need any exaggerated display or special effects to get its point across. Can you think of movies or TV shows that have been extremely vivid even with very few special effects, because they rely on our minds to fill in the gaps with our own visions of horror? Are there movies/TV shows whose impact has been completely dependent on special effects? Does that detract from the story?

Primary Reading

 The Name of the Rose

UMBERTO ECO

Novel, 1980. Translated by William Weaver. Film, 1986. Director: Jean-Jacques Annaud. Screenwriter: Andrew Berkin. Summary and Excerpts.

Usually I do not present a work of fiction as a Primary Reading, but this exception relates to the Aristotle text you have just read. Aristotle's *Poetics* consisted of two books, one on tragedy, and the other on comedy, but the latter has been lost since before the Middle Ages. We know, however, that Aristotle admired the theater, and that book would probably have paralleled his book on tragedy, outlining the proper plot type for a good comedy and so forth. The novel *The Name of the Rose*, by the Italian philosopher and novelist Umberto Eco, is a murder mystery set in the High Middle Ages. It features the resurfacing of a copy of Aristotle's book on comedy, and speculates that if a work by Aristotle had been available in those days that legitimized comedy and laughter, Western culture might have developed differently. It was made into a movie with Sean Connery as the monk/detective William of Baskerville—a literary reference that isn't lost on anyone who is a fan of Arthur Conan Doyle's Sherlock Holmes stories, because one of the most famous stories of the British private detective is the one called *The Hound of the Baskervilles*. William of Baskerville pays a visit to the monastery where serial killings are taking place, accompanied by his trusty young helper Adso, the narrator of the story (played by Christian Slater in the film version). Having originally come to the monastery as a participant in a theological disputation, William is getting sidetracked by the killings, and begins to add up the facts, using logic, rather than the fear and superstition that drive the suspicions of the monks. The murdered monks have met their demise in different ways, but all of them had in common that the index fingertip was blackened, and their tongues were black. The resident monks as well as the visiting clergy believe the murders are due to witchcraft, and the symposium spins into a witch trial conducted by a visiting member of the Inquisition, Bernardo Gui, targeting not only a young woman from the local village who is accused of being a witch, but also two monks known as political radicals. In the meantime William follows the trail of evidence to a book—an ancient lost work of philosophy that has resurfaced from the depths of the monastery library's archives: Aristotle's *Second Book on Poetics*, the book about comedy (as you know, the book has never been found). And William's suspicion is now focused on the librarian, the old blind monk, the venerable Jorge. William confronts Jorge who magnanimously lets him read a section of the book (and although the piece below is Eco's imitation of Aristotle's style, there is a very good chance that the lost book on comedy had a passage that sounded just like this):

> "As we promised, we will now deal with comedy (as well as with satire and mime) and see how, in inspiring the pleasure of the ridiculous, it arrives at the purification of that passion. . . . We will then define the type of actions of which comedy is the mimesis [imitation], then we will examine the means by which comedy excites laughter, and these means and actions and speech. . . . We will then show how the ridiculousness of speech is born from the misunderstandings of similar words for different things and different words for similar things. . . ."

While William is reading from the ancient text it becomes clear that Jorge assumes he is doing what all the murdered monks have been doing: licking his finger and then turning the page. But William has taken precautions and is wearing a glove, and is thus spared the death that Jorge has intended for anyone reading the book, since the pages are laced with poison. William now asks Jorge why this book in particular seems so dangerous that Jorge has decided to kill anyone who reads it? Jorge responds,[*]

> "Because it is by Aristotle."
>
> William: "But what is so alarming about laughter?"
>
> Jorge: "Laughter kills fear, and without fear there can be no faith. And without fear of the devil there can be no more need of God."
>
> William: "But you will not eliminate laughter by eliminating that book!"
>
> Jorge: "No, to be sure. Laughter will remain the common man's recreation. But what would happen if, because of this book, learned men were to pronounce it permissible to laugh at everything? Can we laugh at God? The world would relapse into chaos."

And Jorge flings an oil lamp into a stack of scrolls, starting a fire that will soon engulf the library, while condemned heretics are being burned at the stake in the courtyard.

So what happens to Aristotle's book in the story? Alas, it perishes in the library fire, along with Jorge. I will leave it up to you to read the book or watch the movie and find out whether William and Adso escape the flames.

Study Questions

1. Compare the real Aristotle text on tragedy and Eco's pastiche (attempt at writing something similar). Has Eco done a good job, in your view?

2. Compare Plato's view on comedy and laughter with what Eco believes to have been Aristotle's view. Which comes closer to your opinion? Explain why. (Also, whom do you think Eco would side with: Plato or Aristotle?)

3. Is Jorge right that fear of God is the source of moral laws, and laughter is a distraction from fear, so laughter is dangerous? Compare Jorge's and Plato's comments on laughter. (Remember that Jorge is a fictional character.)

4. Could Eco be right that if Aristotle's book had survived, it might have changed the course of Western culture? Why or why not?

---

[*]This section is quoted from the film, *The Name of the Rose,* because the text of the novel was not available for this edition of *The Moral of the Story.*

Primary Reading

The Simple Art of Murder

RAYMOND CHANDLER

Excerpt from an article in the* Atlantic Monthly, *November 1945.

Raymond Chandler (1888–1959) is considered one of the all-time great American authors of detective/crime/suspense fiction. His style is straightforward and "hard-boiled," but his main characters are rarely one-dimensional, and we get to know not only their façades but also their innermost feelings. His stories usually take place in Los Angeles in the 1930s and 1940s and have set the pattern for countless other detective/crime stories. His primary character, Philip Marlowe, is a private detective, with a love-hate relationship with the LAPD. In 1945 Chandler wrote a nonfiction piece for *Atlantic Monthly* that was to become a classic: "The Simple Art of Murder," primarily about his colleague, the crime-fiction writer Dashiell Hammett (the author of the classic *The Maltese Falcon*). Chandler's own best works include *The Big Sleep* and *The Long Goodbye,* and his novels have been made into movies, sometimes more than once. This excerpt from "The Simple Art of Murder" contains his analysis of the most compelling kind of detective story, and of the character of the detective.

> . . . The realist in murder writes of a world in which gangsters can rule nations and almost rule cities, in which hotels and apartment houses and celebrated restaurants are owned by men who made their money out of brothels, in which a screen star can be the fingerman for a mob, and the nice man down the hall is a boss of the numbers racket; a world where a judge with a cellar full of bootleg liquor can send a man to jail for having a pint in his pocket, where the mayor of your town may have condoned murder as an instrument of moneymaking, where no man can walk down a dark street in safety because law and order are things we talk about but refrain from practicing; a world where you may witness a hold-up in broad daylight and see who did it, but you will fade quickly back into the crowd rather than tell anyone, because the hold-up men may have friends with long guns, or the police may not like your testimony, and in any case the shyster for the defense will be allowed to abuse and vilify you in open court, before a jury of selected morons, without any but the most perfunctory interference from a political judge.
>
> It is not a very fragrant world, but it is the world you live in, and certain writers with tough minds and a cool spirit of detachment can make very interesting and even amusing patterns out of it. It is not funny that a man should be killed, but it is sometimes funny that he should be killed for so little, and that his death should be the coin of what we call civilization. All this still is not quite enough.
>
> In everything that can be called art there is a quality of redemption. It may be pure tragedy, if it is high tragedy, and it may be pity and irony, and it may be the raucous laughter of the strong man. But down these mean streets a man must go who is not himself mean, who is neither tarnished nor afraid. The detective in this kind of story must be such a man. He is the hero, he is everything. He must be a complete man and a common man and yet an unusual man. He must be, to use a rather weathered phrase, a man of honor, by instinct, by inevitability, without thought of it, and certainly without saying it. He must be the best man in his world and a good enough man for any world. I do not care much about his private life; he is neither a eunuch nor a satyr; I think he might seduce a duchess and I am quite sure he would not spoil a virgin; if he is a man of honor in one thing, he is that in all things. He is a relatively poor man, or he would not be a detective at all. He is a common man or he could not go among common people. He has a sense of character, or he would not know his job. He will take no man's money

dishonestly and no man's insolence without a due and dispassionate revenge. He is a lonely man and his pride is that you will treat him as a proud man or be very sorry you ever saw him. He talks as the man of his age talks, that is, with rude wit, a lively sense of the grotesque, a disgust for sham, and a contempt for pettiness. The story is his adventure in search of a hidden truth, and it would be no adventure if it did not happen to a man fit for adventure. He has a range of awareness that startles you, but it belongs to him by right, because it belongs to the world he lives in.

If there were enough like him, I think the world would be a very safe place to live in, and yet not too dull to be worth living in.

Study Questions

1. Chandler writes about the writer of crime/detective stories of the mid–twentieth century. Cop shows are the most frequent kind of television shows these days and have been for decades. Do you think his analysis holds true even today, or have the major themes in crime and suspense stories changed?

2. What does Chandler's analysis of the detective say about Chandler's view of moral values? Would you agree that the detective in a crime story (either a police detective or a private investigator) has to have those qualities, or are we looking for a different kind of hero today?

3. Could you imagine this description of the heroic detective applied to a female detective? Why or why not?

4. Compare this analysis of a good dramatic crime story with Aristotle's template for a good tragedy. Do you see any similarities?

 Narrative

Medea

EURIPIDES

From a fifth-century-B.C.E. play. Summary and Excerpts. Euripides, **Three Dramas of Euripides,** *translated by William Cranston Lawton. Boston: Houghton, Mifflin and Company: 1889.*

The Greek dramatist Euripides (ca. 485–406 B.C.E.) was considered an eccentric and an intellectual radical. Nineteen of his eighty-eight plays have survived into modern times. In fifth-century B.C.E. Athens, the annual festival held for Dionysus had developed into an established tradition of competitions among playwrights of tragedies, satyr plays, and comedies. Although the tragedies were originally supposed to deal with the life, death, and resurrection of the god Dionysus (Bacchus) and stories of the gods in general, they quickly developed into stories about human failings and revenge. The tragedy *Medea,* written in 451 B.C.E., is unusual in that it doesn't follow the established tragic pattern of the triumph of divine justice, but Euripides rarely followed the established patterns of tragedies. He won only four first prizes at the festivals in his lifetime, but after his death his plays became immensely popular. Toward the end of his life he left Athens; he died in Macedonia (where Aristotle was born in 384 B.C.E., twenty-two years later). In the preceding excerpt from Aristotle's *Poetics,* you may have noticed that Aristotle specifically praises Euripides and his unique style.

Greek mythology tells of Jason and his Argonauts, who captured the Golden Fleece from the king of Colchis and brought it back to Corinth in triumph. That is a heroic story, one of Greece's legends of the golden age. Jason was helped in his quest by the daughter of the king of Colchis, Medea, who betrayed her father, her brother, and her country to help Jason, the man she loved. So Medea followed him to Corinth. That was the old myth—and Euripides tells us "the rest of the story."

Years have passed, and Medea is in a deep depression. She won't eat, she can't sleep, she weeps incessantly. Jason has tired of her—she is no longer young, and Jason has fallen in love with another woman, the young blonde princess of Corinth. He has taken her as his second wife without so much as asking Medea's permission. Now the king, the princess's father, is about to banish Medea from the kingdom, together with her and Jason's two sons, because he fears that this woman, an unpredictable foreigner, may take revenge on his daughter. But Medea cannot go home because she caused her brother's death and betrayed her father in helping Jason. She forsook everything for him, including her ties to her homeland, and, without a homeland, one was barely considered a person in the ancient Greek world.

But Medea has a plan, and the old king has seen it coming with a sure instinct: Medea plots to poison both the princess and the king. She has one last, horrible argument with Jason, who comes to make sure she won't be destitute, because he has heard that she has been expelled from the country. She reminds him that he owes her everything—she helped him get the golden fleece, she abandoned her family for him, and even used her magic powers to slay a dragon for him. And she is the mother of his children. But Jason is not moved by her pleas.

Jason and Medea part with bitter words, and now Medea is in luck: King Aegeus of Athens pays her a visit and hears of her marital problems and banishment. He finds Jason despicable and admires Medea for her righteous anger. He himself is looking for a wife to bear him children and offers Medea a refuge as his wife as soon as she is "done with her business."

Medea now pretends to be submissive when Jason comes back and asks that the children be allowed to take gifts to his young bride. The enormity of what she is about to do is beginning to envelop her, and she finds it hard to control herself. After Jason leaves, she hands the gifts to the two young boys and can't stop weeping—because she not only plans to kill the princess but also plans to *kill her own children,* to hurt Jason the only way she knows how.

She sends the children away, and after a while, a messenger tells the gruesome details about how the children's gifts were received: The princess put on the golden diadem, Medea's gift, and instantly the poison began to work:

> Taking the well-wrought robes she put them on,
>
> Upon her ringlets set the golden crown,
>
> And at a shining mirror dressed her hair,
>
> Smiling upon her soulless counterfeit.
>
> Then rose she from her seat and crossed the room,
>
> Daintily treading with her fair white feet,
>
> Exulting in the gifts; and evermore,
>
> On tiptoe rising, backward cast her eyes.
>
> —But now a grewsome sight was there to see!
>
> For, changing color, back she sped again
>
> With trembling limbs, and hardly gained her seat

To fall thereon instead of on the earth.

An agèd servant thought a fright from Pan

Or other god had come on her, and raised

A prayerful cry, before she yet had marked

The white froth coming from her mouth, or saw

Her rolling eyes. the pallor of her face.

Then she responsive to that cry sent forth

A mighty wail. One sought the father's halls,

And one pursued her newly wedded lord,

To tell the bride's mishap; and all the house

Rang with the sound of many a hurrying tread.

Already a rapid walker in all haste

The limit of a stadium might have reached,

When she, who lay with close-shut speechless eyes,

Aroused herself with a shrill shriek: poor wretch!

For twofold agony made war on her.

The golden circlet on her head sent forth

A wondrous stream of all-devouring fire;

The delicate robes, the gift thy sons had brought,

Gnawed the white flesh of the ill-fated one.

Burning she started from her seat and fled;

This way and that she tossed her head and hair,

And fain would cast the crown away: but close

The gold did hold its clasp, the while the flame

Blazed doubly, as she shook her flowing locks.

Prone at the door she fell, o'ercome by woe,—

Save to her sire, most ghastly to behold.

The expression of her eyes was seen no more,

Nor comely was her face, but from her head

The blood with fire commingled trickled down;

And under the drug's teeth unseen her flesh

Slipped from her bones like teardrops from the fire.

A grewsome spectacle! And all did fear

To touch the corpse; her fate instructed us.

The princess's old father rushed to the scene and took her in his arms, and that was how the poison spread to him; within minutes he, too, was dead.

The news galvanizes Medea into action: Now she feels she must kill her children so nobody will take their revenge on them, and she rationalizes,

> Be armed, my heart! Why do we hesitate
>
> To work this dread inevitable ill?
>
> Come, my unhappy hand, seize thou the sword,—
>
> Seize it, and steal to life's grim race-course forth.
>
> Weaken not, nor recall how thou didst bear
>
> Thy children well-beloved, but for this one
>
> Brief day at least do thou forget thy sons,
>
> And mourn them then; for though thou slay them, yet
>
> Dear are they, and a wretched woman I.

From inside the room, we hear the cries for help as she stabs her two sons to death.

Jason returns, devastated at the turn of events. Medea gloats because now she knows she's "got under his skin." To the end, they quarrel over whose fault it is and who is to blame for the children's death. Jason didn't seem to care much for his sons while they were alive, but now that they are dead he loves them with all his heart. He invokes the power of the gods to avenge his children—but the gods don't help him. No divine lightning bolt strikes Medea down—she leaves him to become the wife of Aegeus.

Study Questions

1. This tragedy seemed nothing short of immoral to many critics in Athens because Medea gets away with quadruple murder. Can we defend Medea's actions in any way? Is Jason free of blame? What do you think Euripides intended the "moral of the story" to be?

2. How would Plato evaluate *Medea*—as a moral learning tool or a dangerous temptation to be irrational? How would Aristotle evaluate it? Does it meet his criteria for a well-written tragedy? (Tragedy has to happen to ordinary people as the result of some grave error in judgment of theirs and preferably should happen between family members.) In other words, if Aristotle is right and a good tragedy is the story of an ordinary person—not good, not bad—who makes a major mistake and suffers for it for the rest of his or her life, then who is the main character in *Medea*? From whose viewpoint is the story told? Medea's—or Jason's?

3. Sadly, the phenomenon of parents killing their children is not unusual at all; it may be done in anger, or for insurance purposes, for convenience, or out of some peculiar sense of responsibility ("I won't allow my children to become fatherless/motherless when I kill myself, so I'll take them with me"). Rarely is it done for revenge, as in the case of Medea. Susan Smith, who in 1994 strapped her two little boys in a car and let it roll into a lake, killing both of them, wanted to be unencumbered so her former boyfriend would come back to her. Andrea Yates, who drowned her five children in 2001, was diagnosed as suffering from severe postpartum depression and said she heard voices telling her to take their lives. But one murder case seems like a true Medea scenario: Susan Eubanks killed her four sons in 1998 specifically to get back at their fathers. Now remember that in the play, Medea isn't punished; she leaves for a new life as the queen of Athens. How do you feel about that, considering that Smith is serving a life sentence, and Eubanks is on death row? (Yates's life sentence was overturned and in 2006 she was found not guilty by reason of insanity and committed to a mental institution.)

Narrative

The Sorrows of Young Werther

JOHANN WOLFGANG VON GOETHE

Novel, 1774. Translated by Elizabeth Mayer and Louise Bogan. Excerpt.

The hypnotic power of Goethe's book about young lovesick Werther may be hard to imagine today, but the fact remains that many young readers in Europe took their own lives after suffering along with Werther. Goethe presented the story as though he had found Werther's letters to a friend—in the so-called epistolary (letter) style—and then told about the final days in narrative form. From May to December, Werther undergoes all the highs and lows of falling in love, but in the end his beloved Lotte marries someone else. Shortly after writing this letter to his friend Wilhelm, Werther takes his pistol and shoots himself in the head.

> December 4
>
> I beg you—you see I am done for; I cannot bear it any longer. Today I sat near her as she played the clavichord, all sorts of tunes and with so much expression. So much! So much! What could I do? Her little sister sat on my knee and dressed her doll. Tears came into my eyes. I bowed my head and caught sight of her wedding ring. The tears ran down my cheek—and suddenly Lotte began to play the heavenly old melody. All at once my soul was touched by a feeling of consolation, by a memory of the past, of the other occasions when I had heard the song, of the dark intervals of vexation between, of shattered hopes, and then—I walked up and down the room, my heart almost suffocated by the rush of emotions. "For God's sake," I said, in a vehement outburst, "for God's sake, stop!" She paused and looked at me steadily. "Werther," she said with a smile that went deep to my heart, "Werther, you are very sick. You dislike the things you once liked. Go! I beg you, calm yourself!" I tore myself from her sight, and—God! You see my misery and will put an end to it.

Study Questions

1. Evaluate Werther's reaction from your own point of view: Is suicide because of rejection a realistic scenario? Is it emotionally understandable? Is it morally defensible? Explain your viewpoint.

2. Apply Plato's and Aristotle's views to this excerpt.

3. Analyses have suggested that certain Internet television series such as *13 Reasons Why* may have had a similar effect on some young viewers. It is known as the "Werther Effect." Do you think something should be done to prevent such influence in the future? Explain your viewpoint.

4. Goethe gives the story credibility by pretending that he found these letters of Werther's (although he of course made the whole story up, including the character of Werther himself). The format of letting a story unfold within a frame of a letter, or an ancient manuscript in the loft, or a videotape, dates all the way back to the fifteenth century and lives on because it is such a good way to lend credence to the story. This format was used in the 1990s in the popular film *The Blair Witch Project,* as well as in the film *Cloverfield,* to make the films look like documentaries. Can you think of other stories—novels or films—that use the same trick?

Narrative

Red Dead Redemption 2

DAN HOUSER (director)

Videogame, 2018. Rock Star Games. Summary

The videogame *Red Dead Redemption 2* is a prequel to the 2010 game *Red Dead Revolver*, and at the time of writing this it has become one of the most popular videogames ever, especially since going online in 2019. It has received praise for its dialogue and graphics, and for its rich plot containing 23 possible storylines, one for each character, with each having his or her own backstory and character development. It has been praised for its soundtrack, with its music video being featured on *Good Morning America*. It is also one of the most violent games to date, according to reviewers. (As I am not a gamer, and I am relying on Internet spoilers to get a handle on how the game works, I hope you will bear with this brief, sporadic summary! I apologize beforehand if I have revealed too much.) The plot takes place in the Old West in 1899, where lawmen are tracking down and confronting the last of the outlaw gangs. Players take on the role of Arthur Morgan, a member of Dutch van der Linde's gang of outlaws. After a failed robbery attempt the gang regroups and robs a train, but finds itself pursued by Pinkerton detectives, led by Agent Miller. Miller tries to persuade Arthur to betray his gang, to no avail, and a gunfight breaks out. The gang is on the run again.

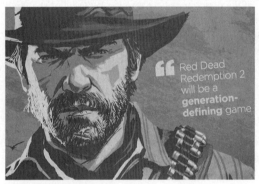

Ink Drop/Alamy Stock Photo

In their quest for riches, the gang finds itself in the middle of a range war between two families, the Grays and the Braithwaites. Dutch and the gang devise a plan to play the two sides against each other, but in the process a young boy, Jack, is kidnapped by the Grays. Jack's father is gang member John Marston, and gamers know he will be the main character in *Red Dead Revolver*. Will Jack get rescued? I would assume that gamers would prefer not to have that revealed! Further adventures involve a bank robbery where several gang members are killed and others make off with the gold. Their escape takes them to exotic locations, including an island which they in turn need to escape from. Will they get off the island? And what are their further adventures? Who will reveal themselves as ultimate bad guys? And what is Arthur's ultimate fate?

At this point those readers who are gamers will probably prefer to explore the plot on their own, but one final hint needs to be dropped: A key character has a fundamental choice to make, and the story lines will diverge, based on that choice. It is of course up to the player how he or she will choose to play the character. And the choice hinges on whether the character is honorable or dishonorable—because choices have consequences.

It is this feature that makes *Red Dead Redemption 2* a candidate for a narrative with a moral, even though the point of view is that of the outlaws, and not of the lawmen: Arthur Morgan—the eyes through which we experience the story—shows himself early on to refuse to betray his gang, and throughout the game he struggles to develop a moral compass, torn between his loyalty to the gang and his emerging conscience. And the theme of honor vs. dishonor is carried through the entire game. If you go back to the section on Westerns earlier in this chapter, you'll recognize the main point in classic as well as newer Westerns: *the hard choices.* Is the protagonist making a choice that will reveal himself, or herself, as a loyal friend, a courageous individual, an honorable person—or is he or she taking the easy way out, abandoning their friends as well as their values? And what exactly is an honorable person? One who is loyal at all costs, or one who follows his or her conscience? Since this is a game, points accumulate according to whether the player acts honorably or not. If the player chooses to be an outlaw, it has consequences, but if he or she chooses to play as a "good guy," it has other consequences, and the game is *not* set up as a moralizing narrative. It is not an easy morality tale of good guys and bad guys. Rather, it simply presents options for choices and their consequences.

But I have to mention that contrary to traditional Westerns, we don't just *observe* the choosing. As players, *we* make the choice. In that respect it resembles real life. But contrary to real life, it is a *game*, and the game will allow us a "do-over" if we don't like the consequences of our choice. Real life is usually not so generous.

Study Questions

1. If you are a gamer and have played this game, outline incidents where the themes of honor and loyalty are prominent in the game. Is loyalty always a virtue? Is honor? Why or why not?

2. If you are not a gamer, does a summary of a game make you want to try to play? Why or why not?

3. The ending is depending on choices you as a player make. Do you like that kind of openness, or do you prefer stories that are pre-written, with a message?

4. Not only is *Red Dead Redemption 2* a very violent game—its main character hangs out with outlaws and commits acts of violence, and since that is the character the player identifies with, then essentially the player takes on the identity of an outlaw. Do you think that is a legitimate form of entertainment, or do you see a problem with it? What would Plato say? What would Aristotle say?

5. Do you think the critics are right that the "do-over" function of videogames may lure young minds into thinking that life also has a "do-over" function, and that no choices are serious or binding? Why or why not?

Narrative

The Education of Mingo

CHARLES JOHNSON

Short story from **The Sorcerer's Apprentice,** *1977. Summary and Excerpt.*

The story of Mingo's "education" is a golem tale—not about an artificially created person, but about a human being whose mind becomes a mirror of the subconscious drives of his "master." We can read this story as an indictment of slavery in the old South, about an unusual relationship between a slave and his master—about affectional bonding and moral responsibility. Or we can read it as a story of a creator losing control over his creation. Or we can read it as a psychological story of what really goes on in the mind of old Moses. But we can also read it as a tale about the dangers of teaching! You never know what the student gets out of your lessons. . . .

Old Moses Green drives his one-horse rig into town and buys himself a slave; we're in the antebellum South, in 1854. The slave that Moses buys, Mingo, is new to the New World, a prince of the Allmuseri tribe, according to the auctioneer. Moses doesn't need a farmhand as much as a companion, because he is a lonely man. But Mingo speaks no English and knows no social customs other than his tribal ways, so Moses sets out to teach him everything: the English language, farming, table manners, ciphering, cooking, and so forth.

Moses has mixed feelings about the young man. Sometimes he feels like a father toward him, and sometimes he feels that he is an artist, shaping a work of art out of clay. But he soon discovers that Mingo, who is a fast learner, picks up not only on what Moses teaches him intentionally but also on what Moses himself does on his own time, such as swearing, dunking cornbread in his coffee, and other bad habits. He copies even Moses' mannerisms and way of being. Within a year, Mingo has become a shadow of Moses—acting out not only what Moses wants him to do but also what Moses himself would subconsciously like to do.

Moses' lady friend, Harriet Bridgewater, has a wry wisdom of her own, and Moses is a little bit afraid of her. She is highly critical of his project of educating Mingo and tries to make Moses understand that he is bound to fail; Mingo's background is too different. Moses argues that Mingo is doing fine and has become a sort of extension of himself—except for one thing: Mingo is supposed to treat strangers with respect and kill chicken hawks. But Moses has observed Mingo treating chicken hawks as if they were human and calling them "Sir." So how deep does this mix-up go? Soon Moses discovers the horrible truth: Mingo has killed old Isaiah Jenson—because Mingo has picked up on Moses' stray remarks about what an old fool Isaiah is. And since Mingo believes that he is supposed to act the way Moses *wants to act,* he kills old Isaiah. This is the moment of realization for Moses: His attempt to teach Mingo everything he knows and, in effect, create a person in his own image has failed—or it has worked too well.

When Moses confronts Mingo about the murder of Isaiah, Mingo points out that he was just doing what Moses wanted done, just thinking what Moses wanted him to think. And Moses realizes that now Mingo even stands in the same way he does, walks the same way, holds his head the same way. His voice even has the same inflection as Moses'. And Moses shrieks in terror—but so does Mingo. They have become two sides of the same coin.

In deep distress, Moses drives his horse and buggy over to Harriet's, yelling to her as he climbs down the rig that Mingo has killed Isaiah—but, he says, it wasn't altogether Mingo's fault. He needs Harriet to help him work things out, but she seems dazed all of a sudden.

> There was suddenly in her features the intensity found in the look of people who have a year, a month, a minute only to live. "I think I'd better sit down." Lowering herself onto her rocker, she cradled on her lap a volume by one M. Shelley, a recent tale of monstrosity and existential horror, then she demurely settled her breasts. "It's just like you, Moses Green, to bring all your bewilderments to me."

So Harriet is no help. Moses goes off to ponder the situation. He can't turn the boy in, because that would be like turning part of himself in; and any way he looks at it, he and Mingo have become part of each other. But he realizes that the person he needs now is Harriet, and he returns to her farm to ask her to marry him—only to find, to his horror, that in the meantime, Mingo has committed another murder. Harriet herself lies dead over by the water pump—Mingo has responded to a stray remark from Moses the day before, about Harriet's being a talkative old hen.

Courtesy of Charles Johnson and used by permission of Humanities Washington.

Charles Johnson has a Ph.D. in philosophy, and has now retired from teaching literature at the University of Washington. He is the author of four novels, *Faith and the Good Thing* (1974), *Oxherding Tale* (1982), *Middle Passage* (1990), and *Dreamer* (1998); two collections of short stories, *The Sorcerer's Apprentice* (1986) and *Soulcatcher and Other Stories* (2001); over twenty screenplays; and numerous articles and books on the African American experience. Johnson has published four short story collections. The most recent two are Dr. King's Refrigerator and Other Bedtime Stories and Night Hawks. His works have won many awards, including the 1990 National Book Award for *Middle Passage.*

This is the moment of truth for Moses: Whatever Mingo has done, he, Moses, bears the responsibility. He finds Mingo and forces him down on the ground while he goes into Harriet's house and retrieves her flintlock rifle. Holding the barrel against Mingo's neck, he cocks the hammer—but he can't shoot:

> Eyes narrowed to slits, Moses said—a dry whisper—"get up, you damned fool." He let his round shoulders slump. Mingo let his broad shoulders slump. "Take the horses," Moses said; he pulled himself up to his rig, then sat, his knees together beside the boy. Mingo's knees drew together. Moses's voice changed. It began to rasp and wheeze; so did Mingo's. "Missouri," said the old man, not to Mingo but to the dusty floor of the buckboard, "if I don't misremember, is off thataway somewhere in the west."

Study Questions

1. Does the ending of the story indicate that Moses takes responsibility for how he has trained Mingo, or does he refuse to take responsibility? Explain. Does it make any difference? How is this story an indictment of the institution of slavery?

2. Is Mingo a golem? Is he a Frankenstein's monster? Is he a Pygmalion's statue? Is he "Mr. Hyde" to Moses' "Dr. Jekyll"? Or is he perhaps a Pinocchio? Explain the similarities and the differences.

3. What is the significance of the book Harriet holds in her lap moments before she dies?

4. Can you think of other stories in which a moral lesson is misunderstood or taken too literally, to the detriment of the characters in the story?

Narrative

 Pulp Fiction

QUENTIN TARANTINO (DIRECTOR AND SCREENWRITER)

Screenplay, 1994. Film, 1994. Summary and Excerpt.

In this summary (with a short excerpt) we focus on one aspect of a complex story. *Pulp Fiction,* which shocked its first audiences with its graphic violence and strong language, has now acquired the status of an instant classic, often referred to in educational contexts precisely because of its casual attitude toward death and violence—up to a point. Here we look at the point where violence suddenly seems to have lost its appeal for one of the main characters, Jules.

Jules and Vincent have had a rough morning. Hit men for a mobster, they have just murdered two young men, with Jules quoting a passage supposedly from Ezekiel, but heavily embroidered with Jules's own words of doom, to them before he kills them, as he usually does; it is his style. Completing the job, they retrieve a briefcase for their boss. What Jules and Vincent don't know is that another man is hiding in the bathroom. When he bursts out, emptying his Magnum at the two hit men, they fire back, and he dies—but neither Jules nor Vincent is hurt. Vincent wants to label it a stroke of good luck and get out of there, but Jules is profoundly shocked and sees it as something else: divine intervention.

Marvin, a young friend of Jules's who has helped him set up the hit, follows them out of the blood-stained apartment into their car; while Vincent is discussing the incident of the bullets that missed, his gun accidentally goes off and shoots the young man in the face. Terribly upset, Jules worries that they are now driving on the highway with a bloody car and a dead body—his concern is not for the untimely death of Marvin.

Later they are having breakfast in a coffee shop, coming down from the morning's events. Jules is still contemplating what he thinks of as a miracle, the fact that he wasn't killed, and he announces that he now considers himself retired from "the Life."

Something else is going on in the coffee shop. A young couple, Pumpkin and Honey Bunny, are now rising up out of a booth, pointing guns at the patrons and the waitresses: They are going to rob the place. Vincent has gone to the restroom and is unaware of the developments, but Jules witnesses the entire holdup. The young couple take the money from the cash register and move in to rob the patrons. When Pumpkin points his gun at Jules, he gives up his wallet but flatly refuses to hand over the briefcase. He lets Pumpkin look inside (we don't get to see the contents, only its mysterious glow), but that is as far as it goes. When Pumpkin points his gun at Jules, Jules quickly twists his arm, and now Pumpkin is the one staring into the gun. The girl attempts to help her lover but realizes that Jules will shoot if she moves. Now Vincent comes back to the table and takes in the situation. Together, Jules and Vincent keep the young couple under control, and Jules tells them that under normal circumstances they would both be dead now—but today he is in a "transitional period" and doesn't want to kill them. He instructs Pumpkin to go into the loot bag, fish out Jules's wallet, take out the cash, $1,500, and just go away. And he tells Pumpkin:

> Wanna know what I'm buying? . . . Your life. I'm giving you that money so I don't hafta kill your ass. . . . You read the Bible? . . . There's a passage I got memorized: Ezekiel 25:17. "The path of the righteous man is beset on all sides by the inequities of the selfish and the tyranny of evil men. Blessed is he who, in the name of charity and good will, shepherds the weak through the valley of the darkness. For he is truly his brother's keeper and the finder of lost children. And I will strike down upon thee with great vengeance and furious anger those who attempt to poison and destroy my brothers. And you will know I am the Lord when I lay my vengeance upon you." I been sayin' that shit for years. And if you ever heard it, it means your ass. I never really questioned what it meant. I thought it was just a coldblooded thing to say. . . . But I saw some shit this morning made me think twice. Now I'm thinkin'. It could mean you're the evil man. And I'm the righteous man. And Mr. .45 here he's the shepherd protecting my righteous ass in the valley of darkness. Or it could be you're the righteous man and I'm the shepherd and it's the world that's evil and selfish. I'd like that. But that shit ain't the truth. The truth is you're weak. And I'm the tyranny of evil men. But I'm tryin'. I'm tryin' real hard to be a shepherd.

United Archives GmbH/Alamy Stock Photo

Pulp Fiction (Miramax, 1994) appears to many people to glorify violence, but educators have discerned a deeper intention: a strong statement against violence. Here Honey Bunny (Amanda Plummer) and Pumpkin (Tim Roth) are preparing to rob the customers and staff of the diner.

Jules lowers his gun and puts it on the table; Pumpkin looks at him, at Honey Bunny, at the $1,500 in his hand, and then he grabs the trash bag full of cash and wallets, and he and Honey Bunny walk out the door.

Study Questions

1. What does Jules mean by suggesting that he might be the "righteous man"? What does he mean by suggesting that he might be the shepherd?

2. What does Jules mean by saying that he is giving Honey Bunny and Pumpkin the money so he won't have to kill them?

3. What do you think is the point of talking about being "righteous" and "being evil," given that the scene we are witnessing is a confrontation between robbers and hit men?

4. If you have seen the film, you will know that the dialogue is laden with profanity (as is evident in the excerpt from Jules's monologue). Do you think the foul language serves a purpose in this context? Why or why not? You might want to discuss the issue of profanity in contemporary speech styles.

5. Do you believe this particular film might inspire more violence (as Plato would believe), or do you think that, in some way, it might serve as a "cleansing" experience (as Aristotle might say) or perhaps as a warning against wholesale cultural acceptance of violence?

6. You may have wondered what the briefcase contains. It is not revealed in the film, but rumor has it that it contains the soul of the gangster boss. Would such an interpretation make a difference to the story? Explain.

Chapter Three
Ethical Relativism

Picture the Indian Ocean and a canoe approaching a remote island. Paddling the canoe is a young man, an American. On the island is a population of natives who dislike strangers and who have a reputation for hostility. The young man is determined to reach the island and take his chances because he has an important message to the inhabitants: He wants to save their souls by bringing them to Christ. This could be a movie plot, or an early twentieth-century novel, but it is an actual, contemporary scenario of a story that didn't have a happy ending. In the fall of 2018, 27-year-old John Allen Chau from Washington State, a former Oklahoma soccer team manager, made the final of three journeys, trying to do missionary work among the inhabitants of North Sentinel, an island in the chain of Andaman and Nicobar Islands off the Bay of Bengal. He had gone through a missionary program in 2015 and had his heart set on bringing Jesus to indigenous non-Christians ever since. So in 2016 he made his first journey to Asia, and was back again in 2017 without being able to fulfill his dream, and so tried again in 2018. But the Sentinel Island is prohibited territory for strangers. Having previously been part of the British Empire (within the territory of India) and seen their tribe decimated, the remaining inhabitants of the island had opted to remain without contact to the modern world, and Indian legislation had made it illegal to approach and enter the island. In 2006, the tribespeople had killed two local fishermen from the mainland whose boat had drifted onto the island. John Chau was aware of all the facts, but even so, he hired local fishermen to take him to Sentinel Island in November of 2018. He made it ashore, with gifts for the Sentinelese, including fish and a soccer ball. At first the encounter seemed to be going well, but then the inhabitants started firing arrows at him, and one arrow hit his bible. John managed to escape, and the fishermen brought him back to the mainland where he wrote a letter to his family saying that he felt the chance was worth risking his life for, and asked them not to be angry if it resulted in his death. And the next day, he was on his way back to Sentinel, with the fishermen towing his canoe. The fishermen stayed on the boat and watched what happened next: John paddled his canoe to the island and went ashore, and tried to communicate with the inhabitants who were gathering at the beach, but they appeared very hostile. Bows were raised, and immediately John was hit by several arrows, and collapsed. The inhabitants destroyed his canoe, and the fishermen reported that they saw John's body being dragged around in the sand and later being buried on the beach.

The international reactions were mixed, of course: sympathy for the young American and especially for his bereaved family, but also condemnation of his action of breaking the law and trying to contact the natives. The Indian officials, after some deliberation, decided not to attempt to retrieve his body, and the U.S. government made the decision in 2019 not to pursue any legal action against the islanders for murder. The decision to go ashore had been John Allen Chau's exclusively, and the U.S. government concluded that risking the consequences was his own choice and his own responsibility. (In the Narratives section, you can read a summary of a novel by American novelist Barbara Kingsolver, *The Poisonwood Bible*, about an American missionary in Africa and his family, and you may want to revisit the story of John Allen Chau for comparisons.)

The attempt by Chau to visit another culture, uninvited, and attempt to affect it brings up a fundamental question: Is it at all acceptable, in this day and age, to impose one's view, familiar in one's own culture, on another culture, even if the intention is to do them good? And to what extent can a culture defend itself against unwelcome interference? As a matter of fact, is there such a thing as a universal set of values which we can (or should) all recognize, or does one's perception of morals and values exclusively depend on which *culture* one has been raised in? For John Chau, the right thing was to keep trying to get in contact with the islanders to teach them about Christ. For the islanders (I assume), the right thing was to prevent cultural contamination at all cost. And we can take the question even further: Is there such a thing as a universal set of values, or is it up to the *individual* to choose her or his value system? And what happens when different value systems collide? So that is the philosophical challenge: How should we deal with moral differences?

We don't even have to imagine clashes between cultural attitudes, religions, and values; we can even perceive moral differences between people within the same culture. You may wait at the movie theater for a friend who never shows up because she is on the phone with another friend and it doesn't occur to her that it is important to keep her date with you. Such actions usually can be dismissed as merely bad manners or callousness; still, you probably will not want to make plans with that person again. Or, in a more drastic example, suppose you are dating someone to whom you feel very attracted. During dinner at a nice restaurant, your date casually mentions that he or she supports a political candidate or cause that you strongly oppose on moral grounds. The fact that your date has a different idea about what constitutes moral behavior will probably affect the way you feel about him or her.

We regularly read and hear about actions that are morally unacceptable to us. A young foreign girl is killed by her brother because she is pregnant and unmarried or perhaps merely going out with an American boy. To the Western mind the brother's act is an unfathomable crime. But the brother believes he is only doing his duty, unpleasant as it may be; he is upholding the family honor, which the sister has tainted by her act of unspeakable immorality (according to the traditional code of his culture—hence the term *honor-killing*). The world is full of stories about people who feel duty-bound to do things others find repugnant. People in some cultures feel it is their moral obligation, or moral right, to dispose of their elderly citizens when they become unproductive. Pretechnological cultures, in particular, have had a tradition during times when food was scarce of exposing their oldest members to the elements and leaving them to die. Often the decision would rest with these older people, who felt morally obliged to remove themselves from the tribe when they believed it was time. Some cultures have felt a moral right or duty to dispose of infants in the same way—usually cultures with no safe medical access to contraception. Other cultures believe it is a sin to seek medical assistance—they believe life should be left in the hands of God. Some people believe it is a sin to destroy any life, even by inadvertently stepping on an insect. Some people think they have a moral duty to defend themselves, their loved ones, and their country from any threat; others think it is their moral duty to refrain from resorting to violence under any circumstances. Box 3.1 explores the cultural relationship between moral values and waylegislation.

Box 3.1 THE INTERSECTION OF MORAL AND LEGAL ISSUES

Do a nation's laws reflect some basic universal moral values, or are they relative to their time and place in history? Philosophy of law generally speaks of two viewpoints concerning the relationship between ethics and the law. The viewpoint of *legal naturalism* (or *natural law*) holds that the law reflects, or ought to reflect, a set of universal moral standards; some naturalists consider those standards given by God, and some see them as part of human nature. The other viewpoint is referred to as *legal positivism* and holds that the law is based on consensus among legislators; in other words, there is no ultimate moral foundation for our laws; they are relative and merely reflect shifting opinions over time.

Whether we prefer naturalism or legal positivism as an explanation of the relationship between moral values and the law, or perhaps a hybrid form that acknowledges some universal values but otherwise sees laws as being contextual and relative, the assumption of a relationship between morals and legislation is ancient. From the Code of Hammurabi (developed by Babylonians in approximately 2000 B.C.E.) to the legislation of today, some laws have reflected the moral climate of the time. Not all laws have done so, though some scholars argue that because laws tell us what we ought to do or ought not to do, all laws have a moral element to them; if nothing else, they promote the idea that it is morally good to uphold the law. However, sometimes the law does not seem to be morally right. The Athenians followed the law when they executed Socrates, but it didn't seem right to his followers, and it doesn't seem right to us today. When times change, what seemed right before may not seem right anymore, and if the legislative power is sensitive to that fact, the law will change. Sometimes it takes a civil war for such laws to be changed; sometimes it takes an act of defiance; sometimes it takes only a simple vote. We can't, therefore, conclude that all laws are morally just, because experience tells us this is not so. Some laws may not even have an obvious moral element. A traffic law that allows us to turn right on red hardly addresses a moral issue.

Legislators, though, are naturally interested in the public's opinion of right and wrong, because, in Western-style democracies, that opinion will be represented by the laws of the country. Not all moral issues are relevant for legislators, however; whether you go home for Thanksgiving may be an important moral issue in your family, but it is hardly the business of anyone else, let alone the state legislature. Whether you choose to download copyrighted music off the Internet without paying for it *is* the business of the courts, and many would also consider it a moral issue (like stealing), while some would not. Some issues are clearly considered both immoral and illegal within a culture, while others tend to be viewed as strictly a matter of legality, or morality, but not necessarily both.

If we look at the relationship between the moral codes and the laws of various societies, we find that they differ dramatically: One society's legislation may reflect the belief that the law should not dictate people's moral choices as long as no harm is caused. Another society's laws may be anchored solidly in the moral code of that society, usually derived from the society's religion. The first type of society reflects a popular Western contemporary viewpoint; an example of the latter would be a Muslim society such as Iran, where a code of law inspired by Islam, the *Sharia,* is enforced. Over time, societies have opted for various combinations of the law, morals, and religion, with a close connection between the three being very common until the twentieth century. However, as some philosophers point out, our postmodern culture is increasingly focused on *what is the law,* rather than on *what is morally right*—possibly because many consider the idea of moral right or wrong an individual choice (*subjectivism*) or a cultural matter (*ethical relativism*).

But it is also possible that some decide to focus on the law rather than morals because they think it lets them off the hook: If a behavior isn't illegal, it must surely be okay, right? Wrong, because we also have *civil codes of ethics,* such as rules for employees in a workplace, politicians in local government, and professors and students on a campus, and because we have a tacit understanding of *moral expectations* among professionals, among friends, and among family members. You may not be arrested for making inappropriate comments to coworkers, or for using your company computer during work hours for transactions on eBay or finding dates, or for dating someone you are supervising, but such behavior can surely get you fired. And betraying the trust of a friend or a family member will usually not get you arrested, either, but it may have irreparable consequences for your relationship. Reducing it all to what is legal is a misunderstanding of the nature of ethics, whether inadvertent or deliberate.

How to Deal with Moral Differences

How do we approach this phenomenon of moral differences? There are at least four major paths to choose.

1. **Moral Nihilism, Skepticism, and Subjectivism** We may choose to believe that there are no morally right or wrong viewpoints—that the whole moral issue is a cultural game, and neither your opinion nor mine matters in the end, for there is no ultimate right or wrong. This view is called *moral nihilism,* and at various times in our lives, especially if we are facing personal disappointment, we may be inclined to take this approach. This is a difficult position to uphold, however, because it is so extreme. It is hard to remember, every minute of the day, that we don't believe there is any difference between right and wrong. If we see somebody steal our car, we are inclined to want the thief stopped, regardless of how much our jaded intellect tells us that no one is more right or wrong than anyone else. (But we can still call the cops! See the box discussing the difference between moral and legal issues!) If we watch a child or an animal being abused, we feel like stepping in, even if we tell ourselves that there is no such thing as right or wrong. In other words, there seems to be something in most of us—instinct, or socialization, or reason, or compassion, or maybe something else altogether—that surfaces even when we try to persuade ourselves that moral values are but an illusion.

   Related to the attitude of moral nihilism is *moral skepticism,* which holds that we can't know whether there are any moral truths, and *moral subjectivism,* which holds that moral views are merely inner states in a person and that they can't be compared to the inner states of another person, so a moral viewpoint is valid only for the person who holds it. Both skepticism and subjectivism are more common than nihilism, but they seem to be equally difficult to adhere to in the long run, because at crucial times we all act *as if* there are valid moral truths that we share with others—we criticize a friend for being late, a politician for being a racist or a sexist, a sibling for not pitching in when the family needs help. We praise a stranger for coming to our aid when we are stuck on the freeway, we praise our kids when they come home on time—so it seems that even if we believe ourselves to be nihilists, skeptics, or subjectivists, we still expect to share some values with others of our own culture.

Although moral subjectivism generally seems a more flexible and appealing theory than categorical moral nihilism or moral skepticism—to the point that some thinkers choose to treat subjectivism as a subcategory of ethical relativism—the three theories have something in common that makes all of them less than successful: *They have no conflict-solving capacity.* How would you persuade the car thief to leave your car alone on moral grounds if you are a nihilist? a skeptic? or a subjectivist? In each case, you have given up on the idea of finding common moral ground. The best you can do is tell the car thief that he is behaving in an illegal fashion; you can't claim that you have a moral argument that he ought to listen to.

" I'm good or bad depending on the circumstances, the situation, and the people involved. "

CartoonStock.com

Roy Delgado/www.CartoonStock.com

Many of us go through life with a sense that moral values are situational–relative to the time and the place. Why does the little girl's response seem problematic? Do you agree with her? Are values relative to the situation? Should they be? What would a moral subjectivist respond? What would an ethical relativist say?

2. **Ethical Relativism** We may choose to believe that there are no universal moral values—that each culture has its own set of rules that are valid for that culture, and we have no right to interfere, just as they have no right to interfere with our rules. This attitude, known as *ethical relativism,* is not as radical as skepticism because it allows that moral values exist but holds that they are relative to their time and place. Ethical relativism is viewed as an attitude of tolerance and as an antidote to the efforts of cultures who try their best to impose their set of moral rules on other cultures. Can ethical relativism solve conflicts? Yes, quite effectively, under limited conditions: within a culture. Whatever the majority deems to be the moral rule is the proper rule to follow. However, intercultural moral disagreements can rarely be solved. The ethical relativist can claim that it was wrong for John Chau to try to influence the culture of the Sentinelese, but the relativist can't claim that one culture is more morally correct than another. This theory is discussed in detail in the next section.

3. **Soft Universalism** We may believe that deep down, in spite of all their differences, people of different cultures can still agree on certain basic moral values. We may think it is a matter of biology—that people everywhere have basically the same human nature. Or we may view this agreement as a process of acculturation, whereby people adjust to the normal way of doing things in their culture. If the native peoples of harsh climates put their unwanted babies out in the wild to perish, it need not mean that they are cruel but, rather, that they want to give the babies they already have a chance to survive, and they know that having another mouth to feed might endanger them all. In this way, we find common ground in the fact that we, and they, do care for the children we are able to raise. If we believe that somehow, under the surface of antagonism and contradiction, we can still find a few things we can agree on, even if we choose to act on them in different ways, then we believe in the existence of a few universal moral values. I call this attitude *soft universalism—universalism* because it perceives that there are some universal moral rules; *soft* because it is not as radical as hard universalism, or absolutism.* Can soft universalism solve conflicts? Perhaps it can do so better than any other approach, because the main goal of soft universalism is to seek common ground beneath the variety of opinions and mores. But what exactly *are* those core values? Soft universalism speculates that they are grounded in our common humanity, but what does that mean? Later in the chapter, you'll see a suggestion from philosopher James Rachels, who speculates that there are three such universal moral values.

4. **Hard Universalism** *Hard universalism* (sometimes called *moral absolutism*) is the attitude that most often is supported in ethical theories. It is an attitude toward morals in everyday life to which many people relate very well. Hard universalism holds that there is one universal moral code. It is the viewpoint expressed by those who are on a quest for the code ("I know there must be one set of true moral rules, but I would not presume to have found it myself"), by those who make judgments based on its analysis ("After much deliberation I have come to the conclusion that this moral code represents the ultimate values"), and by those who put forth the simple sentiment that moral truth is not open for discussion ("I'm right and you're wrong, and you'd better shape up!"). While moral nihilism, with its claim that there are no moral truths, represents one end of the spectrum in dealing with moral differences, hard universalism represents the other end: It does not acknowledge the legitimacy of more than one set of moral codes. Can hard universalism/moral absolutism solve moral conflicts? Yes, in a variety of ways: If you accept someone telling you that you must be wrong because you don't agree with him or her, then that conflict is solved right there; more frequently, an absolutist will try to show you, on the basis of reasoning and evidence, that his or her moral conclusion is better than yours. Appeals to evidence and reasoning are the common problem-solving approaches among most absolutist philosophers, not

---

*Some readers have asked me if I am the originator of the term *soft universalism,* and I have to confess that I simply don't know; I have used it for more than three decades. I may have read it in someone else's book many years ago, or I may have simply constructed it in contrast to hard universalism, as may be the case with other philosophers—it's a handy, straightforward term. If anyone remembers encountering the term *soft universalism* before the publication of the first edition of *The Moral of the Story* in 1994, please let me know! I would like to be able to give credit where credit is due.

appeals to force or fallacious arguments such as "I'm right because I'm right." Being a hard universalist thus doesn't equal inflexibility or dogmatism as much as a firm moral conviction—although such a conviction can of course also be dogmatic.

The first set of viewpoints will not be discussed much in this book, interesting as it may be, because of their lack of ability to solve moral conflicts. The second one, *ethical relativism,* has greatly influenced moral attitudes in the West since the early twentieth century and is the main topic of this chapter. The third, *soft universalism,* and the fourth, *hard universalism,* will be discussed in this chapter as well as subsequent chapters.

The Lessons of Anthropology

In the late nineteenth century, cultural anthropology came into its own as a scientific discipline and reminded the West that "out there" were other societies vastly different from those of Victorian Europe. Anthropological scholars set out to examine other cultures, and the facts they brought back were astounding to the nineteenth-century Western mindset: There were cultures that didn't understand the male's role in procreation but thought that babies somehow ripened in the woman with the help of spirits. There were people who would devour the bodies of enemies killed in war to share their fighting spirit. There were cultures that believed in animal gods, cultures that felt it appropriate for women to bare their breasts, cultures that felt it utterly inappropriate to let your in-laws watch you eat, and so on. It was easy to draw the conclusion that there were cultures out there whose moral codes differed substantially from those of the West.

That conclusion, the first step in what has become known as ethical relativism, was not new to the Western mindset. Because people had always traveled and returned with tales of faraway lands, it was common knowledge that other cultures did things differently. Explorers in earlier centuries brought home tales of mermaids, giants, and other fantasies. Some stories were truer than others. There really were, for instance, peoples out there who had a different dress ethic and work ethic. The Arabian messenger and Islamic scholar Ibn Fadlan traveled north into Russia in 922 and watched a Viking burial; he wrote with disgust about how different and primitive the Viking customs were (his story was the theme of the film *The 13th Warrior*), so not all such reports come from Western travelers commenting about non-Western ways. But what we're most familiar with is of course the tales about non-Western, exotic lands. The (mostly inaccurately portrayed) lifestyle of the South Sea islanders became a collective fantasy for Europeans of the eighteenth and nineteenth centuries; imagine not wearing any clothes, not having to work all the time, living in perpetual summertime, and not having any sexual restrictions! Depending on their ethical predisposition, Westerners considered such peoples to be either the luckiest ones on this earth or the most sinful, subhuman, and depraved. Reports of cultural diversity were also supplied by Christian missionaries who, over the centuries, confronted more or less reluctant cultures with their message of conversion. The death of John Chau would be a recent example of such a culture clash.

The idea of cultural diversity even in early historic times is well documented. The Greek historian Herodotus (485–430 B.C.E.) tells in his *Histories* of the Persian king Darius the Great, who from the borders of his vast empire, which at the time stretched from the Greek holdings in the West to India in the East, had heard tales of funerary practices that intrigued him. The Greeks were at that time in the habit of cremating their dead; Darius learned that a tribe in India, the Callatians, would eat their dead. In Darius's Persia, burials were the norm. Herodotus wrote:

> Everyone without exception believes in his own native customs, and the religion he was brought up in, to be the best . . . [Darius] summoned the Greeks who happened to be present at his court, and asked them what it would take to eat the dead bodies of their fathers. They replied that they would not do it for any money in the world. Later, in the presence of the Greeks, and through an interpreter, so that they could understand what was said, he asked some

Indians, of the tribe called Callatia, who do in fact eat their parents' dead bodies, what they would take to burn them. They uttered a cry of horror and forbade him to mention such a dreadful thing. One can see by this what custom can do, and Pindar [a Greek poet] was right when he called it "king of all."

Usually, the sound bite condensing Herodotus's observation is "Custom is king"—we all prefer what we are used to.

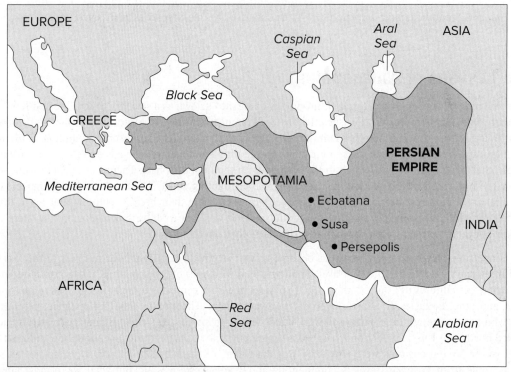

It was not so strange that King Darius might have heard of peoples living as far apart as the Greeks and the Callatian tribe of northern India, because they were in fact his neighbors. At the time of its greatest expansion, Persia (today, Iran) covered a territory stretching from Greece in the west to today's Pakistan in the east. Until the time of Alexander the Great, this was the greatest empire in the ancient Western world.

When anthropologists point out that moral values vary enormously from culture to culture, they are describing the situation as they see it. As long as those anthropologists make no judgments about whether it is *good* for humanity to have different moral values or whether those values represent the moral truths of each culture, they are espousing a **descriptive theory** usually referred to as *cultural relativism*. The theory itself was launched in 1906 by the anthropologist William Graham Sumner, who coined the term "Folkways." For Sumner, each culture has its own set of values, and the anthropologist is supposed to describe it. Let us look at an example. An anthropologist acquaintance of mine came back from a field trip to Tibet and told me the following story: In the little Tibetan village where he had been "adopted" by a local family and was doing his fieldwork, the children worked hard and had very little leisure time. The concept of competition was totally alien to them. One day the anthropologist thought he would give them a treat, and he arranged for a race. All the kids lined up, puzzled and excited, to listen to his directions: Run from one end of the compound to the other and back again, and whoever comes in first wins. The race was on, and the children ran like mad to beat each other and "win." As one beaming kid came in first, the anthropologist handed over a prize—some little trinket or piece of candy. There was dead silence among the kids, who just looked at each other. Finally, one of the children asked, "Why are you giving a gift to our friend who won?" The anthropologist realized that because the children had no idea of competition, they had no knowledge that winning often is connected with a prize. To them, this new idea of "winning" was great all by itself, and there was no need to add anything else; indeed, the prize made them feel very uncomfortable. (The anthropologist said it also made him feel very stupid.)

What the anthropologist was doing by telling this story was relating an example of **cultural relativism**—describing how customs differ from culture to culture. Suppose, though, he had added, "and I realized that they were right in their own way." (In other words, suppose he had made a *judgment* about the validity of the tribal way of life.) In that case, he would have moved into the area of ***ethical relativism.*** Cultural relativism is a *descriptive* theory that states that different cultures have different moral codes. Ethical relativism is a *normative* theory that states there is no universal moral code and that each culture's codes are right and valid for that culture. It is a subtle difference, but philosophically it is an important one. (See Box 3.2 for more on descriptive ethics, normative ethics, and metaethics.) The cultural relativist sees the cultural differences and describes them: There are many moral codes in the world. The ethical relativist sees the cultural differences and makes a judgment: We can never find a common code, and what seems right for one culture *is right for that culture.*

Box 3.2 DESCRIPTIVE ETHICS, NORMATIVE ETHICS, AND METAETHICS

The terms *descriptive* and *normative* are important terms for any ethical theory, not just relativism. When we talk about a theory being *descriptive,* we mean that the theory merely describes what it sees as fact, such as, In the United States it is, in general, not considered immoral to eat meat. In other words, a descriptive theory describes what people actually do or think. A *normative* theory adds a *moral judgment,* evaluation, or justification, such as, It is okay to eat meat because it is nourishing, or a criticism, such as, Eating meat *should* be considered immoral. In addition to descriptive ethics and normative ethics, there is a third ethical approach, *metaethics.* Metaethics does not describe or evaluate but analyzes the *meaning* of the moral terms we use. Some typical questions would be, But what do you mean by immoral? What do you mean by meat—beef, horse, or snake, perhaps? A few years ago, Europe was shaken by a scandal concerning horse meat which had turned up in supermarkets under the label of "beef." But horse meat has had a place on European menus much more so than in American households, so the debate was centered not so much on the issue of unethical consumption of horses, but on the issue of false labeling.

Most ethical systems involve judgments, criticisms, evaluations, and justifications, and are thus normative, but many systems also require an awareness of the terms used to justify the theory. Any time a moral debate moves into a discussion about the meaning of terms, it moves into the area of metaethics. An example of the vital importance of metaethics in the political debate of the first decade of the twenty-first century is the discussion of the meaning of the concept of *torture.* In the first decade of the 2000s, Congress engaged in a debate about what should be permissible as "aggressive interrogation techniques," as opposed to "torture." The underlying assumption was that we, as a civilized nation, are bound by the Geneva Convention and can't allow ourselves to engage in torture, but must allow for access to harsh interrogation methods in extreme situations, to save American lives. It became apparent that what for some debaters constituted aggressive interrogation techniques within accepted limits—such as exposure to cold temperatures, constant light or darkness, and loud noises, including loud music—was for others clearly torture. Most debaters agreed that inflicting physical pain was a clear example of torture, but what about sleep deprivation? The most controversial technique was probably "waterboarding," subjecting prisoners to having water poured over their covered faces while they are tilted backward until they believe themselves to be drowning. In 2008 it was revealed that the CIA had used this technique on at least three occasions with multiple applications, including an interrogation of a captured high-ranking al Qaeda member, and had obtained important information thereby, although that claim remains controversial. For the CIA this constituted an aggressive interrogation technique, not torture, but for several debaters, including members of

the media, this technique should clearly be classified as a form of torture, even if it doesn't involve any actual danger of drowning. While waterboarding during the Bush administration was viewed as a rare but legitimate "aggressive interrogation," under the Obama administration, it was classified as torture and excluded as an acceptable method. During the Trump administration (currently, at the time of this writing) bringing back waterboarding appears not to be on the agenda, but might become an issue according to commentators.

Regardless of the question of the moral acceptability or even the effectiveness of torture as such (which would be normative questions), this example merely serves to show that without a discussion of the definition of key words in a debate, we cannot hope to reach any consensus. In Chapters 5 and 6 we return to the question of the moral acceptability and effectiveness of torture.

The anthropologist Ruth Benedict (1887–1948) was a student of the German physicist Franz Boas, who had pioneered the field of cultural anthropology and declared that cultures around the world should not be judged by the standards of Western civilization, and that moral standards are not universal, but relative to each culture, a concept launched by Sumner a few years earlier, but frequently attributed to Boas. Sharing her teacher's viewpoint, Benedict did most of her writing toward the end of the era in which one could still speak of "uncontaminated" societies—cultures that hadn't yet been overwhelmingly exposed to Western civilization. The term *primitive* still was used for some cultures, and Benedict used it too, but she was quick to point out that the attitude that Western civilization was at the top of the ladder of cultural evolution was—or should be—outdated. In a famous paper, "Anthropology and the Abnormal," from 1934, she says that "modern civilization becomes not a necessary pinnacle of human achievement but one entry in a long series of possible adjustments." With that emphasis she established herself as an advocate of cultural and moral *tolerance,* implying that Western civilization has no right to impose its codes of conduct on other cultures. Ethical relativism has remained popular ever since as a tool of cultural tolerance, although there is some indication here in the twenty-first century that the theory seems less attractive than before. Below we look at some reasons why.

In the same paper, Benedict tells of a number of cultural phenomena that may seem morally odd, to say the least. In the Primary Readings, you'll find an excerpt focusing on the custom of extreme paranoia on an island in Melanesia. Here in the chapter text, another example will have to suffice: Among the Kwakiutl Indians of the Pacific Northwest in times past (a culture studied by Benedict's teacher, Boas), it was customary to view death, even natural death, as an affront that should be retaliated against in one way or another. In one tribe, a chief's sister and her daughter had drowned on a trip to Victoria. The chief gathered a war party. They set out, found seven men and two children asleep, and killed them. Then they returned home, convinced that they had done the morally right thing.

What intrigued Benedict most about this story was not that the chief and the members of the war party viewed their actions as morally good, but that most of the tribespeople felt the same way. In other words, it was *normal* in the tribe to feel this way. Benedict concludes, "The concept of the normal is properly a variant of the concept of good. It is that which society has approved."

Two things are worth mentioning here. First, Benedict is taking a giant leap from expressing *cultural* relativism to expressing *ethical* relativism. She moves from a description of the people's behavior to the statement that it is normal and *thus good* for them to behave that way—in their own cultural context. They are doing the right thing. Second, Benedict is saying that normality is culturally defined; in other words, cultures, especially isolated cultures, often seem to develop some behaviors to an extreme. (For Benedict the range of possible human behavior is enormous, extending from paranoia to helpfulness and generosity.) Those individuals who somehow can't conform (and they will always be the minority, because most people are very pliable) become the abnormals in that culture.

Bettmann/Getty Images

Ruth Benedict (1887–1948), American anthropologist and defender of ethical relativism. Her best-known work is *Patterns of Culture* (1934).

Is the behavior of the Northwest Coast people totally alien to us? Benedict thinks not, because it constitutes *abnormal* behavior in our own society, not *unthinkable* behavior. We might illustrate her idea with some examples. The postal worker who has been fired and who shows up the next day with a shotgun and kills a number of his coworkers is "crazy" to us, but he actually is following the same logic as the chief: His world has been torn apart by powers over which he has no control, and he is retaliating against the affront. The driver who cuts you off on the freeway because she had a fight with her husband is doing the same thing; so was the little girl who ripped a button off your coat in grade school because someone else ripped a button off her coat. There is no question of vengeance, because neither the driver nor the little girl was looking to punish a guilty party. The seven men and two children had nothing to do with the deaths of the chief's relatives, and the chief never said they did. It is not a matter of seeking out the cause of the problem, of gaining retribution; rather, it is an experience of healing a wound by wounding someone else. (What if the strangers who were killed had been American or Canadian loggers who had grown up in a culture that believes it is proper to find and punish whoever is guilty? Then we'd see retribution.) Perhaps we all take it out on someone innocent from time to time; some of us probably do it more often than others. The difference is that we've chosen to call what the Northwest Coast people did *abnormal,* whereas they, in the context of their tribal civilization, considered their actions to be normal and good. How do such choices evolve? Usually it is a matter of habits developing over time. If there is such a thing as a "normal" way for humans to behave, it is to adjust to the pattern of normality that prevails in their particular culture. Today, sociologists would call this process *acculturation.*

Although Benedict obviously wants her readers to approach other cultures with more tolerance for customs alien to them, her choice of examples may seem odd to a modern, culturally sensitive reader: Is Benedict, in giving this account of a tribe of American Indians, actually helping to cement the old notions popular in white Western culture of the "savage Indian"? If so, she is not furthering any mutual intercultural understanding.

There are two things to say here: (1) Benedict herself might answer with something like, "If you read this account as a criticism of Indian customs, then it is just because you are seeing it through the eyes of a preju-diced Westerner. The whole point is to recognize cultural differences as being equally meaningful within their cultural contexts." We should not shy away from noticing differences—but we should not judge them either. (2) As readers looking at the disadvantages as well as the advantages of ethical relativism, we must conclude that relativism does not have as its goal any mutual *understanding*—merely noninterference. Trying to achieve an understanding requires us to find some common ground, and relativism does not allow for any intercul-tural common ground. We return to the question of common ground later in this chapter.

For Benedict, there is no sense in imposing Western morals on another culture, because Western morals are just one aspect of the range of possible human behavior that we have chosen to elaborate; they are no better or no worse than anyone else's morals. Whatever is normal for us we think of as good, and we have no right to claim that our choice is better than any other culture's. A novel that in many ways advocates this approach to other cultures is Barbara Kingsolver's *The Poisonwood Bible,* and you will find a summary and brief excerpt from it in the Narratives section of this chapter.

Problems with Ethical Relativism

Bjoern Kaehler/AP Images

The young Danish mother who parked her baby outside the restau-rant in Manhattan and claimed that she was only doing what parents frequently do in Denmark managed to shine the spotlight on an actual, time-honored tradition: to this day, Danish babies (and dogs) are parked outside of stores and restaurants while their parents are shopping and dining. However, the tradition rests on two general assumptions, (1) that the neighborhood is safe and (2) that strangers will alert the parents if the baby is crying.

Given the overwhelming intolerance for other cul-tures and customs that has been displayed from time to time by Western civilization (a stance some refer to as "cultural imperialism"), many people find something very appealing and refreshing about ethical relativism. And we shouldn't forget to see it in its proper historical perspective: It served as an antidote to nineteenth-century "Eurocentrism" and Western colonialism, in which the notion of West-ern religious and moral superiority (in addition to the technological superiority of the West) had been considered an obvious truth. Ethical relativism broke away from that self-congratulatory attitude and became the inspiration for a shift toward cul-tural tolerance in the early part of the twentieth cen-tury, an attitude that continues in today's United States, with its plurality of cultural and ethnic her-itages. Increasingly, throughout the twentieth cen-tury, it seemed of doubtful virtue among American intellectuals to impose a particular brand of accul-turation on another group that believed it was doing just fine with its own set of moral rules. So many cultures in the nineteenth century had suffered precisely because of that attitude, from American Indians to Asian Indians, and many non-European cultures in between. For many Americans, the fundamental acceptance of the fact that other cultures have a right to be different is so ingrained that when people on social media reacted to the story of John Chau losing his life trying to bring Christianity to a non-Christian population in self-imposed isolation, many condemned Chau for being an intruder rather than condemning the natives for killing him. And ethical relativism cuts both ways: When people from elsewhere visit the United States, we expect from them that they respect our ways of life: A young single mother from Denmark visited her American boyfriend with her baby in New York City some years back and did what she was used to doing in Denmark: The couple had dinner in a New York restaurant at ground level, and she put the baby carriage outside *with the baby in it* and got a table by the window so she could watch the baby. (It was a mild day, and the baby was in no danger of freezing or overheating.) When she was arrested for reckless child endangerment, she was puzzled: "But we do this all the time at home!" she said. I can attest to that personally, having grown up in Denmark. Indeed, babies (in their carriages) and dogs on their leashes are left outside stores and restaurants all the time, at least in the smaller towns. But not in New York City! What has become known as the *cultural differences argument* didn't cut it with the judge—her lawyer's argument that she should have a right to do what she used to was dismissed, and she was sent back to Denmark with her baby, presumably never to come back.

So it appears that we have taken the method of problem solving suggested by ethical relativism to heart. And yet some people (who aren't necessarily hard universalists either) have questioned the noninterference ethics of relativism. What if the culture in question sells children into the sex trade? What if it refuses women the right to vote and own property? And, in our post–September 11 world, what if other cultures believe that Americans are fair targets for terrorism everywhere? Are those beliefs and customs just a matter of their moral choices, which should be respected, or do we have a moral right—perhaps even a moral obligation—to step in and effect changes? This is the big issue that is challenging ethical relativism at the beginning of the twenty-first century.

Six Problems with Ethical Relativism

Even if we grant that ethical relativism provided a positive lesson in the early twentieth century, suggesting the suspension of Western judgmental attitudes toward other cultures, there are serious problems within the theory. Here we look at six problems, all of them logical consequences of the basic idea of ethical relativism that there is no universal moral code. (Box 3.3 is an introduction to a standard philosophical approach: the adversarial method.)

Box 3.3 THE ADVERSARIAL METHOD

You may by now have asked yourself, Is this the procedure we'll be following in the rest of this book—to be introduced to an interesting viewpoint, and then be told how to pick it apart logically until it seems to have lost its appeal? What happened to the simple joy of learning about a variety of viewpoints, without having to immediately learn how to dismantle them? Doesn't that seem unnecessarily negative? You may not have asked yourself that, but I did once, as a Philosophy major. The answer lies in the so-called *adversarial method,* a method employed in philosophy ever since Socrates: In order to move forward toward a presumably true statement or viewpoint (which is the goal), you have to treat each theory presented to you as an adversary,

an enemy, and pound it with whatever attacks your logical, rational mind can think of. Whatever remains after the analysis is then a theory worthy of consideration—or a dismantled theory with little or no value. It is not unlike the procedure of testing a presidential candidate. When the going gets tough and all the nasty (but usually reasonable and relevant) questions are asked, we see what kind of character the candidate has. Is he or she arrogant? weak? capable of a sense of humor? vindictive? intelligent? stupid? lying? truthful? honest? strong? What is the breaking point of the candidate? In the same way, we seek the breaking point of a theory. As you will see, almost every theory does have a breaking point, but that does not always disqualify the theory (that is, render it invalid). If the breaking point comes late in the discussion and only when the theory is attacked by an extremely unlikely hypothesis or by trifles, that speaks well for the theory and encourages acceptance or perhaps only a minor rewrite of the theory. Some theories, however, break early in the discussion and can be discarded. Ethical relativism is a theory with a fairly late breaking point; in other words, there are some good things to be said for the theory, which is a good reason not to discard it altogether.

There is, however, another approach: the French philosopher Paul Ricoeur (1913–2005) had, like many students who are first being exposed to philosophy, grown disenchanted with the constant analytical hammering of well-intended theories and viewpoints. He believed that an unintended side effect was the cultivation of a strictly negative attitude among philosophers, posing as "critical thinking": dismantle a theory and move on to the next theory to be dismantled, as if that is a blood sport in itself. The American linguist Deborah Tannen has recently labeled that method of dismantling an opponent's view "agonism." Instead, Ricoeur suggested a compromise: He said that we ought to both "listen to" and "suspect" a theory. We should "suspect" it of trying to mislead us (through the adversarial method), but we shouldn't forget to "listen" to the wisdom and the knowledge it may contain, because we may learn something and become wiser, even if the theory may not hold up in the long run or be wrong about some details. So look for the positive in a philosophical viewpoint while at the same time detect its flaws. And that is the approach you'll find within these chapters: Adopting Ricoeur's suggested approach, we need to look at the weaknesses of the theories, but that's no reason why we can't also appreciate their ideas and visions.

1. **No Criticism or Praise of Other Cultures** Does this mean that it is always wrong to criticize another culture or group for what it does? If we are to follow the idea of ethical relativism to its logical conclusion, yes. We have no right to criticize other cultures, period. But on occasion things happen in other cultures that we feel, either by instinct or through rational argument, we *should* criticize to maintain our own moral integrity. Curiously enough, at the time Benedict wrote her article (1934), one of the most offensive social "experiments" in history was being conducted in the Western world. The Nazis had taken over Germany and Austria in 1933, and their extreme racism was not kept secret, even though the existence of the death camps of later years was not generally known until after the war. A true ethical relativist would have had to stick to her guns and maintain that other countries had no right to criticize what was going on in Germany and Austria in the 1930s and 1940s. (As it happens, that pretty much mirrored the actual attitude of the rest of the world at the time.) Benedict, however, mentions nothing about this issue in her paper.

People often say, in retrospect, that someone should have protested against or intervened in a particular situation while there was still time. Indeed, this was one of the arguments for going into Iraq in 2003: that Saddam Hussein had the makings of a Middle Eastern Hitler and needed to be stopped while there was still time. In the case of the war in Afghanistan, the relativist might have approved, provided the goal was stopping terrorists from attacking other nations, such as our own, but not if the goal was to put an end to the Taliban regime. In the war in Iraq, the issue was even more complex: If the goal was exclusively to find and destroy WMDs, weapons of mass destruction (which were never found, although there was speculation that they had been hidden), the relativist might find the invasion acceptable, because it would stop aggression toward other countries. However, if the goal was primarily a regime change, toppling Saddam Hussein and creating a democracy, the relativist would not approve, regardless of how much the living conditions would improve for Iraqis, in the short or the long run, because it would be interfering with the internal affairs of a sovereign country. Similar issues could be raised about the conflicts in Libya and Syria: From a relativist point of view, helping the rebels topple an oppressive ruler would be acceptable if it made our own country safer, but not if the goal was to make the country safer for its own inhabitants. And the additional question of whether the inhabitants would actually be safer under rebel rule is of course a good one, but irrelevant to the ethical relativist. In the eyes of the relativist, we are against genocide only because it happens to be against the norms of our own culture; for another culture, genocide may be right.

For most people, however, even those believing they ought to be tolerant, there are moral limits to tolerance, and any theory that doesn't recognize this is just not a good theory. Most Western people, tolerant as they might like to be, would prefer to see certain things come to an end. In several cultures, primarily on the African continent, female genital mutilation ("FGM," or "genital cutting," as it is increasingly referred to) is practiced, usually on young girls of 7 to 10 years of age. A 2016 UNICEF report stated that the practice has worldwide implications, affecting 30 countries, and over 200 million women, and it appears to have increased by 70 million women since 2014, partly due to population increase and partly due to increased reporting of cases. However, the report also notes that in some countries the practice is now declining; in Egypt, 97 percent of young women were circumcised 30 years ago, while the number now is 70 percent. Liberia has gone from 72 percent to 31 percent, and Burkina Faso from 89 percent to 58 percent. Traditionally, the procedure is performed within the culture of women in each community, as a ritual act necessary for adulthood and marriageability, involving ritual tools that aren't sterilized and without anesthesia. The physical benefits are nonexistent—the benefits cited are invariably related to social acceptance and supposed enhancement of virtues such as fidelity and chastity. The U.N. Population Fund reported in 2019 that progress has been made in many African countries such as Egypt, Uganda, and South Sudan, where the procedure has been banned, and educational efforts are underway to inform the population of the harmful effects of FGM. But in Malaysia the development has gone in another direction, into the medical clinics where doctors now perform the circumcisions under sterile conditions, and this development is of concern to WHO because it lends the procedure an aspect of legitimacy, as if it is now medically sound. In Indonesia and other parts of Western Asia, the FGM rates have gone up from 16.9 percent to 21.7 percent, according to the journal *BMJ Global Health*. However, a global effort is underway to eliminate the practice by 2030, supported by the African Union, the European Union, and UNFPA-UNICEF. Ironically, it has often been pointed out by Islamic scholars that the procedure of cutting is, in fact, against Islamic law, since it disfigures the body created by Allah. As a side note, the procedure has been banned for years in the United States as a federal crime, but in late 2018 a U.S. District judge voided the ban as being unconstitutional, because FGM should be regarded as a local crime, to be addressed by state law, and not as a federal crime. At the end of this chapter you will find a summary of a novel that deals with the issue of FGM: Alice Walker's *Possessing the Secret of Joy*.

Hearing of such conditions, can one morally remain a relativist, holding that each culture must be left in peace to explore its own values? Many ethical relativists have felt that a line must be drawn between mere cultural preferences and assaults on human rights—*but that means giving up on ethical relativism.* However, when issues such as equal rights for women are raised in the United Nations, representatives of those cultures that do not recognize rights for women often respond with indignation, asserting that the West is merely doing what it has always done, trying to superimpose its cultural and moral values on other peoples in the old tradition of cultural imperialism. Although ethical relativism wanted to put an end to the wholesale export of Western values, the theorists have reached a critical point: Many people may agree with relativists that there is no need or excuse for the West to try to dictate every aspect of what other nations should think or do, but in extreme situations many of us would like to reserve the right to speak up for people in other parts of the world who can't (or aren't allowed to) speak up for themselves. We want to believe that we have the right to complain about governments that do not respect human rights and that abuse a part of their population; and, in fact, pressure on such governments has at times yielded results.

Not only are we prevented from criticizing another culture's doings if we accept the teachings of relativism, but we also cannot praise and learn from that culture. If we find that the social system of Scandinavia is more humane and functions better than any other in the world, the conclusion based on relativism has to be that this is because it is right for them, but we still can't assume that it is right for us. If we happen to admire the work ethic of Japan, we can't learn from it and adapt it to our own culture, nor can Jainism's teachings of nonviolence have anything to say to us. In short, ethical relativism, when taken to its logical conclusion, precludes learning from other cultures because there can be no "good" or "bad" that is common to all cultures. Curiously, that doesn't mean that all ethical relativists would actually *forbid* us to learn from other cultures or to criticize others—on the contrary, ethical relativists think of themselves as very tolerant and open-minded. The problem is in the *logic* of the theory itself: When it is applied to real-life situations as a moral principle, it reveals itself to have certain limitations.

2. **Moral Majority Rule** The isolation of moral values to the conventions of specific cultural groups has another curious effect: It forces us to bow to *moral majority rule* (as opposed to *political* majority rule, which in a democracy doesn't demand that the political minority abandon their ideas and sympathies). Remember that ethical relativism does not say there are *no* moral rules—only that the rules of each society are proper and valid for that society. What if you live in a society and don't agree with the rules? Then you must, *ipso facto,* be wrong, because we know that the rules that are morally good in a society are those rules that are in effect. If you disagree with those rules, you must be wrong. That makes it impossible to disagree with any rules that exist, and therefore civil disobedience is out of the question. In Iran, if you disagree with the fundamentalist Islamic rules of punishment, then you are wrong. It is, in fact, right and proper in Iran to amputate the hand of a thief. If you are an American and disagree with the general attitude against euthanasia and doctors who help patients commit suicide, then you are wrong, and the attitude of the majority is right—not because the attitude has been subjected to moral analysis, but simply because it happens to be the attitude of the majority. It does not work, either, to point to a historical precedent and say that things were not always done as they are now, because ethical relativism cuts through time as well as space. There are no universal values among different time periods, any more than there are common values among different cultures of the same era. In other words, that was then and this is now. For an intellectual tradition such as ours, which prides itself on valuing minority opinions and promotes the idea of moral progress, the idea that the attitude of the majority is always right (which entails that the moral minority is always wrong) simply is unacceptable. And interestingly, as one of my students observed, if one is an ethical relativist, one would have to agree that ethical relativism as a moral theory should never have been voiced, or gained popularity, in a time period when hard universalism was the moral norm of the culture! If all cultures are right in their own way, hard universalism was right for early-twentieth-century America, and ethical relativism, being a minority moral opinion at the time, would be wrong by definition! The irony is that if ethical relativism is implemented, minority views become morally unacceptable at the same time as we allow other cultures to commit atrocities toward their own people.

3. **Professed or Actual Morality?** There is a further problem with the idea that a group's morality is determined by the majority or that a certain kind of behavior is normal, for what is "normal"? Is it the *professed* morality of the group or the *actual* morality? Imagine the following situation. The majority of a cultural group, when asked about their moral viewpoints, claim that they believe infidelity is wrong; however, in that particular society, infidelity is common practice. Does that mean the morality of the culture is what the majority say they ought to do or what they actually do? We might simply decide that it must be the *normative* rules that define the morality and not the actual behavior; however, Ruth

Benedict assumed morality to be the same as majority *behavior*. If Benedict had implied that morality is the same as what people think they *ought* to do, then all our example would amount to would be to show that most people have a hard time living up to their own moral standards, which is hardly a novel observation. However, Benedict's theory of ethical relativism clearly states that "moral" is the same as "normal," meaning how the majority *actually* behave.

4. **What Is a "Majority"?** Ethical relativism involves a practical problem as well. Suppose the question of doctor-assisted suicide had been determined by a referendum and the law against it overturned in your state. (At the time of this writing, the following states allow euthanasia: Washington, D.C. and the states of California, Colorado, Oregon, Vermont, Hawaii, and Washington. Interestingly, Californians did not vote for the law to change; that was decided in 2015 by California's Congress and, in the final end, the governor of California, Jerry Brown, signed it into law.) The majority now believe it is right for doctors to help terminally ill patients die. If we are ethical relativists, we would have had to conclude that was morally wrong the week before, but today it is morally right. By next year people may have changed their minds, and it will become morally wrong again. There is something very disconcerting about moral rightness being as arbitrary as that and depending on a vote, especially since so few people actually vote in elections. So who exactly is the majority? most of the people? the registered voters? or the actual voters? And what about the individual states? They obviously are part of a larger unit, the United States, and the moral standards of this larger unit would define the morals of each singular state. But not all laws and customs are the same from state to state, and what is considered morally wrong by the majority in one state may well be considered morally acceptable by the majority in another (such as abortion or doctor-assisted suicide). Therefore, might we instead want to allow for morally autonomous subgroups in which the majority within each group defines the moral rules, even if they are at odds with the larger cultural group? If we have large minority subgroups *within* a state and their moral values differ from those of the majority, should such groups constitute morally autonomous units that should not be criticized? (See Box 3.4.)

Box 3.4 MORAL SUBJECTIVISM AND ETHICAL RELATIVISM: A COMPARISON

Sometimes the theory of moral subjectivism is listed as a subcategory of ethical relativism. You may recall that we placed it under the general heading of *moral nihilism* at the beginning of this chapter, because such theories deny that there can be any agreement about moral values based on something other than personal opinion. Ethical relativism is not a morally nihilistic theory, because it holds that there are very strong reasons for agreeing about values within a culture precisely because they are values shared by that culture. However, there is definitely something "relative" about moral subjectivism, so we might say that it represents the transposi-tion of "each *culture* is right in its own way" to "each *person* is right in his or her own way." This theory, often referred to in the media as "moral relativism," is an extremely tolerant the-ory, a "live and let live" attitude in which no one has the right to impose his or her moral view-points, including a preference for tolerance, on anyone else. It has its own severe flaws, however: For one thing, it cannot solve moral conflicts because there is no common value denominator to resort to. That means we can't hope to learn from other people's advice or even their mis-takes, because their values and situations will always differ slightly from ours. And because the theory can't solve moral conflicts, we have no moral weapon against what we personally consider unacceptable. How would you argue against Hitler's Holocaust from a subjectivist viewpoint? Against slavery? Child abuse? Female circumcision and other enforced mutilation rituals? The only thing you might say is that you *feel* those actions are wrong—but others can also feel and think any way they like. For most people this way of thinking is so excessively tolerant that it borders on an obscene lack of social responsibility.

Furthermore, appealing as moral subjectivism may seem when we have just escaped the confines of the moral regulations of our childhood, it simply isn't intuitively sound. We may think we can "live and let live," but in actual fact we react *as if* there is a basic appeal to conflict-solving values. If you are a subjectivist and you see an adult at the supermarket repeatedly hitting a small crying child, are you going to be content telling yourself that you wouldn't do such a thing but that the adult in question is entitled to feel he or she is doing the right thing? Or would you try to appeal to some common value system by stepping in? Moral subjectivism is not only counterintuitive and impractical but also downright dangerous as a moral theory because

it provides no social cohesion and no protection against the whims of those in power, whose "feelings" may be as legitimate as yours but whose ability to carry them out is far greater.

To summarize, the criticism of moral subjectivism is different from the criticism of ethical relativism in the following ways: (1) Moral subjectivism cannot solve conflicts, but ethical relativism can (through majority rule), and (2) ethical relativism is problematic because it implies a moral majority rule, but moral subjectivism does not (because each person is right in his or her own way). What the two theories have in common is the relativity of moral values: The moral subjectivist has no right to call anyone else's values wrong or evil, and neither does the ethical relativist (when judging *other* cultures). So the challenge to both moral subjectivism and ethical relativism is the experience of something that is so egregiously against "common decency" or "our sense of humanity" that we must speak up, regardless of our modern tradition of tolerance toward others' life choices. Finding a universal foundation for criticism of traditions of female circumcision or ritual animal torture or child sacrifice is equally impossible from a basis of either moral subjectivism or ethical relativism.

5. **What Is a "Culture"?** Question 4 leads right into question 5, because ethical relativists have not explained exactly what they mean by a culture either. How can we know if something is the norm within a culture if it isn't clear what a culture is? What sets one culture off from other cultures? Is the United States one culture (as most foreigners believe)? Or is it a collective of many smaller cultures, as many Americans see it? Is Europe one culture? Is Africa? Asia? Central or South America? Iraq contains at least three cultures, but it is one country. From the outside, perhaps, but once you see the regional differences, you'll know it's not so easy to focus on common denominators rather than on the differences. The jihadist militant group calling itself Islamic State, and referred to in the media as ISIL, IS, or ISIS, has presented another challenge to the definition of culture, because it changed from being a rebel group to actually occupying extensive territories primarily in Iraq and Syria, in its effort to create a worldwide caliphate. However, in 2019 the final stronghold of ISIS was defeated by Syrian, British, French, and American forces, so while the ideological group still exists, the territorial claim is no longer relevant, at least at the time of writing this.

What unifies a culture? It used to be *geography:* People living within the same area moved around only rarely and acquired the same general characteristics. But now people move all over the globe, join societies across borders as never before, and participate in social media on the Internet. For some people, the life they live online in the computer game *Second Life* (where you can take on another identity, choose your environment, and buy and sell property) is merely entertainment, but for some, that life takes on a reality of its own. And according to my students, so does the online role-playing game *World of Warcraft,* another community of players in a reality of their own. Formerly the most popular of the social media, Facebook, has been attracting young as well as older people worldwide as a way to communicate with others, but young people have tended to migrate over to YouTube, Instagram and other picture media which allow users to continually share their lives with others—maybe to the point where the online presence *becomes* their life. Are these groups "cultures"? Well, why not? They have their own membership criteria, rules for appropriate behavior, and their own sanctions for breaking the rules.

Could "culture" also be a matter of *ethnicity*? Historically people have tended to stick with others of their own ethnic background, but that seems to be partly a geographical limitation and partly a *cultural* choice (and culture is what we are trying to define). People who were brought up not to be bigoted choose partners, friends, and neighbors from outside their own ethnic group all the time, yet they still feel they are choosing within their culture. In my ethnically and racially diverse college classes, it always strikes me that, diverse as we are, we generally have much more in common than we have with some people in our own families and neighborhoods, because the world of academia is our "culture"—our common experiences with classes and grades, studying and research, exams, and so forth create a cultural identity in itself. Is it *race*? When people were less mobile, people within a region generally formed a culture, and there was ethnic and racial cohesion in the group. But now we are (at least in the United States) moving toward a mixed-race society, and biologists and sociologists are beginning to question the very concept of race and to interpret it as an eighteenth-century invention. Therefore, the category of race can hardly be a firm foundation for a definition of culture. Is it *religion*? Places with one dominant (or one permitted) religion seem to be obvious candidates for a culture, but what about places in which people tend to dress the same, see the same movies, buy the same groceries, and drive the same cars but have different religions? Is it (as anthropologists might suggest) how we view *family relations*? Those categories also are not so stable anymore. And if we resort to vague categories of habits, worldviews, tastes, and so forth, all we end up with is a classification of people according to some criteria, whereas other criteria may cut across those same groups. If an ethical relativist insists that as long as we can identify some form of cultural cohesion, then that group should not be interfered with in its moral practices, we run into horrible problems.

Some ethnic groups in the United States differ from the majority in their views about male–female relationships, about using for food animals that others consider pets, about contraception and abortion, about the rights of fathers to punish their families. How large do such groups have to be in order to be considered morally right in their own ways? If we are generous and tolerant relativists, perhaps we'll say that any large ethnic group should be considered morally autonomous. But would that mean the Mafia could be considered such a subgroup? or neighborhood gangs? Would society then have to accept a plurality of "laws," each governing the subgroups, with no higher means of control? The relativist might accept that one set of laws—federal ones, for instance—would be above all other laws, but it would still be an extremely complicated matter, with possible contradictions arising between what the national law says and what the gang law says. Could we eventually end up in a situation in which acts such as looting are morally right for some because of their subgroup affiliation, but not for others? If ethical relativism is to be considered as a viable moral philosophy, ethical relativists need to agree on a clear definition of "culture."

6. **Can Tolerance Be a Universal Value?** One of the best qualities of ethical relativism is its tolerance, although we've now seen that it can lead to problems. However, there is something problematic about the very claim of tolerance coming from a relativist, for is someone who believes in ethical relativism

allowed to claim that tolerance is something everyone should have? In other words, can a relativist say that tolerance is *universally good*? The trouble is of course that the definition of ethical relativism includes the idea that there are no universal moral values—all values are culture-relative. But if all values are culture-relative, then that condition must apply to tolerance as well. Tolerance may be good for us, but who is to say if it is good for other groups! This notion severely undermines the whole purpose of tolerance, which is not usually considered a one-way street. And what if the highest moral dictum of a certain culture is to superimpose its values on other cultures? Does relativism teach that we must respect a moral system that doesn't respect the morals of others? Western cultures of the past—and, some would say, even the present—have exported their own moral systems; the Communist bloc of the twentieth century sought expansion along those same principles; today, Islamist extremism in some parts of the world also pursues this kind of expansion, combined with political ambitions, like IS (ISIS/ISIL) mentioned earlier. One could say, as some ethical relativists have attempted, that as long as they keep their moral (and perhaps even political and religious) expansionism within their own borders, they have a right to think whatever they want—but the problem is that the moral focus of certain cultures is precisely to export itself to other places. Not only does ethical relativism not have a right to claim that tolerance is universally good, since it also claims that there are no universal values, but it also can't even give a practical answer as to how to deal with moral, religious, and political expansionism. Ethical relativism thus is *logically* prevented from achieving its main goal, resolving international moral conflicts through tolerance.

Refuting Ethical Relativism

The "Flat Earth" Argument

Now we have seen why many people believe that ethical relativism doesn't have enough to offer to be adopted 100 percent; it is a theory with immense theoretical and practical problems. For some critics, the *logic* of the key argument proposed by ethical relativism is faulty. Let us assume that the culture "up north" believes that abortion is morally wrong, whereas the culture "down south" believes it to be morally permissible. The relativist concludes that because there is a disagreement between the two groups, neither can be right in an absolute sense. But surely, the critics say, that is not so; some things are simply true or false. We may have had a disagreement in the past about whether the earth is round or flat. (Indeed, the rapper B.o.B. insisted, in a 2016 tweet, that the earth is flat. The Flat Earth Society is claiming that all space reports and photos from space missions are fraudulent and were concocted in a movie studio.) However, that doesn't mean there is no correct answer; the idea that the earth is round is a verifiable fact. We may be able to verify that some moral codes are objectively right and others are wrong.

The trouble with this critique is that it is easy to verify that the earth is round; all we have to do is look at how things gradually disappear over a flat horizon. But how exactly would you go about verifying that abortion is objectively right or wrong? That would bring us into a much bigger discussion of the very nature of moral truths, which would be no help at all in determining whether ethical relativism is right. The flat earth example is, of course, not supposed to be taken that far. All it shows is that you can't conclude, on the basis of there being a disagreement, that both parties are wrong. It is never as easy to find out who is right in a discussion of moral issues as it is to settle questions of geography.

The Problem of Induction

Some critics believe that the very foundation of the ethical relativism theory is wrong; they believe it simply is not true that there is no universal moral code. If relativists were asked how they know that there is no universal moral code, they would answer that they looked around and found none or possibly that, given the diversity of human nature, there never will be one. This raises more questions, though, because we might reasonably suggest that they should look around a bit longer and refrain from making absolute statements about the future. Blanket statements bring on their own undoing, because any theory based on collecting evidence faces a classic problem: *the problem of induction.*

Induction is one of two major scientific methods; the other is deduction. In deductive thinking we start with an axiom that we believe is true, and we apply that axiom to establish the validity of other axioms, or we apply the theory to specific cases. In inductive thinking we gather empirical evidence to reach a comprehensive theory. Ethical relativism is an example of inductive thinking; it bases its general theory that there are no universal moral codes on evidence from particular cultures. The problem of induction is that we never can be sure that we have looked hard enough to gather all possible evidence.

As an example of the problem of induction we're going to look at a phenomenon that is well known to anyone watching court cases on TV or just about any crime show from *CSI* to *Law and Order* and crime scene documentaries: the gathering of evidence at a murder scene. The detectives gather evidence according to a preliminary hypothesis: that this is a homicide, not a suicide or a natural death. (And if they can't determine this from the start, they keep all interpretations open.) They gather what looks to them like evidence, usually casting a wide net, and this evidence goes to the district attorney, who decides whether to file a case. In other words, the detectives reach a theory of the identity of the killer based on the evidence they gather—they don't gather evidence based on a theory of whodunnit, or at least that is the way it is supposed to work. (That theory would have been *deduction.* It would also shape a biased investigation. In other words, Sherlock Holmes was great at not only deduction but also *induction!*) So, theoretically, the evidence is presented in court, and the jury decides whether it points to guilt or whether there is reasonable doubt. But what if a piece of evidence was overlooked? Blood spatter in a corner—or a fingerprint, a hair, blood, or semen—belonging to someone other than the defendant? Or something that, to a forensic scientist decades down the line, would be hard evidence but has no significance for today's scientists? Something like DNA before the mid-1980s? Or an eyewitness who left town without knowing she saw something important? Those are factors that can't be completely controlled. And then there are the ones that *can* be controlled—such as a forensic scientist deliberately skewing the test results in favor of the prosecution. Either way, we are looking at a real problem of induction: Because we are dealing with empirical science—gathering evidence and building a theory—we can't declare any inductive theory to be 100 percent certain. Induction is a fine method and yields magnificent scientific results. We couldn't do without it—but it is not 100 percent ironclad. Fortunately, in natural science as in court cases, even in murder cases, we don't have to be mathematically 100 percent certain in order to have a working theory or to be legally and morally certain: Circumstantial evidence, if there is a great deal of it, and nothing points elsewhere, is the accepted standard for finding someone guilty. Anything can be doubted—but not everything can be the subject of *reasonable* doubt. But as the Innocence Project, headed by Barry Scheck, has shown, there are people on death row who are, in fact, innocent of the crimes they are convicted of, because of the problem of induction: Evidence was overlooked or not available at the time, such as DNA tests, or (in a few nefarious cases) exculpatory evidence was not introduced in court. In Chapter 13, we take a closer look at the death penalty and such problems.

Now what does this have to do with ethical relativism? Everything—because the method of investigation used by the relativist to claim there are no universal moral codes is the method of induction. The Greeks and the Callatians—different codes. The Northwest Coast Indians, the Tibetan noncompetitive people, all point to the absence of a universal moral code. So can we know, with 100 percent certainty, on the basis of collected evidence, that there are no universal codes? No. We have to leave it open; perhaps someday a universal code will appear—or perhaps we will find that it had been there all the time, and we just didn't see it.

And, yet, I can't help adding a comment that may throw a bit of cold water on the critique of ethical relativism: Although ethical relativism is, indeed, a theory based on induction—sampling world cultures and their moral systems and concluding, on the basis of cross-cultural comparisons, that no cultures share any universal values—perhaps we should take a look at Ruth Benedict's final words in her article "Anthropology and the Abnormal." You'll find them in Study Question 4 in the Primary Readings section, and they are a very odd choice for an ending, coming from the most celebrated ethical relativist of the twentieth century: "It is as it is in ethics; all our local conventions of moral behavior and of immoral are without absolute validity, and yet it is quite possible that a modicum of what is considered right and what wrong could be disentangled that is shared by the whole human race." This extraordinary sentence shows that much as we try to pigeonhole Ruth Benedict as an ethical relativist, she herself had a moment of doubt, or even hope: Perhaps, if we look hard enough, we can find a common moral denominator in all cultures. The problem is that what she is expressing here is not ethical relativism, but *soft universalism.* So, was the primary voice for ethical relativism in the twentieth century not a relativist at all? Or might the issue be slightly different—that she indeed is an ethical relativist, but one whose theory is not vulnerable to the problem of induction, because she doesn't say that ethical relativism is a 100 percent certain theory? She says that until now, all cultures have looked different, but we can't speak for the future. And with that remark, Benedict has perhaps rescued her own brand of ethical relativism from the criticism that you can't reach a certain conclusion based on empirical evidence. But that, of course, does not rescue all other forms of relativism. Any theory that claims to be 100 percent certain, based on empirical evidence, is still open to the criticism of the problem of induction.

James Rachels and Soft Universalism

The problem of induction is advanced not by hard universalists but by *soft universalists,* because they are the ones who advocate looking for some core values that all cultures might share. Soft universalism, to which you were introduced at the beginning of this chapter, is not a new idea; it was suggested by the Scottish philosopher David Hume in the eighteenth century. Hume believed that all people share a fellow-feeling, a compassion, that may show itself in different ways but is present in the human spirit regardless of one's cultural background. Today, soft universalism claims that we ought to look for bottom-line moral common denominators rather than what separates us as cultures and as individuals. This idea has an increasing number of followers, among ethicists as well as laypeople. One of the most adamant critics of ethical relativism in modern times, and an advocate for the idea that all cultures have some values in common, was the American philosopher James Rachels (1941–2003). In the Primary Readings at the end of this chapter, you'll find an excerpt from Rachels's last book, published posthumously, *Problems from Philosophy,* where he argues against ethical relativism.

In an earlier book, *Elements of Moral Philosophy,* Rachels points out that the problem of induction gives us a clue to what values might actually be in common for all cultures: Remember King Darius, who tried to get the Greeks to eat their dead and the Callatians to burn theirs? You may have asked yourself why any group would want to eat its dead. You may have wanted to ask Ruth Benedict why the Northwest Coast Indians were so aggressive. (She doesn't say.) We all may wonder why some peoples approve of infanticide or of dismemberment as punishment. As soon as we ask why, though, we have left the realm of ethical relativism. Relativists don't ask why; they just look at different customs and pronounce them fine for those who hold them. In asking why, we are looking for an explanation, one we can understand from our own point of view. In other words, we are expecting, or hoping, that there is some point at which that other culture will cease to seem so strange. And very often we reach that point. For instance, disposing of the dead through cannibalism is not at all uncommon, and it usually is done for the sake of honoring the dead or sharing in their spiritual strength. It would seem, then, that the Greeks and the Callatians had something in common after all: The Greeks burned their dead because they wanted to honor their spirits, and the Callatians ate their dead for the same reason. Some nomad tribes of the Sahara consider it bad manners to eat in front of their in-laws. American couples rarely talk about sexual matters in the presence of their in-laws for the same reason—it is considered bad manners. These cultures share some common values: Both value good family relationships, and both express embarrassment when a transgression occurs.

James Rachels suggests that at least three values are universal:

1. A policy of caring for enough infants to ensure the continuation of the group
2. A rule against lying
3. A rule against murder

We may be horrified to learn about the custom of killing female babies in the old Eskimo (Inuit) culture, Rachels says, but we gain a better understanding when we learn that female babies were killed only because a high death rate among male hunters led to a surplus of females in the community. Why would it be a bad thing for an Inuit tribe to have more women than men? Certainly not because the women were unproductive—in addition to raising children and cooking, they were the ones manufacturing tools and clothing from the animals brought home by the hunters—but because male hunters were the sole providers of food. (The Inuit diet is primarily meat.) Therefore, a shortage of men in relation to the number of women would mean a shortage of food. Another important fact is that babies were killed only during hard times and only if adoptive parents couldn't be found. In such times, if the babies had been kept alive, the lives of the older children would have been in jeopardy. In other words, the Inuit killed some infants to protect the children they already had. Their culture valued what ours values: caring for the babies we already have.

Why do all cultures have a rule against lying? Because if you can't expect a fellow citizen to tell the truth most of the time, there is no use attempting to communicate, and without communication human society would grind to a halt. This doesn't mean, obviously, that humans never lie to one another, but only that, on the whole, the acceptable attitude is one of truthfulness.

The rule against murder derives from similar reasoning: If we can't expect our fellow citizens not to kill us, we will not want to venture outdoors, we will stop trusting in people, and society will fall apart (not, as some might think, because everyone will be killed off, but because of general mistrust and lack of communication). Rachels believes that even under chaotic circumstances small groups of friends and relatives would band together, and within those groups the nonmurder rule would be upheld.

So these three values are Rachels's suggested universal moral codes, to be found in all cultures regardless of religion and other traditions, solving the riddle of ethical relativism. At first glance they do indeed seem incontrovertible. How could we imagine a culture that doesn't care for its babies, that lies and murders? We can't—but perhaps that is not because the values are universal but because Rachels has simply selected elements that ensure a culture's basic survival. Can we be sure that all cultures have rules that dictate caring for as many infants as it takes to keep the culture going? Absolutely; but perhaps that is not a matter of ethics but of *logic*—in particular, *deductive* logic. How does a culture survive? By reproducing, and raising children. So all cultures that exist survive by raising children. Must all cultures subscribe to raising their children? Actually, no, but if they don't, they'll die out. But that is not unusual—some cultures, from time to time, decide that they will not reproduce (such as the Christian group the Shakers in the nineteenth century), and after a while they will no longer be around. So the value of caring for infants is actually not universal in all cultures, just in all *surviving* cultures, which makes it a tautology, a self-evident truth.

The trouble with rules 2 and 3 is that they seem to apply to "fellow citizens" only. As a member of society, you are expected not to lie to or murder members of your own social group, but there is really nothing preventing you from being morally free to lie through your teeth to an outsider or to an enemy government. You may even be free to prey on and murder members of other tribes, gangs, or countries. In many folktales the culture hero actually saves the day by cleverly lying to the stronger enemy, such as in *The Odyssey* where Ulysses lies to the one-eyed Cyclops Polyphemus, saying his name is "Nobody." So there seems to be no rule against lying universally, only against lying to your own people. A scandal in the discipline of anthropology illustrates this phenomenon in a way that is quite significant: The renowned anthropologist Margaret Mead (1901–1978), who was a student of Franz Boas and Ruth Benedict, and like them an ethical relativist, wrote a book about the sexuality of young South Sea islanders, *Coming of Age in Samoa* (1928), which became a bestseller. But in the 1980s it became clear that she had been the victim of a hoax: Her native contacts in Samoa had strung her along to see how many whopping lies she'd swallow before she became suspicious—but she was young and gullible. It appears that with some additional research Mead could have discovered that for herself, but she never did. So even though the Samoans certainly had an overall rule against lying within their culture (which we know because one of Mead's contacts felt she ought to 'fess up when she was in her eighties), it didn't necessarily extend to the inexperienced young anthropologist.

Besides, is it true that we are expected to tell the truth? Many would challenge that idea across the board of world cultures. In some cultures it is considered good manners to lie, to play down one's own accomplishments (such as the Chinese tradition of berating one's own cooking skills), not to tell the whole truth about a friend's appearance if she or he asks your opinion, to lie about sexual relationships to protect those involved (the notion of chivalry is sometimes invoked). The Chinese philosopher Lin Yutang (see Chapter 11) said that "Society can exist only on the basis that there is some amount of polished lying and that no one says exactly what he thinks"—not exactly what Rachels had in mind. In folklore there is even a tradition of telling "whoppers," and American Western folklore contains many prime examples of "tall tales." The frontiersman David ("Davy") Crockett was elected to Congress in 1827 not just because he was a likable and conscientious man but also because he told better whoppers than his opponent (and had the grace to freely admit that he had been lying). So although it may not be true that a rule against lying is universal, if we characterize it as a rule against malicious deception we are closer to what Rachels means: Without that trust, your network of communications will break down.

Another problem with Rachels's three rules lies in the fact that, whatever rules may apply to a given culture, the *leaders* of those cultures, who should embody the cultural standards, are often the ones who break those rules. If it was to a leader's advantage to bend or break a rule, he or she might even consider it a duty to the throne to do so. Only in the twentieth century did the concept of rulers not being above the law become solidified (to the extent that some leaders have to deal with civil lawsuits during their time-limited reign rather than face charges afterward). Even the near-universal ban on incest, which might well qualify as a fourth universal value, has traditionally been broken by leaders such as the pharaohs of ancient Egypt, who would marry their own siblings, and the royal families of Europe in previous centuries, who sometimes matched up first cousins because nobody else with "blue blood" was available. Interestingly, if we go back to the example from Herodotus about the Greeks and the Callatians, we are perhaps as close to a true universal moral value as we will ever come, and one that is not survival-oriented: a respectful disposal of one's dead relatives.

Rachels has not provided us with any rules that apply universally, only with rules that all responsible people seem to be required to stick to *within their own societies*. Rachels has, however, provided all we need to show that ethical relativism is wrong in its assumption that cultures have nothing in common; we don't have to find a universal moral rule, just a universal pattern of behavior. Because Rachels believes that there are at least three such patterns—care of infants, not lying, and not murdering—we can call him a *descriptive soft universalist:* He describes what he thinks is the case, that we actually have some codes of behavior in common. But even if you can't find any codes in common, you might still be a *normative soft universalist*. In that case, you believe we *ought* to have some code of behavior in common and that we ought to work toward establishing or finding such a code. You can, of course, be both a descriptive and a normative soft universalist. In that case you believe human beings around the world do have a few basic moral codes in common; but you also believe that to move toward a world community in which we can respect one another's differences while striving to work together to solve problems, we ought to find some common ground and set up a basic moral code for humanity to live by, a code such as the concept of human rights.

In the end, the soft universalist may point out that since the relativist's position is logically impossible in that he or she wants universal tolerance but can't have it because of not believing in universal values, so ethical relativism is in fact disingenuous, because it doesn't take itself seriously as a theory—it is an armchair exercise. In a clash of cultures where your own culture is under attack, do you choose to defend it just because it's yours? No, you defend it because you believe its values are good. And if you choose not to defend it, is it because you think nobody is right? Probably not—it is probably because you think the "other culture" has a point. And if you find yourself on trial in another country and (truly) consider yourself not guilty, would you want to be acquitted because of your cultural affiliation? Anything that leads to an acquittal will probably be welcome, but in the end, wouldn't you rather be cleared because you are *not guilty?* These basic situations reveal to the soft universalist that even if we may think we profess to ethical relativism, it can't be upheld when push comes to shove. In effect, like moral nihilism, moral skepticism, and moral subjectivism, it involves an internal contradiction, because as a matter of fact nobody really believes that each culture is right in its own way, and there are no common denominators. The bottom line for the soft universalist is the fact that *we are all mortal human beings,* with the same physical limitations and the same capacities for language, relationships, and pleasure and pain. Unless we're sociopaths, we all want what's

Courtesy James Rachels

James Rachels (1941–2003), American philosopher and advocate of human and animal rights. He was the author of *The Elements of Moral Philosophy* (1968), *The End of Life: Euthanasia and Morality* (1986), *Created from Animals: The Moral Implications of Darwinism* (1990), and *Can Ethics Provide Answers?* (1997). He completed his last two books only shortly before he died: *The Truth About the World* and *Problems from Philosophy,* both with the publication date 2005.

best for our loved ones; we all want to live, unless by dying we serve some greater good (some take that further than others). We dread illness, cherish our good memories, and enjoy the company of our friends. We tell stories, and believe that ethics is indispensable to social life. How could we *not* have more in common than what divides us culturally? In other words, some moral values represent common human standards rather than culturally relative standards. In James Rachels's words—some of the last he ever wrote—"The culture-neutral standard is whether the social practice in question is harmful or beneficial to the people who are affected by it." You'll find more of that text, from *Problems from Philosophy,* in the Primary Readings.

In 2018, soft universalism received a major boost from the *Evolution Institute*, in a special issue, "This View of Morality; Can an Evolutionary Perspective Reveal a Universal Morality?" Oliver Scott Curry, Director of the Oxford Morals Project at Oxford University, claimed in his article, "Seven Moral Rules from Around the World," that based on a broad, interdisciplinary study involving game theory, ethology, anthropology, and psychology, it is possible to isolate **seven distinct moral rules** present in cultures around the world. The fundamental common denominator for all cultures, says Curry, is that we are a cooperating species. We have evolved into social beings who rely on each other, and it is our expectation of cooperation that is the foundation of human morality. He and his colleagues examined 60 cultures, and all of them subscribed to the following rules: *(1) Love your family, (2) help your group, (3) return favors, (4) be brave, (5) defer to authority, (6) be fair, and (7) respect others' property.*

Curry concludes his summary of the research paper with these words:

> "'Morality as cooperation' does not predict that moral values will be identical across cultures. On the contrary, the theory predicts 'variation on a theme': moral values will reflect the value of different types of cooperation under different social and ecological conditions. And certainly, it was our impression that these societies did indeed vary in how they prioritized or ranked the seven moral values... And so there is a common core of universal moral principles. Morality is always and everywhere a cooperative phenomenon. And everyone agrees that cooperating, promoting the common good, is the right thing to do. Appreciating this fundamental fact about human nature could help promote mutual understanding between people of different cultures, and so help to make the world a better place."

So here we see not only a new descriptive soft universalism being proposed, but also with a normative element: We humans are fundamentally cooperative, and we praise cooperation in whatever social context we happen to be born into—we have a fundamental human nature that makes us similar, even across a vast spectrum of cultural variations. And if we can recognize that fact about ourselves, we can try to overcome the obstacles of apparent cultural differences. That was, in essence, what James Rachels was hoping to promote.

For a philosophical approach, we have to ask (of course) whether this version of soft universalism suffers from the same problem that ethical relativism did: *the problem of induction*. Rachels avoided that problem by using a deductive approach, focusing on what a culture can't survive without, but Curry is using induction: he has examined 60 cultures—but what about #61? Or #661? Might they have a different set of values that would torpedo the theory? Curry has already attempted to respond to that question: "Crucially, there were no counter-examples—no societies in which any of these behaviors were considered morally bad. And we observed these morals with equal frequency across continents; they were not the exclusive preserve of 'the West' or any other region." So while Curry and his researchers have not examined all cultures, past, present, and future, they have provided an important response to critics: that in none of the 60 cultures did the researchers encounter any evidence of moral rules that were "opposite'—that celebrated being a coward, or not supporting one's group, or not respecting the property of group members. So is that sufficient to produce a functional inductive theory? As we saw in Rachels' three universal values which were limited to one's group, that doesn't mean that *everyone's* property would be respected—just group members' property, and so forth. But soft universalism isn't looking for hard universalist values, existing and being applied across the planet by everyone toward everyone, just values celebrated within each group. And it seems that behavioral sciences have now done sufficient research to undermine ethical relativism, and make soft universalism highly plausible.

In the Narratives section, we look at a film that illustrates clashes between cultures, and possibly a "culture-neutral" set of values: *Avatar.*

Ethical Relativism and Multiculturalism

With the increasingly pluralistic character of modern Western society comes an increasing belief that all cultural traditions and all perspectives represented in the public deserve to be heard—at universities, in politics, in the media, and elsewhere. Sometimes this is referred to as "multiculturalism," sometimes as "cultural diversity."

Let us consider multiculturalism and its goals. America used to be called a *melting pot,* meaning that there was room for anybody from anywhere, that all would be welcomed, and that after a while all individual cultural differences would subside in favor of the new culture of the United States. To many Americans (from many different ethnic backgrounds, in fact), this continues to represent a beautiful image as well as an accurate description of what America is all about. For many people around the world, this is what America seems to be. For others, however, the idea of the melting pot is a travesty, an illusion, and an insult. America may have embraced immigrants from countries such as England, Sweden, Ireland, and Germany, but many other people still feel as though they are living on the fringes of American society; they have not been accepted the way others have been. For such people, who feel that they and their ancestors were excluded from the melting pot because they were too different or simply unwanted, there is no such thing as a *common* American culture, only a *dominant* American culture; and they claim that what has been taught and practiced until the end of the twentieth century has been *monoculturalism* (sometimes referred to as *Eurocentrism*). Today there is an understanding even among those from the "dominant culture" that this damages the very concept of an American culture. The question is what to do about it.

Some proponents of multiculturalism believe that what we must do is listen to one another. The general idea is to integrate everyone—by law, if necessary—into all aspects of our society; to break through the "glass ceilings" that prevent people of color (women and men) as well as white women from reaching top positions; to become sensitized to what others might perceive as slurs; and, if we are on the receiving end of such slurs, today referred to as microinequities, to learn to speak up for ourselves. An increased awareness of the multicolored pattern of our society should, the thinking goes, result in better working relationships, less of a sense that one cultural tradition dominates the country and that everyone who doesn't share it must be left out, and more tolerance and understanding among the groups. However, for multicultural coexistence to work, it requires goodwill from all parties. And it isn't just an American phenomenon. A few years ago, German Chancellor Angela Merkel commented that multiculturalism had failed—that integration of groups from cultures with vastly different habits and values into a new culture simply wasn't working, despite good will from the majority of local governments. In an interesting twist, Germany was the most welcoming of the countries in the European Union in the early days of the great influx of refugees from Syria and elsewhere in the Middle East in the fall of 2015, telling the fleeing individuals and families that Germany was a safe haven for them, but already in 2016 Germany had made a 180-degree turn and closed its borders to the refugees and demanded passport control—something the European Union had abolished many years earlier. Overwhelmed by the influx of hundreds of thousands of refugees, the European nations pondered the standard of living, respect for open-society values, and even safety of their own citizens, especially after a number of sexual assaults in Germany by newly arrived young male refugees. Sweden, which at the onset also welcomed refugees, set up *ad-hoc* border controls between itself and Denmark—a border checkpoint that had not been in existence for centuries. Denmark itself, which already has a very strict immigration law requiring immigrants to learn Danish as well as key elements of Danish culture and history, refused to accept refugees without careful screening, and set up strict border controls between herself and Germany to the south.

However, Europe doesn't have a tradition of immigration. Nowhere in their culture canon does it say, "Give me your tired, your poor, your huddled masses yearning to breathe free," as is inscribed on our Statue of Liberty. And Europe doesn't have a centuries-old debate about integration and citizenship; the different countries are just inventing their own version of it. They don't have a tradition of a "United States of Europe," speaking with one voice (although Hitler did have such aspirations). The EU only dates back to the 1960s, and most European nations don't think of themselves as states in a union, but as sovereign nations. As a matter of fact, with the United Kingdom choosing to leave the European Union, the phenomenon of "Brexit" ("Britain Exit"), the entire concept of a European political and social union has been thrown into doubt. The fact that such a national debate has existed for a long time in the United States means that we are, presumably, better equipped to at least address the issues before problems become overwhelming—because the United States is, of course, also a target for vast numbers of immigrants, be it for political, financial, or other reasons. (Your author is of course a fairly well-integrated immigrant herself!) The common wisdom has generally been that the values of individual freedom and social responsibility are so deeply engrained in the American spirit that subsequent generation of immigrants will grow into those values, rather than maintain and enforce a different set of values brought with them from their home countries, with cultural separatism as a result. Whether that will also be the case in the future is something that remains to be seen. Some are hopeful, while others are skeptical.

B.C.   **BY JOHNNY HART**

B.C. © 2006 Creators Syndicate, Inc. By permission of Johnny Hart Studios and Creators Syndicate, Inc.

In the debate about multiculturalism, the inclusive approach is sometimes perceived to result in the inclusion of non-mainstream ideas and traditions at the cost of mainstream traditions. The artist of the classic comic strip *B.C.,* Johnny Hart, now deceased, excelled in poignant commentaries defending the Christian point of view. Here he defends the traditional greeting, "Merry Christmas." In your view, does he have a point?

In the American debate about multiculturalism, it has for years been **the teaching of the children** that has been in focus.

This awareness is supposed to begin in schools, where children should learn about as many cultural groups in American society as possible. Adding multicultural awareness to the curriculum means there is less time for some subjects that are usually taught, but proponents of inclusive multiculturalism believe that a growing cultural understanding is worth the price. Today, a new image is frequently offered as an alternative to the old image of the melting pot: the *salad bowl*. A metaphor for inclusive multiculturalism, the salad image implies that each group retains its original "flavor" but that the groups also relate to one another; together they make a sum that is greater than its parts. The metaphor can be stretched only so far, though: Critics who believe that inclusive multiculturalism is not doing enough to foster cultural identity can always turn the image around and ask, Who supplies the salad dressing? The "dominant culture"! (Box 3.5 examines how some advocates of cultural diversity apply what appears to be an ad hominem fallacy.)

Box 3.5 CULTURAL DIVERSITY OR CULTURAL ADVERSITY?

The idea that moral viewpoints acquire their importance from the groups that utter them rather than from their content is, to some philosophers, a misguided attitude. In the old days of Western culture, the dominant viewpoint was the one held by some—but not all—white males, and for most white males as well as for others that was enough to make the viewpoint "correct." Churches and political groups occasionally take the same attitude: The identity of the group is enough justification for the correctness of its views. Today we also see this same viewpoint applied socially by certain groups: If you are a member of an oppressed group, your viewpoint on right and wrong is valuable just because you are a member of that group, and if you are not, then your viewpoint is irrelevant. This form of relativism, which grants the importance of a viewpoint on the basis of gender, race, and class, may be as misplaced as one that denies the importance of certain groups just because they are who they are. Such an attitude, the argument goes, reflects the logical fallacy of the *ad hominem argument:* You are right or wrong because of who you are, not because of what you say. In Jim Garrison's words from Oliver Stone's film *JFK,* "I always

wondered in court why it is because a woman is a prostitute, she has to have bad eyesight" (meaning some people think that just because someone is a prostitute, we can't trust her testimony). Whether this attitude is assumed by those in power or by those who are dispossessed, it is equally faulty as a moral principle, according to the rules of critical thinking. However, life is complex, and some perspectives might only be truly comprehended by people who have experienced them. Can you imagine situations in which a person's identity alone would determine whether he or she was right or wrong?

Ethical relativism has frequently been considered the moral philosophy best suited as a supportive argument for multiculturalism; however, that is a misunderstanding. Ethical relativism states that there is no universal moral code—that each culture will do what is right for it, and no other culture has any business interfering. That may work when cultures are separate and isolated from one another, because the moral code in that case is defined as the code of the *dominant population.* Remember problem 2, "moral majority rule"? One of the problems with ethical relativism is precisely that it implies the moral rule of the majority. However, in our pluralistic society, that won't work because the "dominant culture" (white society) is increasingly reproached for displaying cultural insensitivity. Can ethical relativism function, therefore, in a country as diverse as ours, where we may find opposing values ("Looting is antisocial" versus "Looting is a righteous act for the dispossessed," for example) within the same neighborhood? Because a multicultural ethic asks us not to think in terms of one dominant set of rules, some might opt for an attitude of total *moral nihilism* instead: No values are better than any other values because no values are objectively correct. Such nihilism might well result in the breakdown of the fabric of a society, and possibly in a greater cohesion within subgroups, with different groups battling one another. Rather than describe these battles as gang wars, we might call this phenomenon *Balkanization*—when groups have nothing or very little in common except hatred for what the other groups stand for. It seems as though ethical relativism is not the answer to our new ethical problems of multiculturalism.

Suppose we look to **soft universalism** for the answer? The soft universalist hopes to be able to agree with others on some basic issues, but not on all issues. In the case of multiculturalism, we may be able to agree on the promotion of general equity, and cohesion in the nation (in other words, the will and ability to live together); we *have* to agree that what we want is a functioning society we all share in. If we don't agree on that, cultural coexistence is a lost cause, and so is the whole idea of a United States. According to soft universalism, values can't be allowed to differ dramatically, so we wouldn't end up with acts such as looting being morally right for some and not for others, nor would the killing of family members for the sake of honor be acceptable in one neighborhood and not in another. These questions of common values in the context of a multicultural society are particularly burning, for without some values in common we simply won't have a society.

Is it possible to have one overall culture and several subcultural affiliations at the same time? In other words, can we have loyalties to our ancient ethnic roots and also be Americans (or Canadians, or Italians, or Brazilians, or whatever the case may be)? A few generations ago, immigrant parents made sure their children learned English and had American first names, encouraging them to blend in as quickly as possible so that their future as American citizens would have as few obstacles as possible—an obvious ethnic identity being considered an obstacle. A generation of children lost the language of their parents, and in many cases their family history too. But over the past 40 years or so, people have been involved in looking for their roots, to a great extent inspired by Alex Haley's novel and original television series *Roots* (1977), about an African American family's history. This trend has involved a renewed interest in teaching the new generation of children the language of their grandparents as a second language. One's cultural identity has been to a great extent perceived as formed through the original nationality of one's immigrant ancestors: one is "Irish-American," "Polish-American," "Chinese-American," and so forth—to the extent that the nationality to the left of the hyphen has seemed, to some, to outweigh the second identity: American. This is what has spawned the expression "hyphenated American"—someone who sees himself or herself as having a composite heritage and perhaps also a split cultural identity. Does this mean you have to identify with some ancient ethnic heritage because there really isn't any American cultural identity per se? Box 3.6 explores what it might mean to have an American identity. In the aftermath of the terrorist attacks of 2001, a new generation found, for a while, an answer to what it means to be an American—focusing on the common denominator rather than on individual differences rooted in ethnicity or national roots. But soon thereafter the feeling of national unity gave way to other concerns in connection with natural disasters such as Hurricane Katrina, the economic crisis of 2008, and a renewed manifestation of what I in Chapter 1 called a "50-50 nation," a deep political split between the Left and the Right experienced during the elections of 2000, 2004, and again in 2016, continuing during the presidency of Donald Trump, at a level of mistrust and hostility not only among politicians, but displayed daily in the media (in Chapter 13, we look at the phenomenon of media ethic and media bias). The question of what it means to have an American identity seems to be a challenge for each generation in this still relatively new nation of ours. Perhaps the issue of national identity is not a fixed entity as much as a concept that needs revisiting and redefining in times of crisis as well as in less stressful times.

Box 3.6 AN AMERICAN CULTURE?

When discussing the mores and habits of other cultures with my classes, I often hear students claim that there *is* no American culture—and if common denominators do exist, they are considered negative: brashness, ignorance or mistrust of other cultures, materialism, and so on. To many students, the fact that we are a very diverse society means that we have no shared culture; many consider themselves hyphenated Americans: Irish-Americans, African-Americans, Italian-Americans, Arab-Americans, and so forth. A commercial a few years ago lined up a number of people of different races and with different accents, all proudly proclaiming "I am an American." But what does that mean, other than citizenship?

If you agree that an American cultural identity exists, how would you characterize it? Is it founded in our Constitution? Is it a matter of a general outlook on life? Is it the fact that we, as a matter of course, question authority? Does it have to do with common cultural experiences, common holidays and food rituals (such as Thanksgiving), a love of traveling within our country, and perhaps also with an image of ourselves that has been invented by the movies?

Or perhaps it is the very freedom to define one-self that other cultures seem to have only to a lesser degree. After all, if you apply for United States citizenship and you are accepted, you become an American. If you apply for French or German citizenship (which are very hard to obtain), and you are accepted, you don't become "French" or "German," you become a French or German citizen. Many Americans don't realize what it means to be an American until they travel abroad and experience other cultures—or perhaps tangle with legal systems that do not presume one to be innocent until proven guilty! Rather (as in the Napoleonic Law of France), you are presumed guilty until you can prove yourself innocent.

In the event of a common threat from abroad, one's cultural identity seems to loom larger, in the form of an appreciation for everyday things we used to take for granted and for the rights this society grants us—even the right to disagree about this whole issue. The philosopher and novelist Ayn Rand (see Chapter 4), an immigrant from the Soviet Union, called America the only truly moral culture in the world. In the Primary Readings section, you'll read an excerpt of *America and Americans,* the last book by novelist John Steinbeck, about what makes the American character unique—with negatives as well as positive points on his list, one point being that Americans tend to act in the extreme.

Study Questions

1. Describe the four major approaches to moral differences outlined at the beginning of this chapter. Which one comes closest to your own viewpoint? Explain.

2. Discuss Ruth Benedict's claim that what is normal for a culture is what is moral in that culture. Discuss the advantages and problems associated with the theory of ethical relativism.

3. Discuss James Rachels's three suggested universal values: Are they truly universal? Why or why not? Can you think of other universal values not mentioned?

4. Discuss the suggestion by Oliver Scott Curry that since he and his research team have found seven moral rules across all the cultures they've studied, there are a set of core values that we share as human, cooperative beings. Compare his seven universal values with Rachels' theory. Does that mean that ethical relativism has now been made irrelevant?

5. Can one have both an ethnic and a national identity? Explain.

6. Is Steinbeck right that Americans typically act in the extreme? Think of occasions where we have tended to react strongly to perceived threats, environmental as well as human-made—both politically as well as individually. Why do you think that is? And might it be justified? Explain.

Primary Readings and Narratives

The first Primary Reading is an excerpt from Ruth Benedict's famous paper "Anthropology and the Abnormal." The second is an excerpt from James Rachels's book *Problems from Philosophy* in which he argues that some moral values are culture-neutral, which proves ethical relativism wrong. The final Primary Reading is an excerpt from John Steinbeck's *America and Americans,* in which Steinbeck analyzes the pros and cons of the American character. The Narratives include a summary of Barbara Kingsolver's *The Poisonwood*

Bible, a novel pitting a Christian missionary and his family against traditional African customs, written as a critique of absolutist ethics; next, you'll find a summary of Alice Walker's novel *Possessing the Secret of Joy,* which indirectly—but powerfully—criticizes ethical relativism's tolerance toward the tribal practice of female circumcision; a third story explores the clash between two cultures in the science-fiction film *Avatar.*

 Primary Reading

Anthropology and the Abnormal

RUTH BENEDICT

Essay, 1934. Excerpt. **© 1934 From "Anthropology and the Abnormal" by Ruth Benedict. Reproduced by permission of the Taylor & Francis LLC, http://www.tandfonline.com.**

In her famous paper, Benedict talks about a Melanesian culture displaying extreme fears of poisoning. In addition, you'll read in her own words her view that morality is merely what is considered normal in a given society.

The most spectacular illustrations of the extent to which normality may be culturally defined are those cultures where an abnormality of our culture is the cornerstone of their social structure. It is not possible to do justice to these possibilities in a short discussion. A recent study of an island of northwest Melanesia by Fortune describes a society built upon traits which we regard as beyond the border of paranoia. In this tribe, the exogamic groups look upon each other as prime manipulators of black magic, so that one marries always into an enemy group which remains for life one's deadly and unappeasable foes. They look upon a good garden crop as a confession of theft, for everyone is engaged in making magic to induce into his garden the productiveness of his neighbors'; therefore, no secrecy in the island is so rigidly insisted upon as the secrecy of a man's harvesting of his yams. Their polite phrase at the acceptance of a gift is, "And if you now poison me, how shall I repay you this present?" Their preoccupation with poisoning is constant; no woman ever leaves her cooking pot for a moment untended. Even the great affinal economic exchanges that are characteristic of this Melanesian culture area are quite altered in Dobu since they are incompatible with this fear and distrust that pervades the culture. They go farther and people the whole world outside of their own quarters with such malignant spirits that all-night feasts and ceremonials simply do not occur here. They have even rigorous religiously enforced customs that forbid the sharing of seed even in one family group. Anyone else's food is deadly poison to you, so that communality of stores is out of the question. For some months before harvest the whole society is on the verge of starvation, but if one falls to the temptation and eats up one's seed yams, one is an outcast and a beachcomber for life. There is no coming back. It involves, as a matter of course, divorce and the breaking of all social ties.

Now in this society where no one may work with another and no one may share with another, Fortune describes the individual who was regarded by all his fellows as crazy. He was not one of those who periodically ran amok and, beside himself and frothing at the mouth, fell with a knife upon anyone he could reach. Such behavior they did not regard as putting anyone outside the pale. . . . But there was one man of sunny, kindly disposition who liked work and liked to be helpful. The compulsion was too strong for him to repress it in favor of the opposite tendencies of his culture. Men and women never spoke of him without laughing; he was silly and simple and definitely crazy. Nevertheless, to the ethnologist used to a culture that has, in Christianity, made his type the model of all virtue, he seemed a pleasant fellow.

These illustrations, which it has been possible to indicate only in the briefest manner, force upon us the fact that normality is culturally defined. An adult shaped to the drives and standards of either of these cultures, if he were transported into our civilization, would fall into our categories of abnormality. He would be faced with the psychic dilemmas of the socially unavailable. In his own culture, however, he is the pillar of society, the end result of socially inculcated mores, and the problem of personal instability in his case simply does not arise.

No one civilization can possibly utilize in its mores the whole potential range of human behavior. Just as there are great numbers of possible phonetic articulations, and the possibility of language depends on a selection and standardization of a few of these in order that speech communication may be possible at all, so the possibility of organized behavior of every sort, from the fashions of local dress and houses to the dicta of a people's ethics and religion, depends upon a similar selection among the possible behavior traits. In the field of recognized economic obligations or sex [taboos], this selection is as nonrational and subconscious a process as it is in the field of phonetics. It is a process which goes on in the group for long periods of time and is historically conditioned by innumerable accidents of isolation or of contact of peoples. In any comprehensive study of psychology, the selection that different cultures have made in the course of history within the great circumference of potential behavior is of great significance.

Every society, beginning with some slight inclination in one direction or another, carries its preference farther and farther, integrating itself more and more completely upon its chosen basis, and discarding those types of behavior that are uncongenial. Most of those organizations of personality that seem to us most incontrovertibly abnormal have been used by different civilizations in the very foundations of their institutional life. Conversely the most valued traits of our normal individuals have been looked on in differently organized cultures as aberrant. Normality, in short, within a very wide range, is culturally defined. It is primarily a term for the socially elaborated segment of human behavior in any culture; and abnormality, a term for the segment that particular civilization does not use. The very eyes with which we see the problem are conditioned by the long traditional habits of our own society. . . .

. . . . Mankind has always preferred to say, "It is morally good," rather than "it is habitual." . . . But historically the two phrases are synonymous. . . . The concept of the normal is properly a variant of the concept of good. It is that which society has approved. . . . Western civilization allows and culturally honors gratifications of the ego which according to any absolute category would be regarded as abnormal. The portrayal of unbridled and arrogant egoists as family men, as officers of the law, and in business has been a favorite topic of novelists, and they are familiar in every community. Such individuals are probably mentally warped to a greater degree than many inmates of our institutions who are nevertheless socially unavailable. They are extreme types of those personality configurations which our civilization fosters. . . .

The relativity of normality is important in what may someday come to be a true social engineering. Our picture of our own civilization is no longer in this generation in terms of a changeless and divinely derived set of categorical imperatives. We must face the problems our changed perspective has put upon us. In this matter of mental ailments, we must face the fact that even our normality is man-made, and is of our own seeking. Just as we have been handicapped in dealing with ethical problems so long as we held to an absolute definition of morality, so too in dealing with the problems of abnormality we are handicapped so long as we identify our local normalities with the universal sanities. I have taken illustrations from different cultures, because the conclusions are most inescapable from the contrasts as they are presented in unlike social groups. But the major problem is not a consequence of the variability of the normal from culture to culture, but its variability from era to era. This variability in time we cannot escape if we would, and it is not beyond the bounds of possibility that we may be able to face this inevitable change with full understanding and deal with it rationally. No society has yet achieved self-conscious and critical analysis of its own normalities and attempted rationally to deal with its own social process of creating new normalities within its next generation. But the fact that it is unachieved is not therefore proof of its impossibility. It is a faint indication of how momentous it could be in human society.

Study Questions

1. Is it important for Benedict to discover why the members of the tribe on the Melanesian island are afraid of poisoning? Why or why not? Would it make a difference in terms of ethical relativism if we knew the origin of the fear?

2. Is she right in her statement that "the concept of the normal is properly a variant of the concept of good"? Why or why not?

3. Does Benedict's cultural approach facilitate intercultural understanding? Why or why not?

4. Benedict is now viewed as one of the first spokespersons for ethical relativism, although her aim in this paper was to explore the concept of the abnormal. Her paper ends with these rarely quoted words, exploring the possibility of intercultural standards of normality: "It is as it is in ethics: all our local conventions of moral behavior and of immoral are without absolute validity, and yet it is quite possible that a modicum of what is considered right and what wrong could be disentangled that is shared by the whole human race." Does this statement contradict the general view of Benedict as being an ethical relativist? Does it undermine the philosophy of ethical relativism? Is she contradicting herself? Why or why not?

 Primary Reading

Is Ethics Just a Matter of Social Conventions?

JAMES RACHELS

Rachels, James, *Problems from Philosophy*, pages 154–159 Copyright © 2004 McGraw-Hill. All rights reserved. Used with permission.

The American philosopher James Rachels (1941–2003) was a passionate critic of ethical relativism. In the chapter text, you have seen his argument pointing to the existence of three universal moral values; here, in his final book, he argues that there is a culture-neutral standard: *"Whether the social practice in question is beneficial or harmful to the people who are affected by it."*

> The idea that ethics is nothing but a matter of social conventions has always been appealing to educated people. Different cultures have different moral codes, it is said, and it is merely naive to think that there is one universal standard that applies in all places and times. Examples are easy to come by. In Islamic countries, men may have more than one wife. In medieval Europe, lending money for interest was considered a sin. The native peoples of northern Greenland would sometimes abandon old people to die in the snow. Considering such examples, anthropologists have long agreed with Herodotus that "Custom is king o'er all."
>
> Today the idea that morality is a social product is attractive for an additional reason. Multiculturalism is currently an important issue, especially in the United States. Given the dominant position of the United States in the world, it is said, and the way in which American actions affect other peoples, it is especially incumbent upon Americans to respect and appreciate the differences between cultures. In particular, it is said, we must avoid the arrogant assumption that our ways are "right" and that the customs of other

peoples are inferior. This means, in part, that we should refrain from making moral judgments about other cultures. We should adopt a policy of live and let live.

On the surface, this attitude seems enlightened. Tolerance is, indeed, an important virtue, and many cultural practices obviously involve nothing more than social custom—standards of dress, food, domestic arrangements, and so on.

But fundamental matters of justice are different. When we consider such examples as slavery, racism, and the abuse of women, it no longer seems so enlightened to give a shrug and say "They have their customs and we have ours." Consider these two examples, both of which occurred recently.

In a Pakistani village, a 12-year-old boy was accused of being romantically involved with a 22-year-old woman of a higher social class. He denied it, but the tribal elders did not believe him. As punishment they decreed that the boy's teenage sister—who had done nothing wrong—should be publicly raped. Her name is Mukhtar Mai. Four men carried out the sentence while the village watched. Observers said there was nothing unusual in this, but with so many foreigners in the region the incident was noticed and reported in *Newsweek*.

In Northern Nigeria, a religious court sentenced an unwed mother named Amina Lawal to be stoned to death for having had sex out of wedlock. The 60 people in the courtroom shouted their approval. The judge said that the sentence should be carried out as soon as the baby was big enough to no longer need breast-feeding. The woman identified the father, but he denied the accusation, and no charges were brought against him. This was only one in a series of such sentences imposed there recently. Responding to international pressure, the Nigerian government announced that it would not enforce the sentence against Amina Lawal, but it was feared that vigilantes would carry out the stoning. She went into hiding.

The rape of Mukhtar Mai seems to have been regarded as a matter of tribal honor. Her brother was allegedly romancing a woman from a different tribe, and the elders of her tribe demanded justice. The stonings in Nigeria, on the other hand, are the application of the Islamic law of Sharia, which has been adopted by 12 Nigerian states since 1999. Both actions seem horrible. Our instincts are to condemn them. But are we *justified* in saying the rape and the stoning are wrong? Two thoughts stand in the way of this natural response. Let us consider them one at a time.

1. First, there is the idea, already mentioned, that we should respect the differences between cultures. No matter how questionable the practices of another society may seem to us, we must acknowledge that people in those cultures have a right to follow their own traditions. (And, it will be added, our traditions may seem equally questionable to them.) Is this correct? As we have already noted, this thought has a certain superficial appeal. But when we analyze it, it falls apart.

Respecting a culture does not mean that we must regard everything in it as acceptable. You might think that a culture has a wonderful history and that it has produced great art and beautiful ideas. You might think its leading figures are noble and admirable. You might think that your own culture has much to learn from it. Still, this does not mean that you must regard it as perfect. It can still contain elements that are terrible. Most of us take just this attitude toward our own society—if you are an American, you probably think that America is a great country but that some aspects of American life are bad and need to be corrected. Why should you not think the same about Pakistan or Nigeria? If you did, you would be agreeing with many Pakistanis and Nigerians.

Moreover, it is a mistake to think of the world as a collection of discrete, unified cultures that exist in isolation from one another. Cultures overlap and interact. In the United States, there are cultural differences between Irish Catholics, Italian Americans, Southern Baptists, African Americans in Los Angeles, African Americans in Mississippi, and Hasidic Jews in Brooklyn. Texans who happily execute criminals are quite different, culturally, from the Amish in Pennsylvania. In some ways, we think that "live and let live" is the best policy, but no one takes this to mean that you should have no opinion about what happens in another part of the country.

Similarly, in both Pakistan and Nigeria, rival groups coexist. When the Pakistani girl was raped, authorities in the Pakistani government took action against the local tribal leaders who had ordered it. Which group—the local leaders or the national government—sets the standards that we must respect? There is no clear-cut answer. Lacking an answer, the idea that we must "respect the values of that culture" is empty.

This also raises the critical question of who speaks for a culture. Is it the priests? The politicians? The women? The slaves? Opinions within a society are rarely uniform. If we say, for example, that slavery was approved in ancient Greece, we are referring to the opinions of the slave-owners. The slaves themselves may have had a different idea. Why should we take the view of the slave-owners to be more worthy of respect than that of the slaves? Similarly, when Mukhtar Mai was raped, her father and uncle, who were forced to watch, did not think it was right.

Finally, we should notice a purely logical point. Some people think that ethical relativism *follows from* the fact that cultures have different standards. That is, they think this inference is valid:

(1)   Different cultures have different moral codes.
(2)   Therefore, there is no such thing as objective right and wrong. Where ethics is concerned, the standards of the different societies are all that exist.

But this is a mistake. It does not follow, from the mere fact that people disagree about something, that there is no truth about it. When we consider matters other than ethics, this is obvious. Cultures may disagree about the Milky Way—some think it is a galaxy, others think it is a river in the sky—but it does not follow that there is no objective fact about what the Milky Way is. The same goes for ethics. The explanation of why cultures disagree about an ethical issue might be that one of them is mistaken. It is easy to overlook this if we think only of such examples as standards of dress, marriage practices, and the like. Those may indeed be nothing but matters of local custom. But it does not follow that *all* practices are mere matters of local custom. Rape, slavery, and stoning might be different.

The upshot of all this is that, while we should indeed be respectful of other cultures, this provides no reason why we must always refrain from making judgments about what they do. We can be tolerant and respectful and yet think that other cultures are not perfect. There is, however, a second reason why it may seem that being judgmental is inappropriate.

2. The second troublesome thought is that *all standards of judgment are culture-relative.* If we say that the rape of Mukhtar Mai was wrong, we seem to be using *our* standards to judge *their* practices. From our point of view, the rape was wrong, but who is to say that our point of view is correct? We can say that the tribal leaders are wrong, but they can equally well say that we are wrong. So it's a standoff, and there seems to be no way to get beyond the mutual finger-pointing.

This second argument can be spelled out more explicitly like this:

(1)   If we are to be justified in saying that the practices of another society are wrong, then there must be some standard of right and wrong, to which we can appeal, that is not simply derived from our own culture. The standard to which we appeal must be culture-neutral.
(2)   But there are no culture-neutral moral standards. All standards are relative to some society or other.
(3)   Therefore, we cannot be justified in saying that the practices of another society are wrong.

Is this correct? It looks plausible, but in fact there *is* a culture-neutral standard of right and wrong, and it is not hard to say what that standard is. After all, the reason we object to the rape and the stoning is not that they are "contrary to American standards." Nor is our objection that these practices are somehow bad for *us.* The reason we object is that Mukhtar Mai and Amina Lawal are being harmed—the social practices at issue are bad, not for us, but for them. Thus, the culture-neutral standard is *whether the social practice in question is beneficial or harmful to the people who are affected by it.* Good social practices benefit people; bad social practices harm people.

This criterion is culture-neutral in every relevant sense. First, it does not play favorites between cultures. It may be applied equally to all societies, including our own. Second, the source of the principle does not lie within one particular culture. On the contrary, the welfare of its people is a value internal to the life of every viable culture. It is a value that must be embraced, to one degree or another, if a culture is to exist. It is a precondition of culture rather than a contingent norm arising out of it. That is why no society can regard this sort of criticism as irrelevant. The suggestion that a social practice harms people can never be dismissed as an alien standard "brought in from the outside" to judge a culture's doings.

Study Questions

1. In the chapter text, you find references to Rachels' book *Elements of Moral Philosophy* from which the theory of the three universal values was taken. In this book, written over 30 years later, Rachels still argued against ethical relativism, but was he still a soft universalist? Explain.

2. Summarize Rachels's two major arguments for why ethical relativism is mistaken.

3. What does Rachels mean by saying that there are culture-neutral values? Do you agree with him? Why or why not?

4. Compare Rachels' text with the findings of Curry and his team that there are seven core moral values in all cultures. Would Rachels have welcomed that study, do you think? What might Rachels say?

 Primary Reading

Paradox and Dream

JOHN STEINBECK

America and Americans, *1966. Excerpt.*

In 1966 the American novelist and essayist John Steinbeck, whom you may know as the author of the novel *East of Eden, The Grapes of Wrath,* and *Of Mice and Men,* wrote a book about the concept of an American Identity: *America and Americans.* Steinbeck loved his country and its history, but he wasn't blind to the less positive elements of what we might call the American character, pursuing the American Dream and being engaged in the American Way of Life. Remember that this was written in 1966, and the world has changed dramatically in the decades since then. Even so, who among us, native-born Americans and immigrants alike, does not recognize exactly what Steinbeck is talking about, from a twenty-first century perspective? Steinbeck says, in his essay "Paradox and Dream":

> One of the generalities most often noted about Americans is that we are a restless, a dissatisfied, a searching people. We bridle and buckle under failure, and we go mad in the face of success. We spend our time searching for security, and hate it when we get it. For the most part we are an intemperate people: we eat too much when we can, drink too much, indulge our senses too much. Even in our so-called virtues we are intemperate: a teetotaler is not content not to drink—he must stop all the drinking in the world; a vegetarian among us would outlaw the eating of meat. We work too hard, and many die under the strain; and then to make up for that we play with a violence as suicidal.

Mondadori Portfolio/Getty Images

John Steinbeck (1902–1968) is one of America's most celebrated authors of fiction, known for classics such as *Of Mice and Men* (1937), *Grapes of Wrath* (1939), and *East of Eden* (1952). In addition to his many novels and short stories, he wrote books and articles on such topics as politics, history, and marine biology. Scholars have recently begun to recognize that Steinbeck also made considerable contributions to the field of moral philosophy in his writings—fictional as well as nonfictional.

The result is that we seem to be in a state of turmoil all the time, both physically and mentally. We are able to believe that our government is weak, stupid, dishonest, and inefficient, and at the same time we are deeply convinced that it is the best government in the world, and we would like to impose it upon everyone else. We speak of the American Way of Life as though it involved the ground rules for the governance of heaven. . . . We are alert, curious, hopeful, and we take more drugs designed to make us unaware than any other people. We are self-reliant and at the same time completely dependent. We are aggressive, and defenseless. . . .

Americans seem to live and breathe and function by paradox; but in nothing are we so paradoxical as in our belief in our own myths. We truly believe ourselves to be natural mechanics and do-it-yourself-ers. We spend our lives in motor cars, yet most of us—a great many of us at least—do not know enough about a car to look in the gas tank when the motor fails. . . . We believe implicitly that we are the heirs of the pioneers, that we have inherited self-sufficiency and the ability to take care of ourselves, particularly in relation to nature. There isn't a man among us in ten thousand who knows how to butcher a cow or a pig, and cut it up for eating, let alone a wild animal. . . . We shout that we are a nation of laws, not men—and then proceed to break every law we can if we can get away with it. . . . We fancy ourselves as hard-headed realists, but we will buy anything we see advertised, particularly on television, and we buy it not with reference to the quality or the value of the product, but directly as a result of the number of times we have heard it mentioned. . . .

For Americans too the wide and general dream has a name. It is called "the American Way of Life." No one can define it or point to any one person or group of people who live it, but it is very real nevertheless, perhaps more real than the equally remote dream the Russians call Communism. These dreams describe our vague yearnings towards what we wish we were and hope we may be: wise, just, compassionate, and noble. The fact that we have this dream at all is perhaps an indication of its possibility.

Study Questions

1. Identify the key points Steinbeck lays out as being the core of the American character. Do you agree? Why or why not?

2. Is this a positive or a negative image of Americans? Explain.

3. If you are a native-born American, identify what you perceive to be the American character in positive and negative terms. If you are a visitor or an immigrant, compare what you perceive as the American character with the your perception of character of the people of your original culture.

4. Five years earlier, Steinbeck wrote his last novel, *The Winter of Our Discontent*. You'll find a summary of it in Chapter 4. In it, he paints a bleak picture of the values of post-World War II Americans. I suggest you read the summary and compare it to the excerpt above. Did he change his mind within the next 5 years?

5. Is this an example of "profiling," or even "stereotyping"? If no, why not? If yes, is that a problem in itself, or does stereotyping have some merit?

Narrative

The Poisonwood Bible

BARBARA KINGSOLVER

Novel, 1998. Summary and Excerpts.

The Poisonwood Bible is a story whose message of cultural tolerance has deeply affected readers. In some ways it can be said to support an ethical-relativist philosophy, but in others it seems to support soft universalism. Since this is a work of fiction and not a philosophical treatise, the author shouldn't be judged according to whether she presents a unified theory or not: It will be up to you to decide whether she is, at heart, an ethical relativist or a soft universalist; the quality of the story is what counts. (I think we can exclude the possibility of hard universalism right from the start.)

In 1959 Orleanna Price, a housewife from Georgia, travels with her husband and four daughters to the Congo in Africa so that her husband can fulfill his dream of bringing Christ to the natives. We follow their individual destinies all the way into the 1980s, seeing the consequences unfold of Nathan Price's decision to take his family to Africa. The book is structured with biblical overtones, beginning with a Genesis section, and ending with an Exodus section, but we learn fairly early in the story that this is no story of happy missionaries bringing salvation to the heathens. It is instead the story of the clash between cultures, the culture of the (presumably hard universalist) Christian missionary, and his wife and daughters who have grown up in an American world, meeting a culture where just about *everything* is different: the concepts of right and wrong, good and bad, what's food and what's not food, what's clean and unclean, what's near and far—and eventually, what is home and what is not home. All five women react in their own ways, and with their own voices. Nathan Price's voice is not heard except through the reflections of the women, but he is the catalyst of the changes in their lives. Orleanna, a religious, faithful wife who initially just wants to stand by her husband in his work, eventually finds that the affront to the Africans and their culture perpetuated by her husband's cultural and moral arrogance will require a lifetime of atonement from her. Rachel, the eldest daughter, becomes the voice of longing for her lost American culture of affluence and conve-

AP Photo

American author Barbara Kingsolver (b. 1955) has a deep interest in multiethnic issues. In 1963 her father worked as a medical doctor in Zaire (then Congo), and he brought his family along to the Caribbean in 1967 on another medical assignment. Kingsolver is the author of *The Bean Trees* (1988), *The Poisonwood Bible* (1998), *Prodigal Summer* (2001), and *Flight Behavior* (2012), among other novels.

nience. Leah, once her father's strongest supporter, finds her love and life's work in the politics of revolutionary Africa and lives an African life perpetually apologizing for her whiteness; her twin sister Adah comes to terms with a physical disability afflicting her since childhood, seeing herself in light of another culture. And the baby sister, Ruth May—well, you'll have to read the book to find out about Ruth May.

The novel is lengthy and rich in detail, so here we will just focus on two scenes that illustrate the hard universalism of Nathan Price. One scene is from the beginning of the book: When the Price family arrives in the Kilanga village, they notice that there are a number of big mounds in the fields, and Price inquires what they are for. He is told that they are for growing crops, and immediately he is scornful. What a waste of space! That's not the way to grow crops! You need a nice flat field like in Georgia, and you need to plow in nice, straight lines. As it happens, the missionary cabin has a field adjacent to it, and he now plows it so the villagers can see what a real field looks like. Some villagers are fascinated. But the meaning of the mounds becomes apparent during the annual flooding of the river, where the waters reach the mounds and irrigate them, resulting in the growth of the crops, while Price's nice, straight field is inundated, and his little hopeful plants are washed away. The imagery of the different fields serves to show us how different cultures may have different ways, for a reason. Keep in mind that the story is deliberately written by Kingsolver, casting Price as the "bad guy," so the reader is inclined to disapprove of Price's absolutistic moral attitude.

The next scene involves Price's spiritual opponent in the village, the old chief, Tata Ndu. The Price family has been in the Congolese village for a while. Price has been pushing hard, telling the villagers about Christianity, but also about American democracy, attempting to change the tribal form of government—a council of old men—to a democratic majority voting system. So far he has only a few converts, and the family has become accustomed to only a handful of villagers attending Price's sermons. The chief generally disapproves of the decent villagers becoming spiritually corrupt by attending the Christian church, while he doesn't mind the bad-luck people going to church, drawing the gods' negative attention away from the village. But on one particular day the entire village is present at the sermon, even the chief. And in the middle of the sermon Tata Ndu interrupts Price by demanding that the people should have an election, *ici, maintenant* (French for *here and now*). Here Kingsolver indirectly lets us know that the chief speaks three languages: English, his local Kikongo language, and French, while Price speaks only English. Price dismisses it by saying there is a time and place for elections, but that is precisely Tata Ndu's point: He wants an election right now, not about village leaders, but about gods! Who should be the god of Kilanga village, the local gods or Jesus Christ? And he has brought the voting paraphernalia, two big bowls and pebbles to be placed in them. The villagers get up from their seats and proceed to place pebbles in the bowls, over Price's protests that Jesus is exempt from elections.

Price is beginning to lose his cool, and Tata Ndu remarks that the preacher has been talking about the benefits of Jesus and elections, and he can't go back on that now. Price thinks the old man has completely misunderstood both messages and that he must have the mind of a child, so Price tries to tell him, like you would tell a child, that in America you have different houses for church and politics. Tata Ndu replies that may be a wise thing in America, but "in Kilanga we can use the same house for many things." Now Price has had enough, and yells at Tata Ndu and the congregation that they can't even run their own country, and they're being blasphemous. But Tata Ndu has also reached the limit of his play-acting, because that is what his performance was. He knows very well the difference between religion and politics; he just wanted to show his people how little Price understands of their traditions and how little Price cares. He is the picture of dignity and reason as he confronts Price:

> You believe we are *muwana*, your children, who knew nothing until you came here. Tata Price, I am an
> old man who learned from other old men. I could tell you the name of the great chief who instructed

my father, and all the ones before him, but you would have to know how to sit down and listen. There are one hundred twenty-two. Since the time of our *mankulu* we have made our laws without help from white men. . . . White men tell us, *Vote, Bantu!* They tell us, you do not all have to agree. . . . If two men vote yes and one says no, the matter is finished. *Á bu,* even a child can see how that will end. It takes three stones in the fire to hold up the pot. Take one away, leave the other two, and what? The pot will spill into the fire.

So the entire orchestration of the vote about Jesus versus the local gods was a setup, a joke on Price, to show how voting makes no sense to a community where the political decisions are made in unison, like in the Kilanga society where the old men will talk through the night until a unanimous decision has been reached. And when the pebbles are counted, fifty-six pebbles are for the local gods, while Jesus Christ only got eleven votes.

Toward the end of the book, after decades have passed, disasters have happened, and everybody in the Price family has undergone some pivotal change, Leah tells us about her father's fundamental lack of understanding of the Kilanga culture and the Kikongo language which he never bothered to learn. She, on the other hand, has become an African in body and soul, although to her dismay she will always stand out as a white person. She explains nuances of Kikongo, which give us the secret of the book's title. Because every sermon Price ever gave to the villagers he ended with "Tata Jesus is *bängala!*" And all the villagers would laugh. Why? Because *bängala* means not only "most precious," which Price thought he was saying, but also "most insufferable" and "poisonwood."

Study Questions

1. The title of the book itself is a take on mistakes committed by a hard universalist who doesn't try to understand different cultural nuances: Nathan Price tries to tell the local population that "the word of Jesus is beloved," which in the tribal tongue translates as "*Tata* Jesus is *bängala*." The problem is that, in the context, it comes across as "Jesus is poisonwood." What do you think the author is saying with such a title?

2. What is the significance of Tata Ndu's being trilingual and telling Price that he comes from one hundred and twenty-two generations of wise men?

3. Based on this summary and the excerpt from Tata Ndu's speech, would you say the ethical leaning of Kingsolver's book (meaning Kingsolver's own opinion) is primarily ethical relativist or soft universalist? If you have read the entire book, do you find this summary a fair choice in representing the book's viewpoint? Explain.

4. Compare the story of Price's attempt to convert the Kilanga village to Christianity with the event from the beginning of this chapter, John Allen Chau's ill-fated attempt to do the same in 2018. Is there a difference? Why or why not? If seen from a hard universalist point of view, what can be said in defense of Price? And of Chau?

5. Read the next narrative, *Possessing the Secret of Joy,* and compare its message with that of *The Poisonwood Bible:* What if the tradition Price was protesting had been *female genital mutilation*? (The topic actually does appear at some point in the book.) Would you still expect a message of cultural tolerance? Why or why not? Would you draw the line at tolerating certain cultural practices? Explain.

Narrative

Possessing the Secret of Joy

ALICE WALKER
Novel, 1992. Summary and Excerpt.

If you have read or seen *The Color Purple,* the novel, the movie, or the Broadway play, you will recognize some of the main characters in this moving and shocking novel: Olivia, Adam, and Tashi. (Olivia and Adam are the children of Celie, the key character in *The Color Purple,* and Tashi is their best friend in the African village where Olivia and Adam's adoptive parents are missionaries.) However, *Possessing the Secret of Joy* is a story that stands on its own, making a powerful argument

against the ancient practice of female genital mutilation.* The novel weaves its way through the life of the storyteller Tashi. She is now an American, but originally she was of the Olinka tribe in Africa, a tribe Walker invented as a symbol for all African tribes. In real time and flashbacks, we are introduced to the nightmare of Tashi's life: the death of her older sister Dura, at first a vague memory, but in the end a reality so horrible that, to Tashi, it may be worth killing for.

Tashi has always been afraid of bleeding to death, and she has always had a terrifying dream of a dark tower where she is being kept prisoner, unable to move. Her adult life is in complete disarray. Her husband, Adam, and her best friend, Olivia, try to understand and support her as well as they can, but Tashi has periods of mental instability and moments of great, uncontrollable rage. She sees psychiatrists, and she spends time at a mental institution. But in the course of the book, she tells her own story with increasing insight, and we realize that her mental condition is a result of two traumatic events: a terrible experience when she was a child and another when she was a young adult.

Tashi grew up in the Olinka village, the daughter of a Christian woman. Always a sensitive girl, Tashi was never the same after the death of her sister. As a young woman, Tashi left for America with the missionary family and became an American citizen. She and Adam were lovers, and Tashi loved her American life, but, even so, she decided as a young adult to return to Africa for a ceremony. She wanted to be "bathed" like the rest of the women in her tribe. Because of her Christian beliefs, her mother had kept her away from this ritual in childhood when most young girls were "bathed," but Tashi, at this point in her life, felt that as a political and sentimental gesture of solidarity with her people, and in particular their charismatic political leader, she ought to undergo the ritual—without completely realizing its ramifications. She sought out the *tsunga* (medicine woman),

---

*Female genital mutilation, also referred to as "female circumcision" or "female cutting," is a process that can involve cutting the clitoris, removing it, or completely cutting away the inner and outer labia and sewing up the young girl with an aperture only big enough to allow for menstrual flow. The procedure is widespread in Africa, Indonesia, and the Middle East and occurs illegally in the United States among some immigrant groups from those areas. The purpose of the procedure is not hygiene; it is strictly a cultural and religious ritual. Sexual pleasure becomes all but impossible, and a husband is assured of a virgin wife who is also going to remain faithful. In addition, health problems and chronic pain are often a consequence of the procedure. Most critics of the procedure see it as an affront to human rights and a tool for the subjugation and domination of women. Defenders of the practice argue that Western critics have no right to superimpose Western values on other cultures. As such, female genital mutilation presents a challenge to ethical relativism, which argues that nobody has the right to criticize the moral and traditional practices of another culture. World attention has been focused on this practice since the mid-1990s.

M'Lissa, who performs the rituals. "Bathing" is a euphemism for female genital mutilation, and, from that day on, Tashi has experienced daily pain and health problems, in addition to a loss of sexual sensitivity. While still recuperating in M'Lissa's custody, Tashi is found by Adam, who has been frantically searching for her. She returns to the United States, marries him, and has a baby, Benny, under extremely painful conditions because of the mutilation. As a result, Benny is born with a mental disability. Increasingly, Tashi experiences bouts of anxiety and rage. With the help of psychiatrists she has begun to remember the death, the *murder,* of her sister Dura: Tashi was hiding outside the hut where her sister died, screaming and bleeding to death–from a botched procedure. And who performed the ritual? The same *tsunga,* M'Lissa, with the help of Tashi and Dura's own mother.

By the time we read this, we also know that Tashi is now, in real time, on trial in Africa for murder–the murder of M'Lissa. Did she do it? We won't know until the very end of the story. But we learn that after many years of marriage to Adam, with increasing problems due to psychological instability, Tashi has chosen to return to Africa to confront M'Lissa, who by now is a nationally renowned person, symbolizing the Olinka tradition. M'Lissa welcomes Tashi and reveals to her that she now expects Tashi to kill her, because that will elevate M'Lissa to the position of a saint. She also reveals that she finds Tashi naive beyond belief to have come back for the mutilation when she didn't have to–something M'Lissa would never have done herself. Even so, M'Lissa didn't try to stop her but performed the operation just because she was asked to do it, and it was her traditional job. And M'Lissa now recalls Tashi's sister who died–she had abandoned the bleeding little girl because her crying was too much for M'Lissa to bear.

Monica Morgan/WireImage/Getty Images

Alice Walker (b. 1944), American novelist, author of *The Color Purple, The Temple of My Familiar, Possessing the Secret of Joy,* and *The Same River Twice.* Walker's fiction incorporates many of the cultural strands contributing to the lives of American people of color and relates the African American experience to that of the African. Walker focuses particularly on the life experiences of women who are African and African American.

Is M'Lissa the great evil figure in the story? Responsible for the death of Dura and the loss of Tashi's own spirit–Tashi calls it her own death–she is certainly a villain. But she herself is also a victim: Her own procedure was botched, with lameness resulting. She is a tool for the culture, passing the terror along to future generations of young girls as it was passed on to her. Tashi realizes that the true culprit is not the mutilator but the older men of the tribal society who want the mutilations done, who argue that God thinks of woman as unclean if she isn't "circumcised"–the ones who think of an "uncircumcised" woman as "loose" and immoral, as someone who needs to be kept under control. But still, Tashi can't help blaming M'Lissa:

> It is what you told me. Remember? The uncircumcised woman is loose, you said, like a shoe that all, no matter what their size, might wear. This is unseemly, you said. Unclean. A proper woman must be cut and sewn to fit only her husband, whose pleasure depends on an opening it might take months, even years, to enlarge. Men love and enjoy the struggle, you said. For the woman. . . . But you never said anything about the woman, did you, M'Lissa? About the pleasure she might have. Or the suffering.

At the end of the story we learn the source of Tashi's nightmare about the dark tower, the truth about M'Lissa's death, and Tashi's own fate at the hands of the jury. And the secret of joy? On a very concrete level, the secret of sexual joy is to have an intact, unmutilated body and an unmutilated sense of self, of freedom. On a deeper level, the secret of joy itself is something we each have to find. Tashi's loved ones suggest that the secret is *resistance*.

Alice Walker's novel was received with alarm by many people who were unaware of the practice of female genital mutilation and welcomed by many others as a strong statement against excessive cultural tolerance. Walker was also criticized by some for betraying her African heritage in denouncing a traditional tribal practice as something that should not be tolerated in today's world. Her response was that she considered it a duty to speak up for those who can't speak for themselves.

Study Questions

1. Explain how this story can be viewed as an attack on ethical relativism. How might an ethical relativist respond to Walker's attack?

2. In view of the theme of female genital mutilation, do you find ethical relativism to be an appealing or a problematic moral theory? Explain.

3. Can we understand why Tashi went back as an adult to have the operation performed? Is this a realistic idea? Why or why not?

4. In your opinion, is Walker doing the right thing, exposing the practice of female genital mutilation as immoral, or should she show loyalty and solidarity with her African heritage by defending the practice? Is this a true dichotomy (an either-or situation), or is there another alternative?

5. M'Lissa asks Tashi what an American looks like, and Tashi answers, "An American, I said, sighing, but understanding my love for my adopted country perhaps for the first time: an American looks like a wounded person whose wound is hidden from others and sometimes from herself. An American looks like me." What does Tashi mean? Do you agree with her? Why or why not?

6. Now that you have been introduced to both Kingsolver's and Walker's novels, you may want to compare and contrast them. What do they have in common? What are the differences? Which viewpoint (in favor of or against ethical relativism) do you find more compelling? Explain.

 Narrative

Avatar

JAMES CAMERON (SCREENWRITER AND DIRECTOR)

Film, 2009. Summary.

Avatar is one of the highest grossing film ever, and at the time of this writing its many enthusiastic viewers are anticipating the premiere of the long-awaited *Avatar 2.* Part of its success was without a doubt a whole new world of 3-D animated cinematography, but the solid story had a tremendous audience appeal of its own. However, as some reviewers remarked, the plot was hardly new—since it was essentially the same as Disney's *Pocahontas,* and Kevin Costner's *Dances with Wolves:* a young man encounters a woman from an entirely different culture, and slowly adjusts to the values of her culture, discarding/modifying those of his own. Be that as it may, *Avatar,* with or without predecessors, deals in an entertaining way with fundamental cultural differences, and it is possible to detect basic versions of ethical relativism, hard universalism and soft universalism, and even a certain cynical version of moral nihilism weaving in and out of the plot line.

We're in the twenty-second century, on an earth-like planet, Pandora, in the process of being colonized by humans. Young Marine veteran Jake Sully, disabled in a recent war, receives a surprising job offer: a very special job only he is suited for, and the reward at the end will be a new pair of legs—something he would otherwise never be able to afford. The officer in command, Colonel Quaritch, makes it clear that Jake will be working with scientists, but will in fact be reporting to him and be under the colonel's direct command. Jake is flattered and upbeat—he has every intention of doing a good job for the Corps. The reason why he is so well suited for the job is, sadly, that his twin brother, a scientist, just died, putting his research program in jeopardy, because he was supposed to be part of the liaison team between the humans and another culture on Pandora, the Na'vi; for that purpose a new technology has been invented, that of the avatar: a body grown in the lab, specifically tailored to the researcher, of similar looks and stature as the native population on Pandora: tall and blue, with a long tail. In the avatar body the scientist is able to breathe the air, which is poisonous to humans, and through a mind link machine, he or she will move around naturally and interact with the natives, while the real human body lies in suspension in the lab.

Since Jake's brother was his twin, their physical attributes are similar, and Jake can take his brother's place. However, his brother was a scientist, and Jake is a soldier. He will be coming to the research program with a completely different mindset, and the other scientists are skeptical, especially chief researcher Dr. Grace Augustine, who reassigns him as a bodyguard for their avatar excursions into Pandora's world, teeming with ferocious animals. After being transported to Pandora, Jake is ecstatic to be in his new blue body, because now he has regained the use of his legs. But during the very first excursion with Dr. Augustine and the other scientists in their avatar bodies, an animal chases Jake through the jungle into a waterfall. He escapes but has lost his way and only manages to survive the early part of the night through his Marine training—until he is hopelessly outnumbered by things that want to eat him. But someone intervenes, and saves his life by killing some of the animals, a young woman of the Na'vi people. To Jake's surprise she feels sad that she had to take lives. She has nothing but contempt for him, until a strange phenomenon happens: little creatures of light land on him. He tries to brush them away, but she (speaking English, because there has been contact between the cultures for a while) explains that if the little luminous beings accept him, there must be something special about him, because these little beings are deeply connected with the entire spiritual force of the forest and the planet. He doesn't understand, but will happily follow her home, to what turns out to be the central area of the forest, the Hometree, a gigantic tree that is home to her entire tribe. He meets the tribe, including her father the chief and her mother the medicine woman/priestess, and ends up becoming accepted as a liaison between the tribe and the humans, provided he learns their ways and their language, with the young woman Neytiri as his teacher. Seeing it as a great opportunity to fulfill his mission for the Marines, Jake accepts.

Moviestore collection Ltd/Alamy Stock Photo

The film *Avatar* (2009) is a journey into the moral realm of cultural differences. Here the human Jake Sully (Sam Worthington) in his avatar body learns Na'vi customs from Neytiri (Zoe Saldana).

Whenever his avatar body sleeps, he is physically back in the lab at the station, reporting in. Over the months where he is getting deeper and deeper into the culture, learning how to master their riding animals and, the big step toward acceptance, their flying creatures the *ikrans,* his reports are increasingly enthusiastic. Jake is beginning to "get" the culture. But the colonel is becoming skeptical, since the entire purpose for the military is not to make friends with the Na'vi as such, but to gain access to the rare mineral "unobtanium," which lies under their sacred grove and the Tree of Souls. The colonel is afraid that Jake is losing his focus and is essentially becoming a traitor. He has no interest in the values of the Na'vi, but sees them as mainly an obstacle that needs to be overcome, by hook or by crook. As Jake is immersing himself deeper into the Na'vi culture, becoming the chosen mate of Neytiri and mastering not only their language but also bonding with an ikran of his own and flying with the tribe, acquiring a respect for the spirit of the planet, the colonel is working on an alternative plan: devastating the environment, burning the Na'vi out of their Hometree, and proceeding to tear up the jungle of the sacred grove to gain access to the mineral. Dr. Augustine suspects that a plot is afoot and removes the science team to the fabled floating mountains area, believing that common ground can be found between the humans and the Na'vi. And now the disaster happens: The general and his team will wait no longer, and they proceed to bomb and devastate the Hometree, killing many Na'vi and making the rest homeless. The call now goes out to other tribes to unite against the invaders, and Jake is regarded as a traitor in both groups. In the conflict that ensues, Jake must persuade the Na'vi that he is on their side, fighting for their planet. In order to do that, he will need to succeed in a near-impossible task: bonding with and flying the fabled giant ikran creature Mak Tao, and becoming one of the few masters of the Mak Tao, Taruk Mak Tao. You may be one of the millions worldwide who already know the answer. If not, watch the movie. And then you will also find answers to whether Pandora can be saved from exploitation, whether there is a future for Neytiri and Jake, and whether he will be able to live a life on Pandora in his blue avatar body, rather than as a paraplegic on a space station.

Study Questions

1. Is Jake a traitor to his own people? Why or why not? What does the film want us to conclude? Do you agree?

2. Is the underlying philosophy of the film mostly one of ethical relativism or soft universalism? Explain.

3. Identify the colonel's and his team's attitude and explain: Is it predominantly a hard universalist view or one of moral nihilism?

4. Apply Rachels's set of three universal values to the Na'vi on Pandora: Do they take care of enough infants to keep the culture going? Do they have a rule against lying? Do they have a rule against murder? Can you think of some other value that the Na'vi and the human scientists share, such as one or more of Oliver Scott Curry's 7 universal values?

5. If you have also seen *Pochahontas* and/or *Dances with Wolves,* identify the similarities and differences between them and *Avatar.*

6. A series of sequels have been planned for years, with *Avatar 2* pushed back (at the time of this writing) to a December 2020 release date, followed by *Avatar 3* and *4* within the next few years. If you have seen any of the sequels by the time you read this, discuss whether the underlying moral philosophy of the sequels match *Avatar 1.*

Chapter Four
Myself or Others?

If there has ever been a moment when you have found yourself engaged in discussing a philosophical theory, your topic may well have been *psychological egoism*. Perhaps late at night, after a party, the die-hards were gathered out on the patio or in the kitchen, and somebody brought up the subject of selfishness, claiming that all acts are selfish, or as a character put it in a sitcom, "There are no self-less good deeds." (You'll find the sitcom episode at the end of this chapter.) Perhaps you wanted to argue against that view but found yourself at a loss for words because the theory seemed to be disturbingly right. All of a sudden, everything seemed selfish! Psychological egoism is a theory that haunts us from time to time—most of us don't want to believe that everything we do is always selfish. And, as you'll see in the course of the chapter, we need not buy into the theory, because it has severe flaws. Nevertheless, it has been a seductive and persuasive theory since the days of Socrates, and in this chapter we'll take a closer look at what it entails.

We usually assume that moral behavior, or "being ethical," has to do with not being overly concerned with oneself. In other words, selfishness is assumed to be an unacceptable attitude. Even among scholars, though, there is disagreement about what constitutes ethical behavior. Since very early in Western intellectual history, the viewpoint that humans aren't built to look out for other people's interests has surfaced regularly. Some scholars even hold that *proper* moral conduct consists of "looking out for number one," period. Those viewpoints are known as *psychological egoism* and *ethical egoism,* respectively. Both psychological egoism and ethical egoism are examples of absolutist theories; they hold that only one code is the norm for ethical behavior. (See Box 4.1 for an explanation of the difference between *egoism* and *egotism.*)

Box 4.1 EGOISM OR EGOTISM?

The terms *egoism* and *egotism* are part of our everyday speech, and people often use them interchangeably, but do they really mean the same thing? No: *Egoists* are people who think in terms of their own advantage, generally by disregarding the interests of others. *Egotists* are people who have a very high self-opinion and whose language often consists of self-praise; praise an egotist for a good result on a test or for looking nice, and you might receive responses such as "Of course I did well—I always do, because I'm very smart" or "Nice? I look great!" An egoist need not fall into this pattern, although he or she might, of course, be an egotist as well.

Psychological Egoism: What About the Heroes?

On the day of the massacre on the Virginia Tech campus—April 16, 2007—thirty-two students were killed and twenty-one wounded by Seung-Hui Cho, who then killed himself—one of the worst mass murders in U.S. history. Apparently Cho, a resident alien student with noticeable mental health problems, had chosen his victims at random; he had apparently had no particular grudges against or confrontations with any particular person but took out his self-absorbed anger on professors and students who, in his mind, led a more satisfying life than he did, according to the videos he sent to the media in between two shooting sprees. Many more students would have died had it not been for the heroic efforts of their fellow students who barricaded doors to classrooms with desks and even with their own bodies. But perhaps the most memorable story is that of Liviu Librescu, a professor of aeronautical engineering. Originally from Romania, Librescu was a Holocaust survivor who had immigrated to Israel, and then to the United States, and was still teaching at age 76. When Cho tried to force his way into Librescu's classroom, Librescu blocked the door with his body so that all the students in his class could escape out the window; the last student leaving saw Librescu shot and killed by the shooter. He gave his life to save his students, knowing full well the scope of evil that human beings can inflict on one another—and the day of his death, April 16, was Holocaust Remembrance Day in Israel.

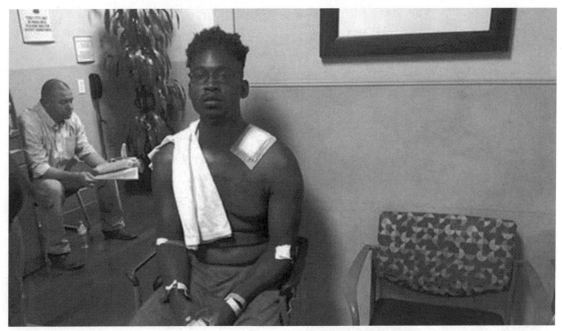

Heather Long/The Washington Post/Getty Images

In October 2017, Jonathan Smith, a father of three children, was attending the Route 91 Harvest Country Music festival in Las Vegas with nine members of his family when a shooter targeted the festivalgoers. He told his family, including three nieces, to run and stick together, and proceeded to help strangers get out of harm's way. He is credited with saving 30 people by pulling them to safety. Fifty-nine people were killed and 500 wounded. Smith himself was hit by a bullet, fracturing his collarbone. After the ordeal, he said that he just did what anyone would do: "Everyone's saying, 'Dude you're a hero, you're this.' I'm not a hero, I'm just someone that just basically decided, you know what, I'll put someone's life before my own."

And as many have observed, during times of great need there will often be ordinary people standing up and doing extraordinary things to help others. Sometimes they live through it, sometimes they perish. During the terrorist attacks of 9/11, 2001, police officers and firefighters died, going far beyond their professional duties to help others survive. In December 2015 in Knoxville, Tennessee, a 15-year-old high school student named Zaevion Dobson protected three young women from apparent random gang shooting by shielding them with his body; he died at the scene, saving their lives. You may remember from Chapter 1 that Jonathan Smith saved 30 people during the Las Vegas shooting while he was looking for his own family—and lived to be interviewed about it later. You may also remember from Chapter 1 that a terror attack was thwarted on a train traveling from Belgium to France when three young American males attacked the terrorist and prevented a tragedy. And there are many more such stories, including the young preschool teacher, Victoria Soto, who died at the Sandy Hook Elementary School massacre in 2012, in the attempt to save her young students by first hiding them, and when they were found by the shooter, then throwing herself between him and the young children. The children lived, but she lost her life.

The news media have used the term *heroes* to refer to such people, and most of us would agree: Risking, and in some cases giving one's life to save others, especially when one is aware of the danger, is something we generally consider to be heroic and admirable.

Liviu Librescu (1930–2007), a professor at Virginia Tech, and Victoria Soto (1985–2012), a teacher at Sandy Hook Elementary School, both gave their lives to protect fellow human beings.
Librescu family/Getty Images; Eastern Connecticut University/AP Photo

And that is why the theory of psychological egoism is disturbing for many of us, since it calmly dismisses the act of someone such as Librescu as an expression of fundamentally selfish human nature. This means that even the person with the most stellar reputation for unselfishness must be reevaluated. From Mother Teresa to Martin Luther King, Jr., from Librescu and the students at Virginia Tech, to Zae Dobson, Victoria Soto, Jonathan Smith, and countless other brave people including local heroes that the world generally will never hear of, all of them are now reclassified as selfish, including ourselves, of course. But what could possibly be selfish about acts of self-sacrifice? Well, says the psychological egoist, since we are all selfish, then the motivation might be any one of a number of things: A person who sacrifices himself or herself for others might have a wish to become famous, or might want to atone for something he or she had left undone in a previous situation, or might simply want to feel good about himself or herself. Or perhaps it is simply an unconscious urge.

Stories about people who have risked and even lost their lives to save others, stories that seem to exemplify selflessness, are precious to most people, because they show us what we might be capable of. We like to believe that humans have a built-in measure of courage that allows us to rise to the occasion and give up our lives, or at least our comfort, for others. Of course, few people perform heroic deeds with the *intent* of getting killed, but if they lose their lives in the process, we only seem to admire them more. (There are those who feel that losing one's life for someone else is stupid, useless, or even morally wrong. Such people may feel more comfortable with the theory of *ethical egoism.*)

If we ask a person who has performed (and survived) a heroic deed why he or she did it, the answer is almost predictable: "I just had to do it" or, perhaps, "I didn't think about it, I just did it." That was essentially what Jonathan Smith said during interviews after the Las Vegas massacre. We take such comments as a sign that we are in the presence of a person with extraordinary moral character. But there are other ways of interpreting the words and actions of heroes. The theory of psychological egoism states that whatever it may look like and whatever we may think it is, no human action is done for any reason other than for the sake of the agent. In short, we are all selfish, or at least we are all self-interested.

The term *psychological egoism* is applied to the theory because it is a psychological theory, a theory about how humans behave. A psychological egoist believes that humans are always looking out for themselves in some way or other, and it is impossible for them to behave any other way. As such, psychological egoism is a **descriptive** theory; it doesn't make any statements about whether this is a *good* way to behave. What does it take for a person to be labeled a psychological egoist? It's not necessary that he or she be a selfish person, only that he or she hold to the theory that all people look after themselves. As we see later, it is entirely possible for someone to be kind and caring and still be a psychological egoist. (See Box 4.2 for an explanation of the difference between *selfish* and *self-interested.*) Suppose, though, that someone insists that all people *ought to* look after themselves—a **normative** view. Then he or she is an *ethical egoist.* We discuss the theory of ethical egoism later in this chapter.

Box 4.2 SELFISH VERSUS SELF-INTERESTED

Psychological egoism is generally described as a theory which states that everyone is selfish at all times. But what does the word *selfish* mean? Some psychological egoists (people who believe everyone is selfish) sometimes emphasize that there is nothing bad or morally deficient about being selfish; all it means, they say, is that we are "self-ish," we are focused on our own survival, which doesn't necessarily imply that we are disregarding other people's interests. However, we use the word in a different sense in our everyday language. According to *Webster's* dictionary, *selfish* means "devoted unduly to self; influenced by a view to private advantage," so if we concede that *Webster's* reflects the common use of the word, we can't deny that *selfish* is a morally disparaging term; it isn't value-neutral, and it certainly isn't a compliment.

Sometimes psychological egoists use the term *selfish,* and sometimes the term used is *self-interested.* There is no consensus among psychological egoists about which term to use. It makes quite a difference which term you choose, but in the end, it may not make the theory of psychological egoism any more plausible. If you say (1), "All acts are selfish," you imply that all of us are always looking for self-gratification and have no feeling for the interests of others. However, if you say (2), "All acts are self-interested," you imply that all of us are always thinking about what is best for us. Is statement 1 true? It may be true that we are always looking out for ourselves in some way, but it is certainly not true that we are always looking for self-gratification; many a moment in a lifetime is spent agonizing over doing what we want versus doing what we ought to do, and often we end up choosing duty over desire. So what if the psychological egoist says, "Doing my duty is better in the long run for me, even if I don't feel like doing it, so I guess I'm self-interested" (statement 2)? But is statement 2 true? Many philosophers over the years have gleefully pointed out that it isn't—we are hardly concerned with what is good for us, at least not all the time. Many people smoke, drink to excess, and take drugs even though they know it is not in their own best interest. So couldn't psychological egoism state that "all acts are either selfish or self-interested"? It could, but it generally doesn't; part of the appeal of psychological egoism is that it is a very simple theory, and putting a dichotomy (an either-or) into the theory makes it much more complicated.

A word of caution: True to the method suggested by Paul Ricoeur (see Chapter 3), I usually present the positive, persuasive elements of a theory before bringing up its weaker points, but here I am deviating from that method, after years of observing student reactions to the theory of psychological egoism. While most students are willing and even eager to find flaws in the theory, I generally encounter students who, reluctantly, feel they have to accept that everyone is selfish, including themselves, just because the theory says so. To those students I say, up front: Beware of being persuaded by the psychological egoist that every one of us is totally selfish! Even if it looks like a persuasive theory, moral philosophers are very critical of it, because logically, it is not a very good theory. Below we take a careful look at what is wrong with the theory, but even before we get there, I want to make sure that you understand that you in no way have to buy into the idea that you and everyone you know is selfish! You may end up liking and supporting the theory, and that is of course your choice; but if you think the theory is too harsh to sound true, hold on to that thought, and we will return to it in the section "Three Major Problems with Psychological Egoism."

Psychological Egoism: From Glaucon to Hobbes

Chapter 2 featured a section of Plato's famous book *The Republic*. The section quoted there is a less well-known discussion about whether going to the theater is a morally worthwhile pastime (and Socrates says it isn't). In this chapter you'll encounter a far more famous part of Plato's *Republic*, the discussion of what makes a good person and whether all people are, or should be, selfish. In Chapter 8 you'll find a more complete exploration of who Socrates was and what role he played in Plato's life, but for now we'll focus on the issue of selfishness.

Socrates is known to us today primarily through Plato's books, the *Dialogues;* Socrates never wrote anything himself, and had it not been for Plato's wanting to keep his teacher's name alive after Socrates' death (at the hands of an Athenian jury, found guilty of crimes against the state, literally "corrupting the young and offending the gods"), we might never have known the name Socrates at all. In most of Plato's books, Socrates has a conversation—a dialogue—with somebody, a friend, a student, or perhaps an enemy. In *The Republic,* Socrates and his young followers have been invited to a dinner party at the house of some old friends, and they are engaged in a discussion about morality, selfishness, and the ideal state, branching off into art theory, gender theory, the nature of reality, and even life after death. In the Primary Readings section you will find an excerpt of that discussion. Plato's brother Glaucon is trying to make Socrates give some good reasons why it is better to be "just" than to be "unjust," or in other words, better to be a decent human being than to be a lying, conniving scoundrel. Glaucon insists that all people by nature look after themselves, and whenever we can get away with something, we will do it, regardless of how unjust it may be to others. Unfortunately, we may receive the same treatment from others, which is highly unpleasant, so for the sake of peace and security we agree to treat one another decently—not because we want to, but because we are playing it safe. Morality is just a result of our looking out for ourselves. (See Box 4.3 for an explanation of psychological egoism in terms of "ought implies can.")

Box 4.3 "OUGHT IMPLIES CAN"

Sometimes a philosophical text will state that "ought implies can." In the civil code of the Roman Empire (27 B.C.E.–395 C.E.), this principle was clearly stated, and Roman citizens knew that *impossibilium nulla est obligatio* (nobody has a duty to do what is not possible). Many philosophical and legal schools of thought today are still based on that idea, and one of these is psychological egoism. "Ought implies can" means that we can't have an obligation (ought) to do something unless it is actually possible for us to do it (can). I can't make it a moral obligation for you to go out and help disaster victims yourself if you don't have the time or the money to travel, but I might try to make you feel morally obligated to help by donating a buck or two. I can't make it a moral obligation for you to take home a pet from the pound if you are allergic to animals (but I might insist that you have an obligation to help in other ways). You can't tell me that I ought to be unselfish if in fact I was born selfish and can't be any other way because it is part of my human nature. This is the point that psychological egoism wants to make: It is irrational to keep wanting humans to look out for one another when, as a matter of fact, we aren't built that way.

What Glaucon is suggesting here about the origin of society is a first in Western thought. His theory is an example of what has become known as a *social contract theory,* a type of theory that became particularly influential much later, in the eighteenth century. A social contract theory assumes that humans used to live in a presocial setting (without rules, regulations, or cooperation) and then, for various reasons, got together and agreed on setting up a society. Generally, social contract theories assume that humans decide to build a society with rules (1) for the sake of the common good or (2) for the sake of self-protection. Glaucon's theory belongs to the second category because he claims (for the sake of argument) that humans primarily look after themselves.

To illustrate his point, Glaucon tells the story of a man called Gyges, a shepherd in ancient Lydia (today's western Turkey). Gyges was caught in a storm and an earthquake, which left a large hole in the ground. He explored the chasm and found a hollow bronze horse with the corpse of a giant inside. The giant was wearing only a gold ring on his finger. Gyges took the ring and left and later, wearing the ring, attended a meeting of shepherds. During the meeting Gyges happened to twist the ring, and he realized from the reaction of the other shepherds that he had become invisible. Twisting the ring back, he reappeared. Realizing the advantages gained by being invisible, Gyges arranged to be one of the elected messengers who report to the king about his sheep. Gyges went to town, seduced the queen, and conspired with her to kill the king. He then took over the kingdom, sired a dynasty, and became the ancestor of the famous King Croesus.

United Archives GmbH/Alamy Stock Photo

If an invisibility ring can provide a perfect outlet for selfishness, will we all grab the chance, as Plato's brother Glaucon speculates, or will we fight temptation? Will we even all be tempted? In *The Lord of the Rings* (trilogy, 2001-3), Frodo volunteers to take the ring of power to Mount Doom and destroy it; but even Frodo, goodhearted as he is, is tempted by the ring's power, and within his small person a great battle is being fought.

Glaucon's question is, Suppose we had two such rings? Let us imagine giving one to a decent person and one to a scoundrel. We know that the scoundrel will abuse the ring for personal gain, but how about the decent person? To Glaucon it is the same thing; their human natures are identical. Decent persons will do "unjust" things just as quickly as scoundrels if they know they can get away with it; furthermore, if they *don't* take advantage of such situations, they are just stupid. In the end, who will be happier, the unjust person who schemes and gets away with everything or the just person who never tries to get away with anything but is so good that people think there must be something wrong with him? Why, the unjust person, of course. (Here Glaucon is in fact arguing not in favor of psychological egoism but *ethical egoism*: It pays to be good at being bad, so it would be stupid to be good—in other words, everyone ought to be selfish.)

This little story may be the first in the literary tradition to explore a theme that has remained popular to this day—and that may be one reason it seems timeless, but it could also be that the moral problem it represents hasn't changed, either. *Arabian Nights* is full of stories about invisibility cloaks, magic rings, and owners making creative uses of them, sometimes to gain a personal advantage and sometimes to spy on and vanquish the bad guys; in 1897 H. G. Wells wrote *The Invisible Man,* which has been made into a movie numerous times and inspired other movies. J. R. R. Tolkien's trilogy *The Lord of the Rings* (1954-6) features an invisibility ring. Usually the moral problem stated is, If you could become invisible, what would you do? Would you still be a morally decent or even halfway decent person? Or would you use your power selfishly if you knew you could get away with it? Harry Potter may have his magic cloak, but most of us don't. Interestingly, in cases where people have been under the impression that they enjoy total anonymity, such as in the days of extensive illegal downloading of music from the Internet, few of those people seemed to have any qualms about breaking the law—which plays right into Glaucon's hands. But does that mean that *everyone* would react the same way, with a cloak of anonymity? Probably not, because many of us have a moral compass that tells us that such behavior is wrong. But the psychological egoist would insist that this is just because we're socialized that way.

With few exceptions, the invisible person in books and films succumbs to temptation and meets a terrible end, as punishment for having a weak or evil character. So most invisible-person stories are *didactic* stories (see Chapter 2), designed to teach a moral lesson: If you let your selfish nature rule, you will surely be punished—if not by others, then by fate. But, as my students have pointed out on several occasions, there is a category of stories that serve as an exception: stories in which invisibility is used not for evil or for gain but for good. *Superheroes* who have invisibility powers (such as those in *Fantastic Four* and *Mystery Men*) are not in the same category as the human whose soul is corrupted by being invisible—they suffer no doubt, they are not corrupted by power, and they are fixated on their goal, to do good for humanity. But then again, that's what makes them superheroes and what separates them from us. And as such, they're simply not as interesting, morally, as the hero who has his or her moments of weakness and doubt. And perhaps the most mysterious superhero of them all, Dr. Manhattan in *Watchmen* (see Chapter 6), is so far removed from his original human nature that human lives no longer seem important to him, because he has lost the human perspective.

So what is the lesson of Glaucon's story? Is he seriously implying that it is foolish and unnatural to be good if you can get away with being bad? No; he is acting as the devil's advocate to make Socrates defend justice as something that is good in itself. However, Glaucon does imply that what he is describing is, in fact, the opinion of most people. He may have been right; a good two thousand years later Thomas Hobbes (1588–1679) agreed with Glaucon's theory of self-interest on all three counts: (1) Humans choose to live in a society with rules because they are concerned with their own safety and for no other reason (a social contract theory); (2) humans are by nature self-interested, and any show of concern for others hides a true concern for ourselves (the theory of psychological egoism); (3) we would be fools if we didn't look after ourselves (the theory of ethical egoism). (We return to this point in the next section; you will find Hobbes's theory in the Primary Readings at the end of this chapter and his view of the selfish basis for pity in Box 4.4.)

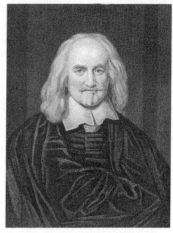

Georgios Kollidas/Shutterstock

The English philosopher Thomas Hobbes was one of the first modern materialists, claiming that all of human psychology consists of the attraction and repulsion of physical particles. As such, the natural human approach to life is one of self-preservation, and the natural life of humans outside the regulations of society (the state of nature) is for Hobbes a filthy and frightening war of everyone against everyone.

Surely we all can remember events in our lives that show that we don't always act out of self-interest. You may remember the time you helped your best friend move across town. The time you sat up all night preparing your brother's taxes. The time you donated toys to the annual Christmas toy drive. The time you washed your parents' car. Did the dishes at Thanksgiving. Or perhaps even helped a stranger on the road or saved the life of an accident victim. Were all those good deeds really done for selfish reasons? The psychological egoist would say yes—you may not have been aware of your true motives, but selfish they were, somehow. You may have wanted to borrow your parents' car: hence, the car wash and the dishes. You helped your friend move because you were afraid of losing her friendship. You may have felt guilty for not helping with your brother's taxes the year before, so you did them this year. The toys? You wanted to feel good about yourself. The stranger on the road? You wanted to rack up a few points in the Big Book of Heaven. Helping the accident victim? You wanted your name to go viral on Facebook, Instagram, and Twitter.

Box 4.4 HOBBES AND THE FEELING OF PITY

Hobbes believed humans feel pity for others in distress because they fear the same may happen to themselves. We identify with the pain of others, and that makes us afraid for ourselves. Therefore, helping others may be a way to ward off bad events. In actual fact we have no pity for others for their sake—only for our own. (He is not the first thinker to have expressed that opinion; Aristotle said approximately the same thing but without implying that we are selfish to the bone.) Hobbes was one of the first modern Western philosophers to ponder human psychology, and we might say that he put his finger on a sore spot. Sometimes we do sympathize with others because we imagine how awful it would be if the same thing were to happen to us. What exactly does Hobbes mean when he says we *identify* with others? It seems that we ask ourselves, If this happened to me, how would I feel? That does not necessarily lead to concern for ourselves but, rather, leads to a concern for others, precisely because we know how they feel. Furthermore, isn't it possible to feel pity for someone or something with which you don't identify so easily? We certainly can feel pity for someone of the other gender or someone of another race or culture, even if what happens to them wouldn't happen to us. But how about feeling pity for dolphins caught in gill nets? For animals caught in traps? For pets used in lab experiments?

When the pictures and videos of the tsunami in Japan 2011 became available, one video in particular went "viral": a dog leading rescuers to another severely injured dog. Many were gratified to read in a blog message that likewise became known all over the world that a pet store owner and animal welfare activist had rescued both dogs. The story tells us that, for one thing, it seems possible that a dog would care about another dog, and for another, that we have no problem extending our empathy to both dogs. And it hardly speaks for a fundamentally selfish human nature, any more than the upcoming story of Abraham Lincoln saving the piglets does.

In a broad sense, perhaps we do identify with other creatures when their lives are in danger and feel that we ward off our own demise by saving their lives. In the final analysis, though, that idea is rather far-fetched, because if Hobbes is right and we fear "contamination" from the misery of others, wouldn't we rather turn our backs on them and flee rather than expose ourselves to their suffering? Given that we don't, perhaps there are forces at work other than selfishness. An easier explanation is that we simply, on occasion, care for the well-being of others.

So what is it that has proved so appealing about psychological egoism? After all, it removes the halo from the head of every hero and every unselfish person in the history of humankind. In fact, that may be part of its appeal, according to an analysis by James Rachels, our acquaintance from Chapter 3: We like to think, in this day and age, that we are honest about ourselves, and we don't want to be tricked into thinking that we are better than we are or that anyone else is either. (1) One reason, then, for this theory's popularity is its presumed *honesty*. Later in this section you'll find an example of this phenomenon in the story of Lincoln and the pigs.

Closely related to the notion of honesty is (2) our modern tendency toward *cynicism*. Somehow, we have a hard time believing good things about people, including ourselves. Refusing to take things at face value may be the mature thing to do, but it may also close our minds to the possibility that not all acts are selfish and not everybody is rotten at heart. (See Box 4.5 for a discussion of modern cynicism.) This possibility doesn't mean we shouldn't view the world with a healthy dose of skepticism and suspicion. Often, we really *are* taken advantage of, people *are* truly selfish and devious, and things *aren't* what they seem. But there is a difference between that kind of prudent skepticism and a universal cynicism that borders on paranoia. Such radical cynicism doesn't allow for the possibility of the existence of goodness and kindness.

Box 4.5 MODERN CYNICISM

There is much speculation about how cynicism began. It's not a new phenomenon. The ancient Greeks invented it: The Cynics (literally, the "doglike ones"), headed by Diogenes, did their best to undermine convention in order to break its hold on people's minds—one of the original "Question authority" movements. In later years, cynicism has questioned authority to the point that misanthropy—automatically believing the worst about everybody—has become a form of authority in itself.

Modern cynicism has a precursor—or even a founder—in French philosopher and author Voltaire (1694–1778), whose sharp remarks about his contemporary France before the Revolution set the tone for the intellectual who rails against double standards and bigotry, trusts no one, including his or her government, and has a never-ending skepticism as far as human nature is concerned. Satire was one of the political weapons of choice in the Age of Reason. But in the last part of the nineteenth century, the Western world experienced a surge of optimism because many believed we were very close to solving all technological, scientific, and medical riddles. It was even assumed that we were too civilized to ever go to war again. You may remember from the section in Chapter 2 on war movies that enthusiasm for war by and large ended with World War I. Often our modern cynicism is regarded as having been born in the trenches of World War I, but there is an interesting precursor: the sinking of the *Titanic* in 1912. The 1997 award-sweeping film *Titanic* reminded us not only of the human tragedies involved but also of the hubris, the cocky assurance that human technology could conquer all obstacles. A ship so well built that it was unsinkable! As we know, it wasn't, and the optimistic belief that now humans were the masters of the universe went to the bottom of the ocean with the great ship. It may not have been the very first blow to human self-assurance in the twentieth century,

but it became the first serious crack in the hull of modern belief in technology.

Cynicism became a way of life in the twentieth century, fueled by the two world wars, the Great Depression, and the revelation of the horrors of the Holocaust. Children who lived through the tragedies and disappointments of the 1960s and 1970s, as well as their children, were all affected by the assassinations of John F. Kennedy, Robert Kennedy, and Martin Luther King, Jr.; by the Korean and Vietnam wars, by fuel shortages; and by the Watergate and Iran-Contra scandals. And then there are the revelations from past decades such as the now infamous Tuskegee syphilis study, in which close to four hundred African American men from 1932 to 1972 unwittingly were reduced to the status of lab rats for government medical experiments. In 2010 it became known that American doctors also conducted syphilis experiments on citizens in Guatemala 1945–1948, for which the Obama administration apologized. Other examples of the use of citizens for some larger purpose without their consent include the nuclear tests of the 1950s, which often involved soldiers and civilians who were given the impression that their lives were not in danger. Inuit people in Alaska were given radioactive medication as part of an experiment. In 1996, the *Los Angeles Times* revealed that in the 1950s the U.S. Army had sprayed chemicals and bacteria over large populations in New York and Washington and even over a school in Minneapolis. Years after the Vietnam War, it became apparent that soldiers had been exposed to a toxic exfoliant, Agent Orange. In 2015–16, a scandal unfolded in Flint, Michigan, where the Flint River turned out to have a high level of lead contamination which was essentially covered up by city officials, claiming that there was nothing wrong with the water supply despite citizens experiencing numerous health problems. And in 2019 the news story erupted in American media: the academic admissions scandal. Some 30 people, famous and wealthy people among them, including Hollywood actors, had conspired to get their children into high-profile schools such as Stanford and University of California, Los Angeles, by engaging in a scam, bribing school officials or arranging for their kids to take a mock entrance exam while someone else was actually taking the test in their place. So perhaps it is understandable that conspiracy rumors appear on a regular basis in response to important news stories; we just have to remind ourselves that although conspiracies do exist, there is a fine line between being a skeptical cynic and a paranoid cynic.

Such revelations by the media are particularly good at reflecting, and often creating, cynicism, but sometimes the scandal erupts within the media world itself. Also feeding our sense of

cynicism are periodically surfacing scandals surrounding politicians caught in sex scandals, breaches of national security, and/or financial irregularities, and the still developing story—global, at this point—of Catholic priests in past decades having molested children and then being reassigned to new areas by the Church as a cover-up.

So is cynicism an appropriate reaction to events and people that disappoint us? Appropriate or not, it is a sign of our times. But perhaps cynicism isn't altogether a bad thing—as it is sometimes said, a cynic is a disappointed idealist. You have a vision of how things ought to be, but you also have a considerable amount of skepticism. So somewhere between hope and skepticism you may be able to deal with the real world.

One more reason that psychological egoism is so popular has to do with (3) *making excuses.* When psychological egoists say, "I can't help myself—it's my nature," they're saying they don't have to worry about remembering Aunt Molly's birthday or texting to the radio station about the mattress they saw blocking the number-two lane on the freeway because humans are selfish *by nature,* and we are not capable of worrying about others—unless, of course, there is something in it for ourselves. But that is nothing but a bad excuse. Psychological egoists who take their own theory seriously never say we can't help being selfish to the bone—they just say there is some hidden selfish motive for whatever we do that we may not even be aware of. Box 4.6 explores the question of whether we, according to the psychological egoist, have freedom of the will to make choices, or whether our actions are determined by nature or nurture.

Box 4.6 PSYCHOLOGICAL EGOISM AND THE CONCEPT OF FREE WILL

It is time to take one step backward and reassess one of the claims of psychological egoism: that we can't help what we're doing. When psychological egoists claim that we can't help being selfish because it is in our human nature, they are of course also saying that we shouldn't be blamed for the selfish things we do (or be praised for the seemingly unselfish deeds either). That lines psychological egoism up with

a famous—some would say, infamous—theory in philosophy: *hard determinism.* A hard determinist believes that since everything is an effect of a previous cause, then we should, in principle if not in reality, be able to predict events with complete accuracy—not only in nature but even in human lives and human decisions. That means that *according to hard determinism, we have no free will* because everything we decide is a result of either our genetic heritage ("Nature") or our experience and environment ("Nurture"). In other words, it may *feel* as if we make free choices, but we really don't; everything is part of the great chain of cause and effect, even our thought processes and moral decisions. That means that when people decide to break a moral rule or even the law, they can't help it and shouldn't be blamed, according to hard determinism. This line of thinking has spawned numerous discussions in ethics as well as in philosophy of law—because (1) we normally assume that people can be held morally accountable for what they do intentionally, and (2) our entire judicial system rests on the assumption that, in most cases, people should be held accountable if they break the law on purpose. Nevertheless, there are individual cases where people truly can't help doing what they're doing, morally and legally. You may want to think of a few such cases and discuss them.

In the sense that psychological egoism traces all human behavior back to self-preservation or self-love as the fundamental cause of all our decisions (such as Hobbes does)—in holding that we can't act otherwise and that we shouldn't be held accountable for being selfish—it can be called a deterministic theory. However, psychological egoism generally assumes that we can choose between several possible courses of action—but all are selfish actions nonetheless. And most psychological egoists would claim that we can be held accountable for choosing wrongly—because it would be in our selfish interest to avoid getting in trouble with the law, just as much as it might be selfishly gratifying to break it. This would speak against classifying psychological egoism as a hard determinist theory. In Chapter 10 we explore further the concept of having a free will in the philosophy of Jean-Paul Sartre.

Three Major Problems with Psychological Egoism

There is something beguiling about psychological egoism; once you begin to look at the world through the eyes of a psychological egoist, it is hard to see it any other way. In fact, no matter how hard we try to come up with an example that seems to run counter to the theory, the psychological egoist has a ready answer, dismissing our example as just another form of selfishness. This is due to several factors.

1. Falsification Is Not Possible

Psychological egoism always looks for selfish motives and refuses to recognize any other kind. For any non-selfish motivation you can think of for doing what you did, the theory will tell you that there was another ulterior motive behind it. It is inconceivable, according to the theory, that other motives might exist. This is in fact a flaw in the theory. A good theory is not one that can't be proven wrong but one that allows for the possibility of counterexamples.

The inability of a theory to allow for cases in which it doesn't apply is considered bad science and bad thinking. The principle of *falsification* was advanced by the philosopher Karl Popper (1902–1994) as a hallmark of a viable theory. It states that a good scientific theory must allow for the possibility that it might be wrong. If it declares itself right under any and all circumstances, it cannot be "falsified." So "falsification" doesn't mean that a theory has to be proven wrong but that it has to be engaged in rigorously testing itself—in other words, it has to consider the possibility that it is wrong and test itself in any way possible. Popper says in his book *The Poverty of Historicism* (1957), "Just because it is our aim to establish theories as well as we can, we must test them as severely as we can; that is, we must try to find fault with them, we must try to falsify them. Only if we cannot falsify them in spite of our best efforts can we say that they have stood up to severe tests." Science itself doesn't always follow the principle of falsification; an example is the eighteenth-century debate about meteorites in which most scientists chose to side with their own theory that rocks couldn't fall from the sky, since outer space, they said, consists of a vacuum. The statements of reliable private citizens who claimed to have seen meteorites fall and land on the ground were consistently brushed aside by scientists as being lies or delusions because most scientists did not question their own theory: It was nonfalsifiable since it didn't allow for the possibility that it might be wrong. As we know, science later had to revise its notion of outer space (the theory was falsified): In 1803, scientists at l'Aigle, France, actually observed a large number of meteorites falling. A similar and more recent story illustrating the same reluctance to accept new data was the dismissal of the existence of "rogue waves" until recent years when the phenomenon has been amply corroborated.

Is the *theory of evolution* a good theory in the sense that it is falsifiable? Scientists today would say yes: The theory is based on empirical research that can be verified objectively (the fossil record), but it doesn't claim that it is correct no matter what happens; it claims that it is the most plausible theory of biology so far, but if new and different evidence should surface, then it is (presumably) open to revision.

Psychological egoism is not a good theory, according to Popper's principle, because it doesn't allow for the possibility that it could be wrong but reinterprets all acts and motives so they fit the theory instead. That is not a theory, strictly speaking; it is a prejudice. It comes across as a strong theory precisely because there seems to be nothing that can defeat it; however, that is not a strength, scientifically speaking. A strong theory recognizes the reality of the problem of induction (see Chapter 3): Any empirical theory (that is, one based on evidence) can't be 100 percent certain.

In addition, the unfalsifiability of psychological egoism demonstrates the logical fallacy of *begging the question*. When an argument begs the question, it assumes that what it is supposed to prove is already true, so the "proof" does nothing but repeat the assumption (such as "your mother is right because your mother is never wrong!"). Psychological egoism works in the same way: It assumes that all acts are selfish and therefore interprets all acts as selfish. So psychological egoism is not the scientific theory it claims to be.

2. Feeling Good About Helping Others May Not Be Selfish

Let us take a look at one of the most devastating of psychological egoism's arguments: that the very act of helping others, leaving our comfort zone and maybe even risking our life, is done not only with the side effect of feeling good afterward, but specifically so that we will feel good—in other words, a self-serving act. Could that really be true? Every time anyone has gone out of their way to help another living being—a human, a dog, or even a pig—and felt relief and joy that their help made a difference, those acts were actually just another form of egoism? Abraham Lincoln seems to have agreed that it is. A famous story tells of him riding on a mud coach (a type of stagecoach) with a friend. Just as he is explaining that he believes everybody has selfish reasons for his or her actions, they pass by a mudhole where several piglets are drowning. The mother sow is making an awful noise, but she can't help them. Lincoln asks the driver to stop the coach, gets off, wades into the mudhole, brings the pigs out, and returns to the coach. His friend, remembering what Lincoln had just said, asks him, "Now, Abe, where does selfishness come into this little episode?" Lincoln answers, "Why, bless your soul, Ed, that was the very essence of selfishness. I should have had no peace of mind all day had I gone on and left that suffering old sow worrying over those pigs. I did it to get peace of mind, don't you see?"

So Lincoln saved the pigs to benefit himself (and here we thought he was just a nice man). That is, of course, the irony of the story: Lincoln is not known to us as a selfish person. But was his theory right? He may have been lying in claiming that he did his good deed for himself—or he may have been joking—but let us assume that he spoke the truth as he saw it—that he saved the pigs to gain peace of mind for himself. He was of course expressing the view of a psychological egoist. But was it really a "selfish" act? That depends on what you call selfish. Is doing things to benefit yourself always selfish, or does it perhaps depend on what the goal is? Wouldn't there be a difference between saving a pig for its own sake and saving it because you want to eat it for dinner? Most people would say there is a substantial difference between the two. If what you want is to save someone, that is surely different from wanting to hurt someone. Lincoln might, of course, interject that saving the pigs was still in his own self-interest, so it wasn't done for them but for himself—but is that true? Why would it have been in his self-interest to know that the pigs were safe if self-gratification was all he cared about? A selfish person hardly loses sleep over the misery of other human beings, let alone that of a sow. A truly selfish person would not even have noticed drowning pigs—or even drowning children. A person who enjoys helping others is not our usual image of a selfish person; rather, as James Rachels points out, that is exactly how we picture an *unselfish* person. (See Box 4.7 for further discussion of Lincoln's motivation.) If what made Lincoln feel good was the thought of the pigs being safe—for their own sake, not his—then his deed of saving them was not a selfish deed. If what made him feel good was that now he would somehow benefit from saving them other than by just feeling good (such as getting points toward going to Heaven), then it was selfish. And how about if it was both? Suppose he saw a certain advantage in people knowing that he was a good guy who cared about pigs (although that's certainly not part of the original story) but he also liked the thought of the pigs being safe. Then it is still a refutation of psychological egoism because there was an unselfish element in an otherwise selfish act. And here we have reached the level of common sense: Some acts are unselfish, some are selfish, and some are a mixed bag. In the Narratives section you will find a classic sitcom episode about a woman who is accused of being selfish because she feels good about helping others, Phoebe from the television sitcom *Friends*.

Box 4.7 LINCOLN: HUMBLE MAN OR CLEVER JOKESTER?

We might ask how Lincoln could have been unaware of the distinction between caring and not caring that becomes apparent when we consider different kinds of behavior. For an intelligent man, his remarks seem unusually dim. It's possible, of course, that the pig story illustrates Lincoln's true nature: that of a very humble and honest man who does not wish to take credit for having done something good. The story makes him all the more endearing, if that is the case, for indeed we know him as Honest Abe. But there is another possibility—that he was joking. According to legend, Lincoln had a pet pig when he was young, so maybe he had a fondness for pigs, too. Lincoln had a fondness for jokes, and this may have been one of them. Knowing full well that he was doing a nice thing, he made use of *irony* by claiming that rescuing the piglets was nothing but a selfish act. Lincoln scholars may have to decide which version they like better. In any event, Lincoln was speaking as a psychological egoist, regardless of how unselfishly he acted, because he expressed the theory that everyone acts selfishly.

Franck Fotos/Alamy Stock Photo

In Taylorville, IL, there is a statue of Abraham Lincoln in the company of a pig. Not exactly the story of Lincoln saving piglets from drowning, it is supposed to illustrate another pig-related event in which Lincoln, while arguing a case at the courthouse, was bothered by squealing pigs under the floorboards, and requested a "Writ of Quietus" (a ruling to quiet someone) to calm the pigs. In that case Lincoln was apparently joking.

3. The Fallacy of the Suppressed Correlative

As we have seen, psychological egoism presents certain problems because it does not always describe the world in a way that allows us to recognize it. One of its flaws may actually be a problem of *language:* If Lincoln's act of saving the pigs is selfish, what do we then call acts that are *really* selfish? The British philosopher Mary Midgley was extremely critical of the theory of psychological egoism and pointed out that since there is such a difference between what psychological egoists call normal selfish behavior (doing something nice for others so you can gain an advantage) and *really* selfish behavior (doing something hurtful to others so you can gain an advantage), it would be illogical to call both selfish. We should reserve "selfish" for genuine self-absorbed behavior, says Midgley (or, as one of my students remarked, shouldn't there be a moral difference between helping an old lady across the street and stealing her cane?). If we, as critics, can get the psychological egoist to admit that there are degrees of selfishness, in a continuum between extremely selfish over somewhat selfish to very little selfish, we have, in effect, disproven their claim that every act is selfish—because what would we normally call an act that is only selfish in the tiniest degree? *Unselfish.* We have in effect reinvented "unselfish." Changing language to the extent that it goes against our common sense (by claiming that there is no such thing as *unselfish* but that it is acceptable to use the term *less selfish*) does not make psychological egoism correct. If the psychological egoist insists that all acts are selfish in some way, critics of psychological egoism point to the linguistic phenomenon known as the *fallacy of the suppressed correlative.* The correlative of the word *selfish* is *unselfish,* just as the correlative of *light* is *dark;* other pairs are *hot/cold, tall/short,* and so on. It is a psychological as well as a linguistic fact that we understand one term because we understand the other: If everything were dark, we wouldn't understand the meaning of *light,* and neither would we understand the meaning of *dark,* because it is defined by its contrast to light; without the contrast there is no understanding. In other words, a concept without a correlative becomes meaningless. If all acts are selfish, *selfish* has no correlative, and the statement "All acts are selfish" has no meaning. In fact, we could not make such a statement at all if psychological egoism were correct; the concept of selfishness would not exist, since any nonselfish behavior would be unthinkable. So not only does psychological egoism go against common sense and preclude a complete understanding of the full range of human behavior; it also goes against the rules of language. (We return to Midgley below in the section *The Selfish Gene.*)

That may sound like a complex argument, but we actually use it frequently in everyday situations. Here are a few examples of suppressed correlatives, situations in which something becomes meaningless if it doesn't have any opposite: (1) If you use a highlighter in your textbook, you may have found yourself studying a difficult text and highlighting many sentences. After a while, when you look at the pages, you find that you've actually highlighted just about everything. The task of highlighting all of a sudden has become meaningless; now *everything* is highlighted (the highlighted areas have lost their contrast), and that is just the same as not having anything highlighted. (2) At Starbucks a small cup of coffee is called "tall," a medium is called "grande," and a large is called "trenta" (Italian for "thirty"—ounces, presumably). Does the designation "tall" really mean anything anymore when it comes to coffees? (3) Sometimes I hear students plead (as a joke, I hope), "Why can't you just give us all A's?" (whether they are deserved or not). The answer is that (aside from the fact that it wouldn't be right) if everybody in the class or the school or the country got A's, the A would become meaningless, since there would be no lower grade to serve as a contrast. If instructors bowed to the pressure to give only A's or B's, the whole idea of grading would be undermined. (4) And how about the line in the movie *The Incredibles* #1, "If everybody is a superhero, then nobody is a superhero"? Any concept, action, or phenomenon that is extended to cover too broad an area becomes watered down; people who curse all the time drain their words of any impact, so there is no way to emphasize a really bad situation; parents who yell at their children constantly have no voice impact left when the time comes for a yell to be effective; kids who "cry wolf" won't be believed in the end. And the psychological egoist who claims that everyone is selfish can't explain what *selfish* means if no behavior is recognized as unselfish.

Proponents of psychological egoism have responded that unselfishness doesn't actually exist, but you can still have the *concept* of unselfishness, which serves as the correlative of selfishness, even if it is imaginary; but critics of psychological egoism reply that the theory still does not make much sense. If it states that everybody is selfish to the bone, then it is a downright false theory. If it just says everybody has a selfish streak, then it is so trivial that it is not even interesting.

The Selfish-Gene Theory and Its Critics

While psychological egoism is generally considered a psychological as well as a philosophical theory, the notion of selfishness has had its own success within the social sciences. The *selfish-gene theory* arose in the 1970s and became popular to the extent that, for decades, many people have taken its viewpoint as an established truth. This theory was introduced by British evolutionary biologist Richard Dawkins in his book *The Selfish Gene* (1976) and at the time supported by the famous American sociobiologist Edward O. Wilson as a way of explaining, scientifically, why some animals as well as humans behave in an altruistic way. In the spirit of psychological egoism, it is not that humans and animals actually behave selflessly, but that such behavior is an instinctive way to promote the survival not of the individual but of his or her genes. Why would a baboon apparently sacrifice herself to leopards so that her "troop" can make a getaway? Because she is closely related to the troop, and her sacrifice ensures that her genes will survive. Why do dogs wake their owners up in the middle of the night to make sure they get out of the house that's on fire? Because they think their owners are the alpha dogs of their pack, and alpha dogs are related to the lower-status dogs, so their genes will survive. In October 2004 off the coast of New Zealand, a group of one adult lifeguard and three teens were herded together in a tight circle by a pod of dolphins—and they didn't understand why, until they saw a ten-foot white shark trying to approach them. The dolphins circled the humans for 40 minutes until the shark got tired and swam off. The whole event was witnessed by another lifeguard in a boat and by people on the beach a hundred yards away. Some years earlier, outside the coast of Sardinia in the Mediterranean, a fisherman had brought his young son with him to go fishing. The little boy fell overboard, and the father couldn't turn the boat fast enough to reach him in time. But up from the depth came a shadow—an old, wild dolphin known to the locals. He propped the boy up so he could breathe and swam with him on his back to the fishing boat, where his father lifted him to safety. In addition, some dolphins were making a ruckus along the beach after high tide in Australia a few years ago, and people noticed they were circling a certain area. Stranded in the water was a dog, who subsequently was rescued, thanks to the loud dolphins. Did the dolphins deliberately help the dog, or were they attacking him? In the past, particularly in the twentieth century, such speculations were dismissed as romantic notions. Now animal behaviorists are beginning to suspect that there can be a variety of motives behind animal behavior, including some form of selflessness.

What would the selfish-gene theorists say to that? That the dolphins rescuing the swimmers, and the old dolphin rescuing the boy use the same maneuvers to protect their own young, and they can't tell the difference between a human in a wetsuit, a small boy, and dolphin babies. (Dolphins, being mammals, have no gills and can't breathe under water, so the mother dolphin will prop up her newborn baby above water until it breathes on its own.) But few animal behaviorists would claim that dolphins, or any animal for that matter, can't tell the difference between humans and their own species, especially since they're excellent at telling the difference between their own babies and other dolphins' babies. (Male dolphins will often try to kill the offspring of other male dolphins.) This phenomenon is of course not limited to dolphins. Other animals have been known to save animals of a different species, including humans. So could we really be witnessing animals making *moral choices?* We will return to that question later.

Courtesy Newcastle University, UK

Mary Midgley (1919–2018) was a British philosopher specializing in ethics. For years she taught philosophy at the University of Newcastle, and she was known for her vigorous critique of scientific theories attempting to reduce the human spirit to sociobiological elements. She is considered one of Richard Dawkins's most vocal critics. Her books include *Beast and Man: The Roots of Human Nature* (1978), *Heart and Mind: The Varieties of Moral Experience* (1981), *Animals and Why They Matter* (1983), *Wickedness* (1984), and *The Ethical Primate: Humans, Freedom and Morality* (1994). In 2005 her autobiography, *The Owl of Minerva*, was published, and *The Solitary Self: Darwin and the Selfish Gene* came out in 2010. In 2016 she had an article on selfishness and science published in *The Philosophers' Magazine*, "The Mythology of Selfishness," and her final book came out in 2018, *What Is Philosophy For?* Despite her advanced age, Midgley was an active, respected scholar until the very end of her life at 99.

As far as *humans* go, does the selfish-gene theory offer any kind of insight? For the originator of the theory, Richard Dawkins, it explains why people sometimes act unselfishly toward strangers: *We make a mistake*. We are preprogrammed through our evolution to help our genes survive, either in our own person or through our nearest relatives, and in ancient times we used to have close contact only with such relatives, and our altruism would benefit only them. But times have changed, and we are now in a complex world of strangers, but our genetic programming makes us act altruistically as if we're still living with a small group of relatives. In his book *The God Delusion* (2006), Dawkins says, "We can no more help ourselves feeling pity when we see a weeping unfortunate (who is unrelated and unable to reciprocate) than we can help ourselves feeling lust for a member of the opposite sex (who may be infertile or otherwise unable to reproduce). Both are misfirings, Darwinian mistakes: blessed, precious mistakes." So Dawkins isn't saying that we shouldn't be altruistic toward strangers—he thinks it is rather wonderful that we are capable of doing such a thing. But he says that, biologically, it makes no sense—it is a misdirection of an original biological purpose.

Many philosophers believe the selfish-gene theory creates more problems than it solves, and even Edward O. Wilson has changed his mind: in an article in the journal *Nature* he explains that he no longer sees the driving force as kin selection (a "selfish gene"), but rather a battle between individual selection (selfishness) and group selection (altruism), regardless of whether the group contains any relatives. This enables Wilson to get beyond the sticky question of why we (and other animals) would choose to help individuals in our group which we're not related to if all we try to do is promote our genes into the next generation. Dawkins, however, continues to maintain that it is a built-in urge to promote one's genes that is the basic explanation of all behavior whether it looks altruistic or not. However, when humans behave altruistically toward strangers, it is often because of the very fact that they are strangers—we don't confuse them with relatives. On the contrary, we may deliberately *choose* to treat them *as if* they are relatives, which is something completely different. The British philosopher Mary Midgley, whom you'll remember from the previous section in this chapter, was a vocal critic of the selfish-gene theory as well as a critic of psychological egoism. Advocating the old principle of parsimony, or *Occam's razor* (choosing the simpler explanation over a more complex one if the simpler explanation works as well or better), Midgley suggests that a much simpler explanation exists for our altruistic behavior than some selfish gene: It's the fact that we've all grown up in groups with other people, and in most cases the people who raised us loved us and cared about our well-being. And when we raise children, we care about them for their sake too. So we have a built-in capacity for caring for our family—and in our human society we just extend that capacity to strangers, who become *honorary relatives* for a time. What makes this different from a version of the selfish-gene theory is that we extend our caring capacity to strangers not for *our* sake (to perpetuate our genes) but for *theirs* (because we care about how they feel), and we make a conscious choice to do so. And let's not forget that most people actually don't choose to go out of their way to help strangers—because most people are probably mostly selfish! If it had been a true instinct to help strangers because we subconsciously believe them to be our relatives, then people would be helping strangers left and right. Dawkins himself has said that Midgley misunderstood his theory: it isn't about people or animals making mistakes about relatives, but a biological hardwiring being misdirected. But here we should remember the argument against psychological egoism that you read earlier in the chapter, that if a concept becomes so broad that it has no opposite (the fallacy of the suppressed correlative), then the concept has become useless. So if all behavior is selfish (instinctually), but some selfish behavior involves altruism, then haven't we watered down the meaning of selfishness?

Here a brief conceptual analysis may be helpful—something that apparently both Dawkins and Midgley have missed, or deliberately disregarded. Dawkins is a biologist, while Midgley is a philosopher, and as such they don't necessarily have the same associations to the same words. *For Dawkins, "selfish" is not a moral, but a biological term,* simply meaning a hard-wired instinct for preservation of the organism or its genetic material—a descriptive term. However, *for Midgley the word "selfish" is a moral term,* and comes burdened with the entire philosophical and social tradition of normative judgment, above all the assumption that if you are being selfish, it is a *moral choice* and you can be blamed for it, because you could choose to be less selfish or unselfish instead. For Midgley, Dawkins is depriving us of one of the finest human traits: the ability to make a conscious choice to help others, even at the cost of our own comfort. As such, there was no way Dawkins and Midgley were going to agree, because their vocabularies are fundamentally different. So Dawkins could be right in his way, that we have a preservation instinct which we share with other animals, and since we are still in our brains the tribal people who are by and large related to everyone in our immediate group, we reach out and help strangers (which is nice) because we're hard-wired to help our relatives. But Midgley could be right in that we also make *moral choices*; sometimes we choose not to help anyone, stranger or relative, and sometimes we engage in elaborate acts of compassion toward total strangers, because we choose to do so, making them as if they were part of our own family for a while. In an op-ed piece from 2016, "The Mythology of Selfishness," published by the Grand Old Lady of British philosophy at the age of 96, Midgley argued that the attempt at explaining human behavior as a predictable evolutionary pattern determined by survival—such as Dawkins's selfish-gene theory—must fail, because of its inability to take human choice and preference into account. She observes in her paper that several biologists such as David Sloane Wilson and Edward O. Wilson (but not Dawkins) have switched gears and are now arguing that it isn't any atomistic, instinctual push for genetic survival that drives the early human communities, but a group selection that favors *social* human existence.

Once in a while we follow stories in the media involving kidnapped and murdered young people and children. Such an interest in the fate of these victims may illustrate this "honorary relative" bestowment: When children go missing, and the story reaches the level of the national media, we frequently see that total strangers volunteer to search for the child, even coming from other states to join in the searches. And many of us keep track of the searches online and on TV with a strange urgency, as if we actually know the families. It may be just part of the Reality Show phenomenon (see Chapter 2), but Mary Midgley may have a point: Occasionally that curiosity becomes one of the finer emotions we are capable of, when a story touches our hearts more deeply than an ordinary news story, and we "adopt" the missing young person as an honorary relative, caring about the welfare of a total stranger, if only for a while.

Ethical Egoism and Ayn Rand's Objectivism

We have already heard amazing stories about heroic acts in this chapter. Here are a few more, with particularly sad and meaningless outcomes: In the winter of 2016, North Carolina resident, 26-year-old single dad Jefferson Heavner was shot to death by the man he was trying to help, a driver whose car had spun out and gotten stuck in a snowstorm. The driver was drunk and apparently perceived Heavner as a threat. Heavner and his family had a tradition of going out in blizzards to help stranded motorists. At a Waffle House restaurant in Florida in April 2019, a man, Craig Brewer, was handing out $20 bills and paying for other people's meals, presumably out of the goodness of his heart. The news media called him a Good Samaritan. But within minutes things went terribly wrong: A woman apparently felt slighted, and started arguing with Brewer; a friend of hers left the restaurant and came back with a handgun, and shot Brewer dead. And finally a story of generosity that didn't involve violence, but was tragic nevertheless: A popular high school principal in New Jersey, Derrick Nelson, decided to donate bone marrow to a complete stranger in need, a 14-year-old teen in France, but died as a result of the ordinarily safe surgery. To these sad stories, the ethical egoist would say that, in effect, these people we call heroes did the wrong thing. For the ethical egoist there is only one rule: *Look after yourself.* The ethical egoist would say you risk throwing your life away if you try to help strangers. Your only moral duty is to yourself and your own life.

Here we should make sure that we have our terms straight. This theory is called ethical egoism simply because it is an ethical theory, a *normative* theory about how we *ought* to behave (in contrast to psychological egoism, which claims to know how we actually *do* behave). The theory implies that we ought to be selfish. Or, to put it more gently, we ought to be *self-interested.* Calling the theory "ethical" does not suggest there might be a decent way to be selfish; it just means ethical egoism is a theory that advocates egoism as a moral rule.

You Should Look After Yourself

Glaucon insisted that if you don't take advantage of a situation, you are foolish. Hobbes claimed that it makes good sense to look after yourself, and morality is a result of that self-interest: If I mistreat others, they may mistreat me, so I resolve to behave myself. That is a rather twisted version of the Golden Rule (Do unto others as you would have them do unto you; see Box 4.8). It is twisted because it is peculiarly slanted toward our own self-interest. The reason we should treat others the way we would like to be treated is that it gives us a good chance of receiving just such treatment; we do it for ourselves, not for others. So the ethical egoist may certainly decide to help another human being in need—not for the sake of the other, but to ensure that "what goes around, comes around." The Golden Rule usually emphasizes others, but for the ethical egoist it emphasizes the self. With ethical egoism we encounter a certain phenomenon for the first time in this book: an ethical theory that focuses on the *consequences* of one's actions. Any theory that looks solely to consequences of actions is known as a *consequentialist theory;* the consequences that ethical egoism stipulates are good consequences for the person taking the action. However, we can imagine other kinds of consequentialist theories, such as one that advocates good consequences for as many people as possible. Such a theory is discussed in Chapter 5.

Box 4.8 THE GOLDEN RULE WITH VARIATIONS

Fifty yard line!
I bet you thought
it was a silly necklace...

Colin Hayes/www.CartoonStock.com

Most people know the Golden Rule: Do unto others as you would have them do unto you, or treat others as you would like to be treated. It is often attributed to Jesus Christ; the Gospel of Matthew cites him as saying, "Therefore all things whatsoever ye would that men should do to you, do ye even so to them: for this is the law and the prophets" (7:12). The law referred to is in Leviticus 19:18 in the Bible (the Old Testament): ". . . thou shalt love thy neighbor as thyself." In the later Talmud, the collection of civil and religious laws in Orthodox Judaism, we read that "what is hateful to you, do not to your fellow man. This is the law: all the rest is commentary" (Shabbat 31a). And other traditions have similar sayings. Brahmanism teaches, "This is the sum of Dharma [duty]: Do naught unto others which would cause you pain if done to you" (*Mahabharata* 5:1517). In Buddhism it reads like this: "Hurt not others in ways that you yourself would find hurtful" (*Udànavarga* 5:18). Islam teaches that "none of you [truly] believes until he wishes for his brother what he wishes for himself" (number 13 of Imam "Al-Nawawi's Forty Hadiths"). In the American Indian tradition, the great leader Black Elk extended the rule to all living beings: "All things are our relatives; what we do to everything, we do to our-

selves. All is really One." And the Chinese philosopher Confucius (551–479 B.C.E.) is known to have taught his students this version, taken from *The Doctrine of the Mean, The Four Books:* "What you do not like when done to yourself, do not do to others." This is sometimes called the "Silver Rule."

The rule teaches that to find a blueprint for treating others, we should imagine how we would or would not like to be treated. (You can see an example of that in the cartoon in this box!) Ethical egoists don't read it that way, however; they read it as a rule for protecting yourself and being as comfortable as possible. The way to avoid trouble with others is to treat them as you'd want to be treated—the path of least resistance. The emphasis on *others* is not a given within the rule. This is the aspect of *prudence* connected with the Golden Rule. But as we see in Chapter 5, the Golden Rule is also used as a blueprint for general happiness, one's own as well as others'. In this case, it is concern for *the other person* that underlies the rule.

Recognizing the wisdom of the Golden Rule is perhaps the most important early stage in civilization because it implies that we see others as similar to ourselves and that we see ourselves as deserving no treatment that is better than what others get (although we would generally prefer it—we're not saints). However, the Golden Rule may not be the ultimate rule to live by because (as we discuss further in Chapter 11) others may *not want* to be treated as *you'd* like to be treated. (You can see an example of that in the cartoon on p. 167!) Then, according to some thinkers, the "Platinum Rule" ought to kick in: Treat others as *they* want to be treated! Proponents of the Golden Rule say that this takes the universal appeal out of the rule. The spark of moral genius in the rule is precisely that we are *similar* in our human nature—not that we would all like to have things our way.

Ethical egoists are themselves quite divided about whether the theory tells you to do *what you want* without regard for others or *what is good for you* without regard for others. The latter version seems to appeal to common sense because, in the long run, just looking for instant gratification is hardly going to make you happy or live longer. Saying that one ought to look after oneself need not, of course, mean that one should annoy others whenever possible, step on their toes, or deliberately neglect their interests. It simply suggests that one should do what will be of long-term benefit to oneself, such as exercising, eating healthy food, avoiding repetitive argumentative situations, and so forth. Even paying one's taxes might be added to the list. In addition, it suggests that other people's interests are of no importance. If you might advance your own interests by helping others, then by all means help others, but only if you are the main beneficiary. It is fine to help your children get ahead in school, because you love them and that love is a gratifying emotion for you. But there is no reason to lend a hand to your neighbor's children unless you like them or you achieve gratification through your actions.

This interpretation—that the theory tells us to do whatever will benefit ourselves—results in a rewriting of the Golden Rule because, obviously, it is not always the case that you *will* get the same treatment from others that you give to them. Occasionally you might get away with not treating others decently, because they may never know that you are the source of the bad treatment they are receiving. Ethical egoism tells you that it is perfectly all right to treat others in a way that is to your advantage and not to theirs as long as you can be certain that you will get away with it. In the Narratives section you will be introduced to one of the classic American novels exploring and exposing ethical egoism: John Steinbeck's *The Winter of Our Discontent*.

Ayn Rand and the Virtue of Selfishness

It is sometimes the case among philosophers that if someone subscribes to a theory that is not shared by most colleagues, politically or religiously, then that thinker risks losing credibility in the philosophical community. So is that why the Russian-born American philosopher and novelist Ayn Rand (1905–1982) has such a low standing among philosophers in this country, or is it simply because her philosophy is untenable or confused? Ayn Rand was born in Russia as Alyssa Rosenbaum and immigrated to the United States at the age of twenty-one because she was deeply dissatisfied with the new Communist regime and its Marxist philosophy, the October Revolution having happened in 1917. Why the United States? Because she considered it the most moral and least Marxist country in the world. Her viewpoints were controversial from the beginning of her career which, other than being a novelist, also included being a playwright.

Ayn Rand is a good example of a philosopher who channels her thoughts into a work of fiction—or a novelist who uses philosophical arguments within the plot of her novels, and as such she is a fine candidate for inclusion in this book where we occasionally look at stories expressing moral viewpoints and debates. But that in itself may actually have been a point in her disfavor among other writers and philosophers: In the mid-twentieth century there were very few American thinkers (contrary to Europe) who also wrote novels, or novelists who wrote philosophical thoughts (in Chapter 3 you met one of them—John Steinbeck). Being a novelist was considered a disqualifying element if one wanted to be considered a philosopher. Also, she was a *woman* writer, and at the time that was a second problem. And to top it off, she neither had an advanced philosophy degree (although she had been an undergraduate philosophy student in Russia), nor was she a *liberal* like most other philosophers (which *per se* shouldn't have counted against her standing as a thinker—there are excellent nonliberal thinkers in the world).

So what was her thinking that so many found unacceptable? She chose to label her primary philosophy **Objectivism**, and it flows through her nonfictional writings as well as in her novels such as the two most famous ones, *Atlas Shrugged* and *The Fountainhead*. In her works of fiction she lets her main characters explain or exemplify the core values of her own theory, such as in *Atlas Shrugged*, where the elusive John Galt addresses the world (in a speech covering sixty pages). Galt has inspired an entire resistance movement among factory owners, entrepreneurs, investors, and inventors, persuading them to go on strike and drop out of society, one after the other, causing financial chaos. He has stayed in the shadows, contacting each person individually, but toward the end he stands forth and explains his philosophy.

"You have heard no concepts of morality but the mystical or the social. You have been taught that morality is a code of behavior imposed on you by whim, the whim of a supernatural power or the whim of society, to serve God's purpose or your neighbor's welfare, to please an authority beyond the grave or else next door—but not to serve *your* life or pleasure. Your pleasure, you have been taught, is to be found in immorality, your interests would best be served by evil, and any moral code must be designed not *for* you, but *against* you, not to further your life, but to drain it.

For centuries, the battle of morality was fought between those who claimed that your life belongs to God and those who claimed that it belongs to your neighbors—between those who preached that the good is self-sacrifice for the sake of ghosts in heaven and those who preached that the good is self-sacrifice for the sake of incompetents on earth. And no one came to say that your life belongs to you and that the good is to live it . . ."

Rand is best known for her novels, but she also published numerous nonfiction works, including an anthology, *The Virtue of Selfishness*, in which she had authored the primary piece, "The Ethics of Emergencies." In that text she defends the concept of **self-interest** and claims that people have a right, even a duty, to look after themselves and seek their own happiness, and that it is "moral cannibalism" to advocate selflessness as an ideal where people are supposed to feel obliged to help those who have no wish to help themselves—in Rand's words, "moochers and leeches." For Rand, altruism, instead of elevating the human spirit to its finest level, pulls people down into a perverted value system. From "The Ethics of Emergencies,"

Everett Collection/Shutterstock

Ayn Rand (1905–1982), the Russian-born American philosopher and writer, developed the theory of *objectivism*, which stresses the right of the individual to keep the fruits of his or her labors and not be held responsible for the welfare of others. She is today best known for her novels, although her philosophy is also gaining recognition as an original twentieth-century contribution.

By elevating the issue of helping others into the central and primary issue of ethics, altruism has destroyed the concept of any authentic benevolence or good will among men. It has indoctrinated men with the idea that to value another human being is an act of selflessness, this implying that a man can have no personal interest in others—that *to value* another means *to sacrifice* oneself—that any love, respect or admiration a man may feel for others is not and cannot be a source of his own enjoyment, but is a threat to his existence, a sacrificial blank check signed over to his loved ones.

Instead, says Rand, we must return to the recognition that an act that focuses on creating happiness for ourselves—and for those we love, because that, too, will make us happy—is of the highest moral value. The duty of the government is to be reduced to a fiscally (financially) conservative *laissez-faire* (hands-off) policy where all it should be engaged in is protecting citizens from dangers coming from other nations and upholding law and order; in the private world of business, the government should stay away and taxes should be reduced to merely cover the basic duties of the government. Any social programs should be financed through charity. Individually, people should feel free to engage in whatever behavior they see fit that will enhance their lives, including helping strangers if that is a joy to them, but it would be far better to spend one's efforts and money helping those one loves, because that will surely mean more to oneself in the long run—in other words, the very core of the philosophy of ethical egoism. Today some members of the Libertarian Party claim intellectual kinship with Ayn Rand, and former Chair of the Federal Reserve, economist Alan Greenspan, once one of the most powerful men in the nation, is reported to respect and admire her philosophy, as do many other conservative culture personalities.

Critics in her own time and in subsequent decades have been quick to point out that (1) Objectivism is nothing but a **blatant defense of capitalism** and stark selfishness. Rand would have agreed to the first part which she saw nothing wrong with, but would have refused to call selfishness "stark"—in her view the world will be better off with everyone minding their own business. Another objection is that (2) Objectivism/ethical egoism simply **doesn't create a better world**—on the contrary, it promotes a ruthless world of Haves and Have-nots, where the Haves prey on the Have-nots and each other to the extent that they can (you may want to compare that to Hobbes's view of life in the State of Nature before the Social Contract). Rand herself would have denied this, pointing to the failed experiments of socialist nations where the mandated shared wealth created nothing but (in her view) lazy, dissatisfied, dishonest people. But (3) if we look at her basic argument that you must either accept fundamental altruism where your only moral duty is to give everything away and lay down your life for others, or accept Objectivism with its liberating right to keep what you earn, take care of yourself and your own, and work for your own happiness without feeling guilty, then we see that she is falling into a common logical fallacy (see Chapter 1), the **fallacy of bifurcation**/false dilemma/false dichotomy: the "Either-Or" which excludes any third option. Many otherwise good thinkers have in their enthusiasm committed the same error, but that is no excuse: There are other alternatives than believing your life is worthless unless you donate it to others and seeing your own right to your own happiness as the only moral duty.

Rand's philosophy which she deemed so clear and incontrovertible that it deserved the name Objectivism was enormously popular some decades ago, especially among college students. Then it faded away. But after the financial crisis in 2008 Ayn Rand's thoughts and books were in vogue again in a major revival with much activity in the social media, her novels shooting to the top of the bestseller charts, and in 2011–14 the trilogy of movies based on her mammoth novel *Atlas Shrugged* came out, in limited release, to mixed reviews. The movie had been in the planning stages under different directors since 1975, and Rand herself had been involved in writing a screenplay. Some philosophers deplore the fact that Rand's theories are once again in circulation, resulting in nothing but muddled thinking. Others welcome the opportunity to have some good discussions and perhaps see things from a different perspective.

Problems with Ethical Egoism

Let us return now to Glaucon and his rings. He assumes that not only will the scoundrel take advantage of a ring that can make him invisible, but so will the decent man, and, furthermore, we would call them both fools if they didn't. A theory of psychological egoism, therefore, can also contain a normative element: ethical egoism (which tells us how we *ought* to behave). Of course, it is hard to see what the point is if we can't help doing what we're supposed to do.

At the end of Glaucon's speech, the reader expects Socrates to dispatch the theory of egoism with a quick blow. The answer, however, is a long time coming; as a matter of fact, Plato designed the rest of his *Republic* as a roundabout answer to Glaucon. In the end, Socrates' answer is, The unjust person can't be happy because happiness consists of a good harmony, a balance between the three parts of the soul: *reason, willpower (spirit),* and *desire.* Reason is supposed to dominate willpower, and willpower, desire. If desire or willpower dominates the other two, we have a sick person, and a sick person can't be happy by definition, says Socrates. Look at the pyramid on page 171. Picture that image as a metaphor for the just person in harmony, a soul in balance, very stable. Now imagine an unjust (selfish) person, steered by his or her desires rather than reason: an inverted pyramid, balancing on its tip! Hardly a stable figure—an unjust person headed for a downfall. We will return to this theory in the Primary Readings of this chapter, with an excerpt from Plato's *Republic.*

In considering the question, Why be just? we must consider justice in terms of the whole society, not just the individual. We can't argue for justice on the basis of individual situations but only in general terms. That makes the question "Why be just?" more reasonable because we don't look at individual cases but at an overall picture in which justice and well-being are interrelated. For Socrates and Plato, being just is part of "the good life," and true happiness cannot be attained without justice.

To the modern reader there is something curiously bland and evasive about those answers. Surely unjust persons can be disgustingly happy—they may seem to us to have sick souls, but they certainly don't act as if they are aware of it or suffer any ill effects from it. The answer to this—that being selfish is *just plain wrong in itself*—is not emphasized by Socrates. For a modern person it seems reasonable to be "just" out of respect for the law or perhaps because that is the right thing to do, but Socrates mentions this only briefly; it is a concern that belongs to a much later time period than the one in which he lived. The highest virtue for the ancient Greeks was, on the whole, ensuring the well-being of the community, and that well-being remained the bottom line more than any abstract moral issue of right and wrong. Today we know this social theory as *communitarianism*. Because justice was best for the state in the final evaluation, justice was a value in itself. In the end, Socrates' answer evokes self-interest and urges us to discern truth from appearance: If you are unjust, your soul will suffer, and so will your community. Furthermore, your community may shun you, ostracize you, banish you (which was common practice in ancient Greece), and if you are nothing without your community, then what will become of you? The interesting implication is that Socrates is saying to Glaucon that the unjust man is out of balance, thus unhealthy, and thus unhappy, because he will be excluded from his network

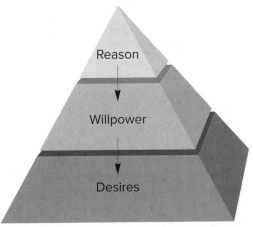

Socrates' answer to Glaucon's suggestion that the unjust man is happier than the just man rests on his notion that a happy person is in balance and without moral virtue (see Chapter 8): you can't be happy, so the unjust man is out of balance, hence sick, and therefore unhappy. Socrates' concept of a morally good, "just" person involves having the right relationship between one's reason, one's willpower, and one's desires. As this illustration shows, reason should control willpower, and together, reason and willpower should control one's desires. And if we flip the pyramid on its head, balancing on its tip, we get Glaucon's unjust man whose desires run his life and who can only keep balancing for so long before toppling over into unhappiness. In Chapter 8 you will see this concept of justice and moral goodness expanded to cover Plato's political theory as well as his idea of virtue.

of friends and associates. That attitude, ironically, may have cost Socrates his life, because he refused to leave his community and flee Athens when he was accused of crimes against the state.

Today communitarianism is alive and well in the United States—it is a political theory best illustrated by the African proverb "It takes a village to raise a child." In other words, individuals are part of the community and derive their identity from that community—and the community members share a responsibility toward one another. A professed contemporary communitarian is former Secretary of State Hillary Clinton, the Democratic nominee in the 2016 presidential election.

Socrates' attitude may not impress people seeking self-gratification (who are unlikely to be concerned about the effects of their actions on their souls or on the people around them), but it may have some impact on people seeking long-term self-interest. It still rests on an empirical assumption, however, that sooner or later you must pay the piper—that is, atone for your wrongdoing. History, though, is full of "bad guys" who have gone to their graves rich and happy. The religious argument that you will go to hell or suffer a miserable next incarnation if you are concerned only with yourself is not really an argument against *egoism* because it still asks you to look after yourself, even to the point of using others for the purpose of ensuring a pleasant afterlife (treat others decently and you shall be saved).

The one type of argument against ethical egoism that has most appealed to scholars insists that **ethical egoism is self-contradictory.** If you are supposed to look after yourself and your colleague is supposed to look after herself, and if looking after yourself will mean hacking her computer then you and she will be working at cross-purposes: Your duty will be to hack her computer and her duty will be to protect her files. We can't have a moral theory that says one's duty should be something that conflicts with someone else's duty, so ethical egoism is therefore inconsistent.

Few ethical egoists find that argument convincing, because they don't agree that we can't have a moral theory that gives a green light to different concepts of duty. Such a view assumes that ethical egoism benefits everyone, even when each person does only what is in his or her best interest. Occasionally, ethical egoism assumes just that: We should look after ourselves and mind our own business, because meddling in other people's affairs is a violation of privacy; they will not like our charity, they will hate our superiority, and we won't know what is best for them anyway. So, along those lines, **we should stay out of other people's affairs because it is best for everybody.** The political theory resulting from this point of view is known as *laissez-faire,* the hands-off policy. Political theorists, however, are quick to point out that laissez-faire is by no means an egoistic theory, because it has everybody's best interests at heart. That is precisely what is wrong with the idea that we should adopt ethical egoism for the reason that it will be good for everybody: It may be true that if we all look after ourselves, we'll all be happier—but who is the beneficiary of that idea? Not "I," but "everybody," so this version is, in fact, no longer a moral theory of egoism but something else.

Another argument against ethical egoism is that **it carries no weight as a solver of moral conflicts:** If you and I disagree about the correct course of action, who is to say who is right? If you favor the course of action that is to your advantage and I favor the course of action that is to my advantage, then there is no common ground. But the ethical egoist generally answers in the same way as to the charge that ethical egoism is self-contradictory: It never claimed to be a theory of consensus in all approaches, merely in the basic approach—that everyone ought to look after himself or herself.

A better argument against the conceptual consistency of ethical egoism is this: **Ethical egoism doesn't work in practice.** Remember that the theory says all people ought to look out for themselves—not merely that *I* should look out for *myself.* But suppose you set out to look after your own self-interests and advocate that others do the same; within a short while you will realize that your rule is *not* going to be to your advantage, because others will be out there grabbing for themselves, and you will have fierce competition. You might decide that the smart thing to do is to advocate not that all people look out for themselves but that all people look after one another while keeping quiet about your own intention of breaking the rule whenever possible. That would be the prudent thing to do, and it probably would work quite well. The only problem is that this is not a legitimate moral theory because, for one thing, it carries a contradiction. It means you must claim to support one principle and act according to another one—in other words, it requires you to be dishonest. Also, a moral theory, in this day and age, has to be able to be extended to everybody; we can't uphold a theory that says it is okay for me to do something because I'm *me,* but not for you just because you're *not me*—that would be assuming that I should have privileges based on the mere fact that I'm *me.*

Logical attacks on ethical egoism have a persuasive power for some—as logical arguments rightly should have. However, perhaps the most forceful argument against ethical egoism involves an *emotional* component. Often, philosophers have been afraid to appeal to emotions because emotions have been considered irrelevant. But as philosophers such as Martha Nussbaum, Philippa Foot, Philip Hallie, and James Rachels point out, what is a moral sense without the involvement of our feelings? Feelings need not be irrational—they are often quite rational responses to our experiences (see Chapter 1). And what seems such an affront to most people is the **apparent callousness of an ethical egoist:** Other people's pain simply doesn't matter as a moral imperative.

One example may speak louder than theoretical speculations: the murder of seven-year-old Sherrice Iverson in a casino restroom in the town of Prim, Nevada. She was being stalked by a young man, Jeremy Strohmeyer from Berkeley, and security cameras showed him following her into the ladies' room. He came out, but she never did. She was found later, murdered. Strohmeyer's friend David knew about the crime taking place, heard the screams, and may even have witnessed it. He never tried to stop his friend, nor did he alert casino security, nor did he turn in his friend afterward.

Psychologically, both college students may have been warped and damaged, but David had quite a rational grasp of the situation and a straightforward explanation for why he didn't step in. It is debatable whether David was an ethical egoist or a moral subjectivist. In an interview he said, "I'm not going to get upset over somebody else's life. I just worry about myself first. I'm not going to lose sleep over somebody else's problems." He seemed to be recommending selfishness, not the tolerance of moral subjectivism's "to each his or her own." If so, is that the kind of practical expression of a moral theory that we should think is legitimate, just because it allows everyone else to be selfish too? Isn't this a case in which we are allowed to feel moral outrage over someone's inhumanity? Why, indeed, should we lose sleep over someone else's problems? *Because they are fellow human beings.*

Perhaps this is a good time to revisit Socrates' argument that the unjust person can't be happy because he (or she) will be socially unacceptable. According to anecdotal reports from Berkeley students, David was given the cold shoulder by other students on campus, although he was not indicted for any crimes. And who is to say whether Socrates might not be right—that being shunned by one's community isn't, in fact, a cause of imbalance and regret in the heart of the person who has transgressed against the moral standards because of selfishness?

Being Selfless: Levinas's Ideal Altruism Versus Singer's Reciprocal Altruism

Now that you have been introduced to the two theories of egoism, including their strong and weak points, explaining human moral behavior as fundamentally selfish (descriptively), and prescribing what human moral behavior ought to be: selfish (normatively), it is time we look at the completely opposite theory: **altruism**, the theory that the only moral duty we have is to look to the needs of other people. Altruism (literally "Other-ism," from Latin *alter* meaning "other") can be viewed as the antidote to both psychological egoism, because it says that is certainly is both possible *and* right to look after other people's welfare and interests for their sake, not just for ours, and to ethical egoism, because it rejects the entire premise that it is morally good to focus on one's own needs. Altruism is thus the theory that would support the actions of those who sacrifice their time, comfort, and in some cases their lives to help others, from the firefighters and police officers during the terrorist attacks of September 11, 2001, to individuals such as Liviu Librescu, Victoria Soto, Jonathan Smith, and Dennis Nelson mentioned previously.

Some of those people we like to call heroes probably went into the perilous situation with the expectation and hope that they might survive, but someone who throws himself or herself on a hand grenade about to explode in order to help their fellow soldiers, or maybe even civilian strangers, is probably aware, at least for a split second, that this is probably their final act. Most of us, despite the persuasive arguments from psychological egoism, admire the fortitude and selflessness of somebody who chooses to die for others. But what about those who sacrifice their lives in a greater cause that involves *taking the lives* of innocent strangers, such as the hijackers of the planes on September 11, 2001, or suicide bombers?

The Western mindset considers self-sacrifice to be noble. Then why do most of us not consider terrorist acts noble? Because self-sacrifice is usually regarded as an act wherein a person dies trying to *help* others, not one that involves deliberately killing innocent people. To discuss this issue further you may want to go directly to Chapter 13, where we address the question of terrorism—but you may also want to consider the concept of *group egoism:* extending your self-interest to the group you belong to, so that if you could help the group survive by giving up an advantage or even sacrificing yourself, then (theoretically) you'd be willing to do that.

A group egoist would not consider members of other groups valuable or as having claims as legitimate as those of one's own group. Suicide bombers do not have the interest of all at heart—just the interests of their own group—at the cost of others.

The traditional definition of altruism is what we today label **ideal (or extreme) altruism**: *Everybody ought to give up his or her own self-interest for others.* In that case we might want to complain (as Ayn Rand did) that we have only one life to live, and why should we let the "moochers and leeches" drain our life away? If we let them take advantage of us, they surely will. Our lives are not things to be thrown away. Only a few philosophers and a few religions have ever held such an extreme altruistic theory. One person in the late twentieth century who did was the Lithuanian-French philosopher Emmanuel Levinas (1906–1995), whom you will meet in Chapter 10. For Levinas, the Other (another human being, the stranger) is always more important than you yourself are (which also means that you are important, as a stranger and an Other, to everyone else), and you should always put the needs of the Other ahead of your own. What readers of Levinas find so remarkable is that he, as a Lithuanian Jew, lost his entire family in the Holocaust and almost lost his own life, and even so (or perhaps because of his wartime experiences), he became a champion of the idea that we should always look after other people, regardless of whether they are friends or strangers. He suggested that we look into the eyes of the stranger and recognize their humanity and vulnerability, and ask ourselves, "How can I help?" People who knew him have said that this is how he lived his own life. But Levinas is an exception among modern thinkers; usually there is a realistic recognition of the fact that humans are apt to ask what's in it for them. (See Box 4.9 for a discussion of psychological and ethical altruism.)

Box 4.9 PSYCHOLOGICAL AND ETHICAL ALTRUISM

The term *altruism* comes from the Latin *alter,* meaning "other." The version of altruism that we are discussing in this chapter is sometimes known as ethical altruism—not because there is a form of altruism that is *un*ethical, but simply because philosophers have seen a parallel to ethical egoism: "Everyone *ought* to disregard his or her own interests for the sake of others." In other words, ethical altruism is a normative theory, like its opposite, ethical egoism. But is there also a counterpart to psychological egoism, *psychological altruism*? I'll let you be the judge of that. As psychological egoism, a descriptive theory, claims that everyone is selfish at heart, psychological altruism would claim that everyone is unselfish at heart: "Everyone always disregards his or her own interests for the sake of others." Now who would hold such a theory? Not many, since it seems to fly in the face of the facts: We know very well that not everyone in this world is caring and unselfish.

As a matter of fact, one might speculate that psychological altruism was invented by a philosopher with a sense of symmetry, just to have a matching pair of altruisms to compare the two forms of egoism with. But if psychological altruism is redefined in the following way, "There is something good and caring deep down in every human being," then the theory sounds quite familiar and plausible to many people.

The concoction of psychological altruism may not reflect any actual moral theory, but it does teach an interesting lesson in ethics: If we think psychological altruism is unrealistic and makes no sense, then we also have to criticize psychological egoism for the same reason, because the theories are based on the same logic and are vulnerable to the same criticisms! Several of astute students at Mesa College have pointed this little tidbit out, and I'm happy to share it with you.

Ideal altruism seems to imply that there is something inherently *wrong* with acting to benefit oneself, and if that is the case, it will never become a widely accepted moral theory because it will work only for saints, or as Larissa MacFarquhar calls them in her book *Strangers Drowning,* "radical do-gooders" who give up everything and even set their own families' needs aside to help strangers. While such sacrifices can be admirable, the apparent humility of some radical altruists sometimes masks a pride in all the good they do and the sacrifices they make that doesn't really belong within our concept of altruism, and brings to mind the argument from psychological egoism that if something makes you feel good, it's selfish (which we have of course dismissed above, but that doesn't mean it can't sometimes be true). Those of you who are familiar with the television series *The Good Place* may recall the character of Doug Forcett, who spends every minute of every day doing good things for others, as well as for the planet. But he doesn't do them because he cares about others—he does good deeds because he wants to earn points to get to the "Good Place" when he dies. So is he really being completely selfless? Here we have to consider not only actions, but also intentions.

According to the Australian philosopher Peter Singer, there is another way of viewing altruism, a much more realistic and rational way: Looking after the interests of others makes sense because, overall, everyone benefits from it. This moderate, limited version of altruism is sometimes called **reciprocal altruism** (or Golden Rule altruism): You are ready to place others' interests ahead of your own, especially in emergencies, and you expect them to do the same for you. Philosophers are in disagreement over whether this position actually deserves the name of altruism.

In *The Expanding Circle* (1981), Singer suggests that egoism is, in fact, more costly than altruism. He presents a new version of a classic example, known as the prisoner's dilemma. Imagine two Pleistocene hunters being surprised by a saber-toothed cat, about 10,000 years ago. They obviously both want to flee, but (let us suppose) they also care for each other. If they both flee, one will be picked off and eaten, so there is only a 50-50 percent chance of survival. If one flees and one stays and fights, the fleeing one will live but the fighting one will die. But if both stay and fight, there is a chance that they can fight off the cat, and increase the survival odds beyond 50/50. So it is actually in the interest of both of them to stay together rather than selfishly run away, and all the more so if they care for each other. Singer's point is that evolution would favor such an arrangement, because trustworthy partners would be viewed as better than ones who leave you behind to get eaten, and they would be selected in future partnerships—so this would also involve a *social* advantage. If you are an egoist and you manage to get picked as a partner by an altruist, you will be the one who benefits from the situation (the altruist is sure to stay, and you'll be able to get away). This will work only a few times, however; after a while the altruist will be wise to you and your kind. In the end, then, it is in your own self-interest not to be too self-interested.

This argument actively defeats not only the everyday variety of ethical egoism that says you ought to do what you want—because in the end that will not improve your survival odds—but also the more sophisticated *rational ethical egoism* that requires us to think of what is to our advantage in the long run. If we look toward our own advantage exclusively, we may not be optimizing our chances, as the example of the hunters shows. Being capable of taking others' interests into consideration actually improves our own survival odds.

Why is this viewpoint not just another version of the ethical egoist's credo of looking after yourself? Because it involves **someone else's interests** too. It says that there is nothing wrong with keeping an eye out for yourself, so long as it doesn't happen at the expense of someone else's interests. In other words, the solution may not be myself *or* others, but myself *and* others. This idea, incorporated in the moral theory of *utilitarianism,* will be explored in the next chapter. Peter Singer, himself a utilitarian, also advocates what is known as *effective altruism,* a form of charity where donations are distributed in terms of where they will do the most good. We also return to Singer in Chapter 5.

So what do biologists, neuroscientists, and psychologists at the cutting edge today think about the idea that humans are born selfish and become moral beings only through reluctant acculturation? It is not nearly as much in fashion as it used to be. The possibility that human evolution has favored the less selfish individuals, as Singer's example claims, has found support in the research of neuroscientists Antonio Damasio · and V.S. Ramachandran, among others (see below in the Hume section). We can now assume that humans not only have a capacity for caring about other people's welfare, but even have a natural feeling of empathy.

A Natural Fellow-Feeling? Hume and de Waal

At this point it may be appropriate to address a question that we have side-stepped until now, except for a brief discussion in Chapter 1: *Where does our sense of values come from?* It is clear that humans living in society have a sense of values, of things that matter to us above and beyond the everyday grind of staying safe and putting food on the table. (And, as Hobbes would say, even staying safe and putting food on the table are values we cherish.) We have a sense of moral right and wrong, of "dos and don'ts," even if they may differ from culture to culture, and even if we may prefer to just look after number one. But where do these internal rules originate? Three major schools of thought have manifested themselves in modern times. (1) Values are a result of *socialization,* a necessary "veneer" over a fundamentally feral and self-oriented human nature. This theory is often referred to as the *Veneer Theory.* You'll recognize Hobbes's philosophy as an early example of this theory. (2) Values are an outcome of the human capacity for *rational thought*: Our reason is capable of seeing through the murk of instincts and emotions to reach impartial, fair solutions, and must be the tool we use to make moral decisions. In Chapters 5 and 6 you'll encounter the two most famous examples of this approach, in themselves very different: utilitarianism and Kantian deontology. (3) Values are naturally embedded in our human capacity for *emotions:* First we experience strong feelings, and then we act on them—and afterward we try to rationalize what we did. And the strong feelings most people have include a natural reluctance to harm other human beings. This theory is generally known as *emotionalism.*

David Hume's Emotionalism

Mary Midgley suggested that human compassion toward fellow human beings should be viewed as something fundamental, based on a love and compassion for extended family. For a more sweeping view of emotion as the fundamental moral characteristic, we turn to David Hume (1711–1776), the Scottish philosopher. Hume believed that compassion is the one natural human feeling that holds us together in a society. For Hume, all of ethics can be reduced to the idea that reason acts as the "handmaiden" to our feelings; there is no such thing as an *objectively* moral act—nothing is good or bad in itself, not even murder. The good and the bad lie in our *feelings* toward the act. For Hume, all morality rests ultimately on our emotional responses, and there are no "moral facts" outside our own personal sensitivity. This theory says that whatever we would like to see happen we think of as morally good, and whatever we would hate to see happen we think of as morally evil. And what is it we would like to see happen? For Hume the answer is, whatever corresponds to our *natural feeling of concern for others.* Contrary to Hobbes, Hume believes that humans are equipped not only with self-love but also with love for others, and this emotion gives us our moral values. We simply react with sympathy to others through a built-in instinct—at least, most people do. Even persons who are generally selfish will feel compassion toward others if there is nothing in the situation that directly concerns them personally. Having the virtues of compassion and benevolence is a natural thing to Hume, and if we are a little short on such virtues, it simply means that we lack a natural ability, as when we are nearsighted. Such people are an exception to the rule.

That means that Hume's theory, far from being merely a focus on how we feel about things, is actually an example of *soft universalism:* We may have many different ideas and feelings about right and wrong, good and bad, but as human beings, most of us share a bottom-line criterion for morality: a fellow-feeling, a natural concern for others.

In Hume's words, from *A Treatise of Human Nature,* Book I, Part 1:

> If morality had naturally no influence on human passions and actions, 'twere in vain to take such pains to inculcate it; and nothing wou'd be more fruitless than that multitude of rules and precepts, with which all moralists abound. Philosophy is commonly divided into speculative and practical; and as morality is always comprehended under the latter division, 'tis supposed to influence our passions and actions, and to go beyond the calm and indolent judgments of the understanding. And this is confirm'd by common experience, which informs us, that men are often govern'd by their duties, and are deter'd from some actions by the opinion of injustice, and impell'd to others by that of obligation.
>
> Since morals, therefore, have an influence on the actions and affections, it follows, that they cannot be deriv'd from reason; and that because reason alone, as we have already prov'd, can never have any such influence. Morals excite passions, and produce or prevent actions. Reason of itself is utterly impotent in this particular. The rules of morality, therefore, are not conclusions of our reason.
>
> No one, I believe, will deny the justness of this inference; nor is there any other means of evading it, than by denying that principle, on which it is founded. As long as it is allow'd, that reason has no influence on our passions and action, 'tis in vain to pretend, that morality is discover'd only by a deduction of reason. An active principle can never be founded on an inactive; and if reason be inactive in itself, it must remain so in all its shapes and appearances, whether it exerts itself in natural or moral subjects, whether it considers the powers of external bodies, or the actions of rational beings. . . .
>
> Thus upon the whole, 'tis impossible, that the distinction betwixt moral good and evil, can be made to reason; since that distinction has an influence upon our actions, of which reason alone is incapable. Reason and judgment may, indeed, be the mediate cause of an action, by prompting, or by directing a passion: But it is not pretended, that a judgment of this kind, either in its truth or falsehood, is attended with virtue or vice. And as to the judgments, which are caused by our judgments, they can still less bestow those moral qualities on the actions, which are their causes.

You'll remember from Chapter 1 that neuroscience has recently weighed in on the origin of the moral sense, and the spotlight has been turned toward Hume once again, because Hume's theory that we are endowed with a natural empathy for other human beings has now found support in neuroscientific findings. Antonio Damasio and other scientists believe they have found a natural tendency in humans to feel empathy toward others—one that can be overridden by rationality as well as pressure from others, and one that may be stronger toward those we feel close to, but a natural tendency nevertheless, and this research has lent support to a new interest in *moral naturalism* (see Chapter 1).

In Chapter 11 you'll find a twentieth-century example of emotionalism in the philosophy of Richard Taylor.

Can Animals Have Morals?

But that leads us back to this question: If humans can truly behave in a somewhat/sometimes selfless manner, what about other social animals with big brains? What about those dolphins saving the group of four swimmers in New Zealand? And the tsunami dog you read about earlier in this chapter, trying to get help for another, injured dog? Throughout history there have been numerous similar examples, and YouTube is full of video clips of animals that seem to be helping other animals, and even humans. Some of those clips are particular moving, and probably unstaged. Is the most plausible explanation that they simply don't know what they're doing and are acting on a "selfish gene" instinct, like Dawkins suggests, or do they make what we would call a moral choice? Consider this story:

Yale Center for British Art

David Hume, Scottish philosopher and historian. Hume believed that human beings are born with a fellow-feeling, a sense of compassion and empathy for others.

Some years ago a small boy fell into the Western Lowland gorilla pit at the Brookfield Zoo in Chicago. The female gorilla Binti Jua, herself a new mother, picked up the unconscious child and shielded him from the other gorillas. Then she carried him over to the doorway, where she was used to zoo personnel going in and out, and a rescue crew came and got the boy.

The story received nationwide attention. Why did Binti Jua show such seemingly "human" concern for the child? Many people were astonished to hear that a gorilla could show signs of compassion, let alone for someone not of her own species. A curator explained that she had been trained to bring her own baby to curators, and she was accustomed to being in close proximity with humans. So some concluded that Binti Jua did not act out of any rational or compassionate decision but simply on the basis of her training. Perhaps she was used to getting a reward for bringing her own baby and expected a reward for bringing the child. Other animal behaviorists who work with great apes didn't find Binti's action very remarkable: Gorillas and chimpanzees have a great capacity for compassion, they said, and will shield and defend an infant ape against aggressive adult apes. But Binti showed not just a compassion that went beyond her own species but also good common sense in carrying the boy over to the place where humans would be most likely to come and get him. So is it possible for a great ape to act unselfishly? Binti may certainly have been expecting a reward, but she also exhibited a gentle concern for the boy himself, so in one gesture this gorilla demonstrated transspecies compassion and rational foresight that seem to go beyond instinct and training. On a side note, a similar story unfolded at the Cincinnatti Zoo in 2016, but with quite a different outcome. A 3-year old boy fell into the gorilla pit, and a Silverback gorilla, Harambe, approached the unconscious boy and started dragging him through the water in the moat. Taking no chances, Zoo officials shot and killed Harambe. It is still debated whether the killing was justified. Harambe's fate has entered into the world of popular memes as a challenge and an inspiration. In the 2016 election, there were reports of over 10,000 write-in votes for Harambe (although that may have been a fake news story), and rappers Young Thug and Dumbfounded have recorded songs about the gorilla. In 2019, entrepreneur Elon Musk joined the artists by releasing "R.I.P. Harambe," performed by Yung Jake.

Science and philosophy have generally assumed that nonhuman animals live in a nonmoral universe of innocence, where what seems cruel to humans is just the natural response of self-preservation: They are beyond the categories of good and evil. But now comes thought-provoking new research, gathering results from years of observing monkeys, apes, dolphins, whales, elephants, and wolves. Contrary to what people have told one another for so long about animals being "beyond good and evil," it turns out that some form of moral code seems to prevail in all these groups of social animals, and "moral code" here doesn't just mean that each animal has an instinct for behaving within the group, because often an individual (usually a young animal) will misbehave and then be punished by the group (with beating or ostracism, but usually not death). After the punishment, there is usually a kiss-and-make-up phase. According to Frans de Waal of

Emory University's Yerkes Primate Center, chimps share food with one another and are indignant when an individual who seldom shares his or her own food expects a share of someone else's. At the Arnhem Zoo Chimpanzee compound where de Waal used to do research, two young female apes came home late one day and held up dinner for all the other apes in the research group; the scientists kept them separate overnight for their safety, but the next day they were beaten up by the rest of the colony. That night they were the first to come home. So the origin of moral rules may have to be sought much farther back in time than the Pleistocene, when Singer's hunters decided whether to run or to fight the saber-toothed cat side by side.

This also means that the psychological egoist's theory that we are "born" selfish needs to be rewritten because it is too vague a statement in light of new research. It is not impossible that each child (and each chimpanzee) is born completely selfish, and that we begin to modify our selfish behavior only when we realize we can't consistently get away with it. But (1) new research has shown that even toddlers seem to display empathy, and (2) even if children act selfishly, the child is not the same as the adult, and some thinkers claim that what I've outlined here is the *genetic fallacy:* confusing the origin of something with what it has become at a later stage. We don't ordinarily claim that children are moral agents, because psychologists tell us that children really don't know the difference between right and wrong before they are about seven or eight years old. So why should the amoral demeanor of a small child be held up as the natural morality of an adult? We don't claim that the talent of a gifted ballplayer, a star chef, a good parent, or a great teacher can be reduced to their skills and knowledge when they were four years old. Children experience *socialization,* and since humans are social beings by nature, the effects on the individual of living in society are part of what we are as human beings. With the right training, we develop intellectually and technically as we grow older; therefore, it should be apparent that we also develop morally. We may start out in life as selfish, but with socialization, most people end up being capable of taking other people's interests into account—not merely because it is the prudent thing to do, but also because they develop an interest in other people's well-being. And that may be the secret behind the immense evolutionary success of human beings.

In his book *Good Natured: The Origins of Right and Wrong in Humans and Other Animals* (1996), Frans de Waal speculates that although humans seem to be the only animals that can take delight in cruel treatment of others, both humans and great apes have the capacity for selfless caring for others. Echoing the thoughts of David Hume as well as Peter Singer and Charles Darwin himself, he writes:

> Human sympathy is not unlimited. It is offered most readily to one's own family and clan, less readily to other members of the community, and most reluctantly, if at all, to outsiders. The same is true of the succorant behavior of animals. The two share not only a cognitive and emotional basis, but similar constraints in their expression.

> Despite its fragility and selectivity, the capacity to care for others is the bedrock of our moral system. It is the only capacity that does not snugly fit the hedonic cage in which philosophers, psychologists, and biologists have tried to lock the human spirit. One of the principal functions of morality seems to be to protect and nurture this caring capacity, to guide its growth and expand its reach, so that it can effectively balance other human tendencies that need little encouragement.

In 2011 a study was published in *Proceedings of the National Academy of Sciences,* in which Frans de Waal and colleagues Victoria Horner, J. Devyn Carter, and Malini Suchak concluded that, contrary to what was previously assumed, chimpanzees turn out *not* to be essentially self-centered animals, but display a high level of empathy-based altruistic behavior. In an interview with Discovery News, Christophe Boesch, director of the Department of Primatology at the Max Planck Institute for Evolutionary Anthropology, said that "All studies with wild chimpanzees have amply documented that they share meat and other food abundantly, that they help one another in highly risky situations, like when facing predators or neighboring communities, and adopt needing orphans." De Waal has already gone on record as saying that empathy appears to be so basic for mammals that we can expect to find it even in dogs and rats. Primatologists seem convinced now that it has at least been established that humans and chimpanzees share the capacity for empathy. The question is, Does that mean the chimpanzees—and other mammals who may share the same neurological structures—have morals? Is fellow-feeling the same as having morals (knowing rules of behavior), or even *ethics* (being aware of the rules, and evaluating them)? De Waal does not commit to a straightforward confirmation, but another scholar does: ecologist Marc Bekoff. In his book *Wild Justice* (2009), co-authored by philosopher Jessica Pierce (see Chapter 13), he argues that not only do apes show a sense of fairness, and are disturbed by unfairness, but so do wolves, dogs, whales, elephants, and just about any highly social mammal all the way to bats and rats. Bekoff's ideas are still considered speculative, but there is far more willingness to consider their merit today than even a decade ago.

So it appears that not only aren't we humans as selfish as we used to think; if our brains have developed within the general realm of normalcy, we have a natural sense of empathy toward other humans, an ability to understand their pain and their joy—and it even appears that we share some of the ability with other highly social mammals. Perhaps the special human trait is that under the right circumstances (see Chapter 1 on Hannah Arendt, Stanley Milgram, and Philip Zimbardo) we are very good at *overriding* those feelings with rational arguments. And while that can create a million bad excuses for causing harm to others, perhaps overriding one's empathy is not *always* a bad thing—an immediate feeling of sympathy without rational thinking may prevent us from seeing the greater picture where harm will be caused to the many if we protect the few. And that takes us into the next chapter on the moral philosophy of Utilitarianism. We will also look more closely at the relationship between empathy and reason in Chapter 11 when we examine the virtue of compassion.

Study Questions

1. What "other human tendencies" is Frans de Waal talking about? Do you agree with him that humans and some apes share the capacity for caring? Why or why not?

2. What are the most powerful arguments in favor of psychological egoism? What are the most damaging arguments against it?

3. Discuss the theory of the selfish gene: Do you find it to be a sufficient explanation for altruistic behavior among humans and animals? Why or why not? Do you think Midgley's counterargument is persuasive? Explain.

4. Discuss the concept of ethical egoism in its most rational form: We ought to treat others the way we want to be treated to ensure our own safety and prosperity. What can be said for this approach? What can be said against it?

5. Outline the most attractive and most problematic points associated with reciprocal and ideal altruism.

Primary Readings and Narratives

The Primary Readings are a discussion about selfishness and justice from Plato's *Republic* and an excerpt from Thomas Hobbes's *Leviathan*. The first Narrative is a summary of John Steinbeck's last novel, *The Winter of Our Discontent*, about a man who finds that everybody is being selfish, and resolves to get ahead by doing the same—an exposé of ethical egoism. The second Narrative is a summary and excerpt from an episode of the TV show *Friends* about whether an unselfish act is possible. The third Narrative is a summary of the film *Force Majeure*, a Swedish story about a father who, when a natural disaster threatens his family, only thinks of his own safety. At the end of the Narratives section is a list of classics and contemporary stories all exploring the concept of selfishness and altruism.

Primary Reading

The Republic

PLATO

Book II. Excerpts. Plato,* The Republic of Plato, 3e. *Translated by Benjamin Jowett. London: Oxford University Press, 1888.

You have already read a section of Plato's most famous Dialogue, *The Republic,* in Chapter 2. Here Socrates and Glaucon discuss the issue of justice and selfishness, illustrated by Glaucon's story of the Ring of Gyges. Glaucon is playing the devil's advocate, provoking Socrates into defending the concept of justice. Socrates is talking about the conversation to friends, so the narrator (the "I") is supposed to be Socrates himself (as written by Plato). Glaucon is advancing three separate arguments in favor of selfishness, hoping to get a reaction out of Socrates: (1) he presents a social contract theory, which you read about in the chapter; (2) he narrates the story of the Ring of Gyges, and follows up with a hypothesis: What if we had two invisibility rings, and gave one to a "just" man and one to an "unjust man"? And (3) he asks if there really is any profit to being good, and if it isn't more profitable to be excellent at being bad (selfish). Eventually we get Socrates' response. The rest of *The Republic* is in a sense dedicated to proving Glaucon wrong.

> I am delighted, he replied, to hear you say so, and shall begin by speaking, as I proposed, of the nature and origin of justice.
>
> They say that to do injustice is, by nature, good; to suffer injustice, evil; but that the evil is greater than the good. And so when men have both done and suffered injustice and have had experience of both, not being able to avoid the one and obtain the other, they think that they had better agree among themselves to have neither; hence there arise laws and mutual covenants; and that which is ordained by law is termed by them lawful and just. This they affirm to be the origin and nature of justice;—it is a mean or compromise, between the best of all, which is to do injustice and not be punished, and the worst of all, which is to suffer injustice without the power of retaliation; and justice, being at a middle point between the two, is tolerated not as a good, but as the lesser evil, and honoured by reason of the inability of men to do injustice. For no man who is worthy to be called a man would ever submit to such an agreement if he were able to resist; he would be mad if he did. Such is the received account, Socrates, of the nature and origin of justice.
>
> Now that those who practise justice do so involuntarily and because they have not the power to be unjust will best appear if we imagine something of this kind: having given both to the just and the unjust power to do what they will, let us watch and see whither desire will lead them; then we shall discover in the very act the just and unjust man to be proceeding along the same road, following their interest, which all natures deem to be their good, and are only diverted into the path of justice by the force of law. The liberty which we are supposing may be most completely given to them in the form of such a power as is said to have been possessed by Gyges, the ancestor of Croesus the Lydian. According to the tradition, Gyges was a shepherd in the service of the king of Lydia; there was a great storm, and an earthquake made an opening in the earth at the place where he was feeding his flock. Amazed at the sight, he descended into the opening, where, among other marvels, he beheld a hollow brazen horse, having doors, at which he stooping and looking in saw a dead body of stature, as appeared to him, more than human, and having nothing on but a gold ring; this he took from the finger of the

dead and reascended. Now the shepherds met together, according to custom, that they might send their monthly report about the flocks to the king; into their assembly he came having the ring on his finger, and as he was sitting among them he chanced to turn the collet of the ring inside his hand, when instantly he became invisible to the rest of the company and they began to speak of him as if he were no longer present. He was astonished at this, and again touching the ring he turned the collet outwards and reappeared; he made several trials of the ring, and always with the same result—when he turned the collet inwards he became invisible, when outwards he reappeared. Whereupon he contrived to be chosen one of the messengers who were sent to the court; where as soon as he arrived he seduced the queen, and with her help conspired against the king and slew him, and took the kingdom. Suppose now that there were two such magic rings, and the just put on one of them and the unjust the other; no man can be imagined to be of such an iron nature that he would stand fast in justice. No man would keep his hands off what was not his own when he could safely take what he liked out of the market, or go into houses and lie with any one at his pleasure, or kill or release from prison whom he would, and in all respects be like a God among men. Then the actions of the just would be as the actions of the unjust; they would both come at last to the same point. And this we may truly affirm to be a great proof that a man is just, not willingly or because he thinks that justice is any good to him individually, but of necessity, for wherever any one thinks that he can safely be unjust, there he is unjust. For all men believe in their hearts that injustice is far more profitable to the individual than justice, and he who argues as I have been supposing, will say that they are right. If you could imagine any one obtaining this power of becoming invisible, and never doing any wrong or touching what was another's, he would be thought by the lookers-on to be a most wretched idiot, although they would praise him to one another's faces, and keep up appearances with one another from a fear that they too might suffer injustice. Enough of this.

Now, if we are to form a real judgment of the life of the just and unjust, we must isolate them; there is no other way; and how is the isolation to be effected? I answer: Let the unjust man be entirely unjust, and the just man entirely just; nothing is to be taken away from either of them, and both are to be perfectly furnished for the work of their respective lives. First, let the unjust be like other distinguished masters of craft; like the skilful pilot or physician, who knows intuitively his own powers and keeps within their limits, and who, if he fails at any point, is able to recover himself. So let the unjust make his unjust attempts in the right way, and lie hidden if he means to be great in his injustice: (he who is found out is nobody:) for the highest reach of injustice is, to be deemed just when you are not. Therefore I say that in the perfectly unjust man we must assume the most perfect injustice; there is to be no deduction, but we must allow him, while doing the most unjust acts, to have acquired the greatest reputation for justice. If he have taken a false step he must be able to recover himself; he must be one who can speak with effect, if any of his deeds come to light, and who can force his way where force is required by his courage and strength, and command of money and friends. And at his side let us place the just man in his nobleness and simplicity, wishing, as Aeschylus says, to be and not to seem good. There must be no seeming, for if he seem to be just he will be honoured and rewarded, and then we shall not know whether he is just for the sake of justice or for the sake of honours and rewards; therefore, let him be clothed in justice only, and have no other covering; and he must be imagined in a state of life the opposite of the former. Let him be the best of men, and let him be thought the worst; then he will have been put to the proof; and we shall see whether he will be affected by the fear of infamy and its consequences. And let him continue thus to the hour of death; being just and seeming to be unjust. When both have reached the uttermost extreme, the one of justice and the other of injustice, let judgment be given which of them is the happier of the two.

Heavens! my dear Glaucon, I said, how energetically you polish them up for the decision, first one and then the other, as if they were two statues.

I do my best, he said. And now that we know what they are like there is no difficulty in tracing out the sort of life which awaits either of them. This I will proceed to describe; but as you may think the description a little too coarse, I ask you to suppose, Socrates, that the words which follow are not mine—Let me put them into the mouths of the eulogists of injustice: They will tell you that the just man who is thought unjust will be scourged, racked, bound—will have his eyes burnt out; and, at last, after suffering every kind of evil, he will be impaled: Then he will understand that he ought to seem only, and not to be, just; the words of Aeschylus may be more truly spoken of the unjust than of the just. For the unjust is pursuing a reality; he does not live with a view to appearances—he wants to be really unjust and not to seem only:—

'His mind has a soil deep and fertile,

Out of which spring his prudent counsels.'

In the first place, he is thought just, and therefore bears rule in the city; he can marry whom he will, and give in marriage to whom he will; also he can trade and deal where he likes, and always to his own advantage, because he has no misgivings about injustice; and at every contest, whether in public or private, he gets the better of his antagonists, and gains at their expense, and is rich, and out of his gains he can benefit his friends, and harm his enemies; moreover, he can offer sacrifices, and dedicate gifts to the gods abundantly and magnificently, and can honour the gods or any man whom he wants to honour in a far better style than the just, and therefore he is likely to be dearer than they are to the gods. And thus, Socrates, gods and men are said to unite in making the life of the unjust better than the life of the just.

I was going to say something in answer to Glaucon, when Adeimantus, his brother, interposed: Socrates, he said, you do not suppose that there is nothing more to be urged?

Why, what else is there? I answered.

This reply of Socrates displays his famous sense of irony. There is much more to be said, and for the rest of the evening, Socrates discusses why the just man is a happier person than the unjust man. He does that by way of imagining an ideal state, governed by justice rather than injustice.

Glaucon and the rest entreated me by all means not to let the question drop, but to proceed in the investigation. They wanted to arrive at the truth, first, about the nature of justice and injustice, and secondly, about their relative advantages. I told them, what I really thought, that the enquiry would be of a serious nature, and would require very good eyes. Seeing then, I said, that we are no great wits, I think that we had better adopt a method which I may illustrate thus; suppose that a short-sighted person had been asked by some one to read small letters from a distance; and it occurred to some one else that they might be found in another place which was larger and in which the letters were larger—if they were the same and he could read the larger letters first, and then proceed to the lesser—this would have been thought a rare piece of good fortune.

Very true, said Adeimantus; but how does the illustration apply to our enquiry?

I will tell you, I replied; justice, which is the subject of our enquiry, is, as you know, sometimes spoken of as the virtue of an individual, and sometimes as the virtue of a State.

True, he replied.

And is not a State larger than an individual?

It is.

Then in the larger the quantity of justice is likely to be larger and more easily discernible. I propose therefore that we enquire into the nature of justice and injustice, first as they appear in the State, and secondly in the individual, proceeding from the greater to the lesser and comparing them.

That, he said, is an excellent proposal.

After having reached the conclusion (to which we will return in Chapter 8) that the just state is similar to the just person, and that a just person's soul consists of three parts—*reason, willpower,* and *desire*—which must all be in balance and governed by reason, Socrates explains to Glaucon and the others the imbalance of the unjust man compared with the well-being of the just man.

And now, I said, injustice has to be considered.

Clearly.

Must not injustice be a strife which arises among the three principles—a meddlesomeness, and interference, and rising up of a part of the soul against the whole, an assertion of unlawful authority, which is made by a rebellious subject against a true prince, of whom he is the natural vassal,—what is all this confusion and delusion but injustice, and intemperance and cowardice and ignorance, and every form of vice?

Exactly so.

And if the nature of justice and injustice be known, then the meaning of acting unjustly and being unjust, or, again, of acting justly, will also be perfectly clear?

What do you mean? he said.

Why, I said, they are like disease and health; being in the soul just what disease and health are in the body.

How so? he said.

Why, I said, that which is healthy causes health, and that which is unhealthy causes disease.

Yes.

And just actions cause justice, and unjust actions cause injustice?

That is certain.

And the creation of health is the institution of a natural order and government of one by another in the parts of the body; and the creation of disease is the production of a state of things at variance with this natural order?

True.

And is not the creation of justice the institution of a natural order and government of one by another in the parts of the soul, and the creation of injustice the production of a state of things at variance with the natural order?

Exactly so, he said.

Then virtue is the health and beauty and well-being of the soul, and vice the disease and weakness and deformity of the same?

True.

And do not good practices lead to virtue, and evil practices to vice?

Assuredly.

Still our old question of the comparative advantage of justice and injustice has not been answered: Which is the more profitable, to be just and act justly and practise virtue, whether seen or unseen of gods and men, or to be unjust and act unjustly, if only unpunished and unreformed?

In my judgment, Socrates, the question has now become ridiculous. We know that, when the bodily constitution is gone, life is no longer endurable, though pampered with all kinds of meats and drinks, and having all wealth and all power; and shall we be told that when the very essence of the vital principle is undermined and corrupted, life is still worth having to a man, if only he be allowed to do whatever he likes with the single exception that he is not to acquire justice and virtue, or to escape from injustice and vice; assuming them both to be such as we have described?

Yes, I said, the question is, as you say, ridiculous.

Study Questions

1. How does Glaucon use the story of Gyges to express a theory of human nature?

2. Is Glaucon right? Why or why not?

3. Plato has Glaucon speculate about the terrible fate of the truly good man. How might Plato's readers interpret that? (Remember that this dialogue was written years after Socrates' death at the hands of the Athenian court.)

4. Has Socrates now proved to you that it is better to be a "just" person than an "unjust" person? Explain. You may want to refer to the graphic illustration of the "Pyramid" on p. 171.

 Primary Reading

Leviathan

THOMAS HOBBES

Excerpt, 1651.

Whereas Glaucon's arguments were the result of playing the devil's advocate, Thomas Hobbes came to the same conclusion in all seriousness some two thousand years later: Humans are selfish by nature, and society is our best way to protect ourselves from one another. Justice is a concept that is to be found in a society only once the rules have been laid down. Before the creation of society, in the "state of nature," where people live in a perpetual state of war against one another, life is "nasty, brutish, and short," and no rules apply except that of self-preservation. To improve our personal condition and for no other reason, we choose to live by the rules of society. Justice is indeed to Thomas Hobbes an invention based on self-preservation, nothing more.

> Hereby it is manifest, that during the time men live without a common Power to keep them all in awe, they are in that condition which is called Warre; and such a warre, as is of every man against every man. For WARRE, consisteth not in Battell onely, or the act of fighting; but in a tract of time, wherein the Will to contend by Battell is sufficiently known: and therefore the notion of *Time,* is to be considered in the nature of Warre; as it is in the nature of Weather. For as the nature of Foule weather, lyeth not in a showre or two of rain; but in an inclination thereto of many dayes together; So the nature of War, consisteth not in actual fighting; but in the known disposition thereto, during all the time there is no assurance to the contrary. All other time is PEACE.
>
> Whatsoever therefore is consequent to a time of Warre, where every man is Enemy to every man; the same is consequent to the time, wherein men live without other security, than what their own strength, and their own invention shall furnish them withall. In such condition, there is no place for Industry; because the fruit thereof is uncertain: and consequently no Culture of the Earth; no Navigation, nor use of the commodities that may be imported by Sea; no commodious Building; no Instruments of moving, and removing such things as require much force; no Knowledge of the face of the Earth; no account of Time; no Arts; no Letters; no Society; and which is worst of all, continuall feare, and danger of violent death; And the life of man, solitary, poore, nasty, brutish, and short. . . .

To this warre of every man against every man, this also is consequent; that nothing can be Unjust. The notions of Right and Wrong, Justice and Injustice have there no place. Where there is no common Power, there is no Law: where no Law, no Injustice. Force, and Fraud, are in warre the two Cardinall vertues. Justice, and Injustice are none of the Faculties neither of the Body, nor Mind. If they were, they might be in a man that were alone in the world, as well as his Senses, and Passions. They are Qualities, that relate to men in Society, not in Solitude. . . .

The Passions that encline men to Peace, are Feare of Death; Desire of such things as are necessary to commodious living; and a Hope by their Industry to obtain them. And Reason suggesteth convenient Articles of Peace, upon which men may be drawn to agreement.

Study Questions

1. What does Hobbes mean by saying that when humans live in a state of war of everybody against everybody, there is neither justice nor injustice? What event creates justice and injustice?

2. Compare Glaucon's and Hobbes's ideas of justice.

3. Hobbes believes we are all selfish by nature; however, since right and wrong for Hobbes don't exist before the creation of society, is selfishness in itself a bad thing? Why or why not?

Narrative

The Winter of Our Discontent

JOHN STEINBECK

Novel, 1961. Summary.

In Chapter 3 you read an excerpt from Steinbeck's essay "Paradox and Dream," from 1966, one of the last things he wrote before passing away in 1968. Five years earlier he had finished his final novel, *The Winter of Our Discontent*, and in 1962 he won the Nobel Prize in Literature. Steinbeck's works of fiction range from social outrage (*Grapes of Wrath*), over psychological analyses of clashes between generations (*East of Eden*) and friends (*Of Mice and Men*), to an anti-Nazi resistance story (*The Moon is Down*) to downright slapstick comedies (*Cannery Row, Tortilla Flat*), but *The Winter of Our Discontent* is possibly his most philosophical and ethically relevant novel, boring deep into questions of selfishness—the theory you know as ethical egoism. It is also one of his least well-known novels. And it is not a happy one; the questions which the main character, Ethan Hawley, asks himself about the value of being good reveal a deeply cynical and disappointed soul whose integrity is about to fall apart. One can almost hear Glaucon's voice (from Plato's *Republic*) in the background: there is much more profit to being selfish and ruthless than to being a good person;

better to seem good than to be good! Steinbeck himself said he wrote the novel in response to what he saw as the deterioration of values and the growing preoccupation with money in the culture of the United States.

A word of warning: In order for you to have a fair experience of the story, I have to include a spoiler: the ending of the novel. A huge change comes over Ethan Hawley in the end, and I don't want you to get the impression that the story is painfully depressing from start to finish—or a blatant defense of ethical egoism.

It is morning in the Hawley home in New Baytown on the East Coast, some year in the mid-twentieth century, on Good Friday. The day starts out well; middle-aged Ethan, Mary's husband and father of their two children Ellen and Allen, is in a good mood and jokes with Mary who doesn't really seem to get his puns, but it is obvious that they care about each other. Ethan is on his way to open up his grocery store; except it really isn't his store, not anymore. He lost the store because of bad investments, and it is now owned by the Italian immigrant Mr. Marullo. In fact, the Hawleys used to own the entire block, and Hawley was an important name in New Baytown, but Ethan's father was reckless with money and lost it all. So now Ethan Allen Hawley is just a clerk in the former family grocery store; he sweeps the floor, places orders, serves customers, and does what Marullo tells him to do. It irks him, because he has pride, but he doesn't really see what he can do about the step down in the social hierarchy. Mary has more social ambitions than Ethan has, and would like for the family to have more money so they can remodel their home, and have a little fun. She has inherited a small sum from her brother, but that is supposed to be a nest egg.

On that Good Friday morning Ethan encounters a number of people who each in their own way will set him on a new, dangerous course where his values will be tested: A friend of his wife's, a woman by the name of Margie Young-Hunt, stops by, and seems to be flirting with him. She is going to visit them later and tell them their fortune with Tarot cards. Next, Ethan meets Mr. Baker, the banker. The Hawleys and the Bakers used to be partners, and of equal status in town, but now there is an obvious social difference between Ethan and Baker who suggests to Ethan that he should make some investments, and take some chances with his wife's inheritance—a thought that is intensely uncomfortable for Ethan. Marullo himself admonishes Ethan to sprinkle the vegetables with water to make them look fresh—which they aren't. When Ethan exclaims that he is not a chiseler, Marullo shrugs it off as plain, good business. Ethan is approached by an acquaintance of Margie's, Mr. Biggers, who is trying to make him purchase goods from another company than the one they have a contract with, and pocket the profit. Essentially, Biggers is trying to bribe him, and whispers to him, "Don't be a fool! Everybody does it!" Ethan, being an educated man, and seeing the Christian symbolism of events on Good Friday, knows that he is being tempted, and that he has been tempted all day long by various people, including Joey Morphy, the bank teller, who is a cynical man. A line from the New Testament comes to Ethan: "lama sabach thani," one of Jesus Christ's seven words on the cross (*Eli, Eli, lama sabachthani?*): "My Lord, why hast thou forsaken me?"

Home again, later in the day, his children tell him about a national essay contest with the topic, "Why I Love America." In particular his son Allen seems interested, and wants to read Ethan's old classics in the attic. Margie Young-Hunt shows up and reads cards to Ethan and Mary, and she predicts that Ethan will soon become very rich. What Mary doesn't know is that the fortune is rigged. Margie already told Ethan that she was going to create a fabulously rich future for him in the cards, so Mary would believe it.

That night Ethan can't sleep; he feels profoundly disturbed at all the dishonesty and selfishness that has surrounded him all day, and he gets up in the middle of the night and walks down to the harbor, where he has a "special place," a little stone cave at the water's edge where he used to hide when he was a boy. Here he sits in the dark and contemplates the day's events. On the way home he meets an old friend, Danny Taylor, who also used to be wealthy, but is now the town drunk. Ethan feels guilty, because he thinks he should have done something to save Danny from himself, so he hands him a dollar, which Danny finds insulting, but he keeps it, anyway, asking Ethan not to give him any more—he'll just drink it up.

The next day Ethan seems different, and even Mary notices. He seems more confident. In the dark place the night before he has become convinced that morals are relative. He impresses Mr. Baker by being willing to consider what they talked about the day before; he calls Marullo by his first name, like an equal. He rejects the bribe that Biggers offered him, and Biggers is impressed, because he thinks Ethan is going for a higher bribe, and is even better at playing the con game than he is. At home he has a talk with Allen and realizes that all his son is interested in is winning the prize for the essay, not the content of the essay. The boy just wants to make money. Just like everybody else.

The night before Easter Sunday Ethan takes stock:

> "It's as though events and experiences nudged and jostled me in a direction contrary to my normal one or the one I had come to think was normal—the direction of the grocery clerk, the failure, the man without real hope or drive . . . caged by habits and attitudes I thought of as being moral, even virtuous. And it may be that I had a smugness about being what I called a 'Good Man.'"

But everybody in town is a crook. The judge fixes tickets. City fathers of high standing commit real estate fraud, and take bribes. And a change has come over Ethan. Why shouldn't he make a profit? What is so great about being good when there is no profit in it? Is it just pride? Or laziness? Ethan resolves to be bold, and push the rules aside, for a while. If he has money, he can take better care of his family—and be respected in town once again.

Ironically, on Easter Sunday (in the Christian tradition: the day of Jesus Christ's resurrection), Marullo rewards Ethan for having rejected Biggers' bribe, thinking that he has finally encountered an honest man. But the new Ethan is anything but honest: he now plans on swindling Marullo out of his store. Ethan has found out that Marullo has been in the country illegally for close to 40 years, which is the reason he has never gone back to Sicily for a visit, so he makes a call to the Department of Justice, anonymously betraying his boss. Joey Morphy, the bank teller, entertains him with a hypothetical story of how to rob a bank and get away with it. So now a plan is hatching in Ethan's mind: he is going to rob the bank. He feels as if he is being carried along by forces he has no control over, in this new life where he has given up on his previous values. In Ethan's subconscious mind the voices of his grandfather, the long-dead Cap't Hawley, and Great-Aunt Deborah, both human beings with a clear moral compass, try to set him straight. But what prevents him from carrying out the robbery is strange turn of events:

At the moment when Ethan is about the carry out the bank robbery a man shows up from the Justice Department, coincidentally, and tells him that Marullo has been arrested and will be deported. Marullo is not going to contest it—and he wants to give Ethan the store because Ethan has always been honest and trustworthy, as Marullo put it to the agent from the Department of Justice, "So the lights won't go out"—so there will still be some goodness in the world.

Earlier, Ethan has given a large sum of money to Danny, from Mary's inheritance, presumably for a rehab stay, but knowing full well that Danny will probably drink himself to death—after bequeathing

Ethan the only thing Danny has left in the world, his family's rural property which Mr. Baker has his eye on as a new municipal airport. And when Danny is found dead from an overdose of liquor and drugs, all of a sudden Ethan is again a well-respected member of the community, a store owner, and a land owner. When the city council members, the judge, and the Town manager are arrested for bribery and fixing tickets, Mr. Baker even suggests that Ethan should run for the position, since he is now too important to just be a grocery store owner, and the town needs a new manager.

So Margie's prophecy is coming true, and Mary is so proud of him, so shouldn't Ethan also be happy and proud? He is not—because deep inside there is still a spark of integrity left in him. Danny is dead, and it is Ethan's fault. Marullo has had to leave the country, and it is his fault. And the only reason why he is not a bank robber is pure coincidence. Somehow, Ethan feels that he needs to do something—to perform a sacrifice.

And what about Allen and Ellen? Allen, Ethan's son, has been working on his essay, and asks his dad if it is cheating to copy something out of a book. Ethan tries to explain to him that there is a big difference between copying with quotation marks and footnotes, and copying without them. Copying without references is, essentially, the same as stealing. And does Allen listen? Ethan isn't sure. The boy sends the essay off without letting Ethan or anybody else read it. And the family is elated when Allen wins honorable mention in the contest, but all he seems to care about is the money, and getting on TV. But Ellen has a different quality about her. She loves reading the old books for their own sake—she is not trying to win an essay contest. One night Ethan observes her sleepwalking. She walks straight to a curio cabinet where they display family keepsakes, and takes out a circular, translucent pink stone with carvings and fondles it, and Ethan sees her as something pure and good, almost with a luminescence. The stone, we hear, has been part of Ethan's childhood, probably brought back from China by his seafaring ancestors, and it represents something very special to Ethan—a family *talisman*, a symbol of good luck. Later he explains to Ellen what the talisman means. The stone will become very important in a short while.

But now the terrible truth comes out: Allen has plagiarized Ethan's old books, a speech by Henry Clay from 1850, and other bits and pieces from famous writings. A representative from national TV shows up and explains the whole thing to Ethan—how Allen committed fraud. But the representative doesn't want a scandal; he says the whole thing will be hushed up, and Allen will probably get a scholarship instead of the reward. When confronted, Allen tells his father that he doesn't care about anything. This, for Ethan, is the last straw. Not only has Allen shows who he really is, but the television channel doesn't even seem interested in making the truth public. Everything seems to crumble. He goes into the bathroom and grabs a packet of razorblades, and puts them in his pocket. He is going to his "dark place" by the harbor. But on his way out, Ellen runs up to him and hugs him fiercely.

Down at the harbor the tide is rising. Ethan struggles to get into the Place. For him, his light has gone out, and he has lost the will to live. He reaches for the packet of razor blades—but instead his hand finds . . . the *talisman*. Ellen managed to slip it into his pocket as she was hugging him.

> "A surge of wave pushed me against the very back of the Place. And the tempo of the sea speeded up. I had to fight the water to get out, and I had to get out. I rolled and scrambled and splashed chest deep in the surf and the brisking waves pushed me against the old sea wall.
>
> I had to get back—had to return the talisman to its new owner.
>
> Else another light might go out."

Study Questions

1. What does it mean, in a Christian context, that Ethan is first being tempted on Good Friday? And that he resolves to become as selfish as everybody else on Easter Sunday?

2. Compare Ethan Hawley's journey into ethical egoism with Glaucon's statement that the "unjust man" who is very good at being selfish will have a happier life than the miserable just man. Does Ethan believe that Glaucon is right? Does Steinbeck?

3. What did Marullo mean—that he wanted to reward Ethan's honesty "so the lights won't go out"?

4. What does the Talisman mean, and how is it the instrument of the change in Ethan at the end of the story? Who is the new owner? And do you think Ethan will make it back to shore?

5. The title of the novel, *The Winter of Our Discontent*, is a borrowed quote from the beginning of Shakespeare's play *Richard III*: "Now is the winter of our discontent made glorious summer by the sun [son] of York," the son of York being Richard's brother, the newly appointed king, the son of the Duke of York. But Richard has designs on the throne himself, meaning that his fine statement is disingenuous. He is a selfish hypocrite. Why do you think Steinbeck chose to borrow that line?

6. Steinbeck is known to be an author with a generally positive outlook on life, without being naive about human nature. Is this book a departure from that positive world view? Do you think it was a fair assessment of America in the 1960s? Would it be a fair assessment of the United States today? Why or why not?

 Narrative

The One Where Phoebe Hates PBS

MICHAEL CURTIS (TELEPLAY)

SHELLEY JENSEN (DIRECTOR)

An episode of **Friends**, *1998-9. Summary.*

Can a television sitcom discuss moral problems in an even remotely significant way? I'll let you be the judge of that. If you've ever sat around the kitchen table after a party with friends discussing whether everyone is selfish, then you can relate to the main story line in this classic episode, one of the most famous of all episodes in the 10 seasons *Friends* was being produced. Just a brief introduction to the characters: *Joey* is an aspiring actor who has a rather blatant tendency to think of himself first, and others second. *Phoebe* is a kindhearted and spiritual (some would say scatter-brained) poet/singer/masseuse who has her own private view of the world. She is the surrogate mother of triplets, given over to her half-brother and his wife, who can't conceive. One morning while some of the friends (Phoebe, Chandler, Ross, and Monica) are having breakfast, Joey comes in, wearing a tuxedo. He has got a gig (he thinks) hosting a telethon for PBS, and he brags that he's doing a good deed for PBS while he himself is getting TV exposure. But Phoebe is appalled: for one thing, she thoroughly dislikes PBS because she had a bad experience with the network some years back. Her mother had just killed herself, and Phoebe was feeling sad, so she wrote to *Sesame Street* because she remembered them fondly from when she was a little kid. But nobody replied—they just sent her a key chain. And at the time she was homeless, living in a box, so she didn't even have any keys! Besides, she says, the only reason why Joey wants the gig is so he can get on TV, not because he wants to do something unselfish.

That gets the ball rolling: Now Joey accuses Phoebe of being selfish, herself, for having triplets for her brother—because it made her *feel good,* and, says Joey, that makes it selfish; we recognize the attitude of a convinced psychological egoist: everyone is selfish, and, in Joey's words, "there are no unselfish good deeds." Phoebe might just as well forget that, because that's like believing in Santa Claus. (Later on she casually asks him what he meant, and when she hears him say that Santa doesn't exist, we see the shock on her face.)

So Phoebe sets out to prove Joey wrong because, as she explains to Monica and her other friend Rachel, she just won't let her babies be raised in a world where Joey is right. Her first attempt involves sneaking over to an elderly neighbor and raking the leaves from his doorstep. But he discovers her and treats her to cider and cookies, which makes her feel great. So, since her good deed made her feel good, it doesn't qualify as a selfless deed, according to Joey's definition.

United Archives GmbH/Alamy Stock Photo

The television sitcom *Friends* (1994–2004) may not seem like an obvious choice for a textbook about ethics, but real life is full of moral problems, and so are many of the *Friends* episodes, such as "The One Where Phoebe Hates PBS," in which Phoebe (Lisa Kudrow, far left) and Joey (Matt LeBlanc, on her right) have a debate about selfishness. The other friends are, from left to right, Courteney Cox, David Schwimmer, Jennifer Aniston, and Matthew Perry.

Meanwhile, to his immense disappointment, Joey finds out that he isn't hosting the telethon after all; talk-show host Gary Collins is; Joey is just going to answer phones, and it looks like he dressed in a tux for nothing. But one of the calls he receives is from Phoebe, who proudly announces that she has found a selfless, good deed: She went to Central Park and let a bee sting her, so it could look macho in front of its friends! And since she's hurting, it's not a selfish deed. But Joey shoots that down instantly: Since the bee probably died from stinging her, the bee didn't benefit (so it wasn't a good deed!).

Joey himself is doing a fine job of demonstrating what his true goal is: TV exposure, rather than helping PBS, thus proving Phoebe's point that he himself is just looking out for number one. He realizes that the place where he is answering calls isn't even within range of the television camera, so he tries to swap places with another volunteer, who is utterly unwilling to comply, to the point where they slug it out between the tables, in the background, while Gary Collins is talking about contributing to PBS's fine programming. So Joey's own quest to gain an advantage for himself isn't doing too great. But now Phoebe makes one last attempt to prove that unselfishness exists.

She makes one more call to Joey, pledging $200 to PBS. She explains that even if she is still mad at them, she also knows that lots of children love their shows, so she is doing a good deed by supporting them, while it doesn't make her feel good at all: $200 is a lot of money, and she had plans for that sum: She was saving up to buy a hamster. Joey can't believe what he's hearing: A $200 hamster? When they normally cost $10? Phoebe implies that it was a very special hamster (and we get the feeling that she was probably being taken for a ride, as often happens). So it looks like she has proved to Joey that selfless, good deeds do indeed exist! But here comes the twist: Because of Phoebe's pledge, the station has now surpassed the sum collected by pledges last year, and Gary Collins steps over to the volunteer who took the pledge—Joey! Who now gets his TV exposure: He is introduced by name standing there in his tux, with a big smile on his face. Phoebe is watching it on TV and is overjoyed that her pledge got Joey on TV—until she realizes what has happened! Her good deed, which was supposed to make her feel bad, now has made her feel good—which again proves Joey's point that all deeds are selfish! So she loses again.

Has Joey now been vindicated? Has Phoebe's failure in proving that she can do a "selfless, good deed" convinced us that psychological egoism is true? Remember that she couldn't have planned on being rewarded with cider and cookies, or that her pledge would get Joey on TV. Those were after-the-fact events. If things we do make us feel good afterward, do they automatically fall into a "selfish" category, even if we didn't plan on feeling good, and the pleasure is an unintended after-effect? Keep in mind the debate about whether Lincoln's act of saving the pigs was selfish or not. A truly selfish person would not feel good about having sacrificed something for others; as you've read, it could be a way to tell unselfish people from the selfish ones that they actually feel good after helping others. However, one might also say that Phoebe had a certain purpose for doing those three supposedly selfless good deeds . . . (see Study Question #1).

Study Questions

1. Some would say that Phoebe's project was doomed from the start, because of the nature of her goal. What might that mean, and do you agree?

2. Discuss Phoebe's attempts at disproving Joey, relating them to the arguments against psychological egoism in the chapter text: the principle of falsification, the Lincoln story, and the fallacy of the suppressed correlative.

3. Is Joey selfish? Is Phoebe? Is everybody? Are you? Explain.

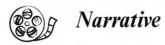 *Narrative*

Force Majeure

RUBEN ÖSTLUND (DIRECTOR AND SCREENWRITER)

Film (2014). Summary. Sweden.

The film *Force Majeure* has a simple plot. Five days at a ski resort where nothing much happens—except for the pivotal event within the first 10 minutes that changes everything, and reveals the fundamental selfishness of one of the main characters. The question is, is he a monster, or is his reaction "terrifyingly normal," as Hannah Arendt might have said? What would you do if you were in a similar situation?

A young family from Sweden is spending five vacation days at a winter sports resort in the French Alps; dad Tomas, mom Ebba from Norway, and the two kids, Vera and Harry. The family spends the first day skiing together on the mountain, and have their family portraits taken by a professional photographer, a happy family like every other family who goes to a ski resort. They all take a nap together in the big King bed in their thermal underwear, the picture of family bliss. Tomas checks his cell phone on the sly when he thinks Ebba isn't watching. At night, the snow cannons go off on the mountainside, to trigger avalanches. On the second day, they are having lunch on the hotel restaurant balcony. Casually, a hotel guest mentions that something is going on over on the mountainside. An ominous cloud of snow is rising, but Tomas assures his family that it is controlled. Everybody gets up to watch the spectacle and take pictures, but the avalanche moves closer and closer with astonishing speed, and soon it is thundering directly toward the resort and the balcony. Ebba reaches out and grabs her young son and her daughter as the moment of danger is upon them. Harry screams for his daddy in a panic, and Tomas gets up from his chair—and rushes toward the exit, shoving a stranger out of the way. The avalanche stops at the foot of the resort, and the balcony is enveloped by a whiteout, but it is only a snowy mist. As the mist clears, everybody checks that their families are okay. Ebba is still holding on to Harry and Vera, and now Tomas comes back, laughing nervously. The family doesn't say a word. They return to their hotel room, and Ebba confronts Tomas in the hallway

> He: You seem irritated.
>
> She: No . . . should I be?
>
> He: I don't think so.
>
> She: No?

Harry and Vera are the only ones who react openly to the event; he is sad, worried, and traumatized. She seeks refuge in her iPad, and they both scream at their parents to leave the room. Outside of the hotel room, Tomas starts crying, but they still don't talk about the event.

AF archive/Alamy Stock Photo

The Swedish film *Force Majeure* (2014) features a young family, Tomas (Johannes Bah Kunhke), Ebba (Lisa Loven Kongsli) and their two kids, vacationing in the French Alps. When an avalanche seems to bear down on the open-air restaurant where they are having lunch, Tomas grabs his cellphone and runs, leaving his family to fend for themselves.

That same evening, Tomas and Ebba are having dinner with a friend of Ebba's from Sweden who has just met a young man, a tourist from the United States. They tell their friends about the avalanche, speaking in English, and we hear Tomas's version: the avalanche grew big, and it looked as if it was going to smash into the restaurant. Quite shocking, even if it was controlled, he says. "Gives me goosebumps!"

Ebba: "It was horrifying."

Tomas: "Yes, you got a bit afraid, but it was controlled. They know what they're doing."

Ebba, laughing: "He got so scared that he ran away from the table."

Tomas, laughing: "No, I did not!"

She insists he did, he insists he did not, and she switches from English to Norwegian, finally confronting him verbally. "You grabbed your iPhone and your thermal gloves and ran as fast as you could, away from me and the kids" she says. Tomas says, "That's not how I remember it." The other couple at the table realize that, despite the laughter, something is not right. Silence and nervous giggling.

Back at the hotel room, out of earshot of the kids, Ebba says she doesn't recognize themselves now, and she doesn't like what she sees. He agrees, but offers no excuse or apology. They hug each other, seeking comfort, but the mood is broken by his cellphone ringing. He tries to convince her that it is possible to have several versions of what happened. She rejects that notion and says they need to agree on what happened, so they agree on the minimalistic version that they all experienced an avalanche.

Next day Ebba announces that she wants to go skiing by herself. She insists on paying her own way. Later, Ebba hangs out with her Swedish friend who has found a new lover while her husband looks after the kids back home in Sweden. Ebba can't relate to her attitude at all—she seeks security and commitment.

An old friend of Tomas's, Mats, shows up with a very young girlfriend, Fanny. As Fanny is telling a long story about work, Ebba, having had a few drinks, blurts out the story of the avalanche. This time she has the narrative down: they were taking pictures of the kids in front of the approaching avalanche, she says, but panic ensued when the avalanche was approaching. She grabs both kids and tries to carry them away, she says, but they're too heavy and she calls on Tomas to help her, but he has just snatched his cellphone and his gloves and is running away from them, leaving them in the path of danger. In the whiteout, she thinks they're going to die, and she calls out to Tomas, but he isn't there. There she is, holding on to the kids, and all of a sudden the sky is blue, and she realizes they weren't trapped by an avalanche after all. Then Tomas comes back, she says, and they just sat down and continued their meal as if nothing had happened. "So my problem," she says, "is that I'm here in this fancy hotel and I'm miserable."

Tomas says nothing. His friend Mats tries to give support to his friend by saying that when you're in survival mode you don't always retain your values; Ebba responds that at least you're supposed to own up to your failings afterwards. Intensely embarrassed, Mats and his girlfriend talk it over with Ebba while Tomas has sought refuge with Harry, playing a videogame. Mats insists on the survival instinct. The enemy, he says, is the image we have of heroes, but the truth is when reality stares us in the face, very few of us are ready to die heroically. Tomas hears every word behind the thin wall of the bedroom. Ebba says, "But my focus is my children who can't fend for themselves, and his focus is away from us."

Tomas is now back in the conversation, and insists that it's a matter of different perspectives. She asks him, again, to give his version of the story. And now the moment of truth arrives, because Ebba realizes that Tomas's iPhone has taped the whole sequence. All four crowd around the phone, to watch. And yes, it looks like Tomas is running away. Mats still tries to come up with an intellectual explanation that will let his friend off the hook, but it is becoming increasingly farfetched.

In the hallway, Mats and his girlfriend talk about what he might have done in the same situation. She: "You and Tomas are the same kind of man. You might have done the same." Another of their friends would never have run away. And it may also be a generational issue. Fanny now realizes that Mats has abandoned his own wife and kids to be with her, so now Mats looks a lot less attractive to her. And Mats is now in an identity crisis, doubting his own commitment to his family and his values in general. The night is ruined for both of them, and Mats keeps Fanny up with endless questions about whether she trusts him. (And at this point we begin to suspect that we are in fact watching a comedy, not a family tragedy.)

Next day Mats and Tomas go skiing together. After a perfect run down the slope, Tomas has a mental collapse, and Mats suggests that he should let out a good, long scream. So the two buddies scream profanities as loud as they can. Afterwards they get drunk, and by the time Tomas gets back to his room it is evening, and Ebba and the kids are not there. She doesn't answer her phone, either. Somehow Tomas ends up at a rave party in the sauna, with other drunk, naked men doing primal screaming. He finally finds Ebba back in their room, and she gives him the cold shoulder. Later that night he breaks down and finally owes up to not having behaved right—but he talks about himself in the 3rd person. And it all comes spilling out: He has also been unfaithful to her, and he cheats at games with the kids, and he can't live with himself any longer—he is a victim of himself. And he cries hysterically.

The last day of vacation is windy with no visibility on the slope. The family is out for one last run, and they try to stay together, but all of a sudden Ebba is missing. Tomas sets out to find her, and leaves the kids in the mist. Will he find her, or has something terrible happened? Will the kids be lost in the snow? Does Tomas redeem himself? I suggest you watch the movie and see for yourself if anything is resolved.

Study Questions

1. The title of the movie, *Force Majeure*, is a legal (originally French) expression indicating a "greater force," something in nature, or in the human heart, that we have no defense against (and shouldn't be blamed for succumbing to, so can't be sued). Is what Tomas experienced a "greater force" that he couldn't fight? Why or why not?

2. What do you think of Mats's defense of Tomas that values only are in effect if one's life is not in danger? And Tomas's explanation that it is all a matter of different perspectives?

3. Is the movie a defense of Psychological Egoism? Is everybody selfish? Does the movie imply that complete selfishness is human nature?

4. If you had been Tomas, what do you think you might have done at the moment the avalanche hit? Are we all at heart like Tomas, or is he just a particularly self-absorbed individual? If you had been Ebba, what would your reaction have been after you'd realized that Tomas had abandoned you and the kids?

5. The movie is categorized as a "dark comedy." If you have seen it, would you agree that it is, fundamentally, a comedy, or perhaps not so funny? Why/why not?

 Narrative

Some Story Suggestions

When selecting narratives for this chapter the problem was not one of locating good stories, but selecting a few from a huge number of well-told classics and new stories. Stories about selfishness vs. unselfishness are about the most numerous in our current world of fiction, in particular on Cable TV, and many such stories could be mentioned and discussed here. I suggest you take some time and think about novels, movies and TV series that focus on selfishness, and ask yourself whether the stories are critical of the selfish characters, or celebrate their selfishness, and if selfishness is considered a positive quality in the story, ask yourself why?

In Chapter 13, you'll see a section about business ethics. It may come as a surprise to you that business ethics does not revolve around ethical egoism, but films that portray the business world as such are numerous.

A very short list of stories within the Western tradition you may want to discuss or research on your own that have a focus on the selfishness of one or more characters; I'm sure you can add to this list yourself:

Television series:

Classics:

Dallas (frequently mentioned as the first television series unabashedly celebrating self-serving behavior); *Dynasty*

Contemporary:

Breaking Bad; House of Cards; House of Lies; Sex and the City; Game of Thrones; Fargo Seasons I and II; *Better Call Saul; The Good Place; Russian Doll*

Films:

Citizen Kane; Fargo; The Shawshank Redemption; Contagion; 2 Days in the Valley; Return to Paradise; Wall Street; The Wolf of Wall Street; L.A. Confidential; American Beauty; Burn After Reading; Dr. Strange.

Novels:

Classics:

The Count of Monte Cristo; Les Miserables; A Christmas Carol; Wuthering Heights; The Picture of Dorian Gray; Vanity Fair; Captains Courageous; The Great Gatsby; Gone With the Wind

Contemporary:

Charlie and the Chocolate Factory; A Clockwork Orange; Gone Girl; Midnight in the Garden of Good and Evil; The Kite Runner.

Chapter Five
Using Your Reason, Part 1: Utilitarianism

In the previous chapter, you read that we may have self-serving tendencies, but that in all likelihood we also have the capacity for fellow-feeling, some limited form of altruism. That means that we can, and perhaps should, look after ourselves and others at the same time, as reciprocal altruism says. This is, in effect, incorporated into one of the most influential moral theories of all time, utilitarianism. However, in utilitarianism it is not only a matter of what we are capable of emotionally, but also a matter of what we ought to do rationally. When deciding on a moral course of action, some of us find it is the potential **consequences** of our choice that determine what we decide to do. Others of us see those consequences as being of minor importance when we view them in light of the question of right and wrong. A student of mine, when asked to come up with a moral problem we could discuss in class, proposed this question to ponder: Imagine that your grandmother is dying; she is very religious, and she asks you to promise her that you will marry within the family faith. Your beloved is of another faith. Do you tell her the truth, or do you make a false promise? This profound (and, I suspect, real-life) question makes us all wonder: If I think it is right to lie to Grandma, why is that? To make her last moments peaceful; what she doesn't know won't hurt her; why should I upset her by telling her the truth? Is that a good enough reason? And if I think lying to Grandma is wrong and refuse to do it, how do I justify making her last moments miserable? You will see that those of us who think lying to her is the only right choice because then she will die happy generally subscribe to the theory of *consequentialism,* in particular the theory of *utilitarianism,* the most widespread and popular form of consequentialism. If you think that lying is always wrong, even if it would make Grandma feel better, then hang in there until Chapter 6, where we discuss Kant's moral theory. (In Box 5.1, you'll find a summary of a particular scene in the film *The Invention of Lying* that comes close to the scenario abut lying to Grandma.)

Box 5.1 IS LYING ACCEPTABLE IF IT EASES SUFFERING?

You have read the (probably) real-life problem presented in the beginning of this chapter, about whether or not it would be morally acceptable to lie to a dying grandmother whose only wish is to see her grandchild marry someone from within the family religion. A recent film has a particular scene that comes close in spirit to that problem, the comedy *The Invention of Lying* (2010). While the movie is a comedy, the scene is surprisingly serious and moving. An elderly woman is dying in a nursing home, and her middle-aged son Mark is by her side. She has a bad heart, and is terrified of death, and of the eternal nothingness she believes it represents. To be there, alive, and then, the next minute, you're gone, that is her deepest fear.

Such a fear in itself may not be unusual, but we have to add that, since it is a comedy, the story has a twist: In the world of the movie, nobody is capable of lying; otherwise the world is just like ours, but everyone speaks the truth, there is no fiction—and there is no religion. Except Mark has recently made a great discovery: he can say things that "are not"; in other words, he has invented lying. And in his mother's final moments, he puts this newfound talent to use. He says to her, "You're wrong about what happens after death. It isn't an eternity of nothingness." And he tells her she will be young again, and free of pain, she will be able to dance like she used to, she will be with all the people she loved who have passed on—and she will get a mansion. There will be no pain, only love. She looks at him in great relief and happiness, closes her eyes, and expires.

So Mark has taken away his mother's darkest fears and given her peace of mind—but what he doesn't realize is that the doctors and nurses have been listening to what he told his mother, and now they are eager to hear more about the knowledge he has about what happens when people die … (because after all, it is a comedy!)

So if we are to apply the principle of utility, *Maximize happiness for the maximum number of people*, to that scenario, would you say that the utilitarian would approve of him telling his dying mother something he makes up on the spot about life after death? What about the subsequent consequences of the nursing home staff having listened in? How does this scenario compare to the example in the beginning of the chapter? Can you think of other situations where it would be acceptable to lie to someone who is afraid, or in pain? (If you don't think it would be acceptable one way or another, you'll find support in Chapter 6.)

In the preceding chapter you encountered the philosopher Peter Singer, who claimed that we as humans are capable of caring for others as well as ourselves. Singer identifies himself as a utilitarian, as do numerous others today—philosophers as well as laypeople. Utilitarians see as their moral guideline a rule that encourages them to make life bearable for as many people as possible. Perhaps we can actively do something to make people's lives better, or perhaps the only thing we can do to make their lives better is to stay out of their way. Perhaps we can't strive to make people happy, but we can at least do our best to limit their misery. That way of thinking just seems the decent approach for many of us, and when we include ourselves among those who should receive a general increase of happiness and decrease of misery, then the rule seems attractive, simple, and reasonable. Small wonder this attitude has become the cornerstone of one of the most vital and influential moral theories in human history.

Utilitarians are **hard universalists** in the sense that they believe there is a single universal moral code, which is the only one possible, and everyone ought to realize it. It is the *principle of utility,* or the *greatest-happiness principle:* When choosing a course of action, always pick the one that will maximize happiness and minimize unhappiness for the greatest number of people. Whatever action conforms to this rule will be defined as a morally right action, and whatever action does not conform to it will be called a morally wrong action. In this way utilitarianism proposes a clear and simple moral criterion: Pleasure is good and pain is bad; therefore, whatever causes happiness and/or decreases pain is morally right, and whatever causes pain or unhappiness is morally wrong. In other words, utilitarianism is interested in the *consequences* of our actions: If they are good, the action is right; if bad, the action is wrong. This principle, utilitarians claim, will provide answers to all real-life dilemmas. (Box 5.2 explores some implications of consequentialism and the word *consequences*.)

Box 5.2 THERE WILL BE CONSEQUENCES!

As you read in Chapter 4, *consequentialism* is the umbrella title for theories that focus on the consequences of an action rather that the intentions or motivations of the agent. As such, the various theories under consequentialism such as ethical egoism, altruism, and utilitarianism all focus on creating *good* consequences for some person or groups of people, but that's where a short sidebar may be in order, because in our colloquial language the term "consequences" has become almost invariably identified with "something bad." When a parent or an educator says, "Didn't you even think there would be consequences to what you just did?", or a film critic complains that violence in a movie "has no consequences" (and is unrealistic), we all know they are implying *negative results* of some action. As it happens sometimes in intellectual history, theories retain an original meaning of a word while our everyday language drifts in a different direction. So when discussing utilitarianism we have to disregard the everyday association with the word "consequences," and remember that it refers to *positive* as well as negative outcomes, because the utilitarian wants to increase good consequences and limit

unpleasant consequences for as many as possible (including animals, as we shall see).

Are all theories that focus on the outcome of actions utilitarian? No. As we saw in Chapter 4, the outcome we look for may be happy consequences for ourselves alone, and in that case we show ourselves to be egoists. We may focus on the consequences of our actions because we believe that those consequences justify our actions (in other words, that the end justifies the means), but that does not necessarily imply that the consequences we hope for are good in the utilitarian sense that they maximize happiness for the maximum number of people. We might, for instance, agree with the Italian statesman Niccolò Machiavelli (1469–1527) that if the end is to maintain political power for oneself, one's king, or one's political party, that will justify any means one might use for that purpose, such as force, surveillance, or even deceit. Although this famous theory is indeed consequentialist, it does not qualify as utilitarian because it doesn't have the common good as its ultimate end.

Jeremy Bentham and the Hedonistic Calculus

Perhaps it is tempting to say that civilization moved toward an appreciation of human rationality in the 1700s, but it would be more appropriate to say that it was moved along by the thoughts of certain thinkers. Such a mover was the English jurist and philosopher Jeremy Bentham. Box 5.3 gives you a quick introduction to the major intellectual movement of the 1700s, the Enlightenment, and Box 5.4 provides you with a brief introduction to Bentham.

Box 5.3 UTILITARIANISM AND THE ENLIGHTENMENT

You may have heard of the time period called *the Enlightenment*. Here is a brief overview of why that time has been so essential for our western culture. The Enlightenment refers to approximately 100 years from the late 1600s (seventeenth century) to the late 1700s (eighteenth century), a time period when both Europe and the American colonies—and of course the young United States, after 1776—saw a general movement toward greater recognition of **human rights and social equality**, of the value of the individual, of the scope of human capacities, and of the need for and right to an education. However, as many people will point out today, not all humans were embraced as being "equals." White women were generally not included, and neither were women and men of color. But, as historians and sociologists point out, the idea of equality spread to other population groups, which were then slowly folded into the concept of a common humanity over the next centuries—even if, for many critics, we may still have a ways to go to reach complete equality and acceptance of each other. Stephen Pinker, whom you read about in Chapter 1, is a vocal spokesperson for the political and moral importance of the Enlightenment.

But how did it start? In the 1600s a great many people, mostly men, were now able to read; a new middle class was forming in the cities, challenging the influence of the royal families and the old nobility; and printing presses were beginning to provide news and debates in local languages, not just religious texts for the educated clergy. And as more people became literate and educated, the demand for political self-determination became stronger, eventually resulting in the revolutions of the 1700s. Some of those revolutions had fundamental changes in their wake, leading to modern democracies. In other places, democracies arose through more peaceful means. But in common for rulers, scholars, and revolutionaries alike in the 1700s was a belief that **human reason**, rationality, held the key to the future—to the blossoming of the sciences as well as to social change. That period is, appropriately, also referred to as the *Age of Reason*, not so much because people were particularly rational at the time as because reason was the social, scientific, and philosophical *ideal*. Utilitarianism is one of the intellectual products of the Enlightenment, with its faith in the power of reason to solve problems, and the belief that each person can engage in rational solutions emphasizing positive outcomes for as many as possible. The commitment to rational thinking has been a staple in moral philosophy to this day, as you read in Chapter 1.

Bentham, author of *Introduction to the Principles of Morals and Legislation* (1789), set out to create not a new moral theory so much as a hands-on principle that could be used to remodel the British legal system. Indeed, it was not Bentham but another philosopher, David Hume, who invented the term *utilitarianism*. Hume believed that it is good for an action to have *utility* in the sense that it makes yourself and others happy, but he never developed that idea into a complete moral theory. Bentham, however, used the term to create a moral system for a new age. So in Hume's version, what is useful is what is morally good. But we have an even earlier, famous reference to the goodness of utility: In Plato's *Republic* (see this book Chapters 2 and 4), Socrates says to Glaucon, "That is, and ever will be, the best of sayings, that the useful is the noble and the hurtful is the base." If a utilitarian is someone who believes that anything useful is good, and anything painful is bad, why isn't Socrates hailed as the first utilitarian? Because there is so much more to Socrates' value theory than a theory of the best outcome, as you'll see in Chapter 8. But also because what is "useful" for Socrates isn't necessarily what is pleasurable! Socrates placed great emphasis on the needs of the community, as you'll remember from Chapter 4, but not as much on the personal needs of the individual; that is a modern concept, and it is precisely during Bentham's era, the time of the Enlightenment, that the needs as well as the rights of the individual become a focal point for moral and political discussions.

Box 5.4 JEREMY BENTHAM, THEN AND NOW . . .

Luise Berg-Ehlers/Alamy Stock Photo

Jeremy Bentham (1748–1832), the British philosopher and jurist, developed together with his friend James Mill the theory of utilitarianism based on the principle of utility: Maximize happiness and minimize unhappiness for as many as possible. Bentham donated his body to medical research and his money to the University College of London, with the provision that after research on his body was complete, it was to be preserved and displayed at university board meetings. That request is not as odd as it might sound: Bentham, a prominent person, hoped that by donating his body to science he would make a statement in support of the medical profession's need for cadavers for research. Most people at the time felt, however, that having one's deceased body cut up was a sacrilege, and so only the bodies of executed criminals were available. As a result, a thriving clandestine business arose, a trade in newly dead bodies stolen from their graves. In one case, the infamous Burke and Hare case of 1828, the body snatchers didn't wait for corpses to be buried but murdered sixteen people in one year and sold them to anatomists. By deciding to donate his body, Bentham took a stand against what he saw as superstition and attempted to put a stop to the practice of body snatching. And he may have thought further, What better way to undo superstitions about dead bodies than for his own to be on display at board meetings? He specified in his will that he was to become an *Auto-Icon,* an image of himself, and he even picked out the glass eyes to be placed in his head after his demise and carried them around in his pocket, according to legend. He had intended for his head to remain on the shoulders of his Auto-Icon, but after his death, the preservation process of his head went wrong, and a wax head was substituted. In this photo you see his wax head, but his real head still exists (with his glass eyes). In 2020 Bentham's body was moved from the mahogany closet where it had been kept to a new, permanent location in the UCL Student Centre, in a glass display case for all to see. Traditionally, he has been wheeled in at annual board meetings where he has been recorded as "present, but not voting."

In Bentham's England the feudal world had all but vanished. Society had stratified into an upper class, a middle class, and a working class, and the Industrial Revolution was just beginning. Conditions for the lowest class in the social hierarchy were appalling. Rights in the courts were, by and large, something that could be bought, which meant that those who had no means to buy them didn't have them. The world portrayed in the novels of Charles Dickens was developing; if you were in debt, you were taken to debtors' prison, where you stayed until your debt was paid. Whoever had funds could get out, but the poor faced spending the rest of their lives with their family inside debtors' prison. There were no child labor laws, and the exploitation of children in the workforce, which horrified Marx some decades later, was rampant in Bentham's day. Bentham saw it as terribly unfair and decided that the best way to redesign this system of unfair advantages would be to set up a simple moral rule that everyone could relate to, rich and poor alike.

Bentham said that **what is good is what is pleasurable, and what is bad is what is painful**. In other words, *hedonism* (pleasure seeking) is the basis for his moral theory, which is often called *hedonistic utilitarianism* (see Box 5.5). The ultimate value is happiness or pleasure—these things are *intrinsically* valuable. Anything that helps us achieve happiness or avoid pain is of *instrumental* value, and because we may do something pleasurable to achieve another pleasure, pleasure can have both intrinsic and instrumental value. (Box 5.6 explains this distinction in more detail.) For this basic rule to be useful in legislation, we need to let people decide for themselves wherein their pleasure lies and what they would rather avoid. Each person has a say in what pleasure and pain are, and each person's pleasure and pain count equally. We might illustrate this viewpoint by traveling back in our minds to nineteenth-century London. A well-to-do middle-class couple may feel that their greatest pleasure on a Saturday night is to don their fancy clothes, drive to Covent Garden in their shining coach, and go to the opera. The woman at Covent Garden who tries to sell them a bouquet of wilting violets as they pass by would probably not enjoy a trip to the opera as much as she would enjoy the bottle of gin she saves up for all week. Bentham would say she has as much right to relish her gin as the couple has a right to enjoy the opera. The woman can't tell the couple that gin is better, and they have no right to force their appreciation of the opera on her. For Bentham, what is good and bad for each person is a matter for each person to decide, and as such, his principle becomes a very *egalitarian* one. At the end of the chapter you'll find an excerpt from Bentham's *Introduction to the Principles of Morals and Legislation,* in which he outlines the principle of utility.

Box 5.5 HEDONISM AND THE HEDONISTIC PARADOX

Often the Greek thinker Epicurus (341–270 B.C.E.) is credited with being the first philosopher to advocate a life in search of pleasure, hedonism. That, however, isn't quite accurate, because what Epicurus seems to have been after was a life free of pain—for if you are free of pain you have obtained peace of mind, *ataraxia,* the highest pleasure. But others have advocated that seeking pleasure and avoiding pain are human nature, and what humans ought to embark on in life is to accumulate good times. Jeremy Bentham believed all humans are hedonists. Everyone wants pleasure, so we search for it. Searching and finding are two different things, however, and the paradox of hedonism often

prevents us from finding what we are looking for. Suppose we set out to achieve pleasure on the weekend. We go to the beach, we take a walk in the woods, we hang out at the mall, we go to the movies, but we're just not enjoying ourselves very much; pleasure has somehow eluded us, and we face Monday with the sense of a lost weekend, telling ourselves that next weekend we'll look harder. Our friend, on the contrary, had a great time; he went with us because he likes going to the beach, loves the woods, wanted to look for a pair of jeans at the mall, and had been looking forward to seeing a movie for weeks. He even enjoyed our company. Why did he have a good weekend while we felt unfulfilled? Because we were trying to have a good time, and he was doing things he liked to do and enjoying being with someone he liked. The pleasure he got was, so to speak, a by-product of doing those things—it wasn't the main object of his activity. We, on the other hand, looked for pleasure without thinking about what we like to do that might give us pleasure, as if "pleasure" were a thing separate from everything else. The hedonistic paradox is this: If you look for pleasure, chances are you won't find it. (People who have been looking hard for someone to love experience a similar phenomenon.) Pleasure comes to you when you are in the middle of something else and rarely when you are looking for it. Sometimes the "Don Juan syndrome" is cited as an example of the hedonistic paradox. A person (traditionally a man,

but there is no reason it can't apply to women) who has numerous sexual conquests very often feels compelled to move from partner to partner because he or she likes the pursuit but somehow tires of an established relationship. Why is that the case? It could be because such people are unwilling to commit themselves to a permanent relationship, but it also may be due to the paradox of hedonism: In each partner they see the promise of "pleasure," but somehow all they end up with is another conquest. If they had been setting their sights on building a relationship with their partners, they might have found out that pleasure comes from being with someone you care for, and you have to care in order to feel pleasure; you can't expect pleasure to appear if there is no genuine feeling—or so the theory says.

Box 5.6 INTRINSIC VERSUS INSTRUMENTAL VALUES

An *instrumental* value is one that can be used as an instrument or a tool to get something else that we want. If you needed to get to class or work on time, a car might be the instrumental value that would get you there. If you didn't have a car, then money (or good credit) might be the instrumental value that would get you the car that would get you to school or to your workplace. How about going to school? If you're going to school to get a degree, then you might say that going to school is an instrumental value that will get your degree. And the degree? An instrumental value that will get you a good job. And the job? An instrumental value that will get what? More money. And what do you want with that? A better lifestyle, a better place to live, good health, and so on. And why do you

want a better lifestyle? Why do you want to be healthy? This is where the chain comes to an end, because we have reached something that is obvious: We want those things because we want them. Perhaps they "make us happy," but the bottom line is that we value them for their own sake, *intrinsically*. Some values can of course be both instrumental and intrinsic; the car may help you get to school, but also, you've wanted the car for a long time just because you like it. Exercising may make you healthy, but you also may actually enjoy it. And going to school is certainly a tool that can be used to get a degree, but some people appreciate training and knowledge for their own sake, not just because those goods can be used to get them somewhere in life.

The Hedonistic Calculus

How, exactly, do we choose a course of action? Before we decide what to do, we must calculate the probable outcomes of our actions. This is what has become known as Bentham's *hedonistic calculus* (also called the *hedonic calculus*). We must, he says, investigate all aspects of each proposed consequence: (1) Its *intensity*—how intense will the pleasure or pain be? (2) Its *duration*—how long will it last? (3) Its *certainty or uncertainty*—how sure can we be that it will follow from our action? (4) Its *propinquity or remoteness*—how far away is it, in time and space? (5) Its *fecundity*—how big are the chances that it will be followed by a similar pleasure or a similar pain? (6) Its *purity*—how big are the chances that it will not be followed by the opposite sensation (pain after pleasure, for example)? (7) Its *extent*—how many people will be affected by our decision? After considering those questions, we must do the following:

> Sum up all the values of all the *pleasures* on the one side, and those of all the pains on the other. . . . Take the balance; which, on the side of *pleasure,* will give the general *good tendency* of the act, with respect to the total number or community of individuals concerned; if on the side of pain, the general *evil tendency,* with respect to the same community.

What do we have here? A simple, democratic principle that seems to make no unreasonable demands of personal sacrifice, given that one's own pleasure and pain count just as much as anybody else's. Furthermore, in line with the scientific dreams of the Age of Reason (see Box 5.3), the proper moral conduct is calculated mathematically; values are reduced to a calculation of pleasure and pain, a method accessible to everyone with a basic understanding of arithmetic. By calculating pleasures and pains, one can presumably get a truly rational solution to any moral as well as nonmoral (morally neutral) problem.

That sounds very good, and yet there are several problems with this approach. For one thing, from where does Bentham get his numerical values? Ascertaining that our pleasure from eating a second piece of mud pie will be intense but will not last long and very likely will be followed by pain and remorse will not supply us with any numerical values to add or subtract: We have to make up the numerical values! That may not be as difficult as it seems, though. It is surprising how much people can agree on a value system, if they can just decide what should count as top and bottom value. If they agreed on a system that goes from −10 to +10, for example, most people would agree to assigning specific numerical values to the various consequences of eating that second piece of pie. What value would be assigned to the aspect of intensity? Not a 10, because that probably would apply only to the first piece, but perhaps an 8. The *duration* of the pleasure might get a measly 2 or 3, and the chance that it would be followed by pleasure or pain certainly would be way down in the negative numbers, perhaps −5 or worse. As for evaluating how many people are affected by the decision, that could take into account friends and family who don't want you to gain weight or the person who owns the second piece of pie (which you stole), who will be deprived of it if you eat it. All such hypothetical situations can be ascribed a value if people can agree on a value system to use for all choices, from personal ones to far-reaching political decisions. (See Box 5.7 for a discussion of pleasure as an indicator of happiness.)

Box 5.7 WHAT IS HAPPINESS?

One of the persistent problems in utilitarianism is the claim that the ultimate intrinsic value is happiness. We have already seen how the search for pleasure can lead to the hedonistic paradox (see Box 5.4), and this paradox is a problem for utilitarians as much as for anyone claiming that the ultimate reason we do things is to seek happiness. But is happiness the same as pleasure? Jeremy Bentham doesn't say, and indeed he doesn't care: For him, happiness is how *you* define it. John Stuart Mill defines happiness as distinct from both pleasure and contentment and views it as an intellectual achievement. Aristotle, who introduced the idea of happiness as a human goal to Western philosophy (see Chapter 9), also believed it was a result of rational activity and not a pursuit of pleasure. In the United States where our fundamental outlook on life has at least to some extent been shaped by the British tradition and the thoughts of John Locke in particular (see Chapter 7), access to *the pursuit of happiness* is considered a human right. In contrast, the German philosopher Friedrich Nietzsche (see Chapter 10), famous for acerbic remarks, once wrote, "Man does not strive for happiness; only the Englishman does!" That tells us in a nutshell what Nietzsche thought of the British....

In recent years there has been a surge of interest in the concept of happiness—among philosophers, but initially by psychologists. "Happiness Studies" have occupied not only intellectual minds, but have spilled over into self-help literature, and frequently publicized polls giving us a picture of which populations consider themselves happy. Again and again the people of Denmark have come out on top of the polls as the "happiest people on earth." But in what way, and why? The trouble with such surveys is that they don't specify what they mean by "happiness": a general feeling of being contented? Some kind of persistent feeling of ecstasy and exuberance? A feeling of deep peace within—akin to what the Greeks called *ataraxia*? Or perhaps a modest outlook on life where one doesn't have too high expectations? Or simply,

as Spanish economist Eduardo Punset suggests, the absence of misery? An interesting perspective comes from French philosopher Pascal Bruckner who argues, in his book *Perpetual Euphoria: On the Duty to Be Happy* (2011), that modern people are now obsessed with being happy, and feel like failures if they are not, as if happiness has become a duty. Bruckner himself sides with the analysis of the hedonistic paradox (Box 5.4) and says that happiness will elude us if we pursue it too vigorously. And what does happiness mean to Bruckner? A fleeting moment of *enchantment*, a "moment of grace," something to cherish when it happens, but you can't expect it to last or be a sustainable condition. And besides, he'd much rather have an adventurous life than a "happy" one, he says.

We are not likely to be able to agree on exactly what happiness means, but the question has occupied many people in many different cultures across the ages. Here is an ancient story which also suggests that happiness has nothing to do with physical comfort or indulgence: A Persian prince was told that to cure his unhappiness he had to wear the shirt of a happy man. The Persian prince now tried the shirts of lords, artists, merchants, soldiers, and fools, but it was to no avail. Happiness seemed to elude him. Finally he encountered a poor farmer singing behind his plow; the prince asked him if he was happy, and the farmer answered that he was. The prince then asked if he could have the farmer's shirt, and the farmer answered, "But I have no shirt!"

What this rating system adds up to is what most people would call the "pros and cons," those lists we sometimes make for ourselves when we are in severe doubt about what to do—what major field of study to choose, whether to go home for Thanksgiving or celebrate it with friends, whether to get married, whether to take a new job, and so on. The only difference is that in this system we assign numerical values to the pros and cons. Can such a list really help us make rational decisions? Bentham believed it was an infallible system for rational choice. A method that quantifies (makes measurable) the elusive qualities of life would certainly be useful, and several workplaces today are actually employing a form of hedonistic calculus in their hiring process: Applicants are rated according to their qualifications, and those qualifications are assigned numerical values (they are quantified); the person with the highest score presumably gets the job. Another area in which the calculus has had a rebirth is in the field of health care, where attempts are being made to create an objective measure for what is known as *quality of life* (see Chapter 7). One person's idea of quality of life may not be the same as another person's, however, and even in workplaces where such a hiring method is used, other, less rational, elements may play a part in the hiring process (such as the looks of the applicant or relation to the employer). People who have given Bentham's system a try in their own personal decision making often find that it may help in clarifying one's options, but the results are not always persuasive. You may end up with 16 items on the con side and four on the pro side and still find yourself getting married or taking a new job simply because you want to so badly. There are parts of the human psyche that simply don't respond to rational arguments, and Bentham didn't have much appreciation for that. Interestingly enough, his godson and successor, John Stuart Mill, did have just such an appreciation, and we will look at his work shortly.

But suppose you actually make a detailed list of the consequences of your actions. How, exactly, do you decide on the values that you assign each consequence? In some cases it is easy, as for example when you compare school fees or driving distances. But if you want to decide whether to stay in school for the duration or quit and get a job and make fast money, how do you choose what things to put on your list? Critics of Bentham's approach say that if we assign a higher value to getting an education than to acquiring fast money, then it is because we are operating within a system that favors higher education; in other words, we are *biased,* and our choice of values reflects that bias. To put it another way, we rig the test even as we perform it. If we were operating within a system that favored making money—for instance, if we already had left school to make money—then our values would reflect that bias. The values, therefore, are truly arbitrary, depending on what we would like the outcome to be, and we can't trust the hedonistic calculus to give us an objective, mathematically certain picture of what to do. That does not mean such lists are useless; they can tell us much about ourselves and our own preferences and biases. However, they can do little more than that, because we can change the numbers until we get the result we want!

The Uncertain Future

Utilitarianism might still be able to offer a less presumptuous system, one designed to give guidance and material for reflection rather than objectively calculated solutions. Even with that kind of system, though, there are problems to be dealt with. One lies in the concept of *consequences* itself (see Box 5.2). Of course, we can't claim that an action has any consequences before we actually have taken that action. The consequences we are evaluating are hypothetical; they have yet to occur. How can we decide once and for all whether an action is morally good if the consequences are still up in the air? We have to (1) make an educated guess and hope for the best, (2) act, and (3) wait to see the results. If we're lucky and wise, the results will be as positive as what we hoped for. But suppose they aren't. Before we learn the results, our good intentions are of course part of the plus side of the hedonistic calculus: If we intend to create beneficial consequences for as many as possible, it is a process that the utilitarian will approve of. But the true value of our action is not clear until the consequences are clear. You may intend to create much happiness, and your calculations may be educated, but your intentions may still be foiled by forces beyond your control. In that case, it is the *end result* that counts and not your fine intentions and calculations. How long do we have to wait until we know whether our actions were morally good or evil? It may take a long time before all the effects are known—maybe a hundred years or more. Critics of utilitarianism say it is just not reasonable to use a moral system that doesn't allow us to know whether what we did was morally right or wrong until some time in the far-off future. Furthermore, how will we ever be able to decide anything in the first place? Thousands—perhaps millions—of big and small consequences result from everything we do. Do we have to calculate them all? How can we ever make a quick decision if we have to go through such a complicated process every time?

Answers to such criticisms were provided by the philosopher and economist John Stuart Mill (1806–1873). For one thing, Mill says, we don't have to calculate every little effect of our action; we can rely on the common experience of humanity. Through the millennia, humans have had to make similar decisions all the time, and we can consider their successes and failures in deciding our own actions. (Because Mill had actually given up on calculating every action to an exact mathematical value, it was easier for him than for Bentham to allow for some uncertainty in future results.) What about having to wait a long time for future consequences to happen, in order to pass judgment on the morality of our action? Mill says all we have to do is wait a reasonable amount of time—a short wait for small actions, a longer wait for bigger actions. Mill relies on us to know intuitively what he means, and perhaps we do. But the problems inherent in utilitarianism are not solved with those suggestions, merely diffused a little.

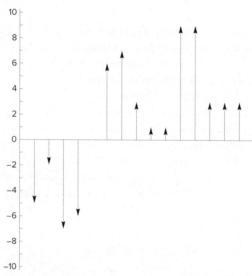

Sheer numbers: If we imagine the horizontal line representing a neutral position in terms of pain and pleasure, 0, the vertical line above 0 representing pleasure, and the line below 0 representing pain, we have a visual representation of the hedonistic calculus. Here all that matters is that the positive numbers outweigh the negative numbers. So if we have a scenario where many (humans or animals) are suffering but not much contentment is generated, the utilitarian would be against it. If only a few are suffering, and the many benefit from their suffering, it is the morally right course of action, according to utilitarianism.

Advantages and Problems of Sheer Numbers: From Animal Welfare to the Question of Torture

Initially, the idea of creating as much pleasure as possible for as many as possible seems a positive one. If we read on in Bentham's writings, we even find that "the many" may not be limited to humans. Bentham's theory was so advanced for its time that it not only gave the right to seek pleasure and avoid pain to all humans, regardless of social standing, but also said that the criterion for who belongs in the moral universe is not who has the capability to speak or to reason but *who can suffer,* and surely suffering is not limited to human beings. (See Box 5.8 for a discussion of suffering and nonhuman animals.) The contemporary philosopher Peter Singer (see Chapter 4) has taken this aspect of utilitarianism to heart and has become one of today's most vocal champions of animal rights and welfare, even to the point where he believes that some animals deserve at least as much moral consideration as some humans, and occasionally more, based on the evaluation of the capacity for joy and suffering in a given animal as opposed to a given human being. His books such as *In Defense of Animals* (1985) and *Animal Liberation: A Practical Guide* (1987) have become controversial classics. In an article from the *New York Times* in January 2007 he says, "We are always ready to find dignity in human beings, including those whose mental age will never exceed that of an infant, but we don't attribute dignity to dogs or cats, though they clearly operate at a more advanced mental level than human infants. Just making that comparison provokes outrage in some quarters. But why should dignity always go together with species membership, no matter what the characteristics of the individual may be?"

Box 5.8 WHO CAN SUFFER?

Jeremy Bentham's insistence that the moral universe be open to any creature who can suffer is still a controversial statement, and in Bentham's own day it was extremely radical. Of his influential contemporaries, only John Stuart Mill took up the idea that humans are not necessarily the only members of the moral realm; it was (and still is) standard procedure to view morality as something only humans can engage in or benefit from. Most arguments that exclude animals are based on the assumption that they can't speak or reason (which is why Bentham says this is irrelevant and asks, "Can they suffer?"). To most people, then and now, it is obvious that animals can suffer—all we have to do is observe an injured animal. But to some thinkers, this is not a foregone conclusion. An argument that used to be popular in theology was that humans suffer because Adam and Eve sinned against God in the Garden of Eden, and suffering was their, and their children's, punishment; since animals have not sinned against God, they can't suffer. A more influential argument in philosophy comes from René Descartes (1596–1650), otherwise known for opening up the gates of modern philosophy with his statement "I think, therefore I am." Descartes argued that only humans have minds; everything else in the world consists of matter only, including animals. If you have a mind, you can have awareness of suffering; if you have no mind, your body may be subjected to physical stress, but you won't know it. The dog whose tail is caught in the door will yelp, but that is no sign of feeling pain, according to Descartes—that is the way the dog is constructed, like a clock with moving parts (in today's jargon, the dog is *programmed*

to yelp). The dog itself has no mind and feels nothing. (Descartes actually was a dog owner; according to legend, his dog's name was Monsieur Grat.) When challenged by Margaret Cavendish, the Duchess of Newcastle, Descartes's answer was that if animals had minds, then oysters would have to have minds too, and he found that ridiculous. Margaret Cavendish was a writer with an interest in science. Like most contemporary readers, she knew that there is a considerable difference between the nervous systems of dogs and oysters, but Descartes's viewpoint has had immense influence on the treatment of animals to this day.

Modern biology generally assumes that mammals and many other animals can feel pain, precisely because there is such a similarity between their nervous systems and ours. In addition, the capacity for suffering seems to be an evolutionary advantage; a being that can feel pain is more likely to be cautious, to survive, and to propagate. And finding support in recent neurological research, there is far more willingness among animal researchers today to accept that animals can feel pain, both physically *and* emotionally. All animals, from humans to reptiles, share a structure in the brain called the *amygdala,* which is responsible for the "fight-or-flight" reaction. It is the amygdala that is activated when our heart starts pumping, our palms get sweaty, and we feel fear or panic, and that reaction is an ancient, primitive, and very useful response to danger that we share with most other vertebrates on this planet. So we can all be afraid—but what is generally less known is that the same, ancient part of the brain, sometimes called the "reptile brain," can also know pleasure, even joy. Life in the wild has never been merely a terrified existence from one dangerous moment to another—it is also full of good times and exuberance! Recent research involving MRI scans have even shown that *dogs* have the emotional sophistication of a 3- to 4-year-old human child, both in terms of their fears and their joys. Suffering and joy are, as Bentham suspected, a part of life not only for humans but for most other animals as well. The utilitarian Peter Singer has argued that there is no reason to assume that *fish* can't feel pain. Where we humans differ from most other animals is that we are *aware* of our own feelings and of our own existence. You can read more about ethical treatment of animals in Chapter 13.

Popperfoto/Getty Images

René Descartes (1596–1650), French philosopher, mathematician, and naturalist, known as the founder of modern philosophy; he is particularly famous for having said, "*Cogito, ergo sum*," or, "I think, therefore I am." Descartes believed that a human consists of a body and a soul; thanks to the soul, humans can be self-aware and conscious of their bodies, including physical pleasures and pains. But since Descartes couldn't imagine that animals have souls, he had to conclude that animals couldn't be aware of their physical condition either, so the inevitable deductive conclusion was, for him, that animals can't feel pain.

If we assume that the capacity to suffer (and feel pleasure) qualifies a living organism for inclusion in the moral universe, and if we believe that each individual's pleasure counts equally, we find ourselves with a dramatically expanded moral universe. Even today, the idea that all creatures who can suffer deserve to be treated with dignity does not meet with the approval of every policymaker. Moreover, if the decrease of suffering and the increase of happiness are all that counts for all these members of our moral universe, what does it mean for our decision if the happiness of some can be obtained only at the cost of the suffering of others? This is where we encounter the problem of *sheer numbers* in utilitarianism, because whatever creates more happiness for more individuals or decreases their pain is morally right *by definition*. If giving up animal-tested household products causes human housekeepers only minor inconvenience, then we have no excuse to keep using them, because major suffering is caused by such testing. Indeed, the focus on animal suffering has become much more prevalent among scientists within the last 30 years: Where countless rabbits would be used in the past in tests on cosmetics and household products, new methods are now being developed in which lab-grown human skin, "Episkin," can be used instead to determine whether the cosmetic ingredients will damage the skin; that is in response to the European Union directive that banned animal testing by 2013. However, if it could be shown that only a few animals would have to suffer (even if they would suffer horribly) so that an immense number of humans would find their housecleaning greatly eased, would it then be permissible to cause such suffering? Yes, says the utilitarian, if the pleasure gained from easy housecleaning in a large number of households could be added up and favorably compared with the immense suffering of only a very few nonhuman animals.

The argument for doing whatever benefits more living creatures, human or nonhuman, is usually advanced with regard to animal testing of medical procedures that could benefit humans. But because sheer numbers are all that matter in utilitarianism, the housecleaning example works too. Curing human ailments is not intrinsically "better" than helping humans clean their houses—what matters is the happiness that is created and the misery that is prevented. Suppose feline leukemia could be cured by subjecting ten humans to painful experiments. The humans would certainly suffer, but all cats would, from then on, be free of leukemia. For some, this type of example reveals the perversely narrow focus of utilitarianism; looking at pleasure and pain and adding them up are simply not enough. For others, examples like this one only confirm that all creatures matter, and no one's pain should be more or less important than anyone else's.

To focus on the problem, let's assume that we are faced with a situation in which some humans are sacrificed for the happiness and welfare of other humans. Suppose it is revealed that governments around the world have for years had a secret pact with aliens from outer space whereby the governments have agreed to deny consistently that UFOs exist and to not interfere with occasional alien abductions of humans for medical experiments. In return, at the end of their experiments, the aliens will provide humanity with a cure for all viral diseases. For a great number of people, that would be a trade well worth the suffering of the "specimens" involved—provided that they themselves would not be among the specimens. Indeed, some humans might even *volunteer* for the experiments, but let us assume, as a condition, that the human subjects are reluctant participants, and no volunteers are accepted. Although some people would gladly commit their fellow humans to death from suffering, others would insist that it is not right; somehow, these humans do not deserve such a fate, and the immense advantages to humankind forever do not really make up for it. In other words, some may have a moral sense that the price is too high, but utilitarianism can't acknowledge such a moral intuition because its only moral criterion is one of sheer numbers. For many, the morality of utilitarianism is counterintuitive when applied to some very poignant human situations.

The UFO example is (or at least it is intended to be) fictional. But recent history has revealed to us a number of real-life, large-scale cases in which a number of people have unwittingly been made into guinea pigs for the sake of some greater cause. What if we could accomplish beneficial results for a large number of people or living beings at the cost of intolerable pain suffered by a few? Whether one sees immediate benefits to a population, such as security measures, or long-term benefits, such as medical knowledge, the price of pain and suffering, even death, was paid by human beings, not by choice but by force, for the sake of some higher goal. The Tuskegee syphilis experiment is a chilling example, but it doesn't end there. Other morally questionable governmental practices have been revealed; see Box 4.5 for some examples. The fictional example of a doctor having to choose whether to cure five terminally ill patients by harvesting organs from one healthy individual may sound outlandish, but on a greater scale the utilitarian idea of maximizing happiness for the many by causing misery for the few has been the guiding principle. Such experiments have reduced people to being mere tools in someone else's agenda. A classic utilitarian will answer that, depending on the greatness and the nature of the goal, the sacrifice and suffering might well be worth the price. But John Stuart Mill added that, in the long run, a population abusing a minority will reap not good results but social unrest, so such practices should be discouraged. (See the subsequent section on act and rule utilitarianism.)

Still, the salvation of humanity is a forceful argument. Let us suppose, however, that we are talking not about salvation from disease but about salvation from boredom. Television is already moving toward showing live or videotaping events involving human suffering and death; home movies are often the source of that footage, and this form of "entertainment" has become increasingly popular. YouTube has a large selection of private videos of young men and women engaging in violent acts toward others. Might viewers choose to watch real-time shows of criminals who are granted one television hour to run through a city or a neighborhood, avoiding snipers and hoping to live through it all and win their freedom? The Romans watched Christians, slaves, criminals, prisoners of war, and wild animals fight each other, with much appreciation for the entertainment value of such events. If they had the ability to televise the events, might we not assume that they would have done so, having recognized that "bread and circuses" (food and entertainment) would appease the unruly masses? According to the utilitarian calculation, a great number of people may be hugely entertained by the immense suffering of one or a few. How far are we allowed to let numbers run away with us in disregarding people's inherent right to fair treatment?

A common utilitarian reply is that under such circumstances, people start worrying about being victimized, and social unrest follows. Until that happens, though, utilitarians must conclude that there is justification in letting a large number of people enjoy the results of the suffering of a few (or even enjoy the suffering itself).

In the Narratives section you'll find several stories illustrating this problem of "sheer numbers": Wessel's satire "The Blacksmith and the Baker"; a selection from Dostoyevsky's *Brothers Karamazov;* Ursula K. Le Guin's story about a child being tortured for the sake of communal happiness, "The Ones Who Walk Away from Omelas"; a summary of the movie *Extreme Measures;* as well as a summary of an episode from the television series *The Good Place,* "The trolley problem." Once we start identifying the utilitarian sheer-numbers problem as one of disregard for the rights of the individual for the sake of the well-being of the many, we tend to be critical of any decision that would favor the happiness of the majority over the rights of a minority, and perhaps rightfully so. However, there are compelling scenarios that make us reevaluate the simple math of Bentham's utilitarianism: When push comes to shove, and hard decisions have to be made in a split second, saving the many by sacrificing the few may be the decision most of us would agree with. Think back to that dreadful day of September 11, 2001, when four airplanes were hijacked with the presumed intent to cause as much damage as possible to people and institutions. Three planes hit their targets: the World Trade Center towers and the Pentagon. But as you may recall, the fourth plane, Flight 93, did not reach its intended target, in all likelihood the Capitol or the White House, because of the heroic resolve of the passengers fighting back, and forcing the plane down. But in the aftermath we also learned that had the passengers not acted, Flight 93 would probably not have reached its target anyway, because U.S. Air Force fighter jets were already poised to escort the plane down or, if necessary, shoot it down. That came as a shock to many Americans, in particular when the government announced that *any* plane on a collision course with a civilian or military structure would be regarded as a threat and would be shot down. Here we see the principle of utility at work in a desperate situation: Sacrifice the few on the plane rather than take a chance and risk the lives of the many on the ground and the security of our institutions. Some might say, "But those people on the plane were going to die when the plane hit the building anyway, so what difference did it make if they died sooner rather than later?" The difference is in the attitude regarding the few as expendable. Furthermore, it isn't a *given* that they would die anyway. So if we could limit terrible consequences for a large number of people by sacrificing a few innocent people, would the decision be acceptable, even if we happened to be among the unfortunate few ourselves? If we say yes, where do we draw the line? How do we define "terrible consequences"? And, if we say no, are we seriously advocating that it is better for the many to perish in the name of fairness than for the many to survive at the cost of the lives of the few?

It is one thing to contemplate the sacrifice of the innocent few to save the many, but how about causing pain to a few people who are not "innocent," such as captured terrorists, for the sake of extracting information? If lives of our soldiers and civilians might be saved, should we engage in **torture of prisoners** who may have the information we need? The hedonistic calculus seems to have a clear answer: We just have to calculate the projected pains involved in administering torture, as opposed to not doing it. But elsewhere the debate has been vigorous among the public, media hosts, and politicians, reaching the Capitol, where new guidelines for torture were established under the Bush administration and revised again by the Obama administration. Here we are looking at a prime example of why a discussion of *metaethics* is important (see Chapter 3): We may have an idea of what torture is and who has been known to commit torture (a descriptive approach), and we may have strong opinions about whether or not torture should be acceptable under certain conditions (a normative approach), but how do we know that we agree on the meaning of the concept of torture (a metaethical approach)? Subjecting a person to methodical, physical pain that leaves permanent or at least long-lasting damage is recognized by everyone as "torture," but what about "enhanced" interrogation methods that leave no physical damage, but do result in psychological scars—such as waterboarding? The Military Commissions Act (Antiterrorism) of 2006 upheld the Geneva Convention for lawful enemy combatants but not for "unlawful enemy combatants"—that is, terrorists. There was some dispute as to whether this might include U.S. citizens. To a great extent, that revised version left the very definition of torture open to interpretation. The Antiterrorism Act did not initially label waterboarding as torture, and the method has been used by the CIA numerous times on at least three prisoners suspected of terrorism (see Chapter 3), presumably leading to valuable information although that has later been contested. However, the Obama administration reclassified waterboarding as torture, and thus made it unavailable as a way to extract information.

In Chapter 6 we look at the viewpoint that regardless of whether torture or "enhanced" interrogation methods yield results, such methods are fundamentally morally wrong in themselves. But for a utilitarian viewpoint the all-important question is, Do they work, and what are the costs compared to the benefits? Senator John McCain (who himself was tortured as a POW during the Vietnam War) argued that the United States should not engage in the torture of enemy combatants/terrorists, because *it doesn't yield reliable knowledge*: The prisoner will say anything to make the torture stop, and sometimes he, or she, has been trained to give out disinformation under duress. Put into a utilitarian formula, the pain caused will not yield sufficiently useful results to justify the pain. Opponents of McCain's view have argued that in an extreme situation we would be remiss if we didn't use harsh interrogation methods as a last resort. The response from McCain and others has been that methods of torture generally don't work, and when employed, may lead to further acts of revenge by the groups whose members have been tortured. All these arguments are, of course, fundamentally utilitarian: The pro-torture argument says that resorting to torture, on rare occasions, will give us the edge we need to survive, so the good consequences outweigh the bad; the anti-torture argument says that torture doesn't yield reliable information, and the counterattacks will escalate as a matter of revenge, so the bad consequences outweigh the good.

Would Bentham be in favor of torturing terrorists who are presumed to have knowledge about a future terror attack, or the whereabouts of their leader? It would depend exclusively on the probable outcome. Critics of Bentham—and of torture—point out that if we can use torture methods as a last resort, what is to stop us from lowering the bar and using such methods in less serious situations? For proponents of using enhanced interrogation methods including waterboarding, there is no doubt that it is a measure to be used only as a last resort, and a necessary one: While we are respecting all other human beings, some of them are preparing to kill us, and we can't afford to lose our vigilance. But, say the critics, in that way we lose sight of what we have cherished the most since the creation of this nation: the fundamental respect for other human beings. The foundation for that respect will be explored in Chapter 6.

Utilitarianism and the Trolley Problem

When you first encountered the trolley problem in Chapter 1, you read about Foot's original version vs. Judith Jarvis Thomson's version with the "fat man" being pushed onto the tracks, stopping the trolley and saving the five people on the tracks, and you also read that experimental philosophers Joshua Green and Jonathan Cohen conducted thought experiments where they concluded that, due to the emotional situation, most test subjects were simply incapable of switching the tracks and saving five people if the price was the life of one person. And you also read that the trolley problem has taken on a life of its own. One might say that it has by now become a "trope" or a "meme" (see Chapter 2), recognizable by most people. Here we take a closer look at the problem from a utilitarian point of view. In the Narratives section, you'll find a summary of Season 2, Episode 5 of the television sitcom *The Good Place*, featuring the trolley problem. Here is Foot's original text from her paper, "The Problem of Abortion and the Doctrine of the Double Effect" from 1967; the trolley problem occupies all of three lines:

> Suppose that a judge or magistrate is faced with rioters demanding that a culprit be found for a certain crime and threatening otherwise to take their own bloody revenge on a particular section of the community. The real culprit being unknown, the judge sees himself as able to prevent the bloodshed only by framing some innocent person and having him executed. Beside this example is placed another in which a pilot whose aeroplane is about to crash is deciding whether to steer from a more to a less inhabited area. To make the parallel as close as possible *it may rather be supposed that he is the driver of a runaway tram which he can only steer from one narrow track on to another; five men are working on one track and one man on the other; anyone on the track he enters is bound to be killed.* In the case of the

riots the mob has five hostages, so that in both the exchange is supposed to be one man's life for the lives of five. *The question is why we should say, without hesitation, that the driver should steer for the less occupied track, while most of us would be appalled at the idea that the innocent man could be framed.*

Foot's original intention was, as you read in Chapter 1, to discuss the concepts of killing vs. letting die, or what philosophers call the *double effect* (see Chapter 13): if an act has two consequences, one good and one bad (and it is wrong to do something bad), the good consequence may outweigh the bad if the bad consequence is done unintentionally, and is unavoidable in order to obtain the good consequence—such as saving the five people by diverting the trolley to the track with the one person. But Foot implicitly criticizes utilitarianism by asking whether it is always the right thing to do to save the many, as long as the end result is more happiness than suffering: why would we be so willing to kill an innocent worker on the track to save five, while we're upset if an innocent person is falsely accused and executed in order to preserve peace? (You may want to read the story in the Narratives section about "The Blacksmith and the Baker," which is essentially the same scenario—from the nineteenth century! Other similar stories have been used by utilitarians and their critics for over 200 years.) Having read about the "sheer numbers" problem in this chapter, you can now identify what it was Foot was getting at with her original example: Yes, it may seem logical to save five lives and sacrifice one, but is it *morally right*? If we don't want an innocent person to get framed and executed, even if the consequences are good for everyone else, we should also feel squeamish about diverting the trolley and kill the worker. Joshua Green calls it the *normative* trolley problem, as opposed to the *descriptive* trolley problem: the descriptive trolley problem asks, "*Could* you kill one person to save five?" but the normative trolley problem asks, "*Should* you kill one person to save five?" You may want to discuss what the difference is between the two questions.

Why is it distasteful to us to sacrifice an involuntary person to help the many? Because we don't want to be that involuntary person? Or because we understand what that involuntary person might feel? Or simply because we feel it is wrong to use a person as a tool to obtain advantages for others? In Chapter 6, we look at that angle.

John Stuart Mill: A Different Kind of Utilitarian

Bentham was not alone in designing the theory of utilitarianism. He and his close friend James Mill worked out the specifics of the new moral system together. Mill's son John Stuart Mill, the eldest of nine children, was a very bright boy, and James Mill's ambition was to develop his son's talents and intelligence as much as possible and as fast as possible through home schooling. The boy responded well, learned quickly, and was able to read Greek and Latin at an early age. Throughout his childhood he was groomed to become a scientist. He was tutored privately and performed marvelously until he came to a halt at the age of 20, struck by a nervous breakdown. His crisis was quiet and polite, in accordance with his nature: He went on with his work, and few people close to him realized what was going on; but internally he stopped in his tracks and in a very modern sense decided to "get in touch with himself," for he had come to the realization that despite his intense studying, one part of his education was pitifully incomplete. He knew much about how to think, but he didn't know how to *feel;* as a child he had been emotionally deprived and had never been allowed to have playmates other than his sisters Willie, Harriet, and Clara, and he now felt totally inadequate in his emotional life. (If you remember from Chapter 2 the emphasis that was placed on feelings during the Age of Romanticism, you'll have an even better understanding of what Mill went through, because he was a young man of 20 when the Age of Romanticism was at its peak.) In the months before his breakdown, he had engaged in debates, published articles, helped edit a major work by Bentham, and was probably beginning to suffer from what we today call burnout—at the very least, he was overworked.

Later in life, Mill described his breakdown in his *Autobiography;* in modern terminology, he put a spin on it that reflected his rebellion against Jeremy Bentham:

> From the winter of 1821, when I first read Bentham . . . I had what might truly be called an object in life; to be a reformer of the world. My conception of my own life was entirely identified with this object. . . . But the time came when I awakened from this as from a dream. It was in the autumn of 1826. I was in a dull state of nerves, such as everybody is occasionally liable to; unsusceptible to enjoyment or pleasurable excitement. . . . In this frame of mind it occurred to me to put the question directly to myself: "Suppose that all your objects in life were realized; that all the changes in institutions and opinions which you are looking forward to, could be completely effected at this very instant: would this be a great joy and happiness to you?" And an irrepressible self-consciousness distinctly answered, "No!" At this my heart sank within me: the whole foundation on which my life was constructed fell down. . . . I seemed to have nothing left to live for. . . . If I had loved anyone sufficiently to make confiding my griefs a necessity, I should not have been in the condition I was.

What Mill read into his breakdown later in life was that his father's intellectual training and Bentham's philosophy had let him down—the utilitarian greatest-happiness principle might lead to happiness for the many, but it didn't necessarily lead to happiness for the utilitarian. Mill, in his *Autobiography,* uses this term to ram a lesson home: You don't find happiness by looking for it but by enjoying life along the way as you focus on other things. "Ask yourself whether you are happy, and you cease to be so." In his crisis, Mill rediscovered the truth of the paradox of hedonism: The harder you look for happiness, the more likely it is to elude you. But what really happened to him psychologically may not have been clear to Mill at all. For one thing, he was overworked, and winter was approaching. For another, he found himself a cerebral intellectual in the midst of the most feeling-oriented period so far in Western history. For a third, he was lonely and became depressed; he had what we've come to know as a severe case of "the blues." But the loneliness problem didn't last long. Neither did his disenchantment with utilitarianism—he just stopped looking for self-gratification in it and focused on the goal of improving the world.

Library of Congress Prints and Photographs Division

John Stuart Mill (1806-1873), English philosopher and economist. Believing that utilitarianism was the only reasonable moral system, Mill nevertheless saw Jeremy Bentham's version as rather crude and created a more sophisticated version of the principle of utility, taking into consideration the qualitative differences between pleasures.

Mill began exploring the world of feelings—music, poetry, literature—and later he went abroad to the European continent and traveled (as did the Romantic painters and poets). In a roundabout way, Mill's personal story illustrates Nussbaum's theory that emotions are not irrelevant for ethics (see Chapter 1). During this period he took time out to reexamine his life and his future, turned his back on the sciences, and decided to "go into his father's business" and become a social thinker and an economist. As a social thinker he became one of the most influential persons of the nineteenth century, laying the foundation for many of the political ideas in the Western world on both the liberal and the conservative sides. Below we look at the three areas in philosophy where Mill has had a profound influence: (1) his theory of the higher and lower pleasures, (2) his theory of the harm principle, and (3) his commitment to equal rights for women.

Mill's Revision of Utilitarianism: The Higher and Lower Pleasures

Mill's aim was to take his godfather and father's theory of utilitarianism and redesign it to fit a more sophisticated age. What had seemed overwhelmingly important to Bentham—a more just legal system—was no longer the primary goal, for he realized that without proper education for the general population, true social equality would not be obtained. Mill also realized that Bentham's version of utilitarianism had several flaws. For one thing, it was too simple; it relied on a very straightforward system of identifying good with pleasure and evil with pain, without specifying the nature of pleasure and pain. (Some say this was actually one of the strengths of early utilitarianism, but Mill saw it as a serious deficiency.) Bentham's version also assumed that people were so rational they would always follow the moral calculations. Mill pointed out, however, that even if people are clearly shown it would give them and others more overall pleasure to change their course of action, they are likely to continue doing what they are used to because people are creatures of habit; our emotions, rather than cool deliberation, often dictate what we do. We can't, therefore, rely on our rationality to the extreme degree that Bentham thought we could. (That doesn't mean, of course, that we can't *educate* children and adults to use their heads more profitably.) We will return to the education question later, but first we look at how Mill decided to redesign the theory of utilitarianism.

Mill seems to have been a more complex person than Bentham, and his theory reflects that complexity. For Mill the idea that humans seek pleasure and that moral goodness lies in obtaining that pleasure is only half the story—but it is the half that is more frequently misunderstood. What do people think when they hear this idea? That all that counts is easy gratification of any desire they may have—in other words, a "doctrine worthy only of swine," as Mill says, repeating the words of the critics of utilitarianism. And because people reject the notion of seeking only swinish pleasures, they reject utilitarianism as an unworthy theory. They get upset, said Mill, precisely because they are not pigs and want more out of life than a pig could ever want. People are simply not content with basic pleasures, and a good moral and social theory should reflect that. Furthermore, says Mill, all theories that have advocated happiness have been accused of talking about easy gratification, but that is an unfair criticism when applied to utilitarianism. Even Epicurus held that there are many things in life other than physical pleasures that can bring us happiness, and there is nothing in utilitarianism that says we have to define pleasure and happiness as mere gratification of physical desires.

Why was Mill so uneasy about being accused of seeking gratification of physical desires? Consider the changing times in which he lived. When Mill wrote his book *Utilitarianism* (1863), the British Empire was 26 years into the Victorian era. Queen Victoria had ascended the throne in 1837, and morals had subtly undergone a shift since Bentham's day; preoccupation with physical pleasures was, on the whole, frowned upon by the middle classes, more so than in the previous generation—it was not considered proper to display such indulgence. For many, that signifies an age of hypocrisy, of double standards, but it would be unfair to accuse Mill of such double standards, because several of his truly innovative social ideas stemmed from his indignation toward this preoccupation with the way other people choose to live. However, it may have been a sign of the times that Mill felt compelled to reassure his readers that they could be followers of utilitarianism and read Bentham without being labeled hedonists.

Some believe there is also a personal side to the story. In his early twenties, Mill, having earlier worried that he didn't have any knowledge of feelings, fell head over heels in love with a young married woman, Harriet Taylor, and the feeling was mutual. They maintained a relationship for almost twenty years, until her husband died, and then they finally got married. Their relationship had become an open secret over the years, even to Mr. Taylor. (Being honest people, they apparently told him of their feelings, but he was also assured that they had no intention of breaking up the Taylor marriage.) It has generally been assumed that they were sexually involved, but judging from their correspondence, it may well have been a platonic friendship until their wedding. Their letters testify to Mill's later version of utilitarianism: The two seem to agree that spiritual pleasures and intellectual companionship are more valuable than physical gratification. John Stuart Mill prepared his book *Utilitarianism* during the years of their marriage, but when it was published in 1863, Harriet was no longer alive. She died (probably of tuberculosis) less than ten years after they got married; however, Mill's moral and political writings were clearly inspired by their intellectual discussions over three decades. (See Box 5.9 for a discussion of Mill's views on women's rights.)

What, then, does Mill propose? That some pleasures are more valuable, "higher," than others. That on the whole, humans prefer to hold on to their dignity and strive for truly fulfilling experiences rather than settle for easy contentment. *It is better to be a human dissatisfied than a pig satisfied, better to be Socrates dissatisfied than a fool satisfied,* says Mill. Even if the great pleasures in life require some effort—for instance, one has to learn math to understand the joy of solving a mathematical problem—it is worth the effort, because the pleasure is greater than if you had just remained passive.

Box 5.9 MILL AND THE WOMEN'S CAUSE

John Stuart Mill is today recognized as the first influential male speaker for political equality between men and women in modern Western history. (In England, Mary Wollstonecraft published her *Vindication of the Rights of Women* in 1792, but already in 1673 the French author Poulain de la Barre, a student of Descartes, had published *De l'égalité des deux sexes,* in which he argued for total equality between men and women because of their equality in reasoning power. That book, however, was largely ignored for a long time.) Mill's book *The Subjection of Women* (1869) revealed to his readers the abyss of inequality separating the lives of men and women in what was then considered a modern society. His exposé of this inequality was a strong contributing factor in women obtaining the right to vote in England, as well as elsewhere in the Western world. In 1866 Mill, then a member of the British Parliament, had tried to get a measure passed that would establish gender equality in England. The measure failed, but Mill had succeeded in drawing attention to the issue. It is often mentioned in this context that Mill was inspired by his longtime friend and later wife, Harriet Taylor, an intellectual in her own right, although he had shown an interest in the women's rights issue in an article from 1824 when he was only nineteen. In the Primary Readings section in Chapter 12, you'll find a text by Harriet Taylor Mill, as well as an overview of the early years of feminism.

Now the question becomes, Who is to say which pleasures are the higher ones and which are the lower ones? We seem predisposed to assume that the physical pleasures are the lower ones, but need that be the case? Mill proposes a test: We must ask people who are familiar with both kinds of pleasure, and whatever they choose as the higher goal is the ultimate answer. Suppose we gather a group of people who sometimes order a pizza and beer and watch *Monday Night Football* or a reality show but also occasionally go out to a French restaurant before watching foreign, subtitled art films on Netflix. We ask them which activity—pizza and football or French food and a subtitled movie is the higher pleasure. If the test works, we must accept it if the majority say that on the whole they think pizza and football is the higher pleasure. But will Mill accept that? This is the drawback of his test—it appears that he will not:

> Capacity for the nobler feelings is in most natures a very tender plant, easily killed, not only by hostile influences, but by mere want of sustenance; and in the majority of young persons it speedily dies away if the occupations to which their position in life has devoted them, and the society into which it has thrown them, are not favorable to keeping that higher capacity in exercise. Men lose their high aspirations as they lose their intellectual tastes, because they have not time or opportunity for indulging them; and they addict themselves to inferior pleasures not because they deliberately

prefer them, but because they are either the only ones to which they have access or the only ones which they are any longer capable of enjoying.

What does that mean? It means if you vote for pizza and football as the overall winner, Mill will claim you have lost the capacity for enjoying gourmet French food and intellectual television (which demands some attention from your intellect), or, to use a modern expression, "Use it or lose it." In other words, he has rigged his own test. This has caused some critics to voice the opinion that Mill is an intellectual snob, a "cultural imperialist" trying to impose his own standards on the general population. And the immediate victim of this procedure? The egalitarian principle that was the foundation of Bentham's version of utilitarianism—that one person equals one vote regarding what is pleasurable and what is painful—collapses under Mill's test. According to him, we have to go to the "authorities of happiness" to find out what it is that everybody ought to desire.

Framed Art/Alamy Stock Photo

Harriet Hardy Taylor Mill (1807-1858) was a chief source of inspiration for her longtime friend and later husband John Stuart Mill. Her views on individual rights are reflected in Mill's book *On Liberty* (1859), published immediately after her death. They did not agree on everything, though: Mill believed that when a woman marries, she must give up working outside the home; Taylor believed that women have a right to employment regardless of their marital status and that no-fault divorce should be available. However, the spouses seemed to be in agreement on most other issues and found in each other what we today call a soul mate. Mill grieved deeply when she died and bought a house close to the cemetery where she was laid to rest so he could visit her grave often.

If we perform Mill's test and ask individuals who seem to know of many kinds of pleasure what they prefer, we may get responses that Mill would not have accepted, because some people may indeed favor physical pleasures over intellectual or spiritual ones; however, a recent study claimed (with no reference to Mill whatsoever) that people who have a spiritual side are happier overall than are people whose lives are completely focused on material pleasures. Now, it is questionable in itself whether it is at all possible to put together reliable statistics on this topic, but Mill would probably have welcomed the survey: It is not merely because higher, intellectual, or spiritual pleasures are somehow finer that he recommends them; it is because they presumably yield a higher form of happiness in the long run than do pleasures of easy gratification. (Box 5.10 explores Mill's attempt at proving that higher pleasures are more desirable and introduces the concept of the naturalistic fallacy.)

Be that as it may, the idea of a "spiritual life" is rather vague and intangible, so let us use an example that is more concrete: learning to play a musical instrument. Anyone who has attempted it knows that for the first few months it usually doesn't sound very good, practicing is hard work, and you'll be tempted to give up. But if you stick with it, there will probably come a day when you feel you can play what you want the way you want and even play with others, giving joy to yourself and your listeners. The same process occurs, of course, with many other skills that take hard work to learn but yield much gratification when acquired: speaking a foreign language, for example, or singing in a choir, or painting with watercolors. So now Mill can step in and ask his question: If you had the choice, would you give up that skill, provided you could get all those hours of practice time back so you could spend them watching sitcoms? I doubt that a single one of us would say yes; identifying our artistic skill as the higher pleasure in spite of all the hours of hard work, tedium, and frustration leading up to it is no challenge at all. It seems that many of us, including Mill, and perhaps also Socrates, would indeed rather be temporarily dissatisfied if it meant we'd put the easy gratifications on hold for something higher and better down the road. But we'd still have to ask whether all skills that have taken an effort to acquire would qualify as "higher pleasures" according to Mill—as well as according to us: How about sports? computer games? or con artistry? At the end of the chapter, you can read a selection from *Utilitarianism* in which Mill gives his version of a happy, meaningful life.

Box 5.10 THE NATURALISTIC FALLACY

John Stuart Mill acknowledges there is no proof that happiness is the ultimate value because no founding principles can be proved, yet he offers a proof by analogy. This proof has bothered philosophers ever since, because it actually does more harm than good to Mill's own system of thought. The analogy goes like this: The only way we can prove that something is visible is that people actually see it. Likewise, the only way we can prove that something is desirable is that people actually desire it. Everyone desires happiness, so happiness is therefore the ultimate goal. Why does this not work as an analogy? It doesn't work because being "visible" is not analogous to being "desirable." When we say that something is visible, we are describing what people actually see. But when we say that something is desirable, we are not describing what people desire. If many people desire drugs, we do not therefore conclude that drugs are "desirable," because "desirable" means that something *should be* desired. The problem, however, goes deeper. Even if it were true that we could find out what is morally desirable by doing a nose count, why should we then have to conclude that because many people desire something, there should be a moral requirement that we all desire it? In other words, we are stepping from "is" (from a descriptive statement that says something is desired) to "ought" (to a normative/prescriptive statement that says something ought to be desired), and as the philosopher David Hume pointed out, there is nothing in a descriptive statement that allows us to proceed from what people actually do to a rule that states what people ought to do. This step, known as the *naturalistic fallacy,* is commonly taken by thinkers, politicians, writers, and other people of influence, but it is nevertheless a dangerous step to take. We can't make a policy based solely on what is the case. For instance, if it were to turn out that women actually are better parents than men by nature, it still would not be fair to conclude that men ought not to be single fathers (or that all women ought to be mothers), because we can't pass from a simple statement of fact to a statement of policy. That does not mean we can't make policies based on fact; that would be preposterous. What we have to do is insert a value statement—our opinion about what is good or bad, right or wrong (a so-called hidden premise)—so we can go from a fact (such as "There are many teen pregnancies today") to the hidden premise ("We believe teen pregnancies are bad for teen girls, for their babies, and for society") and then to the conclusion ("We must try to lower the number of teen pregnancies"). In that case, someone who doesn't agree with our conclusion can still agree with the fact stated but disagree with our hidden premise. Although this idea is occasionally contested by various thinkers, it remains one of philosophy's ground rules.

Mill's Harm Principle

Did Mill achieve what he wanted? Certainly he wanted to redesign utilitarianism so that it reflected the complexity of a cultured population, but did he intend to set himself up as a cultural despot? It appears that what he wanted was something else entirely. Whereas Bentham wanted the woman who sold flowers at Covent Garden to be able to enjoy her gin in peace, Mill wanted to *educate* her so that she wouldn't *need* her gin anymore and would be able to experience the glorious pleasures enjoyed by the middle-class couple who had learned to appreciate the opera. What Mill had in mind, in other words, was probably not elitism but the notion that the greater pleasure can be derived from achievement. We feel a special fulfillment if we've worked hard on a math problem or a piece of music or a painting and we finally get it right. Mill thought this type of pleasure should be made available to everyone with a capacity for it. This Mill saw as equality of a higher order, based on general education. Once such education is attained, the choices of the educated person are his or hers alone, and nobody has the right to interfere. However, until such a level is achieved, society has a right to gently inform its children and childlike adults about what they ought to prefer.

That sounds today like paternalism, and there is much in Mill's position that supports that point of view. To look more closely at Mill's ideas of what is best for people, we must take a look at what has become known as the *harm principle*, sometimes referred to as the *liberty principle.*

Although the principle of utility provides a general guideline for personal as well as political action in terms of increasing happiness and decreasing unhappiness, it says very little about the circumstances under which one might justifiably become involved in changing other people's lives for the better. Mill had very specific ideas about the limitations of such involvement; in his essay *On Liberty* (1859), he examines the proper limits of government control. Because history has progressed from a time when rulers preyed upon their populations and the populations had to be protected from the rulers' despotic actions to a time when democratic rulers, in principle, *are* the people, the idea of absolute authority on the part of rulers should no longer be a danger to the people. But reality shows us that this is not the case, because we now must face the *tyranny of the majority*. In other words, those who now need protection are minorities (and here Mill thinks of political minorities) who may wish to conduct their lives in ways different from the ways of the majority and its idea of what is right and proper. As an answer to the question of how much the social majority is allowed to exert pressure on the minority, Mill proposes the harm principle:

> That principle is, that the sole end for which mankind are warranted, individually or collectively, in interfering with the liberty of action of any of their number, is self-protection. That the only purpose for which power can be rightfully exercised over any member of a civilized community, against his will, is to prevent harm to others. His own good, either physical or moral, is not a sufficient warrant. He cannot rightfully be compelled to do or forbear because it will be better for him to do so, because it will make him happier, because, in the opinions of others, to do so would be wise, or even right. These are good reasons for remonstrating with him, or reasoning with him, or persuading him, or entreating him, but not for compelling him, or visiting him with any evil in case he do otherwise. To justify that, the conduct from which it is desired to deter him must be calculated to produce evil to someone else. The only part of the conduct of anyone, for which he is amenable to society, is that which concerns others. In the part which merely concerns himself, his independence is, of right, absolute. Over himself, over his own body and mind, the individual is sovereign.

So how does this policy go with his statement four years later that higher pleasures are better for people than lower pleasures and that some people aren't capable of knowing what is good for them? Some Mill critics say that they don't go well together at all—that Mill is claiming in one text that people have a right to choose their own poison, and in the other that they haven't. But we can perhaps find a middle way: What Mill is saying in *On Liberty* is that people, if they so choose, should be allowed to follow their own tastes; what he is saying in *Utilitarianism* is that everybody should be allowed to be exposed to higher pleasures through education, so they might be able to make better choices—but he is not going to force anyone who is adult and in control of his or her mental faculties to submit to a life ruled by someone else's taste. At least, that is a possible reading of Mill that brings the two viewpoints together. (See Box 5.11 for an application of the harm principle to the issue of the legalization of drugs.)

Box 5.11 THE HARM PRINCIPLE AND DRUG LEGALIZATION

John Stuart Mill's harm principle, that the only purpose of interfering with the life of someone is to prevent harm to others, has been applied in many social and political debates, with the general result that we see how ambiguous the principle really is. Examples are the euthanasia debate (see Chapter 13), the debate about "victimless crimes" such as (presumably) prostitution, and the discussion about the legalization of drugs.

A general utilitarian view of the legalization of drugs does not take a stand on whether drugs in themselves are "good" or "bad" but on whether more misery (or happiness) in the long run will be created through making them legally available than through prohibiting them. But remember that the harm principle sets limits to the "general-happiness principle" because it keeps us from interfering with people *for their own sake,* unless they are harming others. You can't force someone to try out someone else's model for happiness (and by now you have probably noticed that Mill's own theory of higher pleasures doesn't quite go well with his harm principle, because he believed people ought to be educated so they could enjoy the higher pleasures, even though they might not want to give up their lower pleasures).

Arguments in favor of drug legalization generally include these:

- The war on drugs isn't working—it is costly and clogs the jails with drug offenders; furthermore, drugs are still being brought across the borders.
- If drugs were legalized, they would be safer because they would be controlled by the state, and the black market would disappear. Drugs would become less expensive, and addicts wouldn't have to turn to crime to feed their habit.

- Heavy drug users could be helped by the state, and people who could manage their own drug use could be left to themselves; after all, people who can manage their own drinking are not criminalized.

The harm principle obviously applies here: According to the principle, if a person does no one else harm by a moderate drug intake, then he or she should be allowed to continue using drugs. (This is the drug policy of the Libertarian Party.) This is where advocates of drug legalization usually seek Mill's support. But we should not draw hasty conclusions. If we take a closer look at the issue, do we still have a situation that involves only individuals who are mature enough to manage their own habits?

- The fact that the war on drugs isn't working is no reason to give it up. If jails are being inundated with drug offenders, the solution is not to decriminalize drug use but to educate children about drugs before they start using.
- Will crime go down? Will the black market disappear? Will drugs be safer? Only if you live in a fantasy world. Cigarettes are legal, but there is a huge black market for tobacco, smuggling is big business, and even with cheap drugs there will be some who can't afford them and will turn to crime. If drug legalization involves regulation (safer drugs), then there will surely arise a black market for unregulated drugs, which would begin the cycle again. Case in point: Illegal distribution centers for cannabis still flourish in California, even though recreational cannabis (marijuana) has been legalized.
- Certainly it is a good idea for the state to help heavy users—individual states already

do that. And it is also possible that many people could be completely responsible with a drug habit, just as many are responsible in their enjoyment of alcohol (which is, of course, a drug). But—and this is where the harm principle takes a turn—imagine all those people, young people in particular, who refrain from drugs simply because they are illegal. With drug legalization, that obstacle is removed; this means there will be many more people on the streets who are under the influence, endangering themselves *and* others in traffic, not to mention creating lifelong dependencies.

So opponents of drug legalization are saying that, overall, legalization will cause more harm than continued drug legislation. In addition, even though one individual may not be directly harming anyone else, he or she may serve as a role model of drug use for others less mature or responsible. Mill considered only direct harm to others a reason to interfere, not this kind of indirect harm. (But he would probably have considered drugs a "lower pleasure.") However, later critics as well as supporters of the harm principle have argued that the line between direct and indirect harm is often blurred. A bad role model may cause more obvious and direct harm to an impressionable child than to an adult who

is supposed to be able to distinguish right from wrong. So the harm principle may be used to argue against drug legalization. The issue of medical use of drugs, such as marijuana, may be different, because drugs for medical use are already part of our culture. Given that not only medical marijuana has been legalized in a number of states, but marijuana/cannabis for recreational use has also been legalized in an increasing number of states, at the time of this writing including California, Oregon, Washington, Nevada, Alaska, Michigan, Vermont, Massachusetts, and Maine, the impact of the legalization argument based on the harm principle should be measurable in the near future, and a legal standard has been developed setting the limit for "driving high," driving under the influence of cannabis. The question of legislating alcohol as a drug of course has similarities with the drug issue: Alcohol directly endangers not just the person under the influence but others as well; MADD (Mothers Against Drunk Drivers) and other victims of alcohol-related accidents and their relatives can attest to that. But there is a difference: Most other drugs are taken strictly for their effect; alcohol is very often consumed not for its effect but for its taste, and the intake need not reach a level where a person is a risk to others.

The harm principle has had extremely far-reaching consequences. Built in part on John Locke's theory of negative rights (see Chapter 7), which had great influence not only in the United Kingdom but also on the Constitution of the United States, Mill's theory helped define two political lines of thought that, paradoxically, are now at odds with each other. We usually refer to Mill's view as *classical liberalism* because of its emphasis on personal liberty. The idea of civil liberties—the rights of citizens, within their right to privacy, to do what they want provided that they do no harm and to have their government ensure that as little harm and as much happiness as possible is created for as many people as possible—is also a cornerstone of *egalitarian liberalism*. But the notions of personal liberty and noninterference by the government have also become key in the political theory of *laissez-faire,* the hands-off approach that requires as little government interference as possible, primarily in private enterprise. The idea behind laissez-faire is that if we all look after our own business and no authorities make our business theirs, then we all are better off, which is today considered a *conservative* economic philosophy, expressed in its extreme form by the Libertarian Party.

The limitations of the right to privacy are more numerous than might be apparent at first glance. For one thing, what exactly does it mean that we are accountable to society only for our conduct that concerns others? What Mill had in mind certainly included the right of consenting adults to engage in sexual activity in the privacy of their own homes, regardless of how other people might feel about the issue. In such cases, only nosy neighbors might be "concerned," and for Mill their right to concern would be proportionate to the extent that they would be exposed to the activities of the couple in question. In other words, if it takes binoculars for you to become exposed to a situation (and hence become "concerned"), then put aside your binoculars and mind your own business.

But what about, say, a teenage girl who decides to put an end to her life because her boyfriend broke up with her? Might that fall within the harm principle? Is she harming only herself, so that society has no right to interfere? Here Mill might answer in several ways. First, she is harming not only herself but her family as well, who would grieve for her and feel guilty for not having stepped in. There is also the problem of role models. If other teens in the same situation learn about her suicide, they might think it would be a good idea to follow her example, and more harm would be caused. But when does indirect harm ever end? Doesn't it spread like rings in water? Mill himself would not allow for indirect harm, such as the harm caused by flawed role models, to be an obvious cause for the interference of authorities. To him, an adult should not be prevented from doing what he or she wants to do just because some other adult might imitate the action, but only if his or her action (such as a policeman being drunk on the job—Mill's own example) is a likely cause for direct harm to others. And if someone is *offended* by what another person does, but isn't directly harmed by it, then Mill would dismiss that as being irrelevant; for Mill, offense does not constitute harm. You may draw your own conclusions about current discussions concerning direct and indirect harm, such as the debate surrounding helmet laws, drug laws, and prostitution, as well as contemporary discussions about whether people should have a right not to be offended. It is clear that Mill's interpretation of his own harm principle still engenders heated debate. As for our example of the suicidal teenage girl, Mill would most certainly add the following: This situation does not fall under the harm principle, because the girl is (1) not an adult and (2) not in a rational frame of mind:

> This doctrine is meant to apply only to human beings in the maturity of their faculties. We are not speaking of children, or of young persons below the age which the law may fix as that of manhood or womanhood. Those who are still in a state to require being taken care of by others, must be protected against their own actions as well as against external injury. For the same reason, we may leave out of consideration those backward states of society in which the [human] race itself may be considered as in its nonage. . . . Despotism is a legitimate mode of government in dealing with barbarians, provided the end be their improvement, and the means justified by actually effecting that end. Liberty, as a principle, has no application to any state of things anterior to the time when mankind have become capable of being improved by free and equal discussion. . . . But as soon as mankind have attained the capacity of being guided to their own improvement by conviction or persuasion (a period long since reached in all nations with whom we need here concern ourselves), compulsion . . . is no longer admissible as a means to their own good, and justifiably only for the security of others.

With this addition to the harm principle, Mill certainly makes it clear that children are excluded, but so is anyone who, in Mill's mind, belongs to a "backward" state of society. Again, we see evidence of Mill's complexity: He adamantly wants to protect civil liberties, but he is also paternalistic: Whoever is not an "adult" by his definition must be guided or coerced to comply with existing rules. Individuals as well as whole peoples who fall outside the "adult" category must be governed by others until they reach sufficient maturity to take affairs into their own hands. Critics have seen this as a defense of not merely cultural but also political imperialism: There are peoples who are too primitive to rule themselves, so someone else has to do it for them and bring them up to Western standards. Who are these peoples? We may assume that they include the native-born peoples of old British colonies. Since Mill made his living not as a philosophy professor but as a Chief Examiner at India House, East India Company, the biggest private company in the world at that time, which administered the colony of India (his father, James Mill, had worked for the Company and was the author of a lengthy work on the history of India, and John Stuart himself started working there in 1923 when he was 18), his knowledge of colonial affairs came from the perspective of the colony power. That viewpoint, sometimes referred to as "the white man's burden," is very far from being acceptable in our era, but is it fair to accuse Mill of being an imperialist? Perhaps, especially if we take into account that Mill published his piece in 1859, and two years earlier the British Empire had been shocked by the so-called *Sepoy Mutiny* in northern India, in which hundreds of British officers and their wives and children had been murdered by Indian infantry soldiers (sepoys) in the British-Indian army. That mutiny was the result of long-standing clashes and misunderstandings between the two cultural groups, after a hundred years of British dominion and (as many would describe it) exploitation. In the aftermath of the mutiny, India was taken over by the British Crown and ruled as a part of the empire. Mill was appalled at the mutiny but also at the takeover by the British government, and he retired, declining to take part in the new government. His chief aim seems to have been perpetuating not the British Empire but the utilitarian idea of maximizing happiness for the greatest number and minimizing pain and misery on a global scale. If Mill was biased toward the British way of life, it may be understandable: That way of life was in many ways the best the planet Earth had to offer in the nineteenth century for those with access to a good education. It was, in our terms, an extremely "civilized" culture, at least for the upper and middle classes. Perhaps, then, we can think of Mill not merely as an intellectual snob but also as an educator who wanted to see everybody get the same good chances in life that he got and enjoy life as much as he did. And considering that *On Liberty* was published after Mill had been hit by two major blows, the Sepoy Mutiny and the loss of his job in 1857, and the death of his wife in 1858, it speaks to his resilience that he would redirect his inner turmoil to questions about political freedom and education—in many ways similar to his reinventing himself after his first intellectual crisis when he was 20 years old.

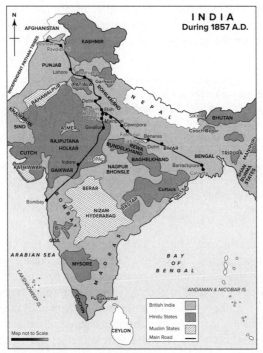

In 1857, the British East India Company controlled vast areas of the subcontinent of India, with John Stuart Mill as its Chief Administrator. The areas indicated by light gray were the areas controlled by the East India Company; the other areas were ruled by local royal families of India. The 1857 Sepoy Mutiny took place across northern India.

One final remark concerning Mill: Sometimes the present forces us to reevaluate things we thought were simply part of history—something we thought we understood pretty well. For at least half a century, it has been considered right and appropriate (at least in this country) to criticize Mill for wanting to govern India until Indians were capable of governing themselves in a democratic fashion. Ethical relativism, being a strong cultural force in the twentieth century, has told us that each culture is right in its own way and that no culture has the right to superimpose its values on other cultures. But wait . . . in Chapter 3 we discussed the types of situations that have made so many people change their minds about ethical relativism. Should we just stand by while little girls are being circumcised? while people are being sold into slavery? Now suppose we add to the list: while people are being tortured and murdered by a dictator, while entire populations are being subject to genocide? Or where a government is denying rights to half the population because they are women? What I am getting at is, of course, the wars in Iraq and Afghanistan in the early twenty-first century. In addition, our military has been actively engaged in aiding rebels topple the dictatorship in Libya and lending support to rebels in Syria, with the intent to help democracy succeed. That puts us at a crossroads: On the one hand, we can stay with the earlier critical evaluation of Mill and say that no matter what the situation, a nation doesn't have the right to try to run another nation or change its regime to something that seems more right, or even just more acceptable or safer. On the other hand, if we agree with Mill that democracy is better than tyranny, and freedom of educated people is better than the superstition of illiteracy—then can we still claim that he is wrong? And if we think he has a point, how does that translate into our engagements in nation-building? For Mill and other British citizens, the Sepoy Mutiny can perhaps be understood as a kind of 9/11/2001 experience. Even if he didn't approve of the way the British government handled the crisis, his conclusion was that nations who aren't "civilized" must be put under the civilizing influence of other nations until they have matured sufficiently to govern themselves. So if we view Mill's attitude through the lenses of our own September 11, 2001 experience, and the subsequent wars in Afghanistan and—in particular—in Iraq, would you condemn his view, or would you instead reevaluate Mill's statement in light of the attempts of the United States and its allies to introduce democracy into a country that has never known a "free and equal discussion," as Mill called it? For a utilitarian such as Mill, the question will eventually become, Can the goal be accomplished, and at what cost? In Chapter 13 you'll read about the theory of just war. For now, I suggest you engage in the thought experiment of taking a look at a nineteenth-century event through twenty-first-century eyes—and then allow yourself to look at today's events from the viewpoint of a nineteenth-century philosopher. It may increase your understanding of the past as well as the present.

Act and Rule Utilitarianism

In the twentieth century it became clear to philosophers attracted to utilitarianism that there were severe problems inherent in the idea that a morally right act is an act that makes as many people as possible happy. One flaw is that, as we saw previously, it is conceivable many people will achieve much pleasure from the misery of a few others, and even in situations where people don't know that their happiness is achieved by the pain of others, that is still an uncomfortable thought. It is especially so if one believes in the Golden Rule (as John Stuart Mill did), which states that we should do for others what we would like done for ourselves and refrain from doing to others what we would not like done to ourselves. Mill himself was aware of the problem and allowed that in the long run a society in which a majority abuses a minority is not a good society. That still means we have to explain why the *first* cases of happiness occurring from the misery of others are wrong, even before they have established themselves as a pattern with increasingly bad consequences. In a sense, Mill tried to address the problem, suggesting that utilitarianism be taken as a general policy to be applied to general situations. He did not, however, develop the idea further within his own philosophy.

Others have taken up the challenge and suggested it is just that particular formulation of utilitarianism which creates the problem; given another formulation, the problem disappears. If we stay with the *classical* formulation, the principle of utility goes like this: *Always do whatever act will create the greatest happiness for the greatest number of people.* In this version we are stuck with the problems we saw earlier; for example, the torture of innocents may bring about great pleasure for a large group of people. The Russian author Dostoyevsky explored this thought in his novel *The Brothers Karamazov:* Suppose your happiness, and everyone else's, is bought by the suffering of an innocent child? (We look more closely at this idea in the Narratives section.)

It is not hard to see this as a Christian metaphor, with Jesus' suffering as the condition of happiness for humans, but there is an important difference: Jesus was a volunteer; an innocent child is not. In any event, a utilitarian, by definition, would have to agree that if a great deal of suffering could be alleviated by putting an innocent person through hell, then doing so would be justified. Putting nonhuman animals or entire populations of humans through hell would also be justified. The glorious end (increased happiness for a majority) will in any event justify the means, even if the means violate these beings' right to life or to fair treatment.

Suppose we reformulate utilitarianism. Suppose we say, *Always do whatever type of act will create the greatest happiness for the greatest number of people.* What is the result? If we set up a one-time situation, such as the torture of an innocent person for the sake of others' well-being, it may work within the first formulation. But if we view it as a *type* of situation—one that is likely to recur again and again because we have now set up a *rule* for such types of situations—it becomes impermissible: The consequences of torturing *many* innocent people will not bring about great happiness for anyone in the long run. Is this, perhaps, what Mill was trying to say? This new formulation is referred to as *rule utilitarianism,* and it is advocated by many modern utilitarians who wish to distance themselves from the uncomfortable implications of the classical theory, now referred to as *act utilitarianism.* If this new version is used, they say, we can focus on the good consequences of a certain type of act rather than on the singular act itself. It may work once for a student to cheat on a final, but cheating as a rule is not only dangerous (the student herself is likely to be found out) but also immoral to the rule utilitarian, because very bad consequences would occur if everyone were to cheat. Professors would get wise in no time, and nobody would graduate. Students and professors would be miserable. Society would miss out on a great many well-educated college graduates. The Golden Rule is in this way fortified: Don't do something if you can't imagine it as a rule for everybody, because a rule not suited for everyone can have no good overall consequences.

Box 5.12 PETER SINGER, A CONTEMPORARY UTILITARIAN

Cindy Ord/Getty Images

In Chapter 4 you were introduced to **reciprocal altruism** and read about the example of the two hunters and the saber-tooth cat. The author of that example was the Australian philosopher Peter Singer. Singer (born 1946) self-identifies as a utilitarian, and his viewpoints come closest to the style we call act-utilitarianism, without incorporating Bentham's numbers-based hedonistic calculus. He has taught at Princeton since 1999. Arguably the most controversial of all contemporary philosophers, Singer has defended his utilitarian views on euthanasia, animal rights, global welfare, and other issues in books, articles, and op-ed pieces, as well as on Twitter. He is a spokesperson for the concept of **effective altruism**, directing one's donations toward where they may do the most good.

His most famous books include *Animal Liberation* (1975), *Practical Ethics* (1979), *The Expanding Circle* (1981), *One World: Ethics and Globalization* (2002), *The Life You Can Save*

(2009), and *The Most Good You Can Do* (2015). In addition, he has created The Great Ape Project in collaboration with Paola Cavalieri, which advocates three basic rights for Great Apes (bonobos, gorillas, chimpanzees, and orangutans): the right not to be killed, the right to liberty, and the right not to be tortured.

Some critics have objected that not everything we do can be made into a rule with good consequences. After all, many of the things we like to do are unique to us, and why should we assume that just because one person likes to collect movie memorabilia, the world would be happier if everyone collected movie memorabilia? That is not the way it is supposed to work, say the rule utilitarians. You have to specify that the rule is valid for people *under similar circumstances,* and you have to specify what *exceptions* you might want to make. It may be morally good to make sure you are home in time for dinner if you have a family to come home to but not if you are living by yourself. And the moral goodness of being there in time for dinner depends on there not being something of greater importance that you should see to. Such things might be a crisis at work, a medical emergency, extracurricular activities, walking the dog, seeing your lover, binge-watching something on YouTube, talking on the phone, or whatever you choose. They may not all qualify as good exceptions, but *you* should specify in your rule which ones are acceptable. Once you have created such a rule, the utilitarian ideal will work, say the rule utilitarians; it will make more people happy and fewer people unhappy in the long run. If it doesn't, then you just have to rework the rule until you get it right.

The problem with this approach is that it may be asking too much of people. Are we likely to ponder the consequences of whatever it is we want to do every time we are about to take action? Are we likely to envision everyone doing the same thing? Probably not. Even if it is wrong to make numerous private phone calls from a company phone, we think it won't make much difference if one person makes private calls as long as nobody else does. As long as most people comply, we can still get away with breaking the rule without creating bad consequences. Even so, we are in the wrong, because a healthy moral theory will not set "myself" up as an exception to the rule just because "I'm me and I deserve it." This, as philosopher James Rachels has pointed out, is as much a form of discrimination as racism and sexism are. We might call it "me-ism," but we already have a good word for it, *egoism,* and we have already examined the merits and flaws of that theory.

This addition to utilitarianism, that one ought to look for rules that apply to everyone, is for many a major step in the right direction. Rule utilitarianism certainly was not, however, the first philosophy to ask, What if everybody did what you intend to do? Although just about every parent must have said that to her or his child at some time or other, the one person who is credited with putting it into a philosophical framework is the German philosopher Immanuel Kant. There is one important difference between the way Kant asks the question and the way it has later been developed by rule utilitarians, though. Rule utilitarianism asks, What will be the *consequences* of everybody doing what you intend to do? Kant asks, Could you wish for it to be a *universal law* that everyone does what you intend to do? We look more closely at this difference in the next chapter.

Study Questions

1. Explain the function of Bentham's hedonistic (hedonic) calculus and give an example of how to use it. Explain the advantages of using the calculus; explain the problems inherent in the concept of the calculus.

2. Evaluate the question of torture used as a last resort in a national security crisis: What would Bentham recommend? Would you agree? Why or why not? (You may want to revisit the question after having read Chapter 6.)

3. Now that you have seen the trolley problem reintroduced in a utilitarian setting, has that changed your mind? Is diverting the trolley onto the track with one person the most sensible, even the most moral course of action? Why or why not? (Remember the problem of "sheer numbers.")

4. Explain John Stuart Mill's theory of higher and lower pleasures: What are the problems inherent in the theory? Overall, does Mill's idea of higher and lower pleasures make sense to you? Why or why not?

5. Evaluate Descartes's theory that only those beings with a mind can suffer and that only humans have minds. Explore the consequences for utilitarianism if we agree that animals (including human beings) have a capacity for suffering.

6. Explore Mill's harm principle: Do you find the principle attractive or problematic? Explain why. Discuss the application of the harm principle to the issue of drug legalization.

7. Are we more likely to accept the idea of utilitarianism in a time of crisis? If so, does that make the theory acceptable? Explain.

Primary Readings and Narratives

The Primary Readings are Jeremy Bentham's definition of the principle of utility and John Stuart Mill's vision of true happiness. The Narratives based on literature include a Danish tale about utilitarianism in action and a pairing of excerpts from Dostoyevsky and Ursula K. Le Guin that look at the happiness of the many in light of the suffering of a few. A summary of the film *Extreme Measures* explores the moral question of performing medical experiments on a few unwanted homeless people to gain knowledge that will save the lives and mobility of thousands of others. Another summarized movie, *Outbreak*, illustrates and criticizes a utilitarian approach to a pandemic situation. And finally, a summary of an episode from the television series *The Good Place* brings up the trolley problem as well as the "Doctor's Choice."

 Primary Reading

Of the Principle of Utility

JEREMY BENTHAM

***From* An Introduction to the Principles of Morals and Legislation,** *1789. Excerpt.*

Jeremy Bentham's primary interests were legislative, and he wrote in a meticulous style suited to the language of the law. In this excerpt Bentham defines the principle of utility and outlines the consequences for individuals, for the community, and for moral concepts.

> I. *Mankind governed by pain and pleasure.* Nature has placed mankind under the governance of two sovereign masters, *pain* and *pleasure*. It is for them alone to point out what we ought to do, as well as to determine what we shall do. On the one hand the standard of right and wrong, on the other the chain of causes and effects, are fastened to their throne. They govern us in all we do, in all we say, in all we think: every effort we can make to throw them off our subjection, will serve but to demonstrate and confirm it. In words a man may pretend to abjure their empire: but in reality he will remain subject to it all the while. The *principle of utility* recognises this subjection, and assumes it for the foundation of that

system, the object of which is to rear the fabric of felicity by the hands of reason and of law. Systems which attempt to question it, deal in sounds instead of sense, in caprice instead of reason, in darkness instead of light.

But enough of metaphor and declamation: it is not by such means that moral science is to be improved.

II. *Principle of utility, what.* The principle of utility is the foundation of the present work: it will be proper therefore at the outset to give an explicit and determinate account of what is meant by it. By the principle of utility is meant that principle which approves or disapproves of every action whatsoever, according to the tendency which it appears to have to augment or diminish the happiness of the party whose interest is in question: or, what is the same thing in other words, to promote or to oppose that happiness. I say of every action whatsoever; and therefore not only of every action of a private individual, but of every measure of government.

III. *Utility, what.* By utility is meant that property in any object, whereby it tends to produce benefit, advantage, pleasure, good, or happiness, (all this in the present case comes to the same thing) or (what comes again to the same thing) to prevent the happening of mischief, pain, evil, or unhappiness to the party whose interest is considered: if that party be the community in general, then the happiness of the community: if a particular individual, then the happiness of that individual.

IV. *Interest of the community, what.* The interest of the community is one of the most general expressions that can occur in the phraseology of morals: no wonder that the meaning of it is often lost. When it has a meaning, it is this. The community is a fictitious *body,* composed of the individual persons who are considered as constituting as it were its *members.* The interest of the community then is, what?—the sum of the interests of the several members who compose it.

V. It is in vain to talk of the interest of the community, without understanding what is the interest of the individual. A thing is said to promote the interest, or to be *for* the interest, of an individual, when it tends to add to the sum total of his pleasures: or, what comes to the same thing, to diminish the sum total of his pains.

VI. *An action conformable to the principle of utility, what.* An action then may be said to be conformable to the principle of utility, or, for shortness sake, to utility, (meaning with respect to the community at large) when the tendency it has to augment the happiness of the community is greater than any it has to diminish it.

VII. *A measure of government conformable to the principle of utility, what.* A measure of government (which is but a particular kind of action, performed by a particular person or persons) may be said to be conformable to or dictated by the principle of utility, when in like manner the tendency which it has to augment the happiness of the community is greater than any which it has to diminish it.

VIII. *Laws or dictates of utility, what.* When an action, or in particular a measure of government, is supposed by a man to be conformable to the principle of utility, it may be convenient, for the purposes of discourse, to imagine a kind of law or dictate, called a law or dictate of utility: and to speak of the action in question, as being conformable to such law or dictate.

IX. *A partizan of the principle of utility, who.* A man may be said to be a partizan of the principle of utility, when the approbation or disapprobation he annexes to any action, or to any measure, is determined by and proportioned to the tendency which he conceives it to have to augment or to diminish the happiness of the community: or in other words, to its conformity or unconformity to the laws or dictates of utility.

X. *Ought, ought not, right and wrong, &c. how to be understood.* Of an action that is conformable to the principle of utility one may always say either that it is one that ought to be done, or at least that it is not one that ought not to be done. One may say also, that it is right it should be done; at least that it is not wrong it should be done: that it is a right action; at least that it is not a wrong action. When thus interpreted, the words *ought,* and *right* and *wrong,* and others of that stamp, have a meaning: when otherwise, they have none.

Study Questions

1. Identify the concept of moral right and wrong as defined by the principle of utility. Do you approve of such a definition? Why or why not?

2. How does Bentham identify the concept of "community"? Evaluate Bentham's statement in terms of possible political consequences. Do you agree with him? Why or why not?

3. In your opinion, is Bentham right in stating that pain and pleasure govern us in everything we do?

4. Some scholars see Bentham as one short step removed from ethical egoism. Why? Is that a fair assessment?

 Primary Reading

Utilitarianism

JOHN STUART MILL

Excerpt, 1863.

In this section Mill outlines the idea of a test of higher and lower pleasures according to the judgment of those who know and appreciate both kinds. He then speaks of the true nature of happiness, as he sees it: a feeling that has little to do with pleasure seeking and much to do with the joy of contributing to the common good.

> It is quite compatible with the principle of utility to recognize the fact, that some *kinds* of pleasure are more desirable and more valuable than others. It would be absurd that while, in estimating all other things, quality is considered as well as quantity, the estimation of pleasures should be supposed to depend on quantity alone.

> If I am asked what I mean by difference of quality in pleasures, or what makes one pleasure more valuable than another merely as a pleasure, except its being greater in amount, there is but one possible answer. Of two pleasures, if there be one to which all or almost all who have experience of both give a decided preference, irrespective of any feeling of moral obligation to prefer it, that is the more desirable pleasure. If one of the two is, by those who are competently acquainted with both, placed so far above the other that they prefer it, even though knowing it to be attended with a greater amount of discontent, and would not resign it for any quantity of the other pleasure which their nature is capable of, we are justified in ascribing to the preferred enjoyment a superiority in quality, so far outweighing quantity as to render it, in comparison, of small account.

> Now it is an unquestionable fact that those who are equally acquainted with, and equally capable of appreciating and enjoying, both, do give a most marked preference to the manner of existence which employs their higher faculties. Few human creatures would consent to be changed into any of the lower animals, for a promise of the fullest allowance of a beast's pleasures; no intelligent human being would consent to be a fool, no instructed person would be an ignoramus, no person of feeling and conscience would be selfish and base, even though they should be persuaded that the fool, the dunce, or the rascal

is better satisfied with his lot than they are with theirs. They would not resign what they possess more than he for the most complete satisfaction of all the desires which they have in common with him. If they ever fancy they would, it is only in cases of unhappiness so extreme, that to escape from it they would exchange their lot for almost any other, however undesirable in their own eyes. A being of higher faculties requires more to make him happy, is capable probably of more acute suffering, and certainly accessible to it at more points, than one of an inferior type; but in spite of these liabilities, he can never really wish to sink into what he feels to be a lower grade of existence. We may give what explanation we please of this unwillingness: we may attribute it to pride, a name which is given indiscriminately to some of the most and to some of the least estimable feelings of which mankind are capable; we may refer it to the love of liberty and personal independence, an appeal to which was with the Stoics one of the most effective means for the inculcation of it; to the love of power, or to the love of excitement, both of which do really enter into and contribute to it: but its most appropriate appellation is a sense of dignity, which all human beings possess in one form or other, and in some, though by no means in exact, proportion to their higher faculties, and which is so essential a part of the happiness of those in whom it is strong, that nothing which conflicts with it could be, otherwise than momentarily, an object of desire to them. Whoever supposes that this preference takes place at a sacrifice of happiness—that the superior being, in anything like equal circumstances, is not happier than the inferior—confounds the two very different ideas, of *happiness* and *content*. It is indisputable that the being whose capacities of enjoyment are low, has the greatest chance of having them fully satisfied; and a highly endowed being will always feel that any happiness which he can look for, as the world is constituted, is imperfect. But he can learn to bear its imperfections, if they are at all bearable; and they will not make him envy the being who is indeed unconscious of the imperfections, but only because he feels not at all the good which those imperfections qualify. It is better to be a human being dissatisfied than a pig satisfied; better to be Socrates dissatisfied than a fool satisfied. And if the fool, or the pig, are of a different opinion, it is because they only know their own side of the question. The other party to the comparison knows both sides. . . .

According to the "greatest happiness principle," . . . the ultimate end, with reference to and for the sake of which all other things are desirable (whether we are considering our own good or that of other people), is an existence exempt as far as possible from pain, and as rich as possible in enjoyments, both in point of quantity and quality; the test of quality, and the rule for measuring it against quantity, being the preference felt by those who in their opportunities of experience, to which must be added their habits of self-consciousness and self-observation, are best furnished with the means of comparison. This, being, according to the utilitarian opinion, the end of human action, is necessarily also the standard of morality; which may accordingly be defined, the rules and precepts for human conduct, by the observance of which an existence such as has been described might be, to the greatest extent possible, secured to all mankind; and not to them only, but, so far as the nature of things admits, to the whole sentient creation. . . .

If by happiness be meant a continuity of highly pleasurable excitement, it is evident enough that this is impossible. A state of exalted pleasure lasts only moments, or in some cases, and with some intermissions, hours or days, and is the occasional brilliant flash of enjoyment, not its permanent and steady flame. Of this the philosophers who have taught that happiness is the end of life were as fully aware as those who taunt them. The happiness which they meant was not a life of rapture; but moments of such, in an existence made up of few and transitory pains, many and various pleasures, with a decided predominance of the active over the passive, and having as the foundation of the whole, not to expect more from life than it is capable of bestowing. A life thus composed, to those who have been fortunate enough to obtain it, has always appeared worthy of the name of happiness. And such an existence is even now the lot of many, during some considerable portion of their lives. The present wretched education, and wretched social arrangements, are the only real hindrance to its being attainable by almost all.

In a world in which there is so much to interest, so much to enjoy, and so much also to correct and improve, everyone who has [a] moderate amount of moral and intellectual requisites is capable of an existence which may be called enviable; and unless such a person, through bad laws or subjection to the will of others, is denied the liberty to use the sources of happiness within his reach, he will not fail to find this enviable existence, if he escape the positive evils of life, the great sources of physical and mental suffering—such as indigence, disease, and the unkindness, worthlessness, or premature loss of an affection. The main stress of the problem lies, therefore, in the contest with these calamities from which it is a rare good fortune entirely to escape; which, as things are now, cannot be obviated, and often cannot be in any material degree mitigated. Yet no one whose opinion deserves a moment's consideration can doubt that most of the great positive evils of the world are in themselves removable, and will, if human affairs continue to improve, be in the end reduced within narrow limits. . . .

As for vicissitudes of fortune, and other disappointments connected with worldly circumstances, these are principally the effect either of gross imprudence, of ill-regulated desires, or of bad or imperfect social institutions. All the grand sources, in short, of human suffering are in a great degree, many of them almost entirely, conquerable by human care and effort; and though their removal is grievously slow—though a long succession of generations will perish in the breach before the conquest is completed, and this world becomes all that, if will and knowledge were not wanting, it might easily be made—yet every mind sufficiently intelligent and generous to bear a part, however small and unconspicuous, in the endeavor, will draw a noble enjoyment from the contest itself, which he would not for any bribe in the form of selfish indulgence consent to be without.

And this leads to the true estimation of what is said by the objectors concerning the possibility, and the obligation, of learning to do without happiness. Unquestionably it is possible to do without happiness; it is done involuntarily by nineteen-twentieths of mankind, even in those parts of our present world which are least deep in barbarism; and it often has to be done voluntarily by the hero or the martyr, for the sake of something which he prizes more than his individual happiness. But this something, what is it, unless the happiness of others, or some of the requisites of happiness? It is noble to be capable of resigning entirely one's own portion of happiness, or chances of it: but, after all, this self-sacrifice must be for some end; it is not its own end; and if we are told that its end is not happiness, but virtue, which is better than happiness, I ask, would the sacrifice be made if the hero or martyr did not believe that it would earn for others immunity from similar sacrifices? Would it be made if he thought that his renunciation of happiness for himself would produce no fruit for any of his fellow creatures, but to make their lot like his, and place them also in the condition of persons who have renounced happiness? All honor to those who can abnegate for themselves the personal enjoyment of life, when by such renunciation they contribute worthily to increase the amount of happiness in the world; but he who does it, or professes to do it, for any other purpose, is no more deserving of admiration from the ascetic mounted on his pillar. He may be an inspiriting proof of what men *can* do, but assuredly not an example of what they *should*.

Study Questions

1. Do you agree with Mill that "a being of higher faculties requires more to make him happy . . . than one of an inferior type"?

2. What might be Ayn Rand's comment on the excerpt?

3. What does Mill mean by "the whole sentient creation"?

4. Comment on the meaning of this passage: "It is better to be a human being dissatisfied than a pig satisfied; better to be Socrates dissatisfied than a fool satisfied." What does Mill mean? Do you agree? Why or why not?

5. In the acclaimed television series *The Wire,* Season 4, a high school teacher takes three of his students to an expensive steak restaurant so they can be exposed to the "finer things in life." For the first time in their lives they're seated by a hostess, and the waitress recites information about the specials of the evening from memory. In the end, they have ordered and eaten items that turned out to be completely different from what they expected, and nobody except the teacher seems to have had a good time. The students ask if they can stop at a McDonald's

afterward so they can get something they actually like. But already next day in school, there is an air of confidence about them, and they joke about the dinner based on experience rather than ignorance. Suppose we now were to ask them what they prefer, a fancy steak house or a fast food burger joint? Suppose they say the burger joint? What would Mill respond? Would you agree? Why or why not?

 Narrative

The Blacksmith and the Baker

JOHANN HERMAN WESSEL

Poem, 1777. Loosely translated from Danish, from verse to prose, by Nina Rosenstand. Summary and Excerpt.

Wessel is famous in his own country of Denmark for his satirical verses. This story (here retold in prose) may have been inspired by a real newspaper story or possibly by British fables.

Once upon a time there was a small town where the town blacksmith was a mean man. He had an enemy, and one day he and his enemy happened to meet at an inn. They proceeded to get drunk and exchange some nasty words. The blacksmith grew angry and knocked the other man out; the blow turned out to be fatal. The blacksmith was carted off to jail, and he confessed, hoping that his opponent would forgive him in Heaven. Before his sentence was pronounced, four upstanding citizens asked to see the judge, and the most eloquent of them spoke:

"Your Wisdom, we know you are thinking of the welfare of this town, but this welfare depends on getting our blacksmith back. His death won't wake up the dead man, and we'll never find such a good blacksmith ever again."

The judge said, "But a life has been taken and must be paid for by a life. . . ."

"We have in town an old and scrawny baker who'll go to the devil soon, and since we have two bakers, how about taking the oldest one? Then you still get a life for a life."

"Well," said the judge, "that is not a bad idea, I'll do what I can." And he leafed through his law books but found nothing that said you can't execute a baker instead of a blacksmith, so he pronounced this sentence:

"The Blacksmith and the Baker," illustration by Nils Wiwel, 1895. Utilitarianism taken to an extreme: The baker is led away to be executed for what the blacksmith has done, because that is more useful to society. The policeman's belt reads "Honest and Faithful," and the building in the background is the old Copenhagen courthouse with the inscription "With Law Must Land Be Built."

"We know that blacksmith Jens has no excuse for what he has done, sending Anders Petersen off to eternity; but since we have but one blacksmith in this town I would be crazy if I wanted him dead; but we do have two bakers of bread . . . so the oldest one must pay for the murder."

The old baker wept pitifully when they took him away. The moral of the story: Be always prepared to die! It comes when you least expect it.

Study Questions

1. Do you think this is a fair picture of a utilitarian judge?
2. How might the utilitarian respond to this story?
3. Return to this story after reading Chapter 6 and consider: How might a Kantian respond?

Narrative

The Brothers Karamazov

FYODOR DOSTOYEVSKY

Novel, 1881. Film, 1958. Summary and Excerpt.

(This excerpt should be read in conjunction with the narrative "The Ones Who Walk Away from Omelas," which follows.)

The story of the brothers Karamazov, one of the most famous in Russian literature, is about four half-brothers and their father, an unpleasant, old, corrupt scoundrel. The brothers are very different in nature; the oldest son, Dmitri, is a rogue and a pleasure-seeker; the next son, Ivan, is intelligent and politically engaged; the third son, Alyosha, is gentle and honest; and the fourth son, Smerdyakov, was born outside marriage and never recognized as a proper son. When a murder happens, each son in turn finds himself under suspicion.

Here, Ivan is telling Alyosha a story:

> It was in the darkest days of serfdom at the beginning of the century. . . . There was in those days a general of aristocratic connections, the owner of great estates, one of those men—somewhat exceptional, I believe, even then—who, retiring from the service into a life of leisure, are convinced that they've earned absolute power over the lives of their subjects. There were such men then. So our general, settled on his property of two thousand souls, lives in pomp, and dominates his poor neighbors as though they were dependents. He has kennels of hundreds of hounds and nearly a hundred dog-boys—all mounted, and in uniform. One day a serf boy, a little child of eight, threw a stone in play and hurt the paw of the general's favorite hound. 'Why is my favorite dog lame?' He is told that the boy threw a stone that hurt the dog's paw. 'So you did it.' The general looked the child up and down. 'Take him.' He was

taken—taken from his mother and kept shut up all night. Early the next morning the general comes out on horseback, with the hounds, his dependents, dog-boys, and huntsmen, all mounted around him in full hunting parade. The servants are summoned for their edification, and in front of them all stands the mother of the child. The child is brought forward. It's a gloomy cold, foggy autumn day, a perfect day for hunting. The general orders the child to be undressed. The child is stripped naked. He shivers, numb with terror, not daring to cry. . . . 'Make him run,' commands the general. 'Run, run!' shout the dog-boys. The boy runs. . . . 'At him!' yells the general, and he sets the whole pack of hounds after the child. The hounds catch him, and tear him to pieces before his mother's eyes! . . . I believe the general was afterwards declared incapable of administering his estates. Well—what did he deserve? To be shot? To be shot for the satisfaction of our moral feelings? Speak, Alyosha!

"Tell me yourself, I challenge you—answer. Imagine that you are creating a fabric of human destiny with the object of making men happy in the end, giving them peace and rest at last. Imagine that you are doing this but that it is essential and inevitable to torture to death only one tiny creature—that child beating its breast with its fist, for instance—in order to found that edifice on its unavenged tears. Would you consent to be the architect on those conditions? Tell me. Tell the truth."

"No, I wouldn't consent," said Alyosha softly.

"And can you accept the idea that the men for whom you are building would agree to receive their happiness from the unatoned blood of a little victim? And accepting it would remain happy forever?"

"No, I can't admit it," said Alyosha suddenly, with flashing eyes.

Here Ivan and Alyosha are engaged in a discussion about the meaning of life: If God does not exist, then what? Then everything is permissible. But what if our highest moral aim is to make the majority happy? Do the means always justify the end? If the suffering of a child could somehow create general happiness and harmony, should its mother forgive those who caused it to suffer?

Study Questions

1. Answer Ivan's question: Would you agree to make humankind happy at the cost of a child's suffering? Explain how a utilitarian might answer, and then explain your own answer.

2. Should the mother ever forgive the general for murdering her son?

3. Return to this story after reading Chapter 6 and consider: How might a Kantian respond?

 Narrative

The Ones Who Walk Away from Omelas

URSULA K. LE GUIN

Short story, 1973. Summary and Excerpt.

There is a festival in the city of Omelas. The weather is beautiful, the city looks its best, and people are happy and serene in their pretty clothes. This is a perfect place, with freedom of choice and no oppressive power enforcing the rules of religion, politics, or morality—and it works, because the people know they are responsible for their actions. This place is a Utopia, except for one thing: The happiness of the citizens is bought at a high price, with the full knowledge of every citizen.

> In a basement under one of the beautiful public buildings of Omelas, or perhaps in the cellar of one of its spacious private homes, there is a room. It has one locked door, and no window. A little light seeps in dustily between cracks in the boards, secondhand from a cobwebbed window somewhere across the cellar. In one corner of the little room a couple of mops, with stiff, clotted, foul-smelling heads, stand near a rusty bucket. . . . The room is about three paces long and two wide: a mere broom closet or disused tool room. In the room a child is sitting. It could be a boy or a girl. It looks about six, but actually is nearly ten. It is feeble-minded. Perhaps it was born defective, or perhaps it has become imbecile through fear, malnutrition, and neglect. It picks its nose and occasionally fumbles vaguely with its toes or genitals, as it sits hunched in the corner farthest from the bucket and the two mops. It is afraid of the mops. It finds them horrible. It shuts its eyes, but it knows the mops are still standing there; and the door is locked; and nobody will come. The door is always locked; and nobody ever comes, except that sometimes . . . the door rattles terribly and opens, and a person, or several people, are there. . . . The people at the door never say anything, but the child, who has not always lived in the tool room, and can remember sunlight and its mother's voice, sometimes speaks. "I will be good," it says. "Please let me out. I will be good!" They never answer.

All this is part of a greater plan. The child will never be let out—it will die within a short time—and presumably another child will take its place, for it is the suffering of this innocent being that makes the perfect life in Omelas possible. All the citizens know about it from the time they are adolescents, and they all must go and see the child so that they can understand the price of their happiness. They are disgusted and sympathetic for a while, but then they understand the master plan: the pain of one small individual in exchange for great communal happiness. Because the citizens know the immense suffering that gives them their beautiful life, they are particularly loving to one another and responsible for what they do. And what would they gain by setting the child free? The child is too far gone to be able to enjoy freedom, anyway, and what is one person's suffering compared with the realm of happiness that is achieved? So the people feel no guilt. However, a few young people and some adult visitors go to see the child, and something happens to them: They don't go home afterward, but keep on walking—through the city, through the fields, away from Omelas.

Study Questions

1. Where are they going, the ones who walk away? And why are they leaving?

2. How does Le Guin feel about the situation? Does she condone the suffering of the child, or is she arguing against it? Is the story realistic or symbolic?

3. How would an act utilitarian evaluate the story of Omelas? Would a rule utilitarian reach the same conclusion or a different one? Why?

4. Return to this story after reading Chapter 6 and develop a deontological critique of the people of Omelas (those who don't walk away).

5. In the film *Swordfish* a similar question is raised: "Would you kill a child to save the world?" However, in Omelas it is not a question of saving the world, just the happiness of all. In light of the discussion about "sheer numbers," would it make a difference to you if the torturous death of the child did indeed save the world and not just people's contentment? If yes, explain while focusing on where you would draw the line. If no, explain why not.

Narrative

Extreme Measures

TONY GILROY (SCREENWRITER)
MICHAEL APTED (DIRECTOR)

Film, 1996. Based on a novel by Michael Palma. Summary.

A young British emergency room doctor, Guy Luthan, is faced with a terrible moral and professional choice: In his emergency room, two patients need urgent care. One is a police officer who has been shot, and the other is the man who shot him, a troublemaker who pulled a gun on a bus. He was in turn shot by the cop. The officer is barely stabilized, whereas the gunman is in critical condition. There is only one surgery slot available. Whom should Guy choose? He needs to decide immediately. He sends the police officer into surgery and lets the gunman wait his turn. As it happens, they both survive, but a young nurse, Jodie, blames Guy for making an unprofessional moral choice: The gunman's medical needs were more urgent than the cop's. Guy explains, "I had to make a choice; on my right I see a cop with his wife in the corridor and pictures of his kids in his wallet, and on my left some guy who's taken out a gun on a city bus! I had ten seconds to make a choice, I had to make it—I hope I made the right one. I think I did, oh shit, maybe I didn't . . . I don't know."

This sets the scene for what could be just a run-of-the-mill hospital suspense story but turns out to be an honest exploration of the principle of utility as a social, moral, and psychological justification.

Guy has just received a fellowship in neurology at New York University. This means much to him and his family, because his father in England, once a medical doctor, lost his license to practice after euthanizing an old friend—another moral choice with consequences.

Meanwhile, a patient is brought to Guy's emergency room from the street, half naked and in complete physical and mental breakdown. He has a hospital bracelet on, and, in a lucid moment before he dies, he says two things to Guy—the word *triphase* and the name of a friend. Not understanding the cause of death, Guy orders an autopsy, but the hospital loses track not only of the autopsy but also of the body itself. Guy feels that something is terribly wrong and pursues the dead man's records on his own. The man had been admitted to the hospital previously for a neurological examination. Other patients turn up in the computer with the same profile: homeless, without relatives, having lab work done, and all files on them deleted.

But Guy is in for another shock: His apartment has been burglarized, and the detectives investigating the burglary find a stash of drugs in his place. Guy is arrested. Since Guy doesn't do drugs, he realizes that the burglary was a ruse and that the drugs were planted to discredit him, to get him out of the way—by whom? Whoever it is, their plan succeeds; Guy manages to raise bail, but once out of jail, he is suspended from his hospital position—his colleagues and supervisors assume that he is guilty. This also means that his fellowship to NYU will be lost because he will no longer be able to practice medicine—just like his father. Compelled to seek the truth, Guy locates a patient of his among the homeless and soon finds himself in a world underground in the subway system, where the homeless and destitute have made a world for themselves. Here he finds another piece of the puzzle: Doctors have been preying on the homeless, subjecting them to experiments leading to great suffering and death. But Guy himself is now being hunted in a prolonged chase, and just as he thinks he has found refuge with a friend, he is rendered unconscious.

United Archives GmbH/Alamy Stock Photo

The film *Extreme Measures* (Castle Rock, 1996) notes that sometimes we must make hard moral choices; the question is, What criterion should we use? Should we do what is right, regardless of the consequences, or should we try to obtain the best result for as many as possible with the least harm caused? This is the dilemma facing Dr. Guy Luthan (Hugh Grant), not only in his own career, but also as the pawn in a greater plot orchestrated by a famous doctor: to use homeless people as guinea pigs. Here Guy has to choose whether to save the life of a police officer with a wife and kids or the gunman who shot the officer in cold blood.

Guy wakes up in a hospital bed—and to his horror, he finds himself paralyzed from the neck down. He is told that the blow he sustained to his spine severed it, and he will be a quadriplegic for life. Realizing the enormity of what has happened to him, Guy feels that, having no hope of recovery, he might as well be dead. The famous neurologist Dr. Myrick now pays him a visit, talking enigmatically about hope. What if there were hope for him after all? What would it be worth to him to return to his old life? What would he risk if a procedure were available? Guy answers, "Anything!" Myrick replies, "You'd better think about that."

Who is responsible for the burglary, the planted drugs, the disappearance of the homeless, and the attempt on Guy's life? The answer lies within Guy's own hospital environment. When Guy's paralysis miraculously wears off after 24 hours, he realizes he'd been drugged, and that it is Dr. Myrick, passionately engaged in helping victims of spinal cord injury, who has undertaken research into spinal cord regeneration by using homeless patients as guinea pigs for the good of humanity.

Guy now tries to escape from the hospital. This is a pivotal scene in the film, and I will not spoil the surprise twists for you. During a dramatic moment, Myrick tries to explain his actions to Guy: The homeless men he experimented on were useless beings—but now they are heroes, since their deaths have given hope to so many injured people. "Good doctors do the correct thing. Great doctors have the guts to do the right thing. . . . If you could cure cancer by killing one person, wouldn't you have to do it? Wouldn't it be the brave thing to do? One person, and it's gone tomorrow?" Guy replies that perhaps the homeless people he used weren't worth much, but they didn't choose to be heroes—he never asked for volunteers. To Guy, doctors can't do that—Myrick has been playing God.

One final confrontation remains—one that solves some issues but raises others. In the end, Guy is given all of Myrick's files from his research into spinal cord injuries . . . and Guy does not reject the files.

Study Questions

1. Discuss the opening scene. Did Guy make the right professional choice? the right moral choice? Should there be a difference? Explain your position.

2. Is Dr. Myrick's experimentation a noble quest to help humanity or a perverse abuse of human beings? Is there a third alternative? Explain your position.

3. Dr. Myrick asks Guy what he would be willing to do to regain his mobility at a time when Guy believes himself to be paralyzed for life. What does Guy answer, and why is this scene so important?

4. Guy accuses Myrick of playing God. Guy's own father lost his license to practice medicine because he euthanized a friend. Do you think there is a connection here, or is this a coincidence in the film?

5. In the end, Guy takes over Myrick's research papers. Is this gesture an acceptance of Myrick's utilitarian principles, or is there another possibility? By accepting the papers, have Guy's hands now been dirtied? Why or why not?

6. Is this a pro-utilitarian or an anti-utilitarian film? Explain.

7. The scene where Guy makes his decision in the ER and Myrick's explanation of his medical experiments are deliberately set up as parallels. What are the similarities, and what are the differences? Does the discussion in the chapter text about the hedonistic calculus as a *last resort* provide us with a tool for distinguishing between Guy and Myrick?

8. Scientists have announced that they believe great strides can be made toward curing paralysis through stem cell research. Assuming that the stem cells originated in a human embryo, do you think there is a difference between Myrick's experiments on homeless people for the sake of helping patients with paralysis and using stem cells from an embryo to accomplish the same thing? Explain similarities and differences.

 Narrative

Outbreak

LAURENCE DWORET AND ROBERT ROY POOL (SCREENWRITERS)
WOLFGANG PETERSEN (DIRECTOR)

Film, 1995. Summary.

Outbreak is now considered *the* classic film about a fast-spreading pandemic, although in 1995 the world had not yet dealt with the virus scares of recent years such as SARS, MERS, the Bird Flu, the H1N1 flu strain, the concerns over the Zika virus, the 2019 outbreak of measles in several parts of the world, including several states in the United States, and the 2019 Coronavirus. The film imagines an Ebola-type virus spreading across the world, and the 2014–15 Ebola outbreak in several African states, with close to 30,000 cases and a death count of over 11,000 people, with infected medical personnel from other parts of the world being shipped home to face treatment (successfully, in some cases), brought back the *Outbreak* scenario as particularly prophetic. At the time of writing this, Ebola cases were once again on the rise in Africa. The connection to utilitarianism is the subplot which (seen from an anti-utilitarian view) exposes a conspiracy to withhold a vaccine.

WARNER BROS/Allstar Picture Library/Alamy Stock Photo

The film *Outbreak* (Warner Brothers, 1995), a medical thriller which is now considered a classic, pits concern for the safety of the many against the rights of the few. In a situation where a contagious, fatal disease is spreading, is it acceptable to adopt a utilitarian policy of isolating and "terminating" the infected? Here Walter (Cuba Gooding, Jr.) and Sam (Dustin Hoffman) are dressed in protective gear, moving among the infected.

It is 1967 in Motaba, Zaire; a camp of mercenaries is struck by a deadly and unknown virus that is 100 percent lethal. Doctors from an American military unit come in, investigate, draw blood samples—and leave. The next thing we know, the camp is annihilated by a bomb blast.

We move on to the present day (1990s) and are introduced to Colonel Sam Daniels and his ex-wife Robby Keough, both medical scientists at a military center for disease control, cleared to work with pathogens at the most contagious levels. Sam has to go to Zaire to investigate an outbreak of what looks like a new virus, 100 percent lethal, which kills its victims within three to four days.

In the lab, Sam and his superior officer General Billy Ford investigate the virus; Sam wonders why Ford does not seem surprised by this virus and does not wish any measures taken to prevent it from entering the country. But behind Sam's back Ford is in touch with his own superior officer, General Donald McClintock, and now we learn that the new virus is the same as the one from 1967, that Ford knows of an antidote, and that McClintock was responsible for the bombing of the mercenary camp in order to contain the virus—and perhaps also for another reason. To prevent Sam from finding out, they assign him to another case ... but when news comes in of a viral outbreak in Boston and in Cedar Creek, California, Sam defies orders and goes to Cedar Creek. Here he encounters Robby, who has been assigned to do research on the outbreak.

How did these outbreaks occur? We are told the story in flashes: A monkey is caught by animal dealers in Zaire, brought illegally to San Francisco on board a ship, placed temporarily in an animal research facility, and taken from there by an animal trader, Jimbo Scott, to a pet store in Cedar Creek. The pet store owner doesn't want the monkey (wrong gender), especially after the monkey scratches him. So Jimbo takes the monkey out in the woods and releases it. Meanwhile, the pet store owner gets very sick; the lab assistant at the hospital dealing with his blood test gets sick and infects an entire movie theater full of people; Jimbo gets sick while flying home to Boston and infects his wife. Within three to four days, everybody infected dies from symptoms much like those associated with the Ebola virus: bleeding from all orifices. In Boston the only ones infected were Jimbo and his wife, but the infection is rampant in Cedar Creek, because a mutation has occurred: The California strain is now airborne. And so the army moves into Cedar Creek and isolates the town. No one goes in or out. Sick family members are rounded up and taken to a camp from which nobody is expected to return. Ford tries to use the old antidote here (and this tips Sam off to the fact that Ford knew about this virus all along), but it doesn't work, because the virus has mutated.

This crisis reaches to the level of the president of the United States. How fast can the disease spread? Within days the entire country could be infected. What must be done to help the people of Cedar Creek and to save the lives of other Americans, perhaps the world? The solution, reached with much hesitation and soul-searching, is "Clean Sweep": an eradication of the town of Cedar Creek in the same manner the mercenary camp was bombed in 1967. In McClintock's words, "Our procedure must be viewed objectively. Be compassionate, but be compassionate globally." As the president's aide remarks, the firebombing of Cedar Creek is unconstitutional because nobody should be deprived of life, liberty, or property without due process—so if the decision is made to go ahead, everyone should know what price is being paid for the safety of the world. Ford and McClintock have their own conversation where Ford points out that you can't treat the people of Cedar Creek like that—they are Americans. McClintock replies that the rest of America may be dying; the people of Cedar Creek should be regarded as casualties of war.

Back at the isolated town, Robby is infected by accident, and Sam confronts Ford: Why was the antidote not given in time, before the mutation happened? Because, as Sam guesses, there was an ulterior motive: The virus presented the perfect biological weapon and had to be protected, so the antidote was withheld. Ford defends the decision as a matter of national security: "At the time it was felt that we could afford a certain amount of losses." And now Ford reveals that Clean Sweep will take place in twenty-four hours.

With the help of young Major Salt, Sam commandeers a helicopter: Quick action must be taken. They now know that the virus came into the country with a monkey as a host. They break into a local television newscast with a warning and a picture of the monkey. This has immediate results: a mother knows her daughter has been playing with a monkey in the woods, not far from Cedar Creek. Sam and Salt capture the monkey and send immediate word to Ford, but to their horror they find out that McClintock has no intention of calling off Clean Sweep, even if serum can now be made from the monkey to save the people of Cedar Creek and Robby. He still wants to protect the virus as a future biological weapon. The pilots of Clean Sweep are in the air, and McClintock is telling them to do their duty. Sam gets on the intercom and pleads with them to reconsider; he tells them the entire story, but they don't respond. In a last-ditch effort, Sam tries to make Ford stop the bombing, but all Ford can do is to send an indirect message to Sam by telling him that he must "get out of the way," because the mission will have to be aborted if his chopper is in the flight path of the incoming bomber....

Will Sam and Salt succeed in stopping the firebombing of Cedar Creek? Will McClintock win? Will Robby live? Will she and Sam get together again? I'm not going to tell!

Study Questions

1. How would Bentham evaluate McClintock's decisions? Do you think Mill would respond any differently? Compare the possible responses from an act- and a rule-utilitarian point of view.
2. Can Ford's action as a co-conspirator acting on the orders of his superior officer be defended? Why or why not?
3. In the case of an outbreak of a pandemic virus, either natural or manufactured, would you approve of governmental measures that would involve sacrificing the few to save the lives of the many? Why or why not?
4. After you read Chapter 6, you may want to re-read the summary and apply Kant's prohibition on treating human beings "merely as a means to an end."

Narrative

The Good Place, NBC television series

CREATED BY MICHAEL SCHUR

Season 2, Episode 5: *"The Trolley Problem,"* 2017

A brief introduction, with a spoiler: In the very first episode Eleanor Shellstrop, a young woman, wakes up in the Afterlife after having been killed in an accident involving out-of-control shopping carts, and is told that she has arrived in the Good Place as a reward for her righteous, moral life. She is teamed with another deceased person, a young African professor of moral philosophy, Chidi Anagonye, because they are supposedly soul mates. But things aren't quite working out; Eleanor is convinced that she is being mistaken for someone else, because she has not led a particularly moral life; she is selfish and egotistical. Chidi turns out to have problems of his own: he is incapable of making decisions, and he and Eleanor seem utterly incompatible. But their guide, Michael (assumed to be an angel) assure them that there are no mistakes. They belong in the Good Place. However (here comes the spoiler), during Season 1 they realize that they are actually not in Heaven, but in a "fake Good Place" run by demons preparing them to be transferred to the Bad Place, from which they will never escape, and Michael is the demon in charge. Their time in the fake Good Place has actually been designed by Michael for them to torture each other.

Fremulon, 3 Arts Entertainment, Universal Television/ Album/Alamy Stock Photo

The fantasy-comedy television series *The Good Place* (NBC) has introduced many viewers to classical concepts in moral philosophy. Here the philosophy professor Chidi Anagonye (William Jackson Harper) and his friend and occasional student Eleanor Shellstrop (Kristen Bell) are discussing the pros and cons of utilitarianism.

In Season 2, Michael has developed a genuine interest in understanding humans, because Eleanor and two other companions, the "soul mates" Tahani and Jianyu, are inspired by Chidi to become better people, even after death. Chidi is now giving classes in ethics to the three others in the hope of getting into the "real Good Place," and Michael is sitting in, because he claims that he wants to learn how to think ethically. In Episode 5, Chidi is teaching his little class about the trolley problem. First he presents a model of Foot's classical version of five workers on one track vs. one worker on another (see p. 213). Eleanor wants to know who the people are, and Chidi answers that they are anonymous; in that case, Eleanor suggests to divert the trolley to the track with the one person. But the students are frustrated because it seems like a lose-lose situation. Either way, somebody has to die. Michael, on the other hand, is trying to solve the problem as he sees it: How can we kill all six at the same time? He hasn't quite mastered the ethical thinking of humans yet.

As a moral philosophy professor, Chidi is acquainted with all the versions of the problem such as, What if the one person is someone you know? Michael wants to know "the answer," but Chidi tells him that the great thing about the trolley problem is that there is no right answer. Michael's reply: "This is why everyone hates moral philosophy professors!" For Michael that is frustratingly abstract, so, being a demon with magical powers, he instantly transfers Chidi and Eleanor to a trolley without breaks ("The Ethics Express"), with five workers on the track ahead, and one worker on another track. And now Chidi has to make a decision! We already know that making decisions is not his strong point. He freezes, and the trolley plows straight into the five workers, killing them. Michael explains that it is just a simulation, and they aren't real—but "their pain is real." (In effect, Chidi's indecision is very similar to Green and Cohen's test subjects in Chapter 1.) And Michael now puts Chidi through many different variations, including having one of his friends being the one person on the other track. Every scenario entails some horror story, and Chidi gets blasted with gore from the virtual victims. So is there really no solution to the trolley problem? Michael instantly transfers Chidi and Eleanor to an operating room at a hospital (another famous moral conundrum illustrating utilitarianism). Now Chidi is the doctor, having to make a terrible choice: He has five patients who are dying, but they can be saved with organ transplants—and Eleanor is healthy, so now Michael says he has to kill Eleanor and harvest her organs. Chidi refuses on moral grounds, but is devastated when a little girl begs for her father's life (he is one of the patients—incidentally one of the workers hit by the trolley!). And all of a sudden it dawns on Eleanor what is going on: Michael is simply being his old demon self, having found the most exquisite way to torture Chidi! Through hard, practical, moral decisions which is Chidi's weakness. Michael laughs and confesses: Yes, that was the whole point.

So do we get an actual solution to the trolley problem? Not in Episode 5—but in Season 2, Episode 10 we do, and this time Michael isn't laughing.

Michael has become convinced that the four don't deserve eternal damnation, so he is willing to take them to the Judge, an eternal being called Gen, so she can evaluate their situation. Michael's own existence is in danger too, because if he fails as a demon, he will himself be tortured for an eternity. But in order to get to the Judge's quarters, they have to navigate through the Bad Place, in danger of being discovered by the local demons. To get through the portal to the Judge's neutral zone, each has to wear a badge. Michael secures badges for everybody—but in the final moment, at the portal to the Judge's place, Michael reveals to Eleanor that he has found a solution to the trolley problem: *self-sacrifice.* And he pins the last badge on Eleanor and pushes her through the portal. He could only secure four badges, and he now has to face the demons.

Will Eleanor, Chidi, Tahani, and Jianyu finally get to the real Good Place? What will the Judge say? And what happens to Michael? Find out for yourself!

Study Questions

1. Interestingly, Michael's solution of self-sacrifice has been suggested in connection with Judith Jarvis Thomson's example with the "fat man": Perhaps the only way that the the two totally disagreeable solutions (push the big guy over or do nothing) can be bypassed is if we imagine

ourselves being the "fat man" whose bulk can stop the trolley, laying down our life for the five people on the track. But that doesn't actually answer Foot's original question of whether we should ever sacrifice the few for the many, it evades it by suggesting a third option. Is that a good answer to the trolley problem? What if self-sacrifice is not an option?

2. If Michael is just torturing Chidi by forcing him to experience variations within the trolley problem, might Foot have designed the trolley problem to torture philosophy students?

3. Do you think there is a connection between the creator of the series sharing his first name with Michael, the "creator" or architect of the fake Good Place? If you are familiar with the Judeo-Christian tradition, can you see another (biblical) connection?

4. In a YouTube original, "Greater Good," *Mind Field* S2 E1, created by Michael Stevens (a third Michael! Think of that!), the thought experiment of the trolley problem is brought to life: Stevens sets up an experiment where a group of individuals believe they are scheduled for an interview about a high-speed rail project. One by one they are allowed to wait in what looks like a control booth with cameras showing various train tracks, supposedly in real-time, and the controller teaches them how to divert a train to another track, just as a show-and-tell courtesy. "Coincidentally" the controller has to leave his post. He doesn't come back. In the meantime they watch, by themselves, in horror, as a train approaches five workers with headphones on a track—and they see that another track has only one worker. Will they divert the train, or will they freeze, like Chidi? Spoiler: two out of five chose to divert the train. The others froze. Of course nobody got hurt, because the control booth was all fake, and the screens were showing videos taped earlier, all designed to make the test subjects believe they were watching a real event unfold—in effect, very much reminiscent of the Milgram shock obedience experiment. You may want to watch the episode, if it is still available when you read this, and compare it to the Foot's original thought experiment, and Green's depiction of a "descriptive" trolley problem on p. 213 (*Could* you pull the lever?) vs. a "normative" trolley problem (*Should* you pull the lever?). Which one is Stevens's version?

Chapter Six
Using Your Reason, Part 2: Kant's Deontology

On the whole, we might say that there are two major ways in which we can approach a problem. We might ask ourselves, What happens if I do X? In that case we're letting ourselves be guided by the future consequences of our actions. Or we might ask ourselves, Is X right or wrong in itself, regardless of the consequences? Just think back to the example at the beginning of Chapter 5, about "lying to Grandma." Do we think, overall, that lying is the best course of action if it gives Grandma peace of mind, and it doesn't create any further problems? Or do we think that lying is simply wrong, because you are betraying trust and showing Grandma disrespect? The first approach is utilitarian, provided that we are looking for good consequences for as many as possible. The version of the second approach that has had the most influence is Immanuel Kant's *duty theory*. (See Box 6.1 for a summary of Kant's life.)

Kant's moral theory is often referred to as *deontology* (the theory of moral obligation, from the Greek *deon*, "that which is obligatory"). Kant believed his theory was the very opposite of a consequentialist theory, and his moral analysis was, in part, written to show how little a moral theory that worries about consequences has to do with true moral thinking. Let us look at an example to illustrate this fundamental difference.

Box 6.1 KANT: HIS LIFE AND WORK

Some famous and influential people lead lives of adventure. The life of Immanuel Kant (1724-1804) seems to have been an *intellectual* adventure exclusively, for he did little that might in any other way be considered adventurous. He grew up in the town of Königsberg, East Prussia (a city on the Baltic Sea, now Kaliningrad in Russian territory). He was raised in an atmosphere of strict Protestant values by his devout mother and by his father, who made a meager living as a saddler. He entered Königsberg University, studied theology, graduated, and tutored for a while until he was offered a position at the university in his hometown. In 1770 he became a full professor in logic and metaphysics, and that was when the philosophical drama began, for Kant achieved influence not only in Western philosophy but also in science and social thinking—an influence that was never eclipsed by anyone else in the eighteenth century. He developed theories about astronomy that are still considered plausible (the so-called Kant-Laplace nebular hypothesis has to a great extent been corroborated by the Hubbell Space Telescope); he laid out rules for a new social world of mutual respect for all citizens; he made contributions to philosophy of law and religion; he attempted to map the entire spectrum of human intelligence in his three major works, *Critique of Pure Reason* (1781), *Critique of Practical Reason* (1788), and *Critique of Judgment* (1790), as well as in smaller works such as *Prolegomena to Every Future Metaphysics* (1783) and *Grounding for the Metaphysics of Morals* (1785). He continued working until late in life; one of his most influential works from that period is *The Metaphysics of Morals* (1797).

When Kant calls a book a "critique," he is not implying that he is merely writing a negative criticism of a subject; he is, rather, looking for the *condition of possibility* of that subject. In *Critique of Pure Reason* he asks, "What makes it possible for me to achieve knowledge?" (In other words, what is the condition of possibility of knowledge?) In *Critique of Practical Reason* he asks about the condition of possibility of moral thinking, and in *Critique of Judgment* he examines the condition of possibility for appreciating natural and artistic beauty. In all those fields his insights helped shape new disciplines and redefine old disciplines. Kant was never an agitator for his ideas, though; on the contrary, he was famous for his extremely quiet and highly regulated routine. He remained single throughout his life, and his sole interest seems to have been his work. His students reported that he was in fact a good and popular teacher.

Consequences Don't Count—Having a Good Will Does

ullstein picture Dtl./Getty Images

This painting shows the German philosopher Immanuel Kant, second from the left, dining with friends. Kant was reportedly a popular guest at dinners, and his own dinner parties were legendary. He even included a guide to the perfect dinner party in *Anthropology from a Pragmatic Point of View,* specifying the ideal number of guests: No fewer than three, and no more than nine; moderate use of wine will help the conversation flow; what is said at the table in confidence should stay at the table; the conversation should start with talking about the news, then a discussion should follow, and the dinner should end with jokes. Among the other rules were: no dinner music, and no extended silences. The end result should be a good time, with cheerful respect of each others' varied viewpoints. And the entire point of a good dinner party? It is part of the path to happiness. Which stage of the dinner do you think the dinner guests in the painting have reached?

Some years ago, newspapers reported an accident somewhere in the Pacific Northwest. A family had gone away for a short vacation and had left their keys with their neighbor so that he could water their plants and look after the place. On Sunday afternoon, a few hours before they were due to arrive home, the temperature was dropping, and the neighbor thought he would do them a favor and make sure they would come home to a nice, toasty house. He went in and turned on the furnace. You've guessed what happened: The house burned down and the family came home to a smoking ruin. That was the extent of the newspaper coverage, but suppose it had been reported by a classical utilitarian. Then the article might have ended something like this: "The neighbor will have to answer for the consequences of this terrible deed." Why? Because, given that only consequences count, the act of turning on the furnace was a terrible one, regardless of the man's good intentions. As it is sometimes said, the road to hell is paved with good intentions. In other words, only your deeds count, not what you intended by them.

Suppose, however, that a Kantian had written the article. Then it might have ended like this: "This good neighbor should be praised for his kind thought and good intentions regardless of the fact that the family lost their home; that consequence certainly can't be blamed on him, because all he intended to do was the right thing."

Let us continue speculating. Suppose the house didn't burn down, but instead provided a warm, cozy shelter for and saved the lives of the entire family, who (shall we say) had all come down with pneumonia. The utilitarian now would have to say that the act of lighting the furnace was a shining example of a morally good deed, but Kant would not change his mind: The neighbor's action was good because of his intention, and the consequences of the act don't make it any better or worse. It is not just any good intention, however, that makes an action morally good in Kant's view: One must have *a respect for the moral law* that is expressed in the intention. It isn't enough for the neighbor to be a kind man who wants his neighbors to be comfortable; he must imagine it to be a good thing for neighbors to act that way *in general*—not because it would make everyone comfortable and happy, but strictly for the sake of the *principle* of doing the right thing. This is what Kant calls having a *good will*. For Kant the presence of a good will is what makes an action morally good, regardless of its consequences. Therefore, even if you never accomplished what you intended, you are still morally praiseworthy provided you tried hard to do the right thing. In his book *Grounding for the Metaphysics of Morals* (1785; also commonly referred to as *Groundwork* or *Foundations*), Kant assures us that

> [e]ven if, by some especially unfortunate fate or by the niggardly provision of stepmotherly nature, this will should be wholly lacking in the power to accomplish its purpose;* if with the greatest effort it should yet achieve nothing, and only the good will should remain (not, to be sure, as a mere wish but as the summoning of all the means in our power), yet would it, like a jewel, still shine by its own light as something which has its full value in itself. Its usefulness or fruitlessness can neither augment nor diminish this value.

The Categorical Imperative

How do we know that our will is good? We put our intentions to a test. In *Grounding for the Metaphysics of Morals,* Kant says we must ask whether we can imagine our intentions as a general law for everybody. That means that our intentions have to *conform to a rational principle*. We have to think hard to determine whether we're about to do the right thing or not; it can't be determined just by some gut-level feeling. However, we don't have to wait to see the actual consequences to determine whether our intentions are good—all we have to do is determine whether we could imagine others doing to us what we intend doing to them. In other words, Kant proposes a variant of the Golden Rule—but it is a variant with certain specifics, as we shall see—and it illustrates that Kant is also a *hard universalist,* perhaps the hardest one ever to write a book on morals.

For Kant, humans usually know what they *ought* to do, and that is almost always the opposite of what they *want* to do: Our moral conflicts are generally between our duty and our inclination, and when we let our desires run rampant it is simply because we haven't come up with a way for our sense of duty to persuade us

---

*To modern readers without much experience with older literature in English, the term *niggardly* generally gives pause because it bears an unfortunate resemblance to a racial epithet and people have in recent years been fired for using the word; however, the two words are unrelated in etymology and meaning, and there is no racial undertone in the word used by Kant's translators. The term means "avaricious" or "stingy." The original German word is *kärglich*. But even though *niggardly* doesn't associate to bigotry and discrimination, how about the term *stepmotherly?* That is Kant's own term in translation.

to do the right thing. Kant therefore proposes a test to determine the right thing to do. He refers to this test as the *categorical imperative*. But because it is a matter of doing the right thing not in terms of the outcome but in terms of the intentions, we must look more closely at these intentions.

Suppose a store owner is trying to decide whether to cheat her customers. She might tell herself, (1) "I will cheat them whenever I can get away with it" or "I will cheat them only on occasion so nobody can detect a pattern." We can all tell, intuitively, that this merchant's intentions aren't good, although they certainly might benefit her and give her some extra cash at the end of the week. In other words, the consequences may be good, yet we know that cheating the customers is not the right thing to do. (We'll get back to the reason in a while.) Suppose, though, that the owner decides *not* to cheat her customers because (2) she might be *found out,* and then she would lose their business and might have to close shop. This is certainly prudent, but it still is not a morally praiseworthy decision, because she is doing it only to achieve good consequences. What if the store owner decides not to cheat her customers because (3) she *likes them too much* to ever do them any harm? She loves the little kids buying candy, the old ladies buying groceries, and everyone else, so how could she ever consider cheating them? This, says Kant, is very nice, but it still is not morally praiseworthy, because the merchant is doing only what she feels like doing, and we can't be expected to praise her for just wanting to feel good. (If you want to reexamine this argument, go back to the section in Chapter 4 on psychological egoism, where a similar argument is analyzed in detail.) And indeed, what if some day she should stop loving her customers or just one of them? Then the reason for not cheating is gone; so, Kant cannot approve of motive 3, regardless of how much we generally approve of people who help others because they enjoy it; it really isn't based on a *principle* any more than motive 1 or motive 2.

The only morally praiseworthy reason for not wanting to cheat the customers would be if the store owner told herself, (4) "It wouldn't be right," regardless of consequences or warm and fuzzy feelings. Why wouldn't it be right? Because she certainly couldn't want everybody else to cheat their customers as a universal law.

If the store owner tells herself, "I will not cheat my customers because otherwise I'll lose them," then she is not doing a bad thing, of course. She is just doing a prudent thing, and Kant says our lives are full of such prudent decisions; they are dependent on each situation, and we have to determine in each case what would be the smart thing to do. Kant calls these decisions, which are *conditional,* because they depend on the situation and on one's own personal desires, *hypothetical imperatives—imperatives* because they are commands: *If* you don't want to lose your customers, *then* you should not cheat them. *If* you want to get your degree, *then* you should not miss your final exam. *If* you want to be good at baking biscuits, *then* you ought to bake them from scratch and not use a prepared mix. But suppose you're closing down your shop and moving to another town? Then you might not care about losing those customers. And suppose you decide to drop out of school—then who cares about that final exam? And if you and everyone you know hates biscuits, then why bother worrying about getting good at baking them? In other words, a hypothetical imperative is dependent or conditional on your interest in a certain outcome. If you don't want the outcome, the imperative is not binding. We make such decisions every day, and, as long as they are based merely on wanting some outcome, they are not morally relevant. (They can, of course, be morally bad, but, even if they have a good outcome, Kant would say that they are morally neutral.) What makes a decision morally praiseworthy is that the agent (the person acting) decides to do something because it might be applied to everyone as a *universal moral law.* In that case that person has used the categorical imperative.

What makes a categorical imperative *categorical* is that it is not dependent on anyone's desire to make it an imperative; it is binding not just in some situations and for some people, but always, for everyone. It is absolute. That is the very nature of the moral law: If it applies at all, it applies to everyone in the same situation. Although there are myriad hypothetical imperatives, there is only one categorical imperative, expressed in the most general terms possible: *Always act so that you can will that your maxim can become a universal law.* In ordinary language that means: Ask yourself what it is you want to do right now (such as making the house next door toasty for your neighbors, skipping classes on Friday, or lying to Grandma about dating someone outside her religion). Then imagine making that action into a rule (such as, Always make sure your neighbors come home to a toasty house; Always skip Friday classes; Always lie to Grandma to spare her pain). Now you've identified your *maxim,* or the principle or rule for your action. The next step is to ask yourself whether you could want that maxim to become a universal rule for everyone to follow. And, if you can't agree to that—if you don't think it makes sense that *everyone* should, under similar circumstances, light their neighbors' furnaces, skip classes, or lie to Grandma—then *you* shouldn't do it either. It's that simple, and for Kant this realization was so breathtaking that it could be compared only to his awe of the universe on a starry night. Let us use Kant's own example to illustrate.

> [A man] in need finds himself forced to borrow money. He knows well that he won't be able to repay it, but he sees also that he will not get any loan unless he firmly promises to repay it within a fixed time. He wants to make such a promise, but he still has conscience enough to ask himself whether it is not permissible and is contrary to duty to get out of difficulty in this way. Suppose, however, that he decides to do so. The maxim of his action would then be expressed as follows: When I believe myself to be in need of money, I will borrow money and promise to pay it back, although I know that I can never do so. Now this principle of self-love or personal advantage may perhaps be quite compatible with one's entire future welfare, but the question is now whether it is right. I then transform the requirement of self-love into a universal law and put the question thus: how would things stand if my maxim were to become a universal law? He then sees at once that such a maxim could never hold as a universal law of nature and be consistent with itself, but must necessarily be self-contradictory. For the universality of a law which says that anyone believing himself to be in difficulty could promise whatever he pleases with the intention of not keeping it would make promising itself and the end to be attained thereby quite impossible, inasmuch as no one would believe what was promised him but would merely laugh at all such utterances as being vain pretences.

Do we know why this man wants to borrow money? Perhaps he wants to buy a speedboat. Perhaps he wants to pay a hit man for a contract killing. Or he needs to pay the rent. Perhaps his child is ill, and he has to buy medication and pay the doctor's bill. We don't know. Is knowing his reason relevant? If we were utilitarians, it would be very relevant, because then we could judge the merit of the proposed consequences. (Saving his child generally has more utility than buying a boat or hiring a hit man.) But Kant is no utilitarian, and the prospect of the man in the example wanting to do good with the borrowed money is no more relevant than the prospect of his wanting to buy a boat or even to hire a hit man. The main issue here is, *Does the man have a good will?* Would he refuse to follow a course of action if he couldn't agree to everyone else having the right to act the same way? At the end of the chapter you'll find an example from Kant's *Grounding* that illustrates what he means by having a good will.

If we analyze the excerpt above, then the **maxim** is that whenever he is broke, he will borrow money and promise to pay it back without having any intention of doing it. His **universalized maxim** is that it is okay for everybody else to do the same thing. And his evaluation of **whether it is rational** is that of course it is not, because in that case nobody would lend him money, because everybody knows that nobody is going to pay back any loans!

Let us go over the structure of the proposed test of right and wrong conduct again: What is it you're thinking of doing? Imagine that as a *general rule* for action you'll follow every time the situation comes up. You have now expressed your *maxim.* Then imagine everybody else doing it too; by doing this you *universalize your maxim.* Then ask yourself, Would this be rational? Could I still get away with it if everyone did it? The answer is no, you would *undermine your own intention,* because nobody would lend *you* any money if everyone were lying about paying it back. So it is not just the fact that banks would close and the financial world would be in chaos—it is the *logical outcome* of your universalized maxim that shows you that your intention was wrong. This means that it is your *duty* to refrain from following a self-contradictory maxim, simply because your reason tells you it can't be universalized. (Box 6.2 illustrates the categorical imperative with a classic episode of the animated sitcom *The Simpsons.*)

Box 6.2 BART SIMPSON AND THE CATEGORICAL IMPERATIVE

Sometimes we can find illustrations of famous philosophical theories hidden like gems in unlikely fictional settings such as sitcoms. You saw one in Chapter 4 with an episode of *Friends*. In a classic episode (S5E7) of the extremely long-running animated comedy series *The Simpsons*, "Bart's Inner Child," Bart's antics provide a perfect illustration of a Kantian "bad maxim," either deliberately or inadvertently written into the episode by the writer George Meyer. You may be familiar with the characters, and Bart in particular: an obnoxious kid with a good brain and no respect for anything at all. Bart's parents, Homer and Marge, and their kids are at an event at the school auditorium with a self-help "guru," Brad Goodman, who teaches people to "do what feels good," and "let loose their inner child." Everybody in Springfield is packed into the auditorium. Bart, being bored, starts heckling the speaker, but instead of getting angry Goodman calls Bart up on the stage, and shows him off as the ideal "inner child" whom everybody should strive to be like—someone with no inhibitions, always doing what he feels like. And now the whole town of Springfield decides to follow Goodman's advice, and overnight everybody becomes like Bart, following their impulses, just doing what feels good. But that unfortunately has a detrimental effect on Bart,

because he can't get away with doing the selfish things he normally does: he usually stops on the footbridge over the freeway and spits on the cars below, but that morning hundreds of people are lined up along the railing, spitting on cars, so he can't get to the railing. He likes to climb a tree in the park and throw water balloons at people, but now he can't even find a tree to climb that doesn't have people already in it, throwing water balloons. And at school, where he usually irritates the teacher with his smart-alecky remarks, now all the other kids beat him to it with their own jokes. Defeated, he sighs, "Everybody is a comedian." Later, after a parade float goes awry, Springfield realizes that it isn't so great to just follow one's impulses, but the point has been made much earlier, for the viewer who is familiar with Kant: Bart's maxim is "Always do what you feel like doing." Universalized, it becomes, "Everybody should just do what they feel like doing, just like Bart." But is that rational? Not according to the formula of the categorical imperative, because when Bart's maxim is universalized, it undermines his intention of doing what he feels like doing! And he has to give up on his maxim because everybody else is doing the same thing. That is, in essence, how we can identify a bad maxim, according to Kant.

The categorical imperative asks us, in effect, Would you want others to treat you the way you're thinking of treating them? The association to the Golden Rule (see Box 4.8) is almost inevitable: How should we treat others? The way we would want to be treated. And yet Kant had harsh words for the old Golden Rule. He thought it was just a simplistic version of his own categorical imperative and that it could even be turned into a travesty: If you don't want to help others, just claim you don't want or need any help from them! But the bottom line is that the categorical imperative draws on that same fundamental realization that I called a spark of moral genius in the Golden Rule: It sees self and others as fundamentally similar—not in the details of our lives, but in the fact that we are human beings and should be treated fairly by one another.

Does that mean that the categorical imperative works only if *everyone* can accept your maxim as a universal law? Not in the sense that we have to take a poll before we decide to act; if everyone's actual approval were the final criterion, the principle would lose its appeal as an immediate test of where one's duty lies. There is an element of universal approval in Kant's idea, but it lies in the reflection of an *ideal* situation, not an *actual* one. If everyone put aside his or her personal interests and then used the categorical imperative, then everyone would, ideally, come up with the same conclusion about what is morally permissible. Kant, who belonged to an era of less doubt about what exactly rationality means, believed that if we all used the same rules of logic and disregarded our personal interests, then we all would come to the same results about moral as well as intellectual issues.

This immense faith in human rationality is an important factor in Kant's moral theory because it reflects his belief that humans are privileged beings. We can set up our own moral rules without having to seek guidance by going to the authorities; we need not be told how to live by the church or by the police or by the monarch or even by our parents. All we need is our good will and our reason, and with that we can set our own rules. If we choose a certain course of action because we have been told to—because we listen to other people's advice for some reason or other—we are merely doing what might be prudent and expedient, but if we listen to our own reason and have good will, then we are *autonomous lawmakers*.

Won't this approach result in a society where everyone looks after himself or herself and lives by multiple rules that may contradict one another? No, because if everyone has good will and applies the categorical imperative, then all will set the same, reasonable, unselfish rules for themselves because they would not wish to set a rule that would be impossible for others to follow.

In this way Kant believes he has shown us how to solve every dilemma, every problem where desire clashes with duty. When the categorical imperative is applied, we automatically disregard our own personal interests and look at the bigger picture, and this action is what is morally praiseworthy: to realize that something is right or wrong in itself. In the Narratives section you'll find a selection of stories that explore, each in its own way, the principle of doing the right thing regardless of the opinion of others or the consequences for oneself: Two Western films are placed together because of their common focus on doing the right thing as a matter of principle: the classic *High Noon* and the 2007 film *3:10 to Yuma*. In addition, a summary of the graphic novel *Watchmen* illustrates (with a spoiler) the clash between the utilitarian and the deontological worldview.

Criticism of the Categorical Imperative

Some people are immediately impressed by the idea that one's intentions count for more than the outcome of one's actions and that the question of right or wrong in itself is important; we can't consider only the consequences if it means violating the rights of others. Others claim that no matter how much you say you're not interested in consequences, they still end up being a consideration. Critics have raised five major points when finding fault with Kant's theory.

1. **Consequences Count**   Doesn't the categorical imperative actually imply concern for consequences? That is the criticism of John Stuart Mill, who had some sharp things to say about Kant's example of borrowing money and not keeping promises. If that was the best Kant could come up with to show that consequences don't count, he was not doing a very good job, said Mill, because what was he appealing to? By asking "What if everybody does what you want to do?" wasn't Kant worrying about *consequences?* What will happen if everyone borrows money and doesn't pay it back in spite of their promises? Then no one else can take advantage of promising falsely, either. In Mill's view, that is as much an appeal to consequences as regular utilitarianism is. That caused Mill to conclude that we all must include consequences in our moral theory, no matter how reluctant we are to recognize their importance. This appears to be a valid point against Kant. The only thing Kant might say in response to this (he never did, of course, since he was long dead by the time Mill criticized his point of view) is that his viewpoint does not look at actual consequences but at the logical implications of a universalized maxim: Will it or will it not undermine itself? Whether Mill has successfully criticized Kant or misunderstood him is still

a topic of discussion among philosophers, but that is only when we focus on the Categorical Imperative in its original version. If we read further in Kant's *Grounding* (as you will in a few pages) we find that Kant indeed has a related theory about duties that in no way refers to consequences of one's actions. On the contrary, the theory of "ends-in-themselves" states that no matter what the consequences, a person should always be treated with respect for his or her humanity. We return to "ends-in-themselves" on p. 256.

2. **Conflict Between Duties**   Can we be so sure that the categorical imperative is always going to tell us what to do? Suppose we have a conflict between two things we have to do—and we don't particularly want to do either of them. Kant's system assumes that a moral conflict is one between duty and inclination—between what we have to do and what we want to do. In that case it is entirely possible we may be persuaded to do the right thing by imagining our maxim as a universal rule for everyone. But suppose we have a conflict between two duties, such as having to take inventory at our workplace the night before we have a final exam for which we should be studying. Kant would assume that we probably want to do one thing more than the other, and in such a case we should do what we feel like doing *the least*, because that would represent our duty. But in this case we can't say we want to do one thing more than we want to do the other—anyone who has done both will probably agree that they are both rather unpleasant tasks. How might the categorical imperative help us decide what to do? All it can tell us is that failing to show up for the inventory would not be rational, but neither would skipping the final, because both are duties that everyone ought to fulfill under the same circumstances. The amount of help offered by the categorical imperative is at best limited to cases where duties are not in conflict. (Of course, in a situation where we have a conflict between duties, we already know of another approach that might answer the question of what to do: Bentham's hedonistic calculus. All we'd have to do is put numbers on the importance of doing inventory versus the importance of taking the final, and we'd know what to do! But most philosophers agree that you can't just mix and match theories according to your needs. In Chapter 11 we return to the question of combining the best of various moral theories.)

3. **The Loophole**   Might it not be possible to find a loophole in the imperative? The categorical imperative tells us that it would be irrational (and thus morally impermissible) for anyone to even think about robbing a bank if he needs money because we wouldn't want everyone in the same situation to take that course of action. But what exactly *is* the situation we're talking about? Let's imagine that a young man named Joe is broke because he is out of work and has been for seven months. He is 20 years old and has a high school diploma. He worked at a bowling alley, but now it is closed because of gang violence. Joe likes to wear denim. His parents are divorced. He is dating a girl named Virginia who works at a supermarket and goes to the local community college, and he needs money so that they can get married and rent a small apartment. Let's assume that Joe applies the categorical imperative and that his maxim is: Every time I (who am in a certain situation) am broke and cannot get a loan, I will rob a bank. Then he universalizes it: Every time someone who is 20, and whose name is Joe, who has divorced parents, used to work in a bowling alley, likes denim, and is dating a checkout girl named Virginia who goes to a community college—anytime he feels like robbing a bank because he is broke, it is all right for him to do so. Now is that rational? Will Joe's maxim undermine his intention because everyone else will do the same thing he is planning to do? No, because he has described his situation so that "everyone" is reduced to only *one person*: Joe himself. In that case it is perfectly logical for him to rob a bank, because he won't undermine his own intention. This is hardly the kind of ironclad philosophical proof of doing the right thing that we were looking for. This argument, which also works against rule utilitarianism, is of course not a valid excuse for doing the wrong thing, and Joe shouldn't run out and rob the bank because he thinks philosophers have shown it to be okay. It is, however, an attempt to show that if we work with a principle that is as general as the categorical imperative, we just can't expect it to answer all our moral questions without a doubt. Of course, it isn't an example Kant himself would have

appreciated. Kant would have complained that we are making the example too specific. But the fact remains that the categorical imperative needs some further clarification and definition to avoid the "escape clause" that the loophole provides. You may think this example is rather far-fetched, since it's pretty obvious that nobody designs a moral rule you can get away with breaking if it applies only to yourself. However, the story of Joe, be it ever so outlandish, is our own story, in all those situations where we ask for lenient treatment because "we're special." We know we're supposed to send our taxes in on time, and to show up for the final, and so forth, but it's been a hard year, we just had the flu, our family's falling apart, and we'd really like some special consideration. And, if the special circumstances apply only in our case, well, then, we've found a loophole. The example of Joe is just a little more extreme.

4. **What Is Rationality?**   Who is to say when something is irrational? This is an issue that might not have occurred to Kant. He, as a product of his times and a coproducer of the Age of Reason, believed that if we use our reason without looking to self-interest, then we will all come up with the same idea and result. Actually, Bentham believed the same thing, even though his moral vision was quite different from that of Kant. Today, after garnering a century of knowledge (since Sigmund Freud's theories about the unconscious were published) about the workings of the subconscious mind and realizing that people just aren't rational all or even most of the time, we are more inclined to believe that our individual idea of what is rational may depend greatly on who we are. If we use a very broad definition of rational, such as "realizing the shortest way to get to your goal and then pursuing it," we still may come up with different ideas about what is rational. Suppose that our Joe not only is broke but also is a political anarchist who believes that the sooner society breaks down, the better for all humanity and for himself in particular. Why then would it be particularly illogical for him to rob a bank, given that the downfall of society, including banks, is what he is longing for? And why should we refrain from lying to one another if what we want is to create social chaos and alienate our friends? Why refrain from hurting one another, if we are sadomasochists and believe it would be great to live in a world of mutual harmdoing? Although Joe is a fictional example, the real world provides examples of people who most of us believe to have acted irrationally although in their own minds they followed a sure rational path toward a goal. Consider Timothy McVeigh, the man responsible for the bombing of the Alfred P. Murrah Federal Building in Oklahoma City in 1995, which killed 167 men, women, and children. McVeigh was convicted of multiple murders of federal agents and was executed in June 2001. What kind of reasoning process did he go through to decide that taking human lives—the lives of strangers who had never done him any harm, the lives of toddlers and children—would somehow further a goal? If we ask whether he seriously considered the categorical imperative—Could he want others to do the same thing? Could he agree to a world in which someone did such things to him and his family?—then the Kantian tradition would probably claim that he could not, that his decision was irrational. But McVeigh already believed he did live in such a world, in which the *government* kills innocent people. (McVeigh was highly influenced by the federal raid on the Branch Davidian compound in Waco two years earlier.) In an interrogation before his execution, he admitted that he thought his actions would start a revolution. So, if the rationality of one's decision depends on one's personal interpretation of the situation, how can the categorical imperative be a guarantee that we will all reach the same conclusion if only we use logic? Would using the categorical imperative have stopped any of the terrorists committing acts of mass murder on American soil and around the world in the last couple of decades? Is it conceivable that they might have asked themselves, Would you want your action to become a universal law? and answered Yes, I am doing the morally right thing.

Kant seems to assume that we all have the same general goals, which serve as a guarantee of the rationality of our actions. Change the goals, though, and the ideal of a reasonable course of action takes on a new meaning. (Box 6.3 further explores the issue of rationality.)

Box 6.3 WHAT IS RATIONALITY?

Philosophers often refer to conduct and arguments as being *rational* or *logical*. Since the Age of Reason (the Western Enlightenment) in the eighteenth century, the emphasis has been particularly strong, the assumption being that as long as you use your reason, you can't go wrong. If you do go wrong, the implication is that you have been applying faulty logic: One part of your conduct or your statement has been at odds with another part. For both Bentham and Kant, products of the Enlightenment, there is a staunch belief in the infallibility of properly applied reasoning. That belief was eroded considerably in the twentieth century, partly because of Freud's theories of the Unconscious as a powerful factor in our decision making but one fundamentally outside the control of our rational mind. In the last decades of the twentieth century, other criticisms were raised against the concept of rationality. If we choose a basic definition of rationality that says, "Decide on a goal and select the most direct method to achieve it," then critics of the philosophical emphasis on reason may point out that this method is above all a *Western* cultural ideal and is not indicative of a worldwide method of conduct. Some cultures prefer *indirect* methods of achieving goals and consider direct methods rude. Some feminists point out that the direct method of rationality is a predominantly *male* approach, whereas many women prefer an indirect way of achieving a goal; in

addition, they say, women make use of a special way of knowing: knowledge by emotion and intuition. Could it be true that men, having developed rational skills from millennia of being hunters, think in hunters' terms—going straight for the prey and killing it? And women, after millennia of being gatherers, think more in terms of picking and choosing and comparing? A comedian, Rob Becker, built this into his act illustrating man the hunter going shopping at the mall, single-mindedly tracking down a shirt—and his wife, the gatherer, shopping around until all items have been compared. It was a very funny routine—and it may actually come close to an evolutionary truth. But many feminists, such as Alison Jaggar, argue that the highest kind of knowledge incorporates both traditional rational thinking and emotional thinking—for both men and women. Although some rejoice in the possibility of there being several legitimate ways of being rational, some women thinkers worry that this view might turn back the clock and revive the old prejudice that "women can't think logically." And some advocates of traditional rationality as a universal philosophical method speculate that although it is possible that several different ways of conducting oneself rationally may exist, the rules of mathematics and logic are universal examples of applied rationality: The basic rules for pure, logical thinking are not culture- or gender-dependent.

5. **No Exceptions?**   Does it really seem right that we can never be morally correct in breaking a universal rule? In other words, can the categorical imperative always assure us that sticking to the rule is better than breaking it? Let us say that a killer is stalking a friend of yours, and the friend comes to your door and asks you to hide her. You tell her to go hide in the broom closet. (This is a slightly altered version of one of Kant's own examples which is generally considered one of the worst examples in the history of philosophy.) The killer comes to your door and asks, "Where is she?" Most of us would feel a primary

obligation to help our friend, but for Kant the primary obligation is to the truth. You are supposed to answer, "I cannot tell a lie—she is hiding in the broom closet." This is what is meant by an *absolutist* moral theory: A moral rule allows for no exceptions. But why? Most of us would assume that the life of our friend would at least be worth a white lie, but for Kant it is a matter of principle. Suppose you lie to the killer, but your friend sneaks out of the house, and the killer finds her; then it is your fault. If you had told the truth, your friend might still have escaped, and the killer could have been prevented from committing the murder. (Perhaps you could have trapped him in the broom closet.) This far-fetched argument follows Kant's own reasoning for why we should always stick to the rule: because if we break a rule we must answer for the consequences, whereas if we stick to the rule, we have no such responsibility. If we tell the truth, and the killer goes straight for the broom closet and kills our friend, Kant insists that we bear no responsibility for her death. But why should we accept Kant's idea that consequences don't count as long as you are following the rule but that they do count when you are not? Philosophers tend to agree that you can't make such arbitrary choices of when consequences count and when they don't. At the end of the chapter, the second Primary Reading shows how serious Kant was about not accepting any exceptions to his moral principles: To the end of his days, in *The Metaphysics of Morals,* he insisted that even white lies are unacceptable. You may remember Martha Nussbaum in Chapter 1 complaining that philosophy abounds with little, dry, unrealistic examples that are written, "cooked," to illustrate a particular moral rule, and that we'd be better off if we instead read a good novel that illustrates that particular moral problem or rule. Kant's story of the killer at the door is precisely the kind of example she was talking about.

If there are all these difficulties with the categorical imperative, why has it been such an influential moral factor? The reason is that it is the first moral theory to stress the idea of *universalizability:* realizing that the situation you are in is no different from that of other human beings. If something will bother you, it will probably bother others too, everything else being equal. If you allow yourself a day off, you should not gripe when others do the same thing. Most important, however, you should think about it before you allow yourself that day off and realize that it won't do as a universal rule. The problem is that on occasion we all encounter special situations when we might actually *need* a day off; perhaps we are sick or emotionally upset. Similarly, on the whole we should not kill, but in certain rare situations we may be called on to do just that, in war or in self-defense. On the whole we should not lie, but there may come a day when a killer is stalking a friend of ours, and we have a chance to save her. In that case we may need to lie. Those are unusual situations, so why should Kant's generalizations apply to them? This issue has caused scholars to suggest that there really is nothing wrong with the format of the categorical imperative, provided that we are allowed to expand our maxim to include situations in which we might accept certain *exceptions* to our rule. As long as they don't expand to become a loophole, the universalization works just fine: We can universalize not killing, with the exception of self-defense and certain other specified cases. We can universalize not taking a day off from work unless we are sick or severely emotionally upset, as long as it doesn't happen very often. We can universalize not lying if it is understood that preventing harm to an innocent person would constitute an exception.

The American philosopher Christine Korsgaard, who has been significantly inspired by Kant's moral philosophy, is also one of the critics of Kant's unyielding hard universalism, and she proposes a solution: that we view Kant's categorical imperative as an ideal solution in an ideal world, but that we must also realize that real life is less than perfect and makes other demands on us. The ideal is still important as a principle, but, she asks, why would we even consider that lying to the killer would undermine our intention to lie, since the killer must surely know that asking where our friend went does not represent a normal situation? In other words, in some situations Kant is right on the mark, such as the example of the man who wants to borrow money, and in other situations we must go beyond the categorical imperative—in cases where we have to respond to actions or people we might characterize as *evil*. As an example of a person making evil choices, or even as an example of an evil person, let us consider the shootings at Sandy Hook Elementary School in Newton, MA, in 2012, where 20 children were murdered by a 20-year old shooter (and where teacher Victoria Soto lost her life protecting the children). Who among us wouldn't have chosen to lie to the shooter on his way to commit mass murder, if he had asked us for directions to the young students, professors, or classrooms and we suspected what he was about to do? We might have been *too afraid* to come up with a good lie, but that doesn't make truth-telling right. This would be a clear case where the truth could be circumvented for the sake of innocent lives, with an exception built into the maxim of not lying. In Chapter 9 we meet a classic theory (by Aristotle) that will suggest that for most actions there is a *right amount*—not too much and not too little, and telling the truth to the shooter would certainly qualify as excessive, if nothing else. But what is particularly interesting is that Kant, a few pages further into the little book *Grounding,* in fact supplies us with the very principle we need to save innocent lives: that no human beings should be treated like stepping-stones or used for other people's purposes.

Rational Beings Are Ends in Themselves

In his book *Grounding for the Metaphysics of Morals,* Kant explores three major themes: the *categorical imperative,* the concept of *ends in themselves,* and the concept of a *kingdom of ends.* In a sense you might say that if we add the idea of people being ends in themselves to the idea of the categorical imperative, then the result will be a kingdom of ends. In the discussion that follows, we look at the ends-in-themselves concept as well as the kingdom of ends.

Persons Shouldn't Be Used as Tools

In *Grounding,* Kant suggests two different ways to express the categorical imperative. The first one we have just looked at; the other, frequently referred to as the "Formula of Humanity," or the "Humanity Formula," goes like this:

> Now I say that man, and in general every rational being, exists as an end in himself and not merely as a means to be arbitrarily used by this or that will. He must in all his actions, whether directed to himself or to other rational beings, always be regarded at the same time as an end.

What does it mean to be treated as an "end in himself"? Let us first look at the opposite approach: to be treated as a "means to an end only." What is a means to an end? It is a tool, an instrument to be used to achieve some goal; it is something that has *instrumental* value in the achievement of something of *intrinsic* value. If someone is used as a means to an end, she or he is treated as a tool for someone else's purpose, in a very broad sense. If someone is being sexually abused or kept as a slave, that person obviously is being treated as a means to an end, but so is the girl we befriend so we can get to know her brother. So is anyone who is being used for other people's purposes without regard for his or her intrinsic value and dignity as a human being, such as in the controversial film *Bumfights,* where young filmmakers persuaded homeless men to fight each other for the camera, for the sake of monetary gain. But Kant would condemn an act of using someone as a tool, even if the purpose is good—such as creating happiness for a large number of people. For Kant this is just another way of expressing the categorical imperative. What made him think this? For one thing, when you use the categorical imperative, you are universalizing your maxim; and if you are refusing to treat others merely as a means to an end, you are also universalizing a maxim, and a very fundamental one. Second, both maxims may be interpreted as expressions of the Golden Rule.

This statement about the immorality of treating other humans as a means to an end was, for the eighteenth century, a tremendously important political and social statement. In Kant's era (although not in Kant's country), slavery was still a social factor; abuse of the lower classes by the upper classes was commonplace; Europe was just emerging from a time when monarchs and warlords could move their peasants and conscripted soldiers around like chess pieces with no regard for their lives and happiness. It was nothing short of a revolutionary idea for Kant to state that it is not social status that determines one's standing in the moral universe, but one thing only: *the capability to use reason*. As one of the leading lights of the Age of Reason, Kant stated that any rational human being deserves respect. Rich and poor, young and old, all races and peoples—all are alike in having rationality as the one defining mark of their humanity, and none deserves to be treated without regard for that characteristic. Here it must be interjected, in case we get carried away with our praise, that Kant himself expressed doubt as to whether women were actually rational beings, or as rational as men; he may have had the same reservations about people of color (see Box 6.4), but we will be generous and look at the *implications* of Kant's theory for human rights, regardless of whether or not he himself saw as the goal that every human being deserves respect. And as you will see below, Kant specifically said that we have to treat all of *humanity* with respect.

Darby Conley/www.CartoonStock.com

Has Bucky treated Satchel as an end-in-himself or has he reduced him to being merely a means to an end—and what end might that be? The ways in which we let ourselves be taken advantage of are of course countless. Products "guaranteed for life" are frequently merely for "the lifetime of the implement," which means that when it breaks, the guarantee is void! Remember that Kant says we should not let ourselves be treated merely as a means to an end, either. So, buyer beware!

Box 6.4 KANT, THE ENLIGHTENMENT, AND RACISM

Over the years, Kant has been considered a primary source of the idea of human rights and equality because of his view that any rational being should be treated with dignity and never merely as a means to an end. This view has inspired Western thinkers, writers, and politicians to the point that we can actually say now that, even if the ideal has not yet been reached, the Western world is denouncing regimes that do not recognize all their citizens as equals, regardless of gender, income, race, ethnicity, religion, and nationality. (See the United Nations Universal Declaration of Human Rights at the end of Chapter 7.) But was that the goal Kant had in mind? It is rather discouraging to find out that it wasn't. Kant himself, as much as he has inspired today's quest for equality, had no philosophical goal of either gender or racial equality. Kant believed himself to be drawing on the cutting edge of biological research (he actually taught more classes in geography than in philosophy); in a rarely quoted text, "On the Different Races of Man" (1775), Kant voices the opinion that there are substantial differences in "natural dispositions" among what Kant sees as the four predominant human races of the world. For Kant and many other eighteenth-century Western thinkers, the European race was more intelligent than other races, and males were more intelligent than females. With no sound scientific evidence, some of the most important thinkers of the Western Enlightenment—which did usher in the first stages of global equality—decided that some humans were more biologically advanced than others. This of course raises suspicion that Kant's "rational beings" may not have included all *humans*, but primarily white males. However, ten years later Kant specified, in *Grounding*, that *all of humanity* should be treated as ends in themselves. It would be grossly unfair to assume that Kant thought only white males were "persons." But Kant's rule of "ends in themselves" only protects humans against abuse—it doesn't guarantee social equality.

Old heroes sometimes topple in the light of new research, and according to some critics this is what is happening to Kant: He may not be the champion of human rights we thought he was. According to some critics, we are even justified in calling him a racist, if we use today's view of racism as discrimination against individuals or groups of people solely based on their race. In my view, however, we should never forget that Kant was, for his day, indeed a champion of human rights. Europe was a place of serfdom, where peasants were treated as the property of the great landowners. Kant's writings did help set in motion the process that we all today have benefited from: the philosophical sea change that resulted in the concept of inalienable human rights. So Kant himself may have been locked in the racial bigotry of ignorance common for his day and age, but his ideas of a kingdom of ends in which *everyone* is treated with respect and dignity have today survived to become a Western political and philosophical ideal. He may fall short of the "minimum qualifications" considered necessary for an open-minded thinker today, but he did leave a legacy that can't be overestimated: the ideal of social and political dignity as a human birthright. That credit should not be taken away from him.

Why are rational beings intrinsically valuable? Because they can place a value on things. What is gold worth if nobody wants it? Nothing. Humans are value-givers; they assign a relative worth to things that interest them. However, as value-givers, humans always have an *absolute* value. They set the price, so to speak, yet cannot have a price set on them. We do, however, constantly talk about people being "worth money." A baseball player is worth a fortune, a Hollywood actress is worth millions. What does that mean? Have we set a price on humans after all? Not in the appropriate sense. It doesn't mean we can *buy* the Hollywood actress for a couple of million. (Well, we might, but in that case she is treating *herself* as a means to an end only, by selling her body.) What we usually mean is that she has a lot of money. And the baseball player? He certainly can be "bought and sold," but hardly as a slave; he retains his autonomy and gets rich in the process. It is his talent and his services that are paid for. Under normal circumstances we don't refer to people as entities that can be bought for money, and if we do, we are usually implying that something inappropriate is taking place (slavery and bribery, for instance). Thus people are value-givers because they can decide rationally what they want and what they don't want. That means that rational beings are *persons,* and the second formulation of the categorical imperative is focused on respect for persons: *Act in such a way that you treat humanity, whether in your own person or in the person of another, always at the same time as an end and never simply as a means.*

Notice that Kant is not talking just about not mistreating others. You have to respect yourself too, and not let others step on you. You have a right to set values of your own and not just be used by others as their key to success. But what exactly does it mean not to treat anybody *simply as a means to an end?* We know that blatant abuse is wrong and that a subtler kind is no better. But what about using someone's services? When you buy your groceries, there usually is some person who bags your items. Truthfully, are you treating that person as a means to get your groceries bagged? Yes, indeed, but not *simply* as a means; he or she is getting paid, and you presumably don't treat these workers as though they were put on this earth just to bag your groceries. Everyday life consists of people using other people's services, and that is just the normal give-and-take of social life. The danger arises if we stop respecting people for what they do and reduce them in our minds to mere tools for our comfort or success. (See Box 6.5.) As long as the relationship is reciprocal (you pay for your groceries, and the bagger gets a paycheck), then there is no abuse taking place. Indeed, students use their professors as a means to an end (to get their degree), but the professors rarely feel abused, provided that they receive a salary. Likewise, the professors use students as a means to their ends (to receive that salary), but the professors surely don't imagine that the students were put on this earth to feed them or pay their mortgage. However, when people truly use others as tools for their own purpose and nothing else, from the phenomenon of "suicide by cop" to sexual abuse and terrorism, we are talking about treating others as a "means to an end only." And that means we have an answer to what Kant might have said about the trolley problem: If the only way you can save the five workers on the track is to take the life of one worker, then you would be using that worker as *merely a means to an end* in order to save the five, and we are not allowed to do that, morally. So the five will die while we are defending the right of the one worker to be treated with respect as a rational human being. However, if the one worker should choose to volunteer to save the others, Kant would have nothing against that, because it would be a free decision.

Box 6.5 MEANS TO AN END VERSUS *MERELY* A MEANS TO AN END?

Kant insists that as long as there is reasonable compensation, or reciprocity, then using other people's time, work, or services is acceptable. A good thing, too, since without the give-and-take of social interaction where people render services for each other, we would have to do everything ourselves. Kant is of course not being unreasonable here. But where do mutual services become abuse of one person by another, or by a group? The world has always been socially complex as long people have been interacting, but our world is far more complex today than in Kant's day. Our spectrum of abuse possibilities seems endless; without going as far as drastic examples of sexual abuse or reduction to slave-like conditions, there is still more than enough disrespect going around. My students were asked to give examples of people being treated "merely as a means to an end," and many have mentioned that being a *server* is an ungrateful job; rudeness from customers is a daily occurrence. Workplace disrespect, especially toward young hires, is not a thing of the past. The #MeToo phenomenon also has come up—usually young women (but it has also happened to young men, of course) being treated as sex objects by (usually) more powerful, older males within their profession. And, as a student, you may recognize this scenario: students helping other students with their homework and finding themselves being taken advantage of, with the other student expecting them to do the work for them, and group work in college where some students let the others do all the work. On the dating front, finding out that someone you thought was your friend really just wanted a date with your brother or sister is not uncommon, either. On a broader scale, victims of natural disasters risk being taken advantage of by Internet or face-to-face scammers. And a fairly new phenomenon is orphaned or abandoned children being used in undocumented immigration scams to facilitate entry into the United States by hopeful adults. The list could go on and on.

So where would Kant draw the line between using someone's service and reducing them to a mere tool? In the #MeToo phenomenon, many young women in the entertainment industry kept quiet for years until the scandal broke, because their careers had actually benefited from their relationship with the abusers—so it may have been a case of what is known as "quid pro quo," something for something. So would that be considered an acceptable, mutual use of services rather than "abuse," according to Kant? No, because he would say that if a person allows herself or himself to be used as a tool, they have no self-respect, and the principle of ends-in-themselves requires that we not only respect others but ourselves as well.

Many critics believe that John Stuart Mill was right when he pointed out that Kant, despite his own insistence that consequences are irrelevant for a good will, ended up including a reference to possible consequences in his categorical imperative in the universalization of the maxim: What happens if I do X? However, when we examine Kant's principle of never treating people simply as a means to an end, we have to conclude that this principle indeed does exclude any consideration of good or bad consequences: Nobody is supposed to reduce another, or themselves, to a mere tool or stepping-stone, regardless of whether it is for a good or a bad purpose, or whether it is based on mutual consent (which is why Kant was also against prostitution). So now we can return to the question raised in Chapter 5 about *torturing terrorists* to obtain vital information that may save lives. We saw that a utilitarian might agree that under specific circumstances it could be the right thing to do. For a Kantian, however, no amount of good consequences would justify the abuse of anyone, including serial killers, enemy POWs, or terrorists. Within a classical Kantian moral system, torture could never be allowed, even if it might save the life of your child, your spouse, your parents, or your country; it is better to suffer with common dignity and respect for other humans than it is to buy the safety and happiness of some with the suffering of others. That doesn't mean we can't punish criminals, including terrorists, with imprisonment or even execution, but the purpose would be *justice* rather than creating good consequences. Indeed, Kant was a strong proponent of capital punishment, and we will take a look at his arguments in Chapters 7 and 13.

Beings Who Are Things

Any rational being deserves respect. We assume that humans fall into that category, but what if there are rational beings who are not human? It is not unthinkable that humans might encounter extraterrestrials who are rational enough to know math, language, and space science; and how about the possibility of AI, Artificial Intelligence? Would Kant respect a thinking android or computer, or a rational alien, or would he advocate treating them like things? If these beings are *rational,* they qualify as full members of our moral universe, and humans have no right to treat them as tools to achieve knowledge or power. Aliens and androids would likewise have no right to cart humans off for medical experiments, because all humans are generally rational beings.

However, Kant speculates that there are beings on this earth who are not rational in his sense of the word: nonhuman animals. In *Grounding* he presents his theory in this way:

> Beings whose existence depends not on our will but on nature have, nevertheless, if they are not rational beings, only a relative value as means and are therefore called things. On the other hand, rational beings are called persons inasmuch as their nature already marks them out as ends in themselves. . . .

That means that nonhuman animals don't belong in the moral universe at all; they are classified as *things* and can be used as a tool by a rational person because animals can't place a value on something—only humans can do that. And an animal is not worth anything in itself; it has value only if it is wanted for some purpose by a human. If nobody cares about cats, or spotted owls, then they have no value. Is it true, though, that animals can't place a value on things? Most people with firsthand knowledge of animals will report that pets are capable of valuing their owners above all and their food bowl second. (Or is it the other way around?) And animals in the wild place extreme importance on their territory and their young. Many people today categorize animal interests as just different in *degree* from human interests and not different in *kind* (Chapter 13). Although Kant and most of his contemporaries (with the exclusion of Bentham) believed that the moral universe should be closed to nonhuman animals, it is just possible today that we not only might include animals as "creatures who deserve respect" but, as you read in Chapter 4, we should also be prepared to encounter instances of *animal morality.* Could the self-sacrifice of a baboon to save her tribe from the leopard be the result of a conscious choice? Did Binti Jua, the gorilla who came to the rescue of the little boy at the zoo, consider her options?

The research into animal cognition (capacity for thinking) and emotions has come very far in the past few decades, and in 2012 the Cambridge Declaration on Consciousness stated that big-brained social animals, such as the great apes, dolphins, elephants, and (to many people's surprise) also the corvids, the group of birds including ravens, crows and magpies, as well as many others, should be included as having states of consciousness and emotions. According to the Declaration,

> The absence of a neocortex does not appear to preclude an organism from experiencing affective states. Convergent evidence indicates that non-human animals have the neuroanatomical, neurochemical, and neurophysiological substrates of conscious states along with the capacity to exhibit intentional behaviors. Consequently, the weight of evidence indicates that humans are not unique in possessing the neurological substrates that generate consciousness. Non-human animals, including all mammals and birds, and many other creatures, including octopuses, also possess these neurological substrates.

But for Kant it was not just a matter of being able to think—one must also be able to show that one has autonomy and can set up universal moral rules for oneself and others; and although certain animals may have some thought capacity, it is doubtful whether they ever can be considered *morally autonomous* in the Kantian sense of the term. But if it becomes clear that an animal such as a bonobo chimpanzee can grasp the Golden Rule, there can be no good reason for modern-day Kantians to deny them at least some kind of partial personhood. (See Box 6.6 for further discussion.)

Box 6.6 CAN ANIMALS THINK?

From the previous chapter you may remember that Descartes didn't believe animals had any mental activity because, according to his theory, they consisted of matter only. Kant does not deny that nonhuman animals have minds; he just does not believe them to be rational minds but, rather, instinctive—in his own words, "depending on nature" (*Grounding*). In *The Metaphysics of Morals* he explains further: Although animals and humans all have wills that propel them toward their goals, only humans have free choice; animals making

choices about what to eat, with whom to mate, and where to sleep don't make use of moral laws, and so their choice is merely brutish (as some people's choices of the same type may be). But when a person makes a choice based on a rational principle of universalizability, then Kant calls it a free choice.

Today the issue of animal intelligence is still controversial. Some ethologists (animal behaviorists) continue to believe that human and non-human animal intelligence are different *in kind*; others now lean toward the assumption that they are different *in degree*. In his book *Self Comes to Mind*, neuroscientist Antonio Damasio (see Chapters 1 and 4) launches the bold theory that every organism that has a brainstem has a basic form of consciousness—a view that has the potential of completely rewriting our perception of animal minds, as well as our relationship to nonhuman animals. The ethologist, Marc Bekoff, suggests in his book *Wild Justice: The Moral Lives of Animals*, co-authored with philosopher Jessica Pierce, that canines such as wolves, coyotes, and dogs have a well-developed sense of fairness (see Chapters 4 and 13), and philosopher Martha Nussbaum (see Chapter 1) suggests in her book *Upheavals of Thought* that many higher animals have a form of cognitive emotion—emotions that are situation-based and have their own rationality. Close observations in experimental situations over years of research and coexistence with animals have led many modern biologists and behaviorists to conclude that at least certain animals, such as great apes, dolphins, elephants, and orcas (killer whales), have a rudimentary capacity for rational thinking and even for linguistic comprehension (as humans define language). In Chapters 7 and 13 we take a closer look at the issues of animal intelligence and animal rights.

Numerous scholars have pointed out, however, that there is a serious problem with Kant's own classification of humans as rational beings, for suppose someone who is genetically *human* can't think rationally? There are many humans who aren't good at thinking or can't think at all because they are infants, toddlers, mentally disabled, or in a coma—or have advanced Alzheimer's. Does that mean that all these people aren't *persons* and should be classified as *things?* As some scholars (such as Peter Singer) have remarked, there are animals who are more like persons (that is, rational beings) than newborn infants or severely mentally disabled humans are. Would Kant really say that such humans are no better than things? The trouble is that Kant never made provisions for any such subcategories of "persons" in *Grounding*. It is either-or. As you may remember from Chapter 1, this is what we call the *fallacy of bifurcation,* or a *false dichotomy:* assuming that there are only two options, whereas there may be three or more. And that is precisely what Kant himself realized.

There is no denying that problems arise if you divide the world into *persons* (with rights not to be abused by others) and *things* (that persons have a right to use). But twelve years after writing *Grounding,* in his long-awaited *The Metaphysics of Morals,* Kant addressed the question of an intermediate category: people who have absolute rights as ends in themselves but who also, for various reasons, "belong" to other persons. Kant calls it "the right to a person akin to a right to a thing"—such persons are legitimately treated *as if* they were possessions, although they cannot be owned as slaves. In our contemporary terminology, we might refer to such a status as a *hybrid* form of personhood. An example would be a small child: She is a person with the right to personal freedom; the child's parents can't destroy her, even if they brought her into the world; but the child does not have full self-determination either, because she is still regarded as a pseudo-possession of her parents until the day she is grown. (If someone takes her, her parents can demand to have her back.) The parents have a duty to raise the child properly, and the child has no duty to repay them. Similarly, servants of a household belong in the intermediate category of being pseudo-possessions: They are free persons, but because they have signed contracts they can't just take off whenever they feel like it, Kant says. On the other hand, they can't be bought and sold either, because then they would be slaves, and slavery is reducing someone to merely a means to an end. Some scholars believe that with this intermediate category between a person with full freedom and a thing with none, Kant has opened the door for the modern category sometimes called "partial rights": A being who is not a rational, human adult may be granted some rights but may still be regarded as under the guardianship of other humans. Vilifying Kant for poisoning philosophy toward the rights of partially rational beings hardly seems fair under these circumstances. But in *The Metaphysics of Morals* we also hear in no uncertain terms from Kant that animals are not rational and have no rights, because for us to have duties to other beings, they have to be capable of having obligations to us. (See Box 6.6 and

Chapter 13 for a continuation of this debate.) Classifying an animal as a thing seemed reasonable to Kant, but, even so, he was concerned that some readers might take that as permission to treat animals any way they saw fit, including being cruel to them. Kant was very specific about condemning cruelty to animals; however, he took that stance not so much for the sake of the animals themselves as for humans, because someone who hurts animals might easily get used to it and begin to hurt people. It appears that Kant was more right than most of his readers could have known at the time; although Kant is not the first person to have claimed that cruelty to animals may lead to cruelty toward people (St. Thomas Aquinas had said the same thing in the thirteenth century), the depth of the connection became apparent only in the late twentieth century, when criminal profiling established that just about every serial killer questioned within the last decades have turned out to have tortured small animals when he was a child. (That investigation focused on male serial killers, since there have been very few female serial murderers so far.) In addition, such individuals would also engage in setting fires and were chronic bed wetters—a configuration known as the "Macdonald triad." That does not mean that a boy who wets his bed, sets fires, and tortures animals will invariably grow up to be a serial killer, but those behaviors are considered warning signs that should be attended to while the child is still young. The point Kant wanted to make, which criminal profiling has corroborated, is that desensitization to—or even enjoyment of—animal pain can lead to deliberately inflicting pain on human beings. In Kant's words (from *The Metaphysics of Morals*):

> It dulls his shared feeling of their pain and so weakens and gradually uproots a natural predisposition that is very serviceable to morality in one's relations with other men. Man is authorized to kill animals quickly (without pain) and to put them to work that does not strain them beyond their capacities (such work as man himself must submit to). But agonizing physical experiments for the sake of mere speculation, when the end could also be achieved without these, are to be abhorred.

It is interesting that Kant, having over the years acquired the reputation of being insensitive to the plight of animals, himself argued against causing needless pain to them. Contrary to Descartes, Kant never thought animals couldn't feel pain; he just thought that within the context of human moral issues it was only marginally relevant. Some issues are thus resolved in *The Metaphysics of Morals,* but not all issues. Even so, the idea that rational beings should never be treated merely as means to an end has been a powerful contribution to a world of equality and mutual respect because it is such a remarkable expansion of the moral universe described in previous moral theories, which tended to exclude social groups that somehow weren't considered quite as valuable as others. Furthermore, Kant placed the foundation of morality solidly with human rationality and not with the state or the church. But for the astute reader it is also interesting to notice that Kant allows for the existence of a "natural predisposition" to avoid causing harm to other human beings. That is what you have encountered elsewhere in this book as "moral intuition" or "fellow-feeling," and Kant is famous for insisting that moral deliberation ought to be exclusively rational, not emotional or intuitive. But that doesn't mean that he completely discounted the notion that we have, embedded in us, a reluctance to hurt other humans—which is what social psychologists and neuroscientists, such as Damasio, have verified recently.

The Kingdom of Ends

That brings us to the third major theme in Kant's *Grounding,* the "kingdom of ends." Applying the categorical imperative is something all rational beings can do—and even if they can't do it exactly the way Kant uses it, the logic of it should be compelling for all people who can ask themselves, "Would I want everybody to do this?" Kant calls this *moral autonomy:* The only moral authority that can tell us to do something and not to do something else is our own reason. As we saw previously, if all people follow the same principle and disregard their own personal inclinations, then all will end up following the same good rules, because all have universalized their intention. In such a world, with everyone doing the right thing and nobody abusing anyone else, a new realm will have been created: the *kingdom of ends.* "Kingdom" poetically describes a community of people, and "ends" indicates that the people treat one another as ends only—as beings who have their own goals in life—never merely as means to other people's ends. Every time we show respect and consideration for one another, we make the kingdom of ends a little more real. In Kant's words from *Grounding,*

> By "kingdom" I understand a system of different rational beings through common laws. . . . For all rational beings stand under the law that each of them should treat himself and all others never merely as a means but always at the same time as an end in himself. Hereby arises a systematic union of rational beings through common objective laws, i.e., a kingdom that may be called a kingdom of ends (certainly only an ideal), inasmuch as these laws have in view the very relation of such beings to one another as ends and means.

> A rational being belongs to the kingdom of ends as a member when he legislates in it universal laws while also himself being subject to these laws. He belongs to it as sovereign, when as legislator he is himself subject to the will of no other. . . . In the kingdom of ends everything has either a price or a dignity. Whatever has a price can be replaced by something else as its equivalent; on the other hand, whatever is above all price, and therefore admits no equivalent, has a dignity.

Here we see how Kant combines the first part of his book, the categorical imperative, with the second part, the idea that nobody should be used merely as a means to an end. People who adhere to the method of the categorical imperative are autonomous lawmakers: They set laws for themselves that, when universalized, become acceptable to every other rational being. When we use that approach, we realize that we can't allow ourselves to treat others (or let others treat us) as merely a means to an end, but recognize that other people should be treated with respect because they are rational beings with dignity, *irreplaceable* beings. We all belong in the kingdom of ends, the realm of beings with dignity. But whatever doesn't qualify as rational has a price and can be replaced with a similar item. (That of course means to Kant that any human being has dignity and is irreplaceable, whereas your dog has no dignity and can be replaced.)

Some readers of Kant believe that he shows a more humane side in his theory of ends in themselves, and indeed we might take this idea and apply it to the problem of whether to lie to the killer who has come to murder your friend. The categorical imperative tells you to speak the truth always, because then you can't be blamed for the consequences. But is that really the same as saying we should treat others as ends in themselves? Perhaps there is a subtle difference; if we apply this rule to the killer who is stalking our friend, would we get the same result? Might we not be treating *our friend* as merely a means to an end if we refuse to lie for her, whether it is for the sake of principle or just so that we can't be blamed for the consequences? If we are sacrificing our friend for the sake of the truth, it might rightfully be said that in such a case we are treating her as a means to an end only. So even within Kant's own system there are irreconcilable differences. That should not cause us to want to discard his entire theory, however; since the nineteenth century, philosophers have tried to redesign Kant's ideas to fit a more perceptive (or, as Kant would say, more lenient) world. Some of those ideas are working quite well—for example, allowing for general exceptions to be built into the categorical imperative itself, and allowing for animals to be considered more rational than Kant ever thought possible.

Study Questions

1. Evaluate the following statement: "Actions are morally good only if they are done because of a good will." Explain what Kant means by a "good will." Do you think the statement is correct or incorrect? Explain your position.

2. Analyze the following statement: "Man, and in general every rational being, should be treated as an end in himself, never merely as a means." What are the moral implications of that statement for humans, as well as nonhumans? How might a Kantian respond to the trolley problem (Ch.1 and 5)? Can you imagine any scenario that would allow a Kantian to pull the lever and deliberately kill one person (treat them merely as a means to an end) to save 5?

3. Explain Kant's position on lying: Is it always morally wrong to lie? What are the implications for the question raised in Chapter 5, "Should we lie to Grandma about something if the truth will distress her?"

4. There is today a growing number of young philosophers who find that Kant, over the past 200 years, has been overrated, considering all the issues and flaws that critics have found in his thinking, in particular his moral philosophy. What is your impression of Kant at this point? A brilliant thinker way ahead of his time, or a pedantic, overrated doctrinarian?

Primary Readings and Narratives

The first Primary Reading is an excerpt from Kant's famous *Grounding for the Metaphysics of Morals* in which he explains the structure of the categorical imperative. The second Primary Reading is an excerpt from Kant's less frequently quoted book, *The Metaphysics of Morals,* in which he explains why lying is wrong. The Narratives are all summaries. Two Westerns each explore the concept of doing the right thing as a matter of principle: the famous *High Noon,* in which the town marshal chooses to face three gunmen alone after having been rejected by the community he is trying to defend, and *3:10 to Yuma,* in which a destitute rancher tries to make a fast buck by putting an outlaw on the train to prison, but ends up making a choice about doing the right thing. The third narrative is a summary of the film *Abandon Ship* about a lifeboat full, to the point of sinking, of survivors from a shipwreck. In order for some to survive, others will have to go overboard—but who? The last summary is of the graphic novel and film *Watchmen,* where a viewpoint based on absolute moral principles is contrasted not only with a utilitarian solution, but also with a viewpoint that is barely human in its objectivity.

 Primary Reading

Grounding for the Metaphysics of Morals

IMMANUEL KANT

Excerpt, 1785.

In this passage Kant introduces the categorical imperative and links it with the concept of the good will as an understanding of doing one's duty in accordance with reason.

> Thus the moral worth of an action does not lie in the effect expected from it nor in any principle of action that needs to borrow its motive from this expected effect. For all these effects (agreeableness of one's condition and even the furtherance of other people's happiness) could have been brought about also through other causes and would not have required the will of a rational being, in which the highest and unconditioned good can alone be found. Therefore, the preeminent good which is called moral can consist in nothing but the representation of the law in itself, and such a representation can admittedly be found only in a rational being insofar as this representation, and not some expected effect, is the determining ground of the will. This good is already present in the person who acts according to this representation, and such good need not be awaited merely from the effect.

> But what sort of law can that be the thought of which must determine the will without reference to any expected effect, so that the will can be called absolutely good without qualification? Since I have deprived the will of every impulse that might arise for it from obeying any particular law, there is

nothing left to serve the will as principle except the universal conformity of its actions to law as such, i.e., I should never act except in such a way that I can also will that my maxim should become a universal law. Here mere conformity to law as such (without having as its basis any law determining particular actions) serves the will as principle and must so serve it if duty is not to be a vain delusion and a chimerical concept. The ordinary reason of mankind in its practical judgments agrees completely with this, and always has in view the aforementioned principle.

For example, take this question. When I am in distress, may I make a promise with the intention of not keeping it? I readily distinguish here the two meanings which the question may have; whether making a false promise conforms with prudence or with duty. Doubtless the former can often be the case. Indeed I clearly see that escape from some present difficulty by means of such a promise is not enough. In addition I must carefully consider whether from this lie there may later arise far greater inconvenience for me than from what I now try to escape. Furthermore, the consequences of my false promise are not easy to foresee, even with all my supposed cunning; loss of confidence in me might prove to be far more disadvantageous than the misfortune which I now try to avoid. The more prudent way might be to act according to a universal maxim and to make it a habit not to promise anything without intending to keep it. But that such a maxim is, nevertheless, always based on nothing but a fear of consequences becomes clear to me at once. To be truthful from duty is, however, quite different from being truthful from fear of disadvantageous consequences; in the first case the concept of the action itself contains a law for me, while in the second I must first look around elsewhere to see what are the results for me that might be connected with the action. For to deviate from the principle of duty is quite certainly bad; but to abandon my maxim of prudence can often be very advantageous for me, though to abide by it is certainly safer. The most direct and infallible way, however, to answer the question as to whether a lying promise accords with duty is to ask myself whether I would really be content if my maxim (of extracting myself from difficulty by means of a false promise) were to hold as a universal law for myself as well as for others, and could I really say to myself that everyone may promise falsely when he finds himself in a difficulty from which he can find no other way to extricate himself. Then I immediately become aware that I can indeed will the lie but can not at all will a universal law to lie. For by such a law there would really be no promises at all, since in vain would my willing future actions be professed to other people who would not believe what I professed, or if they over-hastily did believe, then they would pay me back in like coin. Therefore, my maxim would necessarily destroy itself just as soon as it was made a universal law.

Therefore, I need no fear-reaching acuteness to discern what I have to do in order that my will may be morally good. Inexperienced in the course of the world and incapable of being prepared for all its contingencies, I only ask myself whether I can also will that my maxim should become a universal law. If not, then the maxim must be rejected, not because of any disadvantage accruing to me or even to others, but because it cannot be fitting as a principle in a possible legislation of universal law, and reason exacts from me immediate respect for such legislation. Indeed I have as yet no insight into the grounds of such respect (which the philosopher may investigate). But I at least understand that respect is an estimation of a worth that far outweighs any worth of what is recommended by inclination, and that the necessity of acting from pure respect for the practical law is what constitutes duty, to which every other motive must give way because duty is the condition of a will good in itself, whose worth is above all else.

Study Questions

1. What does Kant mean by a good will?

2. Explain the structure and purpose of the categorical imperative.

3. Can you think of a situation in which it might actually be counterproductive to do a good or a harmless thing if everyone did the same thing? How might Kant respond?

Primary Reading

The Metaphysics of Morals

IMMANUEL KANT

Excerpt from Book I, Chapter II, 1797.

This book was actually printed separately in two parts but is considered one book today. The first part is *The Doctrine of Right,* and the second one is *The Doctrine of Virtue.* This section on lying from *The Doctrine of Virtue* illustrates Kant's talent for careful analysis of even an ordinary kind of experience in order to argue his points that you should not make choices you couldn't wish to become a universal law and that you should not make choices that diminish the dignity of others or yourself.

Man's Duty to Himself Merely as a Moral Being: This duty is opposed to the vices of *lying, avarice,* and *false humility* (servility).

On Lying: The greatest violation of man's duty to himself regarded merely as a moral being (the humanity in his own person) is the contrary of truthfulness, *lying (aliud lingua promptum, aliud pectore inclusum gerere).* ["To have one thing shut up in the heart and another ready on the tongue." Sallust, *The War with Catiline* X, 5.] In the doctrine of Right an intentional untruth is called a lie only if it violates another's right; but in ethics, where no authorization is derived from harmlessness, it is clear of itself that no intentional untruth in the expression of one's thoughts can refuse this harsh name. For the dishonor (being an object of moral contempt) that accompanies a lie also accompanies a liar like his shadow. A lie can be an external lie (*mendacium externum*) or also an internal lie. By an external lie a man makes himself an object of contempt in the eyes of others; by an internal lie he does what is still worse: He makes himself contemptible in his own eyes and violates the dignity of humanity in his own person. And so, since the harm that can come to other men from lying is not what distinguishes this vice (for if it were, the vice would consist only in violating one's duty to others), this harm is not taken into account here. Neither is the harm that a liar brings on himself; for then a lie, as a mere error in prudence, would conflict with the pragmatic maxim, not the moral maxim, and it could not be considered a violation of duty at all. By a lie a man throws away and, as it were, annihilates his dignity as a man. A man who does not himself believe what he tells another (even if the other is a merely ideal person) has even less worth than if he were a mere thing; for a thing, because it is something real and given, has the property of being serviceable so that another can put it to some use. But communication of one's thoughts to someone through words that yet (intentionally) contain the contrary of what the speaker thinks on the subject is an end that is directly opposed to the natural purposiveness of the speaker's capacity to communicate his thoughts, and is thus a renunciation by the speaker of his personality, and such a speaker is a mere deceptive appearance of a man, not a man himself. *Truthfulness* in one's declarations is also called *honesty* and, if the declarations are promises, *sincerity;* but, more generally, truthfulness is called rectitude.

Lying (in the ethical sense of the word), intentional untruth as such, need not be *harmful* to others in order to be repudiated; for it would then be a violation of the rights of others. It may be done merely out of frivolity or even good nature; the speaker may even intend to achieve a really good end by it. But his way of pursuing this end is, by its mere form, a crime of a man against his own person and a worthlessness that must make him contemptible in his own eyes.

It is easy to show that man is actually guilty of many inner lies, but it seems more difficult to explain how they are possible; for a lie requires a second person whom one intends to deceive, whereas to deceive oneself on purpose seems to contain a contradiction.

Man as a moral being (*homo noumenon*) cannot use himself as a natural being (*homo phaenomenon*) as a mere means (a speaking machine), as if his natural being were not bound to the inner end (of communicating thoughts), but is bound to the condition of using himself as a natural being in agreement with the declaration (*declaratio*) of his moral being and is under obligation to himself to *truthfulness*. Someone tells an inner lie, for example, if he professes belief in a future judge of the world, although he really finds no such belief within himself but persuades himself that it could do no harm and might even be useful to profess in his thoughts to one who scrutinizes hearts a belief in such a judge, in order to win His favor in case He should exist. Someone also lies if, having no doubt about the existence of this future judge, he still flatters himself that he inwardly reveres His law, though the only incentive he feels is fear of punishment.

Insincerity is mere lack of *conscientiousness,* that is, of purity in one's professions before one's inner judge, who is thought of as another person when conscientiousness is taken quite strictly; then if someone, from self-love, takes a wish for the deed because he has a really good end in mind, his inner lie, although it is indeed contrary to man's duty to himself, gets the name of a frailty, as when a lover's wish to find only good qualities in his beloved blinds him to her obvious faults. But such insincerity in his declarations, which man perpetrates upon himself, still deserves the strongest censure, since it is from such a rotten spot (falsity, which seems to be rooted in human nature itself) that the evil of untruthfulness spreads into man's relations with other men as well, once the highest principle of truthfulness has been violated.

Remark: It is noteworthy that the Bible dates the first crime, through which evil entered the world, not from *fratricide* (Cain's) but from the first *lie* (for even nature rises up against fratricide), and calls the author of all evil a liar from the beginning and the father of lies. However, reason can assign no further ground for man's propensity to *hypocrisy (esprit fourbe),* although this propensity must have been present before the lie; for an act of freedom cannot (like a natural effect) be deduced and explained in accordance with the natural law of the connection of effects with their causes, all of which are appearances.

Casuistical Questions: Can an untruth from mere politeness (e.g., the "your obedient servant" at the end of a letter) be considered a lie? No one is deceived by it. An author asks one of his readers, "How do you like my work?" One could merely seem to give an answer, by joking about the impropriety of such a question. But who has his wit always ready? The author will take the slightest hesitation in answering as an insult. May one, then, say what is expected of one?

If I say something untrue in more serious matters, having to do with what is mine or yours, must I answer for all the consequences it might have? For example, a householder has ordered his servant to say "not at home" if a certain man asks for him. The servant does this and, as a result, the master slips away and commits a serious crime, which would otherwise have been prevented by the guard sent to arrest him. Who (in accordance with ethical principles) is guilty in this case? Surely the servant, too, who violated a duty to himself by his lie, the results of which his own conscience imputes to him.

Study Questions

1. Why does a liar annihilate his or her own dignity? Is there a connection to the categorical imperative and/or the theory of respect for persons?

2. What is the difference between an external and an internal lie? Is one more acceptable than the other, according to Kant? And according to you?

3. Discuss Kant's own "study question," "Is the servant guilty?" Why? Compare this example with the example of the killer at the door.

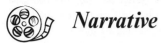 *Narrative*

From *High Noon* to *3:10*: Two Deontological Films

The following two narratives are both Westerns; in both films the basic theme is a man who chooses to do the right thing against overwhelming odds, facing a gang of outlaws, all by himself. But otherwise the stories are very different, as are the lead characters. What I suggest you focus on in discussing these two movies is what motivates Marshal Will Kane (*High Noon*) and rancher Dan Evans (*3:10 to Yuma*), and whether it is appropriate to call their commitment "Kantian" in spirit.

High Noon

CARL FOREMAN (SCREENWRITER)

FRED ZINNEMAN (DIRECTOR)

Film, 1952. Summary.

This film may be the most famous Western of all time, and yet it is not a typical Western. There is very little riding, no cavalry troops or Indians, no cattle, no cowboys—but much talk about the right thing to do. This film was made in the early days of McCarthyism in Hollywood, and Fred Zinneman (the director) has admitted that it is an allegory of the general attitude in 1952 Hollywood of turning your back on friends who were accused (in many cases falsely) of "un-American" (Communist) activities and who might have needed help. When it was produced, it was not considered to have any potential as a classic, but it has soared in public opinion ever since then. It is a Western—but a Western of a different sort—a Western about the problems of a budding civilization in the midst of an era of violence. The film also is very well crafted. The amount of time that elapses from the moment Marshal Will Kane realizes he will have to face four gunmen alone because the whole town worries about the consequences of siding with him to the moment the actual gunfight takes place is the exact amount of time you spend watching it in the theater or in front of your TV or computer: an hour and a half.

The plot is simple. Five years before, Kane brought a killer, Frank Miller, to justice. Miller was sentenced to hang, but "up North they commuted it to life, and now he's free," as the judge says. He is coming in on the noon train to have it out with Kane. Word of his intentions comes just as Kane is marrying his Quaker bride in a civil ceremony. He has already given up his job and is leaving town with his new wife when he turns around to face the gunmen coming in on the noon train. His wife, Amy, asks him why he is turning back—he doesn't have to play the hero for her, she says. He answers, "I haven't got time to tell you. . . . And if you think I like this, you're crazy."

In town, Kane tries to get his former deputies to join him, but everyone is afraid of Miller, except the deputy, who is the boyfriend of Helen Ramirez, Kane's former girlfriend. Helen is the only one who understands Kane's problem because, as a Mexican, she has always felt like an outcast herself—and besides, she used to be Frank Miller's girlfriend too. When Amy leaves Kane because as a Quaker she disapproves of violence as a problem-solver—but also because she watched her father and brother gunned down when she was a young girl– she seeks out Helen because she thinks it is because of her that Kane is staying in town. Amy begs Helen to let him go, and when she hears that he isn't staying because of Helen, she asks, bewildered, what then is making her husband stay. Helen tells her, "If you don't know, I can't tell you." Helen's boyfriend, the deputy, finds Kane and tries to force him to leave town so that he can take over as town marshal. He also asks Kane why he is staying, and all Kane says is, "I don't know."

Desperate, Kane makes for the little church where the Sunday service is still going on, and we remember that an hour ago he was married in a civil ceremony. The service comes to a stop as he enters, and the minister asks him what could be so important since he didn't see fit to be married in church. Kane explains that his wife is a Quaker, and not a member of the town's Protestant congregation, and he knows he is not a churchgoing man, but he needs help. Some of the same men who were deputies with him when they arrested Miller are attending the service—don't they feel the call to duty? Democratically, the congregation plunges into a debate: Why is Kane still here if he is no longer marshal? Why hasn't he arrested the men at the depot? Why must private citizens pitch in every time law enforcement can't handle the situation? But Kane also has supporters who remember that he cleaned up the town and made it a place fit for civilized people. In the end, the mayor speaks: We owe Kane a great debt, he says, so we, the citizens, ought to take care of the situation—and Kane ought to get out of town so there will be no bloodshed. Because (and this is obviously the mayor's real concern) with bloodshed in the streets, investors from up North will shy away from putting money into the town. The support Kane was hoping for evaporates in light of financial concerns.

Mondadori Portfolio/Getty Images

In *High Noon* (United Artists, 1952), Will Kane (Gary Cooper, left) has just been married and has resigned as marshal of Hadleyville, but a killer he helped put in prison and three other gunmen are now looking for him. He tries to get the townspeople to stand by him the way they did when he captured the killer five years earlier, but now they all turn their backs on him, preferring not to get involved. In this scene a former friend, Herb (James Millican), is backing out of his promise to help Kane, having found out that nobody else is coming along.

The "good citizens" want Kane to leave town so there will be no deterrence to progress. The former sheriff wants him to leave, saying that keeping the law is an ungrateful business. Everybody wants him to leave, and at the train depot Frank Miller's three gunmen are waiting for the train that will bring Frank. But Kane feels compelled to stay, even with nobody to side with him. The last man to abandon Kane is his friend Herb. When he realizes that it will be just he and Kane against Miller and his gang, he pleads with Kane, "I have a wife and kids—what about my kids?" And Kane responds, "Go home to your kids, Herb."

The train arrives, a gunfight ensues in the dusty streets of the town, and two of Frank's gunmen are killed. In the end, Amy comes to Kane's rescue and kills the third gunman; Kane kills Miller, and together he and Amy leave town—but not before Kane has thrown his marshal's star in the dust.

Study Questions

1. What makes Kane stay? Is he serious when he says, "I don't know"? Why might we say that this is a "Kantian" Western?

2. Is it fair of Kane to place Amy in a situation where she has to give up her own moral principles?

3. What is meant by the line "If you don't know, I can't tell you"?

4. How would a utilitarian judge Kane's feeling of conscience and duty?

5. Are the townspeople who refuse to help primarily deontologists, utilitarians, or ethical egoists?

 Narrative

3:10 to Yuma

JAMES MANGOLD (DIRECTOR)

HALSTED WELLES AND MICHAEL BRANDT (SCREENWRITERS)

Film, 2007. Summary.

There is more than half a century between *High Noon* and our second Western, *3:10 to Yuma,* but *3:10* is actually a remake of a film from the same decade, the nineteen fifties—a decade where films often dealt with big moral questions. It opened to enthusiastic reviews in 2007, proclaiming that the Western movie was back! A good plot, well acted, well directed, with an intriguing good guy/bad guy dynamic. The fact that it was a remake didn't seem to detract from its freshness. (For those of you who may know the 1957 version, this one is quite different in significant ways that I won't divulge.)

So what was so appealing about the 2007 version? Could it be that both the good guy and the bad guy are sympathetic characters, played by attractive "leading men"? Or that the plot doesn't go where you think it is going to go? Or perhaps that good Westerns are few and far between? You be the judge of that.

3:10 to Yuma is a tale about right and wrong but also, in a secondary way, about good and evil. It is about a man deciding to do the right thing, first for selfish reasons, and then, apparently, just because it's right. Therefore, we can call it a "Kantian" Western.

In *3:10 to Yuma* (2007) the outlaw Ben Wade (Russell Crowe) is being taken to the Yuma train in Contention by a posse of deputies, but at the end of the trip only small-time rancher Dan Evans (Christian Bale) is determined to see it through and do the right thing. An example of the categorical imperative? You decide.

Dan Evans is a small-time rancher with a wife, two sons, and a ranch outside Bisbee, Arizona. The little family is eking out a miserable existence on land without sufficient water for their cattle, since the river is being diverted by the big rancher upstream who is offering Evans water rights for the (then) enormous sum of two hundred dollars. All the while, the rancher's cowboys are harassing the Evanses, stampeding their cattle and burning down their barn. The Evanses are facing impending doom; without the two hundred dollars, they will have to leave their land and everything they have worked and fought for. In addition, Evans is challenged by the fact that he lost a leg in the Civil War—not even in battle, but from "friendly fire," something he hopes to keep from his sons. They have very little respect for him as it is, especially the older boy, who is fourteen.

But by chance, Evans gets the opportunity to make two hundred dollars, which would save his land and his cattle: While rounding up his cattle, he and his boys witness a holdup of the stage by a gang of ruthless men who gun down everyone and take the Southern Pacific Railroad's payroll. One man, a bounty hunter hired by the Pinkerton Agency, survives with a bullet wound to his stomach. The leader of the outlaws scatters Evans's cattle and takes his horses to prevent anyone from riding for help, but we sense immediately that the gang leader is not without a sense of fairness: He promises to leave the horses on the road where Evans and the boys can get to them. And we learn that this unusual bandit is the legendary Ben Wade, a man who has escaped justice over and over again.

Dan and the boys manage to recapture their horses, and they transport the bounty hunter to Bisbee so he can get medical attention. Meanwhile, Wade and the gang have made it to Bisbee, where they report that they have witnessed the holdup. While the marshal rides off toward the holdup spot, the gang members ride off in the opposite direction with the loot—all except Wade, who finds time to have a sexual interlude with a saloon girl he recognizes from another town. He turns out to be a silver-tongued romantic, utterly confident in himself and his own ability to get out of any situation. But his escapade costs him dearly: The marshal has encountered the bounty hunter, Dan Evans, and the boys, and realizes that the man who reported the holdup was one of Wade's gang members—and that Wade is still in town. So Wade is arrested, just like that.

But now the local marshal has a tiger by the tail, because once Wade's gang finds out he is captured, they're bound to come after him. So the marshal and his deputies hatch a plan to get Wade to justice, and railroad representative Grayson Butterfield promises two hundred dollars to any man who will help out. Evans, seeing an end to his financial worries, volunteers to go along with Butterfield, the local veterinarian who doubles as a doctor, the bounty hunter who feels well enough to ride, and one of the rancher's cowboys on the cross-country trail to the town of Contention, where they will put Ben Wade on the train to the Yuma State Prison. There he will be given a perfunctory trial before he is hanged.

The plan consists in a switcheroo to fool Wade's gang: They will make a big show out of putting Wade on a stagecoach with guards. Then, when the stage has reached Dan Evans's place outside town, they'll feign a wheel accident and, in the confusion, switch Wade with one of their own men and spirit Wade away to Dan's ranch. The switch happens seamlessly, the stage takes off again with the fake "Wade" on board, and Wade, in handcuffs, is now a prisoner/dinner guest at the Evans place.

During dinner he charms Alice, Dan's wife, and looks utterly heroic to Dan's older son, William. Wade also manages to hide a dinner fork up his sleeve. Although Dan is disturbed by the fascination Alice and the boys have for Wade, he seems to accept, meekly, that he is not a hero to his own boys. Dan himself finds Wade intriguing, and deserving of respect, because earlier, Wade paid him for the afternoon he and his boys spent looking for their horses and rounding up their cattle a second time.

Dan tells his boys to stay behind with their mother, and rides off with the little posse and Wade toward Contention, hoping to earn the money that will save his ranch. On the trail they are joined by William, who has run away from home to join the posse—and we sense it is also because he feels drawn to the magnetism of Ben Wade. Even so, William comes to the aid of his father and the rest of the little posse when Wade makes a move to escape, so his loyalty is not in question.

A strange camaraderie develops between Evans and Wade. They don't understand each other's motives, but they like to talk. Wade derides Evans for believing in a moral code, but Evans realizes that the outlaw Wade has his own very strong values: He has a sense of fairness, and he will not suffer stupidity, even in his own gang. But Wade emphasizes to Dan that he never does anything unless it benefits himself. Dan can expect no human kindness from Wade. The outlaw proves himself to be a formidable ally as well as a formidable adversary: When a band of Apache Indians attacks in the middle of the night, Wade's battle experience saves them—but with the fork he has stolen, he also kills the deputized cowboy (who, we learn, was the man who set fire to Dan's barn), takes his gun, and succeeds in throwing the bounty hunter off a cliff before he takes off, still handcuffed. The remainder of the posse follows his tracks up into the mountains, through a newly blasted tunnel where the railroad is being pushed through, to the railroad workers' camp. They arrive just in time to rescue Wade from a painful death at the hands of an irate railroad guard who has recognized Wade as his brother's murderer. But during their escape the doctor is shot and dies.

As they approach Contention, the danger of a showdown becomes clear: Wade expects his men to show up any minute, because they will by now have seen through the stagecoach ruse (and we, the audience, have already seen them kill the guard and the "fake" Wade, burning them alive inside the stagecoach). The remaining posse—Butterfield, Dan, and William—take Wade to the hotel to wait for the train, and Butterfield goes to the local marshal's office for reinforcements. Three or four well-armed law-enforcement officers arrive at the hotel, and it looks as if Evans and Butterfield will succeed in putting Wade on the train. But now Wade's gang rides into town, led by his second-in-command, Charlie Prince, a mean-spirited, sadistic character who has 100 percent loyalty for Wade and for nobody else. Prince promises a reward to anyone in town who will kill a member of the posse. The marshal assesses the odds and backs down, telling his deputies that their job guarding Wade isn't worth dying for. But as they exit the hotel, Prince and the gang gun them down in cold blood. Butterfield himself has no intention of dying, so he also leaves, and hides out in the hotel.

Evans finds himself reassessing the situation: Rain clouds are forming over the Bisbee range, which means that his ranch will get water. That means he really won't need the two hundred dollars anymore, so there is no financial reason for Evans to try to get Wade on the train. Now Wade starts bargaining with Dan: He will offer him one thousand dollars in cash, from the stagecoach robbery, if he will let Wade go. For one brief moment Dan considers the offer; then he declines. Wade asks Dan why. Why is it so important to him to keep a promise when everyone else has chickened out? Dan's answer is that when you've been in the war and the only action you've seen is a retreat, and then you lose your leg to friendly fire, that isn't much of a story to tell your boys.

Dan, fearing that he won't make it out alive, sends William away, telling him to remember that his father was the only one who stood up for what's right. Dan also calls Butterfield back and makes him promise that if he doesn't make it back to Bisbee, then his family will receive a thousand dollars as a reward from the railroad. Meanwhile, Wade is watching, and we get a sense that he actually cares whether Dan lives or dies. He makes it clear to Dan that he has been imprisoned in Yuma twice before, and escaped.

It is 3:00, and the train will be in shortly. Wade's gang is spread out from the hotel to the train and the cattle pens. William is waiting by the cattle pens with a rifle. Surprisingly, Wade now seems to cooperate, running and dodging bullets with Dan to get to the station, over rooftops, down alleys, along the cattle pens, until they get to the station—but the train is late!

What will happen? Will Wade get on the train of his own volition? Will Dan survive to get home to his family and the ranch? And what happens to William? As the train pulls up, the gang is approaching . . . You'll have to watch the ending for yourself!

Study Questions

1. Why is Dan Evans doing what he is doing? Is he just trying to impress his son, or does he have another motive? Why is this called a "Kantian" Western in the introduction?

2. Compare Evans's choice to stand alone, doing what is right, with Will Kane's (*High Noon*). Is there a difference? Explain.

3. Why do you think Wade is cooperating with Evans toward his own imprisonment? If you have seen the film, fill in the blanks and evaluate all Wade's actions, including the moment when he whistles for his horse.

4. Would you say that Evans's boys have good reason to be proud of their father? Why or why not? Did Evans make the right choice? Does it depend on whether he lives or dies? What does Evans mean by saying to Wade that until now, he hasn't had a good story to tell his sons? Explain.

5. A "spoiler alert": In a scene that takes the audience aback, Wade guns down members of his own gang. Remember Wade's comment that he will not put up with fools—might it be that the outlaw Wade has principles? Can a truly selfish person have principles?

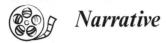 *Narrative*

Abandon Ship!

RICHARD SALE (SCREENWRITER AND DIRECTOR)

Film, 1957. Summary.

Based on a true story, this film opens during the aftermath of an explosion on a luxury liner far from shore. The ship sank so quickly that no S.O.S. signal was sent, and no lifeboats were lowered. Now, some twenty survivors are clinging to the one lifeboat that was launched. It is the captain's dinghy, and it can hold fourteen people maximum. The captain is dying, and he transfers his authority to his first officer, Alec Holmes, admonishing him to "save as many as you can." Holmes is hopeful that help may arrive, but when he realizes that no S.O.S. has been sent, he knows that their only option is to row for the coast of Africa, fifteen hundred miles away. Kelly, an officer and a friend of Holmes, himself mortally wounded, tells Holmes that he won't be able to make it if he tries to keep everyone alive—he must "evict some tenants" in order to save others. When Holmes wants to break the tedium by having the survivors tell their stories, Kelly advises him not to get to know everyone too well—because Kelly knows that sooner or later, Holmes will have to choose who will live and who will die, and such a decision will be much harder if everyone has bonded. To set an example, Kelly throws himself overboard, because he would only be a hindrance to the survival of the "fittest." Holmes at first will hear nothing of this plan, but when a storm approaches, he realizes that he must choose between the death of them all and the death of those who already are hurt and can't pull their weight. When desperate passengers plead with him to at least draw lots, or save the women and children, or call for volunteers, he refuses to consider all approaches other than his own choice: The survivors must be able to row and bail and must be strong enough to stay alive. Under protest and at gunpoint, the others comply by forcing the wounded passengers and crewmen, who are wearing life preservers, overboard, setting them adrift in shark-infested waters. An elderly opera singer, famous in her day, goes to her doom with composure, while a young crew member with his lungs full of oil is begging for his life. One professor remarks, "This is an interesting moral problem," and insists that it is barbarism—the civilized thing to do would be to choose to die together.

Another passenger, moved by seeing a young boy lose both his parents to Holmes's weeding-out process, breaks out a knife and tries to force Holmes to turn around and look for the ones that were adrift. Holmes kills the man in self-defense, but not before the man succeeds in wounding Holmes with his knife. Now the storm hits, and all through the night the remaining passengers and crew struggle to keep afloat. When dawn breaks, and the storm dies down, everyone on board has survived, and there is a general feeling of goodwill toward Holmes—but he is suffering severely from his knife wound. Now Holmes applies his rule to himself and slips overboard so as not to be a burden, but the others rescue him and bring him back on board. Just as the passengers are getting ready to thank him for his foresight and effort, a ship is spotted on the horizon. Miraculously, help has arrived, "too soon," as a feisty woman passenger remarks—too soon for everybody to have decided to support Holmes in his plan to force some of the passengers overboard. The people on the boat are rescued (it is hinted that some of the evicted passengers are rescued too), and Holmes goes on trial for murder. The film concludes with the question, "If you had been on the jury, would you have found Holmes guilty or innocent?"

Glasshouse Images/Alamy Stock Photo

Facing a hard decision, Captain Holmes (Tyrone Power, at the stern) surveys the situation after the shipwreck in *Abandon Ship!* (Columbia Pictures, 1957). Soon he must decide which passengers are fit to row to Africa and which must be thrown overboard, sacrificed so that the others have a chance to survive. The story of *Abandon Ship!* is an illustration of a clash between utilitarian and deontological views.

Study Questions

1. Can this film be seen as a defense of utilitarianism! Explain why or why not.

2. Do you agree that it would have been a more civilized thing for all of the passengers to die together?

3. Would you have convicted Holmes of murder? (In actual fact he was convicted, but he received a short sentence because of the unusual circumstances.)

4. How might Ayn Rand (Chapter 4) have evaluated Holmes's solution?

5. Can you think of another way of solving Holmes's problem?

6. What was Holmes's intention? Might a Kantian accept that as morally good?

Narrative

Watchmen

GRAPHIC NOVEL 1986–87. DC COMIC BOOK SERIES IN 12 VOLUMES. ALAN MOORE (WRITER), DAVE GIBBONS (ARTIST), AND JOHN HIGGIN (COLORIST).

Film, 2009. Adapted from the graphic novel. Zack Snyder (Director), David Hayter and Alex Tse (Screenwriters)

Faithfully summarizing one of the most famous and enduring of all graphic novels in a few paragraphs is a challenge, so I have opted for focusing on the set-up and Chapters 10–12, where the distinct moral philosophies of two major characters come to a confrontation. Consequently, there are several subplots that aren't included here. This summary will also contain **spoilers**. I have decided to refer to the graphic novel rather than the 2009 movie, because for one thing, graphic novel connoisseurs will point out that the novel far outshines the film, but also because *TIME* Magazine has called it not only one of the greatest graphic novels of the twentieth century, but one of the best *novels* since 1923. However, I recommend that you also watch the movie; you will see that the story emphasis is quite different in key episodes. The novel has functioned as a storyboard for the movie, duplicating many iconic scenes from the comic book pages, and the two art forms involving both words and images illustrate how a visual story can be told in dramatically different ways. In 2019, HBO launched *Watchmen* as a long-awaited series, to generally positive reviews. The HBO version, however, is a sequel to the original graphic novel, not a remake.

In our upcoming Chapter 8 (pp. 367–370) there is a mention of Plato's political philosophy, expressed in *The Republic*, where the ideal city-state's government consists of the so-called Philosopher-Kings. Plato also refers to them as Guardians, and assumes that they will be quite capable of guarding themselves and need no oversight, but hundreds of years later the Roman poet Juvenal posed the question, "*Quis custodiet ipsos custodes*?" Who guards the guardians? It is this classic question that underlies Watchmen, and is quoted at the end of Volume 12: "Who watches the watchmen?"

The Watchmen are a select group of American "superheroes," the Minutemen, in the alternative timeline of the novel. Beginning in 1938 and taking us to the 1980s, an alternative world history is laid out. The superheroes don't have superpowers, but are anonymous crime fighters in various colorful disguises—with the one exception of Dr. Manhattan, a blue being who used to be a human scientist, but due to severe exposure to radiation his body is now of a different molecular structure, and he has the ability to look into the future—his own future. The Minutemen helped the United States win the Vietnam War, and propelled President Richard Nixon to a seemingly never-ending presidency, still going strong in the 1980s. The Cold War is moving the Doomsday Clock closer and closer to "midnight," the moment where nuclear war has become inevitable.

RGR Collection/Alamy Stock Photo

In this picture, adapted from a frame from the graphic novel *Watchmen* (1986–87) Dan Dreiberg, formerly the masked crime fighter Nite Owl, has just had a disturbing visit from a former partner, the still active, enigmatic Rorschach, who has told him about the murder of another Minuteman from the old crime-fighting days, the Comedian. Here, in his basement, Dan is contemplating the implications of the Comedian's death, with his own old crime-fighter costume looming over him. Soon he will once again become the Nite Owl, looking for the Comedian's murderer.

When vigilantism was outlawed, most of the original Minutemen retired or were admitted to institutions, and some have been brutally murdered. Ozymandias has gone public under his own identity, the billionaire Adrian Veidt; the first Nite Owl has given his persona and costume to a younger man, Dan Dreiberg, but even he has retired from the hero business. The Comedian, Eddie Blake, has branched off and become a mercenary. Silk Spectre is in a retirement home, and her daughter Laurie is the live-in lover of Dr. Manhattan. Only the enigmatic Rorschach, who wears a mask with changing black-and-white shapes, is true to his crime-fighting persona, because there is evil in the world, and evil has to be punished. And when the Comedian is brutally murdered and thrown out of the window of his apartment as the latest Minuteman victim, his old colleague Rorschach sets out to contact the surviving Minutemen to warn them that they may be future targets of whoever killed Blake, but nobody else believes there is any actual threat to them.

We learn that the Comedian was a cynic and a nihilist who believed that nothing could be done to prevent nuclear war, and that everything was a joke, anyway. We also learn that Dr. Manhattan, who is doing research for a military center and has a number of inventions to his name because of his vast intelligence, has relationship problems with Laurie; when, during a TV interview, he is accused of causing cancer to those who are close to him, he reacts in anger by teleporting the entire audience out of the studio; fearing that he might cause damage to humans, he teleports himself to Mars in order to put human problems at a distance. Meanwhile the Russians, boldened by his departure, invade Afghanistan, and another retired Minuteman is murdered. There is also an attempt on Veidt's life, but he is able to fight his attacker off, and the assailant commits suicide. Rorschach is arrested, and in jail we learn his identity: Walter Kovach. The prison psychologist makes him open up to some degree, and we hear that he donned the mask at some point when he realized that the Comedian was right: humanity is selfish and uncaring. But contrary to the Comedian, Rorschach feels compelled to act according to principles, and attempt to help humanity by doing what is right, regardless of the consequences.

In the meantime, Dr. Manhattan has brought Laurie to Mars, and it becomes clear that as he has lost Laurie, he has also lost the human perspective; he now sees life and the universe "sub specie aeternitatis," under the aspect of eternity—not just without human subjectivity, but the perspective of a god who is too far removed from human life to care about individuals.

We fast forward to the final chapters. Dan (who has again taken on the Nite Owl identity) and Rorschach are zeroing in on what they think is the source of the murders, and they head for Veidt's office in New York City to warn him. But Veidt is away at his retreat in Antarctica, and in his office they realize that Veidt himself must have been behind the murders, including the murder of his old partner Eddie Blake, the Comedian. Rorschach enters the information into his journal which he then drops in a mailbox, addressed to the *New Frontiersman* newspaper, and he and Dan head for the Antarctic.

While Dan and Rorschach are approaching, Veidt pushes a button and celebrates by murdering his associates. What is he celebrating? When Dan and Rorschach enter, Veidt subdues them, and tells the story. Yes indeed, Veidt was behind all the murders, including the attempt on his own life. He was working on a plot, the only way to save humanity from the mutual nuclear destruction predicted by the Comedian: secretly Veidt had developed a formidable weapon to be let loose on New York City, killing half of all New Yorkers, and supposedly set off by aliens—but with the intended result that the Cold War would stop right then and there, and the rest of humanity would be safe, because they would unite against "aliens," a horror fantasy planted in the brains of the survivors of the mass murder. And it was the implementation of that plan he was celebrating, so it is already too late to help the citizens of New York. The weapon has been discharged. Meanwhile, Dr. Manhattan and Laurie have joined them. Veidt warns the four that if they reveal the truth, the sacrifice of millions of New Yorkers will be in vain, and Dan and Dr. Manhattan agree—but Rorschach, believing that where there is evil, it must be exposed, can't support a lie and a hoax, even if it can save the human race.

> Dan Dreiberg: "Rorschach . . .? Rorschach, wait! Where are you going? This is too big to be **hardassed** about! We have to compromise. . . ."
>
> Rorschach: "No. Not even in the face of Armageddon. Never compromise."

I will not give the final pages away; will the world be saved because of Veidt's scheme? Will Rorschach's passion for truth prevail? I suggest you read *Watchmen* and experience the twist ending for yourself.

Study Questions:

1. How can the saying "Who watches the watchmen" be applied to this story?
2. Is Dr. Manhattan capable of acting in the interest of humanity if he has only logic at his disposal, and no human emotions? (See Chapter 1 for the debate about reason vs. emotions.)
3. Identify Veidt's moral philosophy. (Hint: Go to Chapter 5 for the underlying moral theory!) Are his actions in any way justifiable?
4. Can Rorschach's moral stance be viewed as an example of Kantian duty ethics? Why or why not? Can you think of a parallel example from Chapter 6?
5. Would you agree with Veidt, Dr. Manhattan, and the reluctant Dan Dreiberg (we don't really get any commitment from Laurie in the movie or the graphic novel) that the hoax must never be revealed, or with Rorschach that evil must be exposed?

6. Laurie's main contribution here consists of trying to rehumanize Dr. Manhattan, finding a soul mate in Dan, and cry over the New York victims. From a perspective of today, more than 3 decades after the publication of *Watchmen*, could you imagine the daughter of a superhero (maybe even of two superheroes!), herself "Silk Spectre II" in her mother's costume, having somewhat of a more active and heroic role to play? Can you think of movies or TV shows prominently featuring female superheroes in the lead roles?

7. If you are familiar with the HBO series Watchmen, you may want to compare the key elements of the TV series with the original graphic novel: Doe the TV series continue the analysis of the humanity of Dr. Manhattan? Is Veidt's utilitarian solution still an issue? Can the followers of Rorschach be classified as deontologists, or do they have a different function? Who are the heroes of the new *Watchmen,* and what do they accomplish?

Chapter Seven
Personhood, Rights, and Justice

To Kant, any being who is capable of rational thinking qualifies as a person, and (according to Kant's *Grounding for the Metaphysics of Morals*) creatures incapable of rational thinking are classified as things. Today, the debate about what constitutes a person is still with us because the question has lost none of its urgency. At the time when Kant lived, human beings were often treated as things, tools, stepping-stones for the needs or convenience of others. That idea was a legitimate part of public policy in many places throughout the world, and the moral statement that a rational being should never be reduced to a mere tool for another's purpose became part of the worldwide quest for human rights—rights that still have not been universally implemented. That statement is historically important and should not be forgotten, even though many social thinkers today believe that Kant's fight for the recognition that all persons deserve respect must be expanded and that Kant himself didn't have a concept of universal human rights in mind.

In this chapter we discuss issues that reflect several of the theories already studied and that illustrate how such theories can be applied on a social scale in creating policies regarding the rights and duties of citizens. It is thus important that you have studied Chapters 5 and 6 in particular before you proceed.

What Is a Human Being?

If we focus on the rights of human animals, we have to address the question, What does it mean to be human? Are the criteria physical? Does a being have to look human to be human? Does it even have to be organic? A traditional answer coming from Plato, according to legend, is "a featherless biped"—in other words, a creature that walks upright on two legs but is not a bird—but those are hardly sufficient criteria, as his critic Diogenes pointed out, by bringing him a plucked chicken and claiming it was a human being. Nowadays, if we want to use physical criteria, we include not only physical appearance but also genetic information. But with that type of explanation we're faced with two problems: (1) Genetically, there are creatures that are 98 percent identical to the human but are obviously not human: chimpanzees; (2) there are individuals born of human parents who may not have all the human physical characteristics—for instance, persons with multiple physical disabilities (not to mention *mental* disabilities). So is a being born of humans who happens to have some physical aberration—from missing limbs to minor abnormalities such as extra toes and fingers—human? For most people today, the answer is obviously yes, but this was not always so. A worldwide tradition in pretechnological societies has been to dispose of newborns with physical "handicaps" ranging from missing limbs to unwanted birthmarks, and not all of those disposals can be explained by saying that a tribe isn't able to feed those who can't feed themselves. Our culture doesn't follow that practice, but some of us do screen the fetus for severe disabilities and perform abortions if we believe that those disabilities will condemn the child to a less than dignified life. This is not a discussion of the pros and cons of abortion, any more than it is a discussion of infanticide, but it does point out that a good deal of policymaking in other cultures as well as our own depends on how we define "human being," including what a human being, and a human life, *should be like*—a **normative** concept. In Chapter 13 you'll find a discussion of the issue of abortion.

The Expansion of the Concept "Human"

There was a time when people distinguished between friend and foe by calling friends humans and foes beasts, devils, or such. At the tribal level of human history, it has always been common to view the tribe across the river as not quite human, even if members of your tribe marry their sons or daughters. (In fact, the usual word that tribes use to designate themselves is their word for "human," "the people," or "us.") In any geographic area there are people who remain dubious about those from the "other side" because their habits are so different that it seems there must be something "strange" about their general humanity. From the time of the ancient Greeks until quite recently, a common assumption has been that men are more "normal" than women. Interestingly enough, that idea has been held not only by many men but also by many women, who took the men's word for it. (Some still do.) At the nationalistic level, it still is common practice around the world to view foreigners as less than human, not in a physical sense, but, rather, politically and morally in a normative rather than a descriptive sense. And the humanity of a people's wartime enemies almost always is denied, usually because it becomes easier to kill an enemy, either soldier or civilian, if you believe he or she really is not quite as human as you are. Thus the term *human* sometimes evolves into an honorary term reserved for those with whom we prefer to share our culture. Psychologist Daniel Goleman speculates in his book *Social Intelligence* (2006) that the "us versus them" attitude is deeply grounded in our evolutionary history, where it used to be necessary for survival, but that doesn't mean we can't overcome it today with mutual goodwill and effort.

Personhood: The Key to Rights

Many social thinkers prefer the term *person* to *human being* as a philosophical and political concept, partly to avoid the association with the human physical appearance. A person is someone who is capable of psychological and social interaction with others, capable of deciding on a course of action and being held responsible for that action. In other words, a person is considered a *moral agent.* Being a person implies certain duties and privileges—in other words, it is a normative concept: what a person *ought to be and do* to be called a person. Personhood implies that one has certain social privileges and duties and that under extreme circumstances these can be revoked. What was a person to the Greeks? to the Romans? to medieval Europeans? To those groups a person was usually a male adult landowner or tribe member. Different societies have excluded some or all of the following people from their concept of a person: slaves, women, children, foreigners, prisoners of war, and criminals. (See Box 7.1 for a discussion of the personhood of people on the fringes of society, such as prostitutes and drug addicts.) Usually the list of exclusion was extended to animals, plants, and inanimate objects, but other beings might well have been granted personhood, such as gods and goddesses, totems (ancestor animals), and dead ancestors.

Box 7.1 INVISIBLE PEOPLE?

Within two years eleven women disappeared in Cleveland, Ohio, but hardly anyone knew, outside of their families. In November 2009 a local man, Anthony Sowell, was arrested for their murders; he had served fifteen years for attempted rape and had been released in 2005. The women's bodies were hidden in his attic or buried in shallow graves in his backyard, and the neighbors hadn't even reported the smells that wafted from his two-story house. It wasn't the best of neighborhoods, and the women themselves lived what some would call marginal lives: they were drug addicts, and some of them were prostitutes—the preferred type of victim for a serial killer, because they are "invisible" to society, even sometimes to their own families. Many of the women had a long history of disappearing for a while, so some families never even reported them missing, and those reports that were taken were not considered high priority by law enforcement. This is not unusual in itself for a serial killer case, but to that picture should be added the fact that all the women were black (as was their killer). In 2011 Sowell, now dubbed the "Cleveland Strangler," was convicted on eleven counts of murder and is on Death Row at the time of this writing.

Similar scenarios have played out around the country, and even the world: serial killers preying on women and sometimes children who are overlooked by society. Seattle's "Green River Killer" Gary Ridgway was one of the most prolific of them all with at least forty-eight murders on his conscience (for which he revealed, in lengthy interviews, to have very little remorse; he said he didn't consider his victims as any different from trash). He pled guilty to avoid the death penalty. The "Grim Sleeper" terrorized and killed black women in Los Angeles over a period of twenty years, and in 2010 a suspect was arrested, Lonnie David Franklin, Jr. And in Spokane, Washington, Robert Yates pled guilty to nine murders to avoid the death penalty but failed to realize that the deal did not cover the additional two murders he was suspected of having committed in Tacoma. He had to stand trial after all, and he, too, is now on Death Row. Yates's victims were also "invisible" to society—mostly prostitutes and drug addicts—but years before he was captured a radio show in Spokane began speaking up for the women, asking questions such as, "Are these women not human beings with the same rights as the rest of us? Don't they have families who mourn them? Don't they feel pain and anguish in their last moments at the mercy of a murderer? It may be illegal to be a prostitute and to use drugs, but it doesn't carry a death penalty."

Today we in the Western world assume that all humans are persons with inalienable rights (and we also grant personhood to some unlikely entities such as corporations). This is not a recognized truth all over the world, however. "Human trafficking," buying and selling human beings (especially young girls) internationally in the sex trade, is big business. Serfdom still exists in parts of the world, such as Pakistan. In many nations to this day, women are considered the property of their husbands or fathers. Crimes against children are often not punished as severely as crimes against adults, if at all. And even in this country, the equal rights provisions that we take pride in don't always work: The sweatshops that are known to provide us with cheap products from elsewhere in the world are sometimes found to operate on American soil. News stories surface from time to time about undocumented immigrants kept in economic bondage by the people who imported them. Any time we hear a news story of people being abused or taken advantage of, resulting in the loss of their well-being or their lives, we are hearing about people whose *personhood* has been violated—or as Kant would say, they have been treated *merely as a means to an end*—and in general, our court system is capable of dealing with such offenses.

But the lack of respect for other human beings as persons sometimes goes beyond what the law can address. When *discrimination* reaches the level of depriving someone of his or her rights, the law can step in, but when it is merely an attitude, we encounter an interesting problem: Should we outlaw discrimination as an attitude, or is it part of living in a free country that people may choose their viewpoints without being told by the state what to think? There is a fine line here. Most of us would like to see an end to *racism* and *sexism,* but we may also be reluctant to send people who have expressed racist or sexist views to a retraining facility where their minds will be altered, because we believe not only in freedom of speech but also in *freedom of thought*. Perhaps this is where Kant's lesson of treating people as *ends in themselves* has its most profound application in our modern society: With the recognition of every human being as a person with intrinsic value, much disrespect will—at least in theory—fall by the wayside. And racism and sexism are, of course, not the only forms of discrimination that a person can encounter. As an aside, the term "racism" has been broadened over the past decades by the media, including social media, to cover just about any type of discrimination against entire population groups regardless of whether the animosity is grounded in the target group's racial identity. A more traditional term for discrimination against a group of people for their cultural identity is bigotry, and bigotry can take many forms, such as discrimination against the young for their youth as well as the elderly for their age ("ageism"), against the mentally ill or mentally disabled, or the physically disabled ("ableism"), against people of a sexual orientation that differs from one's own, or who are of a different religion or nationality; discrimination of the educated against the less-educated, of the less-educated against the highly educated, of the wealthy against the indigent, and of the less well-to-do against the wealthy. And even of conservatives against liberals, and of liberals against conservatives. Suspicion and resentment are part of the fabric of human society, and in each case, the emphasis on personhood should remind us all that despite our differences, we ought to recognize the personhood in one another. (From Chapter 4 you'll remember the philosopher Emmanuel Levinas, who has a special version of this emphasis, and in Chapter 10 you'll see this theory in detail.)

In recent years the legacy from Kant that all of humanity should be treated never as a means to an end, but always as an end in themselves has been put to the test, in the eyes of many Americans: a number of unarmed African American males have been shot to death by white police officers, some of them under circumstances where the justifiability of such killings has been severely questioned by the media as well as the local communities. In Ferguson, Missouri, in 2014, 18-year-old robbery suspect Michael Brown was shot and killed during a struggle with the police, and his death sparked widespread demonstrations. The police officer who shot him was exonerated, but other cases are pending where police conduct is being investigated. "Black Lives Matter" has become the name for a nationwide activist organization, as well as a rallying cry for demonstrators and critics of perceived police discrimination; according to reports, members of BLM have encouraged targeting police officers, and patrol officers have been gunned down in unprovoked attacks giving rise to another movement, "Blue Lives Matter." On both sides, families have been destroyed, with resulting grief and rage. Aside from the immensely difficult task for the courts and the media of fairly evaluating every one of these highly emotional situations, it seems clear that the twenty-first century so far is not quite ready for Immanuel Kant's "Kingdom of Ends," a world where *all* human beings act rationally and show respect for one another.

Who Is a Person?

What about cases where a person has chosen to disregard the personhood of others, to the point of violating their health, their liberty, their property, or their life? Have such people now opened themselves up to being deprived of their own status of personhood? In other words, is a *criminal* a person? For many people, the more callous the crime, the less human the criminal. Sometimes we even call murderers "animals," although few nonhuman animals have been known to display the methodical, deliberate preying on one's own species typical of human career criminals, serial rapists, and serial killers. In our attitudes toward such criminals, much of our view of what counts as human is revealed: We're not trying to describe their genetic makeup; we're expressing a moral condemnation of their actions and choices. Calling a criminal an animal is a normative statement, not a descriptive one: He (or she) has not lived up to our expectations of what a person ought to be and do, and so we view him as less than human. But genetically as well as legally, serial killers such as Anthony Sowell and Robert Yates (see Box 7.1) are still persons, and the very fact that we choose to hold them accountable in court is proof of that. However, criminals, even convicted ones, don't lose all their rights:

Their personhood status is not revoked, at least not in our culture. They still have the right not to be tortured, for example, although they may have lost their right to liberty. Below we take a closer look at the concept of rights.

Children as a group have not until recently been considered "real people." Until recently, child abuse was not considered a felony. In previous times—in fact, as recently as the nineteenth century and, in some places, the twentieth century—the father of the household had the supreme right to treat his family (including his wife) any way he pleased. That might very well include physically punishing all the family members, even unto death. That right, *patria potestas,* is still in effect in certain societies in the world. The thought of protecting children against abuse, even abuse from their own parents, is actually quite a new idea in Western cultures; even in the recent past, child abuse cases were sometimes covered up or never reported. Current reports reveal that even if we think children are protected in today's society, the reality is quite different: There are stories of children being removed from foster homes and given back to abusive parents who then kill them through abuse or neglect; of parents torturing children to death for wetting their beds or for crying; of children starving to death because their parents or foster parents couldn't be bothered to feed them; of parents or foster parents who are in need of help themselves for severe drug dependency. The heartbreaking numbers tell us that, for whatever reason, authorities charged with the well-being of these children are sometimes not picking up on danger signals. Analysts suspect that the idea that children ought to be with their parents and not in foster care is applied too rigidly, regardless of what is in the child's best interest, and also that because of the notion, left over from a bygone age, that toddlers are somehow not quite "persons" yet, their misery at the hands of their caregivers doesn't merit a criminal investigation.

What has been more publicized, with more visible results, is the now world-wide scandal involving child abuse by Catholic priests, playing out for decades before the revelations by the *Boston Globe* in 2002 of not only the abuses but also the cover-ups by the Catholic dioceses—a scandal that served as the raw material for the Oscar-winning film *Spotlight* (2015). The film is featured as a narrative in Chapter 13. In the terminology of Kant, the children have been used merely as a means to an end. Today the law recognizes not only that children should be protected from abuse but also that children have interests and wishes that they are capable of expressing and that should be heard, such as which parent they wish to stay with after a divorce.

We are now at the point where the conscious interests of children (including everything from having enough food, shelter, love, and education to refusing to go to school in order to play video games or watch TV) must be balanced against what conscientious adults deem to be in the children's best interests, best *in spite of* themselves. In other words, we must remember that what children want is not necessarily good for them. The idea that children are minors who have neither the legal rights nor the legal responsibilities of adults is not about to disappear, even when their interests are taken into consideration. We tend to forget that when a group is excluded from having rights, it is usually also excluded from having responsibilities. In other words, such a group must be given legal protection so that its members, who are incapable of taking on civil responsibilities, will not be treated unjustly.

Persons and Responsibility

Historically, the idea of **children** having responsibilities has shifted back and forth. It was only in the twentieth century that we in the Western world agreed not to hold minors responsible for criminal acts. The legendary German figure Till Eulenspiegel was a mischievous kid who played one too many tricks on decent citizens, and the decent citizens hanged him. The title character of Herman Melville's *Billy Budd* faced the same fate. Billy, a young sailor, was falsely accused of wrongdoing by a vicious officer. Because Billy had a problem articulating and could not speak up to defend himself, he acted out his frustration by striking the officer. Unfortunately, that resulted in the officer's death, and the captain, although aware of Billy's problem, had to follow the law of the sea: mandatory death for anyone who kills an officer. In the end, Billy had to submit to the traditional execution method by climbing up the rigging and slipping a noose around his own neck. Today a crime committed by a person under the age of 18 must reveal an extraordinary amount of callousness and "evil intent" for the court to try the minor as an adult. That is because childhood is considered to be a state of mind and body that doesn't allow for the logical consistency we assume is available, most of the time, to adults; therefore children aren't held accountable for their actions to the degree that adults are.

The United States, however, has seen a shift lately in the attitude toward children who commit crimes. Although most child psychologists still agree that children below the age of seven or eight don't know enough about the difference between right and wrong to be held accountable, public demand is now growing for trying older child offenders as adults. What should the court do with a child who kills another child for his sneakers or his jacket? or who takes a gun to school and kills a number of his classmates and teachers before being stopped? In some states, such as Arkansas, children cannot be tried as adults. In other states, it is the severity of the crime that determines whether the youth will be tried as an adult; we have lately seen teenagers being given hefty prison sentences (although the Supreme Court decided in 2005 that a child under eighteen can't be given the death penalty). In May 2019, two young people, an 18-year old male and a 16-year old friend self-identifying as a male, came to the STEM Schools Highland Ranch in Denver, CO, with the intent to shoot and kill students. They were stopped and disarmed by three classmates, but during the fight one of the three, Kendrick Castillo, was killed defending his classmates. Both the shooters were taken alive, and both would be tried as adults. (In Chapter 11 we take a closer look at the concept of courage and the brave actions of the three classmates.)

In the past, the rights of **women** have followed a course similar to those of children. Women had very few rights until the late nineteenth century—no right to hold property, no right to vote, no right over their own person. That went hand in hand with the common assumption that women were not capable of moral consistency and thus were not responsible. (Mention of women and children in the same breath was no coincidence.) That view often coincided with a male reverence for women and their supposedly higher moral standards, but such reverence was often combined with an assumption that women were idealists with no conception of the sordid dealings and practical demands of the real world.

When it applied to women, the practice of holding only those with rights legally responsible was not strictly adhered to. Many, many women were put on criminal trial. Even so, the general idea was that withholding rights from women *protected* them from the harsh world of reality, whose demands they weren't capable of answering. (In Chapter 12 you'll find a more thorough analysis of the history of women's rights, as well as a discussion of whether there is a specific female form of ethic.) A similar kind of argument kept slaves from having rights throughout most slaveholding societies—rights were denied to provide "protection" for these people because they were "incapable." That did not preclude punishing slaves, of course, as anyone who has read *Huckleberry Finn* knows. In *On Liberty* (see Chapter 5), John Stuart Mill argues that the right to self-determination should extend universally, *provided* that the individuals in question have been educated properly, in the British sense, so that they know what to do with the self-determination. Until then, they are incapable of making responsible decisions and should be protected—children by their guardians and colonial inhabitants by the British. Today, an animal rights activist might argue that we see the same pattern repeated with **animals**: We don't believe them to be fully developed moral agents, and so we protect them—by withholding rights from them. Regardless of whether you would agree that animals should be regarded as *persons* (and we will return to that question in Chapter 13), a subtle shift is already happening in media reporting of accidents and crimes affecting the lives of pets. Where in the recent past a dog being injured or killed in an automobile accident or a home invasion robbery might not even be mentioned by the media, such reporting is now commonplace. It may be because the media has realized that we, the consumers of news, are simply concerned about the fate of other people's pets; it could also be because pets have become part of our families much more than in the past. And it could signify that pets are no longer considered mere property. An interesting concept is evolving; namely, that it is possible for a non-human animal to be considered a person, but a person with *limited* rights, duties, and privileges whose rights are assigned to a guardian. We will return to this idea in Chapter 13.

Science and Moral Responsibility: Genetic Engineering, Stem Cell Research, and Cloning

As it stands now, we must agree that our culture has come a long way in recognizing all postnatal (=born) humans as persons, at least in principle, although that principle sometimes seems to be overpowered by controversy. But what about the future? Genetically engineered children already walk among us, and there will be many more. Your children—and perhaps even you yourself—may be able to look forward to a longer, healthier life span because of genetic engineering. By the time you're reading this, there may be viable human clones among us too, legally or otherwise. Will these new members of our human family be considered persons, or will they encounter some new form of discrimination? In the Narratives section you'll find three stories that explore either end of this spectrum of possibilities: The classic science fiction film *Blade Runner* sets the standard for discussions about the rights of androids, and the long-awaited sequel, *Blade Runner 2049*, picked up where the first movie left off. *Ex Machina* (2015) envisions a near future where a robot will be able to not only act like a human, but have human emotions. The film *Gattaca* suggests a world, right around the corner, where genetic engineering has become mainstream, and it is those who have *not* been genetically "improved" at the embryo stage who will form the new underclass. Who will really be up, and who will be down, in such a "brave new world" (referring to Aldous Huxley's classic 1931 science fiction novel, see below)?

We can ask ourselves two questions here: Given that a future involving a variety of options for genetic engineering and cloning is already upon us, (1) how should we deal with the scientific possibilities opening up for humanity? Should we be phobic about scientific developments and encourage bans and limits to scientific research? Or, should we encourage all such research under the assumption that somehow it may benefit us and that science has a right to seek knowledge for the sake of knowledge no matter the consequences? Or should we, perhaps, take some position in between? (2) Should scientists themselves exercise some form of moral responsibility, taking into consideration that their results will be used in the future, perhaps to the detriment of humans and animals living in that future? In the next section we take a look at one of the most burning issues today: the question of science and moral responsibility.

Science Is Not Value-Free

In 1968 a book came out in Germany that challenged the traditional scientific view that science is value-free, or morally neutral: *Knowledge and Human Interests* by the philosopher Jürgen Habermas. Scientists had claimed—some still do—that scientific research is done for the sake of knowledge itself, not for the social consequences it might bring. As such, scientists' professional integrity hinges on impeccable research; they have no responsibility to the community for what problems—or even benefits—their research might lead to in the future. Habermas claimed that science might attempt to be objective but that an element of vested interest is always present. Society will fund only those projects it deems "valuable" for either further scientific progress, prestige, or profit. Political concerns, social biases, and fads within the scientific community often influence the funding of scientific research projects. Researchers often choose projects for similar reasons. Furthermore, the data selection (choosing research materials according to what the researcher finds relevant to the project) is influenced by the interests of the researcher—whether we like it or not. Habermas's point is that we may think science is conducted in a value-neutral way, but it is not. In addition, having seen what harm irresponsible scientists can cause to a society, wouldn't it be appropriate for scientists to conduct their research with a sense of obligation to the future? and for the community to monitor scientific research? Habermas himself has taken the issue further in a book from 2003, *The Future of Human Nature*. In a version, written in January 2002 specifically for the American bioethics debate as a postscript to the original German edition of 2001, Habermas argues that some forms of eugenics should be allowed, while others should be prohibited, based on Kant's principle of never treating a rational human being merely as a means to an end. Habermas refers to genetic manipulation decided by the parent of the child as **"liberal eugenics,"** staying within the British/European definition of liberal as the philosophy of hands-off/*laissez faire* politics implying individual, personal liberty (see Chapter 5). But reviewer Mary Rorty suggests that a better translation for an American audience would have been "libertarian eugenics," indicating that the parents have the full freedom to decide for their child. Habermas refers to genetic manipulation that *removes* predispositions toward illness for the sake of the child as **negative eugenics**, or also referred to as "therapeutic genetic intervention." This is the only kind of genetic intervention he approves of. **Positive eugenics**, in his terminology, is genetic manipulation that *adds* features to a child's DNA in order to alter its future, also referred to as "eugenic enhancement." He sees positive eugenics as a danger to the child's future options for self-determination, since the child's future has already in some way been determined by others. (You may want to go to pp. 304–307 and read about the concepts of *negative and positive rights* as they are used in a political context.) Whether genetic intervention should be permitted depends, theoretically, on whether the person who is being treated would, in the future, agree to and be thankful for the intervention. You'll recognize the obvious reference to Kant here: People should never be used merely as a means to an end, but should always be treated as an end in themselves. In Habermas's own words,

> As citizens in a democratic community, which must legally regulate practices of eugenic intervention, we surely will not be able to disburden ourselves from the task of anticipating the possible agreement or refusal of those affected by eugenic practices—not, in any event, if we want to permit therapeutic genetic interventions (or even selections) in cases of serious genetic disorders in the interests of the handicapped themselves. The pragmatic objections to the entire project of separating positive from negative eugenics which insist on the fluid boundary between both are based upon plausible examples. And it is as plausible to predict an effect of cumulative familiarization that will push the limits of tolerance for genetic interventions already regarded as "normal" ever further toward more and more demanding norms of health. However, there is a regulative idea that establishes a standard for determining a boundary, one which is surely in need of continuous interpretation, but which is not basically contestable: All therapeutic genetic interventions, including prenatal ones, must remain dependent on consent that is at least counterfactually attributed to those possibly affected by them.

On p. 297 we revisit Habermas's vision of genetic intervention. The problems raised by genetic manipulation are of course only in their infancy, and we take a closer look at such problems within genetic engineering, stem cell research, and cloning in upcoming pages. But medical doctors of the past had their own share of moral problems: An army surgeon would have to decide which of the wounded soldiers he should operate on and which ones should be left to die. A nineteenth-century family doctor might have to choose between saving a young mother dying in childbirth and saving the infant being born. But today, technology allows medical procedures that would have been unimaginable a few generations ago. Life can be prolonged artificially; pregnancies can be terminated with comparative safety for the woman; genetic engineering can save babies from a life of illness while they are still in the womb; women can give birth after menopause; stem cell research promises to cure diseases; and the Human Genome Project, completed in 2003, has put us on the threshold of a future in which we will have mapped human DNA to the point of understanding and preventing a vast array of medical problems. In addition, the old science fiction dream (or nightmare) of creating children completely outside the womb of the mother now looks as if it might become a reality, with recent experiments at Cornell University involving an artificial womb. With the increased knowledge, however, comes an increase in moral problems.

In this new era of medical possibilities, there are few established rules to guide those making the decisions. For that reason, the medical profession has a vested interest in supporting the creation of a viable set of ethical procedures to follow in the gray areas of decision making. If healthy babies can one day be created in an artificial womb environment, what will that mean for the concept of *viability,* a concept that is essential to the abortion debate? Viability means that a fetus could, with medical assistance, survive outside the mother's body; at present, viability is set at the third trimester (so abortion becomes problematic at this time because the fetus will at that point be considered a person). But if viability can be extended backward into the second and even first trimester, does that mean that an early fetus thus becomes a person, not just in a religious sense, but in a legal sense as well? And what will that mean for the abortion debate? Further questions abound when we turn to DNA-related issues: When we finally have the complete ability to interfere purposefully with the human DNA code, how much is too much interference? Should we interfere strictly to prevent terminal diseases, or is it acceptable to interfere with nature to determine the shape of the baby's nose, for example? And given the limited resources of medicine, who should benefit from organ transplants—first come, first served? The young, the wealthy, the famous? Those who have waited the longest?

In the seventeenth and eighteenth centuries, the early years of modern science, the moral sensitivity that accompanied research seems to have differed from that which prevails today. The main concern of scientists then was how to proceed with research without violating the values believed to be expressed in the Bible. In modern times, scientists have occasionally diverged from the path of ethical behavior. In Nazi Germany the ultimate value was success for the Party and the realization of that abstract concept, "the Fatherland." Scientists in Nazi Germany engaged in painful, humiliating, and eventually fatal experiments on human subjects, primarily women and children. Even now, we occasionally learn that, since World War II, scientists have subjected people to experimental medical procedures or have withheld treatment from them—without their knowledge or consent. The Tuskegee Syphilis Study is one of the best known of these experiments. Less well known is the forced sterilization of about 7,500 people in Virginia from 1924 to 1979 based on the ideology of *eugenics,* the presumed improvement of the human race. California was also active in the eugenics project, sterilizing over 20,000 people.

Most scientists and laypeople today would agree that knowledge can come at a price in suffering that is too high; yet we have a credo that says science is value-free/value-neutral: Scientific research is supposed to be objective, and scientists are not to be swayed by personal ambitions and preference. But does that mean they are not supposed to be swayed by ethical values either?

Genetic Engineering

Medical and general scientific researchers now have capabilities that could only be dreamed of in previous generations. We are only slowly developing a set of ethical rules by which to judge those capabilities, however. Genetic manipulation makes possible a future such as the one Aldous Huxley fantasized about in his *Brave New World,* one with a human race designed for special purposes. (See Box 7.2.) Agriculture has for several years been making use of genetic engineering to create disease-resistant crops. Milk and meat are being irradiated before they hit the stores. GMO (genetically manipulated organisms) is a controversial element of the twenty-first century, with perhaps the most controversial aspect being *transgenic* animals, such as pigs that have had human genes placed in them to facilitate organ transplants, cats that glow in the dark, and goats that have been genetically manipulated to contain spider silk proteins in their milk to be extracted and combined to produce materials of unprecedented strength. Although it may be to humankind's ultimate advantage to have access to these wonders, failure to contain such laboratory-generated genetic material, or failure to foresee the overall consequences of such genetic tinkering, could have disastrous results if no sense of ethics or social responsibility is instilled to guide the decision of researchers. After all, the infamous killer bees (which have now settled comfortably in the southwestern United States) are the result of a lab experiment gone out of control.

Box 7.2 A CULTURE OF QUICK FIXES?

Aldous Huxley's science fiction novel *Brave New World* from 1931 is famous for predicting that cloning of humans may be a future option, but even more timely is Huxley's prediction that humans in the future will be so oriented toward an easy life that they will, in essence, be unable to handle any form of emotional stress without medication. The drug of choice, *Soma,* is available to everyone, and it is considered a breach of decorum to handle one's own problems without being drugged into oblivion. The prediction rings true in several ways: For example, many people in this country now seek help from prescription drugs, not just from genuine, serious physical discomfort, but also from emotional stress; rather than working their way through certain emotional problems—the quest for the *quick fix.* Helped along by a powerful medical industry and pervasive advertising campaigns,

some doctors are all too willing to prescribe medication that will dull the pain of life in their patients. Depressed? Take a pill. Can't sleep? Take a pill. Too tense? Take a pill. Too relaxed? Take a pill. Some people are, of course, in genuine need of medication for severe mental stresses as well as physical pain; but our twenty-first-century culture seems to have lost its view toward long-term solutions. Ethicists bemoan the tendency: If we can't get instant gratification or solve a problem in short order, we lose our focus and our resolve. What's more, we lose touch with what is a *normal state of affairs*: life with some pain, some grief, some problems—which you then work through and incorporate into your life story or put behind you. In Chapter 13 we take a look at the philosophy of telling one's life story.

In Europe there is now a general mistrust of the entire idea of genetically engineered food products, or GMOs, from grain to farm animals. But what about genetically engineered humans?

In 2000 a little boy was born specifically in order to try to save the life of his older sister. Six-year-old Molly Nash had a congenital blood disease that would, in all probability, take her life before the age of ten. Doctors used "preimplantation genetic diagnosis" (PGD) to select an embryo in vitro that was both free of the disease and a good match as a blood cell donor. A month after the baby, Adam, was born, stem cells from his umbilical cord blood were transplanted into his sister. Molly was given the transplant while she held her little brother in her arms. Three months later she was allowed to return home from the hospital to her parents and her new brother, with her chances of survival improved to 85 percent. Out of the public eye until 2010 when she turned 15, she was then reported to be a healthy active girl with a normal family life, including a younger brother who knows he helped his sister.

Such are the possibilities opening up to us with genetic engineering. Then why are some people worried about the social consequences of this miracle cure? Because we, as a society, have not decided where we'd draw the line: Do we endeavor to create healthy babies, or should we go further, such as customizing babies according to their parents' specifications—or even to society's needs? Will babies be genetically engineered for sex, height, eye color, and skin color? And will those "designer babies" who have been genetically engineered be the new society's favorites, leaving the natural-born children behind as a new underclass? Molly and Adam Nash's doctor was quick to emphasize that the parents' use of PGD was acceptable because "they were not selecting in a eugenic sense," just looking for a donor baby. The doctors also outlined what they would consider unacceptable uses of the PGD technology, such as aborting selected implanted embryos just to collect tissue or putting the baby up for adoption after using its cord blood—in other words, using such babies merely as a means to an end, as Kant would say. (Another aspect of creative technology involves artificial intelligence, and Box 7.3 explores the specter of robots in our culture of the future.) However, a now-famous movie, *My Sister's Keeper* (2009), based on a 2004 book, outlines a darker scenario, where a baby is conceived specifically to become a kidney donor for her older sister who will otherwise die young–but when the older sister needs a new kidney, the younger sister, now 11, refuses to be a donor, because she, in effect, doesn't want to be treated "merely as a means to an end." The story explores concepts of self-sacrifice and moral responsibility, but at the same time it provides insight into the world at our doorstep where genetic engineering opens up entirely new scenarios and moral issues. These were the concerns during the first decade of the twenty-first century, but the American public has begun to relate to such issues in a somewhat less troubled and confused way: According to the Associated Press-NORC Center for Public Affairs Research, a 2018 poll shows that two-thirds of Americans support human gene editing that results in protection against diseases, but not the kind of gene editing that would allow parents to have their babies genetically engineered for intelligence or athletic ability, or even physical characteristics such as eye color. Also in 2018, Chinese researchers claimed to have altered the genes of twin girl babies in order to protect them from HIV. An Associated Press report on the poll concludes that,

> Indeed, the poll uncovers a lack of trust in science: About a third think this kind of gene editing will be used before it's adequately tested, as many scientists say happened in China. Nearly 9 in 10 people think the technology will be used for unethical reasons, including 52 percent who say this is very likely to happen.

Skepticism concerning scientific results as well as the motivation of governments using new technologies seems to be a solid part of our twenty-first century attitude. The *Crispr-Cas9* technology, which will presumably allow scientists to alter specific genes to prevent diseases, is already in use on a small group of test subjects, attempting to cure their cancer, but the results will not be made public for years to come.

Box 7.3 THE ROBOTS ARE COMING!

Sometimes the future arrives with a fanfare, and sometimes it sneaks up on you. When astrophysicist Stephen Hawking (1942–2018) announced in 2014 that we should beware of creating artificial intelligence (AI) and robots, because it might mean the end of the human race, some critics thought that Dr. Hawking might have watched *I, Robot* and *Terminator* a few times too many. For one thing, isn't the creation of robots many years into the future, if it indeed will ever happen? And for another, why would we assume that artificial beings of our own making would be a treat to us? As far as the first question goes, we already have robots, and they vacuum our floors, and even converse with elderly patients in nursing homes, giving them a (false) sense of comfort. Children who are allergic to dogs (or who live in no-pets apartments) can have a dog-bot, and can teach it

tricks. An industry of *sex-bots*, robots for sex, is already in the making, and some people already seem more comfortable about the idea of having sex with a machine than having sex with another human being. We have refrigerators that communicate with the supermarket about when we're going to need more milk, eggs, and cheese. We have cars that are run by computers—and in 2015, the future did arrive with a fanfare, because we saw the first self-driving cars on our roads (one of them collided with a bus in Silicon Valley, CA), and ABI, a marketing firm, predicted in 2018 that by 2025 there will be 8 million self-driving cars on the road, driver-operated as well as fully driverless. We have drones buzzing around in our airspace, creating new legal problems, and Amazon.com is delivering books and goods per drone. The flying car may actually not be far away, and it will probably be driverless. And Boston Dynamics has announced the production of robots to take on heavy manual labor. The existing robots are of course not self-aware at this point, and the *I, Robot* rebellion against humans seems unlikely at this point, but that takes us to the other question—why worry? Well, all you have to do is think back to Chapter 2 and the Golem stories. Our electronic devices, such as Alexa and Google, are already recording the sounds in our homes, and legal minds are speculating that not only should such recordings be hard to obtain by the courts, but perhaps the concept of *free speech* should even be included as a right of robots. It is an ancient dark fantasy of humans to worry about uncontrollable consequences of our creations—but with an additional letter from 2015, signed by Hawking, the entrepreneur Elon Musk and other scientists focusing specifically on the potential of robots to turn weapons on humans, the science fiction scenarios are brought into the realm of a plausible, dystopic future (see Chapter 2). AI weapons can be inexpensive and readily available around the globe, says the statement:

"The key question for humanity today is whether to start a global AI arms race or to prevent it from starting. If any major military power pushes ahead with AI weapon development, a global arms race is virtually inevitable, and the endpoint of this technological trajectory is obvious: autonomous weapons will become the Kalashnikovs of tomorrow."

The robotic future may have sneaked up on us, but it is here. Frequently, a philosophical discussion will focus on the rights of these artificial beings who may someday achieve self-awareness (and that is what the films *Blade Runner* and *Ex Machina* focus on in the Narrative section), but it may also be time for us to think about protecting ourselves from our own creations, as foreshadowed by science fiction stories.

Stem Cell Research

Although still controversial to many, stem cell research holds great promise as a means of repairing and replacing damaged organs. Stem cells are general cells, not yet specialized, and they apparently have the capacity to become any organ in the body, with the intervention of medical science; these cells can then be used to repair or replace sick organs in a person. The controversy arises from the practice of harvesting and cloning stem cells from *embryos,* which involves taking the life of the embryo. If one is against abortion at any time during pregnancy because one considers the embryo a person from conception, one will also be against any form of stem cell research involving human embryos. However, contrary to what some people think, stem cells can't be harvested from aborted fetuses (yet) because they are too old; the stem cells have to be harvested within the first two weeks of fetal development at the zygote stage. Those who view early abortion as a reasonable option for women generally take little moral issue with the notion of zygotes being harvested and used for research; but for many who find the notion of taking the lives of fetuses objectionable, the stem cell question is particularly challenging—because even if one views the life of a fetus as intrinsically valuable, one also has to consider the importance of born humans who have lives, and people who love them, and who could be saved from a premature death with stem cell research. While restricted under the Bush administration, stem cell research was released from the federal restrictions by the Obama administration in 2009, but in June 2019 the research into fetal tissue by government scientists was again restricted, this time by the Trump administration. However, the existing research has begun to yield results; the first experiments attempting to cure spinal cord injuries were commenced in 2010 based on successful experiments on rats, and tentative results in 2011 seemed positive. Researchers also hope to be able to cure some forms of blindness through stem cell research, and in 2016 British researchers reported having restored eyesight to rabbits through stem cell growth and implantation of a cornea; clinical trials on humans yielded their first results in 2018, when two patients suffering from age-related macular degeneration had their eyesight restored; this was considered a major breakthrough in fighting a dreaded disease, and an "off-the-shelf" treatment is predicted to be available within a few years. In addition, stem cells appear to be obtainable from sources other than embryos such as skin tissue, bypassing the controversy of taking the life of an embryo.

While stem cell research was moving ahead in the United States, the European Union decided, in the fall of 2011, to ban research resulting in the death of the embryo. The impact of this on European research has yet to be seen, including a particularly controversial type of research conducted in the United Kingdom: In 2008 the last legal obstacles to a new kind of research were removed: *Human-animal hybrid stem cells* would be created for the purpose of studying genetic diseases and eventually growing new tissue in the lab; the embryos would be destroyed after two weeks and would not be implanted in a surrogate womb. British medical teams have expressed excitement about this development, but others, including religious groups, have found the development ethically repugnant and scientifically unnecessary.

One of the most controversial scientific experiments in the U.S. has been the development of minibrains, clusters of lab-grown human brain stem cells, for the purpose of understanding early brain development. However, in 2019 it was reported that the little brain clusters were not developing as normal brains would, appearing "stressed." Even so, the study is ongoing. However, ultimate goal of stem cell research is not knowledge for the sake of knowledge; it is curing illness and prolonging life. This process involves what is known as *therapeutic cloning,* our next topic.

Therapeutic and Reproductive Cloning

The three areas of genetic engineering, stem cell research, and cloning are often confused, and there are in fact overlapping areas between the three, but the primary goals of these methods are different. *Genetic engineering* consists in altering/manipulating a person's DNA, either during his or her lifetime or before birth, to avoid certain congenital problems or to enhance a certain biological trait. As we have seen, *stem cell research* allows for stem cells to be used in organ repair. *Cloning* involves creating more individuals, identical to the first one. The overlapping comes into the picture with the stem cells: To create more stem cells, the cells have to be cloned. That means that they are chemically manipulated so that they create duplicates of themselves—in other words, twins. The question is, what are these duplicates used for? That depends on whether we're talking about *therapeutic* or *reproductive cloning.* Therapeutic cloning involves duplicating stem cells to insert them into an organ, or regrow the organ, to improve a person's health or to save his or her life. It is a form of medical *therapy,* in other words. The California stem cell research program is oriented exclusively toward therapeutic cloning, a means to the end of finding cures for human illnesses.

The phenomenon of *reproductive cloning* is far more controversial, because it involves a duplication of an entire individual, not just cells. The excitement and concerns over reproductive cloning began in 1994, with the announcement that researchers had successfully split a fertilized (but nonviable) human ovum into twins (which is what happens naturally to produce identical twins). But since then the cloning issue has taken off with a speed not predicted even by science fiction authors: In rapid succession, labs around the world have succeeded in cloning sheep, calves, goats, mice, dogs, cats, and wolves, using a variety of techniques, including creating a copy of an adult individual using a cell from that individual with a technique pioneered by the creators of Dolly the sheep—raising the specter of genderless reproduction. (See Box 7.4.)

Box 7.4 BRAVE NEW WORLD: THE SPECTER OF DESIGNER HUMANS

As you'll remember from Chapter 2 and Box 7.2, science fiction has experimented with the notion of an artificially designed humanity since Aldous Huxley's *Brave New World* (1931). Huxley speculated that humans would be able to clone other humans within six hundred years, but the ability was on the horizon already before the end of Huxley's own century. In the third decade of the twenty-first century, the technique is available and known as CRISPR, clustered regularly interspaced short palindromic repeats, a natural antiviral defense mechanism which researchers can use to deliver new genetic information to cells, or in other words: to edit DNA. But what is it that we fear so much from the idea of humans creating a new twist to humanity in the lab? The fears are many and varied. One type of anguish arises from a *religious foundation:* Only God is supposed to create life, and types of life, and the fear is that if we play God and create human variations deliberately, we have somehow transgressed and will be punished, as Dr. Frankenstein was punished for creating his monster. Another is that we may be *unleashing powers* that we will lose control over, also in the manner of Frankenstein's monster: New human variations may let loose diseases and deformities that we haven't foreseen (cloned mice became obese, and cloned sheep were born with premature aging), or the new breed may outcompete the garden-variety human being. But a third worry is extremely concrete and down-to-earth: that a designer variation of humans will lead to discrimination. This could take the form of discrimination against the new breed, which could end up being treated like a slave population (as in the film classic *Blade Runner,* see the Narrative section), or of discrimination against the part of the population who has *not* been genetically altered (as in the film *Gattaca,* in the Narrative

section). A discriminatory side effect of doing DNA profiling was, in fact, anticipated in the 1990s by federal legislation and in 2008 Congress passed a bill prohibiting insurance companies and workplaces from using genetic tests to discriminate against persons based on the risks inherent in their DNA profile. An increased risk of cancer or heart disease should not hurt a person's chances of obtaining employment or insurance—but it isn't hard to imagine a future where such rules could be sidestepped.

But now new worlds of possibilities are on the horizon: First, **cognitive enhancement.** We are already used to drinking a cup of coffee or some stronger caffeine drink to stay awake and alert. A variety of drugs exist to make people feel hyper, mellow, aggressive, visionary, and so forth, and when taken for nonmedical purposes they are mostly illegal. But what if our very intelligence could be enhanced through drugs or genetic manipulation? Brain-boosting drugs may seem like the thing to consider before taking a final exam, but should we be cautious because of the possible side effects, or social consequences (utilitarian concerns), or because it wouldn't be *right* (a Kantian concern)?

In 2019 Chinese and American researchers worked together, creating intelligently enhanced monkeys by inserting a gene, Microcephalin, into 11 rhesus monkeys. The purpose of the experiment was to understand human intelligence better, but the moral implications reach all the way to concerns over a *Planet of the Apes*-kind of future, as well as human social and political consequences.

Add to that the possibility of what is now called **moral enhancement:** new research into drugs that can manipulate people's behavior morally, increasing the feeling of belonging to a group, reducing aggression toward other groups, and feeling more generous and selfless. The possibilities of using such drugs in the criminal justice system as part of a criminal's rehabilitation program are being explored. But, ask the ethicists, what use is it if these feelings are drug-induced and not genuine? Do they have any moral value if they come in a little pill and are perhaps even court-mandated as a form of punishment or preemptive treatment of violent criminals? Would we feel grateful for someone who is helpful because he or she receives brain-altering therapy? Would we want to marry someone who feels he or she loves us because they've taken a pill that makes them feel in love? In other words, don't we want to respond to other people's feelings because we assume (1) those feelings are *genuine*, and (2) that people are willing to take responsibility for actions they have chosen to undertake of *their own free will*? Proponents of such enhancement programs respond with a simple question: But wouldn't you rather live in a world where people are friendlier and less violent? You can evaluate such approaches on your own in terms of whether they are predominantly utilitarian or Kantian.

Xinhua News Agency/Newscom

In 2019 a celebrated Chinese police sniffer dog, Huahuangma, was cloned, and the puppy, Kunxun, underwent police training. The potential for cloning working animals as well as pets seems to be limitless, as long as the buyers of the animal realize that they are only getting a genetic copy, not a trained animal whose behavior matches the original, unless every effort is made to duplicate the training of the original animal.

In 2004 we had the first report of a successful cloning of a cat for commercial purposes: Not the first cat to be cloned, this little kitty was the first *made-to-order* clone. It cost her owner $50,000. In 2015, a British couple paid nearly $100,000 for the successful cloning of their deceased Boxer Dylan. Two puppies were created from his DNA by a South Korean pet cloning company. In February 2016, the couple went to South Korea and picked up their two puppies who indeed looked just like Dylan. And in 2019, Chinese researchers announced that they had cloned a top police sniffer dog, 7-year old Kunming wolfdog Huahuangma, resulting in a genetically near-identical puppy, Kunxun, who at the age of 3 months had already started intense police training to see if Huahuangma's talent for K-9 police work has carried over. The intention is, supposedly, to "mass-produce" top police dogs if the experiment is a success.

The notion of cloning pets and working dogs in particular doesn't seem nearly as alien or outlandish as it did a decade ago, even if the price is still out of most pet-lovers' reach. The world of horse racing expects that cloning of particular race horses will become big business in the future. And Korean researchers announced a few years ago that they intended to clone a now-extinct Ice-age lion based on viable, retrieved DNA, which opens up a whole new aspect of cloning extinct animals—a Jurassic World in the making.

But we shouldn't forget that the animal/pet-cloning venture has another side to it: We may be able to get our pets or race horse champions back in the flesh, so to speak, but we can't replicate their spirit or personality, because that would take duplication of the formative experiences of the original animal—meaning, we would need to replicate their childhood. Living beings don't just consist of their DNA but also are the sum of their experiences—and that goes for humans too. There are lessons to be learned about the entire notion of cloning: To get the "same" individual as its DNA donor, we would have to create a completely identical environment for the individual to grow up in—*nature* plus *nurture.* And even if that were accomplished, we would have to factor in what we might call *situation awareness,* what some would call *free will* (see Chapter 4), at least for humans: When a cloned child finds out he or she has been cloned, will he or she decide to be as similar as, or as different from, the original as possible? I would assume the latter, but you never know. This means that very little can, in fact, be predicted about how a clone might develop as an adult.

There is widespread reluctance to envision *human* reproductive cloning, and it is condemned in most countries, although a successful human cloning has yet to be announced and verified. The general assumption has been that scientists who attempt to clone humans for reproductive purposes are playing God and that there is no acceptable reason why anyone would want himself or herself cloned. Some have questioned the entire idea of human cloning from a religious point of view and have asked whether cloned children will have souls. One might even trace the fear of cloning all the way back in time to the fear of the artificial human being which you read about in Chapter 2, from the ancient Jewish concept of the Golem through the medieval fears of magically created tiny people or "homunculi" all the way to Frankenstein's monster and a myriad of sci-fi stories of robots rebelling against their makers. The assumption here has generally been that such beings have no souls, but they are creatures of fiction. What about real-life clones created by nature—identical twins, triplets, and quadruplets? Scientists have responded that if twins have individual souls (which is, of course, a matter of faith, not of science), then surely clones will have their own individual souls too. Other arguments against cloning include these:

- Overpopulation threatens the planet as it is, so why add more people artificially?
- Why create people who, as copies of someone else, will have to struggle to find their identity?
- Clones might be considered expendable people, a new slave population—or perhaps so valuable that they would become a preferred population group. In other words, cloning might lead to a new form of discrimination.
- Animal cloning has led to the birth of individuals with abnormal physical traits. Aren't we risking the same thing making human clones?

Those are good questions, but before we become too "sciento-phobic," we should reconsider the issue. What does reproductive cloning entail? Some imagine that a cloned embryo can be frozen and later "activated" for spare parts. Others focus on human cloning as the answer to being childless. But why would anyone want to have himself or herself cloned? Why not opt for adopting an already existing child who needs a home? Well, for some people the whole point is to have a child who is *related* to them, and cloning would provide that. Also, for a clone to be the offspring of two parents instead of just one of them; research is even in place now that allows for a combination of *three* parents. Science is anticipating social changes—or social changes have opened the door for the application of new developments in science. The reasons people want babies are complex: Some people want children so they can love them and raise them to be good citizens; others want an additional hand on the farm, an heir to their name, a tax write-off, or a status symbol to parade in front of their friends. We have yet to set up legal rules to determine what are *good* reasons to have children (although we already have an idea of which reasons count as *morally* good reasons). Excluding some prospective parents from parenthood because they'd like a kid who looks like themselves will exclude many more people than those lined up to be cloned. Some say, If it can be done, it will be done, so why make an issue of it? Supply and demand will rule! An alternative approach probably lies somewhere in the middle: The day will indeed come when we have human clones, from occasional individuals created to carry on the family name or be the bearer of the cherished face of a departed loved one to the nightmare "Brave New World" scenario of mass-produced "worker ants." We need to think carefully about the implications of this technology for society and about the need for legislation. We have to consider the differ-

360b/Shutterstock

Jürgen Habermas (born 1929), German philosopher and sociologist. Always engaged in the ethics of society and politics, he has been called "the last European," fighting for the ideals of the European Union which he sees as dwindling. He is the first major philosopher to have pointed out that science, despite its assumed objectivity, is not value-neutral. Major works include *Knowledge and Human Interests* (1968), *Moral Consciousness and Communicative Action* (1983), *The Future of Human Nature* (2003), and *The Crisis of the European Union* (2012).

ence between a cloned child who would be loved and cared for by its parents and one who might be used or enslaved for society's purposes. Perhaps the bottom line, as with any planning involving a child, is whether that child can reasonably expect a stable, loving home—not the circumstances of the child's conception. There is a wide variety of issues for legislators and ethicists to consider in the twenty-first century.

Finally, a word from the original author of the idea that science can't be value-free, Jürgen Habermas. As you read on p. 287, he contributed to the debate about genetic manipulation in a lecture from 2000 which was then expanded into a publication in Germany, and translated into English in 2003 with added material as *The Future of Human Nature*. The German attitude toward such subjects reflects the collective memories of the Holocaust and its reduction of human beings to "merely a means to an end," and Germany now has a tradition of strict legislation against any form of genetic manipulation. Habermas has himself been a powerful voice against such research for years, but in his 2003 book he reveals a somewhat modified attitude. As you saw earlier, genetic interventions (negative eugenics) could help individuals overcome physical/health obstacles, and be of the kind that a person would opt for if you could ask them, so with caution, Habermas could allow for such research if it benefits the person whose genes are being interfered with. Genetic enhancements (positive eugenics), on the other hand, would determine a person's future life without their consent and lock them into a life where, essentially, they would be used as a part of other people's agenda, and their very humanity might be altered, which means that their whole engagement in the world as a moral person might be terminated, so Habermas warns against such research. As a reviewer of his book, Mary V. Rorty, has remarked, such caution seems extreme to an American reader these days, and may in fact blind us to the possibility that one can be something other than a human being and still have ethics as well as morals—such as some of the science fiction characters of *Star Trek*. Furthermore, on a more down-to-earth level, Habermas's view precludes any research whatsoever on embryos, because they will then be treated as a means to an end, and that would put an end to embryonic stem cell research and not only reproductive cloning, but also any kind of therapeutic cloning, as well as selecting for/genetically engineering specific traits in human fetuses. If Habermas's moral vision of permissible research had been in effect in the nineteen nineties, Molly Nash would probably not have been able to celebrate her 15th birthday. In the Narratives section the film *Gattaca* deals with the subject of embryonic enhancement.

Questions of Rights and Equality

We have already referred to the concept of rights several times; now we are going to take a closer look at what it entails. In Western culture today, it is generally assumed that all people have rights; the nature and extension of those rights is continually being disputed, however. In the seventeenth century some European thinkers began to advocate the idea of *natural rights,* and that idea became very important in the eighteenth century with its many social revolutions. A natural right was defined as a right one was born with as a human being (or as a male human being, as it was most often argued). Sometimes the concept of natural rights is intended as **descriptive** (as in, "We are actually born with rights"), and sometimes its intention is **normative** ("We ought to have such rights because we are human"). A powerful theory of natural rights comes from Thomas Hobbes, whom you met in Chapter 4. For Hobbes (1588–1679), as you may remember, laws and moral rules have no place prior to a social contract, in the "State of Nature," but even before the contract there is the *natural right* and the *natural law:* The natural right is the right for anyone to do what it takes to stay alive, and the natural law is a built-in prohibition against doing harm to ourselves. Once we have entered into a social contract, the natural right becomes modified, because social and moral laws now kick in for mutual self-protection; but in Hobbes's political philosophy, we never give up our right to defend ourselves and we never have to consent to actions that will harm us, even under the reign of an absolute monarch. A generation later the British philosopher John Locke (1632–1704) introduced his version of the natural rights concept: Anyone, even in the State of Nature, has three inalienable rights of nature, based on our very nature as rational beings: the rights to *life, liberty,* and *property.* Later in this chapter we return to Locke's theory of natural rights. But at the end of the 1700s, the utilitarian Jeremy Bentham had his doubts about the concept of natural rights. His response to the Declaration of the Rights of Man (1789) of the French Revolution—and implicitly also to the American Declaration of Independence (1776)—was that all men are obviously *not* born free, and they are *not* born or do not remain equal in rights. (Nor should they—someone has to give the orders, he says. We can't have associations between equal members, such as equality in marriage—Bentham believed that would never work out!) People are not born with rights, because the concept of rights is a human invention and does not occur in nature. One might wish it did, he says, but it doesn't. So for Bentham, the concept of natural rights is "nonsense upon stilts." That doesn't mean we can't operate with the concept of rights though; we must just recognize it as a legal principle (not a natural one) and identify its goal as being the creation of as happy a society as possible—in other words, maximizing happiness for the maximum number of people (the basic utilitarian principle).

From Chapter 5, you'll remember John Stuart Mill's insistence that there ought to be such a thing as a personal right to be left alone if you are not harming anybody else (the "harm principle"). As in so many other areas, Mill is here redefining utilitarianism from within, but he still remains a utilitarian; his ultimate reason for setting limits on government involvement in people's private affairs is the overall happiness of the population. There is no such thing as a concept of "rights" or "justice" for its own sake in utilitarianism, even in Mill's version: The ultimate goal is still the general happiness, not an abstract principle of justice. We have to go to another theory to find a defense of the concept of rights for their own sake, not for what good social consequences may come of enforcing them: to Kant's deontology. As you have read in Chapter 6, he insists that human beings are ends in themselves and may not be treated merely as a means to an end. That means that even if treating a person as a means to an end might be useful for the majority in a society, it is still not permissible to do so. Good overall consequences for a majority do not provide a sufficient reason to do away with the rule that every person deserves respect. The question of whether decisions affecting many people in a society should be made on the basis of social utility or individual rights is still very much part of the contemporary debate, as we shall see.

What Is Equality?

When we try to define equality, we sometimes feel as much confusion as Saint Augustine did in trying to define time: "When you don't ask me, I know what it is; when you ask me, I don't know." We tend to think equality has something to do with treating everybody the same way—but since all people are not the same, or even similar, how can that be fair? And we know that equality and fairness are supposed to be linked. There are actually several definitions of equality:

1. **Fundamental equality** is the concept we know from the American Declaration of Independence and the French Declaration of the Rights of Man and of the Citizen. The American Declaration reads, "We hold these truths to be self-evident, that all men are created equal, that they are endowed by their Creator with certain unalienable Rights, that among these are Life, Liberty, and the pursuit of Happiness." The French Declaration begins, "All men are by nature free and equal in respect of their rights." However, these declarations do not say that people *are* factually equal—such as equally tall, strong, pretty, or smart—just that people *should be treated as* equals by their government and their legal system: no special privileges, just an entitlement to respect and consideration as human beings.

2. **Social equality** refers to the idea of people being equal within a social setting, such as politics or the economy. Today, most Western political theories are in tune with the idea of fundamental equality, but what exactly social equality (and indeed "people") can mean is variable: The French Revolution did not see women as socially or politically equal with men, and neither did the American Declaration of Independence, although Thomas Jefferson himself has been quoted as being opposed to viewing women as second-class citizens or as property. People of color were generally not considered included in the social equality of the Declaration of Independence either, although Jefferson seemed to have had some second thoughts about that too. Social equality today is generally obtained through such formal rights as the right to vote and to stand for public office; however, that doesn't mean that everyone's social status or income is supposed to be equal.

3. **Equal treatment for equals** is an ancient idea, in glaring contradiction to the fundamental equality principle; we find it in Aristotle's *Politics*. Justice means treating people of the same, usually social, group in the same way. But since we don't know from the definition what it would take to be considered an "equal," it is generally assumed to be an elitist principle with no underlying intent to recognize equality as a fundamental human right.

4. **The social equity principle:** Lately the term *equity* has been heard in the debate about social justice and fairness, especially within the world of American education. It is often presumed to mean the same as *equality*—just a more modern, updated version—but there is a substantial difference between the two terms. As we have seen, Fundamental Equality has everything to do with social goods and opportunities

being equally available to citizens, whoever they may be, but *social equity* (not to be confused with other forms of equity, such as financial equity) has sometimes been described as the principle of "treating equals equally and unequals unequally." That may sound like elitism and bigotry, but it is actually meant to indicate quite the opposite: Creating a "level playing field." Let us say that "equals" according to this definition are people who are in a similar situation under similar circumstances. Imagine the freeway at rush hour: We are all out there in our cars, either moving at high speeds or simply stuck. We don't know one another, but we all deserve respect and decent treatment from one another, no more and no less. Now imagine a person trying to change lanes so he can reach the next exit, because he has some kind of emergency—a flat tire, a sick passenger perhaps. He signals, and you let him go in front of you. Because of his situation he is in fact an "unequal," in special need of assistance. Now imagine that someone else up ahead is impatient and wants to get off the freeway, so she cuts in front of someone else and causes him to brake hard, resulting in a couple of fender benders that include your car. Now that person has also become an "unequal" and deserves special, "unequal" treatment that others don't get unless they have transgressed: punishment. So the principle states that under ordinary circumstances we are just "equals" and deserve the usual decent treatment and respect. When someone has special needs, he or she becomes someone who needs assistance to reach the level of those who are "equals." And when someone breaks the rules, he or she also becomes an unequal and deserves special punishment, according to the principle. However, within the application of the social equity principle we also find a discussion of whether punishment is the right way to approach such a situation, or whether *rehabilitation* in the form of training and education might not be a better path to equality. (See the later section on criminal justice.) According to some scholars, the social equity principle is in harmony with the fundamental equality principle, but it is more elaborate because it recognizes that we sometimes have special needs or sometimes transgress and so sometimes deserve special treatment. The principle supports affirmative action, if people who have experienced the effects of discrimination are considered to be "unequals" in the sense that the "playing field" is not yet level and that some "players" need special assistance before everyone on the field will actually have equal opportunities. However, the risk is that there is no clear definition of the criteria under which someone might need assistance, and critics have pointed out that anyone deemed to be somehow infringing on other people's "equality" may be classified, temporarily or permanently, as an "unequal" whose services, or assets, might be enlisted or even confiscated in the cause of the common good. For some critics, the concept of *redistribution of wealth* is a good example of the principle of "treating unequals unequally" for the sake of overall equity.

One thing the principle of equality in any version usually does *not* imply is *sameness.* What would it be like if we were required to treat others and to be treated in exactly the same way, even if we are physically different? Kurt Vonnegut's short story "Harrison Bergeron" (1970) is a scathing parody of a future society in which it is politically incorrect (years before the term became popular) to be smarter, stronger, or more beautiful than anyone else. In Bergeron's future the smart people wear caps with buzzers that prevent them from thinking a thought through; the beautiful people wear bags over their heads so the less-than-pretty people won't feel bad. Dancers are weighed down with lead so ungraceful people won't feel left out, and strong people wear many bags of lead so they won't have an advantage over the weaker ones. Vonnegut doesn't write about how the truly disabled might feel about such artificial disabling or about what constitutes "normal" sameness, but the story does effectively question the identification of sameness and equality. And perhaps inadvertently, it illustrates an extreme version of the principle of social equity 50 years before it became the preferred pathway toward social equality in certain contexts.

Dworkin: Rights Can't Be Traded for Benefits

A thinker who used Kant's approach to the issue of rights was the American philosopher Ronald Dworkin (1931–2013), professor at the New York University School of Law and the University College of London (the place where Bentham sits in his mahogany closet). For more than three decades, Dworkin contributed to the debate about social rights and equality; some of his most famous works include *Taking Rights Seriously* (1977) and *Freedom's Law* (1996), and he frequently weighed in on current issues in *The New York Review of Books*. For Dworkin, the importance of rights becomes apparent precisely at the moment when social considerations might justify the violation of those rights; we may think that our rights are protected by the Constitution, but there is such a thing as a constitutional amendment. Could we imagine a situation so serious that horrible social consequences will ensue if certain rights are not set aside for the common good? In other words, when push comes to shove, should we adopt a utilitarian view that social benefits outweigh the rights of the individual, or should we, along with Kant, hold the rights of the individual higher than social benefits? Dworkin asks us to consider an example: the right to free speech. Suppose someone, angered by some personal or collective experience, gets up and speaks in public, in an emotional manner, advocating violence as a way to secure political equality. Suppose the emotional speech starts a riot, and suppose people get hurt or even killed. Many would say that if such a situation can be prevented by making such a type of speech illegal, then that is the course we have to take. Dworkin would not. He argued that we can use one of two models for our political thinking about rights:

1. The first model says we have to find a balance between the rights of the individual and the demands of society. If the government *infringes* on a right, it does the individual wrong; but if it *inflates* a right, it does the community wrong (by depriving it of some benefit, such as safe streets). So we should steer a middle course and take each situation on a case-by-case basis. Well-behaved discussion groups can have more freedom of speech than unruly demonstrators because there is more social risk involved in the demonstration. This model of balancing the public interest against personal claims sounds reasonable, but it is not, says Dworkin. If we adopt the model, he asserts, we will have given up on two very important ideas: One is the idea of human dignity (Kant would say, Don't treat people merely as means), and the other is the idea of political equality (if one person has a certain freedom, then all persons should have that freedom, regardless of the effect on the general good). In Dworkin's words (from his book *Taking Rights Seriously*):

   So if rights make sense at all, then the invasion of a relatively important right must be a very serious matter. It means treating a man as less than a man, or as less worthy of concern than other men . . . then it must be wrong to say that inflating rights is as serious as invading them.

   So we can't balance individual rights against social goods; what we *can* do is balance individual rights against each other when the claims collide, because then each individual still retains his or her dignity. But the best proof that the first model doesn't work, says Dworkin, is that it is *not* applied in actual cases in which the stakes for the individual are the highest: in criminal processes. Social benefits don't determine the outcome of a trial. The adage says, It is better that many guilty people go free than that one innocent person be punished, and this is Dworkin's choice for his second model.

2. The second model says that invading a right is far worse than inflating it. If people are prevented from expressing themselves freely and in any way they like, then that is an assault on human autonomy, and all the more so if the subject of a speech is morally important to the speaker. The government might actually be allowed to step in only if the consequences of such a speech would very certainly be grave. But when is anyone that certain? According to Dworkin, the risk involved is speculative; someone's right to free speech should not be abridged just because someone else might harm others as a result of that speech. This is the only way to protect the rights of individuals and in particular the rights of the few against the many. For a discussion of Dworkin's model and the second amendment, see Box 7.5.

Box 7.5 DWORKIN'S MODEL AND THE SECOND AMENDMENT

Dworkin's discussion involving his two models is directed specifically toward the First Amendment, which includes the right to free speech. His first model says we have to find a balance between the right of the individual and the needs of the community, and his second model (which he favors) says that invading or restricting a right for the sake of the needs of the community is wrong and should be done only in very rare cases. In the chapter text you find an analysis of the second model and freedom of speech—but how might Dworkin's model work if we apply it to the Second Amendment, the right to bear arms? The Second Amendment says that "a well-regulated Militia being necessary to the security of a free State, the right of the people to keep and bear Arms shall not be infringed." This amendment has been considered controversial for decades; for many liberals the right to bear arms is (1) outdated, (2) dangerous, and (3) a misinterpretation of the Bill of Rights, which, according to some interpreters, says only that militia members should have the right to be armed. For many moderates and conservatives, there is no doubt, however, that the amendment addresses individuals ("the people") and their right to bear arms, not just

militia members. This interpretation is, supposedly, the classical one before the twentieth century and was upheld by the Supreme Court in the Heller Decision of 2008. Furthermore, many supporters of the Second Amendment quote Aristotle: "Both oligarch and tyrant mistrust the people, and therefore deprive them of their arms." Regardless of what Dworkin might have said about the right to gun ownership per se, how would his principle apply to the Second Amendment? If we apply the *first model,* balancing the right to own guns with the need of the community for security, Dworkin would have to conclude that individual rights shouldn't be balanced against social goods—individual rights can be balanced only against other individual rights. His *second model* would state it in even stronger terms: Someone's right to bear arms should not be abridged just because someone else might choose to harm others because of that right. Would this example of Dworkin's principle used on another amendment make you agree with his principle all the more, or less? In Chapter 13 you will find a discussion of gun rights vs. gun control.

Dworkin seems to imply that freedom of speech (which might lead to violence) is typically used to defend the idea of human dignity; in other words, most decent people might agree with the content of the speech, if not with its emotional character. That may not always be the case. You might want to consider Dworkin's second model in the scenario of an inflammatory racist hate speech being delivered on your campus or on TV. Would you say that the right of the speaker to express a personal opinion is more important than the harmful effects on the group being targeted for hatred or even the harmful effects on the audience being stirred up? The demonstrations Dworkin referred to in his 1977 book were, in particular, the demonstrations (with subsequent riots) against the Vietnam War in the late sixties and early seventies, but if a principle is a principle, it should hold up under any kind of scenario. And freedom of speech is, of course, not just a matter of the actual physical presence of a speaker in front of a group of people—the greater audience in front of the TV as well as today's interactive online audience need to be included also. (In Chapter 13 we address the issue of *free speech and the media,* with an eye to recent controversies.)

According to Dworkin's principle, the free speech of the second model should extend to speakers and demonstrators in general. Demonstrations should be allowed to take place because the rights of demonstrators should not be invaded. (The First Amendment allows not only freedom of *speech* but also freedom of *assembly*.) But the Constitution grants no right to create a public disturbance. So critics of Dworkin's second model suggest a middle course: Certainly we have freedom of speech and freedom of assembly—but that doesn't entail an automatic police permit to march in a demonstration. So let those who want to exercise their freedom of speech assemble someplace, in a hall or on a street corner, but limit the possibility of harm to the public if the issue is volatile. The tendency in our society is increasingly to move toward protection of the public rather than protection of the individual's right to freedom of speech, assembly, or movement. Some years ago judges were generally reluctant to issue restraining orders against domestic abusers because of their right to freedom of movement; today such restraining orders are much more common. You might want to argue about rights within this scenario from the viewpoints of Dworkin and John Stuart Mill. Box 7.6 further explores the concept of civil rights versus the security of citizens.

Box 7.6 CIVIL LIBERTIES VERSUS SECURITY

In the fall of 2001, as a step in the war against terrorism, Congress passed the U.S.A. Patriot Act of 2001, directed at preventing future terrorism through increased powers of wiretapping, including "roving wiretaps" that zero in on a person rather than a telephone number, and intercepting e-mails, faxes, and so on. The purpose was to find and arrest any terrorist, foreign or domestic, who might threaten the security of U.S. citizens at home and abroad. In the wake of September 11, 2001 such measures seemed welcome and reasonable to many, but there were also voices who warned that they might undermine our civil liberties.

Interestingly, those voices have come from both the Left and the Right within American politics: Liberals saw these measures as a threat to political dissidents in an era of conservative government. Conservatives saw them as a danger to individual freedom—especially under some possible future liberal administration. And both pointed out that it in effect undermined the Fourth Amendment of the Bill of Rights, the search-and-seizure amendment, which says officers have to demonstrate *probable cause* (that a crime has been/is being committed) before entering and searching the premises of a citizen without that citizen's permission. The Patriot Act was intended to be in effect for four years, until 2005. In March 2006 a reauthorization bill was signed into law by President Bush, and in 2011 President Obama extended three sections of the Act by another four years: roving wiretaps, library records, and surveillance of possible terrorist loners. In 2015, the Patriot Act expired, but was restored until the end of 2019, except for the phone data collection program. At the end of 2019, the program was again extended.

In addition, September 11 inspired sweeping measures to try foreign terrorists in military tribunals, so as to keep the proceedings—and especially the evidence—secret and thus out of reach of other terrorists.

How far are we willing to go in giving up our civil liberties, and even our constitutional rights, to obtain security? What are we willing to do? In the days following September 11, many Americans would have said, "Anything, just so we're safe," but others have reminded us that having an open, free society carries with it some inherent risks. If we put up too many safeguards to protect our society, we may lose our freedoms in the process. Benjamin Franklin wrote, "Those who would give up essential liberty to obtain a little temporary safety deserve neither liberty nor safety." It is not unusual, however, for a country to enact strict legal measures in wartime that then will be lifted when the war is over.

In the aftermath of the terror attack in San Bernardino on December 2, 2015, a new question of privacy versus security arose: the cellphone of one of the deceased terrorists was assumed to contain information of other terrorist actions and contacts, but the phone could not be unlocked by the FBI without the help of Apple—and Apple refused to cooperate and appealed a court order demanding it assist the Federal government. The rationale was that if

that right were to be lost, it might open up further government intrusions into the lives of private citizens. The FBI sought access to the phone, as a means of protecting citizens from harm and FBI investigators were eventually able to open the cell phone without Apple's assistance. Further issues concerning electronic records of personal information such as may have been recorded by home security devices or personal data management systems such as Alexa (see above) only add to the complications of our modern world. This conflict is a demonstration of the entire debate between civil liberties versus security.

Negative Rights

Some social thinkers believe that although we do and should have rights, those rights should be only of a certain kind: *negative rights,* so called because they specify what ought *not* to be done to you (they are rights of noninterference). Earlier in this chapter you read that John Locke introduced a concept of three natural rights that everyone has as a birthright of a rational human being: the rights to life, liberty, and property. (It is no coincidence that this sounds so similar to Thomas Jefferson's famous emphasis on our rights to *life, liberty, and the pursuit of happiness.* Jefferson was deeply influenced by John Locke's political philosophy.) For Locke, a social contract thinker, these rights are rights people have against the government and one another: Nobody's life should be interfered with for no good reason, nor should anyone's liberty or property be interfered with. The only limit to each right is the right held by other people to their own life, liberty, and property. But even outside a social contract, these rights are in effect, says Locke, because we are rational beings and these rights are rational rights, but they are easier to enforce within a society with democratic laws. In his *Second Treatise on Government* (1690) Locke specifies that "the State of Nature has a law of Nature to govern it, which obliges everyone, and Reason, which is that law, teaches all mankind who will but consult it, that being all equal and independent, no one ought to harm another in his life, liberty, health or possessions." So even before a society is formed with all its rules and laws, says Locke, there is a law of nature guiding our rational thinking toward realizing that everyone is equal by birth, and everyone should be able to live his or her life in liberty without the interference of anyone else. In many ways Locke's philosophy was an inspiration to the founders (traditionally known as the "Founding Fathers") of the United States. Ayn Rand (see Chapter 4) expressed the conviction that the United States was the first moral society in history because it set limits on the power of the state and respected the concept of the rights of the individual. In an essay, "Man's Rights," from *The Virtue of Selfishness* (1965), she says, "All previous systems had regarded man as a sacrificial means to the ends of others, and society as an end in itself. The United States regarded man as an end in himself, and society as a means to the peaceful, orderly, *voluntary* coexistence of individuals."

So what are these individual rights? There is only one fundamental right, says Rand: the right to your own life and to act free of coercion. In that sense it is a positive right. But as for your neighbors, they have negative rights against you: the right not to have their right to life and liberty violated. How do we maintain our life? By our own effort, Rand says; that means you have the right to make money or own property without having it taken away. So the right to property is also a negative right. Are these rights absolute? Do you always have a right to your life, liberty, and property? Not if you have violated someone else's right to life, liberty, or property. In such a case your rights have been forfeited; so the limit of your own liberty is the liberty of the other person. But does that mean you have a right to be kept alive if you can't provide for yourself? Do you have a right to be given property and to be provided with the means to enjoy your liberty? No, says Rand. If you can't fend for yourself, then society has no obligation to help you (but others may want to, because they are caring people). For this philosophical approach, there is no such thing as a right to a job, a home, or fair wages—nor a right to be made happy, only the right not to be interfered with if you don't bother others in your own pursuit of happiness.

The American philosopher John Hospers expresses the same sentiments in defending the political viewpoint of libertarianism in his book *The Libertarian Alternative* (1974):

> Each man has the right to life: any attempt by others to take it away from him, or even to injure him, violates this right, through the use of coercion against him. Each man has a right to liberty: to conduct his life in accordance with the alternatives open to him without coercive action by others. And every man has the right to property: to work to sustain his life (and the lives of whichever others he chooses to sustain, such as his family) and to retain the fruits of his labor.

Both Rand and Hospers emphasize the right to life; does that mean they are part of the right-to-life movement? If we identify the right to life as an anti-abortion viewpoint, then it is not the same as the libertarian negative right, because libertarians are generally concerned with the right of people who are already born not to have their lives taken away. The Libertarian Party platform of 1994 specified a pro-choice stand, as a logical consequence of its view that the right to liberty includes the right for women to choose for themselves; however, the platform also specified that libertarians are against public funding of abortion clinics because forcing others to pay for abortions violates the right to property. (Box 7.7 explores the right to privacy.)

Box 7.7 A RIGHT TO PRIVACY?

In the United States of America we generally assume that we have a right to privacy, based on the Fourth Amendment (see Box 7.6). And our Bill of Rights certainly provides us with protection from undue interference from the government without probable cause, but as you know from the previous box, the probable cause may be defined differently for different urgent situations such as terrorism. Even so, the assumption that we ought to be in control over our own space (home, car) and everything in it, including our personal information, is very deep-seated in most of us, and the assumption extends to wherever our personal information is stored, such as in our doctor's office. Of course there are legal protections in place, so anyone violating our space and privacy illegally can be brought to court, but what about our privacy rights in the age of the Internet and social media? In the recent past there has been an erosion of what is considered private; medical records have turned out not to be so secure, once they are stored electronically; bank records and other financial information are not only sometimes hacked into, but even traded, legally as well as illegally; and in social media such as Facebook the personal information you choose to share with "friends" may, despite your efforts, end up being public. But Facebook and other social media are *private* organizations, like clubs, and are not subject to the Fourth Amendment. You agree to their terms if you want to join—otherwise you're out. And the founder of Facebook, Mark Zuckerberg, has been widely quoted as saying that he thinks privacy is an outdated concept—though in 2019 he seemed to reverse that view, saying "The future is private," emphasizing the importance of Facebook users' right to maintain a level of privacy and control of their information, in response to numerous international investigations of Facebook's privacy violations. In Chapter 13 we take a closer look at social media and ethics.

Accordingly, the right to life is simply a right not to have your life interfered with. What if you are not capable of working to sustain your life? Then you have a problem, because Rand and Hospers do not believe you have a right to receive other people's property without their consent. In practical terms, that means you should have saved up or taken out insurance while you were able to work; for those who never have been and never will be able to work, libertarianism advocates private charity, not government interference, because the only role for the government, say both Hospers and Rand, is to protect the negative rights of the citizens against violation. Anything else is, in the colorful language that Hospers echoes from Rand, "moral cannibalism." Critics of that philosophy—and there are many—sometimes invoke the Golden Rule and ask of the libertarian, Is this the way *you* would want to be treated if stricken with a personal catastrophe that you could not have prepared for? Should the goods of this world be reserved for those who are strong, healthy, and capable of securing them for themselves, or should weaker individuals who lack such abilities also have a right to share in the goods in a civilized society? In the upcoming section on distributive justice, we meet an American philosopher who argues in favor of a fair distribution: John Rawls.

Positive Rights

Library of Congress Prints and Photographs Division [LC-USZ62-16530]

Karl Marx (1818–1883), German political philosopher, social scientist, and economist. Best known as a revolutionary socialist, and author of *The Communist Manifesto* (1848), and *Das Kapital* (1867–1894). He was the founder of a socio-economic theory of *dialectic materialism*, envisioning an ideal society based on workers' rights. Today we refer to that theory as Marxism.

Views in opposition to libertarianism can be found in several areas of modern social thinking. The most extreme alternative would be provided by Marxism, which holds, on the basis of the ideal of social equality, that everyone in society has the right to have his or her life sustained, "to receive according to need, and to give according to ability." That makes the right to live and have your life sustained a *positive right* (a right to receive something from somebody, usually the government). As has often been pointed out, the politics of communism exclude the negative rights just described: It rarely recognizes any right as not to be interfered with by the government. Socialist viewpoints (which are generally not as radical as communist views about government control) also support positive rights (entitlements) such as the right to work, to have shelter, and possibly also to have health care, education, clothing, and food.

According to the German political philosopher Karl Marx, the communist state will take care of the needs of the individual: The individual has a positive right to have his or her needs met. But *needs* is an amorphous term. What does it mean to have your needs met? Marx had in mind the basics: food, shelter, clothing, meaningful work, education, and health care. The needs of your family, however, might stretch the definition of basic needs. Wanting and needing are, after all, not the same. What about braces for your daughter's teeth? What about a Kindle for every student? You may argue that young people really *need* those things to secure their future, but who is to judge? And who is to pay for them? Those who have the ability to work.

In Marx's vision of the communist state—the final stage of political development after feudalism and capitalism—the world will have changed. The capitalist concept of profit will have disappeared because profit is the "surplus value" that the factory owner adds to the product on top of the wages paid to the factory worker—in Marx's view, value stolen from the worker and created on the worker's time and through the worker's effort. In the world of communism, people no longer go to work to make wages or make a profit—they go to work because they have certain abilities that they put into the service of the state. And since they are allowed (ideally!) to work with whatever their talents dictate, they are not bored: The compensation for hard work is the joy of having meaningful work in itself. So society can require a person to work for the good of the community to the extent that he or she is able to do it (willingness is simply assumed). In compensation, the workers will be paid in goods according to their needs. In the early stages of the new world, Marx envisioned a monetary system, but within the completed communist system, money would be abolished. In *Atlas Shrugged,* Ayn Rand (who fled the Soviet Union for the United States) creates a wicked parody of the fate of a factory run on communist principles. The workers with needs soon outnumbered those who were able to put in long hours of work. Those workers with bright ideas and abilities were put on overtime without compensation, so that very soon they were out of ideas and discovered that they were able to put in only a feeble amount of work. But everybody was quick to think up new needs. . . . Marxists have responded that Rand misunderstood the Marxist philosophy: it is only within capitalism that people are greedy and selfish, because each economic system (the base) creates its own culture (the superstructure). According to Marx the communist base will alter human nature and generate goodwill and empathy rather than greed and selfishness. Many a critic has been known to be skeptical about that claim.

The concept of positive rights need not take on such extreme proportions. Most liberal philosophies, such as that of John Rawls (see the next section), include the view that negative rights are not of much use if one's health or the country's economy prevents one from making a living. What good is the right to vote, to express yourself freely, and to hold office if you are so sick or destitute that you can't feed your kids or give them a safe place to grow up? To enjoy negative rights, one must be assured of having basic needs met. The first Primary Reading at the end of the chapter is the United Nation's Declaration of Human Rights. You may want to study it specifically for its emphasis on negative as well as positive rights—rights of noninterference as well as entitlements.

Distributive Justice: From Rawls to Affirmative Action

In modern social philosophy we talk about two kinds of justice. One is the kind that is upheld by the law; it is generally referred to as *criminal justice,* and we will return to it at the end of this chapter. The other kind is *distributive justice,* theories of how to distribute the goods of society fairly. This distinction dates all the way back to Aristotle, who says in his *Nicomachean Ethics* that "a just thing . . . will be (1) that which is in accordance with the law, (2) that which is fair; and the unjust thing will be (1) that which is contrary to law, (2) that which is unfair."

For some social thinkers in the past, distributive justice depended on who could grab how much and hold on to it, but in modern times a clear understanding has emerged among social philosophers that for society to be a functioning system, it must offer both some recognition of needs and some way to meet those needs.

Rawls: Justice as Fairness

One of the most influential arguments against exclusively negative rights and in favor of positive rights—an argument that is also directed against a utilitarian view of rights as merely a means to happiness for the majority (*social utility*)—comes from the American philosopher John Rawls (1921–2002). This is usually identified as a *liberal* argument, not in the sense of Mill's *classical* liberalism (which comes close to today's libertarianism), but in the sense of the modern *egalitarian* liberalism, which believes that everyone should have equal access to social goods, in some way or other. A liberal generally believes in some positive rights as well as some negative rights: You need the right to life and liberty (such as freedom of speech), but without positive rights you may not be able to enjoy those negative rights, so you also have a basic right to be taken care of by society if you can't take care of yourself.

To envision a society that is as fair toward everyone as possible, Rawls suggests a thought experiment: Imagine, he says, that we are about to make rules for a brand-new society and that we are all in on it. (This is one of the most modern versions of the old *social contract theory* that you'll remember from Chapter 4.) Then, he says, imagine that you don't know who or what you'll be when the rules take effect; you may be rich, you may be poor, young or old, male or female, of another race. You pretend you are ignorant of your position in the future; you have now lowered a *veil of ignorance* over your mind's eye. This Rawls calls the *original position,* because it is from this position that we should imagine making rules for all of society. Rawls was deeply inspired by Kant's idea that all of humanity should be treated as ends in themselves, never merely as means to an end. If you don't know who or what you will be, you will want to make certain that whatever rules you help make about fair distribution of the goods of society (such as jobs, food, shelter, child care, health care) don't place you at the bottom of the pile. If you end up being poor and ill, your new rules should be as fair to you as to anyone else; if you end up being rich, you would want fairness too. This is, of course, a form of rational self-interest—but in the bigger picture it transforms itself into an understanding of other people's needs. In Rawls's own words, from his influential work *A Theory of Justice* (1971),

> Thus we are to imagine that those who engage in social cooperation choose together, in one joint act, the principles which are to assign basic rights and duties and to determine the division of social benefits. . . . This original position is not, of course, thought of as an actual historical state of affairs, much less as a primitive condition of culture. It is understood as a purely hypothetical situation characterized so as to lead to a certain conception of justice. Among the essential features of this situation is that no one knows his place in society, his class position or social status, nor does any one know his fortune in the distribution of natural assets and abilities, his intelligence, strength, and the like. . . . The principles of justice are chosen behind a veil of ignorance. This ensures that no one is advantaged or disadvantaged in the choice of principles by the outcome of natural chance or the contingency of social circumstances.

An example may help illustrate this (it is not an image that Rawls uses, but one that he might use): Think of a birthday party for a little girl. There is a big birthday cake, and she would like to cut a big piece for herself before any of the guests get some of it. But her parents tell her, "You may cut the cake, but you get to choose last!" She is a smart girl; what will this force her to do? Cut pieces as evenly as possible, because a tiny piece is likely to be rejected by her guests and thus be the last one remaining for her. In a sense she is in the original position, creating a system of fair distribution for the future.

That analogy works well for the original position, but real life is different. The needs (or wants) of the party guests were for a piece of cake, but in real life some may need more food, shelter, and health care than others, and some have talents that others don't have. So a completely fair distribution of goods would be one in which, as a result, no one is in need of the bare essentials. Justice, then, consists in equal liberty (having the same rights and duties as everyone else) for persons within a society. That doesn't mean that everyone should be treated the same way. As a matter of fact, some inequality is permissible, says Rawls, provided that the end result is *everyone* in society benefits from that inequality (and not just some majority, as in utilitarianism). When Rawls launched his theory of justice, the reader's imagination was what was needed in order to make Rawls' point, but with the current computer technology we might be able to visualize his notion of the Original Position quite graphically: A narrative videogame might be quite useful in bringing home the concept of Original Position and the veil of ignorance as a tool to achieve social justice!

Two American philosophers who are often quoted as criticizing Rawls are the communitarian and pluralist Michael Walzer (born 1935) and the libertarian Robert Nozick (1938–2002). We will meet Robert Nozick's theory of property in the Business Ethics section in Chapter 13. Walzer's philosophy is closer to Rawls's liberal social philosophy than that of Nozick, but there are substantial differences between Walzer's and Rawls's ideas of distributive justice. For Rawls we are, essentially, social atoms, theoretically without affiliations, and that means we can imagine a veil of ignorance hiding our knowledge of who we are to ensure a fair distribution. For Walzer, on the other hand, we live in "spheres of justice" (the title of one of his books from 1983) where we are essentially connected to our communities and what we consider "social goods" depend on what our community values, which means we can't be reduced to social atoms. Walzer identifies himself primarily as a pluralist; to him our affiliations take on special meanings according to our community, and these separate spheres of meaning can't be reduced to a common denominator. In the next section we look at two other, less often quoted American philosophers arguing against Rawls: Elizabeth Wolgast and Marilyn Friedman.

Wolgast and Friedman: Reactions to Abstract Individualism

Rawls's viewpoint has helped immensely in identifying goals within liberal politics; as you can imagine, he has critics among thinkers who identify themselves as being either to the left or the right of Rawls, politically, but he also has them even among thinkers who are generally in favor of social equality involving fair distribution of goods. Here we look at viewpoints from two American philosophers, Elizabeth Wolgast (b.1929) and Marilyn Friedman (b.1945); each in her own way has pointed to a lack in Rawls's approach: the understanding that humans are not just "social atoms," separate individuals who might imagine themselves to be someone else entirely, but persons already existing in a web of interrelationships.

The idea of individualism has a long and important history, says Elizabeth Wolgast, and it has helped make this country what we perceive it to be: a place for individual achievement as a result of competition. It began with René Descartes daring to assert that humans all have the capacity to reason and are equal in their intelligence. Since everyone has this capacity, there is no need for any religious or political authority: We can figure things out for ourselves. This is the beginning of the egalitarianism, as well as the anti-authoritarianism, of Western individualism, says Wolgast, the source of a "do-it-yourself science and theology" that lets everyone play a part. Other thinkers, such as Thomas Hobbes and John Locke, emphasized the right of the individual as a "self-motivated unit" to decide his or her own social destiny, at least in extreme circumstances. One of the modern thinkers who has the most influence in supporting this idea of the individual as a separate unit is John Rawls. If we imagine a society in which everyone is an equal atom, then those atoms are interchangeable, and so ideally each person should be treated the same. But since we are not the same, a policy of justice should take that into consideration, and this is what Rawls's original position policy is all about. It is ingenious as an abstract ideal, but what about real life? asks Wolgast. This model of thinking, beginning with Descartes and culminating with Rawls, presupposes that all human relationships are entered into by separate "atomic" individuals as if they are entering into a contract, as if they weren't in any binding relationships already. According to Wolgast in *The Grammar of Justice* (1987):

> The atomistic model has important virtues. It founds the values of the community on private values; it encourages criticism of government and requires any government to answer to its original justification; it limits government's powers, as they may threaten to interfere with the needs of atomistic units. . . . But it leaves a great deal out. . . . In it one cannot picture human connections or responsibilities. We cannot locate friendliness or sympathy in it any more than we can imagine one molecule or atom moving aside for or assisting another; to do so would make a joke of the model. . . . we need to loosen the hold that the atomistic picture has on our thinking, and recognize the importance that theory has on our judgments and our moral condition.

What is Wolgast saying? She is siding with the much older political theory of *communitarianism,* which stems from the ancient Greek tradition (see Chapter 4). For the Greek thinkers, and Aristotle in particular, an individual does not understand himself or herself as a separate entity but as a social being. We understand ourselves, and others understand us, through the connections we have to our community. A society is not just a collection of individuals but also part of the very purpose of the life of an individual. We are all someone's daughter or son; we have parents and children and siblings; we have friendships and trade relations and other community ties; and stripped of those we are nobody (which is why, to many Greeks, banishment from the community was a horrible threat, as we shall see in the next chapter). As Wolgast says, "the whole makes the part comprehensible." This is the view that was popularized with the title of former Secretary of State Hillary Clinton's book *It Takes a Village* (to raise a child, an African proverb). So Rawls's thought experiment is bound to have limits in this real world because we are not simply atomic units, individuals alone in the universe. We have responsibilities to our community, and a good theory of justice must take such community ties into account.

Marilyn Friedman agrees with much of Wolgast's criticism of the "abstract individualism" of Western modern philosophy and social thinking. She points out that many women thinkers in particular are now critical of this approach because they don't see themselves or people who depend on them and on whom they depend as utterly separate individuals but, rather, as a network or a group of individuals relying on one another. And the solution of communitarianism is tempting and reasonable, says Friedman in a paper from 1989, "Feminism and Modern Friendship: Dislocating the Community"—but we should be careful, because it may take us places we don't want to go. What do we mean by "community"? Very often what is meant is the *family,* the *neighborhood,* and the *nation;* communitarianism teaches that the traditions and demands of our community are highly important and should be a defining factor in each person's sense of self. But if we look at such communities in a historical sense, we find that most often they have been very oppressive toward women; so if we choose communitarianism over Rawls's idea of people as social atoms, aren't we risking going backward and accepting traditions dictating, for instance, that women are the property of their husbands, that children have no rights, or that men have no place in the kitchen or the nursery? Traditions may be a wonderful legacy for a community, but not all traditions are necessarily so. And suppose some of the old traditions were to blame for divisions and resentment among people today; ought we not be morally obligated to overcome those traditions? We can't just celebrate our community attachments uncritically, as some modern communitarians suggest, says Friedman. And how can we get to a point at which we can allow ourselves to be critical? By not throwing out the concept of the modern self without affiliations (what Wolgast called a "social atom"), a self who has learned to be critical of society's claims that we have social and moral obligations.

Furthermore, communitarians seem to believe that we are always a part of a community from the beginning; we have not chosen it, and yet we have responsibilities as members. But, says Friedman, that is true only when we are young; an adult person can generally choose many of his or her community affiliations. Does she want to belong to a union? Does he want to move to this or that neighborhood? Does she want to emigrate? Does he want to join a new church? We choose affiliations based on our personal needs, wishes, and critical sense, and they don't even have to be live-in communities. Today it's possible to belong to communities that don't really have a location, such as Facebook and other social media. (When Friedman wrote her paper, the Internet was still in the future.) So Friedman concludes (in "Feminism and Modern Friendship") that looking to community ties to expand traditional abstract individualism is a good idea, but it should not be done uncritically: We must develop communitarian thought beyond its complacent regard for the communities in which we once found ourselves toward (and beyond) an awareness of the crucial importance of "dislocated" communities, communities of choice. Box 7.8 introduces an additional critique of Rawls's atomistic impartiality concept, Carol Gilligan's ethic of care.

Box 7.8 AN ALTERNATIVE TO JUSTICE ETHICS

John Rawls is considered perhaps the greatest American social philosopher of the twentieth century, and his contributions to the philosophy of justice are considered by many some of the most meaningful in human intellectual history. You have read in the chapter that not everyone agrees that justice should be an impartial ideal; sometimes we can't separate a case from its context, and impartiality seems a ludicrous demand: Why should it be immaterial if a person is a friend of ours, a relative, or a total stranger? Some of us feel that we have greater duties toward those who are near and dear to us than to strangers halfway around the world.

Feminist and psychologist Carol Gilligan introduced a concept in the 1980s as an alternative to Rawls's and other (male) thinkers' ethics of justice: **an ethic of care**, of networking and concern for those in one's immediate social sphere, as a particularly feminine form of ethics. You can read more about Gilligan and her ethic of care in Chapter 12. The concept of an ethic of care has inspired some contemporary American philosophers to focus on a moral philosophy of care with political overtones, and you can read more about that in Chapter 10.

Forward- and Backward-Looking Justice and Affirmative Action

In the debate about the nature and goals of justice, it may seem confusing that legal experts sometimes talk about improving things in the *future* and sometimes talk about making up for mistakes and evils of the *past,* as if the two approaches might exclude each other. And to some legal minds they effectively do, because the issue of justice can be defined in two ways: as *forward-looking* and as *backward-looking.* One concept focuses on future consequences; the other is a rights-based concept centered on responding to conditions in the past. Here it is essential that you have studied Chapters 5 and 6, because this section relies heavily on your understanding of the goals of utilitarianism and other consequentialist theories, as opposed to the ideals of a Kantian viewpoint.

A **forward-looking view of justice** sees the purpose of justice as creating a fair system of distribution of social goods in the future. (Social thinkers use "social goods" to mean access to opportunities such as jobs as well as material things available to citizens in a community.) Regardless of what in the past has brought us to where we are today, our focus must be on creating consequences as good as possible for as many as we can—for everyone, if possible—in the future. A utilitarian would concentrate on creating a functional society of equality and access to opportunities for the majority, under the assumption that that's the best we can do. Of course, a utilitarian might also consider instituting social *inequalities,* provided that the overall outcome is considered beneficial for the many.

A **backward-looking view of justice** requires us to look to conditions in the past and ask, What has brought us to where we are today in terms of inequality and unfair distribution of social goods, and how can we make amends? In the backward-looking view it is essential that we identify both the root causes of today's inequalities and the people in the past who have been affected by them, as well as their descendants and those still living today. Whether compensation for past wrongs done to those people will actually accomplish a system of fair distribution of goods in the future is not relevant—the main concern is to rectify the past wrongs.

An interesting hybrid form is John Rawls's theory of the original position. The Rawlsian focus would be on creating a fair system for *everyone,* using the original position to create rules of distribution of social goods so that no one falls through the cracks. As you'll remember, the original position is a thought experiment requiring that we forget about who we are and have been in the past, in order to imagine a fair and just society of the future where everyone is equal and no one will be sacrificed for the convenience of anyone else. As such it is future-oriented, forward-looking. But Rawls himself is not a consequentialist; rather, he is a follower of Kant's philosophy that nobody should be used as merely a means to other people's ends, even if it might create good consequences. So Rawls's theory of justice in effect looks forward, but drawing on a concept of rights and fairness, not on good social consequences as such. Later we look at Rawls's own theory of combining forward-looking and backward-looking theories of punishment.

In the field of *affirmative action,* the views of forward- and backward-looking justice have determined the way many issues have been raised and solved. Although the entire concept of affirmative action—a term coined by President Lyndon B. Johnson in the 1960s in connection with the Civil Rights Act—is now undergoing scrutiny by politicians, the media, and citizens for its overall results and possibly negative impact on public jobs and education, the goal of affirmative action ("preferential treatment," as it has been referred to by critics) was to level the playing field for disadvantaged citizens. But exactly who the disadvantaged citizens are and how the playing field is to be leveled depend on whether one adopts a forward-looking or a backward-looking view.

A *forward-looking* approach identifies those in society who, at this point, seem disenfranchised, and those who in the near future may be in danger of being caught up in a socially disadvantaged situation, and will focus on making access to public jobs and education easier for that group, regardless of why the situation has arisen or whether the beneficiaries or their ancestors were discriminated against in the past. Thus it is the present needs of disenfranchised individuals and groups that would determine the measure of help required, not their experience with discrimination in the past. A forward-looking view has to determine how far into the future such programs will have to exist to level the playing field—forever, or a few generations—because there will always be needy individuals.

A *backward-looking* view will focus on the history of disenfranchised groups and seek some form of compensation or restitution to those groups—living members or their descendants—based on the past experiences of group members regardless of whether everyone in that group today has in fact experienced discrimination in his or her lifetime. A backward-looking view will also have to determine how far into the past one must go to rectify old wrongs—should it be limited to living memory, meaning about a hundred years at the most, or should it go back several more generations? An extreme backward-looking view that has emerged recently is the notion that laws of property rights should be cast aside if persons from disenfranchised groups commit property crimes, under the philosophy that it is due to societal pressures that such persons commit "crimes," and that they should not be held accountable. In effect, such a view advocates two separate legal systems, one for the "haves" and one for the "have-nots." Critics have responded that (1) that would undermine the entire concept of being equal for the law, and (2) understanding of hardships and past oppression can be accommodated within the legal system that we already have—and it frequently is.

Regarding the question of compensation to African Americans for past injustices caused by slavery, the issue of backward-looking justice is extremely relevant: Assuming that one finds the idea of reparations at all reasonable (which many don't, but a new generation of members of Congress have recently brought the subject to the forefront), a living memory criterion would include compensation not for slavery itself but for the consequences of slavery. And a broader criterion would have to seek compensation not just from descendants of American slave owners but also from descendants of Arab slave traders, and so on. At the end of the chapter, you'll find two op-ed pieces by American philosopher John Berteaux in which he evaluates the status of race and gender equality in contemporary life. And in the Narratives section, you'll read about the film *Mississippi Burning,* based on the true story of the murders of three young civil rights activists in Philadelphia,

Mississippi, on June 21, 1964. In 2005 a separatist Baptist minister and Ku Klux Klan member, 79-year-old Ray Killen, was arrested and charged with engineering those murders, one of the most infamous events of the civil rights movement of the 1960s. He was convicted on all three counts and sentenced to 60 years in prison. Consider how the criminal charges against Ray Killen, 41 years after the murders, are an example of a backward-looking view. Finally. the movie awarded the Oscar for Best Picture in 2019, *Green Book*, tells a story of race discrimination experienced by a gifted African American artist during the same time period as *Mississippi Burning*.

The very different approaches of forward- and backward-looking justice can be found not only within the realm of what we call distributive justice, the distribution of social goods, but also as an important part of what we refer to as *criminal justice.*

Criminal Justice: Restorative Versus Retributive Justice

As a society, we believe that law-abiding persons should be treated equally, *ceteris paribus.* The Latin expression means "everything else being equal," so if you just go about your business, you deserve the same decent treatment by the government that anyone else deserves, no more and no less. But sometimes everything else is not equal: You may come from a historically deprived group, and legislation may state that such persons deserve special benefits (such as affirmative action). Or you may have experienced personal hardship that couldn't be anticipated and may need special help, perhaps in the form of welfare (all depending on which government system is in effect and what kind of rights its legislators may believe in: negative rights, positive rights, both, or none). Or you may have actually benefited society in some way, so the government believes you should be rewarded. (Some governments will pay families bonuses or give them tax breaks for having children, for example.) But suppose you have broken the law. Then, according to criminal justice, the government is entitled to treat you differently from the rest of the population—by depriving you of benefits and sometimes also of certain rights, by punishing you for the crime committed. You may recognize a version of the social equity principle.

The concept of punishment is as old as human history, but only in the past two hundred years has it acquired the face we see today. In past eras around the world, punishment often involved banishment (temporary or permanent), financial restitution to the victims or their families, or loss of body parts—or execution. The principle of "an eye for an eye," today referred to as the law of retaliation, or *lex talionis,* has been in effect for the past four thousand years, since the Babylonian Code of Hammurabi. Incarceration as a form of punishment is a fairly modern idea; in centuries past imprisonment was considered a form of keeping dangerous individuals under control, but not necessarily proportional to what they had done—it was just a way of dealing with a problem, not a matter of justice.

Although most people today think punishment (in some form) is an appropriate response to crime, the viewpoint has been advanced, particularly in the latter half of the twentieth century, that punishment is a demeaning and inhumane approach. The question was raised, Who are we, law-abiding citizens, to pass judgment on people who have perhaps been deprived of the chances in life that have resulted in our being law-abiding? And who is to say that punishment will actually deter them from further criminal activity? Rather than punish people for what they have done, we ought to educate them and supply them with the chance they may never have had before to become good citizens. In other words, the purpose of incarcerating criminals or subjecting them to other restraints has been viewed not as *punishment* but as *therapeutic rehabilitation.* This fundamental philosophical difference between viewing punishment as something deserved and viewing it as something superimposed by a power structure that, somehow, has helped create the problem has led to the distinction between *retributive* and *restorative* justice. In defense of *restorative* justice, Pat Nolan of the Justice Fellowship says,

If all we do is focus on the broken law, then all you can do is enforce the power of the government, the fist of government, and lock people up, to punish them. If, on the other hand, you look at crime as "victim harming," the solution should bring repair to the harm done to the victim. And when you repair the harm done to the victim through restitution and reparation, generally the victim becomes very forward looking and doesn't want to harm and further punish the offender, but says, "I don't want you to do this again." "What can we do to make you not do this again?" "How can we change your life?" Transformation becomes important.

Nolan served 15 years in the California State Assembly—and 25 months in a federal prison on racketeering charges. So perhaps he has an insider's understanding of the issue. He believes the solution lies in religion and in teaching morals. Those who focus on restorative justice emphasize that the balance in society is not restored by locking perpetrators up or executing them. The balance can only be restored if their criminal propensities can be transformed.

A recent op-ed piece in *Aeon Magazine*, "Does the Desire to Punish Have Any Place in Modern Justice?," by Neil Levy, Professor of Philosophy at Macquarie University, Sydney, argues that humans are essentially punishment-happy, but that the feelings of revenge associated with punishment are primitive and outdated in today's world, so retributive justice should be replaced by restorative justice. However, retributive justice advocates will be quick to point out that retributivist punishment is not supposed to include any kind of vengeful feelings, as you will see below. Retributive justice sees a crime as a violation of rules and relationships, whereas restorative justice sees it as harm caused to people; retributive justice sees the state as the victim, whereas restorative justice sees people as victims. Retributive justice focuses on the past, whereas restorative justice focuses on the future. The courtroom is a battle situation for retributive justice, but for restorative justice the model is a dialogue. And for retributive justice, the debt is paid through punishment; for restorative justice, the debt is paid by "making it right."

The most influential, and perhaps also the most comprehensive defense of retributive justice to this day may have been supplied by Immanuel Kant. For Kant, justice *must* focus on the past, because that is how we identify the criminal and the severity of the crime; it must be seen as a violation of rules because it is by the rationality of rules that we justify our moral system—but Kant would not conclude that only rules and not people are victims. On the contrary, respecting the inherent dignity of another human being—victim as well as criminal—is the foundation of his retributive justice. Among contemporary supporters are the philosopher Igor Primoratz and the author Robert James Bidinotto. In the section on retribution we look at Kant's argument in favor of *retributivism*.

So even though most social thinkers believe there should be an institution of punishment within society, there is widespread disagreement on not only *what kind of punishment* people should reasonably be subjected to but also *why* they should be punished. It should not be hard for you to guess at some of the major disagreements.

Five Common Approaches to Punishment

Among all the different reasons people might give for punishment to be an option for society, five appear most often. Four of them are classics in the law books; the fifth one, although popular, is not considered legitimate by most legal experts.

Deterrence   It is often argued that punishment, provided it is swift and strict, is a good deterrent against crime. It may make the criminal change his or her mind about breaking the law again (specific deterrence), and it may make others think twice before turning to crime (general deterrence). Statistics indicate that in places where severe forms of punishment are the norm, such as Singapore, where disturbing the peace is punished by caning and political dissidence can lead to the death penalty, streets are noticeably safer than in free, Western-style societies. We must, of course, ask ourselves what price we are willing to pay for safe streets—a question we explored in Box. 7.6. It appears that here in the United States, crimes against property may be deterred by the knowledge of likely punishment. Who knows how many people refrain from stealing cars only because they know they'll face prison time if they're caught? It has been reported that some juvenile criminals deliberately scale down their criminal activity when they reach the age of 18 because they know their punishment will be harsher—meaning that the concept of punishment *can* have a deterrent effect. But violent crimes seem not to be deterred much by the threat of punishment. California's controversial three-strikes law, which sends felons to jail for 25 years to life when they're convicted of a third serious crime, may serve as a deterrent in cases where two strikes are already on a person's record—but other factors may be at work too, such as shifts in the economy.

Rehabilitation   Some social thinkers see the purpose of punishment as making a better person out of the criminal (see the previous section); having undergone some form of appropriate punishment (generally incarceration), the criminal will have learned not to turn to crime again. This viewpoint generally presupposes prison programs that offer the inmate alternatives to a life of crime.

Incapacitation   If punishment keeps the criminal off the streets, the public is safe and a social good has been achieved. But the proponents of the incapacitation, or protecting the public, approach don't specify *how* a wrongdoer should be incapacitated. Locking someone up is usually considered sufficient for protecting the public, but in the case of an individual who is a flight risk, conditions may have to be tightened, such as placing him or her in a high-security prison. A convicted rapist may be required to submit to chemical castration (although that does not address the problem of violence and aggression underlying the rape), so he is incapacitated in terms of his offense but may still be released into society. The ultimate incapacitation is of course executing the criminal, which eliminates the chance that he or she will prey on innocent people again. We return to this issue in Chapter 13.

These three approaches to punishment have one important thing in common: They all focus on the future social consequences of punishment; in other words, they are *forward-looking.* If there are no future benefits to be had from punishing someone, then a forward-looking theory will not recommend punishment. Because the primary forward-looking social theory today is utilitarianism, these three approaches are often labeled utilitarian.

By now you may wonder why these viewpoints don't address what for many is the best reason for punishing someone: the fact that he or she is *guilty of a crime.* But that is, in effect, a separate reason for punishment; because utilitarianism approves of punishment only if there is social good involved, it is theoretically possible that the overall benefits of punishing some guilty person are minimal, whereas the benefits of punishing someone who is *not* guilty may be considerable—instantly punishing a scapegoat may have a deterrent effect that far outweighs that of catching and convicting the real perpetrator some time in the future (and it may even deter the perpetrator from doing it again). In addition, setting an example by punishing someone with disproportionate harshness is a utilitarian possibility. If, however, we think that it ought to be of some importance whether a person is actually guilty and that we should take the magnitude of the crime into consideration, we must look to the fourth theory.

Retribution   A person should be punished because he or she has committed a crime, and the punishment should be in proportion to that crime. Social utility does not enter into the picture. The most influential thinker advocating retribution as the only proper reason for punishment is Kant. The principle he applies is *lex talionis,* the law of retaliation. Kant would not approve of the three forward-looking approaches because they allow us to use a person *merely as a means* to achieve social utility. When we use a person to set an example, others may be deterred from committing a crime; the goal of incapacitation is to keep the public safe; rehabilitation does indeed make a better person out of the criminal, but who decides how the criminal ought to be? We, society. So even here Kant implies that society is using people for its own purpose, which to him is demeaning, because it means that people are reduced to being a means to an end only. The only acceptable reason for punishment is to show the criminal the respect any person deserves: It is to assume that he or she decided freely to commit the crime. With freedom comes responsibility, so if we want the freedom of never being treated merely as a means to an end, we must also accept the responsibility that goes with it. If we transgress, we should be punished for our transgressions.

As I mentioned earlier, these four reasons might be found in a legal text on retributive justice. But if you ask a person without any legal training why a criminal should be punished, she or he might answer in the following way: "Well, it just makes us feel better to see the murderer (or rapist, or burglar) get punished." And as you saw above, a scholar arguing in favor of restorative justice such as Neil Levy makes the same assumption that punishment is accompanied by feelings of revenge and gratification.

In Chapter 13 we return to the issue of vengeance and justice in the sections on the concept of just war and on the death penalty. For now it will suffice to outline the fundamental difference between a vengeance approach and a justice approach, as some scholars see it.

Vengeance   Vengeance and retribution have something in common: They are both *backward-looking* theories, looking to the past (asking, "Who did this?") in order to punish the guilty. Like retribution, the approach based on vengeance seeks to punish the criminal because of the crime committed, but according to most retributivists there are three major differences between retribution and vengeance:

1. Retribution is based on *logic,* whereas vengeance is an *emotional* response: It is possible for people bent on vengeance to take their anger out on individuals other than the guilty person.

2. Retribution is a *public* act, done with the authority of the government, whereas vengeance is a *private* enterprise, undertaken by private citizens (vigilantes).

3. Retribution wants punishment to be proportionate to the crime, but vengeance may go beyond that and exceed the damage done by the criminal.

Generally, people who are in favor of the death penalty but who are critical of utilitarianism emphasize that there is a big philosophical difference between revenge and retribution, since they see retribution as legally and morally acceptable, but vengeance as unacceptable. A small minority of scholars who are in favor of the death penalty claim that revenge is indeed the overriding emotion behind the support for capital punishment and that it is also an appropriate reason. However, a growing number of scholars and other critics of the death penalty voice the opinion that as much as we think we can find reasons why revenge and retribution are different, it comes down to the same thing: a wish to get back at the criminal, to even the score. In Chapter 13 we take a closer look at the death penalty debate.

We have now considered three forward-looking and two backward-looking arguments for punishment, although the last one (vengeance) is rarely considered legitimate by philosophers of law. But are forward- and backward-looking theories always destined to be opposite? We know that utilitarians and Kantians don't agree on the basic moral motivations, but in real life most of us believe that sometimes people ought to be punished because it will deter others from doing the same thing; sometimes we want the wrongdoer incapacitated; and sometimes we think a first-time offender can be saved from a life of crime and rehabilitated with the proper form of punishment. And sometimes we think a criminal should be punished by the book simply because the crime warrants it and for no other reason. If we as individuals can hold such different views, does it mean we are just inconsistent, or does it mean we have some deeper, if inarticulated, understanding of the issue?

John Rawls has a suggestion that may shed some light on this phenomenon. In his paper "Two Concepts of Rules" (1955), he says utilitarians and retributivists are both right—but in different ways. In *individual* court cases we appeal to retributivism: A burglar goes to prison because he or she has committed a crime, and the crime determines the length of the sentence. But why do we send people to prison *in general?* To make society a better place—which is the point utilitarianism makes. So the *judge's* reason for sending a person to prison is retributivist, but the *legislator's* reason for making laws is utilitarian. The danger, as Rawls sees it, is that this definition might allow the utilitarian to make laws that might sacrifice the innocent for the sake of social benefits for the many—the problem of "sheer numbers" which you encountered in Chapter 5. Thus the application of utilitarianism must be very careful; in other words, a system of checks and balances is needed.

Is Anger Ever Appropriate?

A utilitarian, forward-looking penologist (someone interested in theory of punishment) or an advocate for restorative justice usually sees no difference between retribution and vengeance: *Retributivism* is just a fancy word for the emotional demand for revenge. A retributivist will argue that the difference between vengeance and retribution is that *vengeance is based on an emotion, anger, whereas retributivism is based on a wish for a proportional, logical response.* That would imply that if we feel anger toward a perpetrator, whether as victims or as other members of society, we are merely being emotional and should set aside those emotions for the sake of logic. But is that desirable, or even possible?

In *For Capital Punishment: Crime and the Morality of the Death Penalty* (1979), Walter Berns argues that anger has a deep connection with justice that modern penology hasn't understood. Berns says,

> If men are not saddened when someone else suffers, or angry when someone else suffers unjustly, the implication is that they do not care for anyone other than themselves or that they lack some quality that befits a man. . . . Punishment arises out of the demand for justice, and justice is demanded by angry, morally indignant men; its purpose is to satisfy that moral indignation and thereby promote the law-abidingness that, it is assumed, accompanies it.

(In 1979 gender-neutral language hadn't yet become the norm in academic publications, but I assume Berns is talking about morally indignant men *and* women.) If we are not angry, says Berns, it is because we are selfish utilitarians who are concerned only with *compensations,* but you can't compensate victims for the loss of their physical integrity resulting from rape or for the loss of their life. Not all crimes can be balanced by compensation, but without righteous moral indignation we won't have an understanding of that.

The British philosopher P. F. Strawson argues, in his paper "Freedom and Resentment" (1962), that it is normal and appropriate to react emotionally to other people's actions toward us. We feel *resentment* if we are directly harmed, and we feel *moral indignation* if our involvement is indirect. To that the philosopher of law Diane Whiteley adds in her paper "The Victim and the Justification of Punishment" from 1998 that we must also take human *empathy* into account, because it is "by virtue of human beings possessing the three natural capacities of moral understanding, self-evaluation, and empathy that they have the capability to be moral agents." That means the demand for justice and punishment becomes society's communication of the victim's resentment and the community's moral indignation. In this way, the community stands up for the victim and shows the person respect. If there is no (or too lenient) punishment, the community sends out two messages: that it feels no "retributive sentiment" (or, as Berns would say, anger) toward the criminal and no respect for the victim. And a victim who feels no resentment and doesn't insist on punishment has too little self-esteem. A battered spouse who doesn't want her (or his) spouse punished may have internalized the spouse's claim that she has deserved being beaten. And the community that feels no moral indignation over a crime being committed against one of its members fails to stand up for that member and fails to show the respect for the victim that she deserves.

But, says Whiteley, that is not merely a blindly emotional response. (You'll remember Martha Nussbaum in Chapter 1 arguing that emotions can have their own inherent logic and can be rational responses to situations.) Provided that the victim's resentment is directed toward the right person, and for the right reason, it is an appropriate sentiment, and the community's moral indignation is an endorsement of the victim's resentment as well as a condemnation of the criminal act that has attempted to deprive the victim of moral value (because if you value someone you don't commit a crime against him or her—committing a crime against someone is reducing her or him to merely a means to an end of instrumental value only). Resentment and indignation are proper elements in the process of justice and punishment if they lead not to pure revenge but to retribution based on a natural fellow feeling within a community.

Berns's, Strawson's, and Whiteley's arguments have been considerably strengthened by the recent findings in brain research. As you'll remember from previous chapters, Antonio Damasio and other neuroscientists have found that humans have a natural capacity for empathy, within an area in the brain that, if undamaged, will make them feel reluctant to harm other people, in particular when the harm requires a physical, immediate contact. The twentieth-century favorite analogy to brain function, the *computer model*—utterly rational and unemotional—is slowly being abandoned in favor of a deeper understanding of how our mind works, and scientists across the field are coming to similar conclusions: The human cognition isn't just rational but also deeply emotional, and proper thinking requires a healthy emotional brain.

However, there is a big difference between regarding an emotion such as anger as relevant and allowing emotions to decide for us. As you know, Nussbaum argues in favor of viewing emotions as morally relevant but not morally all-important: Reason has to play the main part in our moral decisions. Some social commentators have pointed out that in recent years, emotions seem to have become more legitimate as a deciding factor in public situations, whereas previously reason would have the final word, increasing the danger that we may lose the calming influence of rationality—the influence that Plato and Kant so staunchly defended (as indeed most philosophers always have). Case in point: the trial of Scott Peterson in Modesto, California, accused and found guilty of murdering his pregnant wife, Laci Peterson, on Christmas Eve 2002 and dumping her in the San Francisco Bay, where her body and that of her unborn baby, Conner, floated ashore months later. This case gripped the nation for two years. Whereas the guilt phase of a trial is supposed to lay out the facts, the penalty phase allows family members and others to make emotional "victim impact statements" for the jury to consider. During the penalty phase, emotions ran high, as is customary, when Laci's mother talked on the witness stand about her grief and anger at her daughter's murderer. After the jury came back with a death penalty recommendation in December 2004—a surprise to most pundits because Peterson did not have a prior criminal record—individual jurors explained that Scott Peterson's *lack of emotion* during the trial was the primary reason for their recommendation. Some commentators asked, Is this allowing emotions to go too far within the legal system? I'll let you be the judge of that.

Study Questions

1. What are Dworkin's two models? Explain, and apply his second model to the issue of protecting a country against terrorism.
2. What does it mean that science is supposed to be value-free? Do you agree? Why or why not? Apply the theory of value-free science to contemporary issues such as cloning and genetic engineering.
3. Explain the four principles of equality. Which one do you find most reasonable? Why?
4. Explain the concepts of negative and positive rights, and identify supporters of each theory.
5. What is the "original position"? Explain the pros and cons of Rawls's theory.
6. Explain forward-looking and backward-looking justice and apply both to the issue of affirmative action.
7. Explain forward-looking and backward-looking theories of punishment. Which approach seems the most reasonable to you? Why?
8. Can anger ever be justified as a reason for punishment? Explain, referring to Berns and Whiteley.

Primary Readings and Narratives

The Primary Readings are the United Nations Universal Declaration of Human Rights; an excerpt from John Rawls's "The Priority of Right and Ideas of the Good"; and two newspaper op-ed pieces by John Berteaux, "Defining Racism in the 21st Century," and "Unheard, Unseen, Unchosen." The first Narrative is a summary of the film *Blade Runner,* with an addendum in reference to the sequel, *Blade Runner 2049.* The next is the film *Ex Machina* from 2015, which also raises the question of who and what is a person. The third is a summary of the film *Gattaca,* about genetic engineering creating a human super-race as well as an underclass. The fourth Narrative is a summary of the 1988 film *Mississippi Burning,* about the murders of three civil rights activists in 1964. The fifth is a summary of the film *Green Book* (2018), also reflecting a true story, the experiences of racism in the American south in the 1960s seen through the eyes of an African American pianist and his Italian American chauffeur.

 Primary Reading

The United Nations Universal Declaration of Human Rights

1948. From the Universal Declaration of Human Rights, © 2016 United Nations. Reprinted with permission of the United Nations.

Now, Therefore, The General Assembly proclaims

This universal declaration of human rights as a common standard of achievement for all peoples and all nations, to the end that every individual and every organ of society, keeping this Declaration constantly in mind, shall strive by teaching and education to promote respect for these rights and freedoms and by progressive measures, national and international, to secure their universal and effective recognition and observance, both among the peoples of Member States themselves and among the peoples of territories under their jurisdiction.

Article 1: All human beings are born free and equal in dignity and rights. They are endowed with reason and conscience and should act towards one another in a spirit of brotherhood.

Article 2: Everyone is entitled to all the rights and freedoms set forth in the Declaration without distinction of any kind, such as race, colour, sex, language, religion, political or other opinion, national or social origin, property, birth or other status.

Furthermore, no distinction shall be made on the basis of the political, jurisdictional or international status of the country or territory to which a person belongs, whether it be independent, trust, non-self-governing or under any other limitation of sovereignty.

Article 3: Everyone has the right to life, liberty and security of person.

Article 4: No one shall be held in slavery or servitude; slavery and the slave trade shall be prohibited in all their forms.

Article 5: No one shall be subjected to torture or to cruel, inhuman or degrading treatment or punishment.

Article 6: Everyone has the right to recognition everywhere as a person before the law.

Article 7: All are equal before the law and are entitled without any discrimination to equal protection of the law. All are entitled to equal protection against any discrimination in violation of this Declaration and against any incitement to such discrimination.

Article 8: Everyone has the right to an effective remedy by the competent national tribunals for acts violating the fundamental rights granted him by the constitution or by law.

Article 9: No one shall be subjected to arbitrary arrest, detention or exile.

Article 10: Everyone is entitled in full equality to a fair and public hearing by an independent and impartial tribunal, in the determination of his rights and obligations of any criminal charge against him.

Article 11:

1. Everyone charged with a penal offence has the right to be presumed innocent until proved guilty according to law in the public trial at which he has had all the guarantees necessary for his defense.

2. No one shall be held guilty of any penal offence on account of any act or omission which did not constitute a penal offence, under national or international law, at the time when it was committed. Nor shall a heavier penalty be imposed than the one that was applicable at the time the penal offence was committed.

Article 12: No one shall be subjected to arbitrary interference with his privacy, family, home or correspondence, nor to attacks upon his honour and reputation. Everyone has the right to the protection of the law against such interference or attacks.

Article 13:

1. Everyone has the right to freedom of movement and residence within the borders of each state.

2. Everyone has the right to leave any country, including his own, and to return to his country.

Article 14:

1. Everyone has the right to seek and to enjoy in other countries asylum from persecution.

2. This right may not be invoked in the case of prosecutions genuinely arising from non-political crimes or from acts contrary to the purposes and principles of the United Nations.

Article 15:

1. Everyone has the right to a nationality.

2. No one shall be arbitrarily deprived of his nationality nor denied the right to change his nationality.

Article 16:

1. Men and women of full age, without any limitation due to race, nationality or religion, have the right to marry and to found a family. They are entitled to equal rights as to marriage, during marriage and at its dissolution.

2. Marriage shall be entered into only with the free and full consent of the intended spouses.

3. The family is the natural and fundamental group unit of society and is entitled to protection by society and the State.

Article 17:

1. Everyone has the right to own property alone as well as in association with others.

2. No one shall be arbitrarily deprived of his property.

Article 18: Everyone has the right to freedom of thought, conscience and religion; this right includes freedom to change his religion or belief, and freedom either alone or in community with others and in public or private, to manifest his religion or belief in teaching, practice, worship and observance.

Article 19: Everyone has the right to freedom of opinion and expression; this right includes freedom to hold opinions without interference and to seek, receive and impart information and ideas through any media and regardless of frontiers.

Article 20:

1. Everyone has the right to freedom of peaceful assembly and association.

2. No one may be compelled to belong to an association.

Article 21:

1. Everyone has the right to take part in the government of his country, directly or through freely chosen representatives.

2. Everyone has the right of equal access to public service in his country.

3. The will of the people shall be the basis of the authority of government; this will shall be expressed in periodic and genuine elections which shall be by universal and equal suffrage and shall be held by secret vote or by equivalent free voting procedures.

Article 22: Everyone, as a member of society, has the right to social security and is entitled to realization, through national effort and international cooperation and in accordance with the organization and resources of each State, of the economic, social and cultural rights indispensable for his dignity and the free development of his personality.

Article 23:

1. Everyone has the right to work, to free choice of employment, to just and favourable conditions of work and to protection against unemployment.

2. Everyone, without any discrimination, has the right to equal pay for equal work.

3. Everyone who works has the right to just and favourable remuneration ensuring for himself and his family an existence worthy of human dignity, and supplemented, if necessary, by other means of social protection.

4. Everyone has the right to form and to join trade unions for the protection of his interests.

Article 24: Everyone has the right to rest and leisure, including reasonable limitation of working hours and periodic holidays with pay.

Article 25:

1. Everyone has the right to a standard living adequate for the health and well-being of himself and his family, including food, clothing, housing and medical care and necessary social services, and the right to security in the event of unemployment, sickness, disability, widowhood, old age or other lack of livelihood in circumstances beyond his control.

2. Motherhood and childhood are entitled to special care and assistance. All children, whether born in or out of wedlock, shall enjoy the same social protection.

Article 26:

1. Everyone has the right to education. Education shall be free, at least in the elementary and fundamental stages. Elementary education shall be compulsory. Technical and professional

education shall be made generally available and higher education shall be equally accessible to all on the basis of merit.

2. Education shall be directed to the full development of the human personality and to the strengthening of respect for human rights and fundamental freedoms. It shall promote understanding, tolerance and friendship among all nations, racial or religious groups, and shall further the activities of the United Nations for the maintenance of peace.

3. Parents have a prior right to choose the kind of education that shall be given to their children.

Article 27:

1. Everyone has the right freely to participate in the cultural life of the community, to enjoy the arts and to share in scientific advancement and its benefits.

2. Everyone has the right to the protection of the moral and material interests resulting from any scientific, literary or artistic production of which he is the author.

Article 28: Everyone is entitled to a social and international order in which the rights and freedoms set forth in this Declaration can be fully realized.

Article 29:

1. Everyone has duties to the community in which alone the free and full development of his personality is possible.

2. In the exercise of his rights and freedoms, everyone shall be subject only to such limitations as are determined by law solely for the purpose of securing due recognition and respect for the rights and freedoms of others and of meeting the just requirements of morality, public order and the general welfare in a democratic society.

3. These rights and freedoms may in no case be exercised contrary to the purposes and principles of the United Nations.

Article 30: Nothing in this Declaration may be interpreted as implying for any State, group or person any right to engage in any activity or to perform any act aimed at the destruction of any of the rights and freedoms set forth herein.

Study Questions

1. Find examples of negative and positive rights, and explain the difference.

2. Evaluate these articles from a libertarian approach and from Rawls's approach.

3. In your opinion, are there any rights that should be on the list but aren't included? Are there any rights you disagree with? Explain.

Primary Reading

The Priority of Right and Ideas of the Good

JOHN RAWLS

Essay, 1988. Excerpt.

John Rawls is generally considered the most influential American social thinker in the twentieth century. Influenced by Kant's philosophy of never using another person simply as a means to an end, Rawls outlines a theory of justice based on the ideas that utilitarianism is unacceptable, and that it is possible to agree on basic principles of justice if we agree to see one another as equals. In this excerpt from a paper written years after his most famous book, *A Theory of Justice* (1971), Rawls describes how a theory of justice as fairness also needs to include what people would accept as "the good," a conception of citizens as free and equal, with room for people to pursue their various interests and needs.

> By way of preface, the following general remark: in justice as fairness the priority of right implies that the principles of (political) justice set limits to permissible ways of life; hence the claims citizens make to pursue ends that transgress those limits have no weight (as judged by that political conception). But just institutions and the political virtues expected of citizens would serve no purpose—would have no point—unless those institutions and virtues not only permitted but also sustained ways of life that citizens can affirm as worthy of their full allegiance. A conception of political justice must contain within itself sufficient space, as it were, for ways of life that can gain devoted support. In a phrase: justice draws the limit, the good shows the point. Thus, the right and the good are complementary, and the priority of right does not deny this. Its general meaning is that although to be acceptable a political conception of justice must leave adequate room for forms of life citizens can affirm, the ideas of the good it draws upon must fit within the limits drawn—the space allowed—by that political conception itself.
>
> . . .
>
> One aim of the idea of goodness as rationality is to provide part of a framework for an account of primary goods. But to complete that framework that idea must be combined with a political conception of citizens as free and equal. With this done, we then work out what citizens need and require when they are regarded as free and equal persons and as normal and fully cooperating members of society over a complete life. It is crucial here that the conception of citizens as persons be seen as a political conception and not as one belonging to a comprehensive doctrine. It is this political conception of persons, with its account of their moral powers and higher-order interests, together with the framework of goodness as rationality and the basic facts of social life and the conditions of human growth and nurture, that provides the requisite background for specifying citizens' needs and requirements. All this enables us to arrive at a workable list of primary goods. The role of the idea of primary goods is as follows. A basic feature of a well-ordered political society is that there is a public understanding not only about the kinds of claims it is appropriate for citizens to make when questions of political justice arise, but also about how such claims are to be supported. This understanding is required in order to reach agreement as to how citizens' various claims are to be assessed and their relative weight determined. The fulfill-

ment of these appropriate claims is publicly accepted as advantageous and thus counted as improving citizens' situation for the purposes of political justice. An effective public conception of justice involves, then, a political understanding of what is to be mutually recognized as advantageous in this sense. In political liberalism the problem of interpersonal comparisons of citizens' well-being becomes: given the conflicting comprehensive conceptions of the good, how is it possible to reach a political understanding of what is to count as appropriate claims? The difficulty is that the state can no more act to maximize the fulfillment of citizens' rational preferences, or wants (as in utilitarianism), or to advance human excellence, or the values of perfection (as in perfectionism), than it can act to advance Catholicism or Protestantism, or any other religion. None of these views of the meaning, value, and purpose of human life, as specified by the corresponding comprehensive religious or philosophical conceptions of the good, are affirmed by citizens generally, and so the pursuit of any one of them through basic institutions gives the state a sectarian character. To find a shared idea of citizens' good that is appropriate for political purposes, political liberalism looks for an idea of rational advantage within a political conception that is independent of any particular comprehensive doctrine and hence may be the focus of an overlapping consensus. In justice as fairness the conception of primary goods addresses this practical political problem. The answer proposed rests on identifying a partial similarity in the structure of citizens' permissible conceptions of the good once they are regarded as free and equal persons. Here permissible conceptions are comprehensive doctrines the pursuit of which is not excluded by the principles of political justice. Even though citizens do not affirm the same (permissible) comprehensive conception, complete in all its final ends and loyalties, two things suffice for a shared idea of rational advantage: first, that citizens affirm the same political conception of themselves as free and equal persons; and second, that their (permissible) comprehensive conceptions of the good, however distinct their content and their related religious and philosophical doctrines, require for their advancement roughly the same primary goods, that is, the same basic rights, liberties, and opportunities, as well as the same all-purpose means such as income and wealth, all of which are secured by the same social bases of self-respect. These goods, we say, are things that citizens need as free and equal persons, and claims to these goods are counted as appropriate claims The basic list of primary goods (to which we may add should it prove necessary) has five headings: (i) basic rights and liberties, of which a list may also be given; (ii) freedom of movement and free choice of occupation against a background of diverse opportunities; (iii) powers and prerogatives of offices and positions of responsibility in the political and economic institutions of the basic structure; (iv) income and wealth; and finally, (v) the social bases of self-respect. This list includes mainly features of institutions, that is, basic rights and liberties, institutional opportunities, and prerogatives of office and position, along with income and wealth. The social bases of self-respect are explained in institutional terms supplemented by features of the public political culture such as the public recognition and acceptance of the principles of justice.

. . .

What is crucial is that in introducing these further goods we recognize the limits of the political and practicable: first, we must stay within the limits of justice as fairness as a political conception of justice that can serve as the focus of an overlapping consensus; and second, we must respect the constraints of simplicity and availability of information to which any practicable political conception (as opposed to a comprehensive moral doctrine) is subject.

To conclude: given the political conception of citizens as free and equal, primary goods specify what their needs are—or if you like, what their good is as citizens—when questions of justice arise. It is this political conception (supplemented by the framework of goodness as rationality) that enables us to work out what primary goods are needed. While an index of these goods may be made more specific at the constitutional and legislative stages, and interpreted even more specifically at the judicial stage, the index is not intended to approximate to an idea of rational advantage, or good, specified by a nonpolitical (comprehensive) conception. This last in particular is what political liberalism tries to avoid. Rather, that more specific index specifies for more concrete cases what is to count as citizens' needs as seen by the political conception. Alternatively, the specification of these needs is a construct worked out from within a political conception and not from within any comprehensive doctrine. The thought is that this construct provides, given the fact of pluralism, the best available standard of justification of competing claims that is mutually acceptable to citizens generally. In most cases the index will not approximate very accurately to what many people most want and value as judged by their comprehensive views. Nevertheless, they can endorse the political conception and hold that what is really important in questions of political justice is the fulfillment of citizens' needs by the institutions of the basic structure in ways the principles of justice, acknowledged by an overlapping consensus, specify as fair.

. . .

Political liberalism can be understood as the view that under the reasonably favorable conditions that make constitutional democracy possible political institutions satisfying the principles of a liberal conception of justice realize political values and ideals that normally outweigh whatever other values oppose them. The two desiderata of a political conception that follow from completeness strengthen its stability: allegiance to it tends to go deeper, and so the likelihood that its values and ideals will outweigh those against it is that much greater. Of course, there can be no guarantee of stability. Political good, no matter how important, can never in general outweigh the transcendent values—certain religious, philosophical, and moral values—that may possibly come into conflict with it. That idea is not being suggested. Rather, we start with the conviction that a constitutional democratic regime is reasonably just and workable, and worth defending. But given the fact of pluralism—the fact that a plurality of conflicting comprehensive religious, philosophical, and moral doctrines are affirmed by citizens in a modern democratic society—how can we design our defense so as to achieve a sufficiently wide support for such a regime? We do not look to the comprehensive doctrines that in fact exist and then draw up a political conception that strikes some kind of balance between them. To illustrate: in specifying a list of primary goods, or any measure of advantage for a political conception, we can proceed in two ways. One is to look at the various comprehensive doctrines found in society and specify an index of such goods so as to be near to those doctrines' center of gravity, so to speak—that is, so as to find a kind of average of what those who affirmed those different conceptions would need by way of institutional claims and protections and all-purpose means. Doing this might seem the best way to ensure that the index provides the basic elements necessary to advance the conceptions of the good associated with those doctrines and thus increase the likelihood of securing an overlapping consensus. But this is not how justice as fairness proceeds. Instead it elaborates a political conception working from the fundamental intuitive idea of society as a fair system of cooperation. The hope is that the index arrived at from within this idea can be part of an overlapping consensus. We leave aside those comprehensive doctrines that now exist, or that have existed, or that might exist. The thought is not that primary goods are fair to comprehensive conceptions of the good associated with such doctrines, by striking a fair balance among them, but rather that they are fair to free and equal citizens as persons affirming such conceptions.

Study Questions

1. What does Rawls identify as "primary goods"? (Hint: look for the five headings!)
2. What are the social bases of self-respect, according to Rawls?
3. How does Rawls suggest we can best specify the needs of citizens?
4. How does Rawls identify the concept of political liberalism?

Primary Reading

Two Texts on Discrimination

John Berteaux is an American philosopher who specializes in social ethics and philosophy of race. In addition to teaching and lecturing, he pens a column in the *Monterey County Herald.* For Berteaux, racism in the United States is no longer a blatant, in-your-face offense; it is more subtle, and in some cases even unconscious, based on the phenomenon of "privileged race." Most white people don't question their race or its privileges; they simply take them for granted—not necessarily in a haughty sense but because they have never lost or had to question the privileges of whiteness. In the first text, Berteaux, in a nonhostile manner, makes a point of raising white America's awareness of this subtle everyday form of discrimination. In the second text, he asks himself if he may not be perpetuating another kind of discrimination, against *women,* in his job as philosophy professor.

Defining Racism in the 21st Century

JOHN BERTEAUX

Op-ed essay from the **Monterey County Herald,** *January 17, 2005.*

With Martin Luther King's birthday approaching, some things occurred recently that got me thinking about what racism means in the twenty-first century. For instance, typically, Sundays, my wife Susie and I set out to the Monterey Sports Center to swim laps. Three weeks ago I stood at the end of the pool twiddling my thumbs waiting for a lane to become available. Someone left one of the lanes to my right. As I prepared to get into the water a white lady strolled past me, jumped into the pool, and started to swim laps. Was she ill-mannered? Maybe she didn't see me? Should I say something or forget it?

A couple of months ago, I was waiting to be seated at a restaurant. I had been there for a couple of minutes. As a result, a line started to form behind me. Looking up from my newspaper I saw the hostess walking my way. She smiled at me—I thought. I replied with a smile. She strode past me and began talking to the fellow behind me in line. After chatting for a second she asked him "are you here for breakfast?" She led him to a seat. Am I invisible? I guess being at the front of the line doesn't mean you can count on being seated first.

I stopped in at the Community Hospital of the Monterey Peninsula to see Joanne Sherrill-Drummer. Joanne works at the hospital, was born in Seaside and has lived on the Peninsula most of her life. During our conversation she spoke of things she has learned not to count on. She does not count on being able to open the newspaper and see people of her own race positively represented. If a traffic cop pulls her over she doesn't count on it not being because of her race. She does not count on her skin color not affecting her in financial situations. Joanne did not list these points with resentment. Rather, she said she was not intimidated by these differences and, in fact, they have helped her develop a sense of self.

I drove over to Mel Mason's office to solicit his thoughts about these events. Is any of this racism I asked. Mel responded, "If you were a white man would the woman at the pool have failed to see you? If the hostess were a black woman and you were in front of the line would she have seated you first?" While it isn't cross burning or lynching and no one yelled a racial epithet, it sure speaks to a sense of privilege.

Interestingly, after that woman seized the lane I was about to swim in, I marched to the other end of the pool. I reached an empty lane at about the same time as another fellow—a white man. He said, "You take it. You've been waiting a while." And that hostess reappeared a couple of minutes later, guided me to a table, and asked if I wanted coffee.

Courtesy of Dr. John Berteaux, California State University Monterey Bay

John Berteaux, American philosopher, professor at California State University Monterey Bay, and columnist for the *Monterey County Herald.*

Unseen, Unheard, Unchosen

JOHN BERTEAUX

Op-ed essay from the **Monterey County Herald,** *March 6, 2006.*

Usually I am ambling along across campus when out of the blue I am overtaken by a niggling uncertainty. In the distance I see Bridgett, Shannon, Vanessa, Rachel or one of the many coeds taking one of my classes. I stop and call out. I call out because I recall that they tried to ask a question or comment on something during the class period and I fear I overlooked them—didn't see their hands—thought I would get back to them and didn't. "Sorry I missed you in class today," I confess. The standard response is, "You answered all my questions." The problem is: that particular response doesn't help.

About four or five years ago, in a class at San Diego State University, I brought up the problem of the invisibility of women in the classroom. I was surprised at the number of women in the room who had developed techniques for dealing with just this issue.

Sadly, most of the techniques were like that of Danusia. Danusia was a returning student, with two young daughters. She was a hard worker, bright, and I would guess in her early thirties—a budding philosopher. During the discussion she said that generally she gave a professor a couple of chances. The second or third time that she was ignored in the classroom she simply stopped raising her hand. Of course, within the period of a half an hour after the discussion, she raised her hand. I said, "Give me a second let me finish this thought." As I finished the thought I promptly called on a young man whose hand was up. He was sitting right behind Danusia. Realizing what I had done I stopped the young man in mid-sentence and allowed Danusia to ask her question.

As I remember, everyone in the class, including Danusia and me, laughed. Certainly the laughter and my apology changed little. Women suffer because of the unconscious assumptions and actions of well meaning people in everyday interactions—assumptions and actions that are invisible to us.

"Was your hand up," I ask? "No," she replies. I go on talking and then three, four, five hands go up at once. As I speak, I mull over, "Whose hand went up first?" I am not sure.

Study Questions

1. Would you agree with Berteaux that the two incidents of being "invisible" in the first text reflect a subtle form of modern racism? If yes, what can be done about it? If no, do you think Berteaux misread the situation? Explain. What significance do the last two incidents in the first text have?

2. Define racism, as opposed to bigotry. In your view, is racism always directed from white people toward people of color, or can racism go in other directions?

3. Do you find that it is harder for women to get their point across in the classroom? If yes, is that due to the same kind of unconscious discrimination that Berteaux points out in the first text? Is Berteaux discriminating against the women in his classroom? Why or why not?

 Narrative

Blade Runner

RIDLEY SCOTT (DIRECTOR),

HAMPTON FANCHER AND DAVID PEOPLES (SCREENWRITERS)

Film, 1982. From the novel **Do Androids Dream of Electric Sheep?** *by Philip K. Dick. Summary.* Blade Runner 2049, **film, 2018. Summary.**

The film *Blade Runner* has become one of the definitive philosophical explorations of personhood in the movies, both in the futuristic sense of granting rights to self-aware androids/Artificial Intelligence, and also at a deeper level, in terms of recognizing every thinking being as an end-in-himself or herself, and not merely a means to an end. This summary was a staple in the first four editions of this book, and it has been brought back at the requests of students as well as professors—partly because the film's emphasis on personhood has only deepened through the years, but also because the long-awaited sequel was released in 2018, one year before the original story takes place. *Blade Runner* is generally recognized as one of the finest science fiction films ever made. Whether the sequel has done it justice is a matter of opinion, but the reviews were generally positive. A postscript to the original *Blade Runner* reflecting the sequel can be found at the end of this section.

At its premiere the critics weren't impressed with *Blade Runner;* it was too weird for most moviegoers' taste at the time. Over the years, though, the film achieved a near-cult status among film lovers for its "film noir" style and prophetic theme of asking, Who counts as a person? What looked like cultural mishmash in 1982 is now recognized as an accurate depiction of life in the inner cities—not only in the far-distant future, but even today.

This is Los Angeles as the movie imagines it in the future year of 2019: dirty, perpetually rainy because of pollution, and populated with people from all cultures, all of whom are looking out for themselves. The language of the streets is a mix of Japanese, German, and English. Giant blimps cruise the skies advertising "a new life off-planet," away from the hopelessness of earth life. There are almost no nonhuman animals left on earth, so humans are manufacturing mechanical pets—robotic owls and ostriches and snakes and what have you. In addition they are also manufacturing artificial humans, replicants to take on hazardous and difficult work off-world. The latest series of replicants is particularly advanced. Stronger and more intelligent than humans, they already have become a danger to them: They are rebelling and have already killed some humans. Private detective Deckard is assigned the job of hunting them down and destroying them. He meets with their manufacturer, who tells him that these beings have a built-in self-destruct mechanism; four years is as long as they can live. Deckard has no sympathy for these beings; as far as he is concerned, they are mere things to be terminated. A young woman, Rachael, is staying at the house of the manufacturer. Deckard is attracted to her, and his view on replicants begins to change when he realizes that she,

Album/Alamy Stock Photo

Considered by some to be the best science fiction film ever, *Blade Runner* (1982) has stood the test of time, which can be particularly hard for a visionary sci-fi film. The world it envisions is not yet upon us; we don't yet have androids, or off-planet colonies to escape to, but we do have crowded polyglot (multi-language) big-city downtowns, with bad weather generated by pollution, and dwindling wildlife species. Here, in one of the most memorable scenes in the movie, and in film history altogether, the android Batty (Rutger Hauer) is nearing the end of his short life, and bemoans the fact that all his experiences are about to disappear—"like tears in rain."

too, is a replicant, although she herself is unaware of it. She is an experimental model, and her "brain" contains implants of someone else's childhood memories, which make her seem more human and make her believe she is human. Given the existence of such extraordinary features, who can say for sure who is a replicant and who isn't? Might Deckard himself also be one?

Eventually, Deckard catches up with the runaway replicants one by one. Their leader, Batty, the strongest and most intelligent of all of them, engages Deckard in a fight to the death. (The replicant's death is approaching anyway, because his lifespan is almost up.) In the fight, when Deckard is close to losing his own life, he realizes that what the replicant wants is what all humans want—just a little more time to live, to sense, and to breathe. Dying, Batty speaks of his life: "I've seen things you people wouldn't believe . . . attack ships on fire off the shoulder of Orion. . . . I've watched c-beams glitter in the dark near the Tanhauser Gate. All those moments . . . they'll be lost, in time . . . like tears in rain. . . ."

In the 2018 sequel, *Blade Runner 2049,* the focus is less on the rights of replicants and more on the fate of the Earth and the characters of Deckard and Rachel 30 years after they met in the original

Blade Runner. Since going into the plot will reveal spoilers as to the ending of the original *Blade Runner,* I will not do that, but just refer to Study Question #4 below.

Study Questions

1. What statement does *Blade Runner* make about humanity and human rights, if any?

2. Are the runaway replicants persons? Is Rachael? Is Deckard? Is the manufacturer? What makes someone a person?

3. What might Kant's position be concerning the question of rights for the replicants of *Blade Runner* (or concerning any question of future rights for self-aware artificial intelligence)? (Remember his criterion for who should never be treated merely as a means to an end.)

4. A question containing a moderate spoiler: In the 2018 sequel, the issue arises of whether it might be possible for a human and replicant to produce a viable offspring—to have a baby. If that were the case, do you think it would change the attitude of the authorities in 2049 toward replicants as being non-human? Would it matter for your attitude toward a cyborg person?

 Narrative

Ex Machina

ALEX GARLAND (DIRECTOR AND SCREENWRITER)

Film, 2015. Summary.

In Chapter 2, you read about the *Golem* trope, exemplified by the story of Frankenstein's monster, the artificially created person who destroys everything it is supposed to protect, including its master. But you also read about the *Pygmalion* trope, the male artist who creates a beautiful artificial woman who falls in love with him and becomes his lover. One is the dark, fearful fantasy of one's creation being out of control, and the other is the happy fantasy of one's creation behaving as planned, or even exceeding expectations. *Ex Machina* is both a Pygmalion and a Golem story. In order to make this point, I'll have to include a spoiler at the end of the summary. The film was nominated for Best Original Screenplay and won an Oscar for Best Visual Effects. The title is taken from the Roman theater where a *Deus ex Machina* means "a god from a machine," a solution to a conflict coming out of nowhere.

A young programmer, Caleb Smith, can't believe his luck when he finds himself the winner of a one-week stay with the founder and CEO of the Internet search engine company where he works, Nathan Bateman. The Bateman property is up in the mountains, so far off the grid that the only means of transportation is by helicopter. Upon arrival, Caleb finds out that for one thing, the compound consists of several segments that have electronic locks, so only Bateman's own key card can give access to the entire home/facility; Caleb's own key card only allows him access to his room and general living quarters of the house. For another thing, he finds out that the reason he has been brought to the Bateman estate is so he can administer a test to Nathan's latest computerized creation, a genuine Artificial Intelligence—a turning point in AI research. Furthermore, he realizes that the lottery was rigged, so there was no question of anyone else winning the one-week stay. Bateman wanted him in particular. The test in question is the famous *Turing Test* (named for the mathematician Alan Turing) which is designed to test whether a computer will be able to mimic a human's responses to the degree that the interviewer mistakes it for a human—but as Caleb remarks, the premise is wrong, because he already knows that he will be working with an AI. Nathan Bateman explains that the robot already has passed the test, but Caleb's task is to engage in conversation and interaction with the robot to evaluate to what degree it could pass for a real human being. Caleb is introduced to the robot, Ava, who has a human face (a very beautiful one), and a robotic body with the shape of a young female. She seems willing to cooperate, and they begin to converse, while Nathan is watching through one of the many surveillance cameras throughout the facility. It turns out that Ava draws pictures, but doesn't know what she is drawing; she has never left the building, which consists of segments that are separated by glass walls, and she really doesn't have a sense of the real world. She is on one side of the glass wall, and Caleb is on the other—to begin with. After a while their conversation becomes less strained, and during a power outage (where Nathan supposedly can't observe them) she tells Caleb not to trust Nathan—that he is a liar.

There is a woman living with Bateman, on the "person" side of the glass walls, Kyoto. She doesn't speak any English, and Caleb can't communicate with her. She seems to be both servant and girlfriend—and perhaps even a slave in her extreme subservience. Nathan is rude to her, and screams at her when she spills some wine. She doesn't seem to have any interaction with Ava.

Over the next few days Ava undergoes a change. She puts on a wig and clothes, and begins to flirt with Caleb who is obviously attracted by her, but also disturbed about the situation, of having a robot come on to him. Nathan himself is behaving erratically, getting drunk and passing out. Caleb gains access to Nathan's private lab where he sees video footage of Nathan abusing Ava and tearing up a drawing of hers. During another power outage—which it turns out that Ava herself is causing—she asks Caleb to help her escape. In addition, Nathan tells Caleb that if Ava turns out not to pass the test, she will be reprogrammed—in other words, killed. Caleb plots to steal Nathan's key card and reprogram the door locks, and during one of the CEO's binges Caleb pockets the card and finds himself in the lab where he discovers Ava's predecessors, deactivated AI women with a wide variety of looks. Kyoto reveals that she herself is a robot, by peeling skin off her face. And Caleb has an "episode" in his own quarters where he desperately tries to reassure himself, by cutting into his arm, that he is not just another robot.

The last night before Caleb is due to be picked up by the helicopter—and is preparing to make his getaway with Ava—Nathan lets him know that he knows all about their escape plans, and that Caleb shouldn't believe Ava's attempts at seduction, she is just using him to get away from Nathan; but Caleb has a surprise for his host and employer: he didn't wait until the last minute to reprogram the locks—he already did that the night before, and all the doors are now open. Nathan, in a rage, knocks Caleb out and runs off to find Ava and deactivate her. Confronting her, he destroys her arm, but now Nathan encounters an unexpected enemy: Kyoto stabs him in the back with a knife—which shows that it isn't just Ava who has developed emotions. And as he tries to get away, Ava takes the knife with her good hand and plunges it into his chest. Next, she locks Caleb in Nathan's soundproof room.

Will Ava make her escape? Will Kyoto? And what happens to Caleb? I won't give the last minutes of the film away, but just point out that the Pygmalion trope, in a nightmare twist, has turned out to be a Golem trope.

Study Questions

1. Has Ava passed the Turing Test that Caleb was supposed to administer? In other words, is deviousness and killing (even if it is in self-defense) part of being a person?

2. Is it necessary for an AI to be granted personhood that he/she/it acts emotionally like a human being? What would Kant say?

3. Who is using whom as "merely a means to an end" in this story?

4. Why do you think Nathan is creating these artificial women? And why does he need Caleb to prove Ava's personhood?

5. What does the title mean?

6. Compare Ava and Rachael (*Blade Runner*), and describe some fundamental differences and similarities between them.

 Narrative

Gattaca

ANDREW NICCOL (SCREENWRITER AND DIRECTOR)

Film, 1997. Summary.

Gattaca is also a science fiction film, but there are very few special effects or futuristic inventions. The science fiction element is almost exclusively one of a thought experiment, a mind game: What if . . .? What if babies could be designed in the lab, eradicating birth defects, nearsightedness, high cancer risk, and so forth? Wouldn't that be wonderful? Perhaps not. Exploring the possible human future of genetic engineering (reminiscent of Huxley's *Brave New World*), *Gattaca* tells the story of a near-future society in which each child is the dream child of its parents, the best combination of their genes—if the child is legitimately conceived in the lab, that is. Children conceived the natural way are considered flawed and will never rise above being manual laborers.

Vincent Freeman is such a child, the firstborn son of young parents. He is born with myopia and a high probability of heart failure before the age of thirty; even so, as a young adult he outpaces his younger brother, a more socially acceptable individual conceived in a petri dish with all the good genes. At the beginning of the film, we witness Vincent's parents' visit to the clinic where they and the doctor discuss the future genetic characteristics of Vincent's brother-to-be, as yet an embryo. We see how reluctant the parents are at first, being resigned to following custom and merely having the embryo screened for diseases, but the doctor persuades them that life is hard enough as it is, so why not give him all the advantages that are possible? "He will still be you—only the best of you." But growing up, the one with the ambitious goals is not the perfect boy conceived in the lab, Anton, but his imperfect older brother. Vincent dreams of becoming an astronaut and leaving for the outer solar system, but as a natural-born individual he has no chance—legally. So he embarks on acquiring an illegal identity, not just a new name and history but new DNA, an entirely new genetic profile. An identity broker sets him up with a genetically perfect individual, Jerome Eugene ("good genes"), who has no use for perfection. Jerome is disabled after a suicide attempt that was never registered, so Vincent pays him "rental" on his identity and moves in with him. The transformation involves surgery to add height to Vincent's legs, but otherwise the two young men are fairly similar. Vincent, now "Jerome," acquires a dream job at the Gattaca complex, where future space programs are planned and astronauts trained, by submitting urine and blood samples from Eugene. Every morning Eugene prepares samples of more blood, urine, hair and skin cells, and so forth for Vincent to use for the ongoing tests so that no trace will reveal the identity of the impostor. In the process, Vincent and Eugene become close friends.

Everything is working smoothly, and Vincent/ Jerome is valued at work for his high intelligence, his physical stamina, and his flawless genetic code. He meets a young female coworker, Irene, who also longs for the stars but has a heart disease probability that restricts her future as an astronaut. Vincent tries to make her realize that such preset probabilities are nothing but that, probabilities. They are not set in stone. He himself is overdue for his heart attack. He has apparently overcome all social obstacles handed to him by his low birth, but an unforeseen event happens: A Gattaca executive hostile to the current space program is found murdered. Although there is no evidence linking him to the murder, one of Vincent's eyelashes is found near the scene of the crime. The police run a genetic analysis on it and come up with Vincent's original identity; but since he as "Jerome" has a different genetic profile, nobody makes the connection. Even so, he fears he will be found out on the threshold of his dream: He has been slated for the next launch to Titan. As the police detectives move closer to his personal life and his girlfriend herself is beginning to suspect that "Jerome" is not what he seems to be, his audacious attempt at breaking out of the social hierarchy seems to be failing and his true identity seems about to be revealed.

PictureLux/The Hollywood Archive/Alamy Stock Photo

Gattaca (Columbia Pictures, 1997) posits a future world where respectable persons are conceived and genetically designed in vitro; only slobs and destitute people have children the natural way. Here Vincent/Jerome (Ethan Hawke) and Irene (Uma Thurman) are hiding from the police, and his false identity is in danger of being revealed.

Will Vincent go to prison for the murder, or will he go to Titan after all? Will his heart give out? Will Irene guess his identity? What happens to Eugene? Who killed the executive? And where is Vincent's brother? The ending of this interesting film offers many surprises.

Study Questions

1. What elements in the *Gattaca* plot are already a reality, or seem like they might become a reality in the near future? Should we welcome them or fight them? Is there a third alternative? Explain your position.

2. The film addresses first and foremost the discrimination against Vincent and others who are being excluded from having a happy, productive life because of their genes. But there is also an underlying angle: a criticism of the *predictable* future society in which there are no surprises because they have been bred out of the population. What is your opinion? Does society need genetic "surprises," unforeseeable genius, and generosity as one side of the coin and unpredictable criminal pathology as the other? Or are we better off with the vast majority of the population falling into a predictable norm?

3. Do the characters' names add something to the story? Explain.

4. When the film came out, very few people caught on to the significance of the title. Now that the Human Genome Project has been completed, it may not seem so mysterious to us. GATC are the initials of materials in the DNA code: guanine, adenine, thymine, and cytosine. What do you think the moviemakers wanted to say by calling the film, and Vincent's workplace, *Gattaca?*

5. The scene with Vincent's parents in the lab, discussing the future characteristics of Anton, was originally longer, providing an understanding of their switch from skepticism to enthusiasm when they hear that they can determine the boy's height and even a musical talent! But the addition of the talent turns out to be too expensive, so they settle for having a strong, smart, healthy, tall kid. This is the only time we hear that acquiring good genes is also a matter of money. In a future where genetic engineering is the order of the day, do you think the scenario of *Gattaca* is realistic? Does the outtake make a difference to the story? Should it have been left in?

 Narrative

Mississippi Burning

CHRIS GEROLMO (SCREENWRITER)
ALAN PARKER (DIRECTOR)

Film, 1988. Summary.

On June 21, 1964, three young civil rights activists were murdered in Philadelphia, Mississippi, an event that has haunted and divided the community to this day. Michael Schwerner, James Chaney, and Andrew Goodman—one black and two white men—had come to the small Mississippi community to register black voters. They were reported as missing and later were found murdered. The Ku Klux Klan was implicated. Some Klan members were brought to trial and found guilty, and others were acquitted. This film is a fictionalized story based on the actual events, and at the end of the summary you can read about an additional feature added to the story in 2005.

It is the early 1960s, in Jessup County, Mississippi, a time of racial segregation—made clear in the opening shot: one modern water cooler for whites and another, older model for blacks. Into this community come three young activists to ensure that black Americans will be able to exercise their right to vote, but in the dead of night their car is chased and overtaken by men in three vehicles, one of them a police car. They force the young men out of the car and shoot them. When the news spreads in the following days that the young men are missing, riots break out, and two FBI agents arrive in town: Rupert Anderson, himself a former sheriff from a small town in Mississippi, and Allan Ward, a go-by-the-book FBI man. Right away we sense that the two men are very different, with clashing personalities and outlooks. When paying a visit to the office of Sheriff Stuckey, Anderson treats the hostile officers like good ol' boys up to a point—and then we realize that he can get very confrontational. Ward, on the other hand, goes by Bureau regulations. The sheriff's story is that the three young men were arrested for speeding, released, and drove off.

The difference between Ward and Anderson is accentuated when they try to have lunch in the local restaurant: The hostess tells them there are no tables available, but Ward sees empty seats in the section for "Coloreds only." He heads straight for a seat next to a young black man and starts questioning him about what he may have heard regarding the activists. The young man is frightened and doesn't respond to Ward. Everyone is shocked, blacks and whites alike; and Anderson appears to be embarrassed that Ward is not only causing a scene but also approaching the issue in the wrong way. Later we see the indirect consequences of Ward's approach: The young black man is thrown from a car onto Main Street, beaten up as a warning.

In the meantime, we learn more about the antagonism between Anderson and Ward. Anderson says he believes the activists are being used politically, by cynical people, but for Ward it is a matter of doing what you believe in and sometimes risking death to do the right thing. When Ward speculates about where all this hatred comes from, Anderson tells him a story: When he was a kid in the South, his father was a poor man, but their black neighbor Monroe was a little better off because he got himself a mule. Shortly thereafter, somebody poisoned the mule, and Anderson's father later admitted to being the poisoner. For Anderson the culprit is poverty, not race. He wants to handle the situation his way, but Ward wants a whole investigative FBI team to become involved, and so they take over the movie theater for their operations. Anderson, though, follows his own nose, and goes to the barber shop, where he finds the sheriff and the mayor. Still acting like a small-town southern sheriff, he engages the mayor in a conversation about the situation. The mayor tells him the blacks in the community ("the nigras") were happy until the civil rights activists showed up. He believes that there are two cultures in the South, a black culture and a white culture, and that any effort of the federal government to effect change is an intrusion.

Next, Anderson heads to the beauty salon, to get the women's point of view. The salon is managed by Deputy Pell's wife, Mary. She is uneasy about the situation, and we sense that she knows a good deal more than she's saying, about the Klan as well as the disappearances.

The missing activists' car is found in the river on the Choctaw Indian Reservation, but there are no bodies. However, it now seems certain that the boys are dead, so Ward arranges for a full-scale dredging operation, to no avail. But the Klan responds with burnings of churches and homes in the black community. Ward and Anderson know that Sheriff Stuckey has an alibi, but they find Deputy Pell's alibi questionable, so they pay him a visit. While Ward confronts Pell with the allegation that he holds a high position in the Klan, Anderson seeks out Mary in the kitchen; and on several subsequent occasions, he makes a point of chatting her up, bringing her flowers, and just exchanging small talk, gaining her trust. And Mary is very different from her husband—we see her having a genuinely good time talking with a local black woman and her baby, people her husband has nothing but scorn for.

In the meantime, the national news media have descended on Jessup County, interviewing white locals. Most of the people interviewed think the whole thing is the fault of the civil rights activists, that Martin Luther King is a communist, and that the three young activists were asking for whatever they got. Some are convinced it's a hoax—a publicity stunt. A Klansmember, Clayton Townley, makes no bones about it: A white supremacist, he doesn't accept Jews, Catholics, or communists, and he wants "to protect Anglo-Saxon democracy and the American way." At the same time a KKK leader rallies the white community against racially mixed relationships, the "mongrelization" of America. Things are escalating, and Anderson now shows his true colors: As much as he comes across as a "redneck," his loyalties are to the FBI, and he single-handedly confronts Pell and his henchman Frank when they claim that no blacks will be allowed to vote. Moreover, he is discovering a new ally in Mary, who lets him know about an upcoming Klan meeting.

Ward and Anderson stake out the "meeting," which turns out to be a manhunt: A young black man is released from prison, then hunted down by the sheriff's men and driven away. The two FBI agents try to follow but lose sight of the sheriff's cars; later that night, they find the young man lying in the woods, alive but castrated. They failed to stop the sheriff's men, but now they suspect that the civil rights activists met their end the same way: released and then hunted down by the Klan.

When the farm belonging to the family of the young man who was Ward's first unwitting contact is torched, things come to a breaking point. The young man, Eric, rescues his mother and siblings and, then witnesses their cows burn to death. His father is captured when he tries to defend his home and then lynched. Eric manages to release the rope before his father chokes to death, and the next day Ward and Anderson help them leave the county for Detroit, where they have family.

This development disturbs Mary immensely, and during a quiet moment with Anderson while Pell is at one of his "meetings," she tells him how things are: Hatred, she says, isn't something you're born with—it is taught, every day, by your surroundings. And she wants it to stop—so she tells Anderson what she knows: Her husband shot the civil rights activists, and she knows where they are buried.

Now that the bodies are retrieved, Anderson and Ward have a heated argument about methods—Anderson's questioning of Mary has resulted in Pell's beating her to within an inch of her life. In a surprising change of attitude, Ward decides to back Anderson: They have the authority, and they'll do it his way. They need someone to talk—and they find somebody who will talk to protect himself. It is the mayor. In a stunning reversal of events, the mayor is kidnapped, by a hooded man. Gagged and bound, the mayor is offered a choice by his captor, who turns out to be a black man—an FBI agent with special talents: Either he talks, or he will be castrated, the same way KKK members have castrated black men. And the mayor talks.

Now Ward and Anderson know who was involved, but since the mayor's story was extracted under duress, they can't use it in court. Instead, they manipulate Pell and his men, making them think each one has been talking to the FBI, and one of them gives up the others. A series of arrests and trials follow, but we also have a feeling that some of the culprits are never going to be held accountable.

Anderson pays a visit to Mary, whose house has been ransacked, and apologizes for having essentially ruined her life. But she explains that she'll stay on, because there are enough people in town who see things her way. Finally, at the burned-out church, black and white citizens gather together for a service.

The film was met with mixed reviews: Some reviewers found that it was a fine, well-crafted, moving story, but others thought it was a manipulative misrepresentation: Blacks were reduced to one-dimensional victims; Klan members were portrayed as degenerates; FBI Director J. Edgar Hoover was portrayed as a civil rights supporter, whereas he, in fact, kept extensive files on Dr. Martin Luther King, Jr.; and FBI agents were depicted as people with questionable ethics. Yet other movie critics pointed out that films are not supposed to be historically accurate social documentaries, but well-told narratives with their own message and their own reality. This film is, of course, not a documentary—it is fictionalized, with invented characters.

But history wrote another chapter to the story: In January 2005, a 79-year-old man was arrested after a county grand jury indictment for being the mastermind behind the deaths of Schwerner, Chaney, and Goodman: Edgar Ray Killen, an alleged Ku Klux Klan leader and a Baptist preacher. Killen was tried on federal charges in 1967 but released after one juror refused to convict him (others were convicted, and some were acquitted); he is a known separatist and has been quoted as saying that God didn't create blacks and whites equal. A jury found Killen guilty on three counts of manslaughter in June 2005, and the judge sentenced him to sixty years in prison. Killen passed away in 2018, in prison. He was 92.

Study Questions

1. Do you agree with Anderson's approach? With Ward's? Or perhaps with another viewpoint expressed in the film? Explain.

2. Is this film an example of forward-looking or backward-looking justice? Explain.

3. Is this film a fair representation of the FBI? of the civil rights movement? of the locals in the small Mississippi county? Some reviewers called the film itself unethical. Can you imagine why?

4. What is the message of this film? Explain. Could there be several messages? Discuss.

5. Assess the current situation in the area of the United States that you know best: What are race relations like today, as far as you can discern? Is there general goodwill and understanding, are there underlying animosities and hidden racism, or is there an open racial conflict? What would you consider progress in race relations in this country?

Narrative

Green Book

PETER FARRELLI (DIRECTOR)
NICK VALLALONGA, BRIAN CURRIE, AND PETER FARRELLI (SCREENWRITERS)

Film, 2018. Summary.

The film *Green Book*, based on a true story about the pianist Dr. Donald Shirley and the memoirs of Tony Vallalonga, has won a number of prizes, including the 2019 Academy Award for Best Picture, Best Original Screenplay, and Best Supporting Actor for Mahershala Ali, playing Don Shirley. Viggo Mortensen, playing Tony Vallalonga, was nominated for Best Actor.

The setting is New York, 1962 (the same time period as in our previous narrative, *Mississippi Burning*). Tony "Lip" Vallalonga is a bouncer at the famous nightclub the Copacabana. After an altercation involving Tony, the club is closed down for renovation, and Tony is temporarily out of a job. Tony is an Italian American blue-collar family man with traditional family values and a talent for BS-ing, hence the nickname "Lip." He loves Italian food and food in general. We see him win a hot dog eating contest, scarfing down 26 hot dogs and winning $50, right before his wife Dolores serves dinner at home.

Reacting to a job offer of being a driver for a doctor, Tony shows up for an interview at an address that turns out to be Carnegie Hall. The famous pianist Dr. Donald Shirley needs a driver for his concert tour. His trio, consisting of himself, the Russian cellist Oleg, and the bassist George, is scheduled for a tour of the Deep South, and Shirley will need not only a driver but a personal assistant who will take responsibility for the tour's completion, an 8-week engagement. Tony is introduced to Dr. Shirley in his apartment above the concert hall—an elaborate abode full of mementos from travels around the world, including an elevated throne. Dr. Shirley enters—a distinguished, elegant African American. He interviews Tony while sitting on the throne, and it is clear that the two have very little in common. Tony doesn't like the prospect and holds out for higher wages, without success, and next we see him pawn his watch; he's broke. However, Dr. Shirley makes a call to Tony's home, and talks with Dolores: Will she be comfortable with her husband being on the road for two months? He offers Tony the job at the price Tony asked for. All Dolores is asking is that he write to her and that he will be home for Christmas.

The tour about to commence, Tony gets instructions; one of his tasks is to ensure that a Steinway grand piano is present at all concert venues (Tony isn't into the terminology of the music world and writes it "Stainway"). In addition, he is instructed in the use of a pamphlet, *The Negro Motorist's Green Book*. The tour is going into the Southern states, and racial segregation laws are the order of the day: people of color can't use the same facilities, eat in the same restaurants, or stay in the same hotels as whites.

Collection Christophel/Alamy Stock Photo

The film *Green Book,* the winner of the 2019 Academy Award for Best Picture, tells a true story (albeit somewhat fictionalized) about the budding friendship between two men from very different backgrounds, a famous pianist on a concert tour, Dr. Don Shirley (Mahershala Ali, who also won the Academy Award for Best Actor), and his driver and subsequent friend Tony Lip (Viggo Mortenson), a New York nightclub bouncer with an Italian American background.

With Tony in the driver's seat and Don Shirley in the back, they immediately start disagreeing. Tony wants to smoke in the car, Shirley prohibits it; Tony seems to be constantly eating, messily, while Shirley only eats using a knife and fork; Tony wants to have the radio on a pop music station, and Shirley hates it. Tony has totally misunderstood the cover of one of Shirley's vinyl records, "Orpheus in the Underworld," based on a light opera with the theme of a Greek tragedy, and assumes it is a story about orphans. But when the radio plays rhythm and blues performed by famous black artists of the 1950s and 60s, Shirley is equally ignorant of the style and the songs. There is an obvious cultural divide between the two—not along racial, but along class lines. Shirley complains about Tony's "Bronx" style of speech, and wants to help educate him and improve his diction, and even suggests that Tony should change his last name to something more pronounceable for the sake of the tour and its highly cultured hosts, and Tony is deeply offended. Tony, on the other hand, offends Shirley by suggesting that he should know more about "his people," in terms of music, but also about stereotypical notions such as foods and manners, introducing him to eating fried chicken with his bare hands.

On the tour, going south from Pittsburgh, PA, to Hanover, IN, to Louisville, KY, the two get to know each other better. Tony realizes that Shirley is a lonely person, not even socializing with his two other trio members during their time off. But he is a world-famous pianist, having performed at the White House twice (in the Kennedy administration), and his education is in classical music, as the first black student at the Leningrad Conservatory of Music in (then) the Soviet Union. And Tony realizes that what was a respectful reception of a famous pianist in Pittsburgh becomes a travesty the further south they go. In one venue only a dirty, cheap piano is available for the concert, and Tony has to flex his bouncer muscles in order to procure a Steinway. The *Green Book* becomes a necessary guide in Kentucky. Shirley has to stay in a rat trap of a hotel, "for colored only," and when he goes out for a drink later on—in a bar for whites—Tony has to extricate him from a physical confrontation with bar guests. At a clothing store, Shirley wants to buy a new suit, but the store manager won't allow him to try the suit on—he has to buy it untried. At a concert in a private home in North Carolina, Shirley is directed to an outhouse when needing the bathroom, while the white audience uses the indoor plumbing. Shirley has a moment where he blames Tony for his difficulties, because Tony down South belongs to the privileged race, but Tony points out that he has nothing in common with southern white people. But a far worse situation arises, in Georgia, when Tony is called to the local YMCA after Shirley's concert. Shirley is being arrested for being in the company of a young man, both of them naked, and obviously having been engaged in a sexual encounter (illegal in 1962). Tony gets him out of the jam by bribing the police officers, in classic mob style. Shirley is not happy about Tony's action of rewarding the cops and admonishes him that "dignity always prevails." Later Tony explains to Shirley that he has been working nightclubs for years, and "knows that life is complicated." Shirley understand that he won't be judged by Tony for being gay.

Two more confrontations are in store for Shirley and Tony: In Louisiana, on a rainy night, Tony loses his way in the dark, and the car is stopped by the police. They are in violation of the "sun-set" law: Blacks have a curfew after dark—and when one of the cops hear that Tony is an Italian American, he calls him half a black person (using a racial slur, the so-called N-word). Tony hits the cop, and they are both thrown in jail. But this time around it is Don Shirley who comes through, with one legally allowed phone call. And begrudgingly, the chief of police lets them go. Whom did Shirley call? Robert (Bobby) Kennedy, Attorney General, the brother of President John F. Kennedy. But Don is not proud that he had to call Washington; humiliated, he doesn't feel that he belongs anywhere—not among blacks, or whites, or heterosexuals—so what is he? That night they both check into a hotel from the *Green Book* list, as friends.

The final insult happens at the last venue, in Birmingham, AL, where the trio is scheduled to play a Christmas concert at a resort with a concert hall and a fancy restaurant. When the trio and Tony want to have dinner before the concert, management steps in: The star of the evening's performance is not allowed to eat in the restaurant, but can go down the street to a place called the Orange Bird. And this is the last straw. Don, standing up for himself, gives them an ultimatum: No dinner, no concert. And when the manager tries to bribe Tony, Don grabs Tony and walks out, breaking the contract. On their way out of town they decide to stop for food at the Orange Bird Cafe. It is a swinging place, full of blues music enthusiasts and diners, mostly black people. Tony and Don have dinner, and the waitress invites him to play a piece on the upright piano on stage. And he does—a classical piece from his repertoire at the Christmas concert. But one piece leads to another, the local blues band joins in, and Don ends up happily playing a Christmas concert at the Orange Bird.

In the night they head north, trying to make it home by Christmas, because Tony promised Dolores. The heavy rain turns to snow further north, and they head into a blizzard. A traffic cop stops them and they fear the worst, after all they've been through—but all he wants is to tell them they have a flat tire. He helps steer the traffic away whole Tony changes the tire, and wishes them a merry Christmas.

Will they make it home safely to New York? Will Tony make it home by Christmas? Will Don Shirley spend Christmas alone among his collections at Carnegie Hall? You'll have to watch the movie to find out! Just one spoiler: As they are headed further north, Tony is at the end of his endurance, and needs sleep—and Don switches places with him, driving his driver toward home.

Study Questions

1. Throughout the trip Tony has been writing letters to his wife; at first the letters are written exactly the way he talks—plain words with flawed grammar, and not very romantic. But then the style changes, and the letters become little works of art. So what happened? Shirley has dictated romantic letters to Dolores, to help Tony out. But toward the end of the trip Tony has learned to write sweetly poetic letters all by himself. What Dolores says to that you'll have to watch the movie to find out, but would you call the letters a fraud? Why or why not?

2. Is Tony a racist, trying to fit Don Shirley into the mold of what he knows about African Americans? Is Shirley a bigot for trying to educate and elevate Tony above what Shirley considers low-class behavior?

3. Is Don Shirley doing the right thing, ditching the Christmas concert despite having a contract at the venue where they wouldn't serve him dinner, and spending the evening playing with the blues band at the Orange Bird instead? Is he breaking his own rule that "dignity always prevails"? What would a utilitarian say? What would a Kantian say? (That could get complicated, so think about your response!)

4. How can we tell that Tony and Don are becoming less prejudicial toward each other during their 8-week journey?

5. Is the story fair to the culture of the South in the 1950s and 60s? Should it be? Why or why not?

6. Compare *Green Book and Mississippi Burning*: Do they have a similar or a different message? Point out the similarities and the differences between the two stories.

Chapter Eight
Virtue Ethics from Tribal Philosophy to Socrates and Plato

Throughout most of Western civilization and most of the history of ethics, scholars have tried to answer the question, *What should I do?* In Chapters 3 to 7 we have explored that quest. Theories that consider what proper human conduct is are often referred to as *ethics of conduct*.

There is a more ancient approach to ethics, and in the past few decades this older approach has experienced a revival. This form of ethics asks the fundamental question, *How should I be?* It focuses on the development of certain personal qualities, of a certain behavior pattern—in other words, on the development of what we call *character*. Because its foundation is in ancient Greek theories involving the question of how to be a virtuous person, this approach usually is referred to as *virtue ethics*. However, virtue ethics as a phenomenon is far older than the Greek tradition and is encountered in many other cultures. On pages 343–346, you'll see some examples of non-Western virtue ethics.

What Is Virtue? What Is Character?

The concept of virtue (Greek: *aretē*) is complex. For one thing, it carries certain associations, which it has acquired over the centuries; thus, in English, we may think of virtue as a basically positive concept—a virtuous person is someone you can trust. We also may experience, however, a certain negative reaction to it; sometimes, a virtuous person is thought of as being rather dull and perhaps even sanctimonious. (Being called a "Goody Two-Shoes" is not a compliment.) In everyday language, "virtue" often refers to sexual abstinence, and that can, of course, be a positive concept as well as a negative one, depending on one's viewpoint. A book titled *Raising Maidens of Virtue* was published in 2004, advocating raising teenage girls according to biblical principles of purity, modesty, cleanliness, and other traditional virtues.

However, the ancient Greek concept of *aretē* differs considerably from what we today associate with "virtue." For one thing, it has its origin in the name of the Greek god Ares, the god of war, and must originally have meant having warrior-like qualities. (Here we can add that the term *virtue* itself comes from Latin, and its origin is *vir*, or "male"!) But regardless of origins in deep antiquity, the word *aretē* would have had no negative connotations for a Greek-speaking person at the time of Socrates and Plato, because it signifies a different kind of person altogether: not a person of untainted thoughts and behavior, but a person who does what he or she does best and does it excellently, on a regular basis. We still have a trace of the ancient meaning of *aretē* in the word *virtuosity*. Originally, a virtuous person was a *virtuoso* at everything he or she did, because of proper choices and good habits but, above all, because such a person had succeeded in developing a good character.

Is Character Innate?

Today we often take a deterministic view of the concept of character. It is something we are born with, something we can't help. If we try to go against our character, it will surface in the end. That viewpoint may or may not be correct, but in any event it is shaped by modern schools of thought in philosophy and psychology. Not everyone shares that view; it often is pointed out that we may be born with a certain character but our character can be molded to a certain extent when we are young, and it certainly can be *tested* throughout our lives. This point of view comes closer to the prevailing attitude toward virtue among Greek philosophers: Character is indeed something we are born with, but it is also something that can and must be shaped. We are not the victims of our character, and if we let ourselves be victimized by our own unruly temperaments, then we are to blame.

Non-Western Virtue Ethics: Africa and Indigenous America

As I mentioned in Chapter 1, Socrates gets credit for introducing the topic of ethics as a philosophical discipline in the Western intellectual tradition, meaning that he engaged in, and encouraged his students to engage in, theoretical discussions about values, good character, and good behavior. But, of course, that doesn't mean that Socrates invented morals, values, or even ethics. It is inconceivable that a culture can exist, and persist, without having some system of values, some moral rules identifying good and bad social behavior, so as far back as we can trace *Homo sapiens* cultures—according to current scientific views some 300,000 years or more—there must have been moral codes. (Even earlier forms of hominins may well have had basic rules of coexistence, such as "Be generous and don't hoard food," "Show respect toward the Old Leaders," and "Be loyal to your tribe.") And it is also almost certain that these ancient groups (as you read in Chapter 2) had stories—myths and legends—that would explain how everything came into being and why humans ought to behave in this way and not in that way. So if we identify ethics as explaining or questioning the moral rules (see Chapter 1), then ethics, too, has been part of the human social fabric for a very long time indeed. Some of those stories are part of the human memory banks to this day in the form of folklore, as well as ancient surviving religions or the surviving written works of dead religions. What is interesting in this context is that in some cultures (such as China; see Chapter 11), the moral value systems have emphasized *conduct*—doing the right thing—but the overwhelming number of ancient stories that we have, as well as examples of tribal cultures around the world, seem to have favored the *virtue ethics* approach: focusing on developing a good character.

Even if the main topic of this chapter is the philosophy of Plato and his teacher Socrates, we'll take a brief look at the phenomenon of *tribal virtue ethics* from two non-Western traditions: African and indigenous American tribal cultures.

African Virtue Theory

For the Akan people in West Africa (in the Ghana region), morality consists of having a good character. Although one probably cannot classify the Akan people of today as "tribal" in the classic sense, their cultural origin is that of a tribal community where religion, moral values, and folklore all help determine the common outlook on life. In his book *An Essay on African Philosophical Thought: The Akan Conceptual Scheme,* the philosopher Kwame Gyekye (1939–2019), himself an Akan, emphasized that Akan ethics is not perceived as something commanded by *Onyame* (God); the Akan people regard their ethics as having a humanistic origin. Gyekye says that insofar as religion is involved at all, the Akan people have a natural law approach to morality: If something makes sense morally, then that is its reason for being a moral law, not its connection to a supernatural being.

Gyekye describes the Akan ethics as focused on virtue and character; whenever a person commits an act of wrongdoing, it is said not that "he/she did something wrong" but that "he/she is a bad person." How does one become a good person? As in every theory of virtue, that is a difficult question, because "character" tends to be something we are born with. However, the Akan ethics assumes, like the Aristotelian theory of the Golden Mean (see Chapter 9), that we can work toward acquiring a good character through good habits. And the best way to teach those good habits is through *storytelling.* Contrary to most traditional Western ethicists, the Akan thinkers have not forgotten that it is through stories that children get their first and perhaps their best exposure to the concepts of right and wrong. Those stories and proverbs habituate the children to moral virtues. Gyekye points out that people still have a choice of behavior and can be held accountable for that behavior because if they act in a morally wrong way, it means that they have not built up their own character the way they should have.

This forms a link between an ethics of conduct and an ethics of virtue, says Gyekye: It is because of what you do that you become a good person; you don't start out doing good things because of who you are. Originally, a human being is born morally neutral, according to Akan moral philosophies.

What kinds of virtues are favored by the Akans? Kindness, faithfulness, compassion, and hospitality are among the key virtues. Akan values are utilitarian in the sense that anything that promotes social well-being is a good thing. Even if God approves of virtue, the bottom line is that it is good for the people. The most important thing in Akan moral thought is the well-being of the community. The community thrives when the people cultivate social virtues. In *An Essay on African Philosophical Thought,* Gyekye says:

> Akan thought . . . sees humans as originally born into a human society (*onipa kurom*), and therefore as social beings from the outset. In this conception it would be impossible for people to live in isolation. For not only is the person not born to live a solitary life, but the individual's capacities are not sufficient to meet basic human requirements. For the person . . . is not a palm tree that he or she should be complete or self-sufficient.

The Akan view of storytelling as a path to moral understanding comes close to the premise of this book: that we, as socialized humans, can explore our ethical systems by listening to and making up stories. In every culture the first moral lessons seem to be taught through stories (see Chapter 2), and in the moral universe of the Akan people myths and legends guide the young toward becoming responsible members of the community. Similarly, you'll remember how the character of Tata Ndu (*The Poisonwood Bible,* Chapter 3) emphasized the importance of the community. This *communitarian* philosophy, with close ties to storytelling, can be found in the virtue ethics of ancient Greece as well.

Native American Values

The value system of North American Indian tribes has itself acquired a mythological status in America and indeed around the world. The values of the Native American have come to stand for *ecological virtue,* because it commonly is believed that these tribal people lived in harmony with nature, without abusing their own resources. One reason for this perceived harmony is the American Indian idea of what constitutes a *moral community;* for the traditional Native American, this community consists of the tribe, but also of their immediate nonhuman neighbors: the animals, and the spirits of the rocks, the trees, the winds, and the waters. In their compilation of Indian myths and legends, Richard Erdoes and Alfonso Ortiz include the White River Sioux account of the old days before Columbus when "we were even closer to the animals than we are now; many people could understand the animal languages; they could talk to a bird, gossip with a butterfly. Animals could change themselves into people, and people into animals."

The ecologist J. Baird Callicott says in his paper "Traditional American Indian and Western European Attitudes Toward Nature: An Overview" that although there is no such things as *the* American Indian belief system, there is still a predominant view shared by tribal Indians toward nature. According to Callicott:

> The Ojibwa, the Sioux, and if we may safely generalize, most American Indians, lived in a world which was peopled not only by human persons, but by persons and personalities associated with all natural phenomena. In one's practical dealings in such a world it is necessary to one's well-being and that of one's family to maintain good social relations not only with proximate human persons, one's immediate tribal neighbors, but also with the nonhuman persons abounding in the immediate environment. For example . . . among the Ojibwa "when bears were sought out in their dens in the spring they were addressed, asked to come out so that they could be killed, and an apology was offered to them."

It does appear that most Indigenous peoples of North America had a quite different relationship with their environment than did the settlers from Europe or even from Asia. The hunter would evoke the spirit of the animal before the hunt, asking its permission to kill it and promising it some kind of sacrifice in return; the hunter would not kill in excess; the hunter would not let anything of his prey go to waste; the women of the tribe would utilize every bit of material from the kill; the women would supply a large percentage of food for the tribe by gathering tubers, berries, and so on; and because theirs was a nomadic existence, the people would not stay in one place long enough to deplete its resources. There is evidence of a close spiritual relationship between the tribal people and their environment, of an understanding of the seasons, of animal movements, and of interrelationships between animal and human spirits—an understanding that humans have only a small part to play in the general order of things and are by no means all-important. There is evidence of a reverence for the mother of all (the earth) in the rejection of plowing by nineteenth-century Indians on the grounds that you don't plow furrows in your mother's breast. A Navajo chant praises the beauty of this world, "beauty before me, beauty behind me," not just empty land ripe for development.

Those values may seem very attractive to a modern, Western, nature-loving person in a world where there is little appreciation of the environment as an autonomous whole and where the word *development* seems to indicate that before the housing area there was "nothing," or at least "nothing of value." However, it may be another matter for a modern person to adopt Native American values. Callicott himself stresses that the American Indian attitude toward nature is not *conservationist* in the true sense, because it is not scientific but an integrated part of a moral and social order. We can't go to the American Indians and copy their way of life, because it involves social concerns that aren't ours anymore (such as taboos and hunting practices), but we can see it as an ideal, available as an option. So what is this option? In Callicott's words:

> The American Indian, on the whole, viewed the natural world as enspirited. Natural beings therefore felt, perceived, deliberated, and responded voluntarily as persons. Persons are members of a social order (i.e., part of the operational concept of a person is the capacity for social interaction). Social interaction is limited by (culturally variable) behavioral restraints, rules of conduct, which we call, in sum, good manners, morals, and ethics.

Does that mean that all American Indians have had a sense of a social order in their natural neighborhood? We can't assume that. It now seems clear that the reason the Anasazi culture of Arizona and New Mexico abandoned their cliff cities after several hundred years was partly because of a drought but also because they had exhausted the environment: There was no more wood, no more topsoil, and so they had to move. It also is a fact that although the Plains Indians did not hunt more animals than they could process (and the animal population did not suffer as a consequence), part of their success was due to the fact that the hunters were not very numerous. Had they been *able* to process large numbers of prey, we might have seen a decline in the animal population back then. It is now speculated that the woolly mammoth disappeared from the face of the earth in part because of very well-organized human hunting in North America as well as in Eurasia.

Humans, regardless of their tribe, have the potential for great care and great greed; we should be careful not to label whole populations "saints" and others "sinners." But if we look to the Native American tribes today, in the southwestern United States and elsewhere, we do find an attitude toward life and the role of humans in nature that indeed is based on a system of values that looks to the *balance* of things: Humans can be physically and mentally fit only if they are in harmony with their surroundings, and nature has to be in similar harmony for humans to stay healthy. The idea of internal and external harmony, which at one time seemed to be disappearing with the decline of American Indian culture, is on the rise again, along with an interest and pride in cultural traditions. In Box 8.1, you can read about an early Canadian environmentalist whose ideas are still relevant. In Chapter 13 we return to the idea of respect for nature as a virtue and take a look at the ethics involved in the debate about climate change.

Box 8.1 ARCHIE GREY OWL AND THE QUESTION OF VALUES

As you have seen, virtue ethics is an original form of value theory which focuses on the question of character rather than on conduct and social policies. As you will see in Chapters 9 and 10, sometimes virtue ethics can supplement ethics of conduct, and sometimes the two approaches stand in sharp contrast. An interesting case study in the contrast is that of a man who once was one of the most celebrated of Canada's environmentalists, but who "fell from grace" and was all but forgotten until recently when his environmental efforts are once again becoming acknowledged: Archie Grey Owl.

In the 1930s much of the Canadian forests were the focus of development, and habitats for wildlife were shrinking. Grey Owl, presenting himself as having been adopted by the Ojibwa Indians, but having had a Scottish father and an Apache mother, became one of the first Canadian conservationists to raise awareness of the intrinsic value of wild nature. Starting out as a trapper, he changed his mind about killing wildlife for profit, deeply influenced by his Ojibwa wife Gertrude/Anahareo, and together they adopted two young beavers and raised them. He went on lecture tours, including a highly publicized tour of the United Kingdom, and wrote a number of bestselling books on the Canadian wilderness, books that were

translated into many languages and sold all over the world. His voice for the environment was treasured because he was very eloquent, and spoke from the perspective of the indigenous peoples. But when he died in 1938 it was revealed that he was not a Canadian Indian at all: he was Archibald Belaney from Hastings, England. When he was a child he had loved stories about the Canadian and American West and above all stories about Indians, and when he was 18 he boarded a ship for Canada and faded away into the forests of Northern Ontario where he worked as a trapper and guide, living the life he had dreamed of as a boy. And he did indeed live with the Ojibwa Indians for a while, but everything else that he told the media and his biographer was fabricated. On his tour of England he had actually paid a visit to his two elderly aunts. So all the work Grey Owl had done for the preservation of the Canadian wilderness seemed tainted, and his name and his books became an embarrassment.

But time has worked in Archie Grey Owl's favor; today his strong defense of the wilderness is again recognized as a valuable contribution to Canadian history, and the fact that he took on a fake identity and "pulled it off" seems somewhat amusing rather than offensive to many. (Perhaps it also has something to do with the fact that most of the people he conned have passed on.) But here is the question, relevant for this chapter: According to ethics of conduct, Archie Grey Owl did lie about his background, but accomplished very important things; for a *Kantian* the lie is unforgiveable, but for the *utilitarian* Grey Owl deserves much praise for his efforts. For *virtue ethics* the all important thing is that Grey Owl adopted the value system of the First Nations culture he so deeply wanted to be a part of, and saw the social relations as being not just between humans, but also between humans and the inhabitants of the wild, and the wilderness itself, mirroring the statement by J.

Baird Callicott on p. 345. But as you can also read in the chapter text, the indigenous people's respect for nature is not traditionally conservationist. This is where Grey Owl provided a new form of thinking, because he reached out to the "white" Canadian community with ideas of conservationism, based on the Ojibwa virtue ethics, a true bridge builder, knowing both the value system of his adopted culture and the language and thinking of the Western world. In your view, what is more important? That Archie Belaney lied about his background, or that he made the Western world aware of the value of conserving wild nature and its inhabitants?

Virtue Ethics in the West

What happened to virtue ethics in ancient times in the West, and why has it been revived by scholars of ethics recently? By and large, what happened was Christianity—with its emphasis on following God's rules and conducting oneself according to the will of God. The ancient world had taught for many centuries that virtue is a matter of shaping one's character, the implication being that once one has succeeded, one can justifiably be proud of what one has become—one can take a legitimate pride in being a self-made virtuous person. (We shall see how that is an important part of Aristotle's virtue theory in the next chapter.) But in Christian thinking, one can accomplish nothing without the help and grace of God—meaning that one just can't take credit for having become a good person, for the credit or glory goes exclusively to God, *Soli Deo Gloria*. A chasm appeared between the teachings of the classical tradition and the moral and philosophical viewpoints of the rising religion. Disagreements exceeded verbal argumentation and turned violent for the first time in Christian history (but unfortunately not for the last time). See Box 8.2 for some examples of that violence. One result, nonviolent but with important symbolic consequences, was the closure of both Plato's and Aristotle's schools in Athens by the Roman emperor Justinian in 529 C.E., after those schools had been in existence for over eight hundred years. (In comparison, the oldest European university was founded in Bologna, Italy, in 1088. The University of Paris opened in 1160, and Oxford University in 1190. Harvard University was founded in 1636, and Columbia University in 1754.) Later in this chapter and in the next chapter, we return to the significance of the closing of Plato's and Aristotle's old schools.

Box 8.2 VICTIMS OF RELIGIOUS FANATICISM

Since 2001 we have heard much about fundamentalist Muslim terrorism and fanaticism, and devastating results of that fanaticism have been felt around the world, from September 11, 2001, in the United States, to the bombings in Bali and elsewhere, to the beheadings of foreign civilians in Iraq and Pakistan. As most people are aware, that does not mean that all Muslims are violent fanatics. What most people don't know is that in the early days of Christianity, small groups of Christian fanatics set out to strike terror in the hearts of non-Christians, because those groups refused to accept the values of the traditional pagan Greco-Roman world. Two such examples of what could be called ancient fundamentalist Christian terrorism took place in the Egyptian city of Alexandria. In the year 415 C.E. a mob of fanatical Christian monks, possibly inspired by the Bishop of Alexandria, attacked and murdered one of the first women philosophers on record, Hypatia, leader of the Neoplatonic Institute in Alexandria. As far as we know, Hypatia lectured on Plato, Aristotle, and Pythagoras, and thus the radical Christians associated her with paganism. As she was riding through town in her chariot during one of the many religious riots, the mob dragged her out of her cart, tore off her clothes, and flayed her alive with clamshells. Hypatia had done her research in the great library at Alexandria (or what was left of it), which was founded by one of Alexander the Great's generals, Ptolemy I, who became the founder of an Egyptian dynasty (fourth century B.C.E.). The library was expanded over the centuries and probably contained most of the works of Greek philosophy, literature, and science, either in the original or copied by hand.

During the reign of Queen Cleopatra, one of Ptolemy's descendants (around 30 B.C.E.), a part of the library was burned down by the Roman army, possibly by mistake. When another section of the library went up in flames in 391 C.E. (along with a pagan temple), there was no doubt that the destruction was caused by Christian extremists. It is, of course, important to note that those small groups of fanatics were an exception. Most Christians in the Roman Empire were not extremist, nor did they advocate terror, any more than they do today. In 380 Emperor Theodosius had made Christianity the official religion of Rome; Emperor Constantine had converted already in 312 C.E., and at the Church Council in Nicea in 325 the Christian bishops had established what were to count as official Christian sacred writings of the Old and the New Testaments.

One last word about the library in Alexandria: Its ultimate destruction came at the hands of Islamic fundamentalist invaders in 646 C.E. Scholars estimate that science suffered a setback of perhaps a millennium from the loss of the library; humanity's loss in works of art—philosophy, literature, drama, and artifacts—cannot be measured. And there is a further lesson, that religious fanaticism is not the monopoly or invention of one religion, past or present.

To *do the right thing* became the main imperative of Christian ethics; however, the concepts of virtue and vice became main elements. Within the Christian tradition and within every aspect of our Western outlook on life that has been shaped by this tradition, the idea of virtue is central, but scholars of ethics point out that it is not so much the question of *shaping your own character* that is important in this tradition as it is recognizing the *frailty of human character in general* and believing that with the help of God one may be able to choose the right thing to do.

From the time of the Renaissance to well into the twentieth century, questions of ethics were less a matter of doing the right thing to please God and more a matter of doing the right thing because it led to general happiness—because it was prudent or because it was logical. However, present-day scholars interested in virtue ethics have put forth the following argument: You may choose to do the "right thing" to please God or to escape unpleasant consequences or to make some majority happy or to satisfy your inner need for logic—but you may still be a less than admirable person. You may give to charity, pay your taxes on time, remember your nieces' and nephews' birthdays, hold the door for physically challenged people, and still be a morose and mean person. As we saw in the chapter on psychological egoism, you may be doing all the "correct" things just to get a passport to heaven or to be praised by others or to make sure they owe you a favor. So "doing the right thing" doesn't guarantee that you are a good person with a good *character*. However, if you strive to develop a good character—to be courageous or protective or tolerant or compassionate—then, on the basis of this character trait, you will *automatically* make the right decisions about what to do, what course of action to take. In other words, virtue ethics is considered to be more fundamental than ethics of conduct, yielding better results.

In today's discussions on ethics, opinions are divided as to the merits of virtue versus conduct; however, no virtue theory is complete without recognition of the importance of conduct. We can have a marvelous "character," but if it never translates into action or conduct, it is not of much use—and how do we develop a good character in the first place if not through *doing* something right? Also, one of the most conduct-oriented ethical theories, Kant's deontology, has the question of virtue and character embedded in it. For Kant, a good character in the form of a *good will,* a fundamental respect for other people, and respect for the nature of the moral law itself is essential to the moral decision process. Indeed, one-half of the book he wrote late in life, *The Metaphysics of Morals,* focuses on a doctrine of virtue (in Chapter 6 you read the section concerning *lying*), and what he used to call the good will is here renamed a *virtuous disposition.* The question of whether we should choose ethics of conduct or virtue ethics is a bifurcation fallacy or a false dilemma (see Chapter 1); we can certainly decide that there is room for both approaches.

Hypatia (370–415 C.E.), the leader of the Neoplatonic Institute in Alexandria and one of the first female philosophers that we know of, was driving through the streets of town in her chariot when she was intercepted, tortured, and killed by Christian extremists.

In the rest of this chapter and in the next chapter, we look at the classical virtue theories of Plato and Aristotle. We then move on to some examples of modern virtue theory.

The Good Teacher: Socrates' Legacy, Plato's Works

The saying goes that a good teacher is one who makes herself or himself superfluous. In other words, a good teacher lets you become your own authority; she or he does not keep you at the psychological level of a student forever. As a matter of fact, great personalities who have had considerable influence on their followers often have failed in this respect. For a teacher it is hard to let go and consider the job done (whether one is a professor or a parent), and for a student it is often tempting to absorb the authority of the teacher, because life is hard enough as it is without having to make your own decisions about everything all the time. This is what the good teacher or parent prepares the student for, however—autonomy, not dependence.

The teacher-student relationship between Socrates and Plato would probably not have become so famous if Plato had remained merely a student, a shadow of the master. Indeed, we have Socrates' own words (at least through the pen of Plato) that the good teacher does not impose his ideas on the student but, rather, serves as a midwife for the student's own dormant intellect. In many ways Socrates has become a philosophical ideal. As we shall see, he stood by his own ideals in the face of adversity and danger; he believed in the intellectual capacities of everyone; he strove to awaken people's sense of critical thinking rather than give them a set of rules to live by, and, above all, he believed that "the unexamined life is not worth living."

Socrates, Man of Athens

What do we know of Socrates? There is no doubt that he lived—he is not a figment of Plato's imagination, as much as Plato may have made use of poetic license in his writings. Aristophanes, the author of comedies in Athens, refers to Socrates in his play *The Clouds* (albeit in a rather unflattering way). The fact is that we don't have any writings by Socrates himself, for his form of communication was the discussion, the live conversation—what has become known as the *dialogue*. From this word is derived the term for Socrates' special way of teaching, the *dialectic method* (sometimes also called the *Socratic method*). A method of teaching that uses conversation only, no written texts, is not exactly designed to affect posterity, but posterity has nevertheless been immensely affected by our indirect access to Socrates through the writings—the *Dialogues*—of Plato.

What we know of Socrates is that he lived in Athens from approximately 470 to 399 B.C.E. The son of a sculptor and a midwife, he was married to Xanthippe and had three children. He was one of several teachers of philosophy, science, and rhetoric in Athens at a time when internal politics were volatile (aristocrats versus democrats) and when Greece, which had experienced a golden age of cultural achievements in the wake of the Persian wars, including the construction of the Parthenon at the Acropolis of Athens, was actually on the verge of decline. The most important political element of the time was the city-state, the *polis* (the origin of the word *politics*). With the peculiar features of the Greek countryside—the inland features of tall mountains and the seaside features of islands—the stage had been set for centuries for a specific power structure: small, independent, powerful realms warring and/or trading with one another. Two of the main areas were Athens and Sparta. Each area, a state in itself, considered itself to be geographically Greek but politically specific to its particular *polis*. Thus, it meant more to an Athenian to be a citizen of Athens than it meant to be Greek. Being a free citizen of a particular *polis* carried with it an inordinate pride. Today some might condemn such a pride as being overly nationalistic; for a Greek of the time it was a reasonable feeling. When Socrates was younger, he had been a soldier in the Athenian infantry and had distinguished himself as a courageous man. The loyalty to Athens that was expected of him then was something he lived up to his entire life; indeed, when he returned from the war, he stayed put in his hometown.

In one of Plato's dialogues, *Phaedrus,* Socrates and a friend, Phaedrus, have ventured outside the city walls, and Socrates carries on about the beauty of nature, the trees and the flowers, to such a degree that Phaedrus remarks that Socrates acts like a tourist. Socrates agrees, because he never ventures outside Athens, not even to go to the Olympic Games. The city of Athens is everything to him. It is the life among people, the communication, the discussions, the company of friends that are important to him, not nature, beautiful as it may be: "My appetite is for learning. Trees and countryside have no desire to teach me anything; it's only the men in the city that do."

It is not unusual to hear a big-city person say the same thing today—that New York or Paris or Rio has everything they could ever want. Most of us think such people are missing out on a few things, but Socrates' attitude becomes crucial to our understanding of his conduct toward the end of his life.

The Death of Socrates and the Works of Plato

Many cultures take the position that someone's life cannot be judged until it is over, that the ending helps define—sometimes even determine—how we think of the life spent. That may seem terribly unfair, for few of us are in full control of our lives, and we would prefer not to have our accomplishments judged primarily by circumstances beyond our control. In the case of Socrates, though, it seems fitting that his life is judged in the light of his death, for in the face of adversity, in the ultimate "situation beyond his control," he seems to have remained in full control of *himself.* This is another reason that Socrates has become not just the philosopher's ideal but also a human role model—because he did not lose his head but instead faced injustice with courage and rationality.

Sara Krulwich/The New York Times/Redux Pictures

In April 2019, Michael Stuhlbarg portrayed the Greek thinker in the play *Socrates* at the Public Theater in New York. In the audience was the British-Ghanaian philosopher Kwame Anthony Appiah, who remarked that "If Athens had had our technology, I'm sure Socrates would have been widely blocked on social media."

After what in antiquity passed for a long life (he was nearing age seventy), Socrates found himself in a difficult political situation, brought about by several factors. First, Socrates had great influence among the young men of Athens—those young men who might be of political influence in the future—and many were the sons of noblemen. Second, Socrates conducted his classes in public (this was customary at the time in Athens, before the formalization of classes, schools, and academy life), and his method was well known to his students, as well as to any city council member who might cross the *agora* (the public square) while Socrates was teaching. Socrates used a certain method of *irony* to get his point across, and it often involved engaging politicians in a discussion under the pretext of ignorance to trick the speaker into revealing his own ignorance or prejudice. His students adored him for it, because it was the ultimate "questioning of authority." The fact that Socrates himself may have been serious in a roundabout way about claiming his ignorance was something his listeners may not have realized. Socrates did not adhere to any one conception of reality unless it could be tested by reason; in other words, he would not profess to "know" anything for certain before investigating it and discussing it. That attitude, which was essentially one of humility rather than arrogance, seems to have been lost on his enemies, and over the years he acquired a considerable number of such enemies. Third, the most elusive factor but perhaps also the most important one: Athens was changing; what had been a place of comparatively free exchange of ideas, the undisputed center of the intellectual Western world, was becoming a place in which people expressed themselves more cautiously. Old laws against impiety were now more thoroughly enforced, and people were being banished for offenses against the state. The reason was complete exhaustion after thirty-seven years of war with Sparta, political upheavals, and an ensuing suspicion of dissidents. Most important, in Socrates' case, he had expressed reservations concerning the democratic government (not "democratic" in any modern political or partisan sense of the word, but a form of government in which male citizens of the city-state had a political voice, as opposed to the oligarchic form of government by the few). For most of Socrates' life Athens had a democratic constitution, but during a brief, troubled time after Athens lost the long Peloponnesian War to Sparta, a group of aristocrats seized power and overthrew the constitution. The leader of this group of "Thirty Tyrants," Critias, had been a member of Socrates' circle, and although Socrates himself fell into disfavor with the tyrants, scholars speculate that some of his enemies had old scores to settle, even though the new Athenian democratic government had given amnesty to all involved in the affair after the fall of the tyrants. Another of Socrates' earlier associates, Alcibiades, had been responsible for a major naval expedition that went terribly wrong: He deserted, and the expedition was destroyed. Those connections may also have contributed to the downfall of Socrates.

Eventually his enemies took action. There was no way of getting rid of Socrates by political means, so they resorted to what appears to be a standard charge: that Socrates was "offending the gods and corrupting the youth." Socrates was tried and convicted by a jury of five hundred male citizens of Athens. The Athenian court would vote once for conviction or acquittal, and once again if the verdict was guilty, in what we today would call the "penalty phase," determining the punishment. Socrates himself gave two speeches, one in his defense and one concerning his punishment. His speech during the penalty phase featured an in-your-face suggestion that the proper punishment would be not death but a *reward* for services to the state, much like a sports hero: to be feted by the city of Athens.

The verdict was determined by a simple majority, not by a unanimous vote. The jury was almost split down the middle as to Socrates' guilt: Some speculate that if Socrates had 30 more votes in his favor, he would have been acquitted. It seems that 280 voted for conviction, and 220 voted for acquittal. A tie vote—half the difference between 280 and 220—would have been resolved in favor of the accused. But the votes in favor of the death penalty after Socrates' "reward" speech were considerably higher than for his conviction—which means that some people who had thought him innocent were now so outraged at his behavior that they voted for capital punishment.

It seems possible that his enemies did not intend to get rid of Socrates by actually executing him. The standard reaction to such charges by accused citizens was to leave the city and go elsewhere within the Greek realm, and there were many places to choose from, because that realm extended from Italy well into the Middle East. But because Socrates chose to stand trial, arguing that by leaving he would be admitting guilt, his fate appeared sealed. Even so, to the last minute there were powers working to free him; his friends, many of whom were of considerable influence, conspired to spring him from jail and bring him to safety in exile. In Plato's dialogue *Crito* we hear how Socrates' good friend Crito pleads with him to listen to his friends and take their offer of escape and life, because "otherwise people will say we didn't do enough to help you." Socrates answers:

In questions of just and unjust, fair and foul, good and evil, which are the subjects of our present consultation, ought we to follow the opinion of the many and to fear them; or the opinion of the one man who has understanding? . . . Then, my friend, we must not regard what the many say of us: but what he, the one man who has understanding of just and unjust, will say, and what the truth will say.

When Crito suggests that Socrates ought to escape because he has been convicted by unjust laws, Socrates replies that two wrongs don't make a right, and the laws of Athens have supported him throughout his life; even though unjust, they are still the laws of Athens. If he, Socrates, had been a less faithful citizen of Athens, he might choose to leave, but because he never left the city, he believes he has to live by his own rule of respecting the laws and the rules of reason and virtue and not turn his back on them.

So Socrates, the citizen of Athens, could not envision a life away from the city, even when the alternative was death.

Could Socrates have done a better job defending himself? Given that only a narrow majority of the five hundred jury members found him guilty, it seems clear it wouldn't have taken much for that small majority to change their minds. In Plato's dialogue the *Apology* (an excerpt of which appears as a Primary Reading at the end of this chapter), Socrates isn't exactly expressing himself cautiously or diplomatically in his address to his judges. He is assuming they will use rational judgment and see his point of view; he doesn't seem to understand the considerable animosity many feel toward him. The end result is, of course, a conviction. Since we can see in retrospect that another style of argumentation, or even just being slightly apologetic, might have saved his life, many have speculated that perhaps he didn't try too hard because he *wanted* to die and make a point. This theory goes all the way back to Plato's contemporary Xenophon, who thought Socrates deliberately antagonized the jury to get a conviction. Others are convinced that he didn't and claim that he was arguing in a style completely true to his personality and outlook on life, that he fought in court, in his own way, until the very end. Box 8.3 speculates that the world we live in might have looked quite different had Socrates not been executed.

Everett – Art/Shutterstock

The Death of Socrates (1787) by Jacques-Louis David shows Socrates still exploring issues of life and death with his friends, even though he will soon drink the cup of poison prepared for his execution by the distraught jailer.

Box 8.3 WHAT IF SOCRATES HADN'T BEEN EXECUTED?

What might have happened if the jury had been convinced of Socrates' innocence—or if Socrates had been convinced by Crito and had allowed himself to escape? If Socrates hadn't been executed, chances are Plato wouldn't have become a writer or a philosopher, for he wouldn't have felt compelled to preserve Socrates' name for posterity and give him philosophical immortality. And without Plato's writings we would have no Platonism, no school influencing antiquity for nine hundred years and beyond, into Chris-

tianity. And without Plato's school the young man from Stagira who came to the big city of Athens to get an education—Aristotle—might never have become a philosopher. And without Aristotle's philosophy? Universities would probably be structured differently, sciences would have other categories, ethics would be different, and elements of Christianity would be absent. Our world might look substantially different today if Socrates had died a natural death.

In the Narratives section you will find another historical figure, Sir Thomas More (*A Man for All Seasons*), who apparently made the same choice: that standing up for the truth is more important than staying alive. But that doesn't mean he, or Socrates, *wanted* to die. You might say they chose integrity over personal concerns, and that is probably what makes the Socratic example so compelling.

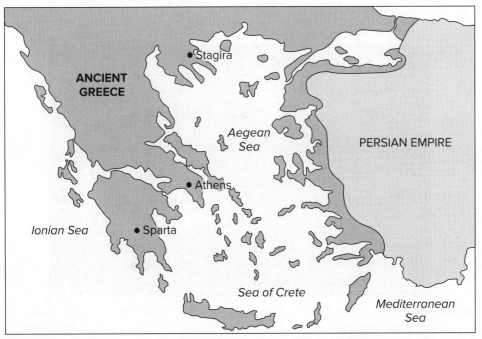

During the time of Socrates (fifth century B.C.E.) the Greek cultural realm stretched from Italy in the west to Asia Minor in the east; although people would consider themselves citizens of the Greek culture, their most important affiliation was with the city-state (*polis*) in which they were born. Both Socrates and Plato were native citizens of Athens, while Aristotle (see Chapter 9) came from the Macedonian town of Stagira.

Was Socrates guilty? His accusers may have believed so, although we may find it hard to imagine why. Did he offend any gods? He seems to have been a religious man; he often made the traditional sacrifices to the gods, and Plato has him referring to gods or "the god" often in his dialogues. But Socrates also referred to what he called his *daimon* (spirit), a little voice inside him telling him what to do. It is hard to know whether he was just talking about his conscience or whether he believed in some guardian spirit, but it may have seemed to his accusers that he was trying to introduce new gods. Did he corrupt the youth of Athens? Well, yes, if you believe that teaching young people to think for themselves, to use their reason in search of the truth, is corrupting them. In his speech in his own defense (see ***The Apology*** in the Primary Reading section), Socrates asked those young people to come forth if they felt they had been corrupted; of course, none of the young people of his own circle did.

Plato tells us about the last, dignified minutes of Socrates' life, thereby giving history and philosophy the legacy of someone who chose to die for a rational principle. The scene is vividly described in the dialogue *Phaedo*. Plato writes that he himself wasn't present because of illness, and the story of Socrates' death is told by another student, Phaedo, but others have speculated that Plato may have already left Athens as a precaution, fearing reprisals against Socrates' supporters. In the end, Socrates' friends and students are gathered to say goodbye. They are on the verge of breaking down, while Socrates does his best to keep their spirits up. Even the jailer who brings in the poison apologizes to the old philosopher for having to cause him harm and hopes Socrates will not hold it against him. Socrates assures him that he will not and swallows the poison, an extract of hemlock. He continues talking, but the end approaches quickly. He lies down and a blanket is placed over him, covering his face. But then—it must have been a dramatic moment for his friends—he removes the cover from his face for a final statement. And what are the last words coming from the Master's mouth? None of the wisdom they were used to hearing him speak, such as "The unexamined life is not worth living." No, he says to his old friend Crito, "I owe a rooster to Asclepius—will you remember to pay the debt?" Crito promises that he will, and asks if Socrates has any more he wants to say, but he replaces the cover over his face, and within minutes Socrates is dead. The meaning of that request has been discussed by philosophers ever since. Was Socrates driven by the memory of an unpaid debt, or was he talking in symbolic terms? Asclepius was a common Greek

Bettmann/Getty Images

Plato (427?–347 B.C.E.) was the son of Ariston and Perictione. They named their son Aristocles, but he became known as Plato, literally "broad." Some people speculate that it meant "broad forehead," referring to his wide knowledge, but others trace the term back to—wrestling! Plato was a wrestler in his youth, and his nickname traveled with him into his career as a philosopher. It seems to have indicated that he had broad shoulders. His father died when Plato was a young boy. His mother, Perictione, was apparently a philosopher in her own right, although women in ancient Greece had virtually no independence.

name but also the name of the *god of healing*. Did he want his friends to sacrifice the rooster to the god because Asclepius had "cured" him—that is, released his soul from the prison of the body? We can only guess, but Plato seems to have favored the latter version rather than the more down-to-earth explanation of owing a debt, because Plato himself believed, in later years, that the body was a prison for the soul.

The effect of Socrates' death on Plato was profound. Born in about 427 B.C.E., Plato had been Socrates' student, in an informal sense, for thirteen years, and the death of his teacher caused him to take leave of Athens for another twelve years, during which he traveled to Egypt and Sicily, among other places. Eventually he returned to Athens, and some time before 367 B.C.E. he founded his own school of philosophy, the Academy (Plato's own home—which he opened up to his students—named after the Greek sports hero Academus). This school appears to have been the beginning of a more formalized teaching institution, with regular lectures and several professors associated with the school. It remained open until 529 C.E., when it was closed by Christians. As Plato took on the mantle of his teacher, he began to reconstruct Socrates' intellectual legacy by writing the *Dialogues*. These books remain some of the most influential writings in philosophy, but they also are works of literature, as brilliant as any drama written in antiquity. That Plato from the very first dialogues reveals himself to be a great storyteller is all the more interesting, for, as you may remember from Chapter 2, he himself was not in favor of the arts, because he believed they spoke to people's emotions and made them forget the cool balance of reason. And, yet, Plato's own writings are works of art in themselves. And as you also may remember from Chapter 2, that storytelling talent had an interesting origin: Before Plato met Socrates, he was a playwright, engaged in the Athenian annual playwrights' competitions. So we may conclude that his talent got channeled into writing some of the most enduring pieces of philosophical literature, his *Dialogues,* which for all intents and purposes are dramatic pieces—while ironically, in *The Republic*, attempting to dissuade others from going to the theater. In his dialogues, Socrates and his friends and students come alive. We understand their way of talking, and we gain insight into their thinking, which, on occasion, is rather alien to our own day and age. The early dialogues of Plato give a picture of Socrates that is very fresh and probably quite accurate. However, scholars believe that in later dialogues Socrates changes into something that is more Plato's image of an ideal philosopher than Socrates himself. Indeed, in the last dialogues, Socrates appears as Plato's mouthpiece for his own advanced theories on metaphysics—theories that Socrates probably never held himself. That may mean that Socrates was indeed a good teacher who did not hinder Plato from "graduating" intellectually. It also means that through this lifelong tribute to Socrates, Plato showed that you can kill a thinker but not his thoughts; so in a sense Plato made certain that Socrates, long dead at the hands of the Athenian judges, lived on to affect the history of thought long after his accusers had turned to dust. (It may of course also have been a safe way for Plato to express his own radical ideas, by having the character of Socrates express them in his books. After all, the citizens of Athens could only put Socrates to death once.)

The Good Life

Socrates' statement to Crito that some things are more important than life itself, such as being true to your principles no matter how others may feel about it, holds the key to what Socrates seems to have considered the "good life" or a life worth living. You may remember from Chapter 1 that Socrates was quoted as having said, "The unexamined life is not worth living." So what is an examined life? That would be a life in which one is not ruled by the opinion of others or even by one's own opinions, those ideas of ours that may or may not have some basis in the truth but that we haven't bothered to examine closely. If we stop for a minute and examine such opinions, we will probably discover that they constitute the basis for the majority of our viewpoints: We think we live in a great country, or perhaps we think we live in a deceitful, oppressive country. We think that chicken soup is good for colds. We may think that what scientists say must be true as long as they are wearing white lab coats. Perhaps we think that people who believe in UFOs are nuts, or we think that UFOs abduct humans from time to time. We hear actors weighing in on politics, and if they are our favorite actors, perhaps we value their opinion—but how exactly do actors get to be experts on politics? Some are indeed very well informed (and some actors also happen to be politicians); others just have *opinions*. And it is the opinion issue that interested and irritated Socrates. We think many things, and if we allow ourselves to examine those opinions, we will usually find that they are based on very flimsy evidence. Of course, on occasion we feel strongly about something precisely because we *have* examined it, but, in that case, Socrates would say, we are not talking about **opinion** (*doxa*) anymore—we are talking about **knowledge** (*epistēmē*). This, for Socrates, was the test of truth: Can it stand up to unprejudiced scrutiny? If so, it must override any sort of opinion we may have, even though it may hurt the feelings of others; if they see the truth, they, too, will understand, for *only ignorance leads to wrongdoing.* For Socrates as well as for Plato, this is a truth in itself: No one is willfully evil, provided that he or she understands the truth about the situation. And if a person still chooses the wrong course of action, it must be because his or her understanding is faulty.

For a modern person the response to that seems inevitable: What if there is more than one way of looking at the situation? In other words, what if there is more than one truth? We are so used to assuming there is more than one way of looking at something that we sometimes assume there is no truth at all. That, however, is very far from the intellectual attitude of Socrates. For Socrates, as well as for Plato, each situation has its Truth, and each thing can be described in one way that best captures its true nature, its essence. That does not mean that this was a common attitude among Greek thinkers. In Socrates' own time, contact with other cultures had brought about a certain amount of cultural relativism, and Greece was sufficiently heterogeneous to foster a tolerance of different customs. Accordingly, for many of Socrates' contemporaries, such as *the Sophists*, relativism became the accepted answer to the search for absolute truth. For Socrates, the theory that virtue might be a question of personal preference or relative to one's own time and culture was the epitome of misunderstanding, and much of the Socratic quest for the true nature, the essence, of a thing or a concept is a countermeasure to the prevailing relativism of the Greek intelligentsia. This also implies a fundamental Socratic principle: that truth should not be confused with appearance. The external appearance of something—a person, or a situation—is not necessarily the same as its true nature. Just as *doxa* must be discarded for *epistēmē*, appearance must yield to knowledge of the inner truth. So for Socrates (and indeed also for Plato), seeking the truth, and examining one's life in the process, should lead to an understanding and knowledge of essential reality beyond the world of change and appearance. Later in the chapter we return to the idea that the truth is somehow not to be judged by our senses but by our rational mind: Plato's theory of Forms.

Virtue for Socrates means to question the meaning of life and to keep one's integrity while searching, to not be swayed by one's physical longings or fear of unpleasant situations or concern for comfort. This ideal is attainable because the Truth can be found—in fact, it can be found by *anyone* who has as a guide a teacher with integrity. In other words, Socrates says we can't hope to attain virtue without the use of our *reason*. Later on (in particular during the Middle Ages), the link between virtue and reason was weakened, but for Plato and Socrates, as well as for Greek antiquity as such, the connection was obvious. Using our reason will make us realize what virtue is and will actually make us virtuous.

The good life, therefore, is not a pleasant life in which we seek gratification for the sake of having a good time. The good life is strenuous but gratifying in its own way, because one knows that one seeks and sees the Truth, and one is in control of oneself.

The Virtuous Person: The Tripartite Soul

Let us now focus on what makes a person good. You'll remember from Chapter 4 that Plato's brother Glaucon told a story about the Ring of Gyges, stating that if you had the chance to get away with something and you didn't, you had to be stupid. For Socrates this matter was of grave importance, and this was his answer: **A person who does something unjust to others is either ignorant or sick**. If we inform that person that he is being unjust, he may realize his ignorance and improve himself. But there is the chance that he will laugh in our face. In that case, Socrates said, he is simply not well—he is out of balance. Glaucon's argument that an unjust person is happier than a just person carries no weight with Socrates, because an unjust person can't be happy at all; only a well-balanced person can be happy. But what is a well-balanced person?

Everybody has desires, and sometimes those desires can be very strong. We may want something to drink when we are thirsty, something to eat when we are hungry; we have desires for sex, for power, and for many other things. We also have desires to get away from things, as when we move away from a fire we're too close to. Those needs and wants Socrates calls *appetites,* and they are what we must control if we are to achieve the good life. Appetites may rule a person's life, but that is not good, because the things we desire aren't necessarily the things that are good for us. So sometimes we pull away from what we want because we realize that it will be bad for us. The power that pulls us back is our *rational element,* our *reason.*

There is a third element at play; Socrates calls it *spirit.* Sometimes he calls it *willpower.* We feel it when we sometimes let our appetites win out over our reason; afterward we feel disgusted with ourselves, and the anger directed at ourselves is our spirit. When we fall off our diet, our reason may have lost the battle, but our spirit will be angry at our weakness and will keep bothering us. What, then, should a person do? Establish a good working relationship between reason and spirit; let reason be clear about what it wants to do, and then train the spirit to help control the appetites. Reason and spirit will, side by side, keep the body healthy and the soul balanced. In Plato's dialogue *Phaedrus,* Socrates describes the three-sided relationship by the following metaphor: A charioteer has two horses to pull his chariot; suppose one is well-behaved, whereas the other is wild and unruly. He is stuck with both and can't choose another horse, so he must make the well-behaved horse help him control the unruly horse and subdue it. So which roles do these figures play? The charioteer is Reason, the well-behaved horse is Willpower, and the wild horse is Appetites. Notice that a "balanced" individual to Socrates does not have one-third of each element—he or she has total control by reason and willpower over appetites. When reason rules, the person is *wise;* when spirit controls the appetites, that person is also *brave* (because it takes courage to say no to temptation and yes to a painful experience); and when the appetites are completely controlled, the person is *temperate* (using self-control and moderation in his or her desires). Such a person is well balanced and would not dream of being unjust to anybody; on the contrary, he or she would be the very picture of *justice,* and justice is the virtue that describes the well-balanced human being who is wise, brave, and temperate. Only that kind of person can be happy in the true sense of the word; Glaucon's idea that an unjust person is happier than a just person can be discarded, because such a person is off balance. (For another thinker's view of the tripartite soul, see Box 8.4.)

Box 8.4 THE TRIPARTITE SOUL: PLATO AND FREUD

PLATO		
Elements of the Soul		*Virtues*
Reason	—corresponds to—	Wisdom
Willpower	—corresponds to—	Courage
Appetites	—corresponds to—	Temperance

FREUD

Theory of the Psyche

Superego

Ego

Id

If an individual has succeeded in mastering his or her appetites by using reason to guide willpower, then a fourth virtue comes into play: *justice*. In that case Socrates and Plato would say we have encountered a truly virtuous individual: a just person, a person of internal balance and integrity.

In the early twentieth century Sigmund Freud suggested a theory about the human psyche that has some parallels to Socrates' theory: Freud's psyche comprises the Id (the Unconscious), the Ego (the conscious self), and the Superego (the codes and rules we have been taught). Can the Id be compared to appetites? Yes, as long as we remember that, for Freud, the Id can't be accessed, whereas Socrates believed a person could understand his or her own appetites. As for the Ego and the Superego, they don't match the Socratic schema too well: The Ego is part reason but also part willpower; the Superego has elements in common with both too. The similarity between Socrates' theory of the soul and Freud's theory of the psyche is not a coincidence: Freud was a great admirer of Plato's dialogues.

Who corresponds to *reason?* Wise rulers, says Plato, "philosopher-kings" who would rather not rule; they will get the job done without fuss and with reason as their principle of guidance. Who corresponds to *willpower* in a state? The "auxiliaries," soldiers and law enforcement. And what about all the rest of the population—merchants, businesspeople, educators, entertainers, private citizens? They correspond to the *appetites* and must be thoroughly controlled. If they are not—such as in a democracy—then that society is off balance and sick. This restrictive social plan did not correspond to democratic Athenian society at all, and Plato has been vilified by democratically minded thinkers ever since. See Box 8.5 for Plato's idea of a well-balanced society.

Box 8.5 A WELL-BALANCED PERSON IN A WELL-BALANCED SOCIETY

On page 358, you'll find a graphic illustrating Plato's notion of a well-balanced soul—not Plato's own illustration, mind you, but a shortcut that to me gathers some of Plato's key ideas: The well-balanced person's reason rules; it is aided by his or her spirit or willpower; and the person's desires are controlled at all times. Here we expand it to cover Plato's theory of the ideal society, Plato's the *Republic* (and it is because of Plato's social theory that I thought of using the pyramid as an illustration in the first place, since Plato says that society is simply the structure of the soul, in a large format). So, following the pyramid structure of the ideal balanced soul, we have the ideal balanced society ruled by philosopher-kings (reason) at the top, a small but powerful group. Next we have the auxiliaries, meaning the soldiers and law enforcement, helping the philosopher-kings keep law and order, and protecting everybody from unrest and enemy onslaughts (compare willpower or spirit). And at the bottom? "The people," what Plato calls merchants and tradesmen, meaning everybody who doesn't get to be in law enforcement or the military, or in government (appetites or desires). *That would mean most of us.* And following the parallel of the individual pyramid, the people never have a say about anything at all that goes beyond their own personal and professional lives—but they are not oppressed (supposedly), since the government is looking out for their interests and the interests of society as a whole (just as reason looks out for the interests of the entire body). This social model is what has caused critics—fairly or unfairly—to call Plato a supporter of totalitarianism, and the *Republic* the first blueprint for a totalitarian society.

Among modern Plato scholars there is some disagreement about Plato's intentions in his social theory of the ideal state. Its radical principles include not only a strict hierarchy but also rules about marriage and children among the philosopher-kings. For one thing, Plato advocates that anyone would be eligible as a guardian (a ruler or a soldier), depending on his or her talent and regardless of *gender;* to his contemporaries (and even to some of our contemporaries) the idea of a woman ruler (or president) is outlandish or even outrageous, but Plato apparently found it a completely reasonable thought. (For a different take on Plato's presumed egalitarian view of women, see Chapter 12.) Most people today, however, find his rules about childbearing among the guardians too extreme and certainly both outlandish and outrageous: For the sake of eugenics (creating a superior breed of people by mating selected men and women), guardians would be paired off and mated during their childbearing years, but the children would be removed from the mothers and raised in common so that no parent would know his or her own child. Plato envisioned such a plan to allow personal preferences and affiliations to be held to a minimum so that the guardians could focus on what was good for the state.

Those radical thoughts have caused some Plato scholars to say that Plato may not have meant one word of his political theory—it was all tongue-in-cheek, a big joke on his students told at a dinner party. Women in government! He couldn't possibly have been serious. However, at least two things speak for taking Plato seriously: For one thing, at some point he left his teaching position in Athens to return to Syracuse, presumably to tutor the young tyrant Dionysius II. Apparently Plato used his own principles as outlined in the *Republic* to try to groom Dionysius into a guardian, with disastrous results: according to legend, Plato became so unpopular that he was captured and sold into slavery. Fortunately for him, he was purchased by an old friend, set free, and put on a ship to Athens. Even though Plato's family had intended for him to go into politics, it is obvious that Plato was much more a scholar and a writer than a successful politician. For another thing, Plato's student Aristotle had no doubt that Plato was serious, and who could be a better judge than a contemporary source who had heard Plato discuss his theories?

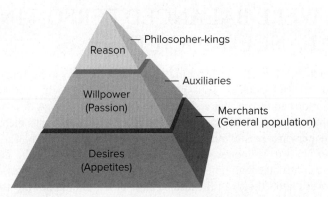

Plato himself never suggested that one might illustrate his theory of the balanced soul and the good state with a pyramid, but the image works, for several reasons. Plato imagines his ideal society to be a hierarchy of power, with the philosopher-kings on top, the auxiliaries in the middle, and the general population at the bottom. But Plato also insists that the ideal society has the same structure as the ideal soul. So when the pyramid illustrates the mind of a just person, the configuration looks like this: At the top of the pyramid we have Reason—the smallest part of our mind, but the most important one. Reason has to dominate and seek the aid of Willpower (sometimes called Passion or Spirit) to control the Desires (Appetites). The result is a very balanced person, a "just" individual who will not be swayed by his or her emotions—just as a pyramid is a very stable structure. Imagine placing the pyramid on its tip—then you'll have the image of a person who is out of balance, because his or her reason is ruled by desires. You may want to revisit Chapters 2 and 4, and apply the pyramid image to Plato's reluctance to go to the theater for fear of losing control, and reread Socrates' argument against Glaucon that a person who lets desires control him is sick, and a sick person can't be a happy person.

There is little evidence that Socrates himself ever had such political visions; his main interests seem to have been getting individuals to improve their thinking and become better persons. Examining the concept of virtue, he would begin with a concept, a word of common usage, such as *justice* or *piety,* and ask his partners in the dialogue to define it, under the assumption there would be one, and only one, description that would be the true one. At some point in the Platonic dialogues, we begin to lose the sense that it is Socrates talking, for another theory develops that is Plato's own: the theory of Forms.

Plato's Theory of Forms

When we ask about a person's view of reality, we generally want to know whether that person is religious or an atheist, pessimistic or optimistic about other people and events, interested in a historical perspective or mainly looking to the present and the future, and so on. Philosophically speaking, however, a person's view of reality is what we call *metaphysics.* What exactly is the nature of reality as such? In philosophy the answer will be one of three major types: Reality is made up of things that can be measured (*materialism*); or Reality is totally spiritual, all in the mind (*idealism*); or Reality consists of part matter, part mind (*dualism*). (These three theories of metaphysics are described in Box 8.6.) What, exactly, was Socrates' philosophical view of reality? The early dialogues indicate that he seems to have believed in an immortal soul that leaves the body at death, which would make him a dualist. In later dialogues, though, Plato chooses to let Socrates speak for a theory—which was obviously Plato's own—that says reality is very much different from what our common sense tells us. What we see and hear and feel around us is really a shadowy projection of "true reality." Our senses can't experience it, but our mind can, because this true reality is related to our mind: It is one of the Ideas, or *Forms.*

What exactly is a Form? Today it is hard to grasp Plato's concept, but for the Greek mind of Plato's own day it was not so alien. In early times the Greeks saw each good thing as represented by some divinity; there was a goddess for justice, another for victory. There were the Muses, lesser goddesses representing each form of art. The Olympic gods each had their own areas of protection. At the time of Plato many intellectuals, including Plato himself, had left traditional Greek religion behind. Some of the ancient tendency to personify abstract ideas, though, may have survived in his Forms. A Form is at once the ideal abstraction and sole source of each thing that resembles it. Let us look at an example. There are all kinds of *beds* today—king and queen beds, twin beds, bunk beds, futons, air mattresses, hammocks. Plato would ask, What makes these things beds? We, today, would approach the question in a functionalistic manner and say something about them all being things to sleep on. Plato would say they are all beds because they all participate in the Form of Bed, a kind of ideal "bedness" not only that they have in common as a *concept* but also that actually *exists* above and beyond each singular bed. It is this quality that gives the bed its share of reality, as a sort of dim copy of the true Bed Form. This realm of Forms is true reality, and the entire world in which we move around is only a dim copy of the ideal Form. Where exactly *is* this world of Forms? It is nowhere that you can see and touch, because then it would just be another example of a copy. It has to be "out of this world," in a realm that our body does not have access to but that our mind does. So it is through our intellect that we can touch true reality, and only through our intellect. That is why Plato has Socrates tell Phaedrus that trees and countryside can't teach him anything—because there is nothing to be learned from the senses except confusion. The only true lesson in reality is achieved by letting the mind, the intellect, contemplate the Forms, because the world we see changes constantly, but the world of Forms never changes. The Forms are eternal, and for Plato (and for many other philosophers), the more enduring something is, the more real it is.

Box 8.6 THREE THEORIES OF METAPHYSICS

In philosophy we encounter three major theories of the nature of reality, or of metaphysics: *materialism, idealism*, and *dualism*. Through the ages people have leaned toward one or the other, and today the prevailing theory in the Western world is overwhelmingly *materialistic*. That does not mean people are overwhelmingly interested in accumulating riches, although that may be the case. Metaphysical materialism has nothing to do with greed; it merely means you think reality consists of things that are *material*—they or their effects can be *measured* in some sense. This category includes everything from food to briefcases to brainwaves. It follows that a materialist doesn't believe in the reality of things supposedly immaterial, such as souls or spirits. Typical philosophical materialists are Thomas Hobbes, Karl Marx, and American contemporary philosophers Paul and Patricia Churchland.

Idealism is the theory that only spiritual things have true existence and that the material world is somehow just an illusion. Again, that has very little to do with the colloquial use of the word, which we associate with a person with high ideals. Few people in philosophy define themselves as idealists today, but this theory had a certain influence in earlier times. Bishop George Berkeley was an idealist, and so was the German philosopher G. W. F. Hegel. The Hindu belief that the world we see is a mere illusion, *maya,* is also an example of idealism. The theories of materialism and idealism are also referred to as *monistic* theories—they only recognize one aspect of reality.

The theory of *dualism* combines materialism and idealism in that a dualist believes reality consists of a matter-side and a spirit-side—in other words, that although the body is material, the soul/spirit/mind is immaterial and perhaps immortal. Although this theory seems to appeal to our common sense, it poses several logical problems, which philosophy has not been able to solve, for how exactly does the mind affect the body if the mind is immaterial and the body is material? René Descartes is the most famous of the dualists, but Plato also is often counted among them, although some might prefer to call him an idealist because of his theory of Forms.

But how did Plato conceive of such a theory? And how does he propose to persuade us that he is right? One example answers both questions: Think of a circle; now think of a perfect circle. Have you ever drawn one? No. Have you ever seen one? No. Can you imagine one? Yes. Can you describe one mathematically (if you have the training)? Yes. If you have never experienced it, then how can you imagine it and describe it? Because your mind understands that the perfect circle really exists—not just as a mathematical formula, but in a higher, mental realm of reality. From this higher realm the perfect Form of a circle (and all the other Forms) lends its reality to imperfect circles and other things in our tangible world; if the Form of a circle didn't exist, then you wouldn't have a notion that a circle could be perfect! Today we would say we understand the perfect circle because we can describe it mathematically, but that doesn't mean it exists somewhere else. (See Box 8.7 for a discussion of how we can know Forms.)

Box 8.7 THE THEORY OF ANAMNESIS

How do we know about the Forms if we can't learn about them by observing the world around us? Plato believed that we remember the Forms from the time before we were born, because during that time the soul's home was the realm of the Forms themselves. At birth the soul forgets its previous life, but, with the aid of a philosopher "in the know," we can be reminded of the nature of true reality. This is one of the functions of Socrates in the literature of Plato: to cause his students to remember their lost knowledge. The process is known as *anamnesis,* a rerememebering, or, literally, a nonforgetting. In Plato's dialogue *Meno,* Socrates shows that this knowledge is accessible to everyone, as he helps a young slave-boy "remember" truths of math and logic that he has never learned in this life.

Plato, furthermore, believed in *reincarnation* (transmigration of souls). Reincarnation was not a common belief among the ancient Greeks, who seem to have believed in a dreary, dark Hades to which all souls were destined to go, regardless of whether they had been good or bad in life. But Plato apparently saw it differently: Toward the end of the *Republic,* Socrates tells an evocative story of the soul's long journey after death, called "The Myth of Er." He claims that the soul must undergo several cycles of life before it is purified sufficiently to go back to the Forms to stay forever. We know that Plato was influenced by Pythagoras, who believed in reincarnation; but some scholars also speculate that Plato may have been under the direct or indirect influence of Hindu theories of karma and reincarnation, which had existed in India for at least five hundred years before Plato's own time. However, other scholars point out that Hinduism hadn't yet spread beyond isolated groups in India.

Because the world of Forms is purely spiritual and immaterial, some philosophers choose to call Plato an idealist; however, more prefer to call him a dualist, because the world of matter is not "nonexistent" but merely of a lesser existence than the world of Forms.

Does everything have a Form? Concepts such as justice, love, and beauty have their natural place in the realm of Forms; they may be on this earth incompletely, but their Forms are flawless. Cats and dogs obviously have Forms; things of nature have a perfect Form in the spiritual realm, which gives them reality. Manufactured objects have Forms too, so in the realm of Forms there is a Form of a chair, a knife, a cradle, and a winding staircase. What about a Form of something that has not "always" been—such as a computer, an iPad, or a microwave oven? Here we are moving into an uncomfortable area of Plato's theory, because even if microwave ovens are a new invention, presumably their Form has always existed. But what about Forms for dirt, mud, and diseases? Plato gives us the impression that the Forms are perfect and somehow closer to goodness than things on this earth; however, it is hard to envision perfect dirt, mud, and diseases, even though the theory of Forms certainly implies they exist. (A generation later, Plato's student Aristotle was to criticize the theory of Forms for assuming that every phenomenon has a Form. Aristotle asserted that some phenomena are merely a "lack" or deficiency of something. A doughnut hole doesn't have a Form—it is just the empty middle of a doughnut.)

The Form of the Good

For Plato the world of Forms represents an orderly reality, nothing like the jumble of sensory experience. Forms are ordered according to their importance and according to their dependence on other Forms. Certainly worms and dirt have Forms, but they are very low in the hierarchy; at the highest level are abstract concepts such as justice, virtue, and beauty. At the very top of the hierarchy Plato sees the Form of the Good as the most important Form and also as the Form from which everything else derives.

In Plato's "Myth of the Cave," a group of prisoners are placed so they can see on the wall of the cave only reflections of objects carried back and forth in front of a fire behind them. Since this is all they see, they assume it to be reality. Had Plato been acquainted with movie theaters, he might have chosen the movie screen as a metaphor for the shadow world of the senses.

Is the Form of the Good a god, in the final analysis? Followers of Plato around the fourth and fifth centuries C.E., the *Neoplatonists,* leaned toward that theory, but it is hard to say whether Plato himself had specifically religious veneration for his Forms; it is certain that he had intellectual respect and veneration for them and for the Form of the Good in particular.

The Form of the Good allows us to understand a little better what Plato means by saying that evil acts stem from ignorance, because, according to the theory of Forms, if a person realizes the existence of the Forms and in particular the highest Form of them all, the Good, it will be impossible for that person to deliberately choose to do wrong; the choice of wrongdoing can come only from ignorance of the Good. The choice to follow the Good is not an easy one, though, even when we have knowledge of it, because we have desires that pull us in other directions. Besides, Plato says the first time we hear about the Forms, the theory sounds so peculiar that we refuse to accept our own recollection of it. Plato tells a story to illustrate this, "The Myth of the Cave." (See **the excerpt from Plato's *Republic*** with the story of the cave at the end of this chapter.) In a large cave a group of prisoners are kept chained to their seats so they can look only in one direction, toward a huge wall. Behind them there is a fire that casts shadows on the wall. The prisoners, having never seen anything else, believe these shadows are all the reality there is. One prisoner gains his freedom and now sees the cave, the fire, and the world outside the cave for what they really are—but will the others believe him when he returns?

Because the cave is our everyday world of the senses, and because we are the prisoners who see only two-dimensional shadows instead of a multidimensional reality, we have the same problems the prisoners have when one prisoner stands up and claims that he or she has "seen the light" and knows that reality is totally different from what we think. How do we respond to such "prophets"? We ignore them or ridicule them or silence them and continue to live on in our illusion. And what is the duty of the philosopher who has seen "the light" of true reality, the Good and the other Forms, according to Plato? To return to the cave, even if it would be wonderful to remain in the light of the Truth and forget about the world of shadows. The philosopher's duty is to go back and tell the others, and that, Plato believed, was what he himself was doing with his dialogues. For Plato, Truth was not something relative that differed for each person; it was an absolute reality beyond the deceptive world of the senses, a reality that never changes and that we, when we shed the chains of our physical existence—either intellectually or through death—will be able to see and be in the presence of. (For a contemporary Cave allegory with a twist, go to the Narratives section and read the summary of the film *The Truman Show*. Truman Burbank lives in a Cave of his own, unbeknownst to himself, but on live television to the rest of the world.)

Box 8.8 STOICISM: VIRTUE IS A LIFE OF REASON

In the third century a new moral philosophy arose in Greece, founded by Zeno of Citium, and it became particularly influential among philosophers of the Roman Empire such as Seneca and Epictetus, culminating with the Emperor Marcus Aurelius, who was a philosopher in his own right. (If you have seen the movie *Gladiator*, you have been introduced to Marcus Aurelius as a deep thinker in his final days. The "deep thinker" part was correctly portrayed, but his death scene was not!) The school of thought derived its name after the place where Zeno and his students met, the Painted Porch, a decorated colonnade (*Stoa Poikile*) in the public square (the Agora) in Athens—the same Agora where Socrates used to meet with his students some 200 years earlier. We only have room for a brief introduction here, so if Stoicism interests you, I would recommend a bit of research on your own.

Since the days of the Roman Empire, Stoicism has never completely gone away. Over 2000 years it has morphed into something in popular Western imagination that the ancient Stoics would barely recognize as their philosophy. It has even entered into our language as a concept: to be *stoic* about life and events means to not let life's ups and downs touch you—to maintain an inner balance regardless of what happens, and to stay unemotional. But that is not what the Stoics taught. They based their virtue-ethics on Socrates' and Plato's virtue philosophy of *wisdom, courage, and temperance* (see p. 355), and added the virtue of *justice*, which Socrates thought was the virtue that a person had achieved if he or she was wise, brave, and temperate. They believed that the point of being virtuous is to be free of suffering, and that the way to achieve that is to follow the path of reason, as a daily practice. The Stoics believed that the world is fundamentally rational and that we become true to our human nature if we listen to the voice of reason rather than our base, hostile emotions. Stoicism is thus a way of life in addition to being a philosophy about life, and it is easy to see how it has perpetuated Socrates' legacy of the "good man in balance" to whom nothing bad can happen.

In early Christianity, Stoicism was considered a pagan philosophy to be shunned, but nevertheless it seemed so reasonable and attractive to many Christian thinkers that they adopted its ideology of remaining aloof from earthly passions.

Plato's Influence on Christianity

Plato's momentous influence on Western thinking is not measured by how many people took his theory of Forms to heart. As a matter of fact, not many scholars followed Plato's metaphysics to the letter; however, his idea of a never-changing realm of goodness, light, and justice to which our soul can have access made its way into Christianity, along with the Platonic disdain for the physical world as an obstruction to that access. Many early Christian thinkers had been trained in the Platonic and Neoplatonic schools of thought (which were probably taught by Hypatia in Alexandria, for one, before she was murdered), and the view of true reality as something that is not of this world came naturally to them; controlling the desires of the body and focusing on the afterlife are elements that Platonic philosophy and early Christian thinking have in common. Saint Augustine (354–430 C.E.), for example, had received a thorough pagan spiritual education before his conversion to Christianity at age thirty-two. He had studied Manichaeism, the then-popular Persian philosophical religion that taught that the powers of light and the powers of darkness are locked in battle until the final day and the powers of light will not win unless we humans help them in their fight for goodness. He had studied Neoplatonism, a philosophy developed by the thinker Plotinus on the basis of Plato's philosophy, which taught that this tangible, material world is unimportant compared with the world of the spirit and even that the material world is godless and should be shunned. This intellectual and religious legacy that Augustine brought with him subtly changed the direction of Christianity forever, according to historians. It is, of course, the ultimate irony that Plato's Academy in Athens was closed in 529 by the Christian emperor Justinian, as you read earlier in this chapter, presumably to stop the pagan influence of the ancient school or simply as a symbolic gesture that antiquity had come to an end—but the most influential of all Christian thinkers in the early centuries of Christianity, Augustine, was already well acquainted with the philosophical principles of Plato's metaphysics by the time he converted to Christianity. In the writings of Augustine, Christianity became a religion that, even more than previously, looked to the afterlife as the true reason for human existence and shunned earthly concerns and earthly pleasures. (Box 8.8 explores the ethics of Stoicism, another inspiration for early Christianity.) That disregard for the physical world and our physical existence has been heavily criticized since the end of the nineteenth century by scholars such as Nietzsche (see Chapter 10), who believe that it shows an abysmal contempt for what Nietzsche saw as the only true reality there is: the ever-changing reality of our physical existence on this earth.

Study Questions

1. What are the mental elements that constitute a person, according to Plato? What is the proper relationship between those elements? (In other words, what is a virtuous person?)
2. You read that Socrates' last words referred to paying a debt to Asclepius. What do you think he meant?
3. Explain Plato's theory of Forms, using his story of the cave as an illustration. Is Plato's theory of reality (metaphysics) materialistic, idealistic, or dualistic? Explain.

4. Imagine that you were assigned to be Socrates' legal counsel. What would you advise him to do or say to escape a death sentence? Do you think it might make a difference? Why or why not?

5. Compare African and American Indian tribal virtue ethics with the virtue ethics of Socrates. What are the similarities? What are the differences?

Primary Readings and Narratives

The first two Primary Readings are excerpts from Plato's dialogues: one from his *Republic,* the wrap-up discussion about the virtuous person in the good state; and one from his *Apology,* his version of Socrates' speech in his own defense. The third Reading is an excerpt from a piece by philosopher Ronald Dworkin, "What Is a Good Life?" The first two Narratives have Socratic themes: a summary of the film *A Man for All Seasons,* whose title character finds himself falsely accused by advisers to King Henry VIII and defends himself in a manner reminiscent of Socrates, and an excerpt from Plato's *Republic,* "The Myth of the Cave," in which people have been imprisoned all their lives so that the only reality they know is the shadows on the wall. The third Narrative is a summary of the film *The Truman Show,* a story that questions the nature of reality. The fourth narrative is a summary of a Cold War–era science fiction story, "The Store of the Worlds," about what truly constitutes a Good Life.

 Primary Reading

The Republic

PLATO

Excerpt from Book IV, The Republic, fourth century B.C.E. **Plato, The Republic of Plato, 3e. *Translated by Benjamin Jowett. London: Oxford University Press, 1888.***

In this excerpt from *The Republic,* you get the conclusion of Socrates' conversation with Glaucon about what constitutes a good, virtuous, or, in Socrates' terminology, *just* man. Like the ideal state, the ideal person must be controlled by reason and use the spirited element (willpower, passion) as its helper to control the appetites. And when the soul works according to this principle, he or she will be wise, courageous, and temperate. With these qualities of virtue, the just person will be highly unlikely to engage in behavior that will be harmful to others or harmful to the state: It is not a matter of mere external behavior but a matter of an inner character.

> And so, after much tossing, we have reached land, and are fairly agreed that the same principles which exist in the State exist also in the individual, and that they are three in number.
>
> Exactly.
>
> Must we not then infer that the individual is wise in the same way, and in virtue of the same quality which makes the State wise?
>
> Certainly.

Also that the same quality which constitutes courage in the State constitutes courage in the individual, and that both the State and the individual bear the same relation to all the other virtues?

Assuredly.

And the individual will be acknowledged by us to be just in the same way in which the State is just?

That follows of course.

We cannot but remember that the justice of the State consisted in each of the three classes doing the work of its own class?

We are not very likely to have forgotten, he said.

We must recollect that the individual in whom the several qualities of his nature do their own work will be just, and will do his own work?

Yes, he said, we must remember that too.

And ought not the rational principle, which is wise, and has the care of the whole soul, to rule, and the passionate or spirited principle to be the subject and ally?

Certainly.

And, as we were saying, the united influence of music and gymnastic will bring them into accord, nerving and sustaining the reason with noble words and lessons, and moderating and soothing and civilizing the wildness of passion by harmony and rhythm?

Quite true, he said.

And these two, thus nurtured and educated, and having learned truly to know their own functions, will rule over the concupiscent, which in each of us is the largest part of the soul and by nature most insatiable of gain; over this they will keep guard, lest, waxing great and strong with the fulness of bodily pleasures, as they are termed, the concupiscent soul, no longer confined to her own sphere, should attempt to enslave and rule those who are not her natural-born subjects, and overturn the whole life of man?

Very true, he said.

Both together will they not be the best defenders of the whole soul and the whole body against attacks from without; the one counselling, and the other fighting under his leader, and courageously executing his commands and counsels?

True.

And he is to be deemed courageous whose spirit retains in pleasure and in pain the commands of reason about what he ought or ought not to fear?

Right, he replied.

And him we call wise who has in him that little part which rules, and which proclaims these commands; that part too being supposed to have a knowledge of what is for the interest of each of the three parts and of the whole?

Assuredly.

And would you not say that he is temperate who has these same elements in friendly harmony, in whom the one ruling principle of reason, and the two subject ones of spirit and desire are equally agreed that reason ought to rule, and do not rebel?

Certainly, he said, that is the true account of temperance whether in the State or individual.

And surely, I said, we have explained again and again how and by virtue of what quality a man will be just.

That is very certain.

And is justice dimmer in the individual, and is her form different, or is she the same which we found her to be in the State?

There is no difference in my opinion, he said.

Because, if any doubt is still lingering in our minds, a few commonplace instances will satisfy us of the truth of what I am saying.

What sort of instances do you mean?

If the case is put to us, must we not admit that the just State, or the man who is trained in the principles of such a State, will be less likely than the unjust to make away with a deposit of gold or silver? Would any one deny this?

No one, he replied.

Will the just man or citizen ever be guilty of sacrilege or theft, or treachery either to his friends or to his country?

Never.

Neither will he ever break faith where there have been oaths or agreements?

Impossible.

No one will be less likely to commit adultery, or to dishonour his father and mother, or to fail in his religious duties?

No one.

And the reason is that each part of him is doing its own business, whether in ruling or being ruled?

Exactly so.

Are you satisfied then that the quality which makes such men and such states is justice, or do you hope to discover some other?

Not I, indeed.

Then our dream has been realized; and the suspicion which we entertained at the beginning of our work of construction, that some divine power must have conducted us to a primary form of justice, has now been verified?

Yes, certainly.

And the division of labour which required the carpenter and the shoemaker and the rest of the citizens to be doing each his own business, and not another's, was a shadow of justice, and for that reason it was of use?

Clearly,

But in reality justice was such as we were describing; being concerned however, not with the outward man, but with the inward, which is the true self and concernment of man: for the just man does not permit the several elements within him to interfere with one another, or any of them to do the work of others,—he sets in order his own inner life, and is his own master and his own law, and at peace with himself; and when he has bound together the three principles within him, which may be compared to the higher, lower, and middle notes of the scale, and the intermediate intervals—when he has bound all these together, and is no longer many, but has become one entirely temperate and perfectly adjusted nature, then he proceeds to act, if he has to act, whether in a matter of property, or in the treatment of the body, or in some affair of politics or private business; always thinking and calling that which pre-serves and co-operates with this harmonious condition, just and good action, and the knowledge which presides over it, wisdom, and that which at any time impairs this condition, he will call unjust action, and the opinion which presides over it ignorance.

You have said the exact truth, Socrates.

Very good; and if we were to affirm that we had discovered the just man and the just State, and the nature of justice in each of them, we should not be telling a falsehood?

Most certainly not.

May we say so, then?

Let us say so.

Study Questions

1. Compare this section of *The Republic* with what you have read in Chapters 2 and 4. What are the characteristics of a just person, according to Socrates and Plato? What are the characteristics of a just state? Do you agree? Why or why not?

2. Why do we need to control our appetites or desires at all times, according to Plato? Do you agree? What are the political ramifications of comparing the rule of reason over appetites to the rule of the guardians over the general population?

 ## *Primary Reading*

Apology

PLATO

Dialogue excerpt, fourth century B.C.E. *Plato,* **The Republic of Plato, 3e.** *Translated by Benjamin Jowett. London: Oxford University Press, 1888.*

In the *Apology,* presumably the very first of Plato's dialogues, Socrates argues in his own defense while on trial. This is not a typical "dialogue," since Socrates does most of the talking, but we know he has listeners because he begs for their attention and asks them not to heckle him. Is this a true retelling of what Socrates actually said, or is Plato here (as often elsewhere) making things up? Scholars have speculated that Plato, being present at the trial, must surely have remembered every word of this traumatic, horrible event; however, the account was probably not written until some years later, perhaps as much as ten years, so we must assume that Plato tells it not only the way he remembers it but also the way he believes it *ought* to sound. Since Plato's account of the trial is not the only one in existence, we can assume that the general gist of Socrates' defense was the way Plato presented it.

I have said enough in my defense against the first class of my accusers; I turn to the second class. They are headed by Meletus, that good man and true lover of his country, as he calls himself. Against these, too, I must try to make a defense. Let their indictment be read; it runs like this: "Socrates is a doer of evil who corrupts the youth, and who does not believe in the gods of the state, but has other new divinities of his own." Such is the charge; now let us examine the particular counts. He says that I am a doer of evil and corrupt the youth; but I say, men of Athens, that Meletus is a doer of evil, since he pretends to be in earnest when he is only joking, and is so eager to bring men to trial from a pretended zeal and interest about matters in which he really never had the smallest interest. And the truth of this I will try to prove to you.

Come here, Meletus, and let me ask you a question. You think a great deal about the improvement of youth?

Yes, I do.

Tell the judges, then, who is their improver; for you must know, since you care so much.* You say you have discovered their corrupter, and are citing and accusing me before them. Speak then, and tell the judges who their improver is. Observe, Meletus, that you are silent and have nothing to say. But is not this disgraceful, and a clear proof of what I say, that you have never cared about this? Speak up, friend, and tell us who their improver is.

The laws.

But that, my good sir, is not my meaning. I want to know who the person is who, in the first place, knows the laws.

The judges, Socrates, who are present in court.

What, do you mean to say, Meletus, that they are able to instruct and improve youth?

Certainly they are.

What, all of them, or some only and not others?

All of them.

By the goddess Hera, that is good news! There are plenty of improvers, then. And what do you say of the audience—do they improve them?

Yes, they do.

And the members of the Council?

Yes, they improve them.

But perhaps the members of the Assembly corrupt them? Or do they too improve them?

They improve them.

Then every Athenian improves and elevates them except me; and I alone am their corrupter? Is that what you affirm?

That is what I stoutly affirm.

I am very unfortunate if you are right. But suppose I ask you a question. How about horses? Does one man do them harm and all the world good? Is not the exact opposite the truth? One man is able to do them good, or at least not many; the trainer of horses does them good, and others who have anything to do with them rather injure them. Is that not true, Meletus, of horses or of any other animals? Surely it is; whether you and Anytus say yes or no. Happy indeed would be the condition of youth if they had one corrupter only, and all the rest of the world were their improvers. But you, Meletus, have sufficiently shown that you never had a thought about the young; your carelessness is seen in your not caring about the very things you bring against me. Now, Meletus, I will ask you another question—by Zeus I will. Which is better, to live among bad citizens or among good ones? Answer, friend, I say; the question can be easily answered. Do not the good do their neighbors good, and the bad do them evil?

Certainly.

And is there anyone who would rather be injured than benefited by those who live with him? Answer, my good friend, the law requires you to answer—does anyone like to be injured?

---

*A play on Meletus's name, which means "one who cares" in Greek. [Ed.]

Certainly not.

And when you accuse me of corrupting the youth, do you allege that I corrupt them intentionally or unintentionally?

Intentionally, I say.

But you have just admitted that the good do their neighbors good, and evil do them evil. Now, is that a truth which your superior wisdom has recognized so early in life, and am I at my age in such darkness and ignorance that I do not know that if one of my associates is corrupted by me, I am very likely to be harmed by him? Yet I corrupt him, and intentionally too? So you say, although neither I nor any other human being is ever likely to be convinced by you. Either I do not corrupt them, or I corrupt them unintentionally; and in either case you lie. If my offense is unintentional, the law has no cognizance of unintentional offenses; you should have taken me aside privately and warned and admonished me. For if I had been better advised, I would have stopped doing what I only did unintentionally—no doubt I would; but you had nothing to say to me and refused to teach me. Instead you bring me up in court, which is a place not of instruction, but of punishment. It will be very clear to you, Athenians, as I said, that Meletus has no care at all, great or small, about the matter. But still I would like to know, Meletus, how you think I corrupt the young. I suppose you mean, according to your indictment, that I teach them not to acknowledge the gods the state acknowledges, but some other new divinities instead. These are the lessons by which I corrupt the youth, you say.

Yes, that I say emphatically. . . .

I have said enough in answer to the charge of Meletus; any elaborate defense is unnecessary. But I know only too well how many are the enmities I have incurred, and this is what will be my destruction if I am destroyed—not Meletus or Anytus, but the envy and detraction of the world, which has been the death of many good men, and will probably be the death of many more; there is no danger of my being the last of them.

Someone will say, "Are you not ashamed, Socrates, of a course of life which is likely to cause your death?" To him I may fairly answer: There you are mistaken; a man who is good for anything should not calculate the chances of living or dying; he should only consider whether in doing anything he is doing right or wrong—acting the part of a good or a bad man. . . . Wherever a man's place is, whether he has chosen it or has been placed in it by his commander, there he should remain in the hour of danger; he should not think of death or of anything but disgrace. For so it is, men of Athens, in truth.

Strange indeed would be my conduct, men of Athens, if I who, when I was ordered by the generals you chose to command me at Potidaea and Amphipolis and Delium, remained where they placed me, like any other man, facing death, and if now, when I believe the god orders me to fulfill the philosopher's mission of searching into myself and other men, I were to desert my post through fear of death or any other fear. That would indeed be strange, and I might justly be arraigned in court for denying the existence of the gods, if I disobeyed the oracle because I feared death, fancying that I was wise when I was not. For the fear of death is indeed the pretense of wisdom and not real wisdom, being a pretense of knowing the unknown; for no one knows whether death, which men in their fear think is the greatest evil, may not be the greatest good. Is not this ignorance disgraceful, the ignorance which is the conceit that man knows what he does not know? In this respect only I believe I differ from men in general, and may perhaps claim to be wiser than they are—that whereas I know but little of the world below, I do not suppose that I know; but I do know that injustice and disobedience to a better, whether god or man, is evil and dishonorable, and I will never fear or avoid a possible good rather than a certain evil. Therefore if you let me go now, and are not convinced by Anytus, who said that since I had been prosecuted I must be put to death (for otherwise I should never have been prosecuted at all), and that if I escape now, your sons will all be utterly ruined by listening to my words—if you say to me, "Socrates, this time we will not listen to Anytus and we will let you go, but upon one condition, that you do not inquire and speculate in this way any more, and that if you are caught doing so again you will die"—if this was the condition on which you let me go, I would reply: Men of Athens, I honor and love you; but I will obey the god rather than you. And while I have life and strength I will never cease from the practice and teaching of philosophy, exhorting anyone I meet and saying to him in my manner, "You, my friend, a citizen of the great and mighty and wise city of Athens, are you not ashamed of heaping up the greatest amount of money and honor and reputation, and caring so little about wisdom and truth and the greatest improvement of the soul, which you never regard or heed at all?" And if the person with whom I am arguing says, "Yes, but I do care," then I will not leave him or let him go at once, but will interrogate and examine him, and if I think he has no virtue in him, but only says he has, I will reproach him for undervaluing the greater and overvaluing the less. And I will repeat the same words to everyone I meet, young and old, citizen and alien, but especially the citizens, since they are my brothers. For this is the command of the god; and I believe no greater good has ever happened in the state than my service to the god. For I do nothing but go about persuading you all, old and young alike, not to think of your persons or properties, but first and chiefly to care about the greatest improvement of the soul. I tell you that virtue is not given by money, but that from virtue comes money and every other good of man, public as well as private. This is my teaching, and if this is the doctrine which corrupts the youth, I am a mischievous person. But if anyone says this is not my teaching, he is speaking an untruth. Therefore, men of Athens, I say to you, do as Anytus bids or not as Anytus bids, and either acquit me or not; but whichever you do, understand that I will never alter my ways, not even if I have to die many times.

Men of Athens, do not interrupt, but hear me; there was an understanding between us that you would hear me to the end. I have something more to say, at which you may be inclined to cry out; but I believe that to hear me will be good for you, and therefore I beg you not to cry out. I would have you know that if you kill such a one as I am, you will injure yourselves more than me. Nothing will injure me, not Meletus or Anytus—they cannot, for a bad man is not permitted to injure one better than himself. I do not deny that Anytus may perhaps kill me, or drive me into exile, or deprive me of civil rights; and he may imagine, and others may imagine, that he is inflicting a great injury on me; but there I do not agree. For he does himself a much greater injury by doing what he is doing now—unjustly taking away the life of another.

Study Questions

1. What does Socrates mean by saying, "The fear of death is indeed the pretense of wisdom and not real wisdom"?

2. What does he mean by saying that if the Athenians put him to death, they will hurt themselves more than him?

3. It has been speculated by philosophers that Socrates in his heart really wanted to die, and for that reason he said things in his argument for his defense that would irritate the jury of five hundred citizens (who voted guilty with only a small majority); however, newer research points toward Socrates being serious about defending himself. In your opinion, based on this excerpt, should Socrates have argued for his defense in some other way?

4. Socrates has been called a martyr to the principle of seeking the Truth. Could you imagine any principle so important to you that you would be willing to give up your life for it? Alternatively, can you think of any circumstances that to you would override even the most important principle?

Primary Reading

What Is a Good Life?

RONALD DWORKIN

Essay, 2010, **The New York Review of Books.** *Excerpt.*

For American philosopher Ronald Dworkin (1931–2013), the idea of living well—with happiness as a life goal—can't be achieved through the theories of Hobbes (too selfish), Hume (too feeling-focused), Mill (too consequentialist) or Kant (too duty-oriented). Religious moral rules will only work if one is religious. Plato and Aristotle have a better overall approach, says Dworkin, because they're looking at the big picture—what Dworkin calls an *interpretive account of morality.* So finding out what a good life is can't be just getting what we want, because the Good Life is normative: living the way we *should* live. Living a good life involves two separate moral standards: an ethical contemplation of one's own role in life, and some kind of fulfillment. In the end, Dworkin concludes that it isn't the end result that counts as much as how we got there—as some people have put it, it's the journey, not the destination. But the journey has to *shine,* as a work of art. (I have heavily abbreviated the first few paragraphs so I could include a larger section of Dworkin's article. I hope you will look up the original and read Dworkin's argument for the Good Life in its entirety.)

> Plato and Aristotle treated morality as a genre of interpretation. They tried to show the true character of each of the main moral and political virtues (such as honor, civic responsibility, and justice), first by relating each to the others, and then to the broad ethical ideals their translators summarize as personal "happiness." Here I use the terms "ethical" and "moral" in what might seem a special way. Moral standards prescribe how we ought to treat others; ethical standards, how we ought to live ourselves. The happiness that Plato and Aristotle evoked was to be achieved by living ethically; and this meant living according to independent moral principles. . . .

> But there is an apparent obstacle. This strategy seems to suppose that we should understand our moral responsibilities in whatever way is best for us, but that goal seems contrary to the spirit of morality, because morality should not depend on any benefit that being moral might bring. . . . We are, most of us, drawn to the more austere view that the justification and definition of moral principle should both be independent of our interests, even in the long term. Virtue should be its own reward; we need assume no other benefit in doing our duty. . . . But that austere view would set a severe limit to how far we could press an interpretive account of morality. . . . That would be disappointing, because we need to find authenticity as well as integrity in our morality, and authenticity requires that we break out of distinctly moral considerations to ask what form of moral integrity fits best with the ethical decision about how we want to conceive our personality and our life. The austere view blocks that question. Of course it is unlikely that we will ever achieve a full integration of our moral, political, and ethical values that feels authentic and right. That is why living responsibly is a continuing project and never a completed task. But the wider the network of ideas we can explore, the further we can push that project.

> . . . We need, then, a statement of what we *should* take our personal goals to be that fits with and justifies our sense of what obligations, duties, and responsibilities we have to others. We look for a conception of living well that can guide our interpretation of moral concepts. But we want, as part of the same project, a conception of morality that can guide our interpretation of living well.

. . . We can, however, pursue a somewhat different, and I believe more promising, idea. This requires a distinction within ethics that is familiar in morals: a distinction between duty and consequence, between the right and the good. We should distinguish between living well and having a good life. These two different achievements are connected and distinguished in this way: living well means striving to create a good life, but only subject to certain constraints essential to human dignity. These two concepts, of living well and of having a good life, are interpretive concepts. Our ethical responsibility includes trying to find appropriate conceptions of both of them.

Each of these fundamental ethical ideals needs the other. We cannot explain the importance of a good life except by noticing how creating a good life contributes to living well. We are self-conscious animals who have drives, instincts, tastes, and preferences. There is no mystery why we should want to satisfy those drives and serve those tastes. But it can seem mysterious why we should want a life that is good in a more critical sense: a life we can take pride in having lived when the drives are slaked or even if they are not. We can explain this ambition only when we recognize that we have a responsibility to live well and believe that living well means creating a life that is not simply pleasurable but good in that critical way. . . .

We have a responsibility to live well, and the importance of living well accounts for the value of having a critically good life. These are no doubt controversial ethical judgments. I also make controversial ethical judgments in any view I take about which lives are good or well-lived. In my own view, someone who leads a boring, conventional life without close friendships or challenges or achievements, marking time to his grave, has not had a good life, even if he thinks he has and even if he has thoroughly enjoyed the life he has had. If you agree, we cannot explain why he should regret this simply by calling attention to pleasures missed: there may have been no pleasures missed, and in any case there is nothing to miss now. We must suppose that he has *failed* at something: failed in his responsibilities for living.

What kind of value can living well have? The analogy between art and life has often been drawn and as often ridiculed. We should live our lives, the Romantics said, as a work of art. . . . We value great art most fundamentally not because the art as product enhances our lives but because it embodies a performance, a rising to artistic challenge. We value human lives well lived not for the completed narrative, as if fiction would do as well, but because they too embody a performance: a rising to the challenge of having a life to lead. The final value of our lives is adverbial, not adjectival—a matter of how we actually lived, not of a label applied to the final result. It is the value of the performance, not anything that is left when the performance is subtracted. It is the value of a brilliant dance or dive when the memories have faded and the ripples died away.

We need another distinction. Something's "product value" is the value it has just as an object, independently of the process through which it was created or of any other feature of its history. A painting may have product value, and this may be subjective or objective. Its formal arrangements may be beautiful, which gives it objective value, and it may give pleasure to viewers and be prized by collectors, which properties give it subjective value. A perfect mechanical replica of that painting has the same beauty. Whether it has the same subjective value depends largely on whether it is known to be a replica: it has as great subjective value as the original for those who think that it is the original. The original has a kind of objective value that the replica cannot have, however: it has the value of having been manufactured through a creative act that has performance value. It was created by an artist intending to create art. The object—the work of art—is wonderful because it is the upshot of a wonderful performance; it would not be as wonderful if it were a mechanical replica or if it had been created by some freakish accident.

It was once popular to laugh at abstract art by supposing that it could have been painted by a chimpanzee, and people once speculated whether one of billions of apes typing randomly might produce *King Lear*. If a chimpanzee by accident painted *Blue Poles* or typed the words of *King Lear* in the right order, these products would no doubt have very great subjective value. Many people would be desperate to own or anxious to see them. But they would have no value as performance at all. Performance value may exist independently of any object with which that performance value has been fused. There is no product value left when a great painting has been destroyed, but the fact of its creation remains and retains its full performance value. Uccello's achievements are no less valuable because his paintings were gravely damaged in the Florence flood; Leonardo's *Last Supper* might have perished, but the wonder of its creation would not have been diminished. A musical performance or a ballet may have enormous objective value, but if it has not been recorded or filmed, its product value immediately diminishes. Some performances—improvisational theater and unrecorded jazz concerts—find value in their ephemeral singularity: they will never be repeated.

We may count a life's positive impact—the way the world itself is better because that life was lived—as its product value. Aristotle thought that a good life is one spent in contemplation, exercising reason, and acquiring knowledge; Plato that the good life is a harmonious life achieved through order and balance. Neither of these ancient ideas requires that a wonderful life have any impact at all. Most people's opinions, so far as these are self-conscious and articulate, ignore impact in the same way. Many of them think that a life devoted to the love of a god or gods is the finest life to lead, and a great many including many who do not share that opinion think the same of a life lived in inherited traditions and steeped in the satisfactions of conviviality, friendship, and family. All these lives have, for most people who want them, subjective value: they bring satisfaction. But so far as we think them objectively good—so far as it would make sense to *want* to find satisfaction in such lives—it is the performance rather than the product value of living that way that counts.

Philosophers used to speculate about what they called the meaning of life. (That is now the job of mystics and comedians.) It is difficult to find enough product value in most people's lives to suppose that they have meaning through their impact. Yes, but if it were not for some lives, penicillin would not have been discovered so soon and *King Lear* would never have been written. Still, if we measure a life's value by its consequence, all but a few lives would have no value, and the great value of some other lives—of a carpenter who pounded nails into a playhouse on the Thames—would be only accidental. On any plausible view of what is truly wonderful in almost any human life, impact hardly comes into the story at all.

If we want to make sense of a life having meaning, we must take up the Romantics' analogy. We find it natural to say that an artist gives meaning to his raw materials and that a pianist gives fresh meaning to what he plays. We can think of living well as giving meaning—ethical meaning, if we want a name—to a life. That is the only kind of meaning in life that can stand up to the fact and fear of death. Does all that strike you as silly? Just sentimental? When you do something smaller well—play a tune or a part or a hand, throw a curve or a compliment, make a chair or a sonnet or love—your satisfaction is complete in itself. Those are achievements within life. Why can't a life also be an achievement complete in itself, with its own value in the art in living it displays?

Study Questions

1. What is the difference between "living well" and having a "good life"?

2. What is the difference between "product value" and "performance value," and how do these concepts relate to living a good life, according to Dworkin? Is he right, in your opinion? Is there more to a good life?

3. Compare Dworkin's idea of a good life lived critically with Socrates' statement that the unexamined life is not worth living. Are they saying the same thing? Why or why not?

4. Give three examples of people you think have lived the kind of life that Dworkin considers meaningful, and explain why.

Narrative

A Man for All Seasons

ROBERT BOLT (SCREENWRITER)
FRED ZINNEMAN (DIRECTOR)

Film, 1966. Based on a 1960 play by Robert Bolt. Summary.

This film, which won multiple Academy Awards, including best picture, best director, and best actor, portrays a real event in England's history. It is the sixteenth century; Henry VIII is king, and he has a problem: His wife, Catherine, whom the pope gave him dispensation to marry because she was his brother's widow (and as such, a relative), has not borne him any sons, and since he is concerned about the line of succession, he is looking around for another queen. The problem is that since England is Catholic, the king has no legal access to divorce, unless clever lawyers can find a loophole in his marriage. Churchmen, government officials, and legal experts, concerned with their own future, put together a strategy: to declare the marriage annulled on the grounds that the pope had no authority to grant the permission to marry in the first place. However, there is one legal expert who refuses to go along with the scheme: Sir Thomas More, a man whom the king considers a friend. Hoping to win him over, King Henry appoints him chancellor and shows up in person at More's estate on the River Thames to persuade him, but he leaves in anger when it becomes clear that More considers the word of the pope to have a higher authority. Why is it so important for the king to get More on his side, when he has the support of everyone else? Because, as the king himself remarks, More is an honest man who would not choose convenience over his conscience, and receiving More's blessing would make the plan legitimate to the king. But More refuses to budge, even though he knows that incurring the king's wrath can be a dangerous thing; indeed, this is the beginning of the end for More, as his erudite daughter Margaret soon realizes.

When Henry VIII institutes the English Reformation and outlaws Catholicism so he can divorce Catherine and marry his new love, Anne (who herself will be executed to make way for another queen a few years later), More withdraws from his position as chancellor in silence, never uttering a word in public or in private about the king's activities. A brilliant lawyer, More is trying to protect himself and his family by following both his conscience and the law to the letter, believing that his silence will be a shield, but he discovers that his silence does not protect him, as it should according to the law. As the king's man Thomas Cromwell remarks, More is an innocent and does not envision the schemes being prepared by his adversaries. A young man, Richard, who used to be part of the circle around More but believed he could find glory and fortune by attaching himself to Cromwell instead, now serves as an informant on More. But there is truly nothing to report: More is a man of integrity, the only lawyer in London who has not accepted bribes on a regular basis, says More's friend, the Duke of Norfolk. Since More refuses to sign a new oath of allegiance to the king and to accept the new rules of succession according to the Protestant Church of England, he is called in for a hearing, during which his sharp legal mind outwits Cromwell; but from now on he is considered an enemy of the court, and being his friend becomes dangerous. Norfolk tries to persuade him to do as everyone else, do the convenient thing to save himself and his career, but following one's principles is more important to More than life and safety. To save his friend Norfolk from the danger and embarrassment of their friendship, he provokes a quarrel that leaves Norfolk hurt and angry, so that he turns his back on More.

Soon More finds himself a prisoner in the Tower of London, the last stage in the lives of many political prisoners; through several seasons he languishes in the damp cell without being allowed to see his family, under constant pressure from Cromwell to either sign the oath or speak up against it. We see how his posture has deteriorated; his hair is gray, and his face shows the hardship of imprisonment. One day he is surprised and overjoyed to see his family—his wife, Alice, his daughter, and her husband—but when he realizes that they have been ordered to come just to put pressure on him, he understands that he will not be seeing them again and that staying in England will endanger their lives; he makes them promise that they will flee the country, by different routes, on the same day, and very soon.

His daughter asks him why he can't just sign the oath to save himself—speak it with his mouth and speak against it in his heart—and More answers,

> What is an oath, then, but words we say to God? Listen, Meg, when a man takes an oath, he is holding his own self in his own hands, like water—and if he opens his fingers then, he needn't hope to find himself again.

John Springer Collection/Corbis Historical/Getty Images

In the 1966 film *A Man for All Seasons* we meet Sir Thomas More (Paul Scofield), a lawyer associated with the court of King Henry VIII. In this true story, More becomes a victim of his own high moral standards: The king wants More's support in annulling his marriage, but More's professional integrity won't allow him to give it. In this scene paralleling Socrates' speech in his own defense (see the ***Apology***), More argues for his viewpoint and his life, well knowing that he is already condemned.

But Margaret is not satisfied; to her, it is not her father's fault if the state is three-quarters bad, and if he elects to suffer for it, then he elects himself a hero. More replies:

> That's very neat. If we lived in a state where virtue was profitable, common sense would make us saints, but since we see that avarice, anger, pride and stupidity commonly profit far beyond charity, modesty, justice and thought, perhaps we must stand fast a little, even at the risk of being heroes.

More knows that his daughter will understand, but his wife, Alice, is tormented by the suffering he is putting her through—she says she is afraid that when he is gone, she is going to hate him for what he has done to them; and, for once, at this moment, Thomas More begins to lose his composure. It means so much to him that his wife understand why he may be going to his death. He begs her to say she does, for without her understanding he might not be able to endure what is going to happen to him. And now she looks at him, embraces him, and tells him she understands that he is a good man and that he must do what his conscience tells him to do. Sad but relieved, he hugs his daughter and his wife one last time.

At last More stands trial; he has often told his family as well as his adversaries that there can be no trial because they have nothing on him; silence can be used only to signify tacit consent and not dissent. But now there is a witness: A man in fancy clothes, a rich and powerful man, approaches the bench. It is Richard, the young man who sold out to Cromwell, More's former friend who now holds a high public office, a position received in return for the perjury he is about to commit. He swears that he has heard More speak his mind, against the king and the new Church of England. Cromwell asks the questions, and his instructions to the jury consist of saying that the jury hardly need deliberate. Thus we know that they, too, must have been "instructed" before the trial. And indeed the verdict is "guilty." Almost deprived of his right to speak, More now rises, a condemned man, and breaks his silence, arguing that he is being executed for not agreeing to the king's divorce, which he certainly was against, because it nullified the authority of the pope. Cromwell decries this as treason; and soon after, on a sunny day in summer, More is executed by beheading.

Study Questions

1. Find similarities between Socrates and Thomas More; are there any significant differences?

2. What does More mean by saying, "When a man takes an oath, he is holding his own self in his own hands, like water—and if he opens his fingers then, he needn't hope to find himself again"?

3. If you were in More's position, what might you have chosen to do? If you had been in the position of More's daughter or wife, would you have understood and accepted his actions? Why or why not?

4. Virtue ethics, as you know, focuses not on what to do but on how to be; the film shows More as a man of honesty and integrity, two very important virtues. But would it be possible to criticize More for having failed the test of the virtues of family loyalty and flexibility? Why or why not? (This question actually reveals one of the problems with virtue ethics: What do we do about conflicting virtues?)

Narrative

The Myth of the Cave

PLATO

Excerpt from the **Republic,** *fourth century* B.C.E. ***Plato,*** **The Republic of Plato, 3e.** *Translated by* *Benjamin Jowett. London: Oxford University Press, 1888.*

There is no better fictional narrative that illustrates Plato's theory of Forms than the Myth, Fable, or Allegory of the Cave itself. Here you have it in its entirety; the two persons talking are Socrates, telling the story, and Plato's brother Glaucon, listening.

> And now, I said, let me show in a figure how far our nature is enlightened or unenlightened:—Behold! human beings living in an underground den, which has a mouth open towards the light and reaching all along the den; here they have been from their childhood, and have their legs and necks chained so that they cannot move, and; can only see before them, being prevented by the chains from turning round their heads. Above and behind them a fire is blazing at a distance, and between the fire and the prisoners there is a raised way; and you will see, if you look, a low wall built along the way, like the screen which marionette players have in front of them, over which they show the puppets.
>
> I see.
>
> And do you see, I said, men passing along the wall carrying all sorts of vessels, and statues and figures of animals made of wood and stone and various materials, which appear over the wall? Some of them are talking, others silent.
>
> You have shown me a strange image, and they are strange prisoners.
>
> Like ourselves, I replied; and they see only their own shadows, or the shadows of one another, which the fire throws on the opposite wall of the cave?
>
> True, he said; how could they see anything but the shadows if they were never allowed to move their heads?
>
> And of the objects which are being carried in like manner they would only see the shadows?
>
> Yes, he said.
>
> And if they were able to converse with one another, would they not suppose that they were naming what was actually before them?
>
> Very true.
>
> And suppose further that the prison had an echo which came from the other side, would they not be sure to fancy when one of the passers-by spoke that the voice which they heard came from the passing shadow?
>
> No question, he replied.
>
> To them, I said, the truth would be literally nothing but the shadows of the images.
>
> That is certain.

And now look again, and see what will naturally follow if the prisoners are released and disabused of their error. At first, when any of them is liberated and compelled suddenly to stand up and turn his neck round and walk and look towards the light, he will suffer sharp pains; the glare will distress him, and he will be unable to see the realities of which in his former state he had seen the shadows; and then conceive some one saying to him, that what he saw before was an illusion, but that now, when he is approaching nearer to being and his eye is turned towards more real existence, he has a clearer vision,—what will be his reply? And you may further imagine that his instructor is pointing to the objects as they pass and requiring him to name them,—will he not be perplexed? Will he not fancy that the shadows which he formerly saw are truer than the objects which are now shown to him?

Far truer.

And if he is compelled to look straight at the light, will he not have a pain in his eyes which will make him turn away to take refuge in the objects of vision which he can see, and which he will conceive to be in reality clearer than the things which are now being shown to him?

True, he said.

And suppose once more, that he is reluctantly dragged up a steep and rugged ascent, and held fast until he is forced into the presence of the sun himself, is he not likely to be pained and irritated? When he approaches the light his eyes will be dazzled, and he will not be able to see anything at all of what are now called realities.

Not all in a moment, he said.

He will require to grow accustomed to the sight of the upper world. And first he will see the shadows best, next the reflections of men and other objects in the water, and then the objects themselves; then he will gaze upon the light of the moon and the stars and the spangled heaven; and he will see the sky and the stars by night better than the sun or the light of the sun by day?

Certainly.

Last of all he will be able to see the sun, and not mere reflections of him in the water, but he will see him in his own proper place, and not in another; and he will contemplate him as he is.

Certainly.

He will then proceed to argue that this is he who gives the season and the years, and is the guardian of all that is in the visible world, and in a certain way the cause of all things which he and his fellows have been accustomed to behold?

Clearly, he said, he would first see the sun and then reason about him.

And when he remembered his old habitation, and the wisdom of the den and his fellow-prisoners, do you not suppose that he would felicitate himself on the change, and pity them?

Certainly, he would.

And if they were in the habit of conferring honours among themselves on those who were quickest to observe the passing shadows and to remark which of them went before, and which followed after, and which were together; and who were therefore best able to draw conclusions as to the future, do you think that he would care for such honours and glories, or envy the possessors of them? Would he not say with Homer,

'Better to be the poor servant of a poor master,' and to endure anything, rather than think as they do and live after their manner?

Yes, he said, I think that he would rather suffer anything than entertain these false notions and live in this miserable manner.

Imagine once more, I said, such an one coming suddenly out of the sun to be replaced in his old situation; would he not be certain to have his eyes full of darkness?

To be sure, he said.

And if there were a contest, and he had to compete in measuring the shadows with the prisoners who had never moved out of the den, while his sight was still weak, and before his eyes had become steady (and the time which would be needed to acquire this new habit of sight might be very considerable), would he not be ridiculous? Men would say of him that up he went and down he came without his eyes; and that it was better not even to think of ascending; and if any one tried to loose another and lead him up to the light, let them only catch the offender, and they would put him to death.

No question, he said.

Study Questions

1. To recapitulate: This is an allegory of what Plato sees as reality. What does it mean? Who are the prisoners? Where is the cave? What does it mean to see the sun?

2. What did Plato have in mind when he let Socrates speak the final sentences? What is the reader supposed to conclude?

3. In what way might this worldview correspond to elements in the worldview of the Christian tradition? Are there significant differences?

4. Can you think of a modern story (film or novel) that speculates about the nature of reality? (Does it ask questions such as, Is reality the way we see it? What are we on this earth for? and Is there life after death?) Does it agree or disagree with Plato's version?

 Narrative

The Truman Show

ANDREW NICCOL (SCREENWRITER)
PETER WEIR (DIRECTOR)

Film, 1998. Summary.

This film is one of those stories we can interpret in a number of ways. That it is a satire on the entertainment industry and its mixing of reality and fiction is the easy interpretation, but some also see it as an allegory about the freedom of the human spirit in a world that is overly regulated. It could also be one man's fantasy of being the center of the universe. But in essence *The Truman Show* is about seeking and finding true reality beyond the illusion that presents itself as everyday life, and as such it becomes a story with a Socratic twist, a parallel to Plato's "Myth of the Cave."

Truman (Jim Carey) is on television 24/7, but he doesn't know it. The world is real to him, but everyone else knows it is a soundstage, a world of fakery. The only thing that isn't faked in the show is Truman himself (a *true man,* as opposed to all the other characters in the show) and his emotional reactions. Once he realizes his world is not real, will he try to seek true reality or be content with illusions and safety? Compare the question asked by Socrates in the Myth of the Cave: What is the philosopher supposed to do once he realizes he has been stuck in a cave of illusions all his life?

Truman Burbank is a young insurance salesman who lives with his wife, a nurse, in the small, pleasant island community of Seahaven, the kind of place where everybody knows everyone else—at least they all know Truman. It's a friendly town, and Truman has never been anywhere else. When he was a boy his father drowned during an outing in their sailboat: Surprised by a storm, Truman's dad fell overboard and disappeared in the waves. This traumatic experience gave Truman a fear of deep water, so the mere thought of going on the ferry to the mainland, or driving across the bridge, makes him anxious. Nevertheless, he has travel dreams: He wants to go to Fiji. As a boy he wanted to be an explorer, but his teacher was quick to tell him that all the places have already been discovered, so why would he want to go anywhere? His best friend since childhood does his best to discourage Truman's longing for exotic places, and Truman's wife points out that they can't afford to just take off, they have obligations and must meet house payments, and so on. In fact, everyone seems to be trying to make Truman stay in Seahaven.

When he was in high school, he fell in love with Sylvia, a beautiful, elusive girl who seemed to have something important on her mind, but somehow they were always prevented from seeing each other—until a fateful evening at the library when they were able to sneak out and make a run for it to the beach. But within minutes a vehicle showed up, presumably driven by her father, who snatched Sylvia away from Truman. She wasn't normal, he said, and shouted that they were moving to Fiji. So we understand that the reason Truman wants to go to Fiji isn't just to see a faraway place—it is to look for Sylvia. Before her father took her away, she tried to convey to Truman that something was wrong—but he didn't understand what she meant.

Now, years later, he is beginning to feel that something *is* wrong. His wife is constantly telling him about new household products with unnatural enthusiasm, as if she is acting in a commercial. In his car on the way to work the radio malfunctions, and he hears a voice describing the route he is taking. He walks into a building on the spur of the moment and tries to enter the elevator, only to find that there is no back wall to the elevator—he can see clear through to a backstage area where people are having lunch. But first and foremost, he has a chance encounter in the street with a homeless person who looks awfully familiar to him. He turns, takes a second look—and realizes that it is Dad, returned from the dead! But at that moment, strangers turn up and whisk the older man away on a bus.

This is the turning point for Truman: Is somebody trying to prevent him from talking to his father? Increasingly, he has the feeling that his entire reality is somehow staged and that people are not what they seem. And as viewers we know that he is right: Everything *is* staged except for Truman and his reactions, because Truman is the hero of *The Truman Show,* a live, twenty-four-hours-a-day television series broadcast to the entire world. That was the secret that Sylvia was trying to tell him but never quite managed to convey.

It is a hugely popular show. Truman has been on TV from the day he was born, without having the slightest idea that his reality isn't normal. And in a way it is "normal"—an idealized normality that doesn't exist for anyone else. His mother is an actor, his wife is an actor, even his best friend whom he has known since childhood—everyone is in on it except Truman. *The Truman Show* is the brainchild of the brilliant director Christoph, who watches over everything on the set high above Seahaven, in a control booth disguised as a perennially visible full moon. The control booth makes the sun rise and set electronically, changes the weather, and cues everyone on the set through earphones. The words of friendship spoken by his best friend are lines fed to the friend by Christoph. In a rare interview the great director is asked why Truman has never questioned his reality, and he answers that we all believe the reality that is presented to us.

But Truman's gullibility is coming to an end: When he realizes that the travel agent has no intention of selling him a ticket to Fiji, he packs his suitcase and heads for the bus depot, and buys a ticket to Chicago. But the bus isn't going anywhere—the bus driver is an actor who can't get the bus started—and Christoph isn't about to let Truman leave. There is nowhere to go; the set is enclosed. But Truman doesn't give up. One night, as the TV crew relaxes because they think he is asleep, what they're really watching is a dummy under a blanket, with a tape recorder producing snoring sounds. Truman has sneaked out. For the first time in his life he is not on camera.

Christoph mobilizes the entire island: All the actors are now engaged in looking for Truman, but he is nowhere to be found—until they think to look for him in the unthinkable place: on the water, in a sailboat, headed for—Fiji? All over the world, viewers watch with bated breath. Will Truman succeed in his quest? Will he escape his confining, designed world? Even Sylvia is watching, praying that Truman will make it. Christoph does what he can to thwart Truman, even ordering his reluctant engineers to whip up a nearly fatal storm. In spite of his deep-seated fear of water, Truman hangs in there and outlasts Christoph's rage. He continues on his way toward the horizon—which comes up sooner than expected: All of a sudden the bow of his boat goes right through the sky, a beautifully painted backdrop. He has been sailing around in a huge tank on the soundstage.

Immediately ahead is a flight of stairs, leading up to a door. Truman steps off the boat, walks to the stairs along the edge of the world, and ascends to the door. And now Christoph, desperate, addresses him over the speaker system, a disembodied loving voice coming from above. He tells Truman about how long he has been observing him as a boy and a young man, all the kinds of experiences a parent would remember— and how well he knows him and his fears. Nothing bad can ever happen to him in Seahaven—the real world is a dangerous place. The door is open to the dark, mysterious real world. Is Truman going to go through it and disappear? Or will he act true to his conditioning and go back?

Study Questions

1. What are the similarities between Plato's "Myth of the Cave" and *The Truman Show,* and what are the differences? In Plato's myth the perfect world is outside the cave. Where is it in the film? You may also want to explore the concept of one person being deluded versus humanity as such being deluded. Is this exclusively Truman's story, or are we all "Trumans," stuck on the soundstage as in Plato's cave?

2. What is the significance of Truman's first name? What does it mean in the context of the story?

3. If you could choose, would you rather have a pleasant life based on a lie, or a difficult, unpredictable life founded on a true perception of the world? (If you're familiar with the film *The Matrix,* you may remember that the fundamental question raised by the movie is essentially the same.)

4. If we view the story as an illustration of Socratic virtue ethics, developing one's character and allowing reason to rule, how might the three virtues of wisdom, courage, and temperance be seen to play out in (1) Truman? (2) the director? (3) the others on the island? and (4) the audience?

 Narrative

The Store of the Worlds

ROBERT SHECKLEY

Short story, 1959. Summary and Excerpt.

What is a "good life"? For many people today it means a life of no financial worries, of material goods and successful pursuit of pleasures. Socrates believed that a good life must involve intellectual and moral awareness: "The unexamined life is not worth living," he said. In order to live a full and fruitful life, one should stay aware and alert, not take things for granted, question authority, acquire knowledge, and certainly also make a point of enjoying oneself. For Socrates a good life would be one spent thinking; analyzing; trying to be a fair, just, and decent human being; and not letting the moments of life go to waste.

This little story written at the height of the Cold War, with its constant fear of sudden global nuclear annihilation, offers a version of what a good life is that may come as a surprise to you. And then again, perhaps not. For Mr. Wayne's fantasy of a perfect life doesn't involve fame or fortune, just the chance to enjoy more of an ordinary life that is gone forever. I think many of us understand the moral of this little story—as does anyone who has come face-to-face with the loss of the daily life he or she has taken for granted.

Mr. Wayne is on a clandestine errand: Making certain he hasn't been followed, he slips into a small, obscure shack, clutching a parcel. Inside the primitive shack is the man he has come to see,

Mr. Tompkins. Mr. Tompkins's activity is illegal, and yet word has spread about it; Wayne would like to know more. Tompkins explains.

> What happens is this, you pay me my fee. I give you an injection which knocks you out. Then, with the aid of certain gadgets which I have in the back of the store, I liberate your mind. . . . Your mind, liberated from its body, is able to choose from the countless probability-worlds which the Earth casts off in every second of its existence.

In every second of Earth's existence, Tompkins explains, alternate realities have been created: All the ways things could have happened, but didn't, in our own reality. You can spend a year in any alternate reality you choose! But the fee is high: Just about everything you own, plus ten years off your life. It will have the complete feel of reality, and the method of choosing will not even be conscious; your choice will be guided by your deepest unconscious desires. Tompkins is still working on a way to make it permanent, but so far he can manage only a year, and that is so strenuous to the body that the customer loses ten years of lifetime.

Mr. Wayne is fascinated, and tempted, but the price frightens him, so he asks if he can think it over. All the way home on the train to Long Island he ponders. But when he arrives home, he has other things to think about: His wife Janet needs to discuss household problems with him, his son wants help with his hobby, and his young daughter wants to tell about her day in kindergarten. Janet notices that he seems preoccupied, but he has no intention of telling her that he went to see the weirdo at the Store of the Worlds.

Next day his attention is completely absorbed by things at the office: Middle East events cause a panic on Wall Street, so he has to put all thoughts of the Store on the back burner. On weekends he goes sailing with his son; his daughter catches the measles; the boy wants to know about atomic bombs and hydrogen bombs and cobalt bombs and all the other kinds, and Wayne explains to the best of his ability. Sometimes on summer nights he and Janet go sailing on Long Island Sound, and it is cool and lovely. Occasionally he thinks about the Store; but autumn comes, and there are other everyday things to deal with. In mid-winter there is a fire in the bedroom, and the repairs put all luxuries out of his reach. Working at the office, worrying about the political tensions around the world, taking care of his son when he comes down with the mumps—all of a sudden it is spring again—a whole year has passed. . . .

Mr. Wayne opens his eyes. He is reclined in the chair in Tompkins's shack. Tompkins hovers over him, asking him if he wants a refund. Wayne assures him that the experience was quite satisfactory and inquires if there is any way that the world of his secret desires could be made permanent. Tompkins says he is working on it, and he is eager to hear about what Wayne's inner world turned out to be, but Wayne doesn't want to discuss it. It's too personal.

Now comes the time for Mr. Wayne to pay Tompkins for having given him a year in his own private world that he desires the most—which turned out to be just an ordinary year in the past, with his wife and his son and daughter, and his job, and the precious weekends, and all the little problems and distractions that come with an ordinary existence. It has now cost him ten years of his life and a fortune in goods: a pair of army boots, a knife, two coils of copper wire, and three small cans of corned beef. Tompkins finds the payment to be quite satisfactory, and Mr. Wayne leaves the shack for home—a home where no Janet is waiting for him, and no son or daughter. No sailboat, no job, no house, no normalcy. All he sees on his way back to his shelter are endless fields of radioactive debris from remnants of cities, covered with fine ash that once were humans beings. Wayne's *real* world is the world after a nuclear holocaust, and his worries are not about his daughter's braces, or home repairs, or Wall Street, but about surviving each day.

"With the aid of his wrist Geiger he found a deactivated lane through the rubble. He'd better get back to the shelter before dark, before the rats came out. If he didn't hurry he'd miss the evening potato ration."

Study Questions

1. What was the world of Mr. Wayne's secret desire? What might the author want to convey with this story? Does it seem relevant to you? Why or why not?

2. How might Socrates comment on this story? Has Mr. Wayne examined his life, thus making it worth living?

3. Reviewers have described Scheckley's story as a humoristic piece. Does it seem humorous to you, or didn't the reviewers get the deeper meaning? Might it be both funny and serious?

4. Today we are close to having access to Mr. Tompkins's invention through computerized *virtual reality;* given the choice of alternate realities, which would you choose to spend a year in? Would you consider the lesson of "The Store of the Worlds"?

5. Is this a didactic story? Why or why not?

6. Apply Dworkin's concept of life as having performance value versus life as having product value with this story. Does Mr. Tompkins's one year in the past have performance value or product value, or both? Is that important? Why or why not?

Chapter Nine
Aristotle's Virtue Theory: Everything in Moderation

After Plato's death in 347 B.C.E., leadership of the Academy fell to his nephew Speusippus. History believes that another man had expected to take over, and with good reason, for he was by far the best student ever to be associated with the Academy. That man was Aristotle, who had studied for twenty years with Plato. Scholars now think that because of the amount of traveling Plato did, Aristotle may never have been especially close to his teacher; it seems certain that the closeness between Socrates and Plato was never repeated between Plato and Aristotle.

Empirical Knowledge and the Realm of the Senses

Making claims about someone's influence on history can be a risky business because such claims tend to be exaggerated. In Aristotle's case, however, it is quite safe to say that he is one of the persons in antiquity who has had the most influence on Western thinking and that even in modern times few people have rivaled his overall historical importance. As Plato left his legacy in Western philosophy and theology, Aristotle opened up the possibility of scientific, logical, empirical thinking—in philosophy as well as in the natural sciences.

It is no wonder that Plato made no contribution in that area. He wouldn't have been interested in natural science, because its object is the world of the senses, far removed from the Forms. Although Aristotle was a student of Plato and did believe in the general reality of Plato's Forms (see Chapter 8), he believed that Forms are *not* separate from material things; Aristotle believed the Forms have no existence outside their objects. If we're enjoying the view of a waterfall cascading off a cliff face, we are at the same time, according to Aristotle, directly experiencing the Forms of cliff, of waterfall, and of falling. If we're in love with someone and think the person is beautiful, we are experiencing the Form of beauty right there in the person's face. And if we are studying a tree or a fossil, the Form that gives us knowledge about the history of that tree or fossil is right there. In other words, knowledge can be sought and found directly from the world of the senses. From the previous chapter, you may remember Socrates' remark in *Phaedrus* that he never ventured outside the city because trees and countryside could not teach him anything—in contrast, Aristotle would most definitely look to those trees for knowledge.

This turn in Aristotle's thinking—from Forms being separate to being inseparable from the thing or the experience—is what made it possible for him to think in terms of empirical research (gathering evidence, making hypotheses, and testing theories on the basis of experience). Legend holds that Alexander the Great, on his exploits deep into Persia and Afghanistan, had samples of flora and fauna collected and sent to his old teacher. Aristotle would have been delighted to receive such samples and would have studied them carefully, because he believed in the possibility of empirical knowledge.

Aristotle the Scientist

It is hard for us to imagine that there was an era when a human being actually could "know everything," in the sense of having access to all available knowledge at the time, and yet it seems that Aristotle was such a person. (Box 9.1 explores the career of Aristotle as a foreigner in Athens.) He was instrumental in founding the sciences—not the exact disciplines as we know them today, but sciences in the sense that the concepts of *logic* and *observation* were combined. The extent of his influence, however, goes beyond that. He was the author of what we know as classical logic; he laid the foundations of the classifications in biology; he developed theories of astronomy; he was interested in politics, rhetoric (the art of verbal persuasion), and drama; he wrote books on the proper structure of tragedy and of comedy; he developed theories of the nature of the soul, of God, and of other metaphysical questions. Indeed, the term *metaphysics* derives from Aristotle: He wrote a book on physics and then another book without a title about the nature of reality. Because it came after the book on physics, his followers called it the "book after physics," *ta meta ta physica.*

Box 9.1 WHO WAS ARISTOTLE?

Michele Ursi/Alamy Stock Photo

Aristotle was born in Stagira in Northern Greece in 384 B.C.E. His father died when he was young, and he was raised by his sister and her husband. They were of good family, and his father had been the physician to the king of Macedonia. When Aristotle arrived in Athens at the age of eighteen it was, presumably, to get an education as a physician so he could take over the illustrious position of royal physician at home, but that was not to be: He was drawn to Plato's Academy, and was arguably the brightest student in the school, maturing into his own thinker over two decades. On the side he reportedly made a living giving medical advice to Athenians. When Plato died, Aristotle—thirty-eight at the time—must have assumed that he would be elected as the new leader of the Academy, but he was passed over for Plato's nephew Speusippus. Considering that Aristotle hadn't seen eye to eye with Plato

about a number of subjects, that's perhaps not so hard to understand, but perhaps more important, he was not an Athenian citizen, and did not have the rights of native-born citizens of Athens. So he had no recourse, and left Athens, presumably in anger. He traveled to Asia Minor, got married, and began his studies in biology. In 343 he went to Macedonia, where he became a tutor for the young prince, the son of King Philip. (In three short years, that boy would become the regent of Macedonia and later of an immense realm covering most of the classical world. He would come to be known as Alexander the Great.) Exactly what Aristotle's status was at court is a matter of speculation—some scholars think that his tutoring of Alexander was actually a minor job compared with the real purpose of his stay, which may have been completely political: King Philip hoped to get Aristotle elected as head of Plato's Academy even if he'd already been passed over for Speusippus, because Speusippus was anti-Macedonian, and Philip apparently had expansionist ambitions and needed a pro-Macedonian leader of the most powerful school in the Greek culture. But when Speusippus died, Aristotle was passed over a second time, and King Philip focused on going to war with Athens instead. So Aristotle packed up and left for his home in Stagira, but his connection with the Macedonian court was by no means over: When Philip was assassinated and Alexander became king, Alexander found use for his old teacher and sent him to Athens in 335 to open up a school of his own, in competition with Plato's school. There is speculation that even at that point, Aristotle had hoped to become leader of the Academy, for he traveled to Athens with a huge amount of teaching material and an entire staff to run the school, but it never happened. Instead, Aristotle started teaching at the site of the public horse track, known as the Lyceum after Apollo Lykeion, and for twelve years—not a particularly long span, as academic careers go—he taught students and wrote books about issues that were of interest to him in philosophy, science, and what we today would call social and political science.

Photos.com/Getty Images

During the Renaissance, Raphael painted this vision of Plato's Academy, titled *The School of Athens*—not a true representation of daily life in the school but, rather, a highly symbolic image of two schools of thought. Two figures are approaching the steps in the center: Plato and Aristotle. Plato, the older man, is on the left. On the left side of the painting are some of Plato's students; but most are historical figures, including some from Raphael's own day, who have subscribed to the Platonic way of thought. Plato is pointing upward to the world of Forms, his image of true reality, whereas the younger man next to him, Aristotle, is stretching out his hand toward us, palm downward. He seems to say that it is in this world we can find true knowledge, not in any intellectual realm removed from the senses. On the right we find the Aristotelians of history, the scientists. And on the far right, Raphael has chosen to place himself, peeking straight out at us.

His book about ethics may prove to have the most enduring influence of them all. But he also wrote about the justification of slavery and the nature of woman as a lower being. Aristotle thus presents ideas in his writings that are deeply offensive to most modern Western readers, but philosophers usually choose to read his more controversial writings as historical documents rather than as blueprints for how to live our lives. In many ways Aristotle was not what we call a critical thinker; indeed, Socrates would not necessarily have approved of him, for he often refrains from analyzing a viewpoint (such as the status and nature of women) but, rather, limits himself to mentioning it. He seems to assume that some things are obvious; most people who lived during his time probably agreed with him.

A great many of Aristotle's writings are lost to us, such as his second book of *Poetics,* as you'll remember from Chapter 2. Aristotle, like Plato, wrote dialogues, and the Roman orator Cicero held them in high regard, but only some fragments remain. For the most part, the works we have access to are lecture notes and course summaries that he used in his classes; some were written for general audiences and some for more advanced students. Some of the works are supplemented by notes taken by his students.

Aristotle's Virtue Theory: Teleology and the Golden Mean

Virtue and Excellence

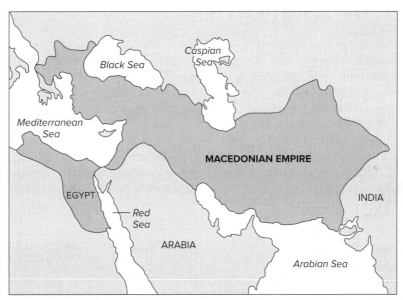

The realm conquered by Alexander the Great (356–323 B.C.E.) was immense by the standards of the time period and even of today; however, it was short-lived. On Alexander's death his generals divided the spoils and had to deal with local insurrections. Nevertheless, the memory of Alexander was kept alive in cultures as far apart as Egypt and northern India; in the mountainous reaches of Afghanistan, Pakistan, and northern India the name "Sikander" (Alexander) became a legend: For example, the Afghan city of Kandahar, which figured prominently in the war in Afghanistan 2001–2014, is named after Alexander. In Egypt a dynasty was founded by his general Ptolemy, and a city was named after him that centuries later would become the new center of civilization, the city of Alexandria.

In the first part of Chapter 8, we saw that the Greek conception of virtue was slightly different from our colloquial use of the word. Although calling someone virtuous may for some imply a certain amount of contempt, no such meaning was implied by the ancient Greeks. If you were virtuous, you would not be considered dull or withdrawn from life, because being virtuous meant, above all, that you managed your skills and your opportunities well. To be virtuous meant to act with *excellence*—we might even say with *virtuosity,* because this term retains some of what the Greeks associated with virtue.

Nowhere is that more apparent than in Aristotle's philosophy: You might say that virtue lies in the difference between doing something and doing it well. To Aristotle, everything on this earth has its own virtue, meaning that if it "performs" the way it is supposed to by its nature, then it is virtuous. For one thing, this means that virtue is not reserved for humans; for another thing, it means that everything that exists, including humans, has a purpose. There is virtue to a sharp knife, a comfortable chair, a tree that grows straight, and a healthy, swift animal. For young, growing entities such as saplings and babies, one might talk about *potential virtue.*

Teleology: The Concept of Purpose

One concept that is essential for understanding Aristotle's ideas on virtue comes from his metaphysics: the concept of *teleology.* In Greek, *telos* means goal or purpose, and a teleological theory or viewpoint assumes that something has a purpose or that the end result of some action is all-important. Examples of teleological theories exist even today; we encounter them often in everyday discussions about "the meaning of life." Modern science, however, has preferred to leave the question of the purpose of the universe behind. Plato also believed in the purpose of things, but Aristotle built his teleology into a complete metaphysical theory of "causes." (For Aristotle's four causes, see Box 9.2.)

Box 9.2 THE FOUR CAUSES

For Aristotle every event has four causes, or four factors that work on it and bring it into being. These are the *material cause,* or the "stuff" the thing is made of; the *efficient cause,* the force that has brought it into being; the *formal cause,* the shape or idea (the Form) of the thing; and the *final cause,* the purpose of the thing. Consider this illustration (for which I give credit to one of my students):

- Material cause: flour, water, and so on
- Efficient cause: me, the baker
- Formal cause: the idea of muffins
- Final cause: to be eaten!

The material cause and the efficient cause are fairly straightforward from a modern point of view: We have a general idea what Aristotle means when he says the material cause of a thing is the actual physical material that makes it what it is. But what about the efficient creative force? For a muffin, the creative force is the baker; for a wolf, it would be the wolf's parents; for a river, it would be mountain springs and precipitation. (Later religious traditions inspired by Aristotle have chosen to read God as the creative, efficient force.) But the formal and final causes are less intuitive. In the formal cause we see the last surviving element of Plato's theory of Forms in Aristotle's philosophy, but the Form is not outside the object in some intellectual realm; it is right there in the object itself. (Consider the painting by Raphael on p. 390: Aristotle is pointing downward, almost as if saying, "*This world* is where you find true reality.") A successful muffin displays the perfect Form of muffin, whereas a misshapen muffin is only a weak representation of the muffin Form.

For Aristotle, the final cause was by far the most important cause from a philosophical point of view, because it allows us to understand the purpose of a thing—in other words, its essential qualities and nature. We do not understand the nature of a thing—natural or manufactured—until we understand its purpose. It follows that Aristotle believed everything has a purpose given to it by nature; if the object realizes its potential, it has fulfilled its purpose and is a success. A sharp knife, a fast rabbit, and a smart human being would be examples of potential purpose actualized because each has become what it was supposed to be.

For Aristotle, everything that exists has a purpose, built into the fabric of reality from the very beginning. The idea of a purpose seems reasonable when we look at manufactured objects, because those objects must surely have started with an idea, a purpose, in the mind of their maker. If a cutler makes a knife, its purpose is to cut well, not just to make a dent. When you bake muffins, you intend them to be edible, whether they turn out that way or not. But can't we have human actions without a purpose? Aristotle would say no, especially if we are creating an object; its purpose is a given thing.

What about nature-made objects? Does a tree have a purpose? Does a wolf? an ant? a river? Today we would hesitate before saying yes, because after all, who are we to make such assumptions? If we say the purpose of a tree is to give us shade, or apples, we are assuming that it is here for us humans and not just for its own sake in the order of things. Even if we say the wolf's purpose is to cull the herd of caribou, we hesitate to say that someone "designed" it that way, with purpose. Today, if we tend to use the term *purpose* or *function* to describe how things work in nature, we should probably remind ourselves once in a while that, scientifically, we are referring to how things work within the ecosystem, without implying that there is an underlying designed purpose to nature. Aristotle, however, had no such compunction about making statements that reflected anthropocentrism (the view that everything happens for the sake of humans) or speculations about the general structure of the universe (for he believed he understood it). For Aristotle, everything in nature does have a purpose, although it may not be easy to determine just what that purpose is. How *do* we go about determining what the purpose is? We investigate what the thing in question *does best*. Whatever that is will be the special characteristic of that thing. If the thing performs its purpose or function well, then it is *virtuous*.

Because of his theory that everything has a purpose, Aristotle is sometimes credited with introducing the idea of *Intelligent Design*, the deliberate creation of the universe by some divine intelligence. That is accurate to some extent, because Aristotle indeed did think that everything was designed, with a purpose, by a vast intelligence. But Aristotle did not believe in a personal god; he seems to have been a *Deist*, believing that a god once created the universe, but contrary to most of his contemporaries who were worshippers of the gods and goddesses on Mt. Olympus, or Dionysis, or the ancient Earth goddess Demeter, Aristotle apparently believed that whatever divinity that created the universe—he calls it "the Unmoved Mover," the force that sets things into motion—was no longer present, or at least outside of human reach, and had no interest in or influence over human affairs or the rest of its creation. So Intelligent Design theories today, suggesting that an all-powerful and omnipresent God surely must have designed nature in all its seemingly purposeful complexity, can only claim a partial connection to Aristotle, because he did not believe that any god was watching over its creation. While scientists today may speculate about the functions of different species in the ecosystems of the natural world, few scientists (regardless of their personal belief systems) will express any professional assumptions about the world being designed by any spiritual being; most scientists believe that such assumptions are a matter of faith, and fall outside the scope of science. And Aristotle, for all his interest in the notion of purpose for every material object and every species, had not yet arrived at the concept of an *ecosystem*, and had no interest in exploring the relationships between species in an ecosystem in balance.

The Human Purpose

For Aristotle, there is no question that a specifically human purpose in life exists. Each limb and organ of the body has a purpose, he says—the eye for seeing, the hands for grasping—so we must conclude that the person, as a whole, has a purpose above and beyond the sum of the body parts. (For Aristotle, that was an obvious conclusion; today we are not so quick to conclude anything about purposes. See Box 9.3 about teleological versus causal explanations.)

Box 9.3 TELEOLOGICAL EXPLANATIONS

We use teleological explanations quite often even today, although generally they are not acceptable as a scientific form of explanation. If we were to explain why giraffes have long necks, we might say something like, "So they can reach tall branches." Saying "so they can" implies that somehow giraffes are designed for that purpose or else that they have stretched and stretched over the ages until they can finally reach those branches. (Such a theory of evolution was proposed in the nineteenth century, before Charles Darwin. Its proponent was Jean Lamarck, and the theory is referred to as "inheritance of acquired characteristics.") Even though we all know that giraffes do eat leaves off tall branches, it would not suit modern science to assume that is their *purpose*. Darwin, with his theory of *natural selection*, proposed a new point of view: that giraffes don't come equipped with a purpose, nor does any other creature, but we all adapt to circumstances, and those who adapt the best survive and have offspring. We therefore must imagine the ancestors of giraffes as being rather short-necked, with some born with longer necks as a result of mutation. Because the ones with long necks could reach the leaves that the others couldn't reach, they were successful during times of hardship when many of the others perished. They gave birth to long-necked offspring, who gave birth to offspring with even longer necks, and so on. This is a *causal explanation*; it looks to reasons in the past to explain why something is the way it is today, instead of looking toward some future goal.

The idea that humans are born for a reason and with a purpose is irresistible even to many modern minds. We ask ourselves, "What is the reason for my being here on this earth?" "Why was I born?" We hope to find some answer in the future—some great deed we will do, a work of art we will create, the children we plan to raise, the influence we will exert on our profession, or the money and fame we plan to acquire. Some believe their greatest moment has come and gone, like an astronaut who has been on the moon—how do you top that? Such people may spend the rest of their lives searching for a new purpose. (See Box 9.4 for a short exploration of the concept of a human purpose.)

Box 9.4 IS THERE A HUMAN PURPOSE?

Aristotle inspired an entire school of thought long after he was dead. The Catholic Church came upon his writings some fifteen hundred years after his death, and Saint Thomas Aquinas incorporated several of Aristotle's ideas into his Christian philosophy in the thirteenth century, including the idea that humans have a purpose. For Aquinas, that purpose included life, procreation, and the pursuit of knowledge of God. Other thinkers are not so certain that humans have a purpose; Jean-Paul Sartre (1905–1980) believed there is no such thing as human nature and that anyone who says there is a purpose is only looking for an identity to hide behind so that he or she won't have to make difficult choices (see Chapter 10).

Our belief in destiny, in one form or another, influences our perception of the purpose of our lives. But that is only half of Aristotle's concept of *telos,* because it applies only on a *personal* level. Aristotle is talking not only about the person becoming what he or she is supposed to become but also about the human being *as such* becoming what human beings are supposed to become. In other words, Aristotle believed not only that a telos exists for an individual but also that it exists for a species. How do we know what the purpose of an individual as a member of a species is? We investigate what that creature or thing does best—perhaps better than any other creature or thing. The purpose of a bird must involve flying, although there are flightless birds. The purpose of a knife must involve cutting, although there are movie prop knives that don't cut a thing. The purpose of a rock? To do whatever it does best: lie there. (That is true Aristotle, not a joke.) And the purpose of a human? To *reason.* We can't evaluate a person without taking into consideration the greater purpose of being human, which is to *reason well:*

> Now if the function of man is an activity of soul which follows or implies a rational principle . . . [and we state the function of man to be a certain kind of life, and this to be an activity or actions of the soul implying a rational principle . . . and if any action is well performed when it is performed in accordance with the appropriate excellence: if this is the case,] human good turns out to be activity of soul in accordance with virtue, and if there are more than one virtue, in accordance with the best and most complete.

> But we must add "in a complete life." For one swallow does not make a summer, nor does one day; and so too one day, or a short time, does not make a man blessed or happy.

Scholars are usually generous here in labeling reasoning the purpose of *humans*—for in Aristotle's terminology it is the "purpose of *man.*" As we go deeper into Aristotle's works, it becomes apparent that he is not using the word inclusively, to cover males and females, as was to become the intellectual habit in the eighteenth, nineteenth, and most of the twentieth centuries: He means *males.* For Aristotle, men are the creatures who have the true capacity for reasoning; women have their own purpose (such as childbearing) and their own virtues. That may seem controversial enough to a modern reader who believes that men and women should have access to the same social opportunities, but the controversy doesn't end there: Aristotle has become nothing short of notorious for proclaiming not only that men and women are fundamentally different but also that, in his own words from his text *The Generation of Animals,* "the female is, as it were, a deformed male." Man is the default gender for Aristotle, because he sees the male as the perfect human being, and since women aren't male, they are less perfect. In a nutshell: Men produce semen, and women don't. Aristotle believed that semen was blood transformed, with the added element of *soul* or essence. It was thus the father who gave the soul to the baby; the mother "only" provided the physical part, the body. (Here it is interesting to recall that Aristotle believed himself to have a considerable amount of knowledge about the human body, probably because he came from a family of physicians. In all fairness, it would have been impossible for him to know that, biologically, the situation is, in fact, reversed: The early human fetus is, by default, *female,* and if it has a Y chromosome, the male characteristics will develop later in the pregnancy.) In believing woman to be a creature fundamentally different from man, Aristotle seems to have joined forces with the public opinion of the times, although not with the opinion of his own teacher, Plato, who believed that the role of women depended on what they were well suited for, individually.

The purpose for man, Aristotle would say, is to think rationally, on a regular basis, throughout his life, as a matter of habit—in other words, to develop a rational *character.* And that, according to Aristotle, is the same as *moral goodness.*

For modern thinkers this is a surprising twist: that moral goodness can be linked with being good *at something* rather than just being good, period. Moral goodness seems for us to have more to do with not causing harm, with keeping promises, with upholding the values of our culture, and so on. For Aristotle, though, there is no difference between fulfilling one's purpose, being virtuous, doing something with excellence, and being morally good. It all has to do with his theory of *how* one goes about being virtuous.

Aristotle recognizes two forms of virtue, *intellectual* and *moral.* When our soul is trying to control our desires, we engage our moral virtues. But when our soul concentrates on intellectual and spiritual matters, we engage our intellectual virtues: When we think about objects of this world that are subject to change and try to make appropriate decisions, we engage our practical wisdom, our *phronesis.* But when we think about higher matters—the eternal questions of philosophy—we use our theoretical wisdom, our *sophia* (you'll remember that *philosophy* is a combination of *philo* = "love of " and *sophia* = "wisdom"). One may excel in other virtues, but the highest virtue of them all is *sophia,* actualizing the uniquely human potential for abstract thought. So the intellectual virtues involve being able to learn well, think straight, and act accordingly. The moral virtues also involve the use of the intellect, because the only way humans can strive for perfection is to engage their intellect in developing a keen sense of the needs of the moment.

The Golden Mean

Ancient Greece gave us the concept of moderation, or the Golden Mean (not to be confused with "The Golden Ratio," a principle of balanced proportions in art and architecture). Over the entrance to the temple of Apollo at Delphi were inscribed "Know Thyself" (*gnothi seauton*) and "Nothing in Excess" (*maeden agan*). Socrates incorporated the idea of moderation in his teachings, as did several other thinkers, but above all it is at the heart of Aristotle's idea of virtue: an action or a feeling responding to a particular situation at the right time, in the right way, in the right amount, for the right reason—not too much and not too little. By using the Golden Mean, Aristotle believes he describes the "good for man"—where a human can excel, what a human is meant to do, and where a human will find happiness. We will return to the subject of happiness shortly.

In his *Nicomachean Ethics,* named for his son Nichomachus, Aristotle compares the Golden Mean to an artistic masterpiece; people recognize that you can't add anything to it or take anything from it, because either excess (too much) or deficiency (too little) would destroy the masterpiece. The mean, however, preserves it. That may remind some readers of a joke among artists: "How many artists does it take to make a great painting? Two—one to paint it, and the other to hit the painter over the head when the painting is done." Why the bash on the head? Because there comes a time, if the work is good enough, when more paint would be too much, and sometimes the artist doesn't recognize that moment. Aristotle would reply that the *virtuous* artist will know that moment—indeed, that is precisely what constitutes a great artist. If that is the case for art, then it must apply to moral goodness: We are morally good if we are capable of choosing the proper response to every situation in life, not too much and not too little:

> Virtue, then, is a state of character concerned with choice, lying in a mean, i.e., the mean relative to us, this being determined by a rational principle by which the man of practical wisdom would determine it. Now it is a mean between two vices, that which depends on excess and that which depends on defect; and again it is a mean because the vices respectively fall short of or exceed what is right in both passions and actions, while virtue finds and chooses that which is intermediate.

Aristotle tells us that every action or feeling must be done in the right amount. In many ways this is quite modern and a very down-to-earth approach to our daily problems. We all have to make big and little decisions every day: How much **gratitude** should I show when someone does a favor for me or gives me a present I didn't expect? How much is the right amount of **curiosity** to express about my friend's personal life? (I don't want to appear to be snooping, and I don't want to appear cold either.) How much should **I study** for my final? (I know when I've studied too little, but what exactly is studying too much?) **How long** should I leave the roast in the oven for it to be done to perfection when the kids like it gray and my spouse likes it bloody? How much **love** should I feel, and show, in a new relationship? We face those types of problems every day, and we rarely find good answers to them. In that sense Aristotle shows a feeling for what we might call the "human condition," common human concerns that remain the same throughout the ages. Very few philosophers have done as much as he to try to give people some actual advice about such mundane matters. Thus, even though

Aristotle's ideas derive from an ancient, alien world of slavery and other policies that are unacceptable to us today, there are features of his works that make his writings relevant for modern times and modern people. At the end of the chapter you'll find two excerpts from Aristotle's *Nicomachean Ethics,* in which he explores the Golden Mean as well as the virtue of courage.

Does Aristotle actually tell us what to do? Not really. He warns us that we each are prone to go toward one extreme or the other and that we must beware of such tendencies, but the only help we can find on the road to virtue is the idea that we must try and try again.

An application of Aristotle's theory of virtue: Three women on a bridge see a drowning child being swept along by the waters. One woman is rash and jumps in without looking; the other is too cautious and frets so much that the time for action is past. But the third one reacts "just right": She has developed a courageous character; she chooses an appropriate action and acts at the right time to save the child. (See Box 9.5.)

There are three questions one might want to ask: (1) If this is supposed to be a theory of *character,* why does it seem to talk about actions and conduct and what to *do?* The answer is that for Aristotle, this *is* a question of character because he is not so much interested in our response to singular situations as he is in our response in general. If we perform a considerate or courageous act only once, he would not call us considerate or courageous; the act must be done on a regular basis, as an expression of the kind of person we strive to be. In other words, we have to acquire some good habits. That means we can't hope to be virtuous overnight—it takes time to mold ourselves into morally good people, just as it takes time to learn to play a musical instrument well. (2) What does this have to do with the specific human virtue of *rational thinking?* The answer lies in the fact that the way we find out what the mean is in every situation is through reasoning, and the more times we have done it and acted correctly as a result, the better we can build up the habit of responding correctly. (3) Does this mean we are supposed to do *everything* in the right amount, not too much and not too little? It is easy to imagine eating in the right amount and exercising in the right amount, but what about acts like stealing? lying? or committing murder? Must we conclude that we can steal and lie and murder too much but also too little? that we will be virtuous if we steal, lie, and murder in the right amount? Hardly, and Aristotle was aware of this loophole; he tells us that some acts are just wrong by themselves and cannot be done in the right amount. Similarly, some acts are right in themselves and cannot be done too often. One such thing is justice: You can't be "too just," because being just already means being as fair as you can be.

How exactly do we find the mean? After all, it is not an absolute mean; we cannot identify the exact midpoint between the extremes the way we would measure the exact number of calories allowed in a diet. It is far more complex than that, and Aristotle warns us that there are many ways to go wrong but only one way to "hit the bull's-eye" in each situation. It takes a full commitment, involving the entire personality, over a lifetime of training. In his lectures Aristotle appears to have covered a wide variety of virtues. Let us look at a few of them.

If someone is **in danger**, that person can react in three ways: with too little courage (in which case he is a coward), with the right amount of courage, or with too much courage (in which case he is being foolhardy). Courage was for Aristotle a very important virtue, and you'll find his analysis of courage in the Primary Readings. Box 9.5 applies the virtue of courage as well as the vices of cowardice and foolhardiness to a specific situation, and two stories in the Narratives section focus on courage as a virtue: the ancient Icelandic *Njal's Saga* and the film based on Joseph Conrad's novel *Lord Jim*. In addition, the theme of courage is explored as a contemporary virtue in Chapter 11.

Box 9.5 THE RIGHT DECISION AT THE RIGHT TIME

Imagine three women on a bridge: Heidi, Jill, and Jessica. Below them a dark river is rushing along, sweeping a little boy toward them, carrying him to certain doom. Heidi looks down at the swirling water and imagines all the things that could go wrong if she were to attempt a rescue: the submerged rocks, how heavy her shoes and jeans will get if she jumps in, the fact that she just got over a bad cold, and the fact that she doesn't swim well. Besides, she remembers, she has to make it to the library before closing time. While she has been doing all this thinking, Jill has already jumped in the river to save the boy. She jumped without thinking, however, and hit her head on one of the submerged rocks and knocked herself out. Jessica sees the boy, and as fast as lightning she calculates the swiftness of the river, the position of the rocks, her own swimming prowess—and she runs down the little staircase to the riverbed, throws in the life preserver that is hanging on the wall, saves the boy, and pulls ashore the unconscious Jill for good measure. Or maybe she sheds her shoes and jumps in and saves the boy. Or shouts to some men who are out fishing and asks them to give her a hand. The main thing is that she *thinks,* and then *acts,* at the right time, in the proper amount. That is courage to Aristotle. Jill acted rashly. Heidi may have had the right intentions, but she did not act on them. You must act on your intentions and succeed in order to be called virtuous.

But what if some time in the future, by some odd coincidence, Heidi finds herself in the same situation again? A bridge, a drowning child—or some other situation where she might be in a position to help by making the right split-second decision. Her previous failure might help her do better this time around. Aristotle believes we become virtuous through doing virtuous acts;

and, if Heidi has learned anything from watching Jessica, then she, too, might do the right thing this time. (But she has to remember that no two situations are exactly alike. In another situation acting exactly as Jessica did could be to act either rashly or too timidly.) Similarly, Jill might have learned from the situation; next time around she might be too timid, but eventually she, too, might get it right. Now Jessica: Can we rely on her to always make the right choice from now on? Most of us would not have such lofty expectations and would forgive her for a future mistake, but for Aristotle it was clear: When you have ascended to the level of a virtuous person, then your future actions will generally also be virtuous, because you have developed virtuous habits. One brave deed does not make a person brave (as one swallow does not make a summer). If Jessica slips and makes a wrong judgment call, then she is not so virtuous after all.

Let's consider the act of **pleasure seeking**. If you overdo it, you are intemperate—but suppose you are not capable of enjoying pleasures at all? That is not a virtue, and Aristotle doesn't know what to call such a person except "unimpressionable." The virtue is to know in what amount to enjoy one's pleasures; that Aristotle calls *temperance.* Thus, for Aristotle, there is no virtue in staying away from pleasures, for "temperance" does not mean "abstinence." The key is to enjoy them *in moderation.*

Suppose we look at the art of **spending money**. For Aristotle, there is a virtuous way to spend money too. If you spend too much you are *prodigal*, and if you spend too little you are a *miser.* Spending just the right amount at the right time on the right people for the right reason makes you *liberal.*

For the Greek mind, for the man of the polis, **pride** is a natural virtue, and so it is for Aristotle. You can, however, overestimate your honor and become vain, or you can underestimate it and become humble. The virtuous way to estimate yourself and your accomplishments is through *proper pride.* (See Box 9.6 for a discussion of the differences between Aristotle's virtues, such as pride, and the traditional Christian list of cardinal virtues and vices.)

Box 9.6 THE CLASH BETWEEN CLASSICAL AND CHRISTIAN VIRTUES

For a modern Western person, the idea that it is legitimate to take pride in an accomplishment is not strange; we understand why Aristotle says we should not humiliate ourselves by making ourselves less than we are. But his idea that we have a right to feel proud about things that aren't our own doing, such as being born of a certain class and race, is more problematic. To the traditional Christian mind, in fact, the entire idea of legitimate pride is a grave misconception. As much as Aristotle became an inspiration to medieval Christianity, there is a marked discrepancy between most of Aristotle's virtues and the Catholic lists of the cardinal virtues and the cardinal sins. For the Christian it is a cardinal sin to feel pride, because our accomplishments come through the grace of God and are not our own doing. This is expressed in the Latin words *Soli Deo Gloria,* the honor (glory) is God's alone. The cardinal virtues are justice, prudence, temperance, fortitude, faith, hope, and charity. The cardinal (deadly) sins are pride, lust, envy, anger, covetousness, gluttony, and sloth.

Is there a virtuous way to feel **angry**? Absolutely—by having a good temper or, as we might say today, being even-tempered. Being hot-tempered is a vice, but so is being meek. If you have been wronged, Aristotle believes, you ought to be angry in proportion to the offense against you. (This may remind you of the highly contemporary debate about the role of emotions in court, which you read about in Chapter 7.)

Let us now consider the virtue of **truthfulness**. We probably would agree with Aristotle that this is a good thing, but what is his idea of a deficiency of truthfulness? Not *lying,* as we might expect, but *irony,* or as it is often translated, "mock-modesty" (in other words, downplaying the situation). Aristotle obviously would not have enjoyed Socrates' use of irony. The excess of truthfulness? Bragging. To the modern reader, the excess of truthfulness might be something different, such as being *rude* by telling someone, "You sure gained weight over the holidays!" But for Aristotle, it is not a matter of not harming others by lying or by being rude but a matter of assessing the situation properly, neither underplaying nor overplaying the truth. Here we touch on a hidden element of Aristotle's virtue theory: *Whom is the theory intended for?* Not necessarily young people who need to get their lives straightened out. It is, instead, directed at future politicians. The young noblemen and sons of wealthy landowners who had the leisure time to go to school were expected to become the pillars of Athenian society. What Aristotle is teaching them is, in many ways, to be good public figures. That is why it is necessary to know how much money to spend, in large sums. That is why it is important to know the extent of your pride and your anger. Of course, Aristotle's virtues are also applicable to other people, but some virtues—such as the virtues of wit or humor—carry a direct message to those young men who plan to enter public life. Most of us probably would like our partners to have **a sense of humor**. But imagine how important it is for a public figure not to be a boor, not to be a buffoon, and to have a ready wit. Aristotle recognized that fact. (See Box 9.7 for additional discussion of virtues.)

Box 9.7 VARIATIONS ON ARISTOTLE'S THEME OF THE GOLDEN MEAN

Below you see an adaptation of Aristotle's original twelve virtues, flanked by vices of excess and deficiency. And Aristotle's approach can be applied to many situations we find ourselves in on an everyday basis; you might want to discuss the additional list of virtues and vices and add your own suggestions.

And so on and so forth! Can you think of a vice (one not mentioned by Aristotle) that has no mean? Can you think of a virtue that has no excess?

In Chapter 7 you read about a theory that it is right and appropriate for a victim of a crime to feel *resentment* toward the perpetrator, as well as for the community to feel *moral indignation* on behalf of the victim. Since Aristotle believes there is a Golden Mean for the feeling of anger—somewhere between being prone to rage and being cold or meek—and he also believes that *righteous indignation* is a virtue, his thinking is in harmony with this theory. Where, within the virtuous middle range, might the proper resentment/indignation response be for a person hit by a computer virus? for a rape victim? for a community targeted by bioterrorism?

ARISTOTLE'S TABLE OF VIRTUES AND VICES

EXCESS (VICE)	MEAN (VIRTUE)	DEFICIT (VICE)
Rashness or Foolhardiness	Courage	Cowardice
Self-indulgence	Temperance	Insensibility
Prodigality	Liberality	Meanness
Vulgarity	Magnificence	Pettiness
Vanity	Magnanimity	Gutlessness
Excessive ambition	Proper Pride	Low self-esteem
Irascibility	Even-tempered	Lack of spirit
Boastfulness	Truthfulness	Mock-modesty
Buffoonery	Humor	Boorishness
Obsequiousness	Friendliness	Cantankerousness
Shyness	Modesty	Shamelessness
Envy	Righteous indignation	Spitefulness

VIRTUES AND VICES, INSPIRED BY ARISTOTLE

EXCESS (VICE)	MEAN (VIRTUE)	DEFICIT (VICE)
Blindly following a leader or a friend	Loyalty	Disloyalty
Passivity	Patience	Impatience
Judgment lacking; intrusion	Compassion	Absence of feelings
Sense of being perpetually indebted	Gratitude	Absence of any gratitude
Excessive studying; workaholism	Sufficient studying to pass test	Insufficient studying; laziness

There are, then, three dispositions: two vices, one on either side, and virtue in the middle. How do we find the virtue? It may be difficult, depending on our own personal failings. If we have a hard time controlling our temper, we might try for a while to be so cool that nothing makes us angry, just to get out of the habit of being irascible; in other words, we might shoot *past* the target of good temper until we feel we can control ourselves and find the mean. If we tend to overindulge in desserts, we might try to lay off sweet things completely for a while. That is not the ideal situation, but Aristotle advises us to experiment until we get it right. Besides, if we find ourselves at one extreme, it is hard for us to see the difference between the other extreme and the virtue: A chocolate lover finds the chocolate hater and the person who has just a few bites of chocolate each week equally dull and unsympathetic. The political extremist may view the political moderate as just another extremist on the opposite front. Indeed, some extremes are closer to the mean, the virtue, than others. Being a coward is probably more opposed to being courageous than being foolhardy is. So if you don't know what path to choose, at least stay away from the extreme that is more opposed to the mean than the other extreme. We all have to watch out for our own personal failings, and we also have to watch out for temptations, because if we let ourselves indulge in too many pleasures we lose our sense of moderation and proportion. These matters are not easy, and Aristotle knew that we must judge each situation separately. At the end of the chapter you'll find the ancient Greek story of the "Flight of Icarus," which illustrates that virtue lies in following a middle course between too much and too little—not because it ensures a bland, average existence, but because it ensures survival.

Does Aristotle then propose a set of guidelines for what virtue is that can be applied in all situations? Nothing beyond the general range of the Golden Mean and an appeal to intuition, reasoning, and good habits. In other words, the virtuous person will know how to be virtuous! That has caused some ethicists to call Aristotle an ethical relativist, because virtue is, in a sense, relative to the situation. But labeling Aristotle an ethical relativist is wrong. He never states that morals are completely culture-dependent or that each social group determines what counts as its moral code. On the contrary, Aristotle is quite adamant about virtues having a rock-bottom value for each situation; it is just that situations may differ, and one may be called upon to do more in one context than in another. If we want to apply a modern term to Aristotle, we might dare to call him a *soft universalist* (albeit with values typical for his day and age): Our responses to situations must remain flexible, and we each have our own ideals and failings, but the right, virtuous response reveals itself in being appropriate to the situation and falls within a range that is recognized by other people of virtue.

Is there such a thing as a perfectly virtuous person for Aristotle? Yes, it appears that he thought it was possible. Furthermore, he seems to have believed that if you are virtuous in one respect but fail miserably in another, then you have lost out completely. If you deviate only slightly, though, you are still a virtuous person—a person who is good at being human and at realizing the human potential.

In the Narratives section, I have included a story that illustrates Aristotle's idea that we become virtuous by doing virtuous things and thus developing good habits: The way to become courageous is to do courageous things, the way to become compassionate is to do compassionate things, and pretty soon it will become part of your character. The story is Isaac Bashevis Singer's short story "A Piece of Advice" about a cantankerous old man who becomes a decent human being by doing decent things.

Happiness

Being virtuous makes you happy—that is Aristotle's sole reason for designing the development of a virtuous character. But if the goal is happiness, why does he warn us about indulging in too many pleasures? Because pleasure and happiness are not identical, as most ancient thinkers would agree. We have to ask what exactly Aristotle means by happiness.

Happiness is what's "good for man," according to Aristotle. For most of us a good life means a happy life (see Chapter 8), but a good person means a moral person. For Aristotle, there was no conflict. We can be happy only if we're good, but in what way? The highest realizable goods are to live well, to be happy, to do well; what is good for man can't be something that harms him, and indulgence in too many pleasures can certainly be harmful. Aristotle labels it *eudaimonia*, being of a "good spirit." A further requirement of true happiness is that it must be steadfast; if we rely too much on pleasures, we'll find that they cease to give us a thrill after a while, so pleasure can't be the same as happiness. Nor can fame or fortune, because those things are certainly ephemeral—we can lose both overnight. So what is the thing that can be ours forever, that nobody can take away, and that is not harmful but beneficial to us as human beings? Good reasoning, or, as the ancient Greeks would put it, *contemplation*. This can be ours forever, and, as anyone who has struggled with an intellectual problem and solved it knows, it can even be exhilarating. For Aristotle, then, the ultimately happy life is the life of the thinker (interestingly, a recent survey declared philosophy professors to have one of the happiest occupations of all!). But Aristotle is a realist too—he adds that, although the truly happy life may be a life of contemplation, it doesn't hurt to have friends, money, and good looks!

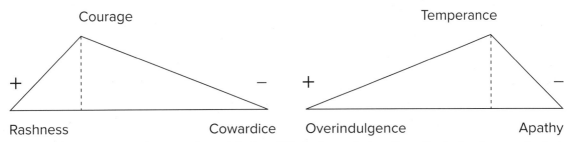

For Aristotle, the mean between the extremes is not an absolute middle; in other words, depending on the situation, the persons involved, and the virtue itself, the mean may be closer to one extreme than the other, and Aristotle advises us to stay away from the vice that is the further from the mean. If you imagine yourself at one of the extremes, you also can imagine that it might be hard to tell exactly where the mean is; that is why Aristotle says we must find it through trial and error. A mean that might be viewed as closer to the vice of excess than to deficiency would be *courage,* which can be said to be closer to rashness than to cowardice; a virtue that is closer to the vice of deficiency than the vice of excess might be *temperance.*

What about happiness as a reward for good behavior, in the afterlife? For Plato, the goal of a human life seemed to be a comprehension of the world of Forms and ultimately a reunification with that world in an afterlife. Aristotle seems to have had a different view of spirituality: As far as we can tell, he had no belief in an afterlife any more than he believes in a god who watches over humanity. He states that the soul is the *form* of a human and the body is one's *matter,* but form cannot exist separate from matter, so when the body dies, the soul ceases to exist in any personal way, even if (as he also says) the form of a human being may be immortal. In any event, whatever we are while we are alive will cease to exist when we die; therefore, happiness for Aristotle is exclusively a phenomenon for the living and must be achieved in this world for a person's life to have fulfilled its purpose. Whereas Plato's metaphysics (as we have seen in Chapter 8) could easily be incorporated into a religion that focused on life after death, Aristotle's metaphysics offers no "pie in the sky." Thus, it is all the more extraordinary that Aristotle's philosophy became one of the great pillars of support for Christianity as it evolved in the high Middle Ages.

Was Aristotle himself happy in his lifetime? It appears that during his twelve years in Athens running his own school, he enjoyed contemplation, he had money, and he had friends. (Whether he was good-looking you will have to judge for yourself (see Box 9.1), but he reputedly liked to dress in the latest styles.) But with the death of his former student Alexander the Great in 323 B.C.E. at the age of thirty-two, it all came to an abrupt end. The anti-Macedonian feelings that were mounting in the realm controlled by Alexander's troops (including the city-state of Athens) no longer could be kept in check, and because Aristotle was considered pro-Macedonian, the Athenian city council decided to get rid of him. Ironically, their method was to charge him with the same offense that had been leveled against Socrates, of offending the gods. But whereas Socrates chose to stay and die for his principles, Aristotle packed up and left Athens for good so that "Athens wouldn't sin twice against philosophy." He took off for his country estate in Chalcis—a place he had inherited from his mother—but he died the year after, in 322 B.C.E., of a stomach ailment.

Here we might want to ask ourselves, According to his own system of seeking the mean between extremes, did Aristotle in the end display courageous behavior, or was his behavior "deficient"? It is tempting to compare his choice with Socrates', and many would probably say that the comparison does not come out in Aristotle's favor. But here we should remember that the relationship Socrates had with the city of Athens was vastly different from that of Aristotle with the city-state; it had been Socrates' hometown, he had been concerned for its welfare all his life, and he had fought for it as a soldier. Aristotle was, for all intents and purposes, a foreigner, a "migrant worker" in the philosophy trade. He may have felt a certain loyalty to Athens from having spent over thirty years of his life in the city, but there was general discrimination against noncitizens, and Aristotle couldn't have been immune to that. He himself might have said that leaving was the perfectly rational, virtuous thing to do: the right action at the right time, for the right reason, not too much and not too little. One might wonder, though, how he must have felt, having never attained what he apparently truly wanted: to take over Plato's Academy.

Aristotle's Influence on Aquinas

Today, Aristotle looms as one of the most influential persons in human history, but several times after his death it seemed as if his writings were destined to be totally forgotten. After his death, his books were collected by the new leader of the Lyceum, Theophrastus, who had been a student of Aristotle's; and subsequent generations of leaders hid the books to preserve them from theft and other threats—especially since the Lyceum was temporarily closed when foreign philosophers were kicked out of Athens around 300 B.C.E. The Lyceum did reopen and stayed open until its official closure by Emperor Justinian in 529 C.E., but it was never the great success story that Plato's Academy had become. Aristotle's own books were damaged in storage and would have been lost had it not been for an avid book collector, Apellicon, who simply appropriated them along with other classic writings and brought them to Rome in 100 B.C.E. Here they were copied, starting a new Aristotle fad among Roman philosophers, but even that was to fade away: When the Lyceum was finally closed in 529 C.E. by the Roman emperor along with Plato's Academy, the scholars working at Aristotle's school feared for their safety and fled to Persia with copies of Aristotle's books. Back in the Roman cultures around the Mediterranean, Aristotle's works were largely forgotten, and even the location of the Lyceum was lost, until its rediscovery in 1997 by archaeologists. Primarily in Alexandria, it was the Platonic spirit that survived to put its mark on the new world religion. In the Middle East, though, Aristotle's works were studied continually. As the scientific spirit declined in the West, Arab scholars kept Aristotelian research alive until the advent of another new world religion, Islam, and early Islamic scholars were influenced by Aristotle's philosophy. It was not until well into the next millennium that an interest in Aristotle was rekindled in the Christian world. Eventually his theories found their way back into Western philosophy through the works of Saint Thomas Aquinas (1225–1274). In the late Middle Ages and through the Renaissance, Aristotle eclipsed Plato as a philosopher and was known in European intellectual circles (as he had been for centuries in the Arab world) as "The Philosopher." You had an example of that in Chapter 2, in *The Name of the Rose*, Eco's novel featuring the imaginary rediscovery of one of Aristotle's lost works. So for a man who for all intents and purposes didn't have an established career by the time he was thirty-eight, whose life's unfulfilled ambition apparently had been to become leader of Plato's school, and who eventually lost his job because of political persecution, Aristotle's posthumous career is nothing short of remarkable: His influence on philosophy itself is immeasurable; his theories of science laid the groundwork for the basic scientific concepts in the Western tradition after the so-called Dark Ages of the early Medieval period; his entire system of classification of sciences and humanities became, to a great extent, the inspiration for the structuring of the first universities in Europe in the high Middle Ages and the Renaissance; he provided inspiration for Islamic interpretations of the Quran; and some of his ideas became the cornerstone of the theology of Catholicism, through the works of Aquinas.

It was Aristotle's concept of *teleology* that became particularly fascinating for Aquinas: If everything has a purpose, then surely it was designed by God. And if we humans, with our free will, decide to follow God's purpose for us, then it must mean we are following God's will, and we are doing right; on the other hand, if we decide to go against God's purpose, we are doing wrong. So what is God's purpose for us? Aquinas identified four specific goals that together made up what has become known as Aquinas's *natural law:* (1) We are obliged to preserve our own lives. (2) We are obliged to procreate within marriage. (3) We are obliged to live as good citizens among other people. (4) We are obliged to seek knowledge, primarily about God and his creation. Those four rules are natural to us because we have been designed that way, says Aquinas. It doesn't mean those rules can't be broken—people commit suicide, people have babies outside of wedlock or take measures to avoid getting pregnant, some people care little about living in harmony with others, and some show no interest in seeking knowledge about God. However, they are going against God's will—a will that, for Aquinas, is knowable and understandable to humans, because that will is rational, and humans have been endowed with reason so we can understand God's rules. So if we decide not to follow our built-in purpose, it is because of a sinful willpower. (Aquinas's natural law is not to be confused with the *laws of nature* we are familiar with from science. Such scientific laws are descriptive, whereas Aquinas's natural law is normative: You can't break the law of gravity, but you can break the law of procreation.)

What happens to people who break the rules of the natural law? Aquinas is convinced that they will not get away with it—they might in this life, but certainly not in the next. That is why there is also *divine law,* for those offenses that God knows about but other humans haven't discovered. On this earthly plane there is also, of course, *human law,* so that criminal offenses that are discovered can be punished. And the entire universe is run by God according to eternal rules, the *eternal law.*

You may recognize some of Aquinas's views on natural law as contemporary Catholic doctrine. For example, it is Aquinas's rule of self-preservation that forbids suicide, and his rule of procreation that forbids abortion, contraception, and homosexual relationships (because all procreation must take place naturally between married couples, without hindrance, and in no other way). This was not always so: Aquinas's teachings were for centuries considered controversial by the Church, and not until a Church council in 1914 was it decided that they would from then on be considered official Catholic doctrine. So we can say that Aristotle long after his death not only made an everlasting mark on Western science and philosophy, as well as Middle Eastern philosophy, but also to this day has been influential within Christianity.

Some Objections to Greek Virtue Theory

As mentioned earlier, the particular brand of ethical theory known as virtue ethics that we find in the Greek tradition by and large disappeared from view with the rise of modern philosophy. That was not merely because the texts were forgotten; it was a concerted effort by scholars to find a better approach to ethics, because as the centuries passed it was becoming clear, for a number of reasons, that the Greek theories of virtue had several shortcomings. For one thing, Thomas Aquinas found it difficult to reconcile Aristotle's virtues not just with Christian virtues but also with the Christian respect for *God's laws.* In the Christian approach to morals, following commandments is far more important than striving toward virtues, and belief in the human ability to shape one's own character autonomously is considered to be a sin of pride. You become what you ought to be by God's grace, not merely by your own effort.

Philosophy, after parting ways with theology in the sixteenth and seventeenth centuries, began to look critically at virtue ethics from a secular point of view, for, as we have seen, Aristotle was talking about the virtues of a ruling class, virtues that could not be disputed by someone with a different point of view. The modern, political vision of equality does not enter into the Aristotelian moral theory, and from both a Christian and a social viewpoint, an egalitarian approach had become indispensable for an acceptable moral theory by the eighteenth century. For those scholars believing in "natural rights" for all people, it was necessary to set up a moral theory that everyone could follow regardless of status, birth, or intelligence, and such a theory could be based only on laws that were clear and reasonable. Virtues were criticized as being too vague and logically problematic, because what happens if two virtuous people disagree about what to do? How can one persuade the other? There is no recourse to reason in that case except to declare one person less virtuous than the other, so *virtue ethics is not a tool in itself for solving conflicts.* Such a problem does not arise if you have a clear set of moral and civil laws to refer to. That is what is needed if we regard each other as equals—not a theory with a static view of what makes a person virtuous. The rejection of virtue theory in favor of a rule- or duty-oriented moral theory was, therefore, considered a step forward in moral egalitarianism.

There is a more fundamental problem embedded in classical virtue theory: its basis in *teleology*. It was natural for Plato and Aristotle to assume that as human actions had a purpose, so did humans themselves have a purpose, and that purpose was to let their rationality shine because that was what human nature was all about. And because this is the human purpose, what is good for humans must begin and end with rationality. But that gives rise to a series of questions: (1) Must what is good for someone always be linked with what he or she does best? Suppose a man is excellent at forging paintings. Does that mean his life should include this as a purpose, to make him happy? Aristotle and Plato would reject this on the basis that forging paintings is bad in itself, but that is not a very satisfying answer because it assumes that we know beforehand which purposes are acceptable and which aren't. However, even if we stick to the idea of rationality, it is not at all obvious that this is the human purpose. Remember that Damasio says we are primarily emotional beings, not rational beings. (2) Why must we talk about a human "purpose" at all? Science and philosophy today do not, as a rule, talk about purposes of nature, including human nature. A purpose requires that *someone* has that purpose; individuals may have purposes, but we hesitate to claim that nature has a purpose or even that there is a higher power with a purpose. This is outside the realm of science and also that of contemporary moral philosophy (see p. 393). (3) Even if humans are very good at being rational, they are not excellent at it, at least not everybody, and even the select few geniuses can't be rational all the time. We are instead good at *being able* to act rationally some of the time, and with those qualifications it is hard to claim that rationality is our overriding purpose. And (4) Why should there be just one purpose for humans? A knife can be used to cut, to throw, to clean your nails (don't try this at home), to hang on the wall, and any number of other things. A tree surely has more functions than to supply humans with shade and fruit—it provides oxygen, its leaves fertilize the ground, it provides a home for birds and squirrels and maggots, it supplies a subject for an art class to paint—and makes more trees. Why should we assume that each thing or species has one function that defines it? Humans surely have a multitude of functions. It is doubtful, then, whether a theory of virtue should, indeed, involve the question of function or purpose at all. Contemporary theories of virtue tend to steer clear of this ancient, problematic issue, as we will see shortly.

Study Questions

1. Explain Aristotle's theory of the four causes.

2. What is Aristotle's Golden Mean? Does it imply that the virtuous person is an average person of average talents and intelligence?

3. Explain Aristotle's theory of virtue in detail, using at least three examples. At least two of the examples must be Aristotle's own.

4. In the end, Aristotle was accused of the same crimes as Socrates, but, unlike Socrates, Aristotle chose exile. Evaluate Aristotle's choice: Was he himself displaying courage? Was he a coward? Was he rash? How do you think Aristotle would have defended his course of action?

Primary Readings and Narratives

The first two Primary Readings are excerpts from Aristotle's *Nicomachean Ethics*. The first is from Book II, in which Aristotle explains the doctrine of the Golden Mean. The second is from Book III, in which he elaborates on the virtue of courage. The third Primary Reading is a piece by Tom Chatfield, a British tech philosopher, on applying Aristotle's concept of balance to a modern world. The first Narrative is the ancient Greek myth of the flight of Icarus, illustrating Aristotle's theory that the virtuous person always seeks the middle way, avoiding the extremes of excess and deficiency: Flying on wings made of feathers and wax, Icarus disregarded his father's advice to take a middle course. The next Narrative explores the theme of courage; it is an excerpt from *Njal's Saga,* the Icelandic epic that takes place in the late Viking Age. In the excerpt, Njal, his wife, Bergthora, and their little grandson face death with stoic courage, choosing to perish together. This is followed by Joseph Conrad's novel and film *Lord Jim,* a story of cowardice, courage, and honor. The fourth Narrative is a summary of a twentieth-century short story by Isaac Bashevis Singer, "A Piece of Advice," in which a nasty, temperamental man learns virtue by developing the habit of pleasant behavior.

 Primary Reading

Nicomachean Ethics

ARISTOTLE

Excerpt from Book II, fourth century B.C.E. **Aristotle, The Nichomachean Ethics of Aristotle,** *translated by F.H. Peters. London: Kegan Paul, Trench & Truebner & Co., 1893.*

This excerpt from Chapters 4, 6, and 7 in *Nicomachean Ethics* contains some of Aristotle's most famous writings on virtue: He explains the relationship between virtue and conduct in Chapter 4, and in Chapter 6 he outlines the general theory of the Golden Mean. The excerpt from Chapter 7 gives us most of Aristotle's own list of virtues as examples of the relationship between the mean flanked by two extremes, too much and too little.

4   But here we may be asked what we mean by saying that men can become just and temperate only by doing what is just and temperate: surely, it may be said, if their acts are just and temperate, they themselves are already just and temperate, as they are grammarians and musicians if they do what is grammatical and musical.

II. 4, 2 We may answer, I think, firstly, that this is not quite the case even with the arts. A man may do something grammatical [or write something correctly] by chance, or at the prompting of another person: he will not be grammatical till he not only does something grammatical, but also does it grammatically [or like a grammatical person], i.e. in virtue of his own knowledge of grammar.

II. 4, 3 But, secondly, the virtues are not in this point analogous to the arts. The products of art have their excellence in themselves, and so it is enough if when produced they are of a certain quality; but in the case of the virtues, a man is not said to act justly or temperately [or like a just or temperate man] if what he does merely be of a certain sort—he must also be in a certain state of mind when he does it; i.e., first of all, he must know what he is doing; secondly, he must choose it, and choose it for itself; and, thirdly, his act must be the expression of a formed and stable character. Now, of these conditions, only one, the knowledge, is necessary for the possession of any art; but for the possession of the virtues knowledge is of little or no avail, while the other conditions that result from repeatedly doing what is just and temperate are not a little important, but all-important.

42   II. 4, 4 The thing that is done, therefore, is called just or temperate when it is such as the just or temperate man would do; but the man who does it is not just or temperate, unless he also does it in the spirit of the just or the temperate man.

II. 4, 5 It is right, then, to say that by doing what is just a man becomes just, and temperate by doing what is temperate, while without doing thus he has no chance of ever becoming good.

II. 4, 6 But most men, instead of doing thus, fly to theories, and fancy that they are philosophizing and that this will make them good, like a sick man who listens attentively to what the doctor says and then disobeys all his orders. This sort of philosophizing will no more produce a healthy habit of mind than this sort of treatment will produce a healthy habit of body.

6   Virtue, then, is a habit or trained faculty of choice, [47] the characteristic of which lies in moderation or observance of the mean relatively to the persons concerned, as determined by reason, i.e. by the reason by which the prudent man would determine it. And it is a moderation, firstly, inasmuch as it comes in the middle or mean between two vices, one on the side of excess, the other on the side of defect; Peters 1893: II. 6, 16 and, secondly, inasmuch as, while these vices fall short of or exceed the due measure in feeling and in action, it finds and chooses the mean, middling, or moderate amount.

II. 6, 17 Regarded in its essence, therefore, or according to the definition of its nature, virtue is a moderation or middle state, but viewed in its relation to what is best and right it is the extreme of perfection.

II. 6, 18 But it is not all actions nor all passions that admit of moderation; there are some whose very names imply badness, as malevolence, shamelessness, envy, and, among acts, adultery, theft, murder. These and all other like things are blamed as being bad in themselves, and not merely in their excess or deficiency. It is impossible therefore to go right in them; they are always wrong: rightness and wrongness in such things (e.g. in adultery) does not depend upon whether it is the right person and occasion and manner, but the mere doing of any one of them is wrong.

II. 6, 19 It would be equally absurd to look for moderation or excess or deficiency in unjust cowardly or profligate conduct; for then there would be moderation in excess or deficiency, and excess in excess, and deficiency in deficiency.

II. 6, 20 The fact is that just as there can be no excess [48] or deficiency in temperance or courage because the mean or moderate amount is, in a sense, an extreme, so in these kinds of conduct also there can be no moderation or excess or deficiency, but the acts are wrong however they be done. For, to put it generally, there cannot be moderation in excess or deficiency, nor excess or deficiency in moderation.

7   But it is not enough to make these general statements [about virtue and vice]: we must go on and apply them to particulars [i.e. to the several virtues and vices]. For in reasoning about matters of conduct general statements are too vague, and do not convey so much truth as particular propositions. It is with particulars that conduct is concerned:† our statements, therefore, when applied to these particulars, should be found to hold good.

These particulars then [i.e. the several virtues and vices and the several acts and affections with which they deal], we will take from the following table.‡

II. 7, 2 Moderation in the feelings of fear and confidence is courage: of those that exceed, he that exceeds in fearlessness has no name (as often happens), but he that exceeds in confidence is foolhardy, while he that exceeds in fear, but is deficient in confidence, is cowardly.

49   II. 7, 3 Moderation in respect of certain pleasures and also (though to a less extent) certain pains is temperance, while excess is profligacy. But defectiveness in the matter of these pleasures is hardly ever found, and so this sort of people also have as yet received no name: let us put them down as "void of sensibility."

II. 7, 4 In the matter of giving and taking money, moderation is liberality, excess and deficiency are prodigality and illiberality. But both vices exceed and fall short in giving and taking in contrary ways: the prodigal exceeds in spending, but falls short in taking; while the illiberal man exceeds in taking, but falls short in Peters 1893: II. 7, 5 spending. (For the present we are but giving an outline or summary, and aim at nothing more; we shall afterwards treat these points in greater detail.)

II. 7, 6 But, besides these, there are other dispositions in the matter of money: there is a moderation which is called magnificence (for the magnificent is not the same as the liberal man: the former deals with large sums, the latter with small), and an excess which is called bad taste or vulgarity, and a deficiency which is called meanness; and these vices differ from those which are opposed to liberality: how they differ will be explained later.

II. 7, 7 With respect to honour and disgrace, there is a moderation which is high-mindedness, an excess which may be called vanity, and a deficiency which is little-mindedness.

II. 7, 8 But just as we said that liberality is related to magnificence, differing only in that it deals with small sums, so here there is a virtue related to high-mindedness, and differing only in that it is concerned with small instead of great honours. A man may have a due desire for honour, and also more or less than a due desire: he that carries this desire to excess is called ambitious, he that has not enough of it is called unambitious, but he that has the due amount has no name. There are also no abstract names for the characters, except "ambition," corresponding to ambitious. And on this account those who occupy the extremes lay claim to the middle place. And in common parlance, too, the moderate man is sometimes called ambitious and sometimes unambitious, and sometimes the ambitious man is praised and sometimes II. 7, 9 the unambitious. Why this is we will explain afterwards; for the present we will follow out our plan and enumerate the other types of character.

II. 7, 10 In the matter of anger also we find excess and deficiency and moderation. The characters themselves hardly have recognized names, but as the moderate man is here called gentle, we will call his character gentleness; of those who go into extremes, we may take the term wrathful for him who exceeds, with wrathfulness for the vice, and wrathless for him who is deficient, with wrathlessness for his character.

II. 7, 11 Besides these, there are three kinds of moderation, bearing some resemblance to one another, and yet different. They all have to do with intercourse in speech and action, but they differ in that one has to do with the truthfulness of this intercourse, while the other two have to do with its pleasantness—one of the two with pleasantness in matters of amusement, the other with pleasantness in all the relations of life. We must therefore speak of these qualities also in order that we may the more plainly see how, in all cases, moderation is praiseworthy, while the extreme courses are neither right nor praiseworthy, but blamable.

In these cases also names are for the most part wanting, but we must try, here as elsewhere, to coin names ourselves, in order to make our argument clear and easy to follow.

II. 7, 12 In the matter of truth, then, let us call him who observes the mean a true [or truthful] person, and observance of the mean truth [or truthfulness]: pretence, when it exaggerates, may be called boasting, and the person a boaster; when it understates, let the names be irony and ironical.

II. 7, 13 With regard to pleasantness in amusement, he who observes the mean may be called witty, and his character wittiness; excess may be called buffoonery, and the man a buffoon; while boorish may stand for the person who is deficient, and boorishness for his character.

With regard to pleasantness in the other affairs of life, he who makes himself properly pleasant may be called friendly, and his moderation friendliness; he that exceeds may be called obsequious if he have no ulterior motive, but a flatterer if he has an eye to his own advantage; he that is deficient in this respect, and always makes himself disagreeable, may be called a quarrelsome or peevish fellow.

II. 7, 14 Moreover, in mere emotions and in our conduct with regard to them, there are ways of observing the mean; for instance, shame (αἰδώς), is not a virtue, but yet the modest (αἰδήμων) man is praised. For in these matters also we speak of this man as observing the mean, of that man as going beyond it (as the shame-faced man whom the least thing makes shy), while he who is deficient in the feeling, or lacks it altogether, is called shameless; but the term modest (αἰδήμων) is applied to him who observes the mean.

II. 7, 15 Righteous indignation, again, hits the mean between envy and malevolence. These have to do with feelings of pleasure and pain at what happens to our neighbours. A man is called righteously indignant when he feels pain at the sight of undeserved prosperity, but your envious man goes beyond him and is pained by the sight of any one in prosperity, while the malevolent man is so far from being pained that he actually exults in the misfortunes of his neighbours.

Study Questions

1. According to Aristotle, can we become virtuous just by doing the right thing? Can a person be virtuous without doing the right thing?

2. Examine the virtue of proper pride. The modern equivalent of humility might be called low self-esteem. Do you think there is such a vice as too much self-esteem? Why is pride considered a sin by the Catholic tradition?

3. Refer to Aristotle's list of virtues and vices in Box 9.7. Are there virtues missing that you think ought to be essential to a virtue ethics? If yes, which ones?

 Primary Reading

Nicomachean Ethics

ARISTOTLE

Excerpt from Book III. Aristotle, **The Nichomachean Ethics of Aristotle,** *translated by F.H. Peters.* **London: Kegan Paul, Trench & Truebner & Co., 1893.**

6   We have already said that courage is moderation or observance of the mean with respect to feelings of fear and confidence.

III. 6, 2 Now, fear evidently is excited by fearful things, and these are, roughly speaking, evil things; and so fear is sometimes defined as "expectation of evil."

III. 6, 3 Fear, then, is excited by evil of any kind, e.g. by disgrace, poverty, disease, friendlessness, death; but it does not appear that every kind gives scope for courage. There are things which we actually ought to fear, which it is noble to fear and base not to fear, e.g. disgrace. He who fears disgrace is an honourable man, with a due sense of shame, while he who fears it not is shameless (though some people stretch the word courageous so far as to apply it to him; for he has a certain resemblance to the courageous man, courage III. 6, 4 also being a kind of fearlessness). Poverty, perhaps, we ought not to fear, nor disease, nor generally those things that are not the result of vice, and do not depend upon ourselves. But still to be fearless in regard to these things is not strictly courage; though here also the term is sometimes applied in virtue of a certain resemblance. There are people, for instance, who, though cowardly in the presence of the dangers of war, are yet liberal and bold in the spending of money.

III. 6, 5 On the other hand, a man is not to be called cowardly for fearing outrage to his children or his wife, or for dreading envy and things of that kind, nor courageous for being unmoved by the prospect of a whipping.

III. 6, 6 In what kind of terrors, then, does the courageous man display his quality? Surely in the greatest; for no one is more able to endure what is terrible. But of all things the most terrible is death; for death is our limit, and when a man is once dead it seems that there is no longer either good or evil for him.

III. 6, 7 It would seem, however, that even death does not on all occasions give scope for courage, e.g. death by water or by disease.

III. 6, 8 On what occasions then? Surely on the noblest occasions: and those are the occasions which occur in war; for they involve the greatest and the noblest danger.

III. 6, 9 This is confirmed by the honours which courage receives in free states and at the hands of princes.

III. 6, 10 The term courageous, then, in the strict sense, will be applied to him who fearlessly faces an honourable death and all sudden emergencies which involve death; and such emergencies mostly occur in war.

III. 6, 11 Of course the courageous man is fearless in the presence of illness also, and at sea, but in a different way from the sailors; for the sailors, because of their experience, are full of hope when the landsmen are already despairing of their lives and filled with aversion at the thought of such a death.

III. 6, 12 Moreover, the circumstances which especially call out courage are those in which prowess may be displayed, or in which death is noble; but in these forms of death there is neither nobility nor room for prowess.

7   III. 7, 1 Fear is not excited in all men by the same things, but yet we commonly speak of fearful things that surpass man's power to face. Such things, then, inspire fear in every rational man. But the fearful things that a man may face differ in importance and in being more or less fearful (and so with the things III. 7, 2 that inspire confidence). Now, the courageous man always keeps his presence of mind (so far as a man can). So though he will fear these fearful things, he will endure them as he ought and as reason bids him, for the sake of that which is noble; for this is the end or aim of virtue.

III. 7, 3 But it is possible to fear these things too much or too little, and again to take as fearful what is not III. 7, 4 really so. And thus men err sometimes by fearing the wrong things, sometimes by fearing in the wrong manner or at the wrong time, and so on.

And all this applies equally to things that inspire confidence.

III. 7, 5 He, then, that endures and fears what he ought from the right motive, and in the right manner, and [83] at the right time, and similarly feels confidence, is courageous.

For the courageous man regulates both his feeling and his action according to the merits of each case and as reason bids him.

III. 7, 6 But the end or motive of every manifestation of a habit or exercise of a trained faculty is the end or motive of the habit or trained faculty itself.

Now, to the courageous man courage is essentially a fair or noble thing.

Therefore the end or motive of his courage is also noble; for everything takes its character from its end.

It is from a noble motive, therefore, that the courageous man endures and acts courageously in each particular case.

III. 7, 7 Of the characters that run to excess, he that exceeds in fearlessness has no name (and this is often the case, as we have said before); but a man would be either a maniac or quite insensible to pain who should fear nothing, not even earthquakes and breakers, as they say is the case with the Celts.

He that is over-confident in the presence of III. 7, 8 fearful things is called foolhardy. But the foolhardy man is generally thought to be really a braggart, and to pretend a courage which he has not: at least he wishes to seem what the courageous man really is in the presence of danger; so he imitates him III. 7, 9 where he can. And so your foolhardy man is generally a coward at bottom: he blusters so long as he can do so safely, but turns tail when real danger comes.

III. 7, 10 He who is over-fearful is a coward; for he fears what he ought not, and as he ought not, etc.

He is also deficient in confidence; but his character rather displays itself in excess of fear in the presence of pain.

III. 7, 11 The coward is also despondent, for he is frightened at everything. But it is the contrary with the courageous man; for confidence implies hopefulness.

III. 7, 12 Thus the coward and the foolhardy and the courageous man display their characters in the same circumstances, behaving differently under them: for while the former exceed or fall short, the latter behaves moderately and as he ought; and while the foolhardy are precipitate and eager before danger comes, but fall away in its presence, the courageous are keen in action, but quiet enough beforehand.

III. 7, 13 Courage then, as we have said, is observance of the mean with regard to things that excite confidence or fear, under the circumstances which we have specified, and chooses its course and sticks to its post because it is noble to do so, or because it is disgraceful not to do so.

But to seek death as a refuge from poverty, or love, or any painful thing, is not the act of a brave man, but of a coward. For it is effeminacy thus to fly from vexation; and in such a case death is accepted not because it is noble, but simply as an escape from evil.

Study Questions

1. Aristotle is often assumed to have said that "a brave man is never afraid." Is this a fair statement?

2. What, according to Aristotle, is the most courageous behavior? Do you agree with him?

3. Would Aristotle consider Socrates' choice to stand trial a brave decision? Why or why not?

4. After September 11, 2001 a debate arose in the media about whether hijacking a plane and deliberately flying it into a building, causing death and anguish to civilians, was a "cowardly act." In many people's opinion the terrorist actions were the very picture of cowardice, using innocent people as weapons against other innocent people. In your view, were the terrorists brave or cowardly? Is there a third possibility? For a solution you might want to turn to Chapter 10 and the section on Philippa Foot, who suggests that a virtue without good intentions is no virtue at all.

5. In Chapter 11 you'll find an expanded discussion of courage, distinguishing between physical and moral courage. Apply Aristotle's Theory of the Golden Mean to both kinds.

Primary Reading

A Balanced Life

TOM CHATFIELD

Essay, New Philosopher May-July 2019.

As you may have discovered already, Aristotle's view of life still has something to offer to twenty-first century people across the time-span of 24 centuries. Here the British tech philosopher, writer, and broadcaster Tom Chatfield applies Aristotle's concept of balance to the contemporary world of technology and our quest to create a balanced life. Since Chatfield ends up opposing Nietzsche's vision of life to Aristotle's, you may want to re-read it after having read the Nietzsche section in Chapter 10, and then you can make up your own mind.

Is balance a self-evident good? It certainly thinks it is. Take a cliché like 'work-life balance'. To be out of balance is by definition to get something wrong. Perhaps you're working too hard, or not enough, or exhibiting insufficient *joie de vivre*. In any of these cases, what you need to do is obvious (even if doing it is difficult). You must weigh up your options and commitments, then find a way to bring your-self back into balance.

Philosophically speaking, the principle of balanced living owes a lot to Aristotle. In the *Nicomachean Ethics*, Aristotle uses the metaphor of a craftsman creating an excellent work to illustrate his ideal of the golden mean. Excellence in art or craft, he argues, describes a point where nothing remains either to he added or taken away — because to do either would diminish the result. The achievement is an equipoise that's the opposite of average.

One objection to this vision of human thriving is suggested by the engineering metaphor itself. Every technology requires a set of assumptions about inputs and outputs: what goes into a system, what ought to come out, and what processes can best ensure this. In this sense, every machine is also a philosophy — the automated embodiment of a set of values. And these values entail fundamental judgements about what does, and doesn't, count.

Writing in *Harper's* magazine under the headline "Home of the Whopper", the essayist Thomas Frank envisions the chain-food restaurants that girdle America's cities in these terms: as technologies of inhumanly impeccable poise, balancing countless components in the service of productive harmony. "The modular construction, the application of assembly-line techniques to food service, the twin-basket fryers and bulk condiment dispensers, even the clever plastic lids on the coffee cups, with their fold-back sip tabs: these were all triumphs of human ingenuity," Frank notes. And yet: that intense, concentrated efficiency also demanded a fantastic wastefulness elsewhere — of fuel, of air-conditioning, of land, of landfill. Inside the box was a masterpiece of industrial engineering; outside the box were things and people that existed merely to be used up.

Inside the box, like a mechanised master craftsman, the system moves in pursuit of a certain perfection — neither too much nor too little of any element; every bottleneck, delay or scrap of waste addressed and improved over time. Outside the box, however, there is only unquantified waste: materials inessential to the balancing act and thus weightless in its terms.

Balance seems a self-evident good precisely because it presupposes the rightness of the system it exists with-in: the virtue of a chosen mean, the value of a chosen task. And the more immaculately engineered the systems we act within, the more their incentives and values can come to seem synonymous with our own — and with those any right-thinking citizen should desire.

Aristotle had strict views about the ends it was, and was not, virtuous to pursue (self-improvement and autonomy featured highly) — but his philosophy can be hard to apply to modern situations without lapsing into lifestyle blandishment. There's no such problem, however, with a more recent thinker, whose work engaged ferociously with the limitations of all systems — and in particular the inadequacy of science and technology when it came to filling the void once occupied by gods.

Friedrich Nietzsche was a sick man for most of his life, plagued by near-blindness, paralysing migraines, and collapses that kept him bed-bound for weeks. As a result, much of his mature philosophy was written in terse, exalted bursts, inspired by days spent walking in the Alps. In her recent biography of Nietzsche, *I am Dynamite!*, Sue Prideaux describes these oscillations as a form of destruction and renewal.

"Every illness was a death, a dip down into Hades. Every recuperation was a joyful rebirth, a regeneration. This mode of existence refreshed him. *Neuschmecken* ('new-tasting') was his word for it. During each fleeting recuperation the world gleamed anew. And so each recuperation became not only his own rebirth, but also the birth of a whole new world, a new set of problems that demanded new answers."

"Nietzsche insisted that all systems proposing an end to questioning were suspect."

Nietzsche's was a philosophy neither of balance nor harmony, but of creative destruction. He refused answers and resolutions, ending his greatest works with an ellipsis rather than a conclusion. "Philosophy as I have understood and lived it," he wrote in the Foreword to *Ecce Homo*, "is voluntary living in ice and high mountains — a seeking after everything strange and questionable in existence, all that has hitherto been excommunicated by morality."

It was a violently hard existence — and Nietzsche's refusal of answers or fixed positions left rich pickings for those who wished to misrepresent him. Yet, in the works he completed in his own lifetime, Nietzsche insisted that all systems proposing an end to questioning were suspect — with a special ire reserved for those that claimed to do so on the basis of scientific certainty.

What's wrong with wishing to live a balanced life? Nothing, so long as you accept that balance implies measures, priorities, and values, all of which can and must be contested if they are not to be hollowed out. While Silicon Valley may have pioneered life's technological quantification, the apotheosis of today's machine-assisted equilibrium is to be found in China, where state surveillance is working steadily towards ubiquitous assessment: the constant algorithmic counterbalancing of approved and unapproved actions, of patriotic and unpatriotic deeds. Under this vision of the near future, each citizen will be constantly rated according to a unified social credit score — with every trip, purchase, action or inaction integrated into the edifice of industrially-engineered harmony. The result: harmonious lives within a harmonious nation. It's a fine principle — so long as you're prepared to presuppose its rightness.

When it comes to systems and their automation of our ethics, Aristotle and Nietzsche would have agreed on at least one thing: without the chance fundamentally to debate the weight of both individual and collective actions, any box you put people inside is ultimately a prison.

Study Questions

1. What do you think Aristotle would say to Chatfield's application of his concept of balance to the fast-food industry?

2. Is it fair to apply Aristotle's concept of balance to a modern technological industry? Is Chatfield applying it fairly?

3. If you are familiar with Friedrich Nietzsche, evaluate Chatfield's use of his ideas as a comment on Aristotle's idea of balance. Nietzsche is featured in Chapter 10, so you may want to return to this section after reading about him, and discuss its relevance.

Narrative

The Flight of Icarus

Ancient Greek Myth. Summary.

This myth illustrates an element in Aristotle's virtue theory that most Greeks were familiar with because it corresponds to the classic Greek ideal of moderation, or what the Greeks called *sophrosyne;* in the *Nicomachean Ethics* we know it as the mean between extremes, not too much and not too little. The story of Icarus, part of Greek mythology, has been used often as a symbol in Western literature over the past several hundred years.

DEA Picture Library/DeAgostini/Getty Images

Pieter Bruegel the Elder, *The Fall of Icarus* (c. 1558). The inventor Daedalus made wings of feathers and wax for himself and his son, Icarus, so they could escape from Crete, but Icarus flew too close to the sun, and the wax melted. If you look closely, you can see the legs of poor Icarus in the water (right-hand corner). Bruegel was so fascinated by this story that he painted it twice, both times with the farmer in the foreground. This is the original painting; the second is nearly identical except that Daedalus is shown flying above the cliffs. The Roman poet Ovid, who retold the story, specifically mentioned in his *Metamorphoses* that the fall was witnessed by a plowman, a shepherd, and a fisherman, and that is why Bruegel put them in his painting. What do you think the significance might be of the artist's having placed the tragedy of Icarus off to the side?

Wanted for the murder of his nephew, the great artisan Daedalus hid out on Crete, where he built King Minos a labyrinth to house the monster Minotaur (a creature with a bull's head and a man's body). Here Daedalus lived for years, fell in love with one of Minos's slaves, and had a son by her, Icarus. When Icarus was a young man, Daedalus decided to leave Crete. But Minos did not want to lose his master craftsman and so locked Daedalus and his son up in the labyrinth; they escaped with the help of Minos's wife. It was difficult to get off the island, because Minos kept all his ships under military guard, but Daedalus had an idea: He fashioned a pair of feather wings for himself and another pair for Icarus. The quill feathers were threaded together, but the smaller feathers were held together with wax. Daedalus was quite emotional when he told Icarus how to use the wings on the perilous journey, admonishing his son not to fly too high to avoid having the wax be melted by the sun and not to fly too low so that ocean water wouldn't soak his feathers. Then he told his son, "Follow me!" and they set out across the ocean toward the northeast. They had already traveled a considerable distance when Icarus, for whatever reason, disobeyed his father. He began rising toward the sun, enjoying the air currents and the sweep of his great wings.

When Daedalus looked back to see if his son was still following close behind him, there was nobody—but far below, on the waves, floated the feathers of Icarus's wings. He had risen too close to the sun, and the wax on his wings had melted, causing him to plummet toward the water below; Icarus had drowned. His father circled around and around until the body of his son rose from the waters; then he picked it up and carried it to a nearby island where he buried it.

Study Questions

1. Is this story meant to be taken literally? Why or why not?

2. Bruegel's painting shows the fall of Icarus, but you have to look hard to find him. Why do you think the artist didn't make Icarus the focal point of the painting?

3. In Western literature the story of Icarus has often been used as a metaphor for overextending yourself, or being overconfident. It has been taken as a warning not to reach above your station in life, to "know your place." Is this lesson exactly the same as the original story teaches? (What would Aristotle say? What lesson might a parent be trying to teach his or her child when telling this story?)

4. Is this a didactic story? Why or why not?

 Narrative

Njal's Saga

Prose epic, ca. 1280. Author unknown. Summary and Excerpt. Burnt Njal, The Story of Burnt Njal, The Great Icelandic Tribune, Jurist, and Counsellor. Translated by Sir George Webbe Dasent. London: Norroena Society, 1907.

This story is set in the latter part of the Viking Age (700–1000 C.E.). It isn't a story of Vikings, however, but of their relatives, who stayed in Iceland to farm the land. The area was settled by the Norsemen (mostly Danes and Norwegians) about 800, and by the time *Njal's Saga* was written it was a land of great unrest; blood feuds and various intrigues led to the Danish takeover of the country, which for four hundred years had been independent. *Njal's Saga* is one of many *sagas,* which are historical epics about past life in Iceland.

Nordic mythology teaches that the world as well as the gods eventually will perish in a natural disaster, Ragnarok. Thus the Norsemen (the farmers as well as the Vikings) held to the belief in a gloomy fate looming ahead. Even though Christianity was by that time the official religion, the old view of life being ruled by fate still had a hold on people's minds.

This very brief outline cannot explain the complex plot of the saga and can only hint at the inevitable tragic ending. Njal, his wife, Bergthora, and their four sons are carrying on a blood feud with neighbors, not because either party is evil, but because over the years events have led in that direction. Through misunderstandings and gossip, the enmity between Njal's family and their neighbors grows, even though Njal does his best to avert it by talking sense to everybody. His negotiations backfire, though, and things get worse. At the *Alting* (the place of arbitration), it becomes clear that all hope of peace is lost, and Njal goes home and prepares for a siege. His adversary, Flosi, arrives with a hundred men, and Njal asks his sons to help him defend the house from inside. The enemy is quick to take advantage of the situation and sets fire to the farmhouse.

> There was a carline [old woman, Ed.] at Bergthorsknoll, whose name was Saevuna. She was wise in many things, and foresighted; but she was then very old, and Njal's sons called her an old dotard, when she talked so much, but still some things which she said came to pass. It fell one day that she took a cudgel in her hand, and went up above the house to a stack of vetches. She beat the stack of vetches with her cudgel, and wished it might never thrive "wretch that it was!"
>
> Skarphedinn laughed at her, and asked why she was so angry with the vetch stack.
>
> "This stack of vetches," said the carline, "will be taken and lighted with fire when Njal my master is burnt, house and all, and Bergthora my foster-child. Take it away to the water, or burn it up as quick as you can."
>
> "We will not do that," says Skarphedinn, "for something else will be got to light a fire with, if that were foredoomed, though this stack were not here."
>
> The carline babbled the whole summer about the vetch-stack that it should be got indoors, but something always hindered it.

Months later, Flosi has now shown up with his force of one hundred men, and Njal has fortified himself and his household inside the farmhouse. Now the vetch (a wildflower) that figured in Sæunn's predictions becomes a weapon:

> Then Flosi and his men made a great pile before each of the doors, and then the women folk who were inside began to weep and to wail.
>
> Njal spoke to them and said, "Keep up your hearts, nor utter shrieks, for this is but a passing storm, and it will be long before ye have another such; and put your faith in God, and believe that He is so merciful that He will not let us burn both in this world and the next."
>
> Such words of comfort had he for them all, and others still more strong.
>
> Now the whole house began to blaze. Then Njal went to the door and said—
>
> "Is Flosi so near that he can hear my voice?"
>
> Flosi said that he could hear it.
>
> "Wilt thou," said Njal, "take an atonement from my sons, or allow any men to go out?"
>
> "I will not," answers Flosi, "take any atonement from thy sons, and now our dealings shall come to an end once for all, and I will not stir from this spot till they are all dead; but I will allow the women and children and house-carles to go out."
>
> Then Njal went into the house, and said to the folk—
>
> "Now all those must go out to whom leave is given, and so go thou out Thorhalla Asgrim's daughter, and all the people also with thee who may."

Then Thorhalla said—

"This is another parting between me and Helgi than I thought of a while ago; but still I will egg on my father and brothers to avenge this manscathe which is wrought here."

"Go, and good go with thee," said Njal, "for thou art a brave woman."

After that she went out and much folk with her.

Then Astrid of Deepback said to Helgi Njal's son—

"Come thou out with me, and I will throw a woman's cloak over thee, and tire thy head with a kerchief."

He spoke against it at first, but at last he did so at the prayer of others.

So Astrid wrapped the kerchief round Helgi's head, but Thorhilda, Skarphedinn's wife, threw a cloak over him, and he went out between them, and then Thorgerda Njal's daughter, and Helga her sister, and many other folk went out too.

But when Helgi came out Flosi said—

"That is a tall woman and broad across the shoulders that went yonder, take her and hold her."

But when Helgi heard that, he cast away the cloak. He had got his sword under his arm, and hewed at a man, and the blow fell on his shield and cut off the point of it, and the man's leg as well. Then Flosi came up and hewed at Helgi's neck, and took off his head at a stroke.

Then Flosi went to the door and called out to Njal, and said he would speak with him and Bergthora.

Now Njal does so, and Flosi said—

"I will offer thee, master Njal, leave to go out, for it is unworthy that thou shouldst burn indoors."

"I will not go out," said Njal, "for I am an old man, and little fitted to avenge my sons, but I will not live in shame."

Then Flosi said to Bergthora—

"Come thou out. housewife, for I will for no sake burn thee indoors."

"I was given away to Njal young," said Bergthora, "and I have promised him this, that we would both share the same fate."

After that they both went back into the house.

"What counsel shall we now take?" said Bergthora.

"We will go to our bed," says Njal, "and lay us down; I have long been eager for rest."

Then she said to the boy Thord, Kari's son—

"Thee will I take out, and thou shalt not burn in here."

"Thou hast promised me this, grandmother," says the boy, "that we should never part so long as I wished to be with thee: but methinks it is much better to die with thee and Njal than to live after you."

Then she bore the boy to her bed, and Njal spoke to his steward and said—

"Now shalt thou see where we lay us down, and how I lay us out, for I mean not to stir an inch hence, whether reek or burning smart me, and so thou wilt be able to guess where to look for our bones."

He said he would do so.

There had been an ox slaughtered and the hide lay there. Njal told the steward to spread the hide over them, and he did so.

So there they lay down both of them in their bed, and put the boy between them. Then they signed themselves and the boy with the cross, and gave over their souls into God's hand, and that was the last word that men heard them utter.

Then the steward took the hide and spread it over them, and went out afterwards.

Study Questions

1. Do you think Njal, Bergthora, and the little boy display courage, or are they just giving up?

2. Would removing the vetch-stack have prevented the arson?

3. For the old Norsemen and -women, the name and reputation you left behind when you died was all-important. How do you think Njal and Bergthora were regarded after they died?

4. Would Aristotle recognize their final act as courageous? Why or why not?

  Narrative

Lord Jim

RICHARD BROOKS (DIRECTOR AND SCREENWRITER)

Film, 1965. Summary. Based on the novel by Joseph Conrad, 1900.

Lord Jim is one of the finest fictional explorations of a human soul trying to do the right thing, at the right time, for the right reason. The film based on Joseph Conrad's classic novel tells the story of a young man named Jim who dreams of doing great deeds. As a newly appointed officer in the British Mercantile Marine, he spends quiet moments on board his ship fantasizing about saving damsels in distress and suppressing mutinies. After having been stranded in a Southeast Asian harbor because of a broken leg, Jim takes a job as chief mate to a crew of drunken, raucous white sailors with an equally unpleasant captain on the rusty old *Patna,* which is transporting a group of Muslim pilgrims to Mecca. Once they are at sea, a storm approaches, and Jim inspects the ship's hull. It is so rusty it is on the verge of breaking up. Back on deck Jim sees that the crew is lowering a lifeboat into the water—just one, for themselves. No measures are being taken to save the hundreds of pilgrims on the ship. Jim insists to the others that he is staying on board, but, at the last minute, as the storm hits, he comes face to face with his fear of death, which causes him to push aside all dreams of heroic deeds, and he jumps into the lifeboat after all.

Believing that the *Patna* is lost already, the men in the lifeboat set course for shore. When they arrive, they see that someone got there ahead of them; in the harbor lies the *Patna* herself, safe and sound. She was salvaged and towed to shore by another crew, and all the pilgrims are safe. Jim is relieved that no one was lost, but his dreams of valor have been shattered—he is tormented by guilt. There is an inquest, and Jim decides to tell all, to the dismay of his superiors, who believe that dirty linen should not be aired in public. His testimony so affects the prosecutor that the prosecutor later kills himself, leaving a note saying that if fear can break even one of us, how can anyone believe himself to be safe and honorable? Jim's officer's papers are canceled. Everywhere he goes from now on, the memory of the *Patna* will haunt him; somebody will recognize him or mention the scandal, and he will have to go somewhere else, to another port and another odd job.

Columbia Pictures/Getty Images

To stay or to jump? Jim (Peter O'Toole) is about to make the decision that will ruin his life: During a storm, he abandons ship and the many passengers who had put their trust in him, in *Lord Jim* (Columbia Pictures, 1965).

Is Jim a coward? Were all the dreams of noble deeds just fantasies? He doesn't know. Months later, in some harbor in Southeast Asia, Jim is now a common dockside worker. One day, while transferring goods from shore to ship, he finds himself in a new, dangerous situation: A worker with a grudge against the shipping company lights a fuse that threatens to blow up the ammo being freighted to the ship, and he calls out to all hands to jump, before it blows. But Jim, on hearing the yell "Jump!," stands fast. The only man remaining on board, he puts out the fire and becomes a hero. The administrator of the shipping line, Stein, offers him a job, which Jim later accepts because he wants to get out of town. The job entails taking the guns and ammunition up river to the village of Patusan to help the local people fight against a tyrant. He becomes the hero of the people, respected and trusted. They call him *Tuan Jim,* Lord Jim. He now believes that he finally has proved himself, but in fact the real test is yet to come. A band of pirates land in Patusan, and with the help of a traitor from the village, they trick Jim into believing that they have good intentions. They are white, they promise they will sail away without harming any of the villagers, and Jim chooses to believe them; he lets them go without disarming them, trusting their word. He vows to the chief of the village that if anyone is harmed because of his decision, he will forfeit his own life. As it turns out, the chief's own son is killed in a fight between the pirates and the villagers. The villagers expect Jim to flee to save his life, and Stein tries to make Jim leave the village with the native woman he loves, but this time Jim stands fast; he explains to Stein, "I have been a so-called coward and a so-called hero, and there is not the thickness of a sheet of paper between them. Maybe cowards and heroes are just ordinary men who, for a split second do something out of the ordinary." In the morning Jim goes to the chief, who is mad with grief over his son, and offers him his life. Does the chief kill Jim? Read the book or watch the film.

Study Questions

1. Is Jim a coward, or is he courageous? Is it possible to be both?

2. Do you think we all are like Jim in the sense that we all have a moral breaking point which, when we reach it, reveals the frailty of our character?

3. How would Aristotle rate Jim? Is he in the end a virtuous person?

4. Although the virtue of *honor* is not on Aristotle's list, it was an important concept in his day. Today it may not seem terribly important to many in the Western world, but in the time period of Lord Jim, the concept of personal honor was at least as important as when Aristotle was alive. Do you agree with the author (Joseph Conrad) that it is more honorable for Jim to

confess his failings during the inquest than to keep quiet and follow the lead of his superiors? Is Jim an honorable man? Why or why not?

5. Compare the plot of *Lord Jim* with Aristotle's prescription for the perfect tragic plot (see Chapter 2): Something horrible happens to an ordinary man, not because of some vice or depravity of his character, but because of a great error in judgment. Does this fit Jim? If so, is Aristotle right that we feel pity and fear because we understand what he is going through—that we might react the same way?

 Narrative

A Piece of Advice

ISAAC BASHEVIS SINGER

Short story, 1958. Translated by Martha Glicklich and Joel Blocker. Summary and Excerpt.

This story takes place in a pre–World War II Polish-Jewish village; Singer (1904–1991), who won the Nobel Prize in literature in 1978 for his "impassioned narrative art," drew on his Polish-Jewish background for most of his stories.

Baruch lives with his wife's family in the village of Rachev; it is a much grander household than his own childhood home was because his father-in-law is a wealthy man and likes to live in style. The father-in-law is a good man in many ways, and a learned man, but he has one major fault: He has a terrible temper. Unwilling to forgive and forget, he harbors resentments over any little offense. One time Baruch borrowed a pen from him and forgot to return it, and that sent his father-in-law into such a fit of rage that he struck Baruch in the face. This upset the family terribly because a father-in-law does not have that kind of authority over his son-in-law, but Baruch, being an easygoing young man, was quite willing to forgive the older man. The differences between the two men are noticeable: The older man is fastidious, and Baruch is lazy; his father-in-law is always sharp and on top of things, whereas Baruch is terribly forgetful and sometimes can't even find his way home because he doesn't pay attention to where he is. But after the incident with the pen, Baruch's father-in-law approaches him—a rare event—and asks his advice on how to control his anger, for he has alienated all his business partners. Baruch suggests that they go to see the Rabbi of Kuzmir, a neighboring town. At first the older man scoffs at the thought, but later he agrees to go.

They arrive in Kuzmir on a Friday afternoon (at the beginning of the Sabbath) after a long journey through the winter snows, and Baruch's father-in-law goes to talk with Rabbi Chazkele; for three-quarters of an hour he is alone with the rabbi, and then he emerges, irate, calling the rabbi a fool, an ignoramus, to the embarrassment of his son-in-law. What was the rabbi's advice that so infuriated Baruch's father-in-law? That he must become a flatterer. For a week he must flatter everyone he meets, going through the motions of saying nice but insincere things to all of them regardless of who they might be. And that, to the father-in-law, is worse than murder. But Baruch suspects there must be a deeper meaning to the odd piece of advice. The older man wants to go home immediately, but since it is the evening of the Sabbath they can't leave for home (because one does not travel on the Sabbath, between sunset on Friday and sunset on Saturday). So they stay in Kuzmir to celebrate the Sabbath and listen to the prayers of Rabbi Chazkele. Both Baruch and his father-in-law are deeply moved by the rabbi's chanting, and by his words.

The rabbi's advice is essentially the same as what he had already told Baruch's father-in-law: It is the deed that counts, not whether you have good intentions. If you are not pious, pretend you are. If you're angry, pretend you're friendly. The Almighty knows your real intentions, so lying to the world is acceptable as long as you do the right thing.

Baruch's father-in-law is now fascinated at listening to the rabbi, and he stays for three Sabbath meals and consults with the rabbi for a whole hour before leaving that Saturday night. On the way home they are held up by bad weather and have to put up at an inn for days. At the inn the father-in-law is being heckled as a Hasid (a Jewish religious sect founded in Poland in the 1700s), but instead of being angry, he takes it all in stride. And in the following days and weeks he stops snapping at people. He is still angry, but he makes an effort not to show it; he is developing new habits of kindness, even if he in his heart doesn't feel it—yet. Baruch says, "One could feel that he did this only with great effort. That's what made it noble." And after a while the external effort works its way inward. The older man becomes a changed person, a kind man. The old habit of rage is broken, and new habits have taken over. Baruch remembers his father-in-law saying, "If you can't be a good Jew, act the good Jew, because if you act something, you *are* it." And Baruch adds,

> "And so it is with all things. If you are not happy, act the happy man. Happiness will come later. So also with faith. If you are in despair, act as though you believed. Faith will come afterwards."

Study Questions

1. Is this an example of virtue ethics or ethics of conduct? Explain your answer.

2. Do you think someone can become a better person by constantly doing the right thing, even if his or her inclination is to do something else entirely? What might Aristotle say?

3. Comment on this quote: "One could feel that he did this only with great effort. That's what made it noble." What might Kant say to that? After you've read Chapter 10, return to this question and discuss what Philippa Foot might answer.

Chapter Ten
Virtue Ethics and Authenticity: Contemporary Perspectives

In the introduction to Chapter 8, I mentioned that the idea of a good character as one of the key elements in a moral theory was eclipsed by the general notion that all that matters is *doing the right thing*. With the advent of Christianity, virtue ethics was rejected in favor of an *ethics of conduct*—asking the kinds of questions explored in Chapters 3 to 7. As we saw earlier, that was in part a result of a greater social awareness: There is more fairness in asking everybody to follow rules of conduct than there is in trying to make people adapt to vague principles of how to be, and there is a greater chance of developing rational arguments for your position regarding rules of conduct than there is of getting others to agree with your viewpoint concerning what is virtuous. In recent years, though, philosophers have turned their attention to the ancient thoughts about character building, and virtue theory is now experiencing a revival. (See Box 10.1 for a brief overview of virtue ethics and character.) This trend has been hotly contested by scholars such as J. B. Schneewind, who believe the original reasons for adopting ethics of conduct are still valid.

Box 10.1 CAN WE CHANGE OUR SPOTS?

Opponents of virtue ethics often claim that for people to be praised for what they do, or blamed for it, it must be assumed that they are *responsible* for their actions. But are we responsible for our character and disposition? Virtue theory asks us to look primarily at people's character. Suppose we ask someone to give to charity, and she doesn't have a generous disposition. Can we then blame her for her lack of virtue? If we can't, then virtue ethics is useless as a moral theory. It may praise people for dispositions that they already have, but it doesn't tell us how to improve ourselves. Virtue theory's response to that is that certain people have certain dispositions, and in that respect some are more fortunate than others, morally speaking; some people are just naturally thoughtful and generous, or courageous, or truthful. The rest of us have to work on these things. Just because we lack a good disposition doesn't mean we can't work on improving it, and just because we have a tendency toward a certain disposition doesn't mean we can't work on controlling it.

The revival of virtue theory has been primarily a British and American phenomenon, and we will look at some of the proponents of this new way of approaching ethics. In continental philosophy (European philosophy excluding the British tradition), there was a separate renewal of interest in Aristotle and his virtue theory in the twentieth century, but in a sense a version of virtue theory has been in effect in continental philosophy ever since the nineteenth century, and we will take a look at that tradition too. Because virtue theory is now associated with the new British/American theory, we will call its continental counterpart the "Quest for Authenticity."

Ethics and the Morality of Virtue as Political Concepts

As we have seen, there is a subtle difference between morality and ethics, and in the debate about virtue that difference becomes very clear. In an *ethics of virtue* the issue is to ask yourself what kind of person you want to be, to find good reasons to back up your view and to listen to possible counterarguments, and then to set forth to shape your own character, all the while being ready to justify your choice of virtue rationally or to change your mind. An ethics of virtue doesn't specify what *kind* of virtue you should strive for, although it is usually assumed that it will be something benevolent or at least nothing harmful. The important thing is that you realize you *can* mold your character into what you believe is right. The question of whether your chosen virtue really is a morally good choice is not necessarily part of the issue.

However, a *morality of virtue* focuses precisely on this issue: Which virtue is desirable to strive for, and which is no virtue at all? Parents of young children generally know that telling stories can be an excellent way to teach moral virtues, but lately politicians as well as educators have also taken notice. The politician, former Secretary of Education, and writer William H. Bennett has published several collections of stories with morals—didactic stories—meant to be read to young children; the best known of those collections is simply titled *The Book of Virtues* and contains stories from the Western cultural heritage, as well as from other cultures, all with a short added moral explanation. (Box 10.2 discusses stories that warn against following nonvirtuous role models.)

Box 10.2 NEGATIVE ROLE MODELS

Virtue theory usually focuses on heroes and saints who are to be emulated, but little attention is given to those characters who perhaps teach a deeper moral lesson: the negative role models. Whether we look to real-life figures or fictional characters, moral lessons can be learned by observing the destiny of "bad guys," provided that they don't get away with their misdeeds. (Twisted souls can, of course, learn a lesson from the evildoer who does get away with it, but that is another matter.) From childhood we hear of people who did something they were not supposed to do and suffered the consequences. Most of these stories are issued as a warning: Don't "cry wolf," because in the end nobody will believe you. Look what happened to Adam and Eve, who ate the fruit of the one tree they were not supposed to touch. Look what happened to the girl who stepped on a loaf of bread so she wouldn't get her feet wet. She was pulled down into the depths of hell (in a Hans Christian Andersen story). When we grow up we learn the lesson of politicians who turned

out to be crooked, of televangelists who didn't practice what they preached, of rich and famous people who have serious drug problems. Movies and novels also bombard us with negative models: Darth Vader (*Star Wars*) sells out to the Dark Side, so we learn to beware of people who have lost their integrity. Charles Foster Kane (*Citizen Kane*) forgets his humanity and dies lonely, his heart longing for the time when he was a small boy. The Count of Monte Cristo loses his own humanity through an obsession with revenge. And Smeagol loses not only his self but even his identity as a "halfling" when he becomes Gollum through allowing the Ring to take over his spirit (*The Lord of the Rings*). Through exposure to such characters we get a warning; we live their lives vicariously and find that bitterness lies at the end. Films such as *Money for Nothing, A Simple Plan, Goodfellas,* and *Fargo* show us that the life of selfish pursuits carries its own punishment. Even a comedy such as *Burn After Reading* brings home the same point, albeit in a roundabout way. And television series such as *House of Cards* have also explored the downfall resulting from a loss of integrity. There are, however, works that fail to bring home the moral lesson because they are either too pompous or simply misinformed. Such a film is *Reefer Madness,* which is now a cult classic depicting the life of crime and madness that results from smoking marijuana. Another antidrug film but with a far superior story and impact is *Requiem for a Dream.* It realistically describes the downward spiral of drug addictions, in this case from diet pills as well as heroin. (If you remember your fallacies from Chapter 1, you'll be able to identify *Reefer Madness* as an example of the slippery slope fallacy, whereas *Requiem* depicts an actual, chilling slippery slope.)

In the latter half of the twentieth century, virtue ethics made another entrance on the stage of British and American philosophy. For some thinkers it was an absolute necessity to make the switch from an ethics of conduct to virtue ethics because, as virtue ethicists say, you can do the right thing and still be an unpleasant person; however, if you work on your character, you will become a good person *and* do the right thing without even having to think about it. For others, virtue ethics has become a much-needed supplement to an ethics of conduct. Some see virtue ethics as a way for people to explore the issue of a good character; others view it as a way to teach what a good character should be all about.

The Political Aspect of Conduct Versus Character

In the last decade of the twentieth century, the political debate in the United States became polarized in a new way—which actually turned out to be a polished and updated version of the older polarization between *conduct* and *character.* Republican politicians brought up the issue of character: Is the candidate trustworthy? Does he or she have integrity? Does he or she keep promises? In short, is the candidate a *virtuous person*—in his or her private life as well? Democratic politicians responded by pointing to the *public policies* of the candidate: What has he or she accomplished politically so far? What social policies does the candidate support, and with what success rate has he or she had them implemented? This is not just an interesting revival of the philosophical question of conduct versus character; it goes to the heart of how we view the importance of values. Do we think the question of personal character and integrity is the most important form of ethics—perhaps even the only form of ethics? Or do we believe that the personal standards of someone who serves the public are less important than his or her social conscience and efforts to change things presumably for the better? For some politicians, the question of character has in itself become a matter of a person's outlook on social policies rather than a question of personal values: A person of good character is a person who supports certain social policies. Regardless of how one feels about national politics, it is philosophically interesting that the revived debate between ethics of conduct and virtue ethics is not always a partisan story—the virtue concept is not in itself a Republican issue, and the policy issue is not by nature Democratic—it all depends on the political needs of the moment.

As with so many of the moral issues we have looked at, an extreme either/or turns out to be a *bifurcation/ a false dichotomy*—a false dilemma with other possible alternatives. If we assume that character is important, why should we assume that a person's stand on social issues is less important? And if we assume that social views count, then why shouldn't character count as well? A person can have a perfectly squeaky-clean character and yet be completely ineffective as a decision maker or a negotiator or even have little grasp of or interest in social policies and the needs of society. And a highly effective politician, well liked and radiating understanding of social and economic problems in the population, can turn out to have a personal life that is in shambles because of a lack of character. At times, though, it does seem all-important that a political leader have character and integrity—even if there is disagreement about his or her policies.

The emerging pattern shows that each group focuses on what it considers most important: Conservatives have typically focused on character and integrity, and liberals on a variety of social policies, such as the right to abortion, affirmative action, gun control, welfare, and other causes related to the general question of what to do. Interestingly, in the 2016 presidential campaign—a very contentious campaign that has had few historic parallels, if any—the question of moral character was at the forefront of the debates. Candidates on both the Democratic and the Republican tickets were blamed for a lack of character, while other candidates were lauded for having a strong character. And frequently supporters of the criticized candidates would point to their good political policies (conduct) if they couldn't point to a righteous character (virtue). During the first years of the presidency of Donald Trump and going into the presidential campaign 2020 (at the time of writing this), the "character vs. conduct" issue flipped from being a Republican focus on character and a Democratic focus on conduct to a Republican focus on political and economic accomplishments (a great economy and presidential promises kept) and a Democratic focus on character (does the candidate have the moral attitude toward the environment favored by most Democrats, and so forth). Whether one focus is preferable to another is of course a matter of both one's politics and one's sense of ethics, but it is an interesting phenomenon that an ancient debate in moral philosophy continues to play out in American politics during different time periods with different concerns.

Have Virtue, and Then Go Ahead: Mayo, Foot, and Sommers

Bernard Mayo

In 1958 the American philosopher Bernard Mayo suggested that Western ethics had reached a dead end, for it had lost contact with ordinary life. People don't live by great principles of what to do ("Do your duty" or "Make humanity happy"); instead, they measure themselves according to their moral qualities or deficiencies on an everyday basis. Novelists have not forgotten this, says Mayo, because the books we read tell of people who try hard to be a certain way—who sometimes succeed and sometimes fail—and we, the readers, feel that we have learned something.

An ethics of conduct is not excluded from virtue ethics, says Mayo—it just takes second place, because whatever we *do* is included in our general standard of virtue: We pay our taxes or help animals that are injured in traffic because we believe in the virtues of being a good citizen and fellow traveler on Planet Earth. In other words, if we have a set of virtues we believe we should live by, we will usually do the right thing as a consequence. However, an ethics of conduct without virtue may not be benevolent at all; it is entirely possible to "do your duty" and still be a bad person—you do it for gain or to spite someone. (A good example of such a person is Dickens's Ebenezer Scrooge in *A Christmas Carol,* who may appear to be a pillar of society but only because it is profitable to him.) You can do something courageous without actually being courageous, says Mayo (although Aristotle would insist that if you do it often enough you actually *become* courageous, and utilitarians would insist that it doesn't matter why you do something, as long as it has good results).

So how should we choose our actions in an everyday situation? Mayo says we shouldn't look for specific advice in a moral theory (Do such and such); we should, instead, adopt general advice (Be brave/lenient/patient). That will ensure that we have the *"unity of character"* which a moral system of principles can't give us. Mayo advises us to select a **role model,** either an ideal person or an actual one. Be fair, be a good American—or be like Socrates or Buddha, or choose a contemporary role model (frequently mentioned by my students) such as Angelina Jolie or Oprah Winfrey. There are heroes and saints throughout history we can choose from, not necessarily because of what they have done, but because of the kind of people they were.

So when Mayo suggests that we learn from factual *exemplars* such as Martin Luther King, Jr., Mother Teresa, or perhaps our parents, he is not saying we should emulate their actual doings but, rather, that we should live in their "spirit" and respond to everyday situations with the strength that a good character can give. This is a much more realistic approach to morality than is reflected in the high ideals of principles and duty that an ethics of conduct has held up for people. People have felt inadequate because nobody can live up to such ideals, says Mayo, but everyone can try to be like someone he or she admires. Critics of this enthusiasm for role models have pointed out that just emulating someone you admire doesn't in itself solve your moral dilemmas: (1) What if your idea of a role model doesn't correspond to what other people consider models of decent behavior? This is one of the traditional problems with virtue ethics: Who gets the final word about what is to count as virtue? It provides no easy method for solving moral disputes. (2) What if your role model turns out not to be so perfect after all? We have seen famous people, role models for many, take dramatic falls from the pedestal of admiration because of personal less-than-admirable choices. And even if your role model is a historical figure (who can't make any new mistakes), there is always the risk that new material will surface, showing another and less virtuous side to that person. Are you then supposed to drop your hero or find ways to defend him or her? (3) The most serious complaint may be the one that comes from several philosophers (from different time periods) who find fault with the very idea that one can be virtuous by just imitating someone else. (Mayo, of course, didn't invent that idea; he just made it part of a modern philosophy of virtue.) One is Kant, who didn't think virtue was a character trait as such, but rather the strength of one's goodwill to follow a moral principle (see Chapter 6), and you can find his thought-provoking criticism in Box 10.3. Another is the French philosopher Jean-Paul Sartre, who insisted that we ought to take responsibility for every single thing we do in order to be true to ourselves and become *authentic human beings.* Taking such responsibility precludes settling for just copying what others do, because that approach would give us a false sense of who we are and a false sense of security—by making us believe we can go through life and be good persons just by imitating others. In Sartre's terminology, we would then be living a life of *inauthenticity.* We look more closely at Sartre's moral philosophy later in this chapter.

Box 10.3 KANT'S REJECTION OF ROLE MODELS

Bernard Mayo points out that Immanuel Kant rejected the idea of imitating others as a moral rule and called it "fatal to morality." Kant deplored holding up an example of an ideal, rather than striving for the ideal itself. Mayo thinks striving for the ideal itself is too much to ask of ordinary people. If we read Kant's *Lectures on Ethics,* we find an interesting argument for why it is not a good idea to point to *people* as worth emulating: If I try to compare myself with someone else who is better than I am, I can either try to be as good or try to diminish that other person; this second choice is actually much easier than trying to be as good as the other person, and it invariably leads to *jealousy.* So when parents hold up one sibling for the other to emulate, they are paving the way

for sibling rivalry; the one who is being set up as a paragon will be resented by the other one. Kant suggests that we should recommend goodness as such and not proffer individuals to be emulated, because we all have a tendency to be jealous of people we think we can't measure up to. So the Kantian rejection of role models is not merely an abstract preference for an ideal but also a realistic appreciation of family relationships and petty grudges. It may even serve as a valid psychological explanation for why some people have a profound dislike for so-called heroes and make consistent efforts to diminish the deeds of all persons regarded as role models by society. Such an attitude may just be another reaction against being told that someone else is a better person than you are.

Philippa Foot

Opponents of virtue theory ask how we can call beneficial human traits "virtues" when some humans are *born* with such traits and others don't have them at all. In other words, human responsibility for those dispositions doesn't enter into the picture at all. Good health and an excellent memory are great to have, but can we blame those who are sick and forgetful for not being virtuous?

The British philosopher Philippa Foot—who invented the famous Trolley Problem which you read about in Chapters 1 and 5—counters that argument in her book *Virtues and Vices* (1978) by stressing that virtues aren't merely dispositions we either have or don't have. A virtue is not just a beneficial disposition but also a matter of our *intentions.* If we couple our willpower with our disposition to achieve some goal that is beneficial, then we are virtuous. So having a virtue is not the same as having a skill; it is having the proper intention to do something good—and being able to follow it up with an appropriate action.

For Foot, virtues are not just something we are equipped with. Rather, we are equipped with some tendency to go astray, and virtue is our capacity to *correct* that tendency. Human nature makes us want to run and hide when there is danger; that is why there is the virtue of courage. And we may want to indulge in more pleasure than is good for us; that is why there is the virtue of temperance. Foot points out that virtue theories seem to assume human nature is by and large sensual and fearful, but there actually may be other character deficiencies that are more prevalent and more interesting to try to correct through virtue—such as the desire to be put upon and dissatisfied or the unwillingness to accept good things as they come along.

But what about people who are *naturally* virtuous? The philosophical tradition has had a tendency to judge them rather oddly. Suppose we have two people who make the decision to lend a hand to someone in need. Person A likes to do things for others and jumps at the chance to be helpful. Person B really couldn't care less about other people but knows that benevolence is a virtue, so he makes an effort to help in spite of his natural inclination. For Kant the person who makes an effort to overcome his or her inclination is a *morally better person* than the one to whom virtue comes easily. But surely there is something strange about that judgment, because in real life we appreciate the naturally benevolent person so much more than the surly one who grudgingly tries to be good for the sake of a principle. As a matter of fact, those are the people we *love,* because they *like* to do things for the sake of other people. Many schools of thought agree that it takes a greater effort to overcome than to follow your inclination, so it must be more morally worthy. Aristotle, however, believed that the person who takes pleasure in doing a virtuous action is the one who is truly virtuous.

Foot sides here with Aristotle: The person who likes to do good, or to whom it comes easily, is a morally better person than the one who succeeds through struggle. Why? Because the fact that there is a struggle is a sign that the person is *lacking in virtue* in the first place. Not that the successful struggler isn't good, or virtuous, but the one who did it with no effort is just a little bit better, because the virtue was already there to begin with. Foot's own example, in *Virtues and Vices,* is honesty:

> For one man it is hard to refrain from stealing and for another man it is not: which shows the greater virtue in acting as he should? . . . The fact that a man is *tempted* to steal is something about him that shows a certain lack of honesty: of the thoroughly honest man we say that it "never entered his head," meaning that it was never a real possibility for him.

In addition, Foot offers a solution to another problem plaguing virtue ethics: Can we say that someone who is committing an evil act is somehow doing it with virtue? Say that a criminal has to remain cool, calm, and collected to open a safe or has to muster courage to fulfill a contract and kill someone. Is that person virtuous in the sense of having self-control or courage? Foot borrows an argument from the one ethicist who is most often identified with an ethics of conduct, even though his work also includes the topic of virtue—Kant: *An act or a disposition can't be called good if it isn't backed by a good will.* Foot interprets it this way: If the act is morally wrong, or, rather, if the *intentions* behind the act are bad, then cool-headedness and courage *cease to be virtues.* Virtue is not something static; it is a dynamic power that appears when the intention is to do something good. The "virtue" value is simply switched off when the good intention is absent. And here we have an answer to the study question raised at the end of Chapter 9, after Aristotle's text on courage p. 411: *Can a terrorist be courageous?* Should we acknowledge that the September 11, 2001, hijackers or the terrorist attackers in Paris 2015 were somehow brave, in spite of their evil intentions? Foot would probably say no: A virtue is nullified if it is done with an evil intention. The hijackers may have experienced some kind of spiritual fortitude, but it doesn't deserve the name *courage* if we view courage as a virtue. And saying that their intention may have been to do something good for somebody other than the victims doesn't count, in any moral theory: not in the religion of Islam, which forbids the killing of innocents; nor in Christianity and Judaism, which forbid the same thing; nor in utilitarianism, which sees the immensity of the massacre and psychological turmoil that followed throughout the world as unjustified by any local cause the terrorists may have had; nor in Kant's theory, which says we should never use any other person merely as a means to an end; nor in virtue theory, which, as we can now see, holds that it is *motivation* that determines whether or not a character trait can be called virtuous.

Steve Pyke/Getty Images

Philippa Foot (1920–2010), a British ethicist, is credited with being one of a handful of twentieth-century philosophers who have revived and modernized the concept of virtue ethics. For years she held the position of Griffin Professor of Philosophy at the University of California, Los Angeles. Her works include *Virtues and Vices and Other Essays in Moral Philosophy* (1978), *Natural Goodness* (2001), and *Moral Dilemmas: And Other Topics in Moral Philosophy* (2002).

We find parallels in other situations in which there may not be any evil or criminal element. *Hope*, for example, is generally supposed to be a virtue, but if someone is being unrealistic and daydreams about wish fulfillment, hope is no longer a virtue. And *temperance* may be a virtue, but not if a person is simply afraid to throw herself into the stream of life. In that case it is a shield and not a virtue.

Critics of Foot's positive attitude toward the person who is naturally good with few selfish inclinations often point to Kant's argument against the storekeeper who decides not to cheat customers (similar to the version of the argument you know from Chapter 6): To say you like your customers so much that you would never cheat them is not enough, because what if you stopped liking your customers? Similarly, the person who has never been tempted because susceptibility to temptation is not in her or his nature may seem a higher moral person to Foot; but perhaps it is just because that person has never come across temptation before, and in that case it is easy enough to be virtuous. True virtue, say Kant's followers, shows itself precisely in the face of temptation—and not in its absence. However, when we have the choice between a store where they have a strict policy against cheating but the personnel are cold and grumpy and the store where they've known us for years and ask us how we're doing, don't we prefer to shop at the friendly place rather than at the unfriendly, but morally correct, place? Kant may think we should choose the unfriendly place, but Foot disagrees: We prefer friendliness, not principles. But what makes being friendly morally superior to being principled, in Foot's view? Remember, Kant rejected the storekeeper's third option because someone who wouldn't cheat his or her customers because of a sunny disposition toward them is really just doing what he or she wants, out of self-gratification, not out of principles. Of course, it is possible to be of a sunny disposition *and* be principled, but that is not the issue here. The issue is whether a sunny disposition is enough to make someone a moral person or whether having a character that isn't tempted is morally superior to being a person who encounters temptation and fights it. Foot says yes: The storekeeper who wouldn't dream of cheating her customers is a better person than the one who has had a moment's temptation and rejected it, because temptation simply wasn't a factor. Foot's assumption is that it takes a weak character to be tempted. But, realistically, perhaps all that was missing was exposure and opportunity. So perhaps Kant has a point after all.

Christina Hoff Sommers

Which, then, are the virtues to which we should pay attention? Foot left the question open to an extent, because people tend to differ about what exactly is good for others and desirable as a human trait. Another ethicist, however, prefers to be more direct; her aim is not so much to defend virtue ethics as such as to focus on specific virtues and moral failings in our Western world. Christina Hoff Sommers tells of the woes an ethics professor of her acquaintance would experience at the end of a term. In spite of the multisubject textbooks they had read and the spirited discussions they had engaged in, the professor's students somehow got the impression that there are no moral truths. Everything they had studied about ethics had been presented in terms of rules that can be argued against and social dilemmas that have no clear solutions. More than half of the students cheated on their ethics finals. The irony of cheating on an ethics test probably did not even occur to those students.

What is lacking in our ethics classes? asks Sommers. It can't be good intentions on the part of instructors, because since the 1960s teachers have generally been very careful to present the material from all sides and to avoid moral indoctrination. (Even this text, as you have noticed, contains sporadic mention of the difference between doing ethics and *moralizing*.) Somehow, though, students come away with the notion that because everything can be argued against, moral values are a matter of taste. The teacher may prefer her students not to cheat, but that is simply her preference; if the student's preference is for cheating as a moral value ("Cheat but don't get caught"), then so be it. The moral lesson is learned by the student, and the chance for our society to hand down lessons of moral decency and respect for others has been lost because of a general fear of imposing one's personal values on others. See Box 10.4 for a discussion on the issue of cheating on tests.

Sommers suggests that instead of teaching courses on the big issues such as abortion, euthanasia, and capital punishment, we should talk about the little, everyday, enormously important things, such as *honesty, friendship, consideration, respect*. Those are virtues that, if not learned at a young age, may never be achieved in our society. Sommers mentions that in ethics courses of the nineteenth century, students were taught how to be good rather than how to discuss moral issues. When asked to name some moral values that can't be disputed, Sommers answered,

> It is wrong to mistreat a child, to humiliate someone, to torment an animal. To think only of yourself, to steal, to lie, to break promises. And on the positive side: it is right to be considerate and respectful of others, to be charitable and generous.

Box 10.4 THEIR CHEATING HEARTS; OR, DO PRINCIPLES MATTER?

Christina Hoff Sommers brings up the question of cheating students and sees it as a problem of students being able to connect personally with the moral theories they have studied.

In 2011 seven high school students were arrested in Long Island for cheating on their SAT scores. One student was accused of taking the tests for the others, with fake IDs, and charging up to $2,500 per test. His lawyer claimed that "Everyone knows that cheating is going on. We're not proud of it, but in some way we've all done it." Another blatant case of cheating was revealed in the spring of 2007 at Duke University, where thirty-four out of thirty-eight students in the graduate business school were disciplined for plagiarism. However, probably the most publicized case of cheating to date was not committed primarily by students, but by their parents. The 2019 college admissions bribery scandal that you read about in Chapter 4 involved thirty-odd parents paying more than $25 million to one organizer who used part of the money to bribe school officials to alter entrance exam scores, and set up entrance exam sessions where hired test takers took the exams instead of the college applicants. In that case nobody claimed that "We're all doing it," because it was a case of very wealthy parents believing themselves and their kids to be exempt from the ordinary restrictions of ordinary people—a case of "affluenza" if you will (see Chapter 4). Ironically, some of the students didn't even seem all that interested in being accepted at the colleges their parents spent fortunes on getting them into, and indeed which many will pay for with months and years of their lives in the form of prison sentences.

The college environment with its set rules of what cheating is applies Kant's ideas of ethics. These rules don't look at the consequences but instead say 'this is always wrong' even if there could be a net benefit to the students and world. If you are a college student who instead prefers Bentham's hedonistic calculus you might conclude that cheating in some situations is actually the 'right' thing to do." But in that case one shouldn't forget that Bentham would take into account *all* the possible consequences, including the pain of likely penalties, and would probably have concluded that, overall, cheating schemes aren't worth it.

In your view, is it wrong to cheat on a test? Is this a black-and-white issue, or are there shades of gray? After having studied a number of moral theories in this book, do you find that one or more theories can clarify such a question for you, or do you regard it as a matter for one's moral instinct to decide? Your answer may go to the heart of the current debate in value theory: Do our moral principles actually matter at all when we make decisions, or are we guided more by other factors, such as personal needs or feelings?

Christina Hoff Sommers

Christina Hoff Sommers (b. 1950), American philosopher, coeditor of *Vice and Virtue in Everyday Life* (1985), and author of *Who Stole Feminism?* (1994), *The War Against Boys* (2000), and *Freedom Feminism: Its Surprising History and Why It Matters Today* (2013) argues for a return to virtue ethics in order for people in modern society to regain a sense of responsibility rather than leave it to social institutions to make decisions on moral issues.

For Sommers, it is not enough to investigate virtue ethics—one must practice it and teach it to others. In that way virtue *theory* becomes virtue *practice*. If we study virtue theory in school, chances are we will find it natural to seek to develop our own virtues. Sommers believes a good way to learn about virtues is to use the same method that both Bernard Mayo and philosopher Alasdair MacIntyre (see Box 10.5) advise: to read stories in which someone does something decent for others, either humans or animals. Through stories we "get the picture" better than we get it from philosophical dilemmas or case studies. Literary classics can tell us more about friendship and obligation than a textbook in moral problems can. For Sommers, there are basic human virtues that aren't a matter of historical relativism, fads, or discussion, and the better we all learn them, the better we'll like living in our world with one another. Those virtues are part of most people's moral heritage, and there is nothing oppressive about teaching the common virtues of decency, civility, honesty, and fairness.

Too often we tend to think that certain issues are someone else's problem; the state will take care of it, whether it is pollution, homelessness, or the loneliness of elderly people. For Sommers this is part of a virtue ethics for grown-ups: *Don't assume that it is someone else's responsibility.* Don't hide from contemporary problems—take them on and contribute to their solution. Do your part to limit pollution. Think of how you can help homeless people. Go visit someone you know who is elderly and lonely. Virtues like those will benefit us all and are the kind we must learn to focus on if we are to make a success out of being humans living together.

Box 10.5 MacINTYRE AND THE VIRTUES

The Scottish philosopher Alasdair MacIntyre believes that our moral values would be enriched if we followed the examples of older cultures and let *tradition* be part of those values. We don't exist in a cultural vacuum, he says, and we would understand ourselves better if we'd allow a historical perspective to be part of our system of values. That doesn't mean that everything our ancestors did and thought should become a virtue for us, but a look back to the values of those who came before us adds a depth to our modern life that makes it easier to understand ourselves. And how do we understand ourselves best? As the *tellers of stories* of history, of fiction, and of our own lives. We understand ourselves in terms of the story we would tell of our own life, and by doing that we are defining our *character*. So virtue and character development are essential to being a moral person and doing what is morally good. But virtues are not static abilities for MacIntyre any more than they are for Philippa Foot. Virtues are linked with our aspirations; they make us better at *becoming* what we want to be. It is not so much that we have a vision of the good life; rather, we have an idea of what we want to accomplish (what MacIntyre calls "internal goods"), and virtues help us accomplish those goals. Whatever our goal, we usually will be more successful at reaching it if we are conscientious and trustworthy in striving for it. Whatever profession we try to excel in, we will succeed more easily if we try to be courageous and honest and maintain our integrity. With all the demands we face and all the different roles we have to play—in our jobs, sexual relationships, relations to family and friends—staying loyal and trustworthy helps us to function as one whole person rather than as a compilation of disjointed roles.

This vision of personal virtues is probably the most direct call to a resurgence of moral values that has been produced so far within the field of philosophy. Sommers, however, is arguing not for a revival of religious values but for a strengthening of basic concepts of personal responsibility and respect for other beings. Her claim is that few ethicists dare to stand by values and pronounce them good in themselves these days for fear of being accused of indoctrinating their students. For Sommers the list of values cited above is absolute: They can't be disputed. Herein lies one answer to why Sommers today remains one of the most controversial of American contemporary philosophers (another answer can be found in Chapter 12: her approach to feminism): In the intellectual climate of the 1990s, it was considered not only customary but even proper to view values as something more or less relative to one's culture and to one's personal life experience; we've explored the issue in Chapter 3. For Sommers, however, the end result has not been what was presumably intended—an enhanced individual moral responsibility—but, rather, the opposite: no sense of responsibility at all, since morals are perceived to be relative. So Sommers digs deeper into who we are as humans and finds a common ground of values.

Harley Schwadron/www.cartoonstock.com

The 2019 college admissions cheating scandal brought several topics into focus, such as the pressures for today's students to gain admission to top universities, the underlying assumption by some parents that all it takes is bribing the right people, and the entire issue of cheating as a way to gain an advantage. You may want to discuss the significance of this cartoon by Harley Schwadron.

But is she right? Can we just pronounce the virtues of decency, civility, honesty, and so forth the ultimate values without any further discussion? Perhaps Sommers is right that most people would agree her values are good, and perhaps not. For many, what Sommers is doing is just old-fashioned moralizing (and some applaud that effort, but others don't). In effect, this isn't just Sommers's problem—it is a problem inherent in all genuine virtue ethics, as you'll remember from the previous chapter: When there is a dispute about virtues, among virtuous people, who gets to be right? How do we determine exactly what virtue is, if virtue is its own answer? How can college students be convinced that cheating is a bad thing? How can teens be convinced that downloading copyrighted material from the Internet is wrong? It can't be done by simply teaching them that honesty is a virtue; that might work for young children, but adolescents and adults need *reasons*. Reasons and reasoning are the key here. What we need is to add **rational argumentation** to virtue ethics: give good reasons why something is a virtue, and a value. The stand-off between Sommers and many of her colleagues might, in this respect, be deflected by seeking an answer in what we've called *soft universalism* and in an approach you're familiar with from elsewhere in this book: looking for the common ground, plus finding good reasons why something is, or should be, a virtue. We return to soft universalism in Chapter 11.

The Quest for Authenticity: Kierkegaard, Nietzsche, Heidegger, Sartre, and Levinas

Within what is called "contemporary continental philosophy"—by and large European philosophy after World War I—one school of thought holds there is only one way to live properly and only one virtue to strive for: that of *authenticity.* That school of thought is *existentialism.* Although existentialism developed primarily at the hands of Jean-Paul Sartre as a response to the experience of meaninglessness in World War II, it has its roots in the writings of the Danish philosopher Søren Aabye Kierkegaard and the German philosopher Friedrich Nietzsche. In this section we take a look at Kierkegaard, Nietzsche, Heidegger, and Sartre. In addition we will look at a philosopher, who in more recent years has emerged as a forceful voice for ethics as fundamental to human existence: Emmanuel Levinas. Whereas Kierkegaard's form of authenticity is ultimately conceived as a relationship between *oneself and God,* Nietzsche's authenticity focuses on the exact opposite, the self's ability to create a *meaning in a world without a god.* Heidegger's authenticity deals with one's relationship to *one's own form of existence,* and Sartre's authenticity deals with *one's relationship to oneself as a person making moral choices,* Levinas focuses on the relationship between *oneself and the Other*—our fellow human beings.

Kierkegaard's Religious Authenticity

During his relatively short lifetime (1813–1855), Kierkegaard was known locally, in Copenhagen, as a man of leisure who had a theology degree and spent his time writing convoluted and irritating attacks on the Danish establishment, including officials of the Lutheran church. Few people understood his points because he was rarely straight-forward in his writings and hid his true opinions under layers of pseudonyms and irony. The idea that there might be a great mind at work, developing what was to become one of the most important lines of thought in the twentieth century, was obvious to no one at the time, in Denmark or elsewhere. As a matter of fact, Kierkegaard was working against the general spirit of the times, which was focused politically on the development of socialism and scientifically on the ramifications of Darwinism. People weren't ready to listen to ideas such as the value of personal commitment, the psychological dread that accompanies the prospect of total human freedom of the will, the subjectivity of truth, and the value of the individual. As it happened, though, such ideas were to become key issues for French and German existential philosophers a couple of generations after Kierkegaard's death.

There are two major, very different ways of approaching the strange writings of Søren Kierkegaard. You can dismiss him as a man who had a difficult childhood and as a consequence developed an overinflated ego with no sense of proportion as to the importance of events. In other words, you can view his writings as simply the product of an overheated brain that pondered the "great mystery" of Søren Kierkegaard's life and times. Or you can view his writings as words that speak to all humanity from a uniquely insightful point of view, which just happens to have its roots in events in Kierkegaard's own life. Among current scholars this second approach has become the prevailing one.

What was so eventful about Kierkegaard's life? Nothing much, compared with the lives of other famous people; but, contrary to most people, Kierkegaard analyzed everything that happened to him for all it was worth and with an eerie insight. He was born into a family of devout Lutherans (Lutheranism is the state religion in Denmark and has been since the Protestant Reformation) and was the youngest boy born to comparatively old parents. Several of his older siblings died young, and for some reason both Søren and his father believed that Søren would not live long either. His father's opinion had an extreme influence on the boy—an influence that Kierkegaard later analyzed to perfection, years before Freud described conflict and bonding between fathers and sons.

When his father was a young shepherd in rural Denmark, he was overcome by hunger and cold one bleak day on the moors, and he stood up on a rock and cursed God for letting a child suffer like that. Shortly after that incident his parents sent him to Copenhagen as an apprentice, and his hard life was over. That was a psychological shock to him, because he had expected punishment from God for cursing him, and he waited for the punishment most of his life. He grew rich while others lost their money, and for that reason he expected God to punish him even more severely. The first tragic thing that happened to him was that he lost his young wife; however, two months later he married their maid, who was already pregnant at the time.

Bettmann/Getty Images

Søren Kierkegaard (1813–1855), Danish philosopher, writer, and theologian, believed that there are three major stages in human spiritual development: the aesthetic stage, the ethical stage, and the religious stage. Not everyone goes through all stages, but true selfhood and personal authenticity can't happen until one has put one's complete faith in God.

Sidney Harris/ScienceCartoonsPlus.com

Kierkegaard is notoriously difficult to understand, whether it is in translation or in his native Danish. He was fond of hiding his personal views under layers of pseudonyms and irony, and many of his ideas are difficult to grasp. This cartoon shows the deep appreciation a philosophy professor may feel when his or her students actually show that they understand Kierkegaard's thoughts!

When Søren's older siblings died, his father thought that God's punishment had struck again, but otherwise his luck held while his guilt grew. It is possible that he then got the idea of letting his youngest son somehow make amends for him—take on the burden and strive for a reconciliation with God. In the Lutheran tradition there is no such thing as making a confession to your minister to "get things off your chest"—you alone must face your responsibility and handle your relationship with God. That means that you have direct access to God at any time, in your heart; you have a direct relationship with God. Your faith is a personal matter, and for Kierkegaard in particular the concept of faith was to become extremely personal.

Søren turned out to be an extraordinarily bright child, and his father devoted much time to his education, in particular to the development of his imagination. The two made a habit of taking walks—in their living room. Søren would choose where they were going—to the beach, to the castle in the woods, down Main Street—and his father would then describe in minute detail what they "saw." It was intellectually and emotionally exhausting for the boy, and scholars have ridiculed the father for his fancy, but today it is recognized by many that the combination of imagination and intellectual discipline is just about the best trait a parent can develop in a child, although one might say that this was a rather extreme way of going about it. At the end of this chapter you can read an excerpt from Kierkegaard's *Johannes Climacus* in which he describes his father's vivid imagination.

Kierkegaard was a young adult when his father died, and he understood full well the immense influence his father had had on him. He wrote the following in *Stages on Life's Way* (1845), though he didn't let on that he was writing about himself:

> There was once a father and a son. A son is like a mirror in which the father beholds himself, and for the son the father too is like a mirror in which he beholds himself in the time to come. . . . the father believed he was to blame for the son's melancholy, and the son believed that he was the occasion of the father's sorrow—but they never exchanged a word on this subject.

> Then the father died, and the son saw much, experienced much, and was tried in manifold temptations; but infinitely inventive as love is, longing and the sense of loss taught him, not indeed to wrest from the silence of eternity a communication, but to imitate the father's voice so perfectly that he was content with the likeness . . . for the father was the only one who had understood him, and yet he did not know in fact whether he had understood him; and the father was the only confidant he had had, but the confidence was of such a sort that it remained the same whether the father lived or died.

So Kierkegaard *internalized* the voice of his father; as Freud would say, he made his father's voice his own *Superego.* This had the practical effect of prompting Kierkegaard finally to get his degree in theology (which his father had wanted him to do but which he hadn't really wanted himself). Kierkegaard also internalized his father's guilt and rather gloomy outlook on life. (See Box 10.6 for another event that may have been influenced by his father.) Kierkegaard believed that everyone, even a child, has an intimate knowledge of what anguish feels like; he believed that you feel dread or anguish when you look to the future—you dread it because you realize you must make choices. This feeling, which has become known by the Danish/German word *angst* is comparable, Kierkegaard says, to realizing that you're far out on the ocean and you have to swim or sink, act or die, and there is no way out. The choice is yours, but it is a hard choice, because living is a hard job. Suppose you refuse to make your own decisions and say, "Society will help me," or "The church will help me," or "My uncle will help me"? Then you have given up your chance to become a real person, to become *authentic,* because you don't accomplish anything spiritual unless you accomplish it yourself, by making the experience your own. Each person is an individual, but only through a process of individuation—choosing to make one's own decisions and take responsibility for them in the eyes of God—can a person achieve selfhood and become a true human individual. The truth you experience when you have reached that point is *your truth alone,* because only you took that particular path in life. Other people can't take a shortcut by borrowing "your truth" they must find the way themselves. We can't, then, gain any deep insights about life from books or from teachers. They can point us in the right direction, but they can't spoon-feed us any truths. In the Primary Readings you'll find a short excerpt from *Either/Or* in which Kierkegaard describes the nature of making hard choices.

Box 10.6 A KIND OF LOVE AND A MARRIAGE THAT WASN'T: REGINE OLSEN

Historic Images/Alamy Stock Photo

Regine Olsen, Søren Kierkegaard's fiancée, a gentle Copenhagen woman who did her best to understand the intellectual scruples of her boyfriend, who could not reconcile his devotion to God with the idea of physical attraction to a woman and a subsequent bourgeois marriage. This photo was taken a few years after Kierkegaard finally broke up with her. (Photo of Regine Schlegel [*née* Olsen] courtesy of The Royal Library, Copenhagen.)

An event of great importance in Søren Kierkegaard's life occurred when he fell deeply in love for the first and only time. The woman's name was Regine Olsen, and she was the daughter of a minister. Regine and Søren became engaged, and he engaged himself in a new intellectual scrutiny: What was this feeling? Was it constant or a fluke? What might go wrong? Was it right for him to try to do something "universal" that everybody did, like get married and have children, or would it somehow interfere with his father's plans for him to be a sacrifice to God? Regine, a kind and loving woman, was utterly puzzled at Søren's reluctance to accept that they were just young people in love. When

they were together, he was in a good mood and was confident about their future together, but when he was alone, the doubts started closing in on him. It appears that he felt he was not quite worthy of her, for some reason—perhaps because in years past he had visited a brothel, or perhaps because he couldn't quite explain his father's influence on him to her. Mostly, though, it was the shock of the physical attraction he felt toward her that distracted him, he thought, from becoming truly spiritual. During this period he began to understand one aspect of the Don Juan character: He realized that he loved Regine the most *when he was not with her* but was fantasizing about her. Once they were together his ardor cooled considerably. Eventually he decided that it was better for both of them if they broke up, but because nineteenth-century mores demanded that the woman, not the man, break off the engagement if her character were to remain stainless, he had to try to force Regine to break the engagement. This he did by being as nasty to her as he could, even though he still loved her. He embarked on a program he himself had devised, alternating between playing the fool and the cynic; once when she asked him if he never intended to marry, he answered as nastily as he could, "Yes, in ten years when I've sown all my wild oats; then I'll need a young girl to rejuvenate me." For a long time he persisted in being rude to her, and she continued to forgive him, because she was very much in love with him. In the end he himself broke up with her, however, and she appears to have talked about killing herself. Kierkegaard wanted her to despise him, and a short time later she actually became engaged to a friend of theirs and married him. After that, Kierkegaard never tired of talking about woman's fickle, stupid, and untrustworthy nature. But here we must remember that Kierkegaard had multiple author-personalities, and beneath the scorn lurked his love, which apparently never died: He approached Regine with the suggestion that they resume their friendship, but her husband wouldn't allow it. After Kierkegaard died, it was revealed in his will that he had left everything he owned to Regine, but she refused to accept the inheritance.

This attitude is reflected in Kierkegaard's cryptic and disturbing assertion that *truth is subjective,* an idea that has been vehemently disputed by scientists and philosophers alike. Some philosophers believe Kierkegaard meant there is no objective knowledge at all; we can never verify statements such as "2 + 2 = 4," "The moon circles the earth," and "It rained in Boston on April 6, 2020," because all such statements are, presumably, just a matter of subjective opinion, or what we call *cognitive relativism.* That would mean that we could never set any objective standard for knowledge. Although other philosophers, such as Friedrich Nietzsche, have actually worked toward such a radical viewpoint, Kierkegaard is not among them. He never says that *knowledge* is subjective, and to understand what he means we have to look more closely at what he says. His actual words are *"Subjectivity is Truth,"* and Kierkegaard scholars believe that to mean the following: There is no such thing as "Truth" with a capital *T* that we can just scoop up and call our own. The "meaning of life" is not something we can look up in a book or learn from anybody else, because *it just isn't there unless we find it ourselves.* There is no *objective* truth about life, only a *personal* truth, which will be a little bit different for each individual. It will not be vastly different, though, because when we reach the level at which we are truly personal, we will find that it corresponds to other people's experiences of individuation too. In other words, the personal experience becomes a *universal* one—but only if you have gone through it yourself. This is the ultimate meaning of life and the ultimate virtue: to become an authentic human being by finding your own meaning. If you settle for accepting other people's view of life, you are no better than the evil magician Noureddin (or Jaffar, in the Disney movie version) in the story of Aladdin; he has no personal magic or talent himself, so he tries to steal it from the one who has, Aladdin.

For Kierkegaard himself, truth is a religious truth: One must take on the concept of sin and responsibility and seek God's forgiveness directly, as an individual. But that is hard for most people to do because we are born with quite another character. Typically humans are born into the *aesthetic stage:* the stage of sensuous enjoyment. Children obviously have a very strong interest in the joys of their senses, but if that persists into adulthood it can result in unhealthy character development, symbolized by the Don Juan type who loves to pursue the girl but loses interest once he has seduced her. She wants to get married, and he wants *out.* He leaves, only to fall in love with and pursue some other girl, and on it goes. Today we would say this is a person who *can't commit.* Kierkegaard makes the same basic observation but explains that this happens because the Don Juan type is steeped in sensuous enjoyment, which sours on itself: Too much of the same is not a good thing, but a person who is stuck in the aesthetic stage doesn't have any sense of what is morally right or wrong. Such knowledge usually comes as people mature and enter the *ethical stage* (although some people are stuck in the aesthetic stage forever).

In the ethical stage people realize that there are laws and conventions, and they believe that the way to become a good person is to follow those conventions. A fictional character from nineteenth-century middle-class Copenhagen becomes Kierkegaard's prototype for the ethical stage: Judge William, the righteous man who tries to be a good judge and a good husband and father. Scholars don't quite agree on how to evaluate this good and kind man, because the fact is that we are rarely certain when Kierkegaard is being serious and when he is being sarcastic. Kierkegaard also cites Socrates (whom he greatly admired) as an example of an ethical person. Although Socrates is commonly recognized as a truly courageous and virtuous man who strove to live (and die) the right way, Judge William doesn't come across as a heroic person; we even get the impression that he is actually a pompous, self-righteous, bourgeois bore who has his attention fixed on "doing the right thing" merely because society expects it of him. So it seems Kierkegaard wants to tell us that it isn't enough to follow the rules and become what everyone else thinks you ought to be; that way you exist only in the judgment of others. You have to take on responsibility for judging yourself, and the way you do that is by making a *leap of faith* into the *religious stage*. It isn't enough to judge your own life in terms of what makes sense according to society's rules and rational concepts of morality; what you must do to become an authentic person is leave the standards of society behind, including your love for reason and for things to make sense, and choose to trust in God, like Abraham, who made that same choice when he brought his son Isaac to be sacrificed, even though it didn't make sense to him (see Chapter 2). Reason and the rules of society can't tell you if the insight you reach as a religious person is the truth.

Popperfoto/Getty Images

Friedrich Nietzsche (1844–1900) is one of the most controversial philosophers in modern times. Frequently writing in aphorisms, he piles scorn on practically every cherished figure and thought in the Western tradition, and an entire post–World War II generation has assumed that his thoughts inspired Hitler's Nazi regime of terror. However, in recent years another image has emerged: that of a passionate thinker who wanted his readers to tear themselves free of what he thought were the shackles of Christian as well as utilitarian thinking and strive for individual greatness.

So why is Socrates not a perfect person? Why did he stay within the ethical stage and make no leap of faith to the religious stage, according to Kierkegaard? Because the leap was not available to him, since he didn't belong to the Judeo-Christian tradition, having lived four hundred years before the birth of Jesus Christ. Socrates is an example of how far you can reach if you stay within the boundaries of reason. However, in the religious stage there is no objective measure of meaning. At this stage you take responsibility for yourself, but at the same time you give up your fate and place it in the hands of God. Finally you can become a true human being, a complete individual and person, because only in the religious stage can you realize what it means to say that "Subjectivity is Truth."

Nietzsche's Authenticity Without Religion

The German philosopher Friedrich Nietzsche (1844–1900), one of the truly controversial figures in Western philosophy, is often credited with being one of the contributors to the French existentialism of the twentieth century (see below). He is an extraordinary character in Western philosophy; some would call him an *enfant terrible*, a "terrible child," roguish and unruly. In the second half of the twentieth century he was often called far worse things than that, because of an association with a part of history that to most of us stands out as the worst which the century, and humanity, could present: The Third Reich, Hitler's regime. However, Nietzsche had been dead for over thirty years when Hitler's theories became popular among the Nazis, and it is still debatable how much of a philosophical kinship there is between them, if any. We return to that question below.

Nietzsche was born in Leipzig, Germany, and several of the male members of his family were Lutheran ministers. His father was a minister, too, but he died when Nietzsche was young, and the boy and his sister were raised by their mother and other women in the family. His upbringing was of the Christian Protestant variety, in which pleasures of this life are considered sinful, and life after death is regarded as the true goal of this life; you'll recognize the influence of Plato and St. Augustine (see Chapter 8). As a young man Nietzsche studied theology for a while; he then switched to classical philosophy and philology for which he proved to have a true talent. He was made professor in Switzerland when he was just twenty-five. He served as a medic during the Franco-Prussian war of 1870, but during that time he became ill. He had presumably contracted syphilis a few years earlier, and bad health followed him for the rest of his life. He was forced to retire from his professorship, and in a sense he retired from life, too, living in seclusion with his mother who took care of him. It was during his retirement, while he was still a young man, that he wrote the works that were to shake up the Western intellectual world in the twentieth century. When he was forty-five, his mental health deteriorated dramatically, although he also seemed to have good days of some mental clarity. He lived on for another eleven years, tended by his mother and when she died, his sister Elisabeth. It has been assumed for many years that his illness was due to the effects of syphilis, but in recent years it has been more accurately determined to be CADASIL (cerebral autosomal dominant arteriopathy with subcortical infarcts and leukoencephalopathy). For those who find that there is some moral stigma attached to dementia caused by syphilis that is an important diagnostic change; however, regardless of the cause, the deterioration of a mind is always a tragedy. Now we just happen to be in a position to diagnose Nietzsche's mental health situation more correctly.

Some people have tried to dismiss Nietzsche's works as the ravings of a madman. But the fact is that Nietzsche's mind was quite healthy and vigorous when he wrote most of the works that were to become so influential after his death. (Only a few European intellectuals outside of Germany, such as the Danish thinker Georg Brandes, were aware of his philosophy during his lifetime. Brandes tried to introduce Nietzsche to Scandinavian readers, without much success.) Besides, a theory must be able to stand on its own, and if it seems to make sense, or at least make interesting observations, it can't be dismissed because of the condition of its author. Nietzsche's works have stood the test of time with eerie brilliance.

Beyond Good and Evil

What is good? What is evil? Nietzsche says that depends on your perspective: If you are a nineteenth-century person, if you belong to the Judeo-Christian tradition, or if you are otherwise inspired by Plato, you might say that a good person shuns physical pleasures, because they are sinful, and concentrates on the afterlife, because that is when true life begins. If you are what Nietzsche would call a socialist, you might say that a good person is not offensive, willful, or selfish, but subordinates his or her will to serve the community. A good person is meek, helpful, kind, and turns the other cheek. An evil person is selfish, gives orders, thinks he or she is better than others, looks to this life and disregards the afterlife, and wallows in physical pleasures. If this is your view of good and evil, says Nietzsche, then you must reevaluate your values, for their true nature is *repressive*, and that realization calls for a *transvaluation of values*. What should be the focus of such a transvaluation? The value system that was common in ancient times, before people began to value weakness: the moral value of strength, of *power*. This means that we must go beyond the common definitions of good and evil toward a new definition.

We can't look to Nietzsche's writings for a systematic account or a point-to-point criticism of the Western value system: His viewpoints are scattered around in his writings, and one must play detective to get the whole picture. Some material is in his speculative work of fiction *Thus Spoke Zarathustra*, and some in his *Genealogy of Morals*, but it is the title and topic of his book *Beyond Good and Evil* that gives us the clue to the clearest version of his cultural critique.

Master and Slave Moralities

In *Beyond Good and Evil* Nietzsche suggests that the old Christian value system of loving one's neighbor and turning the other cheek must be scrapped, because it is the morality of a weak person, a "slave" who fears his "master," the strong-willed, self-made individual. For Nietzsche, the "slave-morality" began in ancient times when slaves hated and feared their masters and resented anyone who wielded power over them. Nietzsche's concern was not the atrocities of slavery; what interested him was the attitude the slaves had toward the masters and each other, and the master's attitude toward other masters and the slaves. He saw it as his task to analyze the two moral systems that grew out of the two strictly separated and yet in some ways intertwined communities of the masters (the warlords) and the slaves (their serfs). In the mind of the feudal warlord, a good person is someone who can be trusted and who will stand by you in a blood feud. He is a strong ally, a good friend, someone who has pride in himself and who has a noble and generous character—someone who is able to arouse fear in the enemy. If the warlord wants to help the weaker ones through his own generosity, he can choose to do so, but he doesn't have to: He creates his own values. The warlord respects his enemy if he is strong—then he becomes a worthy opponent—and values honor in his friends as well as in his enemies. Those who are weak don't deserve respect, for their function is to be preyed upon (the resemblance to Darwin's concept of natural selection and survival of the fittest is no accident: Nietzsche had read, and admired, Darwin's *Origin of Species*). Someone who is not willing to stand up for himself, who is weak, and afraid of you, is a "bad person."

The slave, on the other hand, hates the master and everything he stands for. The master represents *evil*, having the strength, the will, and the power to rule; he inspires fear. *Good* is the fellow slave who helps out—the nonthreatening person, the one who shows sympathy and altruism, who acts to create general happiness for as many as possible. The slaves feel tremendous *resentment* toward the masters, and this resentment ends in revolt. Historically, says Nietzsche, the slaves eventually gained the upper hand, and deposed the masters. The "master-morality" was reversed to the status of evil, while the "slave-morality" became a common ideal. For Nietzsche a slave morality and a *herd morality* are the same phenomenon. The meek have indeed inherited the earth already—but the "herd" has retained their feelings of resentment toward the idea of a master, and everything the master stood for is still considered evil, even though there are no more masters. In Nietzsche's words from *Beyond Good and Evil*,

> The noble type of man regards himself as a determiner of values; he does not require to be approved of; he passes the judgment . . . he is a creator of values. . . . It is otherwise with the second type of morality, slave-morality. Suppose that the abused, the oppressed, the suffering, the unemancipated, the weary, and those uncertain of themselves, should moralize, what will be the common element in their moral estimate? Probably a pessimistic suspicion with regard to the entire situation of man will find expression, perhaps a condemnation of man, together with his situation.

For Nietzsche, this dichotomy (either-or) between slave and master attitude can be found in every culture, sometimes within the same individual. The situation initially developed in early European cultures as well as in the Christian tradition (described by Nietzsche as the "mass egoism of the weak"), which in Nietzsche's eyes clearly displays the herd mentality with its requirement that you must turn the other cheek and refrain from doing harm if you want to partake of "pie in the sky when you die." That mentality has also been prominent in Plato's philosophy, in the moral philosophy of utilitarianism (see Chapter 5), and in socialism, and it has had the effect of reducing everything to averages and mediocrity, because it advocates general happiness and equality at the cost of the outstanding individual. In Nietzsche's view it is the downfall of a culture to put restrictions on such gifted individuals, because it stifles and kills the capacity for individual expression. And for him, that was precisely what Germany and the rest of Europe had become in the late nineteenth century: a population of herd animals who would pick on anyone who dared to be different. The Platonic and the Christian traditions had merged into a world view, and (in Nietzsche's own day) were joined by socialism and Marxism. And even if Marxism is hostile to religion—Karl Marx called religion an "opiate of the masses"—Nietzsche sees a common denominator in Marxism and Christianity, a catering to the meek for the sake of meekness, and a disrespect for life itself.

The Overman   For Nietzsche the slave-morality *says nay to life*; it looks toward a higher reality (Heaven) in the same way that Western philosophy inspired by Plato has looked toward a world of ideas far removed from the tangible mess of sensory experience. This *Hinterwelt* (world beyond) is for Nietzsche a dangerous illusion, because it gives people the notion that there is something besides this life, and thus they squander their life here on earth in order to realize their shadowy dreams of a world to come, or a higher reality. This, for Nietzsche, is to live wrongly, and inauthentically. But there is, to Nietzsche, a value that stands higher than all others, and that is the attitude that *affirms life*: An *authentic existence* consists of realizing that there is nothing beyond this life, and that one must pursue life with vigor, like a "master" who sets his own value. If one realizes this, and has the courage to discard the traditional values of Christianity, one has become an Overman (*Übermensch*), or "Superman." The Overman is the human of the future—not in the sense of a biological evolution, because not everyone in the future will be Overmen, far from it. The Overman is not the result of an automatic, natural selection, but an aggressive seizing of power. For Nietzsche there is one overriding feature of human life: not reason, nor empathy, but *will to power*. The slave-morality will do its best to control or kill this urge, but the man who is capable of being a creator of values will recognize it as his birthright, and will use it any way he sees fit. His right lies in his capacity to use the power, because that power is in itself the force of life. In effect, the right of the Overman is in Nietzsche's philosophy a right created by might, a practical description more than any political statement: You have the right if you can hold on to it and use it. (The gender-specific use of *man* instead of *human* or *person* is intentional here; Nietzsche—at least judging from his writings—mistrusted women and female capabilities, and did not count women among his future Overmen.)

How did readers react to this provocative theory? Aside from the fact that Nietzsche had very few readers in his lifetime, some found it to be an intellectual rekindling of the joy of life, even in the face of hard times, and a critical evaluation of the double standard that existed in Western culture in the past: the condemnation of physical pleasures, combined with tacit acceptance of those pleasures when experienced on the sly. The Victorian Era (see Chapter 5) was particularly steeped in this type of hypocrisy, and many consider this reaction against hypocrisy a *positive* legacy of Nietzsche.

But even so, there is no denying that Nietzsche's most apparent legacy was until recently considered extremely *negative*, because his idea of the Overman was adopted by Hitler's Third Reich as the ideal of the new German Nazi culture. Picking up on Nietzsche's idea that power belongs by right to he who is capable of grabbing and holding on to it (an idea that was taken out of context), the Nazis saw themselves as a new race of Overmen, destined to rule the world. The weak would have no rights, and their sole purpose in life would be to provide fuel for the power of their masters. Here Hitler completely overlooked the fact that Nietzsche's Overmen could only arise as individuals, not as a "race" or even a class of people.

Would Nietzsche have approved of Hitler? Absolutely not. Nietzsche would have seen in Hitler something he despised: a man driven by the herd mentality's resentment against others in power. Nietzsche's writings may be full of acerbic remarks about the English, about Christians, and about Platonists, but he didn't spare the German people, either. He had little respect for his own Germanic legacy, which is why he moved to Switzerland. Furthermore, he was a sworn enemy of totalitarianism, because he viewed it as just another way to enslave capable people and prevent them from using their own willpower. In addition, Nietzsche had no patience or sympathy for anti-Semitism, and had a profound dislike for his brother-in-law, a known anti-Semite (see Box 10.7). The fact remains, however, that Nietzsche's writings include elements that seem to lead to the abuse, or at least the neglect, of the weak by the strong. Because of Hitler's use of his writings, Nietzsche was a closed subject in philosophy for almost thirty years after World War II—he was too controversial to touch. Today we can view his ideas with more detachment, but it is still difficult to reconcile his enthusiasm for life with the disdain for the weaker human beings—a disturbing mixture of free thought and contempt. But how did it happen that Nietzsche's ideas became the house philosophy of Hitler and his associates? In Box 10.7 you can read the astonishing story of the role his sister Elisabeth played.

Box 10.7 ELISABETH NIETZSCHE—HER BROTHER'S KEEPER?

Elisabeth Nietzsche's role in her brother's life has long been recognized as an extremely powerful one, and toward the end of his life rather peculiar: She used to invite scholars to "view" her brother who was by then unable to communicate coherently. However, her influence on him and in particular his philosophical legacy has been far deeper than previously suspected. As children Friedrich and Elisabeth were close, but for a number of years they were not on the best of terms. Elisabeth married a man whom Friedrich despised, Bernard Förster. Förster was a well-known racist agitator, espousing violently anti-Semitic views. He was fired from his position as a teacher because of his racist politics, and soon afterwards he started recruiting Germans of "pure blood" for an emigration plan. He viewed Germany as having betrayed its citizens of Germanic descent by allowing people of "non-Aryan descent" to flourish. (The concept of an "Aryan race" is a misunderstanding, perpetrated by Förster and others, then by Hitler, and eventually by today's Neo-Nazis. "Aryan" refers to a group of languages, not a race.) Elisabeth Nietzsche Förster agreed with her husband on his anti-Semitic views, and helped him distribute racist pamphlets. When Förster heard about land being available in a faraway country, Paraguay, he bought the property unseen and set about to create a "new Germany, *Nueva Germania*, where only pure "Aryans" were allowed. In 1886 Elisabeth traveled with her husband to Paraguay with a small group of hopeful colonists: fourteen families, and their life savings. The land Förster had purchased turned out to be a remote swamp, and three years into the social experiment of restarting the "Aryan" race the colony was falling apart: Elisabeth and Förster had mismanaged the colonists' money, and Förster committed suicide. Elisabeth got word that her brother was ill in Germany and needed her help, so she abandoned the colonists to their own devices and traveled home to Germany.

While the colony was struggling to survive, Elisabeth was back in Germany tending to her brother. During his final years she proclaimed herself curator of his works, and after his death she took on the task of editing his unpublished works. It now appears that her editing was quite "creative": The Nietzsche Archives in Weimar, Germany, has her original inserts of her own writing into her brother's works, with simple cut-and-paste methods. She passed it off as her brother's, giving it an edge of bigotry that would have made Förster proud. Toward the end of her life, in the early years of German Nazism, she managed to get the attention of Adolf Hitler and other prominent Nazis. She inspired them to use Nietzsche's philosophy (with her own edits) as a blueprint for Nazi ideology. Thus, the connection was forged between Nietzsche and the anti-Semitic, totalitarian views of the Nazi regime. Hitler regarded her very highly, and when she died, he gave her the funeral of a "mother of the fatherland." Because of the presumed connection between Nietzsche's philosophy and Hitler, it wasn't until the 1980s that philosophers felt comfortable researching Nietzsche's philosophy and writing about him, mainly thanks to the German-American philosopher Walter Kaufmann. During this research it became clear that much of the supposed pre-Nazi leanings of Nietzsche were in fact infused into his works by his sister. This doesn't mean that Nietzsche was beyond bigotry, or that everything that Hitler used from his writings was invented by Elisabeth; Nietzsche had strong feelings against many thinkers, individuals, and population groups, and he did advocate the theory of the Overman, but Nazism would have been entirely unacceptable in his philosophy of the strong individual.

But what about the colony in Paraguay? *Forgotten Fatherland*, a book published by reporter Ben MacIntyre in 1992, sheds light on the fate of the colonists: Abandoned and forgotten by the world, they struggled to stay alive and racially pure in the Peruvian jungle. Over the decades and into the twentieth century, it persisted with dwindling, new generations of pure "Aryan" blood, because the colonists had transferred their racial hatred from Jews to the local Paraguayan Indians, and intermarriage was not an option for them. The result: massive genetic inbreeding. MacIntyre set out to find the colony in the late 1980s, and found a small German village frozen in time, with inhabitants so plagued by genetic diseases and mental problems that a healthy child was a rarity. However, this is not the end of the story of the Förster colony: A newspaper article reported in 1998 that the colonist descendants had begun to merge with and marry into the local Indian tribes, and speak their language. With a larger gene pool, the inbreeding problem vanished; social ties expanded, and so did commerce. The small village is still there, integrated in the Paraguayan social world, except that families still have German surnames. A road sign is the only memory of Elisabeth Nietzsche, and it is spelled "Elizabeth Niegtz Chen."

The Eternal Return, and the Authentic Life

One of Nietzsche's most infamous/famous statements is that "God is dead"; by that Nietzsche did not mean that Christ had died, or that there is no God *per se*, but that faith in God was waning if not gone altogether, and as a result the guarantees of stable, universal values provided by a faith in God had disappeared. For Nietzsche, *there are no absolute values in the absence of God*; there are no values except those we as humans decide on. Box 10.8 explores the question whether everything is permitted if there is no God. For many people that would mean that morality has lost its sanction, so they lose faith in everything and become *nihilists*. The word *nihilism* is often mentioned in connection with Nietzsche. As you know from Chapter 3, it comes from the Latin word *nihil* (nothing), and usually means that there is no foundation for believing in anything, and that existence is senseless and absurd. On occasion Nietzsche himself has been called a nihilist by critics, but is that correct?

There seem to be two differing views of what Nietzsche really meant by the concept: (1) If God is dead, then everything is permitted, and you soon despair because there are no absolute values, so you become a nihilist, or (2) even if you realize that there are no objective values or truth because there is no God, you must make your own values. By doing so you affirm life and your own strength as a human being, so you are *not* a nihilist. Most contemporary Nietzsche scholars believe that is what he means, not that there is nothing to believe in. For Nietzsche a nihilist is someone who has misunderstood the message that God is dead, and has joined the *nay-sayers*. Above all, as you read above, Nietzsche himself believed in something: In the value of life, and of affirming life, saying *yea to life*.

Box 10.8 WITHOUT GOD, IS EVERYTHING PERMITTED?

An intriguing precursor to Nietzsche's theory of the Overman, and the idea that without God there are no absolute values, was published in 1866 and translated into German: Dostoyevsky's *Crime and Punishment*. However, there is no record of Nietzsche having owned a copy of the book or having referred to it. (Nietzsche's own books, *Beyond Good and Evil* and the *Genealogy of Morals,* were published in 1886 and 1887.) This story of moral and amoral behavior follows the young bright student Raskolnikov in St. Petersburg of the nineteenth century, moving inexorably from philosophical thoughts of the brilliant mind being elevated above the morals of the masses to deciding that he himself, a brilliant mind, is not bound by the morals of society—after which he proceeds to commit murder. In addition, what makes the story of Raskolnikov an interesting comparison is a scene in the book where the young man weeps when he witnesses an old horse being whipped to death; compare that to one of the last lucid days of Nietzsche's life where he came upon a horse being whipped (sadly, a common occurrence in those days), ran up to the horse, and threw his arms around the animal's neck in an apparent attempt to protect it, after which he fainted, and from then on the neurological illness ran its course. Coincidence? Until researchers tell us otherwise, we can only guess.

In effect, Raskolnikov is a harbinger of Nietzsche's Overman: He sees himself as having spe-cial permission to go beyond good and evil, until the magnitude of what he has done brings him back to an appreciation of the common moral law. In a peculiar parallel from the late twentieth century, the serial killer Jeffrey Dahmer was interviewed at length after his conviction, while he was serving a life sentence, before being murdered by an inmate. Dahmer spoke from a state of—presumably—deep contrition, explaining that he had gotten the impression from his teachers that there is no God, so everything is permitted, and he need not heed the common moral (or even criminal) laws, because he would not be held accountable in an afterlife. So he proceeded to do what he wanted: murder young men, and dismember them. Later, after he was caught, he returned to a religious point of view and felt remorse.

The philosopher in the second half of the twentieth century who has been the most influenced by Nietzsche is probably Jean-Paul Sartre, whose existentialism is inspired by Nietzsche's view that there is no God, so there are no absolute God-given moral standards, and we have to rise to the occasion and create our own standards. Sartre's standards are envisioned as a guideline for everyone, though, and not for an elite of Overmen. We look at Sartre later in this chapter.

How did Nietzsche propose to say yes to life? It is easy enough to "love one's fate" when things are going well. Anyone can say yes to life when you're having a good time. The difficulty is to say yes to life when it is at its worst behavior. Nietzsche wants us to love life even at its worst. And what is the worst that Nietzsche can imagine? That everything that has happened to you will happen again, and again, the very same way. This is the theory of *the eternal return of the same*. There is an anecdote of Nietzsche taking a walk one day and being struck by the awful truth: History repeats itself, and all our fears and joys will be repeated. We have experienced them before, and we will experience them again, endlessly. The idea horrified him, and he was forced to consider the question, Even if you know that you will have to go through the same tedious, painful stuff over and over again, would you choose to, willingly?

Bettmann/Getty Images

Martin Heidegger (1889–1976), German philosopher and poet and a member of the National Socialist (Nazi) Party, believed authentic life is a life open to the possibility of different meanings. The feeling of *angst* can help jolt us out of our complacency and help us see the world from an intellectually flexible point of view.

As with the theory of nihilism, there are two interpretations to this problem: (1) One holds that Nietzsche actually believed that everything repeats itself. We're doomed to live the same life over and over again, life is absurd, and our existence is pointless. This is the interpretation that also holds that Nietzsche was himself a nihilist. And, to be sure, such theories surface from time to time. A Hindu philosophy claims that the universe repeats itself endlessly down to the smallest detail, and some astrophysicists believe that the universe will end in a Big Crunch, after which we will have another Big Bang, and so forth. (2) The other interpretation, favored by today's Nietzsche experts, is that Nietzsche had come up with the ultimate test of a person's authenticity and life-affirmation: *What if* everything repeats itself endlessly? In that case, could you say that you would want to live life over again? If you can answer, "Let's have it one more time!" then you truly love life, and you have passed the test.

Which interpretation is correct? Is the "eternal return" real, or is it a *thought experiment* so Nietzsche can make a moral point? Either way, the idea of the eternal return serves as a good test for our love of life. To be sure, Nietzsche's own life wasn't exactly the kind of life one might want repeated: endless illnesses, endless quarrels with people who didn't see things the way Nietzsche saw them, falling out with friends, experiencing war, having to give up his job, getting little public recognition or understanding for his writings, being turned down by publisher after publisher, having no personal life to speak of, living with disturbing thoughts and anxieties the further he got into his mental illness, and finally sinking into a mental darkness that we can barely imagine. And yet he himself believed he passed the test of the eternal return, and became a yea-sayer.

How would you do on Nietzsche's test? The same exams, the same driving tests, the same falling in and out of love, being stood up, having wisdom teeth pulled, being sick, submitting tax returns, losing loved ones, etc., . . . the same vacations, the same marriages and children, the same hopes and fears—would you do it over again, the bad with the good? If yes, Nietzsche congratulates you. You have won the battle against doubt, weakness, lukewarm existence, and nihilism, and you will experience the ultimate joy of life in the face of meaninglessness.

Heidegger's Intellectual Authenticity

Martin Heidegger is an enigmatic and controversial philosopher. He is enigmatic because he aims to make people break through the old boundaries of thinking by inventing new words and categories for them to think with. That means there is no easy way to read Heidegger; you must acquaint yourself with an entirely new vocabulary of key concepts and get used to a new way of looking at reality. In spite of his rather inaccessible style, though, Heidegger has become something of a cult figure in modern European philosophy. He is controversial because he was a member of the Nazi Party during World War II (see Box 10.9).

Box 10.9 HEIDEGGER AND THE NAZI CONNECTION

While we can determine that any connection between Nietzsche and Hitler's regime was established outside of his control and after his death, by his sister, such is not the case for Heidegger. At the time of Hitler's takeover of Germany in 1933, Martin Heidegger's philosophy professor, Edmund Husserl, was head of the philosophy department at the University of Freiburg. Husserl was already a famous philosopher, having developed the theory of *phenomenology,* a philosophical theory of human experience. Its main thesis is that there is no such thing as a consciousness that is empty at first and then proceeds to order and analyze the objects of sense experience; instead, our mind is already engaged in the process of experiencing the world from day one. We can't separate the concepts of the experiencing mind and the experience of the mind, and, because it is impossible for philosophy to say anything about a nonexperiencing mind and the unexperienced object-world, phenomenology sees its primary task as describing, as clearly as possible, the phenomenon of experience itself. Husserl had been the essential inspiration for many of Heidegger's writings; in fact, he had taken Heidegger under his wing when Heidegger was a young

scholar. Husserl was Jewish, though, which meant that he was targeted for persecution by the new Nazi leaders. He was fired from his university position and eventually died as a result of Nazi harassment. Heidegger, his former student and protégé, profited from those events by taking over Husserl's position as department chair; indeed, it seems that he never raised any protest against the treatment of his old professor. At that time Heidegger joined the Nazi Party for, as he explained later, purely professional reasons: He couldn't have kept his university position without becoming a party member. That appears to be stretching the truth, for Heidegger never did anything at all to distance himself from the Nazi ideology during the war years. Today people are divided in their views on Heidegger; some feel that because of his Nazi association, his philosophy is tainted and must somehow contain elements of Nazi thinking. Others believe that Heidegger was essentially apolitical, although he was not very graceful about it; they think his philosophy should be viewed independent of his personal life.

Heidegger sees human beings as not essentially distinct from the world they inhabit, in the same sense that traditional epistemology does: There is no "subject" on the inside of a person and no "object" of experience on the outside. Rather, humans are thrown into the world at birth, and they interact with it and in a sense "live" it. There is no such thing as a person who is distinct from his or her world of experience—we *are* our world of experience. This idea of interaction with the world from the beginning of life is one that Heidegger took over from his teacher and mentor Edmund Husserl, but he adds his own twist to it: What makes humans special is not that they are on the inside and the world is on the outside, but that they experience their *existence* differently than all other beings do. Humans *are there* for themselves; they are aware of their existence and of certain essential facts about that existence, such as their own mortality. So Heidegger calls humans "Being-there" (*Dasein*) rather than "humans." Things, on the other hand, don't know they exist, and to Heidegger neither do animals; an animal may know it is hungry, or in pain, or in heat, but it doesn't know its days are numbered, and that makes the difference. Our humanity consists primarily of our continuous awareness of death, our "Being-toward-death" (*Sein-zum-Tode*). On occasion we let ourselves get distracted, because that awareness is quite a burden on our minds, and we let ourselves forget. We become absorbed in our jobs, our feelings, the gossip we hear, the nonsense around us. According to Heidegger, we often refer to what "They" say, as if the opinion of those anonymous others has some obvious authority. We bow to what "They" say and believe we are safe from harm and responsibility if we can get absorbed by this ubiquitous "They" (*Das Man*) and don't have to think on our own. In other words, we try to take on the safe and nonthinking existence-form of things—we objectify ourselves.

That does not make an authentic life, however, and in any event it is doomed to failure because we can't forget so completely. Humans just can't become things, because we are the ones who understand the relationship between ourselves and things. When we do the dishes, we understand what plates are for, what glasses are for, and why they must be cleaned. We understand the entire "doing dishes" situation. When we prepare a presentation on our computer, we understand what a report is, what a computer is, and why the two have anything to do with ourselves, even if we may not understand what the report is for or how the computer works. In the end, humans are different because we can ask, What is it for? and understand the interconnections of the world we live in. We are asking, thinking creatures, and to regain our awareness of that fact, we must face our true nature. We may pretend to be nothing but victims of circumstances (I have to do the dishes; there is no other choice), but we also can choose to realize that we interact with our world and affect it. In *Being and Time* (1927), Heidegger calls this phenomenon (in his exasperating style) "An-already-thrown-into-the-world-kind-of-Being who is existing-in-relationship-to-existing-entities-within-that-world" (*Sich-vorweg-schon-sein-in [der-Welt] als Sein-bei [innerwelt-lich begegendem Sein-denen]*). But he also describes it, in a slightly more down-to-earth fashion, as the structure of *care.* "Being-theres" always "care" about something, Heidegger says. That doesn't mean humans care *for* others, or *for* things—it merely means we are always *engaged* in something (the state of being engaged in something Heidegger called care—*Sorge*). Sometimes this involves caring for others, but mostly it involves engaging in our own existence: We fret, we worry, we look forward to something, we're concerned, we're content, we're disappointed about something—our health, our promotion, our family's well-being, our new kittens, or the exciting experiences we anticipate on our next vacation. This "Care-Structure" means that we are always engaged in some part of our reality, unless we get caught up in another and deeper element of human nature: a *mood,* such as dread or anguish—*angst.*

Heidegger's concept of *angst* is related to Kierkegaard's: It does not involve fear of something in particular; it is, rather, the unpleasant and sometimes terrifying insecurity of not knowing where you stand in life and eventually having to make a choice—perhaps with little or no information about your options. For Kierkegaard this experience is related to a religious awakening, but for Heidegger the awakening is metaphysical: You realize that all your concerns and all the rules you live by are *relative,* in the deepest sense; you realize that you have viewed the world a certain way, within a certain frame, and now for some reason the frame is breaking up. A woman may feel angst if she loses her tenured job at a university, not just because she is worried about how she will provide for her family, but also because her worldview—her professional identity and sense of security—has been undermined. A young man may feel angst if he learns he has an incurable disease—not just because he is afraid to die, but also because "this isn't supposed to happen" to a young person. Children may feel angst if they are drawn into a divorce battle between their parents. A hitherto religious person may feel angst if he or she begins to doubt the existence of God, because that is the breakup of the ultimate framework. And humans may feel angst when they realize that their worldview is somehow not a God-given truth.

People whose attitude toward the world is *inauthentic* may experience the most fundamental form of angst. Heidegger himself states that if a Being-there is open to the possibility of different meanings in his or her reality, then he or she is living an authentic life. If, however, a Being-there does not want to accept the possibility that something may have a different meaning than he or she has believed up until now, then he or she is inauthentic. A typical trait of those who are inauthentic is that they become absorbed in just reacting to the things in their world—in driving the car, loading the laundry into the dryer, working on the computer, shopping, watching TV. Such persons think the predigested opinions of others or of the media are sufficient for getting by; they let themselves become absorbed in "The They," *das Man.*

But what does authenticity mean? Is it a call to "get in touch with yourself" by pulling away from the world? Or is it just a banal reminder to "stay open-minded"? Even worse, is it a built-in feature of being human, something we can't escape? Some Heidegger scholars see it not just as a call to reexamine yourself or to avoid hardening of the brain cells; to them authenticity is a fundamentally different attitude from one by which we allow the readily available worldviews of others to rule our lives. Being authentic means, for Heidegger, that you stop being absorbed by your doings and retain an attitude that "things may mean something else than what I expect." Only through this kind of intellectual flexibility can we even begin to think about making judgments about anything else, be they facts or people. So authenticity is, in a sense, remaining "open-minded," but it also involves performing a greater task by constantly forcing yourself to realize that reality is in flux, that things change, including yourself, and that you are part of a world of changing relationships. And *this* causes angst, because it means you have to give up your anchors and security zones as a matter of principle. In the end, angst becomes a liberating element that can give us a new and perhaps better understanding of ourselves and the world, but it is hard to deal with while we are in the midst of it.

Sartre's Ethical Authenticity

For some people angst is simply an existential fact, something we have to live with all our days. Jean-Paul Sartre is one of those people. Sartre is the best known of the French existentialists of the mid–twentieth century; others include Albert Camus, Gabriel Marcel, and Simone de Beauvoir.

Sartre studied phenomenology (the discipline of the phenomenon of human consciousness and experience) in Berlin during the years between the two world wars, and he was well acquainted with the theories of Edmund Husserl and Martin Heidegger. In addition, he was familiar with the philosophies of Kierkegaard and Nietzsche. During World War II Sartre was held by the Nazis as a prisoner of war, but he escaped and joined forces with the French Resistance movement. Those experiences in many ways influenced his outlook on politics and on life in general: His political views were socialist and at times even Marxist, to a certain degree. Always politically active, Sartre may well be considered the most influential philosopher in twentieth-century Europe and possibly elsewhere—perhaps not as much because of his philosophical or literary writings (for Sartre was also a dramatist and a novelist) as because of his intellectual inspiration. The existential movement may not have reflected a completely faithful version of the Sartrean philosophy, but it is certain that in his own century Sartre inspired the most extensive philosophical movement ever to reach people outside the academic world—the movement of existentialism.

Although existentialism as a fad in the 1950s became stereotyped as the interest of morose young people who dressed in black, chain-smoked late at night in small cafés, and read poems to one another about the absurdity of life, Sartre's existentialism had a whole other and more substantial content. Partly inspired by his experiences during the war, Sartre also came to believe that there is no God and that because there is no God, there are no absolute moral rules either. The concept that God's nonexistence makes everything permissible was not new at the time; it was well known to Western readers of Dostoyevsky and his novel *The Brothers Karamazov* as well as to readers of Friedrich Nietzsche, as you know. But it was given a new twist by Sartre. Instead of saying, as many other atheists did, that we can find our values in our own human context and rationality, Sartre held that without the existence of a God, there are no values, in the sense that there are no *objective* values. There is no master plan and, accordingly, nothing in the world *makes sense;* all events happen at random, and *life is absurd.* So what do we do? Give a shrug, and set about to make merry while we can? No, we must realize that because no values exist outside ourselves, we, as individuals in a community, become the *source* of values. And the process by which we create values is the process of *choice.* (Here you may be able to detect two major sources of influence in Sartre's philosophy: (1) Kierkegaard's notion that we always have a choice, and that gives us a profound feeling of anxiety about life's indetermined character, and (2) Nietzsche's idea that God is dead, and there is no given design or meaning to our lives.)

Everett Collection Historical/Alamy Stock Photo

French philosopher and writer Jean-Paul Sartre (1905–1980) was recognized as the most influential thinker in the existentialist movement. His best-known works of philosophy are the lecture "Existentialism Is a Humanism" (1945) and the much larger, much more intellectually challenging book *Being and Nothingness* (1943).

When a person realizes that he or she has to make a choice and that the choice will have far-reaching consequences, that person may be gripped by *anguish*–Sartre uses the image of a general having to choose whether to send his soldiers to their death. It is not a decision that can be made lightly by a person of conscience, and such a person may worry about it a great deal, precisely because he doesn't know beforehand whether he will make the right decision. If he realizes the enormity of the situation and still makes his choice as best he can, shouldering whatever consequences may develop, he is living with *authenticity.* However, suppose the general says to himself, "I *have* to send the soldiers out, for the sake of my country/my reputation/the book I want to write." Then he is acting inauthentically: He is assuming that he *has no choice.* But for Sartre, we always have a choice. Even the soldier who is ordered to kill civilians still has a choice, although he may claim he will be executed if he doesn't follow orders and thus has no choice. For Sartre, there are some things that are worse than death, such as killing innocent civilians. So claiming that one's actions are somehow *determined* by the situation is inauthenticity or, as Sartre calls it, *bad faith.* Bad faith can be displayed in another way too: Suppose the general is so distraught at having to make a choice that he says, "I just won't choose–I'll lock myself in the bathroom and wait until it is over." In that case, Sartre would say, the general is deluding himself, because he is already making a choice–*the choice not to choose*–and thus he is in even less control of the consequences of his choice than if he actually had chosen a course of action. In our hearts we know this, and Sartre maintains we can never deceive ourselves 100 percent. There will always be a part of us that knows we are not like animals or inert things that can't make choices, simply because we are human beings, and human beings make choices, at least from time to time. Animals and things can exist without making choices, but humans can't, because humans are aware of their own existence and their own mortality; they have a relationship to themselves (they exist "for themselves," *pour soi*), whereas animals and things merely float through existence (they exist "in themselves," *en soi*). In *Being and Nothingness* (1943), Sartre says:

> Thus there are no *accidents* in a life; a community event which suddenly bursts forth and involves me in it does not come from the outside. If I am mobilized in a war, this war is *my* war; it is in my image and I deserve it. I deserve it first because I could always get out of it by suicide or by desertion; these ultimate possibilities are those which must always be present for us when there is a question of envisaging a situation. For lack of getting out of it, I have *chosen* it. This can be due to inertia, to cowardice in the face of public opinion, or because I prefer certain other values to the value of the refusal to join in the war (the good opinion of my relatives, the honor of my family, etc.). Any way you look at it, it is a matter of choice. . . . If therefore I have preferred war to death or dishonor, everything takes place as if I bore the entire responsibility for this war.

How does bad faith manifest itself? Sartre's famous example involves a young woman on a date. The woman's date makes a subtle move on her–he grasps her hand–and she doesn't quite know what to do. She doesn't want to offend him or to appear to be prudish, but she really doesn't know whether she wants to have a relationship with him either. So she does nothing. She somehow manages to "detach" herself from the situation, as if her body really doesn't concern her, and, while he moves in on her, her hand seems not to belong to her at all. She looks at his face and pretends that she has no hand, no body, no sexuality at all. This, says Sartre, is bad faith: The woman thinks she can turn herself into a thing by acting thinglike, but it is an illusion, because through it all she knows that sooner or later she has to say yes or no. What should she do to be authentic? She should realize that she has to make up her mind, even if she can't foresee whether she will want to have a relationship or not. Making up her mind will then create a new situation for her to react to, even though it is essentially unforeseeable. (As an aside, Sartre doesn't ask us to evaluate whether the young woman's companion may also be in bad faith by attempting a seduction!) This openness to the unforeseen is part of being authentic. When we make a choice, Sartre says, we are taking on the greatest of responsibilities, for we are choosing not only for ourselves and our lives but for everyone else too. Whatever choice we make sends out the message to everyone else that "this is okay to do." Therefore, through our choices we become role models for others. If we choose to pay our taxes, others will notice and believe that it is the right thing to do. If we choose to sell drugs to little children, somebody out there will see it and think it is a good idea. (Interestingly, doing something just because someone else is doing it is not enough for Sartre; as we saw in the section on Mayo's theory of role models, true authenticity must come from personal choices and not from just following role models.) Whatever we choose, even if we think it will concern only ourselves, actually will concern all of humanity, because we are endorsing our action as a general virtue. That is why choices can be so fraught with anxiety—and for Sartre that anxiety never goes away. We must live with it, and with the burden of the choice, forever. We are free to choose, but we are not free to refrain from choosing. In other words, *we are condemned to be free.*

This emphasis on human freedom is one of the strongest in the history of philosophy and one of the most radical, demanding theories of freedom of the will. You'll remember from Chapter 4 that historically, there has been a dispute between supporters of the idea of *free will* and supporters of what we call *hard determinism,* the theory that everything in human life as well as in nature is determined by causal factors: heredity and environment, or nature and nurture. (See Box 10.10 for a closer examination of the idea of hard determinism.) Sartre is one of the strongest critics of the theory of hard determinism, claiming that every kind of explanation of human actions that refers to outside forces or some kind of inner compulsion—in other words, any view that implies that we have no choice—is bunk, a bad excuse, or, in the terminology of existentialism, bad faith. Free will is our only "nature" as human beings; it is in a sense our fate to have no fate, to always be faced with multiple possibilities and the need to make choices, without having control over their consequences—and live with the resulting anguish. That, to Sartre, is living as an authentic human being.

Box 10.10 HARD DETERMINISM, COMPATIBILISM, AND SARTRE'S LIBERTARIANISM

Sartre's entire philosophy of the *pour soi*, the "for itself," the human being who is always free to choose, can be seen as a passionate argument against the viewpoint of **hard determinism**, a theory that has become prominent within the last century with the increasing scientific knowledge of cause and effect. You read about it briefly in Chapter 4, Box 4.6. It claims that nothing happens without a previous cause, and everything is an effect of something else.

Everything in nature is caught up in the causal chain of ever-spreading effects, and since the human brain is part of nature, our very decisions are also part of the great chain of cause and effect. That means that *if* every fact about our lives could be known, *then* in principle every decision of ours could be predicted, because, as hard determinism claims, 100 percent knowledge yields 100 percent accuracy in predictability. We are the results of our *heredity* (our genetics, or "nature") and our *environment* (our upbringing and surroundings, or "nurture"), and therefore our sense of free will is an illusion. Of course that doesn't mean that we *in reality* can predict everyone's behavior, because life is too complex for that, but that doesn't mean that everything *in theory* can't be predicted: in any set of circumstances there will be a tiny germ of things to come—not in a religious sense that a divine mind has predetermined the future, but in the very fabric of causality. As you saw earlier, that has the side effect that, within a system of ethics, we can't blame or praise anybody for any decisions, if nobody can help what they're doing.

The philosophy of hard determinism has its followers today, based on neuroscientific findings that our bodies seem to react even before our brains send out signals to act, but there is also another school of thought known as **compatibilism** which holds that causality need not imply that we don't make free decisions. One thing is when the world puts obstacles in our way that impede our freedom, such as being late for a test because of an unexpected traffic jam, or making a wrong decision because we're sick, or even feeling compelled to act a certain way because we're being threatened. Sometimes we really can't help ourselves. But it's another thing entirely when we make a decision without such factors present, because then we can, and should be held accountable. Aristotle pointed these factors out first, and he can be counted as the first compatibilist. The American philosopher Daniel Dennett is today well known for being a compatibilist, and our legal system works under those same assumptions.

But Sartre had another take on moral responsibility: *We are always accountable*, even if life throws unexpected obstacles our way. If you're late for a test, you could have left home earlier. If you're being forced to reveal the whereabouts of your family to an armed home intruder, you can choose to keep quiet—even if it may cost you your life. His view is known as **libertarianism**, as in "fundamental liberty" (not the political viewpoint which you read about in Chapter 5). If we think that somehow we are in a situation where we have no control over our decisions, we are in bad faith. You may want to do some further research into the topics of hard determinism and compatibilism, and decide for yourself which of the three theories you find to be most plausible.

So can we at least find comfort in the company of other people, close friends, lovers, or relatives who also have to face hard choices? For Sartre, that presents no real solution; the presence of the Other—another person, different from myself—only reminds me of my absolute responsibility to make choices. And besides, the very presence of the Other is problematic in itself: When another person looks at me, and our eyes meet, he or she is always trying to dominate me, as I am trying to dominate him or her. For Sartre every human relationship is a game of dominance using the gaze as a tool of power, and this is especially the case for relationships between lovers. Essentially, we are alone with our choices and responsibilities. In the Narratives section you'll find two stories, each of which in its own way is a wonderful illustration of exactly what Sartre is talking about. The first is a summary of Sartre's own stage play *No Exit*—for Sartre was also a writer of plays and novels—in which three people face one another in their own self-made hell; and next you have a summary of the film *Good Will Hunting,* about a young man who lives in bad faith because he lacks the courage to make choices with consequences.

But how can we make a choice if the world is absurd and all our actions are meaningless? When we first experience the absurdity of existence, we may feel nauseated, dizzy from the idea that reality has no core or meaning. But then we realize we must create a meaning; we must choose for something to matter to us. For Sartre, the social conditions of France became a theme that mattered to him, but you might choose something else—your family, your job, or your Barbie doll collection. Any kind of life project will create values, as long as you realize that the world is still absurd in spite of your project! If you think you are "safe" with your family or your job or your doll collection—if you think you've created a rock-solid meaning for your life—then you've fallen back into bad faith. This is the case with the waiter (another of Sartre's examples) who wants so badly to become the perfect waiter that he takes on a "waiter identity" that provides answers to everything: how to speak, what to say, how to walk, where to go. The waiter has not chosen a project; he has turned himself into a thing, an "in itself" that doesn't have to choose anymore. Living authentically means living in anguish, always on the edge—confronting the absurdity of life and courageously making choices in the face of meaninglessness. When something you care about appears, then you will know what to do. The French philosopher and novelist Simone de Beauvoir, Sartre's significant other and his collaborator on the subject of existentialism, puts it like this: "Any man who has known real loves, real revolts, real desires, and real will knows quite well that he has no need of any outside guarantee to be sure of his goals." (Beauvoir is featured in Chapter 12.)

Suppose you decide you'll do something about your life *tomorrow*. That *next year* you'll write that novel. Or go back to college. Suppose you decide you *should have* married someone else, had children, gone to see the Pyramids, or become a movie actor. Then there is not much hope for your authenticity, says Sartre, because your virtue lies only in what you accomplish, not in choices you make about things you are *planning* to do. If you never start that book, you have no right to claim you are a promising writer. If you never tried to become an actor, then you can't complain that you're a great undiscovered talent. We are not authentically anything but what we *do,* and we are hiding from reality if we think we are more than that. Like Aristotle, Sartre links the value of our virtue with the success of our conduct: Intentions may be good, but they aren't enough.

Levinas and the Face of the Other

Emmanuel Levinas (1905–1995) was born the same year as Sartre, but whereas Sartre became a philosopher of the mid-twentieth century, Levinas was a late bloomer and became one of the leading voices of French philosophy only in the last decades of the twentieth century. His most important works are *Totality and Infinity* (1961; translated into English, 1969) and *Otherwise Than Being or Beyond Essence* (1974; translated into English, 1981). In many ways his experience parallels that of Sartre. He, too, became interested in the philosophies of Husserl and Heidegger in Germany; indeed, his interest preceded Sartre's by more than a decade, and it was Levinas, not Sartre, who introduced those ideas to the French public with books on Husserl and Heidegger. (According to Simone de Beauvoir, Sartre, when reading Levinas's book on Husserl, exclaimed, "This is the philosophy I wanted to write!"—although Sartre afterward claimed he could do it better.) Like Sartre, Levinas was a prisoner of war during World War II, doing forced labor for the Nazis; also like Sartre, he developed a highly personal philosophy based on his early interest in German phenomenology. Both became recognized as distinguished scholars within the field of philosophy. But there the similarities end. Sartre was French by birth, whereas Levinas—born a Lithuanian—became French by choice. Whereas Sartre's Catholic belief in God came to an end, Levinas never lost his Jewish faith. Whereas Sartre developed his existential philosophy based on the fundamental anguish of the choice—an essentially lonely enterprise—Levinas sees the bottom line of all human existence as the encounter with the Other, not in a competition for dominance, as Sartre sometimes would express it, but in coming face-to-face with another human being and realizing that the Other is alive, looking at *you,* speaking to *you,* needing *you* to recognize him or her as someone who is fundamentally different from you and fundamentally vulnerable. Levinas maintains that "ethics precedes ontology": Understanding the needs of the Other and *my* own responsibility for the needs of the Other comes before any philosophy about existence. That is why Levinas has described ethics as "First Philosophy": This is the foundation and the beginning point, which we are normally not even aware of but where we encounter what is really important in life: the face of the Other.

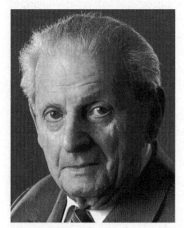

Ulf Andersen/Getty Images

The Lithuanian-French philosopher Emmanuel Levinas (1905–1995) believed that ethics is the deepest and most primary human experience: We see the other person looking at us and we hear him or her talking to us, and we understand that this is someone whose life is precious and irreplaceable. The Other commands us not to kill, and we feel obliged to place his or her needs above our own.

As we have seen, many modern theories of ethics state that everyone ought to be treated as *equal.* Bentham talks about how each person has one vote in terms of his or her pain and pleasure; Kant claims that all persons should be viewed as ends in themselves; Rawls points out that justice consists of treating all persons with fairness regardless of who they are. The Golden Rule is in effect even in philosophical systems that are otherwise opposed to one another. For Levinas, there is nothing wrong with the political quest for equality, but that quest is not fundamental to ethics; what is fundamental is another experience altogether. When I meet another human being, another face, the ethical reaching out to that person consists in realizing precisely that we are *not* equal. Levinas is not saying I am "better" than the Other. On the contrary, the Other counts more than I: The Other, no matter who he or she is, is a person in need, always "poor" and asking for my help and understanding; first and foremost the Other is telling me, "You must not kill." As Levinas says in a dialogue with Richard Kearney:

The approach to the face is the most basic mode of responsibility. As such, the face of the other is verticality and uprightness; it spells a relation of rectitude. The face is not in front of me (*en face de moi*) but above me; it is the other before death, looking through and exposing death. Secondly, the face is the other who asks me not to let him die alone, as if to do so were to become an accomplice in his death. Thus the face says to me: you shall not kill. . . . In ethics, the other's right to exist has primacy over my own, a primacy epitomized in the ethical edict: you shall not kill, you shall not jeopardize the life of the other. The ethical rapport is asymmetrical in that it subordinates my existence to the other.

Of course, that is not really a description of most actual encounters between people; fortunately, we rarely find ourselves in situations in which we are begging for our lives. But for Levinas, that encounter is the underlying foundation beneath all human encounters: The face is naked, the eyes are pleading, the voice speaks. For Levinas, the true ethical moment happens when we are being addressed by the Other. In response, it is not enough to say, "Well, he or she is just the same as I am, we are all humans." That, to Levinas, is not going far enough, or it is going too far: That would be making us all into some collective form of being, some anonymous humanity. Instead, we are supposed to say, "He/she is completely different from what I am, so his/her life is my responsibility." That is the unequal, asymmetrical situation, the *alterity* (otherness) of the Other, which makes the other human individual our responsibility. In particular, it is the Other's voice that calls to us, more so than looking into his or her eyes. Sartre's existential philosophy has often alluded to the power of the *gaze,* the eyes trying to dominate the other person's, but Levinas sees the typical encounter between humans as not only a visual but also an aural experience: You hear the voice speak to *you,* and you respond by being there for the other person. And when you respond with your whole being in acceptance that the Other is there, demanding attention, then you become special to the Other, you become *irreplaceable.* For Levinas, humans in an ethical relationship with each other recognize the Other as irreplaceable, "non-substitutable." The loss of the Other can't be made up for by finding another.

So is that the way things actually are between people, or is it the way Levinas thinks they ought to be? In other words, is he being descriptive or normative? Elegantly, Levinas answers that the encounter is something that happens before we even think in such categories: The encounter with the Other is not merely an actual situation but also the framework within which human encounters take place, so it is the way we actually meet, deep down before we start speculating about existence and responsibility and all the rest, but it is also in a sense the way one ought to meet each individual person—because (sadly) not everyone sees other people as unique individuals who are supposed to be held higher than one holds oneself; some people even see others as "merely a means to an end."

The ultimate disregard for the Other is to Levinas represented by the Nazi Holocaust (in which he lost his entire Lithuanian family). The Holocaust represents the utter evil of putting people through torture and to death not for their convictions but for their ancestry. The fact that Heidegger had been involved with the Nazi Party made Levinas say, in later years, that "one can forgive many Germans, but there are some Germans it is difficult to forgive. It is difficult to forgive Heidegger." And, yet, the dreadful event of the Nazi death camps, where, in Levinas's words, God was not present but the devil was, in some roundabout way did not destroy his belief in God; he says,

> Before the twentieth century, all religion begins with the promise. It begins with the "Happy End." It is the promise of heaven. Well then, doesn't a phenomenon like Auschwitz invite you, on the contrary, to think the moral law independent of the Happy End? That is the question. . . . It is easier to tell myself to believe without promise than it is to ask it of the other. That is the idea of asymmetry. I can demand of myself that which I cannot demand of the other.

> Interview with Wright, Hughes, and Ainley, in Bernasconi and Wood (1988)

So ethics becomes the highest form of religious faith: Without the relief of a promise of heaven, we must be there for the Other, serve the Other for no reward at all. According to Levinas, "Faith is not a question of the existence or non-existence of God. It is believing that love without reward is valuable."

In recent years Europe has experienced wave after wave of undocumented immigrants, many of them refugees fleeing war-torn countries like Iraq and Syria, and the southern borders of the United States have been challenged by the "caravans," large, loosely organized groups of people from Central America in particular trying to make it across the border. While tensions have run high in the debate, some scholars have found support for a compassionate attitude in Levinas's work: Aaron James Wendtland, a Heidegger scholar, points out in an op-ed piece in the *New York Times,* "What Do We Owe Each Other?", that Levinas's philosophy of the Other holds a possible key to overcoming the barrier of cultural differences and stereotypes. We need to see the refugee as a vulnerable Other precisely because of the differences, not because they "are like us." We need to be hospitable.

> Hospitality, according to Levinas, involves curtailing our enjoyment of the world when confronted with another's wants. It is exemplified by the act of welcoming another into our home and sharing our possessions. Welcoming and sharing with others determines who and what we are as specific human beings. Levinas expresses this idea in a discussion of subjectivity in which the self is described as a host and hostage to others. We are hosts to others because welcoming them into our world is a precondition for a relation of identification and differentiation between us. And we are hostages because our personal identity is determined by how we respond to the demands others place upon us. . . . Levinas has taught us that our responsibility for others is the foundation of all human communities, and that the very possibility of living in a meaningful human world is based on our ability to give what we can to others. And since welcoming and sharing are the foundation upon which all communities are formed, no amount of inhospitable nationalism can be consistently defended when confronted with the suffering of other human beings.

While Levinas himself would probably have applauded this application of his philosophy to a current and very volatile political situation on two continents, there are critics who have pointed out that it is one thing to invite vulnerable human beings to share the safety and bounty of one's culture; it is another to open one's gates to large groups of people whose background is extremely hard to vet, and who may include criminals, potential future terror sleeper cells, and radicalized individuals. Levinas might answer that even so, they are still human beings, and their radicalization might be better overcome through hospitality than hostility. Critics might answer that this is a chance few people who care about their homes and the safety of their neighborhoods would want to take. Levinas's philosophy of the Other remains one of the most challenging in modern times.

With his philosophy that we look to the Other as someone we must give our love to but who doesn't have to return it (an ethic that is sometimes used to describe the relationship between parent and child), Levinas's ethics stands as a complete renewal within the European tradition of autonomy, finding personal integrity in a relationship of the individual not to oneself but to someone else. In this he comes closest of all the modern European philosophers to an ethics of virtue, seeing the ultimate virtue as the willingness to serve the Other; as a thinker within the modern tradition of authenticity, he regards the asymmetrical relationship to the Other as the truly authentic relationship. (Box 10.11 explores a new, partially Levinas-inspired American moral philosophy, the Ethic of Care.) Remember from Chapter 4 that Levinas's philosophy was presented as an example of *ideal altruism.* This ethic, which today perhaps more than any other philosophy stands for kindness and sacrifice of one's self for the sake of others, is nevertheless not without further controversy.

Box 10.11 THE NEW ETHIC OF CARE, A POLITICAL VISION

In recent years two American philosophers, Dwight Furrow and Mark Wheeler, have collaborated on an "ethic of care" that includes a liberal political vision of *caring* as the moral standard for human interaction. In his book *Reviving the Left* (2009), Furrow writes,

> The force of morality, its motive, comes from the demands of palpable others who insist that I be responsible, who have the authority to make demands on me, and whose vulnerability and particularity motivate me to respond to their needs. The fact of being in a relationship itself constrains us, generates feelings of obligation and care, a force not unlike the force of gravity, but constantly renewing its hold over us. These fields of force that insist we be responsive to the face of the Other form the basis of couture and gives our lives content, meaning, and purpose.

> Culture is dependent on these relationships of responsiveness and care because they engender social trust, which is the engine of culture. Without the belief that others are responsible and caring, our vulnerabilities overwhelm us, our sense of ourselves as capable persons evaporates, our ability to act is disrupted by doubt and fear. We typically think of culture as made up of institutions such as the law, religion, or the art world, or as patterns of linguistic behavior, shared traditions, or common beliefs. Culture is all of these. But underlying the institutions and patterns of behavior are a network of relationships of responsiveness and care that make the institutions and patterns of behavior possible. . . . Care, as I am

using the term, is both a motive and a practice. To care for someone is to take the good of that person as a motive for my action for her sake. . . . Care is not about having warm feelings or good intentions. It is not fully expressed in merely caring about something. It demands more of us, it demands that we care for something; that we do the labor required to sustain connections and prime the wells of flourishing. . . . Morality inevitably shapes politics because through moral judgment we determine what is fair, cruel, and wasteful and who is worthy of respect, who is needy, and what matters most. . . . Thus, for liberalism to succeed as a public philosophy, it must

Dwight Furrow

Dwight Furrow, American philosopher and author, is pro rata professor of philosophy at San Diego Mesa College.

change culture from the ground up. "Rootstock liberalism" names both the foundation of trust and care that society must cultivate and a political consciousness that aims to build such a foundation.

This political vision of a moral society builds on several theories that you have encountered in this chapter: *Virtue ethics*, as it has been proposed by Philippa Foot, emphasizing character over conduct as the most important ethical element, provides the foundation for an ethic of care that looks to a general attitude of consideration, rather than setting up principles to follow. Heidegger's *Care Structure*, while not similar at all to an ethic of care, still provides another founding piece, inasmuch as it sees human life as always oriented toward something which we are engaged in, and concerned about. But most importantly, Levinas's philosophy of *the face of the Other* who is always in need of our assistance and who should always be regarded as having needs more important than our own, provides

the most solid foundation to the Furrow-Wheeler moral theory. But there is an additional element: Carol Gilligan's theory of an *ethic of care*, as opposed to an ethic of *justice*. For Gilligan, moral philosophers have for many centuries focused on fairness, equality, and impartiality, but what human beings also need from each other is what *women* have typically been used to providing for their families and friends: *a network of caring*—something that doesn't work well with impartiality, because of course we care more about our families and friends than about total strangers. However, the Furrow-Wheeler care ethic does envision expanding our sense of caring to our entire community and maybe even our world, as a political program. You'll be reading more about Gilligan's theory in Chapter 12.

Furrow, Dwight, Reviving the Left. Amherst, NY: Prometheus Books, 2009. Used with permission.

Some critics see his thinking as a kind of throwback to a time when ethics were expressed in personal, even religious, terms, and further, in terms of male and female. And for some critics this throwback is a serious weakness. In a disarmingly innocent way, in his early writings Levinas insisted that the Other is, essentially, feminine (something that Sartre, by the way, has also been criticized for asserting): "The feminine is other for the masculine being not only because of a different nature but also inasmuch as alterity is in some way its nature."

In later years he modified his position, but it still generates discussion. Levinas's critics see this as just another statement in the long line of sexist philosophies in which a male point of view pronounces women to be "deviant" or "different" or "really kind of strange," and which assumes that women accept this as an objective truth. Seen in the light of this old tradition, it is small wonder that many women philosophers, most notably Simone de Beauvoir (see Chapter 12), have accused Levinas of being reactionary, deliberately taking a man's point of view, seeing himself as the Absolute and the woman as the Other.

But even if Levinas could be said to hold the opinion that woman is completely different from man, it does not mean he thinks woman is inferior to man; on the contrary, according to his theory of the Other, if anything is absolute, it is precisely

Christophel Fine Art/Universal Images Group/Getty Images

Dutch painter Johannes Vermeer's famous painting, *Girl with a Pearl Earring,* shows a young woman looking over her left shoulder straight at the painter, which means she is looking straight out of the canvas, at us. She has been looking at us since she was painted in approximately 1665. Do you feel the power of her gaze, across time and space? Is this the face of the Other, as Levinas would say, asking for our human sympathy and aid?

the Other. In his later years, Levinas would talk about the feminine virtues of the home, of the welcoming feminine touch, the quality of "discretion" of the feminine face as opposed to the male face with its authority and self-assertion, but always in positive terms. (However, whether you regard "feminine" as inferior or superior, it is still sexism to a *classical* feminist, see Chapter 12.) A feminist philosopher, Tina Chanter, suggests that Levinas is, in fact, praising the feminine qualities as true *human* qualities; "feminine" does not mean biologically female to Levinas, says Chanter, and "masculine" doesn't mean "male"; rather, each term stands for features in all of us. That interpretation (in some ways similar to the gender philosophy of the psychoanalyst Carl Jung) may give another dimension to Levinas's controversial words about the Other as feminine. In the Narratives you will find a summary of one of the most famous Westerns of all time, *The Searchers,* in which the encounter with the face of the Other is beautifully illustrated.

Study Questions

1. Evaluate the question of character versus conduct in politics. Which do you think is of higher importance for a person running for (or elected to) office to have: personal integrity or a view on government that you agree with? Is there an alternative? Explain.

2. Discuss the question of character versus conduct in personal matters. Philippa Foot claims, with Aristotle, that a person who has a good character is better than a person who has to control himself or herself. Kant would say the opposite. Explain those viewpoints. Which do you agree with more and why?

3. Bernard Mayo wants us to emulate role models. Can you think of a person—a historical figure, a living person, or a fictional character—whom you would like to emulate? Explain who and why. What are some of the problems involved with the idea of emulating role models?

4. Kierkegaard believes that being ethical is not the ultimate ideal mode of existence—one must also have religious faith. Explore his viewpoint: What does he think faith can give that ethics cannot? Do you agree? Can we be ethical without faith? Can we have religious faith without ethics? Explain.

5. Explain Nietzsche's theory of the Eternal Return of the Same. What do you think he meant–that everything will repeat itself endlessly, or is it a test of how much you love life? If you can say Yes to the idea of endless repetition, then you have passed Nietzsche's test.

6. For Sartre, any explanation that deflects one's complete responsibility is an example of bad faith. Do you agree? Are there cases where people should not be held accountable for what they have done? or cases where it is legitimate to say, "I had no choice"? Explain.

7. Levinas suggests that we regard the Other as someone who is always vulnerable and always needs our assistance. Wendtland applies his philosophy to the refugee crisis in Europe. Do you find that to be a perspective that is needed in the current situation of large groups of undocumented immigrants attempting to cross borders, or are there problems associated with such a moral philosophy?

8. Levinas was reluctant to include animals as beings with "faces." Do you agree that ethics can be extended to animals only as a secondary move patterned after ethics toward humans? Or should ethics toward animals be a primary form of ethics? Can Levinas's own theory be redesigned to include animals?

Primary Readings and Narratives

The first two Primary Readings are short excerpts from the writings of Søren Kierkegaard, one from *Johannes Climacus* and one from *Either/Or,* Volume II. The third Primary Reading is an excerpt from Jean-Paul Sartre's lecture "Existentialism Is a Humanism." All four Narratives explore, in one way or another, the existential themes of choice, angst, authenticity, and responsibility. The first is a summary of Jean-Paul Sartre's classic play *No Exit* about three souls condemned to live in one another's company forever, in hell. The second is a summary of the film *Groundhog Day*, selected to represent Nietzsche's theory of the Eternal Return of the Same. The third narrative summarizes existential aspects of the film *Good Will Hunting*. The fourth Narrative is a film summary that takes us to the Old West and issues of racism and the Other: *The Searchers.*

 ## *Primary Reading*

Johannes Climacus

SØREN KIERKEGAARD

Written 1842–1843, first published 1912. Excerpt translated by Nina Rosenstand.

Kierkegaard used to speak through many aliases, and some we are not supposed to take seriously; Johannes Climacus became one of his most serious and personal aliases, and here we read about Johannes's childhood, which exactly resembles Kierkegaard's own.

> His father was a very strict man, apparently dry and prosaic, but under this coat of coarse weave he hid a glowing imagination which not even his advanced years managed to conceal. When Johannes on occasion would ask permission to go out, he was most often refused; however, on one occasion his father offered, as a form of compensation, to take a walking tour up and down the floor. This was at first glance a poor substitute, and yet this turned out to be like the coarse coat: It hid something else entirely. The suggestion was accepted, and the decision where to go was left entirely to Johannes. So they left by the gate, walked to a nearby castle in the woods, to the beach, or up and down the streets, anywhere Johannes wanted, because for his father nothing was impossible. While they were walking up and down the floor, his father would describe everything they saw; they said hello to people passing by, coaches rolled noisily past, drowning out his father's voice; the fruits of the vendor woman looked more inviting than ever. He related everything so accurately, so vividly; he described so immediately in the most minute detail things that were familiar to Johannes, and whatever Johannes didn't know he described in such elaborate and educational manner that he, after having walked with his father for half an hour, was just as tired as if he had been outside an entire day. . . . For Johannes it was as if his father was the Good Lord, and he himself was his favorite who was allowed to come up with silly ideas to his heart's content; for he was never turned down, his father was never perturbed, everything was included and happened to Johannes's satisfaction.

Study Question

1. Do you approve of Kierkegaard's father's teaching technique? Explain.
2. Are there similarities between his technique and virtual reality? Are there differences?

Primary Reading

Either/Or

SØREN KIERKEGAARD

Excerpt from Volume II, 1843. Translated by Nina Rosenstand.

In this text, written shortly after Kierkegaard broke up with Regine Olsen, he speaks with the voice of Judge Williams, admonishing a friend who refuses to make choices (about getting married, in particular). In his friend's words, "Get married, and you'll regret it. Don't get married and you'll regret it." Williams responds,

> The choice itself is decisive for the content of one's personality. . . . If you imagine a first mate on his ship at the moment when it has to make a turn, then he might say, I can do either this or that. However, if he is not a poor navigator, he will also be aware that the ship is all the while moving ahead at its regular speed, and that he thus only has an instant where it is immaterial whether he does one thing or the other. So it is with a human being: Should he forget to take account of the speed, there comes at last a moment when it is no longer a question of an either-or, not because he has chosen, but because he has refrained from choosing—which is the same as saying, because others have chosen for him, because he has lost his own self.

Study Questions

1. Whom do you think Kierkegaard identifies most with: the friend who doesn't want to choose or Williams? or perhaps both?
2. Compare this excerpt with Sartre's theory of the existential choice.

Primary Reading

Existentialism Is a Humanism

JEAN-PAUL SARTRE

Lecture, 1946, published in **Existentialism from Dostoyevsky to Sartre,** *1989. Translated by Philip Mairet. Excerpt.*

In his famous lecture on existentialism from 1946, Sartre expresses the key concepts of his philosophy: Traditionally, philosophers have expressed the thought that humans have an essence, given to us by our creator, or evolved as part of our human nature. But for Sartre, humans don't have a "nature," contrary to all other beings and things in the universe; we exist in the world, with freedom to choose our path, and thus our *existence precedes our essence*. But that puts us in a state of *anguish*, from which we would like to escape (in bad faith), but we cannot, because we are *condemned to be free*.

If, however, it is true that existence is prior to essence, man is responsible for what he is. Thus, the first effect of existentialism is that it puts every man in possession of himself as he is, and places the entire responsibility for his existence squarely upon his own shoulders. And, when we say that man is responsible for himself, we do not mean that he is responsible only for his own individuality, but that he is responsible for all men. The word "subjectivism" is to be understood in two senses, and our adversaries play upon only one of them. Subjectivism means, on the one hand, the freedom of the individual subject and, on the other, that man cannot pass beyond human subjectivity. It is the latter which is the deeper meaning of existentialism. When we say that man chooses himself, we do mean that every one of us must choose himself; but by that we also mean that in choosing for himself he chooses for all men. For in effect, of all the actions a man may take in order to create himself as he wills to be, there is not one which is not creative, at the same time, of an image of man such as he believes he ought to be. To choose between this or that is at the same time to affirm the value of that which is chosen; for we are unable ever to choose the worse. What we choose is always the better; and nothing can be better for us unless it is better for all. If, moreover, existence precedes essence and we will to exist at the same time as we fashion our image, that image is valid for all and for the entire epoch in which we find ourselves. Our responsibility is thus much greater than we had supposed, for it concerns mankind as a whole. . . .

This may enable us to understand what is meant by such terms—perhaps a little grandiloquent—as anguish, abandonment and despair. As you will soon see, it is very simple. First, what do we mean by anguish?—The existentialist frankly states that man is in anguish. His meaning is as follows: When a man commits himself to anything, fully realising that he is not only choosing what he will be, but is thereby at the same time a legislator deciding for the whole of mankind—in such a moment a man cannot escape from the sense of complete and profound responsibility. There are many, indeed, who show no such anxiety. But we affirm that they are merely disguising their anguish or are in flight from it. Certainly, many people think that in what they are doing they commit no one but themselves to anything: and if you ask them, "What would happen if everyone did so?" they shrug their shoulders and reply, "Everyone does not do so." But in truth, one ought always to ask oneself what would happen if everyone did as one is doing; nor can one escape from that disturbing thought except by a kind of self-deception. The man who lies in self-excuse, by saying "Everyone will not do it" must be ill at ease in his conscience, for the act of lying implies the universal value which it denies. By its very disguise his anguish reveals itself. . . . When, for instance, a military leader takes upon himself the responsibility for an attack and sends a number of men to their death, he chooses to do it and at bottom he alone chooses. No doubt under a higher command, but its orders, which are more general, require interpretation by him and upon that interpretation depends the life of ten, fourteen or twenty men. In making the decision, he cannot but feel a certain anguish. All leaders know that anguish. It does not prevent their acting, on the contrary it is the very condition of their action, for the action presupposes that there is a plurality of possibilities, and in choosing one of these, they realize that it has value only because it is chosen. Now it is anguish of that kind which existentialism describes, and moreover, as we shall see, makes explicit through direct responsibility towards other men who are concerned. Far from being a screen which could separate us from action, it is a condition of action itself.

Study Questions

1. What does Sartre mean by saying that, in choosing for oneself, one chooses for all men (= human beings)?

2. Explain Sartre's concept of *anguish*—what is it, and when are we likely to experience it? Is there a difference between being afraid and feeling anguish?

3. The concept of *making a choice* is at the core of existentialism. Compare Sartre's and Kierkegaard's emphasis on making choices—are they talking about the same process, or are there differences?

4. Explain in what way Sartre's existentialism is a theory about moral values.

 Narrative

Groundhog Day

HAROLD RAMIS (DIRECTOR)
DANNY RUBIN AND HAROLD RAMIS (SCREENWRITERS)

Film (1993), summary.

A spoiler alert: I will be giving away the ending of the film, but since this is a movie classic, chances are that you already know the plot. Maybe you've even seen the movie more than once.

Weatherman Phil Conners works for a local Pittsburg television station, and for the fifth time he is assigned to cover Groundhog Day in Punxsutawney where the groundhog, Punxsutawney Phil, will emerge to predict the weather for the next six weeks, according to tradition. Phil Conners doesn't like the assignment, he doesn't like his job, and his main manner of communication is sarcasm and cynicism. New producer Rita's enthusiasm over the project leaves him cold.

February 2, Groundhog Day, dawns in Punxsutawney. The alarm wakes Phil up in his bed and breakfast at 6 A.M., with the old sixties tune *I got you, Babe*. The local radio is blathering about a blizzard coming in. Patchy snow is on the ground. Phil leaves for the event, ignoring or being rude to everyone he meets, including an old high school acquaintance, Ned, whom he hasn't seen in years. Ned is an insurance agent and impossible to get rid of, but Phil manages to escape by being nasty. He insults his TV crew, and Rita realizes that he is an unpleasant, self-centered person. After wrapping up the broadcast—where groundhog Phil sees his shadow—they leave for Pittsburg, but are caught in the blizzard and have to turn back. The cameraman and Rita go to the Groundhog Day party, but Phil is grumpy and goes to bed.

Next morning he wakes up when the alarm plays *I got you, Babe*, at 6 A.M. Patchy snow on the ground. Same local radio show talking about Groundhog Day and the blizzard coming in. And he meets the same people going to the park—the old beggar, Ned—and in the park it is Groundhog Day all over again. He finishes the broadcast, they start for Pittsburg, and are again turned back because of the blizzard. And now Phil begins to worry that he may not ever get home—"What if there is no tomorrow?" he asks—"there wasn't one today!" That night he breaks a pencil and places it on the alarm clock. Next morning, at 6:00, *I got you Babe* is playing, and the pencil is whole again. Now Phil is in a panic. What's going on? He tries to tell Rita that for some reason time seems to be in a loop for him, and she thinks he may be sick. So he sees a neurologist, who can find nothing wrong with his brain, and then a psychiatrist, who tells him to come back the following day. That evening he goes drinking and bowling with two local guys, and says, What would you do if you were stuck in a place, and nothing changes, and nothing you do matters? Which is a fairly accurate description of their lives in a small town. But what if there were no tomorrow? Then, says one of the guys, there'd be no consequences, and you could do whatever you what! So that's what they do—they go driving, hitting mailboxes, and driving on the railroad tracks. Phil ends up in jail—but next morning he's right back in his B&B room, and *I got you Babe* is playing. So now Phil enacts the lesson from the night before, and does whatever he wants. He smokes, eats carbs and fatty foods, punches Ned, makes out with a local woman, and none of it has any consequences. Over the next many repetitions of the day he steals money from a bank transport, dresses up like a Clint Eastwood Western character, and gets Rita to talk about her interests and describe her idea of the "perfect man" so he can (the next many February 2 evenings) quote her back at herself without her realizing that he is playing her. But every time he seems to get close to her, she sees through him, and slaps him. Finally he has had enough, and wants to put an end to it. He kidnaps Punxsutawney Phil and drives to his fiery death in a stolen truck—only to wake up the next morning in his B&B bed, with the same music playing. He can't die. Over and over again he tries to kill himself in all kinds of ways, but to no avail. In a quiet moment he sits at the diner where he has been sitting every day since the loop started, and tells Rita he is immortal and all-knowing. He knows everything about everybody, because he has observed them for an endless row of February 2s—and she says, maybe it isn't a curse? They spend a nice evening together, just as friends, and when he wakes up next morning, back in yet another 2/2, something has changed in him.

He is friendly to the hotel manager, he gives money to the old beggar, he brings coffee to the TV crew, he learns to play the piano from the local piano teacher, he learns how to make ice sculptures, he catches a boy falling out of a tree, he helps people all over town. And when he finds the old beggar dying in an alley, he brings him to the hospital—but he can't keep him alive. And next rerun of 2/2 he sticks with the old man, feeds him a great meal, and hopes to save his life, but he can't—the old man dies in the alley, anyway. So during the next day's Groundhog Day broadcast he speaks into the microphone—saying that if he had to spend every day for the rest of his life in a bleak winter, this is where he'd want to be—and for the first time we get a sense that he is being serious. He is beginning to accept that this is his life, an endless return of the same, and he is ready for it. Rita is moved by his speech, but he has no time for her—he has to make his daily rounds, helping people in town in their predictable predicaments. That same evening Rita goes to the Groundhog Day party, and is surprised to see Phil playing with the band, a skilled pianist after a multitude of one-day piano lessons. Phil has now made a life for himself out of the repetition of a single day. Everybody in town shows up and has something to thank him for, and he is not being snide or sarcastic—he seems genuinely happy for them. When he is asked to join a charity auction—the ladies bid on the bachelors, who then will be "theirs" for the evening, Rita bids top dollar for him. They have a wonderful evening together where he creates a snow sculpture of her face, sensitive and beautiful. And Phil is now happy in the moment, even if it may not last beyond the night.

So next morning he wakes up. It is 6:00, and *I got you Babe* is playing on the alarm—is this just another 2/2, and yesterday is lost, again? No, Rita is there with him, and the town is covered in snow, and it is February 3.

Study Questions

1. Explain why the seemingly endless return of the same Groundhog Day finally comes to an end. What has changed? And what is the moral of that story?

2. Would it make a moral difference to you if there were no consequences to your actions? Why or why not?

3. Explain what is "Nietzschean" about this film. Also, which features (if any) would you say are not compatible with Nietzsche's philosophy? Explain.

 Narrative

No Exit

JEAN-PAUL SARTRE

Play, 1944. Translation by S. Gilbert (1989). Summary and Excerpt. The first presentation of the play was in Paris in May 1944.

For Sartre, there is no life after death, for there is no God to send the soul to one realm or the other. But as a dramatist and a novelist, Sartre played with the idea of hell nevertheless. In the drama *No Exit,* three characters find themselves in a locked room with no windows: a middle-aged man, Garcin; a young woman, Estelle; and a lesbian woman, Inez. They all know that they are dead and in hell, and they are highly surprised that there is no torture chamber—merely a room decorated in bad taste. They don't know one another, but they are forced to spend an unforeseeable amount of time together in this room, interrupted only occasionally by a prison guard, the "valet." For a while they can "glimpse" the life of the living, but that soon fades, and all they have is one another. Each pretends to wonder what the others have done to be sent to hell, but, as Inez says, they are all "murderers." Estelle killed her baby, Inez killed her lover's husband (or at least drove him to his death), and Garcin killed the spirit in his wife by his cruelty to her.

Inez points out that they are in hell because of their selfishness, causing suffering and death to others who cared about them, and now they must pay the piper. But their punishment is not going to come from some devilish torturer; it is already in progress, simply by some power having put these three people together in a closed room, forever, tormenting each other by their nagging as well as their insight into each other's flaws—a self-serve torture chamber, as Inez says.

Of course each of these characters is also adept at torturing themselves, having endless regrets and resentments. Garcin's thoughts keep returning to the fact that he was a deserter, despite always having thought that he would be an honorable human being, and live and die with courage. But he sees his death as a cruel twist of fate, depriving him of his life too soon. Had he lived longer, he would have redeemed himself, he says. But Inez shrugs it off:

> It's what one does, and nothing else, that shows the stuff one's made of. . . . One always dies too soon—or too late. And yet one's whole life is complete at that moment, with a line drawn neatly under it, ready for the summing up. You are—your life, and nothing else.

Estelle is beginning to find Garcin attractive (she is used to men fawning over her). Inez is falling in love with Estelle, and Garcin is himself attracted to Estelle but prefers that each of them stay in their own corner rather than hurt each other. But the stage is set, and they can't help interacting. All three try to manipulate one another; they team up, two against the third one. They constantly scrutinize one another (for in hell you have no eyelids you can close). They need each other for comfort and support, but they have no trust in one another. They realize that there is no need for torture instruments and devils—they are each other's torturers. The room and the other two people in it *are* hell for them: Their punishment is spending an eternity with one another in a hostile triangle. In the end Garcin succeeds in opening the locked door to their room, but now all three are reluctant to leave, because for each that would mean the other two had won the dominance game. All three stay to torment each other, forever.

On the symbolic level Sartre is—probably—not talking about any real life after death but about the human condition. He is saying we make life a hell for one another, because we are so very good at manipulating one another, and every human relationship, even that between lovers, has at its core a battle for power and dominance. Sartre concludes with one of his most famous lines: "Hell is—other people."

Study Questions

1. Would you agree with Sartre that "hell is other people"?

2. Do you think Garcin, Estelle, and Inez might apply Sartre's own principles of existentialism to cope with their life in hell? How?

3. Identify some of Sartre's existentialist concepts in this summary. Can you find examples of bad faith, authenticity, and anguish over having free will?

 Narrative

Good Will Hunting

GUS VAN SANT (DIRECTOR)

MATT DAMON AND BEN AFFLECK (SCREENWRITERS)

Film, 1997. Summary.

Harvard math professor Gerald Lambeau challenges his students to prove an advanced theorem written on the board in the hallway; the following day someone has proved it. In high anticipation, students crowd the auditorium, expecting the math genius to step up, but both they and Lambeau as well as the students are disappointed: Nobody takes credit for the feat. However, we, the audience, know who the genius is—the young janitor Will. We've seen him stop, look at the board, ponder the problem, and work it out. And then we've seen him after work hours interacting with his friends, playing baseball, going to bars, getting drunk, getting into fights, and eventually being arrested for hitting a police officer—a hands-on, violent physical existence that seems light-years away from the cerebral life at Harvard.

But when Professor Lambeau adds a more advanced problem to the board, the young janitor is almost caught red-handed. At first, Lambeau thinks he is defacing the board, but as the young man slinks away, the professor realizes that he has solved the problem. Thinking Will is a student who has taken on part-time work at the school, Lambeau sets out to find him.

Meanwhile, Will's life is taking a new direction: In a bar, his friend Chuckie tries to pick up two female college students by pretending to be erudite, and a male college student steps in and does his best to expose Chuckie as a fake. But the college student must now deal with Will, who exposes the student's knowledge as nothing more than sophomoric parroting of textbook material. Will doesn't understand only math—he shows himself to have a profound knowledge of American social history as well. And as we get to know him better, we realize that his knowledge extends to just about any field of research, and all of it learned through visits to the library, not from any college classes.

One of the girls Chuckie tried to impress has noticed Will. Later that evening she comes up to Will, introduces herself, and tells him she has been waiting for him to make a move. Since he hasn't approached her table and she has to go home, she gives him her phone number. The young woman, Skylar, is in her final year of college and shows no reluctance to go for what she wants. Will, however, has not shown any initiative toward her, even though he likes her, and this becomes one of the pivotal themes in the story.

Next morning Lambeau tracks Will down and finds him in court, at his arraignment for assault. Will defends himself eloquently, but we hear that he has a rap sheet that includes grand theft auto, mayhem, theft, and physical abuse. And we learn that he has been in and out of foster homes for years. This time there will be no mercy, because the person he assaulted was a cop. But Lambeau steps in and makes a deal with the court: Will is released into his custody with the provision that Will agrees to work with him on math theories and agrees to see a therapist.

MIRAMAX/Album/Newscom

The film *Good Will Hunting* (Be Gentlemen Limited Partnership, 1997) shows us that you can be extremely intelligent, and yet have much to learn about life. Will Hunting (Matt Damon) is a mathematical genius, but everything he knows is from books, and he is unwilling to use his math skills to improve his prospects. When the chance presents itself for him to create a future with a woman he is attracted to, Skylar (Minnie Driver), his courage fails him—because who knows if she will reject him? His close friend Chuckie (Ben Affleck) tries to teach him that he should not shy away from reaching out to an uncertain future.

Working with Lambeau amuses Will, because he truly is a self-taught math genius—far brighter than Lambeau himself, who is a Fields Medal winner. But Will chews up five therapists by running circles around them intellectually and emotionally until they give up. Lambeau, worried that the terms of Will's release will be violated, finds him a final therapist: Lambeau's old friend from school, the psychologist Sean Maguire. Will, doing what he is good at, sizes Maguire up and finds his weak spot: He is still grieving over the loss of his beloved wife, who died of cancer a few years earlier. Even so, Sean Maguire takes Will on, seeing the real person behind the mask of intellectual mastery—a person who is afraid of life, afraid of friendship, love, and commitment, because of the abuse and abandonment he experienced in childhood.

Skylar and Will go out on a date, fool around in a novelty store, and eat fast food on what it seems more like a two buddies' night on the town than a romantic date, and when they kiss, it is on her initiative. Our impression of Will as a smart but somewhat inexperienced human being is enforced during his next session with the psychologist. Sean tells him that he has much learning but no experience and that he is a genius but also a terrified orphan—terrified that someone might get power over him if he opens up too much, and abandon him. Even when Will tells a joke, it is about people and places he has only read about. Does he even date? Has he had sex? Sean whistles the tune "People" ("People who need people are the luckiest people in the world")—a little comment to Will that his choice of not needing people is the wrong choice. And Will's dating is certainly in question—he has called Skylar, only to hang up on her before saying anything. Sean calls him on the carpet: Will doesn't want to ruin their budding relationship by finding out that she is not perfect—or by letting her find out that *he* is not perfect. And Sean tells Will that his deceased wife was not perfect—she would fart—but when you love each other, he says, the imperfections become precious, and the question is not, Is he or she perfect? but, Are we perfect for each other? You'll never find out unless you take the chance, he says. On the other hand, as Will is quick to point out, Sean has not remarried. Is he afraid of engaging in life himself? Will presses Sean: How did he know his wife was the right woman for him? Sean tells the story of the great Red Sox game he chose to miss because he wanted to go on a date with her instead. In other words, the value of what you are willing to give up to be with the one you love will tell you how much you love him or her.

Meanwhile, Will takes Skylar out on dates, and they do have sex but never at his place, always at hers, because he doesn't want her to see his squalid living quarters. He tells her elaborate stories about being one of thirteen brothers and having no privacy. But he does share his three friends with her, including Chuckie, and to his delight she gets along with them. But Chuckie realizes that Will is not being up front with his girl.

Old tensions are coming to the surface between Sean and Lambeau: Lambeau wants to recruit Will for a think tank, which would make him both rich and famous, and Sean believes it is more important for Will to find himself and become an authentic human being. We realize that Lambeau is developing an inferiority complex over Will's genius but that he has always believed that Sean felt intellectually, or at least financially, inferior to *him*. But Will has no intention of being manipulated by Lambeau. He sends Chuckie in his place to do a tongue-in-cheek job interview while he himself goes on a date with Skylar, who gives him what amounts to an ultimatum: She is leaving for Stanford University to go to medical school, and she wants him to come to California with her—she loves him and wants to have a life with him. But what if she changes her mind, he asks? What if he changes his? She: "You're afraid I won't love you back!" He: "You don't want to hear I was abused, I was an orphan, I don't need help!" And Will leaves her, saying he doesn't love her.

It appears that Will is reaching a breaking point: He insults and alienates Lambeau, making it clear that he doesn't want his job offer or his help. He refuses a job offer from the NSA, saying he doesn't want to be responsible for his research killing strangers. And when Sean asks him if he has a soul mate, and he refers to dead philosophers such as Plato, Nietzsche, and Kant, Sean confronts him with his analysis: Will sees only the negative possibilities, so he doesn't dare take chances.

Skylar leaves for California, and Will violates his parole, ending his sessions with Lambeau. He goes back to his day job with Chuckie as a construction worker and tells him that it's all over—with the girl and with the fancy job offers—and thinks Chuckie will approve. But to his surprise, his friend now takes him to task: He has the opportunity to do something better than manual labor, his math genius gives him a winning ticket, and he doesn't dare cash it in?

Will now goes back to Sean and arrives in the middle of a ferocious quarrel between Sean and Lambeau, who accuses Sean of having chosen to be a failure. When Lambeau leaves, Sean shows Will that he has Will's old file documenting the horrible abuse he had suffered at the hands of his father.

Sean understands, because he was a victim of an abusive father himself. Finally, Will breaks down in tears, his defenses crumbling.

The following day he goes to a prearranged job interview in Cambridge. There is a sense of change in the air—Sean decides to take some time off and go traveling, and while he is packing, Lambeau shows up, and the two old friends patch up their differences. It happens to be Will's birthday; he is now twenty-one, and his friends spring a big surprise on him: They've scraped enough money together to give him his own wheels—a beat-up old car, but it has a good engine.

So now Will is looking at a future in which his math genius will come to fruition, as a researcher in Cambridge. He has a car, and he has friends—but he also loves a woman on the other side of the continent. What will he do? Will he choose the secure future, or will he follow Sean's example and choose love, even if he can't be sure it is going to work out? The lesson Sean tried to teach him was that the value of what you are willing to give up to be with the one you love will tell you how much you love him or her. So what does Will decide? See the movie for yourself and decide if he made the right choice.

Study Questions

1. Explore the similarities between Will and Sean: How do those parallels help Will find himself? Is Will also helping Sean?

2. Compare the relationships between Will and Skylar and between Kierkegaard and his girlfriend Regine. What are the similarities? What are the differences?

3. How do Will and his friends illustrate Kierkegaard's "three stages of life" theory?

4. How do scenes between Will and Sean display aspects of Sartre's ideas about choice, authenticity, and bad faith?

5. Explain the title of the film. How might it have an existential meaning? Might it also refer to an element in Kant's ethics (see Chapter 6)?

 Narrative

The Searchers

JOHN FORD (DIRECTOR) FRANK S. NUGENT (SCREENWRITER)

Film, 1956. Based on a novel by Alan le May. Summary.

The Searchers was considered a run-of-the-mill Western when it first came out in 1956, but since then it has acquired a reputation for being perhaps the best Western ever made. It is without a doubt one of director John Ford's finest works, and one reason for its current high standing in American film history is that the actor playing the lead, John Wayne, gives a performance that puts an end to the story that he really wasn't much of an actor. Another is that its theme is unusually frank for its time period, displaying one of the less romantic, less palatable sides of the Old West: the prevailing racism directed against American Indians. *The Searchers* appears in a chapter that is otherwise predominantly European in its philosophical themes because of the pivotal scene in the film, which could have been concocted as an illustration of Emmanuel Levinas's theory of the "face of the Other." A word of warning: I will be giving away the surprise ending of this film, because it is in one of the final scenes that the "Levinas" moment happens.

A lone rider approaches a small ranch somewhere in West Texas; it is Ethan Edwards, returning home from the Civil War. He is still in what remains of his Confederate uniform, even though the war ended years before. The ranch belongs to his brother and his family—Martha, his wife; their teenage daughter, Lucy; a son of about thirteen; the youngest daughter, Debbie; and a grown foster son, Marty, who is one-eighth American Indian. We realize that Ethan has had a hard time adjusting to the fact that the South lost the war, and that he has taken his own time returning home because he has strong feelings for Martha—feelings that are reciprocated, in a shy, discreet way. That first evening, Ethan gets reacquainted with his brother's family, but we also hear him belittle Marty for his Indian heritage and looks: "Fella could have mistook ya for a half-breed!"

The following day, a raid on a neighbor's cattle by Comanche Indians lures Ethan and Marty away from the ranch; a troop of Texas Rangers ask them to come along in pursuit, but Ethan's brother stays behind to look after his family. This is the last time Ethan sees his blood relatives alive, except for one. Too late Ethan and Marty realize that they have been tricked into leaving the ranch. In the meantime, the Comanches attack the little ranch and murder Ethan's brother, Martha, and their son, and take the two girls captive. When Ethan and Marty return, all that's left is the burning ranch and the three bodies. Realizing that Lucy and Debbie have been abducted, Ethan and Marty join forces with Lucy's fiancé, Brad, and take off in pursuit. They soon come upon the Indian camp, where they think they see Lucy in her blue dress, but Ethan finds Lucy's body hidden in a canyon—she has been raped and murdered—and buries her with his bare hands. An Indian warrior took her dress and is now wearing it. Brad goes crazy from grief and rage, and rushes into the Indian camp, where he is promptly killed. Ethan and Marty back off and lose sight of the tribe. Weeks turn into months, and the Comanche band continues to be elusive. Their search takes them all over the Southwest, where they find sporadic clues as to the whereabouts of the Indians and hints that Debbie is still alive. Months turn into years, but Ethan has no intention of giving up. "That'll be the day," he says. The two men have one of their most grueling experiences when they come upon a cavalry post after the cavalry has conducted a raid on an Indian village. The soldiers have rescued white captive women and have left a number of Indians dead. Ethan looks on in dread—not at the slaughter of the Indians, but at the blank stares from the white captive women who have lost their minds from years of deprivation, and we sense that he is coming to a resolve about Debbie's situation. If she is still alive, she is now reaching puberty, and since Indian women marry early, she may have married one of the warriors. The search has changed Ethan; he wants to find the Indian tribe who killed his brother—and Martha—to take revenge, but to Marty's horror Ethan now also intends to kill Debbie, who he believes has been "contaminated" by living with the tribe.

Warner Bros/Kobal/Shutterstock

In the film *The Searchers* (Warner Brothers, 1956) Ethan Edwards (John Wayne) ruthlessly pursues a Comanche Indian band that has murdered his brother, sister-in-law, niece, and nephew, and kidnapped his other niece Debbie. Ethan initially intends to kill the Indians and rescue his niece, but the pursuit lasts years, and Ethan later searches for the band with a different purpose: not to save Debbie but to kill her because he believes she has been "contaminated" living with the Indians. When he finds Debbie as a young adult woman, his racism is overwhelmed by sheer human empathy—what Levinas calls "the face of the Other." In this scene, Ethan finds evidence that his niece has been kidnapped and plots revenge.

After years of obsessive searching, they finally catch up with the band of Comanches led by a chief called Scar, who is quite aware of the two searchers and their quest. Ethan and Marty pretend to be traders and are invited into Chief Scar's teepee, where his three wives huddle in a corner. One of them gets up, and Ethan and Marty recognize her instantly: It is Debbie, all grown up. They have to control themselves so as not to give themselves away, and they find a pretext to leave camp so they can make plans—but Debbie has also recognized them and follows them. She wants to warn them of an ambush planned by Scar, but she has no intention of coming with them—she needs to get back to "her people," as she says to Marty. Ethan, true to his word, draws his gun and tries to kill her. Marty steps in to protect her, but at that moment they are attacked by the Indians, and Debbie gets away.

Ethan and Marty barely escape with their lives. Severely wounded, Ethan dictates his will, leaving the ranch and his cattle to Marty, "having no blood kin." "But," says Marty, "Debbie is your blood kin!" Ethan's reply—"She's been living with a buck . . ." ("buck" was a derogatory term for an Indian warrior)—shows us how he has completely written Debbie off as a relative, perhaps even as a human being.

Ethan and Marty return to the little homestead community in Texas to regroup but receive information that the Comanche band is camped not too far away, and with the company of Texas Rangers they set out for one last attempt. Marty has a talk with his girlfriend, Brad's sister Laurie, and to his surprise she says she agrees with Ethan, "and Martha would have wanted it that way": Debbie should be killed, because she is now an Indian, and no longer a white woman. It is clear that Ethan is not alone in his view; it is, in fact, the prevailing view in the little pioneer community. But Marty, who still loves his sister—and who is of course one eighth Cherokee Indian himself—is set on rescuing her. He sneaks into the camp and smuggles Debbie out unseen, to prevent Ethan from killing her, while the rangers are preparing an attack on the village. Scar discovers him, and he kills Scar. During the attack, Ethan locates Scar's tent and, robbed of his revenge for the murders of his brother and Martha, he scalps the dead chief. Now he looks around for Debbie. Debbie is running toward the hills as fast as she can, but Ethan is on horseback; Marty, on foot, tries to intercept Ethan but is summarily brushed aside, and Ethan starts up the hill after Debbie. There is now no way Marty can save her from Ethan. Ethan jumps off his horse, confronting the terrified, cowering young woman. He looks at her face, sees her humanity and vulnerability, and instead of killing her he scoops her up into his arms, and tells her, "Let's go home, Debbie."

So Ethan puts her on his horse, and together with Marty they ride back to the homesteads, where Debbie is welcomed and Marty is met by Laurie. Nobody seems to notice Ethan. We see him framed by the doorway, with the desert behind him; he is alone, and he turns around, away from civilization, and returns to the wilderness.

The moment when Ethan sees Debbie for what she is, and his own humanity takes over, has been called "one of the most moving moments in film history" by the French film director Jean-Luc Godard. Here we might also call it a "Levinas moment."

Study Questions

1. Is Ethan Edwards a racist? Is Laurie? Explain.

2. Evaluate the character of Marty, being of one-eighth American Indian heritage. What does he bring to the story?

3. Why is Ethan trying to kill Debbie? What happens to him at the moment he decides against it?

4. Why might that moment be called a "Levinas moment"? Explain, referring to Levinas's theory of the "face of the Other."

5. Does Ethan's acceptance of Debbie mean that he is now no longer the racist that he was (if he ever was a racist)? In other words, do you think he now views *all* other humans as an "Other" in need? The common interpretation of Ethan returning to the wilderness alone has been that he has been away from civilization too long to belong with his own people—but another interpretation is possible: He *can't* join the family, because he now knows they were wrong about Debbie and her "contamination." He stands in the light of the doorway, and they are in the darkness of the room. He has seen the light, in other words.

6. A few years later, John Ford made another Western, *Two Rode Together,* about a white captive woman rescued and returned to the white settlements, a woman who is *not* welcomed by the bigoted settlers because she is too "contaminated," and who wishes to return to the Indians. The story is similar to what happened to Cynthia Parker, the white captive woman who was the mother of the great Indian chief Quana Parker. What do you think Ford wanted to say in choosing to tell both stories?

Chapter Eleven
Case Studies in Virtue

This chapter presents three classical virtues—*courage, compassion,* and *gratitude*—for closer examination. We look at how they have been perceived by some philosophers of the past and present and how they may affect our lives. Why these virtues? Why not also loyalty, honesty, honor, and other virtues held dear by various traditions? Just for the simple reason that the topics of courage, compassion, and gratitude have provoked some fascinating contributions to the study of ethics, and I would like to share these with you. And there is another simple reason: We have to limit our discussion to just a few samples. However, a few boxes contain brief discussions of additional virtues, and if you should feel inspired to continue the debate with other virtues as topics, I would wholeheartedly encourage it!

Courage of the Physical and Moral Kind

In 1933, during the Great Depression, President Franklin D. Roosevelt reassured the nation when he said, "The only thing we have to fear is fear itself." Those words helped millions of Americans, not only through the Depression but also through the trying times of World War II, to find courage to carry on, but is it true that fear and courage exclude each other? You'll remember that the first virtue Aristotle had on his list was courage—the proper Golden Mean response to danger. But in the Primary Readings for Chapter 9, you also saw that even Aristotle believed that courage is not synonymous with the absence of fear—that would be foolhardiness. Rather, it is an appropriate response to fear, at the right time, and in the right place, and for the right reason. Just to recap: Aristotle says (see pp. 411–412), "Properly, then, he will be called brave who is fearless in face of a noble death, and of all emergencies that involve death; and the emergencies of war are in the highest degree of this kind. Yet at sea also, and in disease; the brave man is fearless. . . . The man, then, who faces and who fears the right things and from the right motive, in the right way and at the right time, and who feels confidence under the corresponding conditions, is brave." As you can tell from the excerpt, Aristotle himself does not say that the brave man has no fear but that properly managed fear distinguishes a courageous person.

Of course, fear can be paralyzing when we are faced with a difficult choice and a dangerous task, but many a brave man or woman has decided to do the courageous thing precisely because of being afraid, not just in spite of being afraid. In many ways, courage has been the exemplary virtue for many philosophers, often in a rather abstract sense, because they were most often speculating about other people's response to dangerous situations. Interestingly, we know that Socrates indeed had the reputation for being a courageous man in battle when he was a soldier in the war against Sparta, but courage in battle just isn't one of Socrates' primary themes. Perhaps that is in itself significant: Those who are courageous generally don't talk about it. In this section we explore some of the many faces of courage. Courage in battle may seem like the most obvious example, and perhaps that is where the most extreme forms of courage manifest themselves; but not all defiant acts under fire qualify for the term *courageous*—some are pure instinct, some are done because one fears a worse consequence (such as being tried for desertion), and some are done for the sake of some future advantage (medals, a political career, and so forth). But even outside the battle situation, we of course encounter courageous people—"ordinary people in extraordinary situations," as they are often described.

What is courage, and why is it a virtue? You already know that Kant says a quality such as bravery is not virtuous unless it is backed by a good will (Chapter 6). That means we can't just declare somebody who is brave a virtuous person—it takes more than simple fearlessness. In Chapter 10, you saw Philippa Foot add her opinion to what makes an admirable character trait a virtue—not the character trait alone, but also the intent behind it.

Stories of Courage

In the first decade of the 2000s, the confluence of several things led to a renewed debate about courage, especially courage in war. Stories coming out of the Iraq and Afghanistan wars have been giving us a picture of what courage is. In Iraq in 2003, Army Sgt. 1st Class Paul R. Smith held off an attack with his machine gun until he was mortally wounded. He posthumously earned the Medal of Honor for organizing a defense that held off a company-sized attack on more than one hundred vulnerable coalition soldiers. Marine Cpl. Jason L. Dunham received the Medal of Honor posthumously; he died in 2004 in Iraq shielding soldiers in his care from a grenade thrown by an insurgent. And in 2011 President Obama awarded the Medal of Honor to Dakota Meyer of the Marine Corps for saving 36 lives after an ambush in Afghanistan in 2009. During a six-hour firefight with the Taliban, Meyer, himself wounded, provided cover for the troops and picked up both wounded and dead soldiers by going into the "killing zone" five times. President Obama noted that Meyer had been haunted by the lives of four fellow soldiers that he wasn't able to save. And in March 2016, the Medal of Honor was awarded, for the first time, to a member of the secretive Seal Team 6, Navy Senior Chief Edward Byers, for a hostage rescue mission. Byers has been reported as also being exceptional in the respect that he is, at the time of writing this, still in the service and has expressed a wish to get back into combat. While most Medal of Honor recipients have left the service by the time they are awarded the medal, things were different in the past: The World War II Medal of Honor recipient John Basilone returned to combat by his own choice, and it cost him his life.

Since the Medal of Honor was established by George Washington in 1782, more than 3,500 men and women have received the honor, but the medal is not given lightly: At the time of writing this, only 18 Medals of Honor, reserved for "the Bravest of the Brave," have been given to soldiers in the Iraq and Afghanistan wars.

But often courage involves more than heroic actions in battle. Pat Tillman, a safety for the NFL's Arizona Cardinals, enrolled in the army after September 11, 2001, giving up fame and fortune because he wanted to make a difference and fight for his country. That act itself is for many a shining example of courage: giving up a rewarding, exciting life to do what one considers the right thing. When Tillman was killed in Afghanistan in 2004, the nation heard that he died bravely in battle. That he did, to be sure—any volunteer soldier who dies in battle deserves to have that said about him or her—but what the nation wasn't told immediately was that he died as a result of "friendly fire," accidental fire by another Army Ranger, and that Tillman was awarded the Silver Star on the basis of a concocted battle scenario. In 2010 a documentary premiered, the Tillman Story, depicting Tillman's family's quest for the truth.

A book that focuses on the concept of courage in general is John McCain's *Why Courage Matters.* For Senator McCain, himself a Vietnam War veteran and a POW who passed away in 2018, the notion of courage has been "defined down": We tend to confuse courage with fortitude, discipline, righteousness, or virtue; we call athletes courageous when they play a good game, we call people courageous if they just do their job—but real courage takes more. What is virtue without courage? he asks. We need courage to keep being virtuous even when our virtue is being tested. In McCain's words, "We can admire virtue and abhor corruption sincerely, but without courage we are corruptible."

PictureLux/The Hollywood Archive/ Alamy Stock Photo

In thirteen episodes, the acclaimed HBO television series *Band of Brothers* follows E Company from D-Day (June 6, 1944) to the end of World War II in Europe (May 1945). One of the frequent themes explored is courage, of both the physical and the moral variety. In the episode summarized in the Narratives section, "Carentan," you'll meet this man, Private Albert Blithe (Marc Warren), who must face his paralyzing fear of combat.

Such courageous people are not just the heroes of famous battles or political struggles but also ordinary people who do their best, following their convictions even to the point of losing everything, including their lives, says McCain. One such person is Angela Dawson, a mother who decided to stay with her children in their neighborhood and fight the drug dealers—a decision that cost both her and her children their lives; the dealers burned her house down, trapping her and the kids inside. Some of the other examples McCain turns to include the Navajo chief Manuelito; John Lewis, a disciple of Dr. Martin Luther King, Jr.; Hannah Senesh, the young Jewish woman who worked to establish a Jewish homeland; and Aung San Suu Kui, the oft-imprisoned political activist in Burma (Myanmar). McCain tells their stories, and lets us see wherein their courage lies. Echoing Aristotle, he emphasizes that courage comes from doing courageous things—but in one important respect McCain and Aristotle differ: Consider the case of Angela Dawson. She certainly had the courage to stand by her convictions and stand up to the drug dealers, but the result was that her home was torched, and she and her kids were burned alive. Did she have courage? It would certainly seem so. But what would Aristotle say? She had too much of it—she was being foolhardy, stubbornly risking her own life and the lives of her children. Aristotle might have said that Dawson misjudged the situation, and because of that (although it is a harsh thing to say) she was not virtuous. So McCain's theory that courage is the foundation of virtue perhaps needs to take into account Aristotle's theory of the Golden Mean—we can often discern when someone has too little courage, but can we also discern when someone has too much? Aristotle's criterion was, Did they succeed? Then they were virtuous. And how did they succeed? By using their *reason* in determining when something is too much and when it is too little. These are two different views of what courage means, and it is up to us to decide if they speak to us, if we prefer one over the other, or if we think it would make sense to modify one with aspects of the other.

Physical and Moral Courage

Your adrenaline is pumping, your heart rate is accelerated, you may even experience tunnel vision and a sense that time has slowed down. But it isn't a movie—it's you, in a dangerous situation, making split-second decisions. You do what you are trained to do, perhaps what seems the logical thing to do, or perhaps you just act out of instinct. Then, if you're lucky, you'll live to talk about it. So now people are calling you a hero—but you didn't feel that you were doing anything heroic; you just responded to the needs of the moment. Do you recognize the situation? If you do, I salute you. Most of us don't, but we have all heard of people who, after having done something that looks extraordinarily heroic, deny having done anything special. As a matter of fact, when is the last time you heard such a person stand up afterward and say, "Yeah, I'm a hero!"? So the title of hero, and the admiration of bravery, is usually something that is bestowed upon an individual by *others*. As we have seen in Chapter 4, we really can't look into the hearts of people and see their true motivation for the deeds they do. As long as it looks like an unselfish act, and involves physical danger, we're generous with our praise and call it courage. Box 11.1 explores the concept of "hero."

Box 11.1 WHAT IS A HERO?

In the chapter text, you have read a discussion about what makes a person courageous. Another aspect of that discussion is the concept of *hero* itself. Is anyone who displays courage a hero? Does it matter what the end result of a courageous deed is, or is it the display of courage that counts? Some critics have pointed out that we are much too quick to pronounce somebody a hero these days—the word has been inflated. If someone has displayed courage but hasn't done much more than simply survive an ordeal, the media will often slap a "hero" label on the person. But that label is offensive to people who set their standards for heroism higher: Saving the lives of others, with courageous disregard for one's own safety, is a suitable criterion for some. For others, a true hero is someone who rises above what he or she has been hired or trained to do and performs an extraordinary deed that helps others—"ordinary people doing extraordinary things." In that case, some of the individuals you met in Chapter 4 who lost their lives helping others survive a mass shooting, such as Victoria Soto and Liviu Librescu, would qualify as heroes. The same criteria would apply to the Thai Navy SEALs who went into the flooded cave in Indonesia to save the stranded boys in 2018 (see Chapter 4)—and the effort cost two of the SEALs their lives. Mostly we tend to assume that courage is part of the picture—unless we choose to think that celebrities are heroes just because they are celebrities, or good at their job, like the so-called sports heroes or movie heroes. In your view, is it true that we have inflated the concept of hero? Can you be heroic without courage? What would be your definition of a hero?

Indeed it may be courage. It could also be luck, or a misinterpretation of motive—in the film *Hero* (1992) a small-time con artist enters a crashed airplane, and in his quest for loot he manages to save every passenger on board. (The utilitarian would say, "Good job!" The Kantian would find his actions deplorable, even with a stellar outcome for all the passengers!) But disregarding physical danger for the sake of others' lives, liberty, property, or simply happiness is generally identified as courage. What we shouldn't forget is that this is only one of many types of courage: the *physical* kind. Although most of us will perhaps never be in a situation where we can prove to ourselves and the world that we can be physically brave, the other type of courage works in the shadows, is rarely recognized, and is perhaps so common that most of us don't even realize when we've had a courageous moment of the *moral* kind: the kind where you stand by your friend when it would be more convenient to distance yourself from him or her; the kind where you don't allow the powerful clique at school to exclude a newcomer, or someone who is a little different from them; the kind where you stand up to your boss because you know you're right, even if you may lose that job. A whistleblower such as Erin Brokovich certainly must have had physical courage, but the very thought of blowing the whistle takes moral courage to begin with, the kind of courage Rosa Parks displayed when she, in 1955, refused to give up her seat to a white bus passenger. Moral courage may not result in the spectacular saving of lives, yet we recognize it in particular when it is *absent*. We may understand, and forgive, friends who failed us when we really needed them, but we rarely forget. And if we have failed a friend in her or his moment of need—if we are decent human beings, that will come back to haunt us even long after our friend has assured us that it was okay, that he or she understands. McCain believed there isn't much difference between physical and moral courage when push comes to shove, and it may certainly be true that the person who has one kind also is likely to have the other; but even so, there is one big difference that we should take into account: Physical courage is *visible,* whereas moral courage often is not—it is often lived through without a sense of accomplishment, or reward, or even acknowledgment. In the Primary Readings section, we take a look at McCain's address to the Senate in 2017 after his brain cancer diagnosis.

We don't even have to search for moral courage in big, publicized media events; there's plenty of moral spine to go around: Calling the doctor's office to get the result from a medical test can be a test of courage all by itself, and so can deciding to tell something to your best friend that she ought to know but won't appreciate your telling her. And even going online and logging into the information on final grades in college can require a certain amount of courage. Everyday occurrences that require us to step up to the plate and do things we generally don't enjoy doing can bring home the immediacy of the moral challenge and remove the notion that courage happens only on faraway battlefields or in rare, life-threatening situations. As Ayn Rand enjoyed pointing out (see Chapter 4), if we reserve our moral challenges only for extremely unlikely situations, we get into the habit of thinking that we may not be called upon to act morally on an everyday basis.

A controversial topic within the discussion of courage is the topic of *suicide.* Is a person who decides to commit suicide courageous or a coward? Or perhaps those categories don't apply at all. In Box 11.2 you'll find a discussion of the subject.

Box 11.2 IS SUICIDE COURAGEOUS OR COWARDLY?

The issue of suicide has come up on occasion in this book; in Chapter 2 you read about young Werther, who killed himself out of unrequited love, and in Chapter 5 we used suicide as an example in the debate about John Stuart Mill's harm principle. Shocking to most of us, statistics show that suicide is the second greatest killer of American college students, more than all illnesses and birth defects *combined,* and takes a back seat only to accidents. So within a college environment, the debate does tend to gravitate toward the subject from time to time, and the issue sometimes comes up: Is committing suicide a courageous act, or is it cowardly? The question assumes there is one clear answer. If we grant that suicide can sometimes be attempted by sane people, then we can apply the issue of virtue and vice, of morally right and wrong (because we wouldn't use moral condemnation on mentally ill people who don't have a choice in their actions), and then the question of courage versus cowardice will have to do with the how and the why. Much of our attitude toward suicide is rooted in religion; Catholicism

sees suicide as a deadly sin, condemning a soul to eternal damnation. Buddhism views suicide as a personal failure to deal with one's karma—a failure that will have negative results in the next life. But some moral systems, whether religious or secular, such as those in Imperial Japan and Imperial Rome, have had great respect for the suicide solution. It is hard to rise above the ethics of one's culture and upbringing in this regard, but if we can for a moment forget the issue of whether or not we have been taught that suicide is plain wrong, we can focus on the courage/cowardice issue.

What if a person allows himself or herself to die, or downright commits suicide so that others may live? Self-sacrifice is usually not even labeled suicide in our language, so that gives us a clue: There is supposedly something *selfish* in suicide. The question is, How much? And of what nature? If a person commits "suicide by cop," by forcing a situation where a police officer has no choice but to shoot, the selfishness extends beyond that person's own wants and usually is met by heavy condemnation because it also inflicts misery on others (the police officer will face a hearing, might lose his or her badge, and will have to live with having killed another person to the end of his or her life). If people kill themselves because they can't face the shame of some personal situation being disclosed, the world usually pities them for their mental agony but would have admired them more if they had stayed alive to face the music—so there is some sense that suicide is an "easy way out." Generally, the only type of suicide that is met with a kind of silent acceptance or even admiration in this culture (where euthanasia is illegal in all but eight states at the time of writing this) is the decision by a terminally ill person to cheat the reaper and

take matters into his or her own hands, shortening the time of torment. However, all these cases surely require a definite amount of personal guts, just to stand up and go through with it. So is there courage in the suicidal act? Undoubtedly, in the decision and in the act itself—but might there be more bravery in staying alive? That may be a very individual judgment call, but our willingness to call the act of suicide both brave and cowardly shows not only that we have mixed feelings about it but also that we may be referring to different aspects of the act: We judge the immediate decision to die, but we also judge the decision to avoid the future.

Let us suppose that we now have a better understanding of courage. It involves taking action, or just standing up for something or someone you believe in, when doing so may involve a risk to yourself, your job, your well-being, even your life—instead of remaining silent because it is easier or less risky, or because speaking up might be considered politically incorrect by some. It involves doing the right thing when it is difficult, not when it is easy. (In the Narratives section, the film *True Grit* (2010) illustrates the courage of a young girl determined to bring her father's murderer to justice.) But here we run into a new problem: When do we know whether our "cause" is actually morally righteous? Can we just trust our moral intuition? As you'll see later in this chapter, Hitler's right-hand man, Heinrich Himmler, thought he was doing the right thing by setting in motion the "Final Solution"—the mass extermination of the German Jews—and he found it a very hard thing to do. Did that make it right? Of course not. In the next section you'll see what virtue can be added to "courage" to make it less likely that courage is misspent: compassion. In addition, we'll look at the role of reason and reexamine why emotions may be morally relevant, but why we also need reason to moderate and give direction to the moral feelings. (Box 11.3 examines some of the complications of assuming that loyalty is a virtue or a vice.)

Compassion: From Hume to Huck Finn

A story that is familiar to most people raised in the Christian tradition is the parable of the Good Samaritan: A victim of a robbery and an assault is passed over by several so-called upstanding citizens and is finally helped by someone who is moved by his plight: the Good Samaritan. You'll find the story in the Narratives section. It is generally recognized that people *are capable of* showing compassion—the debate usually centers on *why:* You'll remember Thomas Hobbes's view that humans are by nature self-centered and that compassion is something humans show toward others in distress because they are afraid the same calamity might happen to them. In other words, when people show sympathy and pity toward one another, either it is to make sure that others will help them if the same thing should happen to them, or else it is a kind of superstition, a warding off of the fate of others. There are scholars who think Hobbes's viewpoint was fostered by the political unrest of the seventeenth century, which might well have caused a thinker to focus on his own survival and to believe that self-love is the primary driving force.

Box 11.3 IS LOYALTY A VIRTUE OR A VICE?

You may remember that the introduction to this chapter listed some concepts that are generally considered virtues but don't have a chapter section of their own. One such concept is *loyalty*. As it happens, loyalty is a word that is considered a positive quality by some but a negative one by others. We all want our friends and family to be loyal, to have our backs when the going gets rough, and to stand by us when the world turns harsh, don't we? When Aristotle mentions "friendship" as one of the virtues on his list of 12, he is in essence talking about loyalty—but in typical Aristotelian fashion, a virtue can be overdone and then it becomes a vice. *Blind loyalty* beyond all reason is no longer a virtue.

So when is loyalty a virtue? Think about it. One thing is how you want your friends and family to behave toward you, with unwavering support—but another thing is, how far are *you* willing to go to show loyalty, while still feeling that your moral integrity is intact? Movies and TV series are full of relatives who are willing to stick up for their criminal family member no matter what—brothers who "take the rap" for their murderous siblings, mothers who swear by everything that is sacred to provide a fake alibi for their criminal offspring, spouses and lovers lying to the law to save their wayward partners. The notion that "blood is thicker than water" sets a moral standard: it implies that there is nothing more important than family; all other moral considerations pale compared to the absolute demand: family comes first. But is that a universal concept? In the Greek tragedy *Antigone*, by Sophocles, the young woman, Antigone, deliberately breaks the law by burying her brother who has been executed, and it is clear that we are supposed to see her action as morally righteous (and the law as flawed). In one of Plato's famous dialogues, *Euthyphro*, young Euthyphro, a student of Socrates', is charging his own father with the murder of a servant. And Socrates is

incredulous, because such a charge would usually only come from the relatives of the dead person, not the close relative of the accused—a breach of loyalty. And yet, in real life we have examples of relatives choosing what they think is right over supporting their relatives, such as the Unabomber's brother, who gave his name to the authorities once he realized the identity of the bomber. If you knew that someone in your close family, or a very good friend, was involved in serious illegal activity, what would you do? Would you turn a blind eye to their activity, would you help them or even join them—or would you let them know you are not "on board," and try to persuade them to change their ways? Or would you contact a tip line and turn them in?

Let us assume that we're not talking about illegal activities, but involvement in a social cause, such as joining a movement working to reduce global warming, or saving animals on the brink of extinction—or simply being passionate about joining a legitimate political group. Is there such a thing as too much loyalty toward one's group? How would you identify the moment when "enough is enough"? For Aristotle it would be when passion overrides reason, and facts are disregarded in favor of political expediency—in other words, when the message becomes more important than doing a reality check now and again.

And then there is loyalty toward a group one feels some connection to, but doesn't really "belong" to. Particularly in times of change such loyalties can become questionable, seen with the eyes of a new era. The loyalty many people have felt toward their employers and their companies was a common and valued thing in the past, while today's employees rarely stay in the same positions for decades, and frequently don't develop deep ties to their workplace. But such emotional ties could, in the past, extend all the way to slaves feeling deep loyalties toward the families that owned them. Some might explain that as a "Stockholm Syndrome" phenomenon, a psychological identification with one's captors, named after the infamous hostage situation after a bank robbery gone wrong in Stockholm in 1973, in which the four hostages began to sympathize and identify with the hostage takers—a psychological survival defense mechanism. But a simple explanation might be that people simply develop emotional ties to the people who employ them, as a kind of pseudo-family. The Mexican movie *Roma*, winner of Best Picture Award at the Oscars in 2019, depicts a young woman who develops such close ties to her employer and her family, even though she is a paid servant without any equity status in the family. In the Narratives section, you'll find *Roma* as an example of both courage and loyalty, and in our context it is interesting to note that while most reviewers found the film to be both moving and beautiful, there were voices complaining that the young maid's loyalty was misplaced because she belonged to another class, the working class, and that she should have stayed loyal to her own class rather than to the upper class of her wealthy employers. So what seems like a virtue to some may appear as a vice to others.

In the eighteenth century, the Age of Reason, two philosophical giants shared a different idea. Both the Scottish philosopher David Hume and the Swiss philosopher Jean-Jacques Rousseau believed that humans are naturally compassionate toward one another. As you read in Chapter 4, Hume held that even a selfish person will feel benevolence toward strangers whenever his self-interest is not involved. Rousseau claimed that the more we are corrupted by civilization, the more we tend to forget our natural inclination to help others and sympathize with them, because it is not an aberration of nature that makes people selfish—it is *civilization* itself. Rousseau certainly agreed that there are people who show compassion only because they are afraid something might happen to them and because they have only their own interests at heart, but that is not a natural thing, he said; it is caused by human culture. If we would seek only the natural capacities in ourselves, we would find the natural virtue of compassion still intact. The best way to reestablish contact with our original nature is to educate children as freely as possible so that they don't become infected with the evils of civilization.

Philosophers in the Western tradition were not the only ones to speculate about human nature and compassion; in the third century B.C.E. the Chinese philosopher Mencius claimed, as Rousseau would some two thousand years later, that humans are compassionate and benevolent by nature but have been corrupted by the circumstances of everyday life. In an upcoming section we take a look at the philosophy of Mencius as well as those of Confucius and Lin Yutang.

Scientists Agree: Compassion Is Hardwired

As you have read in Chapter 1 as well as in Chapter 4, new research in neuroscience has revealed that, contrary to what most philosophers have emphasized for over two thousand years, it is not natural for the human brain to approach moral problems with logic only and without feelings. For those of you who remember the original *Star Trek* television and film series, and/or have seen the new film series, that idea—which most people outside the field of philosophy would consider mere common sense—is illustrated beautifully in the character of Mr. Spock, the half-human, half-Vulcan character. With his brilliant mind, Spock attempts to control his emotional human side and cultivate his Vulcan all-rational heritage, but it doesn't work that way: Spock finds himself to be quite emotional from time to time. One might say that aside from Hume and Rousseau, most philosophers have, for a very long time, attempted to do the same thing: downplay the emotional element under the assumption that it will lead to corruption and favoritism, and perhaps even a slide backward to a less refined, more animal-like existence based on instincts (which is amusing, considering that some of those same thinkers have claimed that animals have no emotional life). But in several distinct studies released in recent years, neuroscientists and other scholars have presented their findings (although there is generally little meta-ethical discussion of whether there was a difference between empathy, sympathy, compassion, or pity—concepts that a philosopher would generally like to keep separate):

1. **The Brain Is Wired for Empathy** University of California neuroscientist Antonio Damasio (see Chapters 1 and 4) pointed out that our brain is wired for empathy, and is generally reluctant to make decisions that are likely to harm other humans; persons with damage to certain brain areas feel less reluctance to make decisions that may benefit the many but will harm a few people. (And, I suppose, such impaired brains might also be less reluctant to make decisions that will benefit the few but harm the many.)

2. **Mirror Neurons** Italian researchers as well as University of California neuroscientist V. F. Ramachandran have found that we have a natural capacity for understanding what others feel through certain neurons labeled *mirror neurons.*

3. **Thoughts of Harm Cause Negative Emotions** Harvard psychologist and philosopher Joshua Greene has, with brain imaging, shown that thoughts of hurting another human being generate negative emotions in the normal brain.

4. **Feeling Versus Thinking Empathy** Researchers from University of Southern California have found, through brain scans, that we humans do experience empathy for each other, but in two different ways: We "feel" intuitive empathy for those we know, and whom we find it easy to relate to in some way; however, when we find it harder to relate to people, for whatever reason, we "think" empathy—we engage our rational part of the brain to achieve an understanding of their plight. But either way, most people automatically make an attempt to empathize.

5. **Toddlers Are Born with an Urge to Help** Recent research from the Max Planck Institute in Leipzig has shown that toddlers are born with an urge to help. Dr. Michael Tomasello has found that infants from the age of 12 months will try to help adults and other children by pointing to things they have lost, or handing them items they have dropped. Claiming that "Children are altruistic by nature," Tomasello says this phenomenon happens across cultures, and independent of what the children have already been taught. (Another thing is that the toddlers don't stay altruistic—around the age of four they start thinking about their own advantage!) Similar studies have been conducted by Hillary Kaplan, an anthropologist at the University of New Mexico, and primatologist Frans de Waal, whom you'll remember from Chapter 4.

6. **Altruism Feels Good** Neuroscientists Jorge Moll and Jordan Grafman have, through brain imaging, found that doing good things for others makes the pleasure area in the brain light up, in the same manner that we respond positively to food and sex. Rather than being a sophisticated override of selfish interests, it is an ancient, basic neurological response that may even predate *Homo sapiens.*

The common conclusion is that, contrary to what most philosophers, psychologists, and biologists thought, the bottom line for our moral universe is *empathy,* or, as David Hume called it, "fellow-feeling." We have instant emotional responses that seem to be universal, such as Greene's brain-imaging experiment in which volunteers were asked to imagine hiding in a cellar in a village with enemy soldiers hunting down all survivors. If a baby cries, should the child be smothered to protect everyone in the cellar? (This scenario was in fact the plot for the final show in the long-running and very successful television series *M*A*S*H.*) Everyone agrees that the baby should not be killed—but also that it is wrong to risk the lives of everyone else. Greene's conclusion is that, in essence, the "emotion" part and the "reason" part of the brain are in conflict, and that the emotional response (don't hurt the baby) is far older than the cooler evaluation of saving everyone else. That, says Greene, explains why we're more willing to help our neighbor than someone starving halfway around the world—our brains evolved in a tribal society where we needed to respond to those around us, and we had no information about distant places.

So the consensus is in among the scientists: We have feelings of empathy that engage when we are making moral decisions. Interestingly, for Greene that doesn't mean that it is always more morally right to go with our emotions rather than with our reason, and the philosopher Peter Singer agrees: We have been tribal people for such a long time, and those responses were appropriate then, but we're in a different world now, and we can't just assume that we can trust our intuition. *Sometimes the right thing to do may be to override our moral intuition.* We get back to this question below, but for now we can consider it scientifically established: The normal human brain is hardwired for empathy. Now we have to see what philosophers make out of that—because even if scientists tell us we're naturally empathetic, it should come as no surprise that a great many people over the years have turned out either to be so brain-damaged that they have no empathy or to have a considerable talent for overriding their empathy and causing deliberate harm to others (and the banality of evil may be part of that phenomenon). And, as philosopher Jesse Prinz comments, having empathy doesn't mean that we are likely to actually *act* on it; it is entirely possible for a person to feel strong empathy for someone in trouble, and yet walk/drive right by and hope someone else will help them (we return to Prinz's theory below). That brings up the philosophical question of *when* we choose to, in very traditional terms, listen to our *heart,* and when to listen to our *head,* and *why.*

Philip Hallie: The Case of Le Chambon

We can now see that Rousseau was more right than he could have imagined when he speculated that we have a natural inclination to help others. But was he also right that it is *civilization* that causes evildoing, or does "civilized" mean "compassionate"? An indirect answer was given years ago by the American philosopher Philip Hallie (1922–1994), whom I once had the privilege of meeting. Hallie was an unusual philosopher, as philosophers go, because he was never afraid to talk about his own feelings and the feelings of others. One might even say that he was way ahead of his time. You cannot understand evil unless you understand how it feels to those who are being victimized, he said, and you cannot understand goodness unless you ask those to whom goodness has been shown. Having been a U.S. soldier in World War II, Hallie had seen his share of bloodshed and cruelty, including the revelations of the Holocaust death camps. Deeply depressed about the apparent inability to fight evil without becoming as violent as one's enemy, Hallie was profoundly moved by learning about a concrete example of compassion that occurred in the midst of a civilization under the heel of barbarism. In the southern part of France, there is a small village called Le Chambon-sur-Lignon, where the population has had a long history of being persecuted for their Huguenot faith. During World War II the people of the village came to the aid of Jewish refugees from all over France in a rescue effort that was matched only by the prodigious efforts of Danish citizens to save the Danish Jews by smuggling them across the water to neutral Sweden, and the extraordinary courage and conviction of the Japanese consul-general in Lithuania, Chiune Sugihara, and his wife, Yukiko, who, against orders from their own government, hand-signed six thousand visas in twenty days for Lithuanian Jews, thus allowing them to travel to Japan and escape death at the hands of the Nazis. The people of Le Chambon also saved about six thousand lives (more than twice the number of their own population). The majority were Jewish children whose parents had already gone to the extermination camps. This took place all during the German occupation of France, even when southern France ceased to be a "free zone" governed by French collaborators.

As a contrast to the compassion of the French villagers, Hallie points to the sadism displayed during the Nazi reign. The Nazis regularly humiliated their prisoners; during marches prisoners were not allowed to go to the bathroom and had to perform their physical functions while on the march. Hallie describes this as an "excremental assault" and calls it an example of *institutionalized cruelty.* Hallie defines this type of cruelty as not only physical but also psychological. When a person's or a people's self-respect and dignity are attacked on a regular basis, the victims often begin to believe that somehow that cruelty is *justified* and that they really are no better than dirt. That is especially true when one population group commits this offense against another group. Thus cruelty becomes a social institution, endorsed by the victimizer and tolerated by the victim. Such instances of institutionalized cruelty can be seen not only in oppressive wartime situations but also in race relations throughout the course of history, in relations between the sexes and discrimination of people not fitting into the standard male-female categories, and in certain parent-child relationships. The general pattern is a demeaning and belittling of one group by another, so that soon such behavior becomes routine.

Why does institutionalized cruelty occur? Because one group is more powerful than the other, either in physical strength (it is bigger, is more numerous, or has more weapons) or in economic, educational, or political clout (as when one group can hold property, get an education, and vote, and the other group can't). Power can even be verbal, as when one group has the monopoly of using slurs against the other.

How can it be helped? By changing the power balance, says Hallie. That, of course, is hard—it is hard to acquire the right to vote, to own property, to get an equal education. It is hard to build up physical strength. And it is hard to reverse the trend of slurs and other insults. Even if all that is achieved, though, the insidious effect of institutionalized cruelty is not over when the cruelty ceases, because *it leaves scars.* The prisoners who were liberated from Nazi extermination camps were never truly "free" again; they carried their scars with them forever. And just being "kind" to a victim doesn't help—it only serves as a reminder of how far he or she has sunk. What truly helps is a gesture similar to what the people of Le Chambon did for the Jewish refugees in the face of the Nazi occupation.

Hallie heard of Le Chambon and went there to talk to the people; most of them didn't think they had done anything exceptional. What these people did for the refugees was to show them compassion in the form of *hospitality.* They showed the refugees that they were equal to the villagers themselves, that they deserved to live in the villagers' own homes while their escape across the mountains to Switzerland was being planned. This, says Hallie, is the only effective antidote to institutionalized cruelty: hospitality offered as an act of compassion, in a way that makes it clear to the victims that their dignity is intact.

The story of Le Chambon has a twist that makes it even more exceptional. How did the rescue effort succeed in an occupied country with Nazi soldiers everywhere? It wasn't that the villagers were tremendously discreet—no group can hide six thousand people who pass through over a five-year period. It was because of the courage of the town minister, André Trocmé, and his masterly organization of the smuggling operation that Nazi curiosity was deflected for the longest time. Trocmé's cousin Daniel Trocmé was arrested and executed by the Nazis, but that did not stop the rescue effort, because the villagers had an ally in a very unlikely person: the Nazi overseer of the village, Major Julius Schmäling. Schmäling's task was to keep the peace in the region—meaning, in Hallie's words, "to keep the French quiet while Germany raped the country and went about its business of trying to conquer the world." And Schmäling did keep the peace, but not through terror. Instead, he chose to ignore the steady stream of refugees and did not report the incidents to his superiors. One victim of the Nazis whom Schmäling could not save was one of the two doctors of Le Chambon, Le Forestier, who himself was not engaged in the underground movement. But one day he gave a ride to two hitchhikers from the underground, who hid their weapons in his Red Cross ambulance. When the ambulance was later searched by Nazi soldiers, the weapons were found and Le Forestier arrested. Intervention by Schmäling led the doctor's family to believe that he would only be sent to a work camp in Germany as a doctor, but in actual fact the Nazis intercepted the train taking the doctor to Germany. They took him off the train and executed him the following day with about 110 other people. The Trocmés found out the truth from Schmäling years after the war and realized that Schmäling, ever since that day, had agonized about the one life he hadn't been able to save.

In his posthumously published book *Tales of Good and Evil, Help and Harm* (1997), Hallie writes about the complex character of Schmäling: He and his wife tried for the longest time to avoid membership in the Nazi Party, but when it was finally imminent, Schmäling joined the army so that he wouldn't have to be a party member. Originally a schoolteacher in Munich, he had told his students that decency has no price, no market value, but as an overseer he was very efficient; otherwise he couldn't have stayed on the job. So that makes him a morally ambiguous man, says Hallie. "He served a government that systematically persecuted defenseless people, but he would not persecute them himself." And that refusal to persecute the weak did not go unnoticed by the people of Le Chambon: After the liberation of Paris in 1944, when Nazi officers were held accountable for their atrocities in trials all over France, Schmäling's trial was most unusual. As he walked up the aisle toward the judge, everyone rose to pay tribute to this man who had saved so many at the risk of his own life. When asked why he had not reported the Jewish children hiding in the village, he responded, "I could not stand by and watch innocent blood be shed." Schmäling spent some time in prison in France but later returned to Germany, where he lived in modest circumstances until his death in 1973. (See Box 11.4 for Hallie's views on one of the major Nazi leaders.)

Box 11.4 IS IT BETTER TO CRY OVER YOUR VICTIM THAN NOT TO FEEL SORRY?

In a celebrated paper the philosopher Jonathan Bennett claims that it is better to be a person guilty of wrongdoing who has compassion than it is to be an innocent person who has no compassion. An example of the first kind of person is Heinrich Himmler, who, as head of the Nazi SS (an elite guard unit), developed stomach troubles because of what he felt he had to do. The seventeenth-century American Calvinist minister Jonathan Edwards was the other type of person; although he presumably served the needs of his flock, he believed everybody deserved to go to hell. Philip Hallie responds to Bennett's point of view by referring to an incident in Lewis Carroll's *Alice in Wonderland*. The Walrus and the Carpenter lure some little oysters to take a nice walk with them along the beach. After a while they all sit down on a rock, and the Carpenter and the Walrus begin to eat the oysters. The Walrus feels sorry for them and weeps, but he eats them nevertheless. The Carpenter couldn't care less about the oysters and is just concerned with eating them. Hallie asks, Are we really supposed to believe that the Walrus is a better creature than the Carpenter because he has sympathy for his victims? The Walrus ate as many oysters as he could stuff into his mouth behind his handkerchief. Likewise, Himmler killed more than 13 million people even though he was "feeling sorry" for them. For Hallie sympathy is no redeeming quality at all if it isn't accompanied by compassionate action.

To Hallie, virtue is this: the compassion one shows in reaching out to save others at the risk of one's own life. It is not necessarily the result of logical thinking—it may be an act of the heart. For Hallie, there are degrees of moral behavior, though. If you just refrain from doing harm, you are following the *negative command* "Do not cause harm." That is commendable, but there is a stronger command, a *positive command:* "Help others in need." It is much harder to follow a positive moral rule than a negative one, which just requires you to do nothing. The people of Le Chambon followed the harder path of the positive rule. In your opinion, what did Major Schmäling do? Did he follow the negative rule of no harmdoing, or did he, under the circumstances, also follow a positive rule of actively helping? At the end of this chapter we look at a powerful story of compassion similar to that of Le Chambon, Steven Spielberg's film *Schindler's List,* and in the Primary Readings, you'll find an excerpt from Hallie's *Tales of Good and Evil, Help and Harm* as well as one from his essay "From Cruelty to Goodness".*

Richard Taylor: Compassion Is All You Need

In Chapters 3 through **7** we looked at a number of rules and principles regarding the nature of moral good-ness and the proper conduct of human beings. Even in this section on virtue, most of the theories we have discussed involve using *reason* to evaluate the proper moral action. But on several occasions you have encoun-tered a suggestion that, in the last decades of the twentieth century, seemed extremely controversial but that has gained considerable interest and acceptance lately among philosophers and scientists alike: the notion that reason isn't everything when it comes to moral evaluations and decisions, that *moral feelings* are highly important too. You'll remember Martha Nussbaum's claim that emotions can have a reasonable side that makes them indispensable to moral decision making (see Chapter 1). In his own way, Philip Hallie considers the virtue of compassion as an *emotion* that is essential for the moral makeup of a decent human being. How-ever, neither Hallie nor Nussbaum suggests that we can dispense with reason. Such a radical view isn't held by many, but some thinkers do believe that the way to do the right thing and have virtue is very simple: We do the right thing *when our heart is in the right place;* moral goodness is simply a gut feeling that we all have, a conscience that speaks without words, an empathy that leads us to reach out in compassion to others. If we don't have that, we have no morality at all. For Richard Taylor (1919-2003), an American philosopher, rea-son has *no* role to play in making the right moral choice. Taylor's theory belongs to a school of thought that says *moral principles are, in effect, useless,* because we can always find exceptions. But Taylor doesn't believe the alternative is a moral nihilism. On the contrary—in his book *Good and Evil* (2000) Taylor says:

> Moral principles are nothing but conventions, but they have the real and enormous value to life that conventions in general possess. They help us to get where we want to go. Without them social life would be impossible, and hence any kind of life that is distinctively human. Their justification is, therefore, a practical one and has nothing to do with moral considerations in the abstract. The moment such a principle ceases to have that value, the moment its applica-tion produces more evil than good, then it ceases to have any significance at all and ought to be scorned.

So if rational principles aren't the basis of ethics, then what is? It is the virtue of compassion, a phenomenon of the heart, not the brain. The eternal focus in ethics on reason needs an antidote, and Taylor finds it in an analysis of *malice versus compassion.*

Imagine a series of atrocities. A child pins a bug to a tree just to watch it squirm. Boys set fire to an old cat and delight in its painful death. Soldiers make a baby girl giggle before they shoot her, and force an old man to dig his own grave before they beat him to death. What is so awful about these stories? It is not just that the victimizers did not live by the categorical imperative, says Taylor (referring to Kant). It is not that they didn't try to maximize general happiness for everyone involved (referring to utilitarianism). It is not that they were ignorant (Socrates) or didn't follow the Golden Mean (Aristotle). The horror we feel—and for Taylor it is the *same kind of horror* in all three cases—stems from the fact that these incidents are simply malicious. The acts are horrible not because the consequences are so terrible (the death of one bug, one cat, and two war victims may not have widespread effects) but because the intent was to cause suffering for the sake of someone else's pleasure or entertainment. These are not crimes against *reason* but crimes against *compassion.*

True moral value, then, lies in compassion, Taylor believes, and he illustrates this with three more tales. A boy comes up to an attic to steal something and rescues some pigeons that are trapped there, despite his father's strict command to leave the birds alone. When his father returns home he gives the boy a beating. A white sheriff beats up a black rioter during the race riots of the 1960s and then, breaking down in tears, cleans the man up and takes him home, after which he goes and gets drunk. An American soldier who is trapped on an island with a Japanese soldier during World War II finally finds the Japanese asleep but is not able to kill him. In each of these cases, Taylor says, the people had been taught moral principles that told them to do one thing ("Obey your father"; "Uphold the law through violence"; "Kill the enemy"), but their heart told them something else, and *their heart told them right*. According to Taylor,

> There are no heroes in these stories. . . . Goodness of heart, tenderness toward things that can suffer, and the loving kindness that contradicts all reason and sense of duty and sometimes denies even the urge to life itself that governs us all are seldom heroic. But who can fail to see, in these mixtures of good and evil, the one thing that really does shine like a jewel, by its own light?

In the end we can't trust our reason, but we can trust our heart; compassion is all we need to be moral human beings, compassion toward all living things. Even people who do the right thing can't be called moral if they don't have compassion—in other words, if they don't have the right intention.

Box 11.5 WHEN EMPATHY IS ABSENT: WELCOME TO CYBERSPACE

You've just seen that neuroscientists and philosophers are beginning to agree that humans aren't nearly as self-centered as we used to think; we are hardwired for empathy for other human beings. But in that case, why are all human societies throughout history burdened with people who prey on other humans? Or who simply ignore the pain of others? For one thing, you saw already in Chapter 1, and now with the examples provided by Philip Hallie, that ordinary people can be put in situations where their empathy can be overridden by authorities demanding that they follow orders, or telling them that it is normal to put other people through hell. And some people simply have less empathy than others. Besides, in big cities there seems to be less empathy to go around than in smaller communities—perhaps because we're on emotional "overload" in the city, receiving too many signals from our fellow human beings, or because it is easier to be anonymous in the city, and much harder not to step up to the plate and help in a smaller community. Because, as Jesse Prinz points out, there is still a difference between *feeling* empathy and *doing* something about it.

But there is a new phenomenon that is catching the attention of educators: an increase in the level of callousness in *cyberspace*, sometimes resulting in cyberbullying. A theory that has surfaced recently is the role of the Internet and cell phones in the lives of young people. Where it was customary a generation ago to spend most of the time with your friends in face-to-face situations (although landline phones were popular for late-night conversations), much social activity today takes place electronically, such as through texting and posting on Facebook, Instagram, and other social media. For most of human history we have been used to looking at the person we are talking to; eye contact has been an important element of communication. And, says the theory, eye contact engages the empathy in our brain (you'll recognize elements of Levinas's philosophy of *the face of the Other* here). But what if there is no eye contact? Are we then less inclined to feel compassion for other people? Perhaps. Is it possible that with less eye contact in one's social life one feels less bound by the rules of behavior, and more inclined to be rude and aggressive, on the phone, while texting, on Facebook—hence cyberbullying? In Chapter 13 we take a closer look at the pros and cons of today's rapidly growing phenomenon of social media.

This is a much more radical view than Hallie's because it tells us to *disregard* our reason. Let us look at how that might work in practice. Taylor assumes that we all have this compassion in us—he appeals to our *moral intuition.* But what about the boys who set fire to the cat? Where was their natural compassion? And what about soldiers who kill defenseless civilians? Obviously, not everyone has this compassion, not even the people in Taylor's own examples. In Box 11.5, we take a look at the current phenomenon of dwindling compassion in cyberspace. What can we do about people who have no compassion? Well, we can try to tell them stories about malice and compassion, but chances are that they will think it is a great idea to set fire to a cat and that the boy in the attic should have left the pigeons trapped. How can we appeal to people who are not responsive to compassion? If we were to ask Kant, Mill, Aristotle, or just about any moral thinker, he or she would say we must try to appeal to their *reason.* If we all had compassion, there might not be any need for reason, but as we have seen, not everyone has it, and not everyone has it at the right time, at the right place, and for the right people. Therefore we must have something that might convince people who are lacking in compassion, and this is where reason has to come in. What arguments can we use? We might say, "How would you like it if someone did that to you?" In other words, we might appeal to their logical sense of universalizability and invoke the Golden Rule. Or we might say, "If you do this you will get caught and punished." In that way we appeal to their sense of logic and causality; they can't possibly get away with any wrongdoing. If those two arguments don't convince them to do right, we might just lock them up—protect them from themselves, and us from them—until they display enough rationality to understand our arguments. Reason, then, is not a substitute for moral feeling (compassion), but it becomes the necessary argument when the moral feeling is absent or deficient. A moral theory that leaves room for only compassion is powerless when it comes to enforcing moral values and virtues.

There is one more problem with Taylor's idea that compassion is all we need, and to illustrate it we will turn to Mark Twain's novel *Huckleberry Finn.* In the story Huck, a young boy, helps Jim, a slave, escape from his owner, Miss Watson. British philosopher Jonathan Bennett analyzes this famous literary incident—and Bennett is a thinker who believes in reason as an important part of ethics. He concludes that Huck certainly did the right thing in helping Jim, but it still wasn't good enough because he did it for the wrong reason. Let's review what happens in the story. Huck wants to help his friend Jim, but he realizes that by doing so he will be going against the morals of the town, which require him to return stolen property, which is what a runaway slave is. Because nobody has ever told Huck that owning people is wrong, he has no principle of equality to hold up against what Bennett calls the "bad morality" of the nineteenth-century town. So in the end Huck ends up lying to protect Jim without understanding exactly why, and he resolves not to adhere to any moral principles from then on because they are too hard to figure out. Bennett's conclusion is that Huck did the right thing but for the wrong reason; he should have set up a new principle of his own, such as "It is wrong to own people" or merely "Jim is my friend, and one should help one's friends." That way Huck's sympathy for Jim would have been supported by his *reason,* and he would not have had to give up on morality because it was too puzzling.

But let us think beyond Bennett. Mark Twain himself probably wouldn't have shared Bennett's conclusion, because for Twain, Huck is a hero who does the right thing for the best of reasons—because he has compassion for a fellow human being (a human being whom many educated readers of Twain's own day and age might have chosen to turn in). Huck has virtue, even if he doesn't think very well. So Twain and Taylor would be in agreement there. But that doesn't make Huck's attitude any better, philosophically speaking, because it is just a stroke of luck that Jim is a good guy and worthy of Huck's compassion. Suppose the story had featured not the runaway slave Jim but a runaway chain-gang prisoner, Fred the axe murderer? Huck still might have felt compassion for this poor, frightened man and decided to help him go down the river and get rid of his irons. But later that night, Fred might have repaid Huck by killing him and an entire farm family farther down the river to get money and take possession of Huck's raft. In other words, natural empathy is not enough. What Huck lacked was not compassion but *reason* to shape it, reason to help him choose when to act and when not to act—because surely not all people are deserving of our compassion to the extent that we should help them escape what society has determined is their rightful punishment. We may sympathize with mass murderers and understand that they had a terrible childhood, but that doesn't mean we should excuse their actions and help them go free.

This example serves another purpose too. Not only does it show that we can't dispense with reason; it also shows that there is something else missing in virtue ethics: If we focus solely on building a good character and developing the right virtues, such as loyalty, compassion, and courage, we still have to decide what to do once we've developed the virtues. We may have a wonderfully virtuous character but still be stuck with deciding between several mutually exclusive courses of action. Huck might ask himself (once he has decided to be loyal to Jim) what exactly is the best way to enact that loyalty: Is it to take Jim up north where nobody can own slaves, or is it to hide him until his owner stops looking for him? Might it be to help him escape with his family, hire him a lawyer, or what? Philosophers who object to virtue theory complain that even if we are virtuous, we still may not have a clue as to what to do in specific situations. A possible answer is that virtue ethics need not necessarily stand alone; even Aristotle talks about finding the right course for one's actions, not just for one's character. But if virtue ethics needs some rules of conduct to be a complete theory, then surely an ethics of conduct would do well to include elements from virtue ethics. In a paper, "Is Empathy Necessary for Morality?," Jesse Prinz argues that empathy is in danger of becoming morally overrated. Different from concern (a caring approach to living beings as well as things one values) and also different from sympathy (a conscious fellow-feeling), empathy is an emotion that makes us feel, to some extent, what another person feels, a "vicarious emotion." What used to be called sympathy is frequently called empathy today, and because of the input from neuroscientists we get the impression that you can't be moral without empathy. Prinz argues that while empathy can be a valuable part of making moral judgments, it is by no means necessary, and may sometimes obscure the real issues involved. Good emotional motivators for moral action are anger and guilt, he says (compare what you read about anger in Chapter 7), but empathy can end up being selective and unfair (the "cuteness effect"), easily manipulated, and prone to in-group biases. And the more we hear about the plight of some strangers, the more empathetic we will be, while news stories that are hardly covered leave us with much less empathy. Besides, says Prinz, you can only empathize with individuals, not with large unfortunate groups of people. If we want to make lives better for others, we should use other emotions such as anger, and combine it with the logic of estimating what can be done about it.

In other words, Prinz agrees with Bennett that it's better to use one's head, plus feelings, than use one's heart exclusively. And even if Martha Nussbaum (see Chapter 1) argues that emotions have their valuable place in ethics, she doesn't say we should skip our reason and only act on feelings. We will take another look at the possibility of a combination of theories at the end of this chapter. In Prinz's words,

> What we really need is an intellectual recognition of our common humanity and combined with a keen sense that human suffering is outrageous. If we could cultivate these two things, we would achieve greater commitment to global welfare. . . . I do not want to suggest that we should actively suppress empathy. Perhaps it enriches the lives of those who experience it, and perhaps it helps to foster close dyadic relations in personal life. But, in the moral domain, we should regard empathy with caution, given empathetic biases, and recognize that it cannot serve the central motivational role in driving prosocial behavior. Perhaps empathy has a place in morality, but other emotions may be much more important: emotions such as guilt and anger. When confronted with moral offenses, it's not enough to commiserate with victims. We should get uppity.

In other words, Prinz agrees with Bennett that it's better to use one's head, plus feelings, than use one's heart exclusively. And even if Martha Nussbaum (see Chapter 1) argues that emotions have their valuable place in ethics, she doesn't say we should skip our reason and only act on feelings. We will take another look at the possibility of a combination of theories at the end of this chapter.

Gratitude: Asian Tradition and Western Modernity

The Russian writer Ivan Turgenev tells the following story in his *Prose Poems* (1883): Once upon a time there was a party in heaven, and the Most High had invited all the virtues. Big and small virtues arrived, and everybody was having a good time, but the Most High noticed that two beautiful virtues didn't seem to know each other, so He went over and introduced them: "Gratitude, meet Charity; Charity, meet Gratitude." The two virtues were very surprised, because this was their very first encounter since the creation of the world. . . . Gratitude as a virtue usually implies that it is something that is *owed* to someone. The question is, Are we obliged to feel or show gratitude just because someone expects it, or are there guidelines for when we should express gratitude?

For one thing, gratitude is a feeling, like love (see Box 11.6). Either you feel love or you don't, and nobody can make you feel it if you don't. (This is something that is known by anyone who has experienced unrequited love.) Similarly, we can't make people feel grateful to us for something we have done for them; indeed, the more we point out how grateful they should be, the more distant and uncooperative they may become. So perhaps we should not talk about making people *feel* gratitude; perhaps we should talk instead about encouraging them to *show* it. Even if you don't *feel* grateful for the socks you got for your birthday, it would be virtuous to *show* gratitude to the person who gave them to you. Not everyone agrees with that viewpoint—I knew a European pedagogue who taught his children that they never had to say thank you or show gratitude for presents given to them, because they had not asked for those presents and to show gratitude without feeling was, in his view, hypocrisy. He may have been right, but life must have been hard for those children when they realized that few others play by the same rules as their father. There are limits to how far you can place yourself and your family outside the mainstream of your culture without getting your nose bloodied from time to time.

Box 11.6 LOVE AS A VIRTUE

When we talk about love as a virtue, we usually are not talking about passionate love. Passionate love does involve virtue; the passionate lover should not be self-effacing or too domineering, for example. However, that is not the issue here. The issue is love that we can *expect* of someone, and we usually can't expect to receive passionate love on demand. During the marriage ritual, when we promise to love and cherish each other, are we promising our partner that we will be passionately in love with him or her forever? Some undoubtedly see it that way, and they often are in for terrible disappointment if the passionate love of their relationship turns out not to last forever. Of course, there are fortunate couples who remain passionately in love over the years or whose passion develops into even deeper feelings, but that is not something every couple can count on. The promise to love each other is, rather, a promise to *show* love, to show that you care about the other person's welfare and happiness and are 100 percent loyal to that person. That we *can* promise to do, even if passion might not last. So love can be a virtue between people who love each other. The Christian virtue of love does not imply any marital promises but is, rather, an impersonal reverence for other people. Because it also does not involve romantic passion, it can be a requirement in an ethical system too.

We Owe Our Parents Everything: Confucius, Mencius, and Lin Yutang

Most of the topics we have discussed in this book are part of the Western philosophical legacy, but other cultures around the world have their own philosophical traditions and moral values, as you saw in Chapter 3. In Chapter 8, also, you saw some examples of virtue ethics in the African and American Indian traditions. Here we take a look at the moral philosophies of Confucius (latinized version of Kǒng Fūzǐ) and his student Mencius (Mengzi) and carry the theme into the twentieth century with the Chinese philosopher Lin Yutang. The subject is gratitude, and the natural recipients of our gratitude are the elderly.

Chinese culture was already ancient in 551 B.C.E. when Confucius was born. When he died in 479 B.C.E., his thoughts on the *superior man* had already changed life and politics in his country, and they were to remain influential, even during periods of opposition, until the twentieth century in China. For centuries the common Chinese attitude toward virtue and right conduct had been to ask the advice of the spirits through divination. However, a certain practical vision had by and large replaced that view by the time of Confucius—a realization that human endeavor was more effective than spiritual guidance. The more important questions became What exactly is a good person? and What is the best kind of human endeavor? The questions were important because whoever was best—a "man of virtue"—was considered to be the person best equipped to rule the country. Before Confucius, such a man was presumed to be a nobleman, but Confucius redefined the man of virtue, the superior man, as someone who is wise, courageous, and humane; someone who thinks well and acts accordingly; someone who models his behavior after virtuous men of the past; and someone who understands that life is a long learning process. The man of virtue exhibits his humanity by being benevolent, and he seeks not profit or revenge but righteousness. Right conduct may show itself in rectifying what is wrong or in particular in rectifying *names,* or titles (in other words, using the proper words to address others, in particular one's superiors). Studying proper conduct and developing proper character are the same as studying *the Way* (*Dao,* or *Tao*). The Way means the way to proper conduct and proper character—wisdom—and only through studying the Way do people become superior. How do we practice the Way? By developing good habits and continual good thinking. The evils to watch out for are, in particular, greed, aggressiveness, pride, and resentment. It truly is possible to become a superior man, according to Confucius, because people can be transformed by learning. Once we have learned enough about the Way to recognize it, we will know that there is virtue in *moderation.* (Like the Greeks, Confucius believed in the virtuous nature of the *mean* between the extremes of deficiency and excess; see Box 11.7.)

Confucianism is closer to virtue ethics than to an ethics of conduct, although proper conduct is also part of Confucius's philosophy. For the Confucian philosopher, ethics is not a matter of rigid definitions of what to do or how to be but a matter of virtues and behaviors that depend on circumstances. To know whether an action is appropriate, you must know how it affects others and whether it might be conducive or detrimental to the harmony of society. Virtue, *te,* consists of both personal character formation and good use of power by a government with good intentions. A person or a government that has achieved *te* is living according to *tao* (*dao*) and has also attained the basic virtues of *jen, li,* and *yi.* As with the term *tao,* there are no easy Western translations for these concepts: *Jen* means having a caring attitude toward others, including nonhuman beings; *li* means understanding and performing rituals correctly, but *li* is empty without *jen* (just knowing how to perform ceremonies correctly is meaningless if you don't have a caring approach); and *yi* is the understanding of what is proper and appropriate, not just in terms of etiquette but also in terms of whether something is reasonable and rational. So to have *li* (the understanding of rituals) you have to have *jen* (caring), but you must definitely also have *yi* (reasoned judgment) so you know what rituals are important and why. The classical Chinese society was burdened with many elaborate rituals and ceremonies, and Confucius allowed for one's critical sense to cut through and determine what was essential and practical and what was not, depending on the circumstances.

Box 11.7 CONFUCIUS AND ARISTOTLE

There are some extraordinary parallels between the virtue theory of Confucius and that of Aristotle; both men greatly influenced posterity, each in his own way. For both thinkers, good habits are the proper way to develop a good character. Both Confucius and Aristotle emphasized the link between good thinking and subsequent action, and both believed that the virtuous human being is one who recognizes the *mean,* the middle state of moderation. But there are also considerable differences. For Confucius, the superior man is one who shuns pride and strives for humility; Aristotle would have considered such a man to have insufficient self-appreciation. Confucius also seems to have reached out to a more inclusive moral universe than Aristotle did, and that has caused some scholars to compare him to Christian thinkers.

Confucius is known to have expressed a version of the Golden Rule: Don't do to others what you wouldn't want them to do to you, sometimes called the "Silver Rule." (See Box 4.8.) We don't find this attitude in Aristotle's writings, because the general idea of *moral equality,* which is essential for the Golden Rule, is absent in Aristotle's code of ethics. Confucius's superior man also must appreciate *cooperation*—both between people and between people and Nature—whereas Aristotle stressed the hierarchy of rule. Both men, however, envisioned a state that is run according to the model of a well-functioning family, with the ruler as paterfamilias at the head, deciding what is best for his family.

Confucius's ideas of the virtuous man and the well-run state became so influential that they were adopted as state religion in China for a period of several hundred years (618–907 C.E.) even though Confucius didn't concern himself with religious questions. He believed that because we know very little about death and any life after death, we must focus our effort on this life and our relationships with other human beings. (Box 11.8 explains some differences between Confucianism and Taoism.)

Mencius (371–289 B.C.E.) followed in Confucius's footsteps but took Confucianism one step further. He believed not only that humans can learn to be good but also that they are good from the beginning; they just have been corrupted by life and circumstances. Mencius thought the proper method of finding our way back to our lost goodness is to look inside ourselves and recapture our nature—our conscience and our intuition. If we pay proper attention to our own good nature, it will grow and take over. Only through ourselves can we find the right way, and that process requires a certain amount of suffering. When we suffer, our character is developed. Mencius doubts that someone who has led an easy life can be truly virtuous. The virtues we are supposed to develop through suffering are independence, excellence, mental alertness, courage, and quietude of spirit. When we have reached such a mental equilibrium, we can help others achieve the same, because benevolence is the prime virtue.

The following admonishments are quoted from *The Book of Mencius,* a collection of sayings probably compiled by his followers. This excerpt shows that for Mencius the development of one's character is fundamentally the most important moral task. Although one has duties (which is why there are rules for *conduct,* which one ought to follow), one is not able to fulfill those duties without being *virtuous*—in other words, without having retained one's moral character:

Box 11.8 TAOISM

The Chinese philosopher Lao-Tzu (Laozi) was a contemporary of Confucius. The two men knew each other and disagreed politely on several essential points, the most important one being the usefulness of social action. For Confucius, the superior man must try to effect change, to make life better for others. For Lao-Tzu, that is a useless endeavor, because humans can't effect changes. Nature is a complex duality of opposite forces working together, the forces of yin and yang, he believed. These forces work according to a pattern that can't be observed by most humans, and things happen in their own time. The best humans can do is to contemplate that fact. This is the only access to the Way, or Tao (Dao): By doing nothing, by letting nature take its course, we are not obstructing this course; we are emptying our minds of the constant question What should I do next? And by letting our minds become still and perfectly empty, we are opening ourselves to the truth of the Way. The Tao of Lao-Tzu is far more mystical than that of Confucius, which is why his ideas have acquired their own label, Taoism (Daoism). Virtue and proper conduct meld together in the concept of "doing nothing," or rather "not overdoing it," *wu wei,* which entails unselfishness and mental tranquility. Interestingly enough, that doesn't mean that you deliberately should refrain from doing things like taking a box of matches out of the hands of a 3-year-old; indeed, not to do so would be a selfish, willful act. You *should* take the matches away from the child but without congratulating yourself that you've saved her life; after all, she may head straight for your medicine cabinet next. Do what you have to do, but don't think you can make a difference; eventually that will give you peace of mind. That is the hard lesson of Taoism.

What is the most important duty? One's duty towards one's parents. What is the most important thing to watch over? One's own character. I have heard of a man who, not having allowed his character to be morally lost, is able to discharge his duties towards his parents; but I have not heard of one morally lost who is able to do so. There are many duties one should discharge, but the fulfillment of one's duty towards one's parents is the most basic. There are many things one should watch over, but watching over one's character is the most basic. . . . Benevolence is the heart of man, and rightness his road. Sad it is indeed when a man gives up the right road instead of following it and allows his heart to stray without enough sense to go after it. When his chickens and dogs stray, he has sense enough to go after them, but not when his heart strays. The sole concern of learning is to go after this strayed heart.

The tradition of Confucius and Mencius continued into twentieth-century China and is noticeable to this day. A modern voice of that tradition is Lin Yutang (1895–1976). Aside from Mao Zedong, Lin Yutang may be the most influential of all twentieth-century Chinese writers in the West. He traveled extensively in the United States but never lost touch with his Chinese heritage and values. Even more than by Confucius, Lin Yutang was inspired by Mencius. Lin Yutang himself believed that Western philosophers were too fixated on the idea of reason and had forgotten what the ancient Greek thinkers saw as the most important element of their philosophy: human happiness. In his 1937 book *The Importance of Living,* he mentions with much modesty that he is uneducated in philosophy. His knowledge of both Chinese and Western philosophy is considerable, however. What is the importance of living? Knowing when to take things seriously and when to laugh at the solemnity of life; being so fortunate and living so long that one can become a serious intellectual and then return to a higher level of simple thinking and simple ways.

In several books Lin Yutang attempted to bridge the gap between East and West, especially at a time during the first half of the twentieth century when there wasn't much understanding between the two worlds. Writing about family values in a transitional period during which Chinese values were changing (the later Communist takeover forced a transfer of authority to the people as the feudal system was dissolved), Lin Yutang saw the greatest difference between East and West not in the area of politics or gender issues but in the way we treat our elderly—our parents in particular.

Corbis/Getty Images

Lin Yutang (1895–1976), the author of *The Importance of Living* (1937) and *The Wisdom of China and India* (1955), may be the modern Chinese thinker best known in the Western world. He worked hard to create a cross-cultural understanding between East and West, but he himself believed that some traditional Eastern values, such as respect for the elderly, are fundamentally different from modern Western values.

Whereas a Western man might think most about helping women and children, a Chinese man would think primarily about helping his parents and other elderly people. That is not because the elderly are thought of as being helpless; it is because they are *respected.* In the Chinese tradition, the older you are, the more respect you deserve. Lin Yutang describes this in *The Importance of Living:*

In China, the first question a person asks the other on an official call, after asking about his name and surname, is "What is your glorious age?" If the person replies apologetically that he is twenty-three or twenty-eight, the other party generally comforts him by saying that he still has a glorious future and that one day he may become old. But if the person replies that he is thirty-five or thirty-eight, the other party immediately exclaims with deep respect, "Good luck!"; enthusiasm grows in proportion as the gentleman is able to report a higher and higher age, and if the person is anywhere over fifty, the inquirer immediately drops his voice in humility and respect.

Just as people under twenty-one in our culture may lie about their age to get into clubs that serve liquor, Chinese young people may pretend to be older to gain respect. But in the West there is a point at which most people don't want to seem older than they are; in fact, they might like to appear *younger* than they are. The Chinese traditionally want to appear *older* throughout their lives, because it is to their advantage. Lin Yutang saw the quest for youth in American culture as alien and frightening—and he was writing in the 1930s, when American teens still attempted to dress and act as "adults." Today, in the exaggerated youth cult that is part of the baby boomer legacy, the phenomenon has become even more extreme. As respect grows with age in the Chinese traditional culture, it seems to *diminish* with age in the West: Somehow we perceive ourselves and others as less powerful, beautiful, and valuable as we reach the far side of fifty or even forty. Lin Yutang quotes an American grandmother who says that it was the birth of her first grandchild that "hurt," because it seemed to be a reminder of the loss of youth. (Box 11.9 discusses our attitude toward aging and how it affects retirement.)

Box 11.9 SELF-WORTH AND RETIREMENT

Lin Yutang chastises the West for its "throw-away" attitude toward the older generation. He praises respect and love for one's parents and grandparents as virtues that have to be learned. The West, however, has not always discarded its citizens at the onset of old age. In earlier farming communities in particular, elders not only were respected but also were considered an important part of the community because of their *usefulness.* Perhaps they couldn't knead bread or plow the field anymore, but they still could share their wisdom and look after the children. In some parts of the Western world, we still can find that type of relationship within a community. But as most people would agree, it is not the case in the larger cities of the West, where it is not customary for grandparents to live with their children. The general attitude seems to be that showing signs of aging is somehow a flaw. A British writer once wrote of Americans that they think death is optional—that if you die you must have done something wrong, such as not having taken enough vitamins.

It would appear that part of our problem with accepting the aging process is that as Westerners we have developed the attitude that when we stop being *productive,* we stop being *valuable* as human beings. When a person retires, that feeling often is reinforced, because the person is all of a sudden excluded from part of his or her habitual environment—the workplace. Especially during the early and middle years of the twentieth century, when people would stay in their jobs for over forty years, retirement forced a reevaluation of the person's identity, and all too often the retiree felt that he or she had been *reduced* in value, had been deemed useless by

society. And as you read in Box 11.3 on loyalty, losing one's "work family" might also create a personal crisis. That may be one reason it is not uncommon for people to fall ill and even die a short time after retirement, even if they had initially looked forward to it.

There are signs that this trend may change; there is a growing awareness that older people are still people, and because nowadays people usually don't stay at the same job as long as they did in previous generations they may depend less on their jobs for their sense of identity. Also, many retirees reenter the workforce part-time, either because they want to or, sadly, because they can't afford not to. The baby boomers, born between 1945 and 1960, are now mostly in retirement and they have not gone away quietly: second careers have been a common option, not just out of financial necessity, but also from personal choice. With potential for longer life spans and a growing understanding that mental powers don't automatically decline after sixty, one's eighties may truly be becoming the "new sixties"—provided that there is some form of health insurance, no devastating pandemics or other major disasters, and that the seniors do their part to stay in shape. Besides, the world of retail is beginning to realize that though it may be sexy to appeal to teens, their buying power doesn't even come close to the buying power of their grandparents. So the "Gray Gold" has indeed been courted more than we have been used to in the past—even if it may largely be in ads for easier living for seniors.

American parents are afraid to make demands on their children, says Lin Yutang. Parents are afraid of becoming a burden, of meddling in their children's affairs, of being nosy. But in whose affairs would we meddle if not in the affairs of those who are closest to us? he asks. Parents do have a right to make demands of their children, he says; they do have a right to be cared for by their children. That is because *their children owe it to them.* We owe a never-ending *debt of gratitude* to our parents for raising us, for being there when we were teething, for changing those diapers and taking care of us when we were sick, and just for feeding and clothing us. (See Box 11.10 for further views.) Among Chinese who immigrated to the United States, for example, the guilt over not being with their parents in China is enormous, even if they have brothers and sisters who can perform the duty in their homeland. (Having had many conversations with my Chinese exchange students over the years, my impression is that the tradition has not changed much even in the twenty-first century.)

Box 11.10 THE DUTY TO TAKE CARE OF ONE'S PARENTS

For Lin Yutang, the duty to take care of one's parents is a quintessential feature of Chinese culture; as a legacy of Confucian virtue theory, which stresses respect for older people and caring for one's parents, it is a powerful cultural tradition even in today's China. However, the duty to care for aging parents is a near-universal moral rule, except in the less family-oriented lives of many modern city-dwellers. In more traditional cultures it is usually the oldest son who is expected to take care of his parents, as in China, but other traditions exist: The family tradition of the youngest daughter's staying unmarried to take care of her mother or her aging parents is, in fact, widespread in several parts of the world. Whether we might call it a new tradition or simply the demands of circumstances, in our society it is quite often the daughter living closest to her aging parents who takes on the task of caring for them; this frequently places a particular strain on such middle-aged female caregivers, since they, in today's world, also are likely to work full-time outside the home and, in addition, may be in the process of raising teenage children. In the Narratives section, we take a look at a Japanese classic novel, *Kokoro,* where the issue of taking care of one's elderly parents is in focus.

According to the Chinese conception of virtue, letting his parents grow old and die without his support is the gravest sin a man can commit. That is true for a woman too, but less so, because it is the duty of the first-born boy to take care of his parents. Whom is the daughter supposed to take care of? Her *husband's* parents. Herein lies the secret as to why it is so important for Chinese families to have male offspring. The state may take care of you in your retirement, but even so, life is not complete without a son to lean on in your old age. Since 1970 with the introduction of the one-child-per-family rule, a measure to attempt to combat overpopulation, the pressure to have male babies has been so intense that occasionally female babies have been killed at birth so that the parents could try again to have a male child, if the parents hadn't already opted for a prenatal sex test, and an abortion in case the fetus was female, or the birth of a girl was simply kept a secret: a difficult choice, since pregnancies are monitored by the state and abortions have been forced on women who already had one child. One alternative was paying a hefty fine for the second child. Another, a twenty-first-century twist has been to take fertility drugs that increase the chance of twins or triplets. If parents have chosen to keep a little girl, the response from friends and colleagues is quite different from what it would be if they had a boy. A boy is cause for celebration; a baby girl could prompt friends and colleagues to send cards of condolence to the parents. From January 1, 2016, the one-child-per-family rule was revised, and two children per family are now permitted; one reason is that the rule has now been in place for sufficient time that long-term consequences are emerging: There are simply not enough young girls in China now to "go around" and become sexual partners and wives in the next generation—and a shortage of women may have far-reaching consequences. Stories have been circulating about female babies being purchased from neighboring countries or downright stolen—and the specter of a culture with a large number of "surplus" young males raises more questions: How will these young men cope, and what will the Chinese state do for its bachelor citizens?

So far, the system has provided for its elderly citizens. Much to the shame of traditional Chinese, there are now some nursing homes for the elderly in the villages of China, but they are presumably more humane than the "human storage tanks" we have in our Western civilization because the elderly are still part of the community, and the problems of the village are presented to them in their capacity as advisers. In this manner the traditional respect for the older people is maintained, at least on a symbolic level, even though the family patterns have been disrupted.

We Owe Our Parents Nothing: Jane English

A young American philosopher, Jane English (1947–1978), proposed a solution to the constant and very common squabbles between parents and their grown children. It seems rather radical: She suggested that we owe our parents nothing. That idea is not as harsh as it appears, however. English believed the main problem between grown children and parents is the common *parental* attitude that their children somehow are indebted to them. This "*debt-metaphor*" can be expressed in a number of ways, such as, "We are paying for your schooling, so you owe it to us to study what we would like you to study"; "We've clothed you and fed you, so the least you could do is come home for Thanksgiving"; or "I was in labor with you for thirty-six hours, so you could at least clean up your room once in a while." The basic formula is "You owe us gratitude and obedience because of what we have done for you." For English, that attitude undermines all filial love, because the obvious answer a kid can give is "I didn't ask to be born." And there is not much chance of fruitful communication after that. (As one of my students remarked, a parent can always fire back with "And you weren't wanted, either," but that would surely be the end of any parent-child friendship.)

So what should parents do? English said they should realize that there are appropriate ways of using the debt-metaphor and that applying it to a parent-child relationship is not one of them. An appropriate way to use the debt-metaphor is shown in the following example given by English in her essay "What Do Grown Children Owe Their Parents?":

> New to the neighborhood, Max barely knows his neighbor, Nina, but he asks her if she will take in his mail while he is gone for a month's vacation. She agrees. If, subsequently, Nina asks Max to do the same for her, it seems that Max has a moral obligation to agree (greater than the one he would have had if Nina had not done the same for him), unless for some reason it would be a burden far out of proportion to the one Nina bore for him.

English labels what Nina does for Max a "favor"—and favors incur *debts*. But once you have paid your debt—once Max has taken Nina's mail in—then the debt is discharged, and the matter is over. This is *reciprocity,* and it means that you must do something of a similar nature for the person you are in debt to. But what if Nina never goes out of town, so Max never has an opportunity to take in her mail and pay off the debt? Then he might mow her lawn, give her rides to work, or walk her dog. If she has no lawn or dog and likes to drive to work, then he might figure out something else to do for her, and chances are that they might become friends in the process. In that case another type of relationship kicks in, one that no longer is based on a reciprocal system of favors and debts. Instead, the relationship is based on a system of duties relating to *friendship.* (See Box 11.11 for further discussion.)

Box 11.11 DATING, DEBT, AND FRIENDSHIP

Many of the problems of dating stem from a difference in attitude, says Jane English. One person thinks of the date in terms of a friendship, and the other one sees it as a debt-metaphor situation. Suppose Alfred takes Beatrice out for dinner and a movie, and at the end of the evening Alfred expects "something" in return for his investment. Alfred has chosen to view the situation as a favor-debt situation; he sees Beatrice as being indebted to him. Beatrice, however, is upset, because she viewed the situation as a friendship situation, with no favors and debts. In essence, Beatrice doesn't owe Alfred a thing, because Alfred's gesture was not presented as a "quid pro quo" situation to begin with but as an overture to friendship. The situation would have been more complex had Beatrice *agreed with Alfred* in the beginning that the dinner and movie were to be a "business arrangement" to be "paid off" later in the evening. A survey from some years back showed that, shockingly, a majority of California high school students, females as well as males, feel that dating is in fact a favor-debt situation. In that case, we must say that if both participants agree, then so be it. There is, however, a good old word for when someone sells physical favors for material goods; that word is *prostitution*. In such a situation the one who is "bought" becomes merely a means to an end.

What can you do if you want to make sure to avoid a favor-debt situation on a date? For one thing, you can insist on going dutch. The two of you probably make the same kind of money these days, so why should one of you pay for the other? Remember, nobody should expect payment for doing someone an unsolicited favor (if the people involved aren't friends), and nobody should expect payment for doing any kind of favor if the people involved are friends. So either way you shouldn't expect anything of your date, and you shouldn't feel pressured by your date to repay anything. Be careful not to abuse this rule, though. One girl commented that "it's great to be able to be taken to a dinner and a movie and not have to do anything in return!" With that attitude, she reduces her date to becoming merely the means to an end, and that's not the idea.

In friendship, according to English, the debt-metaphor ceases to be appropriate, because friends shouldn't think they owe each other anything. Although debts are discharged when a favor is reciprocated, friendships don't work that way; just because you do something for your friend who has done something for you doesn't make the two of you "even." Friendships aren't supposed to be "tit for tat," and if they are, then the people involved aren't real friends. Friendship means that you are there for each other when needed and that you do things for each other because you *like* each other, not because you *owe* each other. The fact that there can be no debts doesn't mean that there are no obligations, however; on the contrary, friendship carries with it the never-ending obligation to be there for each other, at least while the friendship lasts. It implies a mutual sense of duty toward each other. With friendship, instead of reciprocity, there is *mutuality*.

Let us speculate a bit beyond what English herself writes: Suppose you borrow fifty dollars from a friend, and then you have a falling-out with her. Because there are no debts in a friendship and because obligations last only as long as the friendship does, you don't have to pay back the money, right? Wrong, because owing money is a true debt in our society and money must be paid back regardless of whether it is owed to friends or strangers. Similarly, you have to fulfill your part of a contract, regardless of whether it is with a friend, business partner, or a stranger. Such transactions come under the proper use of the debt-metaphor and persist beyond the extent of friendships. (In fact, they often are the cause of the breakup of friendships.)

English believes we often fall into the trap of regarding friendship duties as debts. Most couples find themselves saying things like, "We've been over to Frank and Claire's four times now, so we owe them a dinner." For English, that is a gross misunderstanding of what friendship is all about. You can go visit Claire and Frank a hundred times, and you still don't owe them a thing because they aren't doing you a "favor"; they ask you over because they like you. To most readers, that may seem a trifle idealistic; after the twentieth dinner, Claire and Frank surely will think something is wrong and won't ask you over again. But English's idea is that you will be there if they need you and that you should contribute to the friendship in *some way or other*–she doesn't say how much you should contribute or in what way; how you contribute is up to you.

English says the relationship between parents and grown children should be modeled after the friendship pattern and not after the debt-metaphor pattern. Parents don't do their children a favor by raising them, and, accordingly, children don't owe any debt to them. But that doesn't mean grown children don't have *obligations* to their parents–they have the same obligations as they have to their friends. Those obligations are limitless as long as the relationship lasts; they cease when the relationship ends. No reciprocity can be evoked, such as "You fed and clothed me for eighteen years, so I'll take care of you for the next eighteen but not a minute longer." *Mutuality,* however, is expected at all times.

What is the basis for a good parent-child relationship, then? Above all, love and friendship. If those are present, all that must be considered are (1) the need of the parents and (2) the ability and resources of the grown child. The parents may be sick and in need, and their son may love them, but he also may be out of work and unable to help with the medical bills. In that case, helping to pay the bills would *not* be part of his obligations, but other things would, such as providing cheerful company, taking the trash out, or making other contributions.

Suppose the parents need help but there is *no friendship* between the parents and the child. Then, essentially, the grown child is not obliged to help, especially if the end of the friendship (if in fact it ever existed) was the parents' choice. One might imagine that this would be the time for the parents to approach their estranged child and ask for a favor in the hope of reestablishing the friendship. English seems to assume that all the parents have to do is announce that they are sorry and would like to be friends again–but what if they follow that approach with immediate requests for support? Then their son or daughter might soon get the idea that there is a calculated reason behind this renewal of friendship. (That works both ways, of course; if the son or daughter has left home in anger and later decides that he or she needs help from home, an approach of remorse and offers of renewal of friendship followed by requests for support will look equally suspicious to the parents.)

For a solution, we might want to turn to the American philosopher Fred Berger (1937–1986), whose theory we discuss in more detail shortly. In assessing the extent of the gratitude you ought to show others for acts of kindness toward you, Berger says you should look for the *motivation.* Were those acts of kindness done for your sake? for the doer's? or both? If done for your sake alone, you should show gratitude; if done for the doer's own sake, you have no obligation; if done partly for your sake and partly for the doer's own sake, you should show some gratitude, but there is no need to go overboard. In a similar manner, we might ask why the parents are approaching their grown child (or the children their parents). Is it because of a genuine wish to reestablish contact, is it solely because they want assistance, or is the truth somewhere in between? If the approached party can determine the motivation with reasonable accuracy, then he or she can decide how to react.

What should parents say if they very much would like their grown child to take a certain course of action but realize that he or she does not owe it to them to do so? Not "You owe us" but something like "We love you, and we think you'd be happier if you did x." Or, suggests English, "If you love us, you'll do x." But is the second example a very good one? To most people, that alternative would set off a tremendous guilt trip, because it plays on the notion that if you don't comply, you don't love your parents. Few people are able to follow their parents' advice all the time, no matter how much love and friendship there may be between them. One alternative approach, which was suggested by one of my students, is for the parents to explain the whole situation: "Because of our past experience, we believe it is best for you, but it's your choice."

Jane English never lived to develop her theory further; she died at the age of 31 while on a mountaineering expedition in Switzerland. In her short life she published several other thought-provoking papers, and one might wonder how that bright person might have felt about the same issue had she lived to become a parent of grown children.

Friendship Duties and Gratitude

English supplies some guidelines for how we should consider *friendship* as a virtue that applies to the relationship between parents and grown children; Lin Yutang believes the virtue that should be applied to such relationships is *gratitude.* But what about both friendship and gratitude in other types of relationships, such as those between friends, or lovers, or neighbors? How far do our duties of friendship go? Are we obliged to help our friends in every way? to help them cheat on their tax returns? to lie to their spouse about where they were last night? to hide them from the police? to buy them drugs? (Here you may want to refer to our previous discussion about loyalty in Box 11.3.) The answer is, of course, no—even if they would do those things for us. Friendship may be a virtue, but it doesn't entail giving up one's other moral standards merely for the sake of friendship; besides, your friend is hardly displaying the virtue of friendship toward you, since by helping him or her you may be considered "aiding and abetting" someone in trouble with the law. A good friend doesn't ask that of another. But that doesn't mean you can't do *something* for your friends when they are in trouble, such as being there for them to talk to or finding them an appropriate counselor. (Box 11.12 discusses how the Golden Rule applies to such issues.)

Box 11.12 DOES THE GOLDEN RULE ALWAYS WORK?

The Golden Rule has been mentioned several times in this text, such as in Chapter 4, and it is certainly one of the most widespread rules of ethics in existence, finding expression in religions and moral teachings throughout recorded history. But is it always the best solution to do unto others as you would have them do unto you? Suppose a friend wants you to put her up for a few weeks. She tells you she has been involved in a hit-and-run accident, and now she wants to hide from the police. You are reluctant to let her stay, but she assures you that she would do the same for you or even that you would want her to do the same for you if you were in trouble. But that may not be the case;

you may see the situation in quite a different light. If you were in trouble you might need a friend, but you might not ask that friend to hide you; chances are you wouldn't have left the scene of the accident in the first place. (Staying at the scene is, of course, the only ethical course of action—besides, it's the law.) Your friend's perception of what she wants done for her is not the same as what you might want a friend to do for you. In everyday life we find many examples of this type of situation: Maria gives Cheryl a bread machine for Christmas because that's what Maria would like to get. But she didn't think to find out whether Cheryl might also like one, and in fact, Cheryl doesn't like kitchen gifts. Even an episode of the television series *The Simpsons* has dealt with the phenomenon: Homer Simpson shops for a present for his wife, Marge, and ends up giving her a bowling ball, because that's what *he* wants! Often, such misplaced acts of kindness are caused by a self-centered attitude or a lack of perception, but they also may happen because of a fundamental difference in the approach to life. In her book *That's Not What I Meant,* the linguist Deborah Tannen describes a classic situation of misapplied Golden Rule approaches between partners who have different visions of correct behavior (or what Tannen calls different "styles"):

Maxwell wants to be left alone, and Samantha wants attention. So she gives him attention, and he leaves her alone. The adage "Do unto others as you would have others do unto you" may be the source of a lot of anguish and misunderstanding if the doer and the done unto have different styles.

It appears that if we are to act on the Golden Rule, we have to make certain that the others really want to "be done unto." You may want to revisit Box 4.8 in Chapter 4 for a discussion of "The Platinum Rule."

A more mundane but equally tricky situation arises when someone does something nice for us that we didn't ask for and then expects something in return. Jane English states that such "unsolicited favors" do not create any debt, so we don't have to reciprocate. However, the situation may be more complex than that: The favor extended may be in an emergency in which a person is not capable of requesting help (such as someone picking up a wallet a person has dropped and returning it, or giving someone first aid after an accident). Jane English doesn't address such issues. And what if a person doing an unsolicited favor for a stranger is truly trying to be nice? In that case, doing nothing in return seems rude, even if we didn't ask for the favor. Here Fred Berger answers that certainly we have an obligation, and that obligation is to *show gratitude.* A simple thank-you, verbal or written, may be all it takes. In some situations the person who did us an unsolicited favor (offered to give us a ride or gave us a present) may *insist* that we show gratitude and reciprocate by doing business with them, going out with them, or even having sex with them. In that case, Berger says, we have to look at the giver's *intentions:* Did he give us something or do us a favor just so that we would be indebted to him? In that case, we don't owe the person anything, not even gratitude, because he did it for *himself,* not for us.

So how do we know when we owe people gratitude? Certainly we owe it when we have *asked* them to do us a favor. As far as unsolicited favors go, though, we should express gratitude when we can be reasonably certain that (1) they did it for our own sake—because they like and respect us, as Kant would say, as *ends in ourselves,* not because they viewed us as the *means to an end.* We also should make certain that (2) they did help us *on purpose* and didn't just blunder into the situation. Moreover, we have to ascertain that (3) they did it *voluntarily,* that no one else forced them to do it. In Berger's words, gratitude should be a response to benevolence, not benefits, and that applies to all relationships, even those between parents and children. We should express gratitude in proportion to the things that are done for our sake. (To be sure, not everything parents do is done for the sake of the child.) If something is done for other reasons, our duty to show gratitude diminishes proportionately. And, says Berger, when we do show gratitude to people who have done something for us, we show that we appreciate *them* as intrinsically valuable persons—as ends in themselves and not just as instruments for our well-being.

Suppose the people who do things for us like us and respect us but still hope to get something out of being nice to us? You'll recall that we discussed the issue of selfishness versus altruism in Chapter 4, and we can apply that lesson here. We shouldn't disqualify others from deserving our gratitude just because they were hoping for some little advantage themselves; it is when we were considered solely a means to an end that our duty to show gratitude disappears.

Suppose you have good reason to feel grateful for something someone has done. Let's assume you are a poor student and your neighbors have seven kids. They cook up a huge dinner every night, and at the end of the month, when you are broke, they always invite you over for dinner. They say, "We have to cook anyway, so come on over." And you do, month after month. You keep waiting for the moment when the family may need your invaluable assistance with something, but the time never comes. So you keep eating their food and feeling like a moocher. What can you do? Well, you might do the dishes once in a while or help babysit. In other words, you can contribute to the mutuality of a friendship even if you aren't specifically asked to do so.

Let's return to the question *How much gratitude should I feel?* The answer, says Berger, lies in Aristotle's theory of virtue: just enough—not too much and not too little. Vague as it is, it is still the guideline most people instinctively use when they try to figure out how to respond to an act of kindness. We know that enslaving ourselves for the rest of our natural lives, giving up our firstborn, and other such measures would be too much. We also know that being rude and doing or saying nothing to show our appreciation is too little. But where exactly lies the right amount? That is, as with all the Aristotelian virtues, a case-by-case matter. Sometimes the right amount consists of a thank-you note, a bottle of wine, or a batch of chocolate-chip cookies. Sometimes it is house-sitting for six months, and sometimes it is going across country to give someone a helping hand. If we manage to hit the bull's-eye and find the right response, perhaps Aristotle is right, and we are on the way to becoming virtuous. In the Narratives section, the film *Pay It Forward* suggests that gratitude should be handed on, as a favor to someone else, who then in turn shows her or his gratitude by doing something for someone else—"paying it forward."

How to Receive Gratitude?

One aspect of the question of gratitude rarely touched on by philosophers is a matter that, in everyday life, is almost as important as the questions of when to be grateful and how much gratitude to show, and that is the virtue of gracefully *accepting gratitude.* Just as it takes skill to be a good giver, so it takes skill to be a good receiver, regardless of whether we talk about gifts, favors, or reciprocation. What if you are the person who did someone else a favor without expecting anything in return? In other words, you treated that someone as an end in himself or herself, and the mere fact that you were able to help is enough reward for you. But now the other person wants to thank you and do something for you in return. What do you do? Saying you don't want any thanks may be telling the other person how you feel, but it may not be enough, because the other person may feel he or she *needs* to reciprocate; so you must be able to sometimes allow the other to do so, with the implicit understanding that it is not going to lead to a game of one-upmanship with returned favors. Sometimes a simple "You're welcome" is enough, and sometimes the proper way to accept gratitude may be to gracefully accept a favor or a gift in return, even if you did not do the original favor to be rewarded. And here Aristotle comes in handy again: Your guideline as to how big a favor you can accept in return for a favor should be the extent of the original favor ("just right").

Virtue and Conduct: The Option of Soft Universalism

In Chapters 3 to 7 we explored the most influential theories of what has become known as ethics of conduct, and in Chapters 8 to 11 we have looked at classical and contemporary versions of virtue ethics. The majority of ethicists over the years have perceived their task as defining in the simplest terms possible, and with as few rules as possible, a moral theory that would have universal application, one that would be valid in all situations. As we have seen, no theory so far can be said to work equally well in all situations; all theories, when put to the test, show some flaws or problems. For all its positive elements, **ethical relativism** allows for a tolerance that objects to nothing, not even crimes against humanity; **egoism**, though recognizing the right of the individual to look after his or her own interests, fails to recognize that humans may actually be interested in serving the interests of others; **altruism**, especially the ideal version, seems too demanding for most people; **utilitarianism**, though seeking general happiness for all sentient beings, seems to allow for the few to be used, and even sacrificed, for the sake of the many; **Kantian deontology** wants to do the right thing, but is so focused on duty that it may overlook bad consequences of doing one's duty—consequences that otherwise could have been avoided. And **virtue ethics**, which is intended as an alternative to those theories of conduct, hasn't quite solved the problem of when and how to use one's reason and rational argumentation in defining moral standards, and it hasn't succeeded in coming up with a theory of action in which the general ideas of virtue can be brought into play in particular situations or in solving disagreements between people who consider themselves virtuous. For those who look for a good answer to moral problems, that can be more than discouraging, and some might even decide, like Huck Finn, that moral speculations are too confusing and it's better just to follow their gut feelings. But that would be taking the easy way out, and actually it is not a very satisfying solution. On occasion we all may have to *justify an action*, and "It seemed like a good idea at the time" is not an adequate answer. Furthermore, we may decide that ethicists haven't come up with a complete solution to moral problems, but that doesn't mean we don't have to keep on trying to solve them on an individual basis. Just because the experts haven't given us all the solutions on a silver platter doesn't mean we're exempt from seeking solutions on our own. There *are* alternative answers.

Most of the theories we have looked at originated in time periods when it was assumed that humans would someday know all the answers to everything. It also was assumed, from a scientific viewpoint, that a simple explanation was better and more pleasing than a complex one. To a great extent that is still true: A theory gains in strength if unnecessary elements are cut away. (This phenomenon is often referred to as *Occam's razor*, from the British medieval philosopher William of Occam.) But the late twentieth century's focus on postmodernism also taught us that simple solutions may not always be available, or even desirable, because there may be many possible ways of looking at each situation. (A case in point is Deborah Tannen's example of different "styles" of behavior described in Box 11.12.) So we are not focused on seeking simple answers to complex issues in ethics any longer.

I often hear students remark, Why do all these philosophers have to be so single-minded about everything? Why can't their theories allow for nuances? It is a good question—but it is a question that is possible only because we have become a culture that allows for nuances and different perspectives. Many theories do, in fact, allow for nuances, but it is unfortunately in the nature of introductory courses that some of those nuances tend to fall by the wayside in the effort to express a theory as clearly, and as briefly, as possible. Some moral theories are strong and straightforward precisely because they don't allow for nuances and exceptions, as we have seen in previous chapters. But with the complexity of today's world, what may serve us best could be a moral approach that assumes the possibility that we can have certain basic values in common and at the same time allows for a relativistic tolerance of other values. We may be looking for what was introduced in Chapter 3 as **soft universalism**: the theory that deep down, we can agree on certain core values that are based on our common humanity. However, that is not going to be easy, because we have to agree on *which* values are supposed to be the ones we have in common, and here our different cultural upbringing and ethnic diversity may come into play.

Some philosophers have been trying for a long time to redesign the traditional theories (such as utilitarianism, deontology, or virtue theory) to make them more logical, more responsive to present-day sensitivities, or more tolerant of exceptions. But we can choose another path: seeking the best advice from a multitude of theories. The approach of Fred Berger to the question of compassion is an example of that approach: He uses both Aristotle's theory of the mean between extremes and Kant's theory of ends in themselves to explore the subject of compassion. In other words, he allows for several different theories to be used at the same time, letting them work together to achieve a functional solution. This is a very pragmatic approach, and some might even call it a very American approach, because Americans are (presumably) typically interested in whether or not something *works.*

Berger's approach may work if we don't expect too much. Letting the vast spectrum of ethical viewpoints and traditions become available as options will certainly be no easy road, primarily because we can't just decide to take the best elements of all theories and lump them together in the hope that they may work. For one thing, they may well contradict one another; for another, if we choose a theory for its advantages, we're stuck with its disadvantages too. We can't just decide to add deontology to utilitarianism, for example, and assume that a smooth theory will emerge; we may have doubled our range of solutions, but we have also doubled our problems.

It is, however, probably the only solution for a future theory of ethics. We need theories of conduct, and we need theories of virtue, from more than just a few cultural groups; besides, most of us already use an approach that combines theories on a day-by-day basis. Sometimes we consider *consequences* as vitally important (especially in matters of life and death); sometimes we think *keeping promises* and other obligations is more important than worrying about consequences; sometimes we feel we're entitled to *look after ourselves* and our own interests; and sometimes we are focused on developing a *good character*–based on compassion, courage, or another virtue. Sometimes what we really need is to listen to that "little voice," our moral intuition, which neuroscientists tell us is an innate capacity. Often we do combine those views in specific situations. But we have to be able to decide when one viewpoint or aspect is more appropriate than another, and we have to try to avoid contradicting ourselves by putting together principles that are in obvious opposition to each other. You can't claim at the same time that consequences don't count and that consequences are all-important. What you *can* claim is that there are times when consequences are supremely important (such as calling and waiting for the ambulance to come for your neighbor who keeled over with a heart attack, even if you have to break your movie date to do that), and at other times a principle may be more important than certain consequences (such as a jury turning in a guilty verdict based on clear evidence, even if it may result in rioting). So despite the reluctance of many ethicists to mix and match moral theories, we do it on an everyday basis, and we can train ourselves to do it better by making sure we don't just make loopholes for ourselves, but genuinely try to address and evaluate the various aspects of real-life ethics as they arise in real situations: duty theory, consequentialism, virtue ethics, respect for other moral traditions—and, on occasion, some legitimate self-interest (provided that it doesn't seriously disregard the interests of others).

For many ethicists today the answer lies in what is called *ethical pluralism,* multiple ethical viewpoints coexisting on our planet and within the same culture. At least that was the viewpoint of many before September 11 and other terrorist attacks around the world; some still see ethical pluralism as being the only civilized way for all of us to live together, whereas others, such as Stephen Pinker, have taken a second look at our Western ideals and traditions and found them to be worth supporting and offering to the world as a sensible moral code. Where does soft universalism stand? That depends greatly on what we call ethical pluralism. If it simply means that our culture consists of disparate and mutually exclusive viewpoints—individuals and groups not conversing, isolating themselves within their group identities, whether they be religious, political, or just based on different ethnic traditions—then soft universalism and ethical pluralism have little in common. But if an ethical pluralist can support the idea of a diverse society that wishes to create an environment with mutual respect and interest in sharing the responsibilities and joys of the community, then soft universalism can lend a hand, with its credo that we can show respect for a variety of moral viewpoints, as long as we agree that we can find some common values underlying the differences. Because, contrary to ethical relativism, moral subjectivism, and ethical pluralism (sometimes simply lumped together as "moral relativism" by its critics), soft universalism recognizes that **there are, or ought to be, basic moral truths** such as respect for others and a love of freedom—moral ideals that our nation and the Western civilization in general are based on, even though those ideals have not always been held in equally high regard by everybody. (You may want to revisit James Rachels's Primary Reading text in Chapter 3 for an expression of that viewpoint.) So a soft universalist will be able to profess pride in the traditions and values that promote such a respect for other human beings and an ideal of individual freedom while at the same time recognizing the value of diversity—as long as it is a diversity that accepts the notion of a common ground in shared democratic values. Is that less "tolerant" than ethical relativism? Yes, it is, and I suppose it is one of the philosophical legacies of September 11 and of living in the shadow of terrorist threats that the thinker who wants to be at peace with the world and accept diversity is more willing to draw the line at what he or she is willing to accept.

In the end, the view of soft universalism is that those common values are *founded in our common humanity,* in the fact that we live in groups and bond with other human beings but are also competitive individuals within our groups. So the challenge of soft universalism is to provide justification for why certain values are to be considered common ground. It must begin with the recognition that we share a common human moral intuition, a reluctance to cause direct harm. Next, it must set up a system of justification for which moral values should be considered valid at all times (such as the United Nations' list of human rights, for example), which values should be considered a matter of cultural preference and tradition, and which values should be considered globally unacceptable (such as "Some people are born to be free, and others are born to be slaves" or "People of a different religion/race/gender should be considered as having no rights"). Given that there are, in these times, schools around the world where young boys learn to hate everything Western and prepare for a life dedicated to destroying Western values and human beings, a system of ethics for the twenty-first century must look for the common ground we share as human beings, while balancing on the razor's edge of respecting others' traditions and at the same time cherishing and holding on to the best elements of our own. Whether soft universalism can provide genuine solutions to the problems of our highly complex world remains to be seen.

Diversity, Politics, and Common Ground?

It is time to gather a few threads that have been spun at various times in this edition: In Chapter 1 you read about the division experienced by much of the nation in times when we vote about issues with a moral component, and find ourselves divided—the "50-50 Nation" concept. The outcome of such a division is occasionally the assumption that people who do not share one's moral and political views must be *ignorant or stupid or willfully evil.* That attitude can be found among liberals and conservatives alike, and if we subscribe to that attitude, it entails that people whose views differ drastically (or even moderately) from "ours" essentially have no right to think what they think, because they are by definition wrong. *We* are the reasonable, sensible people, and those who disagree with us must be taught the error of their ways—retrained, perhaps even rehabilitated. They must be taught to see the light. If they resist, they are people of bad faith. But is that really the world of democracy, diversity, and tolerance that most people believe the United States is supposed to exemplify? The belief that one's own attitude is the enlightened one and that the others just refuse to face the facts can evolve into dogmatism, whether it is from the right or the left.

We have focused on *diversity* in this culture for a couple of decades now: People of different ethnic and racial backgrounds have found a place and changed what we now see as mainstream America. Women have found a place in public life and changed the face of the nation. People of color have found that not only can they run for high office, they can *win.* People of different sexual orientations have, in many contexts including the U.S. military, been included as part of the mainstream and the diversity within the realm of gender identification is now also including transgender individuals. But some of us tend to forget that diversity is not just a matter of race, ethnicity, and gender but also a matter of *convictions.* An environment that welcomes diversity must also include *moral and political diversity.* That means that a traditional, conservative environment must learn to accept that liberal members in its midst are liberal because they believe their own values are good and rational—not just because they are too stupid or narrow-minded or immoral to accept other values. And liberals, likewise, must rise above the notion that a conservative is someone who has not revised, or refuses to revise, his or her traditional opinions about values and politics. They must realize that "conservative" is not a derogatory term, and a conservative is not someone who is ignorant, stupid, or evil, but someone whose choice of values can develop with as much rationality and critical soul-searching as the development of liberal values. We must get to a point where we *respect the fact that other people may have different convictions*—but we don't necessarily have to *respect* those convictions! I am allowed to try to change your view, and you can try to change mine. But in recognizing your right to have a different opinion, and in your recognition of mine, we will live up to the quintessential American attitude, voiced by Patrick Henry in the eighteenth century: "*I may disagree with what you have to say, but I will fight to the death for your right to say it.*" (even though that attitude seems to have been by-and-large forgotten in the current political climate). And thus we will share the fundamental value of this democracy: That people have a right to think what they want and speak their mind about it, and when decisions have to be made, *we will take a vote.* Whoever wins (and it goes without saying that the voting must be above-board and can't be rigged or hacked, and so forth) gets to determine the policies—and those who didn't win still have the right to their conviction and to try to change the course of the future in a democratic way. We don't all have to agree that late-term abortions should be banned or that same-sex marriage should be allowed. But we should be able to acknowledge that those who don't agree with us on the issues we care about are, in general, not evil scoundrels but people who also have good will and who also are trying to create the best nation possible—as long as their agenda does not allow deliberate harm of others. So within the setting of a democracy, we all must agree to draw the line somewhere: We don't want to have a thought police, but we can't allow the enactment of political and moral views that entail some people being less than persons. The core value of respect for others' humanity and human dignity is the bottom line.

In Chapter 3, I speculated that the issue of finding common ground in our American culture might have a great deal to do with whether we perceive an outside threat, or whether we choose to focus on internal differences. Suppose we look at the issue in light of the previous discussion about soft universalism. How do we distinguish this proposed moral and political diversity from moral relativism? Precisely through the realization that we must choose and agree on some core values. We shouldn't ask for tolerance of all political and moral views. Some views seem offensive, or ludicrous, to me, and I will not hesitate to say so if someone asks me. But I am suggesting giving people the benefit of the assumption that they, too, make rational decisions based on their worldview, and that is what soft universalism entails: a respect for a diversity that respects our common humanity.

Study Questions

1. Define McCain's concept of courage. Do you agree with him?

2. Should we trust our moral intuition, or should we listen to our voice of reason? Explain your position with concrete scenarios.

3. What does Philip Hallie mean by negative and positive commands? Explain. Do you agree with him that positive commands are harder to live up to than negative commands?

4. Evaluate Richard Taylor's view that morality is a matter not of rational principles but of having your heart in the right place. Explore the pros and cons of such a view.

5. Evaluate the respect for the elderly as expressed in the philosophies of Confucius, Mencius, and Lin Yutang. Are such values completely alien to Western culture? Do you think modern Western culture would be improved by incorporating such ideas? Why or why not?

6. Contrast the conclusions of Jane English and Lin Yutang concerning the parent–grown child relationship.

7. Discuss the issue of dating: Is it a favor-debt or a friendship situation? Is there a way of resolving the problem of different expectations for dating partners in the twenty-first century?

Primary Readings and Narratives

The first Primary Reading is an excerpt from John McCain's July 25, 2017 address to the Senate; the second consists of two excerpts by Philip Hallie, one from his paper "From Cruelty to Goodness" and one from his book *Tales of Good and Evil, Help and Harm*. Next, we have summaries of films illustrating the virtue of courage: an episode from the television series *Band of Brothers,* "Carentan," and the film *True Grit.* We follow this with a summary and excerpt of a classic novel from Japan, *Kokoro,* exploring the theme of fundamental lack of virtue, in particular, courage and loyalty. And the film *Roma* has been selected to illustrate the concept of loyalty in particular—whether or not we identify it as a virtue.

To illustrate the virtue of compassion, praised as the true universal virtue by Western as well as non-Western thinkers, I have chosen the parable of the Good Samaritan and the film *Schindler's List.* These stories explore not only when one should show compassion but also whom one should show compassion toward—in other words, who counts as a member of one's moral universe. And lastly, we have a summary of the film *Pay It Forward* that illustrates the virtue of gratitude.

 Primary Reading

John McCain's July 25, 2017 Address to the United States Senate

JOHN McCAIN

Excerpt, 2017.

In this excerpt from the July 25, 2017 speech by John McCain to the Senate, the first after his brain cancer diagnosis, McCain calls for bipartisanship in political decision making. While the speech can be construed as somewhat partisan in and of itself, with its admonition to the president, we can also read it as a call for courage of the moral kind, for the Senate to set aside political differences and work for what McCain considered the common good. And the subtext is of course McCain's own display of courage in facing his diagnosis and its implications.

> Let the Health, Education, Labor, and Pensions Committee under Chairman Alexander and Ranking Member Murray hold hearings, try to report a bill out of committee with contributions from both sides. Then bring it to the floor for amendment and debate, and see if we can pass something that will be imperfect, full of compromises, and not very pleasing to implacable partisans on either side, but that might provide workable solutions to problems Americans are struggling with today.
>
> What have we to lose by trying to work together to find those solutions? We're not getting much done apart. I don't think any of us feels very proud of our incapacity. Merely preventing your political opponents from doing what they want isn't the most inspiring work. There's greater satisfaction in respecting our differences, but not letting them prevent agreements that don't require abandonment of core principles, agreements made in good faith that help improve lives and protect the American people.

The Senate is capable of that. We know that. We've seen it before. I've seen it happen many times. And the times when I was involved even in a modest way with working out a bipartisan response to a national problem or threat are the proudest moments of my career, and by far the most satisfying.

This place is important. The work we do is important. Our strange rules and seemingly eccentric practices that slow our proceedings and insist on our cooperation are important. Our founders envisioned the Senate as the more deliberative, careful body that operates at a greater distance than the other body from the public passions of the hour.

We are an important check on the powers of the Executive. Our consent is necessary for the President to appoint jurists and powerful government officials and in many respects to conduct foreign policy. Whether or not we are of the same party, we are not the President's subordinates. We are his equal!

As his responsibilities are onerous, many and powerful, so are ours. And we play a vital role in shaping and directing the judiciary, the military, and the cabinet, in planning and supporting foreign and domestic policies. Our success in meeting all these awesome constitutional obligations depends on cooperation among ourselves.

The success of the Senate is important to the continued success of America. This country – this big, boisterous, brawling, intemperate, restless, striving, daring, beautiful, bountiful, brave, good and magnificent country – needs us to help it thrive. That responsibility is more important than any of our personal interests or political affiliations.

We are the servants of a great nation, 'a nation conceived in liberty and dedicated to the proposition that all men are created equal.' More people have lived free and prosperous lives here than in any other nation. We have acquired unprecedented wealth and power because of our governing principles, and because our government defended those principles.

America has made a greater contribution than any other nation to an international order that has liberated more people from tyranny and poverty than ever before in history. We have been the greatest example, the greatest supporter and the greatest defender of that order. We aren't afraid. We don't covet other people's land and wealth. We don't hide behind walls. We breach them. We are a blessing to humanity.

What greater cause could we hope to serve than helping keep America the strong, aspiring, inspirational beacon of liberty and defender of the dignity of all human beings and their right to freedom and equal justice? That is the cause that binds us and is so much more powerful and worthy than the small differences that divide us.

What a great honor and extraordinary opportunity it is to serve in this body.

It's a privilege to serve with all of you. I mean it. Many of you have reached out in the last few days with your concern and your prayers, and it means a lot to me. It really does. I've had so many people say such nice things about me recently that I think some of you must have me confused with someone else. I appreciate it though, every word, even if much of it isn't deserved.

I'll be here for a few days, I hope managing the floor debate on the defense authorization bill, which, I'm proud to say is again a product of bipartisan cooperation and trust among the members of the Senate Armed Services Committee.

After that, I'm going home for a while to treat my illness. I have every intention of returning here and giving many of you cause to regret all the nice things you said about me. And, I hope, to impress on you again that it is an honor to serve the American people in your company.

Thank you, fellow senators.

Mr. President, I yield the floor.

Study Questions

1. Why do you think McCain would suggest a bill that is "imperfect, full of compromises, and not very pleasant"?

2. How might working across party lines toward a political compromise involve moral courage?

3. Do you think McCain's moral (and even physical) courage is illustrated in this speech, given that he knew his diagnosis was potentially fatal?

4. For five years, McCain was a POW in Vietnam. At one point he was offered his freedom but chose to stay behind with his fellow soldiers. That decision resulted in torture by his captors. Evaluate McCain's decision to stay in terms of physical and moral courage.

 Primary Reading

From Cruelty to Goodness; Tales of Good and Evil, Help and Harm

PHILIP HALLIE

Excerpts, 1981 and 1987.

In this chapter, you read about Philip Hallie's encounter with people in Le Chambon who saved six thousand Jews from Nazi death camps. Here Hallie speculates that doing good is morally superior to refraining from doing evil.

> The French Protestant village of Le Chambon, located in the Cévennes Mountains of southeastern France, and with a population of about 3,500, saved the lives of about 6,000 people, most of them Jewish children whose parents had been murdered in the killing camps of central Europe. Under a national government which was not only collaborating with the Nazi conquerors of France but frequently trying to outdo the Germans in anti-Semitism in order to please their conquerors, and later under the day-to-day threat of destruction by the German Armed SS, they started to save children in the winter of 1940, the winter after the fall of France, and they continued to do so until the war in France was over. They sheltered the refugees in their own homes and in various houses they established especially for them; and they took many of them across the terrible mountains to neutral Geneva, Switzerland, in the teeth of French and German police and military power. The people of Le Chambon are poor, and the Huguenot faith to which they belong is a diminishing faith in Catholic and atheist France; but their spiritual power, their capacity to act in unison against the victimizers who surrounded them, was immense, and more than a match for the military power of those victimizers. But for me as an ethicist the heart of the matter was not only their special power. What interested me was that they obeyed both the negative and the positive injunctions of ethics; they were good not only in the sense of trying to be their brothers' keepers, protecting the victim, "defending the fatherless," to use the language of Isaiah; they were also good in the sense that they obeyed the negative injunctions against killing and betraying. While those

Hallie, Philip. "From Cruelty to Goodness." The Hastings Center Report 11, no. 3 (1981): 23–28. doi:10.2307/3561320.
Hallie, Philip, Tales of Good and Evil, Help and Harm: The Eye of the Hurricane. New York, NY: HarperCollins Publishers, 1997.

around them including myself-were murdering in order presumably, to help mankind in some way or other, they murdered nobody, and betrayed not a single child in those long and dangerous four years. For me as an ethicist they were the embodiment of unambiguous goodness. But for me as a student of cruelty they were something more: they were an embodiment of the opposite of cruelty. And so, somehow, at last, I had found goodness in opposition to cruelty. In studying their story, and in telling it in *Lest Innocent Blood Be Shed,* I learned that the opposite of cruelty is not simply freedom from the cruel relationship; it is hospitality. It lies not only in something negative, an absence of cruelty or of imbalance; it lies in unsentimental, efficacious love. The opposite of the cruelties of the camps was not the liberation of the camps, the cleaning out of the barracks and the cessation of the horrors. All of this was the end of the cruelty relationship, not the opposite of that relationship. And it was not even the end of it, because the victims would never forget and would remain in agony as long as they remembered their humiliation and suffering. No, the opposite of cruelty was not the liberation of the camps, not freedom; it was the hospitality of the people of Le Chambon, and of very few others during the Holocaust. The opposite of cruelty was the kind of goodness that happened in Le Chambon.

. . . .

If evil has to do with the twisting and diminution of human life, then the government [Schmäling] ably served was evil. In a mountainous part of France where there were many French guerrilla fighters, he helped keep the French from stabbing his fellow Germans in the back and hindering the cruel march of Nazism. He helped an evil cause ably, and importantly.

But if goodness has to do with the spreading of human life, and the prevention of hatred and cruelty and murder, then he was surely good. Good and evil have much to do with perspectives, points of view. If you want to know whether cruelty is happening and just how painful it is, do not ask the torturer. Do not ask someone like Obergruppenführer [Lieutenant General] Otto Ohlendorff, the head of the special troops assigned to kill unarmed civilians in Eastern Europe. The victimizer does not feel the blows, the victim feels them. Do not ask a sword about wounds; look to the person on whose flesh the sword falls. Victimizers can be blinded by simple insensitivity, by a great cause, by a great hatred, or by a hundred self-serving "reasons." Victims too can be desensitized, but usually they are the best witnesses to their pain. They feel it in their flesh and in their deepest humiliations and horrors.

And if you want to know about goodness, do not ask only the doers of good. They may be doing what they do out of habitual helpfulness or for some abstract cause. They may not realize exactly how they are helping the people they have helped: They may not be looking deeply into the eyes and minds of the beneficiaries of their good deeds.

But usually the beneficiaries of those deeds know. Usually they have this knowledge in their flesh and in their passions. And usually if they do not have this knowledge, goodness is not happening, the joy of living is not being enhanced and widened for them. Do-gooders can in fact do great harm. The points of view of victims and beneficiaries are vital to an understanding of evil and of good.

Study Questions

1. What does Hallie mean by the people of Le Chambon obeying both positive and negative injunctions of ethics?

2. What, according to Hallie, is the opposite of cruelty? Do you think his response is a meaningful way of combating cruel treatment of innocent people? Could it be an antidote to the "banality of evil" (see Chapter 1)?

3. Would you agree that in order to understand goodness, we must ask the beneficiaries of goodness, not just the "do-gooders"?

4. What is Hallie's final verdict on the German officer (Schmäling) who looked the other way while the people of Le Chambon helped Jewish refugees escape to Switzerland while at the same time serving as a Nazi officer (see chapter text)? Was he good or evil? Explain.

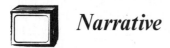 *Narrative*

Courage: Band of Brothers, Third Episode, "Carentan"

TOM HANKS AND STEVEN SPIELBERG (PRODUCERS)

Television series, 2001. Summary.

The highly acclaimed HBO television series *Band of Brothers* is, in effect, a sequel to the film *Saving Private Ryan* not in the sense that we encounter the same characters, but because we move within the same time frame and subject: American soldiers on D-Day, June 6, 1944, and further into the final year of World War II. *Saving Private Ryan* star Tom Hanks and director Steven Spielberg wanted to explore in more depth the war experiences of real American soldiers on D-Day and afterward. In the series, we follow "Easy" (E) Company's campaigns, with each episode's prologue delivered by real survivors from that unit. In this narrative I've chosen to focus on a story that is part of, but by no means all of, the third episode: the story of Private Albert Blithe. I intend for it to illustrate the concept of *physical courage,* but that is an issue you may want to discuss afterward.

It is the day after D-Day and the soldiers of Easy Company, having parachuted through a storm of anti-aircraft fire, are still scattered around the Normandy countryside. Some soldiers were shot before they hit the ground; others head toward their objectives despite the loss of most of their equipment. As these stragglers from many different units encounter one another, they form impromptu teams to engage the enemy while they try to locate their brethren. Except Private Albert Blithe. When some E Company wanderers come across Blithe, we sense that something is dreadfully wrong with him—not physically, but psychologically. He stares up at the sky, as if he's a young bird fallen from its nest looking back up at the peaceful, safe haven from which it tumbled. His gaze is fixed, he barely hears his buddies' questions, and yet there is nothing wrong with him physically.

After rejoining E Company, and surviving a firefight with German soldiers in the streets of the town of Carentan, and after seeing fellow soldiers drop dead from bullets or have limbs torn from their bodies, Blithe sinks to the ground—not wounded, but struck blind by fear and the horrors he has seen. His superior officer, Lieutenant Winters, assures him that he will be sent back to England and treats him with kindness and understanding, even though there doesn't seem to be anything physically wrong with his eyes. Winters's compassionate words are enough to bring Blithe around; his vision apparently returns, and he rejoins his platoon. It is during a quiet moment with another officer that Blithe confesses what is troubling him. We learn that after he hit the ground on D-Day, he hid in a ditch and fell asleep, rather than seek out his comrades and pursue the enemy. He feels his own fear is greater than his brain can handle. At this crucial time in his universe of terror, the brave Lieutenant Speirs (who later in the series performs acts of unfathomable courage) offers Blithe a piece of advice: You hid, he says, not because of fear, but because you still had hope—hope of survival. That hope will paralyze your actions. The only way to do your job and be a soldier is to tell yourself you're already dead.

Another battle ensues: German tanks roll over American soldiers, gunfire is cutting down the soldiers of Easy, bullets whiz and splat around the screaming Private Blithe. But now something happens to him: He raises his rifle, and as if to shoot back at the madness assaulting him, he finds the trigger and fires (and we sense that this is the first time he has fired his gun in battle) and blindly fires again, and again. At the end of the battle when he spies a German soldier on the skyline, he stands up, and without regard for his own safety, *carefully* aims this time, shoots, and sees his enemy fall. Standing over his vanquished foe, Blithe notices the man he killed is wearing an *Edelweiss*—an alpine flower that denotes its wearer as a great warrior. He takes the Edelweiss and affixes it to his own tunic. From somewhere deep within himself, Private Albert Blithe has found courage in battle. Later when a necessary and dangerous mission calls for volunteers, he is the first to step up. But this act of selfless courage is his undoing: He is shot in the neck; and though he is saved by a medic, we learn at the end of the episode that he never recovered from his wounds, and died in 1948, three years after the end of the war. The last we see of Albert Blithe, he is lying in his hospital bed, eyes staring upward, toward the peaceful sky from which he tumbled.

Study Questions

1. What happened to Blithe? Did he lose his fear? Is loss of fear necessary to find courage?

2. Does Lieutenant Speirs's advice seem wise to you? Why or why not? Does such a piece of advice apply only in battle, or is it relevant in other dangerous situations too? Is there a downside to such a piece of advice? Explain.

3. If you are a veteran, you may want to share your reaction to this story with the class or in an essay: Does it ring true? Why or why not? If you have seen the entire *Band of Brothers* series, you may want to put this episode into the greater context of the series.

4. Imagine what John McCain might say to the story of Blithe. Was Blithe courageous? Why or why not? What would Aristotle say?

  Narrative

Courage: True Grit

JOEL COHEN, ETHAN COHEN (SCREENWRITERS AND DIRECTORS)

Film, 2010. Based on the book by Charles Portis. Summary.

The 2010 film *True Grit* was a remake of an earlier Western by the same name from 1969, which earned John Wayne an Academy Award as one-eyed U.S. Marshal Rooster Cogburn. The new version received an Oscar nomination for best film, and has been viewed by critics as in some ways superior to the original: It comes closer to the original novel by Charles Portis; it is harsher and more historically correct; and the character of 14-year-old Mattie shows more "grit." Created by the Cohen brothers who are famous for off-beat movies such as *Fargo,* the film lived up to viewer expectations. But some reviewers found that the 1969 version had a charm of its own that the new one didn't quite measure up to. Be that as it may, we get introduced to the meaning of *true grit,* or courageous gumption. Who has grit? Marshal Cogburn, obviously, but young Mattie also displays her own version of courage and initiative, and is in effect the main character of the movie—rare for a Western. To add to the unusual features of the movie, Mattie was played by another 14-year-old girl, Hailee Steinfeld.

It is Arkansas in the year 1878. Mattie Ross's family has a small farm in Yell County, and her father has gone to Ft. Smith with their hired hand, Tom Chaney, to buy horses. When word reaches the family that Frank Ross has been murdered by Chaney and his two gold pieces and horse stolen, 14-year-old Mattie comes to town with their foreman, Yarnell, to see to it that her father's body is shipped back to Dardanelle for burial. And she has every intention of seeing that Chaney pays for what he has done. As she says in an early voiceover, "We must pay for everything in this world—there is nothing free, except the grace of God." On the day they arrive in Ft. Smith, Judge Parker is conducting one of his multiple hangings. First Mattie and Yarnell visit the funeral parlor where her father lies. The undertaker is taken aback that the first thing she asks is why the

Paramount Pictures/Alamy Stock Photo

True Grit, 2010. 14-year-old Mattie Ross (Hailee Steinfeld) has hired U.S. Marshal Rooster Cogburn (Jeff Bridges) to go into the Indian Territory to apprehend Tom Chaney, her father's murderer, and bring him to trial. Mattie insists on coming along to see that she gets her money's worth.

embalming was so expensive. Mattie gets her father's body shipped out, and sends the foreman home to tell her mother that she'll be delayed, because she must settle her father's affairs. Next, Mattie goes to watch the public executions. Three men are being hanged. Mattie shows little fear, and is most interested in finding out about Chaney's whereabouts. She asks the sheriff, and finds out that Chaney has fled into the Indian Territory (today's Oklahoma) on the other side of the river, and is no longer in the jurisdiction of the sheriff. Now she means to take Chaney to justice and hang him, since the local law failed to do the job. The best U.S. marshal, she asks? The sheriff gives her three choices—a superb tracker, a very mean, fearless marshal, and a very fair and just one. She asks where she can find the mean one, Rooster Cogburn. She is looking for someone with true grit.

We're introduced to one-eyed U.S. Marshal Reuben Cogburn first as a voice in an outhouse, and the next day in a courtroom where he is giving testimony. We learn that he will do just about anything to catch killers, including killing them if they resist—twenty-three men in four years. Not remotely interested in Mattie's story, he dismisses her, unless she comes up with the $50 she has offered him for bringing in Chaney.

Mattie has other business to attend to: She bowls the livery stable owner over with a series of logical arguments that she should be paid for her father's horse that Chaney stole because it was in the livery stable, and furthermore she wants the deal her father made for four ponies to be nullified. When the stable owner tries to brush her off, she drops the name of her lawyer, J. Noble Daggett. The following day she buys one of the ponies at a bargain price, and even secures her father's saddle. Happy with her new horse, she calls him Little Blackie. She retrieves her father's old Colt's Dragoon pistol from the boardinghouse where he was staying, and spends two nights—not in a room of her own, but doubling up with an elderly lady whose cold she promptly catches. So in a fever she sees a man, in her bedroom, smoking a pipe. And he is really there—a Texas Ranger, LaBoeuf, who, as it happens, is also hunting for Chaney, who is wanted for having shot a Texas senator. La Boeuf has been hired by the family to bring the senator's killer to justice—in Texas. But that doesn't sit well with Mattie—she wants her father's killer to stand trial in Ft. Smith, to answer for what he has done. She will have nothing to do with him, and proceeds to make plans with Rooster Cogburn.

Cogburn lives in back of Chen Lee's general store, and sleeps in a Chinese rope bed. The place is filthy, and he is drunk. Even so, they reach an agreement: She pays him $50 up front, with another $50 due when the job is done. At first he will hear nothing of her joining him, but finally agrees to take her along, worn down by her persistence and her assurance that she is used to camping out—she was on a coon hunt with her dad the year before. But next morning when she comes to join him, he is already gone, with LaBoeuf, who has contacted him. They are joining forces because they have common cause—getting the reward from Texas—and they have already left for the Territory on the ferry across the river. Angrily, and fearlessly she rides Little Blackie into the water and swims the wide, swollen river to the other side.

LaBoeuf promptly takes a switch to her, but Cogburn takes her side, and the team splits up—she now rides with Rooster, and LaBoeuf strikes out on his own. Rooster, who has brought a supply of liquor, tells stories from his wild life, and we get the impression that he is a lonely man. He used to have a family, but his wife left him with their son who never really cared for him, anyway. Seeking shelter from a snowstorm they reach a dugout where two men refuse to let them in, and Rooster and Mattie smoke them out with a coat placed over the chimney. In the gunfight that ensues, one young man is wounded, and Mattie persuades him to tell what he knows about her father and Ned Pepper—that Ned is due later that evening—after which he is knifed by the other man, who is then shot point-blank by Rooster, a gruesome burst of violence that leaves Mattie shocked. But she is quick to refocus, and they set up a stake-out where Rooster hopes to capture Ned Pepper and his gang, and Rooster tells Mattie an unlikely story about the time he faced down seven men and took the reins of his horse in his teeth and rode at them with two Navy Colts, and they all ran. But now LaBoeuf inadvertently walks in on the approaching gang, and the ambush is botched. LaBoeuf is wounded, but they have learned the whereabouts of Pepper and his gang, and Chaney, too: the Winding Stair Mountains.

The three are now riding together again, in an awkward truce. They arrive at the hideout and find it abandoned. This discourages both Rooster and LaBoeuf, who each decide to give up, because they consider Chaney to be long gone, and Mattie's relentless sense of righteousness can't persuade them to change their minds. LaBoeuf is leaving for home, and extends his hand in respect to Mattie: He misjudged her. Next morning Mattie goes down to the river to fetch water. To her astonishment she finds there is someone else there—Chaney himself, watering the gang's horses. She brings forth her father's old pistol and tells him he is now under arrest, and when he won't comply, she shoots him—in the shoulder, not being used to handling the gun. The gun's formidable kick sends her flying back in the water, and Chaney manages to capture her when her gun misfires. And now she is the prisoner of Ned Pepper's gang. Yelling out to Rooster that they will kill her if the marshal doesn't leave, Rooster pulls out.

Ned Pepper decides to leave Mattie in Chaney's charge, and leave with his gang for his other hideout. Mattie is highly upset because she of course doesn't trust Chaney, and Chaney is upset because he thinks Pepper is abandoning him. Pepper and his gang depart, and soon after Chaney attacks Mattie with a knife; but up from behind him comes LaBoeuf, who knocks Chaney unconscious with his rifle stock. Meanwhile, down below the cliff, Ned Pepper and his gang are stopped by Rooster. The following dialogue ensues, in a direct quote from the Portis book:

Rooster Cogburn: "I mean to see you killed in one minute, Ned, or see you hanged in Ft. Smith at Judge Parker's convenience. Which will you have?"

Ned Pepper: "I call that bold talk, for a one-eyed fat man!"

Rooster Cogburn: "Fill your hand, you son-of-a-bitch!"

Taking his reins in his teeth like in the story he told Mattie, Rooster rides against the four men with his two guns blazing, and manages to kill three of them and hit Ned—but Ned manages to shoot and kill Rooster's horse. And now Rooster's leg is trapped under the dead weight of his horse. But La Boeuf, being a marksman, manages to shoot Ned from the cliff high above at a distance of four hundred yards, before he can kill Cogburn. So, a happy ending? Not so fast. Chaney has come to, and knocks LaBoeuf out. Mattie grabs LaBoeuf's powerful rifle and shoots and kills Chaney—but the recoil pushes her down in a deep pit, with rattlesnakes. And one sinks its teeth into her arm.

Will Marshal Cogburn be able to save Mattie? You must see the film for yourself and find out what happens to Mattie, Cogburn, and LaBoeuf. And if you already know the 1969 film, don't count on the ending being the same in the Cohen brothers' version!

Study Questions

1. Would you consider Mattie's courage to be of the physical or moral kind, or both? Explain.
2. Would you describe Rooster Cogburn as a brave man? Why or why not?
3. In the 2010 version of the story Mattie is the main character, while in the 1969 original Cogburn is clearly the center of attention. Do you think it makes a difference, inasmuch as the story focuses on having "grit"?

  Narrative

Courage vs. Cowardice
Kokoro

NATSUME SŌSEKI

Novel, 1914. New English translation 2010 by Meredith McKinney. Summary and Excerpt. Film adaptations in 1955 and 1973, and a television production in 1995, as well as anime and manga productions.

The Japanese author Natsume Kinnosuke, who wrote under the name Sōseki, gives us in *Kokoro* a glimpse into a Japan in transition from being a traditional, Confucian society to a modern world of individualism and Western technology. That transitional Meiji period—the reign of the emperor Meiji—ended with the emperor's death in 1912, and the beginning of a new era, the Taisho period, is the time of Sōseki himself, as well as the main character in the novel, Sensei. The translator points out that the title of the novel is a complex word that means "the thinking and feeling heart."

The novel falls in three sections; the first part focuses on the meeting and friendship between a young man (who is never named) and the older Sensei, a recluse who seems to be a philosopher, but without any academic affiliations—indeed, without any professional affiliations at all. Sensei is not his real name, either, but means "teacher," an honorary title given to him by the young man. In the second part, the young man is torn between tending to his dying father in his home village, and longing to return to Tokyo and his contact with Sensei. The third part consists of a long letter sent to the young man from Sensei, "Sensei's Testament," because by the time the young man receives the letter, Sensei has committed suicide.* In the letter, we find that the underlying reason is a feeling of guilt because of selfishness, but we may also attribute it to guilt over a lack of courage—a general lack of virtue—in moments where it counts.

The young man, a freshman student at the university in Tokyo, encounters Sensei on the beach at a summer resort. The young man finds himself drawn to the older man's serious demeanor, and after some days of observing him taking a swim, the student finds an opportunity to talk with him. They take a swim together, and become friends, but Sensei seems aloof. Upon returning to school in Tokyo, the student looks Sensei up, and finds that the older man is married, to a beautiful woman. Sensei isn't home, she says—he has gone to the cemetery to pay his respects. Later we find out that the grave he visits every month is the last resting place of his friend, K, who killed himself many years ago. And we also learn, through the letter at the end of the story, that Sensei carries with him a profound guilt. But he shares none of that with the young student in the beginning, and expresses surprise that the young man seems to enjoy their friendship. Sensei comes across as a self-effacing man of wisdom—but is it because he is wise, or because he carries a secret? One day he confides in the student that his wife doesn't understand him—and if he really was the kind of person she thinks he is, he would not be suffering so terribly. And later he confides that he thinks of love as a sin, which leaves the young man confused, because the marriage of Sensei and his wife seems like a happy one. He also has several opportunities to speak with Sensei's wife, Ojōsan, who confides in him that Sensei changed when his friend killed himself.

But there is something else that nags at Sensei: when he was young, he lost his parents to typhoid fever, and his uncle cheated him out of his inheritance. That left him with a misanthropic world-view: when it comes to a crunch, people turn bad, he says. So now he keeps insisting that the student should settle inheritance affairs legally before his own father passes away. The student, now a graduate, leaves for his home village where his father lies sick, and says goodbye to Sensei and his wife, not knowing that he will never see Sensei again.

All summer long, the young man is preoccupied with his father's physical and mental condition. His father is depressed because of the death of the emperor, and thinks that his own time is up. He finds it strange that his son could even think about leaving him and returning to the city, because in his day, children took care of their parents. The young man sends letters to Sensei, but it is only when his father's condition takes a turn for the worse that, coincidentally, he receives a long response. And that makes him drop everything, turn his back on his dying father, and take the train to Tokyo—while knowing it is too late.

The letter contains Sensei's story, and his deep guilt. When he himself was a student, he used to be a lodger, and his hostess had a beautiful daughter, Ojōsan. But he also had a friend, K, who was going through a crisis and needed his help, so he suggested that K move into the same house. Over the next months, K fell in love with Ojōsan and eventually confided in Sensei, who himself,

---

*Kokoro contains many references to ritual suicide, and as you'll remember from earlier in this chapter (Box 11.2), the act of suicide is generally considered morally questionable in the Western tradition, but not in the Japanese culture.

unbeknownst to K, had fallen in love with the young woman. But despite several attempts where he just couldn't get his courage up, Sensei did not share that with K; instead, consumed by jealousy, he asked Ojōsan's mother for her hand in marriage, and got her consent without talking with either K or Ojōsan.

> Two or three days passed. Needless to say, I remained very apprehensive. What made matters worse was the changed attitude of Okusan and Ojosan towards me. It acted as a constant and painful reminder of the fact that the least I could do was tell K the truth. It added to my feeling of guilt. Moreover, I was fearful lest Okusan, who had a directness of manner rarely found in women, should one evening decide to tell K the happy news when we were all gathered round the dinner table. And I could not be sure that K would not begin to brood on Ojosan's manner, which seemed to me to have conspicuously altered. I was compelled to admit that K had to be informed of the new relationship between myself and that family. Knowing the weakness of my own position, I thought it a terrible hardship to have to face K and tell him myself.

> In desperation, I began to toy with the idea of asking Okusan to tell K of our engagement. (She would speak to him when I was out of the house, of course.) However, if Okusan were to tell him everything truthfully, my action would seem no less shameful than it would if I were to break the news to him myself. It did not seem so much about me indirectly. Moreover, Okusan was sure to demand an explanation from me, if I were to ask her to give K a conveniently false account of how here daughter and I had become engaged; and I would then have to expose my weakness not only to my future mother-in-law, but to the person that I loved. In my naïve and earnest way, I believed that such an exposé would seriously affect the ladies' future opinion of me. I could not bear the thought of losing even a fraction of my sweetheart's trust in me before we were married.

> And so, despite my sincere desire to follow the path of honesty, I strayed away from it. I was a fool; or, if you like, a scheming rogue. Apart from myself, only heaven knew me for what i was. Having once done a dishonest thing, I found that I could not redeem myself without telling everyone of my dishonesty. I wanted desperately to keep my shame a secret. At the same time, I felt that I had to win back my self-respect. Finding myself in this dilemma, I stood still.

> It was five or six days later that Okusan suddenly asked me: "Have you told K about the engagement?" "Not yet," I answered. "Why not?" she demanded. I felt my whole body stiffen. I said nothing.

> "No wonder he looked so odd when I told him," she said. Her words shocked me. I remember them clearly still. She continued: "You ought to be ashamed of Yourself. He is, after all, a very close friend, isn't he? You really mustn't treat him so callously."

> "What did K say?" I asked. "Oh, nothing of great interest," she said. But I pressed her to tell me in detail what K had said. Okusan of course had no reason to hide anything from me. Saying that there was really nothing much to tell, she proceeded to describe K's reaction to the news.

> It would seem that K received his final blow with great composure. He must have been surprised, of course. "Is that so?" he had said simply when told of the engagement of Ojosan and myself. Okusan had then said: "Do say that you are pleased." This time, apparently, he had looked at her and smiled: "Congratulations." Just as he was leaving the morning room he had turned around and said: "When is the wedding? I would like to give a present, but since I have to money, I am afraid I can't."

> As I sat before Okusan, listening to her words, I felt a stifling pain welling up in my heart.

A few days later, Sensei finds K dead in his room, having cut his throat. He has left a letter for Sensei thanking him for his friendship, and explaining that the future holds nothing for him. There is no mention of Ojōsan. And Sensei, knowing that it was his action that killed his friend, spirals into self-hatred for his own weakness that will stay with him until he ends his own life.

A final comment: So Sensei betrayed the loyalty of the two people who meant the most to him in the world, his friend K, and Ojōsan, by accepting K's confession that he was in love with her, but without telling K about his own feelings for her. And then he went behind K's back and proposed to Ojōsan through her mother. He kept Ojōsan in the dark about the situation for their entire life together. So for Sensei his life has been spent in sin, not wisdom, or virtue. Meanwhile, when the young man hurries to Tokyo in the desperate hope that Sensei might still be alive, he, too, becomes a betrayer, abandoning his parents when they need him the most. So maybe Sensei was an effective teacher after all?

Study Questions

1. How might Sensei be regarded as a *teacher* to the young man? Is that an appropriate title?

2. What does Sensei mean by saying that if his wife really knew him, he wouldn't suffer so much?

3. Are there parallels between Sensei's moral failings and the student's? Explain.

4. You've read Lin Yutang's statement about the Chinese tradition of children caring for their elderly parents. How does that compare to the student's situation? What do you think we are supposed to conclude?

5. What would have been the courageous thing for Sensei to do vis-à-vis his friend K? What does Sensei think he should have done? What do you think?

 Narrative

Loyalty:

Roma

ALFONSO CUARÓN, DIRECTOR AND SCREENWRITER

Film, 2018. Winner of Best Foreign Language Film and two other Academy Awards, 2019.

Roma, a black-and-white foreign-language film, gathered much attention before and at the Oscars in 2019, being released simultaneously in the theaters and on Netflix. It is a slice of life of a young indigenous (Indian) woman, Cleo, in Mexico City in 1970 and 1971, and her family—not her blood relatives, but the middle-class family that has hired her as a housekeeper. In order to explore the virtue of loyalty in this movie, I'll have to reveal the ending, so there will be spoilers ahead.

The family consists of a doctor, Antonio, his wife Sophia, a biochemist who is a stay-at-home mom, and Grandma Theresa. They live in the nice neighborhood of Colonia Roma (where the director grew up). They have four children, Toño, Paco, Sofi, and Pepe. Cleo is indispensable; she picks up the youngest boy from kindergarten, does the laundry, keeps track of keys, cleans up dog poop, plays games with the kids, and tucks them in at night and prays with them. She sings songs about being poor, but we don't get the impression that she thinks they apply to her. She even watches TV with the family—in-between cleaning up after dinner. At night she shares a small bedroom with another maid, Adela.

Carlos Somonte/Participant Media/Shutterstock

On their night out, Adela and her boyfriend Ramon choose to neck in the theater, but Ramon's cousin Fermin and Cleo rent a hotel room. Apparently after they have made love, Fermin demonstrates to Cleo his passion for martial arts with the rod from the shower curtain as his weapon. He seems like an interesting, serious young man—but we will soon learn more about his true character.

The youngest boy, Pepe, tells Cleo strange things. He says, "When I was old..." and then he proceeds to talk about when he was a fighter pilot and was shot down, and later we hear that he was a sailor, and drowned. He says to her, "When I was old, you were there, but you were someone else." Cleo just smiles and shrugs it off, and goes about her business.

The doctor is leaving for a conference in Quebec, and we sense that there are tensions between him and his wife. And Cleo has problems of her own: at the movies she tells Fermin that she thinks she is pregnant. Immediately he gets up, claiming he has to go to the bathroom, and vanishes, even leaving his leather coat behind.

By the time Christmas rolls around, the doctor is still in Quebec—and Cleo is still pregnant. She finally breaks down in tears and tells Sophia, dreading that she may be fired. But instead Sophia takes her to the hospital where the pregnancy is confirmed, despite Cleo's inability to say even a few words to the doctor because of shyness and embarrassment.

The family, minus Antonio, leaves for Sophia's cousin's place in the country to celebrate the holidays. Cleo likes it in the country because it reminds her of her own village, but she is not on vacation—her work continues, carrying suitcases, looking after the kids, and so forth. A strange interlude disrupts the New Year's celebration when part of the woods by the manor house go up in flames, and New Year's revelers with wine glasses in their hands try to put out the fire.

After New Year's, Cleo embarks on an important journey: she travels to Ramon's and Fermin's town, ostensibly to return Fermin's coat to him. Ramon tells her where to find Fermin—at the martial arts training grounds—and Cleo finds him there, along with hundreds of other young men who are being trained. When she lets him know that she really is pregnant, he refuses to believe he is the father, and says, "What's it to me?" He shrugs off all responsibilities and threatens her physically. Again, he runs away to join his friends. Meanwhile, back in Roma, the doctor isn't living up to his responsibilities, either. He has been in Acapulco with a mistress, not in Quebec, and he is leaving his family. Sophia is distraught and tells Cleo, "No matter what they say, we women are always alone."

As Grandma and Cleo are shopping for a crib for Cleo's baby, their shopping experience is interrupted by a dreadful incident: riots have broken out in the city, and a group of young men with guns is chasing a young couple into the furniture store. They corner the young man and shoot him point-blank in front of his girlfriend/wife. Cleo watches in horror—and realizes that one of the shooters is Fermin. The shock of the event starts her contractions, and she gives birth prematurely, to a still-born baby, a little girl.

Back home with her "family," Cleo suffers from depression. Sophia announces that they are going on a vacation to Vera Cruz before selling their car, and Cleo is invited as a guest, not to do any work (and later we find out that it isn't so much for the kids' sake or even Cleo's, but because Antonio wants to pick up his stuff and doesn't want to see his family). Arriving at the seaside, the kids are overjoyed and run to the beach right away. Cleo can't swim so she stays in the background, at the beach chairs, and watches the kids.

The final day before returning home, they're at the beach for the last time. Sophia has to check the car, and takes Toño along, and the little kids are told not to go too far out in the water. Pepe is cold and tired, and Cleo takes him back to a beach chair and wraps him in a towel—but as she turns around, she realizes that Sofi and Paco are no longer visible, and that the surf has swept them away. So Cleo, without hesitation, walks out into the surf, struggling against the tall waves, despite not being able to swim. She manages to catch sight of Paco, and grabs and holds on to him as she looks for Sofi, but Sofi has gone under. Finally the girl reemerges in the surf, still alive, and Cleo manages to reach out and hold on to her, too. Struggling, she makes it back to the beach with both kids, and they all collapse on the sand. The boy and girl are shouting that she has saved their lives, and they love her—but Cleo breaks down in tears, and blurts out that she didn't want her baby to be born.

In the car, on the way home to Mexico City, Cleo is in the back seat with her arms full of children, her "family." They say they love her. There is a little smile on her face. Back at the house they are greeted by Adela, Theresa, and the dog. The rooms look different because Antonio has removed his bookshelves and other things, and the kids' rooms have been changed, but Cleo is now back at work, gathering laundry. Life is back in its old groove for her—and yet? Maybe things have changed somewhat? As she climbs the stairs to the roof to hang laundry, three words appear on the screen: "Shanti shanti shanti."

Study Questions

1. Why do you think Cleo broke down and confessed that she didn't want her baby at the moment when she has just saved the lives of two other children?

2. One could say that Cleo shows both courage and loyalty, saving the two children at the risk of losing her own life. What do you think Aristotle would say? What might McCain say?

3. The three final words on the screen, "Shanti shanti shanti," are a Buddhist prayer for the body, for speech, and for the mind: "Peace, peace, peace." What do you think? Has Cleo obtained peace of the body, speech, and mind? Is Cleo happy?

4. Might there be a connection between the Buddhist prayer and Pepe's "memories" of past lives that also involved Cleo? Or do you think the hint at reincarnation is a coincidence?

5. While most critics found *Roma* moving, telling a story from the perspective of an indigenous person, a servant, whose life might not have looked like movie material for a traditional Hollywood screenplay of the past, the socialist philosopher Slavoj Zizek commented that the director made a wrong choice, making Cleo a hero because she is willing to give up everything for her *employer's* family, not of her own class. In other words, her solidarity and loyalty are socially misplaced. What do you think? Is Cleo's loyalty to the family a beautiful, heroic deed, or is it a sign of traditional class (and even race) oppression?

 Narrative

Compassion: The Parable of the Good Samaritan

From the New Testament, Luke 10:30-37, King James Version.

For readers with a Christian background, the story of the Good Samaritan is the archetypal story of compassion. The Good Samaritan is one of the parables of Jesus of Nazareth, and it is intended to be taken as an allegory.

> A certain man went down from Jerusalem to Jericho, and fell among thieves, which stripped him of his raiment, and wounded him, and departed, leaving him half dead. And by chance there came down a certain priest that way: and when he saw him, he passed by on the other side. And likewise a Levite, when he was at the place, came and looked on him, and passed by on the other side. But a certain Samaritan, as he journeyed, came where he was: and when he saw him, he had compassion on him. And went to him, and bound up his wounds, pouring in oil and wine, and set him on his own beast, and brought him to an inn, and took care of him. And on the morrow when he departed, he took out two pence, and gave them to the host, and said unto him, Take care of him; and whatsoever thou spendest more, when I come again, I will repay thee. Which now of these three, thinkest thou, was neighbor unto him that fell among the thieves? And he said, He that shewed mercy on him. Then said Jesus unto him, Go and do thou likewise.

To the modern reader, the story illustrates that the Good Samaritan is the one who is truly good because he acts with compassion, whereas others, who are supposed to know the difference between right and wrong, do nothing. For contemporaries of Jesus, however, the story may have meant something slightly different. A Samaritan was, for the Jews of Israel, a social outcast; the Samaritans were a population politically and ethnically distinct from the Hebrews, and people from Samaria were not held in high regard. The Jews, then, would have seen Jesus' purpose in telling the story as not so much instructing us to be compassionate as instructing us to recognize who our *neighbor* is (our neighbor is any person who acts with compassion toward us). The lesson is, "Even" a Samaritan can be our neighbor. But of course the overriding lesson is to "go and do likewise."

Study Questions

1. Explain what Jesus seems to mean by using the term *neighbor*. Is this story meaningful for Christians only, or might it also appeal to people of other faiths, agnostics, and atheists? Explain.

2. What might an ethical egoist say about this story? Why? Would you have a critical response, or would you agree? Why?

3. A university study conducted years ago tested people's willingness to stop and help someone in distress. A group of students were told to go to a lecture about the parable of the Good Samaritan, and on their way they encountered a man who appeared to be in severe pain. Apparently, the topic of the lecture didn't make any difference: Many of those students who thought they were early for the talk stopped to help, whereas few of the students who thought they were late stopped. Do you think it would make a difference to you, if you found yourself having to choose between helping or hurrying on, whether you remembered this story?

 Narrative

Compassion: Schindler's List

STEVEN ZAILLIAN (SCREENWRITER)

STEVEN SPIELBERG (DIRECTOR)

Film, 1993. Based on the 1982 book by Thomas Keneally. Summary.

All the story summaries in this book come with a strong suggestion: that you experience the stories in their original version because the summaries are intended only to highlight certain moral problems and can in no way do justice to the experience of reading the book or watching the film. That is especially true of the award-sweeping *Schindler's List,* based on a true story from Poland in World War II. The historical fact of the Holocaust is (or ought to be) familiar to everyone, but even if we think we know what happened, the experience of *hearing and seeing* people suffering (even in a Hollywood version) is more powerful than any words can convey. For the sake of the moral of the story, I have to tell you the entire story line, but I have, of course, omitted a great many details.

The year is 1939; the place is Kraków, Poland; the Nazi army has by now taken Poland, and Polish Jews are being moved to the 600-year-old Kraków ghetto. Deprived of the right to make a living, the Jews are trying to adjust. A German Gentile, Oskar Schindler, approaches the *Judenrat* (the Jewish Council) with a suggestion: Their investments and his business sense could make the start of a new factory. But Itzhak Stern, a member of the council, turns him down. We see Schindler getting cozy with top Nazi officials, showing himself to be a high roller and making friends, all for the sake of future business connections.

Two years later the overcrowded ghetto becomes a prison for Kraków's Jewish population; everybody of Jewish heritage is moved into the old city, and Schindler profits from the situation: He takes over the beautiful apartment belonging to a Jewish businessman. And now he again approaches the council with his suggestion; this time they are desperate for food and other goods unavailable to them, so investors agree to help Schindler set up his factory, making enamelware crockery. Stern becomes his production manager and immediately sees a way to help people in the ghetto by hiring them as skilled workers for the factory, people who have never done manual labor before—a rabbi, a musician, a history professor—because if they can't prove that they can contribute to the war effort, they will be deported.

Schindler sends for his wife from his hometown and proudly tells her that he is about to get rich—that all his previous failed business ventures lacked an essential ingredient that is now present: war. He is selling his crockery to his Nazi friends and making money hand over fist.

When Stern leaves his identification papers behind and is stopped without them, the Nazis are quick to put him on a train to Auschwitz. As the train pulls out, Schindler turns up and saves him by threatening the young Nazi officers with an end to their careers; Stern is grateful, but it is clear that Schindler didn't do it for Stern's sake. He says, "What if I'd got here five minutes later? Then where would I be?"

For the others being sent to Auschwitz there is no salvation; we see their suitcases opened by Nazi officials, the contents placed on shelves, their jewelry collected—and their gold teeth as well.

Entertainment Pictures/Alamy Stock Photo

Philip Hallie talks about the *institutionalized cruelty* of Nazi Germany and of the antidote of hospitality provided by the people of Le Chambon; another example of an antidote against the Nazi horrors is the true story of Oskar Schindler, told by Steven Spielberg in his 1993 film *Schindler's List* (Universal Pictures). By hiring Jews as workers in his factory, Schindler was able to cheat the Nazi extermination machinery of more than 1,100 men, women, and children. Here Schindler (Liam Neeson) argues desperately with an SS guard at the Auschwitz death camp that the children of his workers are also needed at his factory because their small hands can polish the inside of artillery shell casings.

A new commander arrives at Plazov, the nearby labor camp: He is Amon Goeth, a ruthless and barely sane man who delights in shooting people at the slightest provocation or merely as target practice. On his order the Nazi storm troopers commence the liquidation of the Kraków ghetto: Everybody is rounded up and either shot on the spot or moved to Plazov. From a hilltop overlooking the ghetto, Schindler watches the horror of the mass murder. From afar he notices a little girl in a red coat (*Schindler's List* is a black-and-white film; the girl's coat is one of only a few items of color); we see his reaction when he understands that the girl will not survive.

Back in his factory, Schindler is all alone; the workers are gone. So he goes to Goeth to get his workers back, complaining that he is losing money. Goeth demands a cut of his profit and lets him have his workers back, all except Stern.

Up until now profit may have been the true drive behind Schindler's actions, but when he is approached by a young woman begging him to take in her parents as "workers" so they won't be killed, he agrees (after first refusing). We begin to see a change in him; he is beginning to see his Jewish workers, the "Schindler Jews," as people. Goeth is in no such frame of mind, though—he tells his maid, one of the young Jewish women, that he likes her, even if "she is not a person in the strictest sense of the word." When he is tempted to kiss the frightened young woman, he accuses her of almost seducing him and cuts her up with a piece of broken glass.

More prisoners are arriving at Plazov, and Goeth wants to make room for them; his method is to sort the healthy from the unhealthy, and so he forces the entire camp to take off their clothes and run around in a circle, naked, under the eyes of the camp doctors. Anyone looking less than completely fit is taken aside and shot. When the survivors are allowed to dress, they are elated—but their joy is short-lived: In the meantime, the Nazis have rounded up the children and are now taking them away to be exterminated. A few children manage to hide, some of them inside the latrine.

After a period of more heartbreaks, Stern tells Schindler that he has been put in charge of the final "evacuation" to Auschwitz, with himself on the last train. Schindler is resigned to going home with his money and calling it quits, but as he is packing up all his money, he thinks of a use for it: He approaches Goeth and asks if he can *buy* his workers' lives, to have them transferred to another camp to set up a new factory. Goeth drives a hard bargain and agrees; now Schindler and Stern together must make a list of names of people to be saved: as many names as Schindler can afford. In the end, the list includes more than 1,100 Jews, and Stern tells him, "The list is life"—all around it is death. So the Schindler Jews are taken to the safe haven of Schindler's hometown in Czechoslovakia; but only the men and boys arrive. The train with the women and the girls has been sidetracked, through a clerical error—to Auschwitz.

By bribing the overseer at Auschwitz with diamonds, Schindler buys his women workers back but has to put up a fight to save their daughters. Finally the families are reunited, and for the remaining seven months of the war the factory produces useless artillery shells, for Schindler does not want to contribute to the killing. By the time the war ends, Schindler has no more money; he has spent his entire fortune saving 1,100 people. Saying good-bye to his Jewish friends (he is now considered a war criminal and must flee), he breaks down, thinking that he might have saved just a few more people if he had sold his car and his jewelry, but Stern and the others give him a letter, signed by everyone, and a gold ring with a quote from the Talmud: "Whoever saves one life saves an entire world." They collected the gold by extracting their own gold teeth and melting them down.

Study Questions

1. Explain the quote from the Talmud: "Whoever saves one life saves an entire world."
2. How does the compassion shown by Schindler compare with the virtue of hospitality shown by the people of Le Chambon? (See the discussion of **Philip Hallie**.)

3. Does the fact that Schindler originally hired the Kraków Jews for profit detract from his efforts to save them? Why or why not? (Here you might use Berger's criteria for gratitude.)

4. Compare the scene in which the prisoners are forced to run naked in front of the Nazi officers with Hallie's theory of institutionalized cruelty.

 Narrative

Gratitude: Pay It Forward

LESLIE DIXON (SCREENWRITER)
MIMI LEDER (DIRECTOR)

Film, 2000. Based on the book by Catherine Ryan Hyde. Summary.

This film can be viewed within several contexts in this book: One context is the virtue of gratitude, which is why it is placed in this chapter, but you could equally well view it in light of Chapter 4 and the discussions about selfishness and altruism.

On a rainy winter night, there is a hostage situation in Los Angeles. A young journalist's car is totaled by the fleeing hostage taker's SUV, and he is now stranded in the rain, at night, in L.A. Out of the mist comes a man who hands the journalist the keys to his Jaguar. It's his to keep, says the stranger—"Call it generosity among strangers."

Cut to Las Vegas, four months earlier. It is the first day of school, and social studies teacher Eugene Simonet is giving his usual class introduction to the seventh grade. Simonet's face is disfigured after what looks like a burn accident, and he obviously has a chip on his shoulder. He asks the kids, Are you interested in the world? One of these days the world will be in your face, he says, and you may want to try to change it. So he gives them an assignment—the same he gives every year: "Think of an idea to change the world, and put it into action." An 11-year-old boy, Trevor, takes the idea to heart. On his way home he sees a homeless young man trying to eat garbage. The next thing we see is Trevor having dinner at home—cereal and milk—with the homeless man. Trevor's project is beginning to take shape, the *Pay It Forward* project. But his mother, Arlene, who is a waitress in a casino, comes across the homeless guy, Jerry, in her garage and is not enthusiastic; frightened and skeptical, she questions Trevor, who tells her it is an assignment. She goes to his school to confront Simonet. The meeting doesn't go well: Simonet is standoffish, and she resents him for being conde-scending. Arlene, divorced from Trevor's father, is an alcoholic. She comes home one day to find the homeless man, Jerry, in her garage—repairing her truck so she can sell it. He is already paying Trevor's good deed forward: Trevor gave him money so he could get cleaned up, and he found a job—and he'll try to kick his drug habit. Now Trevor explains his project in class: If we each help three strangers, and they in turn have to help three other strangers, then we will see a very rapid change for the better in the world. But each act of helping has to be a major, difficult thing, or it doesn't count. Simonet is impressed—it is the first new idea he has heard in his years of teaching.

Trevor experiences two setbacks—Jerry has a relapse into drugs, so now Trevor has to find someone else to help. He focuses on a small school friend who suffers from asthma and who is regularly tortured by two older boys; but when push comes to shove, Trevor can't make himself intervene. And the third person he has decided to help? Simonet. He wants him to date his mother, both for the teacher's sake and for Arlene's—because Arlene is an alcoholic and needs someone stable in her life, and if someone is there, then Trevor's father might not try to come back. We hear that Trevor's father, Ricky, has beaten up Arlene on several occasions, and we understand that Trevor is afraid the old pattern is going to repeat itself, in a never-ending circle of alcohol and violence. So now Trevor plays matchmaker for his mom and Eugene Simonet. Slowly the two warm up to each other and begin to understand that they are not trapped in roles where they are unloved and unwanted. For a short while they seem like a happy couple, and all three act like a content, normal nuclear family—until the return of Ricky puts an end to their happiness. Arlene decides to give Ricky another chance, and when Eugene blames her for exposing Trevor to danger, we finally hear the story behind Eugene's disfigurement: His own father was a violent alcoholic, and when Eugene was sixteen, he confronted his father—who beat him senseless, dragged him into the garage, doused him with gasoline, and set fire to him.

In the meantime, we hear more about the journalist who was given a Jaguar by a complete stranger. Intrigued, he has tracked down the owner and made him reveal why he gave away his car. He was "paying it forward"—after an immense gesture extended to him by a very unlikely character: He was in the emergency room with his daughter, who was suffering from an asthma attack, and the nurse wasn't paying attention to her. An injured man, a young black gangbanger, took charge and forced the nurse to help the gasping girl, firing his gun to make a point. The gunman went to prison, but the girl's life was saved. And the gunman told the father that he must pay the favor forward, to three people—so the journalist stuck in the rain was one.

TCD/Prod.DB/Alamy Stock Photo

From the film *Pay It Forward:* For a short while, Trevor (Haley Joel Osment) is happy. He has brought his mother, Arlene (Helen Hunt), and his favorite teacher, Eugene Simonet (Kevin Spacey), together, and it looks as if things might be working out. But Trevor's violent, alcoholic father, Ricky, returns, and Arlene decides to give him another chance.

The journalist seeks out the young black man in prison and gets him to tell his story by arranging an early parole date. The young man explains that he was running away from rival gang members in Vegas when an old white lady gave him a ride and saved his life—she was a bag lady, living out of her car, and she told him to pay it forward. So now the journalist must look for the old lady in Las Vegas, because he recognizes a good story when he sees one.

We meet Jerry one more time; he has left Las Vegas and gone up to the Pacific Northwest, without being able to kick his drug habit. Absorbed in his own misery, he crosses a bridge—and sees a woman about to jump to her death. He manages to talk her down and realizes that he is now paying it forward—Trevor's project is indeed spreading.

The journalist manages to find the bag lady, who tells her story. Her daughter had sought her out in one of the places where she'd normally drink herself into a stupor and spend the night, simply to tell her that she had forgiven her—for terrible things done to her when she was a child, by her mother's boyfriends while her mother was drunk. She will even let her mother visit with her son again, if the old lady can stay sober; and she has decided to forgive her mother because of an invention her son has made, which he calls "pay it forward." The daughter is, of course, Arlene, Trevor's mother. So now the journalist finally meets Trevor, the source of the project that is spreading like wildfire—to Los Angeles, San Francisco, Phoenix, and the Northwest. On his twelfth birthday he is interviewed by the journalist at the school. Trevor is not impressed with himself; he doesn't think he has succeeded, but he does tell the journalist that you have to try to make changes—that some people are so afraid of change, even for the better, that they just give up. Hearing these words, Eugene realizes that he is one of those people, and he and Arlene fall into each other's arms. And that night, Trevor's interview will be broadcast on national TV, and everyone will hear about the Pay It Forward project.

After the interview Trevor is about to leave the school and sees his friend, the asthmatic boy, again being attacked by the two older boys. Trevor wants so badly to make the world better, to make a difference—will he be able to help his friend this time? Will he be able to enjoy the changes he has indeed set in motion and have a real family life with his mother and Eugene? I will not reveal the ending of the film—you will have to watch it yourself.

Study Questions

1. What might Fred Berger say about showing one's gratitude by paying it forward? Would that be an appropriate reaction? Why or why not? What would Jane English say?

2. Could you undertake a project such as Pay It Forward? Whom would you choose to help? Remember the help must be big, and difficult for you, if it is to count. And what if someone chooses to do something special for you, as a Pay It Forward project—would you feel obliged to continue the project?

3. If you do a big favor for someone, would you be content with him or her paying it forward, or would you like a show of gratitude that is directed toward yourself?

4. From a realistic (some would say, cynical) point of view, is this a wise behavior model to follow? In 2003 a young girl was abducted and killed by a homeless man the family had invited home for dinner, and the same year another young woman, Elizabeth Smart, was abducted by a street person her father had hired as a handyman to help him out—but Elizabeth was rescued and returned safely nine months later. Is it advisable to do favors for strangers, as Trevor does? Are we being too cynical if we think of worst-case scenarios?

Chapter Twelve
Different Gender, Different Ethics?

In this book we have examined prominent theories regarding ethics of conduct and virtue ethics, and their applications. As you have seen, both men and women have contributed to those theories, especially since the middle of the twentieth century. But in addition, there is a special branch of ethics dealing with the question of *gender,* and in the 1980s, 90s, and the first decade of the 2000s it was generally labeled *feminist ethics.* In the past ten years, the topic has expanded to include questions concerning the rights of LGBTQ persons and communities. In this chapter we look primarily at the issue of feminist ethics. Feminist ethics asks two separate, but related, questions: (1) Is there a morally correct way for society to approach the issue of gender equality? and (2) Is ethics gender-specific—meaning, is there an approach to ethics that is typical for women, and another for men? In this chapter we look at both issues.

If you ask a woman in the Western world today whether she is a feminist, chances are she will say no; if you ask her whether she believes that women and men should have equal opportunities, that women should not be discriminated against based on their gender, and that women and men should get equal pay for equal work, chances are she will say yes, and so will most men. That, according to classical feminism, qualifies anyone who agrees as a feminist, because those are the goals of classical feminism. But the word has today been weighed down by additional connotations to the extent that many people don't want to be associated with the idea of feminism; the term *feminazis,* coined by talk-show host Rush Limbaugh, hasn't helped any. Are feminists the same as feminazis? Not according to Limbaugh himself, who says he reserves the term "feminazis" for those he considers radicals. But the label "feminism" has caused some people to assume that all feminists somehow want to rule the world. If you believe that we should end sex discrimination and help create a friendly, cooperative working environment as well as private partnership for men and women based on equality, however, you are in fact a feminist, regardless of whether you are male or female according to many contemporary feminists.

Feminism and Virtue Theory

Originally, feminism was associated with acquiring political and social rights for women: the right to work, to own property, to vote, to get a divorce, and other rights considered irrelevant for women by most thinkers with political influence until well into the nineteenth century. Later in the chapter we take a brief look at that development. During its struggle for political equality, feminism rarely regarded itself as a separate moral theory; the male-dominated (often called *patriarchal* by feminists) world would often point to women's sensibilities as those of a higher moral view (think of the role of the schoolmarm in Western movies, exercising her civilizing influence), but because that was usually coupled with an assumption that women were unfit for life in the rough and heartless real world of men, early feminists usually placed little emphasis on that notion. However, a connection not just to ethics as such, but to virtue theory as well has become apparent in the past decades.

For modern virtue theory the important question is, How should I be? In other words, What is the character I should strive for? The moral rules of "doing unto others," of "universalizing one's maxim," of "maximizing happiness for as many as possible," and of "treating everyone with impartial fairness" take second place to virtues such as loyalty to family and friends, generosity, compassion, and courage. A moral vice may, under such circumstances, very well turn out to be related to a famous rule of moral conduct: If you act only when you can imagine others being allowed to do the same thing (Kant's categorical imperative), then your child or friend may die while you wonder about allowing all others to defend their child or friend. If you insist on treating everyone with impartial fairness (John Rawls's "original position"), you have an equal obligation to a starving person on the other side of the world and to your niece down the street; you have no right to prefer helping your niece. Virtue ethics, however, discards that approach as a breach of loyalty and family responsibility and insists that you *should* help your niece before you spread yourself thin helping strangers. And you can be accused of the same vice if you are trying to make strangers happy (the principle of utility) at the expense of the needs of your family.

This is where the connection to modern feminism comes in. You have already read, in Chapter 7, that Rawls was criticized for assuming we can pretend to be just strangers to one another to achieve fairness. In this chapter, we will take a look at the modern feminist theory that is the basis for that criticism, a theory that suggests that women and men tend to view the entire field of ethics from different viewpoints. Whereas men (who have written most of the theories about ethics, law, and justice so far) tend to think of morality in terms of *rules of conduct,* justice, and fairness, says the theory, women tend to think of morality in terms of relationships, of staying friends, and of caring for those who are close to you or for whom you have accepted responsibility. In other words, women tend to think in terms of the *virtues* of caring, loyalty, and compassion. That theory is advanced by the psychologist Carol Gilligan, and we look at her ideas in further detail later. But first we must take a look at the idea of gender equality: What is it? Do we have it now? And what has been done to achieve it?

What Is Gender Equality?

The purpose of feminism throughout its history, with a few exceptions (such as the 1960s women's organization SCUM, Society for Cutting Up Men, which may or may not have been meant as a joke), has been to achieve equality for the sexes. Today many refer to that goal as *gender equality.* (See Box 12.1 for an explanation of "sex" versus "gender.") You know from Chapter 7 that achieving equality does not imply that everyone is the same but that everyone should be treated as equals unless special circumstances apply—in other words, the *equity* principle. But what exactly does that entail when applied to the two sexes? Below we look at the concepts of cultural as well as biological equality.

Box 12.1 SEX OR GENDER?

By consensus, the term that is most commonly used today when people talk about sexual differences that go beyond mere biological functions is *gender.* Although this used to be a strictly grammatical term, it now is used as a sociopolitical term instead of the biological term *sexual.*

Gender and Language

Since the Enlightenment and on into the twenty-first century, it has been customary to use words of the masculine gender to refer to both males and females. For many of us it is surprising to learn that the term *man* in some political statements, such as the American Declaration of Independence ("All men are created equal"), may not have been intended to cover women or people of color—an issue that is being discussed among constitutional scholars today.

It is not true, of course, that the term *men* can *always* be used to include women; it doesn't make any sense to say, for instance, that half of all men have ovaries and half don't. Today, the use of the terms *he* and *men* to include women is considered by many to be discriminatory. And even though very few men or women ever intended discrimination by using the word *he* for a man or a woman and *man* for all humankind, we have for awhile been moving away from what is known as "gender-specific" language toward "gender-neutral" language, because many believe that even when used with the best intentions, gender-specific terms subconsciously tell us that being male is somehow more important than being female and that certain social roles are best performed by men. The real reason for being sensitive about gender and language is, of course, to achieve gender equality. (Box 12.2 provides a discussion of issues involved in gender-neutral language.)

Box 12.2 FRESHPERSONS AND PERSONPOWER?

People often seem to feel that we are getting too radical in our elimination of gender-specific terms. It may make sense to do away with words such as *chairman* and *fireman* and use *chairperson* and *firefighter* instead, but what about all the words in the English language that just happen to include a gender-specific term but for which there is no graceful substitute? Should *freshman* now be *freshperson?* We've already abandoned the term *manhole* cover for *utility* cover, and *manned* space missions have become *crewed* missions. How about *manpower?* And *manhunt?* (And, jokesters might ask, how about *man*-ipulate? and *his*-tory?) Other languages present similar challenges, but some languages have less of a problem finding a common word for humanity. German has a specific term for "human being"—*Der Mensch*—which is different from the terms for man and woman but which still includes a gender-specific term (*Mensch,* which is masculine in gender). In Danish, the word for "human being" is a gender-neutral term, *Et Menneske.* And in Swedish, the term for "human being" is *En Människa,* a grammatically feminine word! To make matters even more

interesting, there is a word in ancient Icelandic, *man,* that means slave/maid/mistress! Apparently that word has no connection with the ancient Germanic word for man (*Madr*), which is the source for the term *man* in English.

So what should we do? Change all such words? Leave them all the way they are? Two things are at stake here: the self-esteem of half the English-speaking population and the comfort of those used to an established language. We can choose from among four major courses of action: (1) Forcibly change language to some degree (and we have seen that this can be done within a generation). (2) Wait until a new gender-neutral terminology evolves by itself, in response to the changing times. We are seeing that happening before our very eyes, due to vocabulary changes in academic environments. (3) Make a distinction between sexist and nonsexist terms and change only the blatantly sexist ones. (4) Insist on keeping the traditional terms. What would you suggest?

Textbooks and cultural documents are continually being reworded to accommodate our new sensitivity toward gender and language. The Catholic Church has officially endorsed the use of non-gender-specific language in religious documents and biblical translations. Gender-specific words such as *mailman, chairman, housewife,* and *maid* have been changed to *mail carrier, chairperson, homemaker,* and *maintenance assistant* to signify that those terms cover both genders. Writers and speakers alike are instructed to avoid the use of *he* as a generic term and instead use *he or she, they, one,* or *you.* College students are urged to avoid gender-specific language in their term papers. Perhaps you think this is a subject of little importance—that it is merely a matter of semantic misunderstanding. But consider this: If you are male and you hear a statement such as "Now is the time for every man to stand up for what he believes in," there is a good chance you will feel somehow compelled to think hard about what you believe in. If you are female, you *may* feel the same way, but chances are you will feel, subconsciously, that somehow that statement does not apply to you; you may even think, "Yes, it is about time *they* pulled *themselves* together!" If even a few women feel excluded when they read or hear language that uses the masculine gender—excluded either in the sense of feeling left out or in the sense of not having to get involved—then that is enough reason to make some changes in the way we phrase things.

It is all the more surprising to many who have advocated gender-neutral language that a new trend is spreading in academic literature: Instead of the neutral "they," a frequently encountered term nowadays is "she," using the female pronoun instead of "he" or "they" / "one" / "you." A contemporary text may say, "Whenever a person contemplates the needs of another, *she* must remember that we don't all want the same," or "The soldier in battle must surely have considered the possibility that she might not survive." The rationale is, presumably, that it provides a counterweight to all the texts that used to say *he,* and makes woman into an exemplar, a typical human being, no matter what the context. Some scholars find this liberating, others deplore the waning of the gender-neutral effort. Recently a new layer has been added to the debate about language neutrality: In academic circles, people—students as well as instructors—are often encouraged to conclude their e-mails with their preferred pronoun (usually he or she), so recipients will know how to address them, regardless of what gender their name or physical appearance might imply. In addition, because of the growing sensitivity toward transgender individuals, or anyone whose gender is not immediately apparent and who might not wish to identify themselves as *either* male or female, a new set of pronouns has been suggested by several American universities, including Harvard and Cornell. With the suggestion that gender falls along a spectrum and can't be defined by just two options, new options are "ze," or "xe," and "Hir," or "Zir," as in "ze/xe is late," or "that is hir/zir lunch." We will have to wait and see to what degree these options are going to be viable on forms and in conversation.

Is Biology Destiny?

When we ask whether sexual equality exists, we really are asking one of two questions: (1) Does cultural and social equality exist? or (2) Does biological equality exist? The first question is relative to the historical time period: Today we have reason to say that we have not reached total equality yet, but we hope to do so in the future. (In the past, in Western society, the answer would have been a flat no.) But if we ask the second question, we have to ask a follow-up question: What do we mean by "biological equality"? Do we mean that men and women are the same? or similar? That they will do similar things in similar situations? Or perhaps that they have a similar genetic makeup, even if there are cultural differences?

The bottom line is the difference between a *descriptive* and a *normative* approach. A descriptive theory of equality compares capabilities and pronounces people to be "similar" or "dissimilar." A normative theory of equality may or may not look at the "facts" presented by the descriptive theory, but states that people *ought* to be treated a certain way—(1) the same, or (2) similarly under similar conditions, or (3) differently. And if a normative theory asserts that equality is a good thing, it will present a theory for how to achieve it.

Sexual equality, as an idea, is a complex issue. (The same is true of racial equality.) We must ask, Is sexual equality a biological fact? What does that mean? And is that important for an ethical policy? Let us look at what it means first. Are men and women biologically equal? We all know that, physically, most men are taller and stronger than most women, but that doesn't mean individual women can't be taller and stronger than individual men. In nature there is such a thing as *sexual dimorphism,* meaning that the two sexes of a species look very different, with one sex usually being much bigger than the other. (A consequence of dimorphism is usually that the bigger sex dominates the smaller sex and that one individual of the bigger sex can have many mates of the smaller sex, but not vice versa. Where the sexes are of the same size there are usually lifelong monogamous relationships and equal partnerships.) So do humans have sexual dimorphism? Not nearly to the extreme that gorillas do but slightly more than bonobo chimpanzees do; gorilla society is male-dominated, but bonobo chimpanzees, our closest relatives on this earth, have a gender-equal society with a tendency toward matriarchy. Biologically, there is no reason to assume that it is natural for one human gender to dominate the other, but neither can we conclude that we have an obvious natural tendency to be completely equal partners.

But are we then biologically equal when it comes to the *intellect*? The viewpoints on male and female intelligence are diverse, stretching from the old assumption that men are logical and women are intuitive, to the assumption shared by many modern people that if we are intellectually different at all it is merely a subtle difference, to the view that women's intellectual style is superior to that of men. What exactly would intellectual equality mean? That we reach the same results when faced with the same problem? Or that we reach the same results *the same way* when faced with the same problem? Recent studies of the human brain have revealed that men and women actually tend to use their brains differently when dealing with the same math problem but that they generally reach the same results in the same amount of time.

But whether we talk about physical or intellectual equality, some philosophers would call out a warning: Looking for actual equality is one thing, and perhaps a positive one, but if we intend our policy of gender equality to rest on a foundation of what we think is *actual biological equality,* then we may be in trouble, because what if scientists someday prove that biologically we really are not the same at all? Then our reason for gender equality has disappeared, and we may slide back into some form of gender discrimination against women or against men. Better to forget about looking for actual similarities and concentrate on making a policy based on *what we would like to see happen:* Instead of using *descriptive* means to make us politically equal, we might use *normative* means, spelling out how we ought to treat each other. Remember from Chapter 5 that if we try to go from fact to policy, from an "is" to an "ought," then we are committing the *naturalistic fallacy,* basing a policy on fact without adding a moral premise. But that doesn't mean we can't take biology into account when we establish policies. The idea of sexual, or rather *gender,* equality is so important now that we have antidiscrimination laws against "sexism." In other words, we believe that regardless of whether equality between the genders is a natural fact, it should be a cultural institution. Box 12.3 explores one aspect of normative equality: The issue of women in combat.

Box 12.3 WOMEN IN COMBAT?

Should women be soldiers? Whether you agree or not, the fact is that women *are* in our armed forces, and have been, in some capacity, since before World War I, starting with the creation of the Army Nurse Corps in 1901 and the Navy Nurse Corps in 1908. It wasn't until 1948, however, that women got permanent status in the armed forces with President Truman's signing of the Women's Armed Services Integration Act. In 1967 President Johnson made it theoretically possible for women to advance to the top. Today women constitute nearly 15 percent of the U.S. Army, but only 6 percent of the Marine Corps. However, those Marine women are a fiercely proud bunch: They boast three generals, and one of them, Angie Salinas, became the first woman leader of a boot camp, as overseer of the San Diego Marine Corps Recruit Depot from 2006 until 2009.

In recognition of the fact that women have actually been serving in combat situations, fighting as well as dying for their country, in both the Iraq and Afghanistan wars, the Military Leadership Diversity Commission, created in 2009, recommended in its report to the Pentagon in 2011 that the "Combat Exclusion Policy" be terminated, and women be allowed to train for and serve in combat. In 2012 the Pentagon issued a revised policy, allowing women increased access to front-line positions. In 2015, *all* combat positions became available to women in a sweeping new regulation, and in 2016 a House Committee voted in favor of requiring women to register for the draft. The Senate approved the bill that was scheduled to take effect in 2018, but it is still under debate at the time of writing this, with members of Congress suggesting an entire revision of the purpose of the Selective Services. However, that doesn't mean the debate over women in combat has been silenced. The classic arguments in the debate are as follows:

Those in favor of allowing women in combat have argued that

- It is a natural progression toward complete gender equality in a modern society.
- Qualified and well-trained women can be as effective, and as brave, as their male counterparts.
- Many women want to serve their country in combat; and if they qualify, it would be unfair to exclude them.

- Since combat experience is necessary for officers' advancement within the military, it is discriminatory to exclude women officers—it maintains a glass ceiling. (That argument seems to be outdated, since combat experience is apparently no longer a requirement for males to advance, either.)

Those against allowing women in combat have argued that

- Women simply aren't "qualified," except for perhaps a very few. The training criteria for a combat soldier include carrying a heavy backpack plus weapon during a forced march, and the vast majority of even very motivated women just can't do that. And if standards are lowered so more women qualify, the effectiveness of the forces will be diminished, and soldiers put in unnecessarily dangerous situations.
- It is dangerous for the male soldiers to have female comrades-in-arms: Because of a natural chivalry and an instinct to protect, the male soldiers will be more focused on protecting their female colleagues and may become distracted from their battle training.
- Women POWs are in greater danger of being raped than male POWs, and threats or violence against the female POWs could become an element in the enemy's interrogation techniques, wearing down the resistance of the male POWs.
- It is simply uncivilized to have women in combat.

In your view, is the new rule allowing women in combat a righteous decision, or a step in the wrong direction for our military? Can you think of additional arguments for or against women in combat?

Women's Historical Role in the Public Sphere

Gender equality is, of course, a novel idea in Western history. Until the mid-nineteenth century, it was common practice in Western culture to assume that male and female natures were essentially different in their functions, aspirations, and potential, and that male nature was somehow more *normal* than female nature. It was not thought of as necessarily *better,* for, as I mentioned earlier, many men seemed to believe that women had higher moral standards; but it was considered more important in the sense that male nature was more representative of the human species than female nature was. What was that assumption based on? Today we might say *prejudice,* but it can't be dismissed as easily as that, because for a great many thinkers, objectivity was an important ideal. They tried to describe things as they saw them, not as they believed things ought to be, nor as they might appear to an undiscerning eye. And what they saw was that few women had any role to play in public life: There were few women politicians, few women artists, few women scientists. But why were there so few women in public life? The answer is tentative; not all the facts are in yet. It seems obvious, though, that a person's contribution to what we call public life is greatly dependent on that person feeling called or welcome as a contributor. If no one expects or wants you to become a good politician or mathematician or sculptor, you might not think of trying. Encouragement and expectation are major factors in such choices. On the other hand, if it appears that you are *destined* for a certain task, you might not question that either. For most women (until the arrival of dependable birth control), motherhood, several times over, was their destiny. And for those familiar with the demands of large families, it does not come as news that the person in charge of the *private sphere,* the home, has precious little time for anything else, unless she can afford domestic help. Indeed, throughout history—Western history as well as world history—most cultural contributions by individual women were made by those who did not play the role of homemaker.

"Woman's Work"

An interesting question is why women's contributions to the private sphere are rarely discussed. It's certainly true that when women could not own property, vote, or hold a job without the permission of a guardian, many women still had considerable power within the four walls of their home. They managed the bookkeeping and purchases, planned and prepared meals for the household, educated the children, and kept things running on the farm—a full-time job in itself. Why were those management skills not considered important? In an odd way, they were; it is probably our modern-day prejudice to think that they weren't. A young woman chosen as a spouse was expected to have those skills, and "woman's work" was a vitally important social factor. But in the public sphere, women had no place and were not considered potential contributors until almost the end of the nineteenth century. (That assertion, of course, refers to women from middle- and upper-middle-class backgrounds; many working-class women have, for as long as there has been a working class, generally participated in the public sphere, simply because they have had no choice. If a widow with small children didn't enter the workforce, her children might starve to death—and she too.) Even today, many people accept the idea that the public sphere is the vital one—perhaps because work in the public sphere is *paid for* and work in the private sphere generally is not. However, asking whether women's work has been valued may in itself be choosing the viewpoint of the public sphere in which men have traditionally determined values; women have traditionally always valued one another's work, learned from it, criticized it, improved it, and shared it. From a traditional woman's point of view, the question of public (male) recognition for her work may not be the most important question: What may matter more is receiving recognition and appreciation for her work from her peers in the community, other women.

Another factor must be mentioned here. In early times, having women remain outside the public sphere was thought by most men (and women too) to be a way of *protecting* women; they were spared the unpleasantness and insecurity of the world of affairs. That is the viewpoint of the Arab fundamentalist culture, where much the same pattern prevails today. Some critics believe it can be interpreted as a way of treating women as *property* (namely the property of their fathers and husbands)—as an investment in the next generation and as a working resource.

The Goddess Theory: Women Before Patriarchy

This pattern of women being excluded from the public sphere may seem so ancient that we believe it has always existed. However, a theory advanced by many feminist scholars today is that the subjection of women to men (which we know as a historical fact going back at least three thousand years) may not have been the ancient order of things. You may remember that John Stuart Mill was a nineteenth-century advocate of women's rights (see Chapter 5). In his book *The Subjection of Women* (1869), he says that we don't know what it would be like for women not to be subjected to men because they always have been. But he may well have been wrong, because archaeological evidence (artifacts and written documents) now points to the possibility of women having had far more influence in early Middle Eastern and African cultures than we used to think. In the area to the west and south of the Black Sea, there appears to have been civilizations more than ten thousand years ago who revered a mother goddess of fertility; in Greek and Middle Eastern legends, we find ancient myths of a creator goddess and powerful priestesses and queens. While Ancient Greece in the days of Socrates, Plato, and Aristotle was clearly a patriarchal culture, as you have been able to glean from Chapters 8 and 9, although Plato himself has become regarded as the "first feminist" in philosophy due to his theory of women's roles in the ideal state, we can now add the perspective that Greek culture at the time had remnants of an earlier time where goddesses were more considered as having a higher status, and that is considered an indication by many, such as the gender activist Riane Eisler and the historian Gerda Lerner (1920–2013), that

Chronicle/Alamy Stock Photo

A copied page from the lost original encyclopedia by Abbess Herrad of Landsberg/Hohenbourg, *Hortus deliciarum* (Garden of Delight). A highly educated and talented woman, Herrad authored parts of the encyclopedia and edited the rest. Here we see her vision of philosophy with the seven liberal arts surrounding the spirit of Philosophy, Socrates, and Plato. The circle says that Philosophy "studies the secrets of the element and of all things. What she discovers, she retains in her memory. And she puts it all in writing, in order to transmit it to her students."

at least some women may have had a higher social standing, too. (Box 12.4 explores the idea of whether Plato was in fact a feminist.) The goddess Hera, Zeus's wife, may have been demoted from being a mother goddess to "just" being a wife. The goddess Demeter (who, in the old tale, loses her daughter Persephone to the King of the Underworld, Hades) may predate all the gods on Mt. Olympus by thousands of years, being an ancient Earth Goddess or Great Goddess.

Similarly, African legends suggest a strong memory of a mother goddess and of women who had much social power in their communities. Whether we should call those ancient cultures *matriarchal* is open to question because we have no evidence that they were *ruled* by women, but there is tentative evidence that until some gradual cultural change toward patriarchy happened around thirty-five hundred years ago, women in the Old World had higher social standing than they did later. Part of that social standing may have derived from the local religions' belief in a creator goddess rather than a creator god.

Further challenges to the universality of patriarchy have come from other parts of the world: In the American Indian tradition, women were considered respected, full members of the community with rights to have their own opinions and to choose a husband and divorce him. Furthermore, in Eastern tribes it was not uncommon for the chief to be a woman. However, according to American Indian historian Paula Gunn Allen (1939–2008), the European settlers rarely reported that fact, and history books have most often referred to those chiefs as being male. At various times and places in human history, women seem to have had considerably more social influence than they have had in the Western world of the past several thousand years except for the past five decades.

A place where goddess worship may have lasted longer than most other places, and where women may have had comparatively more influence, was Ireland before the advent of Christianity with Saint Patrick in 435. And for centuries after Christianity took hold, the high public standing of women that was a legacy of the goddess religion remained a factor in Ireland. Saint Brigit of Kildare (453–525) was raised by the pagan Druid priesthood but was attracted to Christianity. She was ordained as a bishop by mistake, instead of as a nun, as a result of the wrong oath being administered. It initiated a new tradition, and from then on until the Vikings arrived several hundred years later, women in Ireland could become bishops. Irish bishops generally had a more gender-egalitarian view of women than the rest of Europe did, and when in 900 a European bishops' council convened to decide whether women had souls, the yes votes won—by one vote. That vote came from an Irish bishop.

Box 12.4 WAS PLATO REALLY A FEMINIST?

In Chapter 8, you read that Plato, as the first scholar in Western history, suggested that women should be included at every level of his ideal society. In *The Republic*, he imagines that there will be women intellectuals who will join the men in being philosopher Guardians (Rulers), and women who will be excellent at warfare, joining their husbands as soldiers in combat, and even bringing their children with them. He imagines that women should be doctors, philosophers, artists, merchants, and every other role in society held by males in Greece of the fifth century B.C.E., because the only two differences he sees between men and women are that women can give birth and that men are generally stronger. This section in *The Republic* has propelled Plato to the forefront as the

first classical feminist philosopher—and essentially the *only* one in the West until we reach the 1600s and the early Enlightenment. Not that being a Guardian was supposed to be a cushy job: neither male nor female Guardians would be allowed to own anything, so their greed would not outweigh their sense of duty to the State. Personal life for the women Guardians isn't very rosy either, as Plato imagines it. In order not to be distracted from their governmental obligations, they are not allowed to raise the children they will have with their husbands, the male Guardians/Philosopher Kings. All children of the Guardians will be raised communally, and no one will know their own children. The Swiss-French philosopher Rousseau thought that was a bunch of nonsense, because, as he said, Plato had made men out of the women by making them into intellectuals, and so he couldn't allow them to take on female roles. Now Rousseau was anything but a feminist, and he isn't the only one to have criticized Plato. Aristotle was the first one, believing his teacher to be completely wrong about the natural roles of men and women. Aristotle was of course not a feminist, either—but recently Plato has been criticized, not by anti-feminists, but by feminists themselves.

Lynda Lange, a feminist philosopher, argues in her paper, "The Function of Equal Education in Plato's Republic" (2003), that our perception of Plato as a feminist is a mistake. He never had any notion of gender equality in mind. He flat-out says that the female philosophers will be wives in common for the male philosophers—but the males are not to be husbands in common for the wives. In other words, the female philosophers are to be considered a kind of *property* shared by the men. But why would Plato suggest that? Lange says that in Plato's world women *were* property—and Plato knew that he would never be able to entice men to go into government for 30 years without having access to women, and father children. But the Guardians were prohibited from owning anything—so that would mean they couldn't own a wife, either! How to solve that problem? By making women into fellow rulers, as property in common for the male philosophers. In other words, says Lange, Plato made philosopher queens out of intellectual women so the male philosophers would have access to women (and father legitimate children) without breaking the rule of not owning property. Hardly the view of a feminist concerned about gender equality! The idea that Plato was not the feminist many in the twentieth century have made him out to be has been floated by several scholars in the last 50 years, such as Julia Annas and Harry Lesser.

So was Plato then not a feminist at all? He grew up in a household with a mother, Perictione, who was recognized as a thinker, so he was used to the thought of intellectual women. He specifically says to Glaucon that men do everything better than women except give birth, but he also specifies that some differences are simply not relevant when it comes to intellectual skill, and the soul is for Plato much more important than the body. The French-Canadian philosopher Luc Brisson sees that as a clear indication that Plato focused on unisex qualities of both men and women as Guardians. But we should probably be cautious in applying modern concepts to his worldview. He wasn't anything like a modern-day feminist—but he certainly suggested a social change that would allow women to explore their potential and share in political power, and even if the immediate reason for this idea was that he had to overcome the question of wives as property for the Guardians, the side effect has been that Plato's fantasy of an ideal world has opened the eyes of generations of students to the possibility of women being participants in public life—something that was unheard of in Plato's own day, and didn't become a reality until the twentieth century.

Losing Ground: The Middle Ages

Women rulers in antiquity were few and far between; even Queen Cleopatra in Egypt (69–30 B.C.E.) was co-ruler with her 10-year-old brother. But in a brief interlude of some hundred years in late Antiquity, before the fall of the Roman Empire, women in the Roman realm seem to have had some social and personal freedom. They could own business, teach, and move about freely, and some rose to prominence politically. You'll remember from Chapter 8 that *Hypatia* was such a woman. She was the leader of the Platonist/Neoplatonic Institute of Alexandria in Egypt (then part of the Roman Empire) and taught subjects ranging from math and astronomy to Plato's philosophy, and she was highly respected for her wisdom. But because she was associated with paganism in the eyes of Christian fanatics, she was waylaid by radical terrorists, dragged from her chariot into a church where she was murdered—according to legend, "flayed alive with clam shells." (Clam shells also being the term for roof tiles, she may have had her skin cut off with sharp tiles.) Apparently the real reason for the murder was that she got involved in a dispute between the Roman governor and the bishop of Alexandria which had turned deadly. Radical monks acting on behalf of the bishop, but possibly without his knowledge, targeted Hypatia, and with that act of terror, the freedom of women in the Roman Empire began to wane, according to historians.

Bettmann/Getty Images

Hypatia of Alexandria (c. 350–415), leader of the Neoplatonic Institute in the Egyptian city of Alexandria until her murder at the hands of a Christian mob. She taught philosophy as well as astronomy at the Institute.

In the European convents of the early Middle Ages, women received an education that allowed them to become medical practitioners, illustrators, composers, and writers, aside from having clerical powers equal to the male clergy of the monasteries. One such woman was Hildegard of Bingen (1098–1179), a German abbess. She was given to the Church at the age of eight and began having visions at an early age. She wrote a number of books on God's plan for humanity, two about her visions, and another two on science and nature. She composed liturgical songs, and wrote what is recognized as the first morality play about the battle between good and evil, *Ordo Virtuem.* She founded her own convent, Rupertsberg, where her music was performed. Toward the end of her life she offered her writings to the new University of Paris, only to suffer the indignity of having them rejected on the grounds that she was a woman. And in the late 1100s Abbess Herrad of Landsberg/Hohenbourg put together an encyclopedia, *Hortus deliciarum* (*Garden of Delight*), which was to serve young novices at the convent, teaching them about philosophy and theology. It contained songs, poems, and illustrations, some of them created by Herrad herself. The manuscript was destroyed during a fire in 1870, but enough partial copies remain that we get a vivid impression of it (see illustration on p. 533).

Box 12.5 SOR JUANA INES DE LA CRUZ

In seventeenth-century Mexico, still a colony of Spain, the concept of women's rights was advocated and, in a sense, embodied by a nun, Sor Juana Ines de la Cruz (1651–1695). Born Juana Inés de Asbaje y Ramírez de Santillana, she was the illegitimate child of a Spanish father and a Creole mother. A child prodigy, she educated herself by voraciously reading books in her grandfather's library. At the age of fifteen, she was introduced in court to the viceroy and his wife, who took her on as a lady-in-waiting and created an intellectual environment for her as entertainment for the court. At twenty, she entered a convent but continued her intellectual pursuits, and over the years she amassed a library consisting of over four thousand volumes. Sor Juana wrote secular love poetry, songs, and plays, including comedies, received commissions, and lived to see her works published both in Mexico and in Spain. But with the departure of the viceroy and his family for Spain, she lost her protection against the pressures of the Catholic Church to conform to traditional convent life. Her professional struggle for her rights as an intellectual within the Church began in 1691: When attacked by a bishop whose sermon she had criticized, she wrote a statement that has earned her the title of the first feminist in the Americas, *Respuesta a Sor Filotea* ("Response to Sor Filotea," the bishop's pseudonym), in which she referred to the culture of Mexican women and to a woman's right to disagree with authorities. But shortly afterward she gave away all her books and artifacts, and in a statement signed in her own blood she resolved to dedicate the rest of her life to helping the poor. In 1695, when she was forty-four, she was helping infected nuns during an epidemic, caught the illness herself, and died.

In the twelfth to fourteenth centuries, women lost ground within the Catholic Church. New policies deprived abbesses of their right to hear confessions, and convents that had functioned as hospitals and social safety nets for the community were closed down or transformed into isolated cloisters. No secular schools had been founded yet, and young women were now barred from a religious education. The reason may seem strangely arbitrary to a modern person: To be accepted as a student, receive an education, and communicate with God, the young acolyte's head had to be shaved into a tonsure. But according to Scripture (in particular Paul's first letter to the Corinthians), women not only weren't allowed to shave their heads but also were supposed to hide their hair under a veil when in the presence of God. And since you can't have a tonsure, and thus be eligible for a religious education, while having a full head of hair and wearing a veil, the tonsure policy kept women out of schools. Even so, some nuns, such as Sor Juana Ines de la Cruz, rose to intellectual prominence (see Box 12.5).

Heritage Images/Getty Images

Hildegard of Bingen (1098–1179), one of the last influential women in the Catholic Church before the cloistering of nuns in the 1200s. She was an influential advisor in European politics and a well-known composer, in addition to writing works on theology, botany, and medicine.

The Rise of Modern Feminism

We often hear feminism referred to as "first wave," "second wave," and "third wave." Those chronological terms form a timeline for awareness of women's social situation. (Box 12.7 gives a brief overview of this timeline.) The first wave generally refers to the feminist movement in the West from its early beginnings in the seventeenth century to the accomplishment of its most urgent goal, the right for women to vote. In 1869 women in Wyoming gained the right to vote, but general suffrage for women wasn't obtained in the United States until 1920. In the meantime, New Zealand women had been included as voters in 1893; in 1902 Australia followed suit. Norway joined the list in 1913, and Denmark in 1915. So, too, did Canada, England, Germany, and Austria after World War I, in 1918. Sweden gave women the right to vote in 1921, but it wasn't until 1944 that French women could go to the polls, and Mexico followed in 1947. Switzerland waited until 1971, and in 1994 black women gained full suffrage in South Africa. In 2004 Afghani women became voters, and in 2011 women in Saudi Arabia finally acquired voting rights as the last country on earth, and in 2018 Saudi women were allowed to apply for driving licences. However, the detention of a number of women driving illegally prior to 2018 is an ongoing issue at the time of this writing. What began as furtive discussions 400 years ago has still not reached full global implementation.

Early Feminism in France and England

Library of Congress Prints and Photographs Division

English philosopher Mary Wollstonecraft (1759–1797) wrote *A Vindication of the Rights of Women*, which was much ridiculed at the time by male scholars but would have a lasting influence. Wollstonecraft died in childbirth, giving life to a second Mary Wollstonecraft, who, under her married name, Shelley, was to give life to another kind of creature with the story of Frankenstein and his monster.

A very early speaker for the rights of women was the French thinker **Francois Poulain de la Barre**, who in 1673 argued that men and women are fundamentally similar because they have the same powers of reasoning. Poulain believed women should have access to all occupations in society, even as generals in the army and leaders of Parliament. However, few people paid much attention to Poulain; he remained both unique and unknown as a seventeenth-century feminist. During the French Revolution (begun in 1789), things changed considerably in France. Women began to let their voices be heard in the pre-Revolution debate: **Olympe de Gouges** wrote the *Declaration of the Rights of Woman and the Female Citizen* in 1791, in which she argued for complete equality between men and women, including rights to vote, to own property, to serve in the military, and to hold office. During the Revolution, she wrote over 30 pamphlets and considered herself a revolutionary, but since she was against the killing of the royal family, she was targeted as an anti-revolutionary and was beheaded during the Reign of Terror in 1793 at the age of forty-eight. Another high-profile woman was **Madame Louise d'Epinay**, who believed that women and men have the same nature and the same constitution and will display different virtues and vices only if they are brought up that way; any differentiation is due to social pressure, nothing else. Her ideas inspired the philosopher the **marquis de Condorcet**, who in 1792 suggested that education should be available to women because both men and women were, primarily, members of the human race. Condorcet's opponent, Talleyrand, who was inspired by the social critic Jean-Jacques Rousseau, managed to put a stop to those ideas, which, it seems, were too radical even for the revolutionaries. Thus the view of Rousseau, which had become popular in the late eighteenth century—that men should live in a democracy of equals but that their women belonged at home as intelligent but subordinate partners to their spouses—became the official view of the gender issue in France of the early nineteenth century.

In eighteenth-century England there were voices—male as well as female—that argued for the possibility of a different order. The British philosopher **Mary Wollstonecraft** (1759-1797) was one of the few women of the eighteenth century who directly addressed women's situation. (See Box 12.6 for a short list of other women ethicists before the twentieth century.) In *A Vindication of the Rights of Women* (1792), she suggested not only that it is unfair to women to socialize them to be uneducated, unthinking creatures who are only eager to please but also that it is unfair to men, because although a man may fall in love with that kind of woman, he certainly won't want to live with her. After all, what will the two have in common once the seduction is over and they are married? No, Wollstonecraft wrote, women should have the same opportunities as men. If they don't measure up, men will have reason to claim superiority; but to apply two different value systems—one that says what is proper for men and one that says what is proper for women—is to make a mockery of the concept of virtue itself:

> I wish to persuade women to endeavour to acquire strength, both of mind and body, and to convince them that the soft phrases, susceptibility of heart, delicacy of sentiment, and refinement of taste, are almost synonymous with epithets of weakness, and that those beings who are only the objects of pity and that kind of love, which has been termed its sister, will soon become objects of contempt. . . . Besides, the woman who strengthens her body and exercises her mind will, by managing her family and practicing various virtues, become the friend, and not the humble dependent of her husband.

Box 12.6 WOMEN MORAL PHILOSOPHERS

Carol Gilligan is right in saying that the famous and influential moral theories within the Western philosophical tradition have until recently all been expressed by male thinkers. That does not mean, however, that there have been no women moral thinkers in Western history aside from Mary Wollstonecraft and Harriet Taylor Mill; here is a small selection from a list of more than thirty names in the *Encyclopedia of Ethics* of women ethicists (Western as well as Eastern) from the earliest years of philosophy to the nineteenth century. I don't wish to imply that women's contributions to ethics until the twentieth century can be contained in a box. However, most of these names are not generally well known, and before the twentieth century women thinkers had very little influence in philosophy. This list demonstrates that there were women who could and did think and write during times when women were discouraged or even banned from taking part in intellectual life. In all probability there were many more thinking and writing women than history has recorded.

Phintys of Sparta (c. 420 B.C.E.) held that it was not unfitting for women to philosophize and that courage, justice, and wisdom were common to women as well as men; in the tradition of Greek moral thinking (which you will recognize from Aristotle, who was not born yet when Phintys wrote her book, *On the Moderation of Women*), she recommends moderation in all things as a virtue for women.

Makrina of Neocaesarea (c. 300 C.E.) so impressed her brother, the Bishop of Nyssa, that he cited her moral philosophy in his own writings. Makrina was familiar with Plato's philosophy and taught that women were created in God's image and had rational souls; with a rational soul, one is capable of becoming morally virtuous and thus eligible for entry into heaven after death, she believed.

Murasaki Shikibu (978-c. 1031) was a Japanese courtier who, in her novel *Genji Monogatari* (*The Tale of Genji*), which is considered the first real novel, led her main character, the woman

Ukifune, to a realization of freedom and moral responsibility in the face of existential dread. Today this story is seen as an early exploration of the key themes of existentialism as they were later defined in the Western world of the twentieth century.

Christine de Pizan (1365–1431) wrote a book, *Cité des Dames* (*The City of Women*), in which she envisioned women living in a community to protect themselves from physical and moral harm. She argued that oppression of women was counterproductive to the improvement of society and that women should strive to avoid activities that dull their intellect, since they were limited by certain social roles.

Marie le Jars de Gournay (1565–1645) was the editor of Montaigne's *Essays* and wrote in a work of her own, *Egalité des Hommes et des Femmes* (*Equality Between Men and Women*), that women are equal to men in their capacity for moral reasoning and action. She believed that sexual differences are related exclusively to reproduction and have otherwise no bearing on male or female nature.

Mary Astell (1666–1731) worked on a synthesis of the traditions of Locke and Descartes and believed that reason ought to govern our passions. The only way to accomplish that, she said, was to have universal education for women as well as for men.

Antoinette Brown Blackwell (1825–1921) was the first ordained American woman. She was a prolific writer of philosophy and theology and maintained that women and men make moral judgments differently; in a forerunner of Gilligan's argument about an ethic of justice and an ethic of care, Blackwell claimed that women bring compassion to justice and caring to the concept of rights.

In the nineteenth century John Stuart Mill, inspired by his longtime intellectual friend (and later wife) Harriet Taylor, wrote about how women's as well as men's characters are molded by society:

> All women are brought up from the earliest years in the belief that their ideal of character is the very opposite to that of men; not self-will, and government by self-control, but submission, and yielding to the control of others. All the moralities tell them that it is the duty of women, and all the current sentimentalities that it is their nature, to live for others.

Box 12.7 FIRST-, SECOND-, AND THIRD-WAVE FEMINISM: A BRIEF OVERVIEW

We generally talk about the development of feminism in America as a phenomenon in three waves: "first," "second," and "third" wave. The first wave is considered as having its official starting point in 1848 with the Women's Rights Convention in Seneca Falls, led by Lucretia Mott and Elizabeth Cady Stanton, and culminating with the Nineteenth Amendment in 1920, which granted women the right to vote. The philosophy and goals of the first wave of feminism were straightforward: rights for women to self-determination; rights to inherit and own property, even in marriage (as opposed to the ownership of one's inherited or earned property passing to one's husband); rights to raise one's children; and, above all, *suffrage* (the right to vote). Voting rights were achieved for some women in 1919, and full rights were granted in 1928.

The second wave was ushered in with the publication of Betty Friedan's book *The Feminine Mystique* in 1963. (In France, a similar reaction followed the publication of Simone de Beauvoir's *The Second Sex* in 1949; see chapter text.) For most feminists of the second wave, the primary goal was the creation of an equal-opportunity society without discrimination because of one's sex—a society in which women, as well as men, would be able to freely choose their way of life and occupations; a common focus was on the upbringing of boys and girls, attempting to change the stereotypical gender roles to a more egalitarian pattern. (See the discussion of classical feminism in the next section.) For all second-wave feminists, a common goal was a complete and discrimination-free access for women to any education or profession they might be interested in and qualified for. Some feminists see that job as accomplished in the early twenty-first century, but others believe there is still much work to be done to achieve complete gender equality. While the "glass ceiling" has been broken in just about any profession in the United States, it was a huge disappointment to many feminists that the first female presidential nominee, Hillary Clinton (D), was not elected president in 2016.

The beginning of the third wave is sometimes identified with the publication of Carol Gilligan's *In a Different Voice* (1982; see chapter text), and sometimes with the publication of Susan Faludi's *Backlash: The Undeclared War Against American Women* (1991). The philosophy of the third wave is less clearly defined than those of the first two waves: Radical feminism focuses on identifying and eliminating the roots of still-existing discrimination; other third-wave feminists focus on specific issues, such as feminist environmentalism, easier access to child care for working women, and combating racial and economic discrimination.

Under different social circumstances, Mill says, we would see women acting no longer as the full-time slaves of their husbands but as independent individuals with original intellectual ideas to contribute to society. If women are capable of fulfilling social functions, they should be free to do so. If it is impossible for a woman to do certain things because of her nature, then what need is there to prohibit her from doing them? The old saying "'ought' implies 'can'" applies: You can't tell someone she ought (or ought not) to do something unless she is actually able to do it. Mill does believe that male and female qualities in general are not the same—that men and women are usually good at different things—but that from a moral point of view those qualities should be considered equally important. So what might Mill say about the controversy as to whether women soldiers should be in combat? Probably that most women would prefer not to and would not qualify but that those who want to and who do qualify should be allowed to do so. At the end of the chapter you can read Harriet Taylor Mill's own argument for why women should be allowed in the workforce.

Classical, Difference, and Radical Feminism

Today the idea of gender equality has several facets. Feminists generally agree that there should be gender equality, but they don't necessarily agree on what is female and male human nature, or on what exactly our policies should be to combat gender discrimination. The philosophies of feminism are in a process of development, responding to the pressures of the past and present and the challenges of the future. One facet is *classical feminism* (sometimes referred to as liberal feminism), which calls for men and women to be considered as *persons* first and gendered beings second. (Box 12.8 discusses the issue of whether feminism has to be considered liberal, or whether a conservative can be a feminist.) Another is *difference feminism,* which holds that women and men possess fundamentally different qualities and that both genders should learn from each other. A facet of feminism that sometimes has received bad press is *radical feminism;* although some radical feminists indeed seem to be militant or extremist, the main point of radical feminism is not to mount the barricades but to seek out and expose the *root* of the problem of gender discrimination. ("Root" is *radix* in Latin; hence, radical feminism.) And then there is a breakout form of feminism severely criticized by many feminists that labels itself *equity feminism:* An equity feminist holds that the battle for equality has been won, that we should not think of women as victims of patriarchy any longer, and that we can now adopt any kind of gender roles we like because gender discrimination is by and large a thing of the past. (Box 12.9 discusses equity feminism.)

Box 12.8 CAN A CONSERVATIVE BE A FEMINIST?

Feminism has for a long time been considered a liberal phenomenon, a focus on women's right to self-expression and flourishing while at the same time identifying the source of that freedom as a change in government policies, guaranteeing freedoms for women. What you'll see as "classical feminism" in this book is often called "liberal feminism" elsewhere. The standard feminist attitude toward women's rise in public life has been, throughout most of the twentieth century, that such women should always be supported in their effort to break the glass ceiling, because (1) it was considered a positive thing in itself to see a woman achieve a position that would previously have been reserved for men, and because (2) it was a tacit assumption that such a woman would agree with the general liberal views of most feminists. So it has been a challenge to feminists to find that women from other areas of the political spectrum have found a voice in today's politics. Former Governor of Alaska Sarah Palin, presenting herself as having strong conservative values, was the first female Republican vice-presidential candidate in the 2008 election, and Palin has described herself as being a feminist. Michelle Bachman, congresswoman from Minnesota, who ran as presidential candidate for the GOP in 2011, also supports conservative values. Political commentator and author Ann Coulter comes from a conservative point of view and has a large readership. Columnist Star Parker and commentator Michelle Malkin are also eloquent women with conservative values, and Elisabeth Hasselbeck, formerly of the ABC TV series *The View,* was considered the conservative voice on the show. Carly Fiorina, who ran as a Republican presidential candidate in the 2016 primaries, has been a chief executive officer at Hewlitt Packard, and a candidate for senator from California during the 2010 election campaign. If these women, and others like them, are in favor of women participating in public life, women having equal access to education, as well as to the job market in jobs they are qualified for, and women having a choice whether they wish to raise families, be professionals, or both—can such women be feminists? Or does one have to subscribe to liberal moral values in order to be part of the feminist movement? What if such women are pro-life, and not pro-choice? Some have suggested that we are in effect seeing a new "third wave" of feminism, or even a fourth wave: the rise of conservative women. Others see their political influence as not feminist at all, but rather a throwback to patriarchal (male-dominated) ways of thinking. Perhaps we need to distinguish between feminism as essentially a liberal movement, and other kinds of reform movements advocating an equal role for women? If not, then we have to conclude that feminists can come in many kinds of political colors.

Box 12.9 CHRISTINA HOFF SOMMERS'S EQUITY FEMINISM

In a highly controversial book, *Who Stole Feminism?* (1994), Christina Hoff Sommers (see Chapter 10) argues that feminism has been split into two movements: the "equity feminists," wanting equal opportunity for women and men, and the "gender feminists," "resenter feminists," or "feminist radicals," who, as Sommers sees it, have male-bashing as their main agenda. Sommers sees herself as an equity feminist. She also uses the terms "new feminists" and "gynocentric feminism" to describe the type of feminism she believes has done the movement a grave disservice by creating an atmosphere of general mistrust of men and of women who work with, support, or admire them. Here Sommers doesn't align herself exactly with any of the facets of feminism that we have discussed; although radical feminism comes closest to what she calls gender feminism. Sommers also finds that difference feminism has elements of misandry in that women's approaches are considered superior to those of men. And classical feminism, although being the form of feminism that probably comes closest to what Sommers calls equity feminism, also has elements of gender feminism for Sommers: Simone de Beauvoir, she says, had no intention of letting women choose gender roles freely but wanted to dictate the proper upbringing and life choices for women. Among contemporary gender feminists, Sommers counts Susan Faludi, Marilyn French, Carolyn Heilbrun, and Catharine MacKinnon. Sommers writes:

> Once I get into the habit of regarding women as a subjugated gender, I'm primed to be alarmed, angry, and resentful of men as oppressors of women. I am also prepared to believe the words about them and the harm they cause to women. I may even be ready to fabricate atrocities. . . . Resenter feminists like Faludi, French, Heilbrun and MacKinnon speak of backlash, siege, and an undeclared war against women. But the condition they describe is mythic—with no foundation in the facts of contemporary American life.

Since women now have their political and personal freedom, says Sommers, they should be making use of it, instead of judging the authenticity of each other's attitudes:

> But women are no longer disenfranchised, and their preferences are being taken into account. Nor are they now taught that they are subordinate or that a subordinate role for them is fitting and proper. . . . Since women today can no longer be regarded as the victims of an undemocratic indoctrination, we must regard their preferences as "authentic." Any other attitude toward American women is unacceptably patronizing and profoundly illiberal.

The feminists Sommers criticizes generally respond that Sommers herself has misunderstood the goals and nature of feminism; although the overt oppression of previous times is over, it has now become covert and internalized, and it lives in the hearts of the critics of feminism, women as well as men. Although opportunities have opened to women, many women still grow up believing that the masculine cultural world is their only option; it takes a long time for such wounds to heal, and they don't heal without active interference. For that reason, and for their own sake, women must be shown that equality is still far away. So when Sommers says women have the right to choose a life in which they work at home, raising children, or work in a male-dominated environment or when she says they have the right to enjoy romance literature in which men are strong and women are seduced, then Sommers must herself have internalized the traditional male view of what a woman's proper place is, according to some critics.

Sommers responds by claiming that gender feminism simply does not represent the viewpoint

of most women today—women who are politically aware and concerned with gender
equality—in other words, feminists. Most
women today, says Sommers, have access to the
professions of their choice and want to lead
lives in which they have friendly relations with
male coworkers and loving relations with male
partners. Many want families, and some even
want to live the traditional life of a homemaker,
and they are not interested in being represented
by women who tell them they have a false consciousness. As a fellow equity feminist, Sommers cites the author and fellow philosopher
Iris Murdoch, who believed in a "culture of
humanity," not in a "new female ghetto" of
misandric feminism.

Classical Feminism: Beauvoir and Androgyny

For those taking the view that men and women should be considered as persons first, gender differences are
primarily cultural. Biological differences are significant only in terms of procreation, they say; apart from
birthing and breastfeeding infants, which can be done only by women, the sexual differences are irrelevant.
Culture has shaped men and women, and a cultural change could therefore allow for another type of gender:
the *androgynous* type.

In her groundbreaking work *The Second Sex,* Simone de Beauvoir, one of the most powerful voices for equal
education and equal opportunities in the twentieth century, accuses the philosophical tradition of seeing man
as the "typical" human being, so woman thus becomes "atypical." For man, woman becomes "the Other,"
an alien being who helps man define himself through her alienness, and with whom he communicates on an
everyday basis but who never becomes "one of the boys." Woman, who has been placed in this situation for
millennia, has also come to believe she is atypical. The female anatomy is seen as a psychologically determining factor, whereas the male anatomy is not. In other words, women do what they do because they are
women; men do what they do because they are normal. But this is a *cultural* fact, not a natural one, says
Beauvoir. And the only way a woman can become *authentic* is to shed her role as "deviant" and become a
true human being by rejecting the traditional female role. Society can assist in this process by treating little
boys and girls the same—by giving them the same education and the same subsequent opportunities. Here we
must remember that Beauvoir was engaged in issues other than feminism; she was, with her partner Jean-Paul
Sartre, one of the strongest voices in the philosophical existentialist movement of the mid-twentieth century
(see Chapter 10). Existentialism posits that there is no human nature; any attempt at claiming we *have to* do
or be something is nothing but a poor excuse for not wanting to make a choice: *bad faith.* If we carry this
over into Beauvoir's theory of feminism, we understand what she means when she says that a woman must
shed her culturally given role as the second sex: There is no female human nature any more than there is any
human nature in general; we must fight the cultural traps of gender roles and their assumption that this is how
we have to be, because that is nothing but a poor excuse for not making our own choices. (However, if we
should *want to* make the choice of traditional gender roles, Beauvoir would have little patience with us, since
she believed the choice of gender freedom is best made if the traditional option of stay-at-home-mom is not
available to women. Many contemporary feminists find that this hardly constitutes true freedom of choice.)

It is against the background of the traditional male philosophical approach to the gender question that Beauvoir criticizes Emmanuel Levinas and his view of the Other as essentially feminine (see Chapter 10). To Beauvoir, this is nothing but old-fashioned reactionary male-oriented thinking, because for a classical feminist like
her, the attitude of seeing the sexes as fundamentally different also means that one is generally dominating
the other; when Levinas praises feminine qualities as the nurturing and welcoming element in both men and
women, the classical feminist still sees that as discrimination (against men as well as against women) because
it persists in stereotyping the typically feminine as nurturing.

Until women begin to think of themselves as a group, Beauvoir says, they will believe that they are abnormal human beings. And as long as men and women receive different educations and different treatment from society, woman will not feel responsible for the state of the world but will regard herself as men regard her—as an overgrown child. Of course women are weak, Beauvoir says. Of course they don't use male logic (here we must remember that she is talking about uneducated women before World War II). Of course they are religious to the point of superstition. Of course they have no sense of history, and of course they accept authority. Of course they cry a lot over little things. They may even be lazy, sensual, servile, frivolous, utilitarian, materialistic, and hysterical. They may, in short, be all that some male thinkers thought they were. *But why are women all these things?* Because they have no power except by subterfuge. They have no education, so they have never been taught about the cause and effect of history and the relative powers of authority. They are caught up in a never-ending stream of housework, which causes them to be practically oriented. They nag because they realize they have no power to change their situation. They are sensual because they are bored. In *The Second Sex* Beauvoir says, "The truth is that when a woman is engaged in an enterprise worthy of a human being, she is quite able to show herself as active, effective, taciturn—and as ascetic—as a man." Beauvoir furthermore argues against assumptions based on Freudian psychoanalysis (which at the time was almost undisputed) that the subservience of the little girl is natural.

> If, from the earliest age, the little girl were raised with the same demands and honors, the same severity and freedom, as her brothers, taking part in the same studies and games, promised the same future, surrounded by women and men who are unambiguously equal to her, the meanings of the "castration complex" and the "Oedipus complex" would be profoundly modified. The mother would enjoy the same lasting prestige as the father if she assumed equal material and moral responsibility for the couple; the child would feel an androgynous world around her and not a masculine world; were she more affectively attracted to her father—which is not even certain—her love for him would be nuanced by a will to emulate him and not a feeling of weakness: she would not turn to passivity; if she were allowed to prove her worth in work and sports, actively rivaling boys, the absence of a penis—compensated for by the promise of a child—would not suffice to cause an "inferiority complex"; correlatively, the boy would not have a natural "superiority complex" if it were not instilled in him and if he held women in the same esteem as men. The little girl would not seek sterile compensations in narcissism and dreams, she would not take herself as given, she would be interested in what she does, and she would throw herself into her own pursuits.

So if we change our culture, we will change what has for so long been considered female nature—and with it, probably also male nature. We will create people who are responsible human beings above all and who will respect each other for that reason. This philosophy was adopted by many late-twentieth-century feminists, including Germaine Greer, Gloria Steinem, and Joyce Trebilcot. (See Box 12.10 for Beauvoir's influence on modern philosophy.)

But how profoundly can we change who we are? It used to be considered an obvious truth that we can't change or choose our *sex*, but times have changed, and in recognition of the fact that many people feel they are born into the wrong sex, our society now recognizes individuals who are *in transition*, changing not just from one gender role to another, but from one sex to another through surgery and hormonal treatments. Even the sexual identity of young children is no longer considered a given, at least by some pedagogues and pediatricians, and in some communities children, are encouraged to explore their own sexual identity without feeling pressured to conform to social standards. For some critics, including parents, this new openness is not necessarily a good thing, potentially throwing the child into confusion about a sexual identity that usually is settled by itself in puberty. Other parents welcome the tendency toward greater sexual flexibility. Positive or negative, the future will have to judge, but even when the sexual identity of a child is not in question, their *gender* identity may be. Gender identity can of course be explored without involving any physical alterations, because here we are talking about *social roles*, not sexuality.

In Toronto, as I write this, a child is being raised by (presumably) loving parents. The child's name is Storm, and the parents have refused to reveal his or her sex. The child is not an intersex person, and has apparently a clear sexual identity, but for now the parents are deliberately raising a unisex child, at least in the eyes of the world, so that he/she/*ze* can grow up untainted by the social construct of a gender role—and so the world can get a chance to revise its pigeonholing of people into gender roles. That is at least the way Storm's parents present his/her/*zir* case. In 2016 Storm's preferred pronoun was "she," but when the parents dressed her as a boy as an experiment during a vacation, strangers just assumed that she was male. In other words, the experiment is ongoing. So what will happen when Storm's sex is revealed? And maybe more important, how will this upbringing play into his or her (or *zir*) self-identity? Most people who heard of the Storm case have found the parents' choice to be reprehensible, because they are interfering with the social normal development of their child. Perhaps Storm will share his/her/*zir* story with the world when childhood is over.

Box 12.10 THE OTHER: SIMONE DE BEAUVOIR

Everett Collection Inc/Alamy Stock Photo

Simone de Beauvoir (1908–1986), a feminist and an existentialist, was long considered a minor thinker by the philosophical community. One reason was that she was Jean-Paul Sartre's "significant other," and her books, such as *The Second Sex,* show considerable influence from Sartre's ideas. However, most philosophers now recognize that many of the fundamental ideas of existentialism came about through discussions between Sartre and Beauvoir, and many ideas first published by Sartre may well have originated during those discussions. There is even some suspicion that Sartre occasionally published ideas by Beauvoir under his own name. True or not, this new attitude reveals a changing perspective on women in philosophy. In the twenty-first century, Beauvoir's influence in the area of gender inequality has turned out to be just as viable as Sartre's philosophy. Beauvoir is primarily interested in the existence of woman as a cultural phenomenon; she analyzes woman's subjugation in a man's world—a situation that was far more common in the mid-twentieth century than now. She hopes that instead of a world where woman is considered deviant and man normal, we will have a society of *human beings,* not just males and females, and people will interact with each other equally as productive, authentic beings. However, Beauvoir has come under heavy criticism from some feminists for not realizing that she herself regards man as the norm and wants women to be treated and to act like men, rather than rejoice in their inherent female nature. It appears that Beauvoir herself decided to live a child-free life to escape the female stereotype.

Psychologists of the 1960s and 1970s generally assumed that sex roles were purely a matter of upbringing, or *nurture.* The theory of *psychosexual neutrality,* inspired by the theory of behaviorism, which arose earlier in the century, held that a child can be molded into being male or female but is born neither except by virtue of the genitals; if a person seems stereotypically male, it is because of his upbringing, and not a biological fact. This theory also suggests that if we'd like our children to be less stereotypically male or female than tradition expects, we just have to give them a more unisex upbringing. But the theory of psychosexual neutrality has come under severe criticism within the past few years: Cases that had been reported as successful molding of children born with ambiguous genitalia (formerly called hermaphrodites, they're now referred to as *intersexual* children) are now under scrutiny for simply having assigned a sex to the child and assuming that upbringing and hormone treatment would take care of the rest.

A disturbing story is that of David Reimer, who lost his penis to a botched circumcision as an infant in the late 1960s and was raised as a girl, Brenda. In spite of the parents' well-meaning efforts to convince Brenda that she was a girl, she never felt comfortable, and upon discovering the truth at the age of fourteen, promptly discarded the female persona for that of David. He had reconstructive surgery and married a woman whose children he adopted. But the stresses of his abnormal childhood proved to be too much for David, and after being divorced he took his own life in 2004. The case of Brenda/David as well as cases of intersexual children do seem to point toward *nature* as being more important in forming a person's sexual identity than *nurture* is. (See Box 12.11 for a discussion of homosexuality and gender choice.) But we shouldn't discount the influence of nurture completely: The manner in which we express our sexuality and whether or not we become "typically" male or female may well be a matter of our upbringing, at least to some extent.

Box 12.11 IS GENDER A CHOICE? IS SEXUALITY?

In talking about the possibility of choosing gender roles, it is reasonable to discuss the issue of homosexuality and the so-called gay lifestyle. There is still considerable political and moral opposition to homosexuals in Western societies, in some more than in others. In some societies homosexuals can now marry; in others homosexuality is still illegal. Why is there a traditional opposition to homosexuality in Christian countries? It is because of several traditional Christian assumptions, such as (1) homosexuality is a *moral choice,* and one that goes against nature (nature calls for procreation), so homosexuality is morally wrong; and (2) homosexuals are primarily seducers of adolescents, who will then become homosexual. In the early 1990s scientists reached the *tentative* conclusion (based on brain autopsies) that male homosexuality is not a matter of choice but of biology. In that case both of the above objections would be invalid, because (1) gay men don't choose their lifestyle or sexual orientation but are born with it (so it is *natural* for them); and (2) boys can't be seduced to become homosexuals; they either are born that way or not. (Besides, being gay does not imply that one is primarily interested in young boys.) But there is as yet no extensive research about lesbianism or about bisexualism.

The advantage for homosexuals of a conclusive result pointing to biological factors is obvious: There could be no more reason for discrimination based on the belief that homosexuality is an "immoral choice." But such a finding might open the door for new areas of discrimination: Might we see parents take their young children to the doctor to have them "screened" for homosexuality, and if they test positive, ask to have them "cured"? This process is frequently referred to as "gender conversion therapy." In this way homosexuality would be labeled a *defect,* a disease. Some homosexuals might say they would prefer to be heterosexual if that were possible, but certainly not all would. As of January 2020 there were 20 states in the Union that prohibit conversion therapy on minors.

In the first decade of the 2000s the issue of same-sex marriage became headline news in several states around the country, as well as in Europe. In several European countries gay civil marriages had already been legal for years, but in some European communities the issue became one of allowing gays to have church weddings. In the United States the focus was for a while on civil marriages versus civil unions; quickly the debate shifted to "same-sex marriage," and the tendency has been, across the United States, toward an increasing acceptance of the concept. In June 2015, the U.S. Supreme Court overturned all bans on same-sex marriage. Prior to that ruling, thirty-seven states already had legislation allowing gays and lesbians to marry. However, some states continue their opposition, such as North Carolina. Political commentators (usually in favor of same-sex marriage legislation) see the tendency as clear: Same-sex marriage will become a legal nonissue before long. The Democratic Party no longer uses the term, same-sex marriage, but *marriage equality*. And in 2011 the Pentagon officially abandoned the "Don't Ask, Don't Tell" policy, and allowed gays to serve openly in the armed forces. One of the leading Democratic presidential candidates in the 2020 election was openly in a same-sex marriage without (presumably) any voter backlash. It appears that the issue is not as *politically* volatile as in decades past, although a great number of Americans continue to find the idea of same-sex marriage uncomfortable or downright unacceptable.

Difference Feminism: Gilligan and the Ethic of Care

The idea that nature will prevail over nurture has given a boost to the theory of *difference feminism,* which emerged in the 1980s to claim that women and men should be viewed as equal but fundamentally different. By the beginning of the 1980s women had been in the workforce long enough for people to begin to evaluate the situation, and although some women felt good about working in what used to be a "man's world" and conforming to its standards (to a greater or lesser degree), others felt that somehow those standards were damaging to their female identity. Few provisions for child care existed, there was little understanding of family demands, and the overriding atmosphere was one of competition and isolation rather than cooperation and teamwork. For those women, survival in the male-dominated public sphere was possible only if they were willing to give up some of their female values. Difference feminism proposed that the feminist agenda could include not just equal opportunity and equal pay for men and women but also an acknowledgment that many women want something different from what men want and some of women's capabilities lie in areas other than those of most men.

Interestingly enough, that was not the first time such ideas have been advanced—Western history, and certainly the history of philosophy, is rich with statements about the nature of women being different from that of men. Some famous examples include Aristotle, who believed that women were deformed men; Kant, who found it thoroughly improper for a woman to display any interest in intellectual or technological pursuits, even if she might be good at them; Rousseau, who saw a woman as a man's helpmate and little else; and Nietzsche, who admired women for being more "natural" than men, but vilified them for being inconsistent. Theories such as those all state that women and men have different abilities and thus different places in society. However, those theories were not advanced with any notion of gender equality. John Stuart Mill was the first influential philosopher to suggest that although men and women have different capacities, they should nevertheless be given equal opportunities and equal respect for their abilities. It is that concept toward which the new feminism looks. That the question of gender equality is still a very sensitive one was demonstrated by the resignation of Harvard president and economist Larry Summers in 2006 after a 2005 conference speech in which he speculated that the fact that more men than women have successful careers in science and engineering (today referred to as STEM fields) was due not just to social factors but also to innate abilities—in other words, that men and women are fundamentally different by nature in terms of their typical talents. The speech caught the attention of the media, and an outcry ensued, labeling Summers a sexist, even though difference feminists as well as neurobiologists have speculated along the same lines for decades. However, what critics in the media and at Harvard heard was a throwback, a biased attempt to exclude women based on a traditional mistrust of women's rational capabilities.

Sidney Harris/www.cartoonstock.com

Difference feminism assumes that men and women have very different approaches and expectations; classical feminism, on the other hand, assumes that if we minimize gender differences in a child's upbringing, a new generation of people who are persons first and gendered beings second will appear. But when it comes to the fashion marketplace, what seem to be the trends? Are the traditional gender roles still in evidence, or are the boundaries fading away?

In general, the values we've celebrated for so long as good human behavior have been predominantly male values, say the new feminists, because the male person has been considered the "real" person, whereas women have been thought of as slightly deviant. The man is the typical human being. In older textbooks on human development, the earlier forms of hominids, such as *Homo habilis* and *Neandertal,* have usually been depicted as males ("Neandertal man"). Only recently in textbooks and articles have humans been symbolized by both male and female figures. Even recent theories of psychology seem to use boys and men as their research material rather than girls and women, and the medical community must now face the problems resulting from years of conducting research with primarily male subjects. The older statistics regarding women and certain diseases (heart disease, for example) are unreliable, and the administration of medicine to women is often decided on the basis of research on male subjects. This is not just a matter of a slanted ideology; it is a very practical problem. Women have for a long time been judged by the standards of men, as though women were what Aristotle claimed so long ago—deficient males. Difference feminism wants to replace the image of one of the genders being more "normal" than the other with an image of both genders, with all their unique characteristics, being equally representative of the human race. This shift involves upgrading the female tasks of motherhood, housekeeping, caring for family members, and so on, tasks that for some people seemed to fall by the wayside in the first rush to get women into the workforce. Typical female virtues that arise from concentrating on those tasks are considered to be generosity, caring, harmony, reconciliation, and maintenance of close relationships. The virtues that typically have been considered male are justice, rights, fairness, competition, independence, and adherence to the rules.

Psychologist Carol Gilligan has been a major inspiration in the gender debate. Her book *In a Different Voice* (1982) analyzes reactions of boys and girls, men and women, and concludes that there is a basic difference in the *moral attitudes* of males and females. In one of her analyses she uses an experiment by a well-known contemporary psychologist, Lawrence Kohlberg; it is called the *Heinz dilemma.* An interviewer using Kohlberg's method asked two 11-year-old children, Jake and Amy, to evaluate the following situation: Heinz's wife is desperately ill, and Heinz can't afford medication for her. Should Heinz steal the medication? Jake has no doubts; he says yes, Heinz should steal the medication, because his wife's life is more important than the rule of not stealing. Amy, though, is not so sure. She says no, he shouldn't steal the medication, because what if he got caught? Then he would have to go to jail, and who would look after his sick wife? Perhaps he could ask the pharmacist to let him have the medication and pay later. Since the interviewer didn't get the expected response, Amy changed her answer. The interviewer concluded that Jake had a clear understanding of the situation: It would be just that the wife should receive the medication, because her rights would override the law of not stealing. The interviewer thought that Amy's comprehension of the situation was fuzzy at best. Jake understood what it was all about: rights and justice.

Gilligan rereads Amy's answer and comes up with another conclusion entirely: Although Jake answered the question *Should Heinz steal the drug or not?* (in other words, a classical dilemma requiring a choice between two answers), Amy heard it differently: *Should Heinz steal the drug, or should he do something else?* In effect, the children were answering different questions, and Amy's response makes as much sense as Jake's. But Amy is not concerned with the issues of rights and justice as much as she is with what will happen to Heinz and his wife; she even takes the humaneness of the pharmacist into consideration. In other words, she thinks in terms of *caring.* She acknowledges that there are laws, but she also believes people can be reasoned with. The interviewer, Gilligan says, didn't hear that in Amy's answer because he was looking for the "justice" answer. Gilligan concludes that boys and men tend to focus on an *ethic of justice,* whereas girls and women look toward an *ethic of care.*

Gilligan's influence on modern thinking about gender issues has been enormous, although other philosophers, psychologists, and linguists have also approached them in similar ways, and some of them long before Gilligan's book came out. Perhaps the first person to suggest that women tend to think in terms of caring whereas men think in terms of justice was not a philosopher, or a psychologist, but a playwright: the Norwegian Henrik Ibsen, in his monumentally influential play *A Doll's House* from 1879. You can read an excerpt from this play in the Narratives section. Also, you may remember the debate in Chapter 7 about justice, in which John Rawls suggested that we adopt "the original position," pretending that we don't know who we are when our policy takes effect; you may also remember the responses from Wolgast and Friedman that we can't just assume we are strangers who don't know one another, because part of being a social person is precisely that we have caring relationships with others and don't just exist in some abstract legal universe. That is, in essence, similar to Gilligan's criticism of a traditional ethic of justice as being the traditional male approach to moral questions and emphasizes that we can't just pretend we don't have our own gender. In Gilligan's own words from *In a Different Voice,*

> Women's deference is rooted not only in their social subordination but also in the substance of their moral concern. Sensitivity to the needs of others and the assumption of responsibility for taking care lead women to attend to voices other than their own and to include in their judgment other points of view. Women's moral weakness, manifest in an apparent diffusion and confusion of judgment, is thus inseparable from women's moral strength, an overriding concern with relationships and responsibilities. The reluctance to judge may itself be indicative of the care and concern for others that infuse the psychology of women's development and are responsible for what is generally seen as problematic in its nature.
>
> Thus women not only define themselves in a context of human relationship but also judge themselves in terms of their ability to care. Women's place in man's life cycle has been that of nurturer, caretaker, and helpmate, the weaver of those networks of relationships on which she in turn relies. But while women have thus taken care of men, men have, in their theories of psychological development, as in their economic arrangements, tended to assume or devalue that care. When the focus on individuation and individual achievement extends into adulthood and maturity is equated with personal autonomy, concern with relationships appears as a weakness of women rather than as a human strength.

Does that mean Gilligan is claiming that all women are always caring? That is a matter of interpretation. Some readers see her theory as a description of what we might call the "female condition": Because of either nature or upbringing or both, most women *are* caring human beings. Others see that as a preposterous statement. Not all women are caring, and few women, even if they are generally caring persons, are caring all the time. Gilligan's theory of the ethics of care does not have to be read as a description of how women really act, though; with its emphasis on values it is a theory about how most women believe they *ought to act.* It is a theory of women's normative values—we might call it a theory about the *caring imperative*—not a theory about some inevitable female nature.

Psychologists have not found complete supporting evidence for Gilligan's ideas; it doesn't seem certain that women are particularly care-oriented by nature, but what has emerged is a confirmation of the stereotype that women are more empathy-oriented than men. A study from 2006 found that when most men watch someone get shocked for something he or she did, the *reward center* of their brain is activated—it makes them feel good. Most women, on the other hand, have their *pain center* activated, so it makes them empathize with the wrongdoer. And women are less likely than men to agree that one person should be sacrificed to save five, as in the famous trolley dilemma invented by Philippa Foot (see Chapters 1 and 5). Such examples, mentioned by Jesse Prinz (see Chapter 11), don't necessarily show that women are feeling creatures, and men are not, but they do show that we live in a culture that rewards and expects women's empathy more so than men's—at least that is what Prinz thinks. (Gilligan's theory was one of the inspirational sources for Furrow and Wheeler's Ethic of Care which you read about in Chapter 10, but the Furrow-Wheeler theory goes beyond the gender issue, making a caring approach the moral ideal for humans in general, in the style of Levinas's moral philosophy.)

Paul Hawthorne/Getty Images

Carol Gilligan (b. 1936), American psychologist and author of *In a Different Voice* (1982) as well as coauthor of several books on women's and girls' psychology. She became Harvard University's first professor of gender studies. Like Simone de Beauvoir, Gilligan believes that throughout Western history men have been considered the "normal" gender and women have been viewed as not-quite-normal. However, unlike Beauvoir, Gilligan does not argue for a monoandrogynous society, believing instead that men and women are fundamentally different in their approach to life—different but equal.

What does the Gilligan theory add up to? For many women, it means that their experiences of attachment and their focus on relationships are normal and good and not "overly dependent," "clinging," or "immature"; it means an upgrading of what we consider traditional female values. The point of Gilligan's book is to prompt the mature woman to understand rights and the mature man to understand caring so we all can work and live together in harmony. Her hopes may not be realized for decades to come, however, (and it's already been over 40 years since Gilligan's book came out, so some of us are still waiting!) for although some may argue that they know some very caring men and some very justice-oriented women, it seems Gilligan is right in claiming that most women in the United States grow up believing that caring is what is most important, and most men grow up believing that individual rights and justice are the ultimate ethical values. In Northern European countries, the family values have actually drifted in Gilligan's direction, but some analyses see that as a result of ancient traditions and economic structures rather than as a result of difference feminism.

There are risks involved in Gilligan's theory. Some think we may end up elevating female values far above male values. In that case we will have reversed one unfair system but created another unfair system by declaring women "normal" and men "slightly deviant." A more pressing problem is the following: If we say it is in a woman's nature to be understanding and caring, we may be forcing her right back into the private sphere from which she just emerged. Men (and also women) may say, Well, if most women aren't able to understand "justice," then we can't use them in the real world, and they'd better go home and do what nature intended them to do: have babies and care for their man. Similarly, if a job calls for "caring" qualities, employers may be reluctant to hire a man, because men are not "naturals" at caring. So instead of giving people more opportunities, Gilligan may actually be setting up new categories that could result in policies that exclude women from "men's work" and men from "women's work." It is not enough to say that the qualities of one gender are not supposed to outweigh the qualities of the other, because we all know that even with the best intentions, we tend to rank one set of differences higher than the other. We may all be equal, but remember George Orwell's *Animal Farm?* In that novel, which is a metaphor for political despotism, Orwell warns against some being considered "more equal than others." Critics have claimed that what Gilligan is doing is throwing a monkey wrench into the philosophy of gender equality, and her "ethic of care" theory may result in statements such as this: "We need a new executive with a good head for legal rules—but we can't hire a woman, of course, even though she seems otherwise qualified, because science says that women have a lousy sense of justice." In short, there is a danger that a psychological theory of gender may shift from describing what seems to be the case to prescribing a set of rules about who ought to do what.

Although her theory of the ethic of care may raise problems for the concept of equality, there is no doubt that Gilligan touched on something a vast number of women have been able to relate to.

Some years ago, Gilligan and other feminists engaged in a written debate in the *Atlantic Monthly* with Christina Hoff Sommers (see Box 12.9 and Chapter 10), who by then had acquired a solid reputation among some feminists as being no feminist at all. Sommers had just published a book, *The War Against Boys* (2000), in which she claimed that because of what she calls gender feminism, young boys are now facing a hard time in school. Contrary to the standard wisdom that girls are overlooked in the classroom in favor of the more assertive boys, Sommers pointed out that it is in fact the girls who nowadays are getting all the attention from the teachers and are being held up as role models as smarter and better behaved than the boys. That makes boys lose self-esteem. Sommers's claims caused consternation and disbelief among readers of the *Atlantic Monthly,* where her views were first published. But she has also found an audience who agree that conditions in schools have changed dramatically over the past decades to the benefit of girls, and we need to look at the possibility that in some cases it may have come at a price: the shortchanging of boys. Since her book came out in 2000, her claims have, to a great extent, been supported by further studies as well as a growing appreciation in the court of public opinion. An article in *Newsweek,* January 30, 2006, "The Trouble with Boys," echoed Sommers's analysis with statistics and case studies, claiming that the attention given to girls has made boyhood itself somehow questionable and that what is needed is a positive reevaluation of *masculinity* itself. Critics were quick to point out, however, that this is nothing but a backlash, attempting to undo the great strides women made in the twentieth century and to undermine the intellectual and professional gains of women in the twenty-first century. However, it is clear that the observation that boys are being shortchanged in today's educational climate has hit a nerve with parents, and students, based on personal experience, often summarized as "feminization of the educational system." The debate rolls on.

Radical Feminism: Uprooting Sexism

The term *radical* alone is often enough to make some people tune out. We are used to the term meaning "extremism." For some, a radical feminist is a stereotypical male-basher. But we must be cautious here, because much depends on how we interpret the term *radical.* If we read it as "extremist feminism," then it will generally be used by antifeminists to describe anything they disagree with as being too extreme. The feminists themselves who are tagged with the label may think of themselves as mainstream. It is thus a relative concept and often used in a disparaging sense, meaning any feminism that goes further than you're willing to accept. ("Equal pay for equal work" could sound like radical feminism to some traditionalists.) To be sure, there are feminists who think in more sweeping terms than others. Some see sexual intercourse with men as inherently humiliating for women. And there are misandric feminists who assume that all men are incapable of wanting or working for gender equality, just as there are misogynist men who think ill of all women. But most of those who today call themselves radical feminists have a different agenda: They take the term *radical* in its original

Latin meaning, going to the *root* (*radix*) of the matter. Such radical feminists ask, How did gender discrimination arise? What were the structures that kept it in place? And do we still have elements of those structures today? The answers are generally: *It arose in patriarchy;* those structures have kept gender discrimination alive to this day. A child is still considered to be of the father's family more than of the mother's; yet a mother is still considered to be the primary caregiver of a child taken ill at school, even though the father's profession might be less demanding than hers and his workplace closer to the child's school. A woman is still expected to take her career less seriously than a man is, and to adopt her husband's last name, and some continue to consider a woman's career contributions as less important than a man's. Sexual liberty is still considered more acceptable for boys and men than for girls and women. (Box 12.12 explores the #MeToo phenomenon and the double-standard implications.) Little girls' toys are still in the pink section in the toy stores, and little boys' toys are still action figures from a world with practically no equal women participants. The radical feminist doesn't necessarily want boys to play with dolls or girls to play violent video games, but she or he wants us to understand *where those choices are coming from* and to decide to discard any tradition that sees women as lesser beings than men. The "Princess" phenomenon, explored in Box 12.13, would indicate for the radical feminists that the roots of gender stereotypes are deep, but also that changes may be afoot.

Box 12.12 THE #METOO PHENOMENON

In 2017, a concept went viral in a very short time: *#MeToo*. Those of you who use social media will know that the # symbol, in this case to be read as "hashtag," is a Twitter symbol placed in front of a concept so it can be put into a search engine and shared easily. A legal case was evolving, centered around the famous Hollywood producer Harvey Weinstein, founder of Miramax, who was being accused of sexual harassment and assault by one woman after another, totaling over 80 accusers. He was arrested and later released on bail, awaiting his trial which started in January 2020, and concluded in February with a verdict of *guilty* of assault and 3rd degree rape, but *not guilty* of predatory sexual assault. While his accusers were coming forward, others chimed in with sexual abuse and harassment stories of their own, and shared them online under the "Me Too" hashtag. Primarily women but also a number of men have shared sexual abuse stories from sexual intimidation to rape by influential and powerful men, and, figuratively, heads have rolled. Producers, directors, and movie stars have found themselves accused of sexual misconduct by women, and have been fired on the spot, dropped from the film or television productions, and become *persona non grata* in the entertain-

ment industry. In some cases the accusers have been women whose careers began under the protection of those men—a phenomenon which, in the entertainment industry, has been known for ages as "the casting couch," a method for young women to get roles in show business by agreeing to having sex with powerful men in the industry. And the phenomenon extends beyond the entertainment industry to a wide variety of professions. While some of these powerful men may have believed that this was one of the ordinary perks of being in power, and some of the women may have, in their own way, used those men as "means to an end," a career, it has become clear with the #MeToo movement that sexual abuse of another human being, regardless of one's motivation, is no longer acceptable. Thousands of women as well as men have finally found the courage to denounce the sexual misbehavior of mentors, superiors, teachers, and others whom they initially trusted to be ethical human beings willing to help them with their training.

But as with most explosive Internet phenomena, there has been a backlash. The media, especially the social media, fired up by the righteous indignation of victims finally finding their voices, were quick to denounce any man who had an accusation leveled against him, assuming guilt merely based on the accusation, and some men caught up in the web of accusations have vigorously maintained their innocence. In some cases, charges have been dropped. However, their names and careers have been tainted. Some people began labeling it a witch hunt where any accusation will brand the accused for life regardless of evidence. Especially in Europe, the #MeToo phenomenon has acquired a bad reputation as a twenty-first-century example of public opinion running wild, ruining lives in the process.

Box 12.13 THE PRINCESS PHENOMENON

While second-wave feminists were focused on the classical feminist concept of strict gender equality, some feminists took the radical view that any display of traditional femininity was playing into the hands of patriarchy and male dominance: Skirts gave way to pants, jewelry and makeup disappeared, high heels became flat heels, and life became, perhaps, less glamorous, but also more comfortable. Little girls were dressed in unisex coveralls, and the frilly look was retired. So it was quite disturbing for older second-wave feminists to see the princess look emerge in the new millennium with a new push by the Disney corporation to recapture the minds of romantic little girls and their romantically starved mothers. The pink Princess line of merchandise was a hugely successful result, with clothes, bedding, alarm clocks, everything that a little girl might beg to have in her room. Little girls love it—but some parents are worried that the gender brainwashing has started up again, trying to make the girls into conventional women who focus more on being cute than on creating a meaningful future for themselves. So does that mean that the new generation of girls will grow up to be vain robots—or is it simply opening up more possibilities for self-expression, as third-wave feminism advocates? Lately it appears that little girls aren't stuck with the princess identity in the Disney universe; they can also opt to be fairies (like Tinker Bell)—and pirates! Some critics are linking the phenomenon to popular television shows focusing on women as stereotypical females, thinking primarily about finding a husband, preferably while wearing really hip clothes—such as the popular TV series *Sex and the City*.

The hugely popular Disney animated feature film *Frozen* (2013) would be a countermeasure to that stereotype, with the drama not being between the "girl" and her "boyfriend," but the story of alienation and reunion of two sisters. So from within the beloved, and influential, Disney story machine, there are new tendencies at play. For Halloween 2019 the princess costumes were still #1 for girls, but especially the *Frozen* character of Princess Elsa, reflecting the success of *Frozen 2*. Close behind were superhero costumes—but they are not just for boys anymore. Girls can dress up as superheroes, too, so perhaps times are changing just a little bit.

A famous radical feminist, Andrea Dworkin (1946–2005), wrote in her book *Right-Wing Women: The Politics of Domesticated Females* (1983):

To achieve a single standard of human freedom and one absolute standard of human dignity, the sex-class system has to be dismembered. The reason is pragmatic, not philosophical: Nothing less will work. However much everyone wants to do less, less will not free women. Liberal men and women ask, Why can't we just be ourselves, all human beings, begin now and not dwell in past injustices, wouldn't that subvert the sex-class system, change it from the inside out? The answer is no. The sex-class system has a structure; it has deep roots in religion and culture; it is fundamental to the economy; sexuality is its creature; to be 'just human beings' in it, women have to hide what happens to them as women because they are women—happenings like forced sex and forced reproduction, happenings that continue as long as the sex-class system operates. The liberation of women requires facing the real condition of women in order to change it. 'We're all just people' is a stance that prohibits recognition of the systematic cruelties visited upon women because of sex oppression.

Dworkin says that one of the toughest challenges to women is to realize that all women have a common condition, even women you don't like, women you don't want to be compared to. The common condition is that women are, in Dworkin's words, "subordinate to men, sexually colonized in a sexual system of dominance and submission, denied rights on the basis of sex, historically chattel, generally considered biologically inferior, confined to sex and reproduction: this is the general description of the social environment in which all women live."

The goal of radical feminism is thus to raise the individual awareness of what the patriarchal tradition has done to us, men as well as women. We must try to undo the social and psychological damage done by centuries of male-dominated culture—by making women aware of how much in their personal and professional lives has been dominated and designed by men. Radical feminism sees women's minds as by and large shaped by men's accomplishments and thinking, and unless women learn to focus on women's talents and accomplishments, they/we will always have a "false consciousness": We think we understand, but all we have to work with are mind tools and concepts invented by men. Another radical feminist, historian Gerda Lerner, mentioned earlier, says that women have until recently been excluded from the "power of naming and defining." Men have defined the problems deemed worthy of attention, as well as the vocabulary with which they should be described. Being able to put a name to a problem is part of solving it, and if women are deprived of naming their own problems, the problems remain unrecognized. For that reason, sex discrimination isn't uprooted simply by listening to the private wishes and professional ideas of women, because those wishes and ideas may be favored by the male tradition we all grew up within. Radical feminism insists that both women and men must be educated to see that tradition as one of oppression and be encouraged to create a new one based on a female perspective.

Where Do We Go From Here?

You have now seen some of the schools of thought about feminism and gender that philosophers and others interested in gender theory are dealing with here in the first decades of the twenty-first century. Classical (liberal) feminism has had a setback because of its predominant theory that we are all just people if we remove the factors of upbringing and education, or create a unisex educational environment—because as you have seen, there seems to be a certain biological hardwiring of us as sexual beings, even if we may choose to alter the social gender roles. That means that difference feminism has moved to the forefront as the most prominent theory—except that radical feminism will then point out that if we focus too much on hardwiring, then we may end up in old discrimination patterns, not taking into account that with a descriptive view of sexual human nature we very often have a normative view following, a view that may end up pigeonholing people in preexisting categories they are not comfortable with. And equity feminism will point out that it would be better for all of us if we just stop making gender roles into a problem, because these days anyone can choose any role they like, and discrimination will fade away like other outdated attitudes. So what do you think? In this new world where women can become combat soldiers, where we can change not only the socially constructed gender roles but the biological identities we are born with, where transgendered individuals can compete in sports that used to be for one biological sex exclusively, and restrooms in many states are set up to accommodate persons according to the gender roles they identify with, rather than their physical characteristics, are we creating a society where human beings feel welcome and valued regardless of their sex and gender, or are we creating more obstacles and problems for our coexistence?

Study Questions

1. Give a brief account of the similarities and differences between classical, difference, radical, and equity feminism. Can those facets overlap? Explain.

2. Which brand of feminism do you think is the most relevant today? Are you a feminist? If yes, why? If no, why not?

3. Outline the advantages and the problems associated with difference feminism.

Primary Readings and Narratives

The Primary Reading is an excerpt from Harriet Taylor Mill's "Enfranchisement of Women." The first Narrative is a summary of and an excerpt from the classic play by Henrik Ibsen, *A Doll's House,* in which a nineteenth-century housewife, treated as a beloved but mischievous child by her husband, proves to be very much an adult person. The second Narrative is a summary of Margaret Atwood's modern classic *The Handmaid's Tale,* and the final Narrative is a summary of a novel about women in contemporary Afghanistan, Khaled Hosseini's *A Thousand Splendid Suns.*

 Primary Reading

Enfranchisement of Women

HARRIET TAYLOR MILL

Excerpt, 1851.

You read about Harriet Taylor Mill in Chapter 5, as being John Stuart Mill's soul mate and intellectual partner, and in this chapter you read about their collaboration on the philosophy of women's rights in mid-nineteenth-century Great Britain. Here you have an excerpt from Harriet Taylor Mill's text, written in 1851—sixteen years before John Stuart Mill's own book about women's rights, *The Subjection of Women,* was published. In 1851 Harriet and John were also finally married, two years after the death of Harriet's husband and after a relationship of twenty-one years. Until Harriet's untimely death from tuberculosis in 1858, she and John went on collaborating about other projects such as an analysis of domestic violence, property rights, and the work that was to become John Stuart Mill's first book after her death: *On Liberty.*

In this excerpt H. T. Mill dismisses three standard nineteenth-century arguments against women in the workforce: that allowing women in the workforce would (1) go against the duties of motherhood, (2) be unfair competition to men, and (3) mean an unsuitable hardening of the female character.

> Concerning the fitness, then, of women for politics, there can be no question: but the dispute is more likely to turn upon the fitness of politics for women. When the reasons alleged for excluding women from active life in all its higher departments, are stripped of their garb of declamatory phrases, and reduced to the simple expression of a meaning, they seem to be mainly three: the incompatibility of

active life with maternity, and with the care of a household; secondly, its alleged hardening effect on the character; and thirdly, the inexpediency of making an addition to the already excessive pressure of competition in every kind of professional or lucrative employment.

The first, the maternity argument, is usually laid most stress upon: although (it needs hardly be said) this reason, if it be one, can apply only to mothers. It is neither necessary nor just to make imperative on women that they shall be either mothers or nothing; or that if they have been mothers once, they shall be nothing else during the whole remainder of their lives. Neither women nor men need any law to exclude them from an occupation, if they have undertaken another which is incompatible with it. No one proposes to exclude the male sex from Parliament because a man may be a soldier or sailor in active service, or a merchant whose business requires all his time and energies. Nine-tenths of the occupations of men exclude them *de facto* from public life, as effectually as if they were excluded by law; but that is no reason for making laws to exclude even the nine-tenths, much less the remaining tenth. The reason of the case is the same for women as for men. There is no need to make provision by law that a woman shall not carry on the active details of a household, or of the education of children, and at the same time practise a profession or be elected to parliament. Where incompatibility is real, it will take care of itself: but there is gross injustice in making the incompatibility a pretence for the exclusion of those in whose case it does not exist. And these, if they were free to choose, would be a very large proportion. The maternity argument deserts its supporters in the case of single women, a large and increasing class of the population; a fact which, it is not irrelevant to remark, by tending to diminish the excessive competition of numbers, is calculated to assist greatly the prosperity of all. There is no inherent reason or necessity that all women should voluntarily choose to devote their lives to one animal function and it consequences. Numbers of women are wives and mothers only because there is no other career open to them, no other occupation for their feelings or their activities. Every improvement in their education, and enlargement of their faculties—everything which renders them more qualified for any other mode of life, increases the number of those to whom it is an injury and an oppression to be denied the choice. To say that women must be excluded from active life because maternity disqualifies them for it, is in fact to say, that every other career should be forbidden them in order that maternity may be their only resource.

But secondly, it is urged, that to give the same freedom of occupation to women as to men, would be an injurious addition to the crowd of competitors, by whom the avenues to almost all kinds of employment are choked up, and its remuneration depressed. This argument, it is to be observed, does not reach the political question. It gives no excuse for withholding from women the rights of citizenship. The suffrage, the jury-box, admission to the legislature and to office, it does not touch. It bears only on the industrial branch of the subject. Allowing it, then, in an economical point of view, its full force; assuming that to lay open to women the employments now monopolized by men, would tend, like the breaking down of other monopolies, to lower the rate of remuneration in those employments; let us consider what is the amount of this evil consequence, and what the compensation for it. The worst ever asserted, much worse than is at all likely to be realized, is that if women competed with men, a man and a woman could not together earn more than is now earned by the man alone. Let us make this supposition, the most unfavourable supposition possible, the joint income of the two would be the same as before, while the woman would be raised from the position of a servant to that of a partner. Even if every woman, as matters now stand, had a claim on some man for support, how infinitely preferable is it that part of the income should be of the woman's earning, even if the aggregate sum were but little increased by it, rather than that she should be compelled to stand aside in order that men may be the sole earners, and the sole dispensers of what is earned. Even under the present laws respecting the property of women, a woman who contributes materially to the support of the family, cannot be treated in the same contemptuously tyrannical manner as one who, however she may toil as a domestic drudge, is a dependent on the man for subsistence. . . . But so long as competition is the general law of human life, it is tyranny to shut out one-half of the competitors. All who have attained the age of self-government, have an equal claim to be permitted to sell whatever kind of useful labour they are capable of, for the price which it will bring.

The third objection to the admission of women to political or professional life, its alleged hardening tendency, belongs to an age now past, and is scarcely to be comprehended by people of the present time. There are still, however, persons who say that the world and its avocations render men selfish and unfeeling; that the struggles, rivalries, and collisions of business and of politics make them harsh and unamiable; that if half the species must unavoidably be given up to these things, it is the more necessary that the other half should be kept free from them; that to preserve women from the bad influences of the world, is the only chance of preventing men from being wholly given up to them.

There would have been plausibility in this argument when the world was still in the age of violence; when life was full of physical conflict, and every man had to redress his injuries or those of others, by the sword or by the strength of his arm. Women, like priests, by being exempted from such responsibilities, and from some part of the accompanying dangers, may have been enabled to exercise a beneficial influence. But in the present condition of human life, we do not know where those hardening influences are to be found, to which men are subject and from which women are at present exempt. Individuals now-a-days are seldom called upon to fight hand to hand, even with peaceful weapons; personal enmities and rivalities count for little in worldly transactions; the general pressure of circumstances, not the adverse will of individuals, is the obstacle men now have to make head against. That pressure, when excessive, breaks the spirit, and cramps and sours the feelings, but not less of women than of men, since they suffer certainly not less from its evils. There are still quarrels and dislikes, but the sources of them are changed. The feudal chief once found his bitterest enemy in his powerful neighbour, the minister or courtier in his rival for place: but opposition of interest in active life, as a cause of personal animosity, is out of date; the enmities of the present day arise not from great things but small, from what people say of one another, more than from what they do; and if there are hated, malice, and all uncharitableness, they are to be found among women fully as much as among men. In the present state of civilization, the notion of guarding women from the hardening influences of the world, could only be realized by secluding them from society altogether. The common duties of common life, as at present constituted, are incompatible with any other softness in women than weakness. Surely weak minds in weak bodies must ere long cease to be even supposed to be either attractive or amiable.

But, in truth, none of these arguments and considerations touch the foundations of the subject. The real question is, whether it is right and expedient that one-half of the human race should pass through life in a state of forced subordination to the other half. If the best state of human society is that of being divided into two parts, one consisting of persons with a will and a substantive existence, the other of humble companions to these persons, attached, each of them to one, for the purpose of bringing up *his* children, and making *his* home pleasant to him; if this is the place assigned to women, it is but kindness to educate them for this; to make them believe that the greatest good fortune which can befall them, is to be chosen by some man for his purpose; and that every other career which the world deems happy or honourable, is closed to them by the law, not of social institutions, but of nature and destiny.

When, however, we ask why the existence of one-half the species should be merely ancillary to that of the other—why each woman should be a mere appendage to a man, allowed to have no interests of her own, that there may be nothing to compete in her mind with his interests and his pleasure; the only reason which can be given is, that men like it. It is agreeable to them that men should live for their own sake, women for the sake of men; and the qualities and conduct in subjects which are agreeable to rulers, they succeed for a long time in making the subjects themselves consider as their appropriate virtues. . . . Under a nominal recognition of a moral code common to both, in practice in self-will and self-assertion form the type of what are designated as manly virtues, while abnegation of self, patience, resignation, and submission to power, unless when resistance is commanded by other interests than their own, have been stamped by general consent as pre-eminently the duties and graces required of women. The meaning being merely, that power makes itself the centre of moral obligation, and that a man likes to have his own will, but does not like that his domestic companion should have a will different from his.

Study Questions

1. What are Harriet Taylor Mill's counterarguments to the three standard arguments against women in the workforce? Are they convincing to you? Why or why not?

2. Might the three arguments (motherhood, unfair competition, and hardening of the character) be valid in any conceivable modern context? Explain why or why not.

3. Apply H. T. Mill's arguments to the idea of women in combat. Do you see the same arguments supporting the idea? Or is there a difference? Explain.

4. Comment on H. T. Mill's statement that the only reason women have been ancillary (subordinate) to men is that men like it; is that a fair statement within the context of the nineteenth century, as far as you can tell? Would it be a fair statement in the twenty-first century?

Harriet Taylor Hill. "Enfranchisement of Women." *Westminster and Foreign Quarterly Review* no. 4 (1951) https://www.loc.gov/item/93838319/.

  Narrative

A Doll's House

HENRIK IBSEN

Play, 1879. Translated by William Archer. Summary and Excerpt. Two British film versions exist, both from 1973; one stars Claire Bloom and Anthony Hopkins; the other stars Jane Fonda and David Warner.

By the time the Norwegian playwright Henrik Ibsen wrote *A Doll's House,* isolated voices had been speaking out for the liberation of women for over a hundred years, but there was not a single country in the Western world where women had yet achieved the right to vote. When Ibsen's play was performed on the stages of Europe, the final act turned out to be a bombshell; Ibsen allows us to see Nora's situation from her own point of view and shows us that this viewpoint is heroic in its own way. In her quest to be regarded as a mature human being, Nora sent signals to men and women all over the Western world and made a considerable impact on the gender debate in Scandinavia at the end of the nineteenth and the beginning of the twentieth century. The story has been considered so compelling that the play is still performed today.

Some contemporary readers may prefer to look for literature about the condition of women written by *women,* not by *men.* But, for one thing, Ibsen's play has had historical importance in helping men as well as women see the traditional woman's role as a political question; for another thing, good writers gifted with clear powers of observation and an imaginative genius, such as Ibsen, are often quite capable of seeing a situation from the other gender's point of view.

The conflict between the feminine virtue of caring and the masculine focus on justice may seem new to many readers of Carol Gilligan, but in these excerpts you can see the outlines of that very same debate, anticipated by Ibsen more than a century ago.

Nora and Torvald Helmer are a happily married middle-class couple with three young children. Helmer regards his lively wife as another child, always happy and singing; his pet names for her are his songbird, his lark, his little squirrel. He accuses her of being a spendthrift, of always asking for more pocket money, but he forgives her because she is so sweet and amusing. And even to her friends she seems like a carefree, coddled woman with no worries other than choosing what clothes to wear for parties. But things are not what they seem on the surface. An old friend of Nora's comes to visit, and Nora tells her a deep secret of which she is very proud: Some years ago Helmer was very ill, and the doctor recommended an expensive trip to Italy as a cure. Helmer believes that Nora's father lent them the money, and he is now dead, so he can't tell. But Nora paid for the trip all by herself, with no income or fortune of her own: She took out a private loan, with high interest, and that is why she has been asking Helmer for so much pocket money, buying only the cheapest things for herself, and paying the loan off, always on time, with interest. And it won't be long now before the loan will be paid off: Helmer is being promoted to bank manager, and their finances will improve.

But disaster waits in the wings: An employee at the bank, Krogstad, turns up and begs her to ask her husband to let him keep his job. Why might he lose it? Because he has a criminal record; he has forged papers. And why would he come to Nora? Because Nora knows him well—he is the man who lent her the money for the trip to Italy. He threatens to tell Helmer, but what is worse, he has done some research. Nora's father cosigned the loan, as security—but the signature is dated days after her father died. The conclusion is obvious: Nora forged her father's signature, and now Krogstad threatens her with the law and tells her that his crime was no worse than her own.

Krogstad: May I ask you one more question? Why did you not send the paper to your father?

Nora: It was impossible. Father was ill. If I had asked him for his signature, I should have had to tell him why I wanted the money; but he was so ill I really could not tell him that my husband's life was in danger. It was impossible.

Krogstad: Then it would have been better to have given up your tour.

Nora: No, I couldn't do that; my husband's life depended on that journey. I couldn't give it up.

Krogstad: And did it never occur to you that you were playing me false?

Nora: That was nothing to me. I didn't care in the least about you. I couldn't endure you for all the cruel difficulties you made, although you knew how ill my husband was.

Krogstad: Mrs. Helmer, you evidently do not realise what you have been guilty of. But I can assure you it was nothing more and nothing worse that made me an outcast from society.

Nora: You! You want me to believe that you did a brave thing to save your wife's life?

Krogstad: The law takes no account of motives.

Nora: Then it must be a very bad law.

Krogstad: Bad or not, if I produce this document in court, you will be condemned according to law.

Nora: I don't believe that. Do you mean to tell me that a daughter has no right to spare her dying father trouble and anxiety?—that a wife has no right to save her husband's life? I don't know much about the law, but I'm sure you'll find, somewhere or another, that is allowed. And you don't know that—you, a lawyer! You must be a bad one, Mr. Krogstad.

Krogstad: Possibly. But business—such business as ours—I do understand. You believe that? Very well; now do as you please. But this I may tell you, that if I am flung into the gutter a second time, you shall keep me company.

[*Bows and goes out through hall.*]

Nora: [*Stands a while thinking, then tosses her head.*] Oh nonsense! He wants to frighten me. I'm not so foolish as that. [*Begins folding the children's clothes. Pauses.*] But—? No, it's impossible! Why, I did it for love!

Later, Helmer talks to her about what a despicable man Krogstad is, and how vile his crime. Shortly after, Helmer fires Krogstad, in spite of Nora's pleas, and Krogstad shows up again. Now he wants more: Unless Nora makes Helmer reinstate him and give him a promotion, he will reveal all. And if Nora should think of drastic solutions, such as killing herself, her husband will still be told everything. Now Krogstad wants Helmer to know, so he can blackmail the two of them, instead of only her, and he leaves a letter for Helmer, telling him everything. Nora is desperate and tries to distract Helmer when he comes home by dancing for him, and she makes him promise that he will not open the letter until the next day. Meanwhile, she pleads with her friend and confidante to go to Krogstad and persuade him to stop his threats.

The following night Nora and Helmer are at a dance, and Nora dances as if it is her last night on this earth. Coming home, there is still the letter waiting for them, and Nora, deep in despair, is waiting, too: for a miracle, for without it she is going to kill herself.

But Helmer reads the letter, and is horrified: the woman he loved, a liar and a criminal! He blames her weakness of character and her father's bad influence and sees himself as a ruined man. He insists that Nora can no longer see her children—they must be protected from her evil influence. Nora threatens suicide, but Helmer scoffs at it: How is that going to help *him* and *his* ruin? And now it dawns on Nora that her motivation for forging her father's signature is utterly lost on Helmer; the miracle she was hoping for, and dreading, is far from happening.

But now comes the salvation: Nora's friend has succeeded in persuading Krogstad to drop the matter (through a personal sacrifice which Nora knows nothing about). Krogstad returns Nora's I.O.U. with an apologetic letter, and Helmer is ecstatic, exclaiming that now he is saved. And, magnanimously, he now sees Nora as a poor, misguided soul who has not understood what she has done, and he forgives her. All she needs now is his guidance, he says—from now on he'll be her will and her conscience, and everything will be as before.

Meanwhile Nora, stone-faced, has changed out of her masquerade dress and into her ordinary clothes. For her, the masquerade is over, and although he doesn't know it yet, it is, too, for him. She asks him to sit down, for she has much to talk over with him.

Helmer: You alarm me, Nora. I don't understand you.

Nora: No, that is just it. You don't understand me; and I have never understood you—till tonight. No, don't interrupt. Only listen to what I say.—We must come to a final settlement, Torvald.

Helmer: How do you mean?

Nora: [*After a short silence.*] Does not one thing strike you as we sit here?

Helmer: What should strike me?

Nora: We have been married eight years. Does it not strike you that this is the first time we two, you and I, man and wife, have talked together seriously?

Helmer: Seriously! What do you call seriously?

Nora: During eight whole years, and more—ever since the day we first met—we have never exchanged one serious word about serious things.

Helmer: Was I always to trouble you with the cares you could not help me to bear?

Nora: I am not talking of cares. I say that we have never yet set ourselves seriously to get to the bottom of anything.

Helmer: Why, my dearest Nora, what have you to do with serious things?

Nora: There we have it! You have never understood me.—I have had great injustice done me, Torvald; first by father, and then by you.

Helmer: What! By your father and me?—By us, who have loved you more than all the world?

Nora: [*Shaking her head.*] You have never loved me. You only thought it amusing to be in love with me.

Helmer: Why, Nora, what a thing to say!

Nora: Yes, it is so, Torvald. While I was at home with father, he used to tell me all his opinions, and I held the same opinions. If I had others I said nothing about them, because he wouldn't have liked it. He used to call me his doll-child, and played with me as I played with my dolls. Then I came to live in your house—

Helmer: What an expression to use about our marriage!

Nora: [*Undisturbed.*] I mean I passed from father's hands into yours. You arranged everything according to your taste; and I got the same tastes as you; or I pretended to—I don't know which—both ways, perhaps; sometimes one and sometimes the other. When I look back on it now, I seem to have been living here like a beggar, from hand to mouth. I lived by performing tricks for you, Torvald. But you would have it so. You and father have done me a great wrong. It is your fault that my life has come to nothing.

Helmer: Why, Nora, how unreasonable and ungrateful you are! Have you not been happy here?

Nora: No, never. I thought I was; but I never was.

Helmer: Not—not happy!

Nora: No; only merry. And you have always been so kind to me. But our house has been nothing but a play-room. Here I have been your doll-wife, just as at home I used to be papa's doll-child. And the children, in their turn, have been my dolls. I thought it fun when you played with me, just as the children did when I played with them. That has been our marriage, Torvald.

. . . .

Helmer: To forsake your home, your husband, and your children! And you don't consider what the world will say.

Nora: I can pay no heed to that. I only know that I must do it.

Helmer: This is monstrous! Can you forsake your holiest duties in this way?

Nora: What do you consider my holiest duties?

Helmer: Do I need to tell you that? Your duties to your husband and your children.

Nora: I have other duties equally sacred.

Helmer: Impossible! What duties do you mean?

Nora: My duties towards myself.

Helmer: Before all else you are a wife and a mother.

Nora: That I no longer believe. I believe that before all else I am a human being, just as much as you are—or at least that I should try to become one. I know that most people agree with you, Torvald, and that they say so in books. But henceforth I can't be satisfied with what most people say, and what is in books. I must think things out for myself, and try to get clear about them.

. . . .

Nora: I have waited so patiently all these eight years; for of course I saw clearly enough that miracles don't happen every day. When this crushing blow threatened me, I said to myself so confidently, "Now comes the miracle!" When Krogstad's letter lay in the box, it never for a moment occurred to me that you would think of submitting to that man's conditions. I was convinced that you would say to him, "Make it known to all the world"; and that then—

Helmer: Well? When I had given my own wife's name up to disgrace and shame—?

Nora: Then I firmly believed that you would come forward, take everything upon yourself, and say, "I am the guilty one."

Helmer: Nora—!

Nora: You mean I would never have accepted such a sacrifice? No, certainly not. But what would my assertions have been worth in opposition to yours?—That was the miracle that I hoped for and dreaded. And it was to hinder that I wanted to die.

Helmer: I would gladly work for you day and night, Nora—bear sorrow and want for your sake. But no man sacrifices his honour, even for one he loves.

Nora: Millions of women have done so.

So, in the end, Torvald is the one who understands nothing; he promises to love her, to do anything if she will only stay with him. But she sees him now as a stranger and prepares to leave. In her final words to him she says that to get together again, they would both have to change so much that "communion between them shall be a marriage." And Nora leaves, closing the door behind her.

Study Questions

1. What does Nora mean by the final line in this excerpt?
2. If you were in Nora's position, would your reaction be similar or different? Why? If you were in Helmer's position, would your reaction be similar or different? Why?
3. Examine the excerpts and find evidence of virtue ethics as opposed to an ethics of justice.
4. Ibsen refers to his characters as "Nora" and "Helmer" rather than "Nora" and "Torvald." What kind of effect might that have on the reader of the play? Do you think it is intentional?

Ibsen, Henrik. A Doll's House. Translated by William Archer. Boston: Walter H. Baker & Co., 1890.

Narrative

The Handmaid's Tale

MARGARET ATWOOD

Novel, 1985. Film, 1990. Radio adaptations, 2000 and 2002. Numerous stage adaptations, including play, opera, and ballet. Hulu television series 2017–ongoing. Summary and Excerpt.

Sophie Giraud/MGM/Hulu/C4/Kobal/Shutterstock

In Gilead the "handmaids" wear red robes, and white, starched bonnets hiding their faces. For many fans of the story and the television series, the white bonnet and the red robe have become part of popular culture symbolism of patriarchal oppression (see Study Question #4).

Margaret Atwood's modern classic novel was extremely well received by feminist critics in particular, and it has taken on a life of its own through numerous awards and a wide variety of adaptations, including a successful television series by Hulu. Here we stay close to the book, a work within the category of social science fiction.

We are in the near future in New England. A woman is telling her story to us, but we don't know her name. It is only through others in the story that we find out she is called Offred, and that isn't even her real name, because before her arrival in the household where she is employed as a handmaid* there was another Offred. The current Offred finds evidence of her predecessor's existence by a note, scribbled in a hidden spot: *Nolite te bastardes carborundorum.* Later she finds out the meaning of the Latin words, "Don't let the bastards grind you down." Although it is an old college expression and not real Latin, the meaning is clear: somebody is out to grind Offred down—and that somebody is the new world order, at least in that part of the United States that is now known as Gilead, also a Biblical reference. A disaster has happened; the president and Congress have been murdered,

---

* The term "handmaid" is derived from the Old Testament of the Bible where Jacob's wife Rachel can't have children, so she gives her handmaid Bilhah to her husband for him to produce sons with. The same choice was made by Jacob's grandparents Abraham and his wife Sara who couldn't have children, because according to Hebrew law of the time the wife could order her maid, her "handmaid," to have sex with the husband, and when she became pregnant and gave birth, while leaning on the wife, then the wife would be the child's official mother.

and religious opportunists have taken over. Gilead is now a totalitarian, presumably evangelical fundamentalist enclave, living by what they think is the word of the Bible. Other religions and even other Christian churches are outlawed. Political parties don't exist anymore, and neither do schools, newspapers, and all forms of secular entertainment. The birthrate has gone down, so some women are forced into a breeding program. If you are a wife and it is the first marriage for both of you, but you have no children, then a "handmaid" will be issued to produce children. The handmaid will be a woman who has already given birth to one or two children, and who has had them as a single parent or living in a second marriage, or out of wedlock—because she is now considered a fallen woman. Her children are removed, to be raised by childless couples, and her husband is most likely put to death. Offred is such a woman, and her life now consists of wondering what happened to her husband, Luke, and their little girl—and being available for ritualized sex with her employer, the Commander, Fred (hence her name, Of-Fred) with his wife present. Offred has known her before the change: Serena Joy, once a TV star, and now reduced to hoping for a higher status by having a child born to her handmaid.

Offred has gone through retraining with other women, and she has learned that it is dangerous to ask questions. She might be sent to the "Colonies," terrible, harsh places where women have short life spans, or she might be hanged and displayed at the Wall where dissidents are routinely displayed after execution. Even so, when she is issued a new shopping partner, another handmaid, Ofglen, she realizes that she has found an ally. After many meetings where Ofglen is distant and formal, the two women start whispering, and Offred learns that there is a resistance, and the code word is Mayday—derived from French, *m'aidez*, help me.

Things in the household are also changing: the Commander, apparently a very powerful political figure in the new world order, summons her secretly to his private quarters outside of the ritualized sex encounters. What does he want? Not private sex, but just some human interaction: he asks her to play Scrabble with him. So she discovers that he has a human side, but that doesn't mean her situation has improved—it has just become more dangerous, because of course she would be seen as the instigator if they are discovered, and banished or hanged. And since she still has not become pregnant, her position in the household is becoming precarious. The previous Offred didn't get pregnant, either—and Offred finds out what happened to her: She hanged herself from the chandelier. On a routine visit to the doctor, Offred also finds out how the problem of barrenness is sometimes resolved—because it may be that the Commanders of the households are themselves sterile. And the doctor offers to help—by having sex with the handmaid. Offred declines the offer, but when later Serena Joy is getting impatient that Offred is still having her periods, and offers to arrange secret sex meetings between her and the Commander's servant Nick, Offred consents. A pregnancy will save her life and her standing, even if it also risks her life. Serena Joy rewards her for her obedience by showing her a picture of her daughter, taken recently—so she's alive, and well.

In her nighttime musings, we hear about how Offred and Luke tried to escape to Canada with their daughter, but were informed on by someone they had trusted, and captured. Every time she and Ofglen walk past the Wall, she is afraid that she'll find Luke hanging there. But one day Ofglen is no longer there, waiting for her to go shopping—or rather, there is a new Ofglen.

What happened to Ofglen? Will Offred get pregnant? Will her secret meetings with the Commander cause trouble for her? Will she every see Luke and her daughter again? Some issues are resolved in the book, but not all, but the story evolves in the Hulu television series, at the time of this writing in its fourth season. And in the long-awaited sequel to *The Handmaid's Tale, The Testaments* (2019), taking place 15 years later, we also find that some questions are answered, but they in turn lead to new, intriguing questions.

Study Questions

1. Could you imagine that some political turmoil might nullify all rights for women and throw society into a Gilead scenario? Why or why not?

2. Is Offred making the right choices, under the circumstances? Can you think of alternatives that she hasn't explored?

3. Spoiler alert: In the book we never learn Offred's real name, but in the TV show her name is June. Do you think it makes a difference that her identity is hidden in the book but revealed in the TV show?

4. Some critics see *The Handmaid's Tale* as being a metaphor, not for a dystopian future, but for the present. Analyze their viewpoint. Is it reasonable? Why or why not?

 Narrative

A Thousand Splendid Suns

KHALED HOSSEINI

Novel, 2007. Summary.

Some stories can illustrate a number of different moral issues. *A Thousand Splendid Suns* is one such story. It could find an obvious place in Chapter 4, as an example of selfishness and sacrifice. We could place it in Chapter 3, or in Chapter 10, as an example of soft universalism—how fundamental values are cherished both in Western and non-Western cultures, such as compassion and loyalty. But it is primarily a story about women's hardship in a culture that doesn't recognize them as equal citizens, and while it takes place in war-torn late twentieth century Afghanistan, it could be a story of women in any part of the world and at any time where women have been regarded as chattel, property of the men. Here I've chosen to let it illustrate first the value of friendship under such trying conditions, and second an ethic of care as envisioned by Carol Gilligan.

This is Maryam's story—but it is in equal measure Laila's story. Maryam grows up in a tiny hut on the outskirts of a town, Herat, in Afghanistan, with her mother. No brothers, no sisters—Maryam is her mother Nana's entire life, and the adult woman has a very grim outlook on life and men: "Like a compass needle that points north, a man's accusing finger always finds a woman. Always. You remember that, Maryam." But there is one man in the little girl's life—her father Jalil who comes to visit every Thursday, when he can. Sometimes the little girl will wait in vain for him, but mostly he shows up, for a couple of hours, and those are her happy moments. He takes her fishing and teaches her how to clean fish, he brings her little trinkets and pieces of jewelry, tells stories and recites poetry for her, but he never takes her into town to see his home, because he is married to another woman and has children with her, his "real children." While the law would allow him to have several wives, there is no talk of him marrying Maryam's mother, because she is of a different class. Nana's father might have killed her for the sake of the family honor, since she got pregnant out of wedlock, but instead he disowned her and left town, Nana was hidden away with her daughter, and Jalil promised to support them and keep his two families separate.

As Maryam grows older, she becomes more and more intrigued at the thought of her father's life. He owns a cinema and tells her stories of the films, but never takes her to see any of them. She receives no education except for visits to the kind old Mullah Faizulla, who teaches her to read, and teaches her about the Koran. But her mother is opposed to her going to school, because that is not for the likes of them. And, says Nana, without Maryam she would die. Only one skill is necessary for her, says Nana, and that is to *endure*—endure the suffering that awaits her—enduring as Nana herself apparently has done. When Maryam grows impatient one day when her father doesn't show up, she walks to town with the impetuousness of a young teenager, and shows up at her father's house only to be rejected in the most humiliating way. She spends the night outside the house, and is driven back by her father's driver next day. But a horrible sight awaits her: Nana was serious when she said that without Maryam she would die—she has hanged herself.

Now Maryam has no home, and she is taken in by Jalil and his family, reluctantly. Shortly thereafter her father and his wife present her with the "good news" that they have found her a husband. The fifteen-year-old girl is going to marry a businessman in his forties, Rasheed, who has lost his wife and son. Maryam refuses to go, and begs and pleads, but to no avail. She is quickly married to Rasheed and taken to the big city, Kabul, away from everything she is familiar with, without even being given the chance to say goodbye to old Mullah. And from that moment on she regards her father as having betrayed her.

In Kabul, Maryam finds out that her entire status as a wife depends on her producing a son, a replacement of the boy Rasheed lost. When she has one miscarriage after another, her status dwindles to that of a servant. She has no friends, and is utterly dependent on the goodwill of a man whose disrespect for her increases year after year, and who subjects her to both physical and mental abuse.

But in the same neighborhood another story is beginning, *that of Laila.* Laila is born into quite another kind of family. Her father is a teacher, and her mother is an outgoing woman, proud of her children, especially the two older boys. Laila excels in school, and has a good friend, Tariq, with whom she spends most of her free time. In Tariq's friendly home his father and mother welcome her as one of the family. Tariq himself is no stranger to hardship, having lost a leg in an accident, but he is a boy of good cheer and a positive attitude. As the two children grow up, they find themselves falling in love.

Until this point, it could be a story from anywhere in human history where patriarchy is dominant, but the violent recent history of Afghanistan forces the characters to move in a new direction. The rebel forces, the Mujaheedin, are fighting the Soviet occupational forces (who, within a brief period of time, have established equal rights for women in the world of academia). Laila's two brothers join the Mujaheedin, and are eventually killed. Tariq and his family leave for Pakistan along with thousands of other refugees—but not until he and Laila, now in their mid-teens, have professed their love for each other. They spend one night together, and then he leaves. He wants to take her along and marry her, but she thinks her parents need her, and won't leave them. Shortly thereafter Laila's father and mother are killed by a bomb during an air raid, and now Laila is the one who finds herself without a family. In an ominous replay of what happened to Maryam, Rasheed offers to take on Laila as his second wife, over the protests of Maryam. Laila is strangely compliant, because she now needs a husband—she is pregnant with Tariq's child. And a mysterious stranger has shown up and told her that Tariq is dead in a field hospital in Pakistan, so she agrees to marry Rasheed. However, Rasheed represents a kind of man she has never met before, in her relatively privileged existence: He views women as tools, he is violent as a matter of course, and sees his own wives as property who may not show their faces to the outside world. Both women now wear burqas in public, a precursor to what is to come with the Taliban takeover of the country. Laila's status as a wife seems secure because of her pregnancy (which Rasheed of course believes to have happened after their marriage), but when she has a daughter instead of a son, her status plummets within the household. Meanwhile, the two women are at each other's throats and try to avoid each other as much as possible. But as the little girl grows older, Maryam's heart begins to melt—little Aziza takes her into her heart as Aunt Maryam, and for the first time in her life since her father betrayed her, Maryam experiences love for another human being. And when Laila stands up for Maryam against their abusive husband, a friendship begins to form between the two women. They tell each other of their childhoods, and Laila hears the sad story of Maryam's youth cut short by a spineless father and mentally fragile mother.

In Kabul, meanwhile, conditions are deteriorating. The Mujaheedin have won the war against the Soviets, but now the tribes are fighting amongst themselves. Food is getting scarce, violence erupts, and Laila conceives of a desperate measure: They should leave Rasheed and Kabul for a safer place. They attempt to flee from town, but are turned in to the authorities by a stranger they decided to trust, and are returned to Rasheed and conditions that are far worse than when they left. He keeps Laila and her daughter boarded up with no food and water in one part of the house, and Maryam, beaten to a pulp, is locked up in the woodshed. Finally Rasheed lets them out, swearing that if it ever happens again, he'll kill them.

Life goes on for the two miserable women, locked in a virtual prison by Rasheed. With the takeover of the Taliban (1996), new rules are implemented that limit their lives even further: Now women can no longer go outside unless they are accompanied by a male relative; they can't go to school, or hold down jobs. Jewelry, cosmetics, and laughter are forbidden. And now Laila is pregnant again, this time with a child fathered by Rasheed. When she needs to go to the hospital for the birth, no painkillers or sterile equipment are available, and she gives birth to her son through a caesarian, with no medicine.

Even after Zalmai is born, that doesn't raise her standing in Rasheed's eyes—now he is only concerned with the well-being of the boy. And we get the feeling that he has suspected all along that Aziza is not his—the entire neighborhood was used to seeing Laila and Tariq together all through their childhood. The little girl Aziza is temporarily placed in an orphanage because Rasheed claims he can't afford to feed her, and Laila and Maryam have to find ways to sneak out and visit her, since women can't go outside alone, and Rasheed refuses to accompany them.

And now the bombshell drops: Tariq returns. The tale of his death was concocted by Rasheed to wear down Laila's resistance to their marriage, and now that Tariq has found Laila, they resume their friendship through shy, tentative talks while Rasheed is away during the day. Laila learns of the trials and tribulations Tariq has endured before he was able to come back and look for his beloved. But little Zalmai is now two years old, and can talk, and he tells his father that Mommy has a new friend. So Rasheed now proceeds to punish Laila, and is poised to kill her as he had sworn he would do. He has his hands on her throat, and she is losing consciousness. But behind him Maryam comes in from the toolshed, armed with a shovel. She is willing to do whatever it takes to defend the woman who has become her only friend, and who is the mother of the little girl who adores her. And Maryam takes the shovel to their tormentor with all her might, twice: once to disable him, and next, to kill him.

...

At this point we leave the story, and you will have to read for yourself what happens next. It is murder or justifiable homicide? What do they do with the body? Is Maryam charged with murder, or does she get away? Do Laila and Tariq finally have a life together? And do conditions change for Afghan women? The story plays out on the background of an international situation involving the terrorist attacks on the United States on September 11, 2001, and the political situation in Afghanistan is still volatile even as I write these lines. But the friendship between Maryam and Laila is not defined by world politics, but by a common destiny of having a mutual enemy in an abusive husband. And their choice to take care of each other under circumstances that could cost them their lives might be an example of an ethic of care as you have seen it described by Gilligan in this chapter, and Levinas in Chapter 10: higher than the laws of justice, called forth by facing the humanity and vulnerability of the Other.

Study Questions

1. Compare the situations of Nana, Maryam, and Laila: What are the differences, and what are the similarities? If you have read the book, you might also comment on the characters of Laila's mother and Tariq's mother, and the communist female school-teacher, all providing aspects of women's lives in Afghanistan in the late twentieth century.

2. Compare the images of the men that you have just read about: Jalil, Rasheed, Laila's father, and Tariq. What is the author trying to say about the failings of Jalil and Rasheed? Is this a story that views males as inherently violent and selfish?

3. What do you think of Nana's advice to her daughter, "Like a compass needle that points north, a man's accusing finger always finds a woman. Always."?

4. Does this story really illustrate an ethic of care as suggested by Carol Gilligan? Is that a fair assessment? After all, the women don't seem interested in caring for Rasheed, and he is the one who puts food on the table and a roof over their heads.

Chapter Thirteen
Applied Ethics: A Sampler

This final chapter is a result of reader requests for more detailed discussions of issues involving applied ethics, drawing on the previous chapters on ethics of conduct and virtue ethics. In general, this book is not intended as an applied ethics approach but, rather, as a discussion of fundamental theories of ethics, using stories as examples. However, if theories are not applied to issues in the real world, then ethicists can indeed be accused of living in ivory towers. So in this chapter I present to you a sampling of discussions from the field of applied ethics; each topic is intended to be a starting point for further discussions, because space does not allow me to go into great detail about the pros and the cons. The topics featured are *abortion, euthanasia, media ethics, business ethics, just war theory, gun control and gun rights, animal rights, environmental ethics,* and *the death penalty.* The last section will bring the book full circle: the ethics involved with *storytelling*, in particular as a tool for self-improvement.

The Question of Abortion and Personhood

The landmark decision by the Supreme Court in 1972 known as *Roe v. Wade* made abortion on demand a possibility for American women, because it made the decision to seek abortion within the first trimester a matter of privacy for the pregnant woman. For decades the abortion debate, which had been very polarized and very public in the late 1960s and early 1970s, lived on in two marginal arenas: pro-choice and pro-life movements. The groups known as "pro-choice" looked back to the years of struggle as though the right to seek abortion had become a constitutional certainty, like the right to vote. The groups known as "pro-life," generally coming from conservative religious backgrounds, were more vocal in insisting that abortion should be considered murder; they demonstrated in front of Planned Parenthood offices, and extremists occasionally resorted to violence, targeting and on a few occasions murdering abortion doctors. Even so, *Roe v. Wade* looked as though it couldn't be challenged. And yet, within the first decades of the new millennium, new judges were appointed to the Supreme Court who may, if the matter comes up, decide that the abortion issue should be a matter for the individual states, not a federal matter—which would mean a reversal of *Roe v. Wade*. Political candidates no longer regard the right to abortion as written in stone, whether or not they approve of the right to choose abortion, and the debate has heated up toward the 2020s, especially with the concept, launched in 2019, of so-called *postnatal (after-birth) abortion*—killing of a newborn infant, what has traditionally been labeled infanticide. Critics claim that the entire concept has been taken out of context—that the newborn babies referred to were not viable, and that nobody is arguing in favor of killing babies. However, Mary Ann Warren's argument (see p. 572) that babies have no rights per se predates the current debate by 30 years.

In the following section we examine the question of what constitutes personhood (referring to Chapter 7). Next, we apply two contrasting philosophies to the issue: utilitarianism and Kant's deontology (Chapters 5 and 6). Box 13.1 gives a brief overview of the Catholic Church's view on fetal personhood and abortion.

Box 13.1 SOME RELIGIOUS VIEWS ON FETAL PERSONHOOD

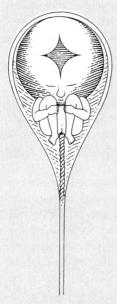

In the seventeenth century Dutch microscopist Hartsoeker drew this image of what he thought was present in the human sperm cell: a small person, a homunculus.

Adapted from Nicholas Hartsoeker. Essay de dioptrique. 1694.p. 230.

The debate over whether abortion should be generally available often focuses on the question of whether the fetus is a person. In some cultures the fetus is not a person at all; even the newborn infant is not considered a person until after a waiting period that usually is imposed to see if the baby will live. In Judaism the baby becomes a person at birth; in Islam, aborting a fetus becomes a serious crime after ensoulment (the soul's arrival in the fetus) which, according to different Muslim schools of thought, can be at 40 days, or 120 days. It is commonly assumed that the view of the Catholic Church is that the fetus is a person from conception, but the story is more complex: In the "Declaration on procured Abortion" issued by the Vatican in 1974, we read that "The tradition of the Church has always held that human life must be protected and favored from the beginning, just as at the various stages of its development." In the Didache [Teachings of the Twelve Apostles] it says, "You shall not kill by abortion the fruit of the womb and you shall not murder the infant already born." But is this the same as saying that the fetus is a *person* from the very moment of conception? Saint Augustine stated that terminating a pregnancy before the fetus is able to *feel* anything should not be considered homicide, because until that time the soul is not present. St. Thomas Aquinas held that the fetus doesn't acquire a rational soul until well into the pregnancy (using Aristotle as a source), and is as such not a person until then (known as the theory of *epigenesis*). The Council of Vienna (1311–1312) concluded that the rational soul isn't identical with the human form (and is thus not present at fertilization). In the secular Western world opinions about the personhood of the fetus underwent a transformation that in effect lasted until the discovery of the human egg, the ovum, in 1847: In the late 1600s the young Dutch microscopist van Leeuwenhock saw a human sperm cell in a microscope for the first time, and that was the beginning of a long-lasting misunderstanding. Other microscopists believed they could see a small person, a homunculus, in the sperm cell (presumably due to the use of different lenses from those that van Leeuwenhock used), and because of what a Flemish doctor had speculated earlier in the seventeenth century, that the soul enters the embryo almost immediately, this was taken to mean that there was a little person already present in the sperm cell. (Contrary to what Aristotle had taught—that the soul and shape of the baby comes from the father and the physical matter from the mother—the assumption was now that the entire human being was contained in the sperm cell, with the mother's womb as nothing but an incubator—the "empty vessel" viewpoint.) It has been debated whether or not this scientific blunder, later completely discredited, had any significant influence on Catholic Church policies. In 1869 Pope Pius IX established what was to become the official Catholic view: that the soul of the fetus enters at the moment of fertilization. However, according to some Catholic theologians the soul is not present in its full complexity at the very beginning of the pregnancy. In 1987 the Vatican stated that while it condemns abortion and contraception, it is not committed to a philosophical affirmation that the fetus is indeed a person from conception. Protestant groups have a variety of views concerning the beginning of personhood, so some are pro-choice and others are pro-life.

The most common argument against abortion is that if it is wrong to kill a human being, a person, then it must also be wrong to kill a fetus, who is either a person from conception or a potential person and should therefore have the same rights as a born person. Within the Catholic tradition it is possible to override the ban on killing a fetus through the principle of the *double effect,* which states that one mustn't take a life under normal circumstances but that it is permissible under very special circumstances: (1) Death must be an *unintended* side effect of accomplishing something else (a primary effect), such as saving a life; (2) the primary effect must be *proportionately* very serious so as to outweigh the death; and (3) causing the death is *unavoidable* and the only way to accomplish the primary effect. Thus, a pregnant woman who has cancer of the uterus will get permission from the Catholic Church to have an abortion because it will be part of the necessary medical process to remove the uterus. The removal of the uterus will kill the fetus, but it is an unavoidable and unintended side effect of saving the woman's life. However, a pregnant woman whose pregnancy itself is in danger of killing her receives no such permission because killing the fetus would in that case be intentional—regardless of the woman's life being in danger. We will meet the double effect again in the section on euthanasia, as well as in the discussion of the just war concept.

Warren and Thomson: Rights and Personhood

What does it take for us to identify a fetus as a person? There are thinkers today who believe that we can surely call the fetus a human being but we can't call it a person because it takes more to be a person than just having human genetic material. The philosopher Mary Ann Warren (1946–2010) argued that a being has to have (1) consciousness and ability to feel pain, (2) a developed capacity for reasoning, (3) self-motivated activity, (4) capacity to communicate messages of an indefinite variety of types, and (5) self-awareness in order to be considered a person; thus even the most developed fetus does not qualify. But neither do newborn babies, according to this viewpoint; so to avoid the specter of infanticide, Warren argued, controversially, that as long as anyone in our culture objects to infanticide, then it should be outlawed—not for the sake of the infant (who is not a person yet), but for the sake of people's feelings in general. Few people in the media are aware of that, but the entire debate about whether it should be legitimate to kill unwanted newborn babies has a precursor in Warren's radical argument as well as in Peter Singer's defense of infanticide of babies who have such severe birth defects that they aren't expected to survive (see Chapter 5).

A slightly less radical view is presented by another philosopher, Judith Jarvis Thomson, who argues for a woman's right to an abortion by saying that it does not matter whether the fetus is a person: What matters is that a woman has a *right to defend her body against intrusions*—even if the fetus should qualify for personhood. Thomson (who wrote her famous contribution to the abortion debate in 1971, just before *Roe v. Wade,* and whom you may remember from the trolley problem in Chapter 1 with the "Fat Man" variation) compares the pregnant woman to a person—any one of us—who wakes up in a hospital bed and finds herself (or himself) attached with intravenous tubes to someone in the next bed, a famous violinist. Suppose, Thomson says, you are told that the violinist can't be moved, or else he will die, so he must be sustained by you for the next nine months (or eighteen years). Do you have a right to unplug yourself? Yes, even if it would mean an innocent violinist's death. For Thomson, there is a small catch, however: You must have tried to take precautions not to be in that situation. Furthermore, if it is only a small sacrifice to you, then you have a moral duty to go through with it—but the violinist still doesn't have any right to demand your life and freedom.

Other positions put forth by abortion rights advocates, based on the view that the fetus may be a person, at least late in the pregnancy, argue that even so, the rights of the fetus as a person do not outweigh the rights of the woman as long as the fetus is not viable (can't survive outside the woman's body).

Utilitarianism Versus Deontology

It is possible to approach the abortion issue from both a utilitarian and a deontological point of view, regardless of whether one is pro-choice or anti-abortion (pro-life). The utilitarian approach focuses on the *consequences* of abortion: The anti-abortion utilitarian will point to the many deaths of unborn children, and the utilitarian who is an abortion rights advocate will point to the back-alley deaths that may occur when women seek illegal and unsanitary abortions. The deontological approach focuses on the issue of *rights:* The anti-abortion deontologist will argue that the fetus, as a person, is being used merely as a means to an end, its life and rights disregarded; the deontologist who is an abortion rights advocate will argue that the rights granted by the personhood and life of the woman outweigh the rights of the fetus, at least until viability (in the third trimester). Box 13.2 explores the broader issue of bioethics from utilitarian and deontological viewpoints.

Box 13.2 BIOETHICS: HUMANS ARE NOT COMMODITIES

One area in which utilitarian and deontological approaches clash is in the moral debate about access to health care. We all want policies to live up to the ideals of equality as well as of justice, but we also know that some people's needs are greater than others'. Since resources seem to be dwindling, it is a question of how to distribute such social goods in a manner that is "fair." In the health care debate the question is becoming urgent, because whatever ethical viewpoint we adopt as the basis for our policies will determine the way in which people with health problems are going to be treated in the future. The utilitarian viewpoint of creating as much happiness for as many as possible was a genuine improvement over the lack of concern for ordinary people that was common in the public policies of Bentham's day, but in Chapter 5 we saw some problems that have arisen from the principle of utility: The majority may be happy, but what if the price of their happiness is the misery of a minority?

Kant's rule that we should never treat a rational being as merely a means to an end has become an antidote to the utilitarian disregard for the minority. In the health care debate the discussion is forming along those same lines: The utilitarian view points to the limited resources of society and the overall capacity for pain and pleasure of the individual and suggests that resources should be directed toward people whose quality of life will be improved in the long run, rather than toward people whose quality of life might not improve dramatically. Bentham's idea of quantifying a qualitative experience (putting numbers on feelings) is in the forefront again, because that may help doctors decide which patient to help: a 35-year-old person or a 93-year-old person (under the assumption that society can't afford to help both). Since the 35-year-old may enjoy life and contribute to society for many years, resources should probably go there instead of to a person close to the end of life whose quality of life might not be improved much; whereas the concept "quality of life" used to refer to extreme situations in which a person was suffering so much that life was no longer enjoyable, it has now come to mean an overall "global" evaluation of a person's life, a concept that has become known as Quality Adjusted Life Years (QALY). Some utilitarian doctors argue that it is the overall QALY calculation that will tell where funding is going to go, and that means that the care of elderly or terminal patients (which has a low QALY yield) will receive less priority than will the care of younger patients whose lives may be saved.

Some doctors and philosophers are disturbed by this development, because they see it as a complete disregard for the respect for *all* individuals (regardless of their age) that Kant argued for and that Rawls was working for in his theory of the original position (in which everyone must have at least minimal care and security, no matter who he or she is). As a modern equivalent of Kant's idea, these philosophers suggest the concept *irreplaceability.* In his essay "Social Justice," the Danish philosopher Peter Kemp (1937–2018) wrote,

> The irretrievable loss of another is one of the most universal human experiences. If I smash a plate I can buy another one. If my house burns down I can build another one in the same style as the old one. Everything we appreciate solely in material terms can be replaced. But another human being can never be replaced. . . . The death of another (which also occurs when e.g. a marriage or friendship breaks down irreversibly) is the fundamental reality from which the irreplaceable ethic springs.

According to the ethics of irreplaceability, each person, no matter how old or how isolated and lonely, is unique and should be respected as a person, never to be sold out to the happiness of the majority. That also means that individuals can't be reduced to a resource for society—their bodies as incubators or their organs for transplants—without their consent. The discipline of bioethics is continually struggling to create policy suggestions for all the areas in which human needs may collide, such as the abortion issue, genetic profiling, euthanasia, and organ transplants; but the underlying philosophy is that human beings and their bodies are not commodities to be used for someone else's purpose, even if that purpose may be the greater good.

A Snapshot of the Debate

So where do we stand at the time of writing this, at the early beginning of the 2020s? *Roe v. Wade* is still federal law, but it is conceivable that abortion rights may, to a great extent, revert to something for individual states to decide. In Missouri, only one abortion clinic is still open. Alabama and Georgia have passed a "heartbeat law" in which abortions are only allowed before the fetus's heartbeat can be detected, which means that most women won't even know they are pregnant when the abortion deadline occurs. In Arizona, new laws are considered at the time I write this in which waiting periods are mandatory. Protesters have marched against the new laws, including in Alabama and Arizona where protesting women dressed up as "handmaids" from the television series *The Handmaid's Tale* (see the Narrative section, Chapter 12) about a near future in which women's reproductive rights—as well as all other rights—have been abolished. Some states, so-called blue states, predominantly democratic, are likely to double down on a woman's right to choose—perhaps not only until the second trimester (the fourth month) as stipulated by *Roe v. Wade*, but on demand for any reason, perhaps until the time of birth. In 2019, following the restrictions in Missouri, Alabama, and Georgia, the governors of the states of Illinois, Vermont, Maine, and Nevada signed increased protections of the right to choose, and California, Massachusetts, and Rhode Island are expected to follow. Vermont and Illinois recognize reproductive rights as fundamental regardless of the fate of *Roe v. Wade*. And the support for reproductive rights isn't necessarily a partisan political issue: Vermont's governor is a Republican.

With the assumption that the Supreme Court now has a majority of pro-life judges, many see the reproductive rights of women as well as available services as being in jeopardy, something that few Americans, including feminists, thought possible a few decades ago. If one believes that abortion is murder of a human being, there is hope, for the first time since the 1970s, that this nation might turn a corner and return to recognizing the rights and humanity of an unborn human. If one is pro-choice and believes that the rights of a woman outweigh whatever rights a fetus may have, there is concern that a future with a decline in women's rights may be a possibility.

Euthanasia as a Right to Choose?

You'll remember from Chapter 7 that the discussion in social and political ethics often has centered on the concept of rights—in particular, *positive* and *negative rights*. Positive rights are identified as *entitlements* and belong to the political spectrum to the "left" of the middle. To the "right" of the middle we find the concept of negative rights, rights of noninterference by the state: the rights to *life, liberty,* and *property*. For many political moderates (such as John Rawls), a mixture of positive and negative rights is essential for the creation and maintaining of a good society.

Below we look at the topic of euthanasia from a "rights" point of view.

The Definitions of Euthanasia

First of all, what is euthanasia? Literally, it is Greek for "good death." There are four major distinctions: *voluntary* and *involuntary* euthanasia and *active* and *passive* euthanasia. "Voluntary" implies that the patient requests euthanasia. "Involuntary" has two meanings: (1) The patient clearly doesn't want to die but is killed anyway (this is the kind of "euthanasia" performed by doctors in the death camps of Hitler's Holocaust); (2) the patient is incapable of communicating his or her wish, leaving the decision to the family (this is also sometimes called *nonvoluntary* euthanasia to distinguish it from outright killing). "Active" euthanasia refers to the patient's life being taken directly, by means such as drugs or the use of a weapon; "passive" euthanasia usually refers to the withholding of treatment from the patient that would otherwise have kept the patient alive longer. At the time of this writing, Washington, D.C., California, Vermont, Hawaii, Maine, New Jersey, Colorado, Oregon, and Washington are the only states in the United States that allow active voluntary euthanasia, under specifically defined circumstances. In Montana the matter is under debate, and in New Jersey the assisted suicide law was temporarily blocked by a judge two weeks after it took effect. Passive voluntary euthanasia is common: The patient wishes life-prolonging treatment to end. Active involuntary euthanasia is not a legal option, whether it means killing someone who doesn't want to die or assisting someone whose family requests assisted suicide for him or her. Passive involuntary euthanasia is common, if we take "involuntary" to mean "nonvoluntary": The family requests a stop to life-prolonging measures.

The Key Arguments for and Against Euthanasia

The key arguments in favor of active voluntary euthanasia (which is what the debate usually focuses on) are that (1) it should be the right of individuals to decide the manner and time of their own death; (2) it should be a person's right to avoid otherwise inevitable suffering (in other words, the right to death with dignity); (3) we help others we love when their lives are at an end and they are facing severe pain—our pets—so we should be able to do the same for our human loved ones; and (4) we might want to have that option ourselves someday.

The most common counterarguments are that (1) it is not up to patients or doctors to play God—there is a time to die for everyone, and we shouldn't interfere; (2) it goes against the Hippocratic oath, by which doctors are sworn to heal, not to take lives; (3) having opened up the possibility of doctors assisting in people's death, the step from voluntary to involuntary euthanasia (the kind where the patient has not given his or her consent) is only as short as the doctor's and family's conscience; and (4) financial pressures might be brought to bear on a terminally ill family member whose insurance is about to run out.

Could the right to die be considered a *negative* right? Yes, if one's body is considered property, then we may argue that we have a right to do with our bodies what we please, provided it doesn't infringe on other people's rights. But it doesn't entail that we have a right to *assisted suicide,* which is the issue. Could the right to die be considered a *positive* right? This is more probable. We may argue that the right to death with dignity is an entitlement all people have, similar to the right to food, shelter, clothing, work, education, and so forth. However, it would be hard to compel others, such as doctors, to help in *taking* lives as a professional duty; nor does a woman's right to seek abortion mean that a doctor is obliged to perform the abortion.

In the euthanasia debate in the United States, it is generally assumed that (1) there is a diagnosis that the patient's condition is not only painful, but terminal, and (2) the patient is of sound mind when requesting doctor-assisted suicide. But in Belgium and the Netherlands where euthanasia has been a legal option since 2002, and a terminal diagnosis is not considered necessary, a new trend is worrying American doctors monitoring the development: psychiatric patients have received euthanasia, presumably without any oversight other than the doctor assisting them. Fifty-five percent of the psychiatric patients who had doctors help them die were suffering from depression, and the others had a variety of issues ranging from posttraumatic stress disorder and anxiety to eating disorders, prolonged grief, and autism. That leads American doctors to ask whether some of those conditions couldn't have been treated, rather than go along with a wish to die that may be caused by the illness? The concern is of course that without oversight, some patients may lose their lives due to causes that themselves may be treatable—or, in a vulnerable frame of mind, by being persuaded by pressures from their family or maybe even their doctor. In the Netherlands, in 2019, a doctor was on trial for having administered euthanasia to a patient who, in a previous declaration, had expressed such wishes—but in the meantime the patient had developed dementia, and had to be held down while the lethal drug was being administered, so she apparently didn't agree to be put to death. The court did not charge the doctor with murder, and agreed that she acted in good faith, but the issue was whether she should have investigated whether the patient, in her current condition, still wanted to die. In the fall of 2019 the doctor was acquitted, and the judge ruled that she had no obligation to ascertain whether or not the patient had changed her mind since the declaration. But it opens up a can of worms, because who is to say that under different circumstances we might not change our minds about something we firmly believed in at a time in our lives when we were younger and healthier? And then what are doctors supposed to regard as the ultimate guideline? The euthanasia option may seem eminently civilized in a society that values the right to choose, but that doesn't mean the legalization is easily accomplished or that the moral difficulties are easily resolved.

Media Ethics and Media Bias

When ethicists say "media ethics," they usually mean the rules of ethical conduct associated with the *news media*, but, to be sure, the issue is broader than that: In the greater area of the media (television and film entertainment, sports, game shows, even magazines of all varieties), we could address issues such as product placement (the "accidental" appearance of products such as soft drinks and alcohol), rigged contests, prizes, and roles and other jobs going to friends and relatives of the producers. Such ethical concerns would come under the general umbrella of *ethics within a profession*. Here we'll focus on the more specific area of *news media* ethics, but we will also take a detour into the new and rapidly developing world of Social Media and the ethics involved (Box 13.3). Why focus on the news media? Because, for one thing, the news media have been part of the heightened focus on controversial issues in applied ethics in the last couple of decades: Stories about people transgressing the moral rules can be "good copy" (news that sells papers or commercial air time), because many people find such stories interesting or just salacious. News stories about the rich and famous being engaged in moral controversies have "legs," but for many people, the truly interesting media focus is on the fundamentally different views on matters such as abortion, euthanasia, the death penalty, gun ownership, and same-sex marriage; and whenever political candidates run for office, their opinions on such matters are closely examined.

Box 13.3 SOCIAL MEDIA AND ETHICS

For quite a while the term "media ethics" has referred to the news media. But another media concept has gained popularity, *social media*. Evolving rapidly from the "chat rooms" and Newsgroups of the 1990s over the popular MySpace website to Facebook, Snapchat, Instagram, and other social e-sites, the Internet gathering places have created entire communities that would have been inconceivable in the past. From groups of people with similar interests, social media now extends past the concept of friends seeking friends to businesses seeking customers, causes seeking supporters, and individuals reaching out to the world in an updated form of a "Kilroy was here" graffiti. While Facebook isn't as popular among young people as it used to be, and has been replaced by other social media platforms, it still remains an important worldwide form of communication. Facebook continues to provide a forum across time and space for people to stay in touch with who, and what, they hold dear. So what could possibly be wrong with that? Many things, say the Facebook skeptics. Look at this list of names: Davidel Mizrachi in Israel, Phoebe Prince in Massachusetts, Holly Grogan in England, Megan Meier from Missouri, Tyler Clementi at Rutgers University. What do they have in common? All of them appear to have committed suicide because of cyberbullying, in most cases involving Facebook and acquaintances posting intimate pictures of them, and/or spreading rumors and derogatory remarks. Perhaps these were young people whose sense of self-worth might have suffered under any kind of bullying in a different day and age, but it just so happens that on Facebook and other social media, bullying can take on a special insidiousness, because it can be done without personal contact, and can more easily bypass whatever innate reluctance to cause harm that most people have.

But even if no harassment is taking place, and no feelings are hurt, Facebook is still a risky acquaintance: The founder, Mark Zuckerberg, claimed a while back (when he was only twenty-four) that privacy is a thing of the past. His Facebook social network is designed to be a place where anonymity is impossible, and personal information is, essentially, available, not just between friends, but to a greater group of unselected readers. Facebook is constantly changing its privacy settings to comply with our concepts of privacy, a concept scorned by Zuckerberg in the early days of Facebook but restored to being a respected and respectable notion, as you read in Chapter 7, but it was also revealed to keep track of its users' websurfing, even after they had logged off, and keeping the information for, presumably, future use. For some users, it's all fair game. Facebook is a private club, so to speak, and it can set its own rules as long as they don't conflict with the laws of the United States; and, as some people would say, if you have nothing to hide, what are you worried about? But others see a dangerous trend: For one thing, even if you have nothing to hide, you may not be particularly interested in mixing work information and private information, and for another, you may not want the entire universe of people trying to sell you something to have access to what websites you like to surf. Let alone the possibility of a government using such information to keep track of citizens with special interests. The specter of political involvement became clear when, during the Presidential campaign of 2016, it turned out that the Facebook list of trending stories had deliberately and routinely suppressed conservative news items. Since then, Facebook has claimed a commitment to less censorship, and more newsworthy stories.

But we can also turn the spotlight on the news media itself: What constitutes ethical reporting, and what is ethical broadcasting? Is it unethical, for example, for a reporter to make public a matter of national security? And does the public always have a "right to know"? Journalists who gain access to sensitive material and publish it may be said not only to report the news but also to create conditions for more "news" to report. In other words, they may play an active role in situations that they supposedly are merely reporting. The film classic *Network* (1976) speculated that a TV network might actually generate news of terrorism for the sake of ratings. In the seventies, that sounded shocking and outlandish, but with the creation of twenty-four-hour cable news, the Internet, YouTube, and the social media in general, such scenarios are not only possible but probable. "Clickbait" methods are frequently used online, tempting readers to click on a shocking or sensationalist headline, and luring them to websites with a different content–a dishonest or even deceptive approach. In the Netherlands in 2007, the network BBN ran a game show in which three kidney-failure patients competed for the organs of a young, dying woman. The show was heavily criticized for being in poor taste—but then the producers admitted that it was, in fact, a hoax. The "patient" was a healthy actress, and the contestants (who were real patients) were in on the hoax from the start. The point of the hoax was to raise public awareness about the dearth of transplant organs. The producers felt that their cause was noble, but many viewers saw it differently: They felt that they had been had—that their good faith had been exploited. This was a game show, not a news show or a documentary, but since the show itself created a news storm, intentionally, it does come under the "media ethics" umbrella, in a broad as well as a narrower, news-related sense. In your view, is such a hoax acceptable if the cause is noble, or is this kind of fake story unacceptable in itself because it disrespects the viewers? You can probably identify the two viewpoints as being a utilitarian vs a deontological approach.

The Right to Know

The public's "right to know" has become questionable in the aftermath of hugely publicized court cases and human tragedies of the 1990s. Televised high-profile trials gathered large numbers of viewers in the last ten to fifteen years, but with the exception of the 2011 murder trial of Casey Anthony in Florida where she stood accused of killing her daughter Caylee (and was acquitted amidst a public outcry) and the Jodi Arias murder trial in 2013 where she was accused and convicted of killing her boyfriend Travis Alexander, the televised trials seem to have dwindled in popularity, for now. However, sensationalism in the mainstream media seems to have become the order of the day. Decades ago, the tabloid ("yellow") press was where you'd find subjects with salacious content, and not much evidence of journalistic concern for verifying facts. But according to some media commentators, the line between mainstream and tabloid media has blurred, to the extent that people have been demonized in the "court of public opinion" with the help of the mainstream media, relying primarily on leaks and rumors. And once the story has hit the press, the genie can't be put back in the bottle. Hasty accusations of wrongdoing published by the media, although later proven to be untrue, may hang over a person's head for years, perhaps for life. When the media decided to go with the story that Richard Jewell, the suspect in the 1996 bombing of Olympic Park in Atlanta, had a history of aberrant behavior, the story was disseminated nationwide. When he was later exonerated (and took the media to court for libel), it wasn't front-page news (but it did eventually become the inspiration for a Clint Eastwood movie, *Richard Jewell* (2019). And most of us just happen to remember sensational headlines on front pages rather than the follow-ups on page 13. While sensationalism generally has a bottom line, the profit generated by the selling of newspapers, magazines, ads, and commercials, sometimes the aggressive path pursued in order to generate stories that sell can backfire: A story out of the United Kingdom has sent a chilly message to sensationalism journalism: In 2011 the famous old British newspaper *News of the World*, owned by the Rupert Murdoch media empire, shut down its presses and called it quits—not because of the "newspaper death" hitting so many other news outlets, but because of ethical and criminal infractions: The story was broken by the British paper *The Guardian* and the *New York Times*: The style of *News of the World* had developed into high sensationalism, ruthlessly getting and printing salient stories before other papers. And the methods used by some of the reporters had escalated to involving hacking into the royal family's phone lines; more hacking stories came out, including actor Hugh Grant having his phone records hacked into. But the shocker story involved the disappeared teenager Milly Dowler, who was later found murdered. Journalists had hacked into her cell phone, deleting messages so there would be room for new incoming calls, which made her parents believe that Milly was still alive. So the paper had in effect also been obstructing justice. The Chief of News International, Rebecca Brooks, was arrested for corruption and conspiring to intercept communications. As a result, Murdoch decided to close the paper at a moment's notice. On the other hand, the news media can of course also champion causes the journalists deem worthy of attention, as watchdogs, and that still epitomizes for many—both reporters and readers—the ultimate virtue of a news reporter. An example of such an effort is the Academy Award-winning film *Spotlight* in the Narratives section, the story of the *Boston Globe* uncovering the scandal of a number of Catholic priests abusing children.

Media Ethics and Free Speech

An aspect of media ethics that has come under scrutiny lately is not the traditional question of what reporters can investigate, or reveal, but what television and radio hosts can *say* without being unacceptably offensive. That raises a new set of issues, especially in cases where media hosts are hired for their abrasive, confrontational style. Should they be censored or even fired for making inflammatory remarks? "Foot-in-mouth" remarks—sometimes deliberately uttered, sometimes caught by an open microphone—have become professional pitfalls for a number of people in the media. At the same time we have an entertainment industry where apparently anything goes in popular lyrics. The concerns are twofold: Are we getting too sensitive about what people in the news can or can't say? And may we be imposing different rules for different groups of people? Is there a problem of *fairness* in what we will allow different people to say in the media? Should there be a separate set of rules for what media personalities of one race or gender can utter, and another set of rules for another race or gender? a certain set of rules for conservative media personalities and another for liberal media people? The philosopher Lawrence Blum stated in his landmark paper from 1991, "Philosophy and the Value of a Multicultural Community," that racial discrimination is unacceptable, no matter who expresses it, but "white" discrimination against people of color is worse than discrimination against white people by people of color because of the historical ramifications of oppression. But the British philosopher Mary Wollstonecraft (see Chapter 12) argued that it is fundamentally unfair to set up separate systems of virtue for separate groups of people (she was talking about men versus women), because, ethically, what is wrong for one group ought to be wrong for the other. Perhaps the recent cases have brought us to the point where we have to decide whether we should have separate standards of virtue in the media or whether we ought to recognize the same sensitivities, live by the same rules, be ready to cut one another the same slack that we would like to be cut if we make mistakes, and be ready to forgive those who later regret using certain expressions, and who apologize for using them. In the end, it ties in with the discussion about *freedom of speech* that you read in Chapter 7: Should this freedom be curtailed for the sake of sensitivities, and if so, should it be curtailed across the board, including art forms such as rap music? Or should the airwaves be available for offensive statements, artistic expressions, and opinions—provided that we can shut off the TV and radio if we don't want to hear them? In Europe, in the aftermath of terror attacks, the issue has been a voluntary self-censoring of stories and views by the reporters themselves—a self-censoring that, to many critics, is equally threatening to the freedom of expression that is valued in most Western cultures.

The News Media and Credibility Problems

The news media have had to face issues of sensationalism and insensitivity, but it is a far graver problem for a news distributor to face accusations of stretching the truth, or downright *lying*. Over the past decades the credibility of mainstream news media has been damaged by instances of journalists inventing characters (Patricia Smith at the *Boston Globe*), plagiarizing material (Mike Barnicle at the *Globe*, Jayson Blair at the *New York Times,* Jack Kelly at *USAToday*), and "inventing" entire autobiographies (James Frey, *A Million Little Pieces,* Misha Defonseca, *A Mémoire of the Holocaust Years,* and Margaret Jones, *Love and Consequences,* in reality written by Margaret Seltzer). In addition, both *CNN* and *Time* magazine brought uncorroborated stories about the United States using nerve gas to kill defectors during the Vietnam War and had to issue retractions; Great Britain's *Daily Mirror* likewise had to issue a retraction after publishing fake photos of abuse of Iraqi prisoners of war. And the career of famous CBS news anchor Dan Rather came to an end after he aired documents two months before the 2004 presidential election, allegedly from 1973, stating problems with President Bush's National Guard service. Internet bloggers pointed out that the documents had to have been forged, since they contained superscript, proportional spacing, and other modern computer features that few typewriters had the capacity for in 1973; Rather later admitted that he had not been careful enough in checking the authenticity of his sources, although he stated that he believed the information to be essentially correct. NBC's anchor Brian Williams was suspended for six months after he was found lying about his experiences as a war correspondent in Iraq. Fox News's Steve Doocy and Anne Kooiman were accused of repeating news stories without any basis in reality. In 2016, a reporter for the website The Intercept, Juan Thompson, was found to have fabricated stories and interviews. And in 2019, MSNBC's Lawrence O'Donnell went on the air with an unverified story alleging ties between Russia and President Trump's finances, a story he later had to retract. It seems that all networks, from the left to the right, have had individuals participating in the embellishment game in more or less serious degrees.

During—and after—the 2016 election campaign the concept of "fake news" became part of our vocabulary, meaning (1) the spreading in both mainstream and social media of deliberately misleading, fabricated news stories, but also (2) publishing unfounded or unverified stories, and (3) dismissing legitimate news stories—ample reason for another wave of public *cynicism* (see Chapter 4).

The phenomenon of WikiLeaks adds another level to the problem of media honesty—with the Golden Mean in mind, we could rightly ask, when is a "truth" too much? In 2006, the whistleblower website and organization WikiLeaks started publishing details and footage of sources behind the news stories as well as political decisions of the decade, and was considered by many to be a "champion of freedom," as the British paper *The Guardian* put it. But public opinion shifted. The founder of WikiLeaks, Australian citizen Julian Assange, was arrested in 2010 for suspicion of espionage and other crimes, and until 2019 he was a resident of the Equadorian embassy in London, seeking asylum and trying to avoid tradition to Sweden as well as to the United States. In 2019, the Equadorian embassy terminated Assange's status and allowed the British authorities to arrest him, and at the time of writing this he is facing charges and extradition.

Over four years, his website had released documents related to the detention of presumed terrorists at Guantanamo Bay, as well as documents concerning the wars in Iraq and Afghanistan, and eventually leaked over 250,000 diplomatic cables to and from U.S. embassies. As it says on the WikiLeaks website, "The documents will give people around the world an unprecedented insight into the U.S. Government's foreign activities." And that is, of course, the problem. British papers (which used to subscribe to Assange's website) have stated that the main driving force behind WikiLeaks was anti-Americanism, and in one writer's opinion in *The Observer*, pure narcissism. Books, essays, and films about Assange, in particular the thriller *The Fifth Estate,* have been released. Assange produced his own documentary, *Mediastan,* in response to *The Fifth Estate.* And in the Presidential campaign 2016, WikiLeaks released a large number of hacked e-mail communications between the Democratic Presidential nominee Hillary Clinton and associates. At the time of writing this, it seems that the Assange story is slowly moving toward a conclusion.

Media Ethics in Wartime

The idea that the public has a "right to know" certain things is at the core of the notion of freedom of the press, a constitutional right embedded in the First Amendment. In peacetime we generally consider the right of reporters to investigate and publish their findings as something fundamental—so much so that reporters generally go out of their way to protect their sources and not reveal them, even under the threat of incarceration. But how about during wartime? All of a sudden, the notion that the public has a right to know takes a back seat to national security. We became engaged in the "war against terror" in 2001. From 2002 to 2014, this nation was at war with the Taliban and al-Qaeda in Afghanistan, and we were militarily engaged in Iraq from 2003 to 2011. (Box 13.4 discusses the subject of terror and violence shown on television.) And since it became clear that CNN and Fox News were watched not only by American audiences but also by the enemy, the issue of national security loomed large even in the everyday details of reporting. Here we are, of course, talking about a fine line: How much information should the journalist have access to, and reveal to the public, without compromising national security?

Box 13.4 HOW FAR WOULD—AND SHOULD—TELEVISION GO?

How far are the news media willing to go to secure an exclusive story—or to provide unique footage? And how far is too far? There is an unwritten rule that TV stations should not show people dying. Over time, live TV has inadvertently shown unexpected deaths, such as the shooting of Lee Harvey Oswald in 1963, the police shooting of a tank hijacker in San Diego in the 1990s, and in the early stages of September 11, TV stations showed footage of people jumping from burning World Trade towers; but such deaths rarely are rebroadcast on the evening news. Does that mean we are not likely to see violent deaths broadcast, live or canned, on network or cable TV in the future? CBS, on *60 Minutes*, chose to air a videotape of the assisted-suicide death of one of Dr. Jack Kevorkian's patients. When *Wall Street Journal* reporter Danny Pearl was executed by terrorists in Pakistan in 2002 and the process videotaped by those same terrorists, CBS aired part of his interrogation, but not his death itself—it was, however, posted to the Internet on several websites. In Iraq during the insurgent phase of the war, several civilians from different nations including the United States were captured by al-Qaeda and beheaded, with videos of their interrogations and executions posted on an al-Qaeda website. And this is where opinions differ: Before, and immediately after 9/11, proper media ethics included not showing violent deaths or other shocking scenes, for the sake of the individuals involved and their loved ones. When Saddam Hussein was executed in late 2006, his execution was videotaped on a cellphone, but only the beginning was shown on U.S. television. In the film *15 Minutes*, the following scenario is suggested: What if the videotaped murder of a famous, popular person is being offered to the networks? Will they take the high road and refuse to air it, or will they air it because if they don't, someone else will? The moral of *15 Minutes* is that airing it would be the wrong, and greedy, thing to do—but what if we are talking about footage of terrorists killing American citizens? For some, that makes no difference—showing the footage plays into the hands of the terrorists and furthers their agenda. But for others this represents a different situation: If we don't actually see how vicious and evil these terrorists are, we may think they can be reasoned with and negotiated with—so the media, by protecting us from shocking footage, may actually be preventing us from judging the situation correctly.

But technology sometimes has a way of circumventing our moral debates: With the introduction of YouTube, where private citizens inside or outside interest groups from around the world post videos, the question of what we should be able to watch on TV has become moot for anyone who has a computer: Saddam Hussein's execution could be seen in its entirety on numerous websites, including YouTube, within hours after it had taken place, and although YouTube has been sued by Viacom over copyright issues, and sets certain restrictions on what can be posted, other Internet venues have already popped up out of reach of censorship. Terrorist organizations have posted videos of mass executions online. Teen gangs post their videos of attacking innocent civilians—*cyberbashing*—and young girls post home videos of other young girls being beaten. Now we have reached beyond the control of regulated news media and are, in a sense, back to the question of personal ethics and character, which was explored in previous chapters.

Since the war in Iraq in 2003, reporters have been permitted at the front lines, "embedded," traveling with the military. While some critics feared that their reporting would be biased, or they would be in the way, the overall results seem to have been a more nuanced picture of war seen from the soldiers' point of view, a challenging of the perceptions of war that proliferated on the home front, and a morale boost for the soldiers who could send greetings home to their loved ones via TV.

But how about the home front? Rumors of terror threats have come and gone, and to this day it is impossible for a layperson to say which were actual terror dangers that were averted by Homeland Security, and which were just rumors. But exactly how much is too much information? When is the media providing vital information, and when is it "crying wolf"?

How much a journalist should report and an editor release, and when, of course depends on the situation. Aristotle's theory of the Golden Mean provides a good starting point for solving the media ethics problem. For each situation there is one correct answer, somewhere within the middle range. Sometimes the media need to freely share information, unpleasant though it may be, in the interest of the public's right to make decisions based on informed consent. At other times the proper amount of coverage called for is the bare minimum, either because no more information is available at the time (and excessive speculation may hurt more than help the public) or because the dissemination of the information might threaten the security of the country. Crying wolf is poor journalistic ethics, but so are apathy and indifference. It is a brilliant journalist or editor who knows the difference in each instance.

In a paper from 1995, *Ethics as a Vehicle for Media Quality,* Andrew Belsey and Ruth Chadwick argue that if the media has too many legal restrictions, *journalists are going to be distracted by trying to get around them, rather than* simply following professional ethics. The fewer legal constraints a journalist has, the higher his or her ethical standards will have to be, according to the authors, because a legal right to publish is not equivalent to a moral right to publish. The authors use the concept of a "virtuous journalist," with a nod to Aristotle, linking the notion of journalism to virtue ethics:

> The virtuous journalist will display a commitment to many virtues, including fairness, accuracy, honesty, integrity, objectivity, benevolence, sensitivity, trustworthiness, accountability, and humor. More important, though, than a list of specific virtues is virtue: the virtuous journalist is one who has a virtuous character, one who therefore has a disposition to act virtuously not only in familiar but also in novel situations. It is in this sense that the competent journalist is the virtuous journalist and is also the journalist with a commitment to quality.

> In such a way, then, can ethics be a vehicle for media quality. As before, it is a vehicle which can travel the ethical route in two ways, a positive aspect emphasizing the ethical requirements for maintaining quality in the media (the virtues, like truth-telling), and a negative aspect emphasizing the prohibitions (the corresponding vices, such as lying).

With the debate about media ethics that has unfolded since the publication of Belsey and Chadwick's paper, from the 24/7 television coverage of the Gulf War as well as the O. J. Simpson criminal trial, to the coverage of the Iraq and Afghanistan wars with embedded journalists, to the coverage of numerous kidnappings, disappearances, and murders of young women, to school shootings, to the current debate about coverage of terrorist acts and national security questions, it is important to question whether having a virtuous character as a journalist is enough, or whether it is appropriate to also consider legal standards for reporting.

Bias in the News Media?

Above we have explored the kinds of issues that media professionals have to deal with regardless of their own political affiliations or those of their news organizations: National security awareness, overall sensitivity, and credibility are demands on the profession that exist for all reputable news outlets. But in addition there is a concern, long considered a suspicion but these days elevated to being considered a fact, that a *bias* exists in the very selecting and reporting of the news. When asked about the choices reporters make when bringing stories to the forefront, reporters often answer that they just report the facts, they don't invent them or doctor them—but that can surely be dismissed as a media myth: Before journalists *report* the facts, they *select* which facts to report (or their network does it for them, with so-called talking points), having already decided what is going to count as newsworthy. Why are some world events reported, and others not? Why do we hear of some disasters (such as the 2016 Zika epidemic in South America and the boys caught in the cave in Thailand in 2018), but others (such as the Darfur genocide tragedy) come to the media surface only slowly, if at all? Conspiracy theorists among us will suggest that it is all nefarious reporting: Some news stories are suppressed, and others are enhanced, for personal or political gain. The truth, however, is often simpler than that. Some news events (such as natural disasters or rebellions) occur while network reporters are already in the vicinity; others simply happen below the radar. And some stories are not picked up because they aren't "sexy" enough for news media that sell ads and airtime.

But we should not be oblivious to the fact that bias does exist in the news media. Some papers and networks find themselves politically to the left of the middle, and some to the right. That, in itself, is not against the rules of media ethics, as long as the political bias is kept within editorials or is expressed by hosts or columnists who are clear about their personal convictions. Often, such hosts have guests who express different viewpoints, and it is all part of the give-and-take of live, and lively, television. The problem arises if it is the presentation of the *news itself* that is preselected on the grounds of somebody's political conviction. When we use a search engine online, we may think we are accessing whatever stories are out there that match our keyword search, but a filter may already have been in place that make some articles available but not others. In 2018, a report confirmed what many users had suspected: the Google News search engine was showing predominantly left-leaning articles. The report was issued by the media technology group AllSides and reported by USAToday among other news outlets. Indeed, Google News listed more articles from a left-leaning perspective than from a right-leaning perspective. Deliberately, as some critics claimed? AllSides said no, it was a matter of a "popularity algorithm" which simply showed what people online searched for the most, but even so, the bias might give a false view of news coverage. Deliberate or inadvertent bias, the scandal added to that public cynicism toward the news media that is already affecting our daily life. Box 13.5 explores the phenomenon of Artificial Intelligence in home electronic devices being used to gather information about us and our habits.

Box 13.5 SPIES IN OUR MIDST? A.I.

In the chapter text you read about Google News prioritizing certain news stories—perhaps on purpose, and perhaps due to automatically programmed algorithms. Here is a related aspect of how pervasive the influence of the electronic world has become, in particular combined with Artificial Intelligence.

In Chapter 7 we briefly touched on the prospect of rights for robots, under the assumption that they might become self-aware and qualify for Kant's definition of a person, someone who should never be treated merely as a means to an end, but we focused more on what might happen to humans in the robotic age. We asked, 'how much on the alert should we be? Are we moving toward a *Terminator/I Robot* world?' Some would say we are already there, but not in the sense that our future robot helpmates are plotting against us—no, in the sense that humans are plotting against each other with the help of ubiquitous Artificial Intelligence, A.I. Do you have a Smart TV at home? Do you talk to Siri on your iPad? Is Alexa listening to your instructions? Do you ever say, "OK Google!"?

These and other similar devices are not self-aware, and they probably will never be in their current form, but nevertheless they open up for a Brave New World (Aldous Huxley's ironic metaphor for a terrible future) where devices are listening to our every word, observing our every move, and recording and reporting them for third party access.

In 2019 the new Google Assistant, Google Nest Hub Max, was released, with a new feature: face-recognition. While it is possible to turn it off with a digital kill-switch, it has no shutter. It will accumulate data about your life at home, accessible to anyone with your password, and even if Google maintains that whenever it sends data to the Cloud, you are still in control of it, skeptics find the whole concept of continuously recording and sharing one's life problematic. Picking up on our privacy discussion earlier in this chapter (Box 13.3), for some people that is not a frightening prospect at all. They already share their life online, and they might say, "If you have nothing to hide, why worry about others listening in on your life?" But for others the very thought of being observed at all times, even in one's most innocent doings, is an abomination, because (1) some of us like the concept of privacy, and (2) since the future is uncertain, one never knows how one's data might be used by authorities with changing agendas. What was legal and acceptable behavior when you were in your 20s may become illegal and unacceptable when you are in your 50s, and now there is a record of that behavior. Is that the world we want?

In an op-ed in the *New York Times*, psychologist Gary Marcus and computer scientist Ernest Davis suggest that the reason we fear A.I. is because we have not given our computers the most basic lessons in what makes a human world: time, space, and causality. If we could program computers to understand how humans understand the world within those three concepts (or what Immanuel Kant would call *categories*), a computer would understand that deaths of organic beings are permanent, and that time can't be reversed. That way they can be taught not to harm or abuse humans. That may be good advice for computer scientists and ethicists, but we humans understand all that perfectly well, and even so we harm and abuse each other. For many of us the threat is not that computers misunderstand us—it is that computers can become the ultimate *weapon of control*, of humans by other humans. We don't even need a smart robot for that—we can do the job ourselves.

The suspicion among liberal viewers and critics is that networks with predominantly conservative hosts (FoxNews and NewsMax) are selecting and twisting the news to fit a conservative agenda; the suspicion among conservative viewers and critics is that the majority of the networks (CBS, NBC, ABC, CNN, and MSNBC) are selecting and twisting the news to fit a liberal agenda. Even in the media this is no longer considered political paranoia: the line between reporting the news and being *activists*, working for a political agenda, is becoming increasingly blurred, as some reporters see it as their professional duty to influence conditions rather than merely report them. The first to bring the question of media bias to viewer attention was media analyst Bernie Goldberg. And during the 2016 presidential campaign, these media biases seemed to be particularly clear—not only in the final stages of the campaign where the "mainstream media" appeared to be rooting for the Democratic nominee, Hillary Clinton, but even in the earlier stages where, at least to supporters of the other Democratic candidate Bernie Sanders, the mainstream media showed a bias in favor of Clinton. That bias has since then been amply documented, and Sanders supporters in the 2020 election were voicing concerns that the same bias against their socialist candidate would influence the election.

Biases don't have to be locked into party politics, but can flavor and maybe determine an election even within a major party. To the viewer who would just like to get some objective reporting, that is intensely disturbing. However, although some of the bias may be part of an underlying scheme, there is a more straightforward explanation: We all have some fundamental worldview, and news that corresponds to that worldview looks to us like "sensible" news. Often, what some viewers call a bias is for the reporter the "default" position of a reasonable person—in other words, the reporter may not even be aware that his or her reporting is grounded in a political viewpoint.

In the aftermath of the 2016 election, the *New York Times* made a promise to their readers:

> As we reflect on the momentous result, and the months of reporting and polling that preceded it, we aim to rededicate ourselves to the fundamental mission of Times journalism. That is to report America and the world honestly, without fear or favor, striving always to understand and reflect all political perspectives and life experiences in the stories that we bring to you.

However, following the election of President Trump in 2016, the American press, including the *New York Times*, did not return to its classic, time-honored standards of reporting the news; on the contrary, to many it seemed as if the entire mainstream newsmedia became engaged in an openly political activist cause against the President. For many, this was an honorable cause, a fight against a government perceived as a danger to our country; for others, nothing less than an attempt to bring down a legitimate government—in other words, a "silent coup attempt." Strong words, but as you'll remember from Chapter 1, we are indeed living in a "50/50 Nation" these days. So what can we do, as news consumers? A website, NewsHounds, has as its tagline "We Watch FOX so You Don't Have To," but that is not an option if you want to be cognizant of the entire spectrum of opinions! You can't delegate the watching to someone else, because you might be misinformed, miss something important, or be the victim of someone else's agenda. Watch and read the news from several sources, every day! Watch CNN *and* FoxNews, listen to conservative talk radio *and* NPR, go on the Internet and read the blogs, be aware of possible "fake news" going viral on Twitter and Facebook, subscribe to your favorite news outlet and then go online and read the competition's viewpoint. That's probably a little too "fair and balanced" for most of us, but at least it allows for critical insight into a variety of views in an increasingly complicated media world.

Business Ethics: The Rules of the Game

In some ways, media ethics and business ethics are overlapping phenomena: Whenever decisions in the media are made with an eye toward profit, we might as well be talking business ethics. And even in other ways there are similarities: Whenever media ethics involve ethics of the workplace, we are also talking business ethics, and whenever the news media ponder moral issues caused by the dissemination of news, we might also be talking about business ethics. All these aspects are part and parcel of responsible decision making within any kind of profession, and the world of business is, of course, an environment of professional standards. The question is, Are these standards different from the moral values we find in personal relationships and elsewhere in our society? In this section we look at the question of whether "business as usual" implies a disregard for moral values; we take a tour of the most common themes in business ethics; and we look at business ethics as grounded in the concept of *property*. (Box 13.6 discusses the melamine pet food scandal of 2006–2007.)

Box 13.6 THE MELAMINE SCANDAL

In the fall of 2006, veterinarians across the country encountered an unusual phenomenon: otherwise healthy dogs and cats were being brought to their offices dying of what appeared to be a kidney ailment. No common denominator seemed to be present—they were from different environments, had not been exposed to any environmental poisons, were of different breeds and species, and had been fed a variety of pet food brands. So what was happening? In the winter and spring of 2007, the scandal unfolded: the animals were dying because of contaminated pet food; unknown to most consumers, much of the pet food sold under various brand names is actually manufactured by just a few producers; and even if the pet food came from other producers, there was indeed a common denominator: a wheat gluten additive from China. To make a long story short: The imported wheat gluten was not completely organic; to stretch the raw materials and increase profit, the Chinese suppliers had added *melamine*, an industrial chemical, to the gluten. Why would the Chinese manufacturers do that? Allegedly because the melamine nitrogen reads as a protein nitrogen in a chemical analysis and thus makes the gluten look as if it has more protein in it than it actually does. Melamine is a material used in making furniture, particularly shelving; it is a nonfood and extremely hazardous to one's health. In low doses, cattle and sheep can convert the nonprotein nitrogen in melamine to amino acids; but with higher doses, even cattle and sheep die. Dogs and cats can't convert the melamine and die much more quickly.

If contaminated gluten can turn up in animal food, how about imported gluten for human consumption? In China, cases of melamine-contaminated baby formula created an additional scandal, and at home we have had cases of tainted toothpaste, also from China. And this assumes that we're merely talking about what we would call shoddy business practices, not a *deliberate* tainting of our food and drug supplies,

as we might see it in a *bioterrorist* attack. So whose fault was the melamine scandal? Pet owners can't be blamed, because most of us try to feed our pets things that are good for them. U.S. and Canadian vets can't be blamed, because they didn't know. Can the importers be blamed? The FDA? Some blame should be shared, yes, because there was insufficient oversight. But the primary blame falls on Chinese companies who rate *profit* higher than respect for business partners as well as consumers. So under normal circumstances, we do expect a certain code of ethics to be upheld by the business world. Whether it is for selfish purposes, such as keeping the profit margin and ensuring repeat customers, or for less selfish purposes, such as recognizing the needs of the community, is a debate that belongs in Chapter 4; regardless of the underlying motivations, the fact remains that we do expect the business community to live by the same general set of values that are in effect elsewhere in our society.

Are Businesspeople Amoral?

For many people, "business" and "ethics" is an oxymoron, as though the concepts are mutually exclusive. Some might say that the business world has not been particularly encumbered by ethical sensitivities for most of its existence—it is almost expected to be a dog-eat-dog type of environment, as if the rules of ethics don't apply. However, Richard T. de George, University of Kansas Distinguished Professor of Philosophy and author of *Business Ethics,* calls this the "Myth of Amoral Business." De George asks, If businesspeople were really expected to do business without an eye to value judgments and ethical standards, then why are we so shocked when a business or a corporation acts immorally or without any regard for moral standards? In other words, we expect an adherence to the general code of ethics that we find in our greater society; that doesn't mean the Myth isn't correct sometimes. Sometimes businesspeople are greedy, and sometimes there are bribes and kickbacks, but it is our outrage at the revelation of such goings-on that shows that this is not the normal or expected state of affairs. Increasingly, businesses recognize that the greater community will react negatively to such revelations, and this is why *business ethics* has become established as a discipline for businesspeople.

"GOSH — THE BUSINESS SCHOOL I WENT TO DIDN'T TELL ME I'D BE FACED WITH ETHICAL DECISIONS."

Sidney Harris/Sidney Harris/ScienceCartoonsPlus.com

This cartoon reflects a very common misunderstanding of business schools—that they somehow are beyond ethics concerns, and that ethics isn't part of their curriculum. But as you can see from this section, business ethics is very much part of the schooling of new generations within the business world. Whether business executives bring their ethics training with them into their profession is of course another question.

As often happens in ethics, we don't notice when things are going right, only when they're going sideways. We pay much attention when managers, executives, and other business leaders break the rules for selfish gain (such as when prominent businesswoman Martha Stewart went to prison for five months for conspiracy and lying to federal investigators about her sale of stocks the day before the stock value fell dramatically); but in the vast majority of cases, businesspeople abide by the rules and provide the normal, smooth business climate that simply works. An infamous case that seems to not have followed that prescription is the financial speculation leading to the collapse of Wall Street in 2007–2008, as depicted in the film *The Big Short*. Box 13.7 gives you a quick overview of the story.

There is a value system *within* the workplaces in the world of business; sometimes this is written down in a code of ethics, and sometimes it is an unwritten set of rules. This can range from rules that one should not take home pens and Post-it pads from the supply room, to rules for dating practices in the workplace, to more serious rules against insider trading. But in addition, there is a value system *for the business as such,* governing the entire business world where capitalism is the norm, and that is the system acknowledging *free enterprise,* with *profit* as the desired result. If you'll recall Karl Marx's critique of the concept of profit in Chapter 7, you already know that Marx and his followers did not consider profit morally justifiable. The discipline of business ethics does ask fundamental philosophical questions, such as the justifiability of profit, but in general, the business world operates under the assumption that there is nothing odious in generating profit. The question more frequently addressed by business ethics is, *how* is the profit obtained? Through fair and honest marketing, or through incomplete or even false advertising? Below we return to a case of dishonest marketing with devastating results.

Box 13.7 HOW TO CAUSE A GLOBAL FINANCIAL CRISIS; *THE BIG SHORT*

The film *The Big Short*, adapted from a non-fiction book with the same title, won an Academy Award in 2016 for Best Adapted Screenplay. It is sometimes listed as a comedy—which is because of the snappy, ironic dialogue—and sometimes as a drama. The drama part would be because of its accurate depiction of the impact of financial speculations in 2007 on the entire world, with the losses of jobs, homes, and life savings for millions of people who were just following the advice of trusted advisors.

The film (the title of which refers to selling something one does not own via a contract, or a "short position") depicts the events that led up to the financial crisis of 2007–2010, leading to a worldwide recession from which the world has been recovering ever since. We are shown that, because of the housing market having overextended itself into so-called subprime loans, banks giving very low interest loans to prospective homeowners who will not be able to pay them, and those loans coming due in 2007, the housing market was headed for a collapse. In 2005, hedge fund manager Michael Burry realizes that he can profit from the collapse if he creates a CDS market, a "credit default swap" which, according to Wikipedia,

> is a financial swap agreement that the seller of the CDS will compensate the buyer (usually the creditor of the reference loan) in the event of a loan default (by the debtor) or other credit event. This is to say that the seller of the CDS insures the buyer against some reference loan defaulting.

The rumors of Burry's transactions spread, other investors are jumping on the bandwagon, and fraudulent AAA ratings of other poor loans are adding to the impending collapse. In 2007, the crisis starts with the dropping of the stock market and the loss of IRA pension funds among other losses, bailout of banks, and the bursting of the housing market bubble, resulting in job losses, foreclosures, and homelessness.

The movie places the blame squarely on Wall Street speculation and greed. Other analyses have pointed to irresponsible home loans given by banks under the assumption that everybody should be able to own a home regardless of ability to pay the mortgage. Pointing the finger of blame may go on for years, but the film insists that when things go wrong, "immigrants and the poor" are blamed.

Often colleges offer courses in business ethics, and often corporations themselves do the same thing for their employees. Is that because there is a general interest among businesspeople in learning about issues in ethics—or it is because companies believe that their employees are in severe need of some guidance when it comes to professional standards? Maybe a bit of both, and sometimes the teachers have to admit that the lessons weren't learned, after all. In Chapter 4, you read about the college admissions cheating scandal of 2019, and it certainly wasn't just students cheating on their applications, but their parents bribing school officials and agreeing to have professional test takers take the admission tests instead of their kids. You'll remember from Chapter 10 that 34 out of 38 graduate business students at Duke University cheated on their take-home exams. What you didn't hear was that all students had agreed to abide by an honor code, posted in the classroom, and that they were, on the average, 29 years old, from many different countries, with six years of work experience on the average, which means they weren't "kids." And even so, they chose to cheat. A study released by the Center for Academic Integrity at Duke University in September 2007 showed that 56 percent of MBA students cheat, compared with 54 percent in engineering, 48 percent in education, and 45 percent in law school, despite having taken ethics courses. Representatives for the Center for Academic Integrity were disappointed, and expressed suspicion that the students were just thinking of themselves, despite the ethics classes. Christina Hoff Sommers (Chapter 10) might reply that perhaps what was taught in those classes was not presented in a way that the students could relate to: Were they taught abstract principles, along the lines of *ethics of conduct?* Or were they given role models, and taken through concrete examples dealing with real people where the student response becomes a matter of having a good character—in other words, according to *virtue ethics?* There is a high probability that the human connection that is at the heart of virtue ethics can bring the lesson home more efficiently than learning about principles. After all, bank and train robbers in the Old West often prided themselves at never having stolen anything from a person; that stealing was wrong in principle didn't impress them as much as the face-to-face realization of the other person's humanity, and a reluctance to violate that humanity. Would the graduate students at Duke have cheated as readily if cheating had been presented to them as a character failing, a breach of trust vis-à-vis their professor? In the Primary Readings you'll find a summary of a report from the Ethics Resource Center, "Critical Elements of an Organizational Ethical Culture," in which the authors, Amber Levanon Seligson and Laurie Choi, argue that being immersed in an "ethical culture" has more of an impact on employees than an actual ethics program.

General Business Ethics Topics

So if you take a course in business ethics, what themes are you likely to encounter? First and foremost the rights and duties of the *corporate world,* examining whether businesses should be responsible for public welfare. When is a corporation liable for damages to the environment? How important is product safety? Is the corporate world responsible to the community for creating jobs and revitalizing low-income sections of town, or do they just have moral obligations to the shareholders? Is there such a thing as ethical investing, or is that an area where ethics doesn't apply? Other questions that involve corporate ethics include marketing and truth in advertising; the entire discussion that has become so prominent in the past decades concerning trade secrets and insider trading; and the ethics of accounting and corporate takeovers. A new area that has received much attention is computer ethics, a morally gray area for many when as long as something is online, it must be fair game; this has led to a series of regulations, concerning both computer privacy and copyright issues, not to mention security issues. An area that promises to become even more prominent in future debates about business ethics is international trade and multinational companies.

Business ethics courses may also focus on *workers' rights.* Above all, the right to fair wages, the right to join unions, and the right to strike qualify as workers' rights issues; but, in addition, the focus may be on protecting against health hazards on the job, discussing conflicts between drug testing and privacy, and determining the proper relationship boundaries between employer and employee, or even among workers. Such discussions might focus on determining what constitutes sexual harassment, or simply outline what the company considers acceptable dating practices. Another set of issues are discrimination and affirmative action.

Whistle-blowing is a sensitive issue in business ethics, contrasting loyalty to the company with the right, and even the duty, to speak up when observing wrongdoing. In the Narratives section you'll find one of the most famous cases of whistle-blowing, as depicted in the film *The Insider,* about one man's moral decision to reveal to the world how the tobacco companies deliberately misrepresented their products.

A business ethics course today may also include a discussion of *personal branding,* becoming your own brand in promotion of your business, or even just promoting yourself as a brand. The phenomenon is explored in Box 13.8.

Box 13.8 SELF-BRANDING, A NEW BUSINESS ORDER

Until a few years ago, business was conducted by, well, businesspeople. Inheriting a business you grew up in, or going to business school and getting an MBA, were pathways to becoming successful. They still are, but the Internet has chanced many things, including the way we do business. Not only do many of us shop online—many of us are also online *sellers*, on a small or a grand scale. A business these days without a website is not taken seriously; most business have a Facebook profile, and many maintain a Twitter account. Personal branding, self-branding, or self-packaging is an element in many successful business ventures these days. In his career as business magnate, President Trump has been considered a master of personal branding. Another name which has become a brand is the Kardashian family, having turned a reality TV show about their family into a self-invented brand franchise selling fragrances, clothes, diet pills, and more, managed by Kris Jenner and with Kim Kardashian as the best-known profile. An online "Celebrity Branding Agency" gives advice about how to sell not your merchandise but *yourself* as a brand. It becomes a matter of raising one's profile online, and if one can partner with a celebrity—or another celebrity—and combine one's impact, all the better. And it is not just an American phenomenon: according to the London School of Marketing,

"Today brands are everything, and all kinds of products and services—from accounting firms to sneaker makers to restaurants—are figuring out how to transcend the narrow boundaries of their categories and become a brand surrounded by a Tommy Hilfiger-like buzz," said Management guru, Tom Peters. "Regardless of age, regardless of position, regardless of the business we happen to be in, all of us need to understand the importance of branding. We are CEOs of our own companies: Me Inc. To be in business today, our most important job is to be head marketer for the brand called You."

Some see the personal branding business model as the wave of the future: we will all have a brand, a persona, which we will market to the world, in resumes as well as in social media. The brand will be who we are in our professional as well as our personal world. Many people find the phenomenon of self-branding to be an exciting, new way of thinking about business and our entire interface with the world. However, some critics regard it as a form of *egotism* (remember the difference between egoism and egotism, Chapter 4!), as well as reducing oneself to a *product*, a form of *reification* (making oneself into a thing). Furthermore, how will "being a brand" affect our lives, our relationships, and our sense of identity? And are those who "buy" our brand, in some form or other, really buying a product or just packaging?

As you can see, many of these topics in business ethics courses display the same tendency that you saw in Chapter 1 about the relationship between ethics and the law: In many cases the ethics of business is just that, ethics—a sense of right and wrong when dealing with coworkers, employers, employees, customers, shareholders, and the general population. But sometimes the question of wrongdoing becomes a matter for the law; as business venues change and technology progresses, new forms of crime also evolve, such as cybercrime, and it is an ongoing task for business ethics theory to identify these new crimes and make them known to the world of business as well as to anyone else who may be affected by them.

The Property Question

As you'll remember from Chapter 7, John Locke pointed out that we have three negative or natural rights: to *life, liberty,* and *property.* This theory of negative rights has become part and parcel of the *laissez-faire* ("hands-off") policy advocated by fiscal conservatives (see Chapter 5), but it has also become a cornerstone of business philosophy. So how does Locke identify property? In his *Second Treatise on Government,* Chapter 5, he says,

> Though the earth, and all inferior creatures, be common to all men, yet every man has a property in his own person: this no body has any right to but himself. The labour of his body, and the work of his hands, we may say, are properly his. Whatsoever then he removes out of the state that nature hath provided, and left it in, he hath mixed his labour with, and joined to it something that is his own, and thereby makes it his property. It being by him removed from the common state nature hath placed it in, it hath by this labour something annexed to it, that excludes the common right of other men: for this labour being the unquestionable property of the labourer, no man but he can have a right to what that is once joined to, at least where there is enough, and as good, left in common for others.

This quotation, and in particular the last line, is known as *the Lockean Proviso.* A famous interpretation from C. B. Macpherson reads into this that we have three restrictions: (1) We can only take and keep as much from nature as we can use before it spoils; (2) we have to leave enough for others, and not take it all for ourselves; and (3) we can acquire property only through our own labor. A debate has gone back and forth over whether Locke implies that you can be a voter only if you own property, and whether you can only acquire your own property or pay others to work it for you; also, the acquisition of property may depend on one's own labor when there is plenty of land in common for all, but once land becomes scarce, and society is well-established, then some will have land and others won't, setting the stage for political inequality. And if you acquire land from the amount of land available to all, do you need everyone else's consent to acquire it? The American libertarian philosopher Robert Nozick (1938–2002) has supplied this interpretation in his influential book *Anarchy, State, and Utopia* (1974)—his so-called Entitlement Theory:

> If the world were wholly just, the following inductive definition would exhaustively cover the subject of justice in holdings:
>
> a.   A person who acquires a holding in accordance with the principle of justice in acquisition is entitled to that holding.
>
> b.   A person who acquires a holding in accordance with the principle of justice in transfer, from someone else entitled to the holding, is entitled to the holding.
>
> c.   No one is entitled to a holding except by (repeated) applications of (a) and (b).
>
> The complete principle of distributive justice would say simply that a distribution is just if everyone is entitled to the holdings they possess under the distribution.

For Nozick, acquiring property is just or fair if others (who used to be co-owners of the land in common) aren't worse off by your acquiring the property. And that leads to the entire realm of business transactions, because if you have acquired property without violating others' right to property, then you also have a right to transfer it. This is the very foundation of commerce. Critics have pointed out that this is hardly a guarantee of fair distribution of property, or of rectification if injustices have occurred. But it is also sometimes pointed out that critics may have been particularly eager to find flaws in Nozick's embracement of the concepts of property and profit, because his critics in academia have usually been further to the left on the political spectrum, preferring thinkers who themselves are critical of the capitalistic ideology, such as the liberal John Rawls and his theory of the Original Position (Chapter 7). Rawls's philosophy strives for social fairness, not only as an abstract idea where property is, theoretically, there for the taking by anyone with the will and skills to acquire it, but also as a continued redistribution of social goods so no one is left worse off than anyone else. And here we should also remember that further to the political left than John Rawls, among socialist and Marxist thinkers, property is itself not a *right* but a *problem,* leading to social inequality. In his *Discourse on the Origin of Inequality among Mankind* (1754), Rousseau said that "the first man who, having fenced in a piece of land, said, 'This is mine,' and found people naive enough to believe him, that man was the true founder of civil society." There are significant differences between Rousseau and Karl Marx, but Marx took Rousseau's cue and in his *Communist Manifesto* (1848) declared property, along with the concept of profit, the cause of social evils. So for some thinkers on the far left to this day, as well as politicians such as Senator Bernie Sanders, libertarian and other defenders of the entire enterprise of business are simply in the wrong no matter how they define and redefine business ethics, because the concept of property for far-left thinkers is fundamentally illegitimate.

Just War Theory

The United States was engaged in two wars for much of the time we have been moving further into the twenty-first century: the war in Afghanistan and the war in Iraq, with the war in Iraq coming to an official end in 2011, and our official engagement in Afghanistan ending in 2014, with a reduced number of troops in place to the time of writing this. To date, the lives of more than four thousand American soldiers have been lost in Iraq, and more than 2,600 lives of coalition soldiers in Afghanistan. Both military conflicts have inspired a renewed discussion of what constitutes a just war. Whether directly or indirectly (an issue that is itself controversial) a result of the terrorist attacks of September 11, 2001, our military engagements in the Middle East have changed how we perceive the phenomenon of war—almost as the rise of the Cold War in the post–World War II years redefined what was then considered typical warfare.

No longer the traditional conflict between armies representing nations, wars in the twenty-first century have been conducted by and against "insurgents," local or imported guerilla forces using terrorist attacks, suicide attacks, roadside bombings, or other forms of ambush. Are these acts of war, or criminal activities? That question has been part of the debate in the new century. A revival of the topic actually predates September 11, 2001, by more than two decades, with the publication of professor of political philosophy Michael Walzer's book *Just and Unjust Wars* (1977).

Is there such a thing as a just war? For a *pacifist,* the answer is no: Nothing on this earth—no attack on our loved ones, no danger to our life or our country—warrants raising our hand or using weapons of any kind against another human being. If you're a pacifist, say critics, you can't make an exception such as "I don't believe in war, but I'd of course want to defend my family," for two reasons: (1) If you have proclaimed that you reject the idea that force can solve a problem, then it doesn't matter if we talk about it on a grand or a small scale: Force is impermissible, period. (2) If you believe that it is okay for you to resort to force to save your family from harm, what about those who don't have family members to save *them* from harm? That is traditionally the state's role: to protect its citizens from enemies, both domestic and foreign. When it is engaged in protection against harm caused by a foreign force, we call it war. And if you find it acceptable for an individual to protect his or her family from harm, then, logically, you should accept that the state takes on a similar action to protect its citizens. Box 13.9 discusses the concept of patriotism.

So, according to the critics, the only consistent viewpoint for a pacifist is to reject the notion of using force to defend one's family against harm. Other forms of defense are acceptable, such as calling 911 (but if you don't approve of violence, you can't allow the police to use violence to save your family, either). Or you can put yourself in harm's way and use passive resistance, hoping that harm to your family will be deflected onto you, or that the harm-doer will think twice. In the 1930s and 1940s, Mohandas K. Gandhi (1869–1948), known by the reverent title of Mahatma, headed a movement to make the British pull out of their colony of India and give it its independence. His method, passive resistance, provided an alternative for countless people—in India as well as elsewhere—who would like to express their disapproval of an idea or a policy without resorting to violence. Gandhi's approach helped bring about Indian independence in 1946, but in 1948 he himself

Box 13.9 PATRIOTISM: TOO MUCH, TOO LITTLE, OR JUST THE RIGHT AMOUNT?

In the weeks following September 11, 2001, we saw flags go up by the thousands in just about every neighborhood in the country, from billboards to bumpers. To some, that was a positive sign of love for one's country; to others, it was an oppressive display of excessive nationalism. A debate about what exactly patriotism is arose, and as the war against terror morphed into the war in Afghanistan, and then the war in Iraq, pro-war and anti-war viewpoints began to differ drastically in their definition of proper patriotism.

But what exactly is patriotism, and when is it too much, too little, or just the right amount? In the 1970s the opinion was voiced among philosophers that patriotism is like racism and sexism: It is an unfounded preference for one's own country just because it is one's own country, just as sexism is a preference for one's own sex and a disregard for the other sex, and racism is a preference for one's own race and a disregard for other races. One of the visions of Marxism, for example, is people shedding their national affiliations and boundaries and becoming international, because the plight of workers is presumably the same everywhere. The final words of the original French song and rallying cry for communism from 1871, *The Internationale,* are "The Internationale unites the human race." Less radical views of patriotism have been suggested, based on the criticism that it makes no sense to say we aren't allowed to love our country more than other countries—just as it would make no sense to say we shouldn't love our own family more than we love strangers. In a paper from 1989, "In Defense of 'Moderate Patriotism,'" Steven Nathanson, an American ethicist, argues against critics of patriotism that "patriotism is a virtue as long as the actions it encourages are not themselves immoral. . . . That a morally acceptable form of patriotism is possible can be seen by comparing patriotism to love or family loyalty. People may (and, one hopes, typically do) have a special interest and concern for their parents, spouses, and children. They really do care more about those 'near and dear' than about strangers. Yet, so long as this concern is not an exclusive concern, there is nothing the matter with it." In other words, it is acceptable to be a patriot as long as one is mainly expressing a love for one's country and homeland and isn't implying that one's country is always automatically right—in other words, this view rejects the notion of "my country, right or wrong" but allows for a personal sense of affiliation and love for one's roots. Part of the American tradition is the right to question authority—to ask good questions and expect them to be answered. One might say that it is a matter of pride in one's tradition, of patriotism, to keep asking good questions. Something that is deeply American and an ingrained feature in both the political left and the political right is to want the United States to be the best that it can be, because we love this country and wish it well. Wherever we find ourselves in this troubled spectrum, it is good to remind ourselves that conservatives don't have a monopoly on patriotism, and neither do liberals.

became a victim of violence, being gunned down by an assassin. Martin Luther King, Jr., met the same fate in 1968 after being a life-long admirer of Gandhi's philosophy of passive resistance and advocating the same method in his civil rights movement. King's commitment continues to inspire people who seek to create political change without resorting to any form of violence.

But critics of pacifism point out: (1) If you put yourself in harm's way to save your family without personal use of force and lose your life, and your act of sacrifice doesn't save your family, nothing has been gained. (2) You may have the right to refuse to use any form of force or violence yourself, but if you have responsibility for others, such as small children, your right does not extend to them, because they are under your protection, morally and legally.

If you are not a pacifist and believe in the concept of a just war, the alternative isn't simply to be a "hawk," a "warmonger," or a belligerent, violent person. On the contrary: The doctrine of just war is based on the assumption that the ideal condition is peace; war is seen as the last resort to restore peace. Once that is a given, several other conditions must be in place to call a war just (*jus ad bellum*). These rules were worked out in the late Middle Ages by the so-called Schoolmen or scholastics, building on Roman law and early Christian thinkers such as Augustine and Ambrose, and they have become the foundation for military ethics in the West ever since. Here we look at an overview of these rules, as they are taught in military ethics courses:

- **Last resort** As stated above, a war can be just only if all other ways of restoring peace have been exhausted, such as negotiations and economic sanctions.

- **Just cause** If going to war is the only way a country can defend its values and lives of innocent citizens against aggression and restoring peace, then the cause is considered just. In modern-day terms, identified by Waltzer in his influential book *Just and Unjust Wars*, this boils down to a response to an aggression and a defense of rights.

- **Legitimate, competent authority** War can be declared only by a competent governmental authority. A clarification may be necessary here: A "competent authority" doesn't refer to the leader's intelligence or lack thereof, but exclusively to whether or not the leader is the legitimate representative of the people and whether he or she has the constitutional authority to declare war. Some overenthusiastic general can't start a war on his or her own.

- **Comparative justice** The values and rights that are being defended must be so important that their defense outweighs the horrors of war.

- **Right intention** The intention must be to defend the rights in question, and not have some ulterior motive, such as gaining territory or enhancing business.

- **Probability of success** There has to be a reasonable assumption that the war will accomplish its goal.

- **Proportionality of ends** The costs of the war must not exceed the presumed benefits. Some victories are too costly, as any utilitarian will tell you. The term for such a victory is *Pyrrhic,* from Pyrrhus, the king of Epirus who won a battle against the Romans in 279 B.C.E. but sustained such huge losses that it put the value of the victory in doubt.

Those are the rules that have to be in place when war is declared; in addition, there are rules that must be followed while conducting the war, "justice in war" (*jus in bello*). Over the past few centuries there has been a tendency to emphasize justice in war rather than just war, because the "just cause" concept is hard to define: After all, any nation (or terrorist group) can claim that its values are at risk and then march off to war. Instead, scholars have focused on limiting the damage done by war through these two rules:

- **Proportionality of means** Although some harm will of course be caused, one should avoid causing unnecessary damage.

- **Discrimination** The term *discrimination* here means discerning, or "discriminating" between combatants and noncombatants. This rule was added to just war theory in the Middle Ages; before then, Western thinking did not discriminate between soldiers and civilians (as some would argue that certain non-Western cultures are still not doing). Since everyone knows that wars usually involve civilian casualties, especially modern wars, the last rule doesn't exclude the loss of innocent noncombatants altogether, but they can't be *deliberately* targeted. Having some civilian casualties—on the enemy side, but also on one's own side—is considered acceptable as long as the overall result furthers the goal of peace. This falls under the principle of the *double effect,* which you read about in the discussion of abortion, a principle based on Catholic theology: An action that is prohibited under normal circumstances can be permitted if part of the outcome is (1) unintended, (2) doesn't exceed the goal in magnitude, and (3) unavoidable in order to accomplish its goal.

Even if two warring nations do follow those rules (which, of course, is not a given), there are still plenty of gray areas where one group can interpret the rules differently than another. And just wars can involve unjust acts. Some would cite the internment of Japanese Americans during World War II as an example of an unjust action during a just war.

A "third pillar" has been suggested in recent years: *jus post bellum,* or justice after war. In recognition that war crimes are often part of the fabric of war, some legal measures are thought to be necessary in the wake of a war. In *Parameters, US Army War College Quarterly,* Autumn 2002, professor of military science Davida E. Kellogg points out that although there may be difficulties setting up an international war-crimes tribunal, it is still a necessity so that injustices committed against citizens can be addressed and so that the citizens don't embark on revenge on their own. A problem facing the new kind of warfare of today is what to do with terrorists who are not innocent civilians but who are not soldiers of a nation either. Kellogg suggests that in the aftermath of a war, such criminals or "unlawful combatants" be treated as prisoners of war with rights, but still regarded as criminals, contrary to the tradition reaching back to the Middle Ages, when such irregular combatants were simply regarded as "pirates" without any rights whatsoever. (Thus, the handful of surviving defenders of the Alamo in Texas in 1836 were executed by Mexican General Santa Anna after the battle precisely because he considered them pirates without the rights of a soldier to honorable treatment.) In "Justice After War" in *Ethics & International Affairs* (2002), Brian Orend argues that the goals for a *jus post bellum* theory would include the following principles:

- There ought to be proportionality and publicity in the postwar settlement, and unjust gains from aggression must be eliminated.
- The settlement should address the basic rights that were violated.
- The settlement must distinguish between leaders, soldiers, and civilians.
- There ought to be punishment of leaders, as well as of soldiers.
- The compensations must be proportional to the losses.
- The aggressor should be rehabilitated under acceptable terms.

The addition of *jus post bellum,* in accordance with the rules of the Geneva Convention, can obviously apply to the aftermath of a war that one nation or coalition of nations has won and the other has lost; but it is harder to apply these principles to the aftermath of a war that has been fought between nations and bands of terrorists.

When we look to discussions of a just war and terrorism by contemporary philosophers, most papers and books written before 9/11/2001 have one thing in common: They imagine a future enemy to be a nation with an identifiable government, rarely a shadowy association of international terrorists. In war-torn eighteenth-century Prussia, Immanuel Kant wrote one of his last works, "Perpetual Peace: A Philosophical Sketch." With a clarity that wasn't apparent to readers until after World War II, Kant envisioned the slippery slope of escalating wars of the future leading to a war of mutual extermination and admonished that the only way civilization will survive is for all governments to become republican, with a system of government that recognizes the division between legislative, executive, and judicial powers. In Kant's words, "A *republican constitution* is founded upon three principles: firstly, the principle of *freedom* for all members of a society (as men); secondly, the principle of the *dependence* of everyone upon a single common legislation (as subjects);

and thirdly, the principle of legal *equality* for everyone (as citizens)." This will prevent various forms of dictatorship that regard their citizens as merely a means to an end. You will remember the concept of the *kingdom of ends* from Chapter 6, and this is what Kant was dreaming of: a world where people respect one another and their laws, where no nation abuses its own citizens, where nations will join together in a federation of free states, and where strangers are considered people too. In his essay, Kant suggests the formation of a "League of Nations" to prevent future wars—a feat that was not accomplished until 1919 on President Woodrow Wilson's initiative. It became a precursor of the United Nations. Although some might say Kant's vision is both a trifle naïve and incomplete, one might hope there is a profound truth to his observation that truly democratic countries, where each citizen knows he or she has constitutionally protected rights, are less likely to generate wars of aggression—or have individuals embark on terrorist ploys against their own government or other nations—than countries where the individual has few or no rights and feels like a pawn in the political games of others. An active global effort toward democracy might thus go a long way toward preventing future terrorist actions as well as future wars. The American philosopher John Rawls, whom you know from Chapter 7, focused in his final book, *The Law of Peoples,* on some of the same issues. He attempts to outline a *realistic utopia* according to the principles of justice, recognizing that peoples should view one another as free and independent. He sees five kinds of domestic societies: *Reasonable, liberal peoples* and *decent peoples* ("nonliberal societies whose basic institutions meet certain specified conditions of political right and justice") together form the category of *well-ordered peoples;* then there are *outlaw states; societies burdened by unfavorable conditions;* and *societies of benevolent absolutisms* (societies that recognize human rights but don't allow their citizens a political voice). Here is a brief excerpt from the section where Rawls explores the right of well-ordered peoples to go to war.

> No state has a right to war in the pursuit of its *rational,* as opposed to its *reasonable,* interests. The Law of Peoples does, however, assign to all well-ordered peoples (both liberal and decent), and indeed to any society that follows and honors a reasonably just Law of Peoples, the right to war in self-defense. Although all well-ordered societies have this right, they may interpret their actions in a different way depending on how they think of their ends and purposes. . . .

> When a liberal society engages in war in self-defense, it does so to protect and preserve the basic freedoms of its citizens and its constitutionally democratic political institutions. Indeed, a liberal society cannot justly require its citizens to fight in order to gain economic wealth or to acquire natural resources, much less to win power and empire. (When a society pursues these interests, it no longer honors the Law of Peoples, and it becomes an outlaw state.) To trespass on citizens' liberty by conscription, or other such practices in raising armed forces, may only be done on a liberal political conception for the sake of liberty itself, that is, as necessary to defend liberal democratic institutions and civil society's many religious and nonreligious traditions and forms of life. . . .

Gun Rights or Gun Control?

"A well regulated Militia, being necessary to the security of a free State, the right of the people to keep and bear Arms, shall not be infringed." These are the words of the Second Amendment of the Bill of Rights of the United States. As you read in Chapter 7, the Second Amendment guarantees the right to "bear arms," to own weapons, but for whom? "Militia." That has been interpreted by some to mean only members of a state militia can own weapons; however, the Supreme Court established in 2008 (*District of Columbia v. Heller*) that the right extends to individuals, reflecting the Founders' concern that a government that doesn't allow the citizenry to own weapons can end up abusing its powers. In the words of the Supreme Court, "The Second Amendment protects an individual right to possess a firearm unconnected with service in a militia, and to use that arm for traditionally lawful purposes, such as self-defense within the home." The decision didn't mean that every single person is entitled to own *any* gun, *anywhere,* however; a tentative list of "presumptive lawful regulations" excludes mentally ill persons and felons, and enables gun prohibition in schools and government buildings, etc., and it is up for debate whether a person has a right to carry a gun with them *outside* the home (either "open carry" or "concealed carry") or whether the right to self-defense only extends to one's home.

In this limited space we can of course not cover all the arguments for and against gun regulation, or as it is commonly known, **gun control**, but I hope this selection of arguments provides a fair overview of key points in the debate, and that it will inspire a class discussion about the extent of constitutional **gun rights** and the likely consequences of gun regulation.

A short list of key arguments in favor of *gun control*:

1. **A staggering number of deaths from guns:** Quoting from ProCon.org, "There were 572,537 total gun deaths between 1999 and 2016: 336,579 suicides (58.8% of total gun deaths); 213,175 homicides (37.2%); and 11,428 unintentional deaths (2.0%). Guns were the leading cause of death by homicide (67.7% of all homicides) and by suicide (51.8% of all suicides)." Those U.S. statistics are viewed as a primary argument why the Second Amendment should be reinterpreted, or even itself amended. Gun control proponents and activists point out that the dreadful frequency of mass murders of innocents including children, such as the 2012 Sandy Hook school shooting in Newtown, Connecticut, with the loss of 26 people (of which Victoria Soto was one; see Chapter 4) including 20 children, and the 2018 Stoneman Douglas High School shooting in Parkland, Florida, in which 17 people lost their lives, and other shootings by individuals with a professed hate for their target group can be stopped if the access to weapons by such individuals can be limited. Gun rights advocates point out that some gun violence can be stopped if so-called "soft targets," currently gun-free zones, (1) have more police presence, and (2) allow trained citizens to carry arms.

2. Gun control advocates believe that **background checks** of gun buyers and limits of legitimate gun sales venues can be a means to that effect. Gun rights advocate are not all opposed to limited background checks, but point out that much gun violence is committed by people who would fail background checks, anyway.

3. Gun control advocates point out that **no civilian needs an assault rifle** for hunting or target practicing. There are somewhere between 245 and 310 million guns in the United States today (a number that is hard to verify), and only some of them are needed for hunting and other sports. The response of gun rights advocates is (1) that some weapons classified as assault weapons are actually common in sports shooting, and (2) that it shouldn't be up to the government to dictate what responsible citizens should prefer.

4. Gun control advocates hold that **the presence of a gun** makes violence more likely. Homicides and suicides seem more likely, statistically, in homes with guns. Gun rights advocates point out that gun owners actually prevent burglaries and assaults in their homes on a regular basis, but that these self-defense cases go underreported by the media.

A short list of key arguments in favor of *gun rights*:

1. Gun control is nothing more than **a euphemism for *gun confiscation***. If certain types of guns are banned (such as military-style assault weapons), it is a short step for a government to ban other types of weapons in increments, known as *incrementalism*, ending in complete confiscation of most if not all types of guns. It may even lead to a ban on other types of weapons, such as certain kinds of knives, as has been seen in other parts of the world, Australia being an example. Some gun control advocates respond that that is a slippery slope argument—no legislators are intent on gun confiscation. However, Democratic presidential candidate Beto O'Rourke, TX, pointed out in a presidential debate in 2019 that he indeed would be in favor of confiscation of certain guns as president.

2. Gun rights proponents point out that gun control will only disenfranchise and disempower law-abiding citizens who will be **deprived of an important means of self-defense and sense of safety.** Gun control advocates argue that defense of the citizenry is the police's business, not individual citizens'.

3. Gun rights proponents argue that gun control will **not keep guns out of the hands of criminals**. Criminals will always have access to illegal guns, and no amount of legislation can prevent that from happening. Some of the worst massacres of civilians by another civilian have been seen in countries with strict gun control, such as Norway, France, and Germany. Some gun control proponents argue that this is why *all* guns should be confiscated, not just regulated.

4. Gun rights proponents argue that **gun control threatens traditional, time-honored gun ownership** in hunting, target shooting and sports shooting. Some gun control proponents respond that gun ownership reflects a world of yesterday where a hunting and target shooting tradition was common, but that the United States of the twenty-first century is no longer such a world, and legislation must adjust to the changing times.

The *utilitarian* response would focus on what is good for the majority in the long run, but this is where opinions differ. For gun control advocates, the predicted lower death toll is the ultimate advantage (and as you'll remember, utilitarianism doesn't hold any rights to be inalienable if they will incur bad consequences for the majority), and gun control activists are arguing in favor of not only gun regulation, but *ammunitions* regulation, as is now in effect in California. However, for utilitarian gun rights advocates, the loss of power of self-defense as well as power to fight a potentially tyrannical government is the ultimate negative consequence.

The *Kantian* response would focus on the principle of inalienable rights of a people regardless of consequences—provided that individuals are not treated merely as a means to an end. So for the Kantian gun control advocate, the gun industry is, overall, using the population as simply a means to an end for its own purpose of gun sales. However, for the Kantian gun rights advocate, it is the entire principle of individuals having rights—or at least the right of adults with a stable mind, and at the very least groups of male and female adults joined in a state-sponsored civilian defense, to own the weapons necessary to meet all such challenges, at home and in public places in defense of themselves and others.

So is there one answer, or even any common ground for gun control advocates and gun rights advocates? The gun debate is not only one of the most emotional debates in the United States today but also one of the most divisive. For gun control advocates, nothing seems more reasonable that making every attempt to curtail senseless violence toward innocent people including schoolchildren, and regulating gun ownership seems like the most obvious path toward that goal. For gun rights advocates (where the great majority also are against gun violence toward innocents, just as much as gun control advocates), the prospect of gun confiscation is nothing less than a fundamental threat to the individual freedom and self-determination guaranteed by the Constitution, a threat to the entire concept of being a free American citizen; for gun rights advocates, the answer is not to take away guns, but to educate the population to the point where a trained, responsible gun owner can defend herself or himself, and even step in and prevent gun violence in an active shooter situation.

In many ways, the gun debate seems to fall along political lines. More Democrats are in favor of gun control than Republicans. However, the right to own guns is also fiercely defended by many Democrats, and the ultimate explanation may be *cultural*: Many Americans, regardless of party affiliation, have grown up in an environment where guns are a normal part of life, for hunting, sports, and defense against wildlife—usually rural areas of the country—and a respect for weapons is taught to the young generation alongside of being taught weapons use. But for the vast majority of people who have grown up in reasonably safe urban neighborhoods, the need for guns as well as a traditional appreciation for weapons and their aesthetics can seem very alien, even unfathomable.

So is there a way in which these antagonistic groups can find common ground? Or are we destined to be in an escalation of disagreement about the issue? The trends can be seen as going both ways: more states and counties in the United States are allowing "concealed carry" with a permit, and "open carry" without a permit, but big retail chain stores such as Walmart are no longer carrying handguns or handgun ammunition, and have issued appeals to their customers to not enter their stores armed with guns. While we may be able to find common ground within the *emotional* issue of wanting life for human beings to be safer—a feeling you'll remember Antonio Damasio (Chapter 1) describing as a natural empathy for others—it by no means entails that we can easily find common ground in how that safety is supposed to be achieved: through legislation, limiting citizens' access to guns, or through supporting the freedom of citizens to be able to defend themselves, their families, and their neighborhoods.

Animal Welfare and Animal Rights

There was a time when animals were considered morally responsible, to a degree. It was assumed, almost as in the fairy tales we knew as kids, that animals have a form of reason, and when they hurt one another or humans, they do it on purpose. Until the mid-nineteenth century, animals could be held legally responsible for their actions (although they had very few recognized rights); all through the European Middle Ages, rats, roaches, and other pests were put on trial (usually in absentia) for the damage they caused to human lives and property. Even in the United States, animals were put on trial for hurting their masters or their own offspring, and they were "executed" if found guilty. Today, when an aggressive dog attacks a small child and is put to death, do we consider ourselves to be "executing" the dog? Some might argue that is exactly what we are doing—we are punishing the dog for transgressing a human law. But legally we are simply disposing of the dog's owner's property not as a punishment against the dog but as a precaution in the public interest. Who *does* get punished? Not the dog, but the *owner*, who receives a fine or even a jail sentence. In San Francisco in 2002, a dog owner even received a second-degree murder sentence after her dogs attacked and killed a neighbor, but a judge later reduced the sentence to four years for manslaughter. Today, we don't consider animals to be legally responsible for their actions, because we don't consider them to be moral agents. A dog who wakes up her owners when the house is on fire may be praised for it afterward, but if she fails to react, nobody will call her "callous" or "evil." (In previous times, when animals were put on trial, the issue of whether they were moral agents still was not solved because it was commonly considered that they had no souls and thus had no free will. Were the people who put them on trial contradicting themselves? Yes. But so do we sometimes, and one of the objectives of discussing these issues is to get into the habit of thinking more consistently.)

Ironically, even if animals in the past were considered as having some form of moral responsibility, they were not considered eligible for rights, or even humane treatment.

In Chapters 5 and 6, we touched on the issue of animals as candidates for moral respect. Chapter 5 introduced you to Descartes's idea that animals cannot feel pain because they have no minds, as well as Bentham's and Mill's view that since animals obviously can feel pain and experience pleasure, consideration for animals should be included in whatever moral decisions we make that might affect them. Today, research by animal behaviorists has established that nonhuman animals are capable of feeling physical pain. In addition, animal studies in the wild as well as under more controlled conditions in labs by animal behaviorists and neurobiologists support the old anecdotal assumption that animals can also feel emotions; and the criticism, raised repeatedly throughout the twentieth century, that animal researchers are just "anthropomorphizing" their subjects is rarely heard now. Animal researchers and writers are increasingly affirming the observations of David Hume and Charles Darwin that if animals act as if they feel emotions similar to fear, joy, and sadness, then it is the simplest and most likely explanation that they do in fact feel such similar emotions—an assumption that has now to some extent been corroborated, at least in the case of the dogs at a research facilities in Hungary and elsewhere trained to sit still during MRIs (see Chapter 5). One might of course also try to talk to the animals themselves and ask them, as some ape researchers are already doing. (The question of animal *intelligence* is considered in Box 13.10.

Box 13.10 RATIONAL ANIMALS?

Michael Nichols/National Geographic Creative

The bonobo chimpanzee Kanzi is today perhaps the most outstanding, and controversial, example of a nonhuman being using and understanding language and demonstrating rational thought—at the approximate level of a human child of three (and occasionally even older). Never having been trained to understand human language or use a lexigram (a talking board with symbols signifying nouns, verbs, and names), Kanzi picked up both skills as an infant from watching his mother in training. Here Kanzi is working with his lexigram.

The question of animal intelligence has been a challenge ever since Aristotle claimed that animals can think in a practical sense, but only humans can think rationally and abstractly. What does it take to think rationally? You'll remember that our working definition of rationality in Chapter 6 was the ability to identify a goal and take the shortest route to it (and that definition itself was questionable). For Kant the true test of a rational being is whether he or she can understand the categorical imperative: Could you allow yourself to do something you wouldn't accept as a universal law? Most of us, however, have a less strict view of what it is to think rationally. If someone solves a problem through trial and error, we usually view it as a rational method, but it is even better if someone can envision a solution to a problem without having encountered the problem before, and solve it on the first try simply by having thought about it abstractly.

Most of us are probably willing to accept that nonhuman animals have some sort of mental activity whereby they associate time and place, link past fears and joys with present persons and places, and anticipate events in the near future, such as dinner. But can nonhuman animals solve abstract problems and even conceive of a kind of categorical imperative? Throughout the twentieth century, that question was so controversial that most scholars steered clear of it for fear of ridicule; in 1900 a horse in Germany, Clever Hans, believed by his owner and numerous scientists to be able to do math because he could thump out the correct answers to math questions when asked, was revealed to be "simply" a good reader of human body language, and research into animal intelligence carried the stigma of Clever Hans with it well into the last half of the twentieth century. But since new research into animal intelligence was made public during the 1980s and 1990s, many researchers have been less reluctant to consider nonhuman animals as having a rudimentary capacity for rational thinking and even for language comprehension. Close observation and interaction with dolphins, orca whales, monkeys, pigs, dogs, and even birds, especially members of the corvid family such as crows and magpies, have led to a new appreciation of the possibility of nonhuman animal reasoning. In particular, research into the behavior and language capacity of nonhuman great apes (bonobo chimpanzees, chimpanzees, gorillas, and to a lesser extent orangutans) has made it conceivable that the great apes have a grasp of abstract rational thinking as well as trial-and-error thinking.

Of the great apes, the bonobo chimpanzee Kanzi may be the most famous example of non-human animal intelligence today, although his sister Panbanisha seemed to surpass him in linguistic talent. Having taught himself how to use a lexigram (an electronic "talking" board with symbols for English words) by watching the humans try, unsuccessfully, to teach his mother its use, Kanzi answers questions or tells his human friends what he wants, including watching videos that feature humans in ape costumes. Kanzi's feats include understanding new sentences and reacting accordingly (such as "Put the key in the refrigerator"), as well as displaying logical thinking, going through a series of actions to achieve a goal (such as cutting a string to get into a box with a key that opens another box with a treat). Panbanisha died from a virus in 2013, but up until her death she had shown a great talent for language. She was copying the words she saw on the computer screen and had reportedly taken up writing words in English on the floor with chalk. In addition, Panbanisha served as an interpreter for her and Kanzi's mother, who never learned the use of the lexigram. Losing Panbanisha was a blow to the entire field of ape language research—as well as to her humans and her Bonobo family.

Would Kant recognize these behaviors as evidence of rational thinking and welcome Kanzi and Panbanisha as persons instead of things? That would depend on whether it is possible for the apes to grasp the concept of universalization: Might they understand the idea of "Don't do that—how would you like it if we did that to you?" Kanzi is in maturity at the level of a 4-year-old human child. Panbanisha's level may have exceeded that. If we are ready to recognize a small child as having some grasp of rational thought and as understanding the preceding sentence, and are willing to call a 3-year-old child a person, why not be as open-minded about the personhood of an ape if he or she is on the approximate same intellectual level? For some thinkers, the entire ape language experiment hinges on whether it's merely some smart animals "aping" human behavior for rewards, or whether apes can really communicate freely (within limits) in a human language. Since one of the first apes who learned American Sign Language, Washoe, taught her son the ASL signs and communicated with him using signs even when they thought themselves to be unobserved by humans, and Panbanisha had been teaching her son, Nyota, how to use the lexigram, the answer seems to be yes.

So are nonhuman animals conscious? According to the Cambridge Declaration of Consciousness (2012),

"The weight of evidence indicates that humans are not unique in possessing the neurological substrates that generate consciousness. Nonhuman animals, including all mammals and birds, and many other creatures, including octopuses, also possess these neurological substrates."

With the new research into animal cognition and sensory perception, it is becoming clear that legislation just hasn't kept up with the new findings, and some administrations are hurrying to catch up. In Italy in 2017 it became illegal to boil lobsters alive, and in 2018 Switzerland followed suit. In addition, lobsters can no longer be transported alive on ice, in recognition of the fact that crustaceans do feel pain. They must now be stunned before they are killed. Other sweeping rules have been added to the Swiss law books in the twenty-first century, such as outlawing puppy mills, requiring new dog owners to take classes in canine care, and requiring welfare officers to be appointed to labs that use animals in their research. In Norway, the mink and fox fur trade will have phased itself out of business by 2025, along with a significant number of other European nations cutting down on or eliminating their corner of the fur business. And in the United States, California became the first state in the Union to ban the retail sales of cats and dogs in 2019. That same year, President Trump signed into law a ban on the trade and slaughter of cats and dogs for human consumption—a practice that had previously been legal in 44 states. "Alt meat," meat alternatives, is so common now that fast food chains serve meat-free burgers.

Is this the direction we want to take, moving toward the twenty-second century? Are we to consider other animals on the planet as fellow travelers through space, to be respected, or are there compelling reasons that humans might feel they have a right to use animals as resources for food, clothing, and entertainment, other than tradition? Below we look at utilitarian as well as Kantian responses.

The Utilitarian Approach

Within the utilitarian philosophy the recognition that animals can feel pain—physically, and even emotionally—obviously doesn't mean we as humans are not allowed to cause animals pain or distress, any more than it means we are not allowed to cause other humans pain: When great results can be obtained for a majority (of humans and/or animals), then causing pain to sentient creatures (creatures that can feel pain and pleasure) is morally acceptable and even commendable. For that reason, classical utilitarians such as Bentham and Mill and most utilitarians today rarely use the term "animal rights." Rather, modern utilitarians talk about "animal welfare." As you'll remember from Chapter 7, Bentham thought the notion of human rights was "nonsense upon stilts," and obviously a utilitarian would view animal rights in the same light, inasmuch as a utilitarian doesn't believe it serves any good purpose to talk about rights that are absolute and can never be infringed on, if the protection of such rights would be detrimental to the majority in a society.

A utilitarian believes we should take animal pain and pleasure into consideration whenever there are no overriding concerns that would justify causing pain for the sake of achieving good consequences for the many. As we saw in Chapter 5, a typical utilitarian response to animal experiments would be to frown on the use of animals in research on household products or cosmetics, because the contentment or protection each individual human would gain from the pain of animal experiments—a safer hairspray, a milder detergent—does not outweigh that pain, especially since humans can choose to avoid products that make your eyes sting and dry out your hands. However, when the focus shifts to medical experiments possibly resulting in the cure for terminal or debilitating illnesses, many utilitarians change their minds: The beneficial outcome of such research, which uses a limited number of animals, could be so overwhelming that there is no excuse not to perform such experiments. (You will recognize the problem from the film *Extreme Measures,* summarized in Chapter 5, even though the film addresses the problem of *human* test subjects.)

The Kantian Approach

As you will remember from Chapter 6, Kant excludes animals from moral consideration as ends in themselves because, to him, they are not rational creatures. Rational creatures are capable of understanding moral rules and, above all, moral duties and responsibilities. Kantians believe that only those who are capable of entering into a mutual relationship involving moral responsibilities are eligible for rights, and since animals are not perceived as having such capabilities, the deontological tradition reserves rights for humans. So what happens to human beings who, for some reason, are not capable of taking on duties and responsibilities? Some modern Kantians, such as the philosopher Carl Cohen, has chosen to solve that problem by saying that as long as most people are capable of rational thinking and understanding duties, then respect should also be extended to the few who aren't. However, even if it may appear as though an animal is capable of understanding its "duties," what that understanding really amounts to is training based on rewards or punishment—not a true understanding of moral duties—so from a Kantian point of view, animals are by their very nature excluded from having rights. This is what Cohen and others refer to as *contractarianism:* If your mind is capable of comprehending the obligations involved in a contract—written or oral—then you are a rational being and should be treated with respect. A creature that doesn't understand the implications of a contract can't have duties and consequently can't have any rights either. That doesn't mean we can't or shouldn't choose to be kind to animals, because there is no excuse for causing needless suffering, but although we may take on the responsibility of caring for an animal, our pet has no moral claim on us.

In an odd twist to the argument put forth by Cohen that only those who can understand fairness should be included in a system that extends rights, several researchers have recently presented evidence that some animals who are very close to us, not genetically but as a matter of tradition, themselves display a sense of justice: *dogs*. In several experiments conducted at the University of Vienna, dogs seem to have an understanding of what fair treatment entails; if one dog gets more treats than another, the other dog will show "inequity aversion" and display stress while asking for treats. Marc Bekoff and Jessica Pierce, in their book *Wild Justice,* have pointed out that the canine sense of fairness is prevalent; not only do they expect fairness from each other, but also from humans. In the Primary Readings section, you'll find an excerpt from *Wild Justice.*

Rights and Interests

From the viewpoint that having rights entails having an understanding of duties, the path to animal rights ought to remain blocked. However, there is an alternative viewpoint linking rights not with *duties* but with *interests.* You were introduced to the ideas of Australian philosopher Peter Singer in Chapters 4 and **5**, and you may remember the title of one of his books, *The Expanding Circle.* The circle Singer would like to see expanded is our moral universe: Who counts as a morally important being? Singer sees our view of who counts as having expanded from the family or the tribe to nations and to all humans. Singer and others would now like to see that circle expanded further to include the great apes and possibly other intelligent, social species, such as whales, dolphins, and wolves, in what is called "the community of equals," as stated in the Declaration on Great Apes. The argument used by many thinkers advocating rights for animals is that if a living being is capable of having interests, then those beings should have at least some moral standing (they should be taken into our moral universe). But what does it mean to have an interest? It may seem as if our cars have an interest in regular maintenance, because otherwise they break down. But presumably our cars don't suffer when they break down (only we, the owners, do). So the capacity for suffering and the interest in not suffering must be included in the basic description of a being with moral standing. But is an interest something that some individual really wants, or is it something that is good for that individual? And if interests imply rights, does it mean that individuals with interests have a right to have the interest fulfilled? For Singer, it is the capacity for interests that makes an individual eligible for rights, but that capacity doesn't mean those individuals have a right to have their wishes (or even their needs) fulfilled; however, they have a right to have their needs taken into consideration as morally relevant. In concrete terms, Singer's suggestions for "rights for the great apes" would include the right not to be tortured, not to be deprived of their freedom, and not to be killed, but it would not include any right to a steady supply of jellybeans (if that's what some individual ape might prefer). Some critics have remarked that it is unusual for a utilitarian philosopher such as Singer to use a concept such as *rights* instead of *welfare,* since traditionally any right for a utilitarian must be superseded by overriding social concerns. But Singer's philosophy of the ethical treatment of animals comes as close to the concept of rights as is possible for a utilitarian, since he believes the possibility that those rights would ever be overridden by other concerns is remote. For Singer, harming an animal would be permissible only in extreme cases, such as saving all of humanity.

Other thinkers sharing Singer's view that beings with interests should have rights include Joel Feinberg (1926–2004) and Steve Sapontzis. For Feinberg, it was obvious that individual animals have interests, perhaps more interests than some humans who are severely mentally impaired, so individual animals should have rights. However, an entire species can't have "interests," so Feinberg doesn't favor the rights of endangered *species,* only those of *individuals,* nonhuman or human. But, says Feinberg, if the criterion for being a member of the moral universe is that you can make moral claims against someone else, then animals already have such rights, because they can be represented in court by humans protecting their interests.

Sapontzis looks at the issue from both a utilitarian and a Kantian point of view: If we agree that animals probably have an overall narrower range of interests than humans, that is still not a sufficient reason to disregard such interests. In "The Moral Significance of Interests," he writes: "It certainly does not follow on utilitarian grounds that because an individual has a narrower range of interests he may be treated as a tool for the gratification of the interests of a being with a wider range of interests. If that did follow, renaissance men could eat specialists and peasants for dinner." Utilitarians aren't obliged to treat humans and animals in *the same* way, just to take their interests into equal consideration (so there won't be a question of giving animals the right to vote or to a good, well-rounded education, as some critics are fond of speculating).

What if we apply Kantianism to the issue of animal interests? Sapontzis points to the wealth of new research in animal intelligence, as well as to our common experiences with animals: It is about time, he says, that we put the debate over whether animals are rational behind us; of course they are—not to the degree of human rationality, but rational nevertheless. They may not be able to use the categorical imperative, but they are courageous, loyal, and devoted, and if we want to extend moral worth to humans with the same qualities, then we must let many animals into the moral fold too. As Sapontzis says, "Anyone still inclined to believe that only humans are rational should adopt a dog and get to know him personally."

What if you still think that granting rights to animals is too big a step, since humans, after all, have such a wide range of moral interactions that animals may never comprehend or participate in? You may consider a solution suggested by the philosopher Mary Ann Warren, whom you met earlier in this chapter: *partial rights*. Because many animals do have the same rudimentary intellectual capabilities as small children and the same (or an even greater) capacity for suffering, they should have some moral standing; but since human capacities for both reasoning and suffering are more extensive, they may override the rights of animals. Animals can probably never be morally autonomous the way humans can, but moral autonomy need not be the only criterion for having rights. It is, however, an important factor. So Warren suggests that humans should be the only beings granted full, equal rights (at least until we find other morally autonomous creatures), but nonhuman animals can be the bearers of partial rights, to be superseded by human rights only in extreme cases. In Box 13.11 you'll find a discussion about whether great apes should be considered *persons*.

Box 13.11 APES AND PERSONHOOD

You'll remember the debate in Chapter 7 concerning the distinction between a human being and a person, and how the term "person" is more useful when discussing rights than "human," because it signifies that the "entity" in question is capable of interacting in a morally and socially significant way with others, whereas the term "human" merely refers to someone having human DNA. A legal case in Austria in 2007 illustrates the need for the term "personhood" in addition to the term "human": Matthew Hiasi Pan was in danger of being sold unless the Vienna Supreme Court granted him personhood, because Pan was a chimpanzee,

and the animal shelter where he had lived for twenty-five years was in bankruptcy. However, the Austrian legislators recognize only the status of a *human* and the status of a *thing*, and Matthew Hiasi Pan had been ruled a thing. (You'll recognize Kant's dichotomy, which we discussed in Chapter 6: Either you are a rational being, or you are a thing.) In England, New Zealand, and Australia, great apes are considered hominids with limited rights, but not so in Austria. The matter was brought before the Austrian Supreme Court, which decided against Hiasi: He was again found to be a thing, with no rights. The problem with the court ruling seems to be that the court has decided against making a distinction between "humanity" and "personhood." It goes without saying that Hiasi is not a human being, genetically, but being a "person" requires (among other characteristics) the capacity for meaningful communication, a sense of purpose, and self-awareness, characteristics that apes share with us at least to some extent. The Great Ape Project, spearheaded by Peter Singer, has undertaken a census of all living great apes, publishing the biographies of individual apes in captivity. The census is intended to be a reminder that apes are not "things" or pets—they are intelligent beings with a long history of abuse by another species of great ape—the humans.

In 2008 the Spanish Parliament passed a bill giving personhood rights to Great Apes, following Germany where apes were granted rights in 2002. In 2014, an appeals court in Argentina declared an orangutan, Sandra, a "nonhuman person," wrongfully deprived of her right to freedom. In 2019 Sandra was finally moved to an ape sanctuary in Florida where she has settled in. In the United States the use of apes in research labs seems to be on the wane, for both financial and ethical reasons, and in 2011 a bill was introduced in Congress, the Great Ape Protection and Cost Savings Act of 2011. In 2015, two chimpanzees in New York were inadvertently granted personhood status, with the order of a judge to show habeas corpus, otherwise only given to humans. That writ was amended later that same day, however. But in 2016 a judge in Argentina ordered a chimpanzee, Cecilia, to be freed from the zoo where she had been kept in confinement, and sent to a sanctuary in Brazil, on the basis of Cecilia having rights of her own simply by being an ape, a landmark decision according to commentators.

Ethics of the Environment: Think Globally, Act Locally

In the 1970s a new concept arose: *environmentalism*. The Western world had suffered an energy crisis, and oil dependency was all of a sudden becoming an issue. Energy consumption in the West had skyrocketed after World War II, outpacing everywhere else on the planet. In addition, it was becoming noticeable that there were fewer bees than before, and fewer birds, and the culprit was tracked down: pesticides sprayed on the fields of grain and on flowering trees and bushes. Birds' eggs had a hard time developing because the shells were thinner and more porous, also because of pesticides. Frogs were disappearing from the wetlands, and indeed the wetlands themselves were disappearing, being drained and turned into farmland or subdivisions. The book *Silent Spring* was a wake-up call for an entire generation, and for a decade or so people scaled back their energy consumption, alternative energy forms were being developed, and people used the stairs instead of the elevator, turned off the lights when they left the room, recycled cans and newspapers, lowered the thermostat in winter, carpooled to work and school, and so forth—all the things that, we hear today, will help us save the environment. The slogan of environmentalism became "Think globally, act locally." And the concerted efforts did indeed make a difference, at least to some extent, in some parts of the Western world: The bees bounced back, and the birds did too. But then oil became cheap again, and we forgot to be energy conscious. For the next decades climatologists debated whether we might be moving toward a "greenhouse effect" because of the steadily climbing levels of CO_2 (carbon dioxide) that are part and parcel of modern energy use. It seemed like a fairly remote theory to most people until reports came in about glaciers melting and the polar ice packs shrinking.

Sidney Harris/ScienceCartoonsPlus.com

For some of us, everyday decisions become a matter of ethical dilemmas, engaging our moral conscience. Should we look for restaurants that advertise serving ecologically raise animals? Should we eat meat at all or go for meatless burgers? What if our salad ingredients are from farms that underpay their workers and/or use pesticides that harm the planet? And so forth. For some of us, limiting our carbon footprint and doing as little environmental harm as possible becomes a kind of sport, like "earning points." For others it is a new and exhausting burden added to all their other worries of the world. And some of us choose not to be affected. When you have lunch at a deli, do you think about ethical matters? Do you think you should?

Climate Change: An Inconvenient Truth?

In the late twentieth century, environmental concerns spawned a variety of approaches. One was a recycling movement, which has had broad success—just look at those blue recycle bins at your workplace, at school, and at the curbside on recycle days. Another was the "save water" approach in American restaurants where ice water is no longer served automatically—you have to ask for it. Some hotels ask you to keep your wet towels for one more use to save laundry water. And some communities experiment with "gray water," cleansed recycled water. But more radical environmentalist viewpoints were already in existence, culminating in the concept of *deep ecology,* coined by the Norwegian philosopher Arne Næss and supported by scientists such as Rachel Carlson and Aldo Leopold: According to the philosophy of deep ecology, humans are only one of many equally worthy species on the planet, without any species having more right to live than any other. The entire land with all its inhabitants is a moral entity. (Box 13.12 explores the concept of respect for nature from the American Indian point of view.) Aldo Leopold (1887–1948) had in 1948 introduced the concept of *land ethic* in his book *A Sand County Almanac:*

> All ethics so far evolved rest upon a single premise: that the individual is a member of a community of interdependent parts. His instincts prompt him to compete for his place in that community, but his ethics prompt him also to cooperate (perhaps in order that there may be a place to compete for).

> The land ethic simply enlarges the boundaries of the community to include soils, waters, plants, and animals, or collectively: the land.

This sounds simple: do we not already sing our love for and obligation to the land of the free and the home of the brave? Yes, but just what and whom do we love? Certainly not the soil, which we are sending helter-skelter downriver. Certainly not the waters, which we assume have no function except to turn turbines, float barges, and carry off sewage. Certainly not the plants, of which we exterminate whole communities without batting an eye. Certainly not

Box 13.12 AMERICAN INDIANS AND LAND ETHIC

Mauro Toccaceli/Alamy Stock Photo

Archibald Belaney, aka Grey Owl, lauded as a spokesperson for Native Canadian peoples in the 1920s and 30s. In a series of well-written books, interviews, and lecture tours, he opened many people's eyes to the value of nature, and what we today call the biosphere. After his death it was revealed that Grey Owl was an Englishman.

As you saw in Chapter 8, traditional American Indian values include a respect for the environment—or, rather, for the spirits of the environment. Since all features of nature are thought to be inspirited (what historians of religion call *animism*), then every living and every natural thing deserves to be treated with respect. That doesn't mean you can't hunt animals, or pick berries, or cut trees, but it does mean that you must do it responsibly, without waste of resources, and that you must engage the environment in a dialogue, asking for permission to hunt or to cut firewood, and giving thanks once your mission has been accomplished. This attitude toward nature was thought by the American philosopher J. Baird Callicott in the late twentieth century to be the ideal *land ethic* (a concept coined by Aldo Leopold; see chapter text): a respect for the entire environment as a whole. But critics (including your author, in a paper titled "Everyone Needs a Stone") have pointed out that (1) this could be just a modern version of Jean-Jacques Rousseau's eighteenth-century concept of the *noble savage;* tribal peoples such as eighteenth- and nineteenth-century American Indians were no more "noble" than they were "savage"—they were people dealing with their environment the best they could, in their own way; and (2) the assumption that the Indians were some early form of environmentalists is a *romantic misrepresentation:* Indians had, in tribal days, respect for the land and its inhabitants, not because they appreciated the interconnectedness of everything, but because nature was dangerous, life was precarious, and if you didn't stay on the good side of nature/the spirits, it/they could destroy you. And it actually shows more respect for the American Indian cultures to view their cultural history from a more realistic and less romantic viewpoint. But that doesn't mean we can't learn from their understanding of nature as a functioning whole that must be respected. Indeed, perhaps the real lesson is here *that if you mistreat nature, it will come back to bite you*—which is quite similar to what many environmentalists are teaching today about the climate change issue. In an ironic twist (which you may remember from Chapter 8), the story of Archie Grey Owl is the story of a land ethic. Grey Owl deserves credit for spreading awareness of the value of wild nature at the same time as Aldo Leopold—but as you'll also remember, Grey Owl claimed to be of aboriginal ancestry, which he wasn't, having been born and raised in Great Britain. He was, in essence, an impostor, but he and his Ojibwa wife Anahareo opened many people's eyes to environmentalism. You decide—is the content of the message more important than the misleading (or even offensive) packaging, or with the modern term, "personal branding" ?

the animals, of which we have already extirpated many of the largest and most beautiful species. A land ethic of course cannot prevent the alteration, management, and use of these *'resources,'* but it does affirm their right to continued existence, and, at least in spots, their continued existence in a natural state.

In short, a land ethic changes the role of *Homo sapiens* from conqueror of the land-community to plain member and citizen of it. It implies respect for his fellow-members, and also respect for the community as such.

This ethic of respect for the land inspired and invigorated many people, but for others, the problem with environmentalism was that it became an "ism." Like any other ideology, it has turned many people off because of its radicalism: Ranchers and farmers saw their rights to use their streams, fields, and woods diminish because of the presence of endangered species on the premises, such as rare mice and birds, and the almost notorious spotted owl. And when activist movements such as the Earth Liberation Front (ELF) and the Animal Liberation Front (ALF) arose, commonly referred to as eco-terrorist groups, environmentalism itself acquired a tainted reputation among many people.

Enter climate change theory: By the early 2000s the idea that the planet's temperatures are heating up because of industrial and vehicle emissions of CO_2 gases, creating a "greenhouse effect" that, in turn, will force temperatures even higher, was a theory advanced by groups to the left of the political spectrum. From 1997 to 1999 the Kyoto Protocol was established, with more than 160 countries as members, and coming into force in February 2005. The purpose of the Kyoto Treaty was to reduce the emissions of carbon dioxide and other greenhouse gases to a level where "anthropogenic" activity (caused by humans) will not present a danger to the world climate. The United States and Australia did not ratify the treaty. The United States was in 2005 the top emitter of carbon dioxides, but we were bypassed in 2007 by China, which is allowed certain exemptions from the Kyoto Protocol. Those exemptions were one reason the United States did not want to ratify the treaty. Other reasons cited were an unfair strain on the U.S. economy and scientific ambiguity as to the effect of greenhouse gases. But in April 2016, on Earth Day, all 196 parties to the United Nations Framework Convention on Climate Change signed the Paris Agreement on Climate Change. The signatories agreed to attempt to limit carbon emissions so that the global temperature of the Earth does not rise above 2 degrees Celsius (approx. 3.6 degrees Fahrenheit) above preindustrial levels, and no more than 1.5 degrees Celsius (approximately 2.7 degrees Fahrenheit) by year 2100. In October 2016, the Paris Agreement was ratified by the European Union, going into effect 30 days later. However, in June 2017, President Trump pulled the United States out of the Agreement, citing that the Paris Accord would undermine the United States' economy, starting a four-year exit process, scheduled to end in November 2020. Twenty-four states have joined in a United States Climate Alliance, upholding the Paris Agreement at the state level despite the federal withdrawal. The perception that climate change is real, whether partially or exclusively *anthropogenic* (caused by humans), is becoming more widespread around the world. So how has the debate unfolded over close to twenty years, from 1997 to 2016? Here is a brief overview:

If you remember the discussion in Chapter 1 about the "50-50 nation" phenomenon where citizens of the United States appear to be divided, sometimes down the middle, on both political and moral issues, and some consider those of a different opinion to be stupid, ignorant, or evil, you have a blueprint for how the global warming debate has developed in the recent past. A subtle shift has happened: Until recently the phenomenon was generally referred to as such, "global warming." But now, the referred term in the media as well as among scientists has become "climate change." And that shift itself says something about perceptions. When former Vice-President Al Gore's documentary *An Inconvenient Truth* came out in 2007, showing with what looked like incontrovertible evidence that the polar caps are melting, the glaciers receding, and deserts spreading at an alarming rate, that became the alarm bell that was finally heard by the greater public in the United States and elsewhere in the Western world. The implication was that not only are we in for major climatic changes, but they are by and large *anthropogenic,* with excess levels of carbon dioxide being released from human industries, creating a greenhouse effect that is likely to trap the heat, and accelerate the process of heating up the globe. But then came "Climategate" (a conspiracy theory, borrowing the term from the infamous Watergate break-in that destroyed the presidency of Richard Nixon), the 2009 revelation of e-mails obtained through hacking into the Climatic Research Unit at East Anglia University in England, indicating that researchers were playing up the warming without having the actual numbers. Since then the implication that global warming was a concoction has been vigorously denied, and the e-mails investigated by several committees who found no conspiracies or fraud, but the ground was laid for climate skepticism. Even so, a growing number of scientists point to the ever-increasing ferocity of storms, increases in water temperatures, and the rapid melting of ice shelves in the Antarctic as well as the ice sheet in Greenland as evidence of major changes. So are these just fluctuations in an ever-changing environment, or signs that we humans have mismanaged our only home, perhaps irreparably? We can't go into the evidentiary details here, but merely notice that there is a deep disagreement and mistrust of ulterior motives in this debate, to the point that a law has been proposed by California Senator Ben Allen (D) to make climate change denial a crime. The bill is directed specifically toward fossil fuel companies. Clearly, the climate change debate has reached a point where it is no longer a matter of personal opinion (and freedom of speech) but of legislation, which reaches a whole new level of ethical issues. In 2018, newly- elected Congresswoman Alexandria Ocasio-Cortez and Senator Ed Markey proposed the *Green New Deal* (an expression used already in 2007, bringing to mind President Franklin D. Roosevelt's New Deal of the Great Depression), a sweeping vision originally intended as a program for clean energy and job security, but redirected as a program combating climate change. In its popularized version, the Green New Deal involves a ban on combustion engines, a reduction in meat consumption, and a subsequent reduction of farm animals. Critics both on the left and the right have called the plan unrealistic and prohibitively expensive; House Speaker Nancy Pelosi (D) dismissed it as the "Green Dream or whatever." But many, especially on the political left, have applauded its visionary quality and have found that while it may be overly ambitious, it sends a signal that drastic measures may be necessary. The concern for the planet is felt in many parts of the world; limiting one's carbon footprint has become both a way of life and a moral issue for many people, especially in Scandinavia. In Sweden, environmental activist teenager Greta Thunberg has inspired many of her generation to become more environmentally responsible, but critics point out that she has also contributed to the anxiety level of many young persons, making them feel powerless and depressed. Also in Sweden, a concept has begun to affect the entire airline industry: "Flight shaming," *flygskam*, using social media to publicly shame individuals who choose to fly rather than opt for other means of transportation. The phenomenon has spread to the UK, Germany, and France. According to BBC, the movement has the potential of cutting airline traffic in half. (Here I should add that in Europe, trains are an affordable and speedy alternative. It is much harder in the USA to opt out of air travel in favor of driving, or taking the train or the bus due to the vast distances between destinations.)

The climate debate has acquired a new term, embraced by many in the western world of today: *sustainability*. The term refers to the policy of redesigning and reconfiguring our use of natural resources to maintain or even restore an ecological balance, while still taking the needs of humans into account, for tomorrow as well as today. In the words of the UN World Commission on Environment and Development: "*Sustainable* development is development that meets the needs of the present without compromising the ability of future generations to meet their own needs." The University of California, Los Angeles has a website dedicated to sustainability which reads, "Sustainable practices support ecological, human, and economic health and vitality. Sustainability presumes that resources are finite, and should be used conservatively and wisely with a view to long-term priorities and consequences of the ways in which resources are used." Many universities and colleges now offer classes and degrees in sustainability, frequently an interdisciplinary effort, involving disciplines such as geography, psychology, economics, biology, statistics, business, and indeed also environmental ethics, under the assumption that sustainability can't be achieved without the expertise of many disciplines working together.

To summarize: For those of us who find the climate change scenario to be straightforward, overwhelmingly corroborated science, the stubborn refusal of others to acknowledge it seems to be because they just don't understand any better (stupidity), or they are misinformed by others with a nefarious agenda (ignorance), or they just don't want to face the facts because it is more convenient, or profitable, to pretend it isn't happening, and continue with business as usual, and perhaps even denying the validity of science itself (evil). And for those of us who believe the climate change story is (1) a hype, or even a new form of neopaganism, a "green religion," and isn't happening at all, or (2) it is happening, but it is just one of planet Earth's many fluctuations and isn't caused by humans, the climate change voices seem like alarmists and easily duped by other alarmists (stupid), or they haven't looked at the actual data (ignorant), or they have a political agenda worth billions of dollars creating a "green" industry for profit, almost like a new religion (evil).

You will have to make up your own mind about our climate, what may be in store for us globally, and what we may or may not be able to, or willing to do about it.

Ethics of the Environment: For Us, or for Itself?

For the header of this section I chose "Ethics of the Environment" rather than "Environmentalism" because of the controversial undertone of the latter. Ethics of the environment implies, in a very broad sense, that we consider the environment as something that should be included in our moral deliberations—for the sake of either *the human beings* whose existence depends on the environment, or *the humans and nonhuman animals* who make this planet their home, or *the humans, the animals, and the organic or even inorganic elements of nature*. The concern about climate change can imply all three. We can choose to be concerned because of immense changes in store for human beings—changes that, according to some scientists involve rising temperatures and increasing droughts in some places, and increasing rainstorms elsewhere, but possibly also involving a risk of dramatically *falling* temperatures as a result of ocean currents slowing down because of melting glacier freshwater—in other words, perhaps another ice age (such as depicted in the film *The Day After Tomorrow*). But we can also choose to be concerned for the plight of animals around the world whose habitats will change, and shrink—at a time when extinction is threatening most of the large mammals in the wild. And we can certainly also choose the *Gaia* philosophy (Gaia was Mother Earth in Greek mythology) and be concerned for the entire planet, whose ancient forests and rivers and deep waters face climate changes of the human or nonhuman kind. This is in essence the viewpoint presented in E. O. Wilson's book, *Half Earth*. A far more radical view, voiced infrequently but definitely present in the debate, is the notion that Planet Earth would be better off *without* humans—that humans are "a plague upon the land," and that the planet would benefit from a dieback of *people,* a view explored in the classic science fiction film *Twelve Monkeys.*

Environmentalism, in its holistic, deep-ecology version, implies that all elements of nature have a right to exist, but that, in itself, raises new questions, drawing on what you have read about rights in Chapters 6 and **7** and in the preceding section on animal rights in this chapter: Can a being or a thing have rights without having responsibilities? Should trees have rights?

In 1974 Christopher D. Stone wrote a paper, "Should Trees Have Standing? Towards Legal Rights for Natural Objects" (in *People, Penguins, and Plastic Trees*). Many dismissed the paper as complete nonsense at the time. However, it has gained in influence since then. In the paper Stone states that every time we have opted to include another group in our welfare concern, such as slaves, women, minorities, children, or animals, the decision has been met with ridicule before it has achieved common acceptance. He proposes that we now expand our moral universe to cover not only individual animals but also entire species and natural objects such as lakes and streams, mountain meadows, marshes, and so on (who really can't be said to have interest since they are not "alive"):

> Whenever it carves out "property" rights, the legal system is engaged in the process of *creating* monetary worth. . . . I am proposing we do the same with eagles and wilderness areas as we do with copyrighted works, patented inventions, and privacy: *make* the violation of rights in them to be a cost by declaring the "pirating" of them to be the invasion of property interest. If we do so, the net social costs the polluter would be confronted with would include not only the extended homocentric cost of his pollution [. . .] but also cost to the environment *per se.*

What Stone suggests here is a grand solution not only to the problem of whose rights should be protected but also to the problem of *how* they should be protected. He proposes fining polluters because pollution is *bad for nature,* regardless of whether it might affect a local human population or visitors to a polluted wilderness area. It would take us too long to discuss in detail the concept of giving rights to plants and natural objects such as rocks and streams (and of course we'd want to include cultural objects such as historical buildings, old baseball fields, statues, and favorite movie locations). The question is how far we want to go, not in assigning protection for the environment—because we can take that as far as we want to go—but in assigning rights per se, regardless of human interest in the subject. If nobody cares about a certain meadow or about the building in downtown Los Angeles where they filmed the sci-fi classic *Blade Runner* (the Bradbury building, incidentally), then should we give it rights on the basis that someone may someday care, or because it has acquired those rights just by hanging around?

If we do assign rights to plants, where do we stop? It is all well and good to preserve a good-looking row of trees, but what about preserving a scraggly row of carrots on the grounds that they have a right to life? What we have here is a *slippery slope argument,* the logical fallacy, you'll remember from Chapter 1, claiming that some idea will lead to a series of increasingly unacceptable consequences (such as: "If you refuse to wear fur because of concern for living creatures, then you shouldn't eat meat, either; as a matter of fact, you shouldn't fight the roaches and ants in your kitchen because they, too, are living creatures, nor should you use antibiotics or antibacterial mouthwash out of concern for the living bacteria"). A slippery slope is usually advanced as a satirical criticism of some idea (here, refusing to wear fur) by pointing to ridiculous consequences. (Another term for this type of slippery slope is a *reductio ad absurdum,* a reduction to absurdity.) To respond to a slippery slope, we can take one of three paths: (1) abandon our original idea, because the consequences now seem silly; (2) agree that we should take the consequences seriously; or (3) *draw the line* between one part of the slope and another by arguing that there is a moral difference between, for example, eating meat and killing roaches that spread disease. Concerning the question of giving rights to trees, one could argue that there is a moral difference between granting rights to trees (if that is one's conviction) and granting rights to carrots. However, if we choose to draw the line, it is up to us to have good arguments as to why there is a moral difference between one step of the slope and the next.

The Death Penalty

In 2014 two executions, one in Oklahoma and the other in Arizona, brought the death penalty discussion to a new level of concern—not because there was any doubt as to the guilt of the two condemned prisoners, or the fairness of their trials, but because the executions were botched.

Clayton Lockett, convicted of rape, kidnapping, and murder among other charges, and sentenced to death in 1999, was scheduled to be executed by lethal injection in Oklahoma in April 2014. The drugs used were untested, due to the standard drugs being unavailable. Despite being declared unconscious, Lockett remained alert during the execution process, trying to raise himself up, calling out, and clearly in pain. After 20 minutes the execution was halted, and a stay of execution given, but Lockett died of a heart attack half an hour later. Oklahoma's lethal injection method of execution was evaluated in 2015 by the Supreme Court that, in a 5-4 ruling, held that Oklahoma could continue with the practice.

In July that same year, Joseph Wood was executed in Arizona. He was convicted of a 1989 double murder, and sentenced to death. The chemicals here were also virtually untested. His execution by lethal injection took an hour, not the scheduled 10 minutes, and he gasped and gulped for air (as described by a reporter) the entire time. The drug cocktail had been administered to him not once, but 15 times. The state of Arizona subsequently halted its executions, pending a review. These cases rekindled the debate over capital punishment, and here we look at the most frequently raised objections as well as the arguments in defense of the practice. To get the most out of the debate, it is recommended that you have the punishment discussion from Chapter 7 fresh in your mind, particularly the five categories of punishment: deterrence, rehabilitation, incapacitation, retribution, and vengeance.

THE WIZARD OF ID   **Brant parker and Johnny hart**

With a particularly dark sense of humor, this *Wizard of Id* strip deals with capital punishment—a topic that isn't usually a source of laughter. The strip creates a perverted application of a utilitarian principle of punishment: As long as punishment has good consequences (such as deterrence or rehabilitation), then the issue of guilt or innocence is of minor importance.

Two Philosophers on Capital Punishment

Until the twentieth century, most philosophers had no compunction about arguing in favor of the death penalty. Two voices coming from two different traditions have been particularly influential, and you are familiar with both of them: John Locke, in seventeenth-century England, stated that humans have rights even before the social contract, in the state of nature. These are the three negative rights, to *life, liberty,* and *property.* But since there is no government in the state of nature to enforce those rights, one must take on that task oneself. Therefore, if a person has infringed on your rights, you are free to punish the perpetrator (if you can catch him or her, that is). And, says Locke, if someone in the state of nature has taken a life, then he has given up his own right to life and can be hunted down and killed like a wild animal. Locke believes such action will have two effects: (1) *deterrence*—those who see how a killer is treated will think twice about doing the same thing—and (2) *retribution,* restoring the balance that was disrupted by the murder. So Locke uses both a forward-looking and a backward-looking argument in favor of killing a killer.

The other familiar voice in favor of the death penalty is Immanuel Kant, speaking to us from eighteenth-century Prussia. Kant argues that capital punishment is a rational response to a capital crime—and he argues exclusively in favor of *retribution:* If we execute a criminal to obtain some good social consequences, such as safe streets, then we are in effect using the killer as merely a means to an end—we are using him or her as a stepping-stone to safe streets. Indeed, executing an *innocent* person would probably have the same kind of deterrent effect. Instead, Kant insists that there should be one reason, and one reason only, for punishing a person: because of his or her *guilt.* And for us to proceed according to the principle of *lex talionis,* we should punish the guilty in proportion to the crime, not with an eye toward any further social consequences. That means the only proper punishment for murder is death—even if good social consequences might actually come out of imprisoning the killer for life or letting him or her go free after a period of rehabilitation.

We see how seriously Kant takes this principle by his example: If a society decides to disband but still has people waiting on death row, then the last action of that society should be to execute its convicted murderers, even if there will be no society afterward to enjoy the safer streets. Furthermore, it is only right and proper to execute a murderer for his crime—and in a sense it is showing the convicted killer the utmost *respect* as a human being: Instead of using him for some social purpose (such as deterrence), or trying to rehabilitate him under the assumption that he didn't know what he was doing, we give him credit for actually having made up his own mind to commit a crime—and then we hold him accountable for it.

It wasn't until the nineteenth century that strong voices began to speak up against capital punishment as such, and not merely in opposition to executions for lesser crimes such as burglary. In the twentieth century, opposition to the death penalty became known as *abolitionism* (whereas "abolition" in the nineteenth century referred to abolishing slavery in America).

Today's Capital Punishment Criteria

From 1968 to 1976, there was a moratorium on the death penalty in the United States, but since 1976 individual states have been able to decide whether they want to make certain crimes punishable by death, as long as their laws meet guidelines established by the U.S. Supreme Court. A moratorium on executions by lethal injection was lifted in 2008, and executions were resumed. In 2019, 30 states still allowed capital punishment, while 20 states didn't. Among the 30 was California, but in March that same year, Governor Gavin Newsom ordered a moratorium on executions in the state, and the death chamber at San Quentin was closed indefinitely. Prior to that, in 2018, a man was charged with eight counts of first-degree murder and 30 counts of kidnapping/abduction in California. His crime spree had extended over 40 years, from northern to southern California, and involving more than 50 rapes and burglaries in addition to at least 13 murders. Today we know him as the Golden State Killer, Joseph James DeAngelo, but he has previously been known as the East Area Rapist, the Original Night Stalker, and the Visalia Ransacker, among other names. His victims included women living alone as well as couples. In May of 2019 the Sacramento prosecutors announced that they would seek the death penalty; at the time of writing this, the trial has yet to get underway; despite the moratorium, he could still be sentenced to death if found guilty, but whether death penalties in California will be carried out in the future remains an open question.

What crimes are today punishable by death in the thirty states that allow capital punishment? Theoretically, treason is, but the death penalty is evoked only under rare circumstances, as with the execution of Julius and Ethel Rosenberg for espionage in 1953—still a controversial judicial decision, especially since 2001, when a witness for the prosecution admitted that he lied on the stand. In previous decades, murder, even if committed in a state of rage or panic, might lead to the gas chamber or the electric chair, but today one or more "special circumstances" have to apply, depending on the state legislation. In California, for example, some of the special circumstances are killing more than one person; raping and killing a person; stalking a victim before killing him or her; killing a police officer, a judge, or a jury member; killing with poison; and killing while carjacking. In other death penalty states, other rules may apply. In the state of Washington, for example, a killer of multiple victims must be shown to have had a "common scheme" in killing them, such as robbery. The simple fact of there being more than one victim isn't enough in itself to warrant the death penalty; Washington legislators have been debating changing the law in the wake of the capture of several serial killers.

Abolitionist Arguments

Abolitionists make the following general arguments:

1. Cruel and Unusual Punishment The death penalty is an uncivilized, cruel, and unusual form of punishment, depriving the criminal of the ultimate right: the right to life. Abolitionists often cite the fact that among Western nations, the United States is the only country that still executes its citizens, and abolitionist nations around the world usually refuse to extradite a murderer to the United States if he or she may be executed.

Proponents of the death penalty, called *retentionists* because they want to *retain* the penalty, reply that of all Western nations, the United States is the only country in which serial killers operate on a regular basis and that the homicide rate is generally higher than in other Western nations, so special measures have to be taken. In the Primary Readings section, you'll find an excerpt from an article discussing Justice Stephen Breyer's view that capital punishment is, in fact, not only cruel but also "unusual."

2. State-Sanctioned Murder Executing a murderer is no better than stooping to the level of the murderer, making murder state-sanctioned. Retentionists reply that this is a false analogy: The murderer kills innocent people, whereas the state executes someone who has been found guilty.

3. Discrimination As it is administered today, at least in certain states, the death penalty shows patterns of discrimination: The poor, the uneducated, and African American men are more likely to receive the death penalty than are people from other population groups, regardless of the crime rate. Retentionists reply that this is not an argument against the death penalty as such, only against the way it has been adminis-tered—which admittedly has been discriminatory. But such slanted approaches can be avoided in the future, and according to a recent report from the Justice Department such approaches are virtually a thing of the past, at least in federal cases. Be that as it may, the general perception among abolitionists as well as many retentionists is that the discrimination issue is still far from having been resolved.

4. Innocents Executed Mistakes have been made and innocent people executed—23 known innocents in the United States in the twentieth century. A person wrongly incarcerated cannot have the years he or she spent behind bars restored, but he or she can be compensated financially. An innocent person who has been exe-cuted can't be compensated in any way, because everything has been taken from him or her. To many, this argument is the strongest abolitionist point, leading to the adage that it is better that many guilty go free than that one innocent person be punished.

5. Political Ambition An aspect that is rarely brought forth, but that may be very important, is the influence of politics. As Mark Fuhrman mentions in his book *Death and Justice* (2003), as long as the death penalty is a factor in local and state politics, there is a danger of its being abused, to secure votes and look "tough on crime." Because judges, sheriffs, and district attorneys are *elected* in many states and have to run election campaigns, their stance on the death penalty and their history of convictions will be part of those campaigns. Deliberately or inadvertently, isn't there a risk that this external factor may slant the view of what is "the worst of the worst" among criminals—those cases deserving the death penalty? Fuhrman cites examples in Oklahoma to that effect: While Bob Macy was District Attorney, executions were at an all-time high, with 21 executions in 2001 alone. When there is even the slightest suspicion that a political factor may play into seeking the death penalty, there is reason for caution.

6. Primitive Emotions Some abolitionists argue that you can choose to be a retentionist only if you are igno-rant, sadistic, or emotional, and that if you bothered to examine exactly what goes on at an execution, and to distance yourself from your emotional response to the victims, then you would become an abolitionist. (These arguments are set forth in the abolitionist book *Who Owns Death? Capital Punishment, the American Con-science, and the End of Executions* (2000) by Robert Jay Lifton and Greg Mitchell.) Retentionists answer that even botched executions are no argument against the death penalty as such, only against incompetence; that most retentionists don't *like* the thought of putting people to death and regard capital punishment as a nec-essary evil; and relating to the suffering of the victims is extremely relevant to the entire issue of punishment. You'll remember the argument from Berns, Strawson, and Whiteley in Chapter 7 that if we are incapable of feeling some form of morally righteous indignation and anger on behalf of the victim—and all the more so on behalf of a murder victim—then we have in effect lost respect and empathy for other human beings.

7. Cost Across the board, abolitionists and retentionists agree with the stark numbers: It costs more to put a criminal to death than it does to keep him or her alive in prison without the possibility of parole. These are some statistics from the Death Penalty Information Center: In California, having the death penalty costs

$114 million per year more than keeping convicts in prison for life. Each of the state's executions has cost the taxpayers more than $250 million. A Duke University study showed that North Carolina taxpayers pay $2.16 million for the death penalty over what life sentences would cost. In Florida, having the death penalty costs $51 million more, and the bill for each execution amounts to $24 million. Now, why would it be more expensive to execute someone than to keep him or her alive for perhaps forty years? Not because of the cost of a rope or bullets, obviously. That was way back when, in the Old West. It is the cost of the *appeals,* which can go on for fifteen years or more. Abolitionists hope to appeal to people's wallets and purses through this argument; retentionists reply that (1) justice should have no price tag and (2) the disparity in costs can be fixed easily enough by limiting the access to appeals. Abolitionists reply that without the appeals system, more innocents are sure to become the victims of a flawed legal system.

Another angle is the *emotional cost* of the death penalty: Abolitionists point out that with the many appeals, the families of victims will be expected to be present in court, reliving their tragedy again and again, whereas if a killer is sentenced to "life without," he or she disappears into the prison system, and the family will never have to face the killer again.

8. Lack of Closure Perhaps one of the emotionally most powerful arguments from the abolitionists is that the assumption that the victim's family will find closure after the execution of their loved one's murderer simply isn't true. Closure is a myth, they say. The majority of murder victims' relatives who witness the execution of the murderer say that nothing "feels better" after the execution, and it doesn't bring back the murder victim. Retentionists argue that to some bereaved family members, the only thing that can bring about some measure of justice and peace of mind is the knowledge that the murderer is no longer breathing the air that he or she deprived the victim of.

Retentionist Arguments

Just because the list of retentionist arguments is shorter than the list of abolitionist arguments, you shouldn't jump to the conclusion that retentionists don't have powerful arguments on their side. It is not a numbers contest. Remember that for each abolitionist argument you have just read, the retentionist has a counterargument. But the strongest retentionist arguments can be concentrated within three major areas:

1. A Matter of Justice Only capital punishment can fit the severity of the crime of murder, and a person who murders has forfeited his or her own right to life. In other words, the issue for many retentionists is *justice,* and the only adequate justice they see for a capital crime is one of retribution. The murderer deserves to die; the victim's family deserves closure; and society deserves to have the books balanced: Commit a crime, and you will pay for it in proportion to the crime. Abolitionists reply that the whole issue of proportionality ("an eye for an eye") has been distorted by retentionists. Only in murder cases do they invoke the principle—does anyone ever talk about "an eye for an eye" when the issue is burglary? Does the court go in and take something from the home of the thief as punishment? Or how about carjacking, embezzlement, or prostitution? How do you punish someone proportionately to that?

2. Elimination of the Murderer The only way to protect the public effectively from future killings is to eliminate the murderer (the argument of *incapacitation*). An abolitionist may argue that keeping a murderer in prison for life without the possibility of parole is just as effective, but the retentionist will answer that the prison has not yet been built that is 100 percent escape-proof. Even science fiction contains escape scenarios from asteroid penal colonies! And even if prisons were escape-proof, we may still have gubernatorial decisions pardoning murderers. A serial killer of children may appear to be completely rehabilitated in prison and given a pardon, but recidivism in these cases is very high. Here an abolitionist may point to the slippery slope, implying that perhaps any criminal who can't be rehabilitated should be executed regardless of his or her crime. Or perhaps we should even try to anticipate what criminal tendencies a first-time offender has and execute him or her on the basis of what he or she will probably do later on! But though some retentionists would welcome a broadening of capital punishment to cover rapes and child molestation, no serious philosophers of law argue that a person should be punishable for something he or she has not done yet, and most retentionists reserve capital punishment for murders with special circumstances.

3. General and Specific Deterrence Some retentionists argue that a conviction followed by execution is a deterrent (whereas almost everyone agrees that the longer the time lag between conviction and execution, the less deterrent effect the execution has). It will certainly be a specific deterrent for that criminal, because he or she is not going to commit murder again! In the general sense of the word, others will be deterred by the threat of sure and swift punishment. Some retentionists cite swift justice as a formidable deterrent in countries where civil liberties are not on the main political agenda: If you know you will have your hand amputated if you steal, are you really going to take the chance? But other retentionists claim that the loss of civil liberties and rights is too high a price to pay for safe streets. The effectiveness of general deterrence is undecided statistically: Some statistics show some deterrence factor after an execution; other statistics actually portray the crime rate as going up after executions. (Deterrence seems to be a fact in noncapital crimes. However, it is hotly debated whether the "three strikes and you're out" law in California and similar laws in other states have had any deterrent effect.) Abolitionists sometimes point out that if a person has killed once and knows that he or she is likely to get caught, convicted, and executed, then what is to deter the murderer from killing again, perhaps witnesses? They can suffer the penalty only once. And retentionists answer back by saying that a murderer in prison for life might well (and often does) go on murdering in prison, knowing that there can be no stricter penalty than the one he or she is already suffering, so the only way to prevent further killings is to retain and use the death penalty.

The five reasons for punishment discussed in Chapter 7 all have a role in the death penalty debate. As we just saw, *deterrence* can be used as a retentionist argument. The effect is usually assumed to be that others are deterred from committing the same crime; the intention is less to deter the criminal from doing it again (specific deterrence). (See *The Wizard of Id* on page 613, a spoof of a retentionist utilitarian argument: The wrong man may be executed, but the real killer learns a valuable lesson.) *Incapacitation* can likewise be a retentionist argument, but what about *rehabilitation*? Rehabilitation is not relevant here, for obviously an executed person doesn't learn not to commit the same crime again. *Retribution,* on the other hand, is highly relevant, for a retributivist will usually argue that the death penalty is the ultimate form of justice: It fits the crime, provided that society can be certain it has caught and convicted the guilty person. *Vengeance,* the supposedly nonlegitimate reason for punishment, is generally the most prevailing retentionist view among laypeople, who often argue that a murderer ought to die because he or she ought to suffer the way the victim suffered and that the suffering of the murderer will make society feel better. An abolitionist will generally argue that a life term can be as effective a deterrent as death, that a life term also incapacitates a murderer, and that there is always a chance that a murderer can be rehabilitated. Few retributivists are abolitionists, but it is possible to argue that a life term is the proportionate punishment for a murder, so we can have proportionality and still have respect for life, even the life of a murderer; vengeance is never an option for an abolitionist, who generally sees the death penalty as an expression of primitive social revenge.

It has been customary among scholars to view this insistence on how we *feel* as a primitive trait, but before we reject all references to emotions in the death penalty debate outright, we should remember that several philosophers have recently argued that emotions are not altogether irrelevant in our moral decision process. Martha Nussbaum (Chapter 1) argues that emotions can have their own logic; Richard Taylor (Chapter 11) says that the fundamental morality of compassion comes from the heart, not the brain; Walter Berns and Diane Whiteley (Chapter 7) agree that a society that punishes without feeling anger toward the criminal doesn't care for its victims; neuroscientists point out that it is *natural* for us to consult our emotions when making moral decisions. And while Prinz (Chapter 11) warns against empathy, he suggests using anger and guilt when making moral decisions. No thinkers today argue that punishment should take place along exclusively emotional lines, because in that case we'd probably quickly see the punishment exceed the severity of the crime, but maybe justice should not be completely separated from emotions either. Should we be seeking a Golden Mean between impartial justice that punishes according to a set scale with neither rage nor compassion and a system of justice that allows a measure of emotion to enter into the picture, as an outlet for society's righteous anger against an identified and justly convicted perpetrator, as well as an opening for mercy when an unusual set of circumstances warrants it? Or is that a dangerous step toward legitimatizing revenge? In the Narratives section, you'll find two stories dealing with the death penalty; one is Larry Niven's science fiction short story "The Jigsaw Man," and the other is the 2003 film *The Life of David Gale.*

The DNA Issue

Recently, a number of people serving life sentences or waiting on death row have been exonerated and released as the result of DNA testing. According to the Innocence Project website, 337 convicted prisoners have been exonerated through DNA testing since 1989; 20 of those were on death row. These reversals have prompted both retentionists and abolitionists to question the procedures that convicted these people in the first place. But a retentionist will state that such cases still don't provide a compelling argument against the death penalty as such, only against the way it has been administered, and retentionists as well as abolitionists are generally in favor of introducing mandatory DNA testing of suspects in a wide array of criminal cases so the risk of convicting an innocent person can be minimized.

However, not all crime scenes contain DNA from the perpetrator; only if the criminal leaves blood, saliva, hair with follicles, body tissue, or semen at the crime scene can DNA be used to rule out other suspects and point to one suspect in particular. And it is equally important to realize that DNA is not the only important evidence that can convict a criminal. Eyewitnesses *can* be reliable and, contrary to the popular conception, circumstantial evidence can sometimes be extremely strong.

When Gary Ridgway was apprehended in December 2001 in Seattle and charged with the Green River serial killings of the early 1980s, most people who had followed the case were astonished that an arrest had actually been made. The case had dragged on so long, with several suspects but not enough evidence, that only a few dedicated police detectives were still on the case. But those clear-thinking officers had collected a saliva sample from one of the suspects years earlier on the off chance that science at some time in the future could do something with it, and in the late 1990s, the DNA technology was available. When the Washington State lab got around to testing the sample in 2001, the perseverance of the detectives paid off: There was a DNA match between semen found on three Green River victims and the saliva sample. Confronted with an overwhelming amount of evidence and a possible death sentence, Ridgway confessed to 48 murders after a long series of chilling interviews with the police, in which he talked, in extremely callous terms, about the individual victims and their deaths. The confession was part of a plea bargain, and thus Ridgway exchanged a trial and a near-certain death sentence for life imprisonment without the possibility of parole. It seems that with the new, faster DNA tests, there is no legal or moral downside: Innocent people are being set free, and killers are being matched up with their victims even decades after their murders. In addition, it isn't just the criminal's DNA left at the crime scene that can help convict him or her—the victim's DNA speaks loudly too. If the victim's blood, for example, has been found in the suspect's home or on his or her clothes, it provides important evidence.

If the American criminal justice system in the future *can* eliminate most of the doubt as to someone's guilt or innocence through DNA analysis, would that also eliminate the abolitionist argument that the death penalty sometimes kills innocents? In cases where no DNA evidence exists, there would still be a danger of an innocent person being executed. And it is the principle of the state taking a life that the abolitionist is protesting more than anything. But for reluctant retentionists, the increased certainty of guilt might pave the way for a *greater* confidence in the justification of capital punishment. Proposals of mandatory DNA tests for all criminals and even a DNA profile for all children born in the United States might go a long way toward helping to solve crimes and avoid wrongful convictions.

Even with these new scientific safeguards against convicting the wrong person, there is a growing unease in the United States about the very nature of the death penalty, at least at the legislative level. An editorial in the *New York Times* in January 2016 speculated that since executions are down all over the United States with the exception of a few states, and public opinion seems to be less in support of capital punishment than before, down from 80 percent in the 1990s to 60 percent, the end of the practical use of the death penalty and perhaps even capital punishment as an option may be in sight. However, California voters decided in 2016 to keep the death penalty as an option—but they also voted against expediting existing death penalties. Be that as it may, it is a moot question in California since the 2019 moratorium ordered by the CA governor.

The Ethics of Self-Improvement: Narrative Identity

The final sampling of applied ethics brings us full circle to Part 1 of this book: "The Story as a Tool of Ethics." As you read in those chapters, philosophers and scholars from other academic fields have lately been turning to stories and storytelling to add meat to the bones of their professional theories. But storytelling has perhaps had its most dramatic impact, psychologically as well as philosophically, in the area of *personal ethics,* and that is the concept of becoming the raconteur of one's own life. It has become clear to philosophers as well as psychologists that we humans are storytelling animals (an expression coined by the Scottish philosopher Alasdair MacIntyre). Therapists observe that patients with mental disorders, or simply in need of some structure to their chaotic lives, get a better grasp of their past, their present, and their future if they try to tell about their life in story-form, sometimes even in the third person. Neuroscientists such as Mike Gazzaniga realize that people strive to *make sense* of events, and thus look for *cause and effect* so they can predict future events of the same kind. And philosophers focus here on two areas: *ontology* (theory of being) and *ethics.* Ontologically, we understand ourselves as strung out between our beginning and our end, our birth and our death. As the French philosopher Paul Ricoeur (1913–2005) says, we don't remember our beginning, and we won't live to tell about our ending, but while we're living in the middle we look back and look ahead, and try to find a direction, so we insert the missing pieces from family stories, and our hopes and dreams. For Ricoeur, we have a *narrative identity,* a self that is the central figure in our own story. But even more important, we *ought to* work on our narrative identity, so storytelling becomes a normative, moral imperative for Ricoeur: We must learn to see our life as a story, to make ourselves better people, and to connect with others, who then become part of our story, as we become part of theirs. Thus, we become *accountable* to one another. In 2004, at the age of 91, Ricoeur received the Kluge Prize for his life's work in philosophy, and in his acceptance speech he said,

> . . . Change, which is an aspect of identity—that of ideas and things—reveals a dramatic aspect on the human level, which is that of a personal history entangled in the innumerable histories of our companions in existence. Personal identity is marked by a temporality that can be called constitutive. The person is his or her history. . . . In this vast panorama of capacities affirmed and exercised by the human agent, the main accent shifts from what seems at first a morally neutral pole to an explicitly moral pole, where the capable subject attests to himself as a responsible subject. . . . The "power to recount" occupies a pre-eminent place among the capacities inasmuch as events of every kind become discernable and intelligible only when recounted in stories; the age-old art of recounting stories, when applied to oneself, produces life narratives articulated in the works of historians. . . . We can then speak of a narrative identity: it is that of the plot of a narrative that remains unfinished and open to the possibility of being recounted differently, and also of being recounted by others.

A few examples: Have you ever been in a situation where someone you have just met asks you to talk about yourself? You may have found yourself answering, "Oh, there isn't much to tell," and then immediately felt that this was a poor answer—especially if you were trying to make a good impression. And perhaps later, when alone, you thought of all kinds of things to say about yourself. This is a common experience, and the good thing about it is that it serves as a wake-up call: That time around you were caught by surprise, but next time you will have a story to tell, because we all do. It is sometimes said that we could all write one good novel, the novel of our life—although the saying assumes a great deal about our ability as storytellers. Most of us aren't very good at telling our own story and must develop a talent for shaping it and adjusting it to our audiences. Talking about ourselves makes us realize that, as much as we may try to be completely accurate, it's not possible. We simply can't remember everything that has happened to us; we also realize that even if we could remember, it would not all be equally interesting. So, according to Ricoeur, *selectivity* is part of the secret of effective storytelling. And we select different things to tell depending on the audience. If you are telling your story to a new boyfriend or girlfriend, you will emphasize certain things in your life, but if you are describing yourself in front of a panel of strangers during a job interview, you will most definitely emphasize other things. And if you are updating your parents about recent events in your life, you will probably choose quite a different story to tell.

Another feature of telling one's own story is a result of being alive: The story is *incomplete*. We are always in the middle of it; we may be closer to the beginning than to the end or closer to the end than the beginning, but we never view our own story from the same point of view as that of an author telling a story—because our story is not finished yet. We don't know how it will end.

A third feature is that, contrary to what we might think, the telling of our own story is to a great extent *fictional,* put together with *poetic creativity.* We may try to remember to be objective, but telling a story generally involves not only a beginning, a middle, and an ending but also a movement from one situation to the next. We don't just say, "And then this happened, and then that happened"; we say, "And *because* this happened, *then* that happened." We assume causality—and since we rarely know all factors involved, we make use of interpretations and make assumptions. (And then, of course, we may be outright lying, but that is a different story!)

So if telling one's own story is such an unreliable enterprise, why bother? Because it is good for us; it helps us find out where we have been and where we are going. As you read in Chapter 2, storytelling is now part of many therapy sessions, and it involves not only listening to stories but also telling them, mostly about oneself. If we see our past as a story, we might be able to identify things to be proud of and things to improve upon. In other words, we may get a better grip on our identity. And when we realize that we are also part of other people's stories, and they are part of ours, then we begin to see ourselves as part of a much bigger story, that of our community and culture.

Searching for Meaning

The psychoanalyst Erik Erikson believed that if we are lucky enough to have become psychologically mature, we will have developed *ego integrity* (see Box 13.13), and we will stop asking useless questions such as "Why did I do that? Why didn't I do such and such?" We will learn to accept the events in our lives, those we are responsible for and those that just happened to us, as facts with which we must contend. Knowing individuals who have attained this peace of mind may help us along the way.

One challenge to our ego integrity occurs when something happens in our life that we didn't expect and that we find grossly unfair. A man works hard and saves his money so he can enjoy his later years, and then he dies six months after retiring. Parents give up everything they have so that their daughter can go to college, and she ends up on skid row because of drug abuse. A promising young football player is gunned down in gang-warfare crossfire, although he isn't a gang member.

Box 13.13 PERSONAL IDENTITY AS AN ETHICAL ISSUE

The question of *Who am I?* is something you may encounter in a philosophy class focusing on metaphysics, or theory of knowledge (epistemology), but you don't find it often within a discussion about ethics. The assumption is, presumably, that once we start worrying about how to behave with *others,* we're already fairly sure who *we* are. But that is, of course, not necessarily the case, and even if we are familiar with ourselves, there is more to the sense of self than just a descriptive level: We shouldn't forget the normative level. William Shakespeare says, in *Hamlet,*

> This above all: to thine own self be true,
> And it must follow, as night the day,
> Thou can'st not then be false to any man.

Here Shakespeare assumes that we're fairly familiar with who we are but that this awareness also carries a moral virtue, and a duty: to have integrity and be true to ourselves—the best in ourselves, that is. (Presumably it doesn't imply that once you know your weaknesses, you should cultivate them!) Understanding who we are *so that* we can become better persons is an idea that dates back to Socrates—he interpreted the inscription "Know Thyself" at the Apollo temple in Delphi as meaning just that: introspection with self-improvement as a result. Let us take a look at three examples:

(1) For the existentialists such as Sartre (see Chapter 10) the concept of *authenticity* captures the moral value of knowing oneself; it isn't merely a question of being comfortable with who you are, or even of constantly questioning yourself and your role in life; more important, you must be able to act out of a sense of integrity, and with absence of bad faith, in everything you do. (2) For American psychologists, the idea of knowing oneself has been labeled as having *ego integrity* ever since the influential German-born analyst Erik Erikson (1902–1994) coined the term. Erikson, who also identified and named the phenomenon *identity crisis,* saw ego integrity as having inner harmony and balance of the mind; you don't dwell on what might have been, or how others have done you wrong, but accept things you have no control over. (3) For the thinker who is interested in storytelling, such as the French philosopher Paul Ricoeur (1913–2005), the quest for personal identity becomes a quest *for self-comprehension through telling one's own story.* Finding one's narrative self doesn't mean that we remember everything and then put it into words, or that we tell everything exactly like it was, but that we find our *character arc* in the process of connecting the dots in our life—seeing a pattern in the events leading up to the present time. In all these cases we are talking about a normative approach to personal identity: First we must understand who we are, and then that understanding must make a difference in the rest of our lives. In that way the quest for personal identity becomes an ethical journey.

Is there a good way to deal with such calamities? One approach that has provided comfort to many people over the ages has been to view such an event as an act of God or of Fate: It had to happen, we don't know why, but to God it makes sense. Now, we see "through a glass darkly" (1 Corinthians 13:12) but later, in heaven, we will see why it happened. Another source of comfort for some is to view it as *karma:* It is the consequence of something you did earlier or in a previous life. In other words, it is your own fault, and it will do you no good to rage about it or blame someone else. The best you can do is to realize it and try to create good karma for next time around.

A popular modern Western way of approaching the problem is to assign guilt, or blame. We say the retiree brought on his death himself; he never exercised, and his cholesterol level was too high. The parents of the girl who became a drug addict must have done a terrible job of raising her. And the football player's parents should have moved to another neighborhood. Our accusations are sometimes justified, but they can also be unnecessarily cruel. Sometimes, common sense will tell us, people really can't be blamed for what happens to them or to those they love. But it is reassuring to bystanders to blame the victim—it's a way of believing that if they're careful to avoid the victim's mistakes, they'll escape disaster. Although it may be true in some cases that a person's conduct contributed to what happened to him or her, that is far from being a universal pattern. In any case, we have no right to infer *guilt* from *causality;* in other words, just because someone's conscious or unconscious conduct led to some problem, we can't automatically conclude that he or she is guilty of some *moral wrongdoing.* Such an attitude often reflects a double standard: If it happens to strangers, they must have done something "wrong"; if it happens to me or to one of my heroes, we are just unfortunate victims.

An enormously popular self-help book and CD with the enticing title *The Secret,* by Rhonda Byrne, claims that anything is within reach if you make an effort to visualize it. This idea is the latest version of the old concept that positive thinking can make good things happen, and there is surely something to that. It is better to take charge of your life than to leave the control to others. However, some caution is appropriate. What if people try to visualize good things, and nothing happens? or bad things happen? Is that just a sign that they aren't following the program—that they're somehow not putting enough effort into it? That is what we call the *fallacy of begging the question:* a circular definition. And does that mean that if bad things happen to people, they are somehow to blame for it because they didn't focus hard enough on good things happening? Then what happens to our compassion for people down on their luck—or our hope of receiving compassion from others when it is our turn at the bottom of the barrel? Those are disturbing questions about a popular phenomenon, showing that if we choose to view life's good things as being within our control, then (1) we're buying into magical thinking and (2) we display a certain heartlessness toward people who are truly the victims of circumstance.

An alternative way of dealing with life's crises is to see them in the light of *stories.* Humans—at least modern humans in the Western world—seem to have a need for history and their own lives to make sense; we need to understand *why* something happened. Even people in traditional cultures with little written history have the same concern about a life well spent. In such cultures, the models are usually the myths and legends of that culture: Do as the cultural hero did, and you will have lived well. In our pluralistic culture, the emphasis is much more on doing something *new*—blazing a trail, inventing something, writing a paper about an idea nobody has thought of before. We like our children to be different from their friends, to be individuals. Martha Nussbaum says that stories teach us to deal emotionally with the unexpected. Of course, the unexpected situation in our own life is not likely to be the same as the one in our favorite story—then it wouldn't be unexpected. But we can react to the unexpected in the same way our favorite characters do, and in that way we may be able to rise to the occasion. Persons from a traditional culture might find such efforts at being ready for the unexpected, as well as efforts at being different, incomprehensible, for what makes persons good in their culture is precisely that they do the *same* as their ancestors. The urge to act well, however, is the same for members of both modern and traditional cultures. To live an accomplished life, you must follow a pattern ("Do like the ancestors" or "Do something new"), and others will deem it a good thing if you succeed. *Havamal,* "The Word of the High One," the ancient Norse poem of rules for living, says, "Cattle die, kindred die, every man is mortal. But the good name never dies, of one who has done well." That doesn't just mean that good people will be remembered—but also means that *we pass judgment* on people according to how they handled themselves in life.

When things go our way, we don't ask about the meaning of life. We find that the whole development makes sense. The mythologist Joseph Campbell compares it to being at a fun party: You don't stop and ask yourself what you are doing there. But at a boring party you might ask yourself that question. Similarly, when things go wrong in someone's life, he or she may question the meaning of life—because somehow, life doesn't make sense anymore. An unexpected element interrupts our life's story, and we lose the thread—we experience an *identity crisis* (an expression introduced by Erikson). So how can stories help?

When we change direction in life, we change our future; we don't know what it may be, but we can assume that if we decide to have a child or switch majors or move to another city, our future will at least contain elements different from what it would have otherwise. But when we change direction in our life, we also change our past, because we now see it in a different light, *redescribing* and *reinterpreting* it. When our viewpoint shifts and we interpret our past in the light of the present, we rewrite our own story and sometimes even the story of our community and our culture. When I decide to major in pre-med instead of business because of my sister's illness, I rewrite my story from then on. If my uncle dies just after retiring, I rewrite his story, and it *does* become a moral lesson; I tell myself I will try not to do what he did or try to avoid what life did to him, or at least to make every day count. (In that way I rewrite my own story as well.) If I lose my money because of a financial crisis or bad investments, I may rewrite the story in a number of ways: I was victimized, but now I'm smarter; or I was too concerned with money, but now I'm smarter. (Of course, we are not always smarter, but it makes us feel better to think so.) At any rate, we rewrite our past so it will make sense to us in the present and give a new, meaningful direction to our future. It is when we feel incapable of finding a new story line in our life—when the change has been so dramatic that there seems to be no new purpose lurking among the rubble—that the identity crisis may be hard to shake. In that case, it takes courage to choose to view the world and human life the way the British philosopher Bertrand Russell described it—as a collection of atoms brought together at random, with no rhyme or reason other than the rules of science and biology. But even that is a story: It is a story of natural forces and how each human fits into the greater whole of biology—rather a romantic notion. In the face of meaninglessness, we also might choose, with certain existential philosophers, to say that life is its own meaning. In that case, the force and will of life in any shape or form become a story we can relate to when no other stories present themselves. We may, of course, choose to say that we just don't know. We would like to think that there is some story, some purpose, but we don't know what it is or whether there is one at all.

When we tell our own story and the story of our culture, it is most often an attempt to see the overall pattern, or impose one, to find some sense behind chaotic events. But we tell personal and cultural stories to try to improve ourselves and perhaps to make up for cultural errors or wrongdoing of the past, essentially on a quest for meaning, whether it may be based on a conservative or a liberal vision. This level of storytelling doesn't just *describe* the situation but also *prescribes* what we ought to be doing next. That is Paul Ricoeur's point in suggesting we work on a narrative identity. This *normative* element contains what may be the deepest moral dimension of the so-called true stories of oneself and one's culture: looking forward to the future, trying to shape it into an ideal image, and reshaping the past so that it appears to lead toward the ideal. (Fictional stories that warn against an unwanted future are part of this moral effort.) Do we have any guarantees that such stories, told to make the future better, actually match reality at all? (One of the characters in the HBO television series *True Detective,* Season 1, expresses a radical viewpoint about that, and you can read about it in the Narratives section.) An actress says she has had a drug problem, but now she is clean and wants to teach others about the dangers of drugs. A schoolteacher tells his class that their culture has elements of discrimination and persecution in its past but that this will never happen again if they will all work together. A politician tells of the hardships we have endured and of the great things we can accomplish if we stand together and vote for her. Or a couple get together again after having broken up and tell each other how they were both wrong and how this time it is going to be different. In some cases those projections are, of course, just wishful thinking, or they are expedient "spin." But well-told stories have a power all their own: *They can make the future happen.* So while we listen to, and create, great stories that can change our lives and our culture, we should remember to retain our critical sense and our sense of moral responsibility: Do our stories prescribe a future that we would actually want to happen?

Living in the Narrative Zone

We humans are temporal beings. We live in the present, but we are always reaching back to the past and forward to the future, in a constant state of tension between memory and anticipation. We live our own story, which has its own beginning and its own end, although we can't describe them. Furthermore, we live the stories of our culture; we identify with them or criticize them or rewrite them. We seek moral lessons in our own stories and in the stories of our culture. We also just like to hear stories, watch stories, and tell stories; and when we do, the time period we experience multiplies. We are still living our own life, but there is a new element: *narrative time,* a concept also introduced by Paul Ricoeur. Narrative time is the compressed time of a novel or a movie, the time it takes for the story to unfold. So although it may take us three days to read a book, its narrative time may span generations. Two hours at the movies, and we may have lived through years of narrative time, following the lives of the characters from youth to old age. In this way we share multiple experiences with fictional characters and expand our moral horizons, as Nussbaum suggested in Chapter 1.

There is a story, "Mantage," by the science fiction writer Richard Matheson, about a man who wanted his life to be the way things are in the movies, because he thought his life was extremely dull. His wish was granted, and this is what happened: He found that time had sped up, and before he knew it he had fallen in love, was married and had kids; now he found himself making money, living in style, and having love affairs, but when he looked at his watch, only an hour had passed. He found that he was living out his life in abbreviated chunks of time, the same as in a movie. After two hours he was old and dying, and the last thing he saw before his eyes was the letters DNE EHT—"The End" to the audience watching him. As the saying goes, when the gods want to punish us, they give us what we wish for.

Obviously that is not what the man truly wished for—he wanted a life with an exciting story line, not a life lived in the time it takes for a film audience to watch a movie. We readers and viewers are luckier, because we can have the best of both worlds. We can retain our own real-life time while we share in the accelerated, telescoped time of books and movies. When we open a book or sit down in a movie theater, we enter what we might call the *Narrative Zone,* where we can live other lives vicariously, acquire skills and experiences that we might never know of otherwise.

We may be emotionally cleansed by experiencing the strong feelings in a story, as Aristotle suggested. We may get an idea of what it feels like to be a member of the other gender or another race, of another time and place, or of another species entirely—and those experiences may help us decide how to live once we leave the Narrative Zone. Nothing else provokes our empathy as effectively as a good story: We weep and rejoice with our friends in the novel or in the movie, even if we know that it is only make-believe. They are not wasted tears or smiles, for they are, ultimately, the building blocks of our character.

If we happen to read the story of the Good Samaritan, there is a chance that we will stop to help the victim should we happen to see a mugging in progress. There is also a chance that the "victim" will end up mugging us, but that doesn't mean we should not have read the story or that we should not have come to the victim's aid; it means that life doesn't always conform to the stories we read, and we shouldn't think it does.

So sometimes we get hurt when we are inspired by stories, and sometimes we are inspired by the wrong stories. The essayist and science fiction writer Ursula K. Le Guin (1929-2018) has compared our existence as readers and listeners to the hoop snake that bites its own tail: It hurts, but *now you can roll!* What is the moral? If the hoop snake doesn't make a hoop, it won't move, and it will be as though it never lived. So we must take chances—we mustn't shy away from taking part in the listening process, in becoming engaged in the story—and we mustn't shy away from becoming engaged in our own story. For Le Guin, telling stories and listening to stories was a kind of life affirmation and an incentive to live life to the fullest.

As a final comment, I'd like to make a full circle myself, figuratively speaking, and remind you of Nussbaum's words from *Love's Knowledge* in Chapter 1. Why do we need *stories* on this journey toward becoming more morally responsible persons? Because "we have never lived enough." Even if our life span stretches into the three digits, there will always be experiences we haven't had, places we haven't traveled to, and lives we haven't lived. Great authors, and filmmakers, help us broaden our horizon so we understand a little more about what it means to be a traveler on Planet Earth, and even beyond—and see other lives in a broader perspective. With the help of great storytellers, you may be able to understand what life must be like for someone born in another time period, on another continent, into the body of someone of another gender, race, or perhaps even species. And perhaps you will be able to tell your own story along the way.

A Final Word

I hope that you will make use of the theories we have explored throughout this book to embark on discussions of some of these other issues as well, since you now have the theoretical background to weigh in with more than how you *feel* about an issue. As we have seen numerous times in this book, feelings about moral issues need not be irrelevant, but feelings can't take the place of rational arguments—primarily because an appeal to feelings rarely solves conflicts, but an appeal to reason might. In addition, I hope you will approach the world of stories with an enhanced appreciation for issues raised in television shows, in movies, and in literature, be they stories about cloning and genetic engineering, media ethics and responsibilities, human relations involving compassion and gratitude, or perhaps courage in wartime and peacetime. In this book, we've used summaries and excerpts of such stories to illustrate and explore some intricate moral issues, and I hope you've felt inspired to seek out and experience the original stories in their entirety by yourself, because a summary or even an excerpt doesn't do a good story justice. My hope is that as the access to a moral theory has perhaps been made easier or more relevant by a movie or a novel, so, too, might a good background knowledge of moral theories enhance your enjoyment of a fictional story. I know it has for me. There are many issues out there, nationally and globally, and many stories about them. Enjoy the exploration!

Study Questions

1. Give an account of the most prominent pro-life and pro-choice arguments. In your view, which is the strongest argument on each side? Why?

2. If you were a journalist, how might you describe the proper balance between the public's right to know and the need for national security? Would it make a difference if you were not a journalist but a member of law enforcement? or a schoolteacher? or a military person?

3. Evaluate the concept of privacy in the context of social media: How much private information should a person be willing to put on Facebook, for instance, and how much control should a person retain over his or her information? Explain.

4. In your view, is the "Myth of Amoral Business" true? Why or why not?

5. In your view, can a war be just? Explain in detail, referring to the text.

6. Should animals have rights? If no, explain why not. If yes, explain whether your view is based on their ability to suffer, their ability to think, both, or neither.

7. What do you find to be the most powerful argument in the gun debate? What do you think is the most persuasive *logical* argument? What do you find to be the most compelling *emotional* argument? Should we favor one kind over another? Why or why not?

8. Do we have a moral responsibility to try to interfere with the expected climate changes? Explain why or why not. If your answer is yes, how would you propose we do that?

9. Which, in your view, is the strongest argument in favor of the death penalty? Which is the strongest argument against it? In your view, should we retain or abolish capital punishment? Explain.

10. Have you tried to tell your own story to a new friend? Did it make you think differently about yourself? Do you think there is any value to the idea that we can make ourselves better people by telling our own story?

Primary Readings and Narratives

The Primary Readings are many in this chapter, reflecting the many topics; they are not intended to reflect the complete debate but merely to be a collection of ideas that may whet your appetite for more. The first two short Readings come from the field of business ethics: "Critical Elements of an Organizational Ethical Culture" by Amber Levanon Seligson and Laurie Choi, a 2006 Ethics Resource Center report summary, and an excerpt from the U.S. Food and Drug Administration's presentation of the FSMA (FDA Food Safety Modernization Act) from 2011. On the animal rights issue, the Great Ape Project is represented by *The Declaration on Great Apes* and an excerpt from Marc Bekoff and Jessica Pierce's *Wild Justice* (2009). In addition, you'll find a text by Rachel Gandy discussing the 2015 status of the death penalty in the United States. The Narratives are the film *Spotlight,* about media ethics; the film *The Insider,* a true story about a man accusing the tobacco companies of misrepresenting their products, which also serves as an illustration of business ethics; the short story "The Jigsaw Man," about a utilitarian rationale for capital punishment; the film *The Life of David Gale,* about an abolitionist activist on death row for murder, and a focus on storytelling from the HBO television series *True Detective,* Season 1.

 Primary Reading

Critical Elements of an Organizational Ethical Culture

AMBER LEVANON SELIGSON AND LAURIE CHOI

Ethics Resource Center Report, 2006.

Executive Summary

In the 2005 National Business Ethics Survey® (NBES), the Ethics Resource Center (ERC) finds that a formal ethics and compliance program alone does not substantially impact outcomes. Additional analysis reveals that ethical culture often has more of an impact on achieving an effective ethics and compliance program than do program inputs and activities.

NBES measures eighteen dimensions of ethical culture by asking employees if their top and middle management, supervisors, and coworkers demonstrate various "Ethics Related Actions" (ERAs) in the workplace. ERC found that employees who perceive their managers, supervisors, and coworkers displaying ERAs are more likely to observe outcomes expected of an effective ethics and compliance program than those whose colleagues and managers exhibit fewer ERAs. This paper builds upon the NBES findings on ethical culture and explores which ERAs have a greater impact on program outcomes. In addition, this paper presents new analysis on whether ethics training is more useful for junior employees than for senior employees.

Key Findings

1. Three ERAs have an especially large impact on outcomes expected of an ethics and compliance program: Setting a good example; Keeping promises and commitments; and Supporting others in adhering to ethics standards.

2. Formal ethics training does not have the same impact on all levels of employees.

Key Conclusions

- Actions speak louder than words. Results regarding the three ERAs with the greatest impact on outcomes imply that having a general organization-wide ethics communication strategy is not enough to create desired outcomes. Employees need to see their superiors and peers demonstrate ethical behavior in the work they do and decisions they make every day.

- Training needs to be different for management versus non-management employees. Ethics training is more useful in helping junior employees feel prepared to handle situations that invite misconduct than it is for senior employees. This does not suggest eliminating all ethics training for top and mid-management employees. What it does suggest is developing training curricula that take these differences into account.

Study Questions

1. Why do you think setting a good example works better as a training tool in business ethics than learning about principles? How does virtue ethics play into this phenomenon?

2. Why do you think training needs to be different for management and non-management employees?

 Primary Reading

Background on the FDA Food Safety Modernization Act (FSMA)

FDA U.S. FOOD AND DRUG ADMINISTRATION

The FDA has been broadly criticized over the past decade for lack of oversight with the American food and drug supply, including the lack of oversight of pet foods. Former FDA deputy commissioner Scott Gottlieb commented in 2007 that (1) the numbers of inspectors were insufficient; (2) FDA simply lacks the cultural and linguistic expertise needed to monitor imports; (3) distributions of goods can happen very rapidly as soon as products cross our borders; and (4) FDA needs to improve its information sources about goods coming in, which requires more cooperation with foreign agents. (5) In addition there needs to be a focus on the risks of bioterrorism.

In 2011, President Obama signed the new FDA Food Safety Modernization Act which is intended to address some of those concerns. You see here an excerpt from the FDA website, http://www.fda.gov/NewsEvents/PublicHealthFocus/ucm239907.htm.

About 48 million people (1 in 6 Americans) get sick, 128,000 are hospitalized, and 3,000 die each year from foodborne diseases, according to recent data from the Centers for Disease Control and Prevention. This is a significant public health burden that is largely preventable.

The FDA Food Safety Modernization Act (FSMA), signed into law by President Obama on Jan. 4 [2011], enables FDA to better protect public health by strengthening the food safety system. It enables FDA to focus more on preventing food safety problems rather than relying primarily on reacting to problems after they occur. The law also provides FDA with new enforcement authorities designed to achieve higher rates of compliance with prevention- and risk-based food safety standards and to better respond to and contain problems when they do occur. The law also gives FDA important new tools to hold imported foods to the same standards as domestic foods and directs FDA to build an integrated national food safety system in partnership with state and local authorities.

Building a new food safety system based on prevention will take time, and FDA is creating a process for getting this work done. Congress has established specific implementation dates in the legislation. Some authorities will go into effect quickly, such as FDA's new authority to order companies to recall food, and others require FDA to prepare and issue regulations and guidance documents. The funding the Agency gets each year, which affects staffing and vital operations, will also affect how quickly FDA can put this legislation into effect. FDA is committed to implementing the requirements through an open process with opportunity for input from all stakeholders.

The following are among FDA's key new authorities and mandates. Specific implementation dates specified in the law are noted in parentheses:

Prevention

For the first time, FDA will have a legislative mandate to require comprehensive, science-based preventive controls across the food supply. This mandate includes:

- **Mandatory preventive controls for food facilities**: Food facilities are required to implement a written preventive controls plan. This involves: (1) evaluating the hazards that could affect food safety, (2) specifying what preventive steps, or controls, will be put in place to significantly minimize or prevent the hazards, (3) specifying how the facility will monitor these controls to ensure they are working, (4) maintaining routine records of the monitoring, and (5) specifying what actions the facility will take to correct problems that arise. *(Final rule due 18 months following enactment)*

- **Mandatory produce safety standards**: FDA must establish science-based, minimum standards for the safe production and harvesting of fruits and vegetables. Those standards must consider naturally occurring hazards, as well as those that may be introduced either unintentionally or intentionally, and must address soil amendments (materials added to the soil such as compost), hygiene, packaging, temperature controls, animals in the growing area and water. *(Final regulation due about 2 years following enactment)*

- **Authority to prevent intentional contamination**: FDA must issue regulations to protect against the intentional adulteration of food, including the establishment of science-based mitigation strategies to prepare and protect the food supply chain at specific vulnerable points. *(Final rule due 18 months following enactment)*

Inspection and Compliance

The FSMA recognizes that preventive control standards improve food safety only to the extent that producers and processors comply with them. Therefore, it will be necessary for FDA to provide oversight, ensure compliance with requirements and respond effectively when problems emerge. FSMA provides FDA with important new tools for inspection and compliance, including:

- **Mandated inspection frequency**: The FSMA establishes a mandated inspection frequency, based on risk, for food facilities and requires the frequency of inspection to increase immediately. All high-risk domestic facilities must be inspected within five years of enactment and no less than every three years thereafter. Within one year of enactment, the law directs FDA to inspect at least 600 foreign facilities and double those inspections every year for the next five years.

- **Records access**: FDA will have access to records, including industry food safety plans and the records firms will be required to keep documenting implementation of their plans.

- **Testing by accredited laboratories**: The FSMA requires certain food testing to be carried out by accredited laboratories and directs FDA to establish a program for laboratory accreditation to ensure that U.S. food testing laboratories meet high-quality standards. *(Establishment of accreditation program due 2 years after enactment)*

Response

The FSMA recognizes that FDA must have the tools to respond effectively when problems emerge despite preventive controls. New authorities include:

- **Mandatory recall**: The FSMA provides FDA with authority to issue a mandatory recall when a company fails to voluntarily recall unsafe food after being asked to by FDA.

- **Expanded administrative detention**: The FSMA provides FDA with a more flexible standard for administratively detaining products that are potentially in violation of the law (administrative detention is the procedure FDA uses to keep suspect food from being moved).

- **Suspension of registration**: FDA can suspend registration of a facility if it determines that the food poses a reasonable probability of serious adverse health consequences or death. A facility that is under suspension is prohibited from distributing food. *(Effective 6 months after enactment)*

- **Enhanced product tracing abilities**: FDA is directed to establish a system that will enhance its ability to track and trace both domestic and imported foods. In addition, FDA is directed to establish pilot projects to explore and evaluate methods to rapidly and effectively identify recipients of food to prevent or control a foodborne illness outbreak. *(Implementation of pilots due 9 months after enactment)*

- **Additional recordkeeping for high risk foods**: FDA is directed to issue proposed rulemaking to establish recordkeeping requirements for facilities that manufacture, process, pack, or hold foods that the Secretary designates as high-risk foods. *(Implementation due 2 years after enactment).*

Imports

The FSMA gives FDA unprecedented authority to better ensure that imported products meet U.S. standards and are safe for U.S. consumers. New authorities include:

- **Importer accountability**: For the first time, importers have an explicit responsibility to verify that their foreign suppliers have adequate preventive controls in place to ensure that the food they produce is safe. *(Final regulation and guidance due 1 year following enactment)*

- **Third party certification**: The FSMA establishes a program through which qualified third parties can certify that foreign food facilities comply with U.S. food safety standards. This certification may be used to facilitate the entry of imports. *(Establishment of a system for FDA to recognize accreditation bodies is due 2 years after enactment)*

- **Certification for high risk foods**: FDA has the authority to require that high-risk imported foods be accompanied by a credible third party certification or other assurance of compliance as a condition of entry into the U.S.

- **Voluntary qualified importer program**: FDA must establish a voluntary program for importers that provides for expedited review and entry of foods from participating importers. Eligibility is limited to, among other things, importers offering food from certified facilities. *(Implementation due 18 months after enactment)*
- **Authority to deny entry**: FDA can refuse entry into the U.S. of food from a foreign facility if FDA is denied access by the facility or the country in which the facility is located.

Study Questions

1. Has Scott Gottlieb's concerns been addressed? Why or why not?
2. Do you feel safer today about the American food and drug supply than if you thought of these matters in 2010, or in 2006 when the pet poisonings occurred?
3. Would you wish to add anything to the list in light of global events having happened since 2011?

 Primary Reading

The Declaration on Great Apes

GREAT APE PROJECT

1993.

The Declaration on Great Apes came out of the Great Ape Project commenced in 1993 by philosophers Peter Singer and Paola Cavalieri, as expressed in their book, *The Great Ape Project: Equality Beyond Humanity* (1994). Your author was herself an advance reader on the GAP FAQ website and had occasion to review and evaluate many of the moral problems arising from the declaration.

We demand the extension of the community of equals to include all great apes: human beings, chimpanzees, bonobos, gorillas and orangutans.

The community of equals is the moral community within which we accept certain basic moral principles or rights as governing our relations with each other and enforceable at law. Among these principles or rights are the following:

1. The Right to Life

The lives of members of the community of equals are to be protected. Members of the community of equals may not be killed except in very strictly defined circumstances, for example, self-defense.

2. The Protection of Individual Liberty

Members of the community of equals are not to be arbitrarily deprived of their liberty; if they should be imprisoned without due legal process, they have the right to immediate release. The detention of those who have not been convicted of any crime, or of those who are not criminally liable, should be allowed only where it can be shown to be for their own good, or necessary to protect the public from a member of the community who would clearly be a danger to others if at liberty. In such cases, members of the community of equals must have the right to appeal, either directly or, if they lack the relevant capacity, through an advocate, to a judicial tribunal.

3. The Prohibition of Torture

The deliberate infliction of severe pain on a member of the community of equals, either wantonly or for an alleged benefit to others, is regarded as torture, and is wrong. . . .

Study Questions

1. What are the implications of this declaration for apes as well as for humans? What will happen to apes in zoos? apes in medical research labs? apes in behavior research labs? apes used in movie productions?

2. Do you agree that apes should be granted legal personhood, at a time when not even all humans on the planet are treated like persons? Why or why not?

3. Some people see this as a positive first step toward protecting all animal life; others view it as a dangerous slippery slope. Where do you stand on this issue?

 Primary Reading

Animal Rights

WILD JUSTICE

MARC BEKOFF AND JESSICA PIERCE

Excerpt. 2009.

Marc Bekoff is Professor Emeritus of Ecology and Evolutionary Biology at the University of Colorado, with a special interest in animal behavior, including animal cognition and emotions. Jessica Pierce is a bioethicist with a special interest in animal welfare. She is a faculty affiliate with the Center for Bioethics and Humanities, University of Colorado, Denver.

In *Wild Justice*, Bekoff and Pierce argue that social animals display a sense of fairness on various situations, such as self-handicapping themselves in play with a smaller member of their species, displaying behavior of apologizing and forgiving, and even having "inequity aversion," when they discover that a distribution they expected to be fair was not fair at all. Bekoff and Pierce are arguing that not only do we have moral duties toward animals, but some animals even have the capacity to recognize fairness and act on it. And as we become better at understanding animal morality, we gain insight about human morality. (Below, Frans de Waal is mentioned. You may remember that you have met him before, in Chapter 4, as a proponent of the idea that animals have morals.)

Inequity Aversion: I'll Have What She's Having

An additional area of research sheds light on animals' sense of fairness and equity. Several primate studies have focused attention on "inequity aversion," a negative reaction arising when expectations about the fair distribution of rewards have been violated. There are thought to be two basic forms of inequity aversion: the first is an aversion to seeing another individual receive more than you do; the second is an aversion to receiving more yourself than another individual receives. Only the first type of inequity aversion—the "That's not fair, she got more than I did" variety—has been explored in animals.

Sarah Brosnan and Frans de Waal tested five female captive capuchin monkeys for inequity aversion. Capuchin monkeys are a highly social and cooperative species in which food sharing is common; the monkeys carefully monitor equity and fair treatment among peers. Social monitoring for equity is especially evident among females. Brosnan and de Waal note, "Females pay closer attention than males to the value of exchanged goods and services."

Brosnan first trained a group of capuchins to use small pieces of rock as tokens of exchange for food. Pairs of females were then asked to barter for treats. One monkey was asked to swap a piece of granite for a grape. A second monkey, who had just witnessed the rock-for-grape trade, was asked to swap a rock for a piece of cucumber, a much less desirable treat. The short-changed monkey would refuse to cooperate with the researchers and wouldn't eat the cucumber and often threw it back at the human. In a nutshell, the capuchins expected to be treated fairly. They seemed to measure and compare rewards in relation to those around them. A single monkey who traded a rock for a cucumber would be delighted with the outcome. It was only when others seemed to get something better that the cucumber suddenly became undesirable.

Skeptics have argued that these monkeys are not exhibiting a sense of equity, but rather a sense of greed and envy. And indeed they are. But greed and envy exist as counterparts to justice; unless you feel short-changed, why would you feel envious? And why would you feel short-changed unless you thought you deserved more?

Brosnan and de Waal speculate that monkeys, like humans, are guided by social emotions or "passions" that modulate an individual's response to "the efforts, gains, losses and attitudes of others." Passions such as gratitude and indignation have evolved to nurture long-term cooperation, and seem to exist in monkeys as well as in humans, and they may exist in other species.

Another study by Brosnan, de Waal, and Hillary Schiff suggests that chimpanzees also display a sense of inequity aversion. As with the capuchins, chimpanzees in a similar experimental setup showed negative reactions to inequity in reward. This study went a bit further than the capuchin study, and made initial forays into some fascinating nuances of fairness behavior. Although chimpanzees responded to discrepancies in level of reward, they seemed indifferent to discrepancies in level of effort. Like the capuchins, the chimpanzees did not seem bothered when they received a superior reward (they didn't show the second form of inequity aversion). Also, the strength of chimps' reactions to inequity varied according to social context, including group size and relatedness. In long-term and tightly knit social groups, the chimpanzees showed more tolerance for inequity. Perhaps this is because individuals keep track of who does what to whom and, as predicted by renowned evolutionary biologist Robert Trivers in his theory of reciprocal altruism, we would expect such patterns of social behavior to arise in long-lived groups in which individuals recognize one another over time. It's important that individuals remember who did what to whom and who should preferentially be repaid in the future.

These studies suggest that justice is situational. What's acceptable in one social context might be unacceptable in another. So, in order to learn more about justice in animals, we need to take into account the specific context in which behaviors are expressed, for example, the size of the group, the longevity of social relationships, and the stability of group membership, which is related to nonsocial environmental conditions. One shoe doesn't fit all.

Study Questions

1. What is the difference between the first and the second form of inequity aversion? Describe in detail. What does it mean for our understanding of animal cognition and emotion that chimpanzees have been shown to have the first kind, but not the second kind?

2. If animals can be shown to have a sense of morality, like the authors suggest, how would that be relevant for our treatment of animals?

3. In your view, do highly social pets (primarily dogs) show a sense of "animal morality"? Describe in detail.

 Primary Reading

Justice Breyer Argues the Death Penalty Isn't Just Cruel, It's Unusual Too

RACHEL GANDY

July 2, 2015. Prison Policy Initiative.

In the *Prison Policy Initiative*, Rachel Gandy, at the time a graduate student at University of Texas at Austin scheduled to graduate in 2016, as well as a volunteer for the Prison Policy Initiative, argues that Justice Breyer's argument against the death penalty shows that the "Cruel and Unusual" aboli-tionist argument, which generally is interpreted as "cruel beyond acceptance" can be taken literally, because the death penalty is, indeed, also becoming unusual.

> On Monday, the U.S. Supreme Court narrowly upheld the constitutionality of a drug used to carry out executions, but one of the dissenting judges raised a more fundamental question: Is the death penalty itself constitutional? In his dissent to the *Glossip v. Gross* decision, Justice Stephen Breyer fiercely argued that, by today's societal standards, capital punishment is both cruel and unusual.

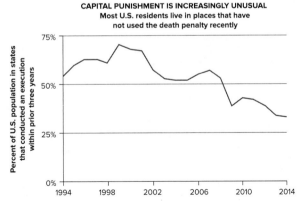

CAPITAL PUNISHMENT IS INCREASINGLY UNUSUAL
Most U.S. residents live in places that have
not used the death penalty recently

> The death penalty is on its way out. The portion of the country that lives in a state where the death penalty was recently used has been in consistent decline for 15 years. In 1999, 70% of the U.S. population lived in a state that used the death penalty within the last three years, but by 2014, only 33% of the U.S. population lived in such a state.

Gandy, Rachel, "Justice Breyer argues the death penalty isn't just cruel; it's unusual too" Prison Policy Initiative, July 2, 2015.

To prove the cruelty of capital punishment, Justice Breyer reviewed three key points. First, death sentences lack reliability because they are frequently (and erroneously) given to two types of people: those who are innocent and those whose convictions must be thrown out due to constitutional errors in their trials. Shockingly, courts and state governors are 130 times more likely to exonerate a defendant when a death sentence is imposed than when one is not. Second, capital punishments are arbitrary. Judge Breyer summarized the evidence showing that race, gender, and geography are often more influential than the severity of a crime in determining if people will be sentenced to death. Third, the long delays necessitated by due process both harm defendants and undermine any deterrent or retributive effects of the death sentence.

To me, the most intriguing part of Justice Breyer's dissent was his argument that capital punishment is unusual. He presented data to show that the death penalty has fallen out of favor nationwide. For example, the number of death sentences imposed and the number of executions conducted have sharply declined in the last 15 years. (See Appendices A and B in the dissent for the graphs that correspond with these facts.) Justice Breyer then makes a powerful point about how rare the death penalty has become by calculating the percent of U.S. residents who live in states that have recently conducted an execution. His findings are striking, so we used the data he provided to illustrate his argument with this graph:

To be sure, public opinion polls show consistent theoretical support for the death penalty, but the reality is that capital punishment is rarely used. Today, 19 states (and the District of Columbia) have formally abolished the death penalty, but the map below shows that a death sentence can hardly be considered "usual" punishment in the remaining 31 states.

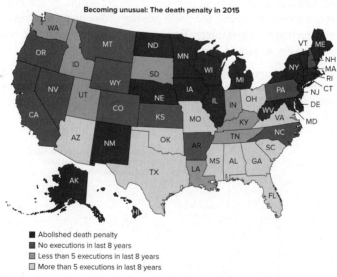

Becoming unusual: The death penalty in 2015

■ Abolished death penalty
■ No executions in last 8 years
■ Less than 5 executions in last 8 years
□ More than 5 executions in last 8 years

Gandy, Rachel, "Justice Breyer argues the death penalty isn't just cruel; it's unusual too" Prison Policy Initiative, July 2, 2015. Copyright © Prison Policy Initiative. All rights reserved. Used with permission.

In the 31 states that do not legally forbid the death penalty, more than a third have not actually conducted an execution since 2007. (Therefore, in total, 30 states have eliminated the death penalty either through legislative action or by common practice.) Another nine states have conducted fewer than five executions since 2007. That leaves only 11 states where the death penalty cannot be deemed "unusual."

That leaves 83% of the U.S. population living in places where the death penalty is unusual either by law or by practice.

Even in the 11 states where the death penalty isn't "unusual," three states conduct an overwhelming majority of the total executions. In 2014, 80% of all U.S. executions took place in Texas, Missouri, and Florida, where less than 17% of the U.S. population lived. That leaves 83% of the U.S. population living in places where the death penalty is unusual either by law or by practice.

The Supreme Court's decision shines a spotlight on a decades-old debate that tends to focus primarily on the cruelty of capital punishment. Justice Breyer, however, used his dissent to shift the conversation. He unequivocally showed that the Eighth Amendment's other requirement is being violated—the death penalty is increasingly unusual, and it's time to rethink its constitutionality.

Study Questions

1. What are Justice Breyer's three arguments against the death penalty?

2. Even if the death penalty is becoming unusual, is that a good argument for abolishing it? Why or why not?

3. Can you think of other legislative features that are becoming unusual, but are maintained, even so, because they are considered good to have in an extreme situation?

 Narrative

Media Ethics:
Spotlight

TOM MCCARTHY (DIRECTOR AND SCREENWRITER)

JOSH SINGER (SCREENWRITER)

Film, 2015. Summary.

There are many movies about unethical journalists, but here is one about journalists having done what generally has been considered *the right thing*. In 2003 the newspaper *The Boston Globe* won the Pulitzer Prize for Public Service. The prize was awarded for a series of articles by *the Globe's* "Spotlight" team of investigative journalists, revealing that some Catholic priests in Boston and elsewhere in the United States had been abusing children for years, and the crimes had been covered up by the church by moving the priests to other dioceses. The movie *Spotlight*, which itself earned the 2016 Oscar for Best Picture as well as for Best Original Screenplay, is thus based on a true story. The summary here contains the plot line including the ending, because it is important to the story, so it is a "spoiler" summary.

The story starts in early 2001; the editor of the "Spotlight" team, Walter (Robby) Robinson, meets with his new boss, the new editor of *The Globe*, Marty Baron. Baron is from Florida, not Boston, and knows nothing of Boston culture, not even baseball (i.e., the Red Sox, the usual conversation topic around town). At their very first meeting, Baron brings up a story about a Boston lawyer, Mitch Garabedian, who claims that a local priest, John Goeghan, has molested 80 children, and he would like Spotlight to investigate the case. This investigation would involve looking into a possible involvement by Cardinal Law, the archbishop of Boston. Robby Robinson is not enthusiastic, because he doesn't think the story has "legs," and it is a very sensitive area: *The Globe* has many Catholic readers; besides, Spotlight is committed to other stories, and each story takes months to investigate. And Robby finds that Baron doesn't quite yet understand the style of Spotlight. But Baron perseveres, and another Spotlight member, Mike Resendez, tries to get an interview with the lawyer, who represents the abused children. He is suspicious and stand-offish, but gradually Mike gets him to open up—partly because they, as members of immigrant families, are somewhat on the outside of the traditional Boston family cliques. Otherwise, says Garabedian, nothing will get done—it has to come from outsiders like Baron. Mike gets an interview with one of the victims, Phil Saviano, now an adult and head of SNAP (Survivors' Network of those Abused by Priests), and hears from Saviano about the priest's grooming of children, and the devastating experience and consequences of sexual abuse: it isn't just physical abuse, says Saviano—it is spiritual abuse as well, often leading to suicide.

During their research, the Spotlight team finds four more Boston priests having been inexplicably moved to other parts of the state or the country after child abuse cases, or rumors. Marty Baron himself gets an interview with Cardinal Law who answers all questions indirectly, and gives Baron a gift, a fine edition of a Catechism—which has a double meaning, because Baron is Jewish.

Pictorial Press Ltd/Alamy Stock Photo

The Spotlight team at the *Boston Globe* discusses the sensitive issue of going public with the story of child-molesting priests and subsequent cover-ups. From left: Sacha Pfeiffer (Rachel McAdams), Mike Rezendes (Mark Ruffalo), Matt Carrol (Brian d'Arcy), Robby Robinson (Michael Keaton) and Ben Bradlee Jr. (John Slattery). (Courtesy of Kerry Hayes/Open Road Films)

Phil Saviano leads them to more priests involved in what the team now sees as a true and growing scandal, and a former priest who is attempting to rehabilitate pedophile priests has an estimate that the team finds hard to believe: that 6 percent of all priests are in fact, or have been, preying on children, both boys and girls. That would mean 90 priests in Boston alone. By researching old files the team does in fact come up with 87 names, and Sasha, one of the team members, does some research into individual priests; she finds out that there are stories behind the stories, such as one priest who was a rape victim himself. But now September 11, 2001 strikes, and all attention is redirected to the terrorist attacks on New York City and the Pentagon. The story is put on hold for six weeks. The team now gets access to public court records that had been spirited away by the Church, and they show that Law knew about Goeghan already in 1984. City leaders are leaning on *The Globe* to kill the story—and as it turns out, history seems to be repeating itself, because years before, in 1995, *The Globe* was made aware of the very same story by Phil Saviano, and chose to ignore it. But this time Robby pushes ahead, at the advice of Baron not to go for the priests themselves, but to go for the Church itself, the Archbishop, as the one who knew about the situation the cover-up. Finally, the team gets the green light from Baron to publish the story after New Year 2002. Robby succeeds in getting the lawyer for the church, Jim Sullivan, to corroborate the report of 70 priests. And why is Robby now so anxious to get the story out? Because he was part of the problem back in 1995. He was the one who rejected Saviano's story.

As the paper is being printed (in a classic Hollywood scene of newspaper reels running, and stacks of papers being distributed) we see some of the effects of the story: team member Sasha's Catholic grandmother is reading the story, and is very upset. And even on a Sunday the phones at *The Globe* start ringing, with calls from other victims who want to tell their story.

Study Questions

1. The introduction stated that the Spotlight journalists *did the right thing*. Do you agree? Why or why not? Evaluate it from a Kantian and a utilitarian point of view.

2. You probably remember the section on "Cynicism" in Chapter 4. Is this a story that will make you feel more cynical, or less? Or indifferent? Explain.

3. Why is it such a devastating story, for Catholics in particular, but also for anyone who cares about children and their safety, that such abuse could go on for so long without individual priests or the bishops covering for them being held accountable?

4. Are the child-molesting priests evil? What about the bishops who covered the crimes up? Refer to the discussion about evil in Chapter 1.

5. Is this on a par with stories about teachers, or clergy from other churches, abusing young students? Are there different levels of evil when it comes to child abuse?

  Narrative

Business Ethics: The Insider

ERIC ROTH AND MICHAEL MANN (SCREENWRITERS)

MICHAEL MANN (DIRECTOR)

Film, 1999. Based on "The Man Who Knew Too Much," a magazine article by Marie Brenner. Summary.

This film is based on the true story of one man making the decision to go public against the tobacco companies with his expert knowledge of the addictive nature of nicotine. In the context of Chapter 6, the plot illustrates the story of two men's sense of duty, regardless of the consequences, acting for the sake of a moral principle. In light of Chapter 7, you may want to apply theories of respect for persons, and negative and positive rights (the negative right of free speech, and the positive right of receiving truthful information). But, in the context of Chapter 8, you might also view it as the story of a person of integrity choosing to fight for what is right, even if the outcome may cost him everything—a story paralleling that of Socrates. In the context of this chapter, you can choose to view it as a story of business ethics as well as media responsibility: What is the bottom line for a television show doing investigative reporting—doing business or serving the public? Do tobacco companies have moral responsibilities to their customers?

One day in the mid-1990s, Jeffrey Wigand comes home from work early. His wife is horrified when she learns that he has been fired. They live in an expensive home and have lots of medical expenses: Their oldest daughter has asthma, and his wife can't work because someone has to look after the little girl in case she has an attack. Wigand was a corporate VP in charge of research and development at Brown & Williamson, the tobacco giant. He has a severance package, but the future looks grim. It is only as the story unfolds that we realize just how grim it is going to get. By coincidence, at the CBS studios in New York, the producer of *60 Minutes*, Lowell Bergman, is putting together a story about a tobacco study and calls Wigand. To his surprise Wigand won't talk to him—but he faxes him cryptic messages, indicating that he'd like to be able to talk but has a confidentiality agreement with his former company. Later, Brown & Williamson executives let Wigand know that since they suspect he has broken the agreement, they want him to sign a new, expanded one—and if he doesn't, he'll lose all benefits. Now Wigand is furious—at B&W for threatening his family and at Bergman, who he believes has leaked the story. Bergman flies down from New York to Wigand's home to persuade him that he, Bergman, can be trusted, and Wigand then tells him the story: At a congressional hearing on the tobacco industry and nicotine some years back, seven CEOs—the Seven Dwarfs, as Wigand calls them—from the tobacco industry testified that nicotine was not an addictive drug. But Wigand knows that to be false. So why was he working for the tobacco company? The pay was good, and there was good medical coverage, even if he perceived that integrity within the industry was a problem.

Mike Wallace, the investigative journalist for *60 Minutes* who early in the film has been introduced as a man of integrity himself, suggests a way for Wigand to be able to speak on his show: What if he were subpoenaed as a witness in a smoker's lawsuit in Mississippi? Then his statement would be on record, and in this way he could get around the confidentiality agreement. So Bergman links Wigand up with the lawyer for the plaintiffs in the Mississippi lawsuit. Meanwhile, the Wigands have had to move out of their beautiful home and into a more modest house. He begins a new career as a high school science teacher and forces himself to adjust to the situation, but his wife finds the transition hard. When they start to receive death threats, Wigand decides that it is time to go public.

He agrees to an interview with Wallace on *60 Minutes*. During the taping he reveals that the tobacco CEOs perjured themselves when they claimed nicotine isn't addictive: Cigarettes, he says, are "delivery devices for nicotine." In addition, he reveals that Brown & Williamson is enhancing nicotine chemically so it is absorbed more rapidly by the brain and that he was fired because he wouldn't keep quiet. Mike Wallace asks him if he wishes he hadn't blown the whistle. At times, Wigand says, but he'd do it again, because he thinks it was worth it. Now things start to happen quickly for Wigand, but in a way he hadn't imagined: Security guards are moving into his home because of the threats, and his wife is leaving him, taking their children with her. They keep the house, so he has to move into a hotel room. He testifies in the Mississippi lawsuit, specifically stating that nicotine is a drug, but his deposition is sealed, unavailable to the public. And the *60 Minutes* crew is in for a surprise: CBS executives lean on them to cut Wigand's interview, claiming the broadcasting company may be sued by the tobacco company for "tortious interference," a third party interfering in a contract situation, creating damages for the first party (the tobacco company).

Frank Connor/Touchstone/Kobal/Shutterstock

In this scene from *The Insider* (Touchstone, 1999), Jeffrey Wigand (Russell Crowe) is being interviewed by Mike Wallace for *60 Minutes*. When the actual interview between Wigand and Wallace aired in 1998, the impact was tremendous. Wigand told the inside story about nicotine that the tobacco companies didn't want us to know: that it is an addictive drug, and cigarettes are the delivery device for the drug.

Bergman is livid: Why should lawyers be able to determine the content of *60 Minutes,* a program of investigative journalism that has proved its integrity over and over again? Is the priority business or news? To Bergman's enormous disappointment, Wallace caves: In the twilight of his career, he has to consider his legacy, and sides with the corporate lawyers. And now the tobacco company embarks on a smear campaign against Wigand, digging up any old secret they can find, such as a dismissed shoplifting charge, so his word will be discredited. Jeffrey watches the cut, gutted interview air and becomes despondent. Both Bergman and Wigand have so much to lose: one his self-esteem and reputation for professional integrity, the other his family and perhaps his life. After a heated, then conciliatory, talk with Wigand, Bergman decides it is time for desperate measures: He leaks the story to the *New York Times.* When the story appears on the front page of the paper, Wallace changes his mind: He will air the original interview. The CBS executive tries to argue that this story will last only fifteen minutes and then people will forget it, but Wallace reminds him that it is fame that lasts only fifteen minutes—infamy lasts longer than that. So Jeffrey Wigand gets to tell his side of the story on national TV. After the airing, Lowell Bergman quits. What was broken doesn't get put back together again.

Study Questions

1. Apply George's analysis of the Myth of Amoral Business of this case: Does it apply to the tobacco companies? To CBS? Why or why not?

2. Apply the criteria of courage from Chapter 11 to the case of Wigand: Does he have physical courage? Moral courage? Explain.

3. Use Kant's second rule, that people should never be used merely as a means to an end, to evaluate Wigand and Bergman's actions.

4. If you were in Jeffrey Wigand's position, what do you think you would have done? Is Wigand doing his "nearest duty"? Is that important?

Narrative

The Death Penalty: The Jigsaw Man

LARRY NIVEN

Short story, 1967. Summary.

This science fiction story explores a topic that seemed far-fetched in 1967 to most readers, illegal trade in organs. But reality seems to be catching up: For years Chinese dissidents who had escaped to the West told stories about the Chinese organ trade, but it wasn't until 2000 that the rumors were corroborated: Chinese prisons tailor executions of death row inmates according to the organs needed. Kidneys are especially popular; Chinese recipients pay less for them than foreign customers do, and such customers have been traced worldwide, including transplant recipients in the United States. Stories in the West about people turning up with kidneys missing may be an "urban legend," but a five-year-old Russian boy was close to being sold for parts by his grandmother in 2000, for $90,000. Niven not only speculates about the future but also seems to express a viewpoint on capital punishment: Young Lew is in jail, awaiting his trial. He knows that the outcome will be a sentence of death. They have evidence enough to convict him, and many people are being convicted and executed these days. We are in the late part of the twenty-first century (in Larry Niven's "Known Space," a future history of Earth and the universe).

In jail, Lew is confronted with a grisly story: Two fellow inmates tell about their crime of organ-legging. Organs for transplant are in high demand among wealthy people, and high prices are paid for illegally acquired organs. How does one acquire organs illegally? One kidnaps healthy people, murders them, and sells their organs. One of Lew's cellmates is the bodysnatcher; the other is the doctor performing the organ extractions. They are both scheduled for execution.

Are there no legal organ transplants in this future society? Of course there are. By this time a method has been developed to keep organs fresh indefinitely, and worthy recipients are always waiting for life-saving organs, but there are more people needing organs than there are organs made available through accidents. As a result, an alternative method has been in use for almost a century (since the 1990s): On death row are people whose death, some say, doesn't do society any good, so they are made to "atone" for what evil they did in life by having their organs serve others when they die. Organ harvesting of condemned murderers is part of the system of punishment now, so Lew's two cellmates know what awaits them: an injection, instant freezing, death, and organ extraction. However, society needs more organs than the murderers on death row can supply. So, although kidnapping was already punishable by death in some states, now other crimes have joined the list.

Suddenly there is activity in the cell: The two cellmates are pressing themselves up against the bars and invite Lew to join them: They are about to commit suicide in a way that will make the organ banks reject them. The doctor has a hollowed-out space in his leg with a bomb implanted, and in a gruesome display of blood and gore the two inmates are blown to pieces—but so is the outside wall! Lew manages to squeeze out the hole in the wall, but he is very far off the ground, up close to the roof of the building. Driven by fear, he manages to swing himself upward toward the roof, and he lands on a pedwalk moving from the jail to the adjoining building. From there he jumps to a ledge and breaks through a window, into an office. While looking for something he can use to make himself less conspicuous—a change of clothes, shaving gear, anything—he notices what building he is in. A hospital. The hospital where criminals are executed and their organs removed. He has landed in the organ bank. Moving from room to room, he tries to find a way out, but he is being tracked, and beams of tranquilizer sounds are hitting him. Desperately he looks around and realizes that he is in the room of organ tanks. Refusing to die for what he considers nothing, he grabs a chair and starts smashing tanks, and he keeps smashing tanks until he blacks out.

Final scene: Lew is in court, hearing prosecutor and defense argue about his case; to his amazement, nobody mentions the organ tanks. They have plenty on him as it is; extra charges are considered only as a backup. Lew knows that he will lose his life, but at least he also knows that he has put up a fight. And now we learn what Lew is accused of, with plenty of ironclad evidence: "The state will prove that the said Warren Lewis Knowles did, in the space of two years, willfully drive through a total of six red traffic lights. During that same period the same Warren Lewis Knowles exceeded local speed limits no less than ten times, once by as much as fifteen miles per hour."

Study Questions

1. How does this story illustrate the type of argument called a "slippery slope"?

2. In your view, can the harvesting of organs from executed criminals be justified? If so, how? If not, why not?

3. Is this story a criticism of a forward-looking reason for punishment or a backward-looking one? Explain.

4. How would a utilitarian respond to this story? How would a deontologist respond? Explain in detail.

  Narrative

The Death Penalty: The Life of David Gale

CHARLES RANDOLPH (SCREENWRITER)

ALAN PARKER (DIRECTOR)

Film. 2003. Summary.

This film is viewed as a powerful argument against the death penalty—and yet, because of the surprise ending, it is not a one-dimensional abolitionist argument but, rather, an exploration of people's commitment to a cause. For that reason I am summarizing the entire story, including the ending—because the moral of this story lies in seeing the beginning in light of the end.

An investigative reporter at a magazine gets a dream assignment: an exclusive interview with a death row inmate, just days before his execution for murder. The prisoner, David Gale, has selected the young reporter because of her reputation: She has spent a week in jail because she would not give up her source for one of her stories. So Gale knows that the reporter, Bitsey Bloom, has tenacity and integrity. Gale himself has spent six years on death row in Huntsville, Texas, for the rape and murder of Constance Harraway. He has now exhausted his appeals and has only three days left before he will be put to death. He used to be a professor of philosophy at the University of Austin and—what's more significant—he used to be a high-profile death penalty abolitionist, a member of "Death Watch," who debated capital punishment on TV with the governor of Texas. And now, having kept silent for six years, he wants to tell his story. When Bitsey first sits down in front of David Gale, with guards monitoring the interview, he says to her that someone on death row is no longer a person, just a crime—and he wants to be remembered for his life, not just for his death. He has claimed innocence from the beginning, but we also sense that he has no hope that his life will be spared—he is resigned to die. And in three days of interviews we get his story in flashbacks, as he tells it (and as viewers, we should remember that since he tells the story, it is the version he wants us to believe is true).

First we see Gale as a philosophy professor, lecturing on the French twentieth-century psychoanalyst Lacan, summarizing one of Lacan's theories: that we can't have our fantasy and still want it—that our desires must remain unfulfilled for us to still want them—and so to be fully human is to live by ideals and ideas, not through wishes. And, "In the end, the only way we can measure the value of our lives is to value the lives of others." Only later do we, the viewers, realize that this is the blueprint for Gale's entire purpose in life.

RGR Collection/Alamy Stock Photo

In the film *The Life of David Gale,* David Gale (Kevin Spacey) is a philosophy professor who likes to challenge his students. He is a firm believer in the abolition of the death penalty and constructs a way to influence the debate significantly. Here, in the beginning of the film, he is lecturing on the philosophy of controversial French psychoanalyst Jacques Lacan. Study question 5 explores the Lacan angle of the film.

A pretty female student, Berlin, approaches him after class—she is failing the class and will do "anything" to pass. Gale whispers to her, suggestively, that he'll give her a very good grade if she will . . . study hard. That same evening, things take an ugly turn: David is at a party for students and professors. His young son is at home with a sitter, and his wife is in Spain, apparently with a lover. At the party, Berlin shows up, and Gale learns that she has been dropped because of failing grades—she puts up a brave front and makes it clear to Gale that since she is no longer a student, they are now free to have an affair. Gale is drunk, and they end up having rough sex in the bathroom. Next day he relates this folly to his good friend Constance Harraway, a fellow professor and Death Watch member—and the later murder victim. Constance is appalled that David would be so stupid, but she has more important things to focus on: The TV debate with the governor is coming up, David hasn't done his homework, and what they need is an example of an innocent man or woman who has in effect been executed—and they can't come up with evidence to that effect. She says that finding an innocent man on death row will only show that the system works—they need an *executed* innocent man to force a moratorium on capital punishment in Texas. During the debate Gale loses his cool and is caught by the governor because he can't come up with evidence that an innocent person has been executed in Texas. But the day is about to get much worse: Outside the studio David Gale is arrested for rape—Berlin has accused him of sexual assault. As David relates the story to Bitsey, we hear that the charges are eventually dropped, and Berlin sends him a postcard in which she writes how sorry she is for the whole thing. But even so, the consequences are devastating: He loses his job; his wife leaves him and takes his son along to Spain; he loses his house and starts drinking heavily. At some point, in a flashback, we see him reduced to being a drunk on a downtown street, ranting about the Greek philosophers he used to teach in his classes—Socrates was ugly, Plato was fat, and Aristotle was a prissy dresser! And yet, because of a chance he might get custody of his son, he cleans up his act, goes to AA meetings, and gets a blue-collar job—and he keeps on being an abolitionist. But eventually he is even kicked out of Death Watch—he is a liability. The final blow is when he learns that Constance is dying from leukemia.

Bitsey has become engaged in David's story in spite of herself—she prides herself on being objective. Two days earlier she believed that David was guilty and deserved death, but strange things start happening after she and an intern go to Constance's house, which has been turned into a ghoulish museum. A gothic girl shows them around, and Bitsey sees the layout of the kitchen and the chalk marks on the floor where the body was found. Later that night she finds a tape placed in her hotel room, with the actual death scene: Constance, naked on the floor, quietly dying, handcuffed, with duct tape over her mouth and a plastic bag tied around her neck—and according to court reports, with the key to the cuffs in her stomach, swallowed before her death. Bitsey is now convinced that Gale has been framed, to make abolitionists look crazy—but we also hear from the intern that Gale apparently could have received a life sentence had his lawyer not messed up. Even so, Gale stood by him and didn't request another lawyer.

The interview series with Gale continues. On the last day of Constance's life, she and David talk philosophically about death: She is not resigned to go, but she is so tired and frightened—and she regrets not having had more sex than she's had. In his own way David loves her, and they make love—which is why Constance had his semen in her when she was found. A close friend of Constance's and a fellow Death Watch abolitionist, Dusty (who wears a cowboy hat), has shown up from time to time, and he is also there now. And then there is a gap in Gale's story—he meanders around town, sleeps in his car, and is arrested, for the rape and murder of Constance.

What happened that night? Can Bitsey find out before Gale's execution the next day? She is determined to help, but he tells her that she is not there to save him but to save his son's memory of his father. And sometimes, maybe death is a gift . . .

Now Bitsey is on a mission. She goes back to Constance's house with the intern and puts herself in the spot of the victim, to perform an experiment—she cuffs herself and places a bag over her head. Sure enough, after a minute she begins to struggle; it is not a quiet agony. When she is freed, she has found the clue: Constance did it herself, David didn't kill her. But why make it look like a murder? Because Death Watch needs an *executed innocent* person to further their cause! And to Bitsey, Dusty is the only possible suspect. She and the intern lure Dusty away from his home and ransack his place—and find a videotape, addressed to Bitsey herself. This videotape has the whole death scene on it, with Dusty stepping into the frame after Constance's death—but Bitsey wasn't meant to see it until *after* David's execution.

Desperate, Bitsey tries to reach the prison before David's execution; does she make it in time? Outside the prison the crowd is howling, "ugly faces screaming for revenge," to quote a previous Reading. But David is executed right on schedule—Bitsey doesn't manage to save him. Devastated, she believes this to be the end, as we, the audience, do. But there is an epilogue: As the nation watches, Constance's death tape implications hit the news; it becomes clear that an innocent man has been executed—and the debate about a Texas moratorium on the death penalty has begun. As a commentator says, in death David Gale achieved what he worked for in life. But was this the death of a martyr? In the mail Bitsey receives yet another tape—the original, with the final scene. We see who steps up to the camcorder to shut it off, and that man is David Gale himself.

Study Questions

1. What does it mean for our understanding of the whole story that David himself removed the tape? Look for clues in the summary to the ending of the film.

2. Is David a hero, or is he a deceitful conspirator? Can one be both? Is there another possibility? Does the final scene of the tape undercut David's own intentions of sacrificing himself? And what do you think about Constance's decision to participate in her own death, to make a moral point?

3. Is this a film about the death penalty, about believing in a cause, about making one's life count, or perhaps a bit of all of those elements? In the end, is it an abolitionist film? Who, in effect, are we supposed to root for?

4. Would it be fair to say that David Gale believes in the idea that the end (ending capital punishment) justifies the means (faking a murder)? Does that make him a utilitarian?

5. The reference to the French psychoanalyst Jacques Lacan may have intrigued you. It is indeed not just a passing reference but adds a deeper meaning to the film, according to Rose Pacatte, the director of the Pauline Center for Media Studies. In an essay, "Sex, Lies, and Videotape: What Is the Value of a Human Life," she writes,

> If you are familiar with linguistic theory (not as boring as it sounds—honest!), then the script for *The Life of David Gale* takes on deeper levels of meaning and shows an intelligence that goes beyond ordinary entertainment. Why so? Because the reference to Lacan makes the film become an invitation to viewers to examine the structures of language, meanings and values that the powers in our nation, such as government, the news media and the Church, use to communicate. Whether we think that capital punishment "makes sense" or not, it behooves us to examine how we reached that conclusion. Thought and language are inextricably entwined with how we live within our culture. As Alan Parker [the director] hoped, his film offers us a "space" to examine and "deconstruct" the place of the human person in society, especially in relation to capital punishment, and just how "free" we really are.

Is Pacatte right? Is the film an invitation for us to reexamine our thoughts and language about who we are as persons? If you are familiar with Lacan, you may want to engage in a discussion about that.

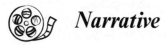 *Narrative*

Telling One's Own Story: True Detective Season 1

CARY JOJI FUKUNAGA (DIRECTOR)
NIC PIZZOLATTO (SERIES CREATOR AND SCREENWRITER)

HBO Television Series, 2014.

The HBO anthology television series *True Detective* broke with the mold of both regular TV series and mini-series, telling one story over eight episodes. The first season of the series won the Golden Globe Award for best Miniseries or Television Film, as well as several other awards. It has been generally recognized as one of the high points so far in the art of television storytelling. Of course we can't go over an eight-episode TV film in detail here, so after a brief introduction the focus will be on one theme that is developed over the season: Rust Cohle's changing view of what the story of one's life is all about. There will thus be a few inevitable spoilers in this summary.

The story has two time lines: One takes place from 1995 to the early years of the 2000s, and the other in 2012, and we see the early events in flashback. In 1995 Rust (Rustin) Cohle and Marty (Martin) Hart are two homicide detectives in Louisiana, investigating the gruesome and apparently ritual murder of a local prostitute. At the same time they're looking into the disappearance of a little girl. They realize, through their investigation, that other women have been murdered, and other children have disappeared. They do zero in on a possible perpetrator, but does that mean the case is solved?

In 2012 we meet the two detectives again, and neither of them is now associated with a police department. Marty Hart is a private investigator, and Rust Cohle is, judging from his appearance, homeless. They are both being interviewed by police detectives in their old district, and it appears that Marty is being *interviewed*, about Rust, while Rust is being *interrogated*, apparently because murder victims have been found that indicate that the ritual serial killings of 1995 have resumed. We learn that Rust has gone through a very bad time, losing his daughter in an auto accident, and having had psychiatric problems, being in an institution for a while. It is also clear that he and Marty are no longer friends, and haven't been for a long time. And in the 2012 time line we now follow Marty and Rust through an uneasy collaboration to the final conclusion of the serial killings and disappearances.

From the beginning, Rust and Marty are very different characters: Rust is a morose intellectual who prefers his own company, while Marty is an outgoing and easygoing (but definitely not unintelligent) character. Their last names are no coincidence: Cohle appears to be a cold personality, while Hart is friendly and emotional—on the surface of it. In episode 1, during a car trip after they have been working together for a few weeks, Marty asks Rust if he can tell a little about himself, and his thoughts, and Rust gives Marty more than he asked for, a monologue about the absurdity of life, and the unimportance of each individual—in other words, that we tell stories about ourselves to escape the fact that there is no meaning.

Rust: "I consider myself a realist, but in philosophical terms I'm what's called a pessimist. . . . I think human consciousness is a tragic misstep in evolution. We became too self-aware. Nature creating an aspect of nature separate from itself with a creature that should not exist by natural law. . . . We are things that labor under the illusion of having a self; these secretions of sensory experience and feeling with the total assurance that we are each somebody, when in fact everybody is nobody. The honorable thing to do is deny our programming and stop reproducing, walk hand in hand into extinction one last midnight, brothers and sisters opting out of a raw deal."

Marty: "So what's the point of getting up in the morning?"

Rust: "I tell myself I bear witness, but the answer is that it's obviously my programming, and I lack the constitution for suicide."

Photo 12/Alamy Stock Photo

In this scene from the HBO series *True Detective*, Season 1, Marty Hart (Woody Harrelson) and Rust Cohle (Matthew McConaughey), partners in the 1995 investigation of serial killings, are teaming up again in 2012 to finally solve the murders.

After Rust's chilling revelation of his inner thoughts, Marty suggests that the car becomes a "silent zone," because he can't stand Rust's attitude.

Later on, in episode 5, Rust develops his theory of the lack of meaning in life in a Nietzsche-style monologue, speculating that everything repeats itself endlessly. Everything is an eternal return of the same (see Chapter 10), all acts and feelings have happened before in the same way, and will happen again. We are doomed to an eternal recurrence, and all the stories we tell are only attempts to make us feel that we have a free will that can escape the pattern of repetition. (Rust shows no Nietzschean accept of the repetition here, however, just despair.)

But in the final episode Rust is a changed man. He has had an experience that has catapulted him from his nihilism about life to something completely different. He still has his old devil-may-care attitude, but we now see that it covers a depth of feelings that he has kept hidden (while, during the show, Marty has revealed himself to be a callous and insensitive man in his own personal relationships). Near death, Rust has found a deeper meaning: He has felt his daughter's presence, as well as his father's, the two people he has loved the most, and lost, and he has felt a profound sense of love surrounding him. Back from the brink of death, he now feels that he again is lost and alone, and the evil of the world and its never-ending crimes weigh on him. But Marty reminds him that when he was young in Alaska, Rust used to look up at the stars and makes stories about them, seeing connections. And Rust answers, "There is only one story. The Oldest. Light against the dark." Marty looks up at the stars and comments, in a moment of cynicism, that it seems to him that the dark has more territory. But Rust responds that darkness used to be everywhere, but it seems to him that *the light is winning*.

John Steinbeck (see Chapter 4) said something very similar in his novel *East of Eden: There is only one story, the story of good and evil.* And thus we have come full circle in the theme of good vs. evil, too, and of storytelling. The ultimate story told in *True Detective* is the one of good vs. evil, of light against the dark. Is this the story that underlies everything we tell each other and ourselves? And is the light winning? I'll let you be the judge of that.

Study Questions

1. How might Rust tell his own story in 1995, based on episode 1? And how might he tell it in 2012, based on episode 8? What is the new sense of meaning that he has arrived at? Has Rust "found religion," or has he found something else? What might Rust of 1995 say to that? How would you evaluate these two different version?

2. Go back to Chapter 10 and re-read the Nietzsche section. Is Rust at that point in time a Nietzschean? Why or why not?

3. If you have watched the eight episodes, you can fill in the missing information here: Why did Marty and Rust have a falling out, and what does it reveal about their personal ethics?

4. How should we tell our own story, in your view? Are there rules for what we should focus on?

Selected Bibliography

Works of Nonfiction

Ammitzbøll, Marianne. *Den skjulte skat.* Copenhagen: Olivia, 1995.

Aristotle. *Nichomachean Ethics.* In *Introduction to Aristotle,* edited by Richard McKeon, translated by W. D. Ross. New York: Random House, 1947.

————. *Poetics.* In *Introduction to Aristotle,* edited by Richard McKeon, translated by Ingram Bywater. New York: Random House, 1947.

Austin, Jonathan D. "U.N. Report: Women's Unequal Treatment Hurts Economies." *CNN.com,* September 20, 2000.

Badinter, Elisabeth. *The Unopposite Sex.* Translated by Barbara Wright. New York: Harper & Row, 1989.

Beauvoir, Simone de. *The Ethics of Ambiguity.* Translated by Bernard Frechtman. New York: Philosophical Library, 1948.

————. *The Second Sex.* Translation by Constance Borde and Sheila Malovany-Chevallier. New York: Knopf, 2009.

Bedau, Hugo A., ed. *Justice and Equality.* Englewood Cliffs, N.J.: Prentice-Hall, 1971.

Bekoff, Marc, and Pierce, Jessica, *Wild Justice: The Moral Lives of Animals.* Chicago: University of Chicago Press, 2009.

Belenky, Mary Field, et al. *Women's Ways of Knowing.* New York: Basic Books, 1986.

Belsey, Andrew, and Chadwick, Ruth. "Ethics as a Vehicle for Media Quality." In *The Media and Morality,* edited by Robert M. Baird, William E. Loges, and Stuart E. Rosenbaum. New York: Prometheus Books, 1999.

Benedict, Ruth. "Anthropology and the Abnormal." *Journal of General Psychology* 10 (1934).

Bentham, Jeremy. *Principles of Morals and Legislation.* In *The Utilitarians.* New York: Anchor Books, 1973.

————. *The Works of Jeremy Bentham,* vol. 2. Edited by John Bowring. Edinburgh, 1838–43.

Berger, Fred. "Gratitude." In *Vice and Virtue in Everyday Life,* edited by Christina Hoff Sommers and Fred Sommers. Fort Worth: Harcourt Brace Jovanovich, 1985.

Bernasconi, Robert, and Wood, David, eds. *The Provocation of Levinas.* New York: Routledge, 1988.

Berteaux, John. "Defining Racism in the 21st Century." *Monterey Herald,* January 17, 2005.

————. "Unheard, Unseen, Unchosen." *Monterey Herald,* March 6, 2006.

Bok, Sisela. *Strategy for Peace.* New York: Random House, 1989.

Billinghurst, Jane. *Grey Owl: The Many Faces of Archie Belaney.* Vancouver/Toronto 1999: GreyStone Books.

Bonevac, Daniel, ed. *Today's Moral Issues.* Mountain View, Calif.: Mayfield, 1992.

Bonevac, Daniel, et al., eds. *Beyond the Western Tradition.* Mountain View, Calif.: Mayfield, 1992.

Booth, Wayne C. *The Company We Keep.* Berkeley: University of California Press, 1988.

————. "Why Ethical Criticism Fell on Hard Times." In *Ethics: Symposium on Morality and Literature* 98, no. 2 (January 1988). Chicago: University of Chicago Press.

Boss, Judith A. *Ethics for Life.* Mountain View, Calif.: Mayfield, 1998.

"Boy Sentenced to Watch *Saving Private Ryan.*" Associated Press, August 20, 1998.

Brickhouse, Thomas B., and Smith, Nicholas D. *Socrates on Trial.* Princeton, N.J.: Princeton University Press, 1989.

The Cambridge Companion to John Stuart Mill. Edited by John Skorupski. New York: Cambridge University Press, 1998.

Carmody, Denise Lardner, and Carmody, John Tully. *How to Live Well: Ethics in the World Religions.* Belmont, Calif.: Wadsworth, 1988.

Chan, W., ed. *A Source Book in Chinese Philosophy.* Princeton, N.J.: Princeton University Press, 1963.

Chandler, Raymond. "The Simple Art of Murder." *Atlantic Monthly,* January 1945.

Cohen, Carl. "The Case for the Use of Animals in Biomedical Research." *New England Journal of Medicine* 315 (October 2, 1986).

Confucius. *The Analects.* New York: Dover, 1995.

Coren, Stanley. *The Intelligence of Dogs.* New York: Macmillan, 1994.

Dawkins, Richard. *The God Delusion.* New York: Houghton Mifflin, 2006.

———. *The Selfish Gene.* Oxford: Oxford University Press, 1976, 1989, 2006.

Dawkins, Richard. "In Defense of Selfish Genes." *Philosophy* Vol. 56, No. 218 (1981). Cambridge University Press.

De George, Richard T. *Business Ethics*. New York: Macmillan, 1990.

Donn, Jeff. "*Company Says It Cloned Human Embryo.*" Associated Press, November 25, 2001.

Douglas, John, and Olshaker, Mark. *Obsession.* New York: Scribner, 1998.

Dworkin, Andrea. *Right-Wing Women.* New York: Perigree, 1993.

Dworkin, Ronald. *Taking Rights Seriously.* Cambridge, Mass.: Harvard University Press, 1977.

———. "What Is a Good Life?" *The New York Review of Books,* February 10, 2011.

"Editor Sacked over Fake Photos." *The Globe and Mail.* May 15, 2004.

Ehrenburg, Ilya. "Bøger." In *Evige Tanker,* edited by Anker Kierkeby. Copenhagen: Westmans Forlag, 1951.

The Elder Edda. A selection translated from the Icelandic by Paul B. Taylor and W. H. Auden. London: Faber and Faber, 1973.

Encyclopedia of Ethics. Edited by Lawrence C. Becker and Charlotte B. Becker. New York: Garland, 1992.

English, Jane. "What Do Grown Children Owe Their Parents?" In *Having Children: Philosophical and Legal Reflections on Parenthood,* edited by Onora O'Neill and William Ruddick. New York: Oxford University Press, 1979.

Erikson, Erik. *Childhood and Society.* New York: Norton, 1964.

Ethics as First Philosophy: The Significance of Emmanuel Levinas. Edited by Adriaan T. Peperzak. New York: Routledge, 1995.

Ethics for Military Leaders I–II. Edited by Aine Donovan, Donald E. Johnson, George R. Lucas, Jr., Paul E. Rousch, and Nancy Sherman. American Heritage Christian Publishing, 1997.

Ethics, Literature, Theory. Edited by Stephen George. Lanham, Md.: Rowman & Littlefield, 2005.

Existentialism from Dostoyevsky to Sartre. Edited by Walter Kaufman. New York: Meridian Publishing Company, 1989.

Feinberg, Joel. "Psychological Egoism." In *Ethical Theory,* edited by Louis P. Pojman. Belmont, Calif.: Wadsworth, 1989.

———. "The Rights of Animals and Unborn Generations." In *Philosophy and Environmental Crisis,* edited by William T. Blackstone. Athens: University of Georgia Press, 1974.

Feinigstein, Alan. "Milgram's shock experiments and the Nazi perpetrators: A contrarian perspective on the role of obedience pressures during the Holocaust." *Theory & Psychology*, October 2015 vol. 25 no. 5.

Foot, Philippa. *Virtues and Vices.* Berkeley: University of California Press, 1978.

Freeman, Derek. *The Fateful Hoaxing of Margaret Mead.* Boulder, Colo.: Westview Press, 1999.

Friedman, Marilyn. "Feminism and Modern Friendship: Dislocating the Community." *Ethics* 99 (1989), University of Chicago Press.

Fuhrman, Mark. *Death and Justice: An Exposé of Oklahoma's Death Row Machine.* New York: HarperCollins, 2003.

———. *Murder in Spokane.* New York: HarperCollins, 2001.

Furrow, Dwight. *Reviving the Left: The Need to Restore Liberal Values in America.* Amherst, NY: Prometheus Books, 2009.

Game of Thrones and Philosophy. Edited by Henry Jacoby. Hoboken: Wiley, 2012.

Genovese, E. N. *Mythology: Texts and Contexts.* Redding, Calif.: C.A.T. Publishing, 1991.

George, Stephen. "The Ethical Dimensions of Richard Wright's *Native Son.*" In *Ethics, Literature, Theory,* edited by Stephen George. Lanham, Md.: Rowman & Littlefield, 2005.

Gilligan, Carol. *In a Different Voice.* Cambridge, Mass.: Harvard University Press, 1982.

Gleason, Kristin. *Anahareo: A Wilderness Spirit.* Tucson, AZ: Fireship Press.

Glenn, Linda MacDonald. "Ethical Issues in Genetic Engineering and Transgenics." June 2004. Retrieved January 13, 2005, from http://actionbioscience.org/biotech/glenn.html.

Gonzales, John Moreno. "Shacks, Tidy Yards and Tight-Lipped Neighbors Surround the Long-Time Home of a Suspect in the Killings of 3 Civil Rights Workers 40 Years Ago." *Newsday.com,* Jan. 10, 2005.

Graves, Robert. *The Greek Myths.* 2 vols. Penguin, 1960.

Grey Owl. *The Men of the Last Frontier* (1931). Dundurn, reprint edition. 2011.

Gross, Hyman. *A Theory of Criminal Justice.* New York: Oxford University Press, 1979.

Guillo, Karen. "*Study Finds No Death Penalty Bias.*" Associated Press, June 7, 2001.

Gyekye, Kwame. *An Essay on African Philosophical Thought: The Akan Conceptual Scheme.* New York: Cambridge University Press, 1987.

Habermas, Jürgen. *The Future of Human Nature.* Polity Press, 2003.

Hallie, Philip. "From Cruelty to Goodness." In *Vice and Virtue in Everyday Life,* edited by Christina Hoff Sommers and Fred Sommers. Fort Worth: Harcourt Brace Jovanovich, 1985, 1989.

———. *Tales of Good and Evil, Help and Harm.* New York: HarperCollins, 1997.

Harris, C. E., Jr. *Applying Moral Theories.* Belmont, Calif.: Wadsworth, 1986.

Hart, Richard E. "Steinbeck, Johnson, and the Master–Slave Relationship." In *Ethics, Literature, Theory,* edited by Stephen George. Lanham, Md.: Rowman & Littlefield, 2005.

Heidegger, Martin. *Being and Time.* Translated by John Macquarrie and Edward Robinson. New York: Harper & Row, 1962.

Herodotus. *The Histories.* Translated by Aubrey de Sélencourt. New York: Penguin Books, 1996.

Hertel, Hans. *Verdens litteraturs historie,* vols. 1–7. Copenhagen: Gyldendal, 1985–93.

Hinman, Lawrence. *Ethics, A Pluralistic Approach.* Austin: Harcourt Brace, 1993.

Hobbes, Thomas. *English Works.* Vol. 3. Edited by Sir W. Molesworth. London: J. Bohn, 1840.

Hohlenberg, Johannes. *Søren Kierkegaard.* Copenhagen: Aschehoug Dansk Forlag, 1963.

David Hume. *An Enquiry Concerning the Principles of Morals.* Oxford: Oxford Clarendon, 1957.

———. *An Enquiry Concerning the Principles of Morals.* In *Enquiries Concerning Human Understanding and Concerning the Principles of Morals,* 3rd ed., edited by L. A. Selby-Bigge, revised by P. H. Nidditch. Oxford: Clarendon, 1975.

Johnson, Charles. "The Education of Mingo," 1977. *The Sorcerer's Apprentice.* New York: Macmillan, 1986.

Kalin, Jesse. "In Defense of Egoism." In *Ethical Theory,* edited by Louis P. Pojman. Belmont, Calif.: Wadsworth, 1989.

Kant, Immanuel. *Grounding for the Metaphysics of Morals.* Translated by James W. Ellington. Indianapolis: Hackett, 1981.

———. *The Metaphysics of Morals.* Introduction, translation, and notes by Mary Gregor. Cambridge: Cambridge University Press, 1991.

———. "On the Distinction of the Beautiful and Sublime in the Interrelation of the Two Sexes." In *Philosophy of Woman,* edited by Mary Briody Mahowald. Indianapolis: Hackett, 1983.

Kaplan, Alice. "The Trouble with Memoir." *Chronicle of Higher Education,* December 5, 1997.

Kearney, Richard. *Dialogues with Contemporary Continental Thinkers: The Phenomenological Heritage.* Manchester: Manchester University Press, 1984.

Kellogg, Davida E. "Jus Post Bellum: The Importance of War Crimes Trials." *Parameters,* Autumn 2002.

Kemp, Peter. *Das Unersetzliche: Eine Technologie-Ethik.* Berlin: Wichen-Verlag, 1992.

———. "Etik og narrativitetens tre niveau'er." *Psyke & Logos,* Copenhagen, no. 1, vol. 17.

———. "Social Justice." In *The Good Society: Essays on the Welfare System at a Time of Change,* edited by Egon Clausen. Copenhagen: Ministry of Social Affairs, 1995.

Kemp, Peter, Lebech, Mette, and Rendtorff, Jacob. *Den bioetiske vending.* Copenhagen: Spektrum/Forum Publishers, 1997.

Kierkeby, Anker, ed. *Evige Tanker.* Copenhagen: Westmans Forlag, 1951.

Kierkegaard, Søren. *Enten-Eller. Anden Deel.* Copenhagen: H. Hagerup's Forlag, 1950.

———. *Johannes Climacus* (written 1842–43, first published 1912). Copenhagen: Gyldendal, 1967.

Kimmel, Michael. "A War Against Boys?" *Dissent Magazine,* Fall 2006.

Kittay, Eva Feder, and Meyers, Diana T., eds. *Women and Moral Theory.* Savage, Md.: Rowman & Littlefield, 1987.

Körner, Stephan. *Kant.* Harmondsworth, England: Penguin, 1955.

Kurtz, Stanley. "Free Speech and an Orthodoxy of Dissent." *Chronicle of Higher Education,* October 26, 2001.

Leake, Jonathan. "Scientists Teach Chimpanzee to Speak English." *The Sunday Times,* UK, July 25, 1999.

Le Guin, Ursula K. "It Was a Dark and Stormy Night." In *On Narrative,* edited by J. I. Mitchell. Chicago: University of Chicago Press, 1981.

Lehrer, Johan. "Hearts and Minds." *The Boston Globe,* April 29, 2007.

Leopold, Aldo. *A Sand County Almanac.* New York: Oxford University Press, 1987.

Lerner, Gerda. *The Creation of Feminist Consciousness.* New York: Oxford University Press, 1993.

———. *The Creation of Patriarchy.* New York: Oxford University Press, 1986.

Levin, Richard. *The Question of Socrates.* New York: Harcourt, Brace & World, 1961.

Levinas, Emmanuel. *Ethics and Infinity: Conversations with Philippe Nemo.* Pittsburgh: Duquesne University Press, 1985.

Lifton, Robert Jay, and Mitchell, Greg. *Who Owns Death? Capital Punishment, the American Conscience, and the End of Executions.* New York: Morrow, 2000.

Lin Yutang. *The Importance of Living.* London: Heinemann, 1937.

Lloyd, Genevieve. *The Man of Reason.* Minneapolis: University of Minnesota Press, 1984.

Locke, John. *Second Treatise on Government.* 1823. Works, 10 vols. London. Reprint, Germany: Scientia, Verlag Aalen, 1963.

MacIntyre, Alasdair. *After Virtue.* Notre Dame, Ind.: University of Notre Dame Press, 1981, 1984.

Mackie, J. L. *Ethics: Inventing Right and Wrong.* New York: Penguin, 1977.

Mahowald, Mary Briody, ed. *Philosophy of Woman.* Indianapolis: Hackett, 1983.

Malinowski, Bronislaw. "Myth in Primitive Psychology." In *Magic, Science, and Religion.* Garden City, N.Y.: Doubleday Anchor, 1954.

Maltin, Leonard. *Leonard Maltin's TV Movies and Video Guide.* New York: Signet, 1996, 2012.

Mappes, Thomas A., and Zembaty, Jane S., eds. *Social Ethics.* 4th ed. New York: McGraw-Hill, 1992.

Mayo, Bernard. "Virtue or Duty?" In *Vice and Virtue in Everyday Life,* edited by Christina Hoff Sommers and Fred Sommers. Fort Worth: Harcourt Brace Jovanovich, 1985, 1989.

McCormick, Patrick T. "Adult Punishment Doesn't Fit the Underage Criminal." *Spokesman-Review,* September 4, 2001.

McLemee, Scott. "What Makes Martha Nussbaum Run?" *Chronicle of Higher Education,* October 5, 2001.

Medlin, Brian. "Ultimate Principles and Ethical Thought." In *Ethical Theory,* edited by Louis P. Pojman. Belmont, Calif.: Wadsworth, 1989.

Mencius. Translated by D. C. Lau. Harmondsworth, England: Penguin, 1970.

Mill, Harriet Taylor. "Enfranchisement of Women." In *Philosophy of Woman,* 3rd ed., edited by Mary Mahowald. Indianapolis: Hackett, 1994.

Mill, John Stuart. *Autobiography.* New York: Columbia University Press, 1924.

———. *On Liberty.* In *The Utilitarians.* New York: Anchor Books, 1973.

———. *The Subjection of Women.* Cambridge, Mass.: MIT Press, 1970.

———. *Utilitarianism.* In *The Utilitarians.* New York: Anchor Books, 1973.

Mitchell, J. I., ed. *On Narrative.* Chicago: University of Chicago Press, 1981.

"Moderates, Liberals Hear Call to Morality Debate." *Los Angeles Times,* November 10, 2004.

Moral Philosophy of John Steinbeck. Edited by Stephen George. Lanham, Md.: Scarecrow Press, 2005.

Morality in Criminal Justice. Edited by Daryl Close and Nicholas Meier. Belmont, Calif.: Wadsworth, 1995.

Morlin, Bill, and White, Jeanette. *Bad Trick: The Hunt for Spokane's Serial Killer.* Spokane, Wash.: New Media Ventures, 2001.

Mulhauser, Dana. "National Group Rallies Students Who Question Campus Feminism." *Chronicle of Higher Education,* October 5, 2001.

Nathanson, Stephen. *An Eye for an Eye? The Morality of Punishing by Death.* Savage, Md.: Rowman & Littlefield, 1987.

———. "In Defense of 'Moderate Patriotism,'" *Ethics,* vol. 99 (April 1989).

Nestle, Marion, and Nesheim, Malden. "Who Knew? Melamine, the Not-So-Secret Ingredient." *BARK: The Modern Dog Culture Magazine,* April 2008.

"News Media's Credibility Crumbling." *Insight Magazine/World Net Daily,* May 8, 2004.

Nietzsche, Friedrich. *Beyond Good and Evil.* Translated by Helen Zimmern. Riverside, N.J.: Macmillan, 1911.

———. *On the Genealogy of Morals.* Translated by Walter Kaufmann and R. J. Hollingdale. New York: Random House, 1969.

Nozick, Robert. *Anarchy, State and Utopia.* Basic Books, 1974.

Nussbaum, Martha. *Hiding from Humanity: Disgust, Shame, and the Law.* Princeton: Princeton University Press, 2004.

———. *Love's Knowledge.* New York: Oxford University Press, 1990.

"N.Y. Times Uncovers Dozens of Faked Stories by Reporter." *Washington Post,* May 11, 2003.

O'Brian, William. *The Conduct of Just and Unjust War.* Westport, Conn.: Praeger Publishers, 1981.

Oden, Thomas C., ed. *Parables of Kierkegaard.* Princeton, N.J.: Princeton University Press, 1978.

Orend, Brian. "Justice After War." *Ethics & International Affairs,* vol. 16.1 (Spring 2002).

Orenstein, Peggy. "What's Wrong with Cinderella?" *New York Times Magazine,* December 24, 2006.

Packe, Michael St. John. *The Life of John Stuart Mill.* New York: Capricorn, 1954.

Plato. *Apology.* In *Dialogues of Plato.* Translated by Benjamin Jowett. New York: Washington Square Press, 1968.

———. *Plato's Phaedrus.* Translated by W. C. Helmbold and W. G. Rabinowitz. New York: The Liberal Arts Press, 1956.

———. *The Republic.* Translated by G. R. U. Grube. Indianapolis: Hackett, 1974.

———. *The Republic of Plato.* Translated by Francis MacDonald Cornford. London: Oxford University Press, 1945.

Pojman, Louis P., ed. *Ethical Theory.* Belmont, Calif.: Wadsworth, 1989.

Potts, Malcolm, "RU-486: Termination of a Pregnancy in the Privacy of One's Home." *North Carolina Medical Journal* Vol. 50, n. 10, October 1989.

Prinz, Jesse J. "Is Empathy Necessary for Morality?" In *Empathy: Philosophical and Psychological Perspectives,* edited by Amy Coplan and Peter Goldie. Oxford University Press, 2011.

Punishment and the Death Penalty: The Current Debate. Edited by Robert M. Baird and Stuart E. Rosenbaum. New York: Prometheus, 1995.

Race and the Enlightenment: A Reader. Edited by Emmanuel Chukwudi Eze. Oxford: Blackwell, 1997.

Rachels, James. *The Elements of Moral Philosophy.* New York: Random House, 1986, 1999.

———. *Problems from Philosophy.* The McGraw-Hill Companies, Inc., 2005.

Rand, Ayn. "The Ethics of Emergencies," "Man's Rights." In *The Virtue of Selfishness.* New York: Penguin, 1964.

Rawls, John. "Justice As Fairness." *Philosophical Review* 67 (April 1958).

———. *The Law of Peoples.* Cambridge, Mass.: Harvard University Press, 2001.

———. "Two Concepts of Rules." *Philosophical Review* 1–13, 1955.

Rendtorff, Jacob Dahl, and Kemp, Peter. *Basic Ethical Principles in European Bioethics and Biolaw.* Vol. 1, *Autonomy, Dignity, Integrity and Vulnerability.* Copenhagen: Centre for Ethics and Law, and Barcelona: Institut Borja de Bioètica, 2000.

Rescher, Nicholas. *Distributive Justice.* Indianapolis: Bobbs-Merrill, 1966.

Ricoeur, Paul. *Interpretation Theory.* Fort Worth: Texas Christian University Press, 1976.

———. "Narrative Time." In *On Narrative,* edited by J. I. Mitchell. Chicago: University of Chicago Press, 1981.

———. *Time and Narrative.* 3 vols. Chicago: University of Chicago Press, 1985–1989.

Rosenstand, Nina. "Arven fra Bergson: En Virknings-historie." In *Den Skapende Varighet,* edited by Hans Kolstad. Oslo, Norway: H. Aschehoug & Co., 1993.

———. "Everyone Needs a Stone: Alternative Views of Nature." In *The Environmental Ethics and Policy Book,* 2nd ed., edited by Donald VanDeVeer and Christine Pierce. Belmont, Calif.: Wadsworth, 1998.

———. *The Human Condition: An Introduction to Philosophy of Human Nature.* New York: McGraw-Hill, 2002.

———. "Med en anden stemme: Carol Gilligans etik." In *Kvindespind–Kønsfilosofiske Essays,* edited by Mette Boch et al. Aarhus, Denmark: Forlaget Philosophia, 1987.

———. *Mytebegrebet.* Copenhagen: Gads Forlag, 1981.

———. "Myths and Morals: Images of Conduct, Character, and Personhood in the Native American Tradition." In *Tribal Mythologies,* edited by Helmut Wautischer. Aldershot: Ashgate, 1998.

———. "Stories and Morals." In *Ethics, Literature, Theory,* edited by Stephen George. Lanham, Md.: Rowman & Littlefield, 2005.

———. "25 years With The Moral of the Story." In *The Next Phase of Business Ethics: Celebrating 20 Years of REIO (Research in Ethical Issues in Organizations, Vol. 21),* edited by Michael Schwartz, Howard Harris, and Debra Comer. Emerald Publishing Limited, 2019.

Rousch, Paul E. "Justification for Resort to Force." In *Ethics for Military Leaders,* edited by Aine Donovan, David E. Johnson, George R. Lucas, Jr., Paul E. Rousch, and Nancy Sherman. American Heritage Christian Publishing, 1997.

Rousseau, Jean-Jacques. *Confessions.* Baltimore: Penguin Books, 1954.

———. *On the Social Contract.* Translated by Donald A. Cress. Indianapolis: Hackett, 1983.

Ruth, Sheila, ed. *Issues in Feminism.* Mountain View, Calif.: Mayfield, 1998.

Sapontzis, Steve F. "The Moral Significance of Interests." *Environmental Ethics,* Winter 1982.

Sartre, Jean-Paul. Excerpt from *Being and Nothingness.* In *Reality, Man and Existence: Essential Works of Existentialism,* edited by H. J. Blackham. New York: Bantam, 1965.

———. "Existentialism Is a Humanism." In *Existentialism from Dostoyevsky to Sartre,* edited by Walter Kaufmann. Translated by Philip Mairet. New York, Meridian Publishing Company, 1989.

Savage-Rumbaugh, Sue, and Lewin, Roger. *Kanzi: The Ape at the Brink of the Human Mind.* New York: Wiley, 1994.

Schmidt, Kaare. *Film-historie, kunst, industri.* Copenhagen: Gyldendal, 1995.

Schneewind, J. B. "The Misfortunes of Virtue." *Ethics* 101, October 1990. Chicago: University of Chicago Press, 1990.

Schwartz, Theodore. "Cult and Context: The Paranoid Ethos in Melanesia," *Ethos, Journal of the Society for Psychological Anthropology,* June 1973.

Seligson, Amber Levanon, and Choi, Lauri. "Critical Elements of an Organizational Ethical Culture." *Ethics Resource Center Research Report,* 2006.

Shaw, William H. *Morality and Moral Controversies.* Englewood Cliffs, N.J.: Prentice-Hall, 1981.

Singer, Isaac Bashevis. *"A Piece of Advice" The Spinoza of Market Street and Other Stories.* Farrar, Straus and Giroux, 1979, New York, NY.

Singer, Peter. *The Expanding Circle.* Farrar, Straus and Giroux, 1981.

———. "A Convenient Truth." From *the New York Times,* January 26, 2007.

———. "If Fish Could Scream." From *Project Syndicate,* September 10, 2010.

Sommers, Christina Hoff. "Teaching the Virtues." *Imprimis.* Hillsdale College, Michigan, November 1991.

——— *The War Against Boys.* New York: Touchstone, Simon & Schuster, 2000.

————. *Who Stole Feminism?* New York: Simon & Schuster, 1994.

Sommers, Christina Hoff, and Sommers, Fred, eds. *Vice and Virtue in Everyday Life.* Fort Worth: Harcourt Brace Jovanovich, 1985, 1989.

Steifels, Peter. "Emmanuel Levinas, 90, French Ethical Philosopher." Obituary, *New York Times,* December 27, 1995.

Steinbeck, John. "Paradox and Dreams." *America and Americans.* New York: Viking Press, 1966.

Steindorf, Sara. "A Novel Approach to Work." *Christian Science Monitor,* January 29, 2002.

Stone, I. F. *The Trial of Socrates.* New York: Doubleday, 1988.

Stone, Oliver, and Sklar, Zachary. *JFK: The Book of the Film.* New York: Applause Books, 1992.

Tannen, Deborah. *The Argument Culture.* New York: Random House, 1998.

Tannen, Deborah. "The Argument Culture: Agonism & the Common Good." *Daedalus,* Vol. 142, No. 2 (Spring 2013).

————. *That's Not What I Meant!* New York: Ballantine, 1986.

————. *You Just Don't Understand.* New York: Morrow, 1990.

Taylor, Mark C. *Journeys to Selfhood: Hegel & Kierkegaard.* Berkeley: University of California Press, 1980.

Taylor, Paul W. *Principles of Ethics: An Introduction.* Belmont, Calif.: Wadsworth, 1975.

Taylor, Richard. *Good and Evil.* New York: Prometheus, 2000.

2004 Child Fatality Report. State of Washington Office of the Family and Children's Ombudsman, May 30, 2006.

Thompson, Shawn. "When Apes Have Their Day in Court." *Philosophy Now,* December 2015/January 2016. Anja Publications, London, United Kingdom.

Tyre, Peg. "The Trouble with Boys." *Newsweek,* January 30, 2006.

"USA TODAY Editor Resigns After Reporter's Misdeeds." *USA Today,* April 20, 2004.

Waal, Frans B. M. de. "Do Humans Alone 'Feel Your Pain'?" *Chronicle of Higher Education,* October 26, 2001.

————. *Good Natured: The Origins of Right and Wrong in Humans and Other Animals.* Cambridge, Mass.: Harvard University Press, 1996.

————. *Primates and Philosophers: How Morality Evolved.* Princeton, N.J.: Princeton University Press, 2006.

Waltzer, Michael. *Spheres of Justice.* New York: Basic Books, 1984.

Warren, Mary Ann. "Human and Animal Rights Compared." In *Environmental Philosophy: A Collection of Readings,* edited by Robert Elliot and Arran Gare. State College: Pennsylvania State University Press, 1983.

————. "On the Moral and Legal Status of Abortion." *The Monist,* vol. 57, no. 1 (January 1973).

Watchmen and Philosophy: A Rorschack Test. Edited by Mark D. White. Hoboken: Wiley, 2009.

Weiss, Rick. "Test-Tube Baby Born to Save Ill Sister." *Washington Post,* October 3, 2000.

Wesley, John. "Reel Therapy." *Psychology Today,* February 2000.

Wilgoren, Jodi. "Death Knell for the Death Penalty?" New York Times News Service, April 15, 2002.

Williams, Bernard. *Morality: An Introduction.* New York: Harper & Row, 1972.

Williams, Ian. "China Sells Organs of Slain Convicts." *Observer* (UK), December 10, 2000.

Wolgast, Elizabeth. *The Grammar of Justice.* Ithaca, N.Y.: Cornell University Press, 1987.

Wollstonecraft, Mary. *A Vindication of the Rights of Women.* Excerpt in *Philosophy of Woman,* edited by Mary Briody Mahowald. Indianapolis: Hackett, 1983.

Wright, Tamra, Hughes, Peter, and Ainley, Alison. "The Paradox of Morality: An Interview with Emmanuel Levinas." In *The Provocation of Levinas,* edited by Robert Bernasconi and David Wood. New York: Routledge, 1988.

Zack, Naomi. *Thinking About Race.* Belmont, Calif.: Wadsworth, 1998.

Zimbardo, Philip. *The Lucifer Effect: Understanding How Good People Turn Evil.* New York: Random House, 2007.

Works of Literature

Andersen, Hans Christian. *Eventyr og Historier.* 16 vols. Odense, Denmark: Skandinavisk Bogforlag, Flensteds Forlag.

Beauvoir, Simone de. *The Woman Destroyed.* Translated by Patrick O'Brian. New York: Putnam, 1969.

Bennett, William J. *The Book of Virtues.* New York: Simon & Schuster, 1993.

Conrad, Joseph. *Lord Jim: A Tale.* New York: Bantam, 1981.

Dostoyevsky, Fyodor. *The Brothers Karamazov.* New York: Signet Classic, New American Library, 1957.

Euripides, *Medea.* In *Classical Mythology: Images and Insights,* by Stephen L. Harris and Gloria Plazner. Translated by Moses Hadas. Mountain View, Calif.: Mayfield, 1995.

Goethe, Johan Wolfgang von. *The Sorrows of Young Werther.* Translated by Elizabeth Mayer and Louise Bogan. New York: Vintage Books, 1973.

Graves, Robert. *The Greek Myths.* 2 vols. Harmondsworth, England: Penguin, 1960.

Grimm's Complete Fairy Tales. Garden City, N.Y.: Nelson Doubleday, 1975.

Huxley, Aldous. *Brave New World.* New York: Bantam, 1958.

Ibsen, Henrik. *A Doll's House.* In *The Collected Works of Henrik Ibsen,* vol. 7: *A Doll's House, Ghosts.* Introductions and translations by William Archer. New York: Scribner, 1906.

Jewkes, W. T., ed. *Man the Myth-Maker.* New York: Harcourt Brace Jovanovich, 1973.

Kafka, Franz. *The Basic Kafka.* New York: Simon & Schuster, 1979.

Kingsolver, Barbara. *The Poisonwood Bible.* New York: HarperTorch, 1998.

Le Guin, Ursula K. "The Ones Who Walk Away from Omelas." In *The Wind's Twelve Quarters.* New York: Harper & Row, 1981.

Matheson, Richard. "Mantage." In *Shock I.* New York: Berkeley, 1961.

Moore, Alan, Gibbons, Dave, and Higgins, John. *Watchmen.* Burbank: D.C. Comics, 2014.

Niven, Larry. "The Jigsaw Man." In *Tales of Known Space: The Universe of Larry Niven.* New York: Ballantine, 1975.

Njal's Saga. Translated by Magnus Magnusson and Hermann Palsson. Baltimore: Penguin, 1960.

Poe, Edgar Allan. *Complete Tales and Poems.* New York: Barnes & Noble Books, 1992.

Rand, Ayn. *Atlas Shrugged.* New York: Signet, 1957, 1985.

Sartre, Jean-Paul. *No Exit.* New York: Random House, 1989.

Sheckley, Robert. "The Store of the Worlds," *Playboy,* September 1959.

Shelley, Mary. *Frankenstein.* New York: Bantam, 1981.

Singer, Isaac Bashevis. "A Piece of Advice." From *The Spinoza of Market Street.* Translated from Yiddish into English by Martha Glicklich and Joel Blocker. New York: Fawcett Crest, 1958.

Soseki, Natsume. *Kokoro.* Translated by Meredith McKinney. New York: Penguin Books, 2010.

Tarantino, Quentin. *Pulp Fiction, A Quentin Tarantino Screenplay.* New York: Hyperion, 1994.

Walker, Alice. *Possessing the Secret of Joy.* New York: Simon & Schuster, 1993.

Wessel, Johann Herman. "Smeden og Bageren." In *De gamle huskevers.* Edited by Fritz Haack. Copenhagen: Forlaget Sesam, 1980.

Selected Website Sources

Abortion

https://www.aclu.org/blog/reproductive-freedom/abortion/waking-sleeping-giant-after-some-states-pass-abortion-bans-other

https://www.cnn.com/2019/05/14/politics/alabama-senate-abortion/index.html

https://www.vox.com/2019/5/30/18645952/louisiana-abortion-ban-heartbeat-bill-edwards

https://www.bostonglobe.com/news/politics/2019/05/14/these-states-have-passed-are-considering-restrictive-abortion-bills-that-target-roe-wade/Ui7Bm4E00ARMpFYw5nojvK/story.html

Abortion and the Catholic Church

http://www.vatican.va/roman_curia/congregations/cfaith/documents/rc_con_cfaith_doc_19741118_declaration-abortion_en.html

http://www.religiousconsultation.org/News_Tracker/moderate_RC_position_on_contraception_abortion.htm

http://faculty.cua.edu/Pennington/Law111/CatholicHistory.htm

"Affluenza" case

http://www.latimes.com/nation/nationnow/la-na-affluenza-teen-prison-20160413-story.html

Aldo Leopold, "The Land Ethic"

http://home.btconnect.com/tipiglen/landethic.html

Altruism

http://mobile.nytimes.com/2016/02/05/opinion/a-question-of-moral-radicalism.html?smid=tw-nytopinion&smtyp=cur&referer=https://t.co/vpU9HItWmN&_r=0

http://www.nytimes.com/2015/10/11/books/review/strangers-drowning-by-larissa-macfarquhar.html

Altruism is innate

http://www.washingtonpost.com/wpdyn/content/article/2007/05/27/AR2007052701056.html

Animal cognition and laws

https://qz.com/1181881/proof-of-animal-cognition-is-recognized-by-new-laws-in-europe/?__prclt=OliehWZ7

Anti-terrorism versus counterterrorism

http://www.tamilcanadian.com/page.php?cat=74&id=4946

AP falsification incident

http://www.worldnetdaily.com/news/article.asp?ARTICLE_ID=40331

Ape language research

http://www.gsu.edu/~wwwlrc/

Ape research may be waning:

http://www.nytimes.com/2011/11/15/science/chimps-days-in-research-may-be-near-an-end.html

Aristotle's biography

http://www.gradesaver.com/ClassicNotes/Authors/about_aristotle.html

http://www-history.mcs.st-andrews.ac.uk/Mathematicians/Aristotle.html

Aristotle's list of virtues

http://www.interlog.com/~girbe/

virtuesvices.html

Aristotle's Lyceum

http://www.newadvent.org/cathen/01713a.htm

Army Sgt. 1st Class Paul Smith, Medal of Honor recipient

http://www.medalofhonor.com/PaulSmith.htm

Artificial Intelligence

https://www.cnet.com/reviews/google-nest-hub-max-the-bigger-nest-hub-isnt-the-better-one-review/

https://www.nytimes.com/2019/09/06/opinion/ai-explainability.html

The Ashley treatment

    http://www.theguardian.com/society/2012/
mar/15/ashley-treatment-email-exchange

Atlantic Monthly websites, Christina Hoff Sommers debate

    http://www.theatlantic.com

Ban on using animals in testing of cosmetics

    http://www.peta.org.uk/issues/
animals-not-experiment-on/cosmetics/

Barbara Kingsolver

    http://www.english.eku.edu/SERVICES/
KYLIT/KINGSLVR.HTM

    https://www.theguardian.com/books/2018/
oct/08/barbara-kingsolver-fells-living-through
-end-of-world

The Big Short (film) and the financial crisis

    https://en.wikipedia.org/wiki/
The_Big_Short_%28film%29

    http://www.investopedia.com/articles/
economics/09/financial-crisis-review.asp

Black men killed by police

    http://www.dallasnews.com/news/local-news/
20150808-cases-of-24-unarmed-black-men
-killed-by-police-this-year.ece

    http://www.alternet.org/civil-liberties/
young-black-men-killed-us-police-highest
-rate-year-1134-deaths

California's same-sex marriage bill

    http://www.mercurynews.com/news/
ci_6069432?nclick_check=1

California's Three Strikes Law

    http://www.rand.org/publications/RB/
RB4009/RB4009.word.html

The Cambridge Declaration on Consciousness

    http://fcmconference.org/img/
CambridgeDeclarationOnConsciousness.pdf

CBS document scandal

    http://www.southerndigest.com/vnews/
displays.v/ART/2004/09/14/41472eba1033d

    http://www.azcentral.com/news/articles/
0910bush-memos10.html

Challenged in House of Lords

    http://news.bbc.co.uk/2/hi/uk_news/politics/
7190530.stm

Charles Dickens

    http://www.worldwideschool.org/library/
books/lit/charlesdickens/ATaleofTwoCities/
Chap1.html

Charles Garner, Abu Ghraib trial

    http://www.msnbc.msn.com/id/6795956/

Chinese pet food scandal

    http://abcnews.go.com/Blotter/toxic-treats
-china-killing-us-dogs-pet-owners/story?
id=15927579

    http://www.cbsnews.com/news/
petco-pulls-chinese-pet-treats-suspected
-of-killing-sickening-thousands/

Chiune and Yukiko Sugihara

    http://www.jewishvirtuallibrary.org/jsource/
Holocaust/sugihara.html

Christianity's development in the Roman Empire

    http://www.roman-empire.net/religion/
religion.html

Christine Korsgaard interview 2003

    http://www.people.fas.harvard.edu/~korsgaar/
CPR.CMK.Interview.pdf

Climate change debate in the UK

    http://www.dailymail.co.uk/sciencetech/
article-2055191/Scientists-said-climate-change
-sceptics-proved-wrong-accused-hiding-truth
-colleague.html

Climate change denial could become offense

    http://insideclimatenews.org/news/29032016/
climate-change-deception-oil-companies-exxon
-california-legislation

Cloned wolves

    http://www.telegraph.co.uk/news/main.jhtml?
xml=/news/2007/03/27/wclone27.xml

    http://www.timesonline.co.uk/tol/news/uk/
science/article1571502.ece

CNN poll on support for the war in Iraq

    http://www.cnn.com/2007/POLITICS/03/19/
iraq.support/index.html

Cognitive enhancement

http://www.nytimes.com/2008/03/09/
weekinreview/09carey.html

Concept of evil

https://plato.stanford.edu/entries/concept-evil/

Congress passes anti-genetic discrimination bill

http://ap.google.com/article/
ALeqM5g9PKo1Dr67gVSZWb-B4tOfMvmg
DwD90D626G0

*Conn. Home Invasion Defendant Read Violent
Books*

http://www.utsandiego.com/news/2011/mar/
14/conn-home-invasion-defendant-read
-violent-books/

Contagion *(film)*

http://www.imdb.com/title/tt1598778/

CSI: Crime Scene Investigation *series*

http://www.cbs.com/primetime/csi/
main.shtml

Criminal justice ethics

http://www.lib.jjay.cuny.edu/cje/html/cje.html

David Hume online, A Treatise of Human Nature

http://www.class.uidaho.edu/mickelsen/texts/
Hume%20Treatise/hume%20treatise3.htm

"The Death of Socrates": video interpretation

https://aeon.co/videos/can-philosophy-and
-morals-be-transmitted-through-a-painting

Death penalty critiques

http://www.deathpenaltyinfo.org/
some-examples-post-furman-botched-executions

http://mobile.nytimes.com/2016/01/17/
opinion/sunday/
the-death-penalty-endgame.html?
smid=tw-share&referer=https://t.co/
11Qk2389Mh&_r=0

http://www.prisonpolicy.org/blog/2015/07/02/
breyer_death_penalty/?gclid=COOrwN
_J7MsCFQeTfgodm8AEGg

Death penalty facts

http://www.deathpenaltyinfo.org/

http://deathpenalty.procon.org/
view.resource.php?resourceID=001172

*Death Penalty Information Center February 1,
2012*

http://www.deathpenaltyinfo.org/
FactSheet.pdf

Debating torture

http://www.pbs.org/newshour/bb/military/
july-dec05/torture_12-02.html

Divided nation

https://www.esquire.com/news-politics/
a26016262/editors-letter-march-2019/

Dogs understand fairness:

http://www.guardian.co.uk/science/2008/dec/
08/dogs-envy-fairness-social-behaviour

*Doing the Ethical Thing May Be Right, but It Isn't
Automatic*

http://www.nytimes.com/2011/11/19/
your-money/why-doing-the-ethical-thing-isnt
-automatic.html?_r=1

Dolphins rescuing humans
http://www.dolphins-world.com/
dolphins-rescuing-humans/
http://worldnewsdailyreport.com/
boys-life-saved-by-dolphins/

http://www.eurocbc.org/page158.html

*"Duke Probe Shows Failure of Post-Enron Ethics
Classes"* (*Update 2*)

http://www.bloomberg.com/apps/news?pid
=20601103&sid=aEL5ZnKhQuXY&refer=u

Dystopia film discussion

http://blogs.takepart.com/2008/02/13/
top-10-dystopian-future-films-telling-us-to-act
-now/

Edward O. Wilson's "Half Earth" Proposal

http://news.nationalgeographic.com/2016/03/
160327-wilson-half-planet-conservation-climate
-change-extinction-ngbooktalk/?google_editors
_picks=true

Elizabeth Nietzsche's Paraguay Colony

http://www.nytimes.com/2013/05/06/world/
americas/german-outpost-born-of-racism
-blends-into-paraguay.html?_r=0

Ethics in space

http://www.cnn.com/2007/TECH/space/05/
01/death.in.space.ap/index.html

Ethics Resource Center Research Report 2006
  http://www.ethics.org/erc-publications/
  organizational-ethical-culture.asp

Ethics Updates, edited by Lawrence Hinman
  http://ethics.acusd.edu/index.html

Euthanasia
  https://www.foxnews.com/world/
  dutch-doctor-euthanasia-trial-netherlands
  https://www.foxnews.com/politics/
  new-jersey-assisted-suicide-law-temporary
  -restraining-order

Euthanasia doctor acquitted
  https://www.theguardian.com/world/2019/sep/
  11/dutch-court-clears-doctor-in-landmark
  -euthanasia-trial

"Existentialism Is a Humanism"
  https://pdfs.semanticscholar.org/2135/
  96e82cf5585801bf66d810342e56d808f263.pdf?
  _ga=2.64465196.284664535.1583019551
  -871028242.1583019551

Ex Machina *(film)*
  http://www.imdb.com/title/
  tt0470752/?ref_=nv_sr_1

Facebook Bias Issues
  https://www.washingtonpost.com/technology/
  2019/08/20/
  facebook-makes-small-tweaks-following-anti
  -conservative-bias-report-theyre-unlikely
  -make-issue-go-away/
  https://news.google.com/news/
  amp?caurl=https%3A%2F%2Ftechcrunch.com%
  2F2016%2F10%2F21%2Funcensoredbook%
  2Famp%2F#pt0-18994
  http://money.cnn.com/2016/05/10/media/
  facebook-trending-topics/

Facebook's Zuckerberg says the Age of Privacy is over
  http://www.readwriteweb.com/archives/
  facebooks_zuckerberg_says_the_age_of
  _privacy_is_ov.php

Fairy Tales are older than previously thought
  http://www.theguardian.com/books/2016/jan/
  20/fairytales-much-older-than-previously
  -thought-say-researchers?CMP=share_btn_tw

  http://rsos.royalsocietypublishing.org/content/
  3/1/150645#F4

FDA Food Safety Modernization Act
  http://www.fda.gov/NewsEvents/
  PublicHealthFocus/ucm239907.htm

Female circumcision
  http://www.nytimes.com/2016/02/05/health/
  indonesia-female-genital-cutting-circumcision
  -unicef.html?_r=0

Fired because of use of word
  http://www.adversity.net/special/niggardly.htm

Flight shaming
  https://www.bbc.com/news/
  business-49890057

Force Majeure *(film)*
  http://www.theguardian.com/film/2015/apr/
  12/force-majeure-film-review-ruben-ostlund
  -avalanche

Gandhi
  http://www.mkgandhi.org/

Gender-neutral pronouns
  http://www.citylab.com/navigator/2015/09/
  ze-or-they-a-guide-to-using-gender-neutral
  -pronouns/407167/
  http://bigstory.ap.org/article/48c986c722ba4e
  5bb8a5a4c1f1d31df1/he-she-ze-universities
  -add-gender-pronouns-alter-policy

Gender-neutral child Storm as of 2018
  https://www.theglobeandmail.com/opinion/
  article-the-brave-new-age-of-gender
  -neutral-kids/

Genetic Engineering and Cloning
  https://apnews.com/
  ef1161deac194f2ca1fd99457dc2cf15
  https://venturebeat.com/2018/11/26/
  designer-babies-are-here-ready-or-not/
  https://futurism.com/the-byte/
  poll-two-thirds-americans
  -support-human-gene-editing
  https://www.engadget.com/2019/04/16/
  human-crispr-gene-editing-trial-begins-in-us/
  https://www.nihr.ac.uk/news/
  stem-cell-treatment-restores-sight-in
  -most-common-form-of-blindness/8142

https://futurism.com/the-byte/
china-clones-top-police-dog

https://www.dailymail.co.uk/news/
article-6828961/China-clones-Sherlock
-Holmes-police-dog-cut-training-times-state
-media.html

https://www.scmp.com/news/china/science/
article/3005772/chinese-scientists-add-human
-genes-monkey-brains-latest-ethics

The Golden Rule in 21 religions

http://www.religioustolerance.org/
reciproc.htm

Good Samaritan, Jefferson Heavner

http://wncn.com/2016/01/23/nc-sheriff-good
-samaritan-fatally-shot-after-stopping-to
-help-driver/

The Great Ape Project

http://www.greatapeproject.org

Grey Owl, Archibald Belaney

http://canadianicon.org/table-of-contents/
grey-owl-white-indian/

http://www.bbc.com/news/
uk-england-sussex-24127514

http://ottawacitizen.com/news/national/
doug-george-kanentiio-impersonators
-have-caused-aboriginal-people-great-harm

Habermas, "the Last European"

http://www.spiegel.de/international/europe/
habermas-the-last-european-a-philosopher
-s-mission-to-save-the-eu-a-799237.html

Halloween Costumes 2019

https://redtri.com/most-popular-halloween
-costumes-for-kids/

https://www.nytimes.com/2019/09/06/
opinion/ai-explainability.html

Halloween Princess Costumes

http://www.cnn.com/2016/10/19/health/
halloween-costumes-superhero-princess/

"Hearts and Minds," on the cognitive revolution

http://www.boston.com/news/education/
higher/articles/2007/04/29/hearts__minds/

Herrad of Hohenbourg/Landsberg

http://home.infionline.net/~ddisse/herrad.html

"How Safe Is Our Food? FDA Could Do Better."

http://blogs.usatoday.com/oped/2007/05/
how_safe_is_our.html

Human–animal hybrid ban lifted in UK

http://news.bbc.co.uk/2/hi/health/
7193820.stm

Human brain wired for empathy

http://news.health.com/2011/07/26/human
-brains-wired-to-empathize-study-finds/

http://www.nytimes.com/2009/12/01/science/
01human.html?_r=1&pagewanted=all

Ibn Fadlan

http://www.luth.se/luth/present/sweden/
history/viking_age/Viking_age4.html

Illinois death penalty report

http://www.cnn.com/2002/LAW/04/15/
death.penalty.report/index.html

Immanuel Kant's Guide to Good Dinners

http://branemrys.blogspot.com/2010/07/
immanuel-kants-guide-to-good-dinner.html

Immanuel Kant's "Perpetual Peace"

http://www.mtholyoke.edu/acad/intrel/kant/
kant1.htm

Islam on fetal personhood

http://www.bionews.org.uk/page_38025.asp

Jeremy Bentham's Auto-Icon

http://www.ucl.ac.uk/Bentham-Project/info/
jb.htm

*John Jay College of Criminal Justice study of child
abuse by priests*

http://www.jjay.cuny.edu/churchstudy/
main.asp

Jonathan Smith

https://www.today.com/parents/las-vegas
-shooting-dad-injured-while-saving-dozens
-t117020

http://btnomb.com/jonathan-smith-helps
-save-30-people-las-vegas-massacre-takes
-bullet-neck/

Journalism or activism?

https://niemanreports.org/articles/where
-does-journalism-end-and-activism-begin/

Jus post bellum

http://www.carlisle.army.mil/usawc/
Parameters/02autumn/kellogg.htm

http://www.cceia.org/resources/journal/16_1/
articles/277.html/_res/id=sa_File1/
277_orend.pdf

Kant on the Highest Moral Good

http://mq.academia.edu/PaulFormosa/Papers/
301499/Kant_on_the_Highest_Moral
-Physical_Good_The_Social_Aspect_of
_Kants_Moral_Philosophy

Kierkegaard and Regine Olsen

http://sorenkierkegaard.org/kw25.htm

Laws protecting cats and dogs

https://www.cbsnews.com/news/california
-to-become-first-state-to-ban-retail-sales-of
-cats-and-dogs/

*Learning from the Japanese Example: What
Makes a Hero?*

http://healthland.time.com/2011/03/17/
learning-from-the-japanese-example%e2%
80%94what-makes-heroes/?iid=WBeditorspicks

Levinas's relevance for refugee crisis

http://opinionator.blogs.nytimes.com/2016/
01/18/what-do-we-owe-each-other/?mwrsm
=Email&_r=0

Life of David Gale, *Analysis*

http://www.daughtersofstpaul.com/
mediastudies/reviews/filmdavidgale.html

Linda MacDonald Glenn

http://www.actionbioscience.org/biotech/
glenn.html

Locke's theory of property

http://plato.stanford.edu/entries/
locke-political/

Lynndie England, Abu Ghraib trial

http://www.usatoday.com/news/nation/
2005-09-26-england_x.htm

*Marine Cpl. James L. Dunham, Medal of Honor
recipient*

http://www.mcnews.info/mcnewsinfo/moh/

*Martin Luther King's "A Letter from (a)
Birmingham Jail"*

http://almaz.com/nobel/peace/MLK-jail.html

The meaning of zombies

http://granta.com/the-meaning-of-zombies/

Medal of Honor recipients

https://www.washingtonpost.com/news/
checkpoint/wp/2016/03/03/the-latest-medal
-of-honor-recipient-wants-to-be-the-first-to
-return-to-combat-since-vietnam/

http://www.defense.gov/News/
Special-Reports/MOH-Special

Media Ethics Issues

http://www.ranker.com/list/
journalists-who-lied/mel-judson

http://www.nytimes.com/2016/11/13/us/
elections/to-our-readers-from-the
-publisher-and-executive-editor.html?_r=0

https://www.cnet.com/reviews/google-nest
-hub-max-the-bigger-nest-hub-isnt-the
-better-one-review/

https://www.nytimes.com/2019/09/06/
opinion/ai-explainability.html

Michael Walzer, Spheres of Justice

http://books.google.com/books?id=dtFbhw7
-wZEC&dq=%22spheres+of+justice%22+
walzer&pg=PP1&ots=hqL0_3RiyP&sig=
_fGe849vRPlL2bPP4Yy2q_qp8cM&hl=en&
prev=http://www.google.com/search?hl=en&
q=%22spheres+of+justice%22+walzer&
sa=X&oi=print&ct=title&cad=one-book
-with-thumbnail#PPR11,M1

Military Commissions Act of 2006

http://en.wikipedia.org/wiki/
Military_Commissions_Act_of_2006

http://www.nytimes.com/2006/09/28/
opinion/28thu1.html?ex=1317096000&
en=3eb3ba3410944ff9&ei=5090&partner=
rssuserland&emc=rss

Mill on suicide

https://ethicsofsuicide.lib.utah.edu/selections/
john-stuart-mill/

Mississippi Burning *reviews*

http://www.cinepad.com/reviews/
mississippi.htm

http://www.law.umkc.edu/faculty/projects/
ftrials/price&bowers/movie.html

The Molly and Adam Nash story

http://www.amednews.com/2001/prse0115

http://www.usatoday.com/tech/science/
columnist/vergano/
2010-01-10-embryo-genetic-screening_N.htm

Moral Enhancement

http://www.guardian.co.uk/science/2011/apr/
04/morality-drugs-improve-ethical-behaviour

Moral responsibility, justice, and vengeance

https://www.psychologytoday.com/blog/
unjust-deserts/201602/moral-responsibility
-and-the-strike-back-emotion#565581

https://aeon.co/opinions/does-the-desire-to
-punish-have-any-place-in-modern-justice

"Movies with a Message"

http://www.jsonline.com/onwisconsin/movies/
oct04/266611.asp

News Media Ethics

http://www.thedailybeast.com/newsweek/
2011/07/17/how-the-guardian-broke-the
-news-of-the-world-hacking-scandal.html

http://www.politico.com/news/stories/1210/
46780_Page4.html

http://www.guardian.co.uk/world/2010/mar/
31/roth-grisham-fake-interview-obama

http://www.guardian.co.uk/commentisfree/
2011/sep/18/
julian-assange-wikileaks-nick-cohen

Narrative identity

https://www.psychologytoday.com/us/blog/
post-clinical/201604/paul-ricoeur-and
-narrative-identity

NASA Workshop for Authors and Scientists

http://www.guardian.co.uk/books/2011/aug/
25/nasa-novel-mission-science-fiction?
CMP=twt_gu

Nietzsche's illness

https://www.ncbi.nlm.nih.gov/pubmed/
18575181

Non-human personhood

http://ieet.org/index.php/IEET/more/
rnhp20110211

*"Obama Awards Medal of Honor to Marine who
saved 36 Lives"*

http://content.usatoday.com/communities/
theoval/post/2011/09/obama-praises
-marine-awards-medal-of-honor/1

Oldest European universities

http://www.unbf.ca/psychology/likely/
scholastics/universities.htm

Olympe de Gouges

http://www.pinn.net/~sunshine/march99/
gouges2.html

The Paris Agreement on Climate Change

http://reason.com/archives/2016/04/22/
earth-day-2016-paris-climate-agreement-s

"https://news.google.com/news/ampviewer?
caurl=http%3A%2F%2Fwww.csmonitor
.com%2Flayout%2Fset%2Famphtml%
2FEnvironment%2F2016%2F1004%2F
With-European-Union-s-ratification
-Paris-climate-deal-to-enter-into-
force"\l"pt0-709000"https://news.google.
com/news/ampviewer?caurl=http%3A%
2F%2Fwww.csmonitor.com%2Flayout%2F
set%2Famphtml%2FEnvironment%2F2016%
2F1004%2FWith-European-Union-s-
ratification-Paris-climate-deal-to-enter
-into-force#pt0-709000

Pascal Bruckner on happiness

http://www.healthzone.ca/health/mindmood/
article/952586—don-t-worry-about-being
-happy-author-says

http://www.guardian.co.uk/books/2011/jan/
23/pascal-bruckner-interview-happiness

Patriot Act extended

https://www.wsws.org/en/articles/2019/11/21/
fund-n21.html

*Paul Ricoeur's acceptance speech at receiving the
Kluge Prize*

http://www.loc.gov/loc/kluge/prize/
ricoeur-transcript.html

Personal branding

http://www.londonschoolofmarketing.com/
blog/bid/388447/
How-to-build-a-personal-brand

https://www.americanexpress.com/us/small
-business/openforum/articles/5-ways-the
-kardashian-family-built-a-65-million-brand/

http://www.celebritybrandingagency.com/
blog/
the-kanye-and-kim-kardashian-lesson-in
-personal-branding-combining-audiences
-for-impact.php

*Peter Singer, "A Convenient Truth;" New York
Times article, 01/26/07*

http://www.utilitarian.net/singer/by/
20070126.htm

*Peter Singer, "If Fish Could Scream." From Project
Syndicate, September 10, 2010.*

http://www.project-syndicate.org/
commentary/singer66/English

*Peter Singer, "Should We Trust Our Moral
Intuitions?" Project Syndicate, March 2007*

http://www.utilitarian.net/singer/by/
200703.htm

Philippa Foot Obituary

http://www.nytimes.com/2010/10/10/us/
10foot.html

Philosophy on the Mesa

http://philosophyonthemesa.wordpress.com/

Police officers fatally shot

https://www.washingtonpost.com/news/
post-nation/wp/2016/04/01/virginia-state
-trooper-becomes-30th-law-enforcement
-officer-killed-in-2016/

The Primates Home Page

http://www.dwebsoft.com/PrimatesWeb/

Privacy

https://www.wired.com/story/
f8-zuckerberg-future-is-private/

Ray Killen's sentencing

http://www.cnn.com/2005/LAW/06/23/
mississippi.killings/index.html

Raymond Chandler, "The Simple Art of Murder"

http://www.en.utexas.edu/amlit/amlitprivate/
scans/chandlerart.html

Recount in Florida

http://www.pbs.org/newshour/media/
media_watch/jan-june01/recount_4-3.html

Retributive and restorative justice

http://www.georgetown.edu/centers/
woodstock/report/r-fea61a.htm

Review of Walzer's Spheres of Justice

http://query.nytimes.com/gst/fullpage.html?
res=9A0CE5DC1738F937A15757C0A9
65948260

Robots in our future

http://mashable.com/2016/02/25/
robot-future-is-here/#YXyU0d4.wGqc

http://www.businessinsider.com/report
-10-million-self-driving-cars-will
-be-on-the-road-by-2020-2015-5-6

*"Robert Nozick, Libertarianism, and Utopia," by
Jonathan Wolf*

http://world.std.com/~mhuben/wolff_2.html

Robert Nozick and Locke's Proviso

http://www.cooperativeindividualism.org/
fremery_nozick_review_of.html

Robert Yates investigation files

http://www.krem.com

Ronald Dworkin's Freedom's Law

http://www.hup.harvard.edu/catalog/
DWOFRE.html

Sandra the orangutan settles in in Florida

https://www.theguardian.com/world/2019/
nov/07/sandra-orangutan-florida-argentina
-buenos-aires

Seven moral rules found worldwide

https://evolution-institute.org/the-seven
-moral-rules-found-all-around-the-world/

Shirley Jackson's 'The Lottery'

http://www.hannaharendtcenter.org/?p=13528

http://sites.middlebury.edu/
individualandthesociety/files/2010/09/
jackson_lottery.pd

The Silent Scream of the Asparagus

http://www.weeklystandard.com/Content/
Public/Articles/000/000/015/065njdoe.asp

The Society for the Study of Ethics and Animals

http://mail/Rochester.edu/~nobs/ssea.html

Sor Juana Inez de la Cruz

http://www.mexconnect.com/mex_/history/
jtuck/jtjuanainescruz.html

http://www.edwardsly.com/ines.htm

Spotlight *(film)*

http://www.latimes.com/entertainment/
movies/la-et-mn-spotlight-review
-20151106-column.html

Stanford Encyclopedia of Philosophy:
Distributive Justice

http://www.seop.leeds.ac.uk/archives/
win1998/entries/justice-distributive/

Stem cell research

http://www.latimes.com/news/local/politics/
cal/la-me-stemcell17may17,1,4139407.story?
coll=la-news-politics-california

http://content.usatoday.com/communities/
sciencefair/post/2012/01/huamn
-embryonic-stem-cell-blindness-treatment
-study-reaction/1

http://www.medicalnewstoday.com/
healthnews.php?newsid=73381

Stem cell research and cloning

http://www.bbc.com/news/
uk-wales-south-east-wales-35763735

http://www.usnews.com/news/articles/
2015-12-29/british-couple-clones
-dead-dog-for-100k

Stephen Hawking warns against AI

http://www.livescience.com/51664
-stephen-hawking-elon-musk-ai-weapons.html

Stephen Pinker's response to John Gray

http://www.theguardian.com/commentisfree/
2015/mar/20/wars-john-gray-conflict
-peace?CMP=share_btn_link

Stoicism

https://en.wikipedia.org/wiki/Stoicism

https://www.iep.utm.edu/stoicism/

https://plato.stanford.edu/entries/stoicism/

Stories of fake memoirs

http://sycamorereview.com/blog/2008/3/4/
fake-memoirs.html

Sudanese Criticize Governor's Decree on Women.
CNN.com, September 6, 2000.

Sustainability

https://www.sustain.ucla.edu/about-us/
what-is-sustainability/

Sue Savage Rumbaugh, William M. Fields

http://www2.gsu.edu/~wwwlrc/

savage-rumb-srcd-mono.pdf

Trolley Problem Psychological study 2010,
"Evolution and the Trolley Problem"

https://psycnet.apa.org/fulltext/
2011-13654-001.html
http://projects.iq.harvard.edu/files/mcl/files/
greene-solvingtrolleyproblem-16.pdf

Torture in Nazi Germany

http://andrewsullivan.theatlantic.com/
the_daily_dish/2007/05/
verschfte_verne.html

Tuskegee syphilis study

http://www.med.virginia.edu/hs-library/
historical/apology/

The 2007 pet food scandal

http://en.wikipedia.org/wiki/
2007_pet_food_recalls

http://www.petconnection.com/recall/
index.php

U.S. Constitution

http://www.nwbuildnet.com/nwbn/
usconstitutionsearch.html

The Victims of Anthony Sowell

http://www.cnn.com/2010/CRIME/10/26/
cleveland.sowell.victims.one.year/?hpt=C1

The Virginia Tech massacre

http://www.latimes.com/technology/
la-na-heroes18apr18,1,2123657.story

Weather Channel Founder: Global Warming
"Greatest Scam in History"

http://icecap.us/images/uploads/
JC_comments.doc

White House press releases on the Patriot Act

http://www.whitehouse.gov/news/releases/
2005/06/20050609.html

*"Who's a terrorist and who isn't?" AP article, 10/
03/01*

http://www.msnbc.com/news/636814.asp

Women in the armed forces

http://thehill.com/news-by-subject/defense
-homeland-security/147889-pentagon
-commission-allow-women-to-serve-in-combat

http://www.signonsandiego.com/news/2010/
feb/20/
truly-female-marines-have-come-long-way/

http://www.womensmemorial.org/
historyandcollections/history/
learnmoreques.htm

http://www.nbcnews.com/news/us-news/house
-committee-votes-require-women-register
-draft-n564166?cid=eml_onsite

http://www.nytimes.com/2016/06/15/us/
politics/
congress-women-military-draft.html?_r=0

Women and the Draft

https://www.military.com/daily-news/2019/02/
26/no-women-dont-have-sign-draft-yet-heres
-whats-next.html

https://www.npr.org/2019/04/27/717756908/
women-and-the-draft

Women's suffrage

http://www.rochester.edu/SBA/history.html

Women's suffrage, global

http://www.womenshistory.about.com/library/
weekly/aa091600a.htm

Glossary

ableism: Discrimination against the disabled.

abolitionism: Today: the viewpoint that the death penalty ought to be abolished. *See* retentionism.

absolution: Forgiveness; usually God's forgiveness.

absolutism: The ethical theory that there is a universal set of moral rules that can and should be followed by everybody. Also referred to as *hard universalism.*

absurdity: The existentialist concept that life is meaningless because there is no God to determine right and wrong (or because we can't know what God's values are, if God happens to exist).

acculturation: Cultural development.

act utilitarianism: The classical version of utilitarianism that focuses on the consequences of a single act.

ad hominem argument: A logical fallacy (a formally faulty argument) that assumes that because a person is who he or she is, his or her viewpoint must be wrong.

ad misericordiam fallacy: Appeal to pity.

ageism: Discrimination against elderly people (or anyone from a different generation) because of their age.

agnosticism: The view that God is unknown or that it cannot be known whether or not there is a God.

altruism: Concern for the interests of others. Extreme (ideal) altruism: concern for the interests of others while disregarding one's own interests. Moderate altruism (also known as Golden Rule altruism or reciprocal altruism): taking others' interests into account while being concerned for one's own interests as well.

ambiguity: Quality exhibited in an expression or statement that can be interpreted in different ways.

anamnesis: Greek: re-remembering. Plato's theory of remembering the truth about the Forms, forgotten at birth.

androgynism: Male and female nature in the same individual, in terms of either sex (biological) or gender (cultural).

android: An artificial intelligence; a robot made to resemble a human being. Literally: manlike. There is no accepted word for a female android, but the equivalent would be *gyneoid.*

angst: Existentialist term for anxiety or anguish, a feeling of dread without any identifiable cause. Most frequently felt when one has to make important decisions. Different from *fear,* where the object of the emotion is known.

animism: The form of religion that sees all elements of nature as enspirited.

Anthropocene Age: The new scientific term for the age where humans have the power to alter their environment.

anthropocentrism: Viewing everything from an exclusively human perspective.

anthropology: The study of humans. Physical anthropology: the study of human biology and biological prehistory. Cultural anthropology: the study of human cultures.

anthropomorphism: Literally: making into a human shape. Projecting human characteristics into the behavior of other animals.

antiquity: Usually refers to the historical time period in ancient cultures around the Mediterranean after the invention of writing (about 6,000 years ago) and before the early Middle Ages (approx. 500 C.E.).

anxiety: *See* angst.

approximation: To approach something with as much accuracy as the conditions allow.

arbitrary: Coincidental, without meaning or consistency.

artificial womb: Medical environment allowing a fetus to grow to maturity outside a mother's womb.

asceticism: Denying oneself physical pleasures and indulgence.

ataraxia: Epicurus's highest form of pleasure, having peace of mind as a result of freedom from pain.

atheism: The conviction that there is no God.

authenticity: Being true to yourself, having personal integrity. Existentialism: not succumbing to the idea that you have no free choice. *See* bad faith.

auto-icon: An image of oneself that consists of oneself. Bentham's term for his own planned future position as a stuffed corpse on display.

autonomy: Independence; a state achieved by those who are self-governing. Autonomous lawmaker: Kant's term for a person using the categorical imperative without regard for personal interest, arriving at something he or she would want to become a universal law. Moral autonomy: being capable of and allowed to make moral decisions on your own.

backward-looking justice: Correcting past wrongs.

bad faith: Existentialist term for the belief that you have no choice; the belief that you can transform yourself into a thing with no will or emotions.

banality of evil: Hannah Arendt's concept of ordinary people being persuaded through pressure from authorities/group pressure to harm innocent people, believing it to be normal/justifiable.

begging the question: A logical fallacy whereby a person who is supposed to prove something assumes from the start that it is a fact.

Being-there: Heidegger's term for human beings, or at least for beings who are self-aware.

benevolence: Interest in the well-being or comfort of others.

bibliotherapy: Using books, usually stories of fiction, in therapy sessions to facilitate patients' understanding of themselves and their situation and options.

bipartisan: "Of two parties," politically neutral or objective.

blog, blogger: From *weblog,* personal websites devoted to opinion and observations, often political.

branding: Creating a brand for one's merchandise. Personal branding: Creating a brand for oneself online.

care: (1) Heidegger's concept of human existence, involving a *Care-structure,* being engaged in living; (2) Gilligan's concept of ethics as it is typically viewed by women—*an ethics of care* rather than an *ethics of justice.* (3) Dwight Furrow and Mark Wheeler's concept of a political ethic of caring.

catalyst: A person or agent that causes something to happen.

categorical imperative: Kant's term for an absolute moral rule that is justified because of its logic: If you can wish for your maxim to become a universal law, your maxim qualifies as a categorical imperative.

catharsis, cathartic: Cleansing. *See* Aristotle's theory of drama, **Chapter 2**.

causality, causal explanation: The chain of cause and effect. Aristotle's theory of causation: material cause (the material aspect of a thing), efficient cause (the maker of a thing), formal cause (the idea of a thing), and final cause (the purpose of a thing).

character arc: A concept used in screenwriting and narrative theory. A character in the story undergoes a certain development leading to a conclusion.

chauvinism: Originally: excessive feeling of nationalism, from the Frenchman Chauvin. Today, it usually means male chauvinism (sexism from a male point of view).

Cinematherapy: Using movies and television series in therapy sessions to facilitate patients' understanding of themselves and their situation and options.

classical feminism: The feminist view that women and men ought to be considered persons first and gendered beings second. Gender differences are due to "nature" rather than "nurture."

cloning: Creating a genetic copy of another individual, either through a process whereby multiple twins are created or through a process whereby a cell nucleus is taken from the original individual, implanted in an emptied ovum, and allowed to develop into an embryo. If the embryo is terminated within ten to fourteen days, *stem cells* may be harvested. If an embryo can survive and be carried to term, a cloned individual is the result. Cloning will not result in a perfect copy of another individual, physically or mentally, because of the variety of circumstances surrounding the growth process that can't be duplicated. *See also* reproductive cloning *and* therapeutic cloning.

cognitive, cognition: The faculty of knowing, examining something rationally.

collateral damage: Unintentional and unavoidable civilian casualties during a war.

communitarianism: A moral and political theory that the individual receives his or her identity from his or her community and can flourish only within the community. The theory is found in the ancient Greek tradition but is also evident in traditional African tribal cultures. Modern communitarians mentioned in this book include Alasdair MacIntyre and Elizabeth Wolgast. In addition, Hillary Rodham Clinton has declared herself a communitarian with the publication of her book, *It Takes a Village.*

compatibilism: A theory claiming that free will and determinism are compatible; i.e., the theories don't contradict each other. *See* determinism.

conceptualize: Make a vague notion into a concept with a clear definition that can be used in a description or an argument.

condition of possibility: What makes something possible, or what makes it come into being.

consequentialism: A theory that focuses exclusively on the consequences of an action. Utilitarianism is the best-known consequentialist theory, but ethical egoism also qualifies as an example of consequentialism.

Continental philosophy: Philosophical traditions from the European continent (excluding British traditions).

contractarianism: The theory that only humans can have rights, because only humans can enter into agreements (contracts) and recognize duties springing from those agreements.

correlative: A term or a concept that is understood in its relation to other concepts. The fallacy of the suppressed correlative: If terms are correlative, like *hot/cold,* and *tall/short,* they help define each other. If one is suppressed, the other ceases to have any meaning.

counterfable/countermyth: A story/fable/myth told deliberately to prove another story, type of story, or idea wrong.

criminal justice: Punishment of people found guilty of crimes.

CRISPR: A gene-editing technology.

criterion: A test, rule, or measure for distinguishing between true and false, relevant and irrelevant. A standard for a correct judgment. Plural: *criteria.*

Crusades, the: Military expeditions undertaken by European Christians from the eleventh through the thirteenth centuries to recover the Holy Land from the Muslims.

cultural diversity: The recognition of a variety of ethnic and racial groups within a given region (all the way from a neighborhood to planet Earth).

cultural imperialism: A critical term for the attitude of imposing one's cultural accomplishments and moral convictions on other cultures.

cultural relativism: The theory that different societies or cultures have different moral codes. A descriptive theory.

culture war: Ideological disagreement between liberal and conservative values.

cyberbullying: Harassment of individuals on the Internet.

cyberpunk: A science-fiction category implying a bad or problematic (see *dystopian*) future.

cynicism: Distrust in evidence of virtue or disinterested motives. Pessimism. Originally a Greek school of thought believing that virtue, not pleasure or intellect, was the ultimate goal of life. Deteriorated into the idea of self-righteousness.

debt-metaphor: English's term for using the terms *owing* and *debt* in situations where they may or may not be appropriate. Appropriate use: a situation in which favors are owed. Inappropriate use: a situation of friendship or family relationship.

deduction: The scientific and philosophical method of identifying an item of absolute truth (an axiom) and using this as a premise to deduce specific cases that are also absolutely true.

deep ecology: Coined by philosopher Arne Næss, it is a radical environmentalist concept that humans are only one of many species on the planet, and that all species have an equal right to live.

deontology: Duty-theory. An ethical theory that disregards the importance of consequences and focuses only on the rightness or wrongness of the act itself.

descriptive: Describing a phenomenon without making an evaluative or judgmental statement. Opposite of normative.

determinism, or "hard determinism": The theory that causality determines everything, including human decisions. Everything is caused by our heredity and/or our environment (nature/nurture), and humans have no free will.

deterrence: A concept of criminal justice: punishing criminals with the intent to deter them (*specific* deterrence) or others (*general* deterrence) from committing the same crime.

dialectic method: Socrates' method of guiding his students to their own realization of the truth through a conversation, a dialogue. Also called the Socratic method.

dichotomy: An "either-or" statement. A false dichotomy: an either-or statement that ignores other possibilities.

didactic: Done or told for the purpose of teaching a lesson.

difference feminism: The feminist view that women and men are fundamentally different, morally and psychologically due to human nature.

dilemma: The situation of having to choose between two courses of action that either exclude each other or are equally unpleasant.

distributive justice: Fair distribution of social goods.

divine command theory: A theological theory that God has created the laws of morality; in other words, something is right because God commands it. Opposed to *natural law theory,* which claims that God commands something because it is right. *See also* natural law.

double effect: A principle primarily found within Catholic ethics: An action that is otherwise prohibited can be permitted, provided that it is an *unintended* side effect to some other, necessary action; that the effect of the primary action is *proportionately very serious,* and the effect of the secondary action is *unavoidable.* The principle is used to justify rare cases of euthanasia and abortion, among others.

dualism: The metaphysical theory that reality consists of matter and mind. Also used as a term for any theory of opposite forces.

dystopia, dystopian: A bad or problematic future; generally a science-fiction genre.

egalitarian: A theory that advocates social equality.

Ego: Freud's term for the human experience of the self. *See also* Superego *and* Id.

ego integrity: Erikson's term for mental equilibrium, accepting one's past, and not playing the "what if" game with oneself.

egregious: extreme, tremendous. "Egregious evil."

Eli, Eli, lama sabachthani?: One of the seven expressions of Jesus Christ on the cross: "My Lord, why hast thou forsaken me?"

elitism: The belief that a certain advantage (for instance, knowledge, education, or wealth) should be reserved for a small part of the population, an elite.

embedded journalist: A journalist who travels with a military force.

emotionalism: The moral philosophy that moral values derive from emotions, not from reason. David Hume is considered the primary emotionalist.

empiricism: The philosophical school of thought that claims humans are born without knowledge, that the mind is an empty slate (*tabula rasa*) at birth, and that all knowledge comes through the senses.

end in oneself: Kant's term for a person. Persons (rational beings) should be regarded as dignified beings who have their own goals in life; they should not be used as a means to an end only. *See* means to an end, merely.

end justifies the means, the: The statement of a consequentialist: Only the consequences count, not how they are brought about.

enfranchisement: Having rights, and thus political power. (*Disenfranchisement* means having those powers taken away.)

Enlightenment, the: In the European and American cultural tradition, the eighteenth century saw a new focusing on the rights of the individual, the importance of education, and the objectivity of science. Also called the *Age of Reason* or the Western Enlightenment; rationality was considered the ultimate cultural goal by scientists, philosophers, and many politicians.

epistemology: Theory of knowledge. One of the main branches of traditional philosophy.

equilibrium: In this book: A well-balanced mind, capable of fair judgment.

equity feminism: The feminist view that the battle for equality has been won and that further insistence on women's inequality only serves to make women into victims.

equity principle: A social fairness principle focused on "leveling the playing field," giving advantages to disenfranchised groups that will allow them to have equal access to social goods.

essence: A thing's inner nature. "Essence precedes existence": the traditional philosophical conception of reality, including human nature; the theory that there is a design or purpose that nature must follow.

ethical egoism: The theory that everybody ought to be egoistic/selfish/self-interested.

ethical pluralism: Several moral systems working simultaneously within one culture.

ethical relativism: The theory that there is no universal moral code and that whatever the majority of any given society or culture considers morally right is morally right for that culture. A normative theory. *See also* cultural relativism.

ethical will: Personal legacy letter summarizing one's values and life lessons.

ethicist: A person professionally or vocationally involved with the theory and application of ethics.

ethics: The study, questioning, and justification of moral rules.

ethics of conduct: The study of moral rules pertaining to decisions about what course of action to take or "what to do."

ethics of virtue: The study of moral rules pertaining to the building of character or "how to be."

ethos: The moral rules and attitudes of a culture.

eudaimonia: Greek: well-spirited, contentment, happiness. Aristotle's term for the ultimate human goal.

euphemism: An expression glossing over a more serious or harsher reality.

Eurocentric: A critical term meaning that American culture is overly focused on its European roots. Possibly a misnomer, since Americans rarely focus on European traditions, politics, and history but, rather, on the European *legacy* for mainstream American culture.

euthanasia: Mercy killing; doctor-assisted suicide. Literally: "good death," from Greek. Voluntary euthanasia: requested by the patient. Involuntary euthanasia: (a) The patient is killed against her or his will; (b) The patient cannot communicate his or her wish, so the decision is made by the family (also called nonvoluntary euthanasia). Active euthanasia: helping someone to die at his or her request. Passive euthanasia: withholding treatment that will not help a terminally ill patient.

evidence: A ground or reason for certainty in knowledge. Usually empirical evidence; facts gathered in support of a theory.

exemplar: A model, an example for others to follow.

existence precedes essence: Existentialist belief that humans aren't determined by any essence (human nature) but exist prior to any decision about what and how they ought to be.

existentialism: A Continental school of thought that believes all humans have freedom of the will to determine their own life.

extrinsic value: *See* instrumental value.

fable: A short narrative with a moral, introducing persons, animals, or inanimate things as speakers and actors.

fallacy: A flaw in one's reasoning; an argument that does not follow the rules of logic.

falsification, principle of: The concept that a valid theory must test itself and allow for the possibility of situations in which the theory doesn't apply. In a sense, part of the verification process of a theory is being able to hypothetically falsify it.

fatalism: The theory that life is determined by a higher power and that our will can't change our destiny.

faux pas: French: a misstep, a social blunder.

fecundity: Being fruitful, having good consequences.

first-wave feminism: Feminism from the eighteenth century until approximately 1920. *See* second- and third-wave feminism.

flygskam: Swedish for "flight shame," the phenomenon of shaming someone on social media for using air transport instead of ground transport.

forensic: Related to the use of scientific or medical procedures to investigate a death.

Forms, theory of: Plato's metaphysical theory of a higher reality that gives meaning and existence to the world we experience through our senses. This higher reality is accessible through the mind. Example: a perfect circle; it doesn't exist in the world of the senses, but it does exist in the intelligible world of Forms.

fortitude: Strength of mind and courage in the face of adversity.

forward-looking justice: Creating good future social consequences. *See also* consequentialism.

free will: The notion that we can make choices that are not completely determined by our heredity and our environment.

fundamentalism: A religious approach to reality that interprets the dogmas and sacred scriptures of the tradition literally.

gender-neutral: Not gender-specific. Usually used when referring to language. Examples: Scientists must do their research well. Nurses should take good care of their patients.

gender-specific: Applying to one sex only. Examples of gender-specific language: A scientist must do *his* research well. A nurse should take good care of *her* patients.

genetic engineering: Scientific manipulation of the DNA code of an individual (human, animal, or plant), usually to enhance certain desired characteristics or eliminate congenital diseases.

genetic fallacy, the: Assuming that something can be fully explained by pointing to its original/first condition.

genocide: The murder of all or most of a population.

genre: A literary type of story (or film), such as horror, Western, or science fiction.

gnothi seauton: Ancient Greek proverb: Know thyself.

Golden Mean, the: The Greek idea of moderation. Aristotle's concept of virtue as a relative mean between the extremes of excess and deficiency.

golem: A Jewish legend of an artificial person that must be controlled lest he overpower his human maker.

good will: For Kant, having good will means having good intentions in terms of respecting a moral law that is rational and deserves to be a universal law.

greatest-happiness principle, the: *See* utility.

hard determinism: The theory that everything can, in principle, be predicted and understood with 100 percent accuracy, because everything is an effect of a previous cause.

hard universalism: *See* absolutism.

harm principle, the: John Stuart Mill's idea that one should not interfere with other people's lives unless those people are doing harm to others.

hedonism: Pleasure-seeking. The paradox of hedonism: The more you look for pleasure, the more it seems to elude you. Hedonistic calculus: Bentham's pros-and-cons system, in which pleasures are added and pains subtracted to find the most utilitarian course of action.

heterogeneous: Consisting of dissimilar or diverse elements.

hierarchy: A structure of higher and lower elements, ordered according to their relative importance.

homeostasis: A biological term for an organism being in balance. Social homeostasis: When a community and its individuals have a balanced existence of well-being.

homogeneous: Consisting of similar elements.

human condition, the: What it means to be a human being, usually in terms of inevitable facts: having physical and spiritual needs, being a social creature, and being subject to illness and aging.

hyphenated: A political term for the distinction between one's national or ethnic ancestry and one's American identity, such as *Swedish-American.* To be "hyphenated" indicates for some people that one's loyalties are divided. Today it is common to omit the hyphen, as in *Swedish American.*

hypothetical imperative: A command that is binding only if one is interested in a certain result. An "if-then" situation.

Id: Freud's term for the Unconscious, the part of the mind that the conscious self (the Ego) has no access to but that influences the Ego.

idealism: The metaphysical theory that reality consists of mind only, not matter.

immutability: The quality of remaining stable and unchanged.

inalienable: Incapable of being taken or given away.

incapacitation: A concept of criminal justice: punishing a criminal with the intent of making the public safe from his or her criminal activity. May refer to incarceration as well as other forms of punishment, including capital punishment.

incrementalism: Deliberately adding to, or taking something away (such as privileges or rights), in small steps, usually so the final goal is less obvious.

incredulity: Skepticism; refusal to believe something.

indigenous: Belonging to an original, or aboriginal, population.

induction: The scientific and philosophical method of collecting empirical evidence and formulating a general theory based on those specific facts. The problem of induction: Because one never knows if one has collected enough evidence, one can never achieve 100 percent certainty through induction.

institutionalized cruelty: Hallie's term for cruelty (psychological or physical) that has become so established, it seems natural to both victimizer and victim.

instrumental value: To have value for the sake of what further value it might bring. Also known as extrinsic value; good as a means to an end. *See* means to an end.

intelligent design: The notion that the universe has been created by a vast intelligence, not by exclusively natural forces.

intersexual: A person with both male and female genitalia.

intrinsic value: To have value in itself without regard to what it might bring of further value. Good in itself, good as an "end in itself." *See* end in oneself.

intuition: Usually, an experience of understanding that is independent of one's reasoning. Can also mean the moment of understanding, an "Aha" experience. Moral intuition: a gut-level feeling of right and wrong.

ipso facto: By the fact itself.

irony: Ridicule through exaggeration, praise, or understatement.

jus ad bellum: Just war: a war conducted in self-defense according to set rules.

jus in bello: Justice in war. Rules for proper conduct of war.

jus post bellum: Justice after war, in terms of punishment of war crimes and compensations for victims.

karma: Originally a belief associated with Hinduism that actions have consequences, either in this life or in the next. Now a modern expression of the concept that "what goes around, comes around."

kingdom of ends: Kant's term for a society of autonomous lawmakers who all use the categorical imperative and show respect to one another.

land ethic: Introduced by Aldo Leopold: Environmentally, humans are members of the entire community of animals, plants, soil and water, and should act responsibly.

leap of faith: Kierkegaard's concept of the necessary step from the ethical to the religious stage. It involves throwing yourself at the mercy of God and discarding all messages from your rational mind or your self-interested emotions.

lex talionis: The law of retaliation; an eye for an eye. A retributivist argument for punishment.

liberalism: A political theory that supports gradual reforms through parliamentary procedures and civil liberties.

libertarianism: (1) A theory of government that holds the individual has a right to life, liberty, and property; that nobody should interfere with those rights (negative rights); and that the government's role should be restricted to protecting those rights. (2) A theory that humans have free will independent of mechanistic causality.

maeden agan/meden agan: Ancient Greek proverb: "Nothing to excess," everything in moderation.

master morality: Nietzsche's view of the morality of strong individuals in ancient times; includes respect for the enemy, loyalty to friends and kin, and scorn for weaker individuals. Leads to the concept of the Overman (Superman), the strong individual who has gone beyond the moral rules and sets his own standards of good and evil.

materialism: The metaphysical theory that reality consists of matter only, not mind.

matriarchy, matriarchal: A society in which women have great social influence and the words of older women within the family carry much weight. Sometimes taken to mean a society ruled by women.

maxim: Kant's term for the rule or principle of an action.

means to an end: Something used to achieve another goal, an end. *See* instrumental value.

means to an end, merely: Kant's term for reducing others to a stepping-stone for one's own purpose.

mental state: Any mind activity or mental image.

metaethics: The approach to ethics that refrains from making normative statements but focuses on the meaning of terms and statements and investigates the sources of normative statements.

metaphor: An image or an illustration that describes something in terms of something different. A figurative image such as "Mrs. Robinson is a cougar."

metaphysics: The philosophical study of the nature of reality or of being.

#MeToo: A popular movement in social media, started in 2017, the hashtag indicating that a person has also been a victim of sexual assault or harassment.

misandry: Misgivings about, hatred of, or lack of trust in men.

misanthropy: Misgivings about, hatred of, or lack of trust in the goodness of human nature.

misogyny: Misgivings about, hatred of, or lack of trust in female human nature.

monism: A type of metaphysics that holds that there is one element of reality only, such as materialism or idealism.

monoculturalism: As opposed to multiculturalism. The concept of a dominant culture, viewing its history and cultural practices as the only significant contributions to the culture in question.

moral agent: A person capable of reflecting on a moral problem and acting on his or her decision.

moral cannibalism: Ayn Rand's description of any moral theory that advocates altruism.

morality, morals: The moral rules and attitudes that we live by, or are expected to live by.

mores: The moral customs and rules of a given culture.

multiculturalism: The policy of recognizing cultural diversity to the extent that all cultures within a given region are fairly represented in public life and education. Sometimes includes gender as cultural diversity. *See also* cultural diversity, pluralism, *and* particularism.

myth: A story or a collection of stories that give identity, guidance, and meaning to a culture. Usually, these are stories of gods and heroes, but they may involve ordinary people too. In common language, myth has come to mean "falsehood" or "illusion," but that is not the original meaning.

narrative: A story with a plot. Narrative structure: perceiving events as having a logical progression from a beginning through a middle to an ending.

narrative time: The time frame within which a story takes place. The experience of sharing this time frame as one reads or watches the story unfold.

naturalistic fallacy: The assumption that one can conclude from what is natural/a fact ("what is") what should be a rule or a policy ("what ought to be"). Not all philosophers think this is a fallacy.

natural law: A view introduced to the Catholic Church by Thomas Aquinas that what is natural for humans (in other words, what God has intended) is good for humans. What is natural for humans includes preservation of life, procreation, socialization, and pursuit of knowledge of God.

natural rights: The assumption that humans (and perhaps also nonhumans) are born with certain inalienable rights.

negative command: Hallie's term for a moral command involving a prohibition, such as "Don't lie" or "Don't cause harm." *See* positive command.

negative rights: Rights not to be interfered with; usually includes the right to life, liberty, and property. Originally an element in John Locke's political philosophy; has become a defining element of modern Libertarian philosophy.

neo-classicism: A style of art and architecture in the seventeenth and eighteenth centuries that revived classical Greek and Roman forms. Also, any spiritual and philosophical movement that tries to recover the classical ideals of moderation and order.

nihilism: From the Latin *nihil,* nothing. The attitude of believing in nothing. Moral nihilism: the conviction that there are no moral truths.

Nolite te bastardes carborundorum: Fake college Latin for "don't let the bastards grind you down."

normative: Evaluating and/or setting norms or standards. Opposite of descriptive.

objectification: Making an object, a thing, out of someone: disregarding his or her human dignity. Also reification, making a thing out of someone.

objective: The kind of knowledge that is supported by evidence and that has independent existence apart from experience or thought.

ontology: A philosophical discipline investigating the nature of existence.

original sin: The Christian belief that the disobedience of Adam and Eve is inherited by all humans from birth, so all humans are born sinful.

Other, the: A philosophical concept meaning either something that is completely different from yourself and all your experiences or someone who is different from you and is thus hard to understand.

Overman, or Superman: Nietzsche's term for the individual who has recognized his will to power and created his own system of values based on an affirmation of life.

pacifism: The belief that war and violence are morally wrong, regardless of the circumstances.

paleo-linguistic: Related to an ancient language.

parable: A short narrative told to make a moral or religious point.

particularism: The branch of multiculturalism that believes people not belonging to the dominant culture should retrieve their self-esteem by learning about the traditions and accomplishments of their own cultural group rather than those of the dominant group or any other group. Also called exclusive multiculturalism.

paterfamilias: The male head of the household.

patriarchy: A society ruled by men, or a society in which men have great social influence.

philanthropy: Greek: loving humans. Doing good deeds, being charitable.

philology: The study of language, its structure and history.

philosophy: Greek: love of wisdom. The study of metaphysics, epistemology, ethics, and other interpretations of patterns underlying everyday life/human mind activities.

phronesis: Aristotle's term for practical wisdom, our everyday decision-making process.

phylogenetic: An origin of a class of phenomena.

pleasure principle: Freud's term for the oldest layer of the human mind, which caters selfishly to our own pleasure. For most people, it is superseded by the reality principle, at least most of the time.

pluralism: The branch of multiculturalism that believes racial and ethnic discrimination in a population of cultural diversity can be abolished by a shared orientation in one another's cultural traditions and history. Also called inclusive multiculturalism. Also: any theory or culture that includes several different viewpoints.

positive command: Hallie's term for a moral command to actively do something rather than merely refraining from doing something wrong (a negative command). Example: "Help another being in distress."

positive rights: Rights of entitlement. The theory that each individual has a right to the basic means of subsistence against the state, such as food, shelter, clothing, education, welfare, and health services.

preconceived notion: An idea that is formed before actual knowledge or experience and that you don't think of questioning.

prerational: Before the use of reason; instinctive; belonging to human nature before the development of reason.

prescriptive: *See* normative.

presocial: Before the existence of society.

principle of utility: *See* utility.

procreation: Having offspring, giving birth.

protagonist: The hero of the story.

psychological altruism: The theory that everyone is always unselfish.

psychological egoism: The theory that everyone is selfish, self-interested.

psychosexual neutrality: The behaviorist theory that human sexuality is a matter of upbringing (nurture) rather than a hardwiring of the brain (nature).

quid pro quo: Latin, something for something; exchanging favors or information. "I'll scratch your back if you'll scratch mine."

radical feminism: The feminist view that the root cause of male dominance of women and discrimination against women must be examined.

rational being: Anyone who has intelligence and the capacity to use it. Usually stands for human beings, but may exclude some humans and include some nonhuman beings.

rationalism: The philosophical school of thought that claims humans are born with some knowledge, or some capacity for knowledge, such as logic and mathematics. Opposite of empiricism.

reality principle: Freud's term for the knowledge that we can't always have things our own way.

reciprocity, reciprocal: Individuals or groups of people agreeing to give each other the same advantages, or doing similar favors for each other.

reductio ad absurdum: A form of argument in which you reduce your opponent's viewpoint to its absurd consequences.

rehabilitation: A concept of criminal justice: punishing a criminal with the intent of making him or her a better socialized person at the end of the term of punishment.

reification: *See* objectification.

relevance: Direct application to a situation; pertinence.

Renaissance: Literally: rebirth. The European cultural revival of the arts and sciences in the fourteenth through sixteenth centuries. This period marked the end of the Middle Ages.

reproductive cloning: Creating an identical individual from an existing person's cells. *See* therapeutic cloning.

restorative justice: Rehabilitation of criminals, and restitution to the victims.

retentionism: The viewpoint that the death penalty ought to be retained (kept as an option).

retribution: A concept of criminal justice: the logical dispensing or receiving of punishment in proportion to the crime. Sometimes known as "an eye for an eye," *lex talionis.* To be distinguished from vengeance, which is an emotional response that may exceed the severity of the crime.

retributive justice: Punishment of criminals in proportion to their crime.

revisionism: Advocacy of revision of former values and viewpoints. Today: refers mostly to a cynical revision of heroic values of the past.

rhetoric: The art of verbal persuasion.

Romanticism, the Romantic movement: A movement among artists, philosophers, and social critics in the late eighteenth and nineteenth centuries, partly based on the idea that emotion is a legitimate form of expression and can give access to higher truths without necessarily involving the intellect.

rule utilitarianism: The branch of utilitarianism that focuses on the consequences of a type of action done repeatedly, and not just a single act. *See* act utilitarianism.

satire: The use of sarcasm in a narrative criticism of conditions one doesn't approve of.

second-wave feminism: Feminism in the United States and Europe from the mid-1950s on. Some consider second-wave feminism to have ended by the mid-1980s; others see it as continuing.

selfish gene: Dawkins's theory that humans as well as animals have a disposition that favors themselves, but also the survival of their genes. Occasionally, animals (or humans) will sacrifice themselves so that their closely related relatives or offspring may survive.

Shanti, shanti, shanti: Buddhist prayer: "peace, peace, peace."

Silver Rule, the: Do not do to others what you would not like them to do to you. A negative version of the Golden Rule, Do unto others as you would have them do unto you.

skepticism: The philosophical approach that we cannot obtain absolutely certain knowledge. In practice, it is an approach of not believing anything until there is sufficient evidence to prove it.

slave morality: Nietzsche's concept of the morality of the "herd," people who in his view resent strong individuals and claim that meekness is a virtue.

slippery slope argument: A version of the *reductio ad absurdum* argument; you reduce your opponent's view to unacceptable or ridiculous consequences, which your opponent will presumably have to accept or else abandon his or her theory. Your opponent's argument must "slide down the slope" of logic. A way to defeat the slippery slope argument is to "draw the line" and defend your viewpoint on the basis that there is a difference between the "top of the slope" and the "bottom of the slope."

social contract: A type of social theory, popular in the seventeenth and eighteenth centuries, that assumes humans in the early stages of society got together and agreed on terms for creating a society.

soft universalism: The ethical theory that although humans may not agree on all moral rules or all customs, there are a few core values we can agree on, despite our different ways of expressing them.

sophia: Greek: wisdom. Aristotle's term for theoretical wisdom, the highest intellectual virtue.

spatial: Associated with space.

stoicism: Originally a Greek philosophical movement claiming that the point of virtue is to be free of suffering, and the method to follow is the path of reason.

Stockholm Syndrome: A hostage or prisoner identifying with his or her captors or guards. Named after a hostage situation in Stockholm, Sweden, in 1973.

straw man (straw dummy) argument: A logical fallacy that consists of attacking and disproving a theory invented for the occasion.

subjective opinion: One that is not supported by evidence, or is dependent on the mind and experience of the person.

subjectivism: Ethical theory that claims that your moral belief is right simply because you believe it; there are no intersubjective (shared) moral standards.

Superego: Freud's concept of the human conscience, the internalized rules of our parents and our society.

sustainability: Focused on maintaining or restoring a balance of the natural resources as well as the needs of present and future generations.

talisman: An item symbolizing or bringing good luck.

teleology: A theory of purpose. A teleological theory such as Aristotle's may assume that everything has a purpose. Also used to designate theories interested in the outcome of an action, that is, consequentialist theories.

temperance: In virtue theory, this means moderation. In a modern context, it may mean abstinence from alcohol.

temporal: Associated with time. Temporal being: a being living in time and understanding himself or herself in terms of a past, a present, and a future.

theology: The study of God and God's nature and attributes.

therapeutic cloning: Generally, duplicating and growing stem cells (cloning) as a form of medical treatment of illnesses. *See* reproductive cloning.

third-wave feminism: Feminism from the mid-1980s to the present day.

totalitarianism: A form of government that views the state as all-important and the lives of its citizens as disposable.

transgenic: Genetic engineering of an animal or a plant (or, theoretically, a human) with some genes from another species.

transition: A term used in today's gender debate, indicating a person transitioning from one gender to another.

trope: A recurring theme in literature.

universal law: Kant's term for a moral rule that can be imagined as applying to everybody in the same situation and accepted by other rational beings.

universalizability: A maxim that is acceptable as a universal law.

universalization: The process by which one asks oneself whether one's maxim could become a universal law: "What if everybody did this?"

unrequited: Unreturned, nonreciprocal.

utilitarianism: The theory that one ought to maximize the happiness and minimize the unhappiness of as many people (or sentient beings) as possible.

utility: Fitness for some purpose, especially for creating happiness and/or minimizing pain and suffering. Principle of utility: To create as much happiness and minimize suffering as much as possible for as many as possible. Also: the greatest-happiness principle.

Utopia: Literally, no place. Sir Thomas More's term for a nonexistent world, usually used as a term for a world too good to be true. Utopia can also mean "good place." A bad place is known as "Dystopia."

veneer theory: The theory that values are merely a thin social veneer covering our basically selfish nature.

vengeance: Revenge. When used as a concept of criminal justice: an emotional response to punishment.

viability: The time in a pregnancy where a fetus could survive outside the mother's body.

vicariously: To experience something through the experiences of others.

Voir dire: The questioning of potential jurors during jury selection.

Way, the: Chinese: Tao (Dao). The morally and philosophically correct path to follow.

yin and yang: The two cosmic principles of Taoism, opposing forces that keep the universe in balance.

Index

Page numbers in **boldface** refer to primary readings and narratives. Page numbers in italics refer to illustrations.